THE UNSEEN POWER:
Public Relations. A History

LEA's COMMUNICATION SERIES
Jennings Bryant/Dolf Zillmann, General Editors

Selected titles in Public Relations (James Grunig, Advisory Editor) include:

Botan/Hazelton, Jr. • Public Relations Theory

Culbertson/Jeffers/Stone/Terrell • Social, Political, and Economic Contexts in Public Relations: Theory and Cases

Grunig • Excellence in Public Relations and Communication Management

Kelly • Fund Raising and Public Relations: A Critical Analysis

Toth/Heath • Rhetorical and Critical Approaches to Public Relations

For a complete list of other titles in LEA's Communication Series, please contact Lawrence Erlbaum Associates, Publishers.

THE UNSEEN POWER:
Public Relations. A History

Scott M. Cutlip
Dean Emeritus, The University of Georgia

LEA LAWRENCE ERLBAUM ASSOCIATES, PUBLISHERS
1994 Hillsdale, New Jersey   Hove, UK

Lawrence Erlbaum Associates, Inc., Publishers
365 Broadway
Hillsdale, New Jersey 07642

Cover design by Jan Melchior

Library of Congress Cataloging-in-Publication Data

Cutlip, Scott M.
    The unseen power: public relations. a history / Scott M. Cutlip
        p.   cm.
    Includes bibliographical references and index.
    ISBN 0-8058-1464-7 (alk. paper).—ISBN 0-8058-1465-5
(pbk. : alk. paper)
    1. Public relations—United States—History.   2. Public rela-
tions—Social aspects—United States.   I. Title.
HM263.C785   1994
659.2—dc20   93-8617
                                                        CIP

Books published by Lawrence Erlbaum Associates are printed on
acid-free paper, and their bindings are chosen for strength and durability.

Printed in the United States of America
10 9 8 7 6 5 4 3 2 1

This book is gratefully dedicated to
my former students who have so greatly
enriched my life.

Contents

Prologue   ix

PART I   THE SEEDBED YEARS OF COUNSELING,
       1900–1919   1

1   The Nation's First Publicity Agency   10

2   The First Washington Agencies   27

3   First Parker and Lee, Then Lee, Harris, and Lee   37

4   The Hamilton Wright Organization—The First
      International Agency   73

5   Pendleton Dudley Starts Fifth Agency in 1909   92

PART II   PUBLIC RELATIONS BOOMS IN THE BOOMING
       TWENTIES, 1919–1930   105

6   Ivy Lee Returns to New York; Joined by T. J. Ross   114

7   Edward L. Bernays: Pioneer, Philosopher, Centenarian   159

8   Bernays: The Counselor and His Genius and
      His Role in the Profession   193

9 John Price Jones Tries to Ride Two Horses 226

10 Steve Hannagan: Super Press Agent 251

11 Harry Bruno: Aviation and Public Relations Pioneer 278

12 William H. Baldwin: Counselor and Citizen 308

13 Ben Sonnenberg: *Sui Generis* 343

14 Clarke and Tyler: Builders of the Ku Klux Klan 372

15 John W. Hill: Builder of an Enduring Legacy 414

16 John Hill's Two Major Battles: Steel and
    Tobacco—and the Person 458

PART III THE DEPRESSION AND THE YEARS BEYOND 525

17 Carl Byoir: The Little Giant of Public Relations 531

18 Carl Byoir: Years of Success and Storm 553

19 Whitaker & Baxter: Architects of the New Politics 589

20 Earl Newsom: Counselor to Corporate Giants 634

21 Earl Newsom and the Auto Giants: Ford and GM 682

22 Earl Newsom and the Ford Foundation 735

Epilogue 761

Index 777

Prologue

Publication of this book is the culmination of more than 40 years of research in the history of public relations in the United States and its strong impact on American society, an impact that generally goes unseen and unobserved. As I have explained elsewhere, my research had its genesis in a series of stimulating conversations over lunch, over dinner, and in the late hours with two long-time friends, the late Merrill Jensen and Merle Curti, two great American historians of the 20th Century. On many occasions, Professor Jensen and I extolled the exploits of Samuel Adams and his hardy band in bringing off the American Revolution. My discussions with Professor Curti focused on the role of public relations in our economic, political, and social history. Like most academics, these and other friends were highly critical of public relations and generally saw it as a corrosive element in our society.

As an author and teacher in this field since 1946, I would repeatedly cite chapter and verse to these critics of the good for society that can be accomplished through ethical, effective public relations. This book presents ample evidence of this good (e.g., Carl Byoir's innovative fund raising that eliminated the fear of polio from parents' hearts). I held, and still hold, that only through the expertise of public relations can causes, industries, individuals, and institutions make their voice heard in the public forum where thousands of shrill, competing voices daily re-create the Tower of Babel. I did not and do not deny the harm done by the incompetent, the charlatan, and those who serve dubious causes. There is also ample evidence in this book of this harm done to the public good. For example John W. Hill's 10-year campaign to deny and obfuscate the damage to a person's health that is caused by smoking cigarettes. This campaign continues to this day, now carried forward by the Tobacco Institute, Inc. and the Tobacco Research Council, successor to the Tobacco Industry Research Committee "front" that John Hill created. Another example of injury to the public interest can be found in Clem Whitaker's and Leone Baxter's $5 millon campaign for the American Medical Association, which delayed national health insurance for a decade and was finally enacted in President Lyndon Johnson's administration as Medicare and Medicaid. The most egregious example of damage done to our society can be found in the story of two Atlanta publicists — Edward Y. Clarke and Elizabeth Tyler — who took a defunct Atlanta bottle club, Ku Klux Klan, and boomed into a national organization with 3 million members from 1920 to 1923. This lasting wound was inflicted on our nation for money, not ideology.

My interest in the early years of public relations history began in earnest in 1955. I joined forces with the late Clifford L. Lord, then director of the State Historical Society of Wisconsin, and we gathered materials for the newly created Mass Communications History Center in that great archive of American history. I wrote many letters and made many trips seeking the personal papers of Ivy L. Lee, Edward L. Bernays, William H. Baldwin III, Harry A. Bruno, Pendleton Dudley, John W. Hill, Earl Newsom, Arthur W. Page, and others. As the result of these efforts, the voluminous papers of Baldwin, Bruno, Hill, Newsom, and Page are now housed in the Mass Communications History Center, which has become a major source of 20th Century mass communications history. This book rests heavily on all of these papers, save those of Arthur Page.

Initially, when I embarked on this project in the late 1950s, I set out to trace the evolution of public relations practice from the Colonial period to the mid-20th Century. The first 10 chapters brought me to only the turn of the 20th Century. A historian friend suggested that I was trying to write a history of the United States. In writing about the history of public relations, it is a difficult task to keep the focus on the practice and not get mired in substantive content of the problem or project with which the practitioner is trying to deal. A call to journalism administration and retirement shelved my original project, one that I return to next.

In 1990, when persuaded to return to this project by the distinguished counselor, Harold Burson, I decided to narrow my focus by profiling the pioneering public relations agencies and their founders. I did this in order to keep the book within tolerable limits. Given its ultimate length, readers may well question whether I achieved this. The persons profiled in this book were chosen for their enduring contributions and by the availability of documentation. This book has been greatly strengthened by the fact that I had access to the private and agency papers of 11 of these pioneers. Given today's social climate, I suspect critics may note the absence of Black counselors and that only two women are included among the pioneers. This is a fact of history, not a choice of mine.

In the 1950s, my research, born of increasing concern about the impact of public relations on society, took two directions. One is what I called at the time "wastebasket" surveys conducted to determine what percentage of the content of newspapers, magazines, radio, and TV was coming from public relations sources — often unedited — and thus being passed on to the public as "news" or "information." This research was carried out over several years in collaboration with graduate students. These studies made it clear that nearly half of the editorial content of the media was being supplied — without cost — by public relations sources. Later scholars, led by Judy Van Slyke Turk and Oscar H. Gandy, Jr., took up this line of research in a more elaborate, refined way. Their works show how industries and institutions in effect subsidize the media and greatly influence their content. This book reveals how this has been the case since the turn of the 20th century, which saw the birth of the public relations vocation. The other way to discern the impact of public relations on our society was to study history. This came naturally to me, a long-time history buff. This book is substantial evidence of this interest in using history to demonstrate the influential role of public relations in our society — its unseen power.

Public relations strategies and tactics are increasingly used as weapons of power in our no-holds-barred political, economic, and cause competition in the public opinion marketplace, and thus deserve more scholarly scrutiny than they have had. This book is the result of my examination of these forces over my career. The increasingly powerful role of the public relations consultant is a major factor in today's political process, as exemplified by the pioneer political consultants Clem Whitaker and Leone Baxter, whose innovations produced a sea of change in America's politics. The escalating power of the political campaign specialist was writ in capital letters in James Carville's role in the election of President Bill Clinton in 1992. Public relations practitioners have inserted themselves into the nation's public information system and thus warrant examination.

Persuasive communication is as old as Plato's *Republic*, but what started in Boston in mid-1900 as a new, ill-defined vocation in our own country has reached the size, scope, and power of an industry. It has now spread around the globe. America's public relations practitioners wield major influence in the public opinion game. Propagandist, press agent, public information officer, public relations or public affairs official, political campaign specialist, lobbyist — whatever their title, their aim is the same: to influence public behavior. All are protected in our democratic system by the First Amendment rights that journalists enjoy, enabling them to play a far more important opinion-making role than the public perceives. It was a lawsuit that Carl Byoir & Associates carried to the U. S. Supreme Court that established First Amendment protection of the public relations practitioner, a case detailed in this book.

A VITAL COG IN THE NATION'S PUBLIC INFORMATION SYSTEM

A democratic nation's public information system consists of all those elements and channels of communication through which a citizen obtains the information he or she needs to make daily economic, political, social, cultural, and philanthropic decisions. The public information system embraces government—federal, state and local, political parties, pressure groups, corporations, nonprofit organizations, public relations personnel, and the channels of communication, manned by reporters, editors, and gatekeepers. Each of these elements performs an influential, integral function in the political and economic and social process. One element works in relation to all other elements, thus all may be lumped together under the rubric of *public information system*. To make their daily decisions, today's citizens must depend on this system. Thus, the same 150,000 public relations practitioners working within the industry have invested themselves with a social responsibility. Not all measure up—as this book reveals.

The social justification for public relations in a free society is to ethically and effectively plead the cause of a client or organization in the free-wheeling forum of public debate. It is a basic democratic right that every idea, individual, and institution shall have a full and fair hearing in the public forum—that their merit ultimately must be determined by their ability to be accepted in the marketplace. To obtain such a hearing, the idea, individual, or institution needs the expertise of the skilled advocate. This becomes truer every day with the multiplication of channels of communication and the growth of clutter and trash in those channels. This can be readily seen in the explosion of "talk show democracy" in which a rabble-rousing talk show host can jam congressional switchboards with 500,000 calls in one day. Thoughtful scholars justifiably fear that Gresham's law of the bad driving out the good is eroding the Miltonian principle of self-righting debate in our democracy. Practitioners have a key role in this process.

The public relations specialist contributes to the Miltonian principle of the self-righting process in a democracy, a principle embedded in historic decisions of the U. S. Supreme Court. The advocate's role is essential in a democracy that must be responsive to the public will and dependent on the reconciliation of public and private interests in a mutually rewarding manner. John W. Hill saw the role of the practitioner as that of the advocate. He once wrote, "We're primarily advocates and we draw upon a deep reservoir of experience in advocating our clients' causes."

In my teaching and writing over these some 45 years, I have repeatedly listed the pluses and minuses of the effects of public relations on society. These are:

Pluses:
1. By stressing to executives the need for public approval, practitioners improve the public conduct of the organizations they serve.
2. Practitioners serve the public interest by making all points of view heard in the public forum.
3. Practitioners serve our segmented, scattered society by using their talents of communication and mediation to replace misinformation with information, discord with concord.

Minuses:
1. Public relations has cluttered our already choked channels of communication with the debris of pseudo-events and phony sound bites that confuse rather than clarify. This is especially true of today's damaged political process.
2. Public relations has corroded our channels of communication on which the public must depend with cynicism and "credibility gaps."

Readers will find ample evidence of these pluses and minuses in the work of the innovative band of pioneers profiled in these pages. The overriding conclusion is the profound impact these counselors and their successors have had on our business life, our political life, our social and cultural life, and still have today. This influence can be seen in the birth of the modern Ku Klux Klan, which torments and divides our people today, in the dominance of today's political campaign consultant, in the popular recreations of contract bridge, motorboating, and skiing, now an "in" sport. The monuments super press agent Steve Hannagan built with his promotional skills dramatically illustrate the impact of this craft: He promoted the Memorial Day auto race at Indianapolis into the dominant Memorial Day celebration in the United States; he built the city of Miami Beach on a filled-in spit of land on the Atlantic Ocean with pictures of pretty girls; and he popularized skiing as a national sport with his promotion of the Sun Valley ski resort. The impact of public relations counseling can be seen in perhaps a more substantial way in the more socially responsible business leadership that emerged in the wake of the Depression and the New Deal. Generally the public responds unaware of the influence of the practitioner. He or she wields an unseen power.

ANTECEDENTS OF TODAY'S PRACTICE

The factors inducing the origin and development of public relations are many and complex. The use of communication to influence public opinion and human behavior is as old as civilization. Farm bulletins telling farmers how to grow their crops were being issued 1,800 years before Christ was born. The Greek theorists wrote about the importance of the *public will*. The Romans believed that "the voice of the people was the voice of God." Machiavelli wrote in his *Discoursi,* "Not without reason is the voice of the people compared to the voice of God." He coldly believed that the people must be either "caressed or annihilated." In medieval England the King had his Lord Chancellor as the "Keeper of the King's Conscience" to facilitate communication and settlement of grievances between the monarch and his people. The word *propaganda* was born in the 17th Century when the Catholic church set up its *Congregatio de Propaganda,* "congregation for propagating the faith." Although propaganda became a pejorative term in the wake of World War I, it continues to be a part of today's public relations in a very real sense. The two terms are still synonymous in many citizens' minds.

Press agentry in the United States is much older than the nation itself. In fact, the American talent for promotion can be traced back to the first settlements on the East Coast in the 16th Century. The exaggerated claims that often characterize publicity began with Sir Walter Raleigh's ill-fated effort to settle Roanoke Island off the Virginia coast. When Capt. Arthur Barlowe returned to England in 1584 from that desolate, swampy area, he reported to Raleigh, "The soile is the most plentiful, sweet, fruitful and wholesome of all the worlds." He even described the Indians as "most gentle, loving and faithful, voide of all guile or treason."

Typical of the use of publicity to lure settlers to the colonies was the extensive program initiated by Lord Oglethorpe and the Trustees of the Georgia Colony from 1732 to 1752. Georgia's publicity campaign included use of print media, pamphlets, sermons, and special events. A scholar's analysis of the Trustees' communication compared with today's principles of public opinion, persuasion, and public relations reveals successful use of target audiences, opinion leaders, and special events. As often is the case today, exaggerated promotional literature and poor communication with the colonists ultimately led to the failure of the Trustees' goals and the collapse of the colony.

Just as publicity was used to lure settlers to America's primitive lands, so was it used to lure their offspring to move West, first to the Alleghenies, then to the broad prairies of the Midwest, and finally, to the shores of the Pacific. Creation of the myth of that brave frontiersman, Daniel Boone, was perhaps the first successful job of "shirt stuffing" of the legion that were to follow. The legend of Daniel Boone was the work of John Filson, a Pennsylvania school teacher who acquired 12,000 acres of land in Kentucke [sic] and then set out to promote their settlement by writing a book, *The Discovery, Settlement, and Present State of Kentucke*, which included as an appendix the hair-raising adventures of the frontier scout. Only 33 pages of the book were given to the Boone narrative, but it was this heroic tale that sent the book into many printings and publication in France and Germany.

Public relations and organized fund raising have evolved together as partners in the efforts to influence public giving. The first systematic effort to raise money on this continent was for Harvard College in 1641 to "educate the heathen Indian." The college sent a begging mission to England to raise 500 pounds. The fund raisers found that they needed a document to make their case, and thus a pamphlet, "New England's First Fruits," became the first in an endless torrent of fund-raising literature.

More sophisticated beginnings of public relations in America are to be found in the American Revolution, which brought the struggle for power between the patrician-led patriots and the commercial-propertied Tories. Later efforts to gain public support were made during the conflict between the trade and property interests led by Alexander Hamilton and the planter–farmer bloc led by Thomas Jefferson, during the struggle between Jackson's agrarian frontiersmen and the financial forces of Nicholas Biddle, and during the searing, bloody Civil War.

The 20th-century developments in this field are directly tied to the power struggles evoked by the political reform movements from Theodore Roosevelt to Bill Clinton. These movements reflected strong tides of protest against entrenched power groups. The jockeying of political and economic groups created the need of each cause to muster public support.

The part played by Theodore Roosevelt in spurring the development of the public relations artillery in political and social battles has been too little noted. The colorful President was a master of the art and power of publicity. He was first to see the White House as a "bully pulpit" and used it to the hilt to vanquish his political foes. Roosevelt sensed the new-found power in the content of the popular muckraking magazines and the mass circulation daily newspapers.

The Publicity Bureau's first major account was to serve the railroads in their effort to defeat Roosevelt's legislation of 1906 to curb the railroads' abuse of the public interest. Then, as now, public relations agencies and officials were called on to promote the passage or defeat of legislation at the national and state capitols. With the growth of mass circulation newspapers and popular magazines in the late 19th Century and early 20th Century, Roosevelt's canny ability to dominate the front pages demonstrated a newfound power for those with causes to promote. Theodore Roosevelt's mastery of public relations profoundly shifted the power from the Congress to the Presidency, another example of the unseen power of this practice.

These political and social struggles intensify in times of crisis. The political and social wars in the Franklin D. Roosevelt era brought large advances in the use of public relations. To win support and compliance with his many New Deal action agencies created to deal with the Great Depression, Roosevelt greatly expanded the machinery of public relations in the Federal Government. His unrelenting attacks on Big Business as the cause of the nation's hard times and the Depression spurred development of public relations departments in corporations. These fierce political struggles born of Roosevelt's Revolution brought about the public relations specialty of campaign management. The story of Clem Whitaker and Leone Baxter, told in chapter 19, brought profound change to American politics and gave birth to a now dominant force in our nation's political process.

Another influential effect of the publicist who operates largely in the shadows off-stage was his or her role in settling our nation and creating the romantic aura that still surrounds the West — an aura that is continually exploited by the movies, TV, magazines, and by the National Rifle Association, which exploits heroic myths of the West to block needed gun control legislation. From the 1850s on, railroads and land developers used publicity, advertising, and free excursions to lure people to settle along their newly laid tracks. Charles Russell Lowell, who directed the Burlington Railroad's publicity campaign, launched in 1858, wrote, "We are beginning to find that he who buildeth a railroad west of the Mississippi must also find a population and build up business." He had good advice for today's practitioners, "We must blow as loud a trumpet as the merits of our position warrants." From then until the frontier closed late in the 19th Century, railroad publicity was a major force in moving people West to new lands and new lives.

The last two decades of the 19th Century brought other discernible beginnings of today's practice. It is here that we find the roots of a vocation that flowered in the seedbed years of 1900–1917.

A VOCATION IS BORN

We somewhat arbitrarily place the beginnings of the public relations vocation with the establishment of The Publicity Bureau in Boston in mid-1900, on the eve of the 20th Century, which brought the function to the scope and impact of a major industry employing some 150,000 persons and exerting great though unmeasured force on American economic, political, and social life. We recognize that to set an arbitrary date for the beginnings of this vocation is arguable. All history, including that of public relations, moves in a seamless web. The history of public relations cannot be fully told by simply saying that it grew out of press agentry. Nor can it be fully told in terms of the Ivy Lees, Pen Dudleys, John Hills, and Earl Newsoms. This effort to partially fill the void of knowledge of public relations' history does not tell the story of its evolution in society's major institutions. Nor does it record the role and influence of such corporate public relations giants as Paul Garrett, who built a strong program for General Motors, or Arthur W. Page, who, from 1927 to 1947, built the nation's most sophisticated and complete public relations program for American Telephone & Telegraph. We narrowed our focus to the pioneer agencies and their founders to keep the book within tolerable limits.

We have long held that the study of how public relations has evolved to meet society's changing needs will provide useful insights into public relations' function and worth. Even today many practitioners do not have a sense of their calling's history. This cripples their understanding of their role and purpose and undercuts their effectiveness. It also diminishes their sense of professionalism, yet professionalism is a goal for which practitioners strive unceasingly.

Published histories have usually telescoped and oversimplified this fascinating and complex story by emphasizing a few colorful personalities and their imaginations. We hope that this book will bring increased appreciation of the evolution of public relations as it was compelled and coerced by the mounting power of public opinion and increased appreciation of those who have gone before us in building this field. Public relations' essential function in managing our institutions of size, profit and nonprofit, becomes clearer with each passing day as we approach the 21st Century. The years ahead will be governed by an increasingly complex technology, instant communication through multiplying worldwide channels, and a resulting powerful and volatile public opinion that must be dealt with. Those issues are set forth in the introduction to Part I.

Historian Alan Raucher, in his seminal *Public Relations and Business 1900–1929,* wrote, "It should be clear from this survey of historical literature that an examination of the origins and development of public relations must proceed from several perspectives. As a business policy, public relations was related to both external and internal problems of modern corporations. The history of public relations must also be a history of a vocation whose practitioners specialized in the use of mass communications." He then commanded his successors, "The study of public relations, therefore, must be a history of ideas and a history of actual practices, an examination of the interrelationship between ideas and action." This your author has endeavored to do in this book.

How all this came about in the 20th Century is told here through profiles of the influential pioneers of today's practice. I can only hope that readers will find these stories of as much interest in their reading as I have had in their telling.

ACKNOWLEDGMENTS

In an effort of this magnitude and over a span of some 40 years, the author has accumulated a long list of large debts to many persons, many of whom are not here to receive my expressions of gratitude. To all who made this book possible, I owe a heartfelt debt of gratitude that these acknowledgments can only partially repay.

My first acknowledgment must go to Harold Burson, founder/chairman of the giant Burson-Marsteller, Inc. firm. Harold had bugged me several times in recent years about getting on with the history of public relations that I had started gathering material for in the mid-1950s. Finally, in early 1990, on a trip to Atlanta, he twisted my arm and brought me back to the typewriter, which resulted in this manuscript. He provided substantial research assistance, wise counsel, and support all the way.

Next I want to acknowledge the thorough, painstaking research that Dr. Karen Miller, then a PhD candidate at the University of Wisconsin, did for me over an 18-month period in the papers of John W. Hill and Earl Newsom, and for the research of secondary sources she did for the Whitaker and Baxter chapter.

I am also deeply grateful to the library staffs of the University of Georgia and the State Historical Society of Wisconsin. University of Georgia librarian William Gray Potter provided me with a convenient home and his congenial staff has been most helpful. The State Historical Society's keeper of the archives, Harry Miller, bent the rules all out of shape to make my work easier. Officials of the Society, which is my sentimental home, lent encouragement and help over these 40 years.

A sweeping salute goes to Mrs. Sandra Gary, who typed the final manuscript.

I owe a special debt of gratitude to Craig Lewis, vice chairman of Ogilvy Adams & Rinehart, New York City, who was the last one to turn off the lights in the Earl Newsom Company, and John R. "Jack" Newsom for their confidence in making Earl Newsom's papers available to me for this book, well ahead of their 1998 time seal on the papers.

In virtually every chapter, I had the assistance and advice of persons knowledgeable on the subject or the research of graduate students. I think it best to acknowledge this debt chapter by chapter:

Chapter 1.   James A. Nafziger and Robert L. Bishop (both of whom are now professors), who assisted with my research in their graduate school days in the 1950s.

Chapter 2. Two able graduate students, Charlotte Wittwer and Felice Michaels Levin, provided help on this chapter.

Chapters 3 and 6. The Ivy Lee chapters were carefully read by his son James W. Lee, now retired, long a member of the Ivy Lee-T. J. Ross firm. He saved me from many errors of fact. For content of these chapters I am indebted to Alyce Weck, a research assistant who worked in the Ivy L. Lee Papers at Princeton University. I also received substantial help from T. J. Ross in interviews and in granting me access to the Lee books, *Matter Sent Out*, and from Joseph Ripley and Carl Dickey for their insights.

Chapter 4. In writing the original article on which this chapter is based, I had an extensive interview with Hamilton Wright II, and extensive correspondence with his widow and with his son, Hamilton Wright III, who closed down the firm. They were most cooperative.

Chapter 5. The Pendleton Dudley chapter is based on interviews, correspondence, and a friendship that extended over several years in the 1950s. Herbert Bain, retired director of public relations of the American Meat Institute, supplied the information on Dudley's role in saving the meat industry in the early 1920s.

Chapters 7 and 8. These chapters are based on Edward L. Bernays' extensive writings, on the voluminous literature about him, a lengthy interview that was recorded by his secretary, considerable correspondence, and a friendship extending over 30 years.

Chapter 9. The John Price Jones chapter is based on my extensive research for *Fund Raising in the United States*, which was facilitated by the kindly, unfailing assistance of the archivists in the Baker Library, Harvard University. More recently, Lizz Frost, library assistant, supplied additional information.

Also I am indebted to Prof. Jack Barbash of the University of Wisconsin-Madison for his reading of the "Johnstown Steel Strike" section in the Jones chapter.

Chapter 10. A graduate student, William C. Adams, now professor at Florida International University, provided the research on Steve Hannagan's handling of Samuel Insull's "defense" when he was brought to trial for his financial peculations.

Chapter 11. This chapter is based on the Harry Bruno Papers in the Mass Communications History Center of the State Historical Society of Wisconsin, a long friendship, numerous interviews, and correspondence.

Chapter 12. Similarly this chapter is based on the William H. Baldwin III papers, numerous interviews, and a long, deep friendship. I am also indebted to a graduate student, then Lt. Col. John H. Forrest (now Lt. Gen. Forrest, USA Ret.) for his master's thesis on Baldwin's career and the correspondence it induced.

Chapter 13. For the accuracy and much of the detail on Ben Sonnenberg's career, I owe a large debt to John Scott Fones, who was his associate for a decade. Mr. Fones kindly read the first draft and saved me from many errors, and improved the chapter's readability.

Chapter 14. As indicated in the notes on sources, information in this chapter rests upon the prodigious research of another former graduate student, Col. John Shotwell of the U. S. Marine Corps. My debt to him is indeed large. Professor Thomas G. Dyer of the University of Georgia supplied the information on the Ku Klux Klan's takeover of Lanier University.

Chapters 15 and 16. The two chapters covering the significant career of John W. Hill are based primarily on the Hill Papers in the Mass Communications History Center and on a series of interviews with Hill and a few of his associates. Another major source was the master's thesis by a graduate student, Col. George F. Hamel, "John W. Hill Public Relations Pioneer," which I supervised and quote from at length. Mr. Hill fully cooperated with Colonel Hamel on this project. Ms. Elizabeth Ann Kovacs, formerly of the Public Relations Society of America, cheerfully supplied the information on the Counselor's Academy contained in chapter 16.

Chapters 17 and 18. For the Carl Byoir chapters I again owe a tremendous debt indeed to a former graduate student, Col. Robert J. Bennett, whose voluminous master's thesis in effect saved the Byoir papers for scholars. Bennett, through my good offices, was given access to the Byoir Papers, which are no longer available to public access. Their disposition is a bit of a mystery. By extensively quoting from these private papers, Bennett served well the cause of public relations history—as well as his mentor. Longtime friend and Byoir successor, George Hammond, also provided information and insights.

Chapter 19. For the Whitaker & Baxter chapter I was cheerfully assisted by Clem Whitaker, Jr., still active in the San Francisco advertising agency that his parents started. His help was crucial because the Whitaker and Baxter Papers are not yet available to scholars. For putting the role of the consultant into perspective in today's politics, I am indebted to a friend of more than 50 years, Prof. Leon D. Epstein of the University of Wisconsin-Madison, internatinally recognized authority on political parties.

Chapters 20, 21, and 22. As already indicated, I owe much gratitude to Craig Lewis for his willingness to break the 1998 time seal on the Earl Newsom Papers (through 1966), now in the Mass Communications History Center, and to Mr. Newsom's son, John R. Newsom, for his careful reading of the first drafts and making additional papers of his father available. I am also indebted to Mr. Lewis and William A. Lydgate for their careful reading of the Newsom chapters and the additional information they provided.

Also, for the chapter dealing with Newsom's counsel to Ford Motor Company and General Motors, I was provided information and guidance by John E. Sattler, long-time director of Ford's New York Office; the late

Paul Burns, long-time Ford public relations executive, a college classmate, and the late Anthony G. De Lorenzo, long-time vice president of public relations for General Motors. Professor David L. Lewis of the University of Michigan and his book, *The Public Image of Henry Ford*, were both helpful in putting the Ford years in perspective. Good friend Harry S. Ashmore, W. H. "Ping" Ferry, and Martin Quigley all provided assistance on the Ford Foundation chapter. Alvie Smith, former student and long-time GM public relations official, was most helpful in his reading of the GM section.

I am also heavily indebted to Prof. James Grunig of the College of Journalism, University of Maryland, and to Professor Ray Hiebert, also of the College of Journalism, University of Maryland, for their thoughtful and critical reading of the manuscript. Professor Hiebert is also editor of The *Public Relations Review*.

Finally, I gratefully acknowledge the guidance and cheerful cooperation of Hollis Heimbouch, senior editor, and Dave Salierno, production editor, of Lawrence Erlbaum Associates for seeing this volume through to publication. As the foregoing acknowledgments make abundantly clear, like most scholars, I am heavily indebted to graduate students who have inspired me, assisted me, and brought me enormous reward over the some 40 years of my academic career.

Scott M. Cutlip

PART I

THE SEEDBED YEARS OF COUNSELING, 1900-1919

The fundamental force setting the stage for the emergence of the first public relations agencies in the early 1900s in the United States was the wild, frenzied, and bold development of industry, railroads, and utilities in America's post-Civil War era. In 25 breathtaking years from 1875 to 1900, America doubled its population and jammed its people into cities, developed mass production, enthroned the machine, spanned the nation with rail and wire communications, developed the mass media of newspaper and magazines, and replaced the plantation baron with the titans of finance and princes of industry and the versatile frontiersman with the factory hand. All of this laid the foundation for a mighty industrial machine and large concentrations of wealth. By 1900, one tenth of the population owned nine tenths of the wealth.

The rise of powerful monopolies, the concentration of wealth and power, and the rough-shod tactics of the robber barons in exploiting human labor and the nation's resources brought a wave of protest and reform in the early 1900s. Contemporary public relations emerged out of the melee of the opposing forces in this period of the nation's rapid growth and emergence from isolationism into an imperial power. Eric Goldman observed in *Two-Way Street*, "Shouldering aside agriculture, large-scale commerce and industry became dominant over the life of the nation. Big Business was committed to the doctrine that the less the public knew about its business, the more efficient and profitable—even the more socially useful—the operations would be"

Not prying into business affairs was accepted as part of the prevailing laissez-faire philosophy of the 19th century. Business historian N. S. B.

1

Gras held, "American business in the Nineteenth Century went back to the exclusiveness of the Medieval Guild in its attitude toward the public". Edward L. Bernays, who opened the eighth agency in the summer of 1919 in New York City, suggested that the public didn't mind this because: "The men who headed the corporations were developing the country. They symbolized America's growth. They were heroes to man."

There are few faint sights of recognition of this need for "the expert in public relations" in the late 19th century. In 1888, the Mutual Life Insurance Company organized a "literary bureau" to put out publicity. In 1889, George Westinghouse, engaged in "The Battle of the Currents" with Thomas A. Edison, ably aided by Samuel Insull, hired a Pittsburgh newspaperman to defend and explain his new system of alternating current. In 1884, the American Medical Association was forced to employ publicists to counter the propaganda of the antivivisectionists, a public relations battle that rages today between scientists and animal lovers.

Even a leading trade journal of that time, *The Journalist*, recognized that a need for press agentry had become apparent. In an editorial of October 18, 1884, *The Journalist* admitted, "Journalism has come to such a state that any enterprise which depends to any extent upon advertising in the public press must have especial men hired solely for the purpose of working the press for notices, free advertising, and the like." It pointed out that not only does "the circus have its Tody Hamiltons and drama its Jerome Eddys, but the railroad and steamboat lines, and even some of the large hotels, employ men whose duty it is to see that the transportation line or hotel they represent is properly looked after in the newspapers." Press agents there were then, press agents there are today in large number. They were and are today a breed apart.

The growing awareness of the need to court public opinion, rather than contemptuously ignore it, emerged in the late 19th century. This was evident in the hard-hitting William McKinley–William Jennings Bryan Presidential campaign in 1896, a development reflecting the growing circulations of mass circulation daily newspapers and popular magazines. That campaign's intensive use of publicists marked the birth of modern political campaigning. Both parties set up headquarters in Chicago, recognition that the American population had moved West. From these headquarters flowed a heavy stream of pamphlets, posters, press releases, and other campaign propaganda, now a standard part of the American political campaign, though now diminished by the dominance of television in politics. William Jennings Bryan, a Democrat with little money, used the campaign train to carry his silver-tongued oratory to the people—an innovation that lasted through President Harry Truman's successful 1948 campaign.

William McKinley's heavily financed campaign won big and was viewed as a triumph of conservative capitalism and laissez faire. This big win for the rich turned to ashes with President McKinley's assassination and the assumption of power by "that damned wild cowboy," Theodore Roosevelt, whose consummate skill in public relations epitomized and dramatized the coming era of the public relations expert. In this fading era of "the public be damned," exploitation of the people and their resources was bound to bring, ultimately, protest and reform once the people were aroused. And aroused they would be with the development of a popular forum in the nation's press and magazines and utilization of this new national forum by the Muckrakers to expose the abuses of people, long hidden from their view. In turn, these attacks created the need for institutions and industries under attack to defend themselves in the court of public opinion as well as in the court of law. In his classic *The Growth of American Thought*, Historian Merle Curti wrote of this development, "Corporations gradually began to realize the importance of combating hostility and courting public favor. The expert in public relations was an inevitable phenomenon, in view of the services he could provide."

NEW CENTURY DAWNS AND A NEW VOCATION IS BORN

When Americans cheered the dawn of the new year on January 1, 1901, they were celebrating knowingly the arrival of a new year and a new century. Little did the celebrants realize that they were ushering in a wholly new era, a century in which travel would move from the horse and buggy and railroad to globe-girdling jets and travel to the moon. The early years of the 20th century were crammed with significant changes, breathtaking in their swiftness, mind-boggling in their scope. The momentous events of this era were to stimulate the birth of the public relations agency as the battle for the public's favor intensified. In fact, the first public relations agency, started in Boston in mid-1900, was born before the new century began. In 1900, the Republicans re-elected President William McKinley in a reaffirmation of the governmental policy of laissez faire. That same year in then faraway Germany, Kaiser Wilhelm made an ominous speech declaring that Germany would no longer suffer "political impotence and economic submissiveness" All these events impacted the development of the public relations vocation.

The dramatic changes that were to come were signaled and symbolized more by the assassination of President William McKinley in Buffalo, NY on September 6, 1901, than by the turn of the calendar. With him the old order expired. President Theodore Roosevelt's succession to the presidency marked, in the words of one historian, "the beginning of a new epoch for a people standing on the threshold of the most momentous century in human history." McKinley's death had ended, at least for a time, what William Allen White called "the alliance between government and business for the benefit of business." This meant that ultimately Big Business would have to win public favor rather than manipulate its way inside government. This brought what at first was called *the publicity business.*

These political, economic, and social changes came with quick-firing rapidity. America, then a nation of 76 million people, had shed its 19th century isolationism and moved into position as a world power. The modern corporation that was to provide the economic engine to pull America was born in 1901 when J. P. Morgan put together the giant United States Steel Company. Unlike his contemporaries, Morgan showed a keen awareness of the power of public opinion then bubbling up by selecting a public relations-minded jurist, Judge Elbert H. Gary, to head this combine and thus escape a government veto on antitrust grounds. Morgan showed the same astuteness when he brought Theodore N. Vail into the management of the American Telephone & Telegraph Co. to halt its deteriorating public position and blunt the growth of independent phone companies then springing up as Bell patents were expiring. With U. S. Steel was born the modern corporation that came to be damned for its abuses of its workers and its customers. In the view of pioneer sociologist E. A. Ross, the corporation permitted "men to commit with a clear conscience crimes which they would have abhorred as individuals."

The year 1901 saw Henry Ford, who was to change the ways of American life forever, build the motor car and market it with great public relations skill. Ford in his younger, more flexible days knew the value of publicity and used it in positive ways to emerge from the pack of automakers now lost in the mists of history. Also the year 1901 brought the Texas Oil Boom that was to provide the gasoline for the 20th century's motor cars, trucks, planes, and trains. The year 1901 saw the Navy give up its carrier pigeons and rely on Marconi's wireless. Two years later the Wright Brothers made their historic flights at Kitty Hawk, NC. Their discovery of powered flight remade the world as Henry Ford's assembly-line manufacture remade America.

A NATIONAL FORUM EMERGES

In the late 19th century and early 20th, a national forum emerged that permitted swift communication of news and a platform for the political reformers and the Muckrakers to expose the abuses of the public by Big Business and corrupt government. The Associated Press (AP), in the modern sense, dates from 1900 though it can trace its history back to 1848. In its first 40 years or so, the AP was a monopoly and thus early begat opposition in Scripps' United Press, started in 1907, and Hearst's International News Services, started in 1909. The advent of the national press association brought a quick exchange of news and opinion across the nation and thus facilitated the agitation for change now abroad in the land. The new AP displaced a series of regional press associations.

The popular, widely circulated magazine was, likewise, a 20th century development. Before 1880, there were only five important magazines, *Harper's Scribner's, Century*, the *Atlantic*, and the *North American Review*. In the 19th century, these magazines had small circulations and were mostly literary, not political, in their content. By 1890, the list of nationally circulated magazines had been augmented by the *Ladies Home Journal*, *Munsey's*, and *Cosmopolitan*. S. S. McClure, who was to play an influential role in the wave of reform that broke across the nation in the 1900s, started *McClure's* on the heels of Benjamin Orange Flower's *Arena* started in 1899. The Weinbergs in their books *The Muckrakers*, termed Flowers "the editorial dean of democracy," a tireless agitator for social reform. Flowers and McClure set off a wave of cheaply priced magazines with large circulations. Frank Munsey once estimated that between 1893 and 1900 the 10¢ magazine increased the magazine-buying public from 250, 000 persons to 750, 000 persons.

The *Ladies Home Journal* broke the million-circulation mark in 1903, the first to reach that pinnacle. But it was the muckraking magazines that stimulated political protest to bring governmental reforms to curb the abuses of the railroads, banks, and corporations and thus give rise to the public reactions counselor. As Arthur and Lila Weinberg wrote in *The Muckrakers*, a collection of the significant writings of this band of crusading journalists from 1902 to 1912, "A nation dominated by laissez-faire, dedicated to the status quo and paying homage to the dollar as a symbol of success, was shocked by a group of writers into awareness that this was not the best of all possible worlds."

The reformers and the Muckrakers now had a national forum, and they used it to the hilt. *Muckraking* has been defined as "the opposing of evils for the purpose of promoting social justice." The term was applied to the crusading journalists of the early 1900s by President Theodore Roosevelt in a moment of pique, despite their paving the way for his reform of the nation's food and drug laws, railroad reform legislation, and trust-busting. These Muckrakers—Lincoln Steffans who exposed the corruption in the nation's cities, Ida Tarbell who exposed the abuses of Rockefeller's Standard Oil monopoly, Upton Sinclair who exposed the foul conditions in the nation's meatpacking plants, and others—underlined the fact that the dominant trends in America were running counter to American traditions of morality, liberty, and equality of opportunity. Perhaps the first of these muckraking articles was published in the *Arena* in August 1901; entitled

"The Great Conflict," described the great disparity of wealth in a day when Andrew Carnegie was netting an income of $23 million in a year whereas the average worker in his steel mill was barely able to earn $500. C. E. Reiger in his *The Era of the Muckrakers* vividly described the abuses of people by Big Business of that period this way:

> It was true that industry was as reckless of human life as it was of natural resources. Some five thousand workers were either killed or badly maimed each year, and yet an inventor declared that he could see a time-saving invention in twenty places but a life-saving device in none. Stockholders did not mean to wear out children, maim workmen, to defraud customers, to pollute the ballot, or debauch public officials; yet thanks to the impersonality of the corporation and to the narrowness of the moral code, they frequently brought about these evils and worse.

A CASE IN POINT

Published in 1906, *The Jungle*, Upton Sinclair's shocking book describing the filthy, unsanitary conditions in Chicago's meat-packing plants, brought swift repercussions from an aroused public. The wave of revulsion that came with *The Jungle's* publication brought new regulatory legislation by the federal government and the first public relations efforts in the meat industry. Sinclair later said that he was aiming at America's social conscience, but he hit the nation in the pit of its stomach. Meat packers claimed that Sinclair "selected the worst possible conditions as typical of the general conditions existing in the Chicago abattoirs." Congress, responding to the public's anger and concern, passed the Federal Meat Inspection Act. President Roosevelt personally campaigned for passage of this act that made federal ante- and postmortem inspection mandatory for all meat in interstate and foreign commerce. The meat packers' response was to form their first national association, the American Meat Packers Association, forerunner of the American Meat Institute formed at the end of World War I, an institute in which pioneer Pendleton Dudley played a major role. His role in bringing stability, sanitation, and profit to the meat industry is told in chapter 5. Here, then, in microcosm is the role of the Muckrakers in stimulating birth of public relations and bringing regulatory government to the nation.

PUBLICITY NEEDED IN MARKETING

Today public relations is intensively used to support the marketing function of those who provide goods and services to the public. In fact, too many in our field see product promotion as *the* main function of public relations, erroneously so. The need for publicity to be used as an adjunct of advertising in promoting the sale of goods became apparent just before the turn of the century when merchandising came into the 20th century. In 1899, the National Biscuit Company decided to take the cracker out of the barrel in country and small-town stores and put it in "a sanitary package." Nabisco retained the nation's oldest advertising agency, N. W. Ayer & Co., to advertise its Uneeda Biscuit in the sanitary package. In its revolutionary ad campaign, Ayer quickly discovered that it was selling more than packaged crackers, it was selling *change*. The Ayer campaign on behalf of what became Nabisco was, to quote its historian, Ralph Hower, "the first to feature a staple food, ready for consumption, and sold in individual packages. It involved creation of an air-tight package, a distinctive brand name, and trade-mark." In bringing this revolutionary change to a frontier America, Ayer quickly realized that it would take a coordinated plan for reaching the general public through newspapers, magazines, streetcar advertisements, posters, and painted signs. It sold sanitation, then sold the crackers. This was the beginning of Ayer's pioneering in the use of publicity to support its advertisers' marketing campaigns. By 1908, the promotional publicity work had become so heavy that it was taken out of the copy department and set up as a separate department. Gradually this work in the Ayer agency grew, and in 1920, a Publicity Bureau was set up, the first in a major advertising agency—A small bore development compared to today's mega combines of advertising and public relations agencies.

Thus was the stage set for the emergence of the publicity agency that evolved into public relations counseling over the next half century, termed by *The Bookman* as "the newly grown bastard of journalism." That publication in its December 1906 issue in an unsigned article continued:

It concerns itself frequently with the efforts of shrewd businessmen to allay public indignation brought upon them by revelation of their unfair dealings.

It is employed to provide for their secret or open representatives in municipal, state, or national governments such real or seeming support in the attitude of the people as to sustain these unliveried retainers against a rising tide of public sentiment.

Pendleton Dudley, venerable public relations pioneer who started the fifth agency in 1909 at the urging of his friend Ivy Lee, argued with the author and in print that it was the emergence of the mass circulation daily newspaper and 10¢ magazine that led to the establishment of the first publicity agencies, not the muckrakers. He wrote, "Doubtless the magazine articles by Ida Tarbell did play their part in creating the new profession . . . however other and more significant developments . . . were more responsible for its initial expression and particularly for its later growth into the function or procedure as we now know it." Perhaps on the latter point he is correct, but his own history, told in chapter 5, gives a hollow ring to his argument. As told in that chapter, his "first client of note" was the Trinity Episcopal Church of lower Manhattan, then being scalded in a series of articles in the *New York World* for its exploitation of the tenants in its large tenement holdings and the housing of prostitutes therein. The histories of the first seven publicity agencies formed in the years 1900–1918 demonstrate that the confluence of the death of laissez-faire government, with the emergence of a popular national forum and its use by the muckrakers to expose the widespread abuses of power on the part of Big Business and Government caused the institutions under public assault to turn to former newspapermen to tell their story to the public and rely less on their lawyers and lobbyists "to fix things".

The basic shift from sole reliance on lawyer-lobbying to influence legislation and regulation can be seen in the history of the railroads in the early 1900s. In 1906, the nation's railroads employed the Publicity Bureau to wage a national propaganda campaign in what proved to be a futile effort to head off President Roosevelt's railroad reform legislation, the Hepburn Act. Roosevelt's skillful use of the press and stump carried the day. In 1910, the Eastern Railroads once again turned to their lawyers to get them a 5% rate increase from the Interstate Commerce Commission. Again to no avail. When Ivy Lee returned to the Pennsylvania Rail Road in 1912 after a 2-year leave in London, he persuaded the railroad executives to take their case to the people to win support for the rate increase. The executives agreed that they had failed because they had not told their story to the public. Lee's campaign for public support won the rate increase in 1914. This was the genesis of the coupling of public relations with legislative relations to attain governmental favors or stay the hand of government. Historian Arthur S. Link summed it up:

> Americans in the early 1900s launched a virtual crusade on all levels of government to revitalize democracy, bring the economic machinery under control, and find an answer to the twin evils of privilege and poverty. The years before the First World War were, finally, a period when Christian moralism subdued the crass materialism of the Gilden Age, and morality and righteousness became the keynotes of politics.

Contagious indeed was the spirit of charge, change, and reform. Public relations was given birth by these forces.

The spirit of the times, a spirit that gave impetus to the importance of public opinion, was caught by President Woodrow Wilson proclaiming his doctrine of "The New Freedom." "We are witnessing a renaissance of public spirit, a reawakening of sober public opinion, a renewal of the power of the people, the beginning of an age of thoughtful reconstruction that makes our thoughts hark back to the age in which democracy was set up in America.

NOTES ON SOURCES

Information for this introduction was based on a wide reading of history of the early 20th Century when public relations first emerged as a identifiable vocation. The following sources were used: Ray Stannard Baker, "Railroads on Trial," *McClure's Magazine,* Vol. 26, March, 1906 (this article also can be found in Arthur and Lila Weinbergs' *The Muckrakers, A Collection of Articles That Fueled the Revolt of the Progressive Era*, Simon & Schuster, 1961); Edward L. Bernays, *Autobiography of an Idea: Memoirs of Edward L. Bernays, Simon & Schuster, 1965;* Merle Curti, *The Growth of American Thought* 3rd. ed. Harper & Row, 1964; Elmer E. Cornwell, Jr., *Presidential Leadership of Public Opinion,* Indiana University Press, 1963 (traces the rise of Presidential Government that started with President Theodore Roosevelt's mastery of public relations); Pendleton Dudley, "Current Beginnings of PR," *Public Relations Journal,* Vol. 8, August, 1952; Eric F. Goldman, *Two-Way Street,* 1948 (a sketchy history of the field's origins), N. S. B. Gras, *Business History of the United States about 1650 to 1950s* (a 3-volume transcript edited by his widow, Ethel Gras, and distributed by Lincoln Educational Foundation, 1967).

Richard Hofstader, *The Age of Reform*, Knopf, 1955, who wrote that "It was muckraking that brought the diffuse malaise into focus", Ralph. W. Hower, *The History of an Advertising Agency, N. W. Ayer & Sons at Work*, Harvard University Press, 1939 (This agency pioneered in use of publicity to supplement advertising), Arthur S. Link, *Woodrow Wilson and the Progressive Era,* Harper, 1954 (traces development of Wilson's New Freedom. Also see his *American Epoch*, Knopf, 1965); Luther B. Little, "The Printing Press in Politics," *Munsey's Magazine,* Vol. 23, September 23, 1900, Peter Lyon, *Success Story, The Life and Times of S. S. McClure*, Charles Scribner's Sons, 1963, biography of the leader of the Muckraking Movement; Alan Raucher, *Public Relations and Business, 1900–1929*, Johns Hopkins Press (details emergence of public relations in its early years); C. C. Regier, *The Era of the Muckrakers,* University of North Carolina Press, 1932 (neglects role of major daily newspapers in fomenting public revolt); Edward A. Ross, *Changing America: Stuidies in Contemporary Society*, CenturyCompany, 1914 (Thoughts of a pioneer sociologist and strong critic of the ways of Big Business).

Upton Sinclair, *Autobiography,* 1st. ed. Harcourt Brace & World, 1962. This remarkable man re-emerges in chapter 19 as the catylst for the modern campaign consultant, today a major field of public relations. William Allen White, *A Puritan in Babylon, the Story of Calvin Coolidge,* Macmillan Company, 1938. White was a colorful Kansas editor of those years.

Chapter 1

The Nation's First Publicity Agency

The nation's first publicity agency, the Publicity Bureau, was organized on the eve of the 20th century that has brought the development and widespread utilization of public relations skills. The firm was founded in Boston, where Harvard University fund raisers and Revolutionary hell raisers had fashioned primitive but effective methods of influencing public opinion centuries before.

The Publicity Bureau lasted some 12 years before it disappeared into the sands of oblivion with the consequence that its history is little known among public relations practitioners. The popular impression in the craft is that the firm founded by George F. Parker, longtime publicity aide to Grover Cleveland, and Ivy L. Lee late in 1904 was the nation's first public relations (PR) firm. The Publicity Bureau left few records in its wake. This may explain its neglect by historians.

The Bureau was started sometime in mid-1900 by George V. S. Michaelis, Herbert Small, and Thomas O. Marvin. Its founding went unrecorded in the Boston press, and no records giving a precise date of organization have been found. *The Fourth Estate*, from June 1900 to July 1901, makes no mention of this journalistic innovation. Nor is it listed in *The New York Times Index* from 1899 to 1905. The *Boston City Directory* does not list the firm in its 1900 edition but does for the year beginning July 1, 1901. A Publicity Bureau advertisement in the 1901 directory lists Michaelis as president, Marvin as treasurer, and Small as general secretary, and gives addresses for the Bureau in Boston, Paris, and Washington.

James Drummond Ellsworth, who subsequently joined the firm, recorded the start of the Bureau as "the early nineteen hundreds." That the firm started in 1900 is certain.

On September 27, 1900, Michaelis, the president, wrote a letter to Harvard President Charles W. Eliot enclosing a publicity release prepared by Herbert Small to publicize Harvard's system of medical visitation for students and its Prospect Union. Michaelis concluded his letter with this assertion: "We have met with very satisfactory success in publication of the articles, and I shall be glad to show you the clippings upon your return."

Although the Publicity Bureau and President Eliot did not conclude a formal contract until early October 1900, it appears from subsequent correspondence that the firm began providing publicity service to Harvard in September. On October 9, 1900, Michaelis wrote President Eliot as follows:

> In the matter of payment, we understand that you are to pay the Bureau $200 a month for our professional services, and those of an artist where drawings seem to be required. That this sum is to include everything except the payment of mechanical work, such as printings and the making of cuts, and the postage necessary to send out the articles themselves to the various papers, which items are to be charged to the University.

This surely is the first fixed fee plus charges for out-of-pocket expenses to be set by a public relations agency, a pattern of charging still used by firms today. President Eliot replied to Michaelis the same day accepting these terms but reserving the right to stop the service at any time. On October 11, 1900, Michaelis wrote Eliot:

> We beg to acknowledge the receipt of your letter of October 9th. It was our understanding also that the charge should begin with the month of September; and we agree that it is quite reasonable that if anything occurs, as you say, to demonstrate the inexpediency of our understanding, you should be at liberty to stop our service before the expiration of the four or five months which we have talked of.

George Vail Sheppard Michaelis who took the lead in founding the nation's first public relations firm was born June 21, 1873, at the U.S. Arsenal in Watertown, Massachusetts, where his father was stationed as a major in the U.S. Army. Michaelis worked at part-time jobs in industry while completing high school. His education ended with his graduation from Augusta, Maine's high school in 1891. He then took a job on the *Kennebec Journal* but was soon lured to Boston where he landed a job on the *Boston Globe* and *Boston Journal*. He held several different jobs in editorial, circulation, and advertising departments of that paper before leaving it in 1900 to launch the Publicity Bureau.

It appears that Michaelis left the Publicity Bureau in 1909, but this is not certain. In August 1914, *Survey* published an article by him entitled "The Westinghouse Strike. 'A Matter of Class-Consciousness and not of Dollars-and-Cents.' " A *Survey* editor's note says Michaelis had been an officer of manufacturing corporations since 1909 and adds that he is "now managing a selling agency," associated with a group working out plans for an "Industrial Peace Movement." In the 1915 *New York City Directory*, a George V. S. Michaelis is listed as a civil engineer at Garden City, Long Island. In the 1917 directory, the same name is listed as secretary of the Bell Products Co. of Garden City. This company apparently made humidors, at least that is what is listed after the firm name in the directory.

There is evidence to suggest that Michaelis changed his name to George Woodbridge during World War I to avoid being confused with the chancellor of Germany, Dr. George Michaelis, who served in that post from July 14, 1917, to November 3, 1917. Such an act would have been understandable in view of the bitter anti-German prejudice of that period. Ellsworth wrote in *Unforgotten Men* that George V. S. Michaelis changed his name to George Woodbridge, the family of his mother, when the other Michaelis became chancellor. The name George V. S. Michaelis reappears in the 1920–1921 *New York City Directory* where he is listed as secretary of Bell Products at 90 West Street. Neither Michaelis nor Bell is listed in the 1922–1923 directory.

Ellsworth, later to make his mark as a public relations pioneer with AT&T, described Michaelis as a man with a "brilliant and restless mind which raced tumultously ahead of the minds of most people. Sometimes he was sound and sometimes he was not, but he was always interesting." According to Ellsworth:

> Being full of new ideas and being a rapid talker, it was he (Michaelis) who persuaded President Eliot of Harvard, Doctor Henry Pritchett of the Massachusetts Institute of Technology, and the heads of shipyards, railroads, steamship lines and various enterprises to employ the services of the Publicity Bureau. The campaigns outlined by Michaelis were perhaps apt to be flamboyant, but the written matter, edited and sent out by Small, was of so high a quality as to be of real value to the periodical which received it.

In another place, Ellsworth asserted that Michaelis "was a young man of many expedients."

Small, the firm's general secretary, brought editorial experience and a scholarly background to this pioneering effort. He complemented the more flamboyant, aggressive Michaelis in many ways. Small was born in Milwaukee, Wisconsin, on May 15, 1869, the son of Simeon and Elizabeth Doane Cogswell Small. He attended the Boston Latin School and was a student at Harvard from 1887 to 1891 but did not graduate. Upon leaving Harvard, he went to work as a reporter on the *Boston Herald*. About 1896, he helped to organize the Small, Maynard, and Co. firm to publish books. It was this firm that brought out the first two Mr. Dooley books by Finley Peter Dunne. The Small publishing house also edited guide books for the Boston Public Library and the Congressional Library. It is worth noting that it was the Small, Maynard firm that published Walter Dill Scott's pioneering books in advertising — *The Theory of Advertising* in 1903 and *The Psychology of Advertising* in 1908. The firm continued for many years past Small's departure.

Small died December 12, 1903, of typhoid pneumonia. His obituary lists him as secretary of the Germanic Museum Association of Harvard University. There is evidence in the Eliot–Publicity Bureau correspondence that this task was taken on as part of the firm's service to Harvard. Ellsworth described Small as "a Harvard man with a fine literary sense."

Just which role the third founding partner, Thomas O. Marvin, played in this pioneering enterprise is not clear. He was listed as treasurer on Bureau letterheads from the start and was associated with the enterprise at least through 1906. Marvin was a New Englander whose career spanned the ministry, newspaper work, public relations, and a long term as chairman of the U.S. Tariff Commission. Born in Portsmouth, New Hampshire, Marvin received a bachelor of divinity degree from Tufts College in 1888 and spent the next 6 years as a minister in the Universalist Church. In 1894, he quit the ministry to become a writer for the *Boston Journal* where he got to know Michaelis.

Marvin served variously as a reporter, a literary editor, and an editorial writer on the *Journal*. Whether he actually quit the *Journal* in 1900 when the Bureau was started is not known; Marvin's *Who's Who data*, presumably furnished and checked by him, does not mention the Bureau and indicates that he worked on the newspaper until 1911 when he became secretary of the Home Market Club. This was a Boston protectionist club organized in 1888. For 2 of the years he was with this organization, Marvin edited its monthly magazine, *The Protectionist*. Marvin's work for the Home Market Club was largely that of propagandist for high tariff protection. A 1913 Congressional Hearing revealed that this organization had distributed more than 100 million pamphlets in a 25-year period. In 1929, Marvin was called before a Senate investigating committee to account for his actions on the Tariff Commission and his work for the Home Market Club.

Marvin left the Home Market Club in 1921 when President Warren G. Harding appointed him to the U.S. Tariff Commission. Marvin, a conservative Republican and protectionist in tariff matters, served as vice-chairman in 1921 and as chairman from 1922 to 1930. He died August 21, 1952, at the age of 84.

Among those soon "drawn into this interesting enterprise was the young reporter from the (*Boston*) *Herald*" — James Drummond Ellsworth. He was one of the first but certainly far from the last of newspapermen to be lured to public relations work by higher pay. Ellsworth was already doing press agentry on the side to supplement his meager *Herald* salary when Michaelis offered him a job. Ellsworth recorded in his memoirs, "Much as I enjoyed my newspaper work at the time, the small pay kept me in hot water and it was only by outside work that I managed to make both ends meet." Ivy Lee gave the same reason for quitting the *New York World* in 1903. It has been ever thus.

Surprisingly, Ellsworth found the editorial standards in the Publicity Bureau more exacting than those at the Herald. He wrote in the third person, "In publicity work he encountered entirely new standards. He must thoroughly understand what he was writing about, a new experience for the average reporter. Moreover his copy must bear the careful scrutiny of say, a professor pyrometry, of the president of the institute, of Herbert Small, and of the editors of the publications which were expected to give it space in their columns." Apparently the standards of the Boston press were not high in those days.

Ellsworth was born in Millford, Massachusetts, on October 14, 1863, the son of Alfred and Angelina Grimke Clementine Cook Ellsworth. He did his preparatory work at Knox Academy, Galesburg, Illinois, and earned his college degree at Colorado College. Ellsworth's father, a Congregational minister, imposed a strict regimen of prayer and church-going on James as a boy, and it was to escape this strict home life that he went to Colorado College. After his graduation in 1884, Ellsworth became editor of the *Coal Creek* (Colorado) Enterprise, a weekly. A year later, in 1885, he took a job as a reporter on the *Denver Republican*, a job he held for 4 years. In 1890, he returned to his beloved New England to work as a reporter on the *Boston Herald*. He supplemented his *Herald* pay by stringing for the *New York Recorder* and taking an occasional press agent assignment. He recorded that he once received $50 for writing a column about Madame Nordica when she came to Boston with the Abbey, Schoeffle, and Grau Opera Company. The next week he did not get as much space, and she cut his stipend to $25. Ellsworth admitted, "Probably I was not much use to my paper in those days, particularly as I had other outside writing on hand."

Late in 1900, Ellsworth quit newspaper work to join the Publicity Bureau and to enter a new field of journalism in which he would spend the next 30 years of his life and, in the process, contribute to the shaping of this new field. Ellsworth was associated with the Bureau until 1907 when he got a job with the American Telephone & Telegraph Co., a Publicity Bureau client since 1903. In 1907, Theodore N. Vail, one of the nation's first public relations-minded businessmen, was put in the presidency of AT&T by the J. P. Morgan led banker group after it had finally wrested control of the bumbling communications giant from its previous owners.

It is apparent from Ellsworth's memoirs that the Bureau landed the then small Massachusetts Institute of Technology as a client shortly after it had got Harvard to sign an agreement. Ellsworth wrote:

President Pritchett (of M. I. T) needed publicity at that time and was willing to pay for it. So did the Boston Elevated, the Fore River Ship Yard, and many other concerns, educational, philanthropic and commercial. As the Herald had educated me in human nature, the Publicity Bureau began my elementary education in science and industry. My first article, which was syndicated gratuitously to a number of Sunday papers throughout the country, went into the matter of pyrometry as taught at Tech, at that time located on Boylston Street. . . . From pyrometry I passed into geology, then into chemistry and finally into what I liked best of all, naval architecture.

This also indicates that the Boston Elevated and the Fore River Ship Yard were among the early clients of the Publicity Bureau. The Boston Elevated was the first American street railway company to establish a publicity bureau. J. Harvey White who was selected to head the department, is among the legion of lost public relations pioneers. A publication, commenting on White's work after he had been in this job 20 years, said, "During the many years in which J. Harvey White as publicity agent has been dealing with the Boston newspapers, his sole idea has been to render service to them. . . . Mr. White furnishes nothing that has not real news value. Nor does he try to use press agent methods . . ." It seems evident that there was wider appreciation of the need for this new function of providing publicity service to the press in Boston than in other large cities in these early years of the new century.

After Small's death in 1903, the Publicity Bureau was reorganized under the name of Michaelis, Ellsworth, & Stegman. The new partner was H. M. Stegman, of whom little is known. His name vanished from the letterheads a year later. Other names listed on the firm's 1904 letterhead are those of Louis A. Coolidge, Frederick G. Fassett, and Earl W. Mayo. Various letterheads were used in the Bureau's correspondence with Harvard, now held in the Harvard University Archives. A 1905 letterhead is headed Michaelis & Ellsworth, Industrial Statistics, and a 1906 letterhead reads, "George V. S. Michaelis, Specialist in Relations With Consumers." The firm name of Publicity Bureau also continued to be used by Michaelis and does not fade from recorded view until at least 1911 when it is listed on the blacklist of the American Newspaper Publishers Association (ANPA) in its antipublicity bulletin. ANPA's antipublicity Bulletin No. 2220, dated June 25, 1910, lists the Publicity Bureau's address as Press Building, Boston, and lists its clients as Boston Elevated Railroad Co., the New England Conservatory of Music, Harvard University, and AT&T.

It is interesting to see the client names of Harvard and AT&T. reappear on the Publicity Bureau list in the ANPA bulletin of 1910 because the Bureau lost both of these clients in the days of Michaelis and Ellsworth. President Charles W. Eliot of Harvard was a shrewd student of public opinion and thus knew the value of public relations. He was also a tough bargainer where Harvard funds were involved. In his inaugural address, Eliot said this of the duties of a university president:

> He must . . . influence public opinion toward advancement of learning; an . . . anticipate the due effect on the University of the fluctuations of public opinion on educational problems . . . (and) of the gradual alteration of social and religious habits in the community. The University must accommodate itself promptly to significant changes in the character of the people for whom it exists.

BUREAU LOSES HARVARD ACCOUNT

President Eliot, who knew the value of publicity, was an exacting and demanding person who insisted on accurate releases. The Publicity Bureau's work for Harvard did not go smoothly, and in 1902 or thereabouts, President Eliot quit paying the Bureau for the work it did for Harvard. Apparently the Bureau kept on providing service for the prestige of having Harvard as a client. Ellsworth said, "For a time the (Harvard) University paid for the bureau's services, but eventually President Eliot said that the prestige of working for Harvard was so valuable that we could afford to do his work for nothing, and we had to agree with him."

Much of the Bureau's correspondence with President Eliot is given to promoting its accomplishments on behalf of Harvard and explaining matters that apparently drew Eliot's ire. On May 4, 1901, Herbert Small wrote Eliot a 17-page letter outlining the concepts guiding the new firm, stressing the value of its services, and apologizing for "certain omissions in the service during the preceding three months." On April 1, 1902, Small wrote Jerome D. Greene, Eliot's secretary, soothing the latter's ruffled feelings over a photo mix-up and concluding his letter with this paragraph indicating that the Bureau was no longer being paid: "I beg that you will pardon the length of this letter written regarding a comparatively inconsiderable matter, but although our relations with the University are not now formal I should be sorry to think that there was less responsibility on our part toward the University in all matters, considerable or inconsiderable, than when we were on the Bursar's books."

Apparently some of the Bureau's continued volunteer efforts were unauthorized. On May 11, 1903, Greene wrote Small in response to the latter's offer to Eliot to assist in publicizing Harvard's School of Education in connection with a forthcoming convention of the National Educational [sic] Association as follows: "As to what the Publicity Bureau might do, or might have done, incidentally for the National Educational Association, the President is not prepared to say. . . . As to the School of Education, President Eliot directs me to say that the announcement to which you refer was unauthorized and premature."

Much of the subsequent correspondence between the Bureau and President Eliot are efforts to see the busy president or to get him to authorize a fee for the Bureau's work. On May 27, 1903, Michaelis wrote, "In accordance with our conversation of this morning I wish to propose that the University make an appropriation of one thousand ($1, 000) dollars for the year beginning 1 June, 1903, in order that we may be in a position to strengthen and enrich our publicity service or work of popular publication for the University." Such a fee was not forthcoming from Harvard because on July 7, 1903, Michaelis wrote again to say, "Our cash outlay on the Harvard service is steadily mounting and we are now facing a rather considerable call for cuts [photoengraving] throughout the country; a call which is to the advantage of the University but which we naturally hesitate to meet on account of the additional expense involved."

These pleas to Eliot were unavailing as indicated in this note from Greene, his secretary, to Michaelis on April 22, 1904, "President Eliot directs me to say, in reply to your letter of April 21, that he will be glad to see you . . . if you think it will be worth your while to have a talk with him. He directs to add, however, that if you have any proposition to make involving the expenditure of money for publicity purposes, the interview will not be worth your while, as such expenditure is absolutely out of the question at present."

Undaunted, Michaelis kept trying for the next 2 years. On January 12, 1905, he wrote Eliot, "It seems almost impossible to break our sympathetic connection with the University. I have not lost hope of its some day being restored to an official connection." In this letter, Michaelis proudly told Eliot, "The new heads of our three offices — Boston, New York, and Washington — are Harvard men. Mr. Frederick Roy Day, '92, in New York, and Mr. Louis A. Coolidge, '83, in Washington. Mr. Martin will also be our Editorial Manager and Mr. Day the head of our Research Department." The last record of communication between Eliot and Michaelis is agreement on an appointment for Friday, May 4, 1906. There the story appears to end.

Harvard may have been the first client lost by a public relations firm, but it was far from the last.

The loss of Harvard as a paying client was offset in 1903 when Michaelis persuaded Frederick P. Fish, the new president of AT&T to employ the bureau's service that same year. Earlier in 1901, Fish had succeeded the tactless John E. Hudson who had brought AT&T much ill will by his public-be-damned attitudes as president of the Bell System. Fish's employment of the Publicity Bureau came some months after Theodore N. Vail had been brought back to the telephone company by the J. P. Morgan interests as a director. Vail's views carried great weight with Fish, and Vail was keenly aware of the importance of good public relationships to long-run business success. He may well have been behind the decision of AT&T to take this historic first step in what was to become, ultimately, one of the nation's most successful and sophisticated public relation programs. Ellsworth sensed this when he wrote:

> Thus a company that had previously been the most secretive, spent good money to have their affairs brought to the public's attention. This right-about change in policy was not, without its underlying causes. The public is inclined to consider any secretive undertaking as mysterious, and as the next step, any mystery as suspicious. This had been true in the case of the Bell Telephone Companies when they concealed perfectly harmless facts. That people thought their secrecy was to cover up discreditable conditions was the management's own fault. And when independent telephone promoters, capitalizing upon the Bell's unpopularity began to build competing and quite unnecessary systems, it was again the management's own fault, because in respect to public sentiment the management had a blind eye. The Bell Companies . . . faced a crisis and Fish, a lawyer rather than business man, fully realized it.

Here we see the wave of revolt, fired by the writing of the muckrakers, then sweeping the country against Big Business bringing one of the nation's large firms to recognize the necessity of systematically dealing with aroused public opinion by having a planned program of public relations.

Ellsworth, assigned to do the Bureau's work for AT&T (at that time still headquartered in Boston), recorded that Fish gave him wholehearted cooperation. This communications giant, which has had its own opinion research department since 1931, early saw the need for systematically gauging public opinion. Walter Allen, who acted as a liaison officer for the company in matters of public information, collected and studied newspaper clippings from the nation's press. When Ellsworth started on this account, he found that about 90% of these articles were antagonistic to AT&T. "After we began to scatter seeds of real information through the press, I kept an eye on Allen's clippings . . . and I was encouraged as those which were antagonistic diminished to eighty percent, then to seventy, sixty percent and still lower." Fish soon started sending Ellsworth on trouble-shooting field trips, and for 4 years he was on the road much of the time.

In 1907, Vail succeeded Fish as president when the Morgan forces gained full control of AT&T. Shortly thereafter Vail dropped the Bureau's services. Vail became angered with the Bureau when he discovered that the Bureau "had carelessly taken credit for publications which had emanated from Col. George Harvey who had been employed on similar lines without the knowledge of the bureau management." Again the Publicity Bureau was perhaps the first public relations firm to lose a client by claiming credit for work it didn't do, but it would not be the last. Loss of the AT&T account was a rough blow to the 7-year-old firm.

By this time, Ellsworth had progressed from writer to manager and then to a limited partnership with Michaelis. He recalled, "The life of the Bureau, like the life of George Michaelis, was a series of ups and downs. George wanted me to invest my savings in the enterprise and as I would not do that, there was nothing for me to do but resign." This he did at the age of 44, but he quickly set to work to get a job with Vail on his own. Vail was reluctant to employ Ellsworth because of the Bureau incident, but when Ellsworth received offers from the presidents of two Western Bell subsidiaries, those around Vail persuaded him to hire Ellsworth to do publicity with the title of "Special Agent." This title was soon erased by Bell's cautious lawyers for legal reasons. For many years, Ellsworth worked with Vail in building AT&T's pioneering public relations program without a title. These two men, working as a team, were to make significant public relations history with Vail's managerial concepts and Ellsworth's implementation of these concepts. This includes the effective Bell System public relations advertising that Ellsworth first used in Rochester, New York, to meet a public relations crisis in that city.

It was the Publicity Bureau's work for utilities that drew the ire of Muckraker William Kittle. Writing in *Arena Magazine* in July 1909, Kittle charged:

> The Publicity Bureau, operated by two men, —Michaelis and Ellsworth—is an effective organ in advancing the interests of a powerful group of gaslight, water, and traction companies, and in prejudicing the public against municipal ownership of any of these utilities. The bureau has offices in Boston, New York, Washington, and Chicago, and from these centers, arguments, half-truths, and edited reports that are very often misleading, are sent out to the press and paid for as regular advertising although they appear as "news."

Mr. Grant of this bureau wrote the following letter, marked "strictly confidential," to the president of the Oconee Telephone Company at Walhalla, SC.

The Bureau has arranged with the American Press Association to furnish a page of plate matter monthly to such newspapers as may be designated. Companies desiring to place such matters in the local papers should communicate with the Bureau — under no circumstances taking up the matter with the American Press Association, or the local paper. All arrangements are made through the Bureau in such a way as the company does not appear in the matter at all. The cost of the service is $20 per paper per year. The great benefit accruing from constant presentation of facts and arguments in favor of private ownership can hardly be overestimated.

THE BUREAU'S CAMPAIGN FOR THE RAILROADS IN THEIR BATTLE WITH TEDDY ROOSEVELT

The Publicity Bureau reached its zenith of size, scope, and feverish activity during the period of 1905–1906 when it was hired by the nation's railroads in a desperate effort to head off regulatory legislation being pushed by President Theodore Roosevelt and his fellow Progressives. The railroads were inviting and proper targets for the sharpshooting attacks of the Muckrakers and the political forces led by Roosevelt, La Follette, and others. Public opinion demanded stricter regulation. In the 5-year period from 1908 to 1913, for example, more than 2, 000 laws were enacted by the Congress and the state legislatures affecting the railroads.

In his annual message of December 1904, President Roosevelt called for legislation extending the power of the Interstate Commerce Commission to the fixing of minimum railroad rates. The House soon responded to Roosevelt's plea by passing the Esch–Townsend bill. In an effort to delay such legislation, Republican leaders in the Senate instructed its Commerce Committee to investigate the railroad problem in the spring and summer of 1905. Instead of applying the whitewash brush to the railroads as expected, this committee exposed a nation-wide propaganda campaign by the railroads against federal regulation. This campaign that was carried out by the Publicity Bureau proved futile in the end.

Threatened by Roosevelt's demands that were supported by growing public clamor for action, the railroads organized a counter-campaign directed by Samuel Spencer, president of the Southern Railroad, F. D. Underwood, president of the Erie, and David Wilcox, president of the Delaware & Hudson. The first concern of this group was to reach the newspapers, and to do this it hired the Bureau.

Ray Stannard Baker wrote of the Bureau at the time, "Their business was not extensive, but both members of the firm were able and energetic; and both had had a thorough training in the newspaper business. They had represented high-class clients; notably Harvard University." Presumably Baker was writing of Michaelis and Ellsworth. Baker continued, "Immediately the firm expanded. It increased its Boston staff; it opened offices in New York, Chicago, Washington, St. Louis, Topeka, Kansas . . . and it employed agents in South Dakota, California, and elsewhere." This had the effect of making the new field of publicity work visible from coast to coast.

The way the firm expanded to carry on the railroads' propaganda against regulation is indicated by the size of the Chicago office. There 43 persons, mostly experienced newspapermen, were employed. This office subscribed to every newspaper published in the Midwest, and these papers were carefully read and clipped in an early if inaccurate effort to get at the state of public opinion toward the railroads. A traveling agent made the rounds of newspaper offices to talk to editors personally to get their views on a host of questions. A card file was set up on each newspaper, an early example of public relations fact-finding. Records were kept on the use of the publicity releases sent to these papers. As Baker observed, "A glance at a card . . . will instantly reveal how many and what sort of railroad articles every paper in the country is publishing, how railroad information is running high in one community and low in another—whether a paper is 'Good' or 'Bad' from the standpoint of the railroads." The card catalog was known in the Publicity Bureau as "The Barometer." Public relations research is not as new as some think.

The Publicity Bureau saturated the nation's press with many articles favorable to the railroads. The bureau also prepared and distributed millions of publications in pamphlet and book form. The then-existing channels of public information were flooded with the railroads' story, but like many a propaganda campaign before and since, the whole effort came to naught when the Hepburn Bill became law on June 29, 1906.

Nonetheless the work of Michaelis and Ellsworth raised questions about the proper role of the public relations agent that nag practitioners to this day. In his critical article, Baker made two points: One, these men conducted their operations secretly instead of frankly appearing before the court of public opinion as railroad employees; two, "against such an organization as this, supplied with unlimited money, representing a private interest which wishes to defeat the public will, to break the law, to enjoy the fruits of unrestrained power, what chance to be heard have those who believe that a present conditions are wrong?"

During the nationwide battle to mold public opinion pro and con, President Roosevelt wrote Baker to ask what he knew of Mr. John R. Rathom and his pamphlet, "The Farmer and His Friends." Baker's reply to the President gives a quick insight to the methods of the Bureau and Baker's appraisal of those methods:

As for John Rathom, I believe what he tells me, that he spends no corrupt money; and I am fair enough to wish that the railroad side may be fully and honestly presented to the people. . . . But they do not present their case frankly as the railroad case. . . . In John Rathom's address — the foundation of the pamphlet you sent me — Rathom appears as the farmer's friend, not the hired railroad agent which he really is. His letterheads declare him to be a lecturer. Thus by deceit these publicity agents not only seek to influence public opinion, but they employ all the great leverage of power of the railroads, their advertising, their passes, their political influence. And when worse comes to worse, as it did last year in Wisconsin, they will buy newspapers outright. It is anything to muffle the truth!

A PARALLEL: THE BYOIR CAMPAIGN

One value of history is to remind people that some things change little. Compare Baker's charge with this one laid down by Federal Judge Thomas J. Clary in his decision, later reversed, in the civil suit of the Pennsylvania Truckers against the Eastern Railroads and their public relations counsel in October 1957, a little more than half a century after the Publicity Bureau's futile effort of 1905 1906:

> The whole tenor of the anti-truck campaign, originated by the railroads in the thirties, abandoned during the war, and thereafter reactivated in 1946, was based upon the use of third parties to "front" for the railroads. As noted, in New Jersey, the New Jersey Automobile Owners, Inc. and New Jersey Tax Study Foundation were two shining examples. In New York, the Citizens Tax League and the Empire State Transport League are two further examples. . . . The above examples are quoted to demonstrate that Byoir (the public relations firm serving the railroads) merely accentuated and accelerated the campaign of the railroads by forming bogus front organizations and perfecting the use of existing ones.[1]

What constitutes a "front" organization remains a cloudy question for practitioners to this day. What is more clear is that the railroads have been the least apt practitioners of public relations in American industry. They seem to have learned little over the years.

Failure of this nationwide publicity and propaganda effort spearheaded by the Publicity Bureau did cause railroad executives to reassess their public relations problems and within a few years, led to establishment of PR departments — the Pennsylvania in 1908 with Ivy Lee in charge and the

---

[1]This latter-day railroad public relations campaign was directed by Carl Byoir & Associates and resulted in public relations' "Magna carta" in this U. S. Supreme Court decision. This is told in chapter 15, "Carl Byoir: The Little Giant of Pubic Relations.

B&O. in 1910 with J. Hampton Baumgartner in charge. As Baumgartner recalled:

> The wave of agitation which swept over the country several years ago . . . was felt keenly by the railroads. In order that they might deal with the situation, the railroads endeavored to establish closer relations with the public, chiefly through the medium of the press and with its cooperation. Departments were established by a few railroads . . . to deal with matters of Public Relations. The offices of these corporations were designated as Publicity Departments. They handled, and they continue to handle matters concerned with public relations.

The output of these proliferating publicity departments in the nation's railroads met with something less than enthusiasm on the part of newspapermen. As part of its full-scale war against "free advertising," the ANPA carried this note in its Bulletin No. 2276, dated September 24, 1910:

> It would appear that free (railroad) publicity is now being sought on an extensive scale. Members are warned to watch for copy issued by Othello F. Andrews under the caption, "W. L. Park on Publicity," which appears to have been sent for the Illinois Central Railroad of which Mr. Park is vice president, and to be a part of the educational free publicity propaganda designed to prepare the public for an acceptance of increased railroad rates.

The railroads also continued their joint public relations campaign to allay public fears and to stem the demands for stricter regulations. The ANPA Bulletin just quoted also noted that general publicity, apparently a part of the same propaganda campaign, was being sent out in 1910 by Parker & Bridge, 20 Broad Street, New York City. This was the firm headed by George F. Parker, Grover Cleveland's campaign publicist and the senior partner in the short- lived Parker and Lee public relations firm.

Meanwhile, back at the nation's first public relations agency, things were not going well. The Publicity Bureau reached its apogee in the intensive but fruitless campaign to head off the Hepburn Act. Shortly after this campaign ended in failure, the Bureau lost the AT&T account. Soon thereafter Ellsworth jumped ship to take a safer berth with the telephone company. By 1909, as indicated earlier, Michaelis had moved his base of operations to New York City and had become "an officer of manufacturing corporations."

ANPA's Bulletin No. 2058, September 16, 1909, lists publicity being sent out by the Publicity Bureau's New York office at 32 Broadway and its Boston office in the Pierce Building. Clients for whom publicity was distributed included the Chicago Board of Trade, Denver Board of Trade,

Seattle Exposition, Elbert Hubbard, Massachusetts Savings Insurance League, and the New England Conservatory of Music. The ANPA noted, "These communications have been variously marked: Ethel Angier, F. W. Coburn, and Frederick Rice, Jr., as well as Publicity Bureau."

This would indicate that the Bureau, after the departure of Michaelis and Ellsworth, became sort of a loose partnership. The F. W. Coburn listed as a sender of publicity by the ANPA in 1911 is probably the same Coburn identified as a writer for the firm as early as 1903. According to the ANPA, clients of the Bureau in 1911 were the New England Conservatory of Music, Massachusetts Zoological Society, AT&T, and Harvard College. The 1915 *New York City Directory* lists a Publicity Bureau of America at 141 Broadway but classifies it as an advertising agency. The 1917 *New York City Directory* lists no Publicity Bureau.

Why was the Publicity Bureau started in 1900 in Boston, Massachusetts? What were the guiding concepts of its founders? It was no mere coincidence that brought the nation's first publicity agency on the eve of America's 20th century. This same year brought the first modern national press association and the large-circulation daily newspaper and saw the first magazine to reach one million circulation—the *Ladies' Home Journal* -nearing that goal. The next year saw the beginning of the Muckraking Era that utilized the power of these new mass media to cause a political revolt against the continued abuse of the public interest by ruthless businessmen—a revolt that crystallized in Progressive legislation reforms. The need for publicists to put one's case before the public had already been reorganized by such business leaders as George Westinghouse, by such utilities as the Boston Elevated Railway, by insurance companies, and by political leaders, notably Mark Hanna whose 1896 campaign for William McKinley set a pattern of Presidential campaigns that was to last for half a century.

The concepts that guided the Bureau's founders were outlined in considerable detail in a letter signed by Herbert Small and addressed to President Eliot of Harvard under a May 4, 1901, date:

> The idea of publicity as we have learned to hold it . . . is entirely distinct from the idea either of advertising or of a press agency. In brief, it is the extension . . . of the proposition that certain public institutions may properly hand to the newspapers certain statements as to the work they have done, or which they hope to do . . . the very fact that the Publicity Bureau had extended this idea so greatly makes its work very different from anything which has ever been attempted before. Publicity, as we conceive it, is not advertising in that it intends to deal only with such subjects as would be suitable and interesting for newspaper treatment.

The Bureau's founders took great pains to distinguish their work from press agentry, born in the American circus in the 19th century and now coming into ill repute as American journalism began to move toward objectivity and responsibility. Small's letter continued, "Press agency work, from which the Bureau would desire to distinguish its service, is evident in all its characteristics . . . in the kind of writing which is offered to the newspapers as reading matter by the theaters." In contrast to the theater press agent "who writes solely with the notion of benefitting his employer," the Publicity Bureau's fundamental idea, Small asserted, was that "no article shall be written except under a definite and constant sense of responsibility to the editor or editors to whom it is to be transmitted."

Thus, Small and his colleagues were the first to advance the principle that the best way a counselor can serve a client is to meet the news requirements of the press. In short, this trio of pioneers saw the need for legitimate, newsworthy publicity and its value in advancing the fortunes of business firms, educational institutions, museums, and so forth, dependent upon public favor to accomplish their objectives. In so doing, they helped shape a new field.

NOTES ON SOURCES

This chapter first appeared in *Journalism Quarterly,* Vol. 43, Summer, 1966, under the title "The Nation's First Public Relations Firm," a bit of overstatement. It is reproduced with the permission of the Association for Education in Journalism and Mass Communication.

The main source for this chapter was the Charles W. Eliot Papers, Harvard University Archives, Box 220. Contains Publicity Bureau's extensive correspondence with President Eliot, a correspondence that reflects the shaky status of this infant field. Eliot's views on public opinion can be found in his "Inagural Address of Harvard College, 1869," in Eliot, *Educational Reforms and Essays,* Harvard.

Another major source was James Drummond Ellsworth's unpublished memoir, "Twisting Trails," in Mass Communications History Center, State Historical Society of Wisconsin, Madison. Also utilized was his unpublished, "Unforgotten Men," also in his papers. This information was supplemented by an interview with his daughter, Mrs. R. H. Scannell, Mt. Vernon, NY, June 8, 1965.

The information on Herbert Small is from the *25th Anniversary Report of the Class of Harvard, '91,* and an obituary in the Boston *Evening Herald* Dec. 13, 1903. Information on George Michaelis' immediate post-Bureau years was found in *Survey,* Vol. 32, Aug. 1, 1914. Information on Thomas Marvin's post-Bureau career can be found, in part, in U. S. Senate Hearings, *Maintenance of Lobby to Influence Legislation,* Vol. 2, 63rd Congress, 1st Session, Washington, DC: U. S. Government Printing Office,

1913. Information on J. Harvey White, comes from "Publicity Among the Bostonese," *Electric Railway Journal,* Vol. 50, Dec. 8, 1917.

Other articles and speeches: Ray Stannard Baker, "Railroads on Trial," *McClure's Magazine,* Vol. 26, March, 1906 (also supplemented by his *American Chronicle,* Charles Scribner's Sons, 1945; Gordon A. Moon, "George F. Parker: 'A Near Miss' as White House Press Chief," *Journalism Quarterly,* Vol. 41, Spring, 1964; William B. Kittle, "The Making of Public Opinion," *Arena,* Vol. 41, July, 1909 provides insight on Bureau's payment for publication of news releases as advertising); J. Hampton Baumgartner, "Railroads on Trails," speech before Virginia Press Association, June 26, 1913 (Baumgartner, at the time, was publicity director for the Baltimore & Ohio Railroad); American Newspaper Publishers Association *Bulletin* No. 2458, June 24, 1911.

For Judge Clary's opinion, see Noerr Motor Freight, Inc. et al. v. Eastern Railroads Presidents Conference *et al.,* No. 14715, *Federal Supplement,* Vol. 155, pp. 768 841. Judge Clary's decision was ultimately reversed by the U. S. Supreme Court, *Supreme Court Reporter,* 523, Feb. 20, 1961.

Chapter 2

The First Washington Agencies

As the waves of the Progressive revolt rose around Capitol Hill in the early months of Roosevelt's presidency, it became apparent to shrewd men that conventional lobbying and legislative fixing would not prove adequate in a time when, in Roosevelt's words, there was "a condition of excitement and irritation in the public mind" The discerning interest groups began to see the need to go beyond the legislator to his constituents to build support for or foment opposition to proposed legislation. Inside government, Roosevelt and his Forester, Gifford Pinchot, were showing the power of publicity in making the nation conservation minded. Outside government, the Anti-Saloon League with its program of political agitation directed toward the defeat of wet and election of dry candidates was showing the way to pressure groups. This new kind of lobbying required communication with a congressman's constituents as well as contacts with him in the Capitol.

Among the first, if not the first, Washington newspaperman to see a profitable calling in this emerging situation was William Wolff Smith, who opened a "publicity business" in the capital in 1902. This agency, too, lasted little more than a decade. Apparently at the outset, the agency was a partnership, Smith and a man named Walmer, but no evidence has been found as to who Walmer was, how long he was associated with Smith, or what his role was. In testifying before the House committee investigating government press bureaus in 1912, Charles W. Thompson, *The New York Times* Washington reporter, recalled, "10 years ago a firm—Smith & Walmer—started a press bureau up here in the capitol, and up to that time I do not think such a thing had been much thought about. They used to solicit press agent employment from anybody who had business before

Congress, and I guess it was legitimate enough; at any rate, the idea apparently struck a number of public officials, and the whole press-agent business sprang up from that." Voicing the newsman's historic disdain of the new publicity man, Thompson added, "I do not think the Washington correspondents make use of these press agencies." Thompson proved to be a poor prophet indeed!

Smith, who would later pioneer in building a public relations program for the U.S. Army, was born in Logansport, Indiana, on December 2, 1874. He took a year's preparatory work and his freshman year at Hanover College, spent his sophomore year at Depauw University, both in his native state, and then enrolled in Johns Hopkins University as a junior. Eye trouble forced his withdrawal from Johns Hopkins after one semester. The next year, 1892–1893, Smith studied law at the Columbian University Law School, Washington, D.C (now the George Washington University Law School). In 1893, he quit school and took a job with the *Baltimore Sun* as a reporter. Subsequently, in 1895, he was transferred to the *Sun* Washington Bureau; in 1897, he also became a correspondent for the *New York Sun*. He quit the *Baltimore Sun* bureau in 1901 to join the *Cincinnati Enquirer* Washington staff, according to a memorandum prepared by him and found in the Department of Army's personnel records.

In 1902, William Wolff Smith quit both the *Enquirer* and the *New York Sun* jobs to establish what he described as a "publicity business at the Capitol." In a form completed on July 9, 1920, to the president of a military examining board, Smith stated his civil experience as "Washington reporter, correspondent, editor and publisher, 20 years. First publicity agent in Washington." Diligent research has failed to find an earlier firm in the publicity business in Washington, thus his 1920 claim stands.

According to this memorandum of May 31, 1918, Smith, from 1902 to 1914, "engaged in publicity business, published a weekly, then a monthly, and acted as correspondent for an number newspapers, the most prominent being the *Buffalo News*, which he represented eight years." In other places, Smith described himself as a "publicity agent" for this period of his career. It appears that during these 12 years Smith mixed his work as a string correspondent for newspapers and his publicity work to the profit of himself and his publicity clients. Each one bolstered the other.

In a long attack on the efforts of Big Business to influence the press in their favor by something less than ethical means, William Kittle, writing in *Arena* of July 1909, cited Smith as a propagandist for the "Interests." In an article entitled "The Making of Public Opinion," Kittle wrote:

> One of the best known of these venal news bureaus is operated in Washington by William Wolff Smith who has his offices in the Munsey Building and employs a number of stenographers and so-called "reporters." Smith is

frequently seen at the New Willard Hotel and at the Capitol. Very few of the leading daily papers can afford the expense of a special correspondent in Washington and most of them readily publish as news letters purporting to come from the direct representative of the paper, but which really emanate from some hired bureau.

As the era of political reform began to fade, presumably the demand for Smith's publicity services began to dwindle. Or it may have been that as he became enmeshed in lobbying work, he came to realize the value of legal training. At any rate, in 1914 Smith quit newspaper and publicity work and returned to school to complete his law studies at the National University Law School. Smith was awarded the degrees of Bachelor of Laws, and Master of Laws, and Master of Patent Law on June 12, 1916, by the National University School of Law. He was graduated with honors and soon thereafter was "admitted to the bars of the Supreme Court of the District, and the District Court of Appeals, and all Government Departments."

It is reasonable to assume that Smith combined his talents in publicity with his knowledge of law to represent business and trade agencies before the legislative and regulatory branches of the federal government until he began his military career as assistant to the Third Assistant Secretary of War on May 15, 1918. Smith was commissioned as a captain in the Sanitary Corps in October, 1918, and was discharged as a regular Army captain in the Quartermaster Corps on November 25, 1922.

Few records remain of Smith's publicity business. At least one client was served the 17 years between his newspaper and military careers—the tobacco industry that today, of necessity, has a large-scale Washington public relations program. In his May 31, 1918, memorandum, Smith recorded, "Now represents the *United States Tobacco Journal* (17 years), and *The Phonograph*, weekly publication issued in New York City, and is under retainer by tobacco interests which he has long represented, supplying them with information such as published in the USTJ (U. S. Tobacco Journal)." Another client for 5 or 6 years in this period was the National Board for Promotion of Rifle Practice. Colonel H. G. Leonard in the Office of the Army Adjutant General noted in a "To Whom It May Concern" letter of June 11, 1920, "When I first knew him (Smith), he was engaged in publicity and newspaper work for the National Board for Promotion of Rifle Practice, of which I was recorder."

It appears that a major source of Smith's income were business firms supporting high tariff barriers to shut out competition of foreign goods. In describing Smith's methods in *Arena* Kittle alleged:

There appeared such an article (a news story purportedly from the publishing newspaper's "special correspondent") in some of the papers of the northwest in January, 1909. It was adroitly and ably written to form public opinion in favor of high tariff. It stated that the annual disbursements greatly exceeded the income of the national government, that President Roosevelt had believed he was right in advocating large appropriations, that if the tariff were lowered a large bond issue would be necessary, that the Standard Oil Company's National City Bank favored such bond issue.

As Kittle pointed out at the time, this column-and-a-half "news story" is loaded with appeals to partisanship, to the then violent antagonism toward Standard Oil Company, a covert attack on President Roosevelt, and was "contrived to have the reader draw the inevitable conclusion that the tariff must not be reduced."

It seems fairly clear that in the 1902–1914 period Smith earned his living as a free lance correspondent, as a provider of information on Congressional developments to affected trade groups, and as a publicist. After he got his law degrees in 1916, he concentrated more on direct lobbying with the new regulatory agencies that had grown up under Roosevelt and Wilson. His law partner of this period, James T. Lloyd, wrote in a letter in a letter dated June 8, 1920:

> His practice was before the Departments and Congressional Committees more than in the courts. In this work he represented at various times a number of clients important in the commercial world, and, apparently to their satisfaction. He frequently appeared before Congressional Committees and Department Officers with success, and his briefs and other papers were ably prepared. He has a faculty of digging into a subject . . . which comes from his combined training as a newspaperman and a lawyer.

In his work in the publicity business, Smith utilized a wide acquaintanceship in Washington he had built as a reporter, his knowledge of law, and, in the words of a former law professor, "adaptability, studiousness, and application, facility of expression, and his analytical and reasoning powers." One-time Presidential aspirant and longtime Senator Oscar W. Underwood of Alabama wrote in a letter of recommendation:

> I have known Major Smith substantially ever since I came to Congress, first when he was on the floor of the House as a representative of the *New York Sun* when I was a member of that body and later as a representative of various newspapers and as an attorney at law. He probably has a wide an acquaintance among public men in Washington as any one and in his long dealing with them has acquired a host of friends who would be glad to see him retained in the service. In my intercourse with him I have found him scrupulously accurate and trustworthy.

In his memorandum of May 31, 1918, Smith claimed that he was earning "over $6, 000 gross and $4, 500 net, from his newspaper work and practice," a reasonably good income in days of no federal income tax and low wages. After the United States entered World War I, Smith caught the patriotic fervor that spread across the land. He put his journalistic and public relations talents to work as a Four Minute Man and as a speaker for Liberty Loan drives. As the war progressed, he became impatient with his civilian role and in May, 1918, he "offered his services to the Secretary of War in any capacity in which they could be utilized, without restriction as to place, title, or emoluments." War Secretary Baker referred Smith to Frederick P. Keppel, Third Assistant Secretary of War, who "tried him out with the result that at the end of six weeks he made Mr. Smith his civilian assistant with an appointment as confidential clerk at $1, 500 per annum." In October, 1918, on the eve of the Armistice, he accepted the offer of a captain's commission in the Sanitary Corps. It was in the Army that Smith left a more lasting mark on the evolution of public relations than did his "venal" news bureau.

THOMAS R. SHIPP AND CO.

The second agency to open in the nation's capital—the nation's sixth—was that organized by Thomas Roerty Shipp in 1914. Like William Wolff Smith and George R. Parker, the senior partner in Parker & Lee that was formed in 1904 Shipp was a native of Indiana and a former newspaperman. Shipp set out on his own after spending 6 years learning the arts of publicity and politics under the tutelage of two pros—Theodore Roosevelt and Gifford Pinchot. Shipp started his publicity company, as he termed it, late in 1914 when he rented an office in the Albee Building. Shipp was opening his shop about the time William Wolff Smith was closing his.

Born in Morristown, Indiana, on August 4, 1875, Shipp received his college education at Butler University. After his graduation in June 1897, he took a reporting job on the *Indianapolis News*. This work led to a job as a private secretary to United States Senator Albert J. Beveridge, which he held from 1902 to 1907. While working for Senator Beveridge, he was paid as clerk of the Senate Committee on Territories. His association with Senator Beveridge resulted in Shipp's being tapped to serve as secretary of President Roosevelt's historic White House Conference of Governors on Conservation, held May 13-15, 1908. This conference—a historic first convening of the nation's governors—made public relations as well as conservation history. It embedded the word *conservation* into the nation's vocabulary. The idea for a "gigantic conference" came from the head of the Reclamation Service. Though the conference was not his idea, Shipp did much of the organizational and publicity work for it. In his *The Conservation Fight: From Theodore Roosevelt to the TVA* Judson King commented, "This sessions of the conference came off successfully under the skillful guidance of its general secretary, Thomas R. Shipp, ably assisted by the alert Dr. (W. J.) McGee. The conference received much publicity." A participant in the conference, President Charles R. Van Hise of the University of Wisconsin, emphasized the historic importance and impact of this staged public relations event — the first in the now traditional annual Governor's Conference and occasional White House Conference — when he wrote:

> Never before in the history of the nation had so representative an audience gathered together. For the first time in the history of the country the governors were assembled to consider a great national question. Even during the extreme stress of the Civil War the governors had not been asked to consult with the President. . . . Apparently President Roosevelt must have thought that the question of conservation was one of fundamental importance before he took so far-reaching a step.

In the article, "The First White House Governor's Conference," in published the *Public Relations Quarterly,* a scholar, Charlotte E. Wittwer, concluded that the conference:

> *Put the issue of conservation on the front pages of the newspapers for the better part of a week,

> *Provided major impetus for discussion of the issue in periodicals and the public forum for many years afterward,

> *Firmly established the term 'conservation of natural resources' in the public vocabulary.

Roosevelt and Pinchot both knew well the value of highly publicized events to dramatize their conservation crusade. To them Shipp gave much and from them learned much. During the 7 months Shipp was working on the White House Conference, he was paid as an editor in the U.S. Forest Service headed by Pinchot. Shortly after the White House Conference, Roosevelt set up the National Conservation Commission composed of 49 prominent leaders in politics, industry, and the sciences. The commission was short-lived because the 61st Congress refused to fund its operation. The commission was immediately replaced by the Joint Committee on Conservation, supported by private funds. In spite of its name, it was not directly connected to the government. It acted primarily as a clearing house for state and independent agencies. Pinchot was president and Shipp secretary of the committee. Because the committee didn't seem to prove effective, these battlers for conservation organized the National Conservation Association in the autumn of 1909 to be "the center of a great propaganda for conservation," in Van Hise's phrase. Charles W. Eliot, venerable Harvard president, was named honorary president, Pinchot the working president, and Shipp once more was given the main administrative burden as secretary. "With the foundation of the National Conservation Association, the great movement for the conservation of the natural resources may be said to have been fairly launched," in Van Hise's opinion.

For the next 3 years, Shipp worked tirelessly to publicize and promote the new word and new cause—conservation. An association pamphlet, presumably written by Shipp, emphasized that "public sentiment, to be effective, must be concentrated upon specific measures and organized for energetic and persistent work." TR, Pinchot, and Shipp all knew well the meaning of each one of these words. Late in 1911, Shipp left the association to become Executive Secretary of the National Conservation Congress, which had its headquarters in Indianapolis. Pinchot reported to the association on January 3, 1912, "Mr. T. R. Shipp, secretary of your association since its organization, has resigned, and is now the Executive Secretary of the National Conservation Congress. . . . A very large part of the achievement of your Association is directly due to the zealous and efficient efforts of Mr. Shipp."

Like President Roosevelt, Gifford Pinchot understood instinctively the necessity of public relations to influence public opinion. He often said, "Nothing permanent can be accomplished in this country unless it is backed by sound public sentiment. The greater part of our work, therefore, has consisted in arousing a general interest in practical forestry throughout the country and in gradually changing public sentiment toward a more conservation treatment of forest lands." Pinchot was the first federal government administrator to make intensive use of public relations and with demonstrable success. One biographer, M. Nelson McGreary, wrote in his *Gifford Pinchot, Forest Politician:*

> No government agency had ever made such extensive use of handouts of stories for newspapers and magazines. Few of the releases attempted to inflate the agency itself. But each one, sometimes openly, sometimes abruptly, got across the forestry gospel. Two or three decades later, when many Washington agencies employed skilled publicity agents, much of the huge bulk of handouts to the press reached the wastebaskets. But at the turn of the century, it was a new device. The press welcomed the canned material and used it extensively.

These lessons Thomas Shipp took with him into his work as a publicity counsel.

Apparently his shift to the new conservation organization was intended to pave the way for Shipp to run for Congress in 1912. He received the

Republican nomination for the House from Indiana's Seventh District but was narrowly defeated in the November election. Early in 1914, Shipp became a member of the Republican National Committee. He continued to maintain close political ties with Gifford Pinchot. In late 1913, the fiery conservationist asked Shipp to make a survey of "Pennsylvania's internal political conditions" to determine whether Pinchot should run for the U.S. Senate in 1914, which he ultimately did. In 1914, Shipp returned to Washington, this time to direct the national GOP publicity campaign in those off-year elections.

After the election, Shipp opened a publicity office, and in his first *Who's Who* (1916) entry, he identified himself as a publicity counsel. He was soon retained to promote the Military Training Camps Association (MTCA), often known as the Plattsburgh Training Camps, organized by his associates in the conservation crusade, Theodore Roosevelt and Henry L. Stimson, as part of the massive Preparedness Campaign then getting under way. Major General Leonard Wood, another close friend of Shipp, was also active in promoting these camps. Publicity on the 1915 encampment at Plattsburgh flowed freely. The *New York Tribune* of August 12, 1915, commented on the favorable publicity that resulted from the prominent personalities participating.

Shortly thereafter the MTCA, through Shipp, started a publicity campaign to recruit for the camps in 1916. In an intensive campaign three and a half million pieces of government literature, 38, 000 illustrated booklets, and 10, 000 photograph albums were distributed throughout the country. Full-page and half-page advertisements were inserted in the larger metropolitan papers, thousands of posters were printed, and a volunteer speakers bureau was set up.

The MTCA also organized the "Preparedness Parades" that started in 1916. By the summer of 1916, Shipp's publicity campaign had fanned such enthusiasm that more than 17, 000 men attended the camps that summer. Shipp's entry in the *Encyclopedia of American Biography* (Vol. 34), states that he conducted the nationwide campaign on behalf of the Plattsburgh Training Camps. The Plattsburgh Training Camps were conceived and pushed by former President Roosevelt and Col. Stimson who were impatient with President Wilson's slowness to prepare for America's involvement in World War I, then raging in Europe.

One of Shipp's proudest achievements as a publicity counsel was his successful promotion of the first American Red Cross fund drive to raise $100 million after the United States went to war in April 1917 with the Central Powers. America's lack of readiness and ultimate all-out response to fighting a world war is exemplified in the story of the Red Cross. When America entered the war, the Red Cross was far from ready to cope with the task that would be assigned to it; when the war was over, it was a strong philanthropic agency of world renown. Publicity played a powerful role in the Red Cross' wartime growth from some 486, 000 members to 20 million members, from a treasury of $200, 000 to the raising of $400 million in 1917–1918.

In May 1917, when the newly organized Red Cross War Council set out to raise the unprecedented sum of $100 million in a national campaign conducted June 18–25, it retained Shipp to promote the giving.

The records of the May 12, 1917, meeting of the Executive Committee of the American Red Cross show that Thomas R. Shipp and Co. had been engaged as publicity agents at a rate of $250 weekly. The exact date when this arrangement was terminated cannot be established, but it apparently lasted approximately 6 weeks. There is a statement in committee records, circa July 1, 1917, that Mr. Shipp was leaving his position as "director of publicity" since the goal of $100, 000 had been reached, according to a letter from Clyde E. Buckingham of the ARC to me dated August 15, 1961. While this first precedent-shattering drive was in progress, Red Cross wartime chairman, Henry P. Davison, drafted Ivy L. Lee as his publicity advisor for the duration of the war. (Lee's role in the wartime Red Cross is told in chapter 3.)

In the years after World War I, Shipp served as a Washington counsel to such major industrial firms as General Motors, Standard Oil Company of New York, the Pullman Company, Swift & Company, and International Harvester. Records of his work for these firms could not be located. Shipp died in Washington on February 10, 1952.

NOTES ON SOURCES

Alerted to the existence of the William Wolff Smith agency by William Kittle's article in *Arena*, I ultimately found most of the information on him in this chapter in his personnel folder, Office of the Adjutant General, Department of the Army, Washington, DC. His application for a commission in the Army was especially valuable. Thomas R. Shipp's work to promote conservation under the direction of President Theodore Roosevelt and Gifford Pinchot is told in the biographies of those two leaders. Particularly helpful was Pinchot's *The Fight for Conservation* (1910), Charles R. Van Hise's *Conservation of Natural Resources* (1910), and M. Nelson McGreary's *Gifford Pinchot, Forest Politician* (1960). Shipp's work for the first American Red Cross World War I drive is found in the records of the ARC, Washington, DC. Also helpful was his obituary in the *Washington Post* of February 11, 1952, 2B. Charles Thompson's testimony about the emergence of the press agent in Washington in the early 1900s can be found in "Department Press Agents," Hearing Before the Committee on

Rules, House of Representatives, May 21, 1912, 62nd Congress, 2nd
Session. "The First White House Governor's Conference," Charlotte Wittwer's article mentioned in the text, published in *the Public Relations
Quarterly*, Vol. 14, No. 4, 1970, spells out the public relations aspect of that
historic Governor's Conference.

Chapter 3

First Parker and Lee; Then Lee, Harris, and Lee

The third public relations agency organized in the Seedbed Era—Parker & Lee—had an even shorter life than the first two; it lasted less than 4 years, but the name of the junior partner, Ivy Ledbetter Lee, lives today as one of the influential pioneers who helped define and build a new vocation. Ivy Lee reappears in our chronicle as one of the influential builders of a new calling in the post World War I era. George Frederick Parker, veteran newsman and political publicist, and the younger Ivy Lee first met in the headquarters of the Democratic Party in 1904. In the Presidential campaign that year, they worked together, Parker in charge, in a futile effort to elect Judge Alton B. Parker, a conservative Democrat. They were up against the astute, colorful, publicity-minded Theodore Roosevelt who was riding the crest of the Progressive wave of reform. Roosevelt was a master publicist in his own right.

Sometime after the election in November, these two publicists formed a partnership called simply Parker & Lee. They rented an office at 20 Broad Street in the Postal Telegraph Building, adjacent to the Stock Exchange, in New York City. (The building was later razed to make room for an addition to the Exchange.) Lee's biographer, Ray Eldon Hiebert, said the firm was founded "late in 1904." Lee's obituary sketch, released by his firm on November 9, 1934, states he "began to engage in public relations in 1905." In January 1908, *Editor & Publisher* refers to the firm as having been started "a little more than three years ago."

The records conflict as to just how and when the Parker & Lee publicity agency was formed. Our research suggests that it was formed in late 1904 after the unsuccessful Presidential campaign. Alan Raucher, a respected historian in this field, said that in March 1904, Lee's office at 20 Broad Street was listed in *The Telephone Directory of the New York Telephone Company* and that Parker was not listed at that address until January 1905. Lee was listed as a "journalist" in 1905 and as an "agent" from 1906 to 1908 by *Trow's General Directory of the Boroughs of Manhattan and the Bronx*.

All evidence indicates that it was Parker who took the initiative. Pioneer Pendleton Dudley later recalled, "Older than Lee and more widely experienced, Parker had quite definite ideas as to the practical functioning of an independent press agency and a sense of urgency about starting one." The older Parker thought that his junior partner would handle "such selling as would be needed." Already Ivy Lee's handsome looks, Southern drawl, and courtly ways had proven to be an asset in his young career. Somewhat to the surprise of both partners who had foresightedly perceived the growing need for an articulate spokesman for the corporations and financial institutions then under heavy fire from the reformers in this Progressive Era, that selling would be needed. "Neither Big Business nor Little Business came running in droves for the services Parker & Lee could provide," Pendleton Dudley, then a close friend of Lee's recalled in an interview with me on March 9, 1959.

Ivy Ledbetter Lee was born in Cedartown, Georgia, on July 16, 1877, the son of a Georgia Methodist preacher and a mother who was just shy of being 14 years old when Ivy was born. Ivy Lee, destined to become the "father figure" in public relations, was very much a product of his parents and his times. From his parents he inherited great intellectual capacity and a wideranging interest in public affairs. Ivy Lee, Jr., said of his father, "My father was constantly on the quest for knowledge. He read unceasingly." Born in the middle of the Civil War and married at the age of 13, Emma Ledbetter was self-educated. Lee's biographer said of her: "Her intellect encompassed such broad interest that later as a preacher's wife she could easily make her household the center of public affairs. After her husband's death she traveled widely as a popular lecturer." Lee's mother died in 1951, 17 years after the death of her first-born and famous son. From his father, Lee heard much about thrift, love, diligence, and moral duties and learned much about the art of conciliation. As a Southern minister, the elder Lee constantly endeavored to conciliate the bitter conflict between the Bible fundamentalists and the Darwinian evolutionists who were cleaving the South in these years. This remains a divisive issue in many Protestant bodies to this day.

A circuit preacher in rural Georgia when young Ivy was born, the Rev. James Wideman Lee in time became a popular minister at Trinity Church and later the Park Street Church in Atlanta before being transferred to St. Louis, Missouri, in 1893 to serve as pastor of St. John's Methodist Church. The Reverend Dr. Lee was brought back to Atlanta for a 3-year pastorate,

1906–1909, and then was returned to St. Louis as Presiding Elder of the St. Louis district. There he died in 1919.

Lee had a close relationship with both parents and was greatly influenced by each one. His childhood in a religious home and one active in public affairs, dominated by two intellectually alive parents, reflected itself in his career, which was cut short by death in 1934. Ivy Lee, Jr. said of his father, the public relations pioneer, that he was "an incessant collector of information and built his own background files or 'morgue," a habit learned from his father who was always in search of sermon material. Lee once recalled in a printed note sent out from Lee & Associates in the early 1920s, "One of my vivid memories of my father was his habit of culling from newspapers, magazines, books, – in fact from every possible source – information of likely interest to his friends. He was constantly sending them clippings on every conceivable subject." Lee had a warm relationship with both parents.

Young Lee grew up in a South that was suffering from the pains of Reconstruction and in a nation with its burgeoning industrial revolution that was rushing headlong into the 20th century and the Progressive Era of reform that would make Ivy Lee's role as a publicist and conciliator essential. In Ivy's youth, Editor Henry W. Grady, who had the vision of the New South, and Joel Chandler Harris, teller of Uncle Remus tales, were frequent guests in the Lee home. From the time Ivy Lee would have been old enough to be aware of the events swirling about him, history was giving him a hand with the career that he fashioned for himself and for countless others to follow. Wealth was being massed on a hitherto unknown scale, laissez-faire was the gospel of the day, and, conversely, the grievances that would be unleashed in the early 1900s were being piled up, one on top of another. In historian Eric Goldman's view, "Ivy Lee was very much a child of the Nineties; to him success meant succeeding in business."

By late 1904, when the Parker & Lee firm got under way, all the forces that had been at work paving the way for Ivy Lee's career and for the "inevitable phenomenon" were in proper juxtaposition. At the same time the forces creating the need for his talent had been at work, so had young Ivy Lee, and by 1904, he was ready to capitalize on the situation. Diligence and application had been a part of Lee's life since childhood, another parental influence. These traits reached their zenith in his public relations career, but the work he would eventually become identified with represented an extension of three interest he had always had: debate, scholarship, and journalism. These had been his strong points since his graduation from high school in St. Louis where he had been an honor student and leader of the debating society.

Lee first enrolled in college in 1894 at Emory College, then located at Oxford, Georgia, and spent two years as editor of the college department of the *Atlanta Constitution* before transferring to Princeton University in 1896. While at Princeton, young Lee studied under Professor Woodrow Wilson among others. In later years, he often referred to times when he and Wilson would take walks in the lovely countryside surrounding Princeton. Ivy soon joined the staff of *Daily Princetonian*, and in his senior year, he served as editor of the alumni *Princetonian*. He earned a good share of his expenses by serving as a string correspondent for the Associated Press, the *Philadelphia Press*, and the *Chicago Record* while in school. Princeton did much to shape the future practitioner. For example, in a Shakespeare course he learned, "There is nothing either good or bad, only thinking makes it so," a thought that stuck in his mind and one he often quoted in stressing the importance of putting a favorable interpretation on a client's activities.

While a student at Princeton and a newspaper stringer, Ivy Lee showed an ingenuity that characterized his career in public relations. He scored a scoop by getting a semipublic appearance and statement from former President Grover Cleveland. Cleveland had retired in Princeton after leaving the White House and had refused to see newspapermen or grant interviews. Lee tried a new approach. He rounded up several students and organized a march to Cleveland's home, where the Princeton men staged an impromptu serenade for the President. Cleveland came out on his porch to thank the students and made a few impromptu remarks. Ivy Lee had his story. Lee remained a loyal, active Princeton alumnus until his death. It was in accordance with his wishes that his papers were deposited there by his family. His longtime partner, T. J. Ross, told me in an interview on March 10, 1959, that he had the feeling that Lee was hurt by never being asked to be a Princeton trustee.

Perhaps because of his work as a news correspondent, Ivy Lee was not an outstanding student at Princeton. His record was marred by a failure in a logic course — something of an irony given the persuasive powers of his logical thinking in later years — and a near failure in a history course. Nonetheless, he was graduated *cum laude* in 1898. In addition to his news work, Lee was active in extracurricular activities. Lee climaxed his exciting 2 years at Princeton by winning the Lynde Debate competition by arguing that the United States should annex Hawaii. He took the $500 prize (paid in gold) and used it to enroll in Harvard for postgraduate work in the fall of 1989, but his money soon ran out, and he returned to New York to look for a job on a newspaper.

Early in 1899, Lee landed a job on the *New York Journal*, a Hearst paper, as a reporter at $12 a week. Ironically, the 21-year-old Lee, later to become the "Minnesinger to Millionaires," was hired by Charles Edward Russell, then editor of the *Journal* but who would later become a Socialist writer and political candidate. Nonetheless, the Socialist crusader and the future counselor to the Rockefellers became and remained close friends. Little did young Ivy realize that when he spent his last nickel for the subway downtown to the *Journal* office that 18 years later, working for the Interborough Rapid Transit, he would be trying to push the rates beyond 5¢. Lee started as a police reporter but soon got a full range of assignments as he proved his ability to handle complex subjects with competence.

Lee, whom Henry Pringle described as a "competent but not brilliant reporter," left the *Journal* after a time, and then worked successively on *The New York Times* and the *New York World*. At *The Times*, he learned much under the tutelage of the famous editor, Carr Van Anda. Along the way he acquired a good education in economics, a natural interest in the stock market, and became a specialist in Wall Street and financial coverage, all of which would stand him in good stead in his public relations career.

Also, said Pringle in a manuscript, "Big Frogs" found in T. J. Ross & Associates file, "Lee . . . was cultivating acquaintances. He never failed to impress his personality and his talents upon the consciousness of the man he met in the grind of gathering news."

In 1901, Ivy Lee married Cornelia Bigelow, a "lovely, intelligent, and proper girl" from St. Paul, Minnesota, whom he had met the year before through her brother, Lewis Bigelow, another New York reporter. In November 1902, their first child, a girl, was born. By 1903, Lee saw that though these were exciting days in journalism, the financial prospects and social status of reporters would not satisfy his ambitions. He quit the *World* that year. A fellow newsman with whom Lee lived before his marriage, John K. Mumford, later recalled, "In 1903 while working on the *World* Lee saw he 'wasn't getting anywhere' so he got a six-month leave from (William) Thayer when he found he 'wasn't getting ahead.' " In an address before students in the Columbia School of Journalism 18 years later, he said that in 1903 he had become tired of newspaper work because he had been married about 2 years and did not like the idea of getting home at two o'clock in the morning. "So I pulled myself up by my bootstraps and got out." In another account, Lee said, "I didn't know what I was going to do, but I knew I was through with reporting." Writing from hindsight, Pringle thought Lee "with rare vision saw the possibilities of press agentry as applied to Big Business."

Typical of Lee's industry and his inquiring mind, while working as a reporter, he enrolled in postgraduate courses at Columbia University and attended classes in the morning before reporting to work in the newsroom.

Lee's eyes, even then, were on the main chance. In his memoir, *This Way to the Big Show*, Dexter Fellows, the famed circus press agent, recalled Lee thus:

Lee had none of the brilliance of (Frank W.) O'Malley, (Irvin S.) Cobb, or (Edwin C.) Hill, but he was a hard worker. Not one of us ever dreamed at that time that he would make a fortune as America's greatest propagandist . . . who would lift the lowly trade of press agentry to the euphonious heights of counselor in public relations.

"Dexter, you're a pretty smart fellow," he told me. Don't you know that you will get nowhere unless you cultivate the right people?"

"What do you mean?" I asked in surprise. "Certainly you are not referring to my colleagues."

"No, but you're wasting your time hanging around with those bums who are sponging on (John) Burke's generosity."

"But I like them," I protested.

"What will they get you? What can they do for you? If you are going to get anywhere in this world you've got to know the right people. Seek them out. Flatter them. If they don't like to lose in a card game, see that they win. If they like golf, learn to play golf. Find out what interests them and make those things your interests. Otherwise you will always be a circus press agent."

Whether it was a vision or pure chance, Lee was quickly caught up in what would become his life's work. Within a day or two after quitting the *World*, he met Captain Arthur Cosby on the street who asked Lee if he could suggest someone to handle the publicity for Seth Low's campaign for reelection as mayor of New York. "How about me?" was Lee's prompt response. Within a week he was sitting in with the campaign committee and preparing the campaign literature. That led to a press job for the Democratic National Committee the following year.

In the Low headquarters, Lee "met big men and began to see a great light." Low was running for re-election as the Fusionist candidate against the then powerful Tammany Organization. As press representative of the Citizens Union, Lee wrote the campaign book for the election, his first major effort as a press agent. The 160-page book, *The City for the People: The Best Administration New York Ever Had* "contained many of the features that were to be common to Ivy Lee's publicity efforts in the years to come." Despite Lee's efforts, Low's Fusion ticket lost. But this campaign experience, in Hiebert's view, "opened up the possibilities of a new career for Lee."

Lee's shrewd understanding of the plight of the inarticulate business man then under heavy cannonading from the Muckrakers, his experience in the Seth Low campaign, and chance opportunities that came his way all served to propel him toward what became the new vocation of public relations. For example, in this interim period, a lawyer friend of Lee asked him for assistance. Lee later recalled to writer for *Success* magazine:

> An important law suit was about to come up for trial in New Jersey, he said, important both to corporations directly interested and to the public. But it bristled with technicalities which the average man couldn't understand. He said that if I would take the papers in the case, go over them carefully and then write a newspaper story in simple terms telling what it was all about, the Newark paper might be glad to print it. . . . I enjoyed doing this, he paid me well for it, and the newspaper used what I had written. Similar work was offered me, which I accepted, and then it occurred to me that there might be a number of large corporations which would be glad to avail themselves of this kind of advice. I have been doing similar work ever since."

In handling this lawsuit, Lee again set a pattern for today's practice. It is now common for litigants to employ public relations specialists to put their particular spin on a case in court to influence public opinion.

PARKER AND LEE FORM PARTNERSHIP

Freelance assignments and some freelance magazine writing kept Lee going financially until George Parker's offer to work for the National Democratic Committee in the 1904 Presidential campaign came along. Working with Parker, "Mr Lee began to meet important national figures and to envision the field of endeavor of which, ultimately, he was to become the leader," his obituary in *Editor & Publisher* of 1934 recorded." That Ivy Lee should have been asked to join forces with a man of Parker's extensive journalistic and political background only 6 years after his arrival in New York City is testimony to the young man's ability to get himself where he wanted to go." George Parker confided to Pendleton Dudley that he saw Lee as a "very lively writer."

The partnership never flourished and the partners didn't get along too well. Ivy Lee told Pendleton Dudley more than once "Parker never brought much to the firm." There was a marked difference in their ages and in their approach to public relations. Parker, schooled in 19th century journalism and political campaigning, represented the old-time press agent and political fixer; by contrast, young Ivy Lee represented the coming of the more sophisticated approach to dealing with public opinion. Further, Ivy Lee, a strong-willed person, did not enjoy his role as a "junior partner" and would never again accept this role. Though the firm did not make money, it did make history.

After his successful campaign to regain the Presidency in 1892, Grover

Cleveland rewarded his publicity manager, George F. Parker, by making him U.S. counsel in Birmingham, England, a post Parker held until replaced by the Republicans in 1889. He stayed on in England 6 more years. During part of this time, he was engaged in private business and was Commissioner in the United Kingdom for the St. Louis Louisiana Purchase Exposition from 1901–1904, the latter largely a public relations job. Shortly after Parker returned to the United States, he accepted an offer to direct publicity for the Democratic National Committee for the 1904 campaign. One of his first acts was to hire Ivy Lee, who had won favorable attention by his work in the New York mayoralty election of 1903. Thus began a relationship that was to last until 1908 when the two men struck out in different directions—one headed for fame and fortune, the other toward the shadows of history.

Parker & Lee boasted of "Accuracy, Authenticity, and Interest" as the credo for their publicity work. Alfred McClung Lee wrote in *The Daily Newspaper in America*, "Parker & Lee decided that secrecy breeds suspicion and that the corporations' great men could be idealized—given suitable 'newspaper personalities'—in such a manner as to inspire popular confidence in their righteousness. After selling these notions to some clients, these astute rationalizers set to work to convince the newspapermen." That these two men were more responsible and honest in their work than most of the flamboyant press agents in these years is seen in the acclaim accorded them by *Editor & Publisher*, the newspaper trade journal, then quite hostile to public relations.

In 1908, *Editor & Publisher* said of Parker & Bridge, successor firm to Parker & Lee:

> This publicity bureau has established itself firmly in the estimation of editors and publishers of the United States. At its birth, this unique institution adopted the motto: "Accuracy, Authenticity, and Interest."
>
> It has never made any attempt at deception; matter is sent to the press with the frank statement that it is in behalf of the client, and that no money will be paid for its insertion in the columns of any newspaper. The aim has always been to present only topics of real interest, phrased so as to attract attention of both editors and readers—never sensational, never libelous, always accurate, always trustworthy, always readable.

Such praise from the press tradepaper that took a dim view of spacestealing press agents in those days was high praise indeed. Or, more likely, it was the uncritical acceptance of what reads like a news release from the Parker & Bridge typewriter. *E&P*, as it is known in the Fourth Estate, averred in 1908 that "the editors soon raised no question of the merit of their matter."

After he had been in the field nearly 20 years, Lee summarized his attitudes of those early years the field nearly 20 years in an interview with Joseph Ripley of *The American Press*, who was later hired by Lee and worked for the firm and its successors until 1965:

> When I started this business, it seemed to me there were two courses open to me. I could tell my clients what they wanted me to tell them. That, of course, would please them. But it would never get me very far. The other course was to tell them what I thought irrespective of their opinion. If my judgment was right, they would come to respect it. If I were wrong, I'd soon find it out. In either case, I'd eventually find my level.

Lee's first crucial test came in 1906 when the anthracite coal operators turned to Parker & Lee for help in telling management's side in the 1906 coal strike. There is no evidence that Parker was involved in this account. On accepting the operators as a client, Lee issued his Declaration of Principles that was, over time, to have a profound influence on the evolution of press agentry into publicity and publicity into public relations. In an era of "the public be damned," his declaration accentuated the positive right of the public to know: As quoted in Sherman Morse, "An Awakening in Wall Street," in the *American Magazine*:

> This is not a secret press bureau. All our work is done in the open. We aim to supply news. This is not an advertising agency; if you think any of our matter ought properly to go to your business office, do not use it. Our matter is accurate. Further details on any subject treated will be supplied promptly, and any editor will be assisted most cheerfully in verifying directly any statement of fact. . . . In brief, our plan is, frankly, and openly, on behalf of business concerns and public institutions, to supply to the press and public of the United States prompt and accurate information concerning subjects which it is of value and interest to the public to know about.

Revolutionary for its time, this profession of practice, though not always lived up to by Lee and his colleagues, stands as an important landmark in the evolution of public relations.

To measure the significance of this unprecedented declaration of public relations principle, one need only contrast the behavior of the anthracite coal operators in 1902 in their efforts to break a strike with their behavior after retaining Lee's counsel. When John Mitchell, head of the United Mine Workers, called a strike in the Pennsylvania coal fields in 1902, the coal owners followed policy of stoic silence in their feudal defiance. They would not respond to press queries nor even urgings of President Theodore Roosevelt, when he intervened in an effort to settle the strike. Their one statement that became the classic epitome of Big Business's prevailing antilabor attitudes was issued by mine owner George F. Baer. Baer, the hard-fisted leader the anthracite and rail companies in the strike, told the press, "The rights and interests of the laboring man will be protected and cared for not by labor agitators, but by the Christian men to whom God in his wisdom has given control the property interests of the country." A blundering statement equalled only by William Henry Vanderbilt's classic, "The public, the public be damned." John Mitchell, on the other hand, saw to it that both President Roosevelt and the press were given every cooperation. Public opinion built solidly behind the miners. George Baer learned his lesson, which led to Lee's retention in 1906 and acceptance of his policy of cooperating with the press.

Although the statement sounds platitudinous today, it was a bold declaration of a new day in Big Business's dealings with the public. Sherman Morse called attention to the sharp contrast between the coal operators' behavior in the 1902 strike and the situation in 1906. Comparing the two strikes, Morse in his *American Magazine* article, noted, How different it was last spring when another great strike was impending!! The Sphinx became talkative. News of importance and interest was easily obtainable from operators as well as miners. Ivy L. Lee, formerly a reporter for The *New York Times*, was openly employed as spokesman for the Trust. For weeks he carried on a campaign of education on behalf of the operators."

Understandably, "The Newspapers, weary of anonymous interviews and underhand methods, welcomed the change." Truly, as *The New York Times* observed years later, "Lee brought something new to the business of publicity."

There is scanty information available on the way the Parker & Lee partnership worked. Contrary to Lee's frequent assertion to Pendleton Dudley that Parker "never brought much to the firm," Parker did have powerful contacts in the world of business and politics; he introduced Lee to an important circle of associates that, like a chain reaction, provided him a lifelong entree to many of the world's leaders in government and industry. Parker was essentially an old-time press agent and political fixer; the more perceptive Lee saw the need for something more. It appears that they worked alone on accounts each one could land in the name of the firm.

Despite Pendelton Dudley's gloomy assessment of the Parker & Lee agency success, the partners found considerable demand for their services in this pioneering venture. Then, as now, institutions and industries turned to this new craft for help in time of crisis. The first of these was the General Asphalt Company, founded in 1903. The so-called Asphalt Trust was troubled by investor resentment over the bankruptcies of two of the asphalt companies in 1901. According to Alan R. Raucher in *Public Relations and Business 1900–1929*, another source of trouble was an undescribed trouble in Venezuela in 1906. This was Ivy Lee's account, and in a publicity pamphlet in 1906, he argued that the Trust "really had intimate relations with the public and was, therefore, undeserving of criticism." He suggested "exposure to true facts about the company would lead responsible people to fairer attitudes."

Another client that turned to Parker & Lee in a crisis was the International Harvester Company, which was the subject of investigation by the Bureau of Corporations as part of President Theodore Roosevelt's battle against "The Trusts." According to Raucher, "To protect the company against possible antitrust action, Perkins [George Perkins of the House of Morgan] started a lobbying campaign. He established cordial relations with representatives of the Roosevelt Administration. And to aid the campaign, International Harvester, in addition to its own publicity bureau, hired the Parker and Lee agency." J. P. Morgan was one of the first financial giants of this period to see that to win their way in Washington, they had to build a supportive public opinion and could no longer rely on pressure and bribery of legislators to gain the day. As part of this campaign to head off the antitrust action against the Harvester Trust, Lee published an article in *Moody's Magazine* of July 4, 1907, entitled "An Open and Above Board Trust." He argued that "enlightened self-interest" made the company "beneficent." As always it is difficult to assess the effect of a public relations campaign, but the fact remains that the Roosevelt Administration dropped its threatened action against the company. However, 3 years later the Justice Department sued the company for violation of the Sherman Anti-Trust Act.

Parker's contacts brought the new enterprise an account with George Westinghouse, who had learned the necessity of a good press in his battle against Thomas A. Edison and Samuel Insull in the "Battle of the Currents" in the late 1880s. Working for Edison who had invented the direct current of electricity distribution, Insull was running a scare campaign against Westinghouse's more efficient alternating current (AC) system. In 1889, Westinghouse had hired a Pittsburgh newspaper reporter, E. H. Heinrichs, to combat Edison's effort to prevent development of the Westinghouse AC systems; this is one of the first instances, if not the first, of a corporation hiring a publicity person. Parker also received an account from Thomas Fortune Ryan, wealthy financier, who had built a $200 million fortune through his New York streetcar and subway lines with fat Tammany contracts. Hiebert asserts, "Ryan came to believe in Parker & Lee so thoroughly that once he wrote out a check for $10, 000 in anticipations of their publicity efforts in his behalf." Lee used the $10, 000 check to persuade journalist Daniel T. Pierce to cast his lot with Parker & Lee in this new field of publicity. Daniel Pierce became a valued assistant to Lee when he organized his own firm in 1916. When Lee returned from a European trip in 1919, he made Pierce manager of Ivy Lee & Associates. According to T. J. Ross, Pierce "left the firm in the middle 20s to work for the anthracite coal operators." He later took a public relations position with the Sinclair Oil Co. (The firm's records show that Pierce left it April 1, 1926.) There is no doubt that Parker landed the Thomas Fortune Ryan account, which disputes Lee's assertion to Pendleton Dudley that "Parker never brought much to the business." But there is doubt as to just what services the firm provided Ryan, who shunned rather than sought publicity for himself. Parker, Ryan, and William C. Whitney had been previously associated in political and business enterprises. Ryan had given $450, 000 to the Democratic National Committee for the Alton Parker campaign the year before, thus he and Parker were associated in that common cause. William C. Whitney, a close friend of Grover Cleveland and George Parker, had been associated with Ryan in the exploitation of New York's new transportation system. Whitney, like Parker, had worked hard to elect Cleveland in the 1892 campaign. Thomas Fortune Ryan was a pallbearer at George Parker's funeral.

It appears that Ivy Lee landed the Pennsylvania Railroad as a client in 1906 and here achieved his first notable success. Two years later, he quit his partnership with Parker and took a full-time job with the Pennsylvania as director of publicity.

The railroad's reasons for hiring the firm and the company's evaluation of Lee's services is indicated by a letter from a Pennsylvania vice-president, M.J.B. Thayer, to a colleague on the Southern Pacific Railroad written in January 1907:

> We came to the conclusion, last June, that the time had come when we must take "offensive" measures as it were, to place our "case" before the public and we engaged a publicity firm — Messrs. Parker and Lee — to perform the work for us under our supervision. The engagement was made, as an experiment, for six months and we afterwards renewed it for an additional six months. Their work has been very satisfactory, and if you are considering making any such arrangements and have not yet completed them, I am inclined to think that an interview with Mr. Lee might be of advantage to you.

Apparently Southern Pacific's executives accepted the recommendation because in August 1907, Lee was touring the West as chief of the publicity bureau of Southern Pacific and the Union Pacific and as personal representative of E. H. Harriman, powerful railroad magnate.

EQUITABLE CRISIS GETS PARKER A "JOB"

During this period, George Parker continued to do political leg work for former President Grover Cleveland, whom he had served as publicist in

Cleveland's three Presidential campaigns. In 1905, a crisis came to the Equitable Life Assurance Society, that brought both President Cleveland's and Parker's talents into play. That year the crusading *New York World* created a furor with its exposure of corrupt practices among the great insurance companies operating under charters issued by the State of New York. According to Schriftgiesser's *The Lobbyists*, "the startling but seemingly well-documented newspaper stories met a favorable response from the people, who had been attuned to the words of the muckrakers and the inflammatory speeches of Theodore Roosevelt." Political pressure forced Governor Francis W. Higgins to call the New York Legislature into session. This resulted in the appointment of special joint Senate-Assembly committee to investigate the insurance companies. The committee was headed by Senator William A. Armstrong of Rochester and became known as the Armstrong Committee.

The insurance companies, particularly the Equitable Life Assurance Company, Mutual Life Insurance Company of New York, Prudential, and New York Life, were shown to have spent thousands of dollars to influence legislation. According to the testimony, these companies were shown to have spent thousands to keep mutual and effective watch over all revenue bills coming before Congress that might affect their revenues. Similar tactics were used on the state level "with the idea that they (the insurance companies) would be protected in matters of legislation. The Mutual and Equitable companies were joint operators of 'The House of Mirth' in Albany where their lobbyists and legislators would meet and enjoy 'entertainment.' " Andrew Fields, who managed the House of Mirth, disappeared before the committee could ask him how he spent $2, 948, 762 for "printing, stationery, and postage." From headquarters in New York City, there passed a steady stream of instruction on bills that should be killed, and on bills that should be supported. Such activities were denounced as "pernicious" by the Armstrong Committee.

In 1905, Parker was retained as an intermediary by Equitable to persuade former President Cleveland to accept the unpaid position of head of the trustees for Equitable, thus dampening down what threatened to be an overwhelming panic in wake of the Armstrong investigation. For his reward, Parker was made secretary to the trustees, a paid post that he held until 1909. Equitable's records indicate that Parker was on the Equitable payroll for this period as secretary to the trustees of the majority stock but that there is "no record of any incidents or activities of Mr. Parker," according to a letter from Equitable to Col. Gordon A. Moon, Parker's biographer, dated December 4, 1960. It appears that this paid job was Parker's pay for persuading Cleveland to lend his enormous prestige to the troubled firm.

Concurrently, Parker continued to do leg work for the ex-President as late as 1908. In 1907, he made a hurried trip through the Western states and reported back to Cleveland on his political observations. At that time, the former President was quite fearful of the threat posed by William Jennings Bryan, who was seeking his third try at the Presidency in 1908. Parker's last interview with the President was on March 12, 1908, not long before the former President's death.

It is difficult to be precise on the full range of Parker's activities after 1905, especially during the 1905–1913 period. He maintained an office during part of that time at the former Parker & Lee office, 20 Broad Street, where he was engaged in "journalistic literary work." Pendleton Dudley, whose public relations career spanned 57 years, said that when the Parker & Lee partnership broke up, Parker came to him with the suggestions that they join forces under the name of Parker and Dudley. Dudley declined, quite probably on the advice of his good friend Ivy Lee, and instead opened his own publicity agency in 1909. Then Parker, according to *Editor & Publisher*, "admitted to the partnership thus vacated" Charles A. Bridge, "hitherto manager."

The article that has the glow of a news release says of Bridge:

"Charlie" Bridge is a newspaper veteran, widely know in the profession. Born in Massachusetts in 1847, of direct lineal Puritan descent, he was educated in the public schools and tutored by his father, a well known clergyman.

In 1876 he started the *News* in Colebrook, New Hampshire, and in 1878 he moved to Boston. In that city he was employed on the staff of the *Herald*, *Advertiser*, and *Globe*, leaving the night editor's desk of the latter in 1888 to come to the *New York World*, on which paper he remained more than ten years. He did much as night city editor of that paper to "create" that position as it is known in the journalism of today.

Mr. Bridge was several years in the employ of Mr. Hearst, holding various executive positions for the New York *Journal* and *Chicago American*. Later he spent five years in the service of the *New York Herald*, as day city editor and on the night desk. . . . A year ago he came to Parker & Lee as office manager.

In its antipublicity campaign, ANPA listed Parker & Bridge, 20 Broad Street, as representing "general railroad and financial interests" as of 1910, and in a 1911 bulletin listing the space-stealing efforts of press agents, the ANPA cited a Parker & Bridge release for Lehigh Valley railroad in regard to its "fuel saving educational work." There is conflicting information on the name of the firm, how long it existed, and the identity of Parker's associates. Few records have been found that show clearly the extent of the firm's business.

Presumably the partnership folded in 1913 because in that year Parker took a job as secretary for press and publicity for the Committee of the General Convention of the Protestant Episcopal Church, a position he held until 1919. Late that year, he returned to the political wars as a counselor to General Leonard Wood, then starting his unsuccessful campaign for the Republican nomination for President in 1920. General Wood and Parker met at the Chicago Club in November 1919, although they might have met when Wood was serving as President Cleveland's physician. Parker still had many contacts in the world of big business and politics that would serve Wood. By then 73 years old, Parker did not become a full time publicity man for Wood but served primarily as a consultant. He followed the old forms of political press agentry, using, for example, handout cards, a technique employed by Parker and Lee 16 years earlier. Though Parker was not active in the day-to-day activities, he was frequently in conference with Wood and spent the last month before the convention in Chicago, according to General Leonard Wood's Diary of May 13, 1920.

In the early 1920s, Parker was paid at least $25, 000 by the Philippine Independence Fund to promote freedom for the Filipinos — an account that may well have come to Parker by way of General Wood. In May 1923, a great furor was created when American correspondent Junius B. Wood revealed that several Americans, in and out of government, had been paid to work for Filipino freedom. Led by Manual Quezon, the Filipinos established a Philippine Press Bureau in Washington to circulate independence literature. What Parker did for his $25, 000 is not clear. The Wood Diary offers no concrete clues as to what Parker did in the Philippines. Michael Onorate, a journalist, "is positive that Parker was not sent merely to ascertain the best means for setting up a campaign." Correspondence in the Wood Papers indicate that the veteran publicist was paid by the Philippine Independence Commission to prepare a long-range publicity campaign designed to bring independence issues to a head.

George Parker died May 31, 1928, in his 81st year, a man more remembered as Grover Cleveland's Boswell than as a pioneer public relations counselor. C. A. Bridge faded into oblivion altogether.

When George Parker and Ivy Lee set out to issue informational news releases and serve as intermediaries between their clients and the newspapers and magazines, then in a muckraking exposé mood, they were operating in a climate in which press agent was a dirty word. In his analysis of the publicity men of 1911, Will Irwin, referred to them as press agents and considered them generally a bad lot. By the end of the first decade, press agents were prominent in the worlds of circuses, Broadway, and other entertainment enterprises. Irwin placed them all unqualifiedly in one category, believing that they were "the only group of men proud of being called liars." But Irwin saw the George Parkers and Ivy Lees as pioneering a "new profession," the members of which were described as being "special pleaders—perhaps fair ones who help create mutual understanding—who are often useful counselors to their employers." Ivy Lee was equally disdainful of the press agent. His onetime classmate John Mumford wrote that Lee told a few corporation heads "that the whole idea was unsound, and the only way to get the respect of the American public or editors . . . was to trot straight with them." Lee made a clear distinction between the press agent and the publicity man, as he described himself in those early days.

IVY LEE EMERGES AS PARTNER IN HIS OWN RIGHT

When Ivy Lee acquired the Pennsylvania account, he persuaded the Pennsylvania executives to hire his brother, James Wideman Lee, Jr., as a full-time publicity writer for the railroad. Ivy Lee counseled on policy decisions and supervised the account through Parker & Lee. Wideman Lee had followed in his older brother's footsteps into journalism. Born at Dalton, Georgia, in 1882, he graduated from Emory College and then entered newspaper work. Wideman, as he was called, first worked on the Columbus, Georgia, *Ledger* in 1904 and 1905. He was state political editor of the *Atlanta Georgian*, a Hearst newspaper, when Ivy persuaded him to also follow him into publicity.

Soon after Ivy Lee had been retained by the Pennsylvania Railroad, he again dramatically illustrated his refreshing policy of the public be informed, not fooled. Prior to his coming to the railroad field, railroads generally tried to suppress news of accidents, then not uncommon, and their costs in lives and property. Shortly after Lee went to work for the Pennsylvania, a wreck occurred near Gap, Pennsylvania. Instinctively the railroad management put its news suppression machinery into motion. Just as quickly, Lee reversed it. Reporters were invited to travel to the scene of the accident at the railroad's expense. Lee promptly set up facilities for reporters and photographers. As Eric Goldman wrote in *Two Way Street*, "Angry protests came from some of the road's highest executives, but when the commotion settled down, Pennsylvania found itself basking in one of the few good presses it had enjoyed since the turn of the century."

The Pennsylvania won still more kudos when, shortly after the Gap accident, a wreck occurred on the New York Central line, the Pennsylvania's biggest competitor. The Central, adhering to standard railroad policy, put restrictions on information about the accident. Newsmen, understandably, were furious. Editorials strongly criticized the Central's action and praised the Pennsylvania's new open policy. Lee saw that a good press was to be obtained by providing journalists information they sought, not in bribing them with railroad passes, then a standard practice among rail-roads.

In 1908, Lee resigned from Parker & Lee and went to work full-time for the railroad with the title of director of the publicity bureau that he organized. Initially, his job and that of his brother, Wideman, was principally publicity. Always eager to broaden his horizons, Lee sought a leave of absence from the Pennsylvania in 1910 to manage the European office of Harris, Winthrop, and Company, a banking firm located in London. The interest he sought to pursue — the techniques of finance — was in line with his interest in the workings of corporations. This was typical of Lee of seeking new knowledge he thought he would need in his career. He was also a great believer in the educational value of travel. Lee's papers at Princeton University contain many folders of information he prepared in advance before going abroad.

Ivy Lee, Jr. explained his father's decision to quit the Pennsylvania in 1909 to gain corporate finance experience in London this way: "In 1909 . . . my father suddenly submitted his resignation. When asked, wasn't he satisfied, or wasn't his compensation adequate, he said: 'That is not the issue. I am resigning because I think international investment banking and finance will play an increasingly major role in world affairs in the years ahead and thus I want to go to Europe and learn how it operates.' " Ivy Lee never slackened in his striving for knowledge of the world about him.

Ivy Lee was not one to burn his bridges behind him; he built them. Before getting the leave of absence to join the Harris, Winthrop firm in London, Lee had a long talk with Pennsylvania executive M. J. B. Thayer in which Lee advocated moving his work to the Pennsylvania's policy level. While Lee was abroad, Mr. Thayer died in the sinking of the Titanic. In a letter from London to the executive who replaced Thayer, George B. Dixon, Lee mentioned his former job as publicity director in asking for a position at the policy-making level if he returned to the railroad. The letter reviewed the conversation he had with Mr. Thayer prior to his going to Europe. "I think Mr. Thayer felt that my brother should continue his present work of supplying to the newspapers such information as the company chooses to make public." The letter reflects a growing two-way concept of public relations as it is known today, although he clung to the term publicity well into the late 1920s.

I think both Mr. Thayer and I saw many ways in which a line of activity could be developed within the company which would be as valuable as it would be novel — a program designed primarily to bring about a greater harmony of understanding between the public and the railroads and the large corporations generally. Mr. Thayer felt, I think, that my experience and training, added to the special study I had made, both of these questions as well as the method of pressing them as an appeal to the public, I could materially assist in interpreting to the public the Pennsylvania Railroad itself—its actions, its motives, and its purpose, as well as seek to bring before the company those aspects of railroad policy and activity in regard to which interest of both the companies and the people are so signally interwoven.

Lee won his case and became executive assistant of the Pennsylvania railroad in 1912, the first known instance of a public relations person being placed at the management level.

His main campaign on behalf of the railroad industry—then in deep trouble with the public—was an effort to win public approval for the Eastern lines' request that the Interstate Commerce Commission allow them to enact a 5% rate increase. The railroads had tried to get this in 1910 and failed. Railroad executives thought that the reason that they had failed was that they had not gotten their story to the public and resolved to correct their mistakes in the 1912 campaign. Reflecting his maturing philosophy, Ivy Lee told them, "I believe in telling your story to the public. If you go direct to the people and get the people to agree with you, you will have no trouble in getting justice from legislatures, commissions, or anybody else." When Lee left the Pennsylvania in December 1914 to work for the Rockefellers, the letters he received from railroad officials and the comments of the press show how highly his work was regarded.

Wrote G. R. Peck, the fourth vice-president of the Pennsylvania, "You have really accomplished the main purpose you undertook in developing a real practical policy for the handling of publicity affairs or rather for the development of proper relations between the corporation and the public." One who could truly appreciate Lee's efforts to turn public opinion about the railroads around was J. Hampton Baumgartner, a pioneer publicist for the Baltimore & Ohio Railroad. Interestingly, Baumgartner used the term *public relations*. He wrote, "I feel that the work which you have devoted to matters concerning the railroads and their public relations have been productive of far reaching results, not only to the Pennsylvania but to all public carriers, by bringing about an intelligent understanding of the problems which confront the railroads and efforts put forth to solve them effectively."

As indicated in chapter 1, "The Nation's First Publicity Bureau," the failure of the railroads in their 1906 nationwide propaganda campaign, spearheaded by the Publicity Bureau, had caused railroad executives to reassess their public relations policies. Thus the executives of the Pennsylvania and the B&O were receptive to the counsel of Ivy Lee and J. Hampton Baumgartner respectively. The B&O established its publicity department in 1910 with Baumgartner in charge. The output of these proliferating publicity departments in the nation's railroad met with something less than enthusiasm on the part of newspapermen.

The constructive approach to dealing with public opinion that Ivy Lee brought to this adolescent field can be seen in the Rockefellers' first and second efforts to deal with the rising tide of protest against John D. Rockefeller's monopolistic and ruthless ways of exploiting the public.

Interestingly enough, the only time John D. Rockefeller, Sr. was moved to admit the need for public relations counsel in his relationships with the public was when his motives for philanthropy were damned in the "tainted money" controversy. He took the step reluctantly and only at the strong insistence of the Reverend Frederick T. Gates. In 1895, the Reverend Washington Gladden, a Congregational minister, had published an article, "Tainted Money," in which he denounced the benefactions of the rich "robber barons" and "pirates of industry" as a transparent means of buying public favor and heavenly salvation. In the article, Gladden mentioned no names but the public thought most of his arrows were aimed at John D. Rockefeller, Sr. In 1905, Gladden renewed the charge and named Rockefeller when the minister violently opposed acceptance of a gift of $100, 000 from Rockefeller to the Congregational Board of Foreign Missions.

John D., Sr.'s tough business mind had long been inured to harsh public criticism of his ruthless business tactics. He never made an effort to reply to public attacks. Once, when questioned by a reporter about Ida Tarbell's attacks on Standard Oil, John D., Sr. replied, "Not a word, not a word about that misguided woman." But the criticism of Gladden and others cast a dark shadow across his philanthropies and cut deeply into Rockefeller's Baptist quick. In the midst of the 1905 dispute, Gates wrote Rockefeller, plainly pointing out to him the error of his policy of secrecy. "While replying frigidly to Gates, Rockefeller gave way. He asked Gates to see [John D.] Archbold; and it turned out that he had sent Gates's letter to the head of Standard, and had frankly yielded the whole question." This led to employment of Joseph Ignatius Constantine Clarke, colorful Irish newsman, as "publicity agent" for the Standard Oil Company in 1906 at a salary of $5, 000 a year, later raised to $6, 000 a year, high wages for the early 1900s. Clarke was assigned to the legal department, a logical move given that department's functions in Standard Oil. In their classic history of Standard Oil Hidy and Hidy wrote, "Quite apart from handling litigation, the department performed the function of keeping well informed on public opinion, projected legislation, and new enactments. A vast correspondence flowed to [Mortimer F.] Elliott's desk from Standard Oil employees, attorneys, and newspapermen." Such duties would fall under the heading of Public Affairs today but reflects the heavy corporate reliance on lawyers lobbying of legislators that prevailed in that day and continues today.

Such reliance on the legal department by the Rockefellers and Archbold proved ironic indeed with the coming of Ivy Lee to counsel the Rockefellers.

Ivy Lee had a strong bias against lawyers being involved in public relations. In an address before the annual convention of the American Electric Railway Association on October 10, 1919, Lee said, "in trying to express yourselves in language which the people can understand, *avoid lawyers.* I have seen more situations which the public ought to understand and which the public would sympathize with, spoiled by the intervention of lawyers than in any other way. Whenever a lawyer starts to talk, he shuts out the light."

Clarke had been Sunday editor of the *New York Herald* from 1903 until he was hired by Archbold in 1906. Before that he had several reporting and reviewer assignments on the *Herald*. Earlier he worked for the *Morning Journal* and the literary weekly, *The Criterion*.

Clarke worked to refurbish the Standard Oil Company's reputation more than to explain and publicize Rockefeller's philanthropies. "My contact was naturally with the Directors, [Henry H.] Rogers and Archbold particularly." One of Clarke's first moves was to promote "an authenticated history of the Standard Oil," that is, one favorable to Rockefeller, to counter Ida Tarbell's the *History of the Standard Oil Company,* published in two volumes in 1904 and which by now, was deeply impressed on the public's mind. "The Reverend Dr. Bacon was engaged," but "he passed away before he had taken the Company far on the road." However, Chancellor James R. Day of Syracuse University, a "booming flagellant of sinners . . . worshiped for his sense of justice," came to Standard's rescue with "a good clear story" but "the press pooh-poohed it." Clarke was obviously referring to the book defending Standard Oil written by Chancellor Day—*The Raid on Prosperity*—published in 1908 by D. Appleton.

In his preface, Day does seem to protest too much: "My convictions have not come to me out of the exigencies of a college presidency or by the contaminating influence to millionaires!" Yet that same year, 1908, Day's Syracuse University dedicated one of the first modern football stadiums in the nation—a gift of Standard Oil President John D. Archbold. Starting with an initial gift of $165 in 1886, Archbold had given Syracuse, through June 1913, a total of $1, 737, 038.57, most of which consisted of gifts for current expenses, and the costs of erecting Sims Hall, and the stadium and gymnasium, both of which bore Archbold's name.

At the same time that Standard Oil was changing its policies on dealing with the press, so was John D. Rockefeller changing his aloof ways. He began to grant reporters interviews and, starting in October 1908, he published in *World's Work* a series of autobiographical articles. The new policies of Standard Oil and Rockefeller brought generally favorable comment from the press. Yet the new concept was not fully accepted at Standard Oil, and by 1911, the officials quit providing information to Clarke. Frustrated, J. I. C. Clarke quit Standard Oil in 1913.

IVY LEE HIRED BY ROCKEFELLERS

During this period, although Lee was using publicity to described his work, his concept of a broader function grew steadily and his success with it. At this time, he was heavily engaged in directing the railroads' campaign for a rate increase, a campaign that involved strategies and tactics well beyond news dissemination. In 1914, an epochal development in the history of public relations counseling came with Lee's appointment as counsel to John D. Rockefeller, Jr. The Rockefellers, father and son, were under heavy verbal assault from the nation's press and public for their brutal strike-breaking tactics in their Colorado Fuel & Iron Co. (C.F & I) strike. This pattern of seeking public relations counsel in a time of crisis set a pattern to be repeated thousands of times from that day to this.

In 1904, the operators of the Rockefeller mine property used State troopers to savagely suppress a strike. After this C.F. & I replaced the strikers with recruitment of immigrants who soon, in the words of one author, "were denied every right and soon reduced to a state of actual peonage." In September 1913, the strikebreakers of 1904 staged a strike against C.F. & I led by the United Mine Workers. George Creel, then a crusading Denver journalist but who would later make history with the Creel Committee in World War I, gave this account of the Ludlow Massacre that aroused the nation's hate against the Rockefellers in his memoir, *Recollections of Fifty Crowded Years*:

> Not more than a fourth of the twelve thousand strikers were members of the United Mine Workers, but the union assumed entire responsibility for the care of all, housing some twenty-one thousand men, women, and children in tent colonies on the mountainsides when they were driven from their company-owned homes. . . . the allied operators organized a private army, and to their aid soon came the militia, called out by a servile governor. Military courts superseded civil authority, the writ of habeas corpus was suspended, and hundred of miners were imprisoned without warrant and held without trial.

> The reign of terror culminated on April 20, 1914 in what came to be known as the "Ludlow Massacre." At a given signal, troops and mine guards opened fire on a tent colony and kept it up until dark. The strikers fought back from arroyos, while the women and children sought the refuge of safety pits dug under the tents. . . . machine guns ignited the flimsy shelters. The flaming canvas then dropped down on the pits, scorching scores and burning two mothers and eleven children to a crisp.

A bewildered John D., Jr., who would later testify that the mine operators had not informed him of any of these illegal activities, turned to Hearst editor and columnist Arthur Brisbane for advice. Brisbane recommended that Rockefeller try to obtain the services of Ivy Lee from the Pennsylvania Railroad. This plea for help came when Lee was enjoying high credibility with the press. For example, the *Philadelphia Ledger* of December 8, 1914, stated "Ivy Lee is what I might call a foremost example of 'Let the Light Shine.' " Lee initially was employed to advise John D. Rockefeller, Jr., but not John D., Sr. In fact, according to Allan Nevins, a Rockefeller biographer selected by Lee, said that the retaining of Lee was initially opposed by the father but his long-standing policy of not interfering with his son's management stayed his hand. Lee's skillful muffling of the criticism of the Rockefellers in the wake of that bloody Colorado strike led to his retention in December 1914 as public relations counsel for the Rockefeller interests. Ultimately Lee worked for both father and son and their widespread interests.

Impressed with Lee in their first conference in May 1914, Rockefeller told him, "This is the first advice that I have had that does not involve deviousness of one kind or another." Rockefeller then sought permission from Samuel Rea, president of the Pennsylvania, to borrow Lee's services. Because Lee was then hard at work trying to build public support for a freight increase, Rea refused but said Lee could advise the Rockefellers. Lee continued to direct the publicity campaign for the rate increase until it was won in December 1914 and took on the Colorado strike problem "in his spare time."

It was brought out in the U.S. Commission on Industrial Relations' hearing in the wake of the Colorado strike that Lee was paid out of John D. Sr's funds. Lee began his work for the Rockefellers on June 1, 1914, and was paid a salary of $1, 000 a month — a very high figure in those times, one that increased the recognition of publicity's importance. A trusted counselor to John D., Jr. for 23 years, Ivy Lee undoubtedly influenced the Rockefeller philanthropic decisions to some extent over those two decades, although the exertion of this influence shrouded their confidential relationships. In major philanthropic decisions, Lee's influence was not primary. For example, his partner of 15 years, T. J. Ross, told me in an interview on March 10, 1959, that he "did not believe that Ivy Lee had any direct influence on the creation of the Rockefeller and Guggenheim Foundations, but he did counsel on their activities." Ross made it clear that Lees counsel for John D., Jr. included his family and his father up to the time of his death. Ross was quite emphatic that Lee did not persuade John D., Sr. to give any dimes to small children. Ross and others have insisted that this was John D.'s idea. Yet the myth persists to this day that this was an Ivy Lee gimmick. For example, writing in 1990, Candice Jacobson Fuhrman, in her book, *Publicity Stunt,* asserted:

> When John D. Rockefeller refused to talk to reporters after a mining accident
> at his company in which many people were killed, he had become one of the

most hated men in the nation. But all that changed in a few years later when he hired Ivy Lee, one of the first press agents to specialize in working for industry. By counseling Rockefeller to give away dimes whenever a crowd gathered (and a suitable number of reporters were there to record it) Ivy Lee is credited with completely transforming Rockefellers' image.

As Practitioners know, truth seldom overtakes fact in the race of events.

When the Rockefellers retained Ivy Lee, this act was widely publicized — as with any event involving the Rockefeller family — and thus brought this new vocation to the attention of the nation, particularly its business and political leaders. In the pre-World War I era when Lee was doing his important work, his emphasis, despite the statement quoted previously, seems to have remained on publicity. Ivy Lee quickly and easily identified himself with the interests and values of Big Business. He tended to believe that business was correct in its works, and if the public only knew of its good works, the public would approve. In one essay, Lee put in bold capital letters this: "I BELIEVE IN TELLING YOUR STORY TO THE PUBLIC. The greatest service public relations could perform was to do for business what Billy Sunday has done for religion — publicize its policies in the language of the man who rides the trolley car and goes to ball games, who chews gum and spits tobacco juice."

Unlike Edward L. Bernays who would follow him into public relations after World War I, Lee made no effort to outline a coherent philosophy for his new-found vocation even though he voiced the two-way concept. He constantly referred to his work as an art. In fact, Bernays was quoted in November 1941 as saying, "He [Ivy Lee] used to tell me that this was an artist's field, that what he was doing would die with him." In fact as late as 1927 at a hearing of the United Transit Commission, the commission's special counsel, Samuel Untermeyer, asked Lee to define his work, to which Lee replied, "I don't know sir, I have never been able to find a satisfactory phrase to describe what I try to do." Nonetheless, he continued to ply his trade by counseling on dealing fairly with the press and public and urging business on its good behavior. As a consequence, his reputation as a sagacious counselor steadily grew. His name became "news."

As Hiebert recounted in *Courtier to the Crowd,* Lee's definitive biography:

The month of December, 1914, was climatic in the career of Ivy Lee. The freight rate advance [a campaign on which he had been working for two years] was passed by the Interstate Commerce Commission. The Colorado strike came to an end. And within a month, the Congressional Commission had revealed to the whole world that Ivy Lee had been personally responsible for those momentous developments. Finally, the Commission hearings revealed that Ivy Lee was now the right hand man to senior John D. Rockefeller himself. In the popular mind, Lee became the man behind the scenes manipulating the world's greatest industrialists and solving their problems.

To understand the magnitude of Lee's first assignment with the Rockefellers, one has to sense the growing public anger over the ruthless efforts of Rockefeller's absentee managers to break the strike that started in 1913.

When John D., Jr. turned to Lee in desperation, Lee counseled, "The first and most important part of any plan should be its absolute frankness; that there should be no devious ways employed." Lee also urged that if the mine operators had a story to tell, "they ought to tell it themselves, and tell it frankly and tell it fully." Rockefeller was really in the dark as to what was going on in Colorado because his managers had been telling him what they thought he wanted to hear, another classic case of failed internal communication; a problem that plagues large organizations to this day. The mine managers also misled Lee, much to his later embarrassment.

After his first conference with Rockefeller in May 1914, Lee had studied the Colorado strike situation and in June 1914, he came up with a plan he outlined in a letter of June 5. He suggested a series of bulletins entitled "The Struggle in Colorado for Industrial Freedom." Lee sent Rockefeller the galley proofs of the first bulletin and suggested a topic for the second. The bulletins contained press notices and articles about the strike situation that put the company in a favorable light. Ray Hiebert maintained that "most of the bulletins contained matter which on the surface was true but which presented the facts in such a way as to give a total picture that was false." Gradually the forces of the union weakened, and by December 1914, after the strike had dragged on for 8 months, the miners voted to go back to work.

When the United States Commission on Industrial Relations charged that Lee had falsified the information he had issued on behalf of C.F &I, Lee lamely replied, "My Job is simply that of advisor and I advise my clients to tell the truth. . . . My idea is that the principal himself should be his own publicity agent. That the function of a person like myself, for example, when acting in that capacity, should be advice with the man who has to take the responsibility for the act itself as to what he should do and what he should say," according to the commission's record of testimony.

Lee, who had been on leave from the Pennsylvania, resigned at the end of 1914 and moved back to New York to work for the Rockefellers full time. Hiebert said, "His departure from the Pennsylvania caused the railroad some unfair publicity when newspaper accused it of being owned by the Rockefellers."

In his work for the Rockefellers and a list of other clients, Lee began adding another dimension to his concept of truthful publicity promptly disseminated. He soon came to realize that in order to win public approval a business or institution must do things that the public perceives as good and beneficial. Again to quote Eric Goldman:

> When the Rockefellers retained Lee, some of their policies ran so counter to general feeling that no amount of semantics could have explained them into any appreciable favor. It was in this circumstance that Lee first conceived of public relations as a two-way function, and by 1916 he was maintaining: "Publicity in its ultimate sense means the actual relationship of a company to the people, and that relationship involves far more than saying — it involves doing. An elementary requisite of any sound publicity must be, therefore, giving the best possible service."

These are the basic elements of today's mature public relations concept.

Lee's experiences as a reporter, political adviser, and publicist for Mayor Seth Low and Judge Alton Parker, his work in Parker & Lee, and for the Pennsylvania and the Rockefellers had, by this time, led him to crystallize his principles of "the psychology of the multitude" to these fundamentals, according to Hiebert:

1. Success of dealing with crowds rests upon the art of getting believed in.
2. Getting believed in requires leaders who can fertilize the imagination and organize the will of the crowds.
3. Since crowds do not reason, they can only be organized and stimulated through symbols and phrases.

Perhaps somewhere in his education he had read and taken seriously Gustave LeBon's *The Crowd*, published in Paris around the turn of the century, a pioneering work in public opinion. LeBon's book also influenced Earl Newsom, a later pioneer whose work is covered in the last three chapters.

IVY LEE SETS UP HIS OWN FIRM — THE SEVENTH

Emboldened by the success of his work for the railroad freight campaign and for John D. Rockefeller, Jr. and Sr., Lee decided to establish his own agency, Lee, Harris, and Lee, the seventh agency and last one to be started in the pre-World War I era. Lee first submitted his resignation to John D. Rockefeller, Jr. at the end of 1915, a resignation the client refused to accept. They agreed, instead, that Lee could form his own firm but would continue to counsel the Rockefellers, father and son, the C.F&I., and the Rockefeller Foundation. One of his partners was his brother Wideman, whom he persuaded to leave Pennsylvania and join him in this new venture, that opened its doors on April 1, 1916. The other partner was W. W. Harris, a former newspaper reporter and editor. Harris, a graduate of the University of Michigan, had been working on the *New York Herald.* Wideman Lee left the firm in the early 1920s to become vice-president and later president of the George L. Dyer advertising agency. It was speculated at the time that he wanted to get out from the shadow of his famous brother. Wideman was replaced by Lee's youngest brother, Lewis. Unlike the early days of Parker & Lee, the new firm, because of Ivy's new fame, had little trouble in attracting clients. Lee wrote his father, "It is very evident that I am going to have all the business I can take care of."

Even before chartering his new firm, he had firm retainers from the Pennsylvania Railroad and John D. Rockefeller, Jr. He quickly acquired two new clients, the Interborough Rapid Transit (IRT) of New York City and Bethlehem Steel. In 1916, the IRT was faced with an employee strike with public opinion firmly on the side of the strikers.

When Ivy Lee opened his own firm, he wrote his father, "My feeling is that I have devoted the whole of my life to the present time in preparing for the work which I am just now undertaking. Of course the whole of my life is an education and my life will continue to be one, but I feel that now I ought to begin to realize on the preparation which I have had." In probably what was the first agency to cite its asset of independence in giving candid counsel to clients, Lee also wrote his father, "It is certainly delightful to be free, to be able to do what you please, and with nobody to tell you what to do. It is what I have dreamed of being able to do for a great many years."

When Ivy Lee decided to establish his own counseling firm in 1916, he took pains to assure John D. Rockefeller, Jr. that his interest would always have first claim on his time. He wrote John D., Jr., "I do want you to feel that you can go away with full assurance that all your interests, insofar as I am watching out for them, are in good shape and receiving adequate attention."

In 1916, Bishop William Lawrence undertook one of the largest fund drives in pre-World War I America when he set out to raise nearly $6,000,000 to start a Church Pension Fund to provide a dignified retirement for the Episcopal Church's priests. In launching this drive, Bishop Lawrence saw publicity as the great problem. He hired two young publicists whose names he graciously did not record and found that "they would not do." In frustration, he took a train to Philadelphia to consult his friend Edward W. Bok, successful magazine editor for the Curtis Publishing Co. Bok gave the Bishop this advice: "Go on as you are: only visualize your individuals; depict, describe your pathetic cases. Money for Belgium stopped flowing last summer; then I happened to see in the paper that Belgian babies wanted milk. We plastered the city with 'Belgian babies want milk' and the flow began again. People give when their sympathies are touched."

Elated by this guidance from a distinguished editor, Lawrence returned to New York and invited Ivy Lee to his office for a conference. Lee rejected Bok's advice, saying, "The sympathies of the American people are bruised and raw with the cry of Belgium; you cannot depict an old parson or his widow or orphan today in such a way as to get people to give. Moreover, in the long run emotional appeals lose their force. The American people, intelligent, just, and generous to a cause that appeals to them, want facts and figures." Over the next week, Bishop Lawrence and Ivy Lee agreed on a campaign of publicity based on facts more than upon emotion. Bishop Lawrence himself possessed a keen sense of publicity. He wisely saw — long before many publicists realized it — that it is the content of the publicity, not the quantity of it, that counts in building public opinion. In the hindsight of his successful Church Pension Fund campaign that raised nearly $9, 000, 000 before it was done, Bishop Lawrence wrote, "Tons of paper and printer's ink are wasted every day. . . . publicity should be so simple and clear that he who runneth may read." Ivy Lee's counsel in this major fund drive would stand him in good stead for his next assignment — war duty with the American Red Cross.

NEW FIRM LANDS STANDARD OIL OF
NEW JERSEY AS CLIENT

Not long after Lee organized his new agency, he landed Standard Oil of New Jersey as a major client. Standard of New Jersey was one of 33 companies organized after Judge Kennesaw Mountain Landis broke up the Standard Oil trust that had been welded together by John D. Rockefeller. The new companies came into being with the clouds of distrust and hate that had led to the government's antitrust action against the original Standard Oil. The monopolistic cartel had reinforced this distrust by bribing the press and not telling the public the truth. The new president of Jersey Standard, A. Cotton Bedford, recognized this and announced at the outset that "I mean to keep my door wide open to every person having a legitimate call upon my attention." Early in 1917 to implement this new open door policy, Bedford retained Lee. Whether this was at the suggestion of John D. Rockefeller, Jr. or not is not known. Rockefeller no longer had any authority in these new companies.

When Bedford sought Lee's advice, Lee told him, according to Hiebert's biography, "He could not carry on in the tradition of subsidizing newspapers to print complimentary stories. It would be useless for him to write and publish articles on his own, appealing to the public to change its view, for the public would not read them. The first step necessary would be for Bedford to set his house in order and then associate himself with the most progressive groups in the oil business." Lee's standard prescription: "Set your house in order, then tell the public you have done so." Bedford's efforts were given a boost along the way when his competitors chose him to head the Committee on Mobilization for the oil industry. In this and other ways, Bedford brought a spirit of cooperation to the oil industry that earlier had known only cutthroat competition.

At Lee's suggestion, the American Petroleum Institute (API) was founded in 1919 by the men and companies who had been active in the Committee on Mobilization. This Institute pattern that Lee originated came to be copied by the iron and steel industry, the meat industry, and other industrial groups needing to present a solid front to the public. Lee's firm was hired by the new Institute to serve as its public relations representative. The Institute became a respected central clearing house for information on the oil industry and central body for dealing with the common problems of all oil companies. The API continues to serve this function today.

Lee faced an uphill battle in bringing a good name and goodwill to Standard Oil of New Jersey. It and its successor companies—Esso, Humble, and now Exxon—despite a heavy investment in public relations have gone from one public relations crisis to another. There are some observers who think Jersey Standard and its successors have never fully recovered from Ida Tarbell's muckrakers exposure in the early 1900s. The late Earl Newsom, leading counselor from the 1940s to the 1960s, once observed, "The Ida Tarbell book fixed a position for decades; it made the oil industry and anything connected with the oil industry a setting duck for criticism." This blemished picture of the oil industry keeps repeating itself one decade to another, whether it is a gasoline shortage bringing long lines at the pump or a quick price jump with the onset of the Crisis in the Gulf. Exxon got a large public black eye in 1989 with its apparent indifference to the damage caused by the largest domestic oil spill in history when an Exxon tanker ran aground in the pristine waters of Prince William Sound in Alaska; this accident cost Exxon billions of dollars and much public anger.

IVY LEE HEADS THE RED CROSS'S WARTIME PUBLICITY

A little more than a month after the United States entered the war, President Wilson created the Red Cross War Council and entrusted to it "the duty of responding to the extraordinary demands which the present war will make upon the services of the Red Cross both in the field and in civilian relief." He added, "The best way in which to impart the greatest efficiency and energy to the relief work which this war will entail will be to concentrate it in the hands of a single experienced organization which has been recognized by law and by international convention as the public instrumentality for such purposes." The recommendation for the war council had grown out of a meeting on April 21 of top Red Cross officials and nationally known civic leaders whom President Wilson had invited to advise him.

The meeting was promoted by Eliot Wadsworth and presided over by Cleveland H. Dodge, the temporary chairman. The president was represented in this meeting by U.S. Secretary of War Newton D. Baker, former Cleveland mayor. Speaking from his Cleveland experience, Baker strongly urged that the Red Cross was the agency that had both national and international recognition and that it would be better to combine all relief efforts and do whatever had to be done through one organization. Baker outlined a long list of services that could and should be provided the armed forces.

The war council brought the leadership and methods of Big Business to the Red Cross. Wilson appointed Henry F. Davison, a partner in the firm of J. P. Morgan, as chairman. At first, President Wilson was quite reluctant to appoint Davison or anyone else from Wall Street but was finally persuaded to do so by Cleveland H. Dodge, who worked through Wilson's confidant, Colonel Edward House. Wilson and Dodge had been warm friends since their student days at Princeton, and Dodge was one Wall Streeter trusted by Wilson. Davison, then 50 years of age, was known to his friends as Harry, the name his parents had given him. He later changed his name to Henry Pomeroy Davison. A member of the Morgan firm since 1909, he was described as "a man with keen insight, ability and courage and one whose judgment was highly respected." Certainly he was a man of action. He took over the day the order was published and gave each member of the war council staff a definite assignment. For himself he kept the publicity responsibility, thus giving public relations top priority.

To direct the tremendous task of raising the money needed to finance the activities assigned the Red Cross by Wilson, Davison summoned the champion money-raiser, Charles Sumner Ward, who served for the duration of the war on loan from the International Committee of the YMCA. Ward was given the title of secretary of the War Finance Committee. Ward then made Harvey J. Hill, already on the Red Cross membership bureau staff, his associate secretary. Early in June, Davison added another future fund-raiser to the staff when he made Robert F. Duncan recorder of the War Council. Duncan, then 27 was secretary of the Harvard Endowment Fund Committee of which Davison's partner at the J. P. Morgan Company, Thomas W. Lamont, was chairman. A minor official in the War Council, Duncan later made his mark with John Price Jones and Kerstin, Brown, & Company.

With war fever obliterating such peace-time pursuits as muckraking, corporation heads, hitherto anemthatized, were called to places of power. Millionaires, supposed to be the only ones to know how to think and act in millions and billions, were given charge of government's 'big business.' " And it "was not uncommon for the dollar a year patriot to have his $1, 000-a-year press agent."

Like many organizations in the nonprofit sector in the early years of this century, the Red Cross had followed a faltering half-hearted publicity policy until 1914 when Austin Cunningham was hired to head the Division of Information. Cunningham followed the limited publicity patterns prevailing prior to American entry into World War I, seeking to accomplish the objectives of his office "through press releases, magazines articles, monthly 'clips,' and monthly advance sheets to 2, 500 newspapers. The news releases were used to solicit funds for the European and Mexican War Relief, and to announce important Red Cross changes."

Cunningham put most of his effort into the *Red Cross Magazine.* He had built a circulation of 300, 000 for this magazine by November 1916 when its publication was transferred to Doubleday, Page, & Company. Cunningham was stricken with tuberculosis in February 1917 and left the Red Cross to recuperate. With his departure, the Division of Information ceased to exist, and with America's entry into the war and the designation of the Red Cross as the nation's relief agency, there was an urgent need for a bold, imaginative public relations program.

Such a program was gradually constructed by Ivy L. Lee, one of the first persons drafted by Davison. For the first few months, Lee served on an informal, unofficial basis, commuting between New York and Washington. This explains why the war council, when announcing its initial staff appointments, provided for only an official photographer and a recorder. However, Lee was quite active in the background. He helped Davison shape his May 10 announcement of his acceptance as war council chairman and at the same time got him to agree to a policy of full disclosure of all information pertaining to the Red Cross. As Lee explained later:

> The first thing I impressed upon him [Davison] was that we were going to handle many millions of the people's money, that we were largely a group of Republicans working under a Democratic administration, and that if the slightest breath of scandal attached to any (of our actions, we might be subjected to a Congressional investigation at the first opportunity. Let us prepare for an investigation now, I said, and then there won't be any. Accordingly we prepared a system of records and checks against these records which covered every dollar. . . . And we took the people into our confidence from the start . . . and we came through clean.

This policy of full disclosure was confirmed by Davison in a statement issued to the public under his name. In a press release dated August 4, 1917, marked for release Sunday, August 5, Davison declared:

> It is the earnest desire of the Red Cross that the American people, to whom the Red Cross belongs, should know all about its acts and its affairs. The people have given a wonderful exhibition of generosity and big heartedness and at their bidding the American Red Cross has undertaken the most stupendous effort in the history of mankind to relieve suffering and distress.

> The accounts of the Red Cross are regularly audited by the War Department and an annual report is made to Congress. But it is the purpose of the War Council to take the people, day by day, as fully as possible into its confidence. Information as to Red Cross matters will accordingly be made public in great detail.

And these were-under the deft hand of the man who probably wrote Davison's statement, Ivy Lee.

Lee consulted with Davison and other members of the war council on questions of basic policy that arose in great number in the early, chaotic days of the council when it was without patterns and precedents. Lee was helpful in shaping the plans for the first big fund drive, contributing the services of his staff in New York City to handle the publicity for the Atlantic Division. But the unofficial, part-time role of Lee did not suit Davison, and he pressed Lee to accept a full-time appointment without salary. Lee did so, and on July 11, 1917, the war council appointed him "assistant to the Chairman of the War Council to give the utmost publicity . . . to the activities of the Red Cross." Lee was given authority, under Davison's direction, over "matters relating to publicity, publications, and the *Red Cross Magazine*. Lee indicated that the choice of title was his and that he eschewed the title of publicity director or press agent because "the public is suspicious." Lee correctly insisted that public relations must function at the policy level. In this Davison concurred. Lee became the right-hand man of Davison, living with him in Washington, eating with him, and traveling with him. A year later Davison told Lee, "I have come to feel a strong affection for you."

Lee's publicity program for the Red Cross soon included:

> The *Red Cross Magazine*. The editorial content was prepared under Lee's direction, picking up where Cunningham had left off; Moving pictures, including their production and distribution, to show the work being done by the Red Cross; News, to disseminate all information about the Red Cross' needs, services, and aims through all news channels; The Red Cross Bulletin, an internal house organ to provide information to the various departments of

the Red Cross, branches, chapters, and others interested; An Information Bureau at national headquarters for the reception of visitors and the answering of routine queries; Speakers' Bureau to arrange for lectures on the Red Cross in cooperation with lecture bureaus, clergymen, school teachers, etc;

Advertising Section to present the Red Cross story through newspaper and magazine advertising, poster, and other forms of advertising that may be found possible.

A general reorganization of the Red Cross Publicity Department along these lines was effected September 1, 1917, after Lee had sufficient time to observe, plan, and experiment with publicity patterns. Under this reorganization, the publicity function was strengthened in subordinate units, and a publicity director was named on the permanent staff in each of the 14 divisions, to work in direct contact with the national headquarters. A year later the Publicity Department consisted of a headquarters group, three main bureaus, and two coordinating divisions. Joseph Johnson was made director of the new department and there served as Lee's chief of staff.

The Red Cross Annual Report issued in June 1918 described the Publicity Department as "the main channel of communication and understanding between those headquarters . . . and the great body of Red Cross workers and the public." In something of an understatement, the report continued, "By presenting to the public the need of an extra-military agency in the winning of the war, the Publicity Department aided in increasing membership and in raising funds." The Red Cross publicity machine, radiating from the "Marble Palace" to local chapters in the nation's more than 3, 000 counties, was greatly augmented by the donated services of Lee's New York staff. Two volumes of clippings in Lee's Matter-Sent-Out archives attest to this contribution to the Atlantic Division and to Red Cross drives in New York City.

Lee himself was not really satisfied with the publicity organization until near the end of the war. On August 27, 1918, he wrote Davison, "Our organization has been very weak, due to lack of personnel and for the past several weeks we have been trying to strengthen that organization. I now feel that we have an ample number of people to cover the whole field and that our staff includes as able a group of persons as it would be possible to get together in the world."

To pave the way for the calls for members, for money, and for volunteer workers, Lee and the expanded Publicity Department bombarded the public from all sides with the Red Cross story. In outlining his program, Lee wrote:

We shall give to the newspapers some kind of story practically every morning and every afternoon; that these stories will be conceived with reference to relating our story as a whole over a given period; that we shall have speakers going all over the country giving our story by word of mouth, by lantern slides and pamphlets which will be placed in the seats of the people who attend the speeches; that we shall have our story told by the motion picture houses all over the country; that we shall have our story carried by preachers, labor leaders; Chautauqua speakers and others in their own particular constituencies.

Lee also frequently used the staged event in attracting public attention. In August, he urged Mr. Davison to make a trip to Europe to inspect the Red Cross work there. The purpose was:

So that you can come back . . . give out a big interview on your arrival in this country, and then make a quick tour of division headquarters, addressing large meetings at all the thirteen cities in quick succession . . . All this program should culminate before December 15 when our Christmas membership drive will start with a great display of posters and specially prepared publicity material to the complement of a greater array of speeches by Four-Minute Men and orators of other kinds and own soliciting organization. We would have a great hip-hip-hurrah time and have the population of the United States enrolled as Red Cross members.

The Four-Minute Men were some 75, 000 civic leaders enrolled by President Wilson's Committee on Public Information to speed war messages to the people in churches, in theaters, in civic groups, in fact to any assemblage of people they might find. Between drives Davison, Lee, and others went on speaking tours to report on the work of the Red Cross.

While Ivy Lee was building and perfecting the Red Cross publicity program to saturation point, his old critic was doing the same thing on an even larger scale for President Wilson's Committee on Public Information, set up to propagate the story of America's war aims and to censor U.S. news media. George Creel, crusading journalist who had bitterly criticized Ivy Lee for his role in the Colorado Fuel & Iron Company strike, created a propaganda campaign unequaled in modern times. The work of the Red Cross Publicity Department and Creel's committee dovetailed, and one agency's output reinforced that of the other. There is no evidence, however, that these old foes ever consulted each other in carrying forward their common effort. The two propaganda machines flooded every channel of communication with patriotic demands that people serve, people give, people believe in the struggle to make the world safe for democracy. In the process, Lee and Creel gave American public relations its greatest thrust forward by their wartime demonstrations of its worth.

After the Publicity Department was functioning smoothly, Lee began to weary of his nonremunerative Red Cross chores. On June 11, 1918, he wrote Dr. Stockton Axson, secretary of the American Red Cross, "I have come to the conclusion that my duties at home compel me to relinquish my Red Cross work . . . there are certain mathematical equations I am compelled to face." Apparently in response to Lee's continuing effort to resign, Davison wrote him on August 31, 1918, "This job as you know demands absolute concentration and continuity and a man better have nothing to do with it if he cannot devote all his time and strength to it. Your service to the Red Cross is incalculable and I should be distressed if it were not to continue." His large ego caressed, Lee stayed to the end. He kept careful account of what his service to the Red Cross cost him. On December 12, 1918, he wrote Mr. Davison:

> The books of my New York office show that I have made an actual outlay in connection with my Red Cross work of approximately $11, 000; this covering the expenses of some 30, 000 miles of travel in this country and Europe, expense of living in Washington, and extra expenses of my department which I have assumed personally. In addition to this my New York office has rendered a very considerable service to the Red Cross. . . . On any fair pro rata basis the actual cost to me on the part of my New York office would amount to $6, 000 to $7, 000 making a total expenditure . . . amounting to approximately $18, 000.

However much he may have grumbled about his sacrifice, Ivy Lee was astute enough to knew he was putting money in the bank in terms of contacts and reputation that would pay off many times in the postwar years. Also, Lee unquestionably learned much from the public relations-minded Davison. Lee once told his Red Cross staff, "Mr. Davison has said time and time again that the publicity was the most important part of the Red Cross and that the Red Cross could not exist except for the interest stirred up in it by its Publicity Department."

Yet Lee himself thought the Red Cross intensive publicity program represented only a wartime need. In bidding farewell to the Publicity Department staff on December 3, 1918, Lee said that "the time has come when we ought to consider, every one of us, the steady demobilization of the Publicity Department. . . . There is no necessity to devote either the time or the money to a continued and active stimulation of the work of the Red Cross; that we ought to let the interest grow out of our work, instead of having a great organization that would merely stimulate that activity." In this talk, Lee showed a lack of perception of the profound change in the Red Cross and proved himself a poor prophet as well. But his prodigious, professional public relations campaign for the Red Cross in wartime does him great credit. It brought in the money. His publicity patterns would be copied in future fund-raising efforts as would his other pioneering concepts forged in the Seedbed Era of Public Relations. I return to the Ivy Lee story in the postwar era.

NOTES ON SOURCES

Unlike so much of public relations' history in which first-hand sources have been lost over time or shrouded in confidentiality, ample records of the work of Ivy L. Lee and T. J. Ross are available to provide a full and fair accounting of their place in this history. The primary sources for this chapter and chapter 6 are the Ivy L. Lee Papers in Princeton University, *The Matter Sent Out Books*, which I examined in T. J. Ross Associates in the Chrysler Building (These M.S.O. books are now with the Lee Papers at Princeton.), and interviews with T. J. Ross, Joseph Ripley, and Carl C. Dickey of the Lee-Ross firm. Also of primary value was an extensive interview my research assistant, Alyce Weck, held with James W. Lee II, and his extensive correspondence with a graduate student, Howard Stevenson. Also helpful was the correspondence with Harcourt Parrish, a member of the firm.

Other primary sources used are the books and speeches of Lee and Ross. Ivy Lee's books, *Publicity Some of the Things It Is and Is Not,* Industries Publishing Co., 1925; *Present Day Russia,* Macmillan, 1928; *The Problem of International Propaganda, a New Technique Necessary in Developing Understanding Between Nations,* issued by his firm in 1934; *Human Nature and the Railroads*, privately printed in 1915, and his many public addresses were a wide window to his intellectual development. T. J. Ross also spoke widely and his addresses were reprinted and distributed widely as part of the firm's promotional effort.

The primary secondary source used was Ray. E. Hiebert's definitive biography, *Ivy Lee: Courtier to the Crowd and the Development of Public Relations*, Iowa State University Press, 1966. This press granted permission for the extensive quotes from this book, based on the Ivy L. Lee Papers.

(Professor Hiebert read my completed manuscript of this volume.) I am also heavily indebted to James W. Lee for a careful reading of this chapter and chapter 6. Lee, now retired in Dorset, Vermont, in a lengthy letter of May 8, 1991, prevented several factual errors in these chapters.

Another primary source was George F. West, United States Commission on Industrial Relations, *Report on the Colorado Strike,* Washington, DC: U. S. Government Printing Office, 1915. Also, The General Leonard Wood Papers, Library of Congress. The correspondence in Box 141 suggests that Parker & Bridge continued into the 1920s with Parker and Roy Mason as partners.

Books

Frederick Lewis Allen, *The Big Change*. Harper & Row, 1952; Joseph I. C. Clarke, *My Life and Memories,* Dodd, Mead, 1925. (Recollections of Standard Oil's first public relations official.) George Creel, *Rebel at Large,* Putnam's Sons, 1947. (Memoirs of early Lee critic and propangandist of WWI.) Dexter W. Fellows and Andrew Freeman, *This Way to the Big Show* (Copyright 1936 by Dester W. Fellows, quoted by permission of Curtis Brown Ltd.); Ray Ginger, *The Age of Excess,* Macmillan, 1965.; Candice Johnson Fuhrman, *Publicity Stunt*, Chronicle Books, 1989; Eric F. Goldman, *Rendezvous With Destiny,* Vintage Books, 1959 (tells of sharp turn in U.S. political history in the early 1900s); Samuel P. Hays, *The Response to Industrialism. 1885–1914,* University of Chicago Press, 1957; William H. Lawrence, *Memories of a Happy Life,* Houghton Mifflin, 1926 (memoirs of an early Lee client); Arthur S. Link, *American Epoch*, Knopf, 1955; Alfred McClung Lee, *The Daily Newspaper in America,* Later ed. Octagon Books, 1973; James O. Mock and Cedric Larson, *Words That Won the War,* Princeton University Press, 1939 (tells of work of Creel Committee); Allan D. Nevins, *John D. Rockefeller the Heroic Age of Enterprise,* Charles Scribner's Sons, 1940, Vol. II (biographer selected by Ivy Lee tells story of Tainted Money controversy); Karl Schriftgiesser, *The Lobbyists,* Little Brown, 1951; John K. Mumford, *A Physician to Corporate Bodies*, Industries Publishing Co., 1925 (favorable publicity for his friend, Ivy Lee, published privately); *Who Who's in America,* 1934–1935. A. N. Marquis Co.

Periodicals

Pendleton Dudley, "Current Beginnings of Public Relations," *Public Relations Journal*, April, 1952; B. C. Forbes, "Rockefellers Make Publicity New Watchword," *New York American,* Feb. 26, 1915; "House of Rockefeller Learns to Talk Under Tutelege of Publicity Mentor," *New York Press,* April 11, 1915; "Ivy L. Lee, New York's Door Opener," *New York City Herald,* Feb. 25, 1917; "Publicity of the Coal Combine," *The Fourth Estate,* Nov. 2, 1907; Ivy Lee, Jr., "About My Father," *Panorama*, publication of Canadian Public Relations Society, November, 1964; "Pennsylvania Railroad Publicity," *Electric Railway Journal, Vol. 45, May 29, 1915; Ivy Lee, "The Technique of Publicity," ibid.*, Vol. 49, January 6, 1917; N.S.B. Gras, "Shifts in Public Relations," *Bulletin of the Business Historical Society,* Vol. XIX, October, 1945; Will Irwin, "Press Agent, His Rise and Fall," *Colliers*, Vol. 48, December 2, 1911; Sherman Morse, "An Awakening on Wall Street," *The American Magazine*, Vol. LXII, September, 1906 (contains Lee's historical decoration of publicity policy.); John K. Mumford, "Who's Who in New York, Nov. 55" New York *Herald-Tribune,* April 5, 1925 (Lee's friend giving him another boost).

Chapter 4

The Hamilton Wright Organization – The First International Agency

The need for foreign governments to explain themselves and to promote trade and tourism in the United States became apparent shortly after the turn of the century when America shed its isolationism and moved onto the world stage in the wake of the Spanish–American War. These needs have intensified through the 20th century as nations grew more interdependent, and a fiercely competitive world economy emerged. These needs have been met and are being met by a proliferation of public relations professionals specializing in the representation of foreign governments and serving variously the roles of promoters, propagandists, and lobbyists.

The stakes involved in this representation are high and often crucial for a South Africa under public opinion siege in the United States for its apartheid policies, for a Canada seeking to gain U.S. cooperation in solving the acid rain problem, or for an Angolan rebel leader seeking U.S. arms.

Despite the important political role these public relations specialists play in our nation's foreign affairs through their provision of information to the news media and their lobbying in Congress, they rarely come under press or Congressional scrutiny. For example, in the decades that followed the Senate Foreign Relations Committee hearings in 1963, the American public was given little public knowledge of these agents as they disseminated foreign propaganda for public consumption.

This public relations representation of foreign governments and foreign interests (e.g., the sugar lobby) first came to public notice in the 1930s when Hitler's Nazi government used two well-known public relations firms as well as its own agents to moderate the hostility being bred by Germany's racial and military policies. These firms were Carl Byoir & Associates, which took the German railroads account to promote tourism in Germany, and Ivy Lee & T. J. Ross and Associates, which represented the interests of I. G. Farben. These stories are told in later chapters. This concern resulted in Congressional passage of the Foreign Agents Registration Act of 1938.

In the mid-1960s, Senator J. William Fulbright of the Senate Foreign Relations Committee held a series of hearings on these "Nondiplomatic Activities." The Fulbright Committee was more specific in defining objectionable public relations tactics and techniques on behalf of foreign governments, for example:

1. Trips and junkets for news personnel paid for by public relations practitioners with foreign governments funds.
2. Failure to label releases as the products of foreign agents.
3. Dishonesty in client–agency relations by "puffing" activities on behalf of client governments.
4. Contributions to U.S. political campaigns.
5. Employment of government officials as part-time "consultants" for a foreign agent.
6. Front or conduit organizations formed to act as cover organizations to keep sources of support for a cause hidden from public view.
7. Failure to identify a foreign agent's association with a foreign principal in dealing with our government or other American public.

One result of the Fulbright hearings was to amend the 1938 act and tighten its enforcement. Under the amended Foreign Agents Registration Act, all persons who are working as agents of foreign governments, companies, or political parties must register within 10 days with the Attorney General and report every 6 months under oath the names of the foreigners for whom they work, the activities they carry out, and where they get and spend their money. *Agent* is defined as anyone in the United States who acts as "a public relations counsel, publicity agent, information-service employee, or political consultant" for a foreign government.

This 1964 amendment, co-authored by Senators Fulbright and Bourke Hickenlooper, provided for greater and more explicit disclosure by agents engaged in political activities on behalf of their foreign principals. It also included a civil injunctive procedure whereby the Attorney General may seek to enjoin persons who are engaged in or are about to engage in an act that violates this statute. This amendment also required the Attorney General to report to Congress on the Act's enforcement, and since 1950, the Attorney General has issued an annual report.

Among those coming under the rather hostile scrutiny of the Senate Foreign Relations Committee in 1963 were Hamilton Wright, father and son, who followed in the footsteps of the first Hamilton Wright in pioneering the publicizing of foreign governments in the United States. The Hamilton Wright Organization, founded in 1908, was greatly damaged by these hearings. The firm subsequently was disbanded in 1969 or 1970. This, then, is the history of the Hamilton Wright Organization from its origins at the turn of the century, when America emerged as a world power, until its demise in the late 1960s.

The Wrights—father, son, grandson, all named Hamilton Mercer Wright[1]—insisted in their long careers that they never engaged in political propaganda, only tourist and trade promotion for their foreign clients. The second Hamilton Wright, then head of HWO, wrote, "We have never contracted for 'political propaganda' in any manner, shape or form. . . . We feel that publicity on the economy of a country—publicity on the industrial opportunities—publicity to attract attention to its natural resources—is all part of a package that says, 'THIS COUNTRY IS ON THE MOVE AND GOING PLACES' " In an earlier letter on February 21, 1967, he wrote, "One thing I want to get straight: At no time since the beginning or to date has any member of the firm engaged in POLITICAL PROPAGANDA. This has been taboo. We always include a paragraph in every contract stating, 'The Organization shall not be obliged to undertake political propaganda in any manner, shape or form.' " In commenting on an earlier draft of this chapter, the founder's widow wrote her son, "Impress him with the fact that never was political propaganda used as a business."

As expressed by a top executive in the atmosphere of the Fulbright hearings, the philosophy of the Hamilton Wright Organization was:

> To sum up—we believe that the people of the United States want and need to know about the peoples of the rest of the world. They can do so largely by having access to legitimate news and/or pictures that authentically transmit how our overseas friends live, work, play. In a constantly expanding world of modern communications—radio or television, the daily and Sunday newspapers, the illustrated magazines or "slick" publications, the trade journals and to some extent the house organs of our major corporations—there is no limit except professional talent and good taste plus a sense of integrity in all undertakings.

What constitutes *political propaganda* becomes a matter of defining some fuzzy, loosely used concepts—propaganda, which became a pejorative term in the disillusionment that followed World War I, political public relations,

---

[1]For the sake of clarification, the grandfather, son, and grandson are referred to as Hamilton Wright I, Hamilton Wright II, and Hamilton Wright III in this chapter. The founder of HWO never used Jr. in his name although his father, too, had been named Hamilton Wright. The son of the founder was named Hamilton Wright, Jr., but dropped the Jr. upon the father's death. His son was named Hamilton Wright III.

promotion, lobbying, and so forth. I shall let the historical record define the Wrights' work.

The founder of the Hamilton Wright Organization was born in New Haven, Connecticut, on December 29, 1884, the son of Hamilton Mercer and Ann Fitzhugh Wright. Wright's father was a neuropathologist and studied and worked in many nations — China, Japan, The Malay States, and England, among others. He worked with the U.S. State Department on several efforts to deal with the opium problem of that time. The family's wide-ranging travels, quite unusual for that era, undoubtedly awakened and kindled the son's interest in these and other countries. The father died in 1917.

Young Hamilton attended the University of Michigan for 1 year and then for health reasons transferred to the University of Colorado, receiving a law degree in 1899. For a year, 1899–1900, he was a law instructor at the University of Southern California. This apparently did not challenge him, so in 1900, he turned to journalism, a field for which he was to demonstrate great talent, especially in pictorial journalism. In turn, this led him into tourist promotion of other lands. Wright worked 3 years as a reporter on the staffs of the *Los Angeles Times, Los Angeles Herald* and *Los Angeles Post*. This work led him to see the possibilities for a publicist in the burgeoning California effort to "promote up building of the whole state" by encouraging immigration of settlers and manufacturers. From 1903 until 1905 or so, working in San Francisco, Wright did publicity for the Bureau of Information California Promotion Committee that had been set up to promote migration. Writing of this work, he said, "The men of the West and South are weaving a magic of publicity and behold! unsettled lands are populated. Almost in a night, as one might say, towns arise and become cities. . . . It is an emphatic tribute to the effectiveness of the widespread use of printer's ink. Hundreds of thousands of dollars are expended by the Chambers of Commerce every year." Wright correctly observed that "the tremendous publicity obtained for California is a result of a conscious effort to call attention to its resources." Making Hollywood the film capital of the world in the early 1900s is but one example of the success of this California campaign.

The promotion of California was initiated by the Southern Pacific and Santa Fe railroads in the 1870s. Kevin Starr wrote, "The railroads brought new varieties of Americans to the Southland; the homesteader, the urban immigrant, the health seeker, the tourist. The Southern Pacific subdivided and sold off its vast holdings. It and the Santa Fe maintained elaborate publicity operations to promote travel to the Southland." In the words of a hired publicist, Charles Nordhoff, this was a "a time, not of gold and speculation, but of plantings, harvests and domestic life."

The late 19th century discovery of the power of publicity brought the emergence of the nation's first publicity firms in the first decade of the 20th century. Hamilton Wright perceived this need and his opportunity.

THE BEGINNINGS

Wright's first venture into the art of promoting Americans' understanding of other peoples was an effort to increase their knowledge of the newly occupied Philippine Island that the United States had taken at the end of the Spanish–American War. Late in 1905, Wright undertook an 1, 800-mile trip through the islands under the announced sponsorship of the Pacific Commercial Museum of San Francisco. The "museum" was ostensibly a front for private interests because a diligent search of published sources failed to find any reference to such a museum. In fact, his widow confirmed this in notes on an earlier draft of this chapter, when she wrote, "1905 – a private enterprise with interest in the Philippines – was paid."

Wright told of the trip in an article that stressed the blessing of American occupation of the Philippines. He wrote, for example, "One American work will probably do more for the Philippines than any other one thing accomplished by the Spanish in their centuries of occupancy – the building of railroads."

Wright's output of propaganda, glorifying U.S. occupation and touting the Philippines' assets was prolific; a check of the *Reader's Guide to Periodical Literature* for 3 years finds titles such as "The Forests of the Philippines," "Philippine Prospects," "Philippines in Prosperity," "Tobacco Raising in the Philippines," and so forth. The essential thrust of Wright's work is found in his argument that "if we do not wish to engage in industry (in the Philippines) under the American flag, then we ought to get out." He argued that "every dollar put into circulation is a humanitarian dollar." Wright's lavish prose about the islands is illustrated in this passage:

> The ardent American in the Philippines is apt to point with pride to our establishment of public schools. The school system, as a system, is a marvel of efficiency and administration. It extends to the furthermost parts of the islands; the schools are crowded to their limits; but the Filipino people pay for the running of the schools; indeed, at the present time, no funds of the United States go to the Philippines, except for running the Army there.

Wright's Philippine promotion culminated with the publication of a book, *A Handbook of the Philippines* (A. C. McClurg), one still in demand in libraries today. The book was dedicated to "My Friends of the Filipino Chamber of Commerce Who Believe that the Commercial Prosperity of the

Philippines Ensures the Solution of Their Political Perplexities and The Abounding Welfare and Happiness of Their Own People."

In view of its dedication, one may fairly assume that this book was underwritten by the Filipino Chamber of Commerce and allied U.S. interests. In 1906, Wright agreed to serve Major General Leonard Wood, commander of the U.S. Army in the Philippines, "by promoting understanding between the Philippine Islands and the United States." The circumstances leading to Wood's employment of Wright are not known. His son, Hamilton II, didn't know. In this assignment, he met General Wood and apparently sold him on the need to promote understanding in the United States of its new possession. He also saw the need to change the attitudes of the bureaucrats who had been sent to the island in the occupation. Wright found, "We have had the appointment of a great herd of subordinate officials . . . who are instinctly hostile to the Filipino. No definite mission or policy has been imparted to these subordinates from the government. Our government has no policy."

The year the handbook was published—1907—Wright became editor of the *Overland Monthly*, a publication devoted to the promotion of California and authored a series of articles on "The Unknown Philippines" in *The World Today*, starting with the December 1907 issue. His approved biography also has him working as a reporter for the *San Francisco Examiner* from 1907 to 1911. His widow recalled in her memo that Wright opened a publicity office in San Francisco for himself in 1908 after he returned from the Philippine assignment. He was a prodigious worker and promoter and probably did publicity on the side, a practice not uncommon in those days. Mrs. Wright also recalled that he was doing some work for Abbot Kinney in 1905 while working on the *Los Angeles Post*. Kinney was one of the pioneer developers of Southern California. The firm Wright started that year carried on its promotional brochures the legend, "Serving Government and Industry Since 1908." This fixes the birth of the HWO agency as the fourth such agency to be started in the first decade of this century.

Wright's strong advocacy of expansion of U.S. trade across the Pacific Ocean led to his being chosen editor-in-chief of the Pacific International Exposition in San Francisco. The title meant he was the chief publicist for this exposition, a position he held from 1915 to 1916. Wright described this enterprise in "Creating an Exposition," in *Overland Monthly*, February 1913. The time had come when these civic promotions had to be publicized vigorously and widely. This fact of life had been discovered before the turn of the century by the promoters of the World's Columbian Exposition in Chicago when they found their plans ridiculed and misrepresented in the European and American press. As a consequence of this bad publicity, the Chicago Exposition quickly set up a Department of Publicity and Promotion and hired a newspaperman, Moses P. Handy, "to utilize the printing press in every possible way."

The promoters of the Pacific Exposition also sensed this:

> Time had been when the leading newspapers of the country detailed their best men to cover the development of an exposition. That day had gone. These undertakings, important as they were, had lost their novelty. But if the newspaper would not come to the Exposition, the Exposition could go to the newspapers; and largely on the suggestion of Director [C. S.] Stanton, who knew the newspaper field, that policy was developed. R. E. Connolly had done work of this sort in 1910. Later, Hamilton M. Wright was engaged as a writer and editor of special articles and general literature for the press.

> It would have been hard to make a better selection. As an independent journalist Wright had formed some good syndicate and magazine connections. He was peculiarly gifted. Editors liked this style and played up his material. . . . Ultimately Wright came to have a small staff under him; and first and last they poured out thousands of stories and descriptive articles and matrices for the papers of the world, and papers of the world gladly took the matter and ran it, sometimes a full page feature; often as column stories of gripping interest.

After the Exposition closed, Wright spent the next 18 months in Central and South America writing articles for the *Pan American Union Bulletin* and other publications, obviously designed to promote trade and investment in those countries. Typical articles were "Through the Marvelous Highlands of Guatemala" in October 1917 and "Through Costa Rica, the Magnificent, on a Motor Car" in November 1917. It appears that Wright had discovered a way of satisfying his keen desire to travel, a desire born as a child of world travelers, and making it profitable to boot. His son said, "Father would earn his way by free-lancing articles when not doing publicity work for a sponsor."

After completion of the Pacific Exposition and his Latin-American travels, Hamilton Wright opened a publicity office in New York City in 1917. He rented an office at 15 Park Row in Lower Manhattan, then the hub of New York's newspaper world. His son recalled that in this early New York period his father did publicity for the Borden Co., Architect Harvey Wiley Corbett, the American Road Builders, the American Institute of Architects, and the Bush Terminal project. The Bush Terminal project was one of Wright's earliest clients. New York City at that time delivered its mail from several post offices through a privately owned pneumatic tube system that Wright publicized. The son further recalled, "Originally the company was involved in two key activities — development of tourist facilities and the protection of prominence, new at that time, of unusual industrial ventures." The senior Wright was catholic in his interest. For example, creative work of designers or architects caught his attention. For many years, he was a personal friend of Ethel Traphagen, a pioneer in fashion.

Early in 1917, Wright landed what promised to be a major account, The United Fruit Co. that would enable the publicist to capitalize on his newly acquired knowledge of Central America. Typical of his work for United Fruit in this brief assignment was this florid piece: "Wonderful Guatemala, with its sky-piercing peaks, its purple mists, its vast forest, great lakes, cool uplands, and cities in the fine architecture of the Spanish renaissance, will well repay the tourist from whatever land. It is easily reached by the fine steamers of the United Fruit Co., from either New York or New Orleans, and is traversed by 50 miles of modern railway."

But America's entry into World War I cut short Wright's burgeoning publicity business. In 1918, he went to Europe to cover the war for Forum magazine and the Central Press, the latter a syndicate begun in 1910 by V. V. McNitt. Work for these agencies broadened Wright's already considerable knowledge of the print and pictorial media. He was now well prepared by journalistic and publicity experience and world travel to launch his agency on solid footing in the postwar era, an era in which publicity and ballyhoo reigned supreme.

FIRM REESTABLISHED AFTER WAR

Wright resumed his publicity business sometime after World War I, either in late 1919 or early 1920. In the early 1920s, he rented offices in the Chrysler Building that he occupied until he moved to Rockefeller Plaza in 1930. This time Wright put his talents to work promoting the state of Florida, California's rival, for tourists, settlers, and tropical fruits. The City of Miami was incorporated in 1896 after an imaginative developer, Julia Tuttle, persuaded industrial tycoon Henry Flagler to extend his railroad from St. Augustine to Miami. The senior Wright served as information director for Flagler's Atlantic Coast Line from 1922 until 1929, the year of the stock market crash. He was also retained to promote the city of Miami to promote tourism from 1927 to 1931.

Henry Flagler, once described as one of the more remarkable carnivores who stalked the American economy in the 19th and early 20th centuries, was a prime promoter of Florida. Flagler became a billionaire in his early partnership with John D. Rockefeller in building the Standard Oil Trust but in the early 1880s shifted his attention to Florida. Through his hotels, then through his railroads and the land purchases that accompanied them, he transformed tiny towns along the Atlantic coast and created new ones, notably Miami and Palm Beach. He knew the power of publicity and fully used it as an engine to build his Floridian enterprises.

In touting Miami, the elder Wright relied heavily on pictures of pretty girls on the beaches and of big game fish. The elder Wright, an ardent fisherman, went to Florida frequently on fishing jaunts, wrote special articles on the excitement of big game fishing of Miami, and brought back pictorial proof of his exploits. He was among the first to capitalize on the power of pictorial publicity. A rival publicist, Steve Hannagan, was using the same kind of publicity to promote Miami Beach as a tourist mecca. Both cities turned to publicity to lure tourists to offset the losses inflicted by the end of the Florida land boom in the mid-1920s. Miami's mayor in 1927, E. G. Sewell, had fought the boom promoters and in that year redirected the publicity campaign to one to attract solid growth as well as tourists. Collecting money from Miami merchants, Wright placed three ads in a Northern newspaper that brought 5, 000 tourists to Miami that winter — more than it could accommodate.

In 1932, Wright's son, also named Hamilton Mercer, took over as director of publicity for the City of Miami and started marching in his father's footsteps. Young Hamilton had been born in Los Angeles in 1901, the first of four sons born to the elder Wright and his wife, Cora Elizabeth Pease. Wright II did not attend college. The son ultimately joined his father in a growing number of foreign accounts and took over the leadership of the firm when the elder Wright died on April 10, 1954. The son was joined in the publicity firm in 1950 by his eldest child, Hamilton Mercer Wright III, who worked for it until its dissolution. Hamilton Wright II died on January 23, 1986, at the age of 85.

One of the Wright's first foreign accounts was Egypt that the elder Wright had persuaded to capitalize on its antiquities to attract tourist dollars to its impoverished economy. From 1932 until 1940, he carried the title of information director in the United States for the government of Egypt, and he served that government again in the same capacity during 1947–1949. In handling this account, the elder Wright toured the Nile Valley Basin in 1933–1935, studying government irrigation schemes and arranging for pictorial publicity of Egypt's tourist attractions. In 1964, HWO handled the opening of the Aswan Dam.

The Egyptian account led the Wrights into the serve of many foreign governments during the life of the HWO firm. Among the nations served over the years were Egypt, Formosa, Morocco, the Ivory Coast, Holland, Luxembourg, Venezuela, Ecuador, Argentina, Italy, Chile, Bolivia, Ceylon, Canada, Mexico, South Africa, and others. A list of former and present clients of HWO, circa 1964, are listed at the end of this chapter. A total of 30 foreign governments were HWO clients at one time or another.

PIONEERS IN PICTORIAL PUBLICITY

The three generations of Wrights taught other practitioners the power of the picture, something the elder Wright first sensed in his Miami promotion in the 1920s. In a day when short subjects were standard fare in movie theaters, the Wrights exploited this medium more effectively than any other firm. By the time of the Fulbright hearings, HWO had produced more than 100 short subjects in black and white, color and Cinemascope, Hollywood-released by 20th Century Fox, Universal, MGM, Paramount, and Warner Brothers to world audiences of more than 200 million. A movie-goer watching with fascination a superbly produced color film on diamond mining in South Africa little realized that it was a film paid for by South Africa. Also, HWO was among the first public relations firms to take advantage of the potent capabilities of television by producing films for this medium from the 1950s on.

Unlike most print-oriented practitioners, the Wrights knew the power of film and quickly adapted their motion picture newsreel technique to TV. By mid-1960 the organization had produced more than 1, 000 newsreels that were distributed in 30 languages to some 40 countries by the motion picture industry. According to one HWO executive, "Regardless of the client, the basic service had always been a solid editorial approach, an interpretation by the written word, in interesting journalese, and a exploitation of the powers of pictorial publicity." As Hamilton Wright II wrote your author, "Almost 80 percent of our effort is in pictures and pictures don't lie — you get the message instantly."

It was Hamilton Wright II who was largely responsible for the lead taken in pictorial publicity in a time when most public relations firms were heavily print oriented. He wrote in an article in the short-lived *Public Relations Independent* in October 1964:

> Many public relations men have journalistic backgrounds or were schooled in the English language. They have been trained to use words to describe events and things. . . . The devotee of pictorial journalism appreciates the value of well-phrased sentences but never resorts to words when he can find the picture that describes at a glance all that he is trying to say. Yet some public relations men still pour out volumes of written words in the attempt to sell a product when one well-executed photo could do the job better.

In 1940, Hamilton Wright II was appointed to direct publicity for the New York World's Fair when its PR director, Leo Casey, resigned to become national publicity director for the Democrats-for-Wilkie Committee. Wright II, 38, was then vice-president and general manager of the Wright firm. He took leave from the firm and handled the World's Fair account independently. The Fair had only 78 days to go, and the younger Wright promised a "blitzkreig of promotion for its last days." He set out to give the Fair a "carnival" and "Broadway" atmosphere, announcing four new "thrill acts" on August 12.

World War II forced the Wright Organization to halt its European and Caribbean activities. But it added another dimension to its services by contacting with the Canadian Film Board and the British Information Service to publicize, through motion picture newsreels, Canadian and British contributions to the Allied war effort. The work for the British government continued through 1946. That year the organization also produced newsreels for the state of Florida and for the government of Chile during 1949–1951.

The family's third generation joined the firm in 1950. Hamilton Wright III brought experience in advertising and marketing to HWO, which boasted that this "ushered in a new era with his concept of 'total' public relations." The Wrights clearly understood the role of public relations in a total PR mix. Hamilton Wright I told the *New York Advertiser*, February 19, 1937, that "businessmen should remember that a paper's revenue comes from ads, not publicity. Publicity cannot sell anything. All it does is to inform and encourage, while ads do the rest. . . . Creative ability is more important today than all the other factors in news publicity. . . . That a publicity man should know what editors want, be able to place it before them and then be thanked for it, is my barometer of true merit in this unique profession." Even then practitioners were referring to PR as a profession, a status it has yet to achieve.

Also in this period, Puerto Rico was obtained as a client. HWO's work for that U.S. commonwealth illustrates the services it provided governmental clients — services that came under fire during the Fulbright hearings.

PUERTO RICO'S "OPERATION BOOTSTRAP"

The Commonwealth of Puerto Rico retained the Wright firm in 1948 to develop a long-range public relations program to create U.S. awareness of its "Operation Bootstrap." Governor Luis Munoz Martin saw the necessity of gaining national prominence and support of his plan to improve the economy of that island. These were the public relations objectives:

1. Create a sympathetic understanding of the economic and social aspirations of the people of Puerto Rico.
2. Develop a "climate" in which industrial investments would feel secure and could prosper.
3. Organize a public relations schedule wherein, at the proper moment, a substantial tourist development program could be launched.

During research on this account, HWO found that for years the mainland press had little news coverage of Puerto Rico and what was carried was mostly negative. HWO set about to counter this lack of coverage by publicizing the construction of large public utilities plants, construction of new factories attracted by the commonwealth's less-costly labor, and improvements in hospitals and public schools. HWO persuaded *The New York Times* to send a reporter, Lee Cooper, to Puerto Rico to do a series of articles on the improvements being made under Operation Bootstrap. Burton Heath of the NEA Service, who had done a series of rather negative articles on the island some years before, was persuaded to return and report on the changes in a series of three articles for Scripps-Howard and NEA. Shortly thereafter, Senator A. S. "Mike" Monroney of Oklahoma wrote in *Collier's* that Alaska and Hawaii "might well consider the commonwealth status as developed by Puerto Rico as more beneficial toward advancement of complete self-government and control over their own affairs." Leonard Bourne wrote in the *Public Relations Journal* of June 1955:

> Basically, the Hamilton Wright program followed a pattern of institutional public relations, free of political implication, but devoted principally toward illustrating the significant advances Puerto Rico was making, largely under its own head of steam. Feature articles, pictorial features, newsreels, motion picture short subjects for theatrical and private audiences were keyed to this concept. The general theme was: These are things we are doing to improve our lot, to become self-supporting in the best possible way.

THE FULBRIGHT HEARINGS

The Senate Foreign Relations Committee, under the chairmanship of Senator J. William Fulbright, began hearings on February 4, 1963. The committee, which held 14 executive and 6 public sessions, heard testimony from U.S. government officials and from 15 agents representing foreign governments. Four public relations agencies were brought under critical scrutiny by the committee. These were Selvage and Lee, Julius Klein, Harry Klemfuss, and Hamilton Wright. The committee also explored how these firms used the media, particularly the Special Service branches of the now defunct International News Service, United Press International, and United States Press Association, which distributed paid-for editorials to newspapers. The committee also focused attention on other public relations agents, lobbyists, and "influence men" and their activities in Washington on behalf of foreign clients.

Undersecretary of State George Ball, the lead-off witness, testified:

> First, it seems to us that the basic approach embodied in the existing law is the correct way to deal with the problem of nondiplomatic foreign agents. That is the approach of full disclosure rather than prohibition.

Second, as far as the Department of State is concerned, we have not found that the activities of foreign agents present any serious problems for the process of policy formulation with the Department. By and large, the Department and its personnel do not constitute the major direct target for those activities.

Third, we recognize the difficulties implicit in the effective administration of disclosure legislation in identification are, by their nature, complex.

Secretary Ball's testimony served to put the issue of U. S. public relations agents' representation of foreign governments in the United States in a sensible perspective. In World War I with the creation of the Creel Committee, in World War II with the Office of War Information, and in the 1950s during the Cold War with the United States Information Agency, the United States government recognized the necessity for a world power to explain its purposes, its policies, and its people to those of other nations. This is a fact of life in today's interdependent world and its public television diplomacy.

This chapter focuses exclusively on testimony involving the Hamilton Wright Organization, the first to develop this area of public relations practice. The Wright firm was called to testify on its accounts for the Republic of China, South Africa, Mexico, Morocco, and the Ivory Coast. The bulk of the testimony concerned the Nationalist China and South African accounts. The Wright firm was paid $300, 000 per year by Nationalist China from 1957 until 1962 and $350, 000 annually by South Africa for several years. In its contracts with these clients, the Wright firm included guarantees of results for the respective public relations campaigns. For the South African government the Wright firm proposed:

As indicated earlier in this letter, we guarantee 5 to 1 publicity results, i.e., five times the lineage one would expect to buy with an advertising budget of the same amount of the contract. This means $1, 750, 000 worth of publicity for $350, 000 — figured on the basis of standard advertising rates for the same material if it were placed in the press and on the broadcast media at standard fees.

Wright offered Nationalist China a somewhat different guarantee:

Every contract this organization signs with a foreign government has a stipulated guarantee of "Six to One." That means $1, 800, 000 worth of publicity — or $6.00 for every $1.00 invested. (All figures are U. S. dollars). I (Hamilton Wright, Jr.) voluntarily increased this figure to $2, 500, 000. I did so because of my belief that the receptivity to our press releases by the newspapers, magazines newsreels, television, etc., will be beyond par, will exceed normal acceptance.

Responding to questions from Senator Fulbright, the son of the firm's founder explained the purpose of Nationalist China's contract this way:

> The contract was bulls-eyed to publicizing the way of life of Free China and this was brought down to a pinpoint expose of their agriculture, their industry, and their way of life to show the American people the problems they had. We also sought to bring into sharp focus how foreign aid money was being spent by the Chinese, and particularly to show that they were getting more mileage out of the dollar than many other countries.

In serving Nationalist China, the Wright Organization produced illustrated feature stories for newspapers and magazines and movie short subjects. Wright testified that it was the practice to make such footage available to movie producers and television networks free to charge, stating that such footage was used by film editors as they saw fit. Committee members questioned whether these editors knew that the film had been paid for by a foreign government. Wright answered that some of them did and indicated such on the released films; others did not and used Hamilton Wright credits or no credits at all. The committee contended, with reason, that it would be difficult for the American public to know that the Hamilton Wright Organization was indeed a foreign agent.

In this connection, the committee turned up evidence that the Wright Organization hired Richard and Robert Kuhne, sons of Jack Kuhne, who was in charge of 20th Century Fox short subjects. The Kuhne sons were free lance cameramen and were paid $259 to $600 per week to work on different film projects. Wright admitted that films the Kuhne sons shot were given to and distributed by 20th Century Fox. The now-senior Wright also testified that he was a close personal friend of Mac Klein, editor of MGM's newsreels, and that he had financed a trip to Mexico for the Kleins. Revealing another aspect of the Wright's work, Hamilton Wright II testified that Don Frifield was paid $1, 333.00 per month to represent the Organization on Formosa and prepare feature articles for U.S. distribution. HWO gave these articles to the North American Newspaper Alliance and the Herald–Tribune Syndicate, which distributed them widely without source identification to newspaper editors or their readers. This is common in general public relations practice.

Wright also testified that he had arranged free trips for editors of King Features Syndicate, editors of United Press International, and others. He argued:

> In the more than 30 years that we have been representing foreign government clients, our news and features, pictures and news material have been available to the press without charge to them or payment by us for its use. It has always been accepted or rejected for use by the individual editor strictly on its news merits. Publication of our materials has never been contingent on friendships,

"free trips," or favors. Our policy has always been and always will be to offer these photographs and articles which to the best of our knowledge, are accurately and truthfully reported.

In the Fulbright hearings and previous congressional hearings in this matter, the investigating committees were attempting to measure the impact of foreign propaganda and public relations activities – a virtually impossible task whether the assessment is of foreign or domestic programs. The 1963 hearings made it abundantly clear that these practitioners had assumed a substantial portion of the news-gathering, news-reporting functions in foreign news, and yet these agencies cannot be expected to report objectively in the public interest. The news media have progressively abandoned their news-gathering function to public relations practitioners. The Fulbright record is replete with examples of foreign news produced by public relations agencies and used in dead-pan fashion by the nation's media. Sophisticated news sources understand this and thus turn increasingly to the practitioner to "tell our side of the story." Studies show that some 40% of media content comes from public relations sources.

The Fulbright hearings concluded without finding the Wright Organization had broken any laws or by censuring it. The only legislative result was the passage of the Fulbright–Hickenlooper Amendment. But the hearings damaged the Hamilton Wright Organization and gave impetus to its ultimate dissolution. However, the Fulbright Committee revelations were not the sole cause of the firm's decline over the next 6 years.

The Wrights had pioneered and excelled in pictorial publicity to exploit the popular movie house newsreel and short subject, the rotogravure and travel sections of Sunday newspapers, and the increased emphasis on pictorial reporting of newspapers, an emphasis that reached its zenith with *Life and Look* magazines. The changes in motion picture fare and the rapidly changing news and TV reporting technology also played a significant part in bringing this firm to a close.

The widow of Hamilton Wright II wrote to me on June 26, 1986:

When Hamilton retired in 1969 or 1970, the Hamilton Wright Organization was legally dissolved. You may remember that the methods of communications had entirely changed and that he was doing public relations for foreign governments mostly through the medium of short subjects for theatrical release, though still continuing editorial work such as the Abu Simbel reconstruction which appeared as cover story in *Life* magazine. His public relations methods were at that time unique . . . and conditions politically in the present world would make it impossible to follow.

Hamilton Wright II, son of the founder who pioneered promotional publicity for foreign governments, understandably took a bitter view of

Senator Fulbright's hearings. In a letter to me dated February 21, 1967, he wrote:

> The U.S. Senate Foreign Relations Committee hearings developed into nothing more than a public smear for the Hamilton Wrights by a Senator whose bull's eye was to eliminate the strong campaign of editorial publicity we were undertaking for the Government of Formosa—and pave the way, in my opinion, for the admission of Red China to the U. N. There was no finale to his hearing—no censure—no nothing.

Wright, then head of the Hamilton Wright Organization, further alleged that after giving representatives of the committee full run of the Wright files, this "turned out to be a 'political knife in the back.' Somewhere, someone had the idea that the Hamilton Wright Organization was a spill-off of the old China Lobby. This did tremendous damage to our reputation."

PRSA'S ROLE IN END OF WRIGHT FIRM

The Public Relations Society of America's (PRSA) decision in March 1964 to censure Hamilton Wright III, then a member, as a consequence of testimony given before the Senate Foreign Relations Committee also played an indeterminate part in the wind-down of the Wright Organization. Article 13 of the *Public Relations Society of America Code for Professional Standards for the Practice of Public Relations*, states: "A member shall not guarantee the achievement of specified results beyond a member's direct control." According to Wright III, it was for violation of Article 13 that he was suspended from membership for 6 months by the PRSA Judicial Council.

Clearly the Wright Organization's guarantee of specified results to South Africa, Formosa, and other foreign clients was a violation of Article 13. Wright's suspension from PRSA membership was the harshest penalty the society had handed down to that point. Wright promptly resigned from the organization, which makes plain the weakness of voluntary code enforcement. In regard to PRSA's action Hamilton Wright II wrote me:

> Regarding the Public Relations Society of American, I was one of 12 men who founded this back in the 1920s. [Wright is undoubtedly referring here to the National Association of Accredited Publicity Directors organized in 1936, not in the 1920s. There was an effort to form such a group in the 1920s, but according to the late Pendleton Dudley who claimed Edward L. Bernays' premature publicizing of it killed it.] As time went on, I spent from eight to 10 months a year traveling in foreign countries. I lost track of PRSA. I seldom attended meetings. As HWO grew, our competitors complained that "they could not bid against HWO because we guaranteed our work. . . . In the foreign field, it is virtually impossible to secure a contract (Egypt, Morocco,

Ceylon, Turkey, Pakistan and other governments) without making specific guarantees. The PRSA requested us to delete these guarantees from our contracts. We refused. The PRSA dismissed my son, who was a member. I was not at the time.

The reasoning behind Article 13 in the *PRSA Code* is this: Practitioners who sell their services on the basis of getting X dollars of "free advertising" for X cents in a publicity fee do themselves, their clients, and the vocation a disservice. Thus, such guarantees of results as the Wrights made in their contracts are damaging to public relations and are claims difficult to substantiate. The American Association of Fund Raising Counsel (AAFRC), a kindred body to PRSA, similarly prohibits acceptance of clients on a guarantee of results or taking a campaign on a percentage fee. The *AAFRC Code* states: "Member firms do business only on the basis of a specified fee, determined prior to the beginning of a campaign. They will not serve clients on an unprofessional basis of a percentage of commission of the sums raised."

On the other hand, Hamilton Wright knew the ways and mores of foreign governments better than any American counselor, and his word that many of these governments insisted on guarantees must be accepted as fact of life in representation of foreign clients, at least in his day.

However, on March 24, 1964, *The New York Times* reported:

> The Public Relations Society of America has suspended Hamilton Wright, Jr., international publicist from membership for six months for alleged violations of its Code. The suspension resulted from disclosures before the Senate Foreign Relations Committee last year concerning distribution by the Hamilton Wright Organization of subsidized news articles and film shorts for Nationalist China and other foreign governments. Mr. Wright was charged with failure to disclose the origins of such material. . . . Mr. Wright denied that there was anything unethical about his concern's practices. He asserted that he did not intend to change his practices, adding "Did not see anything wrong in making it possible for members of the press to visit client countries as guests of that client."

If, as *The Times* reported, Wright III was punished for providing free trips for journalists to visit client countries, PRSA was on shaky ground indeed. Providing junkets for the press has been and continues to be standard practice in many public relations programs. Trips for travel editors to foreign lands are quite common. Airlines commonly take journalists as guests on maiden flights of new routes. Free travel abounds in professional sports. The article of the *PRSA Code* that appears to prohibit such provision of free travel and expense is, Article 6: "A member shall not engage in any practice that tends to corrupt the channels of communications or the process of government." No other member of PRSA to my knowledge, has been cited for the provision of free travel to journalists. It is difficult to ascertain the precise basis on which Wright was suspended from membership by PRSA because the society is not forthcoming in such matters.

Thus, the confluence of the factors of the damaging publicity emanating from the Fulbright hearings, the rapid changes in ways of communicating with large audiences, PRSA's censure and Wright III's subsequent resignation, and Hamilton Wright II's reaching retirement age all served to spell the end of the public relations agency that had pioneered in representation of foreign governments from the dawn of the 20th century—a century that brought the United States from railroad travel to space travel and hurled it into the world community. All this, in turn, made necessary this aspect of public relations practice, then a young, little-recognized vocation in 1908 when the elder Hamilton Wright opened his office in San Francisco.

TABLE 4.1
Representative List of Present and Former HWO Clients (Circa 1964)

British Information Service	Panama–Pacific International
Government of Canada	
(National Film Exposition, 1915, San Francisco Board)	
Alaskan Highway (during construction)	Province of Alberta, Canada
Pan American Airways	
Province of Quebec, Canada	Atlantic Coast Line Railroad
Government of Belgium	Central Railroad of New Jersey
Government of Ceylon	Florida East Coast Railway
Government of Chile	Illinois Central Railroad
Republic of China (Free China)	Seaboard Airline Railway
Government of Colombia	Grace Steamship Company
Government of Cuba (1930s)	United Fruit Company
Government of Czechoslovakia (1938)	American Cyanamid Company
Republic of Ecuador	American Road Builders Association
Egyptian State Dept. of Tourism	Bankers Trust Company
Government of Haiti (1930s)	Bituminous Coal Institute
Government of Holland	Bush Terminal Corporation
Italian State Tourist Office (ENIT)	Corning Glass Company
Government of Libya	Reuben H. Donnelley Corporation
Government of Luxembourg	E. I. duPont deNemours & Co.
Government of Mexico Tourism Dept.	General Electric Company
Government of Morocco	Revere Copper & Brass, Inc.
Republic of Panama	Studebaker Corporation
Government of Poland (1936)	Worthington Pump & Machinery Corp.
Commonwealth of Puerto Rico	Fordham University, New York
Republic of South Africa	St. Lawrence University, Canton, NY
Government of Venezuela	Architectural League of New York
State of Florida	Metropolitan Museum of Art
City of Miami, Florida	Harvey Wiley Corbett (architect) NY
City of Newport, Rhode Island	Eggers & Higgins (architects) NY
City of Sestriere, Italy (Alpine resort)	Reinhard & Hofmeister (architects) NY
City of White Sulphur Springs, West Virginia	John Jacob Astor, New York
New York World's Fair (1940–1941)	

NOTES ON SOURCES

This chapter first appeared in *The Public Relations Review*, Vol. XIII, Spring, 1987. It is reprinted here with the permission of *The Public Relations Review*, now owned by the JAI Press, Inc.

The chapter is based on my extensive interview with Hamilton Wright II in his office in New York City, June 9, 1964, and our extensive correspondence that ensued from that interview. A letter from his widow, Frances Purdy Wright, dated June 26, 1986, was helpful. A major documentary source was the Senate Fulbright hearings, *Activities of Nondiplomatic Representatives of Foreign Principals in the United States,* before the Senate Committee of Foreign Relations, 88th Congress, Parts 1 through 13. Government Printing Office, Washington, DC, 1963.

The story of the early 20th Century promotion of California, in which Hamilton Wright I had a large hand, can be found in Kevin Starr, *Americans and the California Dream*, Oxford University Press, 1973. The story of Florida Coast's development in which Hamilton Wright II played a part, is found in Edward N. Akin, *Flagler Rockefeller Partner and Florida Baron*, Kent State University Press, 1988.

A letter from Leonard Bourne, a feature editor in the Wright Organization, dated February 21, 1967, and his article in the *Public Relations Journal*, June, 1955, provided details of the Wright Puerto Rico campaign. Also see, "Puerto Rico Fights Back," *Reader's Digest*, Vol. 54, June, 1949.

The Code for Professional Standards for the Practice of Public Relations is carried annually in *The Public Relations Register* of the Public Relations Society of America. This Code was adopted in 1988, replacing the Code of Ethics that had been in force since 1950. The code of the American Association Fund Raising Counsel may be found in Cutlip, *Fund Raising in the United States*, Transaction Press, 1990.

Chapter 5

Pendleton Dudley Starts Fifth Agency in 1909

When the public relations firm (DAY) was dissolved into Ogilvy & Mather Public Relations on November 1, 1988, the longest lived public relations agency disappeared into the sands of time that enveloped the first four agencies started in the first decade of this century. The *D* in that firm name that dates from post-World War II stood for Pendleton Dudley, a venerable pioneer in this vocation. Dudley, at the urging of his friend Ivy Lee, opened the nation's fifth agency in 1909 in Wall Street.

[In its latter years, DAY had been owned by two sisters, Jean Way Schoonover and Barbara Hunter. They sold the agency to Ogilvy & Mather in 1983 in the decade of mega agency mergers and the internationalization of public relations services.]

The fifth public relations agency had its beginnings when a young Missourian, Pendleton Dudley, opened a publicity office in New York City's financial district. Over the next 5 years, Dudley, a rugged product of frontier, agricultural America, fashioned a profitable calling out of the complex communication and marketing needs of 20th century urban, industrial America. He saw publicity grow from an uncertain hand-to-mouth business into a large-scale enterprise, and he did much to infuse this new field with respectability.

Pendleton Dudley — known to his close friends as Pen and to associates in his firm as PD — was born on September 8, 1876, in the small, frontier town of Troy, Missouri, the first of four sons of Peter and Cornelia Pendleton Dudley, who had migrated to Missouri from Kentucky by wagon a few years before. The elder Dudley ran a general store in a town of some 800 persons. In this frontier outpost Pendleton Dudley spent his boyhood in what he later recalled in an interview as pretty primitive conditions:

> There were no telephones and the only time a family got a Western Union message was when there had been a death in the family. We had only a four-page weekly newspaper and only a few St.Louis newspapers came to Troy each day. There was no library and in our home we had only a handful of books—the Bible which served as the family registry, a novel, *Ships That Pass in the Night*, and a few others which I cannot recall. Our family did take *Saturday Evening Post* and *Youth's Companion*. Ours was a self-contained community.

Dudley attended grammar school in Troy and then took 2 years of high school work at nearby Mexico, Missouri, before he had to quit school to help out in his father's grocery store because of the latter's ill-health. Shortly thereafter, Dudley took a part-time job on the four-page weekly, the *Troy Free Press*, working as a typesetter and reporter. Even though he had had only what he correctly termed a "sketchy education," he taught country school one term to help keep the family going. His work on the *Free Press* in time led to a job on the *Mexico Ledger* where he worked for 2 years. He reflected in later life that his newspaper work and his teaching excited his curiosity about the larger world beyond the confines of Troy and Mexico but that he felt trapped by his family's financial straits. One of the family's few links with the exploding, exciting developments in the United States was a magazine that showed the young man the way out of his dilemma.

DUDLEY HEADS FOR NEW YORK

In the summer of 1898, when Dudley was nearly 22 years old, he read an article by Jesse Lynch Williams, "Working Your Way Through College," in the *Saturday Evening Post* that fired him with the realization that the education and outside world he dreamed of were within the realm of possibility. "I put down that magazine and vowed 'this is for me,' " Dudley later recalled. In the article Williams cited several examples of men who had worked their way through college and "this so impressed me that I decided to put the William's thesis to the test." He started saving what money he could from his meager pay as a reporter. In early September 1899, he left Troy with the intention of enrolling in Princeton University. Determined to get an education, young Dudley headed East carrying a tin trunk full of clothes and about $100 in his pocket—the year's savings. After he arrived in New York City, he decided to enroll in Columbia University because "I found the earning opportunities better in New York City." Because he lacked a high school diploma, Columbia would admit him only as a special student, but the energetic young man quickly demonstrated his capacity for college work. He was graduated from Columbia in 1903, and from that day until his death he was a proud, devoted alumnus. In his later years, the Columbia University Club in mid-town Manhattan, around the corner from his office at 551 Fifth Avenue, held an important place in his social and professional life. He transacted much business over lunch at his club. For a time he was a lecturer in Columbia's Business School.

Dudley earned his college expenses by organizing a Boys' Athletic Club on New York's upper West Side for the sons of the well-to-do, by tutoring, and by doing freelance work for a newspaper that in those days paid most reporters on a space basis. He earned more than enough. Half a century later he boasted, "When I graduated four years later the sum [$100] was still intact, with several hundred dollars added." While in Columbia, Dudley was a frequent contributor to its humor magazine, *The Jester*.

Soon after he arrived in New York, Dudley received a letter of introduction to Ivy Lee from Russell McClellan, a St. Louis salesman who called at the Dudley store in Troy. McClellan worshipped at the Rev. James W. Lee's (Ivy's father) St. Louis church and from this tenuous connection came what Dudley later described as "one of the controlling factors of my life," —his friendship with Ivy Lee. Dudley and Lee quickly took to one another and became fast friends; soon Dudley was accompanying Lee on his reportorial rounds. Dudley commented that Lee, who was also taking some courses at Columbia at this time, "was obsessed with the importance of communication and some of this rubbed off on me." One of Dudley's vivid memories of this period was that of helping Ivy Lee cover a big fire in Paterson, NJ, when the latter was working for *The Times*. Dudley said that "Ivy threw quite a few freelance jobs my way" in these years.

HIS EARLY INTEREST IN BUSINESS

Already matured by years and experience, Dudley the college student tended to focus his interest "more sharply upon the unusual happenings in the great worlds of business and finance that upon the staid routines of the classroom."

Upon his graduation, Dudley decided to build a career in business and perhaps influenced by his experience in this father's store, chose merchandising as the place to start. He took a job in John Wanamaker's Philadelphia store but after 2 years found that this work bored him. "Next I took a job selling bonds for Barklie Henry but I failed at this and he ultimately fired me, the only time in my life that this ever happened to me." At Ivy

Lee's suggestion, Dudley returned to New York City in 1906 or so (Dudley in later years couldn't recall the exact date) and with Lee's help landed a job on the *Wall Street Journal*. This shift was the result of the converging forces of Dudley's ambitions for success, his reliance on Lee's counsel, and his enthrallment with Big Business of that day. He later recalled:

> Both Lee and I had great zest for people of all sorts, particularly for persons who did things in a big way. As the Wall Street of that day was the central arena for business action and the clash of big business personalities, Lee and I gravitated to it as naturally as small boys to a circus.

> Those were the formative years of many American industries. No week passed without the announcement of a new industrial or financial trust whose operations in effect were working revolutionary changes in the nature of American business. As a *Wall Street Journal* reporter I had a ringside seat, so to speak at this great financial free-for-all.

It was his work on the *Journal* that convinced the cautious Dudley that Ivy Lee had correctly seen the growing demand for the newsman who could serve as a buffer between Big Business and the press. "I knew enough about reporting to realize that Lee had hit upon a tremendous want." Dudley rightly observed that most of the financial and business giants were "most inept fellows" when it came to handling the press and the public. The reason was that most of them grew up on the "environment of man-to-man communication" and business privacy but now "found themselves completely dismayed by the public demands for news and information about their private business." Though this "tremendous need" was not widely recognized in those days, Ivy Lee kept urging Dudley to get into publicity work. "Now, as I review our friendship, I can recall that from the first he was weighing the idea of setting up a press agency or bureau to serve a few clients. Such an agency, as he saw it, would provide expert knowledge of news values and act as an intermediary between the newspapers that were printing the news and the men who were making it."

THE FOUNDING OF DUDLEY'S FIRM

Pendleton Dudley finally took the step at the urging of an unscrupulous speculator whom he wouldn't identify to me. Dudley agreed to publicize a new mining venture for this speculator and promptly quit his job on the *Wall Street Journal*. "The speculator was shocked when I told him that I had quit the *Journal*. He had expected to use the columns of the *Journal* to promote his worthless stock by hiring me. He had the wrong man." Indeed he did. Undaunted, Dudley went ahead with his plans for an agency and opened an office at 34 Pine Street in October 1909, knowing full well that this was "a risky business." The title of the new enterprise was Pendleton Dudley and Associates, the "associate" being a young male secretary. Including associates in PR agency titles came to be quite common. "A few weeks after I had opened my office I heard a rumor about another newspaperman starting a publicity agency and I didn't sleep a wink that night. I just knew that there wouldn't be business enough for both of us." It appears that though Dudley saw the need for the interpreter of institutions then in the news but that he didn't sense its full potential. "There was no precedent for our [Dudley and Lee] thinking we could be making a living by doing publicity work."

Benefiting from his years of experience and hindsight, Dudley, in a 1963 speech, saw the start of public relations this way:

> A few venturesome newspapermen, more imaginative than their fellows, saw an opportunity in the situation to do business with these bold enterprisers by providing them and their companies with a special news service, which in time became known as public relations practice. This service had the aim, of course, of answering their newspaper and magazine critics, and what is more to the point, of satisfying the hunger of the public for news of these newly born companies and their promoters.

> Their [the public relations pioneers] initial efforts in their new work were limited to short news releases which reported the financial operations of their clients. The scope of their work rapidly broadened . . . and other newspapermen, encouraged by what we were doing, left their papers and joined the ranks.

Dudley recalled that when he launched his one-man firm he had not heard of either the Publicity Bureau or William Wolff Smith and could not remember Ivy Lee's ever mentioning their work in the many Lee–Dudley conversations. He wrote, "Let me stress . . . that there was no precedent in Lee's mind when he set up his office in the financial district. His venture grew out of an awareness of a need, gained at first hand in his work as a finance reporter on *The New York Times*, an awareness backed by the courage essential to a pioneering effort. I caught some of that spirit and, following Lee after several years, hung out my own modest shingle." Five years earlier, speaking at the 1960 conference of the Public Relations Society of America in Chicago, Dudley told his fellow counselors, "Ivy Lee was a great man. He spoke the language of business. Most of us came out of newspaper work and we had to learn a new language, the language of business. Ivy Lee paved the way for most of us. We all owe him a great debt." Dudley never ceased to acknowledge that it was Ivy Lee who led him and later colleagues to a challenging, lucrative vocation.

RISE OF THE NEW VOCATION

In his later years, Dudley argued that it was the impact of the mass circulation newspapers, dramatized by the Hearst–Pulitzer war then raging in New York City, rather than the work of the muckrakers that gave rise to this new vocation. He wrote:

> Doubtless the magazine articles by Ida Tarbell et al. did play their part in creating the new profession . . . however, other and more significant developments . . . were more responsible for its initial expression and particularly for its later growth into the function or procedure as we now know it.

> To this public curiosity [about the exciting personalities in Big Business] I would attribute the emergence of the popular influence of the *New York World* of Joseph Pulitzer, and the Hearst newspapers—indeed, of the generally explosive effect of large newspaper circulation upon public sentiment . . . Yet the public hunger was ill fed . . . In this atmosphere financial reporting became a sort of hide-and-go-seek, catch-as-catch-can-affair.

Although Dudley minimized the role of the Muckrakers in goading individuals and institutions under attack to turn to publicity men for defense as giving rise to the new field, his "first client of note" came this way. In fact this client—the Vestry of Trinity Church Corporation of New York—came to him early in 1909 while he was still working on the *Wall Street Journal*, 9 months before he opened his office. The Trinity Church Corporation had been under public fire since the mid-1890s for its exploitation of tenants in its large holdings of tenement property. In 1894, the Parish of Trinity Church, an historic church in lower Manhattan, was the second largest landholder in the city and was receiving an annual income of $600,000 in rents. On December 10, 1894, the *New York World* started a crusade to expose the conditions of Trinity's tenements with a long story—two full columns on page one and nearly two more on page two—headed: "BAD LANDLORD TRINITY. ITS RAMSHACKLE TENEMENT-HOUSE NOT FIT FOR HUMAN HABITATION." The attacks on Trinity were taken up by such noted crusaders as Jacob Riis and Charles Edward Russell, reaching a crescendo in mid-1908.

Trinity's policy in the face of growing public criticism was truly a stony silence in the view of *The New York Times*. "In years past Trinity has adopted towards its detractors a policy of dignified reticence as serene as the faces of the stone saints looking down from her spire into Wall Street" As the attacks became more frequent and were taken up by such respected voices as that of *The New York Times*, Trinity's new rector, Rev. Dr. William Manning, decided new policies were essential. Dr. Manning was aware of the importance of the press and realized that just as the press had served to arouse public opinion against Trinity, it could be used to help Trinity. He persuaded a vestry committee to hire Pendleton Dudley. "My service as public relations counselor began in January, 1909 (I am relying upon the accuracy of the *New York World's* news) and ended with the entrance of the U.S.A. into the first World War, when Dr. Manning and his Vestry, all fervid Anglophiles, went all out for a vigorous support of the Allies, religious garb was cast aside, and austerity made the order of the day." The *World* story to which Dudley referred was published January 22, 1909, announcing that Trinity had "employed a press agent to give out news of its affairs." Dudley was not the first nor the last newspaperman to earn extra money by doing publicity outside his job.

THE FIRST BUSINESS ACCOUNT: A.T.& T.

Dudley got his first big business account "shortly after I set up shop at 34 Pine Street, to offer a special press service to large corporations, a service now known as public reactions practice," the American Telephone & Telegraph Company. The giant utility kept Dudley on a retainer until his death in 1966; in his later years, it was more for gratitude than for business reasons. Dudley related how he got his client:

> The relationship with Telephone grew out of my work as a reporter on the *Wall Street Journal*, one of my assignments being to maintain contact with the President of the System, the late Theodore N. Vail, during his frequent visits to New York, the company's headquarters being at that time in Boston. About the time I launched my modest venture, Mr. Vail shifted the President's office to 195 Broadway, New York.

> On the basis of my acquaintance with Mr. Vail, I proposed a press relationship with the Company, which I discussed one weekend at his dairy farm in the hill country outside Lyndonville, Vermont. . . . We closed the deal . . . on my terms and the modest monthly fee I named as a fateful decision, as I now see, since, alas, it set the financial tone for the future operations of our firm.

> My commitment was to supplement the activities of the Company's own press department; no promises as to volume, no schedule of operations, just a free lancer with an open field.

> At that time the Company's press department was pretty much a one-man show with the late J. D. Ellsworth and a secretary putting on the show.

In the first year of his business, Dudley undertook a mission at the behest of Princeton University alumni in the effort to get Woodrow Wilson out of the Princeton presidency and into the governorship of New Jersey, a matter Dudley refused to discuss in his twilight years. He wrote me on March 26, 1959, "As to the Woodrow Wilson incident, let me say first that this was a highly confidential matter involving very delicate personal considerations and to identify a pioneer public reactions practitioner with a rather devious development . . . would be . . . damaging to our profession." What his mission was must be left to speculation. Dudley was always greatly concerned with protecting and improving the reputation of his field.

With the AT&T account as a financial base to build on, Dudley was soon earning a good living for those days. ANPA's antipublicity bulletin of March 25, 1911, identified him as "press agent" for the Adams Express Co., the National City Bank, and "other financial interests." The firm continued to go by the name of Pendleton Dudley & Associates until 1946 when he converted it to a partnership with Thomas D. Yutzy, who also died in 1966, and George Anderson, the surviving partner. When Dudley died, his firm ranked as one of the nation's largest, employing a staff of 70 writers, home economists, researchers, industrial experts, and account executives. Fifty-seven years from 1909 Dudley's "risky business" had become a respected "profession," at least in his eyes.

PENDLETON DUDLEY'S MAJOR ACHIEVEMENT — STABILIZATION OF THE MEAT INDUSTRY

The end of World War I found the nation's meat industry facing its second major crisis. In 1919 and 1920, bills were introduced in the Congress calling for the government to take full control of livestock and meat marketing. Such legislation had been recommended by the Federal Trade Commission. There were also bills to license packers and to prohibit them from engaging in any business except slaughtering and processing. By this time, the industry, feeling unfairly abused, decided to fight back and hired Pendleton Dudley to counter the industry's critics. Thomas E. Wilson, major meat packer and president of the American Meat Packers Association (AMPA), and Dudley joined forces to switch the industry from a defensive to an aggressive posture. The early public reactions programs devised by Dudley and eagerly approved by industry leaders in the early 1920s have "provided a stimulus for [American Meat] Institute activities ever since," according to Herbert Bain's history of the institute. In a letter to me dated February 2, 1991, Bain wrote, "He [Dudley] did more than a great deal for the meat industry. He transformed it. His is a story that is largely untold in the PR world."

The reputation of meat packers at the end of the war was highly negative, and political leaders responding to public opinion were introducing bills to regulate the industry more tightly, as indicated previously. President Wilson of the meat packers proposed to the board of the American Meat Packers Association, formed in 1906 in the wake of Upton Sinclair's devastating *The Jungle*, be reorganized along lines similar to the American Petroleum Institute and the Iron and Steel Institute. Pen Dudley joined in this plea for a stronger organized voice for the industry. Dudley was now chairman of the AMPA's new Bureau of Public Relations. The board enthusiastically approved this move and the American Meat Institute (AMI) was born. Dues were sharply increased to pay for an expanded public relations program.

G. E. Swift, Jr., another major packer, became chairman of the AMI's public relations committee, and he and Dudley moved quickly to organize "a general news service," a "special news service and publicity department for women," a "special news service for agricultural and livestock papers," a "service for retailers," a "speaker's and lecture bureau," and a "clearing house for publicity material issued by individual members of the institute." Bain added in his 75th anniversary account of the AMI:

> Swift—with Dudley at his side—also proposed that the Institute furnish the public with accurate reports of all appropriate hearings, answer adverse editorial attacks promptly, distribute reprints of favorable editorial matter, prepare printed bulletins, pamphlets and booklets of appropriate matter, prepare a list of about 100,000 names to which should be sent, from time to time, educational materials concerning the packing industry, prepare an educational exhibit for display at expositions, supervise the preparation of motion picture films, and launch an advertising campaign to benefit the industry as a whole.

To implement this expansive and far-sighted program for its day, Dudley hired a woman to handle publicity for women at $300 a month and two men at $200 a month each to staff the agricultural news service and the service to retailers. The estimated cost of this program was put at from $5,000 to $6,000 a month, which did not include the advertising. Dudley was way ahead of his time in recognizing the need to appeal to women and to employ women on his staff. This was 1920—the year women got the vote.

Dudley and his associates had an uphill battle in waging their ambitious program. A general business slump in 1920 hit the industry hard. There was a sharp decline in exports, and the demand for meat slackened at home as unemployment rose. On top of that, the government dumped 100 million pounds of frozen beef it had bought for the military on the market. And on top of that a federal judge had raised the pay of meat workers from 25¢ an hour in 1917 to 53¢ an hour. Nonetheless, the public relations efforts began to pay off by 1921 when Dudley's aide could report "outside pressure on the industry" has eased, that the public generally agreed that meat prices were low, and that agitation for corrective legislation had subsided. The bills introduced in 1919 did not pass. One of Dudley's early PR failures was his effort to change the name of the "hot dog" to "red hots."

In the 1920s, as today, nutritionists and medical experts were raising questions about the healthfulness of a heavy meat diet. In 1927, Pen Dudley convinced the AMI to finance a 2-year diet of just meat and water by Vilhjalmur Stefansson, famed Arctic explorer. It was a great success, and Dudley was credited with having given the relatively new activity of public relations a good name, not by publicity alone, but by educating the public with provable facts. The AMI followed this up with a nationwide educational and advertising campaign, "The Meat Educational Program," which made great use of the Stefansson finding that meat was a good thing to eat. In the 1990s, the meat industry was employing public relations agencies to promote the idea that "beef is real food for real people."

In 1928, Dudley scored another PR coup when he persuaded the AMI to sponsor the 1928 Public Conference of Business and Industry, starring Columbia University's president, Nicholas Murray Butler, as the keynoter. The banquet that night at the Astor Hotel was billed as "Tribute to the Pioneers of American Industry," with Thomas A. Edison, Henry Ford, Harvey Firestone, George Eastman, Charles Schwab, and Julius Rosenwald on the speakers' dais.

Pendleton Dudley continued to counsel the nation's meatpackers in the ways of sound public relations practices that would bring stability, profit, and public approbation to the industry until his death at the age of 90 in 1966. Dudley's AMI program became a model for industry.

In the 1930s, Dudley won the Florida Citrus Commission account, one that remained with the firm at least until it was sold by the Way sisters. Dudley recruited George Anderson from United Press International to handle this account and, as noted previously, Anderson later won a partnership. Anderson often characterized the firm as consisting of people and second-hand furniture. He was responsible for establishing the first professional home economics department and the first test kitchen in a public relations agency. Anderson produced much of his food publicity under the pen name of Dorothy Ames Carter.

During World War II, many of its staff left to join the services; many of those who remained worked on a War Department account. At the end of the war, Thomas D. Yutzy, a former newspaper editor, joined Dudley and Anderson. In 2 years, the firm became Dudley–Anderson–Yutzy, then DAY in 1970, then went off the public relations marquee in 1988.

Kate Yutzy succeeded to her husband's partnership, then in 1970, sold her interest to Jean Way Schoonover and her sister, Barbara Hunter. George Anderson had sold his share of DAY the year before he retired. In 1979, when DAY celebrated its 70th anniversary, it ranked among the top 15 independent counseling firms and had 60 employees.

AN EVALUATION OF PENDLETON DUDLEY

Pendleton Dudley had a lively, vigorous mind and never slacked in his efforts to learn. In his 80s, he was an enthusiastic participant in the Public Relations Society's first [1959] Public Relations Institute that dealt with social, economic, and political trends. He frequently quoted William James's comment, "Compared with what we ought to be, we are only half awake."

> Semantics and psychiatry were especial concerns of his. Dudley came to value research and took the lead in organizing the Foundation for Public Relations Research and Education, once an arm of PRSA. It was primarily Pendleton Dudley, working in cooperation with me, who initiated the PRSA Fellowship program for public relations teachers. Despite his age, he was always looking ahead, worrying about tomorrow; this included concern for sound public relations of education.

Unlike many practitioners of his age and newspaper background, Dudley saw the importance of research in public reactions. He was eternally confronting communications and opinion researchers with a demand to come up with a yardstick to measure the effectiveness of public relations programs. He went to his grave dissatisfied with researchers' efforts in this regard. He also worried much about the standing of public relations with the public. He strove mightily to build a favorable reputation for his craft and contributed to that goal by his durability, industry, integrity, and his venerability here defined by Webster as "calling forth respect through age, character, and attainments."

Dudley was one of the founders and a former president of the National Association of Public Relations Counsel, a group of New York City practitioners who first organized in 1936 as the National Association of Publicity Directors. This organization changed its name in 1944 and was one of the two groups that merged to form the Public Relations Society of America in 1948. Dudley received the predecessor organization's award as the individual considered to have done the most to improve public relations from a professional standpoint. In 1965, he received the Distinguished Service Award presented by the New York Chapter, PRSA.

But like his chum, Ivy Lee, Pendleton Dudley never seemed to doubt the ethics and methods of the businessmen whose story he sought to tell—then or in later years. Both these men, born in humble circumstances, stood in great awe of Big Business and relished their ability to move in these exalted circles of prominence and plushness. Both Lee and Dudley talked much of telling the business story but never appeared too much concerned with the merit of that story. As late as 1965, Dudley wrote, "For business enterprise is the life blood . . . of our nation and unless the nature of business and industry is understood by the people there can be trouble, and big trouble."

Pendleton Dudley labored unflaggingly for 57 years to tell business's story as he saw it.

NOTES ON SOURCES

Substantial parts of this chapter were first published in *The Public Relations Quarterly,* Vol 14, No. 4, 1970, an expanded version was published in *The Public Relations Review*, Vol. 17, No. 4, 1991, and are used here with permission of those publications.

This chapter is based on an extensive interview with Dudley on March 9, 1959, frequent luncheon conversations before and after that date, and extensive correspondence with him from the mid-1950s until shortly before his death in December, 1966. His account of his "first client of note" was told in a letter to me dated March 26, 1959, and one to Major Earl Stover dated December 3, 1963. In both letters he refused to discuss his work for the anti-Woodrow Wilson group in 1909. Other important letters to me which recount his career and his views on current practice are ones of November 22, 1960, January 23, 1961, August 1, 1962, August 19, 1965, and August 26, 1965. (These are in the Scott M. Cutlip Papers, Mass Communications History Center, State Historical Society of Wisconsin.) My last interview with Pen Dudley was in March, 1962.

Three Dudley articles were helpful in shedding light on his concepts of public relations: "What's Ahead in Public Relations," in *Public Relations Comes of Age*, published by National Association of Public Relations Counsel, October 23, 1945; "Current Beginnings of Public Relations," *Public Relations Journal*, Vol. 8, August, 1952; "Counselors Need to Adapt to More Varied Needs," *Public Relations Journal,* Vol. 11, October, 1955; and "A Statement About Public Relations and Its Impact," undated paper in Pendleton Dudley Papers, Mass Communications History Center, State Historical Society of Wisconsin. (These papers are a thin source because Dudley, his successors and heirs turned over only a few of his papers to the Society.)

The story of Dudley's work in stabilizing the meat industry is recounted by Herbert Bain, "The First 75 Years of the American Meat Institute, a commemorative magazine published by the AMI Arlington, VA in 1980. Also helpful on this aspect of Dudley's work was a speech by Wesley

Hardenburgh, "Progress," given September 23, 1957, and published in the *National Provisioner*, October 5, 1957. For a picture of the meat industry at the End of World War I, before Pendleton Dudley came to its rescue, see: U. S. Federal Trade Commission, Summary of the Report of the Federal Trade Commission on the Meat-Packing Industry,": Government Printing Office, Washington, DC, 1918.

The final days of D A Y were told in a letter to me dated November 22, 1988, from Jean Way Schoonover, its last president. Also included was a synopsis of D A Y's later years. Also see: "45 Years of Management-Level Counseling, *TIDE*, Vol. 28, November 6, 1954. Pendleton Dudley's obituary was published in *The New York Times*, December 12, 1966. For an appraisal of his 59-year career, see: Milton Fairman, "A Memoir," *Public Relations Journal,* Vol. 23, February, 1967.

PART II

PUBLIC RELATIONS BOOMS IN THE BOOMING TWENTIES, 1919–1930

The successful mobilization of public opinion in support of World War I by the Creel Committee on Public Information, the spectacular results of the Liberty Loan drives in which John Price Jones got his public relations baptism, and the raising of more than $600 million in Red Cross and other wartime drives created a widespread awareness and blind faith in the power of publicity. This faith that publicity could move mountains was reinforced by the successful culmination of the Anti-Saloon League's campaign for national prohibition and the victory of the Woman's Suffrage Movement in 1920.

Equally impressive was Herbert Hoover's wartime reliance on public relations to encourage food conservation by the nation's households, hotels, restaurants, and food dealers. The Food Administration, under the public relations direction of Ben Allen, former Associated Press correspondent, transmitted appeals about saving food by every available means of communication, including $20 million worth of donated advertising space, a campaign that brought results.

The lesson was more widely observed in business, education, and philanthropy than in the United States government as to the potential of public relations, although Secretary of Commerce Herbert Hoover had learned his wartime lesson well. He built a strong public relations program in the Commerce Department, one that propelled him into the Presidency in 1929. Leo Rosten pointed out that after World War I, there was a heightened consciousness of the value of a "good press." The Creel Committee was particularly influential in spreading the new gospel because of its spectacular accomplishments and because of the large number of persons involved in its operations. For example, it mobilized 75, 000 Minutemen to carry the war message to every city, town, and hamlet in a day when there was no radio and no TV.

George Creel, crusading journalist and strong Wilson supporter, was summoned by President Woodrow Wilson shortly after America's entry into World War I to head the newly created Committee on Public Information (CPI). Organized to unite public opinion behind the war at home and to propagandize American peace aims abroad, the CPI soon became known as the Creel Committee because of the dominating, controversial personality of its chairman. Early on, when confronted with a logjam in the Government Printing Office, Creel drafted Carl Byoir, then circulation director of Hearst magazine. Byoir quickly solved the printing problem and was kept on by Creel as associate chairman. Then only 28, Byoir became the person who kept the organization functioning during Creel's many absences and his work as counselor to President Woodrow Wilson. (Byoir did not return to public relations until 1930 when he established his successful firm, Carl Byoir & Associates.)

Creel and Byoir had faced an enormous task at the outbreak of the war, one for which there were no precedents, no blueprints. Their demonstration of propaganda was to have a profound effect on American culture and on the future of public relations. Creel, Byoir, and their associates, led by President Wilson, had been so successful in building fervent hopes for "a world made safe for democracy" at home and in Europe that when these hopes were crushed in the wake of the Treaty of Versailles, their work led to the corrosion of the word *propaganda*, now used as a derogatory, pejorative term. Consequently, its use was dropped in the worlds of advertising, public relations, and politics. In the immediate postwar years, men who had gained experience under Creel and had observed the efficacy of the propaganda campaigns for Prohibition and Women's Suffrage carried this knowledge back into civilian life. Vigorously nourished by these wartime developments, the public relations, or more accurately the publicity specialty, quickly spread. It showed up in government, business, the churches, social work — now burgeoning in the war's aftermath — the labor movement and efforts to quell it, and in social movements. Because the process of urbanization and industrialization had been pushed ahead several notches during the war, the growth and development of these practices, like much else, was accelerating in society. Industrial executives were discovering that mass distribution of goods and services made possible by greatly expanded mass production facilities required stepped up campaigns of advertising and product promotion. This was particularly true in the now booming automobile industry and the beginnings of commercial aviation.

Walter Lippmann's seminal *Public Opinion*, first published in 1922 and still widely used in college classrooms, reflected the awakening interest in the nature and power of public opinion. In all the years prior to 1917, there were only 18 books published on public opinion, publicity, and public relations; at least 28 titles were published between 1917 and 1925. In his classic statement based upon his World War I observations, Lippmann predicted the need for intermediaries in a complex society. Social scientists have been agreeing with him ever since. More recently, pollster Daniel Yankelovich agreed by stating, "Public consensus depends on bringing competing values into the open to resolve them." In the booming twenties, an increasing number of publicists emerged to facilitate what Lippmann described as the intermediaries' role. Ivy L. Lee was the first to see the need for this role and envisioned a lucrative calling in filling it.

Little wonder that in these postwar years, coming after the several successful demonstrations of the power to mold and move public opinion, that there emerged an overly optimistic belief in the power of publicity. A noted political scientist, Harold Lasswell, observed, "But when all allowances have been made, and all extravagant estimates pared to the bone, the fact remains that propaganda is one of the most powerful instrumentalities of the modern world."

The World War had greatly expanded the nation's industrial capacity and created a shortage of consumer goods. It had also brought new inventions and new ways of producing mass consumer products. These factors created need for experts in advertising, marketing, public relations, and fund-raising. Those who had been schooled in these techniques found a ready market for their talents. Ivy Lee led the way in the rapid expansion of the public relations agency business after World War I. He soon hired T. J. Ross, who ultimately took over the firm when Lee died. With his courtly manner and Southern drawl, Lee moved easily among the power brokers of his time.

Edward L. Bernays, a Broadway press agent before the war, had held a minor post in the Creel Committee. In partnership with his wife, Doris Fleischman, Bernays opened his agency in 1919 and began promoting the term *public relations counsel*. His book *Crystallizing Public Opinion*, was the first to define the mature concept of public relations as interpreting the institution to the public and more importantly, interpreting the public to the institution's executives. John Price Jones incorporated his firm in November 1919 "to give counsel and service in organization and publicity to business houses, institutions of public, semi-public and private character" and "to meet the demand for highly specialized knowledge in these fields." Jones's firm prospered as a fund-raising organization but made few waves in public relations. Similarly Carlton and George Ketchum, schooled in wartime fund-raising, started a publicity agency in Pittsburgh, also in 1919, but in 1923, they decided fund-raising and advertising were not compatible and split. Their beginnings are described later.

Harry Bruno, wartime flier, formed a publicity agency in 1923 in partnership with Richard Blythe after the airline firm Bruno had been working for went broke. Their firm gained national prominence in 1927 when they handled Charles A. Lindbergh's solo flight across the Atlantic. Demonstrating one of the important tasks of public relations, Bruno did much to speed the public's acceptance of commercial aviation. In 1926, when William Baldwin opened an agency to serve corporate and civic clients, there were only six agencies listed in the telephone directory of New York City.

The next year, 1927, John W. Hill, a newsman, opened his office in Cleveland. In 1933, he formed a partnership with Don Knowlton; a short time later, Hill moved to New York to found Hill & Knowlton, Inc., a separate firm. Knowlton remained in Cleveland until he retired in 1964 when the Cleveland office was sold. Public relations' growth from these uncertain early years was dramatically reflected when Hill & Knowlton, Inc. was sold to J. Walter Thompson in 1980 for $28 million.

The Twenties era ended on a jarring note for the new vocation when Congress investigated the propaganda of Samuel Insull's creation, the National Electric Light Association (NELA), and found that since 1922, NELA had been carrying on a campaign of misinformation and bribery of public opinion leaders to fight public ownership of utilities. As Bernays noted, "The new profession received a bad name from which it did not free itself for years." Insull and his ace publicist, Bernard Mullaney, were not the only ones to bring taint to this adolescent vocation.

The postwar twenties also brought the "Red Scare" that provided the seedbed for the hatreds, fears, and bigotry that two Atlanta publicists, Edward Y. Clarke and Elizabeth "Bessie" Tyler, exploited to take a defunct Atlanta bottle club, the Ku Klux Klan, and boom it into a national organization of three million members in 3 years—a legacy of publicity and promotion that divides and scars this nation today. In his memorable book, *Only Yesterday*, Frederic Lewis Allen described that seedbed in this way:

> Those were the days when column after column of the front pages of the newspapers shouted the news of strikes and anti-Bolshevist riots; when radicals shot down Armistice Day paraders in the streets of Centralia, Washington and in revenge the patriotic citizenry took out of jail a member of the I.W.—a white American—and lynched him by tying a rope around his neck and throwing him off a bridge; when properly elected members of the Assembly of New York State were expelled . . . simply because they had been elected as members of the venerable Socialist Party; when a jury in Indiana took two minutes to acquit a man of shooting and killing an alien because he

had shouted, "To hell with the United States." It was an era of lawless and disorderly defense of law and order, of unconstitutional defense of the Constitution, of suspicion and civil conflict, in a very literal sense, a reign of terror.

And in this volatile, suspicious climate of Red-baiting, Clarke and Tyler made their millions and left the vocation a bitter legacy. Also in this climate of hysteria and "union busting," there is Ivy Lee in the early 1920s again defending strikebreaking coal operators as he had done for the Rockefellers in the aftermath of the Ludlow Massacre. John Price Jones and John W. Hill, pioneers both, also lent their talents to breaking the Little Steel Strike of 1937.

A SPATE OF BOOKS

The burgeoning practice of publicity/public relations prompted the publication of several books to describe the emerging vocation. Most influential in defining the mature function of public relations was Edward L. Bernays's *Crystallizing Public Opinion* published in 1923 by Boni-Liveright. This book's influence is discussed in chapter 7. Because of his influence as leader in the new field, Ivy L. Lee's privately published *Publicity Some of the Things It Is and Is Not* (1925) also was influential in clarifying the function. It was Lee's little book that awakened John W. Hill's interest in publicity.

R. H. Wilder and K. L. Buell, former newspapermen who had formed a publicity agency in the early 1920s, authored *Publicity*, published by the Ronald Press Company also in 1923. These publicists defined publicity as "the organized and deliberate effort to enlist the support of the public for an idea, sponsored by any given group for any given purpose," adding, "The word is the only one which includes the entire field of activity involved in such an appeal." These authors recognized, too, "the increasing part played by public opinion the various affairs of life." They made the distinction between publicity and advertising—often confused in those days—by insisting that "advertising is a well-marked field of its own."

A year later, J. H. Long wrote *Public Relations a Handbook of Publicity*, published by McGraw-Hill in 1924. Long, at that time was on the staff of the National Automobile Chamber of Commerce. His title and subtitle reflect the confusion over the two terms then rampant and still evident in some people's minds. Long recognized the growing competition for the public's attention as publicity/public relations agencies were springing up and advertising was booming. "The competition for public attention is . . . enormous. Hence, one finds the modern newspaper or magazine editor, or radio-program director, or whoever controls a medium of communication with the public in the position of the Town Meeting Chairman." He recognized the public's suspicion of the new publicity craft, noting that the function was frequently charged with twisting or misrepresenting facts or concealing the source of information. Long argued that "flat misstatement of fact, or misrepresentation, is not the general practice in Publicity Work." Were that so, then or now!

Religious organizations were also awakening to publicity's power in these years. Richard Beall Niese, news editor of the *Nashville Tennessean*, authored a little book, *The Newspaper and Religious Publicity*, published in 1925 by the George H. Doran Company. It was mainly a handbook on newspapers and how church leaders could use publicity to advance religion.

A year later, 1926, Roger William Riis and Charles W. Bonner, partners in one of the new agencies, authored a book entitled *Publicity* published by the Kingsport Press, Kingsport, Tennessee — presumably a vanity publisher. The book carried a foreword by Richard Washburn Child, another of the 1920s publicists, who wrote, "No other land has developed the art, the science, and, indeed, the ethics of publicity to the extent we see under our noses in America." True, the United States pioneered in the ways and uses of public relations, well ahead of European and other countries. Child saw the role of the publicity expert was to counsel silence as well as dissemination of information.

Riis and Bonner defined publicity as "anything that any of us does to become well-known and to become well-known creditably." They agreed with Child, "When a publicity agent undertakes any specified work, he may counsel either 'telling the world' or maintaining industrious silence." These publicists saw publicity and advertising as twin vehicles to sway public opinion. This book was published by the J. H. Sears Company.

Employee relations was also beginning to gain attention as a subspecialty of public relations. Hayes Robins wrote a book, *The Human Relations in Railroading*, published in 1927 by the General Publishing Company in which he advocated more managerial attention to employees and their motivation. He saw the 1920s as a time of "a deliberate effort to dig to the roots of discord, in so far as they may lie in the everyday human relationships of railroad operations and to find, if possible, what the tangible effects of common interest are, upon which a new era of willing and intelligent cooperation for public service may be built."

Surprising — to me at least — is that the engineering profession was among the first professions to recognize the need for publicity and public approval. The American Association of Engineers sponsored the "First National Conference on Public Information" in 1922. The proceedings of this conference were published by the association that year, entitled *Publicity Methods for Engineers* "to make plain the principles of presenting to the public information about engineers and to show by cases how this is being accomplished." The engineers recognized in this early time that "public opinion influences most undertakings to such an extent that without its support few succeed, while none can withstand opposition." "The best public servants do not allow public opinion to drift . . . they mold and aggressively direct it like any other energy for the public weal," the preface read. The power of public opinion was coming to be widely recognized, thus providing the opportunity to aspiring publicists, many of whom matured into public relations counselors.

THE GENESIS OF KETCHUM, INC.

Of the several public relations or publicity agencies born in the post-World War I era in these fields, only two have survived into the 1990s. The oldest of these, Ketchum, Inc., born in 1919, ranks today as a major agency. The Ketchum story is not told in this volume because I was not given access to Ketchum's records. What is today Ketchum Public Relations, Inc. was born of happenstance, or perhaps luck of the draw would be more accurate.

Charles Sumner Ward and Lyman Pierce, both YMCA secretaries, changed America's philanthropy when they linked publicity and organization to appeals for giving in the early 1900s. They were the originators of the whirlwind, intensive campaign to raise large sums of money by bombarding the public with sure-fire emotional appeals and by recruiting scores of volunteers to solicit many times their number. Professionals still refer to "The Ward Plan" or "The Pierce Plan." These pioneers fused their talents in a whirlwind campaign to raise $300, 000 for a YMCA in Washington, DC, in 1905, the first fund drive to employ a full-time publicist. As a result of their early successes, both men were sought by institutions seeking to raise needed funds.

In January 1914, Chancellor Samuel Black McCormick of the University of Pittsburgh, then in the process of transition from the old Western University of Pennsylvania, sought Ward's services to raise $3 million urgently needed to develop its new campus in Schenley Park. Ward met with the Pitt Alumni Committee in January, and they mapped "a whirlwind campaign" to run for 10 days in May 1914. Ward brought in Frederick Courtenay Barber to publicize the campaign, then asked Chancellor McCormick to provide two student assistants from the university. The students chosen by the Chancellor were Carlton and George Ketchum. Of this campaign, Carlton Ketchum recalled, "The methods of the campaign would now be considered simple, if not naive, but at the time caused a great deal of excitement and amazement because most of the people who served in the campaign or were affected by it had never seen such an operation or anything like it."

Subsequent to the Pitt campaign, Frederick Courtenay Barber started his own fund-raising firm. He had been highly impressed by the energy and ability of the Ketchum brothers and hired both of them. They joined the Barber firm when Carlton was graduated in June 1916. George did not complete the work for his degree but was soon using the lessons Mr. Ward had taught him to raise funds for the Rose Polytechnic Institute in Terre Haute, Indiana. Carlton's first assignment was to serve as publicity man for a campaign for a Salvation Army building in Great Falls, Montana, but he soon moved back to college fund-raising. In the months preceding World War I, Carlton was engaged in one of the very first organized campaigns for a woman's college, Elmira College. After the campaign in Elmira, Carlton worked on a public relations program for Lafayette College to pave the way for a fund-raising campaign and then as director of a fund-raising effort for a woman's suffrage campaign in Illinois.

Carlton and George Ketchum quit the Barber firm in 1917 to go into military service. When Carlton told Barber of his intentions to enlist in the army, Barber gave him a "good round denuciation." Both served as officers in the U.S. Army in World War I.

When Carlton Ketchum was discharged early in 1919, he went to work for the University of Pittsburgh as a publicist and fund-raiser. When George arrived home early in August, he prepared to open the office of Ketchum Publicity—"an organization consisting of George, a stenographer full-time and such part of Carlton's time as could be had on evenings and Sundays." Norman MacLeod, who later formed the Ketchum–MacLeod––Grove advertising and publicity agency with George, joined the firm in 1920. Carlton quit his job at Pitt to work full time in the new firm in 1921. The firm was incorporated as Ketchum, Inc. in 1923—this became Carlton's fund-raising firm. At the same time, Ketchum, MacLeod - Grove was organized as an advertising agency. Ultimately, the two firms became distinct entities, with George heading the advertising and publicity agency, Carlton the fund-raising firm. Both ultimately became leaders in their respective fields.

In a letter to me dated September 6, 1961, Carlton recalled, "We set out to be a public relations firm but when we were only a year old we directed a campaign for the Industrial Home for Crippled Children in Pittsburgh, then one for the Y.W.C.A. in Wilkinsburg, a Pittsburgh suburb." The rest, as they say, is history.

The other firm founded in the post-World War I boom that survives today is Hill and Knowlton, Inc. of New York City. Founder John W. Hill's story is told in chapters 15 and 16.

While these new firms were being born in New York City—the nation's communication center—small firms were springing up across the country. For example, what is today's oldest independent public relations agency—

Edward Howard & Co. — was being started in Cleveland, Ohio. Edward Howard, like John W. Hill who followed in his footsteps 2 years later, quit his job at the Cleveland Trust Co. where he had been editor of the bank's employee magazine and started a one-man agency in 1925. After the founder's death in 1954, his sons Edward Jim took over the business and expanded it. In 1965, Edward Howard & Co. opened a New York City office. In 1969, the Howard firm bought Selvage and Lee — founded in the 1940s by James Selvage and Morris Lee. In 1974, the Selvage, Lee, and Howard operation was dissolved, and Edward Howard & Co. returned to being a Cleveland-based firm. Upon dissolution of the Selvage-Lee-Howard operation, Farley Manning, who had started his firm after World War II, merged with a revamped Selvage and Lee to form Manning, Selvage, and Lee, a large firm today. Morris Lee was still active in the original firm when he and Manning merged.

Also a major factor in the public relations–communications boom of the 1920s was the advent of radio broadcasting that provided an instant and expanded means of communication for alert publicists.

NOTES ON SOURCES

Information on Herbert Hoover's skilled use of public relations in World War I is from an unpublished master's thesis by Leonard P. Deleanis, "Herbert Hoover's Use of Public Relations in the U. S. Food Administration, 1917–1919," University of Wisconsin, 1969. President Hoover was the first president to officially designate a White House press secretary. On this, see Marietta Pane, "George Akerson: First Presidential Secretary," unpublished master's thesis, University of Wisconsin, 1969.

For the unsavory history of the Insull-led propaganda campaign against municipal ownership of utilities, see: *Utility Corporations: Efforts by Associations and Agencies of Electric and Gas Utilities to Influence Public Opinion,* A Summary Report Prepared by the Federal Trade Commission, 70th Congress, 1st Session (Senate Document 92, Part 71-A), Washington, DC: Government Printing Office, 1934; and Frederick Lewis Allen, *Only Yesterday.* Harper, 1957.

The brief account of the Ketchum agency is based on: (a) a letter from Judith Campbell, University of Pittsburgh, after a careful search of the university files, to me dated August 2, 1961; (b) Carlton G. Ketchum in Memorandum dated March 1, 1960, addressed to David S. Ketchum, "Material for Article on the History of Trends in Fund Raising Campaigns for Colleges and Universities," in that firm's files; and (c) a letter from Carlton Ketchum, to me dated Sept. 6, 1961.

Chapter 6

Ivy Lee Returns to New York; Joined By T. J. Ross

Ivy Lee's last service for the American Red Cross came at the war's end when he was asked to accompany Chairman Henry P. Davison to Europe on a fact-finding mission for President Wilson. Lee was somewhat reluctant to take on this assignment because of the demands of a growing list of clients and his desire to make money. Lee did agree in this instance to let the Red Cross pay his traveling expenses. In a telegram to John D. Rockefeller, Jr. dated December 13, 1918, Lee wired:

> Davison sails Monday response to President's request that he undertake international Red Cross mission. Both Davison and War Council consider it important that I serve as a member of the commission on theory great delicacy of presentation vital consequence to ultimate success. . . . Have considered the matter with great earnestness myself, feeling extremely reluctant to leave, in view of the fact that my service to the Red Cross has not only been of great expense directly but has been the cause of losing considerable business I might have had. Opportunities for my activities on substantial scale have been developing with great rapidity ever since prospects of peace loomed up. . . . I have concluded that in spite of the very material sacrifice that this would mean for me I have no right to decline to perform this service if my clients are willing that in my absence my office should care for their affairs.

IVY L. LEE & ASSOCIATES FORMED IN 1920

In 1920, Lee decided to reorganize Lee, Harris, and Lee and rename it Ivy L. Lee & Associates with offices at 61 Broadway in Lower Manhattan. An announcement brochure issued June 10 carried the brief biographies of his professional staff of 13. His brother, Wideman, Jr., who had left the Pennsylvania Railroad to join his brother's firm in 1916, led the list of associates. Wideman, Jr. had spent the last year of the war as Deputy Commissioner to Belgium for the American Red Cross. Perhaps to escape the shadow of his famous brother, Wideman, Jr. left the new firm in 1920. He became vice-president and later president of the George L. Dyer Advertising Agency; in 1931 Wideman, Jr. set up his own company. The U.S. Rubber Company had asked Ivy Lee to recommend an advertising agency. Wideman, Jr. helped Dyer get the U.S. Rubber account, and this got him a position with that agency. Ivy Lee was constantly looking out for his family. When Wideman, Jr. left, he was replaced by a younger brother, Lewis.

W. W. Harris, who had been a partner in the original firm, continued as a key executive in the reorganized agency. Daniel T. Pierce, third in seniority, also was extolled in the announcement of the new firm. He had taken a leave of absence in 1917 to handle public relations for the International Shipbuilding Corp., then Lee had him assigned as director of public information for the American red Cross in Paris until the war's end. Lee had made Pierce manager of the firm upon his return from the Davison mission to Europe in 1919. Harris retired from the firm in 1928 or 1929, T.J. Ross couldn't remember which. Pierce left the firm in April 1, 1926, to work for the anthracite coal operators. His last position was with the Sinclair Oil Co. Thomas E. Orr quit the firm on September 30, 1926. Lewis Lee, Ivy's youngest brother, who had joined the firm when he got out of the Navy in 1919, left the agency on March 31, 1927, to go into the brokerage business. Lewis later became director of the Greater New York Fund.

But then a new name was added to the roster in 1919—that of Thomas J. Ross, Jr. who in time, became Lee's partner and eventually took over the firm after Lee's death in 1934. In 1919, when Ross started to work for Lee, he was 26; it was his first, and as time would tell, his only public relations affiliation.

T. J. Ross by his formal business signature, and Tommy Ross to friends, was born in Brooklyn, NY, on July 27, 1893. He was graduated from St. Francis Xavier College, a Jesuit school, in 1913 and quickly landed a job as a reporter on the *New York Sun*. Ross had gotten his start in journalism while in college by doing night assignments on the *Brooklyn Eagle*. He received $1 a story and later worked the night trick on the *Eagle* Saturday nights. Ross worked on the *Sun* for 3 years and in 1916 covered the Republican and Progressive conventions and Judge Charles Evan Hughes' campaign for the Presidency. In 1917, he was hired by the *New York Herald-Tribune* to cover the New York State Legislature. At the outbreak of World War I, Ross entered the First Plattsburgh Training Camp. He was commissioned a second lieutenant in the Field Artillery and fought with artillery units in France. Although his commission was good for the regular Army, he resigned after the Armistice.

Ross's long and brilliant career in public relations, like that of most practitioners, was happenstance. Upon getting out of the Army, he wrote a friend Lou Palmer, a former Sunday editor of the *Sun*, inquiring about job leads. As Ross recalled later in an interview with *Printer's Ink*, "The day Palmer got my letter, he was lunching with W. W. Harris, a former managing editor of the *Sun*, now a partner in Lee, Harris, and Lee. Palmer showed Harris my letter and that afternoon I got a telephone call from Harris asking me not to make any plans for civilian employment without talking to him. That's how I got in the public relations business." "Ross was actually hired by Wideman Lee, Jr., upon Harris's recommendation. Ivy Lee was in Europe at the time. I return to the Tommy Ross story later.

The announcement brochure also listed Lewis Bigelow, a brother of Lee's wife, who had both a bachelor's and a law degree from Yale University. In the 1890s, Bigelow worked on the *New York World* and as a Washington correspondent for the *Evening Sun*. Ivy hired his brother-in-law for special assignments on the Pennsylvania Railroad, and later, while serving with the American Red Cross, appointed Bigelow as editor of the *American Red Cross Bulletin*. Lee and Bigelow had known each other in the late 1890s through their work on a New York newspaper, and it was Bigelow who introduced his sister to Lee.

Other members of the professional staff listed in the announcement included: William A. Willis, who had worked on the *New York Sun*, the *Evening World*, and the *New York Herald*. His last assignment there had been as acting managing editor, which indicates that Lee's salaries were more than competitive with those on newspapers; William R. Hereford, a Harvard law graduate with extensive newspaper experience, whom Lee had come to know when Hereford served as director of the Department of Publicity and Public Relations for the League of Red Cross Societies in Geneva, Switzerland in 1919–1920; Samuel Morse, who had worked on the news staffs of the *Omaha World*, the *Denver Republican*, the *Milwaukee Sentinel*, and lastly, *The New York Times* as night city editor; Thomas H. Uzzell, whose last journalism assignment was a managing editor of *The Nation's Business*; Thomas E. Orr, who had worked on Philadelphia newspapers before joining the publicity and legal departments of the Philadelphia Rapid Transit; Charles W. Towne, who also had a background in journalism and in public relations; Edwin Lewis, a graduate of the Columbia School of Journalism and a reporter of the *Herald–Tribune*; Francis A. Collins, an author and former newspaper reporter; William L. Dempsey, a graduate of Lee's beloved Princeton and former reporter who also had worked for Lee in the American Red Cross. The business manager for the revamped firm was H. W. Dengler, Jr., whom Lee had come to know and value when Dengler worked for him at the Pennsylvania Railroad. He had been hired by Lee when he started his first firm in 1916. A review of this roster makes clear two things: one, Lee's firm belief that newspaper experience was an essential qualification for public relations, and two, that Lee had brought together the strongest, most experienced staff of any of the fledgling agencies in the post-World War I era. But Lee saw more than the need for newspaper experience; he saw the need for a public relations practitioner to be a broadly educated person who is attuned to the public opinion environment.

Ivy Lee's foresight in developing his concepts of public relations was in seeing that it was an important part of the counselor's function to monitor and interpret the public opinion environment to management so that corporations and institutions could anticipate and adjust to swiftly changing social, political, and economic currents. To serve this function, Lee saw the need for a wide range of reading and traveling, both at home and abroad. Ivy Lee's reading ran the gamut of periodicals, left to right. He made travel an avocation, not vacation, by carefully boning up on the countries on his proposed itinerary. He insisted on the same wide-ranging education on the part of his staff. A veteran staff member, Harcourt Parrish, wrote to me in a letter dated May 28, 1952:

> It seems to me that in any discussion of Mr. Lee's activities, some consideration must be given to his thorough training program for his associates. He insisted that they read and study consistently and continuously on a wide variety of subjects, not necessarily those relating directly to the clients for whom we worked. He insisted that we travel as much as possible, as he himself did. He liked to send his associates on extended trips and he always insisted that they 'see things'. For instance, when he sent me to Europe he told me to take three or four weeks in Paris and France and 'get it out of your system.' Since I was on my way to Poland, he instructed me to stop off in Germany and make several reports for him in Berlin, particularly on the Zeiss Planetarium. He had foresight, because this visit of mine in Germany was productive later when I received a cablegram in Warsaw to go to Berlin to see the I. G. Farben people.

Hearst Editor Arthur Brisbane once said Lee's contribution "to civilization is that he interprets his client to the public and the public to his client."

LEE HELPS REVIVE COPPER INDUSTRY

The war had seriously damaged the copper industry because virtually all its production had to be diverted to the war and its munitions. Builders and other users of copper had turned to aluminum and other substitutes for copper and brass. Consequently when the munitions industries shut down in 1918, copper producers faced a greatly shrunken market. Earlier Lee had done public relations work for the Anaconda Copper Co. and the Phelps Dodge and Company. In this work, he had become acquainted with John Simeon Guggenheim, who retained him to serve Guggenheim's extensive mining interests. When confronted with the crisis facing the industry after the war, Lee again counseled formation of a trade association similar to the one he had proposed to the oil companies, an idea that would be widely copied. As told in the previous chapter, the meat packers, who likewise were confronted with a post-World War I crisis, formed the American Meat Institute on the counsel of Ivy Lee's close friend, Pendleton Dudley, who frankly admitted that he was copying Lee's American Petroleum Institute and that of the Iron and Steel Institute. The trade association or institute, then an innovative idea, is now standard in American industry. It has two functions: to maintain internal discipline on its membership so as not to offend the public and to present the industry's case to the public and governmental bodies.

The Copper and Brass Research Association became the central agency to serve the public relations requirements of 42 major copper producers. The obvious purpose was to help copper regain its share of the market for its products. At Lee's direction, the association launched a major advertising campaign to tout the benefits of copper. Intensive use of advertising in a public relations campaign was another Lee innovation, one that was not widely copied until World War II. Advertisements aimed at the consumer were placed in newspapers and magazines nationwide. Copper dealers were supplied with brochures for distribution to their customers. Architectural, manufacturing, and technical publications were used to target specific groups and specific uses of copper. The advertising program was matched by a promotional campaign. A monthly bulletin was sent to the construction industry, a prime target. Publicity was disseminated suggesting new uses for copper.

The most important development was the creation of a research staff to find new and wider uses of copper and to make surveys of just what was being done with copper and its alloys in industry. The work of this research staff constantly provided news pegs for stories. According to Hiebert, "The Copper and Brass Research Association helped to restore industrial uses of copper after a period of scarcity caused by the war." This association remained a major account for the Lee agency for years to come. It also brought him and his staff work for other farflung Guggenheim interests.

Another account that came to Lee's firm as the war was winding down was that of the steel makers. Secretary of the Navy Josephus Daniels decided that the Government should make its own steel plate for ships.

Charles Schwab, president of Bethlehem Steel, sought Lee's counsel on behalf of the steelmakers to oppose Daniels' plan. He asked Lee what his services would cost; Lee told him that he didn't know; but would investigate and see what could be done on the case. Lee set out to determine a course of action and worked on the case for 3 months, without anything being said about the fee.

Finally, Schwab walked into Lee's offices one day and asked, "With what do you pay your grocery bills at your house?" Lee bantered, "Oh, the neighbors send us in things once in a while." Schwab then asked what the company owed him, Lee answered him, "What you think is right." They finally arrived at an agreement by writing on slips of paper what each of them thought the job was worth and then dividing by two. As it turned out, Schwab had listed an amount twice that put down by Lee. Such was the way counseling fees were set in those still informal days of public relations.

IVY LEE AGAIN DEFENDS STRIKEBREAKING

Even though it appeared that Ivy Lee was getting enough business to support his large, experienced staff, he was not reluctant to return to the defense of strikebreaking as he had done for the Rockefellers' Colorado Fuel & Iron Company in 1914. The agency's records show that the Lee firm had as a client, albeit briefly, the Logan County (West Virginia) Coal Operators from October to December 1921. The Lee firm was retained by the coal operators of West Virginia to counter the ugly publicity that had flowed from their use of a large armed force to crush a miners' march on Logan and Mingo counties, organized to protest police brutality against union organizers. In pitched and running battles over 6 days in what came to be known as the Battle of Blair Mountain, some 70 miners were killed, 3 Army officers died in a plane crash, and an unknown number of police and military soldiers were wounded.[1]

On the night of October 31, 1919, nearly 400,000 soft coal miners struck against the operators of the bituminous mines of the nation, from Illinois to Pennsylvania, despite a temporary injunction obtained by U.S. Attorney General A. Mitchell Palmer. *The New York Times* of November 1, 1920, reported that 394, 600 miners had gone out on strike, though their leaders

---

[1]At the start of Lee, Harris, and Ivy Lee had set up a system of placing a copy of all releases and other matter disseminated in large leather scrapbooks labeled "Matter Sent Out" (MSO). These MSO books, as they became known to the staff, which constitute a documented record of the firm's clients and those of his successors, were deposited with his papers at Princeton University in the late 1980s as the firm reached its denouement. The MSO Book for 1920–1922 records the work the Lee firm did for the Logan County Coal Operators from October to December 1921.

had been silenced by the court order. Coal operators, meeting in Cleveland, vowed to keep the mines running. Thus began one of the bitterest struggles in American industrial history with federal troops and state guards being used, finally, to crush the miners' strikes.

Ivy Lee, staunchly Big Business and conservative, apparently had no compunction against becoming involved in this massive Big Business drive to weaken or, if possible, destroy organized labor and protect the open shop. At the end of World War I, during which many grievances had festered, labor disputes broke out across the nation. In 1919, more than four million workers were involved in labor disputes, quadruple the number the year before. The growing number of strikes and the Recession of 1921 spurred manufacturers' associations and chambers of commerce to mount open-shop drives.

In the unrest that followed World War I, the United Mine Workers (UMW) made a futile effort to organize the coal miners in West Virginia to end their exploitation by the coal operators who paid them low wages for long hours in often unsafe mines and held them hostage to company housing and company stores that charged them dearly for what they bought with company scrip. The grievances of the coal miners were bitter and justified. Scribner's *Concise Dictionary of American History* summarized these grievances: ". . . dangerous working conditions, unsatisfactory wages, abuses by company towns and privatized police, introduction of scab labor, black listing, and yellow dog contracts." The coal companies that in West Virginia could deputize as many deputy sheriffs and put them on its payroll as it chose also used Pinkerton and Baldwin-Felts "detectives" to harass and drive out union organizers. President Warren G. Harding and West Virginia's Governor Ephriam Morgan, both Republicans, put the power of government on the operators' side. Court injunctions against the UMW were frequent in 1920 and 1921. When this struggle began, John L. Lewis' United Mine Workers had a membership of 500,000; by 1929, it had dwindled to 150,000. The Mine Workers' resurgence did not come until President Franklin D. Roosevelt's New Deal legislation. West Virginia did not outlaw the coal company deputy sheriff until 1933.

Lee's staff took on the Coal Operators' account in the wake of the brutal, bloodiest of the operators' strikebreaking tactics. This antilabor campaign culminated in a series of battles in late August-early September 1921, along the Logan County–Boone County line in Southern West Virginia. Precise figures on the number of involved on both sides of the battle line and the toll of dead were difficult to ascertain. The *Encyclopedia of labor Conflict* states there were 6,000 miners arrayed against 2,000 police officers and private citizens and records only the deaths of 3 Army officers in a plane crash. News account put the miners' death toll at least 70.

The coal miners, then some 2,000 in number, began assembling at

Marmet, near the state capital, Charleston, the night of August 27 for the march to Logan and Mingo counties to protest Governor Morgan's imposition of martial law. Sheriff Don Chafin, fierce foe of organized labor, began assembling his forces on the western slope of Blair Mountain. *The New York Times* of August 29 reported, "The flames of warfare in Logan County, fanned by the march of armed miners, flared up today near Sharples, a little mining town across from the Logan County line from Boone. Five miners are believed to be dead and others are reported to have been wounded." As the conflict continued, Governor Morgan sent in a large contingent of State Police, some National Guard units, and President Harding ordered in 1,000 troops from Camp Dix, NJ, (the 26th Infantry), 600 from Camp Sherman (19th Infantry) and 1,4000 from Camp Knox (40th infantry). All left for the battle site by train on September 2. President Harding accompanied his order to the U.S. Army with a proclamation calling upon the rebellious miners to disarm and peacefully disperse. According to The *Times* of September 2, this only brought "a resumption of fighting in both the Blair Mountain and Crooked Creek sectors of the border line between Boone and Logan counties." The sheriff of Boone County estimated that there were from 8,000 to 10,000 miners at the foot of the ridge.

The military used planes to drop copies of Harding's proclamation. In the face of this overpowering force, the miners' defeat and retreat was inevitable. Surrounded by the federal troops, the miners began to surrender or try to escape. *The New York Times* of September 5 headlined: "Miners Disbanding in West Virginia; May Reduce Troops" and reported that the miners were leaving peacefully. The Army commander denied that the Army planes had dropped bombs, saying they were used only for reconnaissance. The 1921 operator–miner struggle is vividly told in a novel, *Storming Heaven*, by Denise Giardina.

It was into this charged atmosphere, fueled by wide national press coverage, that the Lee firm came to refurbish the tarnished reputation of the coal operators. When I examined them, the MSO books did not indicate who had worked on this account nor whether any staffer ever went to West Virginia to get his facts firsthand.

The firm's step was to create a bulletin, *The Miner's Lamp*, carrying a Huntington, West Virginia dateline, and "published weekly by Authority of the Logan County Coal Operators in the Interest of the West Virginia Coal Industry." The second issue, dated November 15, carried this headline: "COURT UPHOLDS OPEN-SHOP MINES IN WEST VIRGINIA TO PROTECT THE PUBLIC." Another story was captioned: "HIGH EARNINGS IN LOGAN MINES ARE MAKING RECORDS." The December 5 issue was devoted to a defense of Logan County's brutal, corrupt sheriff, Don Chafin. It was headlined: "FIRST HAND SKETCH OF SHERIFF

DON CHAFIN REVEALS DIFFERENT TRAITS THAN PUBLIC HAS BEEN GIVEN TO UNDERSTAND." This was a vain effort to make a silk purse out of a sow's ear. Efforts of the UMW to organize the mines in Logan County had been repeatedly beaten back by the notorious Chafin and his army of "company deputy sheriffs." Lee's firm also issued two other bulletins, *Coal Facts*, sent to newspapers as background information. *Coal Facts* No. 1 issued in October 1921 was headed; "THE TRUTH ABOUT MINE GUARDS AND GUNMEN IN WEST VIRGINIA." *Coal Facts* No. 2 issued on October 31, 1921, headlined: "GROUNDS UPON WHICH UNIONIZING OF WEST VIRGINIA MINES AND COLLECTION OF UNION DUES BY 'CHECK-OFF' SYSTEM WERE ENJOINED BY U.S. COURT." *Coal Facts* No. 3, on November 1921 dealt with the question "Why Miners Do Not Own Their Own Homes," an effort to justify the way operators of that day used company housing as a means of controlling their workers. *Coal Facts* No. 4 dated November 18, 1921, extolled the operators under the heading: "WHY COAL PRODUCERS AID WEST VIRGINIA SCHOOLS." The next *Coal Facts* presented the testimony of Walter R. Thurmond, president of the Logan Coal Operators, justifying miners' low earnings. The last such bulletin, No. 7, was an effort to justify the coal company store that operators used to make miners pay higher prices for their groceries and goods and keep them in hock by advancing before paydays company scrip that was good at only the company store. Yet the bulletin touted: "COMPANY STORES PROTECT MINE WORKERS' POCKETBOOKS." The Lee firm issued 5 issues of *The Miner's Lamp* and 10 of *Coal Facts*. It also published a booklet justifying the massive armed attacks on the miners' army, "The Battle of Blair Mountain, Before and After," purportedly from the "Logan District Mines Information Bureau." The bureau's address was listed as the Charleston National Bank Building, Charleston, WV. Lee's firm, like most of its contemporaries, often used the *third party technique*, a public relations tactic that came to be roundly criticized by public relations' critics and spawned lawsuits. The Byoir firm brought this technique to perfection in the Railroad–Truckers Brawl, as is told later in this volume. Lee's last service for the coal operators was to send out a matted feature, "The Florence Nightingale of Blair Mountain."

No amount of skillful public relations would put a favorable interpretation on this bitter, bloody strikebreaking campaign, costly for both the operators and miners. Just as in the case of the Colorado Fuel & Iron Company's crushing of the coal miners in that state in 1913–1914, Lee and his staff did not fully, honestly measure up to his 1906 "Declaration of Principles." Perhaps it was the case with the West Virginia Coal Operators as it was with the officials of the CF&I that he accepted as "facts" those given to him by the client. In the Colorado situation, the operators gave him false and exaggerated information that he published as truth. Later he testified before the United States Commission on Industrial Relations, set up to probe the Colorado strike, that his view of his job that he was simply an adviser, and his advice was to tell the truth. "My idea is that the principal himself should be his own publicity agent," something of a cop-out. If after having been widely criticized for the information he issued on behalf of the Rockefellers in the wake of the Ludlow Massacre, Lee would have been naive indeed to have accepted the West Virginia coal operators' version of the "truth." Realistically, Lee had little choice. The Rockefellers were major stockholders in the Consolidated Coal Co., one of West Virginia's coal giants.

T. J. ROSS RISES TO PARTNERSHIP

T. J. Ross, who had joined the Ivy Lee firm in 1919, grew steadily in Lee's esteem and in the importance of assignments given him, until Lee in August 1933, decided to make him a full partner. The press interpreted this move as a sign that Ivy lee was thinking of retirement. Ross was only 39 at the time. Ross' skillful handling of his two major accounts, the Chrysler Corporation and the Pennsylvania Railroad, had impressed Lee. More than that Ross had become the buffer between the often hot-tempered Lee and his staff. Associates thought Lee had become more temperamental with the passing years and his increased prestige. According to *Time* magazine of August 7, 1933, "When Mr. Lee would summon his staff to meet him in his uptown suite in the old Waldorf, demand to know why a certain letter had not been sent out as directed, then brokingly announce: 'I'm through. You fellows divide up the accounts!'—it was Tommy Ross who quietly herded the office staff back to work." As *Time* magazine put it, Ross was the "public relations man" between Lee and his staff.

In early August 1933, the senior staffers of the Lee firm were called into Lee's elaborate, book-filled office in the firm's suite of offices at 15 Broad Street to hear Ross, now the acknowledged chief of staff, announce that from now on he would be a senior partner of Lee. He then announced that henceforth these account executives were junior partners: Burnham Carter, who had joined the firm 10 years earlier and recently returned from a leave of absence to serve Ambassador Guggenheim in Havana; Harcourt Parrish, veteran Associated Press and *Louisville Courier-Journal* newsman who had, the year before, served in the campaign of banker Melvin Traylor for the Democratic nomination for President in 1932; Joseph Ripley, former editor of the *American Press*, a journalism tradepaper; James Wideman Lee II, 26, the eldest son of Lee who had been working for his father since his graduation from Princeton 4 years earlier; and Ivy Ledbetter, Jr., 24, who had graduated from Princeton the year before.

When Daniel T. Pierce, who had managed the office for Lee, Harris, and Lee and then in the recognized firm, quit the firm on April 1, 1926, to take a position with the anthracite coal operators, Lee set up a three-man committee to manage the firm during his absence. Lee spent his summers in Europe. This troika did not seem to work out. Ross later recalled, "I have never seen a three-man committee work out." "Finally," he told me, "I practically offered to do the work myself," and this ultimately brought him to the partnership.

Many years after their father's death, both of Lee's sons left the firm as signs of strain appeared to creep into their relationship with Ross. Ivy Lee, Jr. took a leave to serve in the armed forces in 1940. Upon his release from the service, he took a job with Pan American Airways but soon was drafted to serve as the press officer for the organizational meeting of the United Nations in San Francisco in 1945. Ivy, Jr. fell in love with that great city and decided to live there. He became assistant to the president of the Bechtel Corporation, a worldwide construction firm, but later on set up his own agency in San Francisco. He retired in the 1980s. The elder son, James Wideman II, did not leave the agency until 1961. James spent most of his later years as the account executive on the Chrysler account and lived in Grosse Point, Michigan. He retired on July 1, 1961, to take over a New England resort, the Barrows House in Dorset, Vermont.

At the time James Lee quit his partnership, Ross' other partners were Carl C. Dickey, who had years before left the Carl Byoir firm under a cloud; William J. Gaskill, who along with other associates, later took over the firm; Richard T. Nimmons; and Joseph Ripley.

The sense of staff morale, hinted at in the *Time* article, is reflected in this letter from Harcourt Parrish, at the time a junior partner, to me dated May 28, 1952: "My whole point in this is that while Mr. Lee was making all those speeches and constructive organizations, especially during the latter part of his career, he did have an organization which was bringing in the money." Parrish was suggesting that Lee had little to do with the firm's accounts. James W. Lee II vigorously disputes Parrish's assertion. He recalled, "George Washington Hill paid Ivy Lee $50,000 a year to advise him while the staff handled the publicity aspect of the account. George Hill said several times that he liked to talk with Ivy Lee because he always got something back for his questions." Jim Lee also said that his father had a similarly close relationship with Walter P. Chrysler after the firm acquired that account. "These Chrysler and Hill associations along with similar ones with Mr. Rockefeller, Winthrop Aldrich, Charles Schwab, and General Atterbury exemplified the relations Ivy Lee had with his clients. A German banker once said to me about Ivy Lee, 'I have never met a man who could understand our problems so quickly.' "

Lee was a demanding boss and for all his emphasis on policy making, he never lost sight of the value of publicity—particularly to the clients. Speaking in a 1925 staff meeting, Lee exhorted, "We are not getting enough stuff into the newspapers today of the material which we could get in. . . . When I pick up the . . . papers and see the small amount of stuff we have in these papers, I am always distressed. . . . You men are all responsible. . . . Let us get our stuff into the papers to the utmost possible extent."

When I interviewed Ross, I found him usually wreathed in halos of smoke from his always present cigar, courtly, pleasant, but far from loquacious. He answered questions briefly but frankly. One writer described him as one "with round face, pink skin, conservatively suited, loyal to a stiff white collar and a gold watch-chain that comfortably spans his vest." Talks with Ross gave the impression of a man who was calm and in control and with a good sense of humor about men's affairs. When I asked him to recount some of the firm's success stories in interviews on March 9 and 10, 1959, he said with a smile, "I would if I could think of one." Strict confidentiality was a hallmark of Lee and Ross, carried to the point that the firm wouldn't release a list of clients even though all major news sources knew where their news releases came from and whom to contact for more information.

Lee and Ross both made confidentiality of their counsel to clients a basic doctrine. This stands in sharp contrast to the practice of many counselors in public relations, a very promotion-minded business. Edward L. Bernays was always a notable example of seeking credit for his ideas. Ross told me:

> Our work must remain anonymous and private. We do not talk about what we do or have done for a client. Our reluctance is not due to any need for secrecy. Like most other corporations, the ones we work for do not have anything to hide. The principle of anonymity evolves from a very simple philosophy of our work: When things go wrong for a corporation in the public relations area, it is the management of the corporation that takes the bumps. We believe that when things go right, they deserve the credit, and it should not be synthetic.

L. L. L. Golden once wrote in the *Saturday Review*, "Corporate public relations directors who have watched Ross in sessions with their top managers have come away with the conviction that Ross is a good listener, but when it comes to giving advice to management he has not been fearful of speaking his mind." Golden quoted one corporate vice-president as saying, "Tommy Ross has never failed to lay it on the line to the boss, nor has he backtracked if he believed that a course of action contemplated by management could hurt the company. He is never rude. I have never seen him lose his temper. But I have never seen anyone more blunt when bluntness is necessary." Undoubtedly it was these qualities that brought Ross to the leadership of the Lee firm and ultimately established him as one of the outstanding counselors of his time.

In elaboration of his philosophy, Ross told the New York Chapter of the Public Relations Society on January 15, 1958:

> I have also found it is essential to be frank, especially with those whom we try to serve. No one is expected to know all the answers. It is good practice to admit this to oneself and to be frank with clients in the same respect. Zeal for learning is important as is acceptance of the need to earn our way to the confidence of others. . . . It is worth remembering that insofar as helping with decision-making goes, our efforts are confined to those areas of decisions having public relations implications. We should guard against "the chairman of the board complex," the delusion that we have the answers to any and all problems that may face a corporate management. Ours is essentially a staff function.

ROSS COULD EVEN HANDLE G. W. HILL

Tommy Ross' ability to handle difficult clients was put to its toughest test when the firm acquired the American Tobacco Co. account in the summer of 1927. This was Ross' first major account. It appears that as Mr. Lee grew more affluent and famous, he spent more time on travel. For the firm, he was mainly occupied by his service to the Rockefellers and Guggenheims. Nonetheless, Lee and George Washington Hill became good friends and conferred frequently. The Rockefeller Foundation had been formed in 1913, the year before Lee was retained by John D., Jr., but "he had a great deal to say about the activities of the Foundation in the 20s and early 30s," Ross told your author. Ross said Lee also spent a great deal of time with the Guggenheim interests and their foundations. *Time* magazine wrote in its August 7, 1933, issue, "No competitor can approach Ivy Lee in wealth and social stature. His friends are the Rockefellers, Mackays, Guggenheims, John W. Davis, the late Senator Dwight Morrow. He lives magnificently in swank East 66th Street." This gave T. J. Ross his opportunity to emerge as "the wheelhorse" of the firm, despite his oft stated disclaimer, "We are all deck hands around here." Ross was proving his ability by his deft handling of the firm's other major accounts — the American Tobacco Co. and the Chrysler Corporation, and often substituting for Lee on the Pennsylvania Railroad account.

By far the most difficult of these was George Washington Hill, president of the American Tobacco Co., whose primary product was Lucky Strike cigarettes. No counselor nor ad agency ever had a more difficult, temperamental, and eccentric client. The legendary Hill, celebrated in novels and motion pictures, electrified employees and advertising men by setting fire to several books of matches during a conference or upsetting pitchers of water on the conference table to make a point, or as he said, "just to get your attention." T. J. Ross landed the Hill account and then set out "to find out all I could about the tobacco business." At this time, Bernays, characteristically, had publicized the fact that he, too, was retained by American Tobacco Co. According to Bernays, when asked why he retained both the Bernays and Lee firms, Hill replied, "If both are working for me, then they can't be working for my competitors." Asked about this unusual arrangement, Ross wrote me on September 26, 1960:

> All I know about it is that our firm, which was then Ivy Lee & Associates, was engaged by George Washington Hill in the Summer of 1927; that at that time Edward L. Bernays had been in Mr. Hill's employ for some time, but just how long I do not know; and that a few years after our firm was employed we were the only public relations firm working for the company, and still are.

Bernays had difficulty keeping clients over a long span of time.

When interviewed in 1959, Ross recounted how he had to meet Hill for lunch every Friday, first at the old Murray Hill Hotel, later at the Vanderbilt Hotel. During lunch, Hill would throw a water glass to the floor to make a point or express irritation with the service. "He was a very dramatic personality, always wore his hat in the office, and smoked constantly." Ross lauded Hill as a great salesman, adding that the wartime slogan "Lucky Strike Green Has Gone To War" was Hill's, nobody else's. Despite Hill's difficult ways, Ross had a fondness for the flamboyant Hill and until his retirement, kept a picture of Hill, autographed to Lee, prominent in the firm's reception hall.

Harcourt Parrish who worked on the American Tobacco account made it clear that the agency's role was mainly to promote the sale of Lucky Strike cigarettes. Selling was George Washington Hill's consuming passion. Parrish wrote me on May 28, 1952:

> Most assuredly, Mr. Hill was much concerned in a basic public relations way with the bitter criticism of his huge salary and the American Tobacco Company's method of executive compensation. We did a lot in this regard for him, but our most important job was to sell Lucky Strike cigarettes through continued publicity on the "toasting" process, and such slogans as "Reach For" almost anything. That's where the money came from — selling cigarettes — and that's what we were hired to promote. Victor Knauth and Joseph Ripley also worked on the American Tobacco account.

It is an unfortunate legacy of the Lee and Ross firm's promotion of Lucky Strike cigarettes that the campaign to encourage women to smoke and thus double the cigarette market has also doubled the number of deaths due to smoking. Albert Lasker's Lord & Thomas advertising agency bears this same nicotine stain.

THE CHRYSLER AND PENNSY ACCOUNTS

Ivy Lee and T. J. Ross obtained the Chrysler Corporation account in 1927 through their work for Dillon Reed & Co., stock brokers, who had been retained by Walter P. Chrysler to win approval of his takeover of the much larger Dodge Motor Car Company facilities by the Dodge stockholders. The theme of a booklet prepared to support the merger prepared by the Lee agency was the genius of Walter P. Chrysler and the Chrysler company. It made these points: (a) foresight and vision of what the public wants in a motorcar — anticipating demand instead of merely meeting it, and (b) ability to supply these wants effectively and economically. The pamphlet was entitled, "The Growth of Chrysler." The validity of this promotional boast was demonstrated in 1930 when Chrysler introduced the Airflow design that ushered in the era of streamlining in America. (Also in 1928, the Lee firm handled other accounts for Dillon Reed — the United Steel Works of Germany, the National Bank of Boliva, and the Ruhr Chemical Co. of Germany. This was the beginning of the agency's international involvement, Germany in particular, that later brought it bitter criticism.)

Walter P. Chrysler insisted that a large majority of Dodge stockholders must approve the merger or that the deal would not go through. Chrysler won by a large majority, and the merger was consummated. Chrysler himself was quite pleased with the work of Lee and Ross and some months later retained the firm for the enlarged corporation. (At the time, Chrysler was building the tall Chrysler building in mid-Manhattan. The T. J. Ross firm moved into it in 1937 and occupied the 40th floor, its last office home.) From 1928 until the mid-1930s, Ivy Lee and T. J. Ross handled all of Chrysler's public relations and publicity. In 1935, Chrysler hired a local newsman, Frank Bogart, to handle announcements in Detroit. After Mr. Lee's death, T. J. Ross took full control of the Chrysler accounts.

After his firm had acquired the Chrysler account, Ivy Lee and Walter P. Chrysler became good friends. In a letter to me, James W. Lee II wrote, "This is exemplified by Mr. Chrysler telling his board, "I believe that the Depression is over' and he was going to expand his facilities." When asked how he knew the Depression was over, he said, "My friend Ivy Lee told me and I believe him." As result, the son asserted, Chrysler "got a jump on his competitors."

At Ross' urging, he was made a member of the Chrysler Operations

Committee and attended its meetings every 2 weeks. "There was a formal docket for each meeting, and everyone had to speak his piece," Ross told me. A public relations counselor cannot ask for more than this. When James W. Lee II returned from Germany in 1935, he was assigned to the account. "I began weekly trips to Detroit, and around 1938 I moved out there and became the residence public relations department. Ross came out for one day every two weeks. Things remained that way until after the war [World War II] when James Cope was hired as director of public relations," according to James W. Lee II. Cope had been with the Automobile Manufacturers Association.

The Pennsylvania Railroad resumed its relationship with Ivy Lee in 1920 after the nation's railroads were released from control by the federal government, a wartime measure. The Pennsy had maintained a public relations department since it hired Lee in 1908.

Thus, there was never a cessation of the Pennsy's public relations activities from that time. W. W. Atterbury, railroad president, held weekly staff meetings that included Lee. Atterbury insisted that every member of the staff have an understudy, and Lee chose Ross to represent him when he could not attend. In time, Ross replaced Lee at the Pennsy management table. This connection brought the firm the account of the American Association of Railroads in World War II. It also involved Ross in the selection of Carl Byoir & Associates as public relations counsel for the Eastern Railroad Presidents' Conference. This ultimately led to the celebrated lawsuit of the Pennsylvania truckers against the Eastern railroads and Byoir; a lawsuit that went all the way to the U. S. Supreme Court and established a "Magna Carta" for public relations practice. This public relations battle between the Pennsylvania truckers, termed a "no-holds-barred" fight by Justice Hugo Black, became known as the "Truckers–Railroad Brawl." As counsel for the Pennsylvania, T. J. Ross was deeply involved in this battle all the way but never received the publicity Carl Byoir and his staff did. (This saga is told in detail in chapter 18.) Ironically, the Lee–Ross house organ, *Public Relations*, No. 21, of April 20, 1925, carried this headline: "MOTOR TRUCK AN ALLY OF RAILROADS, NOT ENEMY, SAYS PRR."

In his interviews with me Ross stressed his policy, "We don't represent anybody, we work for people," a doctrine Ivy Lee enunciated in 1915 before the U. S. Commission on Industrial Relations. Ross also stressed to me, as he often did in his public speeches, the importance of "preventative public relations." He gave this example:

Six months before Pearl Harbor, the Association of American railroads [which by that time had become a Ross client] took a public opinion poll to discover whether the public would favor the Federal Government taking over the railroads in case of a war as it had done in World War I. About half the respondents said yes. A publicity program was then initiated to emphasize that the railroads were doing an extraordinary job and could meet the demands of war transportation if called upon to do so. A second poll asking the same questions taken six months after Pearl Harbor found less than one-fourth of those polled believing the government should take control of the railroads. Polls were taken throughout the war and the results were constantly favorable to the railroads.

As reflected in lengthy interviews in 1959, Ross' basic policy relations philosophy boils down to this: "We work with managements to assist them in establishing sound policies and practices which, if made known to and understood by the public, will be reflected in a favorable attitude toward the institution and its products or services." He made it clear that this was not to look down his nose at the pedestrian work of publicity. He once told *Printer's Ink*, "If it's necessary for me to put on my hat and take a release down to *The New York Times*, I will do it." Actually the firm maintained a two-man office on West 57th Street, to maintain mailing lists and distribute its publicity.

The always tight-lipped Ross never intimated in our many interviews that he had served as counsel to Major General Leslie Groves, director of the Manhattan Project, that developed the atomic bomb that brought World War II to an abrupt halt. Ross counseled Groves on the maintenance of secrecy during the development phase of this difficult, delicate operation at no charge of fee. His involvement came about through his membership in The Wisemen, an elite group of influential corporate counselors started in 1938 by John W. Hill. General Groves sought the counsel of DeWitt Wallace, founder of *The Reader's Digest*, on his delicate, troubling problem. Wallace asked the general if he might consult with his longtime friend and counselor, Pendleton Dudley. Wallace and his wife, Lilah, had started their successful publication in Dudley's pony barn at his Pleasantville, N Y farm. Groves assented and Dudley suggested to Groves that he meet with The Wisemen for advice. After the necessary military clearances, this meeting was brought about. Accompanied by two representatives of G-2 General Groves met with the Wisemen at the University Club in New York City. He gave these men a full briefing on the project (all had been cleared by G-2) and then asked for advice on how to handle the first tests and then if the developers were successful, on how to handle the announcements of the bombing of Japan. The upshot of the discussion was that T. J. Ross was retained at no fee and that William Lawrence of *The New York Times* was drafted to handle the announcements.[2]

---

[2]This information is contained in an informal history of the Wisemen, written by James W. Irwin, an early member and corporate counselor, in March 1978.

IRT: IVY LEE AND PUPLIC RELATIONS UNDER FIRE—AGAIN

One of the first major accounts that Ivy Lee's new firm, Lee, Harris, and Lee, acquired in 1916 was that of the Interborough Rapid Transit Company (IRT), one of the major subway and streetcar operators in New York City. Like that of the Colorado Fuel Company, this account ultimately brought a public hearing that put Ivy Lee and his public relations methods under a white hot news spotlight.

The U. S. Commission on Industrial Relations, set up to probe the facts involved in the Colorado Fuel & Iron Strike that brought Ivy Lee's employment by John D. Rockefeller, Jr. national attention, had focused on Lee's role in settling that bloody strike and on the truth or falsity of information he had disseminated on behalf of CF&I. The IRT public hearings of 1927 focused more on the worth of what he did for IRT and whether a corporation supported by public funds needed a public relations counsel or publicity. Thus, the function, now emerging into the nation's consciousness, was under the spotlight along with Lee.

In the early part of 1916, employee unrest had brought a strike to New York's subways and street railways. This brought IRT to seek Lee's counsel and services. Ray Hiebert recorded Lee's initial success:

> He studied the I.R.T. problems carefully. The company had just taken a big loss as the result of the employee strike. Now uneasiness was setting in again, and another strike seemed imminent. But to Lee the employee representation plan that had worked in Rockefeller's Colorado coal mines could work just as well in the New York subways. After some convincing of both sides, the plan was accepted and it averted a second violent strike.

Lee's "education campaign" that over a 10-year period produced eight large bound volumes of newspaper clippings, magazine articles, posters, pamphlets, folders, and other materials came under heavy fire when the New York Transit Commission opened hearings into the operations of the IRT and Lee's role as its "propagandist." These hearings raised an issue that plagues public relations to this day: "What right did the I.R.T. have to spend taxpayers' money to finance a publicity campaign to push something that was against the public interest, i.e., a raise in the five-cent subway fare?" As reported by *Editor & Publisher* on July 2, 1927, the Transit Commission's counsel, Samuel K. Untermeyer's, questioning of Lee, brought out that between June 30, 1919, and April 30, 1927, Lee had been paid $212,954.19. That caused Untermeyer to ask Lee what he had done for all this money. "Wasn't it," Untermeyer asked, "in the line of putting the company's affairs before the public in the most favorable light?" Lee replied, "That, and also shaping their affairs that when placed before the public they will be approved." Untermeyer followed up, "Are you concerned with shaping the affairs of these corporations?" Lee answered, "I am very often consulted with reference to companies' policies," adding "I have assisted them in development of their labor policy, in their development of their plan of employee representation."

Early in the hearing, an IRT official was called to the stand to justify the firm's hiring a public relations counselor. This is the first time, insofar as it is known, that a client was asked publicly to justify the retention of public relations counsel. Why, asked the interrogator, did the IRT need a public relations man to present it in a good light if IRT had done nothing wrong? And why was the public relations budget so high? The implication was that right, if the corporation possessed it, would prevail without the need of expensive public relations staffs. The debate on this troublesome question for public relations practitioners occupied the press and public's attention first in 1921 and then again in 1927 when the Transit Commission hearings were held. In both instances, the issue was essentially the same: What right did IRT have to spend taxpayer's money to finance a publicity campaign to push a rate increase that was "against" the public interest, that is to raise the nickel subway fare. The 1921 coverage came when Mayor John F. Hylan appointed a commission to look into New York City's transit problems. William Randolph Hearst was a strong supporter of Mayor Hylan, and his newspapers roundly attacked Lee's work for the IRT.

In round one, in 1921, it was *The Subway Sun* and the *Elevated Express* broadsides, that Lee's firm prepared for the subway and elevated cars that were the target of the Hearst papers' fire. On December 8, 1920, the *New York Evening Journal* ran a huge cartoon, captioned: "The Great Subway Mystery: Who is Editor of the Subway Sun?" This was the first of 12 such cartoons by the *Journal* cartoonist, Thomas E. Powers. The perception that the public was being robbed on the matter of fare increases was furthered at the opening of Mayor Hylan's hearings in January 1921. Public Service Commissioner John M. Delaney charged that the IRT had cheated the city out of $423,000 by padding its operating expenses, thus minimizing the firm's profits. The *Subway Sun* was cited as among the items wrongfully charged to operating expenses. On January 31, 1921, the Hearst *New York American* ran a huge headline: "PUBLIC TAXED FOR COST OF 8 CENTS FARE GRAB" and subheaded: "IRT GOUGES–STRAPHANGER FOR PUBLICITY ON RATE FIGHT." *The New York Times* on the same day headlined its story: "DELANEY PROTESTS IRT PROPAGANDA AS OPERATING COST" whereas the *Herald–Tribune* headline charged: "IRT CHARGED WITH PADDING OPERATING COST." In February 1921, the *New York Evening Journal* ran an extensive article on *The Subway Sun*, describing it as "one of the most colossal pieces of impertinence ever devised by the traction trust." The emerging function of public relations and its necessity were now clearly on trial in the press and public forum.

However, it wasn't only the Hearst papers that Lee had to contend with. On February 26, 1921, the *New York Tribune* had its say on *The Subway Sun* and the *Elevated Express*. The article recounted that Commissioner Delaney's testimony included these publications totaling $432,000 that he asserted were "so much padding" in the operating expenses of IRT, then stated this:

> The latest edition of the *Subway Sun* which was posted yesterday took a backward glance at its own career and justified its existence in the following terms: 'If you see it in the *Subway Sun* it's so. People own the subway. This company operates them. We report to our patrons through the *Subway Sun*. Stick a pin right here: every statement of fact in this paper is 100 percent true and can be verified. We print this paper because we believe that car-riders are entitled to information from us bearing on our transit service, present and future.

This assertion of the *Sun* was quickly challenged by Edward T. O'Laughlin of the *Evening Journal*.

> "HOW THE SUBWAY SUN FEEDS FALSEHOODS TO THE PUBLIC" was the headline over this lead: That the *Subway Sun* falsifies facts is borne out by the testimony adducceded before Mayor Hyland's investigating committee as shown by the records of the hearing on February 23, 1921, at City Hall. Ivy Lee, the editor of the *Subway Sun*, was on the stand and he was shown a copy of the poster described as the *Subway Sun* which carried a picture of a vast crowd of people gazing into the focus of the camera with indication that this had been taken at a stockholders' meeting and was offered as proof that stockholders were wrought up by the question of fares and falling revenues.

The *Evening Journal* asserted that this picture was a fake and had no connection to the IRT. The article continued, "Now this statement contained a triple falsehood and before corporation counsel Burr got through with Ivy Lee on the stand he made the editor of the 'Subway Sun' admit that the poster issued for February, 1920, containing this statement was merely a piece of baseless propaganda."

In the wake of the New York Transit Commission hearings in 1927, *Editor & Publisher*, long a critic of both Ivy Lee and the vocation he was instrumental in developing, weighed in with its criticism. The editorial first reported that Ivy Lee had been paid $212, 954 by the IRT between 1919 and 1927 and then continued:

> Is it possible, the people of New York are asking, that a man could receive that stupendous sum, charged to operating expenses, for a such a trifling duty as the writing of those simple car-cards, telling riders, for instance, that there

was a fine zoo in the Bronx, that the red ball was up for skaters at the park lakes, and that the Interborough was the world's safest railroad? It seems incredible, especially in view of the meager pay the company allows a motorman who drives a ten-car train at lightning speed through the dark tunnels, guardian of some 2,000 human lives. What is this great service which Mr. Lee renders which costs more in eight years than a motorman could earn in a hundred years at such nerve-wracking toll? The car-cards might be written by an intelligent stenographer.

The concept as well as the cost of public relations got a thorough going over in the New York Transit Commission hearings under the relentless questioning of Counsel Untermeyer. In June 1927, *Printer's Ink* ran part of the testimony of James Quackenbush, attorney for the Interborough, with this introduction: "The testimony is given here because it represents one of the first endeavors of the client of a public relations advisor to explain the nature of the work done by persons bearing that high sounding title — a title of late has superseded 'press agent' and "publicity agent." The article was headed: "The Difference Between 'Public Relations Advisor' and 'Press Agent'. Is it $4,500 a Year?" This question is explained by the testimony that revealed that Daniel Pierce of Lee's staff was being paid $7,500 a year whereas Lee, the public relations advisor, was receiving $12,000 a year. Untermeyer's questioning of Quackenbush continued:

Q. Who gave him [Lee] that title?

A. He did.

Q. He tries to mold public sentiment, doesn't he?

A. I don't think that is the way he puts himself. Of course, Mr. Lee is a gentleman who undertakes to inform the public concerning things that affect the interests of the people by whom he is employed; no question about it whatsoever.

Q. He seeks to put the company's affairs in the best possible light before the public.

A. Precisely.

When Ivy Lee took the stand in these hearings, Untermeyer pressed him hard to define precisely what his role as an advisor is and what he does for his corporate clients. Lee was less than precise in defining his work and the vocation he was doing so much to pioneer in the 1920s. The questioning went like this:

Q. What is your occupation?

A. I assist various corporations and individuals in any way I can, primarily in reference to publicity and public relations.

Q. How many corporations and individuals do you assist?

A. Perhaps 25 or 30.

Q. You are not exactly what you'd call a publicity agent, are you?

A. I don't think so.

Q. Do you act as a salesman for some of them?

A. No, I act as an advisor, for example, to a number of corporations with reference to their advertising which is distinctly a selling operation.

Q. What is the difference between the vocation you follow and that of the publicity agent?

A. I don't know.

Q. Is there any?

A. I don't know sir. I have never been able to find a satisfactory phrase to describe what I try to do.

Q. When you say advise, what do you mean?

A. Practically every large corporation has, of course, very important relations with the public. It is important to study the operation of public opinion, study the attitude of the public. It is important that the corporation or interest should make known its activities so they will be understood. And my work is to assist, as far as I can, in enabling corporations to do that.

Q. You mean in placing their affairs before the public through publicity methods in the most favorable light?

A. That and also shaping their affairs that when placed before the public they will be approved.

Q. Are they concerned with shaping the affairs of these corporation?

A. I am very often consulted with reference to their policies.

Lee was obviously distressed with the impression Samuel Untermeyer's dogged examination was giving the public of Lee and of public relations. On June 29, 1927, he sent this memorandum to "City Editor" — presumably to the city desks of all of New York's daily newspapers. Found in the MSO Book of 1927, it reads:

City Editor:

At the hearing before the Transit Commission, Mr. Untermeyer tried to put me in the position of having stated in my testimony on Monday that since 1922 I had had nothing to do with the publicity on behalf of Interborough relating to the desirability of increased fares. Then he quoted various documents which had been issued tending to prove that *since 1922* the Company *had* with my assistance, issued certain material. In order that whoever reports the testimony this morning may realize that there was nothing produced this morning in conflict with what was said on the witness stand the other day, (notwithstanding the fact that Untermeyer apparently got an inaccurate impression of what I said). I am quoting on a separate sheet the exact testimony on this point. As this involves not so much a matter of personal honor as it does an accurate recollection of what was said, I would appreciate it if you would ask your reporter to have this in mind in any new news treatment of the subject.

Ivy Lee

The New York Transit Commission hearings, starring Samuel Untermeyer, brought Ivy Lee and the burgeoning field he did so much to advance, much unfavorable publicity coast to coast. This was reflected in the large volume of clippings found in Ivy Lee's papers. Typical is this clip from the *South Bend Tribune* of June 29, 1927:

Inquiring into the affairs of the Interborough Rapid Transit Company of New York, the state transit commission brought out some facts about the new profession of public relations counsel. Ivy Lee, the man who's done more than any other to develop the profession, was on the stand. He had received from the Interborough in salary and in support of his activities about $250,000 in eleven years. . . . The position of public relations counsel appeared about twenty years ago when certain corporations, appreciating that they needed a fuse between themselves and the people, employed former newspaper men to represent their interests. . . . At first this consisted of preparing and giving to the newspapers corporation news. . . .

These representatives are glorified press agents but they differ from the press agent in that their work is not so much to get the names of their clients before the public as to see that their clients are not misrepresented but always put forward in a favorable light. Often their mission consists of preventing undeserved unfavorable publicity. . . . The fundamental reason for the evolution this profession is that corporation heads as a rule are unskilled in newspaper practice. . . . Therefore, they are glad to hire their good will work done.

This editorial was more judicious and enlightening than most of the publicity generated by the IRT hearings. *Editor & Publisher's* comments were more typical. Its story on the hearings of July 2, 1927, read in part:

Ivy Lee, sometimes called America's super publicity man, was paid more than $200,000 by the New York traction interests, it is revealed, to convince the subway riders of that city that their nickel fare wasn't enough. He didn't succeed in convincing them, which is a terrible blow to the publicity business. Publicity men—everywhere—and they are everywhere—will not feel very kindly toward Mr. Lee for this letdown he has given their industry.

Not its failure, because the power of this kind of publicity is very generally overrated and fails more often than not, but because of the publicity that attended its failure. The super publicity man ought to be able to keep his failure from being public. This was the regrettable feature of this particular publicity undertaking. The failure itself might have been anticipated, we think.

As when retained by John D. Rockefeller in 1914 in the wake of the Ludlow Massacre in the Rockefellers Colorado mines, Ivy Lee had, with this "particular publicity undertaking," brought both himself and his new vocation into the nation's news spotlight. The resulting publicity to an incalculable degree increased the nation's awareness of public relations and undoubtedly skepticism about its worth and ethics.

To focus on the year 1927 in Ivy Lee's career is to see a double image. There is the image of Lee and public relations that the press presented: the super publicity man paid big money for press agentry with questionable results. And there is the Ivy Lee in his January 1927 staff meeting articulating this concept of "the new policy oriented leader who wanted to stop doing publicity and who saw the function of his office of developing sound policies for clients and then publicizing them." This Ivy Lee paradox reached its zenith [or its nadir] in the I. G. Farben case that took him to his grave with a badly tarnished reputation.

OTHER MAJOR ACCOUNTS

The limits of this volume do not permit a detailed recounting of all the Ivy Lee–T. J. Ross accounts. However, a few major accounts deserve at least a mention for the insight they show on the work Lee and Ross and their associates.

The contrasting pictures of two Chase Manhattan Bank executives before the Senate Banking and Currency Committee in 1932 when the nation was in the grip of the Great Depression and banks were failing left and right show the wisdom of Lee's counsel. The committee's investigation of banking had been initiated by President Herbert Hoover and was led by committee counsel, Ferdinand Pecora, a tough examiner. The committee examined, in turn, Wall Street leaders and banking executives. According to Hiebert, these hearings indicated that these titans of finance little understood their public responsibilities or the vagaries of public opinion. Lee had been counsel to the Chase Manhattan Bank for some years when this firestorm broke. Its first victim was A. H. Wiggin, bank chairman.

According to Hiebert, "From the beginning Wiggin had not understood the wisdom of Lee's advice. Once during one of the many mergers that had made Chase the world's largest bank, Wiggin had refused to give out information about the merger." When Wiggin was called before the Senate Committee Counsel Pecora, he was hapless on the witness stand, and his public humiliation forced him to resign his chairmanship of Chase. An Ivy Lee–T. J. Ross partner said later, "Wiggin was severely castigated as though he had been dishonest or at best a weak leader. Mr. Wiggin lost his position and his family was greatly harmed by the bad publicity."

Winthrop Aldrich, a brother-in-law of John D. Rockefeller, Jr., was elected to head Chase, a Rockefeller-controlled bank. Aldrich knew Lee intimately and respected his judgment. As Hiebert found:

> When Aldrich became president of Chase National Bank, and he and Lee agreed that "planned publicity" used to cover up banking sins would never cure the unpopularity of bankers nor heal the source of trouble. Rather, Lee advised Aldrich that he must bring his policies into line with the necessities of the times, make his own house clean first, his actions sound, and then open the channels of communication to tell the man on the street about them.

This was standard Lee counsel.

Again, to quote a Lee–Ross partner who requested anonymity, "The result of this self-examination, adopting new policies, and electing a new president resulted in the Chase National Bank's operations being adjudged by the Senate Committee as fair and sound." Ivy Lee and his staff helped prepare the written statements given in the Chase testimony that enabled Aldrich to escape the scorn heaped on A. H. Wiggin.

Perhaps second only to the Rockefeller accounts in bringing prestige and dollars to the Lee firm was its work for the Guggenheims. The firm's work for the Guggenheims included the American Smelting and Refining Co., the Chilean Nitrate of Soda Educational Bureau, the John Simeon Guggenheim Memorial Foundation (which over the year has benefited thousands of scholars and artists with its annual grants), and perhaps most important of all, the Daniel Guggenheim Fund for the Promotion of Aeronautics, created in 1926. The latter fund did much to speed the acceptance of commercial aviation in the 1920s. Ivy Lee's firm, along with Harry Bruno, deserves much credit for gaining public acceptance of flying. Harry A. Bruno and his then partner, Richard Blythe, handled the publicity for Col. Charles A. Lindbergh's historic flight to Paris in May 1927 and his high-pressure schedule when he came home to a hero's reception across the nation. But it was the Guggenheim Fund that sponsored his nationwide tour in support of commercial aviation. The Lee firm handled the tour. The Guggenheim Fund also sponsored regularly scheduled passenger flights to prove them feasible and financed advances in weather reporting and Jimmy Doolittle's blind flying experiments.

In 1925, Lee's firm publicized the Geggenheims' Anglo-Chilean Consolidated Nitrate Corporation. The Lee–Ross firm, like any successful public relations agency, was adept in product promotion to bolster the consumer sales of its clients. Its most successful product promotion came with the creation of the famous and enduring personality of "Betty Crocker." The Washburn–Crosby flour-milling firm of Minneapolis was among the first of food processors to see the need for publicity in support of sales. One of Lee's first moves was to create a distinctive brand name for Gold Medal Flour. Until the 1920s flour, an essential staple in diets, was sold generally as "flour," often in barrels. Housewives were obviously the target audience in promoting Gold Medal and other food products for the firm that grew into General Mills. The Lee staff developed the idea that the best way to communicate with the nation's housewives was through a "typical" housewife, thus was born "Betty Crocker" whose image lives today in food pages and on supermarket shelves. The image has been modernized periodically since the 1920s. The Lee firm made her a household word in America in a few short years.

Another Lee promotion for General Mills was publicizing the need for a hearty breakfast, an idea that sold General Mills' cereals. The Lee staff surveyed a representative group of doctors and reported widely their opinion that a good breakfast was important for energy throughout the day. Lee advised this client that a promotional campaign based on these doctors' opinions would have wide appeal. This idea eventually led to Wheaties, "the breakfast of champions," a campaign that has lasted eight decades. Edward L. Bernays was exploiting the same theme in the 1920s to sell breakfast bacon.

Early in its history, Ivy Lee took on fund-raising campaign promotions and was involved in such campaigns for a brief time. Early in 1920, the Lee, Harris, and Lee firm ran a fund-raising campaign for the newly organized Dobbs School for Girls with a goal of $500,000, a campaign sponsored by the Dobbs Alumnae Association. It issued periodic newsletters under the title, "Do It for Dobbs." The campaign was successful, and the cornerstone of Dobbs' new main building was laid on April 28, 1920, with appropriate ceremony and publicity.

Lee and his associates also promoted the Princeton Endowment Campaign to raise $14 million dollars for his alma mater. The first *Princeton Endowment Bulletin No. 1* was issued on January 12, 1920. Two days later, the firm staged a well-publicized reception at the Waldorf for parents to meet President and Mrs. John G. Hibben of Princeton and sent out a press release on the president's remarks. Ivy Lee's staff was quick to borrow the technique of Charles Summer Ward and Lyman Pierce, pioneer fund—raisers, in glorifying gifts from the "little person." Lee's firm publicized gifts from an African-American janitor at Princeton and one from a high school teacher who promised to send $1 a year for five years. By the end of March, the firm announced that after 6 months the campaign had raised $6,059, 703.63 in gifts and pledges. All releases carried the letterhead of the Bureau of Information, Princeton University.

Also in the early days of the agency, it handled the publicity for a campaign for the Woman's Roosevelt Memorial Association, headed by Mrs. Leonard Wood, wife of the retired general and now Presidential candidate. Lee's staff widely publicized a joint service held on January 4, 1920, to commemorate the first anniversary of President Roosevelt's death. By April 19, Lee's staff could report that the association had raised $175,000 to restore Roosevelt's birthplace at 28 East 20th Street in New York City. This campaign, too, used the Ward–Pierce technique of publicizing gifts large and small. A news release issued on April 15, 1920, reported, "Today's mail at national headquarters brought a $5,000 pledge from Mrs. Willard Straight; a crumpled two-dollar bill sent more than six weeks ago from a U.S. Signal Corps private stationed at KoKrines, Alaska, and a contribution from Miss F. Heisn Siang of Nanking, China." The Lee promotions for the Roosevelt fund drive used the Bolshevik Menace and Americanism as themes in their fund appeals to exploit the current American mood.

However, it appears that as the young firm prospered, it ceased to be involved in fund-raising, leaving that function to the newly organized John Price Jones Corp. founded in November 1919.

FOREIGN ENTANGLEMENTS CLOUD LEE'S REPUTATION

When Ivy L. Lee, then only 57, died on November 8, 1934, in St. Luke's Hospital, New York City of a brain tumor, he died under dark clouds of suspicion and accusation brought on by his representation of the German Dye Trust long after Hitler's Nazis had stormed to power. His partner, T. J. Ross, remain convinced to his death the hounding of Lee by a Congressional committee and taunts of being a "Nazi sympathizer" brought on the brain tumor. Curiously, the doctors agreed that the tumor had started to develop about the time the Farben firestorm broke.

Ivy Lee, a man of insatiable curiosity and a veteran traveler, was an internationalist in an American that was still isolationist. His broad knowledge of Europe and Russia, gained through travel and voracious reading, surely was of inestimatable value to his clients, most of whom had worldwide dealings.

Lee's loyalty to the United States first came under attack after he made a 10-day trip to the Soviet Union in May 1927 and then wrote a book recording his observations of the much-feared "Bolshevik Menace" — this at a time when the United States still did not have diplomatic relations with Russia. T. J. Ross told me in our 1959 interviews that Lee had become fascinated with Russia while he was in London in 1910–1912 — long before the Russian Revolution. In the preface to his account of his 1927 trip, *Present Day Russia* [Macmillan, 1928], Lee wrote prophetically:

> Certain it is that if we accept the phrases and stated practices of the Bolshevik regime as literally embodying the permanent policies of the Russian Government and the Russian people, Western civilization must make definite plans to defeat these purposes. The fundamental question is how can we defeat them. Can they be defeated by isolation and encirclement of Russia, and an attempt to starve the Russian people? Can they be defeated by merely keeping out of our own borders Bolshevik literature and Bolshevik agents? Can they be defeated by trading with Russia or by refraining from trading with her?

It was to determine "the essential facts and the factors with which the world must deal" that took Lee to Russia. Lee concluded, wisely, that the time had come for the United States to recognize the USSR and by so doing open a dialogue with the Russian leaders and the Russian people. This conviction was born of Ivy Lee's faith in two-way communications that he had found and practiced in his public relations career since the early 1900s. These views, understandably brought Lee harsh criticism and unfair accusations in a United States that was still too paranoid to have diplomatic relations with the USSR. Reports began circulating that Lee had become a paid propagandist for the Soviets. This typewritten memo was found in the MSO Book for 1929, then kept in the Lee–Ross offices in the Chrysler Building:

January 10, 1929

> Any report that I have ever received a penny of money from the Soviet Government directly or indirectly is a complete fabrication. Evidently the same forgéry mill which accused the chairman of the Foreign Relations Committee of the United States Senate of accepting a bribe from the Soviet Government has thought it worth while to bring my name into the discussion.

> I have telegraphed the Senate Committee which has been investigating this matter asking that I be permitted to appear before the Committee and answer under oath any questions the Committee may seek to put. In view of all the activities with which I am associated in behalf of large business interests, every

principle of whose operations is opposed to some of the fundamental tenets of the Russian government, it would be absolutely impossible for me to engage in any activity which might in the remotest manner accept financial support from the Soviet Government.

Ivy Lee

Lee's memo was followed in the MSO Book by this wire to Senator Reed:

Hon. David Reed
United States Senate
Washington DC

One of the newspapers advises me that they have a story to the effect that it was revealed today that the Senate was in possession of a document stating that the Soviet Governmenthad paid to me a certain sum of money for some undescribed expenses. The fact is that I have never received one penny or money from the Soviet Government directly or indirectly. I should appreciate the privilege of appearing before your Committee and making this statement under oath and should also be very happy to place at the disposal of you [*(sic)*] Committee the books and files of my office. The whole suggestion is a complete fabrication and utterly without basis in fact.

Ivy Lee

Senator Reed's letter of January 16, 1929, was mimeographed and released to the press with the Senator's permission according to a notation in the MSO Book:

Senator Reed's reply:
January 16, 1929
My Dear Mr. Lee

Answering your telegram of yesterday, the facts are as follows: An individual in Paris who tried to sell us the "originals" of certain receipts which he claimed showed the payment of money to United States Senators, was asked by us what corroboration of his story might be had. He could suggest no corroboration but after a few days appeared with a typewritten copy of a letter (signature typewritten). A copy of this document is enclosed herewith.

I have been hoping that this incident is closed. Our Committee is unanimously of the opinion that the whole affair is a cock-and-bull story and a fake. However, I will show your telegram to the other members of the Committee and if they decide the letter is worth contradiction, I will be glad to let you know. My own impression is that it is not worth the trouble of a trip to New York.

Faithfully yours
D. A. Reed

There is no indication that Senator Reed's Committee pursued the matter further. But the story would not die. Walter Winchell, nationally syndicated gossip columnist, not noted for his accuracy, wrote in his column in November 1930 that Ivy Lee had been dropped from the Standard Oil payroll "because of his Soviet connections." On November 19, Lee wrote Winchell that there was no such thing as a Standard Oil payroll and secondly, he had not been dropped from any of his counseling connections. Lee concluded his terse note to the columnist, "In the third place, I have no Soviet connections, direct or indirect, my interest in Russia being purely personal and having no business aspect, direct or indirect."

Time and events proved Lee right in his observations on the United States' relationship to the young Communist government. Stating that he was not afraid of Soviet propaganda, Lee said, "My own observation of the operation of propaganda has been that nothing so quickly exposes error as to bring it into the open." Sound practitioner that he was, Ivy Lee exposed himself to all points of view, including those with which he disagreed. Nonetheless, a taint and suspicion about his relationship to Russia remained until his death.

THE I. G. FARBEN ACCOUNT HOUNDS LEE
TO HIS GRAVE

Ivy Lee's agreement to serve as counsel to the German Dye Trust, I. G. Farben [Interessen Germeinschaft, Farben Industrie] and through it to the Nazi government of Adolph Hitler dealt Lee's reputation a devastating blow on the eve of his death. It was the last controversy of his career. As indicated earlier, Lee took frequent trips to Europe to confer with business and political leaders. Among the acquaintances made on these trips were the top officials of I. G. Farben, German industrial giant. Generally known as the German Dye Trust from its free translation, "Community of Interests of the Dyestuffs Industries, a Stock Corporation," I. G. Farben in Germany, formed in 1925 as a merger of the country's six leading chemical manufacturers, was among the largest corporations in that nation. Lee had come to know the Farben officials well after he took on the American I. G., a holding company of the German firm, as a client in 1929. As a consequence, he had often discussed the company's policies with the German officials. Several prominent American business leaders — for example Edsel Ford and Walter Teagle, president of Standard Oil (New Jersey) — served on the I. G. board. Lee's retainer for this account was $4,000 a year.

In May 1934, I. G. Farben, concerned about the rising anti-German sentiment in the United States born of Hitler's persecution of the Jews and his rearming of Germany, sought Lee's counsel, and he accepted. He was given an additional $25,000 a year for counseling the parent company. I. G. Farben's directors told Lee that they were "very much concerned about German– American relations" and the "criticism being made" in the United States of Nazi Germany. Lee was asked "what could be done to improve those relations and to do so continuously." As Lee later testified, he stipulated that he would disseminate no information inside the United States and his only function was that of adviser. What Ivy Lee actually did for the I. G. Farben firm soon became lost in a storm of criticism once he appeared before the House Special Committee in May 1934. He was accused of being a propagandist for the Nazis, of being anti-Semitic, and other serious charges.

In May 1934, when brought before the U. S. House Special Committee investigating Nazi propaganda in this country, Lee was asked, "Was the Ivy Lee firm through its relationship with the German firm, I. G. Farben, indirectly advising the German Government?" Lee's testimony was given in a special executive session of the committee on May 19, 1934, and when it was released to the press in July, the storm broke. *The New York Times* ran its account of the testimony on the front page under a double-column headline: "IVY LEE, AS ADVISER TO THE NAZIS, PAID $25,000 BY DYE TRUST." "PUBLICITY COUNSEL HAS YEARLY RETAINER – DRAFTED STATEMENT TO GUIDE REICH – HE PAYS SON IN BERLIN $33,000 SALARY." On July 14, 1934, in his column, "Shop Talk at Thirty," *in Editor and Publisher* Marlin Pew, a longtime critic of Lee's made no comment but ran the following two items as leads: July 1934 bannerline in the *New York Mirror*: "ROCKEFELLER AIDE NAZI MASTER MIND": overheard in a Times Square restaurant: "I see that John D. Rockefeller is behind German Government's attack on the Jews."

A week later, articles about the testimony were run both in *Newsweek* magazine and the *Literary Digest*. On July 21, 1934: "Ivy Lee: An Extraordinary Press Agent Gives Advice to Nazis" and on July 22, 1934: "Ivy Lee's Firm revealed as Reich 'Press Adviser,' " were the respective headlines.

When Lee died in November, the *Jewish Daily Forward*, in noting his death, asserted, "He was an agent of the Nazi government," adding, "His recent adventures in German and Russian propaganda brought little credit to himself or his employers, and most domestic corporations have outgrown the Lee publicity technique."

But these exaggerated, somewhat distorted charges would live on long after Ivy Lee's death. In the 1946 – 1949 trials of war criminals at Nuremberg, Germany, the prosecution, in stating its case against 23 officials of I. G. Farben indicted as war criminals, made the following interpretation of Lee's relationship to I. G. Farben. Brigadier General Telford Taylor, Chief of Counsel for War Crimes, who acted on behalf of the United States and introduced the five-count indictment against the I. G. Farben officials, said on May 3, 1947, "In 1933, Farben's American public relations expert began to disseminate Nazi and anti-Semitic propaganda and literature throughout the United States."

Clearly what Ivy Lee actually did quickly got lost in these damning headlines and indictments. As best as can be determined, here is what he actually did on this I. G. Farben account.

In 1933, the Farben officials along with other German industrialists became alarmed at the world reaction to Hitler's policies of abusing and murdering Jews and his militarist threats against his European neighbors, both of which resulted in a growing boycott of German-made goods, particularly among the Jewish population. In his classic book, *The Rise and Fall of the Third Reich, a History of Nazi Germany*, William Shirer suggested that German business leaders who had welcomed the Hitler dictatorship as representing "a natural reaction to the muddled state of affairs of recent years, and not least to the Marxist–Communist agitation," had come to realize in the early spring of 1933 that there was growing fear of the government they had supported and of its policies as these emerged. In 1933, out of these concerns and its fear of the U.S. boycott, I. G. Farben hired Ivy Lee. James W. Lee II, who was made account executive on the I. G. Farben account, told an interviewer, Alyce Weck, in 1961, that his father had often talked with German businessmen about Germany's general habit of putting her foot in her mouth.

James Lee told Weck that "Ivy Lee posed the question: What do you do to warrant decent publicity" and told the officials that the problem should be studied and that public reaction in this country to German policies should be noted as a way of studying the problem. His father suggested the obvious thing, James Lee told Weck, in her interview of March 29, 1961, in the T. J. Ross offices. Lee told them, "The government should make sound policy decisions, in line with the idea of doing what would warrant decent publicity, then have responsible men in government announce the decisions." This by now was the standard Ivy Lee advice to American corporate clients, but to give such advice to a German giant already enmeshed in the Nazi war machine carries naivete to the point of absurdity. Lee's son said his father didn't see that taking the Farben account would mean problems for him down the road!

There never was any secrecy on Ivy Lee's part on accepting Farben as a client. Before signing the contract, he consulted the U.S. State Department and was told that it had no objection. When he first went to Berlin on this account, Lee called upon American Ambassador William Dodd and told the Ambassador what he was doing. He met with American correspondents in Berlin—Louis P. Lochner of the Associated Press, Frederick Birchall of *The New York Times*, John Elliott of the *New York Herald-Tribune*, and

Emlyn Williams of the *Christian Science Monitor*—and told them about what he was hoping to do to better German–American relations. According to his son, the account executive on the Farben account, "they applauded his effort."

In retrospect, it seems I. G. Farben's reason for hiring Lee was to get his help in urging the German government toward a more acceptable policy with a view toward clearing up its own business problems. The true dimensions and aims of Adolph Hitler were as yet unseen by all parties to this client contract. Ivy Lee testified in executive session before the McCormack Committee on May 19, 1934, 3 days after Hitler was named president of Germany to replace the ailing President von Hindenberg, an election made possible by the support of the German Army. The deal made Hitler's dictatorship supreme and secure. By early summer 1934, what had been done began to dawn on those who had put Hitler in power, including the industrialists. Shirer in his monumental book said that by summer demands were coming from various elements, including the industrialists, that the arbitrary arrests, the persecution of the Jews, the attacks upon churches, and the brutal behavior of the storm troopers be curbed. These steps were also being urged upon the I. G. Farben officials by Ivy Lee.

THE HOUSE COMMITTEE ON UN-AMERICAN ACTIVITIES, 1934

On March 20, 1934, a resolution was passed by the U.S. House of Representatives of the 73rd Congress authorizing the Speaker of the House to appoint a special committee composed of seven members "for the purpose of conducting an investigation of (1)the extent character and objects of Nazi propaganda activities in the United States and (2) the diffusion within the United States of subversive propaganda that is instigated from foreign countries and attacks the principles of the form of government as guaranteed by our Constitution." Two major counseling firms were caught in the crossfire of this committee and their reputations greatly damaged by the resulting publicity and public denunciations: Ivy Lee & T. J. Ross and Carl Byoir & Associates.

The Byoir firm's representation of German interests in the United States is fully told in chapter 17. George Sylvester Viereck testified before the McCormack Committee that the Byoir firm had a contract for $108,000 over an 18-month period from the German railways to promote tourism for Germany. Viereck, an acknowledged pro-Hitler author and publicist, had steered the contract to the Byoir firm and for this was put on its payroll for $1,750 a month. The contract was signed on behalf of the Byoir firm by Carl C. Dickey, then a junior partner of Byoir's. When all this backfired,

Dickey resigned from Byoir and later joined the Ivy Lee–T. J. Ross firm. Apparently his role in the German propaganda effort did not deter Ross from taking him into the partnership.

Representative John McCormack of Massachusetts, later to be elected Speaker of the House, served as chairman of this special committee. He told the committee at its opening session that since the end of World War I "unrest, discontent with the existing order, and a widespread agitation for changes in the form, character, and substance of governments has spread over the world, overturning established governments and resulting in many new and radical experiments in government." There was rising fear of Nazism in the United States much akin to the scares of "The Bolshevik Menace" of the early 1920s, one that was rekindled in the early 1950s in the era of McCarthyism.

These fears are reflected in this portion of McCormack's opening statement:

> In these circumstances, with so large a percentage of its population foreign, usually European origin, the House of Representatives has keenly sensed and fully realized the danger of vicious propaganda of foreign origin aimed at the subversion of those fundamental principles upon which our Constitution rests and seeks to investigate the extent and origin of such propaganda with the ultimate object of protecting this country and its people from its dissemination.

IVY LEE TESTIFIES

Ivy Lee testified on May 19 in executive session, but his testimony was not made public unit July 11. Ivy Lee was in Europe when his testimony was released; ironically he had gone to London to speak on July 3 at the London School of Economics on "The Contacts Nations and a New Technique of Helpful International Propaganda." At the outset Lee testified:

> I have an arrangement with the I. G. As I say, I have been related with them for the past five years. My relationship with them was materially broadened last year, because the directors of the company told me they were very much concerned over the German relationship with the United States. They want advice as to how these relations could be improved. So they made an arrangement with me to give them advice. I stipulated in the beginning that there should be no dissemination whatever by me in the United States.

Lee told the committee that he had been paid $4,000 a year by the American I. G. and that his fee for service to I. G. Farben was $25,000 a year. The finances of this arrangement heightened the committee's suspicion that something was amiss. It was difficult for the Congressmen to understand that Lee was paid this sum just for his advice. Nor could they understand why his 28-year-old son, James W. Lee II, was receiving $33,000 a year from the firm for his work in Berlin. A confidential source in the firm later indicated to your author that the salary may have been listed that way for tax purposes. Lee told the committee that he was hoping his son would eventually succeed him and that he was trying to shift more and more responsibility to him. Ivy Lee explained that his son was in Berlin not only to keep in touch with I. G. Farben but also to serve another Lee account, the Solvay Chemical Co. of Belgium.

Another central issue was whether Lee's firm was disseminating German propaganda in this country. When both Lee and Burnham Carter established that they had not distributed propaganda in the United States and had advised their client to tell the German government not to do so either, the committee then took another tack. A committee member argued that because Lee and his associates were advising the I. G. Farben to recommend to their government that policy statements be made by responsible people in government and then distributed, then wasn't it true that these statements got into the channels of communication. Lee conceded this point.

Carter, another junior partner in the Lee–Ross firm, also testified before this House committee. It was with Carter that the committee was able to force an admission that the Lee firm was indirectly advising the German government and they were aware that they were doing so. Lee confirmed this by testifying:

> I have often discussed with German officials, friends of mine, German relationships with the United States. . . . Since this new arrangement was made, there have been several points that I have urged upon these gentlemen over and over again. In the first place, I have told them that they could never in the world get the American people reconciled to their treatment of the Jews; that was just foreign to the American mentality and could never be justified in American public opinion. . . . In the second place, anything that savored of Nazi propaganda in this country was a mistake and ought not be undertaken. Our people regard it as meddling in American affairs.

> That the only way really to get Germany understood with any accuracy . . . would be if they would establish closer relationships, more authoritative relationships with the American correspondents located in Germany . . . that authoritative utterances of responsible Germans interpreting German policy be given the widest possible publicity in Germany with the American correspondents . . . and always when distributing these authoritative statements of policy always making clear its source.

Lee was giving his standard public relations advice of publicizing sound basic policies and providing the source for all publicity or propaganda — this advice to the Madman who perpetrated the Holocaust! Two or 3 months after signing the contract with Farben, its officials took Lee to meet Hitler "just as a personal matter, just to size him up." He also admitted that in January 1934, he had met with the Nazi cabinet officials. Lee was assured by Joseph Goebbels, the Nazi propaganda chief, that the German government "did not want to interfere with anything in the United States."

The House committee's counsel, Thomas Hardwick, kept pressing Lee on two points — the counsel's inability to understand why a company would pay him $25,000 a year for "advice" and whether or not Lee had distributed German propaganda in the United States. Lee replied to the first query by saying that this "was not the largest contract he had ever had of an advisory nature," and reiterated that he never had disseminated propaganda for the Germans in this country. On the latter point, Lee did admit he had discussed the German situation with American correspondents in Berlin. "American correspondents there knew precisely what I was doing precisely what my relationship was, and what I was saying to those officials with whom I met in Berlin."

At the beginning of his testimony, Burnham Carter gave essentially the same answers Lee had given. Chairman McCormack came to the point quickly: "And in advising them [I. G.Farben] you had in mind that the recommendations and advice which your firm would give to your clients would be ultimately carried to the attention of the German officials for consideration." In subsequent questioning by McCormack on this point, Carter said he knew it was possible "and even probable that such advice as our client approved of might be transmitted to the German Government; yes." McCormack then read back to Carter testimony he had given in executive session: "So that for all practical purposes it is a case of the state of mind on your part in sending this advice over there, that you are in a sense, indirectly at least, advising the present German Government." Carter's reply at that time had been, "I think that is a fair statement" and upon its rereading, said, "All right, I subscribe to that." Carter later asserted that "much of this advice was made with the hope that certain of those policies would be modified." McCormack pursued his original point:

The Chairman: Coming right down to it, Mr. Carter, there is no question but what this contract was made by the German Dye Trust for the purpose of receiving advice, which advice was to be given to the German Government?

Mr. Carter: If they approved it, I would answer yes.

The Chairman: But in submitting it to your client, you know, or had reason to believe, that your client would submit it to the officials of the German Government?

Representative McCormack then introduced a copy of a general report that Carter had given to I. G. Farben and read the following excerpt:

> Could not a suggestion be made that Mr. von Ribbentrop undertake a definite campaign to clarify the American mind in the disarmament question, and that Mr. von Papen undertake a similar effort in reference to the Saar? Could it not be suggested that, first of all, there be a series of press conferences dealing respectively with these two subjects? Also, could not arrangements be made whereby each of these gentlemen should speak over the radio to the American people on these points? Furthermore, each of them should write a considered article for an important American publication, dealing comprehensively with these two subjects.

Lee's and Carter's testimonies made clear that I. G. Farben retained the Lee agency to obtain advice that it could funnel to the German hierarchy in the futile hope of modifying Nazism that they had helped spawn. These hearings also made clear that Ivy Lee clearly understood the purpose of his retention.

The House committee hearings show that the Congressmen were almost totally preoccupied with the fact that Lee and his staff were advising the Nazis, albeit indirectly, and that they showed little concern for the content of that advice. In sum, the most charitable things one can say of Lee's involvement with the German government is that he was "naive in the extreme" in failing to discern the monster-like qualities of Hitler and the Nazis. The U.S. Ambassador to Germany at that time, William Dodd, whom Lee regarded as a friend, put it bluntly, "It is only another of the thousands of cases where love of money ruins men's lives."

Lee was his own worst client. The McCormack Committee chose to release Lee's testimony in July 1934 at a moment when America's revulsion against Hitler's atrocities and "blood purges" had reached a new level of intensity. Even though he had been exonerated of wrong doing by the committee, Lee was being crucified by the nation's headlines. Yet when reporters reached him at Bade, Germany, where he was taking the baths, he refused to make a statement—going against the advice he had been giving clients since 1906. Upon his return to the United States, he would not answer reporters' questions at dockside. Hiebert described this as "a characteristic lack throughout his lifetime; his inability to do for himself what he had done so well for his clients."

LEE'S STORY ANEW IN NUREMBERG TRIALS

Even though he had been dead some 14 years, Ivy Lee's service to the German Dye Trust and to the Nazi Government got a reprise in the nation's press when the Nuremberg Military Tribunals were convened after World War II to try the Nazi war criminals. Among those indicted, tried, and convicted were I. G. Farben's top officials, including Max Ilgner, who had retained Lee's firm in 1933. Deputy Chief Counsel Josiah Du Bois, Jr., speaking on Point G. in Case 6, *U. S. v. Krauch*, argued:

> Some of Farben's foreign agents endeavored to persuade the Vorstand to use its influence to soften the anti-Jewish policies, in the interests of Farben's export trade. But Farben was playing for bigger stakes and its reaction to the American boycott was the launching of a vigorous and insidious campaign which would have done credit to Goebbels himself. They retained a well-known public relations expert, Ivy lee, to devise methods for countering the boycotts and organizing pro-German propaganda.

The prosecution, speaking on Point G. in the indictment, continued:

> Farben's foreign agents formed the core of Nazi intrigue throughout the world. Financed and protected by Farben, and ostensibly acting only as business men, Farben officials carried on propaganda, intelligence, and espionage activities indispensable to German preparation for, and waging of, aggressive war. In Germany, Farben's Berlin N. W. 7 office was transformed into an economic intelligence arm of the Wehrmacht. The Nazi party relied upon Farben as one of its main propaganda machines.

In 1933, the defendant Max Ilgner became a member of the "Circle of Experts of the Propaganda Ministry" and president of the Carl Schurz Association that was active in disseminating Nazi propaganda. In 1933, Farben mailed a report idealizing conditions in the Third Reich to all its representatives abroad and requested them to circulate its contents. In 1933, Farben's American public relations expert began to disseminate Nazi and anti-Semitic propaganda and literature throughout the United States.

An official of I. G. Farben, a Dr. Petry, wrote to me on September 20, 1961, that "Dr. Ilgner read a paper to Allied authorities in Paris in May, 1945, entitled 'The Relationship of I. G. to Mr. Ivy Lee, to "Propaganda" and the Activity of the Carl Schurz Association,'" but I. G. Farben, then in liquidation, did not have a copy of this paper, or so it claimed.

Death, of course, had sealed Lee's lips and he was unable to respond in his own defense, particularly to the last charge. No evidence was ever produced before the House Special Committee on Un-American Activities to refute Lee's assertion that he never disseminated propaganda in the United States for Farben or the German government.

Ilgner was charged with one count in the Farben indictment: "Planning, preparation, initiation, and waging of wars of aggression and invasion of other countries." The prosecution cited Ilgner as a member of Vorstand, chief of the Berlin N. W. 7 office directing intelligence, espionage, and intelligence activities. Ilgner's defense counsel, Dr. Nath, asserted in reply to the charges:, "The American propaganda expert, Ivy Lee, was commissioned by the IG and asked for advice on how this serious obstruction [the U. S. boycotts of German goods] of business could be countered. I shall prove that this activity of the late Ivy Lee in the U.S.A. is unobjectionable and did not in the least have the tendency and the scope the prosection wants us to believe."

Ilgner's closing statement to the Military Tribunal [found on page 1069, Vol. VIII of the Hearings] said of Ivy Lee:

> When in 1933 the boycott campaign was started against the exports of German industry, Farben was exposed to especially severe attacks. . . . One year later, in 1934, when Ivy Lee, the publicity advisor of the Standard Oil Company of New Jersey, who had also advised Farben, was slandered in the American press campaign by a competitor, the press campaign against the IG — this time also again directed against my person — it started again like a heavy thunderstorm.

With reference to Ilgner's testimony, I was never able to find evidence that a competing public relations firm was behind the flood of publicity linking Lee with the Nazi government. Further, T. J. Ross assured me that Ivy Lee & T. J. Ross did not have Jersey Standard as a client but only Standard Oil of New York [Socony]. This was perhaps a distinction without a difference as they were major Rockefeller holdings, and the Rockefeller interests were always tended to by Lee.

Fate did not permit Ivy Lee to live to respond to these ugly and recurring charges. As with the case of the Colorado Fuel & Iron strikebreaking charges and the interborough Rapid Transit investigation by Samuel Untermeyer, Lee did not present a credible defense to the charges against him. As David Rockefeller, then president of the Chase Manhattan Bank and an admirer of Lee, commented, "How ironic it is that he managed to give an honest, genuine, and convincing performance on behalf of his clients and failed for himself. Maybe it's the old dictum that a lawyer should not conduct his own defense."

His son, James W. II, intimately involved in the Farben account from day one, made this defense for his father in a letter to me dated May 8, 1991:

> When it became obvious that Hitler's activities were harming their world trade, these German industrialists tried explaining this to Hitler and they told us that he would not listen. It was then, they said, they thought of hiring the world's leading international advisor and Hitler would pay heed to what he

said. Naive, yes, but the truth. And with that group, which was headed up by Max Ilgner, was the German foreign minister Hans Dickoff, Hjalmer Schacht, and believe it or not, von Ribbentrop. We all know now how Ilgner and von Ribbentrop changed and went completely into the Hitler camp but when we were asked to help them, it was not thus. I believe that Ivy Lee viewed this association as a completely normal and proper thing—a service he could render and if his advice had been followed, the world might have wound up a different kind of place.

Hindsight is easy, but when Ivy Lee took the German job, it is impossible not to believe that he foresaw good in it for the world if his advice was taken and if Hitler had wanted to improve German–American relations.

IVY LEE'S LEGACY

In pioneering the new vocation, Ivy Lee's income was large for its time and because of the grand style of his living and travel, it was widely assumed that he was a millionaire. His friend and fellow pioneer Pendleton Dudley wrote to me on May 8, 1959, that "while it was true that Lee was well paid, and certainly influential, it is quite inaccurate to say that he made millions before he was through." He certainly moved in the circles of millionaires and lived as though he were one, yet when his estate was settled, he had a net worth of $24,000 after his debts and taxes were paid. Fortunately for his widow, he had made an agreement with T. J. Ross in their partnership that either surviving partner should take care of the other's widow for 5 years. Mrs. Lee retained a major share of the firm's profits" until 1939.

But Ivy Lee left a legacy of public relations concepts and practices that endure to this day. *Editor & Publisher*, a newspaper tradepaper that was long a fierce critic of Lee's acknowledged in its brief obituary that Lee was a "public relations counsellor extraordinary, whose methods since 1900 revolutionized the concept and scope of publicity work." Lee, in a sense, wrote his own epitaph in his speech to the London School of Economics on July 3, 1934, only a few months before his death:

Extensive experience in assisting large corporations to adjust themselves to the demands of public opinion in making their purposes and policies understood and in creating for themselves a favorable position in the public mind has shown that no amount of propaganda is any value unless the policy of an institution is in the first place sound and honest, and is responsive to the high demands of enlightened public sentiment.

Ivy Lee was early and quick to see the importance of preventative public relations. In the firm's newsletter of April 3, 1925, he wrote, "What an individual or a corporation tells of its doings, voluntarily and in advance, acts much more favorably upon every mind concerned than in the way of explanation after the fact. It is indeed the best use of publicity to prevent misapprehensions before they appear." Even though a year later Lee was using publicity to describe his new vocation, he had already arrived at the mature, public relations concept. In his interview with Joseph M. Ripley of the *American Press* in December 1926, Lee said, "The great publicity man is the man who advises his client as to what policy he shall pursue, which, if pursued, would create favorable public reaction. The function of the publicity man, once the policy has been determined and the action decided upon, is to draw up the facts so that the newspapers and the public will get the full significance of it" [Lee later hired Ripley who became a valued partner in the Lee–Ross firm until his retirement.] Through his precepts, ceaseless public speaking, and the prominence of his clients, Ivy Lee, did much to define, build, and promote the vocation of public relations. On the debit side of the ledger, surely the controversies that brought Lee to the nation's front pages and were later recorded in magazines and books did much to surround the function with a taint and suspicions that hound practitioners to this day. We know of no other counselor whose judgements and counsel were so widely sought by the movers and shakers of his era.

T. J. ROSS PASSES BATON, FIRM FADES OUT IN LATE 1980s

On October 1, 1961, the name of the founder, Ivy Lee, was dropped from this pioneer public relations firm; on that date it became T. J. Ross & Associates, to operate henceforth as a partnership. T. J. Ross announced that the change in the firm's name was being made at the request of Ivy Lee's widow. Ross stated at the time, "Our partnership agreement provides that if neither of Ivy's sons is in the firm, the continued use of Ivy's name is subject to Mrs. Ivy Lee, Sr.'s consent. Mrs. Lee was informed me that she wishes us to discontinue the use of Ivy Lee's name". Ross continued as president of the company at this juncture.

This erasing of Ivy Lee's name came when James W. Lee, Jr. left the firm to go into the resort business. As indicated earlier, there were undercurrents of strain between Ross and the Lee sons, but none ever commented publicly about their relationships. As Ivy Lee made clear to the House of Representatives committee in 1934, he had hoped that his son would succeed him as head of his public relations firm. Perhaps the father's mistake in making James II the account executive for I. G. Farben tarnished the latter's reputation to the point that it was not feasible to promote him to a senior partnership after Ivy's death. Or perhaps the strong-willed T. J. Ross was the obstacle. The father assigned the son to the Farben and Solvay accounts, he told the committee, in an effort to shift more and more responsibility to him. When James Lee returned from Germany after his father's death, Ross assigned him to the Chrysler account in Detroit.

T. J. Ross served as president of the Ross agency until 1965 when he assumed the post of chairman and was succeeded by William J. Gaskill. When Ross retired in 1971 as chairman of the board, Gaskill succeeded him. Ross died on May 27, 1975, after a long illness. His retirement in 1971 capped a strong, substantial career in public relations during which he served as a close adviser to powerful business leaders, including George Washington Hill, Walter P. Chrysler, John D. Rockefeller, Jr., William Paley, W. R. Grace, and others. In his practice and in his speeches, Ross insisted that counselors must deal with top management so as to be involved in the formation of policies that affect a corporation's public relationships. Although, a strong, dominant personality in his understated manner, Tommy Ross never suffered from "the chairman of the board" complex that has affected many a practitioner. Ross's manner with clients was always serious. One client recalled to *Printer's Ink*, "In all the years we've attended meetings together I don't remember his ever making a joke."

Ross had few hobbies save for golf and spent much of his time on religious and philanthropic causes. A devout Catholic, he worked to advance Catholic education and was a member of many lay Catholic groups. For these efforts, he was awarded honorary degrees by Georgetown University, Manhattan College, and Marymount College.

When William Gaskill took over the leadership of the firm, he and his partners decided to incorporate the business. They also effected a stock-holders' agreement that required the corporation to buy back shares owned by anyone leaving the firm, retiring, or from the heirs of anyone dying. When Gaskill retired in 1978, three senior staff members, David D. Frank, William M. Simpich, and Gordon Sears bought back his shares. Sears, who had become president of the firm in 1971, became the CEO in 1978 and then took the title of Chairman in 1980. David Frank succeeded him as president and CEO, and Simpich was executive vice-president and treasurer. Simpich retired in the early 1980s leaving Sears and Frank as the sole owners of this historic firm. In March 1986, in the words of Sears, "We decided mutually that maybe we should turn things over to younger people and so sold our stock on March 15, 1986, to a group headed by Thomas Little." The Little group, in turn, sold the stock to Golin–Harris public relations agency in early 1988, and it, in turn, was soon lost in one of the mega advertising–public relations agencies that swept this field in the 1980s. Thus, the famous and illustrious names of Ivy Lee and T. J. Ross faded into history, understandable in a business as highly personal as public relations.

TABLE 6.1
Accounts Handled by Ivy Lee and T. J. Ross

John D. Rockefeller, Jr. (also Rockefeller Foundation, General Education Board)
John D. Rockefeller, Jr.'s sons (until 1945)
Copper and Brass Research Association
Dillon, Reed & Co.
United Steel Works Corp. of Germany
National Bank of Bolivia
Cotton Textile Institute
Chrysler Corporation
Pennsylvania Railroad
Simeon Guggenheim and Brothers
Cathedral of St. John the Divine
Cement Information Service
Long Island Railroad
Anthracite Coal Operators
R. H. Macy & Co.
Bethlehem Steel Co.
Otto Kahn of Kahn & Loeb
Dominick & Dominick
General Mills
American Tobacco Co.
Chilean Nitrate Industry (for the Guggenheims)
Chase National Bank
Interborough Rapid Transit Co.
Daniel Guggenheim Fund for the Promotion of Aeronautics
Armour & Co.
The Harmon Foundation, set up by William E. Harmon
Continental Baking Co.
Bakelite Co.
American Brown Boveri Electric Corp.
Princeton Endowment Fund
Clarence Mackay and the Mackay Companies
Lever Brothers
Park Avenue Church
George W. Perkins
Bulgarian Refugee Settlement Loan
Standard Oil Co. of New York
National Diary Products Co.
New York Trust Company
Metropolitan Opera Association
Waldorf Astoria Board

Note: First Ivy Lee and then Ivy Lee & T. J. Ross always refused to make public a list of clients of their counseling firm. This policy was reaffirmed at the time of Ivy Lee's death in November 1934. Based on my perusal of the MSO Books, held in the T. J. Ross & Associates offices in the Chrysler Building in 1959, the Ivy Lee firm and its successors handled these accounts at one time or another.

NOTE ON SOURCES

The primary sources for this chapter were the Ivy L. Lee Papers in the Princeton University Library and the M.S.O. Books, then in the offices of T. R. Ross and Associates, now in the Princeton University Library.

Also valuable in constructing this history were my extensive interviews with T. J. Ross, Joseph Ripley, and Carl Dickey of the Lee–Ross firm and my correspondence with Harcourt Parrish, also a partner in the Ross firm. Alyce Weck's interview with James W. Lee II also provided great insight on the I.G. Farben matter. Correspondence with James W. Lee II saved me from many errors and brought several matters into perspective.

Ray Eldon Hiebert's *Courtier to the Crowd: The Story of Ivy Lee and the Development of Public Relations* (Ames, IA., The Iowa State University Press, 1966), was the primary secondary source for this chapter and chapter 3. It is quoted extensively with permission of the Iowa State University Press. Professor Hiebert of the University of Maryland also read this chapter to insure its accuracy.

Other secondary sources were: Henry Beckett, "Ivy Lee, America's Most Highly Paid Publicist," *New York Evening Post*, January, 1929; Silas Bent, "Ivy Lee: Minnesinger to Millionaries," *New Republic*, Nov. 20, 1929; "Ivy Lee: Extraordinary Press Agent Gives Advice to Nazis," *Newsweek,* July 21, 1934; "Ivy Lee Explains His Press Agent Work," *Editor & Publisher,* July 2, 1927; "Ivy Lee Revealed," *Editor & Publisher*, Nov. 15, 1930; James J. Butler, "$27, 720 for Advertising, $22, 750 for Holding Company Publicity," *Editor & Publisher*, Vol. 68, July 20, 1935; Tells of Lee's firm working to oppose FDR's utility holding bill.; Ivy L. Lee Obituary, *New York Times*, November 10, 1934; "Lee and Company," *Time Magazine*, Vol. 22, August 7, 1933; Ivy L. Lee, "The Black Legend," *The Atlantic Monthly,* Vol. CXLIII, May, 1929; Markey Morris, "Merchants of Glory," *The New Yorker*, August 28, 1926; Wayne W. Parrish, "He Helped Make Press Agentry a Science," *Literary Digest,* Vol. 117, June 2, 1934; Henry F. Pringle, "His Master's Voice," *The American Mercury*, Vol. IX, October, 1925.; Joseph M. Ripley, "Ivy Lee Talks About Publicity and Newspaper Editors," *The American Press*, No. 3, December, 1926. (Lee later hired Ripley who ultimately became a T. J. Ross partner; M. K. Wisehart, "How Big Men Think and Act," *American Magazine*, Vol. CVIII, July, 1929; Ivy Lee an editorial, *Editor & Publisher*, Vol. 67, November 17, 1934.

"T.J. Ross, Pioneering Counselor," *Printer's Ink*, June 13, 1938; "T. J. Ross, Public Relations Counseling at Work," *Printer's Ink*, Oct. 18, 1965; For favorable comment on T. J. Ross' work, see L L. L. Golden columns on public relations in *Saturday Review* issues of March 10, 1962, and Dec. 14, 1968. T. J. Ross, "Public Relations in Industry," *General Management Series No. 132,* American Management Association, New York City, 1937;

"Difference Between 'Public Relations Advisor' and 'press Agent,'" *Printer's Ink*, June 16, 1927; L. J. deBekker "World's Greatest Authority Caught at His Own Game," *Success* Magazine, 1924; "Foreign Propaganda," *Editor & Publisher,* editorial of July 14, 1934; Upon Sinclair, "Poison Ivy," *The Brass Check*, Published by author, Pasadena, CA, 1920.

For information on end of bloody, West Virginia coal strike, see series of stories in The *New York Times*: "Mine Crisis at End, Bandholtz Miners Reports," August 28, 1921; "Mingo Marchers Fight With Police, Five Miners Fall," August 29, 1921; "Mingo Marchers Still Menace Area," August 30, 1921; "Outposts Battle in Logan County, Four Are Killed," September 1, 1921; "400 Miners With Arms as Troops Surround Fighting Area," September 4, 1921; "Miners Disbanding in West Virginia, May Reduce Troops," September 5, 1921.

The account of T. J. ross's selection to counsel Major General Leslie Groves of the historic Manhattan Project is found in James W. Irwin's informal history *The Wisemen,* dated March 10, 1978, Irwin papers, Mass Communications History Center, State Historical Society of Wisconsin, Madison.

Government documents used in this chapter include: *Investigation of Nazi and Other Propaganda*, Washington, D C: U.S. Government Printing Office, 1934; U.S. House of Representatives, *Report No. 153, Special Committee on Un-American Activities, 1934,* 74th Congress, First Session, February 15, 1935, Washington D C: U. S. Government Printing Office; *Trials Of War Criminals VIII, Case Six, U. S. v. Krauch, The I G. Farben Case,* Washington, D C: U. S. Government Printing Office, 1953

Two of my lengthy interviews with T. J. ross were held in his office in New York City on March 9 and 10, 1959. His letter on the firm's relationship with George Washington Hill is dated Sept. 26, 1960.

For a more detailed discussion of Ivy Lee's relationship with Nazi-controlled I. G. Farben, see Alyce S. Weck's unpublished master's thesis, "Ivy Lee's Concept of Public Relations as Seen in Three Cases," The University of Wisconsin, 1963. Contains extensive correspondence with James W. Lee II on this case.

For rounded view of T. J. Ross' concept of public relations, see T. J. ross, "Public Relations—Understanding and Being Understood by the Public," chapter in roger Barton, ed., *Advertising Handbook,* Prentice-Hall, Inc., 1950.

Chapter 7

Edward L. Bernays: Pioneer, Philosopher, Centenarian

Friday night, November 22, 1991, 350 admirers gathered at a glitzy banquet in the Charles Hotel in Cambridge, Massachusetts, to celebrate the 100th birthday of Edward L. Bernays and to sing his praises as "the father of public relations," an honor that he had spent a long lifetime seeking and promoting. The centennial banquet climaxed a week-long celebration of Bernays and his career as a public relations practitioner and philosopher. Bernays was hailed "as one of the most influential figures of the century" — a fact confirmed by Life Magazine in 1989 when it listed Bernays as 1 of the 200 outstanding Americans of the 20th century — the only practitioner so honored.

In his prime, Bernays was small of stature and weighed 160 pounds. His prominent characteristics were his heavy black mustache and a little round belly which he constantly patted when expounding at length about his accomplishments and philosophizing on the ways of "engineering public consent." At the centennial banquet, he was a bit thinner, smaller — "elfin-like" one writer wrote — and with a small wispy grey mustache. But he was in full command of the evening, telling a series of anecdotes picked out of the attic of his memory, anecdotes honed by years of retelling.

Bernays took a rapt audience on a dance through his 80-year career as press agent, publicist, and public relations counselor, reciting his accomplishments in getting Americans to eat bananas, American women to smoke, children to like to wash with Ivory soap, humanizing President Calvin Coolidge, persuading William Paley to make news a strong feature of his infant Columbia Broadcasting System, celebrating Thomas A. Edison's invention of the light bulb, and other public relations coups —

events that Bernays had recited a thousand times before. His was an indefatigable zeal in promoting himself as the father of public relations and in using excessive hyperbole in the retelling of his public relations endeavors. A perceptive *Washington Post* reporter at the Bernays Centennial Celebration recognized that "some of his own image-making has been pumped up through the years."

All these generalizations will come clear as I recount the life of perhaps public relations' most fabulous and fascinating individual, a man who was bright, articulate to excess, and most of all, an innovative thinker and philosopher of this vocation that was in its infancy when he opened his office in New York in June 1919, the seventh agency to be set up in this nation. Bernays was shunned by his peers in his active years but came to be lionized and venerated after his contemporaries had long left the field of battle.

Bernays's view of himself in the nation's public relations history is revealed in this handout from his office issued in 1952:

> Edward L. Bernays is a notable, unique example of how a profession grew up with a man rather than of a man growing up with a profession. For it was Edward L. Bernays who not only created and named the profession of counsel on public relations, but laid down, over three decades, a system of practice and ethics for this profession as valid today as when it was first pronounced. . . . Small wonder *Time* magazine calls him U. S. Publicist No. 1.

Bernays was brilliant person who had a spectacular career, but, to use an old-fashioned word, he was a braggart. His competitors in this new field from the 1920s to the 1960s were put off by what one termed "Eddie's chutzpah," citing the presumptuous title of his autobiography as *The Biography of an Idea.*

Yet persons who were not in competition with him for accounts saw him differently. For example, John T. Flynn, writing in the May 1932 issue of *Atlantic Monthly* in an article generally critical of Bernays' propaganda work, had this to say of him as a person:

> In spite of all this, it must be said that Bernays remains singularly free from swank and make-up. Small of stature, careless in his dress, not always evenly shaved, he resembles rather a diminutive absent-minded professor than the alert business man. What is more, he is utterly without posture when he talks about his profession. He offers no hypocritical explanations about the purposes behind his campaigns; he considers them quite proper.

BORN IN AUSTRIA, BROUGHT TO UNITED STATES AS AN INFANT

Edward L. Bernays was born in Vienna, Austria, on November 22, 1891, the son of Eli Bernays and Anna Freud Bernays. The Bernays family had lived in Hamburg, Germany, for centuries after Bernays' forebears had fled Spain during the Inquisition. Eli Bernays had moved to Vienna at an early age where he found a job as a secretary to an economics professor. There he met Anna Freud, sister of Sigmund Freud, the pioneering psychoanalyst. Freud in turn married Martha Bernays, Eli's sister, that making young Edward a double-nephew of the famous man—a fact that was an over arching presence in Bernays's mind-set and practice. In 1890, Eli Bernays came to America to find a better opportunity for himself and his growing family. The elder Bernays found a place for himself on New York's Produce Exchange and in 1892, brought his family to New York. His brother-in-law, Sigmund Freud, helped with the financial expenses of the move even though the brothers-in-law were not on the best of terms. Young Edward celebrated his first birthday aboard ship.

In an interview with me on March 12, 1959, Bernays recalled, "My earliest recollection is attending kindergarten in New York. Then I attended private and public schools. I went to DeWitt Clinton High School in 1908 and took a classical course, Greek, Latin, and the Like." In the fall of 1908, Bernays enrolled in the College of Agriculture at Cornell University. His high school grades had earned him a state scholarship that would have permitted him to enroll in any college at Cornell. But his parents insisted that he enroll in agriculture—a field for which the young man was totally unsuited. Bernays told me, "My father had been influenced by Theodore Roosevelt's 'back to the land movement' and my mother was a lover of nature, so I went to the Cornell University College of Agriculture." This, as Bernays acknowledged, was a day when parents generally dictated a child's choice of college. Bernays rebuffed my question as to whether the free tuition in a state school was a factor, saying, "My father was a well-to-do Produce Exchange member when I went to college."

Dean Liberty Hyde Baily of the college "was a man who believed that education could be given in terms of specific disciplines and the training I received there undoubtedly aided in the establishment of what I hope are analytical and logical approaches to my work." Bernays' years at Cornell were not particularly happy ones. "Contact between professors and students began and ended with a far-off view of a crowded lecture hall. . . . I had social contact with only two professors in my three- and-one half years at Cornell." "Life on the campus was as rigidly stratified as in Ithaca. The status symbol was a membership in a fraternity. We had very few links with the outside world."

Bernays continued, "When I was graduated from Cornell, I knew I would not become a farmer and went to work on the Produce Exchange with a young former associate of my father's. Office work, copying letters, stamping bills of lading, soon bored me, and I went off to Europe for the rest of the summer."

A CHANCE MEET-UP WITH CLASSMATE
BRINGS A BREAK

After his return from Europe, young Bernays was at loose ends until one December morning he met up with a former schoolmate, Fred Robinson, when they were traveling on the recently electrified Ninth Avenue elevated. Fred was then helping his father, a physician, publish books, booklets, and a journal, *Critic and Guide*, that campaigned against the prevailing prudery of the time. Fred's father had just given him two monthly medical magazines, *Medical Review of Reviews* and *Dietetic and Hygienic Gazette*. On the spur of the moment, Robinson asked, "Ed, how'd you like to help me run the *Review* and the *Gazette*?" Bernays' response was quick and spontaneous, "Sure." Bernays as a school pupil and high school student had found pleasure in working on his school papers. At Cornell, he had worked on the *Countryman*. When the son proudly announced to his parents that evening that he was going to work on medical journals the next morning, the Victorian father asked, "How can you be a competent editor of a medical journal when Cornell University prepared you for an agricultural career?" Little did the father know that his son's job would lead him to his natural metier, press agentry, and promotion. Bernays told me, "I had always liked communications and journalism."

Bernays continued in our interview:

In 1913 I read a manuscript submitted to us about *Damaged Goods*, a propaganda play that fought for sex education. We published the manuscript. Within several weeks I heard that Richard Bennett [then a famous actor] wanted to produce the play. He was unable to because of its strong content for the period, an era Comstockery. I suggested to him and to Fred Robinson that we organize the "Medical Review of Reviews Sociological Fund," selling memberships in the fund. As a result we produced the play.

Bernays expanded on this landmark event in his career in his memoirs:

Suddenly an idea came to me. *Damaged Goods* could be produced by *Medical Review of Reviews* Sociological Fund Committee. We would organize the fund and the committee, made up of distinguished men and women. This would raise the funds necessary for the production. Our office would be headquarters for both. . . . Fund membership of four dollars would entitle a person to a ticket to *Damaged Goods*. This would defray production costs, which were negligible because Bennett's actors were donating their services. . . . My salary would be twenty-five dollars a week. *The Medical Review of Reviews* would make no profit.

This was a pioneering move that is common today in the promotion of public causes—a prestigious sponsoring committee. In retrospect, given the history of public relations, it might be termed the first effort to use the front or third party technique. Bernays was "careful to invite men and women whose good faith was beyond question and who would be responsive to our cause." "Hundreds of checks poured in after our first public announcement." Bernays also solicited testimonials from prominent people and got John D. Rockefeller, Jr. to comment for publication, "The evils springing from prostitution cannot be understood until frank discussion of them has been made possible." The play was presented to a full house on the afternoon of March 14, 1913. Among those in the audience were Mr. and Mrs. Franklin D. Roosevelt. Next morning's papers gave the sensational play full coverage. With the play's success, Richard Bennett took his rights to *Damaged Goods* and ran, telling Bernays and Robinson, "I don't need you or your damned sociological fund any more. I'll start my own fund."

Questioned about this innovation in our 1959 interview, Bernays expanded:

> We used it (the idea of a prestigious sponsoring committee) many times since then because I think it is still the most useful method in a multiple society like ours to indicate the support of an idea of the many varied elements that make up our society. Opinion molders and group leaders have an effect in a democracy and stand as symbols to their constituency. . . . I might add, however, that when this was done, we did it in an open or overt way.

Bernays emphasized the last point because by 1959 use of fronts or third party techniques had come under heavy fire from the critics of public relations and issues in landmark lawsuits.

Building the public opinion that had permitted and funded this then sensational play had been a heady experience for young Bernays, then 22 years old. He found return to the routines of magazine editing boring. Once again bored, he took off for Europe with the money he had saved while working on the magazine and tutoring on the side. His time in Europe included a good visit with his Uncle Sigmund. In the fall of 1913, when Bernays returned to the United States, he decided "to become a newspaperman." But it was to press agentry that he gravitated—an art for which he was a natural talent. He told me, "I decided that I liked the theater, wrote to Klaw and Erlanger for a job, and that started my career in publicity. I became the publicity man for a whole string of actors and plays that kept me busy from 1913 to 1915. Then I was offered a partnership in the Metropolitan Musical Bureau and remained there to handle a concert tour of Caruso and Nijinsky and the Russian Ballet."

This experience, like that of getting *Damaged Goods* on the stage, helped prepare Bernays for his long and successful career. He wrote:

> My years as a press agent for the theater and for music helped me to learn about the New York press, its personnel, and how it functioned, and the press

of that day was the principal medium of millions of readers for information and entertainment. The newspapers represented all shades of opinion, and readers chose the medium that reflected their hopes and aspirations, likes and dislikes, and beliefs and prejudices. . . . I studied the papers to learn how they treated amusements, to what extent they covered theater news.

Bernays found his years from 1913 to 1918 as a theatrical and music press agent exhilarating.

My work as a press agent on Broadway, the entertainment center of the nation, was an ideal existence for a young man of twenty-three who had been judging cows in a cattle ring and passing tests in agronomy. I hobnobbed with actors and actresses whose names shone on the marquees; I went backstage whenever I wanted to, had free run of most theaters to catch a glimpse of an act, had the privilege of writing pieces for the press, worked for glamorous newspaper people, and, best of all, I was independent to think and act on my notion that seemed to have merit as a promotional idea. And for this I received seventy-five dollars a week. Life was one thrill after another.

In those years, he publicized Elsie Ferguson in *The Strange Woman*, Ruth Chatterton in *Daddy Longlegs*, and Otis Skinner in *The Silent Voice*. Among others, Bernays credits his success as a Broadway press agent to Freddie Schrader and Jack Pulaski, crack staff reporters for *Variety*, the trade paper of show business.

BERNAYS GOES TO WORK FOR THE CPI

The dull blanket of war and turmoil fell across this happy existence when President Woodrow Wilson persuaded Congress to declare war on Germany and the Central Powers in April 1917. "Immediately in 1917 when war broke out, I tried every possible way to get into war service, but my eyesight was poor. It was not until 1918 that I went to work with the United States Committee on Public Information (CPI)." Finally a friend, George Cosgrove, introduced Bernays to Ernest Poole, head of the Committee on Public Information's Foreign Press Bureau, and in 1918, after getting military clearance, Bernays went to work in the bureau's New York office.

In his autobiography, *The Bridge*, Ernest Poole, praised Bernays as "one of the ablest and most devoted younger workers on our staff." In their *Words That Won the War*, Mock and Larson wrote, "The two most important figures in the CPI invasion of Latin America were Lieutenant F. E. Ackerman and Edward L. Bernays," adding, "Creel was not uniformly pleased with the post-Armstice work of Bernays, but everyone granted the importance of his contributions while we were still at war."

George Creel, director of the CPI, included Bernays in the official party to accompany President Wilson to the Versailles Peace Conference where the CPI, according to early plans, would provide "technical assistance" to the press covering the conference. The party left from New York on the *Baltic* on November 10, 1918. According to Bernays, Poole instructed him to issue a release prior to the CPI party's departure. As would happen on later occasions, Bernays' penchant for publicity got him in hot water. Bernays' release announced that the Official Press Mission to the Peace Conference was leaving the next day for Paris and instead of the narrow technical press support mission Creel had defined for the group, Bernays inserted this sentence: "The announced object of the expedition is to interpret the work of the Peace Conference by keeping up a worldwide propaganda to disseminate American accomplishments and ideals." Two days later, the *New York World* headlined the story: "TO INTERPRET AMERICAN IDEALS." George Creel was furious; already in a battle with Congress, Creel knew that this would add fat to the fire. He disavowed the story. Nonetheless, it hastened the demise of the CPI.

Mock and Larson reported more blandly that Creel was displeased at the "way Bernays was handling publicity for the group towards the end." Creel's ire was brought about because Republican Senators, already antagonistic toward him, attacked him for this presumptuous release. The upshot of this that the CPI never functioned at the Paris Conference as had been planned. Bernays related, "We never did what it was intended to do. My speculation is that if Creel had insisted on carrying out his original intention, world history might have been different because America would have been informed of the activities at the conference," Bernays insisted to me that "Mock and Larson's conclusion relative to Creel's attitude toward me, was not based on true fact."

Bernays told me in the 1959 interview:

> The work I did for the C. P. I., based upon my publicity experience, aroused some interest at the time. It gave me the first real understanding of the power of ideas as weapons and words as bullets. When I came back from the war, I recognized consciously what we had done to make "the world safe for democracy" in intensifying the attitude of our own people in support of our war aims and ideals, in winning over the neutrals and in deflating enemy morale.

BERNAYS AND CARL BYOIR TEAM UP – BRIEFLY

Bernays and Carl Byoir, who starting in 1930 built the most successful public relations agency of its time, had a somewhat distant relationship during their days in CPI. Byoir was in Washington managing the agency as Creel's deputy, while Bernays was in the New York office in a lesser role. They were together in the CPI delegation Creel selected to go to Paris. Immediately after World War I, Byoir and Bernays came together in a brief association to promote recognition of Lithuania's independence. In that brief time, Bernays envisioned the opportunity to use public relations as a lucrative vocation; Byoir wouldn't. Ultimately, Byoir came back to public relations in 1930 and made his mark as well as millions. His story is told in chapters 17 and 18. The Bernays–Byoir story goes this way.

Shortly after his return from Paris, Bernays was having lunch with Byoir, who suddenly asked him, "Would you like to do publicity on a free lance basis for the (Lithuanian National) Council trying to win support of the American people for Lithuanian recognition?" The next day Byoir, on behalf of the Council, contracted with Bernays to advise the Council on how to meet their objective and write six short articles a week about Lithuania for newspapers.

Aided by Bernays, Byoir's task was to mobilize public opinion that would assure affirmative action by the U. S. Senate on a resolution extending such recognition. They waged a successful campaign, using techniques developed in the Creel Committee. They spread their message through chosen spokesmen in the nation's large cities and the newspapers. They were successful in eliciting editorials and telegrams to U. S. Senators supporting the Lithuanian cause.

In 1919, The Senate duly recognized Lithuania as an independent nation, but formal U. S. recognition did not come until July 1922. Bernays recorded in his 1965 memoirs that this campaign was "the prototype of modern-day public relations techniques." He described it as a "pioneering effort to mobilize public opinion."

To spread these targeted messages, Bernays distributed the articles to newspapers, syndicated feature services, and trade papers. His clipping bureau returned hundreds of stories from newspapers across the country. In a victorious America that had successfully fought a war to make the world safe for democracy, Bernays found a favorable public opinion climate for his propaganda efforts.

The Lithuania National Council paid Byoir $23,000 to defray the costs of the campaign. Byoir paid Bernays a $150 weekly salary but took no salary himself. The success of the Lithuanian campaign persuaded the perceptive Bernays there was money to be made on this new vocation, then burgeoning in the wake of World War I.

In the seeds of Bernays's thinking in 1919 and his innovation of the *segmental approach* to influencing the public were the rudimentary concepts he would refine and enunciate in *Crystallizing Public Opinion* in 1923—the first clear statement of the two-way concept of public relations.

Byoir, in contrast, saw a different vision out of their common experience in the CPI and in promoting Lithuania's demand for independence. He was eager to make millions and went into the import–export business with a wartime ally, Emanuel Voska, who had been Czechosolvakia's propagandist in the United States during the war. Byoir, who had worked 2 years as a $1 a year man for the government, was broke and needed money. In the 1921 Depression, the Byoir–Voska partnership lost its collective shirt, and Byoir was left with $120,000 in personal debt. He paid this off in the 1920s by shilling patent medicines and Blondex, then came back into the public relations fold in 1930.

In later years, Carl Byoir expressed satisfaction in having "given Eddie Bernays his start." Pendleton Dudley told me this and also repeated the thought to Harry Bruno, expressed in a letter from Bruno to me dated May 12, 1965.

In a letter to me dated November 28, 1960, Bernays challenged the assertion I had made earlier that month in an address to the Public Relations Society of America that Byoir had briefly employed the budding young publicist. He wrote:

> This is not the fact. After I came back from the Peace Conference, the War Department retained me to carry on a publicity campaign for the re-employment of ex-servicemen. This was a free-lance activity. I was also retained on a free-lance basis by the Lithuanian National Council to write publicity articles in support of Lithuanian freedom. This assignment was given to me by Carl Byoir on behalf of the Council. In June, 1919, on the basis of these and other clients, I opened an office at 19 E. 48th Street.

Byoir's recollection differed.

Incidentally as the result of that speech, printed in *Editor & Publisher* of *November 26, 1960*, I received several letters, one from a former employee of Bernays that read in part, "From 1945 to 1950, I was employed as senior counselor on the staff of Edward L. Bernays, and you will understand when I say I witnessed a continual outpouring of a rather cloudy and highly abbreviated version of the genesis of public relations."

BERNAYS OPENS OFFICE TO DO PUBLICITY DIRECTION

With his prewar press agent experience and bolder insights gained into the process of public opinion as the result of his wartime work, young Bernays decided to open an office and stake out a future as a publicist and promoter. His only competition was the reinvigorated and enlarged Ivy Lee firm. Bernays rented three rooms on the fifth floor of a large, remodeled house at 19 East 48th Street in June 1919. "My office furniture cost $1, 102, the first month's rent was $255, making a $1, 537 investment in my future." Bernays' first move was to "hire my young friend, Doris E. Fleischman . . . to work with me. She would be my staff writer at $50 a week." Bernays' also hired a secretary and his brother-in-law, Murray C. Bernays, at $75 a week. "My assignments paid for the staff and left me something besides." Bernays claimed in the 1959 that "At that time I did not know that Ivy Lee had done public relations" adding, "I did not know public relations work had been done in public utilities." "Don't forget," he told me, "there were no trade papers or professional papers in the field and a young man starting in the activity we were in New York and nowhere to go to learn what else might be going on outside of personal contacts." Bernays' thinking as he broke out to pioneer a whole new field is recounted in his memoirs:

> My wartime experience showed me that press-agentry had broader applica-
> tions than theater music or ballet. I knew the clients I wanted would
> misunderstand my intentions if I called my work press-agentry, and I was
> determined it would be more than that. I could have called my work
> "publicity" but that seemed only a littler better than press-agentry. "Publicity"
> was then and still is a vague term used to describe the gamut of activity from
> advertising through promotion to press-agentry. I had not then heard of the
> term "public relations," which had been current mostly in public utilities
> during the early years of the century. I called what I did "publicity direction."

Bernays's thinking at this crucial juncture in his career had been heavily influenced by his work for the CPI. In our interview, he said, "There was one basic lesson I learned in the CPI—that efforts comparable to those applied by the CPI to affect the attitudes of the enemy, of neutrals, and people of this country could be applied with equal facility to peacetime pursuits. In other words, what could be done for a nation at war could be done for organizations and people in a nation at peace."

DORIS—MORE THAN A WIFE, A FULL-FLEDGED PARTNER

Much of Edward Bernays' success and fame derived from his full-fledged partnership in marriage and in counseling with Doris E. Fleischman. They met and courted infrequently shortly after Bernays returned to New York City from Cornell. Bernays described her in their courtship days as "beautiful, intelligent, charming and ingenious." She attended *Damaged Goods* with him, a "daring thing for her to do," he thought. After she graduated from Barnard, Bernays helped her get a news job on the *New*

York Tribune. It was rare for a woman to get a news job in those days, but Doris was a free spirit and pacesetter from then on. Shortly after he opened his office of publicity direction, he hired Ms. Fleischman, by then assistant Sunday Editor at the *Tribune.* She became the staff writer at a salary of $50 a week and worked on the Lithuanian and War Department accounts.

In Bernays' words, their relationship "was on two levels. At the office we were fairly businesslike and professional, but after working hours our relationship became highly personal." They were married September 16, 1922, in the marriage chapel in New York's Municipal Building. Doris, an early feminist and member of the Lucy Stone League, insisted on registering at the Waldorf Astoria under her maiden name that night. The next day the press carried boxed items stating that for the first time a married woman had registered at the Waldorf with her husband, using her maiden name. Again when they made their first trip to Europe, she insisted that her passport be issued in her maiden name. The State Department at first refused, then a compromise was worked out.

Their marriage brought them two daughters, Anne Bernays, a novelist and wife of Justin Kaplan, and Doris Held, a psychological counselor whose husband Richard is a professor of psychology at MIT. This partnership of "happy, twenty-fours a day companionship" ended when Mrs. Bernays died on Friday, July 11, 1980, in Cambridge, where the Bernays had moved in 1961. Mrs. Bernays was the author of a best seller, *A Wife Is Many Women*, published in 1955, and many magazine articles. At the time of her death, she was vice-president of the Edward L. Bernays Foundation, Inc., established by the couple in 1946 to better human relations. In 1972, she received the highest honor of the national society Women In Communication. Mrs. Bernays was active in many civic and philanthropic activities.

In a scholarly paper, Susan Henry noted, "Her media visibility extended through the 1970s, when she and her husband continued public relations consulting and advocated such causes as pay for housewives and accelerated advancement for women working in the media. Her 1980 *New York Times* obituary described her as an 'enthusiastic feminist.' " Professor Henry, in her paper entitled, "In Her Own Name? . . . ," writes, "She had no formal contacts with clients. Instead, it was her husband who clients got to know and who was credited with the firm's success. Her role in the business was played down in numerous other ways as well, although she seems to have accepted this uncomplainingly." Nonetheless, in Henry's view "her accomplishments were undeniable."

Doris Fleischman brought a breadth of view, sound common sense, clear writing, and stability to their partnership of 58 years in counseling, a great strength for his agency. As Bernays told me in an interview in his office on March 12, 1959, "She has played an equally important role with mine, except that her insight and judgment are better than mine. Her ability to write is exceptional, as you may know from her book." After her death, he wrote, "These are difficult times, being alone after 58 years of happy twenty-four-hour-a-day companionship. . . . She was a rare woman. . . . And work goes on."

BERNAYS BRINGS UNCLE SIGMUND'S REVOLUTIONARY THEORIES TO AMERICA

Bernays' relationship as a double nephew of the famous Sigmund Freud exerted a profound influence on Bernays' public relations concepts and was a central theme in his indefatigable self-promotion over his long career. More importantly, Bernays' early publicizing of his uncle's revolutionary theories of psychoanalysis in the United States in 1920 had profound impact on American thought. Once again there is the significant impact of public relations practice on American society. Thus, this relationship merits an accounting.

When a person would first meet Bernays, it would not be long until Uncle Sigmund would be brought into the conversation. His relationship to Freud was always in the forefront of his thinking and his counseling. In his profile of Bernays, Irwin Ross caught this quickly when he interviewed him in the 1960s: "Addressing a client or a reporter, he displays the tolerant, unruffled manner of a psychoanalyst—an appropriate resemblance for Bernays' proudest family connection was the late Sigmund Freud, his uncle, and Bernays liked to think of himself as a kind of psychoanalyst to troubled corporations."

The Freudian influence is first clearly evident in Bernays' seminal book, *Crystallizing Public Opinion*, published in 1923 shortly after he had arranged for and publicized Freud's book, *Introductory Lectures in Psychoanalysis* in the United States. For example, in his chapter "The Group and the Herd," Bernays wrote, "We have gone somewhat elaborately into the fundamental equipment of the mind and its relation to the group mind because the public relations counsel in his work in these fields must constantly call upon his knowledge of individual and group psychology."

When I asked if Freud's theories had influenced him, Bernays replied, "I would say very definitely yes to this question. Although I do not qualify as a psychoanalyst, because I was brought up in a background of psychology and my uncle's methods, I have undoubtedly gotten a lot of it by osmosis, and what I didn't get by osmosis, I got from reading his works. As a matter-of-fact, as far back as 1923, in *Crystallizing Public Opinion*, I urged the study of social sciences as underlying a sound approach to public relations."

Little wonder that Henry F. Pringle, writing in the February 1930 issue of *The American Mercury* tagged Bernays with the title "Mass Psychologist." Pringle wrote, "Nephew Eddie can foretell the future. He makes no claim to crystal gazing, as such. He would modestly deny that he is clairvoyant. His science, once understood, is really very simple. What he does is to create a demand by molding the public mind. He creates a desire for specified goods or services. It is not often that mass psychology fails to find a solution."

Illustrative of Bernays' exploitation of the Freud relationship is this paragraph in a news release Bernays issued in 1973 headed: "1973 Marks Fiftieth Anniversary of Academic Public Relations Courses" and "Bernays, now 82, is a nephew of Sigmund Freud. He pioneered in applying the social sciences to the problems of public relationships. In his germinal book, *Crystallizing Public Opinion* (1923) the first on public relations, he laid down its system of practices and ethics. His published books include 7 other titles, including his memoirs, *Biography of an Idea*."

Despite the fact that Bernays' father and his brother-in-law, Sigmund Freud, had a strained relationship for many years, Edward Bernays's early recollections of his uncle are fond ones. Their relationship became more tense and difficult when the young public relations counsel took on the task of having Freud's works published and publicized in the United States in the early 1920s. Biographies of Freud make it clear that he was a very private person, one not easy to deal with.

Bernays' first recollection of his famous uncle was in 1900 when Eddie was nine and vacationing with his mother in the Austrian Tyrol. Freud was very fond of his sister, Anna, Bernays' mother. Freud and his younger brother were on a walking tour and came to visit their sister and her children. Bernays remembered "Uncle Sigi" as being "jaunty and bareheaded and wearing knickers." They renewed their acquaintance when in 1913, Bernays took a vacation trip to Europe after leaving *Medical Review of Reviews*. He visited his uncle at Carlsbad and "my relationship with him resumed as though it had been a continuing one. . . . Freud and I took long walks together in the woods that surrounded Carlsbad, he in pepper-and-salt knickers and Tyrolean hat . . . and I in my Brooks Brother suit. We often lunched together at local restaurants. . . . I recall his pleasant and easy attitude toward me." A much different personality emerged in their professional relationship.

Bernays' role in publicizing Freud's original theories in the 1920s came about this way. As related earlier, George Creel included Bernays in the CPI delegation taken by President Wilson to the Versailles Peace Conference in 1919 to provide "technical press services at the conference." Carl Byoir was in the party. Byoir informed Bernays that he was going to Vienna to work on restoration of diplomatic relations with Austria. Bernays promptly went to a tobacco shop and bought a box of Havana [Corona] cigars for Byoir to take to his uncle.

Upon his return to Paris, Byoir told Bernays that he had been warmly received by the famous psychoanalyst and that Freud appreciated the cigars because his supply had been cut off in the war. To show his appreciation, he sent Bernays an inscribed copy of his *Introductory Lectures* in German, delivered at the University of Vienna between 1915 and 1917—a gift that would have great impact on American psychiatry. Early in his public relations practice, Bernays acquired Horace Liveright, a book publisher, as a client. Bernays urged Liveright to publish Freud's lectures under the title *A General Introduction to Psychoanalysis*.

INTRODUCTION TO PSYCHOANALYSIS

This representation brought difficulties with Uncle Sigmund over a conflict with his English representative and biographer, Dr. Ernest Jones. Nonetheless, it publicized Freud's theories in the United States and popularized psychoanalysis. Bernays' primary motive was to get some money for his uncle, then in dire straits in postwar Vienna where the crown was virtually worthless. Bernays took no payment for his effort. Bernays learned later from Jones's biography that the war had wiped out Freud's savings of $29,000 and his insurance of $20,000. Bernays chose Liveright because he knew he would intensively promote the book, then a rarity among book publishers. Bernays quickly arranged for a translation of Freud's book by a young PhD in psychology at Columbia University, a Miss Hoch. Freud found fault with her hurried-up translation. He next persuaded G. Stanley Hall, editor of the *American Journal of Psychology*, to write a foreword. Here is Bernays' version of what happened next, as told in his *Biography of an Idea*: "Everything was moving ahead smoothly when my uncle sent my father a cable dated September 24: "MONEY DISTRIBUTED. TELL EDWARD STOP TRANSLATION. EXPECT LETTER. FREUD." The money referred to a gift of 1 million crowns made by Bernays' father to a children's home in Vienna. Bernays cabled the following reply: "CABLE RECEIVED. UNDER YOUR AUTHORIZATION PROCEEDED IMMEDIATELY, TRANSLATION FINISHED, INTRODUCTION WRITTEN BY STANLEY HALL, ALSO PRINTING ADVERTISING AND PUBLICITY CONTRACTS ALL PLACED. DISBURSEMENTS AND OBLIGATIONS TO DATE AGGREGATE $3,000 MUST THEREFORE CONTINUE. YOUR PROPERTY RIGHTS FULLY PROTECTED."

Later Bernays received a letter dated September 27, 1919, thanking the nephew for his interest in Freud's cause by saying, "I now believe that such action [approving the publication] was somewhat hasty. Do not take it amiss that I now review the matter." What had happened was that Dr. Ernest Jones had intervened. As told in his biography of Freud, *Life and Work of Sigmund Freud Jones's version is:*

> "When I saw Freud the following October [*sic*] I told him of our plan to produce an English translation of the book and of the difficulty of finding an English publisher if the American rights had already been disposed of; this was a recurrent source of misunderstanding among us. He at once cabled New York to stop translation there. But it was too late. . . . Freud was displeased with the numerous errors and other imperfections in the translation and later on expressed regret at having sanctioned it in spite of the welcome royalties it had brought him during a time of stringency.

In reply to his uncle's letter, Bernays wrote reaffirming what he had said in his cable, adding that the book would sell for $4, that he expected a sale of 3,000 copies, and expressing regret that he had moved so swiftly that he could not withdraw. Bernays sent his uncle $100 as an advance on the royalties and offered to help him find an English publisher if he so desired. But Dr. Jones had this base covered.

Shortly after the disagreement over the book, Horace Liveright asked Bernays to convey an offer to Freud guaranteeing him $10,000 for a lecture series to be given in English under Liveright's sponsorship. Freud turned down the offer writing, "I do not think I should risk it. My health and my powers are not up to the point and I would lose very much by the preparations here." In a letter dated January 4,1920, Freud wrote Bernays to ask, "Would you consider the thought of entering into business relations with our International Psychoanalytic Publishing Co., which is creating a press in London for bringing out a new Anglo-American PSA? You could help us a great deal." The upshot of this was ultimately a news release from the Bernays' firm: "The International Psychoanalytic Press of London and Vienna announced the opening of its New York office at 19 East 48th Street [the address of Bernays' firm]. A quarterly journal, the *International Journal of Psychoanalysis*, directed by Prof. Sigmund Freud and edited by Ernest Jones, M.D. will be brought out by the organization." Jones subsequently wrote Bernays a letter to cut Bernays' commission from $33\frac{1}{3}\%$ to 15% of the $6 subscription price for the *Journal*. Bernays accepted the cut, but this deepened the distrust these two men felt for each other. Later Bernays informed Jones that he could no longer promote the *Journal* for a 15% commission. The relationship fizzled out.

Despite his displeasure with the translation of his book that Bernays had arranged, Freud was pleased with the reception on the book was getting and with his royalties. He wrote Bernays on October 2, 1920, "Now, my appetite getting sharpened, I propose to you the following arrangement which will likely fall in with an offer of yours. I could promise to write, let us say, four popular papers for a certain review chosen by you, and these articles, if successful, could be collected into a small book after some time." Bernays wrote in his memoir, "I discussed the matter with the editors of *Cosmopolitan*, one of my clients. They were interested in several articles, $800 to $1,000 per article but would not contract them in advance. However, they suggested more popular titles, e.g. 'The Wife's Mental Place in the Home.' " To this Freud crustily replied: "This absolute submission of your editors to the rotten taste of an uncultivated public is the cause of the low level of American literature. . . . A German publisher would not have dared to propose to me on what subjects I write" In Freud's biography, Dr. Jones characterized Freud's reply as "a stinging letter of refusal."

At about the same time, Bernays was approached by Scofield Thayer, editor and publisher of *Dial*, offering Freud $10,000 to spend 6 months in the United States treating patients in the morning and lecturing in the afternoon. Bernays relayed the offer saying that $5,000 would cover his expenses while in this country and thus give him a net profit of $5,000. Freud cabled back: "NOT CONVENIENT." Bernays was becoming frustrated with his temperamental uncle: "It was furthermore quite clear that Freud had no idea of how widespread his popular appeal was here; nor did he realize that scientific knowledge could be popularized without diminishing its scientific validity."

Nonetheless, Bernays continued to be a watchdog for his uncle's interests. In August 1923, Bernays read a highly critical article of Freud's theories by Dorothy Thompson, popular syndicated columnist, and then cabled Freud: "AMERICAN WRITER IN AMAZING ARTICLE GIVEN WIDE CIRCULATION AMERICAN PRESS GIVES ABSTRACT ICH UND ES AND DISTORTED VIEW OF YOUR WORK. PRESS ASKED ME CONSTRUCTIVE STATEMENT YOUR FORTHCOMING WORKS. IN INTEREST YOURSELF URGE COMPLIANCE THIS REQUEST." Days later Freud cabled back: "NEVER MIND." Later in a letter he amplified his reluctance to respond to criticism: "I never hitherto reacted to criticism or misrepresentation and I think I did well."

The friction between Dr. Jones and Bernays vying as Freud's literary agents came to a climax in December 1923 when Freud wrote Bernays:

> You know it was my serious intention to give you the agency for the American sale of my books on a business basis. But I am sorry to say as soon as I have made known my decision the International Psychoanalytic Institute Press [directed by Jones] revolted against it, proclaiming it could not exist without

these rights and I had to concede these rights for two years more. I am quite sure that this is no loss for you but I am annoyed to have to retrace my steps.

Bernays' last effort to represent his uncle and broaden his popularity came when he forwarded an offer from Horace Liveright of an advance of somewhat over $5,000 against royalties for his autobiography, but Bernays suggested that the psychoanalyst could get a better offer. Freud replied that the offer was an impossible one. He added, "Incidentally, it is American naivete on the part of your publisher to expect a hitherto decent person to commit so base a deed for $5,000. For me, temptation might begin at a hundred times that sum, but even then it would be turned down after half an hour."

Another Bernays idea for promoting Freud in this country was propounded to Freud when Bernays and his wife, Doris, visited him at his summer home in Semmering in 1925. Bernays proposed that Freud accept the headship of an international psychoanalytic foundation to start collections for a scientific fund for the promotion of psychoanalysis. Bernays, ever the publicist, gave the Vienna bureau of *The New York Times* a release that it carried under the headline: "DR. FREUD TO HEAD WORLD FOUNDATION." The foundation, the story said, was to be devoted to "psychological knowledge along Freudian lines, and combat the fake psychoanalysis said to be rampant in the United States." This idea, too, came to naught because in Bernays' words, "Regrettably, the American public was not yet ready to contribute funds to such an endeavor, and we abandoned the effort."

To strengthen his association with the famous Freud, Bernays and his wife celebrated Freud's 75th birthday by throwing a big banquet at the New York Ritz–Carlton on May 14, 1931. They invited a notable group of people—psychoanalysts and those interested in it or related to the field in some way who cabled greetings to the absent honoree. Among the guests were Clarence Darrow, famous criminal lawyer, and Theodore Dreiser, the novelist. This is the end of the Freud–Bernays saga. Even though he never profited monetarily from his efforts to promote the Freudian theory of psychoanalysis, Bernays gained favorable public attention through this association. More importantly, he publicized and popularized the new science of psychoanalysis in the United States with a profound effect on American mores.

The Bernays-managed publication of his uncle's book and his ceaseless publicizing of Freudian theories had a far-reaching influence on American thought then and to this day. It fully illustrates a basic theme of this volume—the unseen power of the public relations specialist on American political, social, and cultural thoughts. Publication of Freud's lectures was indeed timely—his theories of sexual freedom fit neatly into the context of the Roaring Twenties of post-World War I. Freud's name in the 1920s became inextricably linked with the idea of social reform as well as sexual freedom. Ultimately, it became more. As Dr. E. Fuller Torrey wrote in a harsh book, *The Malignant Effect of Freud's Theory on American Thought and Culture*, "The name Freud, once merely a euphemism for sex with overtones of social reform and liberal political belief, slowly became reified into a broader symbol of nongenetic approaches to human behavior, liberalism, and humanism."

CRYSTALLIZING PUBLIC OPINION

Bernays' most enduring contribution to the development of public relations was his landmark book, *Crystallizing Public Opinion*, first published in 1923 and then republished in 1961 on the occasion of his 70th birthday. In this book, Bernays was the first to set down the rationale for public relations as a function in management, introduce the *two-way concept of public relations* in contra-distinction to one-way publicity, and introduce the term *public relations counsel* in the American lexicon. In this book, Bernays developed the theory of public relations as a two-way mediating–interpretation liaison between an organization and its constituent publics, a theory that has stood the rest of 70 years, though it did not gain the acceptance of management until years later. In this landmark work, Bernays stressed that public relations theory and practice must be based on a full knowledge of the social sciences, another concept new for that time. The book was published by Boni & Liveright and sold for $2.50. Bernays first used the term public relations counsel to describe his work in 1920. Bernays is clearly entitled to fathership of this term, if not of the public relations vocation.

Bernays' introduction of the term public relations counsel and his two-way street concept put him well out in front of his contemporaries. The postwar publicity boom brought not only a growing number of agencies and positions in industry and higher education, but also a spate of books that saw the new vocation as publicity or press agentry. These books were discussed in the Introduction to Part II. Typically, as late as 1927 Charles Washburn wrote a book entitled *Press Agentry* to argue that "the good newspaperman makes the best press agent." Washburn described both Dexter Fellows, celebrated circus press agent, and Ivy Lee as "press agents." That same year, the pioneer counselor of public relations, Ivy Lee, on the witness stand in a New York court, was having difficulty in defining his work. Thus, the Bernays concept stood out as a beacon light to those confused by the terms press agentry, publicity, propaganda, and advertising.

A British government public information office, J. A. R. Pimlott, gave an outsider's view of American public relations in 1951 in his book, *Public Relations and American Democracy*. He said, "Bernays' book . . . though published as long ago as 1923, stood alone among works dealing specifically with public relations in having exerted any influence outside the narrow public relations world or much influence within it."

In his little book *Two-Way Street,* subsidized by Bernays, Eric Goldman wrote:

> The book emphatically disassociated public relations from either press agentry or mere publicity work. The public relation man's primary function, Bernays declared, was "not to bring his clients by chance to the public's attention, nor to extricate them from difficulties into which they have already drifted. . . . "Developing its fullest kind of thinking toward which men of the Lee school had been tending, Bernays declared the primary function to be both the changing of public policy and public attitudes so as to bring about a rapport between the two. . . . He helps to mold the action of his client as well as to mold public opinion.

In effect Bernays was singing out of Ivy Lee's hymn book in his enunciation of the policy of constructive public behavior as the only sound basis of earning a favorable reputation with the public. Bernays enunciated these fundamentals in a clearer, more precise way than Lee had done in those years. Running through Bernays' discussion was an emphasis on the social role of public relations. He challenged the contention that the public relations man was inevitably, or even primarily, the defender of the status quo. The greatest bulwarks of the status quo were the stereotypes of the public mind that prevented people from seeing in terms of experience and thought and hence impelled them to oppose new points of view. Bernays argued that the social value of the public relations counsel lies in the fact that he brings to the public facts and ideas that would not so readily gain acceptance otherwise. Bernays emphasized in this path-breaking work that the public relations man's ability to influence public opinion placed upon him an ethical duty above that of his clients to the larger society. Though these seem like platitudes today, they were revolutionary thoughts in the adolescent vocation.

Much of Ivy Lee's thinking is woven into *Crystallizing Public Opinion* without attribution. Lee may have indirectly been responsible for Bernays' coinage of the term public relations counsel. Bernays and his wife were brainstorming for a phrase that would describe their work as they conceived it. The natural analogy was the legal profession. In 1921, Lee had used this analogy in his firm's promotional newsletter: "There have arisen what are known in many institutions as publicity departments and trained publicity advisers, whose work amounts to a new profession. They have to do with public relationships as lawyers do with legal relationships."

In this seminal work, Bernays, undoubtedly aided by his frequent discussions of their work with his brilliant wife, laid down the fundamentals that govern sound public relations practice to this day. These principles of public relations are set forth in the accompanying boxed insert. Bernays thought through and clarified the function of the public relations counsel in a time when the vocation was in its adolescence, if not puberty. It is a tribute to the minds of Bernays and Walter Lippmann that their books of 1923 and 1922, respectively, are useful guides for students and practitioners some 70 years later.

EDWARD L. BERNAYS – HIS PHILOSOPHY

There is probably no single profession which within the past years has extended its field of usefulness more remarkably and touched upon intimate and important aspects of the everyday life of the world more significantly than the profession of public relations counsel.

The counsel directs and supervises the activities of his clients wherever they impinge upon the daily life of the public. He interprets the client to the public and he interprets the public to the client.

The training of the public relations counsel permits him to step out of his own group to look at a particular problem with the eyes of an impartial observer and to utilize his knowledge of the individual and the group mind to project his client's point of view.

How does the public relations counsel approach any particular problem? First he must analyze his client's problem and his client's objective. Then he must analyze the public he is trying to reach. He must devise a plan of action for the client to follow and determine the methods and the organs of distribution available for reaching his public. Finally, he must try to estimate the interaction between the public he seeks to reach and his client.

Perhaps the chief contribution of the public relations counsel to the public and to his client is his ability to understand and analyze obscure tendencies of the public mind. He first analyzes his client's problem – he then analyzes the public mind.

The public relations counsel is first of all a student. His field of study is the public mind.

Not only did *Crystallizing Public Opinion* set the parameters of an emerging vocation., it stimulated wide discussion of this new adjunct to the nation's public information system. At Bernays' suggestion, Horace Liveright started the discussion by writing many prominent persons of the day asking their comments on a book on the counsel of public relations. Bernays wrote, "The responses indicated general curiosity, interest in and ignorance of the subject. Melville Stone, head of the Association Press, professed complete ignorance of the existence of public relations." The initial reactions to the book were equally pro and con. The *Bookman* praised the book as "a short but remarkably clear study. A book every businessman, as indeed, every artist, should read." The *Dial* told its readers that the book was not about just publicity, but about "the larger aspects of this activity . . . The book delves into psychology, ethics, salesmanship, it undertakes to show, in effect, how people may be divided into groups, how groups may be reduced to herds." Even the *Dry Goods Merchants Trade Journal* wrote, "No book ever before has taken up the idea of influencing public opinion and the building of goodwill."

There was plenty of adverse reaction to Bernays's revolutionary concepts of the ways of dealing with public opinion. Using loaded words, the *Survey* said, "Mr. Bernays writes frankly of the processes by which the herd instincts are exploited in the instincts of a new and far-ranging salesmanship." Ernest Gruening, a social critic of the period and later a United States Senator from Alaska, wrote in a 1924 review for the *Nation*:

> This new sublimation is in response to an obvious need. Mr. Bernays points out that . . . perhaps the most significant social, political and industrial fact about the present century is the increased attention paid to public opinion, "especially by men and organizations whose attitude not long ago would have been "The public be damned". . . . Will the final result be greatly different for the public which, while it no longer tolerates being "damned," guilelessly permits itself to be "bunked"? Is seduction preferable to ravishment?

Further, Gruening pooh-poohed Bernays's claim that the public relation counsel serves as a conscience for his client, writing, "Not only may one doubt that the glorified press agent will fulfill this destiny, but that a public conscience thus created would be useful or desirable." There were other voices of concern about the potential power of this new breed.

The book and the public discussion of it continued on through the years, bringing both public recognition of this new calling and harsh criticism of its practitioners. In a 1924 editorial, the *Chicago Tribune*, a conservative newspaper, urged that the business executive, when he was trying to obtain the public's cooperation, should as a priority extend complete cooperation to the public relations department of his organization. A year later, Abram

Lipsky, in his book, *Man, the Puppet*, saw the public relations counsel only "as a new Pied Piper who was the old press agent in new guise." Yet by 1926, the *New York Herald* editorialized, "The old time press agent has gone and that with the emergence of public relations counsel there was change not only of title but of methods." In his *American Language*, the caustic Henry L. Mencken dismissed Bernays' counsel on public relations as a euphemism for press agent: "A press agent is now called a publicist, a press representative or a counsel on public relations, just as 'realtor' and 'mortician' are euphemisms for real estate salesman and undertaker." Marking the field's progress in acceptance 20 years later, Mencken recognized the validity of the term in his *American Language Supplement No. 1.*

Through most of this period *Editor & Publisher* remained a reconstructed foe of the new field. In its "Shoptalk" of December 7, 1939, *Editor & Publisher* carried this verse that made plain its fear that the press agent was costing newspapers advertising: "Eddie Bernays gets the cash/Gets much cash/And makes the papers cover/Eddie Bernays gets the cash/Gets much cash/Yes, much cash/Eddie Bernays gets large cash/That once went into paid space." E&P's fear was expressed earlier that year on July 27, 1939, when it wrote, "Perhaps some can explain to us why it is that certain publishers who would instantly discharge a reporter for 'making news, 'will accept the synthetic news creations of press agents."

Goldman thought that "the public relations counsel as described in *Crystallizing Public Opinion* marked the third stage in the evolution of public relations thought in the United States." No longer was the public to be fooled in the manner of the press agent or merely informed by the publicity agent; the public was to be understood. Public relations was to be a two-way street in a good neighborhood. This was a time when the new breed of public relations practitioners were heavily criticized on the basis of two false assumptions that (a) they were trying to get pieces in the newspaper as free advertising and (b) public relations counsel was a euphemism for press agent. These false perceptions of the field linger to this day.

Wary of Editor & Publisher's constant attacks on him, Bernays took a full page ad in its issue of January 29, 1927, headlined: "COUNSEL ON PUBLIC RELATIONS — A DEFINITION" (see Fig. 7.1). The ad set out to answer two questions constantly raised about this emerging vocation: What is a counsel on public relations, and what are his relations to the press of this country? Unlike most of his peers, Bernays had no compunction about using advertising to promote himself and his ideas. For example, in 1946, he placed an ad in the *New Republic* headlined: "WATCH OUT, INDUSTRY; HUMAN PROBLEMS AHEAD," asserting that "the social sciences can serve industry's human relationships in the same way that physical sciences serve industry's technologicaL progress."

COUNSEL ON PUBLIC RELATIONS

—A Definition

What is a counsel on public relations
and what are his relations to the press
of this country?

These two questions are asked so often that we desire to answer them
in *Editor and Publisher*

A COUNSEL on public relations directs, advises upon and supervises those activities of his client which affect or interest the public. He interprets the client to the public and the public to his client.

He concerns himself with every contact with the public wherever and whenever it may arise. He creates circumstances and events in advising a client upon his public activities. And he disseminates information about circumstances in helping his client to make his case known to his public.

Essentially he is a special pleader before the court of public opinion.

He uses every method of approach to the public mind—the printed word, the spoken word, the photograph, the motion-picture. In respect to the advertising agency, the counsel on public relations works with it in the solution of the client's problems. He is often called upon by the agency itself to supplement its direct selling effort by a broader

and more general moulding of public opinion in favor of the individual product. Often through his efforts, a new field for advertising is created.

As a creator of events and a bureau of information for his client, he frequently supplies the press with information or expressions of opinion, labeled as to point of origin. His news is naturally given its place in any fair competition for news space at that particular moment.

In his capacity as a crystallizer of public opinion, he is building public acceptance for an idea or product. This usually leads to exploitation through advertising and all the other modern methods used to advance a cause.

His work is comparable to that of any special counsel in the highly organized society of today, the lawyer, the engineer, the accountant.

High ethical standards are imposed upon

him by his work. He owes the maintenance of these standards to his client, to the public, to the medium he deals through and to himself.

The value and importance of a favorable public opinion toward a basically sound product or idea is universally recognized at the present time by the heads of large enterprises of all kinds. To supervise this branch of any enterprise an expert in public opinion is retained. Organizations as varied as nations, governmental departments, educational institutions, scientific foundations, insurance companies, real estate developments, art galleries, food corporations, silk manufacturers, soap companies recognize the value of regular, continuous service of this kind.

"Contact," a publication, is published by us from time to time in the interest of furthering an understanding of public relations and the working of public opinion. It will be sent to you free upon request.

EDWARD L. BERNAYS
9 EAST 46TH STREET
NEW YORK, N.Y.

FIG. 7.1.   An advertisement reprinted from Editor and Publisher, of January 29th, 1927.

Crystallizing Public Opinion was only the beginning of Edward L. Bernays' crusade of some 70 years to bring public understanding and acceptance of the public relations counsel. In the twilight of 1991, he was told *The New York Times*, "Public relations today is horrible. Any dope, any nitwit, any idiot can call himself or herself a public relations practitioner." *The Times* reporter wrote, "Bernays bristled at the misuse of the term, 'public relations.' " He was then past 100 years of age. To describe Bernays as prolific is a master understatement. Through his frequent public speeches and magazine articles, he espoused the cause. In 1951, the F. W. Faxon Company in Boston published a bibliography of Bernays' writings, *Public Relations, Edward L. Bernays, and the American Scene*. This was an annotated bibliography of the writings of and about Bernays, covering the years from 1917 to 1951. Reviewing the publication for *Editor & Publisher* in its June 9, 1951, issue, Roscoe Ellard wrote, "Its nearly 400 references pretty well sketch the development of public relations and changing attitudes toward it." Professor Ellard added with sarcasm, "It is an unusual bibliography. So far as I know, the only somewhat similar compendiums were on Napoleon and Abraham Lincoln." The last bibliography of Bernays' writings and articles and books about him published near the end of his life totaled 755 pages.

He started his public relations campaign for public relations when he opened his firm. He told me on March 12, 1959:

> One of the first things we did to disseminate our point of view was to publish *Contact*. This four-page house organ became a most important element for getting public recognition for public relations, and certainly for our activity. We published 46 issues until 1939. In the 19-year period we were sending out 15,000 copies an issue and it brought us fascinating letters, publicity, and, indirectly, I suppose, many clients. My wife had the judgment and insight to pick little squibs that were published, and with a few words to point them up.

Bernays claimed in this connection—wrongly—that as a result of *Contact*, a study of public relations made by the Metropolitan Life Insurance Co. found "that there were only two firm names generally known in New York: Ivy Lee's and ours." More precisely, the Metropolitan published a book in 1928 through its Policyholders Bureau, *Functions of a Public Relations Counsel*, based on interviews with Bernays and T. J. Ross of the Ivy Lee firm.

SECOND BOOK, *PROPAGANDA*, CONFUSES AND BRINGS CRITICISM

In 1928, Liveright published Bernays' second major book, *Propaganda*, which set back his effort to clarify the function of public relations and, to boot, handed the infant field's critics a club with which to bludgeon it. In this book, Bernays "called public relations the new propaganda and expanded the thesis of *Crystallizing Public Opinion*." His was an inept public relations decision—to put it mildly. Surely by this time, Bernays knew what every seasoned practitioner knows today: The manner in which a disseminated message is interpreted by the receiver is largely determined by the context in which the message is delivered – the prevailing climate of opinion. His timing could not have been more unfortunate.

In the 1920s, in the disillusionment that settled across America when the United States failed to achieve its lofty war aims of World War I, propaganda became a whipping post for the critics and the cynics. The word *propaganda* was once a perfectly respectable word describing a church function. It originated in the 17th century when Pope Gregory XV created the Congregation for Propagation of the Faith. In its original sense the word described the work of propagating a faith, a doctrine, or a cause. Propaganda came to be defined by Webster as "the spreading of ideas, information, or rumor for the purpose of helping or injuring an institution, a cause or a person." America's era of the 1920s made propaganda an ugly, connotative word as writers and political leaders asserted that the United States had been suckered into the war by the false propaganda of the British, for example, "the Belgian Atrocities" and the fervor of the Creel Committee's drumbeating.

And on top of this, that same year, 1928, brought the start of the exposure of the nation's utilities, led by the notorious Samuel Insull, for their conduct of "an aggressive countrywide propaganda campaign . . . measured by quantity, cost, extent . . . probably the greatest peace-time propaganda campaign ever conducted by private interests in this country." According to the Federal Trade Commission that conducted the hearings, this campaign "literally employed all forms of publicity except 'sky writing' and frequently engaged in efforts to block full exposure of opposing news." The commission's published hearings preceded the collapse of the great public utility empires, built by pyramiding, of Insull and others. (The denouement of the Insull saga is told in chapter 10.)

This propaganda campaign, which included the subsidizing of professors and textbooks, came to light as the result of the efforts of Senator Thomas J. Walsh who on February 28, 1927, introduced a resolution in the U. S. Senate calling for an investigation of the financial dealings of the power and light industry. Walsh's resolution did not get out of committee that Congress, so he reintroduced it in the next session, 1928. The utilities' lobbyists and controlled senators, among them Senator Walter F. George of Georgia, were able to shunt the investigation to the Federal Trade Commission. In the course of this debate, Senator George, heavily obliged to the Georgia Power Co., admitted that he thought no investigation was needed. It was. Over the next 3 years, the Federal Trade Commission probe found what Ernest L. Gruening wrote in *The Public Pays* a "far-reaching propaganda campaign of the privately owned utility companies selling electric current, a campaign designed to subvert public opinion so that these companies might maintain their monopolistic *status quo*, as well as conceal and further their excessive profiteering and unsound financial practices."

The Commission found that in the 1920s the utilities, led by Insull and his publicity genius, Bernard J. Mullaney were using the "Red Scare" of the Russian Bolsheviks that had been whipped up in 1919 and 1920 by the then Attorney General A. Mitchell Palmer and his young aide, J. Edgar Hoover. (This same red herring was used to promote the Ku Klux Klan as described in chapter 14.) The Commission determined, "that a favorite method of attack was not to meet the public ownership argument . . . but to pin the red label on their proponents. The advocates of the right of people to own and operate their own public utilities were labeled as 'Bolsheviks,' 'reds,' or 'parlor pinks.' " It was further found that the National Electric Light Association, the leading propaganda organization, boasted that the "public pays" the expenses of this campaign. In the retrospect of the 1990s, the fear of Communism that gripped this nation from 1919 to 1991 makes fools of us. Thus in 1928, cynicism and public deception were corroding the term *propaganda*. Bernays as a student of public opinion should have known this in titling his book. He did learn "how vital in the process of communication is knowledge of words." Understandably, he gives this book short shrift in his autobiography.

A public relations historian, Marvin N. Olasky, in a Bernays perspective, in *Public Relations Review*, Fall 1984, described bernays' purpose in this book: "Bernays was one of the first to realize fully that American 20th Century liberalism would be increasingly based on social control posing as democracy, and would be desperate to learn all the opportunities for social control that it could. Thus his candor in *Propaganda*." Writing in the *Independent* of September 1, 1928, Bernays gave this defense of his book:

> It is altogether fitting and proper . . . to inquire in the light of the last ten years what have been the developments in postwar propaganda, especially as applied to industry—to Big Business. The World War left business astounded at what the technique of propaganda had accomplished in the conflict. Not only had it raised men and money for individual Governments. There had been propaganda in favor of the love of nations, and other propaganda for the hate of other nations—all successful. Big Business was not the first force to recognize what it could mean to it. The war had brought about big money deficiencies in the funds of colleges and other . . . social service bodies. The war technique was turned to the solution of these problems.

In his classic book, *Propaganda and the News*, Will Irwin had this to say of Bernays's touting his brand of propaganda:

> Edward L. Bernays, in his clever book *Propaganda*, described and defended this [public relations] process as regards purely commercial uses. And he gives

examples of press-agentry which rise above routine and achieve real art. . . . These are not culpable instances of the larger press-agentry. The maneuvers of the velvet men, the exploitation of Jackson Heights [a real estate promotion handled by Bernays], we may put down without criticism among the ruses which our sharp modern competition makes inevitable. . . . However, the publicity agents for special and selfish causes inimical to the general interest and disturbing to the Commonwealth use just as much ingenuity and invention plus at least a fair measure of corruption. Security in their trade depends upon permanent silence. Only occasionally does some unforeseen accident, like a Congressional investigation for a moment lift the veil. It is enough here to know that even before 1914 the United States of America which had taken the lead in journalistic technique, had also evolved most expert methods for using journalism to further selfish causes.

Predictably, *Editor & Publisher's* Marlen E. Pew responded, "My pick as the young Machiavelli of our time is Edward Bernays." *Inquiry Magazine* in 1929 criticized *Propaganda* saying, "that we all would be a lot better off if all propaganda were offered undisguised — that is, with full revelation of the promoting interests." In this regard, it will be remembered that Ivy Lee saw no danger in propaganda so long as the source was clearly identified. In the *Survey* of 1929, Leon Whipple wrote of the new Bernays' beliefs:

Somebody "who understand the mental processes and social patterns of the masses" should manipulate these controls so that people can know what to believe or buy. The counsel steps in to help — at a price. He rides here in a world of "high spotting," fashion-making window dressing, blind instincts and artificial habits, where events are created to make news, and indirection is the watchword. . . . The book is worth reading, for the Herr Doktor gives an almost metaphysical exposition of his creed. . . . The general idea is to control every approach to the public mind so we get the desired impression, often unconsciously.

Little wonder, given the context of postwar disillusionment, the exposée of Samuel Insull's use of public relations to build his watery empire, and the onset of the Depression, that Bernays' writings were setting off alarm bells among political, academic, and religious observers. In his 1932 article in the *American Mercury*, Henry Pringle wrote that "Eddie is a stern realist who operates on the demonstrable theory that men in a democracy are sheep waiting to be led to slaughter." Justice Felix Frankfurter, in a letter to President Franklin D. Roosevelt, described Bernays and Ivy Lee as "professional poisoners of the public mind, exploiters of foolishness, fanaticism and self-interest." A sociologist, E. T. Hiller, opined that "such widespread efforts to manipulate public opinion constitute a financial burden, a perversion of intellectual candor, and a menace to political sanity." *The*

Michigan Christian Advocate feared "there is danger in the discovery of the mass mind." A 1934 article by Abraham Cohen in *Opinion* stated, "Now that the art of Ivy Lee and Edward Bernays has been reduced to a science, and is receiving the attention of universities, we may soon look to a new crop of manipulators of the public will." Prophetic! It was inevitable in this period of the rise of Hitler to power in Germany that Bernays's principles of propaganda would be linked to Nazism. *Barron's* did this in 1935: "Hitler by making what Bernays calls 'devils' for the German masses to look down upon, has aroused the acclaim of the more easily swayed masses". In his interview with the *Washington Post* on the occasion of his 100th birthday, Bernays, told the reporter, Paul Farhi, that "Goebbels kept a copy of *Crystallizing Public Opinion* in his desk and there wasn't a damned thing I could do about it." A doubtful story given the Nazis' views of Jews. Books by Jewish authors had long since been burned.

Creditable propaganda for public relations *Propaganda* wasn't!

"THE ENGINEERING OF CONSENT"—ANOTHER CLUB FOR PUBLIC RELATIONS' CRITICS

In 1935, Bernays handed the growing army of critics of the field, now populated in substantial numbers, another weapon to fire at practitioners when he wrote an article, "The Engineering of Consent," for the *Annals of Social and Political Science*. His essay was in a special issue, "Pressure Groups and Propaganda." Bernays explained his purpose, "I first studied books on medicine and law to find whether doctors and lawyers apply a common procedure to every case. I found that they do. I then tried to find a common approach to public affairs—as well as other public relations— problems." He argued, "An engineering approach is essential because of the myriad choices to be made and interests to be dealt with—internal and external publics, their group leaders and opinion molders, the broadcast and print media. Engineering of consent deals both with attitudes and actions of the business man, consistent with coincidence of the public and private interest, and their communications to the publics concerned, to inform and persuade."

From his study of law and medicine, Bernays developed these methodical steps to "engineer public consent":

1. Define goals or objectives.
2. Research public to find whether goals are realistic, attainable, and how.
3. Modify goals if research finds them unrealistic.
4. Determine strategy to reach goals.

5. Plan action, themes, and appeals to public.
6. Plan organization to meet goals.
7. Time and plan tactics to meet goals.
8. Set up budget for out of pocket expenses for the program.

These are perfectly sound principles for public relations but are corroded by the offensive term *engineering of public opinion* that connotes manipulation of the public, a manipulation that most public citizens innately fear; a fear that makes them wary of the work of the practitioner, even today. In Bernays' defense for using this suspicion-arousing term, it must be recalled that Ivy Lee first used this term in a 1917 address, but he never used it a second time. Despite the adverse criticism this term — made to order for public relations critics — brought the field, Bernays stubbornly stuck with it. He wrote an article, "The Engineering of Consent," for *Industry's* December 1978 issue. And to cap it off, he chose it as a title for a book published in 1955 by the University of Oklahoma Press, a series of essays to which he and Doris both contributed.

Despite its manipulative connotation, Bernays stuck to the use of the term *the engineering of consent* into his Golden Years. On March 9, 1959, he wrote to me:

> This is a term that I think is basic to the sound functioning of a democracy. Anti-social causes are continually attempting to gain the consent of the people for their point of view. Unless sound social causes can engineer the consent of the public for their point of view, our democracy may get in a bad way. By "engineering of consent" I mean just that — adopting the engineering approach to the problem of gaining consent for a point of view, ideas or things. Many people today think that public relations is applied common sense. Of course, we know that it is not. American society is so complicated today that it demands an engineering approach to deal with it. Every leader know this. We just put it into simple terms.

In his defense of the term, Bernays begged the question that engineering consent, can be used by the bad guys as well as those wearing white hats. Bernays' purpose here was a laudable one — he was seeking to bring precision to a practice in which definitions were fuzzy and ways of work were generally imprecise, to put it mildly.

In 1952, Bernays reformulated his 1923 definition in a new book, *Public Relations*, published by the University of Oklahoma Press: "I now define the term as: (1) information given to the public; (2) persuasion directed at the public to modify attitudes and actions; (3) efforts to integrate attitudes and actions of an institution with its publics and of publics with those of the institution."

THE BIOGRAPHY OF AN IDEA

In a more than 800-page book published in 1965, Bernays told the story of his life and his career in public relations in *Biography of an Idea: The Memoirs of Public Relations Counsel Edward L. Bernays*. The book brought some harsh criticism from his peers in public relations, quite favorable comments from many reviewers, and increased public recognition of Bernays and the practice of public relations. The book was heavily promoted by its publisher, Simon and Schuster, starting with a full page ad in *The New York Times* of October 29, 1965, headed:

TODAY

You can learn what Henry Ford and Thomas Edison said at a lunch in 1929 . . .

You can discover how Sigmund Freud thanked his nephew for a box of cigars . . .

You can find out why Caruso had his bed made with 18 pillows, 3 mattresses . . .

CONCLUDING

Today you can own and read the book that surely will be the most talked about volume in years.

Bernays' fellow practitioners mostly resented the presumption of Bernays as "the father of public relations," a distinction he started promoting early in his career and kept up beyond his 100th year. William Baldwin, a respected counselor of the period whose career is sketched in chapter 12 wrote another counselor, Harry A. Bruno, on October 16, 1965, in part:

I have had a chance only to dip into the book here and there, but that has been enough to make me feel that its title was conceived in sin and whelped in iniquity. Naturally, I would be very much interested in knowing the context of the quote from me. I have always felt that Bernays did make the first major breakthrough in getting public awareness of public relations, but that this was but a by-product of self-publicizing. His selection of photos and of captions for the sections of illustrations for the book certainly bears out that appraisal.

Harry Bruno passed on Baldwin's copy of the Bernays book to T. J. "Tommy" Ross of T. J. Ross and Associates. Ross wrote Bruno, "I got it yesterday and so far have read only the chapter on George Washington Hill. It is outrageous, as well inaccurate. Even the address of the company is incorrect. (As is told in the next chapter, both Bernays and Ross served George Washington Hill of American Tobacco Co. as counselors.)

Advance copies of the book were sent to 50 influential leaders for comments that could be used as blurbs on the book's jacket and in a heavy schedule of advertising. The favorable ones were used. Typical were these:

> The story of Edward Bernays and public relations is an important part of our culture. It is part of the fabric of American history during the first half of the twentieth century. No serious student of American life can afford to ignore it — *The Washington Star*

> A remarkable compendium of ingenious problem solving by a truly pioneering mind. — *Gerhart D. Wiebe*, Dean of the School of Public Communications, Boston University

> So chock-a-block with people, places, and business campaigns that it is difficult to do justice to it in the space allotted. Bernays' book is as illustrative of American history of the past half-century as many an academic tome, and the fact that he gathered his material in the marketplace rather than an ivory tower makes it all the more valuable — John Barkham, *Saturday Review Syndicate*

> Your insights into the meaning of the new instruments of communication for the shaping of opinion are among the most important of our age. You have made a great contribution in analyzing these instruments and discovering their power — Daniel Boorstin, Eminent American Historian

Not used in the promotion of the *Biography of an Idea* was my response to Bernays' request that read in part, "This autobiography of Edward L. Bernays, long a colorful and controversial figure in American public relations, has added new fuel to fires of controversy that have burned around him in public relations circles for 50 years. Bernays has worked to build a reputation in public relations but has never been able to work in harness with other practitioners in the field."

I also reviewed the Bernays' book and among other comments, wrote that it was too long; Bernays responded in a letter of January 8, 1966, to me, "I was much interested in your comment on length because a number of the reviews from *competent* critics stated that the book wasn't long enough and didn't go into detail enough."

Another *New York Times* ad was headed under a picture of Bernays: "BERNAYS. He invented modern public relations. His memoirs are being greeted with excitement by scholars, critics, and men of affairs." So went the ballyhoo for an illuminating but not always accurate book and further glorification of its author.

In his hundredth year he was working on another memoir, this one entitled *The First Hundred Years.*

NOTES ON SOURCES

This and the next chapter are based on Edward L. Bernays' voluminous writings, many public speeches, and several interviews and extensive correspondence with Mr. Bernays dating from the late 1950s. Our relationship began with an extensive 2-hour interview held on March 12, 1959, that was taken down in shorthand and then transcribed by his faithful secretary, "Krausie" An extensive correspondence with Bernays ensued into the early 1990s. We appeared on several conference programs together and had many long conversations. (The first interview and the correspondence is in the Scott M. Cutlip Papers, Mass Communications History Center, State Historical Society of Wisconsin.)

His autobiography, *Biography of An Idea: Memoirs of Public Relations Counsel Edward L. Bernays* (Simon & Schuster, 1965) was a constant reference as we worked our way through these two chapters.

The amount of material written by and about Edward L. Bernays is, to put it mildly, voluminous, a result of his unceasing self-promotion and his longevity. Bernays, a prolific writer and speaker, left the most complete record of any of the pioneers. This is reflected in the two bibliographies of his written works, the most recent of which totals more than 700 pages. *(Public Relations, Edward L. Bernays and the American Scene, A Bibliography.* comp. Keith A. Larson, F. W. Faxon, Westwood Massachusetts, 1979.) His many books and articles also provide meaningful insight into his philosophy and practice of public relations: The landmark book, *Crystallizing Public Opinion,* published *by* Boni and Liveright in 1923; *Propaganda*, published in 1928; *The Engineering of Public Opinion,* a series of essays to which he and his wife, Doris Fleischman, contributed and edited, University of Oklahoma Press, 1952, *Speak Up for Democracy*, Viking, 1945, and a monograph, *Public Relations,* Bellman Publishing Co., Boston, 1945.

These and other ideas are amplified and elaborated in many speeches and articles: "Uncle Sigi," *Journal of History of Medicine and Allied Sciences,* Vol. XXXV, April 1980. (Outlines his relationship with his famous uncle and onetime client, Sigmund Freud.) "Counseling Not Communication, *IPRA International Review,* Journal of International Public Relations Association, September, 1977. "The Social Responsibility of Public Relations," talk before Independent Citizens Committee for the Arts, Sciences, and Professions, New York City, June 23, 1945. "The Engineering of

Consent," *Industry*, Vol. 43, December, 1978. "American Public Relations, A Short History," *Gazette* (Lieden, Holland) Vol. II, No. 2, 1956; "What Future for Radio Advertising?" *Advertising and Selling,* February 8, 1928; "Mass Psychology," address before Retail Board, Boston Chamber of Commerce, September, 1930; "Emergence of the Public Relations Counsel, Principles and Recollections," *Business History Review,* Vol. XLV, No. 3, Autumn, 1971; *Public Relations as a Career,* George H. Doran Co., 1927; "A Public Relations Counsel States His Views," *Advertising and Selling,* January 26, 1927.

Marvin N. Olasky, a public relations historian, discusses. Bernays' writings and the reaction to them in an insightful article, "A Bernays Retrospective," *Public Relations Review,* Fall, 1984.

Articles and books relied on for information and insights on Bernays in this and the next chapter include: Irwin Ross, *The Image Merchants,* Doubleday & Company, 1959 (quoted with permission of the author), Will Irwin, *Propaganda and the News,* McGraw-Hill, 1956; Eric Goldman, *Two-Way Street,* Bellman Publishing Co. 1948 (a sketchy history of the early years subsidized by Bernays); Alan Raucher, *Public Relations and Business, 1900–1929,* Johns Hopkins, Press, 1968; James R. Mock and Cedric Larson, *Words That Won the War,* Princeton University Press, 1939, Strother H. Walker and Paul Sklar, *Business Finds Its Voice,* Harper, 1938; Ernest Gruening, *The Public Pays,* Vanguard Press, 1931 (tells story of National Electric Light Association campaign based on Federal Trade Commission hearings.) Ernest Poole, *The Bridge.*

John T. Flynn, "Edward L. Bernays, The Science of Ballyhoo," *Atlantic Monthly,* May, 1932. Henry F. Pringle, "Mass Psychologist," *American Mercury,* February, 1930, "PRs' Edward L. Bernays, Creating Acts That Make News That Raises Sales," *Printer's Ink,* December 4, 1959. Wayne W. Parrish, "He Helped Make Public Relations a Science," *Literary Digest,* Vol. 117, June 2, 1934. "A Conversation with Edward L. Bernays," *The Public Relations Journal,* Vol. 47, November, 1991.

The story of the short-lived Bernays and Carl Byoir partnership is told in Cutlip, "Lithuania's First Independence Battle: A PR Footnote," *Public Relations Review,* Vol. 16, No. 4, 1990.

Light on the family and professional relationship with Bernays' uncle, Sigmund Freud, was found in his memoir, *Biography of An Idea,* his article on "Uncle Sigi," and these books: Ernest Jones, M. D., *The Life and Work of Sigmund-Freud* Vol. 3, The Last Phase, 1919-1939, Basic Books: Norman Klell, *Freud Without hindsight: A Review of His Work 1893–1939,* International University Press, 1988; *The Diary of Sigmund Freud, A Record of the Final Decade,* Charles Scribner's Sons, 1992. Also a *New York Times* story, "Freud's autobiography," April 22, 1925.

Notes on sources for this chapter:

Doris Fleischman's supporting role in the Bernays partnership is fully told in Professor Susan Henry's paper presented to the annual meeting of the Association for Education in Journalism and Education, July, 1988, entitled; "In Her Own Name? Public Relations Pioneer Doris Fleischman Bernays."

Story on his 100th birthday party appeared in *The Washington Post,* Style Section, "The Original Spin Doctor," by Paul Farhi, November 23, 1991.

The William Baldwin quote is in his papers, Mass Communications History Center, State Historical Society of Wisconsin.

Chapter 8

Bernays: The Counselor and His Genius and His Role in the Profession

As he stressed in *Crystallizing Public Opinion*, Edward L. Bernays saw himself as counselor to his clients, not as the head of a large public relations service agency like those built by Ivy Lee, Pendleton Dudley, Carl Byoir, and other pioneers of this vocation. As he put in his interview of March 12, 1959:

> Counsel on public relations is a profession. A doctor, lawyer, architect does not work on an account executive basis if he is carrying on true professional activities. He may have partners or associates, but the client knows that he is getting a professional. We regard what we do as a personal service. . . . I do not feel the public relations profession is fulfilling its highest function in satisfying the social and economic needs of the society if it simply functions like a factory. I have no objection to organizations with hundreds of people who write communications material for their clients with news desks, magazine desks, and the like. Instead of working to expand our organization in number of personnel, we have worked to make our services of counseling worth more to the client and society. From an economic standpoint, the public relations counsel earns as much with a few people as thirty.

The client got Bernays' personal attention and with that quite imaginative solutions to pubic relations problems. These following illustrations suffice to document his imaginative and innovative techniques, examples he often recited in his writings and his lectures.

One of Bernays' oft-told tales is how he quelled the rumors that the famous Waldorf–Astoria Hotel was about to close, rumors fueled by talk of tearing down the original structure and building a more magnificent hotel in its place. When the owners came to Bernays to ask if he knew how to stop these rumors, he replied that it was futile to battle rumors head-on. He asked, "What about your famous chef, Oscar of the Waldorf? Do you plan to keep him on? He's an institution on both sides of the Atlantic. You are going to keep him on, aren't you?" Told by the hotel manager that of course they planned to keep him, Bernays then said, "Send a two-stick story to the newspapers. Announce a 10-year contract with Oscar. Give a little of his background — and the total of his 10-year salary. That'll fix things." Denials would merely raise eyebrows." That solved the Waldorf's problem.

One of the few clients that Bernays kept over a long period of time was the large marketer, Procter and Gamble of Cincinnati. Bernays wrote in an article in the *Business History Review*, Autumn 1971:

> Procter and Gamble, leading American manufacturers of soap and vegetable fats, retained us for counsel on public relations early in this period, [the 1920s] and we worked together on diversified projects in close consultation with management. Soap sculpture became a national outlet for children's creative instincts and helped develop a generation that enjoyed cleanliness. We publicized cleanliness. We worked to make guaranteed employment more acceptable in American Industry. We made social science studies of folkways and mores of communities where new plants were to be located, to ensure that acceptable patterns for employment were followed. He helped set up within the company a department of public relations, an example other companies soon followed.

Bernays wrote of this celebrated PR "pseudo-vent": "Kids hated getting soap in their eyes when they were being given baths. I did some research and found that many sculptors used soap instead of wax. I contacted public schools and asked them to participate in soap sculpture contests. Within a year we had 22 million school children doing soap sculptures and loving it. It gratified their creative instincts."

The idea Bernays developed for P&G conducting soap sculpture contests for children became a celebrated example of public relations. Although Bernays' influence on P&G is difficult to assess, at least until 1991 when it stubbed its toe trying to find the source of leaks in P&G to a *Wall Street Journal* reporter, Procter & Gamble has been a sophisticated practitioner of sound corporate relations. A 1991 check of P&G Archives found no record of the length of Bernays' retention as its public relations counsel. On November 29, 1930, *Editor & Publisher* in its continuing campaign against press agents listed a number of accounts and their "press agents." Bernays was listed as representing Ivory Soap and Crisco, also a P&G product. It also listed him as promoting incandescent lamps and Worth Fashions.

Another Bernays feat that has been oft told is his effort to change the image of President Calvin Coolidge, known in his day as "Silent Cal," when in fact he was a very loquacious man. Alice Roosevelt's wisecrack that Coolidge had been "weaned on a pickle," caused his supporters to seek Bernays' help to change the Coolidge "image." Bernays arranged for a breakfast in the White House to "humanize his reputation" by inviting stage and screen celebrities to attract national attention. Al Jolson, "The Jazz Singer," the Dolly Sisters, and other celebrities brought front-page stories in the nation's press. Bernays claimed "it helped to mellow the President's reputation."

In *Business Finds Its Voice*, Walter and Sklar extolled Bernays' work for Philco Radio. In 1934, Philco, a client of Bernays, put on the market a new radio boasting of its "high fidelity reception." No publicity was issued; again Bernays took the indirect approach. He sent letters to a list of well-known music critics, asking what they thought of radio reception. He then persuaded Pitts Sanborn, a noted critic, to edit and issue under his name a symposium of opinions on radio reception using the replies to Bernays's letters. The verdict was that radio reception in 1934 was generally bad. Walker and Sklar observed from this, "Bernays . . . knows that it is better to implant an idea in a group leader's mind and let him spread it than to write up the idea and sent it to the papers as a release. He has developed the technic [*sic*] farther perhaps than anybody else."

Bernays was a pioneer in using art to gain recognition and sales for a manufacturer. Cheney Brothers, a longtime New England silk manufacturer, sought Bernays' counsel on ways for them to establish style leadership for their silks. Bernays somehow arranged for the Luxembourg Museum in Paris—then the center of the style makers—to hold an exhibition of Cheney silks. Bernays saw to it that this exhibition received wide publicity in Paris and in New York. He wrote, "The impact of 'art in industry' was lasting; it changed women's wear and the decorative arts for the better." Today corporate support of and use of the arts in industry is a standard part of public relations. Again, Bernays must be accorded the role of pioneer.

In his *Propaganda and the News*, Will Irwin gives this example of Bernays's use of style-makers to promote a product:

> The velvet manufacturers found that their material was fast going out of fashion. How could they stimulate demand? Paris sets the styles. And behind Paris stands Lyons, where workmen with tradition centuries old make the finest silk fabrics in the world. Someone [Bernays implied] saw the Lyons manufacturers, persuaded them to put out tentatively a few velvets with new colors and weaves. Under persuasive auspices, these were shown to the famous Parisian coutouriers, who created several all-velvet costumes or inserted the fabrics as a detail into others. When they introduced them at their

regular showings, the promoters of velvet saw that these details were noted by the fashion reporters. It was news — in the world of vanities — big news. Across the Atlantic flashed the line "Velvet has come back." The rest was easy.

Because of his work with Lyons manufacturers and the Parisian designers in the promotion of silks and velvet, Bernays was appointed in 1925 as Associate Commissioner to the 1925 Paris Exposition of Decorative Arts by Secretary of Commerce Herbert Hoover. This further enhanced his growing reputation.

One of the continuing and demanding functions of the public relations counselor is to gain public acceptance of new ideas and new technology — a tough assignment given human nature's innate resistance to change. Bernays faced this challenge early in his career when he was retained by the newly formed United States Radium Corporation. Madame Curie had isolated the new element in Paris in her research laboratory, and a short time later, Carnotite ore containing radium had been found in Colorado. Bernays' task was induce doctors and scientists to experiment with and use the new radium technology. One of the uses Bernays promoted radium for was cancer therapy where today it is used extensively. He also promoted its use for luminous gauges and watches, a use that ultimately was outlawed as cancer causing.

One of Bernays' early clients was the Beech Nut Packing Co., then famous for its bacon. To promote the sales of bacon, Bernays again took the indirect route. He conducted a survey of physicians on America's eating habits. One result of this survey was reported as physicians recommending people eat hearty breakfasts. Bernays' publicity encouraged this with the notion that a hearty breakfast consisted of bacon and eggs. Bernays was early among publicists to promote the sizzle, not the steak, sleep, not the mattress. To promote the suggestion that persons should eat heavier breakfasts, Bernays sent letters to 5,000 physicians giving the results of his survey and the opinion of his own physician.

Another long-term account of Bernays was the United Fruit Company's promotion of bananas as a health food, an account Bernays landed in the early 1940s and held for almost 20 years. This promotion started with what Bernays called "the celiac project." Celiac disease is a debilitating digestive disease of children. Bernays' research found that a Dr. Sidney Haas, a New York pediatrician, had reported some years before that a banana diet cured children with celiac disease. His clinical findings had been reported in a medical journal. A friend of Bernays sought him out and said that friends and parents of patients of Dr. Haas wanted to honor him for his 50 years of practice and for his contribution in discovering bananas as a cure for celiac. With United Fruit's money, Bernays put on celebratory event, a Golden Jubilee Tribute lunch at the New York Academy of Medicine.

Robert Moses and Mr. and Mrs. Arthur Hays Sulzberger, owners of *The New York Times*, served as the sponsoring committee. Bernays saw to it that Dr. Haas's paper, "The Value of the Banana in the Treatment of Celiac Disease," published 20 years before, received renewed national publicity. One hundred thousand copies of a small hard-cover book that Bernays edited, describing the Haas luncheon, were sent to editors, publishers, librarians, dieticians, home economists, pediatricians, and physicians specializing in digestive disorders. This discovery and its promotion took Bernays into other medical areas. At Bernays' suggestion, United Fruit started funding research into the relation of bananas and a person's health. Today bananas are a staple item in most persons' diets.

United Fruit was confronted with a difficult PR problem when, in the 1949 polio epidemic, damaging rumors were circulating that bananas had caused the outbreak of the disease. Naturally, the company wanted to put out a denial of this untrue rumor immediately, but Bernays knew that this would have little credence. Instead he sought the cooperation of Basil O'Connor, head of the then National Foundation for Infantile Paralysis. O'Connor got Dr. Van Riper, medical director of the foundation, to issue the requested statement. Bernays followed this up with newspaper advertising in cities where the story seemed alive. The denial was accompanied by a recommendation to "keep food clean." The advertisement stated that funds had been provided by friends of the foundation as a contribution to the educational activities of that organization. The "friends" were United Fruit.

Bernays' work for United Fruit also included counsel on its political and social problems in Central America where the bananas were grown. United Fruit dominated those little republics that in popular parlance became known as "banana republics." Bernays spent much of time on these problems in what he chose to call "Middle America."

Another public relations coup of which he was still boasting in his twilight years was the promotion of national highways to boost the sale of Mack trucks. In an interview with *The New York Times* (December 30, 1991 issue), Bernays said that in the 1940s E. L. Bransome, president of Mack Trucks, sought his counsel in getting more roads paved. Bernays persuaded Bransome to call a press conference and demand Congress build a road across the country. Bernays claims the press conference persuaded Congress to approve funds for Highway 66, the Chicago-to-Los Angeles road of song and legend. Whether this was an accurate claim is open to question.

A STINT WITH DODGE BROTHERS

In 1927, George Harrison Phelps, head of a Detroit advertising agency of that name, phoned Bernays to seek his counsel for the Dodge Brothers

Motor Car Company, which was getting ready to introduce a new model car. The first thing Phelps asked Bernays to do was to find a catchy name for the new six-cylinder car. Bernays sought out an old friend, Frank Irving Fletcher, a copywriter, and asked him to take on this assignment for $15,000. Fletcher came up with a list of names (e.g., Lexington or Concord), but the Dodge officials rejected them and decided on Victory Six. Next Bernays was asked to handle the Victory Six's introduction. In those days, the unveiling of a new car was a widely reported news event. As Frederick Lewis Allen wrote in *Only Yesterday*, "The first showing of a new kind of automobile was no matter of merely casual or commercial interest. It was one of the great events of 1927."

In December 1927, great excitement surrounded the introduction of the Ford Model A car, excitement generated by full-page advertisements that ran 5 successive days in the nation's 2,000 newspaper.

Bernays' challenge was to top this. He came up with a plan for a Victory Hour on the still young National Broadcasting network because radio advertising was still an unknown quantity. Bernays had difficulty in selling the idea to Phelps and the Dodge folks but he finally did. Bernays recalled, "Will Rogers opened the program in Hollywood. In New York Paul Whiteman and his orchestra played *Rhapsody in Blue*, and Fred and Dorothy Stone in Chicago sang hits from their musical comedy successes. E. G. Wilmer [Dodge president] in a short talk announced the new Victory Six from Detroit, and Al Jolson, from New Orleans, sang Mammy.' " This was one of radio's first blockbuster programs. *The New York Times* carried a front-page story.

The Dodge Victory Hour was so successful that Phelps gave Bernays a second assignment in 1928, this time to promote the introduction of the model, the Dodge Senior. Again Bernays used the medium of broadcasting, this time putting together a cast of Hollywood movie star "seniors" — Norma Talmadge, Charlie Chaplin, Douglas Fairbanks, D. W. Griffith, John Barrymore, and others. As a publicity gimmick to promote the show, Bernays had Phelps and Dodge insure Chaplin's voice against stage fright with Lloyds of London, which was well publicized before the day of the show. Phelps also asked Bernays to arrange for local promotion in the nation's 55 largest cities to insure traffic to the Dodge showrooms.

This assignment provided a snapshot of the extent of the public relations and publicity fields [more publicity than public relations in 1928] on the eve of the 1929 Stock Market Crash and the ensuing Great Depression. To accomplish this, Bernays set out to build a list of publicists in these cities and then hire them on a part-time basis. In sending me his file of correspondence with these publicists, Bernays wrote a letter dated March 1, 1961, "What surprised me . . . was to learn there are so many people calling themselves publicity people available." Bernays first sought out the Universal Trade Press Syndicate (UTPS) that had a line on persons doing trade publicity. On May 15, 1928, Bernays sent Henry J. Hoch of the Phelps ad agency a list of representatives in 55 cities, noting that those marked UTPS would have to be engaged through the syndicate. Hoch replied on May 11:

> Enclosed is the list of 56 [sic] cities in which we will want to connect with the correspondents referred to in this morning's telephone conversation. This list represents dealer territories which will absorb 50% of the Senior output. You may recall that one of the campaigns we are developing contemplates use of the photographs of prominent Senior owners, with their endorsements. Ordinarily, such pictures and statements can be obtained but the trouble is that in many instances the dealer won't do it. . . . It is also possible that we may wish to use the endorsement of bankers and other prominent citizens.

Examples of the responses to Bernays's telegram of May 21, 1928, follow: Dudley Glass, who had an agency in Atlanta, GA and billed himself as providing "Legitimate Newspaper Publicity. Advertising Copy That Compels Attention. Special Publications," replied: "CAN ACT AS PUBLICITY REPRESENTATIVE FOR YOUR CLIENT AT FIFTY DOLLARS PER WEEK NOT LESS THAN SIX WEEKS CONTRACT"

Another reply came from Luther P. Weaver who had an advertising agency in St. Paul. His resume indicated that he had left newspaper work in 1922 to become assistant director of the Rust Prevention Association. A year later, he became the first executive secretary of the Minneapolis Publicity Bureau, financed by the city's businessmen. He opened his own publicity and advertising business in 1925.

John W. Oldine who had an advertising agency in Worcester, Massachusetts, replied to Bernays' telegram: "CAN ASSIGN AN EXPERIENCED MAN AT $100 PER WEEK FOR PREPARATION OF PUBLICITY AND DEALER SALES PROMOTION. . . . WE ARE RECOGNIZED ADVERTISING AGENTS AND IT IS SOMEWHAT DIFFICULT FOR US TO ANSWER MORE SPECIFICALLY WITHOUT FURTHER INFORMATION FROM YOU."

In cities where Bernays did not have a name of a publicist, he wired the local Chamber of Commerce. The Grand Rapids Association of Commerce secretary replied, "YOUR WIRE EVEN DATE. RECOMMEND ALLEN G. MILLER & Co. . . . THERE ARE SEVERAL GOOD PUBLICITY MEN IN THIS CITY, SOME SPECIALIZE IN ONE CLASS OF WORK AND SOME IN OTHERS. YOU DID NOT SAY JUST WHAT KIND OF PUBLICITY YOU WERE INTERESTED IN. THE NAME WE HAVE GIVEN YOU IS THE PRINCIPLE ALL ROUND AGENCY OF THIS CITY."

Indicating that it was common in those days for newspapermen to take on publicity jobs on the side was this response from Chic Feldman of Scranton, PA: "AM AVAILABLE FOR IMMEDIATE DUTY MY POSITION IS SPORTING EDITOR SCRANTONIAN ALSO DEPUTY BOXING COM-MISSIONER. . . . HANDLED ENTIRE PUBLICITY LATZO WALKER CHAMPIONSHIP MATCH"

Ned Hastings of Cincinnati, Ohio, wired Bernays: "CAN PROVIDE EFFICIENT PUBLICITY REPRESENTATION YOUR CLIENT FOR TWO HUNDRED AND FIFTY DOLLARS PER MONTH PUBLICITY AND SALES PROMOTION FOR LOCAL DEALERS. . . . TWENTY YEARS PUBLICITY EXPERIENCE WITH NATIONALLY KNOWN CORPORATIONS NOTABLY KEITH ALBEE ORPHEUM CIRCUIT."

Despite all these efforts, the Dodge car did not sell well. Nonetheless, Bernays claimed in his memoirs that at about this time the Chrysler Corporation made an offer to him to handle Chrysler's public relations, but he declined "out of loyalty to Phelps and Dodge," adding, "neither Phelps nor I knew that when this offer was made to me negotiations were already under way for Chrysler to purchase Dodge." As a result of this takeover by Chrysler, the Ivy Lee-T. J. Ross firm held Chrysler's public relations account many years. As explained in the preceding chapter, Lee and Ross obtained the Chrysler account through their work for Dillon Reed and Co., stockbrokers, who had been retained by Chrysler to win the approval of Dodge stockholders to approve the merger of the two car companies.

Another major account lost!

Other major accounts that serve to further illustrate Bernays' ways of work and relationships with the principals follow.

BERNAYS HELPS SHAPE CBS

In 1929, a young William Paley who was just starting to build what became, in time, the powerful Columbia Broadcasting System, hired Edward L. Bernays as public relations counsel. Once again Bernays' employment with CBS was relatively brief. In his time there, he exerted considerable influence on young Paley, an influence that redounded to the public good. Paley had been given the infant company in 1928 by his millionaire father who had made his money in cigars — a business for which the son had no interest. Given Paley's small staff, Bernays found himself involved in many aspects of management.

Paley was the young network's chief salesman, hustling advertising against the older, stronger NBC networks, the Red and the Blue. Bernays helped him to fashion a sales policy based on research and to promote CBS through an advertising program. In other ways, Bernays served a talent scout for a new medium starved for program talent. Bernays helped shape up the one-man publicity department and taught Paley the importance of getting accurate program listings to the newspapers. Most importantly, over the long run of broadcasting, when Paley was uncertain about the role of radio news, Bernays pressed him hard in building a strong news program. At the time, Paley seemed to fear that CBS news policies were being too aggressive, but Bernays'counsel prevailed.

Bernays wrote that his "most effective contribution was to define policy for radio's future and, in effect, for television." On January 17, 1930, Paley appeared before a Congressional committee as a witness on newly proposed legislation to regulate broadcasting. Bernays wrote Paley's script that the sometimes arrogant and egotistical executive accepted without change. Paley testified:

> There is perhaps no other force touching the American people more broadly and vitally than this new form of communication, education, and entertainment. . . . Radio broadcasting is a private business based on the coincidence of public and private interest. It is the part of enlightened business, however, to serve the public, and in doing that we are following in the footsteps of the greatest and most successful industries in America.

The statement welcomed the proposed communications bill to bring about improvement in broadcasting and pledged CBS's fullest assistance. Paley stressed the public service aspect of broadcasting, pointing out that only 22% of CBS's programs were sponsored. Sustaining programs, Paley told the committee, were sent to 75 affiliated stations without cost, a precedent in network broadcasting. Using Bernays script, Paley stressed his devotion to public service because he was trying to defeat a provision in the legislation that would allocate 15% of remaining channels to educational stations.

In her excellent biography of Paley, *In All His Glory*, Sally Bedell Smith confirmed that "Paley 's presentation was entirely scripted by Bernays. . . . Paley gave an effective performance, a cunning blend of apparent candor and high ideals." She continued "Bernays had directed Paley to avoid saying much about the mass appeal programs that enabled CBS to profit handsomely — programs like 'Street and Smith' detective magazine stories that included . . . 'dramatic and bloody murder scenes.' " (That complainant to the FCC ought to see today's TV fare!) Paley shrewdly stressed CBS shows that featured the views of senators and congressmen, who by now were beginning to sense the political value of broadcasting that, of course, came to full flower in the TV politics of 1960s and onward.

Ms. Smith also confirmed Bernays' strong influence on Paley in pushing emphasis on news. "News and public affairs programs formed the cornerstone of the image-building strategy that Bernays and Paley had launched the previous year" At first Paley followed NBC's lead on public affairs, but Bernays kept prodding Paley to build a distinct identity for the CBS news. Bernays's most important contribution to the building of the strong CBS news team came through indirection and cost Bernays the Paley account. In 1929, Bernays hired Edward Klauber, a suitor of Doris Fleischman's sister, whom Klauber soon married. Doris' sister didn't like her husband's night hours, so Bernays got him a job at the Lennen & Mitchell advertising agency. Klauber soon tired of the advertising business, so Bernays took him into his firm, but with misgivings. Bernays found this moody but talented man difficult to work with and recommended to Paley that he hire him for CBS. Soon "Klauber was functioning as Paley's assistant and things there were moving along smoothly. Shortly before my contract was to be renewed Klauber invited me to lunch at the Berkshire. He told me Columbia's budget could not carry two PR advisers—himself and myself." "I told him that if he believed this he should never have accepted the job we got him with Paley." Klauber replied, "Conditions are what they are. It is unjust to saddle two public relations expenses on Columbia." Again, Bernays lost a lucrative retainer after 1 year.

Klauber went on to play a major role in shaping CBS'S dominance in news. Sally Bedell Smith wrote, "Behind the promotional facade, however, CBS was steadily increasing its commitment to news. . . . In 1931 CBS broadcast 415 special events compared with 256 on NBC. These stirrings were the first evidence of Ed Klauber's most important role at CBS." Edward R. Murrow, CBS great, said of Klauber, "Ed Klauber is an intolerant man, intolerant of deceit, deception, and double talk. . . . If there be standards of integrity, responsibility and restraint in American radio news, Ed Klauber, more than any other man, is responsible for them." Again, a lasting imprint on American communications systems by a public relations practitioner.

Later on, Paley ever conscious of his public image, retained Earl Newsom as his public relations counselor. This story is told in chapter 20.

Ironically, shortly after Bernays' dismissal as counsel to CBS, David Sarnoff, president of RCA, retained Bernays to advise the newly installed president of NBC, Lenox Lohr. Lohr, with whom Bernays spent one unfruitful evening trying to discuss NBC's public relations, soon moved on to the Chicago Museum of Science and Industry. "But my relationship with NBC was not entirely fruitless, for I was kept busy with vice presidents, of whom there was a goodly number, and with publicity directors. I learned a lot about corporate structure while at NBC. I found, for instance, that the internecine warfare between executives was always greater than their common action against the competition or to meet other problems the company was facing." Broadcasting has been like that forevermore. Bernays' tenure at NBC was also short lived.

BERNAYS AND GENERAL MOTORS

As was made clear earlier, Edward Bernays was regarded with from skepticism to scorn by his fellow pioneers in his productive years as a counselor. There many reasons for this: his exaggerated hyperbole in boasting of his accomplishments — or claimed accomplishments, his tireless self-promotion; and as a few claimed, a lack of ethics on occasion. Other reasons and views become evident in the chapters recounting the careers of William Baldwin, Harry Bruno, and John Hill. For this chapter, two examples suffice. First is Bernays' 1 year-role in the public relations of General Motors.

Paul Garrett was the second public relations practitioner to earn a corporate vice-presidency and stands as one of the towering figures in public relations' first half-century. When General Motors (GM) began encountering difficulties in the Great Depression, including slumping car sales, Alfred P. Sloan, then GM president and architect of today's corporate giant, sought Paul Garrett's guidance. Garrett was then financial editor of the *New York Evening Post*. When Sloan asked Garrett which title he wanted, Garrett replied, "Director of Public relations" because he "saw the importance of public relations for a large industrial organization." When he joined GM in 1931, Garrett saw his job to interpret General Motors to the public in such ways as will favorably dispose the public toward the purchase of its products. GM, then only 25 years old, was suffering from a sales slump because of the Depression, thus this seemed a high priority to Garrett at the time. Garrett's public relations concepts broadened immeasurably, and in 1940, he was rewarded with a vice-presidency.

Shortly after he had assumed his duties, Garrett was approached by Sloan who told him another key executive thought he ought to have the help of outside counsel. The executive told Sloan, "Paul has a very big job. Why don't we get him outside counsel?" After thinking through the whole situation, Garrett determined that no outside help was needed, but he decided that discretion was the better part of valor. He wisely saw that the solution to this problem was to retain Edward Bernays who, Garrett speculated, would talk himself out of the job. That is exactly what happened. Garrett made the point of bringing Bernays to all major executive meetings. After business-like presentations by Garrett or other GM executives, Bernays would philosophize at length, generally in broad terms. This went on for nearly a year. One morning Sloan came to Garrett's office and told Garrett, "I don't think they like him, Paul. I think you better let him go." With shrewd insight, Garrett had solved his problem with the help of Bernays's endless philosophizing and a major gaffe.

Now hear the Bernays' version as recorded in his memoirs: "In December, Paul Garrett, newly appointed public relation director of General Motors, asked me to promote General Motors in connection with the January auto show at Grand Central Palace in New York. He told me General Motors could not afford my regular fee. I agreed to $5,000." Bernays found the atmosphere at the directors' table "heavy, stuffy, and institutionalized." Bernays quickly grew impatient with these directors' lack of "requisite knowledge or experience on which to base." public relations decisions. He took a like dim view of Garrett. "He had only recently come into the company." Bernays continued, "He was as green about public relations as I was about motor mechanics. Nevertheless he held the job of head of the public relations department." Bernays continued his denigration of Garrett, one of the most respected persons in the history of public relations, "Paul was ambitious and planned to make his future with the company. His pattern of conduct was carefully thought out. He was not going to be a strong no man; no one could object to his tentative negatives or be offended by his opinions. On the positive side he was a quick learner."

The climax of Bernays' counsel to General Motors came—as it often did in his career—when he became the news story instead of the client, a mistake a T. J. Ross, William Baldwin, John W. Hill, or Earl Newsom would never make. In 1932, the nation was on the economic ropes, and banks were failing left and right. Two of Detroit's major banks, the First National and the National Guardian Bank of Commerce, were among the first to fail. The city was in the throes of panic. As a gesture of goodwill and good public relations, General Motors agreed to make these banks a loan of $12.5 million with the assurance that the loan would be repaid by the Reconstruction Finance Corporation (RFC) that had been set up by President Hoover as a Depression measure. Bernays accompanied GM officials to Washington to close the deal with Jesse Jones, head of the RFC. Charles Michelson, shrewd publicist of the National Democratic Party who had been instrumental in tying the millstone of the Depression around Hoover's neck, wrote that release. But then Bernays prepared a release and sent it back to Detroit for the morning papers. It included a statement by GM President Sloan that GM would withdraw from the banking situation as soon as it was stabilized and depositors paid off.

The next morning, Bernays met the two GM vice-presidents at breakfast and they were irate, to put it mildly. They handed Bernays a copy of the *Detroit Free Press* that announced, under an 8-column banner, that Edward L. Bernays, a special representative of Sloan, was bringing a $12.5 million check to Detroit to save the people of the city. Bernays claimed, "Some Washington correspondent has recognized me and made me the hero of the story." Bernays professed that he had absolutely nothing to do with the story's slant, but this didn't wash with GM officials.

Consequently, despite all his contributions to GM's public relations program he claimed in his memoirs, Bernays' contract was not renewed at the end of his first year.

Paul Garrett's view of the unhappy year of Bernays' retention as counsel was told to me in a luncheon at Garrett's favorite University Club in the early 1960s and reduced to writing in a letter dated December 24, 1963, to Colonel Stacy Capers, who was writing a thesis on Garrett's career under my supervision. Garrett wrote Capers:

> Eddy had no impact on me in the development of my public relations philosophy at General Motors. If I were to complete a list of 25 men inside and outside General Motors who had an impact on my development during the early General Motors years, it would not even occur to me to put Eddy on the list. . . . This whole Bernays thing has assumed a dimension that is ridiculous as I think it would be clear from the fact that we dismissed him at the end of his first year.

In this letter, Garrett was responding to an assertion Bernays had made in a letter to me dated June 8, 1963, in which he gratuitously wrote:

> What you say about Garrett brings up recollections. When General Motors asked me to become their counsel on public relations in 1932 . . . they had taken a young financial; editor who had worked on the *Philadelphia Ledger* and then had been transferred by Curtis Publishing to the *New York Evening Post*. He knew nothing about public relations except what he had absorbed as financial editor of the two dailies. And it was my job to indoctrinate him. . . . He was ambitious for advancement, but he knew the labyrinthine ways of a large corporation and always seemed like a demure mousy young man and it paid off!

BERNAYS, HENRY FORD, AND LIGHT'S JUBILEE

One of Bernays' most celebrated feats — one he boasted of for some 70 years — was the staging of Light's Golden Jubilee in 1929, an event originally conceived by General Electric (GE) as "an investment in good public relations" to honor Thomas Alva Edison, the inventor of the incandescent light bulb. GE was then currently under criticism in Congress for its monopolistic practices in lamp manufacture. Westinghouse was also brought into the promotion. GE had neglected to consult Edison about its plans, according to Bernays. "They asked him to play the part they had assigned to him." Edison would have none of this — he had been stung in business dealings with both GE and Westinghouse. Edison appealed to his longtime friend Henry Ford, the auto magnate. Bernays had been retained by GE to "explore ways of demonstrating the contribution the electric light had made to society." Bernays carried on a year-long campaign of publicity, but the main news attraction came in Dearborn on October 21 under Ford's direction and auspices. Ford somewhat reluctantly — given his anti-Semitic views—permitted Bernays to share the press responsibilities for the Dearborn event with Ford's publicist, W. J. Cameron, editor of the notorious *Dearborn Independent*.

Thomas Edison was a highly revered figure in America in those years. Ford was a fervent admirer; on his Greenfield Village in Dearborn he had built the Edison Institute of Technology (a replica of Independence Hall) in honor of Edison. The anniversary was celebrated for months throughout the world in events leading up to October 21. The post office issued a 2¢-stamp in honor of the electric light, a coup for which Bernays took only slight credit. "We merely wrote the Post Office on our letterhead." "I planned elaborate activity that would develop cumulative support for the Jubilee and give almost everyone a chance to participate." George M. Cohan wrote a song in tribute to Edison. A press bureau and speakers bureaus were set up by Bernays to pump out the publicity.

But it was Henry Ford's program at Dearborn that captured worldwide publicity. At Ford's invitation, President Hoover dedicated the replica Edison Institute early in the day. The culminating banquet starred Hoover, Ford, Edison, Harvey Firestone, Madame Curie, and other celebrities on the dias. At the climax of the dinner, Edison spoke to a worldwide audience over the relatively new medium, radio.

The upshot of all this hoopla was great praise of Bernays as a propagandist. Scholar Leonard Doob termed the show "one of the most lavish pieces of propaganda ever engineered in this country in peacetime." In a profile of Bernays in *The Atlantic Monthly* 3 years later, John T. Flynn wrote:

> On October 21, 1929, there occurred the climax of a celebration ostensibly to commemorate Edison's invention of the incandescent lamp. Edison re-enacted this procedure before a distinguished audience in Detroit which included Henry Ford and the President of the United States. Before and after the event praises of Edison were sung all over the world . . . Henry Ford constructed the village in which Edison was born and the original laboratory where the invention had been conceived was reproduced as faithfully as possible. On the surface a truly great man was being honored by a great industrialist. As a matter of fact, Mr. Bernays was the man who managed and directed the series of dramatic episodes. He was working "not for Edison or for Henry Ford, but for very important interest which saw in this historic anniversary to exploit and publicize the uses of the electric light." [General Electric]

Typical of this unending publicity on the "classic" was Stanley Walker's observation in his book, *City Editor*:

> There was, for example, Light's Golden Jubilee. The story of Edison's invention was retold. To Dearborn went Edison, Henry Ford and even the President of the United States as well as a great crowd of other important

figures. It was not Mr. Ford's show, or Edison's, or even the President's. It was simply a publicity stunt pulled off by Bernays, representing powerful and rich interests, to exploit the uses of the electric light. Newspaper editors who might have understood this may have felt sad — but what could they do about it?

An interesting aside: *The New Yorker* in reporting on the Jubilee eschewed the term public relations counsel, referring to Bernays instead as "a specialist in making news events."

In his comprehensive and illuminating book on Henry Ford's pioneering uses of publicity to break out of the early automobile pack, *The Public Image of Henry Ford*, David Lewis cast an entirely different light on Bernays's role in Light's Golden Jubilee. Lewis wrote:

> The event naturally received worldwide publicity. The press was handled by [W. J.] Cameron [Ford's publicist] and Edward L. Bernays, a publicist who had been retained by General Electric to dramatize "Light's Golden Jubilee" during 1929. In later years many writers, in discussing the jubilee [which has become a public relations classic) have greatly magnified Bernays' role in the Dearborn celebration.

> Other authors have claimed that Bernays arranged for Ford to reconstruct the press and, in fact, he would have had nothing to do with the Dearborn celebration had not Ford, who had obtained Edison's promise to attend the dedication of the village on October 21, permitted General Electric to tie in the jubilee with the Ford ceremony. It was Ford's show, and it was he who issued the invitations to the prominent guests. The Edison project was begun before anyone in Dearborn had ever heard of Bernays.

> The publicist as a matter of fact incurred Ford's wrath after the dedicatory party arrived in Dearborn because he tried repeatedly to inject himself into the group picture with Hoover, Edison and the host. Ford took Fred Black aside and told him to "get Bernays the hell out of here or I'll have Harry Bennett's men throw him over the fence." Black told Bernays of the threat and he moved out of camera range.

Again, Bernays forgot who the client was. Little wonder that *Editor & Publisher*, a constant critic of the new public relations practitioners, editorialized about Bernays as "the most audacious, blatant, ponderous, insistent of the self-styled public relations counsel 'profession.' "

GEORGE WASHINGTON HILL AND THE GREEN BALL

In the mid-1920s as the cigarette marketing wars heated up, Edward Bernays first worked for Liggett & Myers, makers of Chesterfields, and then for the stormy, eccentric George Washington Hill at American Tobacco Company, maker of Lucky Strikes. In later years when the damages to a person from cigarette smoke became clear, Bernays would regret this work.

Bernays' counsel was first sought by Liggett & Myers (L&M). R. L. Strobridge of the Newell Emmet advertising agency told Bernays, "American has cut in on Chesterfield's sales. Liggett & Myers have never tried public relations before. I've persuaded them to make a trial run. Would you handle L&M on a six-month basis?" Bernays agreed to a 6-month contract for $8,000 because "the challenge of pitting my experience against a company that annually spent millions in advertising . . . proved too great to resist." Bernays rarely turned down any account.

Bernays decided not to try to match George Washington Hill's millions being spent on advertising but to a slash at Lucky Strikes through ridicule. "I speculated that if the newspapers that carried Luckies' advertising were to ridicule this same advertising in their news and editorial columns, the advertising impact would be weakened." He sought out an old friend, Henry Bern whom he knew would enjoy the publicity, to head a front, Tobacco Society for Voice Culture, Inc. "to awaken the public's appreciation of the numerous commercial organizations that do us good." A New York judge refused to incorporate the society, dismissing it as "frivolous," much to Bernays' delight because this refusal got the spoof organization the desired publicity. He then persuaded a New Jersey judge to approve the incorporation. Bernays' campaign was aimed at the then Lucky Strike campaign, directed by Albert Lasker of Lord & Thomas, picturing Metropolitan Opera stars endorsing Luckies "because they are kind to your throat."

Lord & Thomas made Lucky Strikes the best-selling cigarette, and American Tobacco Company made Lord & Thomas and Albert Lasker very wealthy. By the end of the 1920s, Lucky Strike brought in more business than all other Lasker clients combined; 58% of the company billings came from George Washington Hill, the shrewd but difficult tycoon of American Tobacco. Prior to World War I, it was thought a sign of being effeminate for men to smoke; real men chewed tobacco or smoked cigars. World War I brought cigarettes into vogue for men. After Lasker had taken Hill as a client, another client, Paul Hoffman then with Studebaker, told Lasker, "If you can get women to smoke you can double your market." Lasker set out to do exactly that—with lasting ill effects for the women of America. He was spurred to action when his then wife, Flora, lit up a cigarette in a Chicago restaurant, and the manager told them that they would have to move to a private dining room if she wanted to smoke. Lasker was furious. He determined to break the taboo against women smoking in pubic—and make American Tobacco Co. millions in the process. Thus, he conceived the idea of getting famous Metropolitan singers to give testimonials with slogans like "Cigarettes Are Kind to Your Throat" and "I Protect my Precious Voice With Lucky Strikes."

This became Bernays' point of attack. Henry Bern sent a letter to all newspapers that read in part:

> In these days of tooth, booze, and breath control, we wish to call your attention to a new movement—a CAUSE—may we say a CRUSADE? It is the Tobacco Society for Voice Culture which has been incorporated in New Jersey.
>
> We are told daily that we should smoke cigarettes not because they are good, but because they are good for us, that a cigarette is not a pleasure, but medicine.
>
> The Tobacco Society for Voice Culture will establish a home for singers and actors whose voices have cracked under the strain of their cigarette testimonials.

The publicity caught on. "Our campaign penetrated to many places." This was true enough that the nettled George Washington Hill used a front, David A. Schulte of the Schulte Cigar Stores in New York, to woo Bernays away from L&M. Schulte called Bernays to come to his tower apartment one night and there offered him a $25,000-a-year retainer with the provision that he could work for no other tobacco company. He accepted after being told by Liggett & Myers that it would not make a year's commitment. For the next 9 months, he received only an occasional call from Schulte asking for advice. Nine months later, Bernays was summoned by Hill, whom he labeled "Advertising's Holy Terror," and then was told that Hill's private detectives had learned that he was behind the spoofing of Lucky Strike's current ad campaign and that Schulte had fronted for Hill in retaining Bernays. "You've been on my payroll nine months." Hill bragged to the startled young counselor. This was in 1928. Only later did Bernays learn that Ivy Lee's firm had been retained by Hill a year earlier.

Bernays wrote in his memoirs, "One day at lunch with Ivy Lee, I casually mentioned my client, American Tobacco. 'Your client!' Lee exclaimed. 'American Tobacco is our client.' To our astonishment it was true." Neither of the men had known of the other's work for Hill. When Bernays had the temerity to ask Hill about this, he replied, "If you are both working for me, then neither of you can be working for competitors."

T. J. Ross's version of this unusual situation of a client retaining two major public relations firms was discussed in the previous chapter. In that chapter, a letter from Ross to your author made it clear that the Ivy Lee-Ross Firm held the account as late as 1960, 26 years after Bernays lost his retainer. The reason for his loss of this account is told in a moment. T. J. "Tommy" Ross was the first Lee account executive on the American Tobacco Co. account, a relationship described in the previous chapter.

Over the next 6 years, Bernays joined in Hill's effort to make Lucky Strikes the dominant cigarette in the market. Hill, an irascible genius, ran American Tobacco sales from $153 million a year to $558 million in 20 years. He spared no expense on advertising or public relations. Bernays' first efforts for Hill focused on the slogan, "Reach for a Lucky Instead of a Sweet." He got a young photographer friend, Nickols Muray, to send a letter to influential photographers praising slender women who lit cigarettes instead of eating sweets and asking their support for the ideal of slimness. When his story was sent to the newspapers, photographers and artists took their cue from Muray and "the public soon became more oriented toward slenderness," a fetish that has driven women from that day to this. The sugar industry reacted bitterly. At Bernays' urging, Hill hired a doctor to make a study of the scientific literature showing the effects of excessive sugar use on the human body. In December 1928, Hill asked Bernays to devise a plan to support the new advertising campaign stressing moderation, a modification of the "Reach for a Lucky" theme. Bernays enlisted the Ziegfield Follies beauties in his scheme. They were brought to the Ritz--Carlton Hotel where they pledged themselves to moderation and organized the Ziegfield Contour, Curve, and Charm Club. When the Follies toured the country, "moderation" became part of its publicity pattern.

One of Bernays' celebrated feats for Hill was the "torches of freedom" march down Fifth Avenue on Easter Sunday, 1930. A psychoanalyst had given Bernays the idea. Dr. A. A. Brill had advised him that some women regarded cigarettes as symbols of freedom. With due fanfare, including large ads in the New York papers, Bernays paraded 10 young debutantes lighting "torches of freedom" on Fifth Avenue as a protest against women's inequality. Predictably, this caused a national debate and received wide attention. He recounted, "Front page stories in newspapers reported the freedom march in words and pictures. For weeks after the event editorials praised or condemned the young women who had paraded against the smoking taboo." The wire services carried the story to all the big cities, and he boasted as late as 1984 "women across the country were lighting up in public." A few weeks later, a Broadway theater let women inside its heretofore men's smoking room. Bernays told a St. Petersburg Times reporter in February 1984 that if he had known then what he knew now, he would never have participated in this effort to make smoking in public for women respectable. And for good reason!

What Bernays thought was a great idea, one extolled at length in his memoirs, cost him the American Tobacco account in 1934. Hill's drive to get women to smoke and thus double his market knew no limits. One day, he called Bernays to his office and said, "Women aren't buying Luckies as they should. What do you suggest Mr. Bernays?" (Their relationship was always a formal one: Mr. Hill and Mr. Bernays.) Bernays replied, "Change the color of your package to a neutral color that will match anything women wear." Hill thought this lousy advice, so Bernays' next suggestion was to popularize the Lucky green for women's wear. He came up with the idea of a Green Ball. He approached Mrs. Frank A. Vanderlip, an influential leader and philanthropist in New York City, with the idea of staging a Green Ball to raise money for a favorite charity of hers, the Woman's Infirmary of New York. She accepted.

Bernays explained that an anonymous sponsor would pay the costs and that he would donate his services to promote the event. Next he persuaded the Onondaga Silk Company to bet on the color green. The company's president, Philip Vogelman, gave a "Green Fashions Fall" luncheon that spring for fashion editors and fashion trades at the Waldorf–Astoria to persuade style setters to adopt the Lucky green as the fall color. The luncheon menus were printed on green paper and the food was colored green. Bernays next organized a Color Fashion Bureau — another front — to spew out endless releases.

To obtain the support of Paris designers, Bernays persuaded Mrs. Vanderlip to go to Paris, where Bernays' agent arranged a tea for Mrs. Vanderlip and 40 top French designers plus the editors of *Vogue* and *Harper's Bazaar*, fashion trend setters for American women. Finally, a consultant was hired to handle the mechanics of the ball. "Debutantes flocked to her call; society editors followed her lead." As early as August, the *New York Herald-Tribune* carried a full page headlined: "CHARITY BENEFIT TO STRESS FASHION IMPORTANCE OF GREEN." The dress rehearsals attracted the Hearst and Universal newsreels. Bernays claimed in his memoirs: "Happily, the ball was a great success, from the social fashion standpoint, and it firmly established green's pre-dominance." Bernays did not attend the ball — but Hill did.

According to one writer, the crusty Hill "couldn't see, count, smell or taste what his $30,000 had purchased. He promptly dropped Bernays and returned to his own milieu." In his book, *The Super Salesmen*, Edwin P. Hoyt wrote, "He [G. W. Hill] made some phenomenal mistakes, such as the attempt in 1934 to try to promote the color green in New York as a tie-in for Lucky Strike advertising. He hired a public relations man [Bernays] and gave $30,000 anonymously to promote a charity ball, which would be called the Green Ball. . . . He wanted to establish green that year as the color for women's fashions. *He failed dismally*." Another account lost — this one after 7 years.

Ironically, in his autobiography, Bernays wrote, "I followed a principle I later termed the engineering of consent. Like an architect, I drew up a comprehensive blueprint, a complete procedural outline, detailing objectives, the necessary research, strategy, themes and timing of the planned activities. I wanted to be sure the money Hill had authorized was spent effectively."

GETS FINGERS BURNED IN LANDMARK GE CASE

Bernays became involved in a landmark labor case, *General Electric v. the International Union of Electrical, Radio, and Machine Workers* (IUE) in the early 1960s and came away with his expertise on propaganda in question. The case involved whether GE's employee communications to employees during an IUE strike constituted an unfair labor practice under the Taft–Hartley Act. The case was heard by a trial examiner for the National Labor Relations Board (NLRB) who ruled against GE. Looking at the totality of conduct, the examiner ruled General Electric had "flooded employees with a constant stream of communications plugging the merits of its bargaining position." General Electric appealed first to U.S. District Court and then to the U.S. Court of Appeals for the Second Circuit. Both courts upheld the NLRB ruling that GE had engaged in an unfair labor practice when it combined "take or leave it" bargaining methods with a widely publicized stand of unbending firmness through its communications.

To bolster its case before the NLRB, the IUE retained Bernays as an expert on propaganda. Bernays testified that he had been retained by IUE to review General Electric communications and to make a "content analysis" or "propaganda analysis" of the material. The hearings of the first week in November 1961 were largely devoted to cross examination of Bernays' earlier testimony. He was on the stand from Tuesday through Thursday of that week. He stated that he made his content analysis by studying the communications context (which he defined as grammar, words, and organization of material), the situational context (which he defined as who says what to whom and under which circumstances), and the behavioral context (which he defined as what the writer's purpose was in communicating).

As the cross-examination proceeded, it became apparent that at least as far of Bernays' study of the situational context was concerned, his analysis was open to question. He testified that he studied IUE communications of Pittsfield in addition to GE publications but later conceded that all he had been shown by IUE attorney, Benjamin Siggal, were 14 IUE documents, all but 1 of which were issued in the strike period. He admitted that he had been given no documents issued in the prenegotiations period; neither had he been given copies of IUE's nationally distributed *IUE News* or other IUE booklets to review. He also testified that he had been given a number of IUE handbills that Attorney Siggal had assured him was a "representative sample" of IUE's propaganda.

Under the pressing questions of GE's attorney's, Bernays also admitted that his "analysis" of the situation had not included either an inspection of what was being said about negotiations in the public press in Pittsfield, what was actually happening in the 1960 negotiations in the public press in Pittsfield, what was actually happening in the 1960 negotiations, or the nature of the previous relationship between the company and the IUE. Bernays brushed aside these omissions, stating that none of these had any bearing on his ability to inspect General Electric's communications and determine from them the company's motivation and the probable effect on employees. In its *Employee Relations News* of November 8, 1961, GE editorialized, "Mr. Bernays stands virtually alone in his contention that either intent or effect of communications can be judged without considering the situation in which communication occurred." Experienced counselors know that the context into which communication is received weighs heavily on that communication's interpretation by the receiver.

Not content with its somewhat devastating cross-examination, GE brought to the stand two other communication experts to repudiate Bernays' testimony. The first, Dr. Charles W. Redding, director of the Communications Research Center at Purdue University, testified the first week in January 1962. Dr. Redding told the trial examiner that the intent of the communicator cannot be judged or determined by studying only the *content* of communications, and that no authority in the field would agree that it was possible to do so. Dr. Redding said that scholars have agreed that there are six factors which must be considered in any competent communications study before valid conclusions can be reached as to either intent or effect. Finally, he said, most studies also consider the actual effects—both immediate and long-term—of the communications. Dr. Redding was emphatic in saying that "Bernays is not considered to be an expert in the field of communication study by other scholars in the field, adding, "that he had heard of Bernays as only a public relations man."

The third week in January 1962, Professor Redding returned to the stand to face cross-examination by IUE Attorney Sigal. Throughout 4 hours of questioning, Mr. Sigal failed to shake Dr. Redding's testimony on what he termed the irresponsible nature of the study made by Bernays. Among the reasons cited by the communications expert was that an analysis, if conducted on a scientific basis by a qualified analyst, would have required a minimum of 150 hours of study. Bernays earlier had testified that his study took a total of 40 hours. Citing paragraphs from Bernays' testimony, Dr. Redding contended that Bernays had used merely an "impressionistic" approach and avoided detailed tabulation in his analysis.

Not satisfied with Redding's rebuttal, GE brought to the stand in early February 1962 Dr. Sebastian De Grazia, professor of political science at Rutgers University, who characterized Bernays' study of the General Electric communications as "biased, amateurish, and worthless." Under further questioning, Dr. De Grazia, who served as chief of propaganda analysis of the Federal Communications Commission during World War II, testified that he considered both Bernays' method and conclusions biased because Bernays had set up his categories on the basis of preconceived inferences as to the company's intent in issuing these communications and had then selected only examples that supported these inferences while ignoring examples that were contrary to these preconceived assumptions. As to Bernays' categories (e.g., "Big Lie," "Slanted News," "Name Calling," "Divide and Conquer"), Dr. De Grazia testified that these weren't categories at all but were "charges and accusations."

A former student, then working for General Electric Public Relations, wrote "I am delighted to see 'seat of the pants' research refuted." However vigorously Bernays's IUE study was refuted by more expert witnesses, the fact remains that the NLRB and the courts found GE's communications to constitute an unfair labor practice. In sum, Bernays' reputation as an expert on propaganda was badly dented, if not destroyed.

BERNAYS AND THE PROFESSION

In his some 70 years as a public relations counselor, Bernays progressed from being shunned by his fellow pioneers to being lionized in his late years by a later generation of practitioners who saw him more as a legend than as a competitor. It was a long and sometimes bumpy road he traveled to being hailed and feted as a public relations pioneer. As a mutual friend wrote to me in 1992, "He is still going strong and still collecting awards. Amazing what the combination of good genes and a strong ego can do." Though past 100 years of age, Bernays was insisting in late 1991 that he was still consulting with clients.

Bernays, along with several other pioneer practitioners, early realized the need for a professional organization to set standards and provide a guide on ethics of this new calling. In 1923—the same year Bernays wrote *Crystallizing Public Opinion*—R. H. Wilder and K. L. Buell in their book, *Publicity*, observed that a major obstacle to professional status was the lack of adequate checks on the honesty and behavior of press agents. Three years later, Roger William Riis—son of the noted social reformer, Jacob Riis—and his partner, Charles Bonner, in their book, *Publicity*, published in 1926, urged the establishment of a national publicity association to purge the many "jackals" who were tainting the "profession." They advocated that such an association formulate and enforce a code of ethics.

In 1927, a year later, steps were taken to form such an organization. At a meeting of the Advertising Club on March 23 in New York City, a committee to professionalize public relations was set up. Of the 13 members, 11 were from corporations or trade associations – a reflection how the new function was being accepted. Edward Bernays was named chairman of the committee; the only other independent counselor on the committee was Ivy Lee. Bernays' eagerness for publicity and self-glorification brought this organizational effort to an abrupt halt. A story he released to *Editor & Publisher* was carried in its April 2, 1927, issue under the heading "PLANNING TO 'PROFESSIONALIZE' PRESS AGENTRY" turned off the other independents. This Bernays admitted in our March 12, 1959, interview:

> In the twenties we undertook to organize publicity men but a full-page story in *Editor & Publisher* killed the activity because *Editor & Publisher* was strongly against publicity for reasons of their own. However, it was not this conclusion of *E&P* that affected the next situation; it was rather the fact, I think, that in the article the major attention was given to me. . . . Everybody seemed to be so jealous of the major publicity that had been given to me that the group folded up and was never heard from again.

William H. Baldwin, who had opened his public relations office just the year before, confirmed this in our many conversations, "Eddie's desire for publicity killed that early effort to organize."

The hostile full-page story in *Editor & Publisher* on Bernays' effort to organize the growing band of practitioners in the 1920s was predictable – *E&P*, under the editorship of Marlen E. Pew, was an unrelenting foe of publicists whom it saw as cheating newspapers out of advertising through their "puffery." In an editorial of September 15, 1928, *E&P* asserted, "No matter what virtuous men Mr. Bernays or Mr. Ivy Lee or other professional propagandists may be, the device they seek to establish in public life is dangerous because it is irresponsible and calculated to break down advertising practice, which responds to checks and balances evolved from experience and conscience of a century."

As is made clear in chapter 12, Bill Baldwin was a man of great integrity and thus deeply concerned about the ethics or their lack in the young vocation of public relations. He took the lead in organizing the National Association of Accredited Publicity Directors (NAAPD) in 1936. The group was composed only of New York City-based practitioners; obviously the words "national" and "accredited" were used loosely. Bernays was purposely excluded from this association.

Baldwin acknowledge Bernays' role as an articulate exponent of public relations but the latter's tireless self-promotion offended Baldwin's New England conscience." In fact, the NAAPD had a rule that when a member mentioned Bernays, he had to drop a quarter in a pot. The money was used to buy drinks at the end of the year. Roger William Riis, another pioneer publicity man active in the 1920s, once wrote William Baldwin that the two persons he distrusted most were Edward L. Bernays and Ben Sonnenberg, who is profiled in chapter 13.

Bernays gave this account of the origins of the National Association of Accredited Publicity Directors in our 1959 interview:

> To give you an indication of the interest in public relations in the 1930s, let me relate this incident to you: A man announced himself as an individual who promoted trade associations. I saw him and he told me he was promoting a publicity association and he wanted me to be president of it. I asked him what his profit would be and he said his organization acted as secretary of organizations he helped form. I told him that I was not interested in treating the field on such a basis. That did not deter him and he organized the National Association of Publicity Directors [sic]. I did not want to be a part of any such promotion then, now, or ever, for I do not think that this is the way to develop a professional organization that has criteria of education, skill, know-how and character as a basis for joining.

Bernays made another effort to organize a professional group when he organized the Council on Public Opinion by inviting a number of prominent leaders to dinner at his home in Manhattan in January 1938. Again, he promptly publicized the group in a memo to *Time* magazine, which reported in its January 24, 1938, issue: "Around a dinner table in Manhattan frequently gather some 20 of the top propagandists in the U. S. This unpublicized high-powered group calls itself the Council on Public Opinion. Chairman is the Nation's No. 1 publicist, dark Machiavellian Edward L. Bernays." Among those included was John W. Hill, who had opened his New York office only 5 years before. Hill was offended by the *Time* publicity because to Hill, it was made to appear that other New York counselors were sitting at Bernays' feet as though he were the oracle of public relations. Hill, as is described in chapter 15, did gain two things out of his meeting with the Bernays group—a lifelong friendship with Claude Robinson, pioneer pollster, and the idea for The Wisemen, an elite group of counselors organized by Hill that continues to this day. Bernays' council was short lived. Bernays was never invited to be a member of the Wisemen. He was public relations' loner until late in life.

Bernays was caustic in his criticism of Dr. Rex Harlow, one of the field's pioneers and a prime promoter of its professionalism. Professor Harlow founded the American Council on Public Relations in 1939 as an association of West Coast counselors and in that organization started *The Public Relations Journal* that today is published by the Public Relations Society of America. (The Public Relations Society of America was formed in 1948 by merging the National Association of Accredited Publicity Directors and the American Council on Public Relations. A Washington-based organization of practitioners, the American Public Relations Association, was merged into PRSA in 1961.) Of Harlow, Bernays said this:

> In 1939, there was another incident in the development of public relations which, looking back, I deplore today. Another promoter [Harlow] saw there was something in public relations that he might profit from. He arranged to get space at Leland Stanford University, promoting a course in Public Relations. He wrote to me and Harwood Childs at Princeton University about a summer course at Stanford. He offered us an honorium of $1,000. I accepted because I thought that the University was tied up with the course. Actually, the University had no real relationship to the course. The promoter sold tickets to businessmen on the basis of the reputation of the people he had asked to come out. I went through with the lectures at Stanford University, Reed College in Portland, Oregon, and the University of Washington, Seattle. The promoter [Harlow] thought he would cash in on the interest we had created. . . . When I came East, I found he had carried through his promotion and formed The American Council on Public Relations. But all this is back in the 1930s, and is today relatively ancient history.

From the time the Public Relations Society was organized in 1948 until late in his life, Bernays would have nothing to do with this principal organization of practitioners. In response to my question, Bernays wrote in a letter dated November 29, 1975, "As for PRSA, I have never attended a meeting of this group. In fact, I was a member of the organization for only one year as a gesture of goodwill to a good friend. . . . I firmly believe and still do that the organization should from its start have required the highest standards of character and professionalism of its prospective members. But that was not in the cards for PRSA because the organization depended upon numbers for its existence."

Even though he had stubbornly refused to join the Public Relations Society of America, he was invited to address its 1965 annual conference in Washington, DC. He told PRSA members that they should adopt more rigid standards of membership: "The reputable practicing professional should have as much idealism as the lawyer who seeks justice, the architect who is looking to make the best building. The public relations man should seek to serve the coincidence of public and private interest in terms of social goals." Bernays exhorted the some 1500 PRSA members to have standards for public relations at a level with other professions, requiring examinations as to character and ability, a thought he repeated in many places over many years.

In our interview in 1959, he explained why he thought the Public Relations Society of America was on the wrong track.

> For an organization to be professional, it first has to treat itself as an art applied to science, in which pecuniary motivation is not the primary element. Since there is no state licensing of public relations people, practically anyone can call himself or herself a public relations man or woman. It seems to me that under such conditions, for the profession to grow professionally, it must grow from small beginnings with high standards, rather than emerging big with the promotion object of the association being fulfillment of somebody's profit motive in promotion.

LICENSURE

A critical point of dispute between Bernays and the professionals in the Public Relations Society of America was the issue of licensure of practitioners to separate the competent practitioners from the inept and the charlatans. The last several decades of Bernays' life was spent in a tireless advocacy of licensure. This campaign started in earnest at the conclusion of his talk before the Independent Citizens' Committee of the Arts, Sciences, and Professions at the Waldorf–Astoria on June 23, 1945. After his talk, Bernays proposed the following motion that was adopted unanimously:

> Because our complex civilization demands professional counsel on public relations in order that there may be a better integration between the component parts of our society, we propose that courses on public relations in our universities be extended, that public relations men and women organize a professional group with high standards of social responsibility and that the state provide legal safeguards so that all who practice the profession by the title "counsel on public relations" have the qualifications of character and learning which society demands.

Bernays dreamed for the day when public relations would take its place alongside the older professions of law and medicine and argued that state licensing was essential to this goal. Writing in the *IPRA Review* of September 1977, he argued:

> Public relations will fulfill its greatest function when its practitioners are trained in education and experience to practice their profession. In this writer's judgment, this can be done only if everywhere the profession takes its place with the older professions and supports and acquires registration and

licensing by the state, as a protection to profession and public alike. . . . Only through state registration and licensing can the public relations profession protect all society against possible present-day and future abuses of those who call themselves public relations practitioners and really are not.

In contrast, the Public Relations Society of America has thoroughly debated this issue several times in the past 15 years, and each time the membership has voted against seeking state registration and licensure for their work. The PRSA answer is its voluntary Accreditation Program, based on years of experience and passage of a fairly rigorous examination. The PRSA position fails to recognize that codes of behavior will lack effective means of enforcement until there is legal certification of practitioners dependent on passage of an examination based on a prescribed body of knowledge. PRSA further fails to recognize that controlled access that licensure would provide is the *sina qua non* of an established profession. Voluntary codes do not do this.

In 1981, Bernays argued, "In the entire history of professions, licensing standards and criteria and finally codes of ethics in public conduct have been necessary . . . to exclude those who are not properly qualified." PRSA opponents of licensure argue that state licensing would impair the practitioner's right of free speech guaranteed by the First Amendment, a specious argument. More difficult is the state's requirement that for a group to qualify for state registration and licensure, it must demonstrate a "compelling public interest." This criterion might be more difficult for practitioners to meet. That licensure would *professionalize* the field gets short shrift in law. Licensing cannot be imposed simply to benefit a particular group. Such efforts are often seen by the courts as efforts to "fence" persons out of a particular vocation or calling. Nonetheless, Bernays was adamant on this subject in his zeal to see public relations recognized as a profession, a cause to which he contributed much with his writings and frequent speeches.

EDUCATION

Bernays also saw a sound and proper education as the basis of professionalism in public relations. To promote his new book, *Crystallizing Public Opinion* and further spread the word of what he saw as a new profession, Bernays persuaded New York University's Department of Journalism, then headed by Professor James Melvin Lee, to let him offer a course in public relations, a first he repeatedly recounted. This was the first university course to be labeled *public relations* but it was not the first university course to deal with this emerging vocation. The first effort to teach publicity techniques at the college level came at the University of Illinois in 1920. It was taught by Joseph P. Wright, the university's newly appointed publicity director. Wright wrote the author in a letter dated April 15, 1961, "I thought if more people learned that an honest publicity man—at least in the educational area—dished out news and not propaganda, the climate for my work might be improved." In sum, the desire to bring prestige to the new calling and win his acceptance on a campus where the faculty were highly suspicious of this new function, prompted Wright's pioneer course.

Of his pioneering effort to introduce the subject on the university level—where today it is widely taught—Bernays wrote in a letter dated March 9, 1959, "The original course I taught in 1924 [sic]. It was the first course at any American University. They made me an adjunct professor in 1949, but I resigned my professorship because the boys were interested in only the 'fast buck' and not in theory and an abstract approach to the subject." Or perhaps it was the voluble professor's high-flown theorizing and philosophizing that dulled the students' interest. Bernays taught the one-semester credit course for 2 years, 1923 and 1924.

Bernays' interest in seeking a strong professional education never flagged, even in his declining years. For years he advocated a separate school or department in a university for public relations education, a plea most educators found unrealistic. An article in *Advertising Age* of February 21, 1944, about Bernays stated this:

> Bernays, often called U. S. Publicist No. 1, had not only developed a far more profound concept of public relations, but has pioneered in establishing fellowships at American universities to carry forward the study of public relations . . . It is Mr. Bernays' hope that from the studies of the men and women holding these fellowships will come a body of interpretive material which will help orient public relations thinking of the men in charge of our destinies in the postwar period.

The Centennial Celebration of Bernays' birthday was a vehicle for raising scholarship funds in his name at Boston University, where he frequently lectured after moving to Cambridge in 1961. His support of education and educators was constant. In his twilight years, Bernays' support of public relations education in general and his specific support of Boston University's School of Public Communication after he moved to Cambridge in 1961 were recognized when that university awarded him the honorary doctorate of Humane Letters. Ohio University also awarded him its Honor Award for his work.

IN 1971 THE LIONIZING BEGINS

On November 5, 1971, Bernays, responding to the urging of the PRSA's leadership, joined the profession's major organization, an organization that he had disdainfully refused to participate in after a one-year token membership in 1948. This marked a string of fetes and honors that lasted for two decades. In 1976, Bernays was awarded PRSA's Gold Anvil, its highest award for distinguished service to public relations. He was also given the status of APR — Accredited in Public relations — without examination, an exception made by PRSA only to one other person. As a Gold Anvil winner, Bernays was included in the original class of PRSA Fellows, organized in 1990. The PRSA Fellows, an elite group of that society, celebrated his 100th birthday with a dinner in Phoenix, Arizona, early in November 1991. This was followed by the elaborate Edward L. Bernays Centennial Jubilee in Cambridge later that month, described at the outset of chapter 7. In fact, Bernays' birthdays have been oft celebrated, almost as often as the celebration of the founding of *Public Relations News*.

In 1961, Arthur Pell, president of Liveright Publishing Corp. and Bernays' publisher, organized a celebration of Bernays' 70th birthday in November 1961. This event coincided with the republication of *Crystallizing Public Opinion*. Prior to the celebration, Pell wrote a long list of persons identified with public relations a letter requesting a letter of congratulations to Bernays. Pell wrote, "I am writing to some distinguished Americans to ask for a statement of comment or appreciation concerning the significance of Edward L. Bernays' contribution to the world-wide understanding of the importance of public opinion." Pell's letter included a plug for the Bernays' book as "still the standard authority on the basic concepts, principles, ethics and practices of public relations." *Editor & Publisher*, once Bernays' nemesis, reported, "Edward L. Bernays celebrated his 70th birthday November 22 at City Hall, New York. In the presence of his wife and a few friends, he received the Medallion of Honor of the city as 'U.S. Publicist No 1.,' " a tag pinned on him much earlier by *Time* and one that he used until the end. *Editor & Publisher* saw the event as "a case of PR for a paradox, in that Mr. Bernays had reached this summit of his career as a man of contradictions."

In 1981, a Committee of Ninety, headed by Paul A. Newsom, organized a gala reception and luncheon at the Harvard Club of Boston on Bernays' 90th birthday. Invitations asked the recipient to "join us in celebrating this remarkable milestone in the life of a remarkable man." Remarkable indeed!

The birthday celebration routine was repeated when Bernays reached his 95th year. A Committee of Ninety-Five of leading figures in public relations and civic affairs sponsored a reception and luncheon at the New Marriott Hotel in Cambridge on November 22, 1986.

Countless other honors continued to come his way in his glory years. In 1975, the Distinguished Award of the National Public Relations Council (NPRC) of Health and Welfare Agencies were presented to Bernays at a ceremony in Cambridge. The plaque, presented by NPRC President

Carlton Spitzer, read: "To Edward L. Bernays for his lifelong pioneering efforts in shaping modern communications and public relations to serve human needs." In May 1981, the Publicity Club of Chicago presented Bernays with its Golden Trumpet Award, which the club states recognizes "the highest professional standards in publicity and public relations." Bernays responded with a major address "Yesterday, Today and Tomorrow" that was reprinted and widely distributed.

Bernays was not the retiring type in more ways than one. On March 30, 1987, he wrote to me vehemently denying a statement in the sixth edition of *Effective Public Relations* that he had "retired." He wrote, "In the matter of truth and accuracy this statement is incorrect. I know there will be additional editions of your book, so please know that I am actively engaged in public relations at age 95. And that since I moved to Cambridge in 1961, we have had some of the most intriguing clients, including the U.S. State Department, the U.S. Department of Health, Education, and Welfare, and Massachusetts Law Association." He continued a vigorous program of speaking and writing to the very end.

Like Madam Schuman-Heink, Bernays made a series of "farewell tours." These celebrations and fetes gave him an opportunity for even more publicity. Some examples are: Miami area newspapers were headlining in September 1984, "The Father of PR to speak at FAU" when Bernays gave a lecture at Florida Atlantic University on marketing and public opinion. The *Miami Herald* headlined the next day, September 11, "The father of PR lectures his offspring." The story's lead read: "So far as anyone knows, he was the first bona fide public relations counselor," and continued, "He represented four U.S. presidents, numerous titans of industry, and cultural legends such as singer Enrico Caruso and dancer Vaslav Nijinsky. Sigmund Freud was his uncle. Thomas Edison a client." Of such half-truths a reputation was built.

The *Chicago Tribune* of Monday, October 29, 1984, carried a two-column UPI story from New Orleans where Bernays spoke and was widely interviewed. The UPI lead read: "At 93, Edward L. Bernays, author, philosopher, and 'father of public relations' has the longevity and laurels to do little or nothing at all. Yet the Vienna-born nephew of Sigmund Freud often strayed from his Cambridge, Massachusetts, home to dispense pungent opinions on the industry he created, help young inventors market their products, and even visit a struggling world's fair. . . . He is campaigning vigorously against mandatory retirement."

In the spring of 1985, at the age of 93, Bernays undertook a speaking tour of the Southwest to enhance his legend in that part of the nation. The *Tulsa World* of April 28, 1985, carried an extensive interview with reporter Lane Kelley, headlined: "EDWARD L. BERNAYS: 'THE FATHER OF

MODERN PUBLIC RELATIONS.' " It emphasized his usual patter: "He had promoted four U. S. Presidents, the lectures of Sigmund Freud, the memoirs of Eleanor Roosevelt, the voice of Enrico Caruso, and the ballet genius of Nijinsky. He also turned American on to daily showers and bananas. His name is Dr. Edward L. Bernays, referred to some as 'the father of public relations.' " Bernays was there to be honored at a luncheon by the Tulsa chapter of the Public Relations Society of America. He went to speak in Dallas where he was honored by the North Texas Chapter of the society. Steve Smith of the *Dallas Times-Herald* in an interview headlined: "THE FATHER OF PUBLIC RELATIONS: AT 93 EDWARD BERNAYS BRIMS WITH HISTORY AND ENERGY." Smith focused on the marvel of a person Bernays's age having his vitality and drive. "What they [the audience] did not expect is a literate little man with unflagging energy, who, at 93, still travels alone. The evening before, he had been up until midnight at a similar appearance in Tulsa, then rose at 5 a.m. to catch a plane to Dallas. . . . His only concession to age was that he liked to grasp the hand of a pretty young female escort while he walked about."

Bernays was a prophet with honor in his own country. In a luncheon interview with David Purcell of the *Christian Science Monitor* of August 28, 1984, Purcell wrote, "Edward L. Bernays, the father of public relations, doesn't like the way his child is growing up. What the errant boy needs, he seems to say, is a better sense of identity and a strong dose of discipline." Once again Bernays is lamenting, after 85 years, "ignorance of what public relations is." This interview included a new claim by Bernays. "He advised the Indian Government under Jawaharial Nehru on adopting a Bill of Rights for its Constitution." Again Bernays repeated his current interest of that moment, "My big projects now are to try to modify American attitudes toward the elderly." Bernays' vigor in his later years was a powerful argument for that cause.

Earlier, in 1980 on the eve of his 80th birthday, the *Boston Globe* carried an extensive interview headlined: "Edward Bernays, 'the father of public relations,' will be 80 next November, a fact that bothers him not at all. He rises each morning at 5 a.m. works pretty much non-stop until about 5 p.m. when 'my wife drags me away.' " Bernays often attributed his longevity to the fact that regularly he skipped lunch and worked right through the day.

In November 1983, as Bernays approached his 91st birthday, Clayton Haswell of the Associated Press did a long interview story that the AP papers — the majority of the nation's press — carried across the nation from Cambridge. The *Milwaukee Journal* headlined Haswell's piece: "A LIFE IN PR: THE 'FATHER OF PUBLIC RELATIONS,' EDWARD L. BERNAYS IS 91 AND THRIVING." The AP encapsulated Bernays many oft-recounted feats:

Without him, the great Caruso might not have become the toast of the land. Sigmund Freud's work might not have been translated for American readers for another decade. A generation of children might have grown up with dirty faces, and a generation of women might have gone on smoking cigarettes behind the shed. His clients included the famous and powerful: Presidents Coolidge, Wilson, Hoover, and Eisenhower; Thomas Edison, Eleanor Roosevelt, and the dancer Nijinsky.

This could be Edward L. Bernays' self-chosen epitaph. Its accuracy can be assessed by what has gone before in these two chapters profiling, albeit more sketchily than he would like, his career that almost spanned the 20th century, from the birth of public relations to its maturity.

NOTES ON SOURCES

This chapter, as did the preceding one, continues to rely heavily on my interviews and correspondence with Bernays, and on his voluminous writings. In addition, the following sources were helpful.

Sally Bedell Smith's excellent biography of William S. Paley, founder of CBS, *In All His Glory*, provided useful information on Bernays' counsel to Paley in CBS' infant years. This book, copyrighted by Sally Bedell Smith, (1990) is quoted with permission of the publisher, Simon & Schuster, Inc.

The General Motors account story is based on T. Stacy Capers' master's thesis, "The Public Relations Career and Philosophy of Paul Garrett," University of Wisconsin, 1964; Garrett's interviews and correspondence with Capers, and with me. Garrett's letter to me is dated December 24, 1963.

The story of the Golden Light Jubilee is based in part on David L. Lewis *"The Public Image of Henry Ford,"* published by the Wayne State University Press (1976), Bernays' writings, etc. The Lewis book is quoted with permission of the publisher. The *New Yorker* quote is from its November 9, 1929, issue.

The Bernays' entry in *Current Biography*, H. W. Wilson Co., Vol. 21, September, 1960, was used in this chapter. Bernays' promotion of velvet is from the "Press Agents" chapter in Will Irwin, *Propaganda and the News*. The assessment of his "Green Ball" project is found in Edwin P. Hoyt, *Super Salesmen*, World Publishing Co., 1962. His "study" for General Electric Co. is reported in GE's employee publication, *GE Employe Relations News*. "Communications Expert Testifies Bernays' Conclusions Not Valid," issue 62-1, January 8, 1962; "Bernays Study Tagged as Not Valid," issue 62-5, February 5, 1962.

The New York Times assessment was in a story of December 30, 1991, C6.

Typical of the "farewell stories," is one by Steve Smith in the *Dallas Times-Herald* May 8, 1985, "Edward L. Bernays Brims With History and Energy." Another may be found in *The Tulsa World* of April 28, 1985. *The Milwaukee Journal* story was published November 14, 1981, Part 1.

Chapter 9

John Price Jones Tries to Ride Two Horses

Like many other public relations counsellors who emerged in the burgeoning of public relations agencies in the wake of World War I, John Price Jones had been schooled in newspaper reporting, advertising, and had gained his public relations spurs in the promotion of Liberty Bond sales to finance the U.S. war effort. He was quick to see after two successful college fund-raising campaigns "that there may be a business in this." Jones launched his firm, John Price Jones, Inc., on November 23, 1919, "to give counsel and service in organization and publicity to business houses, institutions of public, semi-public, and private character, and to individuals." Jones set out to build "a business" in both fund-raising and public relations but was never able to harness the two functions effectively. Jones made his mark as a great fund-raiser, but the public relations side of the business never became a major competitor to other agencies. In the view of an early associate, Robert J. Duncan, "We got so labelled in the philanthropy field that our PR business didn't develop." He also saw that the two functions didn't dovetail as neatly as Jones thought.

The same thing held true for brothers Carlton and George Ketchum, who had been schooled in the art of fund-raising by Charles Sumner Ward, another pioneer and highly successful fund-raiser. Carlton and George Ketchum opened a publicity agency in Pittsburgh in 1919, then split in 1923, Carlton building a fund-raising firm that still prospers and George an advertising and publicity agency that ranks as a major agency today. The Ketchum history was told in the Introduction to Part II.

John Price Jones was born on August 12, 1877, at Latrobe, PA, in the heart of the anthracite coal region, the son of a mine foreman. Jones was fired with ambition as a boy and meant to pull himself out of the coal fields. He saved his childhood earnings and managed admission to Phillips Exeter Academy. A neighborhood grocer, admiring the boy's spunk, lent him $150 to round out his preparatory school budget. The lender was astonished to receive an initial installment on the repayment during the first weeks of Jones' stay at Exeter. He had obtained a half dozen jobs, including waiter and campus agent for the tailor. Before he finished school he had repaid the storekeeper's loan. Jones finished Exeter in 1898 and entered Harvard that fall. He earned his way through Harvard by serving as correspondent for several daily newspapers. He was graduated in 1902, and from then on Exeter and Harvard were to play influential roles in his life.

Upon leaving college, he became private secretary to Congressman Samuel L. Powers, for whom he worked in Washington for 2 years "doing also a certain amount of newspaper work." Jones then took a reporter's job on the *Washington Post*, where he stayed until 1911. Realizing the need for the broadening experience of travel, Jones quit the *Post* and took off for Europe. He traveled steerage and returned to New York on December 13, 1912, with one dime in his pocket. He quickly landed a job on the *New York Globe*. Next he "tried some publicity work, and then transferred to the *New York Press*. I worked on that paper until Mr. Frank A. Munsey bought it. As he considered me a too-high priced man, he fired me. I then went to the *Sun*, where I remained for almost four years, until Mr. Munsey bought that paper too. He and I did not meet on the *Sun*, for after a few months, I decided not to let the lightning strike twice in the same place, so I went into the advertising business" Jones took a job in the H. K. McCann Company advertising agency, forerunner to today's McCann-Erickson. It was from the McCann agency that Jones was drafted to handle the publicity for the Liberty Loan drives in New York City, an assignment that was to launch him on his highly successful career. Jones served in the Liberty Loan campaign post for 2 years, on loan from McCann.

Jones was put to work under the direction of Guy Emerson as "assistant director publicity Liberty Loan Campaigns, Second Federal Reserve District, 1917–1919." From this point on, Guy Emerson, Harvard '08, worked closely with Jones, Harvard '02, in pioneering fund-raising, public relations, and philanthropy. Emerson put Jones in charge of the Press Bureau for the Second Liberty Loan drive. The former reporter quickly brought his urge for system, detail, and planned procedures to bear on the campaign, and in the Second Liberty loan campaign a well-thoughtout plan of publicity was coordinated with the vast soliciting effort.

After America entered the war, $13,856, 484,000 was raised in five successive bond drives. Speakers, posters, pamphlets, and press bureau were skillfully coordinated and exploited in developing an emotional reaction that repeatedly sold the bonds. Jones induced leading screen and stage stars such as Douglas Fairbanks, Mary Pickford, Charles Chaplin, and Lillian Russell to promote bond sales. One historian asserted, "Where the movies really helped to win the War was in the Liberty Bond drives when the Chaplin-Fairbanks-Pickford triumvirate loosed the purse strings of an adoring nation." He also persuaded New York's Consolidated Edison to imprint campaign appeals on gas and electric bills, milk companies to put slogans on bottle caps, and banks to insert patriotic appeals with their monthly statements.

For the Fourth Liberty Loan campaign, Jones organized a "Features Bureau," an effort to crystallize and standardize the work of using special events as a means of stirring enthusiasm of both the workers and the public. During the Victory Loan drive after the armistice, Jones took on, in addition to his press and feature bureau work, direction of a speakers' bureau. A great believer in putting down on paper all lessons learned, after each campaign, Jones wrote up lessons that could be utilized in the next drive. "These studies demonstrated conclusively that a new era in fund-raising was at hand," Wolcott Street wrote in his history of the Jones firm. Jones soon put these lessons to work for his alma mater.

Thomas W. Lamont, Harvard '92 and partner of J. P. Morgan & Company, had accepted the plea of President A. Lawrence Lowell to lead a drive for a $10 million teachers endowment fund for Harvard in 1916. Lamont hired a bright young Harvard graduate, Robert F. Duncan '12, to serve as secretary of this endowment fund campaign. Duncan, a native of Clinton, MA, was recruited from the news and circulation department of the *Springfield Republican*. The Harvard drive stopped, of course, with America's entry into the war. Lamont quickly persuaded his partner, Henry P. Davison, to take young Duncan to Washington and give him a job in the Red Cross, where he became recorder for the Red Cross War Council. There Duncan came to know Ivy Lee.

Duncan told the next chapter of this story this way, in his reminiscences:

> The day after the Armistice in November, 1918, I was back at Morgan's. Mr. Lamont wanted to get right at the job. Before the war, I had known that Guy Emerson '08 had had a part in the Episcopal Church Pension Fund. One of my first calls on returning to New York was on Guy. . . . He told me, "There's a man named John Price Jones '02 handling publicity for the Liberty Loans with whom you ought to talk. He'll be finishing up soon at the Liberty Loans and he'd be a great help to Harvard." To make it short, I talked promptly to John Price Jones, saw quickly that Guy was right, talked to Mr. Lamont, brought the two together, and in a few weeks Mr. Jones was on the Harvard Endowment Fund payroll—my recollection is at $7,500 a year.

Jones and Duncan took command of the Harvard Endowment Fund Campaign and began a collaboration that was to last more than 31 years.

Jones was made general manager, and Duncan continued as secretary. Offices were rented at 165 Broadway, and the staff was completed by three wartime Red Cross workers. One was John W. Prentiss '98, a partner in Hornblower & Weeks, who was fund treasurer and did much of the personal solicitation of the big givers. When the campaign to raise $10 million for the Harvard Endowment Fund was launched, it not only made fund-raising history but changed the course of American higher education, for Harvard was dramatically telling the nation and sister colleges that the old methods of financing higher education in America was passe. Guy Emerson observed, shortly after the drive was over, "For years men who undertook campaigns of this kind were obliged to shoot entirely in the dark,"

Not so with the Jones–Duncan directed campaign. Efforts to obtain gifts were preceded by an intensive, intelligent publicity program documenting the service that the university, through the training of young people and the research work of its professors, had furnished the nation. The educational program made clear Harvard's pressing needs as well as her opportunities for greater service, if the money was given to her. The way for the solicitor was paved with forceful publicity. What Jones had learned during the Liberty Loan drives about organization of fund drives mostly from Guy Emerson was utilized. Jones made it clear to his associates that he sought to develop enthusiasm for giving to Harvard by dignified means, "without rough and tumble methods." He wisely saw that the publicity must reflect the nature of the institution and that donors must be shown reasons for giving.

Thorough organization preceded the solicitation; the systematic solicitation provided for a visit to every Harvard alumnus. Stag smokers, luncheons, and dinners were staged in every city with an appreciable number of Harvard alumni. Rivalry—a stimulus always exploited by the shrewd fund-raiser—was stimulated among the classes of Harvard and among the Harvard clubs. Publicity directed specifically to Harvard alumni and more generally to the public stressed that there was a great need for educated men in all important walks of life and that Harvard was producing educated men of the highest culture. "With a gradual crescendo, as the gifts began to pour in, everyone connected with the University was swept into the movement to push the fund over the top. Over the top it went. $14,2000,000 had been raised by November, 1919—and the big movement of organized giving to American education was underway" Wolcott Street wrote.

Smith College was among the first to seek Jones's help in organizing a fund appeal. Duncan recalled that Mrs. Harold C. Greene invited him to her Bronxville home to discuss Smith's needs and the possibilities of a fund drive. Mrs. Greene arranged for Duncan to meet Mrs. Hannah Dunlop Andrews, a Smith alumna, who asked if the "Harvard group" would take on the task of raising funds for Smith.

Duncan reported this to Jones, who mused, "Maybe there's a business in this." On this cue, Jones and Duncan went to see Mr. Lamont to discuss the feasibility of starting a small corporation to specialize in directing fund and publicity campaigns. The Morgan partner lent encouragement to the idea. Next the pair talked with Guy Emerson, who also gave the idea his hearty approval. That was all the young enterpriser needed.

The John Price Jones firm was incorporated under the laws of the state of New York on November 23, 1919. Jones' announcement said it was created "to meet a demand for highly specialized knowledge in these fields." The corporation was formed with these directors: Jones, Duncan, Emerson, George A. Brakeley, H. K. McCann, Parke F. Hanley, Bayard F. Pope, Edward Harding, and Harold W. Thirlkeld. Emerson, his mentor, was at this time vice-president of the National Bank of Commerce. In turn the directors elected Jones president, Brakeley vice-president and general manager, Hanley vice-president, Thirlkeld vice-president, and Duncan secretary and treasurer. Jones rented 5, 200 square feet of office space at 150 Nassau Street, at Printing House Square, in the old *New York Sun* offices. At one time this area was the center of New York's newspaper industry. It was a matter of great pride to Jones to put his desk in the exact spot where his desk as business of editor of the *Sun* had stood. "Jones was always quite sentimental about the old *Sun*," one associate recalled. When the furniture had been bought and the firm was ready to open, there "was still a little money in the bank," Duncan recalled.

Jones's first task was to recruit a staff. Two key workers on his Harvard campaign staff were brought to the new offices on Nassau Street: Harold J. Seymour, Harvard '16, moved over to the Jones payroll immediately; Chester E. Tucker, Harvard '19, joined the Jones staff on December 15, 1919. Both Seymour and Tucker attained vice-presidencies in the Jones firm before moving on to other jobs in fund-raising. Tucker also was president for a time.

Like Duncan, Tucker had worked on a Springfield, MA, newspaper, as Fort Devens correspondent for the *Daily News*, whence he joined the Harvard Endowment Fund Committee staff. Seymour had read proof for the *Harvard Crimson* when in college and was a competent writer with a talent for publicity. Two decades later, he directed the National War Fund drives of World War II. Tucker later became vice-president in charge of development for the University of Pennsylvania, long a Jones client. These three men were Jones's anchor men for a quarter of a century and contributed greatly to his success. In the opinion of those familiar with the situation, Jones never gave this trio due recognition for their contributions, nor did he offer them any substantial part of the business. Consequently, all eventually left him.

To take charge of the public relations services in the new firm, Jones tapped a former newspaper associate on the *New York Sun*, George A. Brakeley, a Princeton graduate. Starting as reporter, Brakeley successively was assistant night city editor, assistant city editor, assistant editor, and Sunday editor in the *Sun*. From there Jones had drafted him for publicity work in the 1918 and 1919 Liberty and Victory Loan campaigns. After the war, Brakeley had taken the job of managing editor of the *Red Cross Magazine*, a job he quit to join Jones. He ultimately returned to his alma mater as treasurer in charge of fund-raising and development. Hanley had managed the Features Bureau in the Liberty Loan publicity department under Jones's tutelage.

Hanley's right-hand man in the Features Bureau — today it would be called special events — H. W. Thirlkeld, was also brought into the new firm. The heavy journalism orientation of this eager young staff naturally resulted in heavy emphasis on the role of publicity.

Heavily influenced by his experience as a reporter, business editor, advertising writer, and Liberty Loan publicist, Jones conceived of his new enterprise as both a public relations and a fund-raising business and envisioned extensive possibilities in both fields. Down through the years, he sought to put equal stress on these two fields in obtaining business and in serving clients; but it was from fund-raising that his principal income came. Postwar America was ready for the commercial fund-raising expert; it was not as receptive to the need for the public relations expert.

In Jones' meticulously drawn plans for the new enterprise, he envisioned a Press Department "to promote properly the interests of the clients of the corporation" with these aims:

1. To create a demand for news and other printable material.
2. To produce news and other material.
3. To adjust the production to the demand and the opportunities.
4. To maintain a high standard of production, distribution, and publication.
5. To make publication as widespread as possible.

He further outlined that the scope of the Bureau shall be as unlimited as the spread of the limited word, listing the channels of publicity which existed at that time. Jones, in his methodical way, then stated, "The publicity campaign must be developed objectively, i.e., keeping the reading public always in the focus of operations." Jones had learned through his prior experience the importance of targeting a specific message to a specific audience. "Therefore, the campaign output must be directed to two channels, viz. the 'Psychological,' and the 'Emotional.'

Early in 1920, Jones issued a pamphlet:

We take pleasure in announcing the organization of a special bureau devoted to publicity for social affairs. In this bureau are competent writers and skilled organizers ready for the instant service of corporation clients. This bureau is prepared to give service as follows: Publicity Advance, Announcements, News Stories, Special Articles, Executive direction in organizing features [special events], meetings, dinners, bazaars, balls, entertainments. Mail service in sending out invitations, announcements, appeals.

In another promotion pamphlet issued in Jones's ceaseless quests for new business, he promoted "A Summary of Services That Will Crystallize an Idea, Advance a Cause, Sell a Product." The pamphlet promoted these services: public relations, publicity, fund-raising, direct mail advertising, and a letter shop.

In 1925, Jones formed a direct mail subsidiary, The John Price Jones Direct Mail Service-By-Letters, and in 1929, the name was changed to Direct Mail, Inc. Jones saw this direct mail service providing for his clients and then selling its services to other advertising and public relations agencies so that there would be no idle time in his shop. This subsidiary, too, apparently failed as the result of Depression for it was dissolved September 30, 1939.

Under the heading "How the Corporation Can Serve," a 1920 pamphlet read: "Does your enterprise need publicity or organization or both? Do you want to secure funds in behalf of a college, school, or some other public enterprise? Do you need advice in campaign organization? Do you need a new and different point of view in your advertising? Do you wish to know the attitude towards your concern or your product? Do you want to win increased confidence from your employees?" Here one sees Jones envisioning the moneymaking possibilities of today's separate and lucrative fields of fund-raising, public relations, public opinion research, advertising, and employee relations services. In a printed "Survey of the Margarine Industry and Its Public Relations"—obviously a presentation designed to land this PR account—found in Jones's papers, 1920–1922, Jones claimed, "The John Price Jones Corporation which in point of personnel and in number of accounts is the largest public relations corporation in America." This was obviously a severe stretching of the essential truth though it may have been literally true. Duncan never shared Jones' enthusiasm for building up the public relations side of the business or his penchant for detailed paper work. This became a perennial topic at the annual staff conference Jones initiated as part of his systematic training of his staff. At the 1935 staff conference, Bayard F. Pope, Jr. was asked an obvious question that eternally bothered Jones executives, "Why, if we are equipped to conduct a public relations account, don't we have a few public relations clients?" Pope answered the question with these reasons:

1. Because most of our staff are engaged in fund-raising and seldom think of the commercial side of our service.

2. Because few members of the staff realize how much commercial experience we really have had and because they try to sell commercial jobs on the basis of our fund-raising experience.
3. Because we are regarded by the public as a fund-raising organization and because the public fails to see the similarity between the two types of work.

In a plans book dated March 1, 1921, Jones set forth this as the purpose of his firm:

The purpose of the Corporation is to originate and promote an idea, to develop an intangible thought into a concrete reality which the public can hear or see or read about and understand and through understanding be moved to a definite course of action or be restrained from action. In the development of this work, the Corporation is much like the selling or promotion department of a big corporation. We originate ideas for our clients, ideas that help in the development of a smoothly running organization, that help in putting that organization in a better light before the public or help that organization sell more goods, or help in the spreading of a munitarian, religious, economic, or education idea that works for the general good of all. *The Corporation, furthermore, serves a client in need of publicity or organization advice in much the same way that a lawyer gives legal counsel.* To carry on this work with the utmost effectiveness requires the application of new methods within the Corporation and the generation of new ideas for general distribution in behalf of its clients.

To carry out these objectives, Jones, in his reorganization plan of 1921, set up six departments: Executive, New Business, Planning, Organization (the fund-raising operation), Production, and Controller. With the new organization plan went a manual of standard practices that Jones laid down for all hands. A great memo writer and rule maker, Jones kept a taut rein on his staff and required them to submit daily reports. One former staff member recalled, "The daily report was a nightmare to the staff but a great boon to the business. It established a system of control which made it apparent from day to day where a job was going. He also required you to report on 'Work to be Done' so you had to plan ahead."

Though he spelled out the plans, the function, and the objectives of the new firm in minute detail in 1919, Jones was to admit a decade later, "At the start of our business we were pretty vague about our task. We were hazy about publicity. We have learned a lot in ten years, and most of what we have learned you will find in Standard Practice."

Jones, the great memo writer, issued a revised memorandum on the firm's Standard Practice on November 15, 1926, in which he repeated the firm's purpose to "offer service which embraces counsel and direct aid in publicity, public relations, direct mail advertising, and fund-raising. In both its policies and its methods of procedure, it may be said to have taken a unique place." Jones' systematic ways put his firm in the forefront of those counsellors who came to see the function of public relations as a problem-solving process involving research, planning communication, and evaluation. He put it this way: "The usual procedure of this Corporation is undertaking a job for a client, involves a *survey*, (a study of the situation involved), a *plan* (our recommendations based on the survey), a *schedule* (guide and time-table for the steps to be taken), a *brief* (a skeleton outlining the development of some idea), and a *report* (a statement of what was done, and possibly what remains to be done)."

Then he sternly admonished, "These five steps of procedure . . . are common to virtually every task undertaken for and by the Corporation. It is therefore of the utmost importance that every member of the staff should understand these five steps, and get into the habit of following them all the time . . . thoroughly." In emphasizing thoroughness of procedure and strict accounting for time spent, John Price Jones was far ahead of most of his contemporaries in the agency business of the 1920s.

Jones was fully cognizant that he was pioneering a new profession. In a small, undated folder (circa 1920) he stated, "Production of publicity and advertising ideas and the distribution of these ideas have recently become a recognized business. The John Price Jones Corporation is engaged in this new business. By training and by experience it has learned how to put speed, power, and direction behind the right idea."

In 1931, Jones formed a partnership with his former advertising agency, McCann–Erickson to set up the Commercial News Corporation. In heralding the new subsidiary, Jones announced, "The present companies bring to the joint venture an unusual combination of talents." These "talents" apparently did not sell during the Depression Years because this firm was dissolved on October 6, 1939.

JONES' FIRST ACCOUNT INVOLVES SUPPORT OF STRIKEBREAKING

The first public relations account obtained by the Jones firm was listed simply as "Coal Operators." Jones' financial records show that the firm started billing the Coal Operators — as it was carried on the books — November 29, 1919. Thus, the fledgling Jones firm joined in the anti-United Mine Workers (UMW) campaign much earlier than did the Ivy Lee agency, which came to fray after its climax in the fall of 1921. The effort to crush the United Mine Workers' effort to organize the coal fields of Southern West Virginia after World War I carried on by the coal operators and other major industries was described in a previous chapter that detailed Lee's firm's participation in this antilabor campaign. Jones, who had grown up in the Pennsylvania coal fields, was an ultraconservative and undoubtedly his infant firm needed the business.

Jones' involvement in this disgraceful chapter of American history was minor and, at least based on available records, consisted mainly in providing biased intelligence on four supporters of the UMW campaign. Background reports, mostly prepared by George Brakeley, were supplied on Roger Baldwin, director of the newly organized American Civil Liberties Union (ACLU) [a cousin of pioneer counselor William H. Baldwin], the Rev. Dr. Harry Ward, a professor in the Union Theological Seminary, Albert DeSilver, and Joseph D. Cannon, a member of the ACLU Board. These reports mostly were made to John B. Pratt of the National Coal Association headquartered in Charleston, WV. (Brakeley later organized his own successful fund-raising firm.)

The flavor of these reports can be tasted in these excerpts:

> Baldwin . . . is the active head of the Civil Union [*sic*] and is the general manager. He spends much of his time at 100 Fifth Avenue, and also circulates considerably among persons of wealth, of the so-called parlor socialist variety. There are all kinds of radicals affiliated with the Civil Union either directly or through groups and small societies which are fed by it. The Union is like the mother ship for a flotilla of submarines. Much of its work is under the surface, and consists of giving aid and comfort to the enemies of corporations. The subsidiary organizations range in color from faint pink to a violent red.

These comments must be placed in the context of the early 1920s when there was great paranoia of the Communist menace in the wake of the Russian Revolution, a fear spurred by the Red-baiting of Attorney General Palmer.

Of the Rev. Dr. Ward, president of the ACLU, Brakeley wrote, "The Rev. Dr. Ward . . . goes about preaching in the leading churches of the country and on account of his good appearance and his suave manner is a major asset for the Civil Union." No effort was made to link him with the UMW organizing effort.

Another Brakeley report asserts that the propaganda work on behalf of the coal mines on the part of Joseph D. Cannon is "underwritten and financed by the American Civil Liberties Union." He is described as having "run for Congress on the Socialist ticket and was once mentioned as a candidate for Vice President on the ticket with Eugene V. Debs." Brakeley's report adds:

> At present Cannon is connected with a Paper Box Makers Union, and he is a part time worker at the Labor Film Corporation." His role in the UMW

campaign is described thus: "Since the first of this year, Cannon has been distributing newspaper mimeographed copy with a date mark indicating that it is mailed from his home. At the headquarters of the Civil Union the investigator was told that the newspaper releases were all sent from there as a convenience to Mr. Cannon, and that the Union, and the United Mine Workers of American [sic] were interested with him in "staging" a mass meeting at Logan, West Virginia. The date was set for February 10, then postponed until February 17, but now the plans for the promoters of the demonstrations are indefinite, although they say they are still working on their program.

On February 9, 1923, Brakeley sent a telegram to John B. Pratt stating: "MAN YOU MENTION [presumed to be Cannon] IS MEMBER EXEC- UTIVE COMMITTEE AMERICAN CIVIL LIBERTIES UNION. VERY ACTIVE AND PROPOSES HOLDING MASS MEETING WEST VIR- GINIA MATTER NEXT WEEK. WILL AMPLIFY REPORT."

Three days later, J. B. Pratt of the National Coal Operators Association, based in Washington, sent a telegram to Brakeley requesting: "PLEASE WIRE COMPLETE REPORT ON JOSEPH D. CANNON ACTIVITIES TO C C DICKINSON FUEL COMPANY AND MAIL SPECIAL DELIV- ERY. HE WOULD LIKE ANYTHING YOU CAN GET ON HISTORY AND ACTIVITIES OF CANNON AND THE AMERICAN CIVIL LIB- ERTIES LEAGUE [sic] ALSO YOU CAN MAIL HIM COPY OF PAM- PHLET WRITTEN BY ALBERT DESILVER ISSUED BY LEAGUE. WOULD APPRECIATE MAILING ME DUPLICATE OF ANYTHING YOU SEND DICKINSON." Brakeley wrote Dickinson that Albert DeSilver was a New York attorney, "counsel for the Civil Union and other red groups and member of its National Committee gathering information on coal situation but unable to get pamphlet. Denied so far he has written one. Are keeping after it." In another report, Brakeley described Cannon as "a pacifist and socialist. He had much to do with the organization of the People's Council, patterned after the Soviet idea."

This now seemingly ancient labor history is recounted here to illustrate the primitive state of public relations counseling in the early 1920s. The evidence makes clear the Jones firm was more interested in massaging these clients' deep-seated prejudices than in counseling them on ways of dealing with their problems, a sample of public relations counsel of this period. The Jones firm would not again become involved in union-breaking activities until the 1937 Johnstown Steel Strike. That episode indicates a more sophisticated ap- proach to this work. Harold J. Seymour, who worked on the Coal Operators account, told me, "I don't think it amounted to much more than the fact that Jones had need of clients even more than money in this commercial field. . . . I'm sure as anything that can be that John L. Lewis was never caused even one extra heartbeat, let alone any loss of sleep."

OTHER EARLY ACCOUNTS

Promotion of adoption of the U.S. Budget Office in the federal government was the second public relations account landed by Jones.

The National Budget Committee represented an effort of big taxpayers to cut costs of government in this year (1921) of "normalcy." The stated goal was "to promote efficiency and economy of government finances" by getting new budget laws adopted by Congress. This campaign was led by John T. Pratt, national chairman, and Henry L. Stimson, a director of the committee. R. Fulton Cutting served as chairman of the New York committee. Conservative businessmen then, as today, were convinced that the nation was headed for financial ruin because of its large debt and "many of the friends of Mr. Jones in Wall Street and State Street, Boston, were positive that the days of great fortunes were at an end." The National Budget Committee campaign was directed by George A. Brakeley.

Seymour wrote a series of editorials for the committee's house organ in the style of Mr. Dooley, but he doubted "if this had any lasting effect on the public passion for thrift and economy." The main effort was the promotion of a National Budget Club chain and a *Fortnightly* magazine. The Fortnightly Clubs were organized to "serve as forums for discussions of public finance." This account was terminated in 1921 with its mission accomplished. Bureau of the Budget legislation that President Wilson had vetoed in 1919 was reintroduced in the Republican Congress at President Harding's request. President Harding signed the Budget Act on June 10, 1921, and soon thereafter appointed Charles G. Dawes as Budget Director. This was one of the few positive accomplishments of the tainted Harding presidency. Jones' supporting campaign undoubtedly played a part in gaining approval of this fiscal management tool after it had been defeated in 1919.

At the end of its first year as a corporation, the Jones organization undertook a 6-month drive to raise a fund for famine relief in China. President Wilson appointed Jones' sponsor, Thomas W. Lamont, as chairman of the relief committee. This was a project with great appeal for churches and similar agencies. In his early history of the Jones firm, Wolcott Street recorded, "The story to be told in the campaign publicity was tremendously dramatic. . . . Through news stories, Sunday stories, magazine articles, direct mail pieces, and posters the public was made thoroughly familiar with the fact that between forty and fifty million Chinese in five provinces were threatened by death by starvation." He added, "The publicity was 'trick stuff.' The direct mail pieces pierced unsuspected cracks in the armor of their readers. The art work was beautifully conceived in the Chinese tradition." The drive raised $7,750,420.32. Unlike Carl Byoir in a later time, Jones was paid for this effort.

In June 1921, under the leadership of Franklin D. Roosevelt, a group of prominent liberals selected the corporation for the establishment of a foundation to bear President Woodrow Wilson's name and perpetuate his ideals of world peace and justice. This foundation has had a long and illustrious history and substantial impact on scholarly research in public affairs. Jones set about organizing a National Founders Committee and a Founders Committee in each of the 48 states. Many groups sympathetic to the ex-President were enlisted—societies that had advocated America's entry into the League of Nations, the Democratic Party, Woodrow Wilson Clubs, and groups of educators approving an association of nations to promote world peace.

The Press Bureau and the Speakers Bureau laid down a heavy barrage of publicity for peace and Wilson across the nation. The campaign was opened with a series of mass meetings from "East to West" in Street's account. The corporation devised many slogans to back up the drive; prominent poets of sympathy with Wilson's cause wrote verses in support; the American Legion sent greetings from its convention to its former Commander-in-Chief; several newspapers conducted symposia on the topic, "Is the World Coming Back to Wilson's Ideals?" Jones again used his effective quota system and exploited the stimulus of organization rivalries. In short, the early drive methods were employed to the hilt. Emotional appeal was the keystone of the campaign arch. The first months of this drive brought in $800,000.

The corporation's annual financial statements for these early years indicate that Jones obtained these clients for the publicity division: The Coal Operators; the National Budget Commission; Chinese Famine Relief, West Virginia Coal & Coke Co., All-American Cables, the Flint Kote Co., American Bankers Association, the Anti-Bonus Campaign, Cosmopolitan Books, Dominion Asbestos Rubber, Johns Manville Co., National Monetary Association, Weekly Review, Bond & Godwin, and the Woodrow Wilson Fund.

Thus, though not a heavy hitter among the new agencies of the 1920s and 1930s, the Jones did a fair publicity business.

Even though the public relations side of the corporation's business never kept pace with fund-raising, Jones was persistent in his effort to get public relations clients. In 1930, recognizing that Big Business was in the public doghouse with the onset of the Great Depression, Jones issued a pamphlet entitled "They Hate Big Business." It stated, "Officers and boards of directors of thousands of sound businesses will undoubtedly be asked to consider spending millions of dollars in these next few years for a thing vaguely known as 'public relations.' Much of this money will be wasted. Worse, much of it will do possible harm. . . . Frankly, no one knows as much about 'public relations.' The John Price Jones Corporation, for one, after seventeen years knows only a few simple things." The pamphlet continued:

> Big business for many years has been reticent in speaking of itself and silence breeds ignorance and rumor. And, finally, big business has been occupied with Men, Money, Management, Materials, Machines, and Markets. Sometimes, let us admit, Big Business has overlooked its manners. The answer, many have found, is that it pays to consult outside counsel, and above all with no axe to grind, counsel that will give you the simple truth, and recommendations based only on its best collective judgment as to what should be done under the circumstances.

The corporation's publicity philosophy was expressed this way by A. C. Gumbrecht at the 1930 Staff Conference: "Publicity is the organized expression of an idea or an institution. Its social value lies in that it brings to the public facts and ideas of public interest and often social utility which otherwise would not become readily known. In the expression of an idea or an institution, ethical principles should guide publicity and the publicity worker" This is rather advanced concept on the social value of publicity for 1930.

Jones' key officers were also fully cognizant that they were in a pioneering venture. Vice-President Harold J. Seymour, speaking at the 1931 Staff Conference, said:

> We are participating in what may appear in future years to have been a critical period in the evolution of a new profession. Publicity no longer men as a battle of wits. It now involves a meeting of minds. The publicity man of the future will not be able to survive on superficial cleverness, or on the measurement of newspaper space and the selling power of a breezy personality. The best publicity man will be an educated and cultured gentleman [this was the day before women had entered the field in any numbers], a recognized expert and a chronic sufferer from an insatiable curiosity.

Seymour was prescient in seeing the practitioner in years to come. He was reflecting the end of the Postwar-Publicity-Solves-Every-Problem years of 1919–1929 to business's awakening to the need to accommodate the public interest if it were to emerge from its Depression doghouse.

The failure of banks and businesses in the Depression brought a new opportunity for profit to the Jones Corporation. Using the skills the staff had developed both in fund-raising and public relations, the corporation was called up to assist in the reorganization of failed businesses. Donald Hammond, an executive, gave these examples of the 1934 Staff Conference:

The reorganization in which public relations played an important part were the Hopkins Place Savings Bank in Baltimore, and the Refunding Operation conducted by a banking group in behalf of U. S. Fidelity and Guaranty Company and the Maryland Surety Company. The problem of the bank was to secure the consent of 25,000 depositors to a plan which required the sacrifice temporarily of 35 per cent of the deposits and induce them to leave as much as possible of the remaining 65 per cent in the bank. The problem of the surety companies was to induce approximately 45,000 individual holders of mortgage bonds by these companies to deposit their bonds under a plan approved by the Reconstruction Finance Corporation. Both of these objectives were achieved.

Hammond told his colleagues, "The parallel between these jobs and a fund raising campaign is not exact, yet in their main essentials the two are pretty much alike. In both cases, just as in fund raising, the first essential is preparation of the case." He could have added that this was also an exercise in persuasive public relations. Another colleague, Harry W. Brown, pointed out at this conference that success with another such account, Globe and Rutgers, "has proven that with certain minor modifications . . . we can apply Standard Practice to good advantage in solving reorganization problems of our commercial clients." Before the day was done, business reorganizations proved a rich lode for the Jones Corporation. When John Price Jones sold the firm to Charles W. Anger in June 1955, he had made a total of $89,755.00 in business reorganization work.

JONES HELPS BREAK A STEEL STRIKE

John Price Jones played a major role in an organized effort to break the strike of the Cambria works of the Bethlehem Steel Co. in Johnstown, PA, in 1937. The strike had been called by the Steel Workers Organizing Committee in the CIO's effort to organize the steel industry. Labor lost the battle in Johnstown but eventually won the war in one of the most violent periods in U.S. labor history. With the passage of the Wagner Act of 1935 creating the National Labor Relations Board, organized labor, led by John L. Lewis, saw the opportunity to create a mass labor movement by organizing industrial rather than craft unions as favored by AF of L's William Green. Lewis created the Steel Workers Organization Committee (JWOC) in 1936, staffed with United Mine Workers staff and provided a $1 million fund.

The SWOC's effort to organize Bethlehem's Johnstown plant began July 21, 1936, and collapsed in failure in late June 1937, when Pennsylvania's Governor, George H. Earle, lifted the edict of marital law he had issued 6 days earlier on June 19 closing the plant. It was apparent that Earle was reacting to the firestorm of public opinion generated by the opponents of organized labor. This chapter of the Jones firm's story is largely based on the hearings conducted by Senator Robert M. LaFollette, Jr. of the U. S. Senate Subcommittee on Labor and Education from March 10–19, 1938.

When the strike was called in mid-June, violence erupted on the picket line between those on strike and those wishing to return to work. President Eugene Grace promptly announced that the plant would remain open for those who wanted to work. These scuffles prompted Governor Earle to declare martial law, close the plant, and send in an augmented State Police force to enforce order. The amount of violence was greatly exaggerated in the public opinion battle that followed.

When Earle declared martial law on June 19, 1937, the Citizens Committee, financed in large part by Bethlehem Steel and led by industrialists and bankers, held an emergency meeting in the Sunahanna Country Club. Chairman Francis C. Martin, a bank president, later told the Senate committee that "Mr. Waters gave it as his opinion that in our utterly helpless condition under the circumstances, it was his judgment that an appeal to the public and turning the light on what the Governor had done was the only thing that could be used in order to accomplish anything." Robert S. Waters was president of the National Radiator Co., also located in Johnstown. There was a consensus that this was the way to go, and later that night, Waters called his uncle, John Price Jones, to ask him to join the fight. Not only was Jones Waters' uncle, he shared his antiunion views as he had demonstrated in handling the West Virginia Coal Operators and West Virginia Coal and Coke accounts, the bloody mine battles of the early 1920s. Jones company records show the National Radiator Corp. of Johnstown as a client, handled by Jones, from June 18, 1934, until 1947 when the list was composed. There is also an entry for Robert S. Waters from January 20, 1939, to January 28, 1939. No explanation of work done is recorded.

Jones took on the Citizens Committee as a personal cause. David M. Church, longtime executive in the corporation, recalled in an interview on February 2, 1962. "Jones was an arch conservative. He regarded the steel companies' cause a just one. To Jones nothing was ever impossible." Church related that Jones set up the advertising firm of Thornley & Jones to keep the committee work out of the Jones firm. Thornley was recruited from the N. W. Ayer & Son advertising agency. Later, after the strike, George Brakeley was brought in as a partner, and the subsidiary was renamed Jones, Brakeley, and Thornley. There is no record in the Jones's papers as to when the advertising agency folded.

Jones went to Johnstown Monday morning where he met first with the Citizens Committee executive group and then later at Waters's home with the full committee. With Waters's endorsement, the committee agreed to Jones's plan for a "publicity campaign." He told the group that he would use the press, radio, and advertising to carry the Johnstown story to the nation. Asked to state the campaign's objective, Chairman Martin said its purpose was to "inform the people of this country what had been done to Johnstown by the Commonwealth's Governor."

Jones' first step was to direct his partner, Thornley, to prepare a newspaper ad headlined: "WE PROTEST." The radio publicity and advertising was subcontracted to the George Ketchum advertising and publicity agency in Pittsburgh; thus, another pioneer counselor was brought into this antiunion campaign. The ad was signed by Martin as chairman and Lawrence W. Campbell as secretary for the Citizens Committee and by Carel H. Shaffer as chairman and James J. Barnhart as secretary for the Steel Workers Committee. Martin and Campbell did not sign the ad but gave their permission. No evidence could be produced that these officers of the "paper" Steel Workers Committee had any part in the ad that read in part:

> We protest to the people of Pennsylvania and to all other Americans against the action of Governor Earle in his use of martial law in the City of Johnstown against the Cambria plant of the Bethlehem Steel Corporation. . . . Up until last Saturday the situation was this: The Cambria plant continued function and those men who wished to work continued to do so. Those who wished to strike continued to picket in the manner prescribed by law. There was no serious disorder and there was no prospect of any. The local authorities with the cooperation of the State Police were in full control in the situation.

The ad was written by Mr. Thornley and his staff. The firm netted approximately $4500 for its work, getting a 15%, commission from the $30,000 spent to place the ad. The "WE PROTEST" ad was placed in forty major newspapers on June 24. *The New York Times's* front page of June 24 carried a June 23 dispatch that read in part:

> The forces which have opposed Governor Earle's policy in the strike of the Bethlehem Steel Corporation's Cambria plant combined here tonight and announced a drive on a nation-wide scale to raise funds to fight "the greatest invasion of the worker's rights ever attempted in this country". . . . The advertisement will appeal for funds for a war chest and conclude "If this can happen in Johnstown, it can happen anywhere. It can happen in your community unless you protest now to your elected representatives."

Thus, this became one of the first in a long line of public relations ads to appeal for funds, a common technique in today's world of many contending causes. The ad brought in $34,850.71 big bucks in the Depression Era. Also the ad foretold a later campaign to take the Citizens Committee national in the battle with the SWOC.

Members of the committee asserted to the Senate committee that the ad's only purpose was "reestablishing law and order through normal governmental agencies." Asked to justify this assertion, Mr. Campbell argued that it was justified "by the violence and intimidation of workers that have taken place in Franklin Boro primarily." Then Senator LaFollette asked Mr. Campbell to square that statement with the advertisement's assertion "That there was no serious disorder and no prospect of any."

Called before the Senate committee, John Price Jones reported that he had told the committee that its first task was to tell its story to the country and that this could be done by a publicity campaign—"I mean articles appearing in newspapers and also by advertising." "I pointed out that this would take money and that they should start a little campaign to raise money." Jones said that he had not been told that the committee, before his employment, had received substantial sums of money from Bethlehem Steel. The strike had been called June 11 and Chairman Martin admitted that he first learned on June 13 that Bethlehem Steel had given the committee $25,000 "to preserve law and order." The committee assured Jones that it would raise the cost of the publicity campaign, and on that basis he ordered his staff into action.

Jones instructed the committee on the fundamentals of publicity. "You must bear in mind, that when you have got a statement to make as to your position, you can put it out in an interview, but you never know how it is going to be handled by the newspapers. When you take paid space you write the statement as you want it to appear before the public. . . . When you buy space from the newspapers, you get just what you pay for." Jones' reliance on paid ads put him in forefront in the use of this public relations tool.

The George Ketchum agency was brought into the campaign apparently because it had worked for Waters' firm before. The day after he had taken on this assignment, Jones was driven to Pittsburgh by Mr. Waters to coordinate plans with Ketchum. Also included were the Rev. John C. Stanton, a Presbyterian minister who was one of the committee leaders, and Mr. Martin. Significantly, Ernest T. Weir, president of the National Steel Co., also participated in this strategy session. Thornley also was there.

To underwrite these campaigns, Jones' subsidiary, Direct Mail, Inc., proceeded to prepare and mail a fund-raising letter to some 30,000 to 40,000 prospects, a list built by the Jones firm in its nearly 20 years of fund-raising. Jones explained that the list had been "accumulated over a period of 20 years that we have actually taken from newspaper reports of people who give away money, and since they have been publishing the S.E.C. reports of stockholders and salaries of individuals, we have gradually added those

names . . . there are over 40,000 names by now." The letter was addressed
to "Fellow American". This salutation put Jones on the defensive before the
committee. Senator Elbert H. Thomas said the inference was that all those
who supported the act of martial law and the strikers were "un-American."
Jones heatedly replied, "Senator . . . from my point of view, it is absolutely
un-American for any Government official, or any group to keep men from
going to work when they want to go to work." Jones defended the letter by
asserting, "We have the right to express our opinion," but Senator Thomas
rejoined, "You were actually trying to hurt these men [the strikers]." Jones
replied, "We were appealing to the public for an understanding of the
situation in Johnstown and for sympathy for the people who were not
allowed to go to work and for the citizens of Johnstown who were being
hurt by the closing of the mills." Then he heatedly added, "I helped in the
composition of that letter and it represents certain convictions which I have
and which I am entitled to hold, whether I am right or wrong." The writer,
Stanley Frank, once wrote: "In the hands of a high powered expert such as
John Price Jones, a mailing list can be made to play Mother Machree on a
comb." The direct mail appeal brought in $18,253.

The Jones firm also prepared a pamphlet, "The Lesson of Johnstown,"
which was widely circulated to opinion leaders across the nation. It was
apparent that Jones was looking to the formation of a national committee
that would provide him continuing fees, but in this he was disappointed.
The pamphlet was signed by the Rev. Stanton, but Jones admitted that all
the copy was prepared in the Jones's firm — SOP in public relations — "but it
was done in conjunction with Rev. Stanton."

For whatever reason or reasons, the Jones-directed campaign of the
Johnstown Citizens Committee appeared to be successful because Governor
Earle rescinded his martial law order late on June 24, and it was lifted early
morning June 25. This broke the strike, and many workers returned to the
reopened plant. Earle was obviously bowing to public pressure generated by
the publicity-advertising campaign. The National Association Of Manufacturers (NAM) *Labor Bulletin*, quoted earlier, asserted, "The text of the
advertising which can be credited with stirring public opinion to greater
indignation than it had already." This was under a subhead, "The Great
Court of Public Opinion Had Broken the Strike and Nothing Could Save
It."

But apparently there was more than publicity and advertising involved.
LaFollette's committee obtained a copy of a telegram sent by John Price
Jones to his staff on July 21 from Cody, Wyoming, where he annually
vacationed on a dude ranch, that read:

"YOU BETTER KEEP IN TOUCH WITH WATERS IF YOU WANT
MONEY FOR ADVERTISEMENT. CAMPBELL DOING DIRTY

WORK. YOU MIGHT ADVISE WITH CHURCH [DAVID M. CHURCH] REGARDING FRIDAY MEETINGS. [Signed] Jones."
Later when questioned by Senator LaFollette about this "dirty work," Mr. Campbell replied:

I don't know how you would qualify "dirty work." I did feel that the representatives of Mr. Jones that were in Johnstown did not show me the courtesy of being secretary of the committee, and certain material in the nature of communications were never given to me unless I insisted upon them—and I so stated that to our committee that I felt it was only fair that they should know what is going on. Now as far as the National Citizens Committee was concerned, it was more or less the impression that the committee could go out and establish itself to merit confidence and thereby gain support of the country, rather than do it professionally.

This dissembling answer to the "dirty work" question harks back to the futile effort to take the Johnstown Committee nationally and the dismissal of Jones as the consultant.

The testimony before the Senate Committee made clear that Jones' helped formulate the policies of the Johnstown Committee. Emboldened by the lifting of martial law and the breaking of the strike, Jones recommended taking the cause nationwide. On his recommendation, a meeting was called for July 15, 1937, in Johnstown to organize a National Citizens Committee to combat the CIO's organizing campaigns nationwide. This proved to be an unsuccessful undertaking from which the Jones firm ultimately resigned or was dismissed. The record is not clear.

On Jones' recommendation, an effort was made to organize a capital labor committee with an agenda prepared by his firm, "Tentative Plan for Johnstown Meeting." The purpose was to "organize a spearhead for a national movement to face the present inequities of the labor situation." Out of that came a Citizens' National Committee. The committee, which never proved viable, was quickly bankrolled by contributions from Mr. Waters, Ernest T. Weir of National Steel, Richard Scaife, a Mellon heir, and other industrialists who hoped to stop unionization of the auto and steel industry. This campaign was kicked off by another ad, this one entitled "COMMON SENSE" that ran in the *The New York Times* of July 16 but was not as widely placed as the "WE PROTEST" ad.

The July 15 meeting passed a resolution, previously drafted by Jones' staff, "to have a temporary continuing national committee to be composed of the following persons: Rev. John H. Stanton of Johnstown; W. C. Woodward, Massachusetts; Ormsby G. McHard, New York; Rev. Rembert Smith, Oklahoma; and Don Kirksey, Washington, D.C." Jones professed no personal knowledge of these persons. President Roosevelt, Governor Earle, and John L. Lewis were bitterly attacked throughout the debate and an open forum discussion. The preamble to the resolution authorizing a National Citizens' Committee left no doubt as to the purpose of this industry-financed public relations campaign: "Certain public officials in high places as well as minor executives of the law throughout the country have refused to use the authority given them as a trust under oath to protect American citizens in their inalienable rights to work without molestation."

The some 200 persons attending this organizing meeting were exhorted by two strong foes of organized labor — T. Y. Williams of the League for Industrial Democracy and Prof. Gustavus W. Dyer of Vanderbilt University, who told the audience that "industrial strife in the nation is a result of the 'breaking down' of the National Government," adding, "the Government in Washington is not our government."

On August 25, Don Kirkley resigned from the committee because, among other reasons, "The Committee has become a 'red baiting' agency and while I am opposed to Communism as any member I feel that 'red baiting' is not the American way to meet the problem." Rev. Stanton dismissed Kirkley's protest as to the course of the National Committee as "wanting to start his own organization." A few weeks later, the Rev. Stanton resigned as acting chairman, claiming the press of "other duties." This proved to be the beginning of the end of this abortive antiunion campaign. Whether it could have succeeded with Jones' continued counsel is a doubtful proposition. Jones told the Senate committee that he was fully paid by the Johnstown Committee, but that when his services ended or were terminated by the National; Committee, the later group owed him $17,597.15.

Jones' role in breaking the Johnstown strike brought him florid vituperation of the Extreme Left. McAlister Coleman, a former journalistic colleague, damned him as a Fascist in an article in the *Socialist Call* of July 24, 1937. In an article headlined: "JONES' FASCISM", Coleman charged, "Fascism American style dragged its slimy length into the open last week at the meeting of the Johnstown Citizens Committee. All the open shoppers, the labor baiters, the nightriders of the Legion and Klan were there at a meeting inspired by the Bethlehem Steel Co. and other strike breaking independents. . . . Now Mr. Jones . . . is going to put over a 'Right to Work' campaign, undoubtedly on a commission basis." This dire prediction of course proved to be a mirage. Coleman, who stated he had worked with Jones on a newspaper, termed him "a likeable, bounding little chap."

Whereas the Lewis-led CIO effort to unionize the auto industry starting with General Motors in February of 1937 through the employment of sit-down strikes was successful, Little Steel was able to crush the strikes in that year. Little Steel included Bethlehem, Youngstown Sheet & Tube, and Republic Steel.

With the passage of the Wagner Act creating the National Labor Relations Board, Big Business, using the NAM, waged a 10-year war on the NLRB and all forces supporting a modern view of industrial relations. One history describes this NAM public relations campaign "as extensive as ever taken by the Association." This antilabor propaganda effort was directed by James Selvage, its director of public relations. [After the war, Selvage formed a public relations partnership with Morris Lee, now Manning, Selvage, and Lee.] The NAM antilabor tactics included the Remington Rand formula for breaking strikes. On the eve of America's entry into World War II, the CIO won contracts from Little Steel. A responsible labor historian, Jack Barbash, saw this period as nothing less than "class warfare." Thomas Girdler of Republic Steel railed against the "communistic dictates of the CIO," whereas McAlister Coleman and his cohorts saw Jones and the other strikebreakers as "fascists." In this war, John Price Jones played his bit part with conviction.

Writing in the *Public Opinion Quarterly* of October 1939, Frank H. Blumenthal concluded, "Johnstown's contribution to the 'Little Steel' strike of June, 1937, consisted of clear and frequent resort to advertising and other forms of publicity by those groups interested in waging battle against the steel union. These devices of propaganda are found in testimony and exhibits evolving out of the investigation of the strike by Senator LaFollette's Civil Liberties Committee." He added, "The keynotes of this appeal — coercion, outsiders, right to work, stoppage of business — are identical with the chief slogans used to break the strike itself." Blumenthal wrote:

> In concluding the survey of Johnstown, it is interesting to note that the N.A.M. *Labor Relations Bulletin* of July 15, 1937, contained an article, "Public Opinion Chief Factor in Ending Johnstown Steel Strike." It credited the steel strike there with demonstrating the most vigorous expression of public opinion ever recorded against a strike. It called the back to work movement "wholly spontaneous." It relied on the economic losses to the community as the main reason for the popular revolt. It concluded by proudly reprinting the first "We Protest" ad of the Citizens' Committee.

John Price Jones had indeed made labor and public relations history. His apparent success at Johnstown set the pattern used by Hill and Knowlton, Inc. in their service to the American Iron and Steel Institute and to Republic Steel in trying to squelch the Little Steel union organization effort across the Midwest. This effort is recounted in chapter 16.

JOHN PRICE JONES BOWS OUT IN MID-1950s

His success and affluence attained, John Price Jones started easing up from his hard-driving work ethic in the early 1950's, spending more and more time on his farm in Pineville, Bucks County, Pennsylvania. He sold the agency in 1955 to Charles W. Anger, a director of the company and then employed as director of development under President Dwight Eisenhower of Columbia University. At the time of Jones' death on December 23, 1964, nearly a decade later, Anger was chairman of the corporation board and chief executive officer. At the time of his full retirement, John Price Jones had supervised the raising of $746,625,351. Added to the $89,755,000 raised in business reorganizations in the Depression, this came to $836,380,351. No figure as to the total brought in by public relations accounts was found in the voluminous Jones Papers at Harvard.

An account check sheet showing accounts handled by the Jones firm from 1919 to about 1947 and who handled the accounts showed a total of 366 accounts. Of this number, it is estimated that 58 were public relations accounts. These accounts included corporations, political committees, and cause groups. This gives a rough estimate of the proportion of fund-raising accounts to public relations/advertising accounts.

Jones held his last staff conference on June 25, 1954, 35 years after the firm's founding. Early conference planning for this meeting called for a review of those 35 years, but for reasons unexplained, this idea was dropped. Jones, an austere man, was not one for frills or great celebrations. As one officer explained, "There was no cutting of a cake." Chester E. Tucker, who had been there at the beginning, did offer this, "It is no exaggeration to say that our Company has come a long way and achieved a stature of which we all have a right to be proud of. . . . The Company itself is 35 years old this year and it is fitting that we have here a new generation of John Price Jones men. What the John Price Jones Corporation is today is the sum of its principles and traditions over this 35 years and of its energy and conscience today." Thus came the end of a pioneering effort in the postwar boom in fund-raising and public relations.

More accurately, the assets, accomplishments, and stature of this Corporation were the result of the vision, determination, and hard work of John Price Jones who had a profound effect America's philanthropy. He was an innovator as well as a hard taskmaster; a "hard bitten Welshman," one officer labeled him. Jones was a precise, punctual man and insisted on the same qualities in his staff. Office Bulletin No. 4, issued January 21, 1920—in the early months of the firm—carried this as its lead item: "LATENESS: A record kept of attendance this morning shows that of 83 employees of the John Price Jones Corporation, 32 arrived after 9:10. It has come to the attention of the Accounting Department that persons arriving at 9:15 or 9:20 have charged the half hour on the time cards from 9 to 9:30 to various clients. This is obviously unfair to our clients. All members of the staff should report promptly at 9 o'clock."

Jones wasted hours of company and employee time in detailed, meticulous record keeping and in reports. Donald Hammond once recorded in a memo, "Some of us, I feel, do a vast amount of futile and unnecessary paper work." A mild understatement indeed. In the opinion of one long-time associate, "Jones had very little sense of humor. He was all business and damn well determined to put his ideas into practice." Another said, "To Jones nothing was ever impossible."

Evidence of Jones' tough-minded ways is also found in the memoirs of William H. Baldwin, who in 1926, established the sixth public relations agency in New York. (Baldwin's story is found in chapter 12.) Baldwin, just released from the U. S. Naval reserve at the war's end in 1919, was hired by Jones to work on the Harvard Endowment Campaign. Baldwin, too, was Harvard, '13. In an interview at the Harvard Club in New York City on March 30, 1960, Baldwin told me that Jones offered him a job in the new firm he was founding. Baldwin replied, "No thanks Jack, I think we'll remain better friends if I don't work for you."

Possession of such qualities and vision usually bring success as they did for this son of a mine foreman who pulled himself out of the coal fields of Pennsylvania to make both fund-raising and public relations history, more of the former than the latter. Though his name and reputation have disappeared into the mists of history, this intelligent, diminutive, and somewhat humorless man brought innovation, methodology, and a strict management concept to public relations as well as to fund-raising. Like his fellow pioneers in public relations, Jones left lasting imprints on society in the money he raised and the causes he served.

Jones and his staff left a rich legacy in the strengthening of institutions of higher education and hospitals, in building public support for the Bureau of the Budget Act in 1921 after it had failed in 1919, in funding the Woodrow Wilson Foundation that has benefitted countless scholars, in advancing the cause of first the Birth Control League and later Planned Parenthood, which today is in the vortex an intensely emotional battle with its opposite numbers, and in other philanthropic and social causes. On the other side of the ledger must be writ his work for the strikebreaking activities of the Coal Operators in the 1920s and the Steel Industry in 1937. He won those battles but eventually lost the war in an era of more prudent management–labor relationships.

NOTES ON SOURCES

This chapter is based primarily on extensive research in the John Price Jones Papers in the Baker Library, Harvard School of Business, Harvard University, which the author utilized in his *Fund Raising in the United*

States, first published by Rutgers University in 1965, and republished by Transaction Press, 1990. Specific references include the following.

A biographical sketch issued by John Price Jones, Inc. November 19, 1959. John Price Jones entry in *Twenty-Fifth Anniversary Report of Class of '02*, Harvard University. Wolcott Street, "John Price Jones Corporation History" unpublished mss. in Jones Papers. Street, a staff member, wrote this as a business promotion piece. Robert F. Duncan's mimeographed memo of reminiscences date September 30, 1939. An interview with Mr. Duncan, March 29, 1960. A letter from David M. Church dated June 6, 1962. Proceedings of annual staff conferences from early 1920s. Jones Plan Books. A confidential report dated June 15, 1935, in Jones Papers. A John Price Jones unpublished mss. A letter from Harold Seymour, dated September 5, 1961. Testimonials prepared by the Jones staff for his 80th birthday, August 12, 1957.

Jones' participation in efforts to break the strike against Bethlehem Steel in Johnstown is documented in *Violations of Free Speech and the Rights of Labor*, U. S. Senate Committee Hearings, 77th Congress, 1st Session. Washington, DC: U. S. Government Printing Office, 1938. Jones' testimony before Senator Robert M. LaFollette Jr.'s subcommittee was given on March 10 and 12, 1938, and is found on pages 8299 to 8525 of the hearings record and is found in pages 280–286 in the summary volume *Violations of Free Speech and Rights of Labor,* U. S. Senate Committee Hearings, 77th Congress, 1st Session, Washington, DC: U. S. Government Printing Office, 1938; and *Violations of Free Speech and Labor*, Report No. 151, 77th Congress, Washington, DC: Government Printing Office, 1941. Events in Johnstown were reported in *The New York Times* for February 18, 19, 20, 22, 24, 25 and March 12, 1937. Frank H. Blumenthal's article, "Anti-Union Publicity in the Johnstown Little Steel Strike of 1937," *Public Opinion Quarterly,* October, 1939, was helpful. *The Socialist Call*, which attacked Jones in its July 24, 1937, issue was then published in New York City.

The Mohawk Valley Formula for breaking strikes developed by Remington Rand and used by Little Steel in the 1937 Little Steel Strikes was spelled out by the National Labor Relations Board in its Remington Rand decision at Rand's Ilion, NY, plant in 1936, NLRB Report, March 13, 1937. The National Association of Manufacturers published, without the NAM imprint, a pamphlet inferentially recommending the Mohawk Valley formula of James Rand, and distributed at a meeting of the National Industrial Council in Chicago on July 16, 1937 — the day after the Citizens Committee meeting in Johntown. The pamphlet was entitled, "Industrial Strife and the Third Party."

Chapter 10

Steve Hannagan: Super Press Agent

The fascinating story of Steve Hannagan, America's great press agent of the first half century, ended when he died of a heart attack in Nairobi, Kenya, on February 5, 1953, just short of his 54th birthday. He was there on a trip for the Coca-Cola Export Corp., a major client for many years. His heart gave out under the racehorse life he had led since going to work on a newspaper at age 14. In *Collier's Magazine* for November 22, 1947, Dickson Hartwell wrote of Hannagan that he was "probably the most unusual press agent who ever drew breath." Given the stars of press agentry such as Richard Maney, Jim Moran, Henry Rogers, and others, this was high praise indeed.

Hannagan, who never pretended to be anything but a press agent, in fact became more and involved in the broader aspects of public relations in his later years after he opened his own office in New York City in 1935. Hannagan built three enduring monuments to his press agentry in today's popular Memorial Day Auto Race on the Indianapolis Speedway, Miami Beach, Florida, which was created by dredging muck out of Biscayne Bay, and Sun Valley, the ski resort. His imagination, energy, and integrity carried him to many successes and the great esteem of newspapermen, a breed not known for its affection for flacks. Hartwell wrote, "He is a loud-shouting, belligerent, whip-smart press agent, who has never been known to pull a phony or a double-cross."

Stephen Jerome Hannagan was born "on the wrong side of the tracks" in Lafayette, Indiana, on April 4, 1899. His father, William J. Hannagan, was a pattern maker earning $18 a week. The inspiring force in Hannagan's life was his mother, Johanna Gertrude Hannagan, who managed to make ends meet for her family of six on her husband's meager pay and still put $2 a week in the local Building and Loan Savings Association. Her frugality came to the fore once when she was visiting her now affluent son in New York in the 1940s. He had put her up in a small, luxurious hotel, but after she found how much her room cost, she moved into his apartment and slept on a couch. "A lot of nonsense," she said tartly, "all that money and all that room just for me."

Whatever the source of the motivation, Steve Hannagan, while still in high school and only 14 years old, applied for a job at the Lafayette *Morning Journal* (now the *Courier-Journal*) as a reporter. The managing editor, understandably, turned him down cold. The brash youth, not to be denied, went to the publisher, Henry W. Marshall. He told the publisher's secretary that he wanted to see Mr. Marshall. When asked his name, Steve replied, "Mr. Stephen Hannagan." Marshall thought this was Steve's uncle, for whom he had been named, who was a saloon keeper of considerable political weight in Lafayette. So he told the secretary, "Show him in." When he recovered from his surprise, he was irritated and unimpressed with the young lad. He, too, dismissed his plea. But Steve Hannagan was not to be denied; he went to see Mr. Marshall 13 times before the publisher offered him a job at $1 a week just to be rid of his pestering.

With his zeal and his bright mind, the young high schooler soon demonstrated a remarkable talent for finding and reporting news. By the time he was 17 and before graduation from high school, he had been promoted to city editor at a salary of $25 a week. He was by now also earning money as a byline stringer for Indianapolis and Chicago newspapers. His meteoric rise in the newsroom matches that of a young Carl Byoir in Des Moines with whom Hannagan competed in the 1930s and 1940s for public relations accounts.

Upon graduation from Jefferson High School at age 18, Hannagan enrolled in Purdue University as a special student and became the local correspondent for the *Indianapolis Star*. With his various stringer assignments, he was soon making more than $55 a week, big money in those days. Like John W. Hill, who bought his firm after his death, Hannagan was not sufficiently challenged by his university teachers, and he left the university after 2 years.

At about this time, he got his first lesson in the practical aspects of press agentry. One of Bill Picken's barnstorming auto races came to Lafayette, and Steve, who had already accomplished the feat of interviewing George Ade in a bathtub, was hired to handle the local publicity on a straight salary plus a percentage of the gate. Some time after the race, he learned that he had been shortchanged at the box office. He tracked down Pickens and found him in an Indianapolis hotel room holding court with Barney

Oldfield and other racers. Hannagan brusquely told him, "I've been gypped; I was short-counted on your Lafayette race." Pickens blandly replied, "You'll be a great success as a promoter, son. Usually they never find out," Hartwell wrote.

Eager to broaden his experience in "the big city," Hannagan at age 20 took a sports writing job on the *Indianapolis Star* for only $30 a week, a sharp cut in his earnings, but the contacts he made in this job changed his life forever and led him to his great success as America's super press agent. His first big break came when he took a job on the side as a publicity assistant for the Memorial Day race on the Indianapolis Speedway. Built in 1911 for auto racing, the speedway had been used by the Army in World War I. Since it had reopened, it had had only mediocre success.

A shrewd promoter and investor, Carl Fisher, had bought the speedway after the war, using a chunk of the $5 million dollars he had been paid by Union Carbide and Carbon for his Prest-O-Lite battery company. In this assignment, Hannagan, who knew little about cars but had a keen news sense, shifted the publicity focus from the cars to the drivers. The nation's editors eagerly used his copy glamorizing such drivers as Oldfield, Ralph De Palma, and Tommy Milton. Consequently, in 1919, the Speedway got its greatest coverage to date for the Memorial Day race. The publicity focus had been on the various cars because the speedway was built for promoting cars, not for a sporting event. Hannagan said that "he didn't know a sparkplug from a crankshaft," so he wrote about the colorful, daring drivers. Publicity focus on personalities became a hallmark of Hannagan's press agentry.

As the result of the success of the 1919 race, Hannagan asked for a raise from Theodore (Pop) Myers, head of the track. While they were arguing about the merits of a pay raise, the speedway owner entered the room and soon demanded to know, "What is this all about?" Hannagan repeated his claim, and Fisher said, "All right, son, from now on you're the publicity boss around here." This meeting proved portentous for Hannagan and Fisher. He continued his publicity themes for the 1920 Memorial Day race and boosted the attendance from 50,000 to 175,000. Today the Memorial Day race is one of the nation's top sporting events, drawing millions at the track and on television—a lasting monument to Steve Hannagan's press agentry.

In his *500 Miles to Go*, Al Bloemaker, a later publicist for the speedway and its 500-mile Memorial Day race, pointed out that the Indianapolis Speedway, scene of the world's best-known auto races, was the first proving ground and the first great center of publicity for America's automobile industry in its first two decades. He paid tribute to Carl Fisher and Steve Hannagan in this book. "It was Carl Fisher, who, with stubbornness and singleness of purpose in the face of great odds pushed through the building of the Speedway. It was Fisher and his associates who helped the automobile builders by forcing through the first East–West paved road—the Lincoln Highway." He wrote of Steve Hannagan, "Prominent drivers made good copy for Steve Hannagan as he tackled his '500' assignment with an enthusiastic freshness welcomed by sports editors throughout the country."

In the early years of the century, Henry Ford had demonstrated that auto racing would sell cars. Racing was also a constant proving ground and publicity for tires, motor oil, batteries, carburetors, and fuel-injection systems. This purpose of the Memorial Day and other races has been intensified with the advent of television.

Deeply immersed in his successful Miami Beach development, Fisher relinquished control of the Speedway to World War I flying ace, Eddie Rickenbacker, who became president in 1927. Rickenbacker, who had come to know Hannagan's prowess years earlier, kept Hannagan on as chief publicist. In both the Miami Beach and Speedway promotions, Hannagan hired Joe Copps as his assistant in 1924. Hannagan relinquished his speedway duties following the 1933 race when he took a job with the Lord & Thomas advertising agency in Chicago; Joe Copps took his place. In 1945, Rickenbacker sold out his speedway interest, and Joe Copps joined Hannagan's staff in New York. Copps was succeeded by Al Bloemaker. It was Wilbur Shaw, the driver who took over after Rickenbacker, who created the immortal command, "Start your engines, gentlemen!" Copps was serving as president of Robinson–Hannagan when the firm was sold to Hill and Knowlton, Inc. in 1955.

In the early 1920s, Hannagan became restless in Indianapolis and moved on to Chicago where he took a job with the Russell Seeds advertising agency. There he wrote copy for everything from Pinex Cough Syrup to the Stutz "Bearcat." In 1921, he flew across the United States with Rickenbacker to promote Rickenbacker's motor car. While working in Chicago, Hannagan met Roy W. Howard, the president of United Press (UP). Impressed by Hannagan's personality and energy, Howard hired him for the UP and directed him to report to the New York headquarters of that press service. At UP, Hannagan covered the waterfront, everything from police news to writing for United Features. He was ultimately assigned to the Scripps-owned NEA syndicate, the same syndicate that John Hill was then writing for. Their public relations paths would cross one day. Increasingly, Hannagan became bored with newspaper work. He often expressed the felling that his newspaper years were "a total loss," yet he recognized the value of newspaper experience in his work and would hire only ex-journalists for his staff. Once when pressed by a journalism student for the secret of his success, he replied, "All you got to have is newspaper training and common sense."

ON TO MIAMI BEACH

In 1922, feeling confident because of his 10 years' experience in journalism and publicity, Hannagan opened his own publicity office and returned to publicizing the speedway and its Memorial Day race. His next big break came when Carl Fisher summoned him in 1924 to Miami Beach where he was developing a whole new city by pumping the muck out of Biscayne Bay into a mangrove swamp. From a swampy sandspit that was home for mosquitoes and water moccasins, Fisher, aided by Hannagan, built what one journalist termed "A Gleaming Babylon by the Sea Inhabited by Millionaires." Miami Beach was built not only with sand but with scads of photos of pretty girls romping about in scanty bathing suits. Hannagan had accepted Fisher's offer after he was offered a salary of $300 a week plus all his expenses.

The next year, Hannagan set up the Miami Beach News Bureau, which became a model for information services and resorts around the globe. In the process, the now standard "Hometown newspaper please note," each one carrying a Miami Beach dateline, was developed. Legend has it that Hannagan would do anything for the Miami Beach dateline in the papers. In his early days there, he wired all news services: "FLASH: JULIUS FLEISCHMAN JUST DROPPED DEAD ON A POLO FIELD HERE. DON'T FORGET MIAMI BEACH DATELINE." Hannagan knew news and saw to it that news from the Beach reached the wires. As *Fortune* wrote of Hannagan's work in 1936, "Hannagan invented the cunning stunts to keep Florida in the rotogravures and newsreels all winter long." Hannagan was guided by the motto, "Anybody from any town that comes to Florida for the winter and could be pictured in a bathing suit" was important for a picture back home. Time proved that these "hometowners" would bring more tourists from those cities and towns the next year. Newspapers around the country (save perhaps California) were printing pictures of pretty Miami Beach high school girls cavorting on the beach in tight-fitting bathing suits, of waiters racing across the sands, and snowball fights on the beach as well as every tourist who came within range of Hannagan's photographers. One theme inserted endlessly in his releases was the fact that Miami Beach's surface was warmer in January than Los Angeles's famed surf was in August.

The miracle Fisher wrought with the help of Hannagan's unending publicity barrage can be seen in the fact that when the first settler landed on Miami Beach in 1880, he bought miles of this swampy, offshore sandspit for 35¢ an acre. Today an acre of Miami Beach ocean front costs millions. One writer in describing the modern Miami Beach wrote, "Even people who have never been to Miami Beach have seen its skyline on a thousand postcards, travel folders and TV shows. Like a fantastic mirage, its shining towers and rainbow hotels rise sheer from the blue Atlantic, bathed in the sunlight of everyone's dream of a tropical vacation." Another observed, "To some, the Beach is an exotic golden paradise, far from the dark northern winter. To others, it is our grossest national product." It was Fisher who made the revolutionary discovery that a steam dredge could use the muck from Biscayne Bay to build cheap land on the 20-mile long sandspit.

During the 1920s, Fisher and Hannagan imported gondoliers from Venice, Italy and polo ponies from California. They tore down the old tacky bathhouses and hired pretty girls to lounge around the new concrete swimming pool. Hannagan's flair for the unusual led to myths about his skill in creating news events. For example, Hartwell, in his *Collier's* article credited Hannagan with inveigling President Warren G. Harding to visit Miami Beach where Hannagan provided him with a baby elephant as a golf caddy. Only trouble with this story is that President Harding died in 1923, and Hannagan didn't go to Miami Beach until 1924.

Along with the fluff of pretty girls and baby elephants as golf caddies, Hannagan was supplying hard news to the nation's press and developing a reputation for integrity and accuracy. One story illustrates this: In 1930, an editor of *Time* doing a roundup on the tourist business in the Depression wired Hannagan for a report on Miami Beach. Hannagan wired *Time* that "business is lousy, down 20 per cent," and followed with details. The *Time* editor told a writer, "Cancel this story, let's do one about an honest press agent." The result was a flattering piece in *Time*, adding to Hannagan's growing stature as a responsible press agent. There are two versions of this story in the Hannagan lore. One says it was an editor of *Time*, another that it was Henry Luce, the founding publisher. Hannagan was savvy enough to know that such a reputation was his greatest asset in dealing with the press. From Miami Beach went all the news good and bad.

Fisher's initial success began to dim when a severe hurricane in 1926 frightened tourists away and brought the end of the Florida land boom, a disaster in which many Northern speculators lost a bundle. Three years later came the Stock Market Crash and ensuing great Depression. Tourism fell off, and in 1930, a new era began when the notorious gangster, Al Capone, strutted out of prison to spend the season at his palatial home on the Beach. This was the beginning of a transition from a great vacation place to an early Las Vegas with the riffraff of the nation flocking to bet on Hialeah's ponies or to play roulette in Miami Beach's new casinos. As the tawdriness and the bilking of tourists began to blight the Miami Beach image, Hannagan, in 1933, dropped the account and left Miami Beach. As Hartwell reported, "As this violated Hannagan's Client Requirement Number One—honesty—Hannagan filed for divorce." The candid Hannagan also told friends there was no money in the account any more.

Yet Hannagan was once accused—falsely his friends insisted—of planting a story of an attempted assassination of Jack Dempsey, the former World's Heavyweight Boxing Champion, in order to promote the Sharkey–Stribling fight in Miami Beach. Dempsey, front man for the bout, was spending the night as a guest in a strange house. Hearing a strange noise downstairs, he went to investigate. As Dempsey came down the steps, he surprised a burglar who panicked and fired a shot at him. A reporter was tipped to the story, and it got a heavy national newsplay. Hannagan vigorously denied any part in this episode; it would have been out of character for him. More likely it was planted by the fight's publicists.

Hannagan's publicity success was particularly galling to Miami Beach's cross-town rival, Miami. Their rivalry for the tourist trade was spirited, to put it mildly. There is no published score of the result, but Hannagan treasured a clipping from the editorial page of a Miami paper that sadly complained that all the good news of the area went out under a Miami Beach dateline, and all the bad news was datelined Miami. In a few years, Steve Hannagan had set up the most elaborate municipal publicity system in the world. Early on, Hannagan's success in promoting Miami Beach forced West Palm Beach, Miami, and Coral Gables to follow suit. Gerry Swinehart, who later became a driving force in the success of Carl Byoir & Associates, was director of publicity for Palm Beach and West Palm Beach from 1926 to 1930. He joined Carl Byoir in Cuba in 1930 to help launch Carl Byoir & Associates. By 1933, Hannagan was ready to move on, the Babylon by the Sea a shining monument to his prowess.

A sad footnote to the Fisher–Hannagan success with Miami Beach: Fisher thought he could create a summer resort off the tip of Long Island, which he named Montauk Playground and sunk $12,000,000 in the 90-acre venture. Hannagan's magic couldn't pull this one off when the nation was hit by the Stock Market Crash of 1929 and the ensuing Great Depression. When Carl Fisher died in 1939, he was down to his blue chip securities, a morose alcoholic.

THE GENE TUNNEY MYTH

In 1928 before his championship fight with Tom Heeney, World Champion Gene Tunney retained Steve Hannagan, a longtime friend, to promote the fight with Heeney. Somehow out of this association came the myth that it was Hannagan who had publicized Tunney's interest in Shakespeare and other good books. The myth was repeated in the long obituaries of Hannagan the press carried after his death in Africa. The Shakespeare stories started flowing out of Tunney's training camp before his historic fight with Jack Dempsey in Philadelphia on September 23, 1926. Most of the stories originated with Brian Bell of the Associated Press who reported that Tunney was reading Emerson, Omar Khayyam, and Shakespeare. These stories shocked boxing fans who were not accustomed to associating boxers with such literary tastes.

Shortly after the Hannagan obituaries appeared, Frank J. Starzel, general manager of the AP, was having lunch with Tunney at the Dutch Treat Club. Tunney told Starzel:

> I noticed the other day that some one mistakenly credited Steve Hannagan with originating those stories. Steve was a good friend of mine and he did help me before my last fight — with Tom Heeney in 1928 — but he had nothing to do with the first news accounts of my interest in good books. Brian Bell deserves all the credit. He got the story first because he was a good reporter, looking for things outside the routine of a fight training camp. Once he broke it, others picked it up and had a lot of fun with it.

AN UNSUCCESSFUL INTERLUDE WITH LORD & THOMAS

In one of the early efforts by an advertising agency to develop a publicity service for its advertisers, Albert Lasker, the father of modern advertising and builder of the giant ad agency, Lord & Thomas (later Foote, Cone, and Belding) offered Hannagan a position as vice-president in charge of new business in 1933. Lasker saw Hannagan's main task as promoting the products and services of Lord & Thomas's clients. Difficulties for Hannagan arose almost immediately. He was one among many vice-presidents and had no staff to assist him — as he had had in Miami Beach and Indianapolis. This, coupled with other problems in finding a place for the publicity function, led Hannagan to resign in 1935 and open his own publicity agency in New York City. His detractors sneered Hannagan "couldn't play in the major leagues" of big-time corporate advertising and public relations — words that his critics would swallow years later.

Given Lasker's unorthodox ways of managing his agency, it is easy to understand why Hannagan had difficulty in finding a place for himself and his function in Lord & Thomas. On top of that, the idea of a publicity division in an advertising agency was relatively new and untried. N. W. Ayer & Son, the oldest agency in the nation, had seen the importance of product promotion as a supplement to advertising at the turn of the century when the National Biscuit Company, with Ayer's help, took the cracker out of the barrel in general stores and put it in a sanitary package. In gaining acceptance of this revolutionary change in merchandising, National Biscuit and the Ayer agency learned that it takes more than advertising to gain acceptance of change. It takes education, now as then a fundamental assignment for public relations. In 1930, J. Walter Thompson developed a publicity capability, primarily to promote its sponsors' radio shows, such as the Kraft Music Hall.

In his favorable biography of Albert Lasker, *Taken at the Flood*, John Gunther said Lasker "was certainly not a conventional executive." He described Lord & Thomas as "eccentrically run," explaining, "Trying to find out exactly the sequence of officers in power during the 30s, I asked one man who had been president of Lord & Thomas for a while who his successor was; he looked puzzled, scratched his head, and replied, 'I don't think we had one.' Lasker hated committees as much as he hated graphs and charts. Gunther found that "Lord & Thomas was not an organization at all, but a series of semi-autonomous pools, with Lasker, the dictator, way up at the top." Little wonder Hannagan had trouble finding his niche there.

Gunther's only mention of Hannagan's association with Lasker involved a humorous incident. Merrill C. Meigs, who had worked for Lasker before World War I and was now a Chicago publisher, was a flier and had his own airplane. Hannagan happened to run into Meigs in Detroit one day after discovering he had just missed a train to Chicago where he had an urgent appointment at Lasker's home in Lake Forest. He explained his plight to Meigs who offered to fly him there. Without warning, Meigs landed his Stinson on Lasker's fairway, near the sixth green and 50 feet from the house. When Hannagan walked in, Gunther reported, "Lasker was overwhelmed with amazement, curiosity, and delight."

THE SAMUEL INSULL SAGA

It would be hard to image two more disparate personalities than Steve Hannagan and Samuel Insull, who skillfully used publicity to build a watery utilities empire in the 1920s. Hannagan was one of the most flamboyant press agents ever to garner a clipping. His Irish black hair, heavy black brows, keen flashing blue eyes, and wide grin were familiar from famous Hollywood night spots to New York's Stork Club, owned by his friend Sherman Billingsly. Insull was a dour-appearing individual with a heavy white mustache and a stern all-business demeanor, the stereotype of an industrial tycoon. In his heady days of success, he was gruff and testy with reporters.

In 1934, while working for Lord & Thomas, Hannagan, with considerable uneasiness, agreed to Samuel Insull, Jr.'s pleas to help his father, now a fugitive from United States justice. Thus began the Hannagan–Samuel Insull saga.

In the mid-1920s, Americans, certain that they had found the key to permanent prosperity, were scraping up or borrowing money to invest in the stocks of American industry and finance. Corporate magnates, Samuel

Insull among them, were riding the crest of this spiraling paper wealth, blissfully ignoring the possibilities of the catastrophe that would overtake them in 1929. Insull had built a pyramiding utility empire as board chairman or majority owner of more than 70 utility companies in some 30 states. His personal wealth was small as he poured virtually everything he earned into his companies. He expected the same of those who worked for him. Insull used every form of media to persuade thousands of investors to buy shares in his giant Middle West Utilities, Commonwealth Edison Company, People Gas, and other utilities. Through his pyramiding of holding company into super holding company, Insull sold electricity to the nation.

One of the most public relations-minded business leaders of his era and a young assistant working for Thomas A. Edison in The Battle of the Currents with George Westinghouse, Insull has learned the importance of publicity. Westinghouse's alternating current system finally triumphed over Edison's direct current system. Early in his career, Insull advocated governmental regulation of utilities and vowed to sell electric energy at the lowest possible rates. A master of the "timed rate cut," Insull used publicity and advertising to tell the public that he was holding the line on prices during times of escalating costs. His innovative publicity program was directed by Bernard J. Mullaney, a former Chicago newspaperman. Mullaney used house publications as early as 1902 and began using the new-found art of motion pictures as early as 1909 to tell the Insull story to employees, customers, and investors. In the 1920s, Insull used the engine of publicity to build his expanding empire. In this campaign, he used many unethical and unsavory tactics that led to an investigation by the Federal Trade Commission in 1928 that cast dark shadows across Insull's reputation. The main thrust of the campaign was to persuade the public of the advantages of private ownership of public utilities. Insull's campaign, which began in 1919, a time when there was much support for municipal ownership of public utilities, is well described in Ernest Gruening's *The Public Pays.*

When Samuel Insull fled from the United States after the collapse of his shaky super holding company structure, public anger rose against him. To many, his self-imposed exile made certain their conviction of his guilt. He was accused of financial mismanagement, stock watering, embezzlement, or worse. Insull hoped that if he could stay abroad for a few years, tempers would cool and then he could get a fair trial. However, the drumbeat of the press wouldn't let the public forget. Hounded by reporters and an unrelenting government, Insull skipped about Europe, Turkey, and Greece, until taken from Turkey by a State Department guard in March 1934.

In the meantime, Samuel Insull, Jr., then in his early 30s, was working for the new management at Commonwealth Edison that had dumped Insull's longtime advertising agency, McJunkin, and retained Lord & Thomas. Along with Britton I. Budd, formerly an Insull public relations aide, young Insull became the liaison between Commonwealth and Lord & Thomas. In the course of events, young Insull met Steve Hannagan, and according to Insull, Jr., they took "an immediate dislike to each other."

There are two versions of how Hannagan came to be involved in the effort to save Insull, Sr.'s hide. Samuel Insull, Jr. has told interviewers that when the father was being brought home to face the many indictments against him that Hannagan, forgetting their past differences, called Junior to offer his help when the "old gentleman returned." More than one writer who had interviewed Hannagan pictured the press agent as responding to Junior's plea for help.

Forrest McDonald in his authorized biography, *Insull*, quoted Junior as telling his father that Hannagan had agreed to help for "free." The author was unable to determine whether this service to the Insulls came while Hannagan was still on the Lord & Thomas payroll or between his leaving the ad agency and opening his office in New York City. However, they came to an agreement; Hannagan and Insull, Jr. met on a Saturday morning in Insull's office. Hannagan made two blunt demands before agreeing to handle the assignment: One, would Junior's father do as his son told him? Two, would Junior do as Hannagan told him? The son agreed to both demands.

Friends quoting Hannagan in later years insisted that it was young Insull who came to Hannagan to plead for help for his father and that Hannagan always "regretted handling the Insull publicity." The hard fact was that the son was now the sole support of his father and under indictment himself; he had been planning his father's defense alone. He needed the Hannagan magic more than Hannagan needed this assignment. A former judge, Floyd Thompson, was retained as the Insulls' counsel. The son, Hannagan, and Thompson, worked closely together with the legal defense becoming an extension of Hannagan's public relations program for Insull. Through all this, Hannagan insisted that he remain in the background. In compliance with Hannagan's conditions that he be in charge of all except the legal aspects of the case, Junior relayed Hannagan's instructions to his father and sternly told him that Hannagan's instructions were to be followed to the letter. The frightened and broken old man complied.

Where once there was a gruff tycoon who had little patience for reporters, there was now the picture of a cooperative, broken, aged former tycoon. Insull started his campaign aboard his ship, the *Exilona*, on the way home from Turkey. Accompanied by State Department officials and several news correspondents, he began to unravel the fascinating story of his life;

a story he unfolded in court 6 months later in an amazing display of recall and delivery. Hannagan pumped this image of a poor, broken old man into larger than life size during the pretrial summer months of 1934.

Insull's arrival in the United States from his self-imposed exile was a big news event. The *Literary Digest* of May 19, 1934, reported that Insull's return on May 7 was a major event for the press. "Tugs and airplanes filled with reporters surrounded the boat and Mr. Insull, who formerly was accustomed to shaking his gold-headed cane angrily at photographers, graciously consented to pose innumerable times in innumerable ways.

Before the army of reporters, Insull, Sr. pulled a crumpled piece of paper from his pocket and read from a handwriting he had never seen before the following statement, speaking in his clear, crisp British accent:

> I am back in America to make the most important fight of my life — not only for freedom but for complete vindication. Two years ago when I left this country there were no charges against me. . . . I have erred, but my greatest error was in underestimating the effect of the financial panic on American securities, and particularly on the companies I was working so hard to build. I worked with all my energies to save those companies. I made mistakes, but they were honest mistakes. There were errors in judgment, but not dishonest manipulations.

Though the reporters were told that this was the son's statement, it was in Hannagan's handwriting — the only statement or release he ever wrote in this case. On the train trip home from New York when Insull and his son had a chance to talk in a washroom away from the security guards, the old man asked, "Who the hell wrote that statement? It's pretty good." Then young Insull briefed his father on Hannagan. "He's running our affairs and I hope that you'll do what he says." Insull, Sr. who had known the importance of public relations before Steve Hannagan was born, looked up from a washbasin and said, "Well, I'll be god damned."

Upon arriving in Chicago, Samuel Insull was booked and placed behind bars in the Cook County Jail with flashbulbs flashing and reporters furiously taking notes. The presiding judge put Insull's bail at $200,000, a very large bail in those days. Hannagan later reflected that the stiffness of the bail and the resultant publicity of the old man behind bars was the turning point of his public relations campaign. As *Collier's* observed after Insull's acquittal, "Americans don't like to see repentant septuagenarians go to jail unless they're convicted." Insull's biographer, Forest McDonald, wrote in *Insull*: "The publicity attending the bail and jailing incident was the first step in transforming the popular image of Insull from that of an evil manipulator and swindler . . . into an infirm aged sometime public benefactor persecuted for the sins of his generation."

Released from jail, the elder Insull took up quarters in the modest Seneca

Hotel on Chicago's famous Gold Coast. Then began the summer's campaign to condition the public in favor of the Insulls. The press agent's hand was easily discernible in that campaign although Hannagan stayed in the background. Basically, Hannagan counseled the elder Insull through the son that he must always be accessible to the press and always let the photographers have "one more" shot. Suddenly, Chicago newspapers began running photos of a kindly, aged, family-loving Samuel Insull. Pilloried in the same newspapers only months before, he was now portrayed in a wholly new light. Along with inviting the press to every possible Insull group gathering, Hannagan made certain the "old gentleman" was seen by Chicagoans all summer long. Where Insull went, the press also went, including frequent trips to Chicago's World's Fair. Meanwhile, Insull, Jr. busied himself making friends with the many journalists who frequented the Seneca, looking for new angles on the upcoming trial. When October 2 came, Thompson's case was ready and public opinion was now favorable to the defendant.

Each day before the trial, Insull met with Hannagan and Thompson as to which tack to pursue during the day's testimony. For 42 days, the case was tried in the courtroom and in the press. Press conferences continued to be called at the Insull residence for any or no reason, anything that would depict Insull as a loving family man. Reporters always responded, not wishing to miss a possible Insull story. On November 24, 1934, Insull was acquitted of all charges 42 days after the trial had begun — a triumph for the legal defense and Hannagan's public relations strategy.

With the mail fraud charge behind him, Insull, Sr. next faced trials on charges of embezzlement and violation of the federal bankruptcy laws. Neither trial lasted long enough to become big news, and Insull and his son were both acquitted. Hannagan was not involved in these latter trials.

Although various civil litigations continued to haunt Insull until his death in a Paris subway station, Hannagan's counseling had brought about a major shift in public attitudes toward the architect of one of the world's greatest financial disasters. A troublesome question: Did Hannagan's strategy serve the cause of justice?

HANNAGAN MOVES TO THE BIG CITY

With the Insull campaign over and his continued dissatisfaction with his situation at Lord & Thomas, Steve Hannagan left Chicago and opened the office of Steve Hannagan & Associates in New York City. The associates at first were Joe Copps and Larry Smits. More than one new client was steered to Hannagan by a grateful Samuel Insull, Jr., who often described Hannagan as a "clear thinker." In New York, Hannagan became a fixture at Sherman Billingsly's Stork Club. Although Billingsly was never a paying client, Hannagan gave him much helpful public relations advice. Billingsly, in turn, steered clients to Hannagan.

ANOTHER MONUMENT — SUN VALLEY

The first major corporate client the new Hannagan firm acquired was the Union Pacific (UP) Railroad. He was in Hollywood in 1936 when he got a telephone call from W. Averill Harriman, chairman of the railroad's board of directors and its major stockholder. Harriman told Hannagan, "I've had an Austrian ski expert combing the country for a winter ski resort that would match anything they have in Europe. He thinks he's found such a place. It's up in Idaho near a town called Ketchum. I want to know what you think of it." Hannagan hurriedly took a train to Chicago.

Indicating that Hannagan and Insull, Jr. had become close friends, the Insull son recorded the fact that Hannagan had called him from the station to suggest that they have dinner. According to young Insull, Hannagan confessed he didn't even know how to get to Ketchum, let alone promote it. As the men talked, Insull, Jr. suggested that they look Ketchum up in the railway guide in the downtown office of the Illinois Central Railroad. "Freight service only—weekly," it read. With this knowledge, he made arrangements to meet William M. Jeffers, vice-chairman of the UP board in Shoshone, Idaho. Hannagan took a plane to Pocatello and there transferred to a train to get to Shoshone. The men visited awhile that night.

The next morning at 5 a.m., Jeffers routed Hannagan out of bed on a bitter cold day. Hannagan was wearing a light, tweed suit, a camel's hair topcoat, and a pair of galoshes he had borrowed from a UP trainman. Hannagan and Jeffers rode on a motorized handcar to Ketchum. There they transferred to a horse-drawn sleigh with a potbellied stove in front for heat. The drive took them over an unending expanse of snow. Before long they were forced to stop and go by foot. Hannagan was a bit disenchanted with this assignment at this point. He felt nothing but cold and saw nothing but snow. Then suddenly the sun came out, flooding the tremendous amphitheater of the valley. Within an hour, Hannagan was down to his shirt—and beaming. "Why a fellow could take a sun bath in the nude right out here in the snow," he exclaimed according to Hartwell's piece. His imagination started to take flight as he visualized the possibilities of this as a ski resort.

Harriman accepted Hannagan's favorable report, and the wheels started turning but quickly got stuck on a name for the resort. Jeffers and other UP directors were determined to name it Ketchum after the nearest UP railroad station. Hannagan told them there might be a few names less sexy, but he couldn't think of any. He had come up with Sun Valley and stubbornly stuck with it. Harriman finally broke the deadlock and chose Sun Valley. Both Hannagan and the Union Pacific officials later regarded this felicitous name as Hannagan's most important contribution to the resort's success. His publicity surely came second.

Hannagan launched the promotional campaign as construction started, and it was so successful that bookings were heavy for the opening of Sun Valley on December 21, 1936. Just one thing went wrong. There was no snow, something that hadn't happened for 45 years! At Hannagan's instructions, the management telegraphed the prospective guests that they would get free transportation to the nearest ski slopes 10 miles away and could stay at the Sun Valley Lodge free of charge until there was snow in its front yard. On December 26—St. Stephen's Day as Hannagan fondly recalled—the snow came, and on the same day a trainload of Hollywood celebrities arrived, and Sun Valley was on the front pages and in the newsreels. Hannagan was enthusiastic about this project after he had seen its possibilities. A few days after his exploratory visit, he called Insull, Jr. to tell him, "It's going to be the greatest ski resort outside the Alps."

And Hannagan would make it so, using the same glamorous beauty photographs and hometown stories he had used to build Miami Beach. A deluge of pretty women in bathing suits wearing skis flooded the nation's press. The Hannagan organization was in its element again. In 1938, *Fortune* devoted four of its king-sized pages to Sun Valley. In 1941, *Life* featured the Sun Valley adventure of the Ernest Hemingway and Gary Cooper families. With these and other stories planted in the national magazines, Harriman's ski-train business was booming. The publicity Hannagan achieved on behalf of what he had first termed when he saw it, "a god damned field of snow," did its work. Today Sun Valley is synonymous with skiing. It put the nation on skis—another monument to his legendary prowess.

Writing in the *Smithsonian Magazine* of December 1984, Peter J. Ognibene suggested the impact of Hannagan's promotion, "Within a few years of its opening in 1936 the resort had radically altered the public's perception of what skiing was all about. It replaced the skier's forbidding old daredevil image with a glamorous gallery of Hollywood stars—gliding gracefully down Idaho's mountains. It made skiing the absolutely 'in' thing to do."

HANNAGAN BECOMES NEWS

With Sun Valley saturating the nation's newspapers and magazines in the late 1930s, Hannagan himself was becoming news. He was featured in national publications with his new girl friend, the model Suzie Brewster, whom he married in 1939. His first marriage to Ruth Ellery in 1931 had ended in divorce. When his marriage to Suzie Brewster ended in divorce in the 1940s, he then began courting Ann Sheridan, the movie actress. They became a frequent gossip column item.

In 1936, *Life, Newsweek, and Fortune* all did stories on Miami Beach with detailed coverage of Hannagan's role in its popularity. *Life* gave a 6-page spread to Hannagan's stunts on behalf of the resort town.

Writing for *Scribner's Magazine* of May 1938, Stanley Jones called Hannagan "a living myth." Of his role in the Insull case, Jones succinctly wrote, "Gradually, the notion grew that no good would come from slapping a seventy-five-year-old-man into the sneezer . . . and Sam was acquitted." It was Jones who asserted that "friends believe he [Hannagan] regrets he ever handled the case." This is put in doubt by the fact that he and young Insull kept in touch over their remaining years. Hannagan also kept an autographed picture of Samuel Insull, Sr. on the wall of his New York office for several years but finally took it down because it drew too many caustic remarks.

Dickson Hartwell's lengthy review of Hannagan's career, published in December 1947 — just 12 years after he opened his New York agency — claimed that Hannagan was turning away a half million dollars worth of business a year. Hartwell wrote, "He refused to take over the second year of the Dallas Fair and similarly turned down the New York World's Fair. When he was asked to give Treasure Island Exposition a shot in the arm he backed away from that, too. He has also refused to publicize chain dance master Arthur Murray. James C. Petrillo, the musician's Feuhrer, appealed to him by telephone for a little popularity, and Hannagan told him to go climb a violin."

BASEBALL'S CENTENNIAL

The year 1939 marked the 100th anniversary of Abner Doubleday's invention of the game of baseball at Cooperstown, New York. In a public relations coup fashioned by Albert D. Lasker, a major owner of the Chicago Cubs, Major League Baseball created the post of Commissioner in an effort to save the game in the wake of the 1919 "Black Sox" scandal that broke in 1920 when it was learned that several members of the Chicago White Sox had thrown the World Series to an inferior Cincinnati Reds team. Judge Kennesaw Mountain Landis assumed the Commissioner's role in 1921 and ruled organized baseball with an iron hand until his death in 1944. Landis had gained national fame as the judge who broke up the Standard Oil Trust in 1911.

The owners of the major league teams decided that the centennial of baseball ought to be celebrated with fanfare. They appropriated $100,000 for the event. Commissioner Landis didn't cotton much to the idea. Someone recommended that he hire Hannagan, whom he had never met, to direct the observance. He called Hannagan from Chicago and told him, "Some damn fools in the baseball industry want to spend $100,000 on a 100-year celebration. They've given me the money. I understand you're honest and won't try to steal it or throw it away. You probably won't be able to do any good, but will you take this money off my hands and spend it?" Hannagan accepted and set about with a season-long celebration.

The final event was an All-Star game in Cooperstown, home of the Baseball Hall of Fame. After the final event, Landis and Hannagan met on the train back to New York. The crusty commissioner put his arm around Hannagan and congratulated him. "I was wrong, the money was spent to achieve splendid results." "I've got some money left over, Judge," Hannagan told him. "I'll send it back to you." Landis looked startled, then smiled, "If it's as much as $500," he said, "that's good." Hannagan beamed, "Judge, I am going to send you a check for $35,000." It took a full minute for Landis to recover. Hannagan never forgot the lessons of frugality his mother had taught him. He was not loose with a buck.

WORLD WAR II BRINGS A LOSS OF ONE AIRCRAFT CLIENT BUT GAINS ANOTHER

When Pearl Harbor came, Hannagan was public relations counsel for Consolidated Aircraft. Soon thereafter Victor Emanuel bought control of Consolidated from Rueben Fleet. He already controlled Vultee Aircraft in Los Angeles, so he merged the two into Consolidated Vultee, the present Convair Division of General Dynamics. Emanuel asked Tom Girdler, former president of Republic Steel, to run the two companies, and he took charge in January 1942. John W. Hill, founder and president of Hill and Knowlton, Inc., New York City, had served as Girdler's public relations counsel since the late 1920s. Girdler took Hill to Los Angeles with him and gave him the unpleasant task of dismissing Hannagan as counsel.

As Hill recalled in his autobiography, *The Making of a Public Relations Man*, written with his staff's help:

> I had met Steve some years before when, as a salesman, for the Lord and Thomas Advertising Agency, he called upon me to solicit the American Iron and Steel Institute account. He had a breezy, winning personality with energy and drive. I imagine he suspected the nature of my visit but, when I arrived, he came to the reception room with a cordial welcome. . . . When I told him what the situation was, he said he quite understood and wished me luck. A

few months later, however, he had his innings when he lured back into his fold a former employee of his I had taken over as our representative in San Diego [John W. Thompson].

Hill's comment tend to confirm the impression that Hannagan was hired by Albert Lasker primarily as a salesman to bring in new accounts.

FORD AND WILLOW RUN

Being 46 years old when World War II came to the United States at Pearl Harbor, Hannagan's main activities during the war years were concentrated on serving the Ford Motor Company's Willow Run bomber plant and counseling John Hay (Jock) Whitney on the latter's wartime service. Before the war, Hannagan had been retained by Whitney to promote a series of minor epic pictures produced by Whitney, mostly known in the media as a wealthy sportsman. When the war broke out, Whitney was commissioned a captain in the Air Force and assigned to Public Information, a subject about which he knew very little. Captain Whitney enlisted Hannagan's counsel after he was assigned to England in the Eighth Air Force. On a regular basis Hannagan sent Whitney analyses of news published in the United States about the air war in Europe, along with suggestions as to which type of stories would interest readers at home. Whitney rose from captain to colonel during the course of the war. Hannagan disclaimed any credit for this, saying, "Colonel Whitney had a very good war record."

But his main energies were focused on putting in perspective the false expectations officials of the Ford Motor Company and the Defense Department had aroused in constructing its Willow Run B-24 bomber plant. Started in 1941, Ford's Willow Run Plant was awarded the glamour plane, the B-24 *Liberator*, for production in its new plant. Ford's public relations at that time were uncoordinated, to put it mildly, and various officials were promising to "build a bomber every hour." The new building was described in one publication as "Henry Ford's miracle." Another boast was that 1,000 bombers would emerge from the plant every 24 hours. Henry Ford had only promised to build 1,000 bombers every month. According to David L. Lewis in *The Public Image of Henry Ford*, "The myth that production miracles were being performed at Willow Run was exploded in August, 1942. Meantime, in June Edsel Ford, dismayed by the company's uncoordinated public relations activities and the 'loose talk' about Willow Run production, appointed Steve Hannagan to be responsible for dissemination of all Ford news and be in all instances the one and only initial liaison with the press." John Hill speculated in his book that Hannagan was chosen by Edsel Ford because of his experience with Consolidated Vultee.

A bit of background from Lewis's first-rate history of the ups and downs of public relations in the Ford Motor Company in the reign of Henry Ford I is enlightening. In his early days as a manufacturer of the Model T Ford, Henry Ford, aided by his then partner Frank Couzens, was promotion minded and used every conceivable tool of publicity and marketing. The chronicler of Ford's public relations history, *The Public Image of Henry Ford: An American Hero and His Company*, Lewis concluded, "The industrialist is revealed . . . as perhaps the most astute self-advertiser in the whole history of a land that has produced its full share of promoters and showmen." From 1908 on, Ford, Couzens, and their associates sought publicity, in sharp contrast to their publicity-shy contemporaries in the automobile business that may explain why Ford prospered as many competitors fell by the wayside. And fall by the wayside they did and still do. More than 4000 different makes of automobiles have been put on the market in the United States, and only a relative handful have survived. Ford used auto racing, started a Ford Owners Club, and was among the first to use the newly invented motion picture. His 1914 motion picture of the Ford assembly line method of car production brought him wide acclaim in business circles.

But with his success and dominance of the auto market, Henry Ford became smug and rigidified and lost interest in publicity or public relations. Consequently, when the war was over, he ordered Hannagan dismissed. It was not until 1945 when his grandson, Henry Ford II, took over the failing company that public relations was restored as an important function in the company. This time it was Counselor Earl Newsom who built an image of young Henry as an industrial statesman, an image that came to be tarnished in his later years as head of Ford. That story is told in chapter 21.

In Hannagan's opinion, the Ford account was the most exciting and challenging of his career. Hannagan was exhilarated by the thought that next to the President of the United States, Henry Ford could reach the nation's front pages faster than anyone else. According to Lewis, "The announcement that Ford had engaged a 'loud-shouting, belligerent whip-smart press agent' whose specialty had been described as 'peddling photos of pretty legs in mid-winter' raised many eyebrows and provided considerable speculation about Hannagan's new assignment." The *Detroit News* stated, "America will expect a lot from Steve Hannagan and Henry Ford."

Hannagan set out to organize a news bureau to get out factual reports on the Willow Run plant operations, knowing full well that swift and accurate reporting of the facts was the best way to offset vacuums of curiosity that would be filled with rumors. In organizing the bureau, he was assisted by his longtime chief assistant, Joe Copps. John W. Thompson, who had worked for Hannagan at Consolidated, was named bureau manager. Four men were recruited from Eastern and Midwestern newspapers to round out the staff. One of them, Charles Carll, ultimately became director of Ford Motor Company's public relations in 1945.

Hannagan persuaded Edsel Ford that nothing, absolutely nothing, be said about the bomber plant's production until bombers started rolling off the assembly line. He also set about to stop leaks on this story and make his bureau the sole source of news on the B-24. Hannagan wrote the Fords, Charles E. Sorensen, and Harry Bennett, Henry Ford's bodyguard and main adviser, "Today the nation has the general impression that bombers are rolling off the assembly line at the rate of one an hour. This is not yet true. When it is, we will tell the story with newsreels, radio, press associations' stories and pictures, in its full bloom." Hannagan's recommendations were accepted, and he spent the rest of the year releasing news to focus on other war productions of the company. Stories on the bomber plant did begin flowing in November and December.

Hannagan took other steps to project a more rounded picture of the Ford Motor Company in time of war. A few weeks after Hannagan came on the job, Ford resumed institutional radio advertising in June 1942. Hannagan hoped that the new program, "Watch the World Go By," would improve public morale by creating a better understanding of Ford's war effort. For 2 months after Hannagan's appointment, there was little criticism of the Willow Run plant's production. But then in mid-August 1942, according to David Lewis, "Willow Run production problems were rudely shoved into the limelight by Ford's aviation nemesis, 'Dutch' Kindelberger," who in an August 13 interview, attacked "the political cowards who are withholding from the American people the full true facts" about the auto industry's production problems. Quickly, within a few hours, a March of Time newscast lambasted Willow Run. A few days later, *Time* 's sister publication, *Life*, using the same data carried a lengthy article, "Detroit Is Dynamite." Detroit's mayor, R. J. Thomas of the United Auto Workers union, and Detroit newspapers all struck back, but this only poured gasoline on the flames of this story. Strangely, neither the Ford Motor Company nor the Defense Department issued a rebuttal. The company virtually closed the plant to public inspection and declined further comment on bomber production.

On January 29, 1943, the War Production Board lifted the veil of secrecy admitting there had been disappointments and that even the other plant was far from full production. It blamed the lack of available manpower for much of the problem. Then on February 13, the Office of War Information (OWI) issued a statement it felt necessary because of "widespread, conflicting stories, reporting [Willow Run] output all the way from ridiculously small to fantastically large numbers. Both reports withheld actual numbers because of "military security." The day the OWI released its report, Hannagan issued a flood of pictures and press releases of Willow Run's operations. Lewis recorded, "Hundreds of newspapers ran stories and pictures of bombers on the assembly line and of employees, many of them attractive girls, working on the aircraft." Hannagan never overlooked the potential of pretty girl photographs.

By January 1944, the Willow Run plant was out of the woods when Ford declared that it was "the largest supplier of B-24s." As the early boasts started coming true, the plant and company officials received widespread praise in the press and from politicians. In the early days before hiring Hannagan, the Ford Company had made a common public relations blunder — creating false expectations in the public, only to reap disappointment. The extravagant premature buildup was the fault of both the company and the Defense Department. In Lewis's opinion, Charles Sorensen "was perhaps more responsible than any person for its buildup and letdown."

According to Lewis, Edsel Ford and Charles E. Sorensen were the two executives most responsible for the company's considerable wartime achievements. Edsel Ford, who had lived always in his father's shadow, died of stomach cancer in May 1943, and Charles Sorensen left the company after Henry Ford and Harry Bennett again gained the upper hand in the company's management. Lewis wrote, "Playing upon Henry Ford's senile spinelessness, he [Harry Bennett] got rid of Steve Hannagan, whose retention by Edsel Ford had the strong support of Sorensen, and who had engineered much of the production executive's favorable publicity." On June 1, 1943, only 4 days after Edsel's funeral, the magnate fired Hannagan. Sorensen was powerless to intervene. John W. Thompson, who had gained Bennett's goodwill, remained as head of the News Bureau. From then on until he himself was fired by Henry Ford II, Bennett, through Thompson, controlled Ford's public relations.

HANNAGAN'S FIRM PROSPERS UNTIL HIS DEATH

In the next decade until his death in February 1953, while on a mission in Africa for Coca-Cola Export Co., Hannagan's firm served such corporate clients as Union Pacific, mainly in promoting UP's Sun Valley ski resort, Libby–Owens–Ford (LOF), Willys–Overland, Cities Service Company, Pan American Airways, the Commonwealth of Puerto Rico, and the Fifth Avenue Bus Company.

More than 2 years after Hannagan's death, his old firm was bought by

John Hill, then chairman of Hill and Knowlton, Inc. for $200,00. The firm had been taken over and renamed Robinson– Hannagan by William Robinson. A short time later, Robinson was tapped by the venerable builder of the Coca-Cola empire, Robert W. Woodruff, to be president of the soft drink giant. Joe Copps, longtime association of Hannagan, was president at the time of the sale in August 1955. More on this in a moment.

Libby–Owen's–Ford retained Hannagan for two reasons: one, to promote the use of bottles for the sale and delivery of milk; two, to promote its new safety glass for installation in automobiles. During World War II, a shortage of milk bottles developed and dairymen started turning to paper cartons. Hannagan and his associates bird-dogged details. His Hollywood staff man learned that the script for the hit movie, *The Lost Weekend*, starring Ray Milland, called for Milland to stumble over milk cartons as he entered his apartment. Hannagan's Hollywood representative, learning of this, quickly rushed to the studio with a quantity of glass milk bottles and persuaded the director that the clatter of bottles would be more dramatic. This assignment also included a campaign to persuade customers to return all the bottles cluttering their basements and back halls, a campaign that benefitted client Coca-Cola as well as LOF.

He had other clients on a less sustained basis in the postwar years. For example, in 1946, the American Tobacco Company paid Hannagan $50,000 to promote Jack Benny's radio programs. Similarly, the Electric Auto-Lite Company retained him for awhile to promote the programs of Dick Haymes, the company's radio singer. In these latter years, his counsel and service became more and more a mix of publicity and public relations.

HANNAGAN HAD HIS FAILURES, TOO

Though great monuments remain to remind us of Hannagan's Midas publicity touch, he, like all practitioners, had his failures. Previously cited was the Fisher–Hannagan failure to make a go of the Montauk Playground off Long Island. Another time a manufacturer of a newly developed electric razor asked him to promote its acceptance. He tried out the razor for a month and told the prospective client, "It won't sell." Given his success with the Indianapolis Speedway, Hannagan was retained to promote the Roosevelt raceways on Long Island, an attempt in the late 1930s to introduce European road racing to the United States. According to Dickson Hartwell, Hannagan "filled the sports pages with advance news of the event. But for various reasons the project laid an egg."

One reason that Hannagan had many more successes than failure was that he was careful as choosing clients as a jeweler is in choosing pearls.

HANNAGAN'S GUIDING PRINCIPLES

There were more fundamental reasons for Hannagan's success as a publicist and sometimes public relations counselor. Hannagan wouldn't compromise, either on the integrity of his output or in his dealings with the media and clients. He eschewed political accounts, saying, "Politics is a compromise and I am not a compromise man." At Miami Beach, Carl Fisher presented Hannagan with several pictures he thought would promote his enterprise. Hannagan told him they were lousy pictures, and he wouldn't use them. He also refused to compromise on the naming of Sun Valley in his dispute with the Union Pacific board.

As this chapter makes clear, Hannagan knew that his honesty was his most precious asset in dealing with the media, a fact that little concerns the press agents operating in Hollywood and along Broadway. As the famous creator of stunts, Jim Moran, once told me, "I play in the brass section of the public relations orchestra." Another friend, a Hollywood press agent, once said, "We stoop to anything, but our stuff gets printed." Hannagan was not of this breed. Staff members going out on an assignment were given a Hannagan stock lecture before leaving. "When in doubt call me, if you can't reach me, take fifteen minutes in the men's room for meditation, then come out and do the honest thing."

Accuracy in reporting that had been hammered into him in his cub days of newspapering was a fetish with Hannagan. His unfailing reputation for accuracy of his releases was no small factor in his ability to publicize his clients. His contracts called for a 60-day cancellation clause by either party. It is asserted that several times he canceled client contracts because he thought he was not doing a good enough job for them. Finally, to insure accuracy and service to clients, Hannagan built a data file of newspaper clips and radio transcripts that kept him in tune with the news context of the day. Finally, he earned the loyalty of his staff. Joe Copps and Larry Smits had been with Hannagan 26 years when he died. His Hollywood executive, Paul Snell, and his secretary, Miss Ray, served him a quarter of a century. Steve Hannagan was quite a guy.

HANNAGAN'S FIRM, LIKE MOST OTHERS, FADES FROM VIEW

Steve Hannagan's faded from view when his firm like all the others founded in the post World War I era, save two, the now Robinson–Hannagan Associates was bought in 1955 for $200,000 by Hill and Knowlton, Inc. and absorbed into H&K a year later. The two exceptions that have survived and flourish today are Ketchum Communications, Inc., which was founded in

1919 in Pittsburgh by brothers Carlton and George Ketchum, and Hill and Knowlton, Inc., which had its genesis in Cleveland in 1927 when John W. Hill opened what was then primarily a publicity business.

William E. Robinson, who had a long career in newspaper publishing including nearly 20 years with the *New York Herald-Tribune* that folded later in 1966, bought the controlling interest in the Hannagan firm in 1954, renaming it Robinson–Hannagan Associations, Inc. In so doing, he took over the principal client, Coca-Cola Company and Coca-Cola Export Corporation. Obviously, Robinson and Robert W. Woodruff, the venerable chairman of Coca-Cola who built the soft drink company into the giant that it is today, hit it off. Less than a year later in 1955, Woodruff made Robinson president of the Coca-Cola Company, a post he held until 1958 when he became chairman of the board and chief executive officer. In 1961, Robinson became chairman of the executive committee, a post he held at the time of his death on June 6, 1969, when he was nearly 69 years old. Joe Copps, long Hannagan's right hand man, became president of the Robinson–Hannagan firm when Robinson went to Coca-Cola.

George Allen, confident of President Eisenhower at the time, was the intermediary in the sale. As John Hill told it in his autobiography:

> Riding back north from Atlanta with the President one day in the Spring of 1954, Robinson discussed his desire to sell his interest in the public relations firm. Allen [who was serving on Hill and Knowlton's board] advised him to get in touch with me. He did, and, after some months of negotiation, we finally took over the old firm of Steve Hannagan. Hannagan was one of the greatest of all press agents, but made no claim to being a public relations man in the broadest sense.

The acquisition was announced August 9, 1955.

In a memo to H&K employees issued the day before, Hill said, "You will particularly want to note that the announcement makes clear that Robinson–Hannagan will be operated as a separate distinct public relations counseling organization, with present management continuing in charge of operations." The memo added, "There are no plans as of now to transfer any Hill and Knowlton, Inc., employees to Robinson–Hannagan, or any Robinson–Hannagan employees to our firm. We anticipate many benefits will accrue to the clients and employees of both organizations as a result of our acquisition."

A confidential memorandum found in the John W. Hill Papers, dated June 21, 1955, gives the status of Robinson–Hannagan's client list as of that date and its assessment by Hill. The memorandum that reflects the fees being charged in the mid-1950s reads as follows:

Confidential Memorandum

Re: Robinson–Hannagan   6/12/55

Accounts Reported Satisfactory: *Fee(Annual)*

1. Bahamas Development Board		$36,000.00
2. Allied Stores		36,000.00
3. Boys Republic		10,000.00
4. Glass Institute of America		40,000.00
5. Venetian Blinds		35,000.00
6. Clary Multiplier Corp.		25,000.00
7. American Potash Corp.		13,000.00
8. Owen Illinois		25,000.00
9. Coca Cola (D'Arcy Agency)		65,000.00
10. Coca Cola Export		25,000.00
11. Fifth Avenue Coach		30,000.00
	TOTAL	$341,000.00

Accounts – Continuance Questionable:

1. Gillette Safety Razor		$36,000.00
2. Olin Matheson		36,000.00
3. Electric Auto-Lite		36,000.00
	TOTAL	$108,000.00

Accounts – Severance Sure:

1. R.C.A.		$35,000.00
2. Union Pacific		25,000.00
3. Cities Service		38, 500.00
	TOTAL	$98, 500.00
	TOTAL	$547, 500.00

Robinson–Hannagan is now serving 17 accounts, of which 11 involve satisfactory relationships, the continuance of three is questionable, and the severance of three others appears to be sure. For two of these – Olin Matheson and Gillette Razor – relations are not good with the firm. The third questionable account is Electric Auto Lite, which may drop out because of business considerations.

Of those for which severance appears sure, one – the RCA account – is for advertising counsel which the company now is not equipped to provide. Another is the Union Pacific and the third is Cities Service, which automatically would be severed if Hill and Knowlton, Inc. entered the picture, because of competing oil company account.

On this basis, Hill and Knowlton, Inc. buying control of Robinson–Hannagan could reasonably count on only 11 accounts, and not 17 as are now on the books.

These 11 accounts would return a fee total of $341,000.

Total fees for the 17 accounts amount to $548,000., total salaries billed to clients on these accounts amount to $356,581., making a total billing for fees and salaries of $904.581. Out-of-pocket expenses and certain other costs are also billed.

The net return before taxes on fees and salaries billed is approximately 7.8 per cent, and about 4 per cent after taxes.

On the basis of the 11 sound accounts, there would be a calculated reduction from present business of around 37 per cent. It is not possible to predict whether billable payrolls would fall in the same proportion. If they fall only half as much, or to around $275,000., total billings to the clients would be $612,000.

Applying the 4 per cent rate, the net return after taxes would be around $25,000.

There are two serious limitations to Robinson–Hannagan business. One is the restricted range of services available to clients. The firm does not go much beyond supplying product publicity in all of its forms. This it does well. The Hollywood office has a high repute, and the firm has a high standing for integrity and service among the various media. Steve Hannagan had a fine reputation for fair dealing with the press and this was backed up by an effective organization. Bill Robinson maintained the firm's reputation and brought to it a wide and valuable range of contacts. But the firm has not greatly broadened its range of services beyond its original concept of publicity.

The second limiting factor is in its arrangements with clients. Bill Robinson has done an excellent job in getting fees on a good basis, but the weakness lies in the failure to charge clients properly for overhead. The result is that the firm last year earned something like 7.8 per cent before taxes on its total business, less out-of-pocket costs, whereas a return of around 25 per cent before taxes is considered as a reasonable return for personal service organizations like public relations.

NOTES ON SOURCES

There is no definitive biography of Steve Hannagan, thus much of this chapter is based on news accounts and articles in the periodical press that began appearing as he gained national fame through his publicity exploits. The most definitive article is that of Dickson Hartwell in *Collier's Magazine*, Vol. 120, November 22, 1947. Another excellent article was the one by Jay Scriba of *The Milwaukee Journal*, March 4, 1970, that described Miami Beach as a "Gleaming Babylon by the Sea." Hannagan's role in building the

Indianapolis Memorial Day auto race into a prime national event is told in Al Bloemaker's *500 Miles To Go, The Story of the Indianapolis Speedway*, Coward-McCann, 1961. Hannagan's brief and none too happy stint with Lord & Thomas, is dealt with briefly in John Gunther's biography of Albert Lasker, *Taken at the Flood*, Harper, 1960. Hannagan's success in promoting Sun Valley as a ski resort is best told by Peter J. Ognibene, "At the first ski spa, stars outshone the sun and snow," *Smithsonian Magazine*, Vol. 15, December, 1984. The debunking of the Gene Tunney myth was told in *The AP Log* (house organ of the Associated Press), January 25–February 3, 1954. Lengthy obituaries in the *New York Times* and New York *Herald-Tribune*, both published February 6, 1953, filled in many details on this fabulous man.

Scholar David L. Lewis's *The Public Image of Henry Ford, An American Hero and His Company*, Wayne State University Press, 1976, was the main source on Hannagan's one-year stint with the Ford Motor Company. His dismissal from Consolidated Vultee is told by John W. Hill in his *The Making of a Public Relations Man*, McKay, 1963. The purchase of the Hannagan-Robinson agency by Hill & Knowlton, Inc. is detailed in the John W. Hill Papers, Mass Communications History Center, State Historical Society of Wisconsin.

Hannagan's recasting of Samuel Insull's reputation is told in Forrest McDonald, *Insull*, University of Chicago Press, 1962, a none too critical biography and in a master's thesis by Professor William C. Adams, written under my direction in 1968. Articles on this episode include "Insullism and Other People's Money, *Literary Digest*, Vol. 117, May 19, 1934. This section is based primarily on Adams's research. The story of the Insull Empire's rise and fall is told in Ernest Gruening's *The Public Pays*, Vanguard Press, 1931. Also used in this aspect of the chapter was Stewart Holbrook's *The Age of the Moguls*.

Permission to quote from the David Lewis book was granted by the Wayne State University Press.

Chapter 11

Harry Bruno: Aviation and Public Relations Pioneer

Harry Bruno, another of the innovative small band of public relations pioneers who opened offices in the post World War I era, demonstrated that a prime function of public relations is to win public acceptance of new ideas and new technology. Bruno not only pioneered in developing this field by maturing from brash press agent to successful counselor but by playing a major role in gaining acceptance of commercial aviation in the United States.

He was born in London, England, on February 7, 1893, the son of Henry and Annie Thompson Bruno. His early education was in a British public school, but this was interrupted for him when the father decided there was a better opportunity for him and his family in the United States. The father came to New York in 1905 and established a marine insurance office. In 1907, he returned to England to bring his wife and their two sons, Harry and Frank, to Montclair, New Jersey. When the young lads arrived here, America was still excited and amazed by the advent of powered flight. The Wright Brothers had made their first powered flight at Kitty Hawk in 1903. Harry felt a responsibility for his younger brother after their parents died on the *Lusitania,* and they had a close personal relationship all their life, cemented by common interests in flying and in journalism. Frank, a newspaperman, died of cancer in 1933, when he was only 32.

Harry Bruno, only 12, was quickly caught up in this excitement, spurred by the almost daily headlines about these new-fangled, boxy flying machines; he gave his heart to flying. In time, this came to dominate his life and career. By the time the lad reached high school, he had become bored with school and much to his father's disappointment and displeasure, quit school. While working as a runner on Wall Street at $9 a week, Harry and his pal, Bernie Mahon, started work on a monoplane, the *Brumah,* a combination of their names. After many missed meals and countless diagrams, on November 26, 1910, the monoplane (actually it was a motorless glider) took off from the top of a barn on the outskirts of Montclair. Bernie was given the honor of the first flight. Tense with expectations, Harry cut the ropes and saw the frail craft glide a few feet off the roof and then fall to the ground a crumpled heap. Bernie was unhurt.

These young enthusiasts were undaunted. They went to work to build *Brumah II,* that they publicized as "the smallest monoplane in the world" to gain press attention. This time they put sled runners on it to give it momentum. Christmas Eve, 1910, with the aid of friends, they hauled the plane to a sandpit outside town, and that night poured buckets of water on the hill. The next morning, they found to their delight snow had fallen and the "runway" glazed with ice; they were ready for their second "flight". This time it was Harry's turn to be the pilot. Bernie and their friends pushed the craft onto the icy runway. As it slid down the icy slope, it gained speed, and at the end of the runway it caught an updraft and sailed, as Bruno later described it, "a beautiful two hundred and sixty five yards before crashing."

More frightened than before, this time Mr. Bruno grounded Harry and extracted a promise from his 17-year-old son that he would not fly again until he was 21. The father thought that by at that time his son would surely have outgrown "that fool hobby." How wrong he was. Not only did this experience wed Harry Bruno to aviation for life; it taught him the power of publicity. Given the news context of keen public fascination with the miracle of flight, *Brumah II* got a heavy news play in New York and New Jersey papers. *The New York Times* headlined: "GOOD GLIDES IN BOYS' AERO." The father was prompted to act when he learned that townspeople had started a collection to buy Harry and Bernie an engine for their next plane. The connection between this and the publicity did not escape young Bruno.

Tired of his Wall Street runner's job, young Bruno sought and got a job on the *Montclair Herald,* which had a circulation of 800. At the urging of a friend, Bruno had taken a correspondence course in advertising. Before long he was earning $35 a week and feeling that newspapers offered a good career for him. A few months later, he got a job on the *News and Graphics* in Greenwich, Connecticut. He started in advertising but soon was made assistant editor. In his newspaper work, he developed an easy, fluent style of writing that was to serve him well in his career as publicist and public relations counselor.

Then when things seemed to be going swimmingly, tragedy struck. His parents went down on the *Lusitania,* when it was sunk by German submarines on May 7, 1915. The Brunos were going to England because her father was seriously ill. The father, Harry related later, had wanted to take an American ship, but the mother held out for the *Cunard ship* because it was faster.

Because of his parent's death at the hands of the Germans, Harry was determined to get into the war effort after the United States declared war on Imperial Germany in April 1917. In May, he sought to enlist in the Aviation Corps but was told that only college men could apply. So in May 1917, Harry and his brother, Frank, who had caught his contagion, enlisted in the Royal Flying Corps (RFC) of Canada. Harry was assigned to Squadron 84 at Camp Mohawk, Deseronto, Canada. There his flight instructor was Vernon Castle, the famous dancer. Harry later ruefully told me that Castle taught him to fly but couldn't teach him to dance. In fact, it was Castle who recruited Harry and his brother for the RFC. Brother Frank decided that he didn't want to be a fighter pilot, resigned from the Flying Corps, returned to the United States, and joined U.S. Marines' first bombing group, soon to go overseas.

When Harry Bruno was demobilized after the war's end, he found that flyers were hard put to find jobs. As one biographer, Princine Calitri, wrote, "Planes were being junked and demolished, as few people (certainly not the government) saw the potential in flying as nothing but stunting at county fairs." Harry Bruno tried to make ends meet by lecturing to clubs about the glamour of flying and aviation's potential for civilian life. One night at a Brooklyn club, a member of the audience, S. W. Huff, sought Bruno out and took him home to dinner. The upshot of this invitation was a job with the New York City Car Advertising Company. The job paid $35 a week and after some discouragement, Bruno came to like the work.

But the siren of aviation beckoned once again. As Bruno wrote in *Wings Over America*, "The vehicle of my return the flying world was a serial, Aveline of the Airmail, ' published in *Ace High*. No great shakes as a serial, it was responsible for an offer from the Manufacturers Aircraft Association to work for them (*sic*) as a publicity man. Now I found myself in the midst of the aviation industry's great battle for survival." Bruno enlisted in that battle and helped win it.

BARNSTORMING FOR AVIATION

Sam Bradley, general manager of the Manufacturers Aircraft Association (MAA), hired Bruno at $75 a week, less than he was making as ad salesman, but of course he could not resist a chance to return to his first love and join in the battle for its survival. Bradley also hired Howard Mingos to win public understanding of the great potential for air transportation. The association had been under bitter attack since its birth in 1917, when it had been labeled an *aircraft trust*. Trust still had a pejorative ring to it from the Trust Busting days earlier in the century. Bruno was assistant publicity director, working under Mingos's supervision. Mingos taught his young assistant much about the techniques of publicity, knowledge that would stand the future counselor in good stead. Both men were acutely aware that within 3 months after the armistice, the aircraft industry had been liquidated to the point that it was down to 10% of its wartime strength. Luther K. Bell, president of the MAA, told the two publicists, "You've got to arouse America to the importance of flying." Bruno told a story that reflected this shaky period of American aviation. A woman admirer of an early flyer was remonstrating with him to give it up "because it is so terribly dangerous." Bruno's buddy replied "Dear, the greatest danger in flying is starvation."

Mingos saw the association's mission as: "The principal work involved a campaign of public education as to the commercial possibilities of aircraft. It appeared rather simple, at first. One told the people all about it, and of course they would believe it, in other words, they would use airplanes." Bruno saw the task this way:

> It fell to the MAA to stimulate the market for airplanes by keeping aviation alive. This was a large order, and the amazing growth of the automobile industry was not making it any easier. This program of advancement was all-embracing. Air meets were to be organized, shows were to be held, new record flights were to be conceived and carried through. The idea was to get people talking about flying, to make them want to fly, and especially important, to make them want to invest money in aviation.

A tall order for a new and somewhat primitive technology that stirred fears as well as awe.

In the coupling of Mingos' education approach and Bruno's barnstorming publicity approach, they had staunch support from General Manager Bradley who directed that "facts be set forth honestly and properly, but interpretation of those facts to influence the slow but steady progress of commercial aviation."

All hands at the MAA understood that they needed more than just airplanes to gain acceptance of aviation. There was a desperate need for airports, runway lighting, navigational aids, accurate weather forecasting, federal licensing of pilots, and other requirements. In *Wings Over America,* Bruno wrote:

> Compared with the efforts of ocean-spanning pilots, my own labors on behalf of the MAA seemed picayune but my job was to keep aviation on the minds

of millions of newspaper readers and newsreel audiences. Some of the stunts we pulled early in the campaign were of value. The coast-to-coast air race of 1919, for instance, taught flyers as much as it thrilled the public. The ballyhoo job we did on the New York Aero Show, held at the 71st Regiment Armory in 1920, was quite different.

For that show, Bruno first demonstrated his flair for press agentry. An LWF Owl, an experimental large bomber, was on display. He persuaded Kathlene Martyn, a Ziegfeld beauty, to pose on "the downiest mattress I could find" in her silken pajamas to publicize "the first sleeper plane in history.". The press fell for it!

While with the MAA, Bruno created another "first", the sort of thing he liked to brag about—the Quiet Birdmen. At Marta's Restaurant in Greenwich Village, a group of wartime fliers—Jimmy Doolittle, Fiorella LaGuardia, Dick Blythe, C. S. "Casey" Jones, and few others—gathered for a reunion. A magazine editor, Harold Hersey, dubbed them the Quiet Birdmen (QB), which they definitely were not. It flowered into a fraternal organization, and Bruno always proudly wore his silver and blue wings of the QB in his lapel.

Mingos stayed on to educate the public for the MAA, but in 1921, Bruno left to take the position of sales and advertising manager for the newly organized Aeromarine Airways, one of the smaller manufacturing firms, located at Keyport, NJ. It was owned by Inglis M. Uppercu, a wealthy Cadillac dealer in that area. He had bought a surplus of HS 2 Navy Coastal Patrol planes and was converting them into aircraft priced at from $6,500 to $9,000. A single Liberty engine plane could carry six persons in an open cockpit, a twin Liberty-engine plane could carry 14 passengers in an enclosed cabin. Bruno was provided a luxurious office in the Times Building.

He recounted in *Wings Over America:*

> The situation called for an organized campaign—a campaign that would see aviation first and our own planes after that. . . . Our job was to sell an apathetic public on the sheer safety of flight, this at a time when most people had not even seen a plane at close range. There was only one thing to do. We had to bring flying—its safety, its beauty, its advantages—to the people themselves. . . . The planes had to be brought to the people.

Consequently, Bruno the pilot and salesman set off on ballyhoo jaunts "to New Haven, to Providence, to Boston, and all points in between that had a harbor, a river, or even a large pond on which we could land. Each hop was a goodwill flight and so publicized in the local press. Every landing was an event." In each city Bruno and his associates was greeted by the mayor, councilmen, community leaders. Bruno made his pitch for the promotion of aviation facilities and claimed that "we left behind us a series of airport booms."

He also kept busy on the publicity front. Aeromarine announced the opening of an air freight service that proved to be premature, to put it mildly. Air freight services did not boom until after World War II. Early in 1922, Aeromarine announced the first regularly scheduled air service when it launched it from New York to Miami to Key West to Havana. The air trip took 2 days whereas the trip by train and boat took 4 days. The Aeromarine managers thought the flight to Havana would appeal to Americans made thirsty by "The Noble Experiment," Prohibition, that had been enacted in 1920 as a result of a masterful public relations campaign by the Anti-Saloon League. Bruno dubbed the flight" The Highball Express."

In June 1922, Aeromarine announced the first daily flight service from Cleveland to Detroit, a two-trip a day service that took only 90 minutes. On the New York Central from Cleveland to Detroit, the trip took $5\frac{1}{2}$ hours. This new service, like the New York–Havana one, was greeted with public skepticism. This, Bruno related, "called for a new bag of tricks." In what has become routine public relations for airlines, he arranged VIP inauguration flights for city officials, club leaders, and reporters. The firm soon found, to its dismay, that most people were still afraid to fly. Bruno wrote, "We tried flying infants. We tried publicizing pet dogs of the pilots. We tried . . . glamour."

From goodwill tours to taking babies aloft to selling aerial rides around the Statue of Liberty for $15, Bruno and the planes stayed busy. He managed to tie Aeromarine into the famed Dempsey–Carpentier flight, and on a more somber note, dropped flowers on the graves of the war dead on Memorial Day. In a more substantive feat, Bruno as commander and with Durston G. Richardson as pilot, flew around the Great Lakes on 7, 500-mile trip, and for this received the Glidden Trophy of the New York Aero Club.

Bruno even used faked news events to promote Aeromarine. Another historic first he engineered was to airlift a Ford Model T from Detroit to Cleveland. The car had to be dismantled before it could be put aboard, and the disassembly was carried out in a freight shed near the dock. The loading of the plane was witnessed by reporters and photographers. The engine accounted for roughly half the weight, Bruno told the press, and it took four men to put it aboard. As the plane took off, the assembled group cheered. The crate of course was empty. Bruno, to his credit, came to regret this deception. All this effort was to no avail. On September 1923, Aeromarine folded, leaving Bruno out of a job.

BRUNO STARTS OWN FIRM IN CUBBYHOLE

Bruno's first thought when he found himself out of a job and broke was to apply to Ivy Lee, then the big name in publicity, for a job. He wrote a persuasive letter to Lee, who agreed to see him. But before that could be arranged, Bruno met a friend on the street who was a friend of Anthony Fokker, the Dutch plane builder whose Fokker fighters the Germans had used against Allied fighters in World War I. This led to a contract with Fokker and a decision to start his own firm. Fokker, an engineering genius who knew little of public relations, was fighting the negative attitudes born of World War I in his effort to sell planes in the United States Fokker told Bruno, "I am sending the Fokker T-2 out to the St. Louis air races. Go out there and get Fokker plenty of publicity—after that, we'll talk business."

At St. Louis, the young publicist quickly ran into a roadblock. He found the Army Air Corps was determined to keep Tony Fokker's name out of print and had placed the plane at the far edge of the show, well out of the line of traffic. First, the Air Corps information officer, Colonel Horace Hickam, refused to give Bruno credentials because he represented the planemaker who was trying to sell the T-2 to the Air Corps. But Bruno quickly got around this by getting press credentials from the Newspaper Enterprise Association and from the Hearst Corporation. By this time, Bruno had wide friendships in the press. Next he found an old friend handling the microphone in the press box. Typically, it was a hot day in St. Louis. Bruno said to his friend, "Lou, you took wilted. Let me spell you while you go get a drink." Bruno got the mike and quickly started touting the T-2 and ordered mechanics to bring it to the middle of the field. Fokker, by plan, walked out in front of it. The crowd roared its approval, and the press the next day ran the story and Fokker's picture on the front page. Fokker, eminently pleased, retained Bruno indefinitely. Bruno had his first client.

The second client came by way of none other than the once outsmarted and angered Colonel Hickam. He called Bruno to say, "I've recommended you to an English friend of mine, Major Jack Savage who has invented a new business, skywriting, and needs publicity." Savage was seeking to sell his new "medium" to George Washington Hill of the American Tobacco Company, who was then pushing the sale of cigarettes to women as well as men. Bruno arranged a showing for the crusty Hill. Bruno, Savage, and Hill watched from the steps of the New York Public Library as Savage's pilot, Capt. Cyril Turner, flew over the library spelling out "Hello USA." Hill, unimpressed, grumped "It won't sell cigarettes." The persuasive Bruno got Hill to agree to a second test the next day, this one from the Vanderbilt Hotel. Bruno instructed Savage to have his pilot spell out the message, "Call the Vanderbilt Hotel," with the number 7200 trailing the command. Bruno suggested that he and Hill visit the hotel switchboard. It was jammed with calls and remained so for $3\frac{1}{2}$ hours. Washington was sold, Major Savage had a million-dollar contract, and Bruno had his second client. The Savage company was still in business as of 1961. But Bruno's days of prosperity were still far in the future.

His third client was Sherman Fairchild, a rich son of one of the founders of IBM, who had invented an aerial camera that he was attempting to lease for aerial mapping and survey work. He needed publicity and sought out Bruno. Again the press agent in Bruno came to the fore. He arranged for the disappearance of a Fairchild camera plane while on an Everglades map-photo survey for the State of Florida. Inspired wire service stories reported the missing plane in the alligator-infested Everglades. Bruno provided pictures of the missing plane, photos of missing pilots and pictures taken by the pilots before their disappearance to reflect the quality of the Fairchild camera. Bruno later confessed "When we thought it was time to end the excitement after four days of hogging every front page in the land — the plane, the crew, and the Fairchild Camera were found in good order by a guide who just happened to get a tip from a friend who was a friend of mine. And so another job was finished." The stunt brought Bruno many letters, expressing cynicism. One reporter wrote, "I wish to hereby take off my hat to a master at the art of publicity." Bruno scored other publicity coups for Fairchild. The inventor showed Bruno some mapping his plane had done in the Hudson River. A light went on; Bruno took them to a photographic studio and created a montage using pictures of a submarine running to New Haven. The product was leaked from the Prohibition Unit in New York City and newspapers soon blared headlines such as: "RUM-RUNNING SUBMARINES IN HUDSON CAUGHT BY FAIRCHILD CAMERA."

A story in the *New York American* indicated that a divisional agent, R. Q. Merrick, did start a search along the shore near Sing Sing to see if liquor caches could be found. The papers treated the whole episode tongue-in-cheek. Young Fairchild next created a cabin monoplane, the first in America, and pursuant to Fairchild's request, Bruno was able to get Gloria Swanson, then the reigning movie star, to christen it. Next, Bruno persuaded young Fairchild to hire a glamorous aviatrix, Ruth Nichols, "who had great stage presence" to fly the new plane non-stop to Miami. This, too, "got a lot of publicity." He was "master of the art of publicity" indeed.

Emboldened by these successes, Bruno decided to rent a small office — he had been operating from his bachelor apartment in Times Square — and hired a small staff. He also brought in as a partner his longtime friend, fellow pilot, and roommate, Dick Blythe — one of the founders of QB and also a veteran of Canada's Royal Flying Corps. The letterhead read H. A. Bruno and R. R. Blythe and Associates. It was funded as a privately held company and later became a partnership, Bruno & Blythe. In one of their first joint tasks, they managed to hog the limelight for the Fokker plane in the first annual Ford Air Reliability Tour. Organized by one the shrewdest industrial promoters of this century, Henry Ford, the event was intended to spotlight the Ford Trimotor plane. Ford, who had broken from the pack of

early automobile makers by this skillful promotions, recognized the brilliance of Bruno and Blythe's work. He hired them to promote the second
and third annual Ford Reliability Tours. These tours, open to all plane
manufacturers. did much to publicize the safety of flying. The planes flew
from Dearborn, Michigan, to Omaha and back without serious incident.

To eke out a living in the early lean days of the new publicity firm, Bruno
also worked part time from 1924 to 1928 as program director and chief
announcer for radio station WEBJ, New York City, a powerfully equipped
radio station owned by the Third Avenue Railway System. This work, like
his earlier newsroom experience, equipped him to utilize a new and growing
medium of publicity.

As the firm expanded and took on more clients, they began to plan and
offer clients somewhat more formal services that included statements of
objectives. These extracts are revealing in the way the firm saw its functions
and represented itself to the clients. After stating that it is the firm's duty "to
continuously safeguard the interest of your company through all mediums
of expression," one statement continued, "We will organize news creating
events which will reflect not only beneficial publicity but strong public
relations interest in your activities." In the plan to promote the second Ford
Reliability Tour, Bruno and Blythe stated their primary objective as "being
the creation of a desire on the part of the public to visit the various air bases
on the route." This statement continued:

> Inasmuch as the function of the public relations counsel is to ascertain the
> state of public opinion towards the projects of his clients and to devote his
> efforts to strengthen favorable impressions or dispel ungrounded prejudices,
> we shall crystallize public opinion in favor of the Second Annual Ford Tour.
> It is an essential part of our services to create the circumstances or the news
> which will themselves eventuate in the desired expression from the public.

It would be interesting to know if the firm's use of the term to "crystallize
public opinion" came from Edward L. Bernays's path finding book,
Crystallizing Public Opinion. Published in 1923, it was the first to make
clear that public relations included understanding and interpreting the
client's publics to the client and interpreting the client's policies and actions
to the publics. Also the previous indicates that by the mid-1920s, public
relations was coming to replace publicity as a term in this burgeoning field.
In a presentation to the Aviation Corporation, Bruno and Blythe promised,
"In addition to the dissemination of information on your behalf, we will
supervise your national publicity in such a way that stories that might be
detrimental to your announced program, would not be published or if they
were the text of the story would be changed so that it would react
favorably."

These promises of course would be impossible for any public relations counsel to keep. To the contrary, one of the problems then and today for the counsel is to make clients understand that he or she can't keep bad news that happens from being printed. Such unwarranted claims have long been a problem for the sensible, ethical counselor. Even today there are firms that purport to offer public relations counseling but, in reality, are primarily overpromising publicists.

Though they were now using the term *public relations*, Bruno and Blythe continued to engage in stunts to attract publicity. In 1925, the firm was hired to publicize the air races at Mitchel Field, Long Island. They organized a sham battle to take place over Wall Street at high noon on a Saturday. When the airplanes arrived, they were so high that they attracted little attention, and the reporters started to leave their watch. But Blythe had foreseen this and transformed the dull event as Bruno related in *Wings Over America*: "Before he could say another word, a series of resounding explosions echoed through the entire financial district. Dick's pal on the roof of 49 Wall Street had touched off a series of giant cannon firecrackers and then vanished. Three fire alarms were turned in, Wall Street, lower Broadway and Exchange Place were filled with a milling mob. Word spread like wildfire that another Wall Street explosion had taken place."

In the mid-1920s, Fokker started using the new Wright Whirlwind Engine in his planes. Charles Lawrence, who had invented the motor for the Wright Aeronautical Corporation, sought to publicize its advantages, a great advance in aviation. On Fokker's recommendation, he retained Bruno and Blythe. From then on, every piece of news about Fokker planes carried this sentence "Powered by 200 HP Wright Whirlwind Engines." In 1925, the firm was hired to handle publicity for Juan Trippe's Colonial Air Transport, forerunner of Pan American Airways. By the end of 1925, Colonial had won an airmail contract and was seemingly on its way, but Trippe's first commercial air service went broke. But he came back to make it big with Pan American that Bruno also acquired as a client.

LUCKY LINDY—LUCKY BRUNO AND BLYTHE

While Bruno and Blythe were busy getting publicity for a growing list of clients, including Pioneer Instruments, many meaningful events were taking place in aviation. In 1922, Jimmy Doolittle flew across the country in less than 24 hours. In 1923, two Army lieutenants made the first nonstop flight across the nation. In 1925, Congress passed the Kelly Air Mail Act that authorized the Post Office to contract with private firms to fly the mail. But it was two historic flights in 1926 and 1927 that put aviation on a solid footing and did the same for Bruno and Blythe and Associates.

On May 9, 1926, Lieut. Commander Richard E. Byrd and his pilot, Floyd Bennett, flew from Spitzenbergen to the North Pole and returned safely, a feat that attracted worldwide attention. Bruno and Blythe were hired to enable Byrd to capitalize on this historic flight. The Byrd flight proved that planes could go to remote places and return safely. Byrd's crew had flown in a three-engine Fokker plane. The trip was financed mainly by Edsel Ford and John D. Rockefeller, Jr. Most of the food, equipment, clothiers, and so forth had been supplied by merchants in return for publicity. After his successful flight, Lieut. Commander Byrd, enroute home to a gala welcome, wired Bruno and Blythe that he was in need of $20,000 to pay off his debts.

The two partners brainstormed the problem and came up with a decision to call their friend, Grover Whelan, New York's famed greeter, and ask him to ask his boss, John Wanamaker, if he would like to display the *Josephine Ford*, the plane, in his show windows in New York and then in Philadelphia. Wanamaker bought the idea for $30,000. The plane, displayed in New York 2 weeks and then 2 weeks in Philadelphia, drew large crowds, and, surprisingly, among them many women. Byrd, who later made history with his expedition to the South Pole, was now out of debt, and the firm had pocketed a nice fee. Their great fame was yet to come.

Raymond Orteig, owner of the Brevoort Hotel in New York, obviously seeking publicity, put up $25,000 for the first person to successfully fly the Atlantic Ocean. Many fliers responded with preparations. Bruno and Blythe were delighted because every pilot entering the competition, with one exception, were flying Fokker planes equipped with Wright Whirlwind engines and Pioneer Instruments, all clients. All of the entrants met with mishap or difficulty with one exception, Charles A. "Slim" Lindbergh, who had been flying a mail route out of St. Louis for Major William Robertson. Lindbergh arrived on Long Island in his "Spirit of St. Louis" already something of a hero. He had broken the transcontinental speed record in a flight from San Diego to New York, a feat that captured the nation's headlines. Wright Aeronautical Corp. had offered the young pilot the services of Bruno and Blythe to enable him to deal with a more and more demanding press. Lindbergh accepted this offer.

After Lindbergh arrived on Long Island, Bruno called Guy Vaughn of the Wright firm and asked, "He's in, what do you want us to do?" "Protect him from the exploiters and the mob," were the only instructions the pair received for the handling of this most famous of all clients. When Lindbergh arrived at Curtiss Field, he had less than $50 in his pocket, carried little except a shaving kit, and wore an old blue serge suit. The partners decided that Dick Blythe would stay with Lindbergh until he took off and that Bruno would start pumping the publicity. He contacted all the newspapers and radio stations that were coming to the fore as a new publicity medium. Already the press was calling him "Lucky Lindy" and "The Lone Eagle." On behalf of Lindbergh's St. Louis backers, Bruno contracted with *The New York Times* $125,000 for exclusive rights to the flier's story if he crossed the Atlantic. In an effort to relieve the young pilot's tension, Bruno and Blythe took him to Coney Island one night and watched him ride the merry-go-round and eat hot dogs like "a youthful teenager." Bruno observed, "He seemed like a big overgrown kid but when the occasion demanded, he was poised, though always reticent." After several days of the publicists taking care of him at Wright's expense, Lindbergh asked them to be his personal representatives, and he would pay the usual percentage fee. They accepted with alacrity.

Waiting for the right weather began to wear on all their nerves, so Bruno arranged to take Lindbergh to dinner and then to the show *Rio Rita*. Before they left the hotel, Dr. James H. Kimball of the U. S. Weather Service called, "You've got your weather, Slim." Lindbergh responded, "I want no delays," and they left for the field to get the plane ready. As Bruno recalled the historic moment to Columnist Bob Considine:

I had to pray harder than I ever prayed before. I stood beside Charles A. Lindbergh and his "Spirit of St. Louis" at Roosevelt Field. The time was about 5 a.m. on a damp, rainy morning. I was there with my late partner, Richard R. Blythe, as Lindbergh's personal representative.

Suddenly, as mechanics finished fueling the plane, a watery sun rose, and its rays lit up the fragile aircraft revealing that it rested on a bed of violets. I silently prayed for the young aviator's success. At the take-off I drove my open roadster behind the lumbering "Spirit of St. Louis." Beside me was Abram Skidmore, chief of the Nassau County Police, who was holding a fire extinguisher. The plane bounced once, and I prayed as I have never prayed before. Twice more the frail undercarriage hit the ground before the plane staggered into the air.

Bruno then turned to Skidmore and exclaimed, "By God, he made it."

Thirty-three hours, 39 minutes, and 3600 miles later, "Slim" Lindbergh circled Paris and landed at LeBourget Field; he was quickly acclaimed the world's hero. This was a turning point in world history but also a turning point in Bruno's and Blythe's concept of their function. The problem of handling a hero taught them that it was no longer a matter of creating publicity, it was a matter of public relations to build the public's confidence in aviation. By this one dramatic flight, Lindbergh had received more publicity than a 100 publicists could produce in a year. Bruno's firm was now charged with seeing that thereafter he would receive no adverse publicity; in doing so they had to hold at bay hundreds of people who sought to exploit the Lindbergh fame, especially women.

HANDLING LUCKY LINDY

Bruno and Blythe were totally unprepared for the barrage of phone calls, telegrams, letters, and invitations that flooded in when the news flashed around the world from Paris. They had promised Lindy's backers that they would not let exploiters use or cheapen him. The first test came quickly. Dick Blythe had arranged to meet the cruiser, *The Memphis*, that was bringing the hero back to New York for his great welcome. Blythe carried with him a colonel's uniform that had been ordered for Lindy by Major General Patrick, chief of the Army Air Service, who had just promoted the flier from captain to colonel in the Air Reserve. Blythe was told to instruct Lindbergh to wear the uniform for his arrival in New York. Lindbergh put on the uniform and was pleased with it. Blythe told him sternly, "Slim, you can't wear that uniform." After 10 minutes or so of heated argument, Lindbergh capitulated and donned his old blue serge suit. One Washington paper commented, "He returned as a plain citizen, dressed in the garments of the everyday man." Other reporters took up this theme. Lindbergh was still a common man who had conquered the ocean with only his determination and skill. After their arrival, Blythe accompanied the hero to Washington where President Coolidge pinned the Congressional Medal of Honor on him in front a cheering Cabinet. Then it was back to New York for a great Jimmy Walker welcome and a Broadway ticker tape parade. This was only the beginning of events and parades that acclaimed Lindbergh for his brave, pioneering flight.

Yet in only 3 years, disenchantment set in, at least from reporters who were frustrated by his antipathy to publicity. As Dixon Wecter wrote in *The Hero in America*, "Later, in 1930, when the first feud between Lindbergh and the newspapers was rife, Morris Markey reported in *The New Yorker* that on the *Memphis* that Lindbergh has thrown the proffered uniform on a chair with the caustic remark, 'I didn't notice the Army took much interest in me before the flight.' Still later, in the *Saturday Evening Post* for October 21, 1933, Lindbergh's press agent, Harry A. Bruno from direct knowledge provided what is the true version of the rejected uniform story." Wecter, taking note of the myth that Lindbergh had no press agent in his Paris flight, said. "It should be noted that in early May the Wright Aeronautical Corp. had presented him with the services of Bruno and Blythe." Wecter asserted that Lindbergh said to these unsought publicity men, "Don't bother about getting publicity because it doesn't interest me. Just make the newspapermen leave me alone." Wecter also asserted that Lindbergh "came to loathe the nicknames 'Lindy' and 'Lucky' and to hate the sight of a camera." Yet the public adulation continued until his secret escape to England and later his praise for the Nazi Luftwaffe.

Throughout all the celebrations, welcomes, parades, and public adulation, Lindbergh remained poised, using a simplicity of words to express his gratitude. Dick Blythe became his buffer, a task made easier by their developing friendship. But his name was not always magic. Lindbergh was persuaded to become technical adviser to Transcontinental Air Transport, the forerunner of TWA, the first airline offering cross-country commercial flights. Bruno nicknamed it "The Lindbergh Line," and it prospered briefly but couldn't compete with cheaper train fares and folded. The manner in which Bruno and Blythe handled Lindbergh won them widespread acclaim and put their business on a solid basis.

General James Doolittle later paid them this tribute, "Bruno and Blythe were the first two people to understand aviation and its potential and the manner and means in which it should be presented."

In a letter dated November 22, 1927, Lindbergh wrote:

Dear Dick and Harry

Now that my affairs have quieted down somewhat . . . I want to thank you both, once again, for the assistance you gave me both in the preparation of my flight to Paris and after my return to New York.

The efficient manner in which you handled things during this period is something that I deeply appreciate.

I have watched with interest your publicity work in relation to the aeronautical industry. Conservative, straight forward publicity will aid greatly in its progress.

Sincerely

Charles A. Lindbergh

NEXT: AN AIR DISASTER AND SADNESS

From the triumph and exultation of Lindbergh's brave feat, Bruno next witnessed an air disaster that doomed the commercial future of lighter-than-air craft. In 1910 when young Harry was building his tiny gliders, Count Ferdinand von Zeppelin was carrying more than 10,000 passengers a year in six giant airships on scheduled runs throughout Germany. In the First World War, the Germans produced 88 airships for the German Army and carried out the first bombing raids on London, creating near panic. American interest in dirigibles was minimal until after the war. In 1924, Goodyear built the first semirigid dirigible, but that event was obscured by the delivery of a German-built warship, the *Los Angeles*, to the U.S. Navy. In 1925, the Aircraft Development Corporation that had retained Bruno and Blythe was building the first all-metal dirigible. Publicized by Bruno and Blythe, the ship was completed and flown in 1928. It was flown 600 miles nonstop to the Naval Air Station at Lakehurst, New Jersey, where after days of testing, it was bought by the U.S. Navy. By the 1930s, Bruno and Blythe were simultaneously representing three companies that were building lighter-than-air ships.

While the American manufacturers were encountering repeated setbacks, the Germans continued to make progress in this field. In 1928, the Germans completed the 772-foot giant, the *Graf Zeppelin*, designed to cruise more than 6,000 miles without refueling and travel at 60 miles an hour. Bruno and Blythe were retained to publicize its maiden voyage from Germany to Lakehurst, a flight it made in just over 111 hours. Bruno had been asked to handle the publicity for this maiden flight by Paul Litchfield, president of Goodyear, and Hugh Allen, Goodyear's PR officer, because they thought it would advance the cause of lighter-than-air craft. "The Navy gave us splendid cooperation and everything was done to assist the press and photographers to work without difficulty. We flooded the papers with pictures and stories about the safety and the luxury of Zeppelin travel. We then suggested that the Graf Zeppelin make a grand world tour," Bruno wrote in a letter.

This idea caught on and newspapers started a bidding war for exclusive accounts of the global voyage. Bruno learned that William Randolph Hearst, the successful bidder, had recommended to the German officials that Carl Byoir & Associates handle the flight. Bruno learned later that Hearst blamed him and Dick Blythe because he was unsuccessful in signing Lindbergh to an exclusive contract. Bruno recalled, "I took a chance and wired the publisher at San Simeon. The next day Hearst cabled his Berlin representative, Von Wiegand, to give me the American end of the publicity job." This flight clinched the financing of regular transatlantic service, but then the worldwide Depression intervened.

It was not until May 1936 that the American Zeppelin was able to inaugurate these flights across the ocean. But now Bruno was torn by doubt whether he should take this assignment. He wrote in *Wings Over America*, "Although I was hired by the American corporation to publicize these flights and the service, I took the job only when friends convinced me that in the long run American and not Nazi aviation would benefit most. The Navy Air Base at Lakehurst was made the American port for the Hindenburg. . . . I never did believe . . . that the operations of the airship were entirely commercial." Bruno told me that he was highly suspicious that the Germans were using these and other flights for espionage purposes but said he decided if the U.S. Navy accepted them, he should not worry about it.

With the acclaim of the success of its inaugural flight, publicized throughout the world, the giant *Hindenburg's* first flight of 1937 promised to be a triumphant reenactment of the year before. The first one had stimulated many editorials and much debate about America falling behind in this phase of aviation. Once again the press fully reported every step of the flight from Germany. The *Hindenburg* was due to land at Lakehurst the evening of May 8. The impending landing was the focus of attention throughout the nation; dozens of reporters, broadcasters, and photographers were on hand. The *Hindenburg's* tragic end became probably the most intensively covered disaster in history.

Again quoting Bruno from the Bob Considine column, "I had gone out to Lakehurst to meet the Hindenburg. I had arranged for its regular captain, Ernest Lehmann, to do a book. I would end up pulling him out of the fire when the Hindenburg crashed and burned. His back was burned down to the vertebrae. I got him a baggage cart and to the hospital. He died the next day." Pathe newsreels of the holocaust are still shown in history recaps and in movies. Those who witnessed the fiery crash marveled that of the 100 persons aboard, only 36 lost their lives. The end result of the worldwide, intensive publicity of this dramatic disaster brought the end of this client relationship with a German corporation. Probably none too soon. As indicated, Bruno had misgivings serving the Zeppelin company after Hitler's Nazis seized control of Germany. Unlike Ivy Lee and Carl Byoir, Bruno escaped criticism on this score.

The event did bring Bruno new stature and respect among newsmen. A letter from one journalist, contained in the Harry Bruno Papers, reads, "At this time I wish to pay belated respects to the splendid job done by your organization last spring at a time when everyone's heart, who was at all interested in aviation, was sick. I had the opportunity of profiting by the unselfish, and perfectly newsworthy services rendered by your men at Lakehurst during that period."

By this time Dick Blythe had retired from the partnership, and it was now H. A. Bruno and Associates. The "happy-go-lucky" Blythe was taken ill in 1932. After hovering between life and death for months, he grew stronger and his doctor urged him to take a trip. He visited England, started to fly again, and regained his strength. In this interval, according to Bruno, Blythe's interest in the firm waned. He retired from the firm in 1934 to make a trip around the world. World War II brought Blythe back to the Royal Canadian Air Force (RCAF). On May 1, 1942, another fateful day in May for Bruno, Blythe was injured in a crash while serving as a flight instructor at the RCAF's Ottawa Airbase. He died in the hospital the next day.

The Bruno–Blythe partnership from 1923 until it ended in 1934 was a happy and productive one. As Bruno's biographer, Princine Calitri wrote, "It was because Harry and Dick understood and agreed upon their concept of public relations that they could mesh their ideas so smoothly and without friction. . . . Their respect for each other allowed the firm . . . to prosper."

They both enjoyed what they were doing and felt proud to be advancing the cause they loved.

The Lindbergh triumph and friendship also ended on a sad note in this period. As Bruno recorded in his book:

> On May 20, 1937, the tenth anniversary of the Lindbergh New York to Paris flight, Lindbergh's remaining claims to the respect and admiration of the aviation men who had been closest to him in 1927 were blown higher than the stars. Two affairs were held in celebration of the flight in New York on that day. Lindbergh refused to come or to speak to either gathering over the Transatlantic telephone. At the Waldorf dinner, Thomas W. Lamont tried to make excuses for him. . . . Many newspapermen snickered at Mr. Lamont's blunder.

It can be speculated that Lindbergh was recoiling from the harsh criticism he had been getting in the press and the halls of Congress for his pro-German sympathies and outspoken support of those who opposed aid to Britain after the war broke in 1939. In 1938, Lindbergh had gone from England for a tour of Germany, during which he was wined and dined by Nazi officials and the German luftwaffe. Herman Goering had decorated him with a medal. As a result of his speeches nationwide and belief in the power of the Luftwaffe, some went so far as to damn this once great hero as "pro-Nazi." In a speech to the Adventurers Club on November 16, 1960, Bruno said of Lindbergh, "I have nothing but the highest regard for him." Yet that same year in an interview with me, Bruno confided that he had become quite disenchanted with his onetime close friend and idol. In *Wings Over America*, Bruno was quite critical of Lindbergh and his family leaving the United States in secrecy and fleeing to England after the kidnap-murder of their infant son. "Neither I nor Ivy Lee (who had replaced Bruno as Lindbergh's counsel) would have counseled such action," he averred.

LINDBERGH'S FLIGHT SPURS EXPANSION

Supported by the swell of acclaim and glamour that followed Lindbergh's heroic flight, commercial airlines expanded their services. In 1929 American Airlines followed Transcontinental in offering coast to coast transportation, air service by day, train service by night. Night flying was still not safe in 1929. Both were promoted by Bruno and Blythe. As in the case of the lighter-than-aircraft clients, the partners seem to have no problem with a conflict of interest in handling competitors. As Bruno explained later, "We were the only public relations firm specializing in aviation publicity so we often were handling competitors."

The Bruno firm also continued to counsel individuals who were taking planes on new and gruelling tests. In 1931, the firm handled the press relations and publicity for Wiley Post's and Harold Gatty's first around-the-world flight. Gatty was Post's navigator. When Post set out to prove that he could repeat this feat without a navigator, Bruno warned him he was headed for disaster and refused to have any part of this flight. Bruno's premonition proved sadly true when Post and Will Rogers, the great comedian and writer who helped finance the second venture, crashed and died in Alaskan waters near Point Barrow in November 1935. Bruno also handled the Lincoln Ellsworth Antartica Expedition. He also helped raise the money for Amelia Earhart's ill-fated flight across the Pacific, getting $20,000 from Vincent Bendix and $10,000 from Floyd Odlum. The Texas Company to publicize its new line of aviation products retained another pioneer pilot, Frank Hawks, who broke one airplane record after another — all properly publicized by Bruno's firm. Hawks was also proving the effectiveness of gliders until he died in plane crash in Buffalo.

It was not only aviation that came to appreciate the need for publicity and public interpretation of their companies. By 1925, the firm was emphasizing public relations and over several years were retained by Beech-Nut Packing Company, Metro-Goldwyn-Mayer, Packard Motors, Royal Typewriter, and Standard Oil (New Jersey).

FROM FLYING PLANES TO MOTOR BOATS

Despite a growing number of accounts, the cash flow didn't always match the firm's payroll and office expenses, including rent. In 1925, in a low moment of red ink, the two kept bouncing ideas around where they might get additional clients. They came up the name of Ira Hand, secretary of the National Engine & Boat Manufacturers. Hand responded, "Harry it's a good thing you called today. We're having the Gold Cup Regata at Manhasset Bay and my publicity firm and I are not in agreement on how it should be handled. If you have some ideas, come on over and I'll listen to them." When Bruno hung up, Blythe said, "Harry, let's do it for expenses. We want a chance to prove that Bruno and Blythe can do the job for him. Let's keep our sights on the National Boat Show at the Grand Central Palace this Winter." Bruno and Blythe got the job and went on to popularize boating as they were doing with aviation.

When the time came for the Regatta, Bruno and Blythe were on the water with a motorboat loaded with material for the press. The press was on a separate barge in the bay. As race time neared, all boats not involved in the race were ordered to clear the course. In order to get their copy ashore the reporters had to go by motorboat. The publicists got a call from the barge from Alan Gould of the Associated Press, "I've got a story to go in. Can you help?" (Alan Gould later became a distinguished sports editor of the AP.) Bruno and Blythe picked up his dispatch and got it to runners waiting for it on the shore. The Gold Cup Regatta received unprecedented publicity, and Bruno and Blythe got the National Boat Show at Grand Central Palace in 1926, an account they kept for the next 40 some years.

The intrepid pair set about to study boats as they had planes and quickly became as enthusiastic about boating as they were about flying. The 1926 Boat Show brought a record attendance and thousands of words of copy went out across the country. The boat show got all kinds of newspaper coverage and Ira Hand was immensely pleased. When the show closed, Bruno sold Hand on retaining his firm on an annual basis. But the publicity didn't sell boats, and that was its purpose. The partners set about analyzing the reason for low boat sales. Their research indicated that many people wanted to own boats but no place to dock them or store them. Dick Blythe went to Miami to study its boat facilities, reputed to be the best in the nation. After a complete study of the Miami operation, he prepared a manual that related in detail how a marina should be built and operated. Thus the word *marina* was introduced into the English language. This book was sent out by the association to all cities on waterways, both on shore and inland, showing municipal officials and private companies on how to build and run a marina. Bruno and Blythe understood the parallel of their task in promoting airport construction in order to increase flying.

Bruno saw an opportunity to expand this promotion of boating by promoting boating facilities across the country. They got support from Standard Oil (New Jersey) and in Esso's offices, met with the artist, Ted Geisel, the famous Doctor Seuss, and with him conceived the Seuss navy with an Admiral's Commission. Seuss drew caricatures for a monthly bulletin sent from the High Chief Admiral to all the Admirals. The Esso logo was in the right hand corner of the certificates. At the 1927 Boat Show, Bruno and Blythe staged an Admiral's luncheon. Those attending got a highball glass with the menu on it in color. By this time, Bruno and Blythe had Pittsburgh Plate Glass as a client, so this was a double promotion. Ted Geisel became famous for his children's books, and Engine and Boat Association members started selling engines and boats. Pittsburgh Plate had retained the firm primarily to promote the use of show windows by merchants to increase the market for plate glass.

The dimensions of the Boat Show account are reflected in an article in *Yachting*, January 1966:

> An extravaganza like the boat show naturally requires sophisticated liaison with the press. This responsibility has been handled by Harry Bruno and his associates or the past 40 years. . . . Actually, the boys from Bruno handle all

the public relations activities for the association, which has some 25-industry-presented projects in addition to the boat show. This, however, is the major operation which involves servicing the needs of some 300–400 members of the press. . . . Russ Gudgeon and Ralph Ianuzzi preside over the press room with the unruffled aplomb of Chief Boatswains Mates with an armful of hash marks.

By 1966, the association had a crew of 140 men who were responsible for arranging some 400 exhibits for the show that, as a package, represented $2.6 million worth of marine merchandise. The expense for staging the show ran to $500,000. (Mr. Hand died in 1949 and was succeeded by Joseph H. Choate, who held the position as late as 1966.)

Successes such as that in serving the Association of Engine and Boat Manufacturers put the Bruno firm on the road to financial success. This was signaled in 1939 when he moved the firm's cramped offices in the Chandler Building at 220 West 42nd Street to luxurious quarters at 30 Rockefeller Plaza, where it remained until Bruno's retirement. The move to Rockefeller Center came about this way. When handling the publicity for the National Air Races, Bruno met Vincent Bendix, an aviation enthusiast, and they watched several races together. When the races were over, Bendix told Harry he would like to get recognition for his company in the growing field of aviation. Bruno came up with the suggestion of the Bendix Trophy transcontinental race. Bendix bought the idea and lent the Bruno firm three members of his staff to handle the legalities of instituting the race and meeting the requirements set down by the National Aeronautic Association. From the Doolittles, Jacqueline Cochrans, and others, Bendix got his publicity—in reams.

In 1939, Bendix called Bruno and told him he wanted to see him in his office at 30 Rockefeller Plaza. Bruno was a half hour getting there. Bendix was highly impatient. "When I need to see you, I can't wait hours. You'll have to move to this building." Bruno repled that he couldn't afford it. Bendix retorted, "I want you in this building and as of now your retainer is doubled." With that Bruno agreed to move to his new quarters, sublet from Bendix, where he enjoyed the view of the city and the Hudson River. A footnote on this move: Bruno moved his old furniture to the new quarters. Shortly afterwards, Lincoln Ellsworth, the explorer, visited him and noticed the shabby furniture. In a few days, a load of new office furniture arrived at Bruno's offices. Attached was a note, "Many thanks for your kind and wise counsel, Lincoln Ellsworth."

Soon Bruno was caught up in persuading American housewives to adopt another new technology—the Bendix automatic washer. Bendix, a creative inventor, was intrigued with this new machine and was anxious to get it accepted by American housewives. In the publicity plan prepared for

Bendix, Bruno suggested pictures of the Bendix home laundry, with Betty Grable, then the nation's pin-up star, alongside; Manhattan College track stars with a pretty cheerleader showing how they used the machine for cleaning dirty track uniforms; pretty American Airlines hostesses praising the machine for speedy cleaning that enables them to make quick turn-arounds, and so forth. The Grable shots got widespread publicity for the new washer. But it developed some serious problems and brought threats of Bendix's ouster from stockholders, already unhappy that Bendix had taken them into an uncharted field. The inventor learned to his chagrin that General Motors had been quietly buying up Bendix stock to gain control of the company and force him out. Bruno was determined to save his patron's face and beat GM's publicists to the wires. He quickly got out a story boasting of Bendix's aviation achievements and citing him as "Man of Vision." Bendix's story ended with his failure to invent a helicopter that would compete with Sikorsky or Boeing. He retired and moved out of Rockefeller Plaza. Bruno remained there.

SERVICE IN WORLD WAR II

With the clouds of World War II hovering ever more darkly over the United States, President Roosevelt set up the Office of Production Management (OPM) in 1941. Floyd Odlum, whose Atlas Corporation Bruno had as a client, was drafted to head the Division of Contract Management of OPM, a familiar acronym throughout the war. He had come under fire from Harry S. Truman for not more quickly helping manufacturers find their place in war production and doing more to expedite the manufacture of parts of planes and tanks. In September 1941, Bruno received a call from Odlum to come to Washington, and he quickly boarded a train for the nation's capital. Before he saw Odlum, a journalist friend, Henry "Hank" Paynter of the Associated Press, told him about Senator Truman's criticism. Truman then headed a Senate Investigation Committee — an idea born in cocktail talk among a party of senators attending Senator Matthew M. Neely's inauguration as Governor of West Virginia in January 1941.

Bruno had gotten the Atlas account through his aviation network. Odlum was married to Jacqueline Cochran, the famous aviatrix. Bruno had reluctantly taken her on as a client when she started her company, Jacqueline Cochran Cosmetics, in 1937. She told him that she could only afford to pay him $50 a week, well below his usual fee, but promised that if the venture paid off, he would be well compensated. It did, and he was. Cochran had gained famed for winning the Bendix Trophy.

Odlum beseeched Bruno to come up with a dramatic idea to spread the word, one that would get off the ground quickly. After some thought,

Bruno devised a plan for Defense Special Trains to fan out across the nation with displays of parts needed by the military. Odlum, armed with a full-scale map prepared by Bruno's staff, presented the plan to Senator Truman and explained that this would give small businessmen a chance to study the parts and decide what if any they could manufacture. Bruno left the conference greatly impressed by the "ordinary-looking Senator" and how quickly he got to the nub of a problem. Truman strongly approved of the plan and recommended it to President Roosevelt, who endorsed it and authorized the funds.

Bruno was appointed Director of Defense Special Trains, and 5 weeks from the President's o.k., three Defense Trains, painted in bright red, white, and blue, were on the road. They were staffed by military personnel from the three services, and thus American material manufacture got a head start before Pearl Harbor came. This work took Bruno to Washington 2 or 3 days a week. Once Pearl Harbor came, he also signed up as a public relations advisor to the New York War Savings staff of New York State and the National Aviation Clinic. On January 13, 1942, Floyd Odlum wrote Bruno:

Dear Harry:

The Special Defense Trains were organized as a project, and from the time they left Washington until their return handled to perfection. You were the person responsible for this, and I want you to know how much I appreciated both the efforts and the results.

To handle these Defense Trains and their personnel under normal circumstances would have been a difficult task. To start with an idea only, and three weeks later to have the trains equipped with so many thousand bits and pieces manned with outstanding official representatives of the Armed Services, and on their way . . . was a masterly feat.

The trains went way beyond my expectations with respect to results obtained.

On behalf of the government . . . please accept my thanks and grateful congratulations. Perfection is the only word that adequately measures the work you did.

Sincerely,

Floyd B. Odlum (signed)

World War II also brought the Bruno firm more business. For example in March 1942, H. R. Sutphen, now president of the National Association of Engine and Boat Manufacturers, asked Bruno to publicize the christening of the first PT boat for the Elco Company, Bayonne, N.J. Lt. Robert Montgomery, the movie star, was persuaded to break the champagne bottle over the PT boat's prow. At that ceremony, Bruno met John J. Hopkins, who later bought Convair Corporation from Floyd Odlum and created General Dynamics. Impressed with the Elco ceremony, Hopkins offered Bruno the new corporation's account. He was also retained by Phelps Dodge Copper Co., which gave him one of his toughest assignments. The British had developed an armored lead pipe that could resist great pressure and wanted to build lines under the English Channel to deliver gasoline to the Allies when the invasion came. The U.S, Corps of Engineers advised British officials that Phelps Dodge was the company best able to do this. Phelps Dodge accepted and forthwith built a plant adjacent to one of its plants in Yonkers, N.Y. Thus, Operation Pluto was born to develop and produce an armored lead pipe that could resist high pressure and yet be flexible. Bruno was called to a Top Secret conference and directed that he should keep all news of Operation Pluto out of the media. Bruno was successful in keeping this pipe production one of the war's best kept secrets. In the immediate postwar years, Bruno landed the assignment from Willys–Overland to popularize the civilian models of the jeep that had become a popular and valuable part of the military effort in the war. A valued vice = president in Bruno's firm, Russell Gudgeon, who had been hired to handle the Boat Show, returned to the firm at war's end after having served in military intelligence.

THE POSTWAR YEARS

Harry Bruno had known James Rand of Remington Rand since 1929 when Rand started the New York Rio and Buenos Aires airline that he eventually sold to Juan Trippe and that became Pan American Airways. Rand brought Bruno to the computer age that came to dominate the world in the postwar years. Rand asked Bruno to come and see him. In the Remington Rand office, Rand told Bruno that he had developed an outstanding innovation — the UNIVAC computer — and that he wanted Bruno to promote it. One of Bruno's first coups was to persuade CBS to use UNIVAC for its election returns. Another assignment was to announce General Douglas MacArthur's selection as chairman of the Remington Rand board. This was done in a tasteful ceremony at the University Club. Incredulously, the general told Bruno, I know nothing about public relations. I shall be guided by your advice." This was the understatement of the century!

Presumably to enable his key associates who had helped build his successful firm, in 1954 the Bruno firm was incorporated as H. A. Bruno & Associates, Inc., still at 30 Rockefeller Plaza. Bruno was elected president,

Russell D. Gudgeon elected executive vice-president and a director of the company and Hudson Phillips and Theon Wright were elected vice-presidents. By 1954, this was one of the oldest firms in public relations. Gudgeon was a newspaper editor and an Associated Press Bureau chief before joining Bruno. Hudson Phillips was also a former AP staffer, specializing in financial reporting, when Bruno hired him in 1946. Theon Wright had been a newspaper reporter, a United Press staff writer, and director of public relations for Trans-World Airlines before joining the firm shortly after World War II. The press release announcing the incorporation read, "This quartet forms a team that combines Bruno's long years and experience with modern-day public relations, not the press agentry of two decades ago, but the complex assortment of relations with all the publics that confront modern industry and business management from stockholders and customers to labor and government." Bruno's concept of his role had indeed come along way from the days of downed aerial mapping planes and rum-running submarines in the Hudson.

Reflecting the maturity of the once shaky enterprise in a cubbyhole office near Times Square, in 1960 a Bruno promotion piece listed these clients: Allied Laboratories, Inc.; Atlas Corporation; the Babb Company; General Dynamics Corp.; Florida-Southern Land Corp.; Goodyear Aircraft Corp.; Curtiss–Wright Corp.; Goodyear Tire & Rubber Co.; Gruman Aircraft and Engineering Corp.; Lovelace Foundation for Medical Education and Research; National Association of Engine and Boat Manufacturers, National Motor Boat Show, Phelps Dodge Corp.; Sperry Rand Corp., and Pan American Airways. This list reflects Bruno's long passionate involvement in the promotion of aviation, yet the Boat Show was his oldest client. A 45th anniversary promotional brochure from the firm listed an even longer list of clients.

A frequent world traveler, Bruno sensed this same year, 1960, the emerging field of international public relations. In the winter of that year in New York, he started talking with Humphrey Berkeley, a British member of Parliament and a director in the public relations firm, Michael Rice & Co., Ltd., about the possibility of a joint working arrangement. The Rice Company had been formed 5 years earlier. In the summer of 1961, the Bruno and Rice firms entered into a formal agreement for an "interchange of ideas and services for clients." Mr. Rice's contribution to the British–American PR alliance brought a greater diversity of clients: Carreras Rothman, cigarettes; British Van Heusen shirts, R. A. Brand, industrial spray packaging and Samuel Montagu & Co., bankers. Unlike Bruno, "who wouldn't touch political accounts with a ten-foot pole," the Rice firm sought and accepted such accounts. Rice, in an interview with *Editor & Publisher* on December 9, 1961, explained the impetus for this deal this way, "Growth of the overseas market, tariff reductions due to the Common

Market, stepped-up European sales savvy are just a few of the factors that
have contributed to whetting the business appetites of American firms."

HARRY BRUNO ON PUBLIC RELATIONS

As Bruno prospered and his concept of the function expanded, he became
increasingly concerned about the ethics and competence of those who were
proclaiming themselves counselors in increasing number. He was one of the
founders and strong voices in organizing the national Association of
Accredited Publicity Directors in 1936, later somewhat more accurately
titled National Association of Public Relations Counsel (NAPRC). He
worked with William H. Baldwin in this endeavor. Bruno served three terms
on the Board of Directors of the NAPRC before it was merged with the
American Public Relations Council, a West Coast organization, to found
the Public Relations Society of America in 1948. Bruno over time became
disenchanted with PRSA and refused to join it.

The root reason, he indicated in an interview with me in 1960, was
PRSA's failure to enforce its code of professional practice against those
using false fronts and the third party technique. These questionable
practices had been a hot topic in public relations circles for some years as
the result of the Pennsylvania Truckers' lawsuit against the Eastern
Railroads, counseled by T. J. Ross and Carl Byoir & Associates. This suit
was still in litigation in 1960 when *Editor & Publisher* on February 27, 1960,
headlined: "DEAN OF PR SEEKS TO RAISE CRAFT LEVEL." The lead
read: "Harry A. Bruno, president of H. A. Bruno & Associates, is leading
a movement to raise the professional level of the Public Relations craft."
Bruno and the other unnamed "prominent practitioners" explained that
they were seeking a way "to prevent every Tom, Dick, and Harry from
becoming a PR counsel by simply hanging out a shingle." Yet Bruno
candidly admitted that is what he had done 37 years earlier.

The month before this story broke, the Public Relations Society had
announced its new code of professional conduct, section 8 of which
prohibits members from making use of "any organization purporting to
serve some announced cause but actually serving an undisclosed special or
private interest of a member or his client or his employer." Ward Stevenson
of PRSA said, "undisclosed" meant "false front" rather than "front" or
"third party technique." Bruno told *E&P* that his group was "waiting to see
how this clause is enforced by PRSA's national judicial council." "What
should happen immediately, in Mr. Bruno's opinion, are some resignations
of those who believe in and use false fronts." Bruno openly favored
licensing of counselors, a move that PRSA and practitioners generally have

stoutly resisted. Oddly enough this allied him with Edward L. Bernays, indefatigable advocate of licensing, yet for whom Bruno shared the generally disdain of his fellow members on the National Association of Public Relations Counsel. In fact, it was Bruno who provided your author a copy of the William H. Baldwin letter to the *Harvard Business Review* pot-shotting Bernays's autobiography, egotistically entitled, *Biography of an Idea*. This was cited in the William H. Baldwin chapter. Yet Bruno was not without his critics. William Riis, son of the social reformer Jacob Riis and a New York publicist, wrote in a memo to Baldwin dated December 17, 1951, that "I got a mind to put a blacklist of PR men in at Pleasantville [presumably to *The Reader's Digest*] but would not know any facts today. All I ever observed cheating were Ben [Sonnenberg], Harry Bruno, and Bernays. All B's no Baldwin. Bill." PRSA became even stronger when the Washington-based American Public Relations Association merged into PRSA in 1961. Nonetheless, Bruno remained aloof from it but his vice president, Russell Gudgeon, became a member.

Harry Bruno's contribution to and impact on society is much easier to discern in the fields of aviation and advancing technology than it is on the practice of public relations. In the words of Maj. Alexander. P. de Seversky in the foreword to *Wings Over America*, for Bruno public relations was "not a business, but a consecration to the aviation cause." Loose use of the word *consecration* aside, it is clear that from his high school drop-out days as a youth of 17 until his death March 21, 1978, Bruno's life revolved around flying and the camaraderie of his fellow pioneers. His writings and his speeches dealt with aviation, not public relations. He made virtually no contribution to the literature of public relations as did say, William H. Baldwin, Ivy Lee, or Arthur W. Page.

Bruno's work in promoting commercial aviation won him an accolade in *Coronet* magazine in November 1942 as one of the nation's six "top publicists" in an article by Ellsworth Newcomb. Other publicists listed by Newcomb were: Edward L. Bernays, Charles Michelson, drum beater for the Democrats in the New Deal era; Paul W. Garrett, who built GM's outstanding corporate program in the 1930s and 1940s; Steve Hannagan, who built the aura around the Indy 500 and Sun Valley, Idaho; and William H. Baldwin. Newcomb wrote of Bruno, "Bruno, who has a keen, earnest face and ready smile, possesses an enormous capacity for work. His new book, *Wings Over America*, is just off the press. . . . The big names of aviation were Bruno's clients."

Charles Washburn, a press agent in the 1920s, singled out only two practitioners of that period for detailed attention in his book, *Press Agentry*, published in 1937, Bruno and Bernays. Of Bruno, Washburn wrote:

From the angle of directing public relations work to the point of actual sales of a product, take the example of the campaign handled by H. A. Bruno & Associates recently for the National Biscuit Company, and its three-hour "Let's Dance" radio show. Here research and survey came into play and a campaign of publicity and direct mail inquiry was directed to the several hundred college and university fraternities and sororities which owned their own chapter houses throughout the nation. . . . All leading and even small, fresh-water colleges were contacted and asked: (1) If they listened to the three-hour dance program; (2) If they had held any house dances to the music; (3) What comments and suggestions they had to better the program. From these replies, it was possible to show local retail dealers just where groups were dancing every Saturday night in the nation.

Washburn concluded: It may be said that the goal set by Bruno's executives is one beyond present-day conception of the press agent or the public relations counsel. Taking the ever important but oft-neglected elements of careful research, principles of advertising and salesmanship, and common sense, this organization aims toward the day when there will be a complete and accepted equality of importance of advertising, public relations work, and general sales promotion. They believe that these are essentially one and the same in their objectives, yet differing radically in their machinery of operation.

Did Harry Bruno see today's world of melding public relations, advertising, and marketing in conglomerate agencies? The record is clear on this point.

He also made a substantial contribution to the knowledge of public relations when he deposited his papers and his memorabilia of his public relations practice to the Mass Communications History Center of the State Historical Society of Wisconsin in 1965. (His aviation materials and memorabilia were given to the Smithsonian Institution.) Bruno until the later stages of his career was essentially a publicist and a damn good one. Dealing with Charles A. Lindbergh's problems after his historic flight brought a wider concept to this pioneer. Based on his papers until at least well into World War II, it seems that Bruno did not have the wide view of the nature of the function as did such contemporaries as Ivy Lee, Arthur W. Page, Garrett, or William Baldwin, to name but a few. In this context, it should be noted that the aviation industry and the press both saw and used publicity and public relations as synonymous terms until the postwar period of the late 1940s. After World War II, it was ever more evident that he fully understood the need for analysis of a problem or public, development of a comprehensive plan of action based on that analysis (e.g., promotion of the Bendix Washer), and finally evaluation of the results of the program.

By 1955, Bruno had put the role of a "good press" in perspective. In response to a query from *Editor & Publisher,*, Bruno wrote, "A good press, ' in the final analysis, reflects the kind of citizenship an industry offers to the people and the nation that sustains it. If industry is to remain part of the solid framework of our country, built to stay and meet the demands of a growing population, to bulwark the standards of living that have made America strong—then a continuing 'good press' is important to industry." Nonetheless, his impact on American society in gaining acceptance of commercial transport and motor boating and on public relations is considerable. Truly, he deserves to be saluted as an aviation and public relations pioneer. His contributions to the advancement of aviation were recognized, in a sense, when the Embry-Riddle Aeronautical University, Daytona Beach, awarded him an honorary doctorate in 1975 in aviation management. His work in paving the way for today's commercial aviation was also recognized when he was inducted in to the Aviation Hall of Fame.

HARRY BRUNO THE JOINER

In his youth, Harry Bruno, who was like filings to a magnet in his attraction to celebrities, met Elbert Hubbard, advertising man–philosopher, and was told by Hubbard, "To have friends you have to be a friend." (Hubbard went to his death on the *Lusitania* along with Bruno's parents.) This became an operating principle for Bruno who developed thousands of friends over a lifetime but never abused these friendships in any way. Bruno was an ebullient, outgoing person, full of the juices of life. A Bruno firm release once described him at age 60 as "thin, balding, and a somewhat slenderized version of the late Robert Benchley." His hallmark was a small mustache he wore all his adult life. He was gregarious in the extreme and was a generous, gracious host to his innumerable friends.

The great love of his life was his first wife, Nydia de Sosnowska, a Polish baroness and beautiful actress, whom he married in New York City in 1930. Dick Blythe had first courted the Ziegfeld star, and it was through him that Harry met her and fell madly in love at first sight. The newspapers carried the headline: "LINDBERGH PAL MARRIES MUSICAL COMEDY STAR." Her stage career concluded with her marriage, and she devoted her life to helping Bruno with gracious entertaining and in other ways. In later years, they had a home, "Green Chimneys," at Montauk, Long Island, as well as an apartment in Manhattan. In 1942, they purchased a ranch in the Coachella Valley at Indio, California, to grow dates and grapefruit, an avocation they both enjoyed. Nydia died in 1970 ending a beautiful, story-book marriage of 40 years. They had no children.

Two organizations, above the many others to which he belonged, claimed much of Bruno's time, energy, and affection: The Lotus Club, founded in 1870 to honor men and women who have distinguished themselves on the national and international stage, and the Air Service Post 501 of the

American Legion, founded by World War I flyers in 1919. Bruno played a dominant role in both organizations most of his adult life. He was never prouder nor more gracious than when entertaining at the Lotus Club and regaling his guest with its lore and distinguished membership. Your author had lunch there with Bruno on May 19, 1960. Bruno was honored at the Lotus Club's 267th State Dinner on February 2, 1960, celebrating his 50 years in aviation and his ninth term as president of what Mark Twain once called "The Ace of Clubs." General James Doolittle, a longtime friend and the principal speaker, described the honoree as a "genius" whose good works are legion.

The Air Service Post, oldest in the American Legion, was organized September 29, 1919, by pilots who had flown in World War I on doped fabric wings, held to wooden fuselages by a network of protesting guy wires. Bruno received the post's William J. McGough Memorial Award in 1950. He was a post commander and served many years on its board. Two other organizations in which he took great pride were the National Aeronautic Association, headquartered in Washington, and the Adventurers Club, which honored him with a state dinner and the Amelia Earhart Medal on November 16, 1960. Also dear to his heart from World War I on were the Quiet Birdmen that he helped organize, and the Early Birds. In short, the gregarious Bruno was a joiner and collected organizations and awards as he collected friends.

Harry Bruno formally retired in 1969 after a 46-year career as a publicist, public relations counselor, and promoter of commercial aviation. That year he sold his firm to Ralph R. Ianuzzi, Sr., whom he had employed in 1958 to handle the National Boat Show. Mr. Bruno recruited Ianuzzi from his position as editor of *Rudder* magazine. Mr. Ianuzzi changed the firm name to H. A. Bruno, Inc. Mr. Bruno continued as outside counsel until his death. Ianuzzi gradually converted the agency to a trade show management firm, building on his experience with the National Boat Show, the Westchester County Fair, and other special events. In 1979, he moved the offices from Rockefeller Center across the Hudson to Englewood Cliffs, N.J. In June 1990, H. A. Bruno, Inc. was merged with Blenheim Exhibitions PLC, a London-based producer of more than 200 trade shows covering a wide range of industries; the firm name was changed to Bruno–Blenheim, Inc. Mr. Ianuzzi served as chairman and chief executive officer of the tradeshow management companies of 1990. Thus did the name of pioneer Harry A. Bruno fade from the public relations marquee.

Harry A. Bruno died March 21, 1978, at the age of 85, in Southampton, Long Island. A memorial service was held at the Montauk Community Church on March 28. He was survived only by his second wife, Evelyn Denny Witten, whom he had married in 1972. Despite his long and meaningful career, *The New York Times* carried no obituary. A sad and final note for one who had generated so much favorable publicity for others!

NOTES ON SOURCES

This chapter is largely based on the Harry A. Bruno Papers in the Mass Communications History Center, State Historical Society of Wisconsin, on several interviews with him, and extensive correspondence (the latter can be found in the Scott M. Cutlip Papers in this depository). Other sources were: Bruno's *Wing Wings Over America,* first published in 1942 by Robert McBride, then republished in 1944 by Halycon Books – an autobiography; a biography, *Harry A. Bruno Public Relations Pioneer,* by Princine Calitri, T. S. Denison & Company, 1968; a chapter, "Harry A. Bruno and Aviation," in Charles Washburn, *Press Agentry,* National Library Press, 1937; Wayne Biddle, *Barons of the Sky From Early Flight to Strategic Warfare,* Simon & Schuster, 1991; *Harry A. Bruno a Lotos Club Tribute,* Lotos Club, Kingsport Press, 1960; *History of the Oldest Air Service Post in the American Legion,* Air Service Post 50, 30 Rockefeller Plaza, 1959. Other tributes were in a Lotos Club press release of February 2, 1960 and the *Lotos Leaf* of March, 1960. That same year his firm issued a revised biography of Bruno. A promotional pamphlet, "Forty Five Years in Public Relations," was issued by his firm in 1968. Harry A. Bruno with William S. Dutton, "Thieves of Thunder," *Saturday Evening Post*, Vol. 206, August 5, 1933. An undated letter, printed as a promotion piece to *Editor & Publisher* newspaper trade magazine,, answering a query, "How important to industry is a good press." Dixon Wecter, *The Hero in America,* Charles Scribner's Sons, 1941.

Other sources included a column by Bob Considine, "3 days in May: Ship Sinks, Zep Burns, Lindy Flies," New York *Journal-American,* May 9, 1965; Philip Schuyler, "Dean of PR Seeks to Raise Craft's Level," *Editor & Publisher,* February 27, 1960; "British Executive praises Objectivity With Client," *Editor & Publisher,* December 9, 1961; Howard Mingos, *The Birth of an Industry,* W. B. Conkey Co., 1930; "Outline Public Relations Program Second Annual Ford Air Tour," 1926, mimeograph in Bruno Papers; Justin Schmiedke, "PR Man Spent 40 years Selling Public on Safety of Aviation," *The Capital Times,* April 28, 1965; "Harry A. Bruno, Early Supporter of Aviation," William Fulton in *Chicago Tribune,* January 25, 1968. The William (Bill) Riis letter to William Baldwin with comments on Ben Sonnenberg and Edward L. Bernays is in both the Bruno Papers and the William H. Baldwin Papers.

Chapter 12

William H. Baldwin:
Counselor and Citizen

William Henry Baldwin III, who opened his "shop" in New York City in 1926 as the tenth agency in the World War I PR boom, was a breed apart from his contemporaries and remained so until he closed his shop in 1960. He remained active for many more years as a part-time counselor and active citizen. "Bill" Baldwin, as he was affectionately known in the wide mover-and-shaker circles in which he moved, was the product of a rich family heritage that led him into a career as an influential citizen as well as a public relations counselor. That he was a liberal Democrat and a tireless worker for the public good somewhat set him apart from other counselors. He was a man of character and integrity who often put principle above profit and who, at times, neglected his business for public service.

This was the result of a proud heritage from his distinguished father and mother. "Evaluated in terms of my heritage from both parents, I am pretty much of a paper tiger," Baldwin once reminisced. Bill Baldwin was born on September 17, 1891, in Saginaw, Michigan, the son of William H. Baldwin, Jr., a rising railroad executive, and Ruth Standish Bowles Baldwin, the daughter of Samuel Bowles, editor of the *Springfield Republican*. Because Bill Baldwin's life and work clearly reflected the interests of his father in African-American education and of his mother in the Urban League, it is important to know these parents.

William Henry Baldwin, Jr. was born in Boston in 1863, and upon graduation from Harvard went to work for the Union Pacific Railroad. He was hired by President Charles Francis Adams upon the recommendation of President Charles W. Eliot of Harvard. At the time of young Bill's birth, the father was general manager of the Flint and Marquette Railroad. From

October 1896 until his untimely death in 1904 at the age of 41, he was president of the Long Island Railroad. Before that, in 1894, while serving as vice-president of the Southern Railway, Baldwin, Jr. became interested in Booker T. Washington and his Tuskegee Institute. He joined the board of trustees at Tuskegee and became Washington's financial counselor.

The public-spirited railroad executive put Tuskegee on the map and advanced education for African Americans when he persuaded Andrew Carnegie to give six $100,000 U. S. Steel bonds as an endowment for Tuskegee. This $600,000 gift to Booker T. Washington's struggling little college attracted national attention. Baldwin, Jr. was indirectly responsible after his death for Julius Rosenwald's first major gift to African-American education. In 1910, Booker T. Washington called on Rosenwald in Chicago but was turned down. Just at that time the eulogistic biography of William Baldwin, Jr. by John Graham Brooks was published. Paul J. Sachs, an investment banker in New York City, sent a copy to Rosenwald. As a result, Rosenwald sent Washington a telegram stating he was making a substantial gift to Tuskegee. This was the forerunner of the Rosenwald School Program in the South. Booker T. Washington was a frequent guest in the Baldwin home. Thus, interest and support for African-American education was deeply ingrained in William H. Baldwin III. Concern for social welfare was another.

In the early 1900s, after Baldwin, Jr. had returned to New York City as President of the Long Island Railroad, New York passed the one million population mark and, as a consequence, was experiencing acute social problems, particularly commercialized vice. Social and economic problems were especially acute among the wave after wave of immigrants. A series of exposures by newspapers had convinced a group of public-spirited citizens that action had to be taken to combat vice and gambling. They formed the Committee of Fifteen to work with city officials on these problems and asked William Baldwin, Jr. to take the chairmanship. He took it. Upon his death, the committee renamed itself as the Committee of Fourteen and left Baldwin's chair perpetually unfilled. In time young Bill Baldwin would join this committee.

When Mr. Baldwin died, *Life* magazine eulogized, "The late William H. Baldwin, Jr. had the greatest talent for being good of any man of a like ability and success that we Americans have seen much of in recent years. He was not only good, but affirmatively helpful, industriously good, and yet no one seemed to lay it up against him. . . . He is dead at forty-one, a lamentable loss to the country." This public adulation was amply reflected in *An American Citizen's Life, William Henry Baldwin, Jr.* by Brooks, published by Houghton Mifflin in 1910. All this made a profound impression upon a grieving son. He often recalled that he was driven to "measure up."

But Bill Baldwin got more than deep social concerns from his father. He got the fundamentals of the public relations philosophy that guided him through the reefs and shoals of his clients' problems. In Baldwin, Jr.'s last years, the muckraking attacks on the abuses of Big Business were in full cry. His personal experiences convinced him that the critics of business had a case. He declared, "Business first of all has a social responsibility."

His mother similarly left him a legacy of interests. Mrs. Baldwin, third daughter of Samuel Bowles and a graduate of Smith College, married Mr. Baldwin in 1889. She quickly became intensely interested in the social work and reform in the many fields in which her husband was occupied. Her obituary in the *Springfield Weekly Republican* of December 20, 1934, recorded, "The cause of those any way oppressed or underprivileged found in Mrs. Baldwin a sure and sympathetic friend."

She picked up her husband's efforts to help African Americans solve their social and economic problems, and probably made her most significant contribution in this field. She was the leading force in organizing the National Urban League on Urban Conditions Among Negroes. The organization was founded at a meeting in her home in 1910. The renamed National Urban League endures to this day as a vibrant force for good, a monument to Ruth Standish Bowles's memory. The Urban League, of which Bill Baldwin later served as president, was another of his influential legacies. In the early 1930s with her health failing, Mrs. Baldwin involved herself, at least through letters and memos with a wide range of problems. She enlisted her nephews, Chester Bowles, later a United States Congressman and Ambassador to India, and Roger Baldwin, who later headed the American Civil Liberties Union, in these causes. One of her last projects was to help found the Highlander Folk School near Knoxville, Tennessee, a school that came under heavy attack in the days of McCarthyism and the Civil Rights Movement.

With this rich inheritance and these legacies, Bill Baldwin set about to prepare for his life's work. Mrs. Baldwin, Jr. sought advice from her father, Samuel Bowles, Talcott Williams, soon to launch Columbia's School of Journalism, and Oswald Garrison Villard, owner of the *New York Evening Post*, as to her son's education. On their recommendation, he enrolled in Harvard in 1909. There the bright scholar completed the requirements for his degree in 3 years. At the end of his junior year, Villard offered him a job on *The Evening Post* after his graduation. But Baldwin wanted to graduate with his class in 1913, so on advice of Villard and others, he enrolled in the University of Wisconsin for the 1912–1913 academic year. Here he was greatly stimulated by the teachings of Charles McCarthy, father of "The Wisconsin Idea," John R. Commons, pioneer labor historian, sociologist E. A. Ross, economist Richard T. Ely, and Lloyd Jones. In one instance, Baldwin wrote, "The Madison experience certainly broke through the curtain of Eastern parochialism." In a letter to me he wrote, "My year at Wisconsin was a real milestone; although I neither received nor pointed toward a degree, I got a stimulation and degree of education that stacked up with my three years at Harvard."

For the next year, Baldwin would complete his education with a year in Europe, that was much a part of the education of that era for sons and daughters of well-to-do families. He went armed with letters of introduction to important leaders from his mentor, Villard. Baldwin later recalled, "Undoubtedly this experience abroad laid the foundation for my later concern for tariff and world trade situations." Both of these issues involved Baldwin clients in a later time. He returned from Europe in June 1914 as "Guns of August" loomed on the horizon. Villard told him that he would start in September in the circulation department of *The Nation*. This left him footloose for the summer, so he picked up the family heritage and worked for the Urban League. "This was to become the first of a variety of non-profit activitie which have absorbed a considerable amount of time and a modest amount of personal cash. Quite aside from the personal satisfactions they have brought *per se*, they have given me information and contacts which have definitely improved my ability to serve business clients in many key situations."

When World War I started in Europe, Baldwin saw a chance to escape circulation duty on *The Nation*, which interested him not a whit, so he went to Editor Villard to see how he might help out in this drastically changed news situation. *The Evening Post* had had no ship reporter but with the rising tide of refugees from Europe's war, this became an important beat. Baldwin was assigned and quickly made the most of it. He rode the Coast Guard cutter with the immigration officials to meet incoming ships and there interview passengers and ship personnel about conditions in Europe. He also took on other assignments from the city editor when there were no ships to meet. Baldwin later recalled that in his 3 years on the *Post*, he concentrated on "a depth and diversity of reporting, rewriting, and copy editing that most young reporters did not acquire in several times that period." This, too, helped prepare him for his career in public relations.

Immediately upon the United States' entry into the World War, Bill Baldwin enlisted in the U.S. Naval Reserve Force. This, too, equipped him for his life's work. He was assigned to duty as press censor in New York, and his office was next to the New York office of the Committee on Public Information. He became interested in this propaganda work and whiled away many an hour in the CPI office. Later, he was promoted to ensign and posted as censor in Key West, Florida. Released from duty in May 1919, Baldwin was given a job in the Harvard Endowment Campaign by John Price Jones. He served in Cambridge as the liaison with the New York headquarters. Here, too, he learned the fundamentals of fund-raising that he put to good use early in his career. At the campaign's end, Jones offered him a job in his new corporation, but as reported in an earlier chapter, Baldwin declined.

Instead, he took a job on the staff of the American International Corporation (AIC). He later described the corporation as a "war baby" that had assembled a complex of shipbuilding, steamship operations, port development, and other heavy construction. At AIC, Baldwin worked under an astute public relations mentor, Thomas F. Woodlock.

Baldwin described Woodlock to me as "an early public relations man." This long, lanky Irishman started out as a partner of Barron in *Barron's Weekly* but later split with Barron. He then took the public relations job with AIC. Woodlock was hired because AIC was in the public doghouse in connection with Hog Island, the producer of World War I Liberty Ships. A presidential inquiry had taken place in November and December 1918. Charges of mismanagement and fraud were publicly made and denied. Woodlock and later Baldwin were hired to blunt this criticism. This was one of the early instances to be oft repeated down through years when a company or individual in crisis turns to public relations as a "fire extinguisher." Indicative of the shaky state of this adolescent field was the fact that Woodlock would not permit the term *public relations* to be used in their work—or even on the office files! Baldwin recalled that Woodlock saw himself as a "troubleshooter," not as a PR man. He seemed to think that this term would hurt his credibility.

Bill Baldwin worked at AIC from the fall of 1919 until December 1922. Bill Baldwin thoroughly enjoyed his 3 years under Woodlock's tutelage whom he considered an experienced and shrewd mentor. Baldwin always considered these years a valuable apprenticeship for his career. Woodlock's basic approach was to say nothing until he had something favorable to say. He had a keen Irish sense of humor and once told Baldwin, "There are times, Bill, when the best public relations is silence, and very little of that." Woodlock completed his career writing a column, "Thinking It Over," for the *Wall Street Journal*.

Baldwin left AIC when a challenge came his way that one of his heritage could not turn down. Through the influence of Paul D. Cravath, a well-known New York attorney and chairman of the Fisk University Board of Trustees, Baldwin was asked to direct a fund-raising drive that would bring the first $1 million endowment fund for an African-American college in the South. Actually, Baldwin had to raise only $500,000; the General Education Board had pledged that amount if Fisk could raise a matching sum. A national campaign for Fisk, Baldwin reasoned, would cost too much. "It would have to be a rifle shooting, rather than a shotgun campaign."

Young Baldwin accepted the Fisk University assignment on condition that he be appointed to the Fisk Board of Trustees. Baldwin thought this would give him more authority with Fisk officials and more status in approaching such major potential donors as Henry Pritchett of the Carnegie Corporation and Julius Rosenwald, Chicago merchant and philanthropist. Baldwin later wrote in the *Public Relations Journal*, "Money was obviously Fisk's target, but interpretation of need in terms of improving race relations was the basic consideration." He added, "It [the drive] included changing the famous Fisk Jubilee Singers from an iterant band singing in private drawing rooms and then 'passing the hat' into a concert group charging admission and seeking and getting artistic approval from the music critics." Baldwin wrote in a letter of October 20, 1959, "Early in the game I accompanied the Singers to the office of Judge Elbert H. Gary, head of U.S. Steel, at 71 Broadway, where they sang some of his favorite spirituals, but I don't recall that he ever gave any substantial sum to Fisk." Baldwin promoted appearances at Carnegie Hall for the singers and afterward a Carnegie Hall concert for Roland Hayes, a Fisk student, who went on to a great musical career. Building respect for the African American and improving race relations was Baldwin's deep-seated goal in serving Fisk then and throughout his active life. The idea of these Fisk students going from rich man's parlor to rich man's parlor was repugnant to him. With his guidance, the singers not only raised money for Fisk but built respect for their race.

Baldwin raised the requisite $500,000 to match the General Education Board's offer. He got $250,000 from President Henry Pritchett of the Carnegie Corporation—and just in the nick of time. Mr. Stone, of Stone and Webster, was on the Carnegie board and tipped off Baldwin that Pritchett was stepping down. Pritchett had closed his last formal board meeting and only then took up the Fisk appeal. Baldwin finished the Fisk campaign in 1924 but continued to serve on its board until near the end of his active life. Advancing African-American education and improving the lot of the African-Americans was a consuming interest of Baldwin as long as he lived.

Baldwin meanwhile was continuing his work with the Urban League and the Committee of Fourteen.[1] One interesting aspect of this work was to help gain recognition for African-American writers. He used his public relations contacts with editors of magazines, notably *Harper's*, to get consideration for qualified African-American writers' works. He got many of their articles published in the early 1920s.

When Baldwin finished the Fisk campaign in 1925, Carl W. Ackerman, former journalist who then had his own public relations office, approached

---

[1]When William Baldwin, Jr. died he was not replaced on the Committee of Fifteen that he had helped organize, thus it became the Committee of Fourteen.

Baldwin to work for 6 months on the fund-raising campaign for the National Episcopal Cathedral in Washington, DC. Impressed with his success at Fisk, Ackerman asked Baldwin to work on attracting individual donations. In later years, Baldwin recalled "I became the Unitarian chaplain to the Bishop of Washington, accompanying him to 'put the bite' on wealthy dowagers and other prospects." One of Baldwin's suggestions to the bishop was adopted years later — to put a flag from each state in the nave of the cathedral with the amount donated by that state. Another suggestion that was not adopted was to have the cathedral apply for a broadcasting license and establish a religious radio station, "The Voice of Religion." Little could the bishop foresee the millions that would later lie at the foot the televangelists' rainbow.

Baldwin's next move was to accept the secretaryship of the Arbitration Society of America, which had been formed to reduce litigation and promote peaceful settlement of labor–management disputes, today a major feature of American law. The society was in a head-on collision with the American Arbitration Foundation, which had the same purpose. Baldwin emerged as the peacemaker; their in-fighting was contained through their joining in the formation of the American Arbitration Association with Baldwin elected as secretary.

Baldwin soon tired of this role and was anxious to get back into public relations. His break came when Ackerman was offered the deanship of the Columbia University School of Journalism and closed his office to accept the job. Ackerman contacted Baldwin and offered to pave the way for him to take over the Seiberling Rubber Company account, that Ackerman had. Baldwin accepted and in June 1926, at the age of 34, he opened a small office in midtown Manhattan. There were only six other agencies listed in the Manhattan telephone directory at that time, he later recalled.

BALDWIN SETS A DIFFERENT PACE

This new firm consisted of one counselor, one secretary, and one account — Seiberling. Baldwin's main work for Seiberling was promoting the "Seiberling Singers" and James Melton as the "Voice of Seiberling." This work gave the new counselor a ringside seat to radio broadcasting as this young medium was groping to find its way. This knowledge, like all the other he had accumulated by now, would be of help as his practice grew. This one account was not enough to keep the energetic Baldwin busy, so he gave more time to his civic interests, his "ward work" as he termed it. He pushed ahead with the Urban League and the Committee of Fourteen. He became secretary of the committee.

These contacts began to pay off for Baldwin. Percy Straus, vice-president of Macy's Department Store, was a member of the committee. Obviously impressed by the young Baldwin, Straus introduced him to his relative, Jesse I. Straus, president of Macy's. Jesse Straus offered Baldwin a vice-presidency, to be in charge of publicity and advertising. Baldwin declined, recalling, "I finally transmuted the offer into retention as outside counsel. This arrangement lasted five or six years and paved the way for a continuing association with retail merchandising." In a letter of October 20, 1961, to Major John F. Forrest, Baldwin wrote, "I had already concluded that a PR counselor should be on the outside of an organization, not part of it, and I frankly felt that I was not competent in advertising."

Jess Straus was not persuaded of the correctness of Baldwin's position and their negotiations continued for months. As is often the case, a Macy's crisis forced Straus to hire Baldwin as a counselor.

BALDWIN SAVES THE MACY THANKSGIVING DAY PARADE

Given the millions who today line the sidewalks of New York City and tune in the TV extravaganza of Macy's Thanksgiving Day Parade, it is difficult to perceive that this event almost died in infancy. Macy's had staged the Thanksgiving Day Parade in 1924 and 1925 to open the Christmas shopping season without complaint. But then in 1926, a storm of criticism arose from the clergy of New York City. Baldwin later recalled, "The parade had not become rooted into New York's traditions and was therefore sensitive to attack." Patriotic organizations also joined the protest of the clergy, arguing that the parade was an offense against a national and essentially religious holiday.

Baldwin counseled Jesse Straus that most of the heat would be dissipated by rescheduling the event from morning to afternoon. Baldwin reasoned that most of the complaints were generated by the conflict with morning religious services that were common in that day. Baldwin argued that an afternoon parade would only compete with football games. Preparations had already started for the 1926 parade, and a stubborn Jesse Straus vetoed Baldwin's solution, saying that arrangements had already been made and rescheduling would cause costly duplication of work.

Displaying his independence, Baldwin would not accept Straus's veto. Baldwin was convinced that he was right and set out to prove it. His ward work paid off again. He got in touch with the Rev. S. Parkes Cadman, a fellow director of the Brooklyn Urban League who was president of the New York Council of Churches. The Rev. Cadman agreed with Baldwin's solution and said if the conflict with church services were eliminated, the opposition to the parade would end. New York Police Commissioner

McLaughlin was visited next. He was a longtime associate from Baldwin's antivice work on the Committee of Fourteen. He, too, approved of Baldwin's plan and said a new parade permit could be obtained for the afternoon. He recounted:

> This time I reported more formally to "Mr. Jesse," armed with the endorsements of the Rev. Cadman and the Police Commissioner, Straus assented to the change. The change was made in time and widely publicized, and the parade was held without further protest." Thus a counselor's "ward work" had paid off and the Macy Thanksgiving Day Parade saved to delight generation after generation of "children." Delighted, Straus retained Baldwin as public relations counsel for the next six years.

Baldwin's next task for Macy's was to set about to change its reputation from that of a store offering low-cost merchandise of good quality to upscale goods. He started a contest among club women in Manhattan, Glen Cove, L. I., and New Canaan, Connecticut, where he had social connections, to come up with ideas to make Macy's more attractive to upscale women. This was a small project with unmeasurable results. Given what is known today of the role of influentials, attracting these style leaders may have been the first step in changing Macy's image. In the same campaign, the counsel encouraged Macy's to sponsor an art show, "Art Industry," and prepared articles boosting the show for the president of the Metropolitan Art Museum. These articles and other layouts were published in *Women's Home Companion*, *Literary Digest*, and *Review of Reviews*. This publicity also assisted in upgrading the public's perception of Macy's. The latter also illustrates how Baldwin could use his social contacts to a client's advantage.

A larger project was published by Macmillan in 1929. It was written for the housewife as a shopping guide. Baldwin envisioned it as a book the "housewife would put on her shelf next to her cook books." It covered rugs, linens, furniture, kitchen appliances, and so forth. Macy's was mentioned only in the preface with its research laboratories cited as an authority on product quality. This book had a long life. The book remained in print until November 2, 1956, when Macmillan canceled Baldwin's contract.

BALDWIN HIRES MAURICE MERMEY

Maurice Mermey, who years later became a partner of Baldwin, early in 1928 applied for a job in Baldwin's small firm. Baldwin said he didn't have the business to warrant hiring him. Three months later, in March, when Baldwin landed the Parke Davis & Co. account, he hired Mermey. Mermey had sought the public relations job because his wife was expecting, and he knew they couldn't make it on his United Press salary. The United Press's Downhold Club has funneled hundreds of journalists into public relations. In 1933, hit by the Depression, Baldwin had to let Mermey go because he was "earning a pretty good salary." Mermey landed a job with Grover Whelan, who was directing the 1939 New York World's Fair. That work done and Baldwin's business having improved, Mermey was brought back to the firm as a partner in 1939.

Baldwin was hurt initially by the Depression, as was every business in America, but after shaking of the initial shock, "I was able to swim upstream and little bit against the tide." He estimated that his business fell off about 10% at the low point of the Depression. Financial statements in the Baldwin Papers in the State Historical Society of Wisconsin indicate that his firm grew rapidly initially, altered a bit in the Depression, and continued to grow in a somewhat uneven pattern. Baldwin charged his clients a variable fee, depending on the size of the job, its length, and so forth plus the normal out-of-pocket expenditures. Baldwin's firm never grew as large as did those of most of his competitors.

This was at least partly by Baldwin's design. Part of it was due to what Baldwin described as "the turbulence associated with opening up and stabilizing any new frontier." By 1929, this individualistic counselor had come to the conclusion that prospective clients look for a counselor who appears to be more than a one-man operation. Consequently, he changed his letterhead to read "William H. Baldwin and Associates." Later on, he changed the name to Baldwin and Beach, even though Beach was only an employee. Eventually, in 1939, a true partnership was formed when the firm became Baldwin, Beach & Mermey.

Perhaps the main reasons that Baldwin's firm did not become a major one in the public relations constellation were his rugged honesty that would not permit him to accept a client in whose cause he did not believe and his strong belief that a client was entitled to the full attention of the counselor he had hired. Indicative of the former was a letter to his cousin, Chester A. Bowles, successful advertising man and public official, asking Bowles' help in landing a foreign account, but "not just any foreign account." In that letter, Baldwin recounted that he had turned down a fee of $250,000 offered by the Chinese government of Chiang Kai-Shek to represent it in the United States. (Presumably this is the account that went to the Hamilton Wright organization and eventually proved an embarrassment in the Fulbright Senate Committee hearings of 1963.) Earlier he had declined to represent the Cuban Dictator Machado, who had brought such pain to the young Carl Byoir agency. He stoutly believed that a practitioner must not accept a client "whose objectives run counter his or her personal code of right and decency." On the other hand, publication of promotional in-house letters and articles authored by Baldwin and Mermey indicate a continuing quest for new business.

Another reason was Baldwin's sound conviction that the principals should be freely available to their clients for counsel and not be shunted off to a lower level employee. He believed that the public relations function is primarily counseling and assistance to the client. He held that if a public relations office advertises the services of a Baldwin or a Mermey, there is an obligation to give a client these men's services and not those of hirelings. Acceptance of this principle limits the growth of any agency. Obviously, today's giant agencies don't hold to this premise.

Baldwin, in his stubborn New England way, had definite ideas about how a public relations agency should be run. He believed in the value of an outside counselor who could be more objective and independent in dealing with management. He had repeated opportunities to join client firms as the public relations executive—Macy's, Coca-Cola, International Nickel, and others—but rejected them all. He also thought that public relations and advertising should be kept separate and refused offers from Richard Compton and J. Walter Thompson to head the public relations department in their agencies. Baldwin thought that if public relations is to be related to advertising, it should be in the superior position.

Baldwin saw these as the advantages of outside counsel:

1. Greater independence.
2. Better perspective and skills.
3. A concentrated effort toward properly determined goals.
4. A better opportunity to develop good media relations.

A 20-YEAR CAMPAIGN AGAINST SUGAR TARIFFS

In 1929, Bill Baldwin enlisted in a 20-year campaign to oppose high tariffs on refined sugar on behalf of two major clients—the Hershey Chocolate Corporation and Coca-Cola, both large users of industrial sugar. When Baldwin was retained, the disastrous (as history proved) Hawley–Smoot Tariff bill was before Congress. It provided for an import tax on refined sugar. To be certain of an independent supply, Milton S. Hershey had formed a corporate company in Cuba to produce refined sugar there. The refinery was just coming into production when the Smoot–Hawley bill was introduced. This plant's 600,000-ton capacity far exceeded Hershey's needs, so Hershey persuaded Coca-Cola to buy its excess production. Because of their common interests, the two corporate giants decided on a joint public relations campaign and retained Bill Baldwin to direct it.

Baldwin was first contacted by a New York banker, who was close to the Coca-cola company, and asked, "Bill, are you interested in a tariff account?" Baldwin, a low-tariff Democrat, replied, "It is up or down?" Told it was "down," he expressed interest. Baldwin's analysis of the problem and his proposed strategy got him the account. In his candid way, Baldwin told these firms that he didn't know Washington and wasn't particularly interested in Washington. Instead, he said, he would take the issue to the country. Hershey was in full accord because he knew from his support of the Anti-Saloon League that the path to lasting legislative support led through the congressman's district. In taking this approach, Baldwin was pioneering a technique quite common in today's special interest-dominated legislation at both the national and state levels.

In March 1929, when Baldwin was hired, the bill was under debate in the House, and with Senator Smoot's interest in protecting Utah's domestic sugar beet growers, it was a foregone conclusion that the sugar tariff would be enacted. Time was limited, but Baldwin quickly lined up several powerful allies for his side.

Some editorial comment had already appeared in opposition to the sugar tariff. Baldwin set out to stimulate more adverse comment and cartoons. He persuaded *The New York Times* to do two in depth articles on the damage such a tariff would do to U.S.–Cuban relations and to U.S.–Latin American relations. His main theme was aimed at the consumers of sugar — corporations to housewives. Representative Fiorella LaGuardia led the opposition in the House. Baldwin next confronted Congress with all this opposing opinion to make a strong impact at the critical moment. This was a 96-page compilation of the opposition views in a booklet, "What Price Sugar?" placed on the desk of every congressman and senator the day the Senate Finance Committee took up the House-passed bill. The Senate committee shelved the sugar provision for later consideration, which gave Baldwin and his clients needed time to continue their fight. It was not until February 1930 that the Senate took up sugar; it then voted a heavy duty on raw sugar but dropped an import tariff on refined sugar. This fight won, Coca-Cola dropped out of the campaign.

Hershey continued to retain Baldwin for 20 years. His counsel and publicity work were needed because the domestic refiners continued their battle for special protection in a succession of hearings before the U.S. Tariff Commission, the Agricultural Adjustment Agency, and Congressional committees. For each of these Baldwin prepared basic memoranda for the testimony of Hershey witnesses. Simultaneously Baldwin embarked on a long-range campaign to influence the affected publics.

A series of pamphlets was prepared outlining the increased cost of sugar to consumers, the selfishness of a small group of refiners, the damage to American relations with Cuba (which then were amicable) and America's historical commitment to a policy of free trade for agricultural products. Alliances with like-minded groups such as women's clubs were consolidated and organized to put pressure on Congressmen and senators.

But in 1934, the domestic refiners got Congress to pass the Jones–Costigan Act, that established quotas in the domestic market for the recognized producing areas. This legislation was passed as "Depression Measure" to get the hard-hit economy moving again.

The Jones–Costigan Act was to be in effect for only 3 years. So in 1937, the fight resumed. Baldwin repeated his earlier fight plan and looked for more allies. He found a more favorable environment this time. The economy had begun to improve, and under the leadership of President Roosevelt and Secretary of State Cordell Hull, the consideration of foreign affairs had become more important in the Congressional scheme of things. "The Good Neighbor" policy had been enunciated by FDR, and Baldwin used this theme to the hilt. But at the same time, FDR was now having difficulty with Congress, mainly because of his effort to pack the Supreme Court. Consequently, the domestic refiners won again; the act was extended. Baldwin always suspected that FDR used the sugar bill as a pawn in the Supreme Court fight with Congress.

But apparently there was a gentleman's agreement that this would be the last extension of the act, thus Baldwin's efforts seemed not wholly in vain. In signing the legislation, President Roosevelt said, "The sole difficulty relates to a little group of seaboard refiners who, unfortunately, for many years have joined forces with domestic producers in maintenance of a powerful lobby in the National Capital and elsewhere. . . . This monopoly costs the American housewife millions of dollars every year and I am just as concerned for her welfare as for the farmers' welfare." It seems that Baldwin's message had gotten through to the administration. However, the gentleman's agreement Roosevelt spoke of apparently didn't exist or hold, for the sugar fight was resumed in 1940 and continued until 1960 when President Eisenhower suspended Cuba's quota as a sanction against Cuban dictator Fidel Castro.

Hershey and Baldwin ended their relationship — amicably — in 1949. Baldwin informed his client that the internal developments in Cuba during this period "made it impossible for Hershey to continue identification of its interests with those of American consumers." This was a time when in Cuba extremists, right and left, were using violence and supporting sabotage in the Caribbean to promote their political doctrines. Baldwin's honest advice cost him a client.

Reflecting on his 20-year battle for Cuban participation in the American sugar market, Baldwin wrote in The *Public Opinion Quarterly* of March 1941, "The urgent need at this time, therefore, is to bring before important groups of the American body politic where their best interests are identified with a reasonable participation of Cuban sugar in the American market, and to urge these groups to make, or have made for them, impartial, fact-finding studies of claims and counter-claims." He saw it as a long-term effort, "It will take leadership and it may take years to build . . . protection around the sugar bowl in Washington." Baldwin, a true democrat with a small *d*, had unyielding faith in the public once it had the facts put before it; a faith in this instance was not warranted. The Sugar Lobby in Washington continues to cost the American consumers millions of dollars as it maintains pegged prices.

INTERNATIONAL NICKEL — ANOTHER MAJOR CLIENT

In mid-summer of 1930, Baldwin was invited to become counsel for International Nickel. He never learned why he was chosen for what became a long and valued relationship for client and counselor. This was another Depression-born account. Nickel had developed into a major industry in World War I and then in the 1920s found a market in the manufacture of cars. The Depression severely cut back auto production, so International's President, Robert C. Stanley, sought to find new markets. Baldwin's imagination did just that. He developed "The Alloy Age" as a theme for promotion and publicity. He initiated a clip-sheet of stories on uses of nickel alloys in industry and homes, the *White Metal Newsletter*. Baldwin exploited newspaper and business publications year-end business reviews by issuing in mid-December "The Nickel Industry in 19 — " This release received wide usage each year he had the account.

Baldwin scored a ten strike for the company's alloy of copper and nickel refined from its Canadian mines and marketed as Monel metal. To promote its use for kitchen sinks, Baldwin invented the term *sink fatigue*. Working with the U.S. Bureau of Home Economics, tests were conducted in the Washington, DC. area of sink usage and its results. He wrote biographer Major John F. Forrest in 1961, "The data we obtained became news and feature copy as a vehicle for making the point that monel sinks never become fatigued and keep their pristine polish."

Platinum and palladium are byproducts of nickel production, so Baldwin sought to widen the markets for these metals. It appears that Baldwin arranged for a platinum medal to be presented to President Herbert Hoover by the George Washington Bicentennial Commission in 1932, the first such medal to be struck in the United States. A platinum tea service was developed by Tiffany's, the prestige jeweler, for the Chicago World's Fair in 1934. Also displayed was a platinum and crystal trophy by Cartier's. Next Baldwin had the company to commission a distinguished Canadian sculptor to design a platinum medal for an award from the Canadian Institute of

Mining and Metallurgy that became in time the highest honor in that Canadian industry.

One evening while playing bridge with Ely Culbertson, world renowned bridge expert, Baldwin persuaded Culbertson to quit using a gold trophy for his World Bridge Olympic and to present a platinum trophy instead. Four miniatures in platinum were presented to the four winners.

At the same time he was pushing this new product publicity, Baldwin was developing a broader public relations program for International Nickel. He initiated quarterly financial reports to distribute to the press and to shareholders. To celebrate the Canadian industry's 50th anniversary, Baldwin arranged a ceremonial dinner at the Royal York Hotel in Toronto. He also developed a two-part series on the history of the nickel industry for the *Journal of Chemical Education* and also a pamphlet issued by the company. Whether Baldwin stimulated it or not is not clear, but when *Fortune* decided to do a major story on the company, Baldwin persuaded Stanley and other corporate officials to cooperate with candor. Baldwin accompanied the writer throughout his work on the piece and provided facts and background in an open manner. The result was a friendly article.

On two occasions, Stanley sought to persuade Baldwin to take a full-time position with the company, but Baldwin stuck to his position that he could be of more help on the outside than from within. It may surmised, too, that his role as a counselor gave Baldwin freedom to pursue his ward work that never went neglected. On the eve of World War II, International Nickel canceled its contract with Baldwin and set up its own internal department; the parting was amicable, and Baldwin was given a generous termination payment. A decade later International Nickel would again seek Baldwin's counsel.

This was prompted when *Fortune* again published an article on the company that this time was quite unfavorable to it. The attack focused on the firm's management. The company's vice-president for public relations sought Baldwin's advice on how to counter this bad rap. Baldwin explored the background and reasons for the attack and suggested a course of corrective action. As a result, he again was retained as outside counsel and held that account until his firm's dissolution in 1960.

An ironic twist to the 1939 termination was that only 3 days before, Baldwin had been invited to meet with Robert Woodruff, the man who made Coca-Cola a worldwide household word, and other Coke executives in Wilmington, Delaware. When dinner was over, Woodruff took Baldwin aside and offered him the Coca-Cola account "if you will tell me it will be your Number 1 account." Baldwin, thinking of International Nickel, replied he could not honestly make such a promise. Baldwin did not get the Coke account.

SAVING MCKESSON-ROBBINS—THE BIG ONE

Perhaps the highlight of Bill Baldwin's success as a public relations counselor came with his role in helping to save the McKesson Robbins drug firm after a headline scandal and financial disaster took it to the brink of dissolution. This epic tale began to unfold December 5, 1938, when this staid, respected, and profitable company unexpectedly filed for bankruptcy. Just the year before, the federation of wholesale drug and liquor companies had reported a profit of nearly $4 million before interest and taxes. When board members got wind of this surprise move by McKesson Robbins' president, they went into federal court in New York to block the move. District Judge Coxe accepted the case and appointed William J. Wardell, an investment banker as federal trustee in what came to be the first important case initiated and completed under Chapter X of the Bankruptcy Act.

At an Urban League dinner in mid-December, Baldwin's cousin, Chester Bowles, a partner in the highly successful advertising agency Benton & Bowles, told him he had been approached by Wardell to handle this public relations crisis, but because his firm had the Colgate account, which could represent a conflict of interest, Bowles had recommended Baldwin. Baldwin & Mermey took the account and plunged into an unfolding tale of bizarre criminal and financial events.

At first the bankruptcy story stayed on the business pages as merely a financial problem story. By December 12, it became known that McKesson Robbins had been embezzled of as much as $18 million, $10 million in missing drugs and $8 million through falsified business records. When this was exposed, the company president, F. Donald Coster, committed suicide as police were arriving to take him into custody for questioning. McKesson Robbins was now front-page news and remained so for months. More bad news the next day—the "scholarly" president of the firm was revealed to have been an imposter and convicted swindler, Phillip Musica.

A typical paper, the *St. Louis Glove Democrat* gave half of its front page to this sensational story. More bad news unfolded. The company was accused of shipping arms to Spain in boxes labeled Milk of Magnesia. Seven McKesson Robbins subsidiaries were found by the trustee to be nonexistent. Coster's claim of a PhD from the University of Heidelberg proved to be a lie. Two vice-presidents were found to be Coster's brothers also using aliases. As more bizarre facts emerged, *Fortune* termed it "the strangest swindle of modern business history." This was further compounded when a third Coster brother was unmasked in the Accounting Department. To cap the bad news, the Federal Drug and Food Administration seized McKesson Robbins products for failure to comply with regulations covering manufacture and labeling. This seizure, coupled with others dug out by reporters, appeared to be an indictment of all the company's products.

Baldwin waded into this crisis on December 21. He decided that he would work exclusively with the trustee while he employed Brewster S. Beach to work with the company executives. He thought it desirable to split the public relations work because of certain conflicts of interest between the company and the trustee.

In a letter of October 24, 1961, Baldwin's analysis of the problem outlined two basic characteristics:

> One was the very nature of the McKesson & Robbins organization. Although it had an old and respected name, it was, in 1938, actually a very loose confederation of wholesale drug firms scattered across the country, each retaining its old personnel, local pride, and traditions. The other was the public's intense concern for its health as symbolized by the drugs which the McKesson name was identified with. Enter on the stage the villain in the form of Coster–Musica, his defalcations of an unknown amount and his subsequent identification as an ex-convict, the villain releasing the public fear and near panic to exert a centrifugal force that threatened to disintegrate the McKesson Robbins structure and drive the component drug houses into independent operations. This was the essence of the public relations problem Wardall faced and its successful solution was primarily public relations in nature.

Wardall moved quickly and dramatically. He put new men in charge of the company books, changed all the locks, and shifted the bank accounts to his name. Next, he ordered a complete audit, a complete inventory, and a spot chemical analysis of all the company's products. Quickly he was faced with a tough question, one that he used to dramatize his intention to keep the firm intact and going. He was presented with a purchase order for whiskey costing $1,250,000. If he failed to sign, the company would lose its competitive position and send the wrong signal to the public. He signed the order.

Two days after Baldwin was retained for a fee of $1,500 a month — all a Federal bankruptcy trustee could pay — he and Wardall called in the press and informed reporters:

1. The company is sound.
2. The business the company does is essential.
3. Manufacturers and retailers have expressed and demonstrated confidence in the company.
4. McKesson & Robbins will continue in business.

On December 29, in the dull news time of the holidays, Baldwin issued an announcement about the thorough investigation of the company's fiances by S. D. Leidesdorf & Co. the thorough inventory by Ford, Bacon, & Davis, an engineering firm, and described the scope of their work. These were Baldwin's first two steps. Next he set in motion events and news releases to accomplish the following:

1. Make clear that the company would carry on.
2. Continue and expand the firm's advertising campaign, especially in the cities of McKesson Robbins affiliates.
3. Keep the press fully informed of progress in reorganization and the recovery of assets. Baldwin hoped that this positive information would counteract the negative press reports then getting a big play.
4. Make a full public disclosure when each phase of the reorganization was completed.

This strategy to communicate with the key publics involved—employees, shareholders, retailers, manufacturers, and the public via the media—was outlined in an undated pamphlet authored by the three partners, "McKesson Robbins: A Study in Confidence."

As is usual in crisis situations, paid advertising was used heavily. Wardall repeatedly placed ads in the 66 cities in which the affiliates were located. These ads made the points that McKesson Robbins services were not affected in any way or even interrupted by the scandal and that the high quality of the company's products would be maintained. In turn, he persuaded the affiliates to publish ads expressing and their full confidence in the parent company. On Baldwin's advice, Wardall also increased the advertising in the trade press. Both newspapers and the trade press pegged new stories on these ads, particularly those of the affiliates.

As the criminal aspects of the company's problems continued to dominate the news, Baldwin and Wardall made every effort to counter with constructive news but deliberately erred on the side of understatement. These defensive measures continued until mid-January 1939 when Baldwin called a press conference for Wardall so he could announce the recovery of $500,000 in assets. A court order transferring these assets to the company was displayed. Wardall eventually recovered $2,485,000 in missing assets, in part from Coster's estate and $600,000 from the board of directors. Coster and his brothers had worked their swindle for 12 years and stolen $2. million from the company. In pursuit of their policy of candor, Baldwin and Wardall issued a financial report that for December, sales were down 4%. Baldwin later made the point that "the trustee adhered to the policy of keeping to the standard form of a financial report." "It was never rearranged to 'put our best feet forward.' The editors soon realized that they were dealing with a man of integrity, and public confidence in him and therefore in the McKesson Robbins organization steadily grew."

In January 1939, Wardall issued a financial report to stockholders and creditors giving a candid report on the firm's status and progress of the reorganization. He reported that sales in January 1939 were a fraction of a per cent higher than the previous January. Thus, a month and 10 days after Coster's suicide, McKesson & Robbins was on the public relations offensive. Baldwin obtained a statement from the director of the Federal Food and Drug Administration that its earlier seizure of McKesson Robbins products had been "strictly technical and routine." Another coup was achieved when several motion picture producers interested in making a movie of the Coster Scandal were persuaded that such a motion picture would be adverse to the public interest, because it would shake the public's confidence in the entire drug industry. On April 29, 1939, the public reactions offensive got another boost when Wardall announced the results of the chemical analyses of all the company's products found them safe and untampered with.

Baldwin later wrote that the turning point "in internal morale came at the convention of the American Medical Association in May, 1939." After Wardall's vacillating on the matter of its traditional exhibit at the AMA convention, Baldwin persuaded Wardall it would be a serious step backward not to have such an exhibit. Brewster Beach came with the idea for an illustrated brochure, "A Camera Tour Through the McKesson Robbins Laboratories," completed just in time for distribution at the convention exhibit. Baldwin wrote of this turning point, "McKesson's representatives at the convention were cordially received and the 'tone' of the McKesson management rose immediately and perceptibly."

The crisis was considered over when the trustee reported that the firm's earnings in the calendar year of 1939 were greater than any previous year, and in 1940, earnings again increased. Also, McKesson & Robbins were reorganized from a loose confederation of 66 wholesale houses into a tight, viable organization. Not only did the company's finances bound back, no major executive jumped ship when it hit the stormy waters of the Coster brothers' swindle. For his part, Baldwin, remembering Thomas Woodlock's admonition to endure the press's aggressive questioning until he had something to report and then go on the offensive appears to be a key in saving this company from failure. Perhaps this was Bill Baldwin's great shining moment in public relations. The Wardell–Baldwin triumph was heralded by *Fortune* in an article entitled "McKesson & Robbins, Its Fall and Rise," in March 1940.

However, the credit was to be shared, Baldwin and his partners set about to get theirs in a series of writings. A pamphlet entitled "McKesson Robbins: A Study in Confidence", undated, was distributed by Baldwin, Beach & Mermey as a promotional piece. Baldwin and Beach authored an article by the same title for the *Public Opinion Quarterly* for June 1940.

Finally, Baldwin wrote a definitive article on this case study, "The McKesson & Robbins Reorganization," for the *Harvard Business Review* of Summer 1952. He noted in this prestigious publication that the *Public Opinion Quarterly* and *Fortune* articles were published when the reorganization was roughly at its halfway mark. In the *Harvard Business Review*, Baldwin summarized, "Within a span of 31 months the country's one really national wholesaling organization in the fields of drugs, drug sundries, wines, and liquor plummeted in respectability and success to the brink of financial disaster and disintegration, only to work its way back to a stronger internal structure, a greater public prestige, and a better earning power than it had ever previously enjoyed."

Baldwin was one of six publicists singled out by Ellsworth Newcomb as the nation's "Top Publicists" in *Coronet* magazine of November 1942. Newcomb wrote, "William Henry Baldwin, who looks faintly professorial and has a gentle New England background . . . paradoxically has, as public relations counsel, dealt with some of the most militant situations of our time. . . . It is for his work on the McKesson-Robbins drug firm reorganization (completed in 1941) that Baldwin is widely famous."

BACK TO THE TARIFF YEARS

Growing opposition to renewal of the Reciprocal Trade Agreements (RTA) that President Roosevelt and Secretary of State Cordell Hull had initiated early in the New Deal brought Bill Baldwin's expertise in this field back into play. In 1943, 1945, and 1948, Baldwin and Mermey was retained by national committees formed to develop public support for extension of this act. The 1943 and 1945 committees were headed by Clark Minor and the 1948 one by Gerard Swope, honorary president of General Electric. The Reciprocal Trade Act, first passed by the Democrats in 1934 to modify the disastrous Sooth-Hawley Tariff Act, had relatively smooth sailing until 1948 when President Truman faced a hostile Republican Congress.

The protectionists saw this as their chance to greatly modify or scuttle the RTA. They went to the country first. News accounts as early as January began to report speeches, forums, and investigations purporting to show the damage the RTA was having on certain segments of the economy. By March, their campaign was in full swing and a call to arms went out from the free traders. Will Clayton, Assistant Secretary of State for trade policy, called Swope and asked him to head a campaign to turn the tide. Swope wanted to think it over and wanted more information. On March 16, John Abbink, chairman of the National Foreign Trade Council, and its president, Eugene Thomas, accompanied by Bill Baldwin, called on Swope. Swope's main question was, "Who will do the work if I accept?" The foreign trade officials said Baldwin would. Out of this came the Citizen's Committee for Reciprocal Trade with Swope as chairman and an employee of Baldwin's firm as secretary.

A crash program was quickly planned because there was no time to lose. Only a year before, in 1937, Baldwin's firm had developed a publication, *Resolved*, devoted to the interests of nonprofit organizations. Through the mailing list developed for this monthly newsletter, Baldwin knew or was known by the leaders of these groups nationwide. Within 3 weeks, Baldwin and his staff had signed up to 280 members for the committee, with organizations paying $1,000 and individuals $250. These members were from 75 cities in 32 states. Baldwin sought a wider and larger membership but decided it was time to move from organization to implementation. Cordell Hull accepted the honorary chairmanship, thereby lending his prestige to the cause.

Baldwin first prepared a 16-page pamphlet, *That Hickory Limb*, for distribution to all members of Congress. This pamphlet asked and answered 20 questions about RTA. It carried the names of the rather formidable committee the group had put together. Fourteen thousand copies of the pamphlet were printed, but before the guns had subsided, Baldwin had received 100,000 requests for it. Persons were charged 7¢ a copy. A weekly newsletter was sent to groups and key individuals to keep them informed and to stimulate their support. Some 8,000 copies were mailed each week. A fact-laden Speaker's Notes were sent to 950 advocates of the act's extension. Secretary of Commerce Averill Harriman was drafted to make a major speech in support of the extension. Leaders of the League of Women Voters, American Importers National Council, and other pro-low-tariff groups were exhorting their members and bombarding congressmen with mail. In late April, President Truman and Secretary of State George Marshall weighed in with strong speeches.

Before the committee hearings opened, Baldwin armed Swope with a brief and secured a statement from Secretary Hull to be read at the hearing and a supporting statement from the American Chamber of Commerce of Cuba, an old ally. Then the Baldwin campaign got a big break. Republican Representative Bertrand Gearhart of California, chairman of the Tariff Subcommittee of the House Ways and Means Committee, who had been leading the campaign against extension, blundered by closing the hearings with this statement, "I can't see any useful purpose would be served by listening to spokesmen for a bunch of ladies' sewing societies reading statements . . . prepared by the State Department." Baldwin quickly exploited this dumb statement by contrasting the "sewing society" with the membership of the Citizen's Committee for Reciprocal World Trade.

As the result of these and other public relations moves, the free trade forces won the war when the U.S. Senate passed the bill without the House version with Rep. Gearhart's amendment requiring Congressional approval of tariff reductions. The House accepted the Senate version, and President Truman signed the new act on June 27. For a modest $31,540, covering fees and expenses, Baldwin had built an aroused public opinion to which Congress appropriately responded.

Bill Baldwin, reflecting on this victory, gave this insight on his philosophy, "The way any society moves reflects the ability of component individuals and groups to get the ear on the controlling power. . . . The more genuine a democracy and the freer its press and other channels of communication, the more does the ear of the public become the prime target. . . . The strength of this approach is that it is out in the open. You have to be a straight shooter because you are under public scrutiny." Bill Baldwin was a straight shooter.

The taste of the Reciprocal Tariff victories turned sour for Baldwin in 1962. October 31 of that year he wrote me, "This has been a tough year for me. I got very thoroughly pushed around and finally aside in my efforts to do a job in support of the Trade Expansion Act, a job for which I was better qualified—on past performance but not on Washington in-fighting—than anyone else in this field."

BALDWIN AND MERMEY'S LAST 20 YEARS

The Japanese attack on Pearl Harbor that brought World War II to the United States imposed profound changes and dislocations on nearly every individual and institution. Public relations agencies were no exception. In 1942, Brewster Beach enlisted in the U.S. Navy, and the firm's name was changed to Baldwin and Mermey, which it remained until the firm was dissolved in 1960. World War II cost the agency the International Nickel account and the newly acquired account to promote the St. Lawrence Seaway. However, it brought Baldwin and Mermey the Sterling Drug Company account. This firm faced a crisis because of its long association with I. G. Farben. A similar problem faced Standard Oil (New Jersey), then being counseled by Ivy Lee for whom the problem was compounded because Lee had accepted fees from I. G. Farben. This story was told in chapter 6.

Typical of Baldwin's approach in such matters, he advised "say nothing, deny nothing, perform responsibly." He advised telling Sterling's story in the present tense and not to rehash ancient history. Baldwin and Mermey set out to publicize Sterling's accomplishments. Articles on aspirin and atabrine appeared in *Collier's* and *Reader's Digest*. (Atabrine was taken daily by servicemen in the South Pacific as a safeguard against malaria.) The company got a big break when it was awarded the Army–Navy E for helping the war effort, a ceremony duly heralded. The furor against Sterling that came with the war against the Nazis soon petered out. Finally, the firm produced *The Sterling Story* to acquaint the company's worldwide organization with the history, policies, and program of the parent company and its subsidiaries. This book later went into a second edition.

In 1943, the Baldwin and Mermey secured an account from a division of Englehard Industries to do a full publicity and promotion job for the use of platinum and palladium in jewelry. Then in 1944, Baldwin and Mermey were retained by Abraham and Straus to cover the range of employee relations, college recruitment, and promotion for the main store and its branches. The firm also started A&S's Junior Angler Fishing Contest, that became a part of the New York City recreation program.

The A&S account probably led to the work for the Retail Dry Goods Association of New York that began in 1945. In devising on all phases of public relations, Baldwin could draw on his long experience with retailing, starting with the Macy account in 1926. In a related field, Maurice Mermey became director of the Bureau of Education on Fair Trade in 1949. This came about as the result of pending federal and state legislation on fair trade that would directly affect retailers by forcing them to charge the manufacturer's "fair price." In the summer of 1942, James C. Petrillo, president of the American Federation of Musicians, demanded royalties from the record companies for new recording and from radio broadcasting stations using broadcast music. To effect his demand, Petrillo enjoined all union members from playing for any kind of mechanical reproduction. As a result, no records were made for 18 months. Baldwin and Mermey was retained by the National Association of Broadcasters and at the end of the "music strike," won for broadcasters freedom but Petrillo did get fees from the recording companies.

Baldwin and Mermey were selected to handle the public relations for the *Crusade for Freedom*, launched in 1950 by the Eastern Establishment to demonstrate American commitment to freedom in Europe and to raise funds for Radio Free Europe—in short a part of the Cold War with the USSR that fortunately now is history. The crusade was triggered by the Berlin Blockade of 1948–49 and headed by General Lucius Clay, who had been Military Governor of Germany. Baldwin explained, "The Crusade was primarily and essentially a public relations operation—to get the voice of the American people registered through the hanging of a replica of the Liberty Bell in beleaguered Berlin." Petitions were circulated throughout the country asking people to sign and contribute a dollar. More than $650,000 was spent in promotion that brought in 15 million signatures and $1,288,044 in contributions—Another public opinion victory.

In the mid-1950s, Baldwin worked with Arnold Michaelis, a radio and TV producer, on the concept of *recorded portraits*. These were taped recordings of informal conversations with outstanding public figures of that day. The idea was to capture the leader's personality and viewpoints on tape to be used as a teaching tool in schools of business. This project was one that didn't meet with success, and when Baldwin and Mermey closed shop, it was, in Baldwin's words, "a piece of unfinished business."

In the 1950s, Baldwin also worked on accounts for Pationo Mines and the St. Lawrence Seaway legislation whereas Mermey handled the Bureau of Education for Fair Trade. But Baldwin's deep sense of citizenship kept pulling him into public-spirited projects, efforts to advance standards of public relations, and to promote what he termed *Civitas*, a merger of the leaders of business and nonprofit organizations for the public good.

CIVITAS—A GOOD IDEA THAT DIDN'T FLY

Reflecting Bill Baldwin's careers as a counselor and as a citizen was the project he chose to call *Civitas* that had both business and public sector objectives. This was an effort to bring together influential and public nonprofit sectors in order to bring more mutual understanding between the public and private sectors and thus more amity to society. Baldwin developed this plan in the 1940s, visualizing a national information service concerning citizen groups "to broaden the area of understanding, respect, and agreement between the business world and Civitas." *Civitas* was the word he coined to describe citizen associations. He planned to collect and catalogue information on the attitudes of all major nonprofit citizen organizations in the United States that were active in public affairs. Armed with this information, Baldwin thought he could then provide a service to the corporate community by informing them of what support and what opposition they would face on a particular issue. Baldwin reasoned that with this basis of understanding, public relations programs could be tailored to merge the interests of the business interests and the citizen groups. He sought a service that would serve both business and Civitas. He saw it as a mutually beneficial proposition.

To implement this plan, Baldwin initiated a four-page monthly newsletter, *Resolved*, to report the activities of nonprofit citizens organizations concerned with public affairs. He saw this as a cooperative publication with its free controlled distribution. In return, he expected recipients to provide information of developments and campaigns in their organizations. The first issue of *Resolved*, published in May 1947, carried this in its masthead: "A newsletter devoted to exchange of information among citizen organizations as an aid to increasing the effectiveness of their programs." The basic mailing list included approximately 1,200 names. He included women's groups, service clubs, parent and youth organizations, civic and welfare groups, and so forth. He excluded farm groups, labor unions, and trade and management associations.

Baldwin later said, "The publication won a quick and broad acceptance, and the volume of incoming mail from organizations with activities to report grew steadily. What gained their confidence was that an Editorial Advisory Council functioned from the very start." The council was made up of 12 men and women representatives of Civitas, and it edited all copy in advance and suggested and approved subjects for each issue. The volume of incoming material far exceeded the space available. All incoming communications were recorded on index cards that became Baldwin's "Catalog of Attitudes." Paralleling this, a master index was created to record the vital statistics of these organizations. Baldwin could then establish a "Dynamic Quotient" reflecting the identification of organizations on either side of an issue.

Thus, Baldwin and Mermey could put together a packet of specialized and unique information to sell to a business interest to gain clients. Baldwin was enthusiastic about this scheme, to put it mildly. He bragged in one of his Harvard Business School seminars that harnessing the power of citizen organizations with business would be "the most significant contribution to the public relations function in American life since the development of attitude measurements." Sadly, the idea never caught on, although Baldwin doggedly tried to push it after Baldwin and Mermey had dissolved. He later admitted to me that the project had cost $40,000. It did provide much-needed help in the 1948 battle to extend the Reciprocal Trade Agreements without the Republicans' crippling amendments. He wrote me on October 31, 1962, "As for the Civitas operation, I have left it on the shelf through lack of time and nervous energy to fight on still another front; but that is a solid concept which can be dusted off anytime conditions are favorable. Meanwhile, I'm keeping my chin up and finding plenty to do in extra-curricular activities." That he did, doubled in spades, until ill health overtook this indomitable man.

THE AMI-OPERATION UNITY — BILL BALDWIN'S LAST HURRAH FOR AMERICA

Bill Baldwin, a man of rugged integrity and a liberal internationalist, had, understandably, been deeply offended by the political Red-baiting and smearing of good reputations and by headline-seeking politicians, led by Senator Joseph McCarthy, in the 1950s. Thus, he "conceived and helped to launch as an essentially a public relations project to develop national unity here at home and understanding and prestige for America throughout the world" — AMI-Operation Unity. In blunter language in an interview with his biographer, John F. Forrest, he said he undertook this large-scale effort "to fight McCarthyism, McCarranism, and for Americanism." As he explained in a letter to me of October 20, 1959:

> This grew out of my having been asked to join the board of the American Scientific and Historic Preservation Society and give free public relations advice in its fight to save Fort Clinton [built to defend New York's Harbor during the War of 1812] from demolition by Robert Moses in his plans for "improvement" of the Battery at the tip of Manhattan. When it became evident that we would be successful in saving the old fort as a National Monument, I began to think what could be done to save it from being a passive relic. Remembering that, as Castle Garden, it had served as the first federal immigration station, I got the idea that it could be developed into a Museum of American Immigration to dramatize for all time the story of immigration in the building of America. The museum idea took hold at once.

And it took hold of Baldwin for most of the remaining years of his life, a passion that brought him much anguish and ultimately satisfaction. The first problem to be met was how to finance the project. Many of those initially involved favored going to Congress for an appropriation. Baldwin, true to his New England ancestry, insisted that the project stand on its own feet. The preservation society created a special committee to develop the campaign as "Operation Unity." Baldwin wrote, "In my eyes AMI-Operation Unity had the makings of a public relations development that would bind us together at home and prove a strong beacon light to the confused peoples of the world." Time would prove the ordinarily realistic practitioner optimistic on both counts.

The organization for the campaign rapidly took shape. Major General U.S. Grant III agreed to serve as chairman, Pierre S. DuPont III as chairman of the executive committee, Alexander Hamilton as secretary-treasurer, and Edward Corsi, George Meany, and Spryros Skouras among the vice-presidents. A pattern of participation and recognition was developed to embrace nationality, veteran, and other patriotic organizations, farm groups, labor unions, business and industrial corporations, foundations, and school children on a countrywide basis. Pete DuPont (whose participation Baldwin had obtained through the good offices of Harold Brayman, du Pont's public reactions officer) and David J. McDonald, president of the United Steel Workers Union, served as cochairman of the national appeal. The group procured the Postmaster General's permission to give it an unprecedented address: "Statue of Liberty, U.S.A."

The National Park Service, heavily involved from the start, suggested that establishment of the museum in Fort Clinton would impair its restoration as an historic fort and suggested that the museum be placed in the base of the Statue of Liberty, which had never been properly developed. The Park Service estimated $1 million for construction of the museum and another $1 million, for assembling and installing the exhibits. On this basis, Baldwin recommended a fund-raising goal of $5 million. General Grant got an agreement from the Secretary of Interior that the museum would include a Hall of Records to inscribe the names of all donors. This, too, was unprecedented for national monuments.

Baldwin's Papers further record, "The project was becoming too time consuming for me to volunteer my services, even though it was my idea. It was therefore arranged to retain Baldwin and Mermey as counsel, I to devote most of my time to developing staff and supervising the program. In view of this professional status, I resigned as trustee and board secretary."

The agreement between AMI and Baldwin and Mermey started early in 1954 and was terminated December 31, 1955, because in the fall of 1955, it was evident that the campaign was in bad shape. Baldwin's firm canceled $33,000 in back obligations. Baldwin noted, "The two great disillusionment of the campaign were the inability of the original volunteer leadership to enroll effective leaders in key centers throughout the country, and the failure of organized labor, which contributed $250,000 of the $2,000,000 publicly pledged by David A. McDonald and later publicly confirmed by George Meany." When his firm resigned the account, Baldwin offered to take a leave of absence from the firm and devote full-time to AMI at reduced compensation. His offer was accepted; AMI reduced its quarters and staff and terminated all contracts with fund-raising firms. In June 1957, the campaign was put in mothballs, save for a full-time secretary and part-time bookkeeper, both of whom were paid by Mr. du Pont.

The campaign had netted some $400,000 and the AMI Board, back-tracking on an earlier refusal, agreed to accept the National Park Service's provision for matching funds raised for national parks or monuments. Thus, in the fall of 1960, it was announced at a public dinner in New York that the Park Service would undertake the first year's phase of construction of the museum. At the dinner, Chairman du Pont presented AMI's check to Secretary of the Interior Stewart Udall. In his letter of November 23, 1961, Baldwin wrote, "These developments mean that the Park Service has faith that the Museum will be established. We have moved into the home-stretch — but still without a jockey! It looks as though I am going to be able to sweat it out and see it through."

Sweat it out, he did. "My position for the past three years has been that the campaign must be reactivated and pushed through to success; that no broad public appeal is required inasmuch as we have a pattern of participation that is nationwide and that we should concentrate on a rifle-shooting job in Metropolitan New York, which we have never really cultivated," Baldwin vouched. In October 1962, he wrote on a more optimistic note:

The Museum would seem to be at long last on its way to reality. This past Sunday its cornerstone was laid in rather impressive ceremonies during which the director of the National Park Service (NPS), which is in direct charge of construction and will be the permanent custodian and administrator, definitely announced the Intention of NPS to have the Museum in operation when the New York World's Fair opens in the spring of 1964. There still is some $700,000 to be raised from the public, but key persons are pretty well committed to seeing it through.

But 5 years later on May 12, 1967, came this pessimistic note from Baldwin: "The case study I would most like to write about I can't — at this time at least. It is that of the AMI-Operation Unity project at the Statue of Liberty. It now looks as if it will limp to completion in another two years. Until it does it badly needs Woodlock's 'silence' — and very little of that treatment. I pray no newshawk gets his talons into it at this time."

Once again Baldwin was a bit optimistic. The museum project continued to languish until President Lyndon B. Johnson came to the rescue and proposed in his 1968 budget that funds be appropriated to complete the museum. AMI officials that year were ascribing the delay in opening the museum to lack of funds and construction difficulties. AMI officials announced later that year that the first exhibit area would be devoted to the Statue of Liberty and would open in November. On May 17, Lady Bird Johnson, wife of the President, opened an exhibit of sketches showing how the museum would look when it was finished. In this connection, the American Scenic and Historic Preservation Society issued a statement lauding citizens for their contributions. Finally after a troublesome 17 years, Bill Baldwin saw his dream realized when the American Immigration in the pedestal of the Statue of Liberty was dedicated September 26, 1972. In his last letter to me, Baldwin wrote with obvious satisfaction:

The American Museum of Immigration, which now encircles the base of the Statue of Liberty, started as my dream in the early Fifties and went through a nightmare of frustration and delay before a reality of its official opening in September, 1972. We trustees of AMI held our annual meeting yesterday when we were advised that the National Park Service is prepared to work out a cooperative development with us of Liberty Island, Ellis Island and Castle Clinton (the first Federal immigration station), as a combined center for telling the story of immigration in our nation's growth.

This letter, dated November 10, 1977, announced his plan to move from his home in New Canaan to Crosslands, a Friends' retirement home in Kennett Square, Pennsylvania, that December and where he died in 1980.

Truly, this was Bill's last hurrah for the nation he loved and for which he did so much. Fortunately for him, he did not live to see the diminution of his dream with the opening of $156 million Ellis Island Immigration

Museum of the National Park Service in September 1990. [Ellis Island is now the focus of the immigration story and many of the AMI exhibits were moved there prior to its gala opening.]

For reasons never fully explained, Baldwin and Mermey dissolved their partnership in 1960, and Baldwin's new letterhead read: "William H. Baldwin, Public Relations Counsel, 60 East 42nd Street, New York 17, N.Y." As he wrote a year later. "There's been a change in course, but there has been no move to drydock! Subject to some unforeseen illness, I shall steam ahead for another five years." Not until ill health caught up with him in the late 1970s, steam ahead he did. Later he gave up his office and moved in with Robert L. Bliss & Company at 60 East 42nd Street as associate counsel. A few years later, he retired to his home in New Canaan, Connecticut.

Perhaps a hidden factor in Baldwin's decision to end the partnership and again operate solo with more time for his public interests was the sale of the *Springfield (MA.) Republican* to Samuel I. Newhouse, who paid $4 million for the 40% interest owned by the 60 descendants of Samuel Bowles. Baldwin handled the sale on behalf of the Bowles's heirs. Determination to sell followed 8 years' frustration with the newspaper's absentee management. On June 25, 1960, *Editor & Publisher* quoted Baldwin as saying, "We have no voice in the determination of dividends or other vital decisions." Baldwin's share of the sale price is not known.

WHB ON PUBLIC RELATIONS AND ITS ADVANCEMENT

In his roughly half-century involvement in public relations, fund-raising, and advancing public causes, Bill Baldwin's relations philosophy steadily expanded and matured. As he wrote in 1958, "The bits and pieces of past education and experience fell into a useful pattern." In a letter to me dated December 27, 1960, Baldwin wrote:

> We had no literature; we had no formal teaching. I, for one, served an apprenticeship under Woodlock, just as an earlier generation "read law" in the offices of distinguished attorneys who had been trained in a similar way; but at least they had their Blackstone. We earlybirds reacted, improvised, and experimented, each in his own isolated way. One of the first groupings toward a meeting of minds was under the aegis of the National Association of Accredited Publicity Directors.

William H. Baldwin did much to advance the craft of public relations through his personal standards, writings, teaching, and through his effort to develop a professional association and, with it, standards for the field. Baldwin never asserted, as many practitioners do today with doubtful validity, that public relations was or is a profession.

In 1939, 20 years after he started in public relations at the American International Corporation, Baldwin gave this concept in a speech, "Public relations has to do with the technique of persons getting on with one anther. One half is making your self understood, one half is understanding the other fellow." In short, he had adopted the two-way street concept first enunciated by Edward L. Bernays in this *Crystallizing Public Opinion* in 1923. If Baldwin were alive, he would bristle at this suggestion, because he had little respect for Bernays. In a letter of November 25, 1945, to John F. Chapman of the *Harvard Business Review*, Baldwin wrote bitingly:

> Bernays' "Biography of an Idea" and its promotion by the publishers constitutes a pretty sorry bill of goods. Public Relations Counseling as a constructive aid to management predates him, will survive him and has developed rootage and quite a bit apart from his self-accreditation as its be-all and end-all. I haven't read the full text and don't intend to do so, but I have done some exploratory drilling and have come up with pretty dry holes.

Baldwin's view of Bernays reflected a general consensus among the pioneer practitioners of that time.

In a promotional pamphlet, *Public Relations in Modern Business* (circa late 1930s but before 1939) Baldwin explained:

> Public relations has two main functions: The first is one of analysis and advice in which getting an understanding of the other fellow's point of view is a most important factor. . . . If you are going to get on with your public you must be prepared to meet it pretty much on its own terms. Lip service won't do the job. The basis for sound public relations is doing the right thing in the right way at the right time. And the right time comes before you are forced to do it. The second function of public relations is presentation of your case at the bar of public opinion. In the intense competition for public attention, your case will necessarily go by default unless it is actively and continually promoted. In such a program both advertising and publicity have their places.

This concept, still valid and frequently voiced, has stood the test of time, demonstrating Baldwin's sound approach to public relations problems.

Baldwin never equated public relations with publicity. In footnotes to *Public Relations*, a promotional letter Baldwin and Mermey published monthly from April 1945 to May 1948, Baldwin observed, "Publicity is hardly a synonym for public relations." He defined public relations as "the conscious reflection of a way of life toward a determined objective. It cannot be picked up and dropped like a tool but is a continuing organic force." He saw publicity as "the creation and dissemination of facts which all promote a particular interest, whether an institution, product, cause, or service."

In an article, "The Public Relations Counselor's Job," in the *Public*

Opinion Quarterly of January, 1939, he further refined his concept, "Public relations is an all-inclusive term which embraces all human relations in the conduct of business, from the impression the switchboard operator gives in handling incoming calls to the impression which the corporation president makes in public hearing of a Senate investigating committee." He explained, "Advertising and publicity, on the other hand, are methods for achieving objectives in public relations."

Bill Baldwin's final effort to define the mature concept of public relations came to him one Saturday in April 1961, "while my dog and I were ingesting, respectively, our usual milk-bone and beer." "Public relations counseling is the disciplined art focused on aiding Management to be ever sensitive and adjusted the world in which it operates."

BALDWIN ON PUBLIC RELATIONS AS A PROFESSION

By the mid-1930s as the number of practitioners was multiplying and the expectations of the "magic" of public relations were mounting, Bill Baldwin became increasingly concerned about the matter of ethics and the need for a professional organization to police the behavior of those labeling themselves public relations counsel. As he and Raymond C. Mayer wrote in the *Public Opinion Quarterly* in the Summer 1944 issue in an article "On Buying Public Relations":

> Public relations is at a dangerous age. It has arrived at that tricky state . . . where almost anything may happen. The public mind, fascinated by its techniques, has been encouraged to expect too much too quickly. . . . All too frequently the business world's conception of public relations is that of an aspirin for an immediate headache. Much of the fault lies within the profession itself, which has yet to build up effective safeguards against over-selling by irresponsible opportunists. Whereas the State polices such profession as law, medicine, and public accounting, the only present controls over public relations are such self-policing as the group itself may develop and such discrimination as the purchasers of public relations services may evidence.

As a consequence of this situation, Baldwin, himself possessed with a high sense of ethics and morality, was one of the leaders in organizing the first association of public relations practitioners. He and a few other leaders came together in 1936 to form the National Association of Accredited Publicity Directors. The group was limited to New York City. Obviously, the words *accredited* and *national* were used loosely. Marking the growing shift from publicity to a more mature public relations, the association changed its name in 1944 to the National Association of Public Relations

Counsel (NAPRC). Edward L. Bernays was purposely excluded from this association. Baldwin always acknowledged Bernays as an articulate and major prophet of public relations, but the latter's indefatigable self-promotion offended Baldwin's "New England conscience." In his view, Ivy Lee was "the high priest" of public relations and his employment by the Rockefellers was the "turning point" in public relations history. Baldwin served as chairman of the NAPRC board in 1941–1942. Out of this impetus for an organization to solidify and provide ethical guidance for public relations came today's Public Relations Society of America, organized in 1948 with the merger of the New York-based NAPRC and the American Council on Public Relations that had been started by pioneer Rex Harlow in San Francisco in 1939.

Even though Baldwin and Raymond C. Mayer, then current president of the NAPRC, used the term *profession* in their *Public Opinion Quarterly* article, Baldwin never engaged in this pretension. He saw the field as an "art" or a "craft." Professionalism to him required an accepted ethical code that could be enforced. He also observed, "There is no association or organization to supervise professional studies in public relations." Later, after the Public Relations Society had been formed and was functioning, Baldwin averred: "PRSA, as the dominant self-governing body in public relations, has put on paper a resounding code of ethics; but, unless and until it takes action against infractors among its members, its code will remain more lip-service to ethics." Ultimately, PRSA did begin to enforce its Code of Professional Standards, although somewhat unevenly in the opinion of its critics.

As of 1961, Baldwin didn't see the field as even growing toward a profession. "It has no licensing requirement and no exact field of effort. Its area of activity is fluid. While lawyers and doctors have precise areas of interest, public relations serves industry's or other client's entire relation with many publics." Baldwin was known for his ethical standards that, in his view, went beyond "misusing public relations techniques by hood-winking communications media and the public." As mentioned earlier he believed and adhered to at some personal cost that the practitioner must not accept clients "whose objectives run counter to his personal views of right and decency."

BALDWIN THE CITIZEN

As indicated at the outset, William H. Baldwin III was the son of two distinguished public-spirited parents, William H. Baldwin, Jr. and Ruth Standish Bowles Baldwin, whose spirit of public service and public concerns he inherited and to which he devoted much of his life and his treasure. He went on the Fisk University Board of Trustees when it took on its fund-raising campaign in 1923 and served on its board and in its cause the rest of his life. He joined the board of directors of the Southern Education Foundation in 1945 and served it diligently until his death in 1980. The Southern Foundation promotes equal educational opportunities for African Americans and seeks to advance their interests in other ways, a cause Bill Baldwin believed in all his adult life. Eleanor Roosevelt served with him as a fellow board member for several years. Dr. John A. Griffin, director emeritus of the foundation, said this of Baldwin's service, "His commitment to the improvement of the status of Negro Americans was a preoccupation of his entire life, particularly his concern focussed on the advancement of Negro Education. Such service called for large investments of time and effort."

He served long and faithfully the Urban League, today a strong force in the nation's public affairs, a dedication that he inherited from his public-spirited, democratic mother. He became a director of the league in 1914, the year after he graduated from college, served as secretary of the board from 1915 until 1942, and as president from 1942 to 1947 during the turbulent war and post-war years. He once wryly commented to me, "The only piece of business I ever got from all these associations was the one from the Committee of Fourteen." World War II, he served as treasurer of the American War Community Services Fund, designed to promote social planning for the postwar period. A similar organization, the United Community Defense Services Committee, was set up during the Korean War, and Baldwin served on this board.

Undoubtedly, one of the public services Baldwin was proudest of was the saving of Sydenham Hospital in New York City after he went on its board in 1943. In a letter to me dated October 20, 1959 Baldwin recounted:

> Situated on the edge of Harlem, Sydenham had become a moribund institution. Its trustees agreed to let several of us, white and Negro, join the board to establish majority control. During the next five or six years we developed so significant a demonstration of integration that other voluntary hospitals in New York began to admit Negro doctors to their visiting staffs, and that representatives of hospital management in other parts of the country, including the South, came to see what we were doing.

The new board had inherited a serious financial condition in unpaid bills, accrued maintenance, and increasing costs of operation. The hospital went from one financial crisis to another; on one occasion, it was bailed out by a campaign initiated by the *New York Post*. Seeing the handwriting on the wall, Baldwin "got a couple of my fellow trustees to join me in calling on the Commissioner of Hospitals for the City of New York." "I gave him the financial picture and said that one morning he would wake up to find

Sydenham on the City's doorstep." About a year later, that morning came. The commissioner courageously took over the institution and made municipal hospital history by assigning two floors to semiprivate and private wards and by permitting private doctors to serve their patients in them. The commissioner appointed several members of the old board to serve as an advisory committee that continued to function as late as 1960. Baldwin concluded in a proud note, "Sydenham still carries the torch with a warming and enlightening influence on hospital policy and administration here and elsewhere." However, in 1980, the year of Baldwin's death, Sydenham was closed as a hospital and converted by the city to apartments for the elderly.

TO SUM UP

William H. Baldwin was one of a handful of former journalists who had served in World War I on several fronts to join the parade of pioneers who brought sense and shape to this still ill-defined vocation. It was a time when, in Baldwin's words, "It began in a Silurian age when formal education in journalism was in its infancy, public attitudes were measured in terms of wishful thinking, and counseling, as an aid to management, was virtually unknown." A pioneer builder of today's mature, established vocation, Baldwin led by precept and by example. He was a tireless worker for the public good as he defined it, both as a citizen and counselor. He left a strong imprint on American society in building support for African-American education, civil rights, and equality of justice for all citizens, in his battles for reasonable trade policies, in his campaigns to stimulate patriotism, and in the institutions he served and saved. The inheritor of a rich legacy from his father and mother, he extended and enriched that legacy for generations to come. Yet in his days of discouragement in the twilight of his career, he told me, "Somewhere along the way—I don't know where—I missed the boat. I had so many opportunities, knew so many people." This modest genial man with whom your author shared many a drink at his beloved Harvard club, "missed the boat" in estimating his impact and influence on his sons, his society, and his profession. Ripples that flowed from his life and deeds affected all Americans. Once again, there is in Bill Baldwin's career, as in the career of other practitioners, the public relations counselor's rather profound impact on American society. The headline in *The New York Times* of May 20, 1980, sums up Baldwin's dual career as counselor and citizen:

W. H. BALDWIN DEAD:
PUBLIC RELATIONS AIDE,
URBAN LEAGUE LEADER

That says it all, Counselor and Citizen. Truly, he was a "Man for All Seasons."

NOTES ON SOURCES

This chapter is based primarily on the William H. Baldwin III Papers, in the Mass Communications History Center, State Historical Society of Wisconsin; on our long period of friendship and correspondence; on an unpublished master's thesis by Major John F. Forrest (now Lt. Gen. Forrest, USA ret.), "William H. Baldwin: A Historical Study of a Career in Public Relations," The University of Wisconsin. This thesis provided much additional information through interviews and correspondence with Mr. Baldwin and the author. Other sources include the following.

John Graham Brooks, *An American Citizen's Life, William Henry Baldwin, Jr.*, Houhgton-Mifflin, 1910. Information on the career of Baldwin's mother, Ruth Standish Bowles Baldwin, was found in her obituary, *Springfield (MA) Weekly Republican,* December 20, 1934. The following articles by William H. Baldwin: "Training for Public Relations," *Public Relations Journal,* Vol. VII, No. 8, September, 1951; "On Lobbying," *Public Relations Journal,* Vol. V, No. 7, July, 1949; "Pressure Politics and Consumer Interests," *Public Opinion Quarterly* Vol. 5, March, 1941; "The McKesson-Robbins Reorganization," *Harvard Business Review,* Summer, 1942; (With Brewster Beach) "McKesson-Robbins: A Study in Confidence," Vol. 4, *Public Opinion Quarterly,* June, 1940; "The Public Relations Counselor's Job," *Public Opinion Quarterly,* Vol. 3, January, 1949; "Public Relations in Modern Business," talk given before St. Louis Chamber of Commerce, March 8, 1939; privately printed pamphlet, "Thirteen Memories for as Many Grandchildren"; "Like Topsy, We Just Growed," *Public Relations Journal,* Vol. 14, September, 1958.

Other periodical articles: "McKesson-Robbins — Its Fall and Rise," *Fortune,* Vol. 21, March, 1940; Hubert A. Kenney, "The Sugar Shortage and Politics," *The American Mercury,* Vol. LXII, No. 269, May, 1946; "Squeeze on Nickel," *Fortune,* Vol. 42, November, 1950; Elliott Newcomb, "The Top Publicists," *Coronet,* November, 1942. Baldwin's final definition of public relations was in a letter to me dated April 18, 1961. Baldwin's letter to the *Harvard Business Review* commenting on Bernays *Biography of an Idea* can be found in the Harry A. Bruno Papers.

Chapter 13

Ben Sonnenberg: *Sui Generis*

The story of Benjamin Sonnenberg, who made the transition from imaginative, flamboyant, and sometimes designing press agent in the middle 1920s to counseling the rich and famous by the 1940s, is another saga of rags to riches in the Horatio Alger mold, a career similar to those of Edward L. Bernays and Carl Byoir.

Born in Brest Litovsk, Poland, in Old World poverty on July 12, 1901, and later reared as the son of a pushcart vendor on New York's impoverished Lower East Side, Sonnenberg died a millionaire on September 6, 1978. In between he was creator of New York's most fabulous mansion, a confidant of celebrities, and very much a celebrity in his own right.

In his colorful heyday, Sonnenberg was tagged "the era's master publicist," and by a French magazine as "the father of public relations." (Public relations, it seems, is a vocation born of many fathers.) In his book, *Merchant Princes* (1979), Leon Harris described him as "American's most successful and most colorful public relations man . . . [who] was paid enormous fees by corporations and by individuals because his advice was unorthodox." Everything about Ben Sonnenberg was unorthodox; truly he was *sui generis* in the history of this field. Yet the contrived aura and glitter he fabricated for his persona has faded. Many of today's oncoming generation of PR practitioners may not even recognize his name.

Unfortunately, the story of this extraordinary career can never be fully told. The Sonnenberg will, written December 7, 1977, when he was terminally ill with throat cancer, directed the executors of this estate to destroy all his files and papers. His decision to leave no trace of his life's work left his friends, associates, and scholars with a paradox: Why did such a person who unceasingly courted public attention by his dress, his flashy lifestyle, and his lavish celebrity parties in his antique-crammed mansion not wish to leave his professional record to open to biographers?

Sonnenberg truly was a self-made man in the literal sense of that oft-used cliché. He decided early in life to escape the taunt of being, in his own words, "a fat little Jew," by adopting a contrived style of Edwardian sartorial elegance and the lifestyles of the English nobility: four-button suits, striped or checked bib-front shirts, a Homburg hat or bowler in winter, boaters with colorful tailored hat bands in summer. As Irwin Ross wrote in the *Image Merchants*, "In all seasons, he is a picture of Edwardian splendor." Another writer described him as having the appearance of a "blimp."

In adult life, Sonnenberg stood 5 feet 7 inches tall, quite rotund, bald, and sported a conspicuous walrus mustache. He acquired over time an ornate lifestyle and spent money fiercely, guided by the conviction that he should "always live better than his clients." As Irwin Ross observed, "He insists that he does not seek personal publicity, though he has devoted much of his career to fabricating a personality which inevitably elicits attention. His motives have been understandable: to attract potential clients, to impress present clients, and revel in his own legend. . . . His flamboyance is atypical only because it is inflated to heroic dimensions."

He developed a lavish lifestyle, dining at "in" posh restaurants, entertaining in grand style, collecting expensive antiques and art, and traveling, mostly to England. Even so, he left an estate of more than $5 million to his widow, the former Hilda Kaplan, who was a supportive helpmate and lived in the shadow of his overpowering personality, and to his two children, Helen and Ben, Jr. His drive for riches and gracious living was undoubtedly born of his impoverished childhood. The inspiration to acquire riches came to him on a trip to Europe with expense dollars to spend for Herbert Hoover's American Relief Administration. As he later told *The New Yorker's* Geoffrey Hellman, "The significance of having a man draw your bath and lay out your clothes burst upon me like a revelation. I realized for the first time what it was to be rich." His son, Ben Sonnenberg, Jr., observed in his autobiography, *Lost Property*, "That to him was like a bolt of lightning on the road to Damascus."

Sonnenberg was the only son of Ida Bedder and Harry Zonnenberg. The Zonnenbergs also had two daughters. As a child, Sonnenberg (the Z was changed to S when the family came to the United States) had known the discomfort of grinding poverty. Born in a garrison town then controlled by Czarist Russia, Ben lived his early years in a small wooden hut. His father, seeking to escape the poverty and pograms of Russia, emigrated to New York City in 1905 to seek a better life. In 5 years, he had saved enough money to bring his wife, Ben, and two daughters to America. They arrived on a hot July day in 1910 when Ben was nine. Sonnenberg the elder set up a vendor's cart on Grand Street, which enabled him to pay the rent on a small apartment on the same street and keep food on the table; yet he rarely earned $20 a week. Ben's mother, Ida, got a job at the Henry Street Settlement House as a cleaning woman. Ben started going with her so she could keep an eye on him while supplementing the family income. This was most painful to her son.

A CHILDHOOD OF LEARNING

It quickly became apparent that young Ben had a wide-eyed curiosity about his new environment and was a bright, quick-study in all that he saw or read. "I was a restless child," Sonnenberg once related. By age 12, he was avidly reading newspapers, magazines, or spending his last 50¢ for a balcony seat in a New Yorker theater. As he told Geoffrey Hellman for *The New Yorker*, "Here is the phenomenon of the young immigrant who, willy-nilly, is dumped on the Eastern Seaboard on the United States through a process of experiences becomes more American than Coca-Cola and assimilates himself to the point of knowing the latest boogie-woogie beat in the propaganda of his times."

This metamorphosis was speeded by his attendance in Public School No. 62 and later DeWitt Clinton High School. Summers young Ben worked as a stock boy in Gimbel's, little realizing he someday would be counseling the elite Bergdorf Goodman fashion emporium. But perhaps it was Lillian Wald and the Henry Street Settlement House that did most to mold this young immigrant in the ways of America and send him on to a fabulous career. Young Ben found most of his recreation at the House, where he took part in dramatics and dances. This bright, earnest lad made such an impression on Miss Wald, the organization's founder and director, that she guided him into forensics and dramatics in an effort to help him rid himself of his foreign accent.

One Sonnenberg biographer, Isadore Barmash, concluded, "It would be difficult to exaggerate the influence Lillian Wald and the Henry Street Settlement had on him. Eager but confused, troubled by language difficulty and by the poverty that surrounded and weighed on him, young Sonnenberg probably found the humanity and the sensuousness of the community house just what he needed to balance him." Barmash described the future publicist's mind set at this juncture this way, "Ambition sprouted in him like a hungry seed. He decided to greatly improve his situation, provide well for his parents, and also seek a life that would be cultured, sophisticated, artistic, and influential, one with perhaps a strong English flavor." But Lillian Wald's idealism had no impact on young Ben. He once told his son on one of their walks in the son's early years, "I'm no reformer, I'm a realist."

Under Miss Wald's watchful eye, young Ben slowly developed self-confidence and the ability to speak with ease and style. His mind was like a sponge, soaking up all the learning and experience that came his way. In 1917, when Sonnenberg was 16, Miss Wald called him to her office and said, "Ben, you've grown up quickly," She offered him a job as leader of the boy's club. She told him that he could continue his schooling and live at the Settlement House. He was delighted by the chance to work more closely with Miss Wald and to ease his family's financial burden. Two years later, she helped Sonnenberg obtain a 1-year scholarship to Columbia College. To pay his expenses for books, lunches, and so forth, Sonnenberg got a job covering Columbia University sports for the *Brooklyn Eagle*. This enabled him to hone his writing skills that he would put to use as a publicist.

Neither his studies at Columbia nor his work for the *Brooklyn Eagle* provided sufficient challenge for the always restless young man. Answering a want ad in *The New York Times*, Sonnenberg got a job with the Chicago Portrait Company as a door-to-door salesman persuading people to have their old portraits enlarged, tinted, and framed. When he made a sale, he sent the portraits to the Chicago company. But he soon became bored with calling on what he termed "frowsy housewives," and quit after 2 months. He next found himself in Bay City, Michigan, with $40 in his pocket. He mailed his resignation and last photographs to the Chicago company and the hitchhiked to Flint, Michigan. There, in that cultural desert, he induced the editor of the *Flint Journal* to give him a job as a $25-a-week reporter and movie critic. Presumably the editor was impressed with Sonnenberg's persuasive ways and his knowledge of the New York theater scene. Sonnenberg found Flint provincial and boring. In 1921, he returned to New York City, where he had a lifetime love affair with the Big Apple.

He went back to the comfort of Henry Street Settlement House and the affectionate interest of Miss Wald. Again she helped him by getting him a job with the Joint Distribution Committee, a charitable organization sponsored by wealthy American Jews. The committee was mainly engaged in helping World War I victims in Europe and the Near East. This job brought him exposure to rich businessmen, one of his tasks was to peddle $50-a-plate luncheons for war relief. In this role he became, in Barmash's words, "an ardent tycoon watcher." He also observed that these business-men, bankers, and merchants seemed to warm to his youthful chutzpah that he possessed in abundance.

Again in 1922, Lillian Wald intervened to further young Sonnenberg's career. The opportunity came when she got a call from Lewis Strauss, the former secretary to Herbert Hoover and director of the American Relief Administration that had been set up by Hoover at the request of the U.S.

Ambassador to Great Britain. The task was to get food and medical assistance to the famine-stricken areas of Russia and Europe. Strauss hired Sonnenberg as staff worker who eagerly absorbed another rich learning experience. Barmash wrote, "He spent six months in the Ukraine, where he observed first hand the degradation of extreme poverty and enjoyed the gracious, well-served life of a humanitarian bringing succor to a foreign power." This luxurious living did much to whet the future publicist's appetite for wealth and the lifestyle that it could bring. At the end of the mission, with cash to spend, Sonnenberg visited Rome, Paris, and finally London, where his lifelong affection for all things British began. He returned to New York in the winter of 1923, his education complete and ready to steer an exciting new course.

A BUDDING PUBLICIST

Young Sonnenberg, now 22, rented a room in Greenwich Village and set about earning a living by providing publicity for Jewish fund drives, the Salvation Army, and night clubs. He also dabbled in acting and writing from time to time. As late as 1926, he tried writing a play, *The White Dove*, about one of his clients, Elizabeth Arden. In March 1924, he married Hilda Kaplan, whom he had met at a Henry Street Settlement dance. She was a social worker, and they had dated off and on for 6 years. Hilda provided him support and love for the next 55 years. Her son, Ben Jr., made it clear in his autobiography that her life was not a happy one. Sonnenberg often claimed that their honeymoon after the City Hall ceremony was a "fifty cent Chinese luncheon." She kept her job at the settlement house, and he continued to hustle publicity work wherever he could find it. He was always nearly broke. He also tried writing for *Smart Set*.

His first big break came when he persuaded Oscar Weintraub, the manager of the new Fifth Avenue Hotel about to open, to hire him to promote the new hotel. Dapper in derby, striped ascot, dark four-button suit, and gray spats, the brash young publicist promised Weintraub that he would make the hotel known to the public through the distinction of its guests. On the other hand, Sonnenberg promised that he would keep the name of the hotel out of the newspapers in case of a guest's suicide or scandal—a promise no reputable practitioner would make today.

Sonnenberg scored his first coup when a hotel guest who went by the name of "Trader Horn," an explorer of uncertain origins from South Africa, bearded and tough, became, through the alchemy of Sonnenberg, a romantic hero who was able to sell 300,000 copies of his book extolling the author's exploits. At the time, much doubt was expressed that this adventurer from the African jungles had actually written his book or achieved all the feats he claimed. But Sonnenberg wrapped Trader Horn in an aura of mystery, then titillated the public by promising that Horn would make a public appearance soon. He then persuaded the Studebaker Motor Company to provide an elaborate open automobile, put Trader Horn on the back seat, and drove the car up and down Fifth Avenue waving to the crowds lured there by newspaper stories. Naturally, the trip began and ended at the Fifth Avenue Hotel. Understandably, Manager Weintraub was delighted.

There are conflicting versions about how Sonnenberg acquired his next client, Prince George Matchabelli, the refugee from Georgia who became a renowned parfumier. Geoffrey Hellman wrote:

> Another hotel guest was Prince George Matchabelli, a Georgian emigre' who had become a perfume manufacturer before Sonnenberg brought the Prince's colorful personality to the notice of editors, columnists, and reporters. The result, a spate of feature articles, some of them widely syndicated, caused Matchabelli to hire him in 1928 as press agent for his perfume company . . . Bergdorf Goodman was a Matchabelli outlet. Sonnenberg saw that his releases on the Prince contained mention of this connection.

Whenever a clipping contained mention of Bergdorf Goodman, Sonnenberg forwarded the clip to Edwin Goodman, the head of this elite store, in an effort to add Bergdorf Goodman as a client.

In Barmash's biography, *Always Live Better Than Your Clients*, (Dodd-Mead, 1983) he quoted Andrew Goodman, Edwin's son, as recounting:

> That summer [1927] Father decided to take a gamble on Ben, who wanted desperately to go to Europe and broaden himself. He gave Ben two thousand dollars, a lot of money in those days, and Ben left. He was gone the entire summer. But when he came back he had two prizes—Prince Matchabelli, the parfumier, and the Grand Duchess Marie Romanov. He told Father that he had hired them for us to help us gain some new glamour with the public. They would be sort of in-house celebrities.

Today with all of Sonnenberg's records destroyed, it is difficult to ascertain which of these versions is correct.

Still another Fifth Avenue Hotel guest emerged as both client and national celebrity through Sonnenberg's magic touch, and there are also two versions of how it happened. *Continent* has this version, "One day the hotel manager said: 'There is a man here who owes us 400 dollars. He claims to have invented a new way of playing bridge. Meet him and see if there is some way of getting our money back.'" Sonnenberg found the man in question was Ely Culbertson, the creator of contract bridge. For that unknown genius, Sonnenberg organized tournaments at Madison Square Garden, eagerly followed by newspapers all over America.

Probably the more accurate version is Barmash's, who wrote that Culbertson, seeking greater exposure, sought out Sonnenberg. At this time, bridge was just coming into its own as a pastime, and it was hard to interest the press in a new version. With his stubborn persistence and abundant chutzpah, Sonnenberg persuaded *The New York Times* to set up a telegraph line when Culbertson staged one of his matches at the Waldorf–Astoria Hotel in New York so that its reporter could report the competition rubber-by-rubber. With Sonnenberg's promotion, Culbertson became a celebrity and a columnist, and contract bridge became a great competitive sport, which it remains to this day.

Manager Weintraub, naturally pleased with Sonnenberg's success in promoting his holstery, retained him to promote his other two hotels, the Half Moon Hotel on Coney Island and the White Hotel on Lexington Avenue. By now, Weintraub and Sonnenberg had become good friends, and Weintraub next introduced Sonnenberg to Joel Hillman, an entrepreneur who was about to open the George V Hotel in Paris. The George V became Sonnenberg's first European account. Thus, in 1926, only a year after becoming a full-time publicist, the publicist had three hotel accounts.

With this increasing success and its concomitant income, in 1927, Sonnenberg persuaded his father to retire from the clothing stand. Now financially secure, Sonnenberg felt that he had "arrived." By 1929, he was able to leave his small digs in Greenwich Village and open a single-room office in a luxurious midtown building at 247 Park Avenue, where his agency remained until just before the building was torn down in 1963. Although he also hired a secretary and a writer, the lone typewriter was rented and the carpet borrowed! Sonnenberg edited all the press releases himself, took needed photographs, and carried his publicity releases in person to the newspapers. During the 1930s, his earnings over expenses climbed to more than $5,000 annually, a handsome sum in those Depression years. In 1934, he raised his fees and rented a larger office on the top floor of 247 Park Avenue. He also incorporated as Publicity Consultants, Inc. He kept his staff small and hired freelancers as needed.

INTO BIG BUCKS AND THE BIG HOUSE

From the time of his move to the top floor of 247 Park Avenue, Sonnenberg's fee income never amounted to less that $250,000 a year and from 1942 until his death, never less than a half million. By the early 1930s public relations was becoming a respected vocation, and Sonnenberg's reputation for successful promotions was becoming widely known. As a result of the Stock Market Crash of 1929 and the ensuing Great Depression, Big Business had lost its credibility and thus its public support. Big Business's need to regain public confidence was providing increased opportunities for the publicist and emerging public relations counselor.

By 1935, there were 10 public relations agencies in Manhattan. In the early 1930s, Sonnenberg was representing Delman Shoes; the Hygrade Food Products Corp., Arvis Gloves; the Book-of-the-Month Club; Viking Press; Ely Culbertson; Morris Guest; J. David Stern, publisher of the *Philadelphia Record* (Stern later switched to Carl Byoir & Associates); Russeks; I. Miller; Charles V. Paterno, the real estate operator; Paul Whiteman, the orchestra leader; William Bloom, a wholesale haberdasher and blouse manufacturer; John Cavanaugh, the hatman; Bollinger Champagne; Elizabeth Arden; and Helena Rubenstein. Although some of these relationships were short lived, others went on for years. Apparently—as the list indicates—Sonnenberg was not bothered by taking accounts with competing interests.

As Geoffrey Hellman observed, Sonnenberg "made extraordinary efforts to please." "For clients who wanted them, he arranged for theater tickets down in front, hotel suites, reservations in caste-conscious restaurants, and other worldly accommodations." Irwin Ross thought, "To a great extend his success comes from his ability to persuade his clients that with Sonnenberg they get press agentry flavored with the elegance of a world they never knew. Many clients look down on press agents; Sonnenberg makes them look up. His operation is interesting as a study in the techniques of dazzling clients quite as much as in the techniques of public relations." Ross also suggested that Sonnenberg had the uncanny ability to persuade his admirers that it was worth his fee for him just to be at the other end of the telephone. Sonnenberg did much of his business on the telephone and was adjudged "a great telephone performer." He was also adept in handling the press—an essential for success in publicity and public relations. Ross wrote, "His stock in trade is exuberant flattery, delivered with an engaging air of roguish humor." He also extended favors of gifts, trips, and other favors, including wine and women. In "Tales of Sonnenberg" in *Fortune* of April 23, 1979, Ross save this example:

> Years ago when David Schoenbrun was chief correspondent for CBS in Paris, he met Sonnenberg and soon found himself hotly pursued. "I flew into New York from Paris," Schoenbrun later recalled," and there was immediately a call at the hotel from Sonnenberg, What do you like—a blonde, brunette, or redhead?' he asked in his kidding way. I told him that I was in love with my wife. The next trip to New York his secretary called to say that unfortunately Mr. Sonnenberg was out of town, but he wanted to send two theater tickets each night of my stay. What shows did I want to see? I explained that I wasn't interested in going to the theater, whereupon she said that she would select the shows. And every day two tickets arrived."

When reminded of this story, Jack Scott Fones, longtime associate of Sonnenberg's, wrote me, "This was a giggle for Ben. He would say it, in fun, to lots of people. In ten years, though, I never knew him to 'provide' a woman to a client or press. It could have happened, of course, but never to my knowledge."

Sonnenberg often remarked that "I have a quality many publicity men don't have. I have warmth. The thing is to approach life with warmth, to approach it affirmatively. I have enthusiasm." These qualities he demonstrated in spades in his lavish entertaining and gift-giving. It was typical of Sonnenberg to end an interview with a young reporter by saying, "You ought to interview my tailor—I'll have him make you a handsome Norfolk jacket." Gossip of the time suggested that many reporters, unlike David Schoenbrun, accepted these gifts. Irwin Ross opined, "Though some reporters regard him with suspicion, there is no evidence that the interests of Sonnenberg's clients have suffered."

The bottom line is that Sonnenberg enjoyed success and affluence because he delivered on his promises, and this stimulated word-of-mouth recommendations. In the latter 1930s, Sonnenberg's business boomed, and the publicist changed with it becoming less a flack and more a counselor. He used less frequently the vernacular of Broadway press agents, shifting to a more formal, Olympian type of speech, even convoluted. He came to describe himself as "a builder of bridges to posterity" and a "a lay psychoanalyst." A more pedestrian line was, "I supply the Listerine to the commercial dandruff on the shoulders of corporations." The profits from his business grew rapidly as he accented the demeanor of public relations counselor, and his fee income rose to $250,000 a year during the last years of the Depression and during the 1940s. To accomplish this, he put more of himself into his efforts to expand his business, sacrificing time he wanted to spend with his wife and two children. Yet, despite the growth of his client list and his affluence, he was not listed as one of "The Nation's Top Publicists" in Newcomb's *Coronet* article of 1942. Though he was always hustling for clients in his inimitable way, Sonnenberg refused to make formal presentations to win new accounts.

As Sonnenberg's client list grew, he developed what, in effect, were two operations, "linked but quite separate, even as to office decor." Sonnenberg the man presided in an elegant executive suite, whereas down the hall there were utilitarian offices where his staff produced the press releases, booklets, and brochures. In his office of rich decor, Sonnenberg received his clients and plotted grand strategies for them.

The Sonnenbergs first lived in Sunnyside, Queens, then moved to Greenwich Village. When Sonnenberg's income increased, they moved to a two-bedroom apartment at 44 Gramcery Park, on the north side. When she walked her dog, Hilda Sonnenberg looked longingly at 19 Gramcery Park.

"My mother used to walk around the park and dreamed of living there someday," her daughter, Helen Sonnenberg Tucker, told *New York* magazine in 1991. Caught in the rain one day, Hilda took shelter in the vestibule of uninhabited No. 19, and a caretaker showed her around. According to an article in the January 21, 1991, issue of *New York*, "He showed her the first two floors, which, with a little imagination, she could see were very grand. She thought it was wonderful and romantic and exciting," her daughter said. This was despite the fact that the windows were all boarded up and the house was in very bad condition. *New York* described what became the fabulous Sonnenberg Mansion this way: "No. 19 Gramcery Park neighborhood, a genteel urban oasis evoking another era. The building's three chimneys rise from its mansard roof; its black shutters are splayed against its chocolate-purple brick. Little about the plain, defined exterior of No. 19 would suggest that it is a landmark and an anachronism, a building rich in social history—and in Brendan Gill's words, 'unquestionably the greatest house remaining in private hands in New York.' "

In his Sonnenberg profile, Geoffrey Hellman described what became the Sonnenberg mansion:

> The Sonnenberg house is . . . thirty-two by sixty, has five stories and thirty-seven rooms, and is air-conditioned throughout. It was built in 1831 for Stuyvesant Fish. Several years ago, Sonnenberg spent three hundred and fifty thousand dollars to remodel and redecorate it. It is probably the busiest house in New York. During eight or nine months of the year, it is, every few days, the scene of a party attended by from twenty to two hundred guests. It is run by a staff of six, who live next door in a house Sonnenberg also owns. It contains so many brass urns, samovars, pitchers, charcoal burners, candelabra, mugs, boxes, plates, and irons, teakettles, coal buckets, mortars, pestles, mirror frames, wall scones, bowls, beakers, salvers, and canisters that polishing these items constitutes the principal occupation of the Sonnenberg houseman. For parties, the regular staff is assisted by an auxiliary body of tail-coated door openers, coat checkers, and waiters engaged for the occasion.

In the Great Depression, during hard times, Sonnenberg had found his affluence and his big house.

The Sonnenbergs moved into No. 19 sometime in 1931, renting the two bottom floors under the condition that they could do any remodeling they chose. By 1945, Sonnenberg was able to afford the entire house and bought it from Stuyvesant Fish, Jr. for $85,000. The remaining tenants, among them Norman Thomas, were evicted and a massive restoration got under way with the renovators clearing out a maze of small rooms to create a massive ballroom and screening room on the top floor.

These details about No. 19 are relevant because the house as both focus of lavish entertaining and museum of artifacts and art played a unique role in the Sonnenberg public relations career. In his illuminating profile, Geoffrey Hellman wrote that despite Sonnenberg's dramatic success as a publicist, the talk centered on his home, his clothiers, and his grand manners. His 1978 obituary, which was distributed by *The New York Times News Service*, recounted that Sonnenberg often called himself a "cabinet-maker who fashioned large pedestals for small statues," then added, "His pedestal was a mansion."

But the House at 19 Gramcery Park was not a home—at least to the two Sonnenberg children, Helen and Ben, Jr. The latter wrote in his autobiography, *Lost Property*, "Our house, *my* home, was a stage for his work; when he was home, he was changed by whatever role he was playing. He wasn't the same as he was on our walks. Giving the provenance of a painting was different from telling the story of a city building."

In his preface, young Sonnenberg wrote:

I am a Collector's Child.

I was born in New York City, on the thirtieth of December, 1936, and was brought up in a very grand house, 19 Gramcery Park. It was crammed with servants, furniture, art. My father and mother were famous for their fabulous parties they gave there. . . . I grew up in a sort of *Arabian Nights*, with extreme attributes being given to all the adults and objects around, which then . . . disappeared.

Until his death in 1978, my father was one of the best known public relations men in America. He described his business as "making giant plinths for little men to stand on." In fact, his clients were often large powerful corporations, and his services to them were different from the flackery which his description implies, more commonplace, more corrupt. For his services he was paid, as he said, "*scandalously* well," and we all lived in a showy, extravagant way.

THE RISE AND FALL OF CHARLES LUCKMAN

One of those plinths Sonnenberg built for little men was the one he fabricated for Charles Luckman, probably Sonnenberg's most famous client and onetime rising star in American business. It illustrates the validity of the oft-stated principle that performance must match one's publicity for enduring credibility and success. Sonnenberg promoted, in the literal sense of the word, Luckman into the presidency of the giant Lever Brothers USA, but neither he nor Luckman's newly acquired in-house PR staff could keep him there because of his ineptness as a chief executive. As *Fortune* observed in "The Case of Charles Luckman" in April 1950, "Ben Sonnenberg, wiliest and wittiest of press agents, gave Luckman consequence and a franchise on the community." However, as Sonnenberg told people when Luckman was fired at Lever Brothers, "It is not my fault that Luckman did not measure up." *Fortune* asked the question, "How did Charles Luckman achieve the eminence he did?" and then answered it this way: "The thread that runs through both is the part played by the press, by Luckman's public relations' men, and particularly by that extraordinary press agent, Ben Sonnenberg. It is difficult to exaggerate their importance; the entire press was taken in. Luckman himself had a flair for publicity and Sonnenberg showed him how to make the most of it. Together they built up the Luckman folklore; small and colorful incidents were puffed up and handed out to the press until the stories almost became legends."

Luckman, born in Kansas City of modestly situated parents, worked his way through the University of Illinois where he earned a degree in architecture, magna cum laude. He was bright, handsome, self-assured, one who "who did all the right things fast and well." When he graduated, he found that because of the Depression, there was little demand for architects. He found a job as a soap salesman for Colgate–Palmolive–Peet, a role for which he had great talent. At Colgate, he was "something of a sensation" but did not, as later publicity claimed even attain the rank of divisional manager. His boss at Colgate later became the Pepsodent account executive at Albert Lasker's Lord & Thomas advertising agency. Pepsodent needed a sales manager; his former boss recommended Luckman for the job. *Fortune* stated, "Pepsodent badly needed a salesman and glad-hander to restore its reputation with the embattled apothecaries. Luckman's genius for putting across his point of view enabled him to do the job beyond anything his employers had hoped." He was made vice-president and general manager of Pepsodent in 1938. In 1939, Pepsodent hired "the then rising and intricately resourceful Ben Sonnenberg as press agent. Ben and Luckman hit it off."

One of the first myths created to build the Luckman legend was that he had discovered Bob Hope when he was shopping for a comedian to sell Pepsodent on the air. Actually, Luckman had nothing to do with hiring Hope for the Pepsodent show nor in changing his style to make himself the butt of his jokes. The Hope show was bought by Pepsodent on the urging of Ed Lasker to his father, Albert Lasker. It was many months later that Hope and Luckman got together. Another heralded Luckman success story was that of his being able to head off a boycott of Pepsodent by the National Association of Retail Druggists, who were angry because Pepsodent was being sold by chain drug stores as a loss leader. He achieved this, so the story goes, by offering the association $25,000 for promotion of a fair trade act. *Fortune* said, "There are several variations of the story (as related by Luckman) and in each he is the hero." At this convention, Luckman was there as a subordinate and had been with the company only a few days. Pepsodent's decision to go fair trade had been made by top management in Chicago. Such were the building blocks out of which Luckman's "towering press reputation" was erected.

Luckman became president of Pepsodent in 1943, and the next year Lever Brothers bought the company. By this time, press agentry had made him a national figure, and it was speculated at the time that one of the reasons Lever Brothers bought the company was to get Luckman's highly publicized talents. Two years later, Luckman was made president of Lever Brothers USA. When he was installed at the company's headquarters in Cambridge, Massachusetts, the admiring press not only repeated all the old myths about Luckman's jet-propelled career but added new ones. His predecessor, Francis Countway, announced that Luckman would be paid $300,000 a year (actually he got much less) and hailed him as one who "had the makings of a business statesmen." Celebration parties were held in several cities, including one at the Waldorf–Astoria in New York City. Among the guests was Bernard Gimbel, president of Gimbel Bros. The next day, Gimbel sent Sonnenberg a note that Ben proudly circulated among his friends. Gimbel wrote, "In your current masterpiece from the moment you went to work on an obscure, little-known person up until last night when you established Chuck as the outstanding businessman of the country, the power of the press was again demonstrated . . . The job was done almost as quickly as Lever Brothers used to make a cake of soap. . . . From here on it's up to your superman to deliver . . . Svengali Sonnenberg."

The astute Gimbel was prescient. In a word, Luckman fell on his face as president of Lever Brothers and was ultimately fired. Before the fall, Luckman was highly publicized as an industrial statesman by Sonnenberg and Thomas Gonser, a former fund-raiser for Northeastern University, whom Luckman had hired to establish a large public relations department at Lever Brothers. Sonnenberg continued to handle outside publicity. Together, they touted Luckman as "a hard-hitting liberal businessman," placing articles under his byline in magazines like *Collier's, Harper's*, and the *Atlantic Monthly*. Luckman also lambasted businessmen for their consistent opposition to social reforms. All this got him favorable attention, including President Truman's. Truman asked Luckman to head up a voluntary food conservation effort to save 100 billion bushels of grain for wartorn Europe. *Fortune* noted, "Luckman somehow got as much personal publicity as did the saving of food, and the fact was noticed." Luckman was constantly on the road making speeches or on assignments such as the one President Truman gave him. The consequence was things were not going well back at "the company store.' Luckman made a number of wrong business decisions, for example, buying the Harriet Hubbard Ayer cosmetics business that lost $3 million in 2 years, moving the company headquarters from Cambridge to New York City, and being most inept in handling Lever's longtime executive staff. In *Fortune's* opinion, the headquarters move "culminated in some of the most inept community relations in years." The move brought wholesale firings of capable executives, effected in a ruthless manner that was termed by Bradley Dewey, president of the Dewey & Almy Company, as "the worst blow American free enterprise has received in years." Yet his publicists, Gonser and Sonnenberg, continued to extol Luckman's greatness. They placed an article in a trade paper, *Soap and Sanitary Chemicals*, praising Lever Brothers' employee relations and quoting Luckman, "The most important asset of our company is the people in it." In January 1950, Luckman was fired by Lever Brothers and later went back to his first love, architecture. *Fortune* concluded, "Astute press-agentry plus salesmanship and pleasant demeanor, which charmed and persuaded all who met him, took him to the mountaintop."

Barmash thought that "if there is one single achievement that public relations men cite Sonnenberg for, it is the media barrage that he engineered for Luckman, beginning with a *Time* cover piece." That exposure did much to cast the former soap salesman into national prominence and make the one-time Republican a favorite in the Truman White House. In great measure, Sonnenberg accomplished this with help from his right hand man, George Schreiber, who had studied at Harvard with former New Dealers Ben Cohen and Tom Cocoran, then top lobbyists lawyers in Washington. Sonnenberg was expert in tapping the "levers of power" he accumulated during his burgeoning career. Yet with all his wizardry, Sonnenberg couldn't keep Luckman on the mountaintop!

THE BUILD UP OF JOHN I. SNYDER, JR.

The late Frank Saunders, a former *Fortune* editor and later a staff associate in the Sonnenberg firm, told this story:

> A client of ours was the late John I. Snyder, Jr. of U.S. Industries, Inc. I remember arranging a dinner at Ben's for a few top editors. The point was to introduce Snyder. Ben did a hell of a job for him. He made him the principal spokesman for industrial workers displaced by automation. Snyder was invited to address the AFL–CIO. I got up some great ads for U.S. Industries. But Ben just dropped them on the floor. He thought up the ad about "The Billion Dollar Board" listing the clout of the directors. That's the lesson I learned from Ben: The biggest factor is corporate ego.

Writing of that dinner for Snyder, Barmash said, "Even the toughest-skinned editors succumbed, somehow walking away with the conviction Snyder was a paragon of the American business statesman," a line

Sonnenberg had used with Luckman. Barmash continued: "U. S. I. climbed a series of notches in journalistic estimation, and Sonnenberg continued to massage Snyder's image." To reinforce the reputation of Snyder being built in the press, Sonnenberg persuaded Snyder to replace his board members with well-known, prestigious industrialists and businessmen. 'We'll call it 'Our Billion Dollar Board' " he told a wide-eyed Snyder. The plan was put into effect, first with the appointments, followed by a series of bold newspaper advertisements proclaiming "Our Billion Dollar Board" in major newspapers and financial journals. Newspaper and magazine stories started appearing in the financial press. In a few seeks U.S. I. stock was being traded more actively and moving up in value. Saunders recalled, "What we were doing was exciting, because somehow U.S. Industries had managed to put together some of the best minds in American industry. It was a brilliant coup. And it cost them nothing." Once more Sonnenberg's fertile imagination had paid dividends for his client—and for himself. In suggesting potential members for the new U. S. I. board, Sonnenberg knew that "Within each powerful man there was still craving for recognition and more power."

SONNENBERG PUTS THE MET ON THE AIR

Opera lovers who enjoy the Saturday afternoon broadcasts from the Metropolitan Opera little know that they have Ben Sonnenberg to thank. In the late 1930s, Sonnenberg had been retained by the Texas Company for a most unusual assignment—to publicize its "clean, sanitary washrooms" in Texaco stations across the nation. Pleased with the publicist's work on that assignment, Sonnenberg was later called back to Texaco headquarters for a much tougher task—responding to charges in the *New York Herald--Tribune* that Torkild Rieber, Texaco's chairman had been a Nazi, sympathizer in 1939–1940. The company, understandably, reacted with shock, acutely aware of the public's hatred of Hitler and Nazi Germany for its brutal invasion of Poland to start World War II and the Nazis' persecution of the Jews. Sonnenberg obviously had mixed feelings on this matter but concluded that the allegations in the muckraking article were unfounded or old hat at best. To counter the damage that had been done, particularly in the New York market, Sonnenberg came out of left field with the suggestion that Texaco sponsor radio broadcasts of the Metropolitan Opera on Saturday afternoons; the suggestion was quickly approved by the nervous Texaco executives. The sponsorship brought wide praise, and Rieber resigned his position at Texaco soon thereafter. Thus began the longest running radio sponsorship in broadcast history; these broadcasts continue to this day, much to the enjoyment of opera buffs in the United States and Canada.

COUNSELOR TO DEPARTMENT STORES

As recounted earlier, one of Sonnenberg's first accounts came to him in 1927 when Edwin Goodman, founder of Bergdorf-Goodman, hired him at $100 a month to publicize the ornate, expensive Fifth Avenue department store. According to Andrew Goodman, less an admirer of Sonnenberg than was his father, "I remember that Ben would always come into the store with a batch of clippings to show us. He had gotten lots of stories, but they were all in papers like the *Tulsa Gazette* or the *Oklahoma Bugle*, not that those were the real names. But I said to him, 'Ben, what do those crappy clippings mean when we sell only expensive, custom-made clothes?' There are only ten to fifteen thousand people in the whole country who can afford our clothes." Young Goodman, who succeeded his father, said his father didn't seem to care because he was fond of Sonnenberg, "especially his *chutzpah*." Goodman, Jr., who admired Sonnenberg's personality and creativity, nonetheless would drop him from time to time but then would rehire him. Their relationship lasted for 25 years.

Edwin Goodman hired Sonnenberg to stage and promote Bergdorf-Goodman's 50th anniversary in 1951. The publicist came up with a plan for a gala dinner dance at New York's fashionable Plaza Hotel, just across the street on Fifth Avenue and 59th Street. Guests were charged $50 per person to attend, a plan that the elder Goodman didn't approve. Barmash reported, "The affair was a sellout, seven or eight hundred people." Andrew Goodman beamed, "Sonnenberg did the whole thing, and wonderfully too." Other ideas Sonnenberg used for this event was to stage a live fashion show for a top designer, the first one to have a scenario and a story line. Another "bright" idea was to scatter buckets of authentic-looking gold dust from the store's entrance across the street to the Plaza, a sure traffic-stopper. Another was to put live manikins in the store windows. The publicists cashed in on this idea when George Weissman, then an account executive, sold *Collier's* magazine on a feature article titled "Oh to be Naked in Bergdorf's"—the joy of a complete new wardrobe from the store.

His Bergdorf-Goodman work led to two other major department store clients—one a nonpaying client! The paying client was Fred Lazarus, Jr., founder of the Federated Department Stores in Cincinnati and operator of such famous emporia as Bloomingdales, Abraham & Straus, Filene's of Boston, and Burdine's in Miami. Leon Harris wrote in his *Merchant Princes*, (1979), "Fred's New York publicity agent was the late Ben Sonnenberg. A public relations genius whose work, in his own unbuttoned phrase, consisted of 'diapering rich men.' Sonnenberg succeeded in getting stories about Fred into *Time, Fortune, Saturday Evening Post* and other journals in the 1940s and 1950s—stories that were an important part of building Fred's reputation for being the shrewdest retailer in America."

Harris added: "Certainly the only thing as obvious at Federated as Fred's genius had been, and still is, its nepotism, characterized by *Fortune* as "the somewhat alarming geometric progression that produced one Lazarus merchant in the first generation, two in the second, and four in the third." Lazarus was not an easy client for Sonnenberg because the merchant "thrived on controversy and attack, both in his business and in his family affairs." One of his children wrote, "We were all terrified of him," Harris wrote. But this was not the face shown to the public by Sonnenberg's publicity.

Another merchant prince whom Sonnenberg often counseled for free was his longtime friend, Stanley Marcus, who built the famed Nieman–Marcus chain of upscale stores. Marcus told Isadore Barmash in an interview, "I learned more from Ben Sonnenberg about life and business than from any other person except my father." Marcus, who left the chain's management to become a consultant and author, added. "And Ben would sometimes chide me that I wasn't even a client." They became close friends and met frequently socially. Sonnenberg respected Marcus who had a solid instinctive feel for public relations. He also found Marcus a good listener, one who took notes and made use of Sonnenberg's expertise. Marcus said of Sonnenberg, "He understood human motivation and often told me stories about his Wall Street cronies. He regarded most of the financial tycoons an unscrupulous lot and a lot of them as stuffed shirts . . . He liked to tell stories how they liked to fight over women and power." They saw each other frequently even into Sonnenberg's retirement, as Marcus spent much of his time in New York firming up his ties with the Seventh Avenue fashion houses. One night when they were having dinner, Marcus told Sonnenberg that some people complained that everything the publicist did was calculated and rooted in making a buck. Sonnenberg responded heatedly, "You son of a bitch. You are the only guy who has milked me for forty years and paid me nothing." Marcus did pay Sonnenberg in respect and affection. Incidentally, Sonnenberg had all his clothes tailored for him by an English tailor, Bernard Weatherill, located on 57th Street, New York City. Ben did not trust zippers, he insisted on fly buttons.

Sonnenberg was always a generous man with his friends, reporters, and clients. Jack Scott Fones, a staff associate for 10 years, told this illustrative story, "On a trip to Dallas in the 50s with Ben to see a client we had a couple of hours to kill and strolled through Neiman Marcus' store. He bought a life-size clown doll for one of his kids, then we went to the jewelry department. 'Pick out something for your wife,' he said to me. 'Here I've taken you away on this trip and she should be rewarded.' I chose a pearl-and-ruby bracelet, which was recently appraised at $2, 500.00."

Though generous, Sonnenberg was not always straight-forward in dealing with people, clients, or the press. Irwin Ross wrote in *Fortune*,

"He . . . did not scruple to play tricks on clients." Fones confirmed this with an incident that took place in the late 1950s. Fones was directed to write a release announcing a change of presidents at the T. J. Lipton Tea Company. Fones wrote a standard news release and then read it over the phone to the retiring president, who exploded. He was irate that the major attention was devoted to the new president instead of him. Fones tried to explain that the press would want to play up the incoming president but got nowhere with the client. He took his problem to Sonnenberg who said calmly, "That's no problem. Revise the release for the old president and send it to him. Send your original release to the newspapers." He thought that this way each release served its own purpose, according to Fones.

PEPPERIDGE BRINGS IN THE DOUGH

Sonnenberg's most lucrative account in his dazzling career was Pepperidge Farm, Inc. It made him a multimillionaire. During the late 1920's, Sonnenberg had met Henry and Margaret Rudkin, who lived on a small farm near Norwalk, Connecticut. Henry was a wealthy Wall Street stockbroker and the prosperous owner of polo ponies until the Great Crash came. One of the three Rudkin sons, Mark, was asthmatic. His doctor told his mother that yeast in commercial bread was one of the foods that set off the son's asthmatic attacks and that he should have rich, homebaked bread. Her first several attempts were failures until she tried her grandmother's recipe for the Pepperidge Farm bread that graces supermarket shelves today. The homebaked bread was "just what the doctor had ordered." The physician asked Mrs. Rudkin to bake loaves that he could provide to other asthmatic patients. She also shared loaves of her bread with her neighbors, who urged her to put it in local grocery stores. She did, and it was an instant success with grocers asking for more loaves almost every day. Soon the family stove gave out under the stress of constant baking. The Rudkins, now broke, asked their friend Ben if he could lend them $300 to buy a second-hand commercial oven. He could and did. They told the publicist they had decided to start a small bakery company and sell the bread more widely. There are two versions of what happened next. In his *You Always Live Better Than Your Clients*, Isadore Barmash wrote that Mrs. Rudkin said, "Because we knew that you would come to our help, we are going to give you one-third interest." Sonnenberg thanked them and asked, "What are you going to name your company?" Mrs. Rudkin replied, "Pepperidge Farm, after our farm." In its article, "The Promoter," *Continent* magazine stated, "Mrs. Rudkin asked Sonnenberg whether he would be willing to publicize her bread, in exchange for 10 per cent of the shares of the Pepperidge Farm corporation. She had no money to offer him. Sonnenberg accepted. She made to perfection the best bread on the market and Sonnenberg took care of making it known everywhere." In either case, Sonnenberg realized millions when the company was sold in 1958 to the Campbell Soup Co. for $28 million according to Barmash ($29 million according to *Continent*). Barmash asserted, "Sonnenberg got one third of his share in cash, the rest in Campbell Soup Co. stock." It is Fones' understanding that Sonnenberg got one third interest in the bread company and thus netted some $9 million.

Sonnenberg earned his windfall by doing a masterful job of promoting Pepperidge and the company's other products as they were added. The company prospered, no doubt due to the barrage of publicity Sonnenberg laid down in the nation's newspapers and magazines. Pepperidge's business went from the initial $20 to more than $50 million a year in two decades. Bread production eventually went from 100 loaves a week to 1 million. Rolls and cakes were added later to the product line. Sonnenberg moved quickly to get the Rudkins and Pepperidge Farm favorable publicity in the *Reader's Digest*, *Ladies Home Journal*, *McCall's*, and other nationally circulated magazines that reach millions of women. The Pepperidge Farm company never advertised in all the years the Rudkins owned the company. Sonnenberg's unceasing publicity efforts and resulting word-of-mouth comments did the job. Such case histories give credence to media owner's complaints that publicity is just a way of getting free attention.

PHILIP MORRIS—A MAINSTAY ACCOUNT—SENDS A SIGNAL

Philip Morris (PM), the cigarette maker, became a Sonnenberg client in 1933 and grew into his major account until he gave it up in 1963 to Ruder & Finn in a somewhat painful parting of the ways. By 1963, Sonnenberg had pared down his staff and was doing mainly consulting as he wound down toward retirement. Philip Morris by now needed a full service agency, and thus Sonnenberg could no longer meet their requirements. He got the PM account in 1933 with typical Sonnenberg flair. He and Alfred E. Lyon were sitting in a hotel lobby one day that year. Sonnenberg sneaked off and gave the midget call boy $1 to "Call for Philip Morris," an act that become a feature of PM advertising. Sonnenberg was doing show biz publicity then. Lyon was impressed and hired both Sonnenberg and the call boy, Johnny Roventini.

George Weissman joined Sonnenberg's firm as an account executive in 1948 and was assigned the Philip Morris account. He left Sonnenberg to join Philip Morris in 1952 as vice-president for public relations. Weissman subsequently became president and later chairman and CEO at PM. In what

Barmash called Sonnenberg's "most durable relationship," they became more then business associates; they became close friends in an enjoyable friendship that endured until Sonnenberg's death in 1978. Weissman was executor of Sonnenberg's estate. Another very close friendship evolved from the Philip Morris account—that with James Bowling. Despite their sharply contrasting backgrounds, Bowling from a small town in Kentucky and Sonnenberg from Manhattan's Lower East Side, they found common interests and a camaraderie that brought both great enjoyment. Bowling told author Barmash, "I would go down to have lunch with him at Gramcery Park, once a month at least, for years, and sit at first in his den and talk. And then we would have lunch in that delightful, little English room he had down on the first floor and talk for hours. We kept in touch at all times. . . . He had a fascinating mind. He had a keen grasp of the human psyche and a great feeling for what motivated the world, people, and politics." Most counselors today would envy this close client–counselor relationship.

Sonnenberg had Philip Morris as a client before the scientific evidence mounted and the public storm against smoking blew into the critical public relations problem that it is today for such companies. In the first decade at least, the work for this client consisted mostly of issuing press releases, preparing annual reports, and suggesting story ideas to the trade and general press. Sonnenberg's staff called the public's attention to important company decisions, new products, acquisitions, new construction, and the work of its research laboratories.

Because of his close friendship with Bowling, Sonnenberg paid close attention to the needs of this client, for a time, no detail, however insignificant, was overlooked. Sonnenberg carried his loyalty to Philip Morris to the extent that every smoker on his staff smoked its cigarettes; Philip Morris cigarettes were also freely offered to visitors.

Ultimately, in 1963, Jim Bowling came to a sad and reluctant decision— the time had come to sever Philip Morris's relationship with Sonnenberg but not his friendship with Ben. Barmash explained the parting this way, "Jim knew that there were people working for Ben whom he literally had not met. Philip Morris was growing steadily and needed all the daily services of a P.R. agency that could function as a direct reflection of the company's growth. But Ben, as Bowling knew, was very busy in other ways, doing things that he enjoyed. . . . He simply was not interested any longer in the mundane, day-to-day details required in servicing a major account." The latter part of Barmash's assertion is true, but by this time Ben had only a few employees and worked with them daily. Jim Bowling told his good friend that his present employees were not capable of providing quality service that had always been his hallmark. He said more bluntly, "What they are doing is trading on your good name and reputation."

After moments of heavy silence and while thoughtfully stroking his walrus mustache, Ben replied, "Young man, I think you've got something." Bowling had persuaded George Weissman, by then CEO of Philip Morris, to provide a generous severance. Philip Morris agreed to treat Sonnenberg's employees as though they were company employees, in terms of severance and related matters. They also agreed to keep Sonnenberg on retainer while seeking another agency for its public relations work. Before Bowling got back to his office at 100 Park Avenue, Sonnenberg had called a columnist at *The New York Times* and told him: "I no longer want to run around in the rain and have to worry about where my rubbers are or my overshoes to keep my feet from getting wet. I am going to concentrate on a different part of my work and life, and I won't have the public relations aspect any more, or the press activities aspects, you see." Thus, the clever Sonnenberg got a favorable story out of what might have been an "end of the road" story. Ruder & Finn (R & F) got the lucrative PM account. Weissman and Bill Ruder had worked together for Sam Goldwyn's studio when Goldwyn was a Sonnenberg client. Ruder and David Finn, an artist and photographer, had formed their firm in 1948. Sonnenberg got another signal when R&F hired Frank Saunders, one of Sonnenberg's few remaining seasoned staffers, to handle the Philip Morris account.

SONNENBERG GETS THE MESSAGE—IT'S TIME TO STACK ARMS

A confluence of signals from associates and friends that Sonnenberg began receiving as early as 1961 finally persuaded him that the time had come to put away the paint brush he had used so sweepingly to paint in bright hues his business clients, Jim Bowling's decision to terminate Publicity Consultants, Inc. in 1963 was probably the clincher. At a luncheon with Sonnenberg in 1961, his top executive at that time, John Scott Fones, raised the question of what Sonnenberg saw as the future of the agency because that impinged on Fones's future markedly. Fones had prepared an elaborate 12-page memo on what he saw for the agency for the next 5 years. Sonnenberg read the first few pages languidly, then flipped over the remaining pages. He told Fones that no one would take over the agency, that he would fold it when he retired, and that it would probably come in the next few years. At this point Fones decided to go into business on his own—which he did successfully. Fones wrote to me, "Most of my reminiscences of Ben are hazy now, but I regard my ten years at his side as the most exciting and interesting of my life."

Another factor driving Sonnenberg to make the change happened the very morning of the day Jim Bowling met with him to tell him the Philip

Morris' sad news. Sonnenberg had received word that morning that his office building at 247 Park Avenue was to be torn down, compelling him to give up the address where his firm had flourished and find new office space. Sonnenberg hadn't had to look for office space in 25 years, and he soon found that rents were astoundingly high. Another emotional factor that led to his ultimate decision was that his longtime righthand man, George Schreiber, had fallen terminally ill with a brain tumor. Schreiber, self-effacing, had never upstaged Sonnenberg's showmanship. Schreiber was a graduate of the Harvard Law School but had not practiced law. At Harvard, he had been a classmate of Ben Cohen and Tommy Cocoran, as indicated earlier. It was through Schreiber that Sonnenberg was able to use these "levers of power" in the nation's capital. In time Schreiber became Sonnenberg's amanuensis. He had a brilliant mind and was an astute student of the nation's political, social, and economic trends, a must for a reliable public relations counselor. Barmash wrote "Schreiber helped Ben in two major ways. Since he read everything and could store it away or discard it, depending on how he evaluated its worth or pertinence, Schreiber slid into a role of alerting the publicist to the thought trends that were stirring American society or Americans at large." In short, Schreiber manned Sonnenberg's radar station on behalf of his clients. Sonnenberg saw no replacement for him in sight, and this was another of the influences leading Sonnenberg to stack arms. During his many conversations with his longtime friend, Alistair Cooke frequently chided Ben for allowing his clients to dominate his life. When the point came that he was no longer having long business meetings or giving big parties, he was, according to Cooke, "terribly proud to it."

Thus, after 36 years of tirelessly hustling clients and building an ever increasing volume of business, Sonnenberg closed down Publicity Consultants, Inc. in 1963. He divested himself of all the clients who required a full-service public relations agency. He became strictly a consultant, primarily in communications, but also on corporate and social behavior. Even though he had been pushed in this direction for several years by the confluence of forces described previously, he was not particularly happy with his new role. Friends found him edgy. He took a small office at 280 Park Avenue.

Later, as he wound down his splashy, fabulous career, Sonnenberg closed his Park Avenue office in the mid-1960s and converted the fifth and sixth floors of his house to his public relations consultancy. According to *New York* magazine, "Gradually, he relinquished many of his clients, but he continued to entertain. In June 1978, at age 76 he went to England for one last collecting jaunt. A visitor that August, Charles Ryskamp, later recounted, I was shocked at how frail he was. His daughter, Helen Tucker, took charge of the house and Ben Jr., who had never truly come to terms with his father, began visiting more often."

Barmash summarized the last years this way, "In his final phase, Ben Sonnenberg worked truly alone. He was still very active, but on a smaller scale. There was no sadness in his home, none, at least, that he would allow anyone to see. And in fact the last decade and a half were, in some ways, the best years of his life and career." In those latter years, Sonnenberg gave up his big parties, his ballroom showings of the latest movies, and even his limousine and chauffeur. In these years, Sonnenberg would often tell some of his closest friends that he had earned between $25 million and $30 million in his professional lifetime. Even if partially true — the figure seems inflated and typical of Sonnenberg's florid hyperbole — it was quite an achievement for the "self-made man" from Manhattan's Lower East Side, the son of an immigrant pushcart vendor.

On September 5, 1978, Sonnenberg, stricken with throat cancer, suffered a heart attack; he died the next day. It was ironic that a publicist who had manipulated so much media attention for his clients would die during a newspaper strike, when major dailies printed only greatly cut obituaries when they resumed publication. *The New York Times*, however, distributed its three-take obituary about him to its news service clients with this lead: "Benjamin Sonnenberg, a Russian immigrant who became a legendary press agent and a friend of the rich and famous, died of a heart attack Wednesday. He was 77 years old." *The Times* obituary, written by John L. Hess, quoted a former employee who spoke of Sonnenberg's publicity technique with admiration this way, "Ben was capable of leading people to the mountaintop. Like getting an advance copy of a cover story in *Time* magazine that he hadn't had anything to do with. He'd send copies around with those big cards of his and a note, 'I thought you might be interested in this.' He wouldn't claim credit for it. Ben had gained insiders at several magazines who would send him advance copies of important stories about corporate leaders."

When Sonnenberg died, his estate consisted largely of his collections and his furnishings. The house by this time belonged to the Gramcery Park Foundation that Sonnenberg had created in the 1950s as way to gain large tax deductions. In the 1950s and 1960s, Sonnenberg donated his home to the foundation; he then rented it back for his own use. The rent, as of 1977, was a modest $58,000 a year and represented the biggest source of income for the foundation that paid all operating expenses of the house. When it was sold, the proceeds went to the foundation. Through this scheme, Sonnenberg saved several hundred thousand dollars in taxes.

Well before his death Sonnenberg had decided that when the time came, his vast collection of art, artifacts, and furnishings would be auctioned off by Sotheby's. His collections were valued at $3.8 million at the time of his death. He told his close friend, Alistair Cooke, "Strike the set, the show is over." His will directed that all his household possessions be sold at auction save for one drawing he had donated to the Metropolitan Museum. The showcase house with its 37 rooms was put on the market for an asking price of $1.9 million. There were no takers until Dr. Walter Langer, creator of White Shoulders perfumes, bought it for $1.5 million in 1979. Langer died in September 1983. As of 1990, the house once again stood empty. As *New York* observed, "No. 19 has had its ups and its downs before, and it might yet have another day of glory."

SONNENBERG: THE PERSON AND HIS PHILOSOPHY

Sonnenberg saw his work as planned persuasion and had a clear understanding of the need for his new PR function in the management of business enterprises in his era of the 1920s to the 1960s. He told Geoffrey Hellman:

> In the olden days, your only forum was a courtroom. At the present time, you are tried in the press or in other public media; you are tried before the bar of public opinion. A man's whole career can be ruined, because of the media of mass communications, by innuendo. The law can't catch up with that. The result is that a man or even a corporation is more and more dependent on public opinion, it is necessary to practice preventive medicine in publicity and to initiate counterattacks. Sometimes you have to make your client change, so that the charges which may have been true at one time cease to be true and he really does become a public benefactor.

This statement showed a remarkable grasp on what has become the mature concept of public relations; His all the more remarkable because it came from a flamboyant publicist at heart.

It is to Sonnenberg's credit that although many of his clients did not measure up to their clippings, he did preach to them the importance of social responsibility, telling them, "It is no longer enough merely for a man to sell his wares at a profit. He must take time out to express a feeling of social responsibility. It is important that . . . he is at all times behaving in the public interest. . . . The public-relations man sees to it that his client puts his best foot forward in the corporate equation."

For example, Sonnenberg's longtime friend, Theodore Kheel, the veteran labor negotiator, got John Snyder of U.S. Industries interested in the problems that would be caused by layoffs resulting from increasing automation in industrial production. It was at Sonnenberg's and Kheel's urging that Snyder established the American Foundation on Automation and Employment. The successful campaign, orchestrated by Sonnenberg and Kheel, was highly successful until halted by Snyder's untimely death in 1965.

Yet Sonnenberg apparently saw no inconsistency with this sound view of public relations against his exaggeration of his client's virtues and his shielding their weaknesses from public view. He created a favorable aura around his clients by dropping hints in influential ears, planting useful rumors, and by giving humanizing anecdotes to columnists, who were a major resource for Sonnenberg. Hellman wrote, "By feeding material to the public prints, radio, and television, he has managed to invest some men whose companies have retained him with characters more colorful than the facts warrant." His buildup of Charles Luckman by attributing to him mythical qualities not justified by the facts is a case in point. One contemporary described Sonnenberg in this way, "Ben is a frustrated artist. He paints with a bold brush. Not all the men he has boosted have quite been able to live up to his portrayal of them."

Ben Sonnenberg and Edward L. Bernays had much in common, including the disdain or worse of their contemporaries. Both were sons of Jewish immigrants, both had brilliant minds, both were driven by an insatiable desire to succeed, and both found their road to success in public relations. Both were loners as professionals and neither was invited to join the first organization of counselors, The National Association of Accredited Publicity Directors. Perhaps this was because both were indefatigable self-promoters. However, their exaggerations of their accomplishments and that of their clients coupled with their self-promotion brought scorn from their contemporaries in publicity and public relations counseling. In a letter to a friend, William Riis, who had a publicity partnership with Charles W. Bonner, Jr. for 19 years, wrote:

> I find that he [referring to an executive of the General Cable Company] has what is known as a public relations man, Ben Sonnenberg. I was in that business for myself for 19 years. I came into competition with Sonnenberg, once dramatically and marvelously in front of a client [Schenley Distillers]. He [the Schenley executive] quizzed us both in our mutual presence. The net result of that, which was about 1935, was that: at no time will I work on any story in which he represents the subject. He's a cheap, prevaricating operator in whom the truth does not dwell. This is not to say that he represents only crooks. Unhappily, he will be bound to get now and then a lamb, who is dazzled and hoodwinked by his vociferous and tawdry front. But for me Sonnenberg kills any story.

In sending a copy of this letter to his friend, counselor William H. Baldwin, Riis appended this note:

The client wanted to know our connections for certain specific reasons. Did we know Arthur Ballantine? It just happened he was an ancient family friend, the Ballantines of the Riises. "Well, very well," says Ben, "but he's in Cuba." "No," says I," he's not in Cuba, I saw him in the Biltmore this afternoon." Turns out Ballantine never heard of Ben. Next name was Roy Howard . . . I am intimate with Roy Howard, says Ben. "He is at this moment in California." "He is at this moment at his home on 63rd street," says I, "and we can verify that by calling his private number." The third name I forget . . . I never saw more boldfaced and unabashed lying, and it never fazed Ben at all. The odd thing was the naming of three close friends, or three definite connections I had.

Riis got the account! Riis had an equally low opinion of Bernays. Bernays and Sonnenberg did have one major difference. The term *press agent* did not bother Sonnenberg, whereas Bernays spent a long lifetime promoting public relations as a profession and seeking to distinguish public relations from press agentry, although he started out as a Broadway press agent and used press agentry for many of his clients.

Another insight into Sonnenberg the man is to look at his relationships with his family. Like many successful persons who drive themselves to the top, Sonnenberg's hectic schedule of phone calls, meetings with clients, luncheons at 21 or Le Pavilion or the Colony, and big dinner parties at 19 Gramcery Park left little time to spend with his wife or children. Barmash said that in the beginning Sonnenberg was a devoted father and husband, "a hugger, a kisser." But as demands on his time grew, he found less and less time for his family. Ben, Jr. (Penny) who today has a fair reputation as an essayist and poet, said of his childhood, "I was a kid at the mercy of angry help." He elaborated later in *The Nation*, "The house was ruled more by the wishes and expectations of its large, exceedingly specialized staff than with thought of my own childish good." Young Sonnenberg also had difficulties with a German governess during World War II. He said of her, "She was openly pro- German." Penny was in many ways in rebellion against his parents' grand style of life and their "worship" of material things—the various art and antique collections. Barmash said, "Although the father loved the son, the lack of real communication between them grew."

Ben, Jr., an intellectual, found his career as an essayist, poet, playwright, and book reviewer; he is an introverted, contemplative person, a total opposite of his extroverted, flamboyant father. No wonder there was a wide gulf between them. In creating a house as an opulent showcase, Sonnenberg failed to build a home. As Ben, Jr. later wrote, his father's passion for collecting suggested that "I was a subordinate to Sheraton, second to George the Second, and not so much fun as a cheerful chintz." The son saw their house as a public place, "like a Cunard liner waiting for passengers. The strongest sense that I had as a child was of living on a stage set."

For 9 years, young Ben edited a literary quarterly, *Grand Street*, but then his illness, multiple sclerosis, forced him to give it up. In 1990, he transferred the magazine to Jean Stein. His memoir, *Lost Property*, was published in 1991 by Summit Brooks. Finally, young Penny, as he was known in the family, said, "To penetrate the mystery of my father, one would have to be as labile and volatile a character as he made himself." In his son's eyes, his father lived a life of make-believe. The son regarded public relations life as a "bitch."

Sonnenberg's wife Hilda, though, was a loving person who provided strong support for all that he did. *The Times* obituary concluded, "Mrs. Sonnenberg who helped her husband in a self-effacing manner for more than half century, survives." Barmash concluded, "There is no doubt that Ben's reach to the social and professional heights was eased by an understanding, patient, even indulgent wife. But toward the end she grew weary of their endless round of entertaining, and increasingly would slip away from a party and go to a neighborhood movie." Barmash notes, "Through the thirties and into the forties, she was a constant and vital part of Ben's social life." Damon Runyon once wrote in a column in the Chicago *Herald–American*: "Benjamin Sonnenberg has lived there [19 Gramcery Park] with his wife, a most charming lady who was his boyhood sweetheart and who still sits in his lap in unabashed affection."

It is indeed difficult to capsule such a dazzling man of complexity and of no little self-fabrication as Ben Sonnenberg. Although he was genius in press agentry, he met all the requirements of a seasoned professional counselor. He knew the importance of assaying current public opinion and interpreting the climate to his client. He once said of the public relations counsel, "He takes the public's temperature and reports it to the client." He knew that the counsel must provide sound advice across a wide spectrum — public opinion, labor unions, publicity methods, international policy, and so forth. Sonnenberg also fully understood that the context in which a message is received determines its interpretation, and thus its effectiveness. "The most important ingredient in public relations is timing. What is heroic one hour may be villainous the next." Contrary to his critics, Sonnenberg insisted that "it is certainly not the business of public relations to try to deceive the public. The merchandise presented must have quality. The message must be solidly based on fact, useful to society and durable in value. Otherwise, the public will reject it." No professional counselor today would quarrel with Sonnenberg's concept of public relations. However, the record is clear that he did not always practice this preachment.

Because so much of his work was shirt-staffing clients — Samuel Goldwyn and Charles Luckman are cases in point — Sonnenberg did not leave the large imprint on American society and life as did many of his contemporaries who were pioneering public relations in the post-World War I era. Yet because of Sonnenberg's press wizardry, today's upscale consumers find Pepperidge Farm products on their supermarket shelves. And because of his counsel to the Texas Company, opera lovers still enjoy Saturday afternoon broadcasts of the Metropolitan Opera in the United States and Canada. Other millions enjoy contract bridge as a pastime or a great competitive sport. Once again the unseen hand of the public relations counselor leaves its fingerprints on the fabric of society.

Denny Griswold, former editor of *The Public Relations News*, once worked for the Sonnenberg agency. She also worked briefly for Edward L. Bernays. She said of Sonnenberg, "His great forte was that he understood people magnificently well. He could discern their weaknesses and their hidden longings and work on them. . . . Everyone has a hidden dream, and everyone has a hidden hangup. He could supply the dream, and he knew how to soothe the hangup. His goal was to be well paid, and he was." He also knew how to make his own dreams come true.

NOTES ON SOURCES

Because of Ben Sonnenberg's desire to leave no traces of his work by ordering his executor to destroy all his files and personal papers, a writer must rely heavily on secondary sources. For insight on Sonnenberg as a father and a person a reader should consult the son, Ben Jr.'s, autobiography, *Lost Property*, published in 1991 by Summit Books. It is sub-titled, *Memoirs and Confessions of a Bad Boy* and one reviewer wrote, "The substance subsists in the subtitle." Young Sonnenberg's agent refused to permit extensive quoting from his book.

Two biographies were heavily relied upon and extensively quoted. Isadore Barmash's unauthorized biography, *Always Live Better Than Your Clients,* (Dodd-Mead, 1983) is quoted with the permission of Mr. Barmash, author and business writer. Sonnenberg's friend, Geoffrey Hellman, profiled Sonnenberg in *The New Yorker* April 8, 1950, under the title "A House on Gramercy Park. This article is used with the permission of the Fales Library, New York University. Equally helpful were the recollections and corrections of errors by John Scott Fones, who was an associate of Sonnenberg's for 10 years. I am also indebted to Mr. Fones, now retired and living in Florida, for his meticulous editing of a rough draft of this chapter. Another oft quoted source was Irwin Ross' chapter on Sonnenberg in his *Image Merchants*, Doubleday & Company, 1959. This is quoted with Mr. Ross' permission.

Other sources used for this chapter include: "The Promoter," in *Continent*, a Parisian journal, Vol. 1 No. 10, May 20, 1961; "The Case of Charles Luckman," *Fortune*, April 1950; Irwin Ross, "Tales of Sonnenberg,"

Fortune, April 23, 1979; Craig Unger, "House Proud," *New York* magazine, January 21, 1991; John L. Hess' obituary in *New York Times News Service*, September 5, 1978; "Dismanteling an Opulent Fossil," *Time* magazine, February 12, 1979; Leon Harris, *Merchant Princes*, Harper & Row, 1979. The William Riis memo is in the Willian H. Baldwin Papers, State Historical Society of Wisconsin, Madison.

Ben Sonnenberg Jr.'s article, "Lost Property," was carried in *The Nation*, June 30, 1979. The quotes by Damon Runyon were in a column, "The Brighter Side: The House That Hot Air Built," *Chicago Herald-American*, May 11, 1946.

Chapter 14

Clarke and Tyler: Builders of the Ku Klux Klan

"EX-KLANSMAN DAVID DUKE NARROWLY LOSES LOUISIANA GOVERNORSHIP"; "DAVID DUKE AN-NOUNCES CANDIDACY FOR PRESIDENT"; PASSING THE TORCH OF WHITE SUPREMACY: NEW GENERA-TION PERPETUATES KLAN'S TENETS"; "KLAN'S CAROLINA MARCH KINDLING FEAR AND UNITY"; "FIVE ARRESTED AS KLAN MARCHES"; "KLAN PRO-TESTS WINDER PRINCIPALS'S DEATH"; "THE KLAN: THEN AND NOW: DRAWN BY HISTORY, FRUS-TRATED BY REALITY"

These current newspaper headlines reflect the bitter legacy of the most disgraceful but albeit successful public relations campaign that gave birth to the modern Ku Klux Klan (KKK) in the 1920s, making it into a powerful national force for terror, bigotry, and racism. The evil effects of the Southern Publicity Association's revival of the Klan live to this day to divide and haunt American society, although the Klan's political power has been greatly diminished from its zenith in the 1920s. The lasting effects of two Atlanta publicists to the ill of society were writ large in 1991 when an ex-Klan leader, David Duke, received nearly 700,000 White votes in his race for governor of Louisiana. This unquestionably is the saddest chapter in public relations' history.

The Southern Publicity Association, the second such agency formed in Atlanta, was headed by Edward Young Clarke, a former *Atlanta Consti-*

tution reporter and son of the *Constitution's* one-time owner. His partner and sometimes bedmate was Elizabeth Tyler, an uneducated country girl but a woman of shrewd instincts. They formed their partnership in 1917 to promote wartime fund-raising drives. By 1920, their business had pretty well petered out.

First a bit of background on the Klan's earlier history: The original Ku Klux Klan was formed in the wake of the Civil War in Pulaski, Tennessee, by six bored and restless Civil War veterans. More than 125 years later, it stands as perhaps the most mysterious and certainly the most feared fraternal organization in American history. In its early stages, the organization's purpose was "to make mischief and play pranks," but it quickly got out of hand. Confederate General Nathan Bedford Forrest, though not one of the organizers, became the Klan's Imperial Wizard in 1867. By this time, the Klan had become a group that found great sport in hazing and harassing African Americans. Under Forrest's leadership, the Klan grew in numbers and in ruthlessness. By the spring of 1868, the Klan was fully launched throughout Tennessee as a vigilante group.

Subsequently the Klan left such a trail of terrorism, lynchings, and hysteria that President Ulysses S. Grant ordered its elimination from American society. Grant, a much-criticized President, took a more aggressive stand against the night-riding Klan than any other President before or after him until President John F. Kennedy. The terrorizing of both White and African-American citizens who incurred the wrath of a Klansman caused President Grant to dispatch the Seventh U.S. Cavalry to South Carolina to eliminate the Klan there. (The Seventh Calvary was so successful in its mission that it was then dispatched to quell the Indians at Little Big Horn under General Custer. That mission was not successful!) In response to President Grant's action, General Forrest ordered the original Klan disbanded early in 1869. However, it took an Act of Congress and the recovery of power by Southern White leaders before the original Klan disappeared into the dustbin of history.

KLAN REBORN AS AN ATLANTA BOTTLE CLUB

Years before Prohibition became the law of the land in 1920, the state of Georgia was legally dry if a bit wet for those with the power to form and operate private clubs. The legislature provided that members of a club could keep liquor in their lockers and drink it on the premises. In 1915, a tall ex-Methodist preacher with a gift of oratory and a penchant for spirits decided to create his own bottle club, the Knights of the Ku Klux Klan. Enter William Joseph Simmons into the saga of the birth of the modern Ku Klux Klan.

Simmons' father had been a member of the original night-riding, hell-raising Klan, and as a boy he heard many a tall tale of its terroristic activities. His family's African-American help also told him of the Klan's scary activities. Simmons later recalled that he was inspired to recreate the Klan when at age 20, he had a dream in which a white-robed Klansman on horseback galloped across his bedroom. "When the picture faded out, I got down on my knees and swore that I would found a fraternal organization that would be a memorial to the original Klan." Simmons' thirst for liquor was probably a more compelling for reason for founding his bottle club. He was also a professional fraternalist. He earned something of a living by selling insurance for Woodmen of the World [WOW] in which he held the rank of colonel. A joiner, he also belonged to the Masons, the Royal Arch Masons, Knights Templar, and other such secret orders. But his dream was to found his own order and model the regalia and ceremony after the Reconstruction Klan. (The work Klan comes from the Greek word, *kuklos*, meaning circle.)

After a brief stint in the Spanish–American War, during which he never advanced beyond the rank of private, Simmons entered the Methodist ministry. He was a hellfire-and-brimstone orator in the pulpit, a talent that would give him power as a Klan leader. He rode the circuit to tent revivals and camp meetings; he also served briefly in several small rural churches. He gained fame as an evangelist in the South, but in 1912, he was bounced out of the ministry by the Alabama Methodist Conference because he continually overspent his allowances and ran his churches into debt. He subsequently moved to Atlanta and started selling insurance for the WOW. In time, he was put in bed by injuries from an auto accident, an event that would bode ill for America. Simmons used his idle hours in bed to work out the complex ritual, ceremony, officer titles, and rules of his new club.

When Simmons recovered his health, he started casting about for the most likely charter members for his new Knights of the Ku Klux Klan and pondered the most propitious time to launch his new order. There were still a few members of the old Klan living in Atlanta, and he persuaded three of them to join him in founding the KKK. Then a tragic Atlanta murder provided the impetus and favorable climate Simmons needed to launch his hate-mongering organization. A 13-year-old Mary Phagan worked in an Atlanta pencil factory, and on a Saturday in April — Confederate Memorial Day — in 1913 when she came to collect her pay envelope, she was brutally raped and murdered. The girl's disfigured body provided ample grist for the city's sensation-seeking newspapers. Her employer, a transplanted New York Jew named Leo Frank, was quickly fingered by the company janitor as the guilty person. In the words of historian Leonard Dinnerstein, this accusation triggered "one of the most lurid displays of intolerance in the Progressive Era." The crime, wrote Dinnerstein in his *The Leo Frank Case*, "channeled the fears and frustrations of the people in Atlanta, themselves victims of the Southern industrial transformation, and Frank emerged as the focal point for resentments endangered by the fledgling industrial society." Frank, only 29, was speedily convicted in a sensational trial that drew national publicity.

The Atlanta newspapers recklessly branded Frank as "the murderer" the day he was arrested even though the evidence brought against the mild-mannered Frank was circumstantial and flimsy at that. (In 1982, an 82-year-old former office boy, Alonzo Mann, came forth with the evidence that finally exonerated Frank. This led B'nai B'rith to lead a campaign for his legal exoneration that a somewhat reluctant Georgia Board of Pardons granted in 1985). Wealthy Northern Jews financed an appeal of Frank's conviction, and thus Frank became a symbol for everything Southerners feared about Jews—"Big Money," Northern capitalists exploiting Southern womanhood, greed, and perversion. The violent reaction served, in Dinnerstein's view, "to highlight the dilemmas and difficulties facing the American South during that Period." These fears, dilemmas, and difficulties the shrewd Simmons sought to exploit. The raging anti-Semitism in Atlanta reached a new level of fury when Georgia's governor, John M. Slaton, commuted Frank's sentence to life imprisonment minutes before his scheduled execution. Goaded by Populist leader Tom Watson (later U. S. Senator), Georgians boycotted Jewish merchants, staged noisy nocturnal demonstrations, and, inevitably, broke into the prison farm where he was held and lynched the hapless Frank.

The lynchers were no ordinary howling mob of angry rabble insane with rage. There were the Knights of Mary Phagan, a well-organized group of prominent citizens from Marietta, the Atlanta suburb where Mary Phagan had lived. They quietly entered the prison late at night, disarmed the guards (probably with little difficulty), abducted their unresisting victim, and transported him back to Marietta where they hanged him at daybreak.

Although this lynching of what history knows to have been an innocent man was righteously decried by decent citizens of Georgia, the Knights of Mary Phagan were the folk heroes to many in Atlanta. Simmons saw his opportunity and took it. He invited the Marietta night riders to form the nucleus of his charter chapter, and his order became the Knights of the Ku Klux Klan. After the group voted to organize, Simmons filed for a charter with the state and Fulton County, and began looking for an opportune time and place for the initiation ceremonies. Simmons had read of a new motion picture, *The Birth of a Nation*, that presented a highly romanticized, sanitized version of the old Klan. When an Atlanta theater booked the movie, Simmons saw, as he recalled later, that the picture's premiere "would give the new order a tremendous popular boost." He scheduled the initiation of his Klan on November 25, 1915, 10 days before the film's opening in Atlanta.

Simmons, a man with a keen sense of showmanship and emotion-arousing appeals, scheduled the initiation ceremony atop Stone Mountain, a large bald slab of granite 16 miles east of Atlanta that can be seen as far as 30 miles away on a clear day; a burning cross atop Stone Mountain at night signaled to all of Atlanta the Klan's birth. (The present-day KKK commemorates the Klan's founding each November 25 with a cross-burning on Stone Mountain.) Simmons rented a travel bus to take his disciples to the base of the mountain, but only 15 showed up on a very chilly evening. Simmons led his shivering members to the top of the mountain where they constructed a makeshift stone altar and a base for the pine cross they had lugged up the slope. They covered the cross with excelsior and soaked it with kerosene before lighting it. While the American flag fluttered in the light of the blazing cross, Simmons read from the Bible and administered the oath of the KKK to his band of 15. Most Atlantans who witnessed the burning cross from afar were more puzzled than awed. Many brushed it off as a publicity stunt for the upcoming showing of *The Birth of a Nation*.

Permission to use the Stone Mountain site was granted by its two owners, the Venable brothers, who were Klan sympathizers. Their nephew, James R. Venable, who died in 1993 at the age of 90, later became an Imperial Wizard of the National Knights of the Ku Klux Klan, one of the many splinter Klan groups, from 1963 to 1987. A Stone Mountain lawyer, Venable hosted for half a century an annual Klan rally the Saturday night before Labor Day in the Stone Mountain area; atop the mountain from 1931 to 1946, thereafter in a pasture he owned nearby. Sometime before his death, James Venable "longed for the good old days when the Klan was a real power."

To tie the Klan in with the emotion-arousing film, Simmons persuaded the *Atlanta Journal* to run an ad for the Klan alongside ads for the movie. The advertisement promoted the Klan as "The World's Greatest Secret, Social Patriotic, Fraternal, Beneficiary Order . . . A High Class Order for Men of Intelligence and Character." Understandably, the cheering crowds that packed the Atlanta theater during the engagement were quick to associate the movie's distorted picture of the old Klan with Simmons's "high class order."

To indicate that the national climate would be receptive to Simmons' newly founded hate organization, when *The Birth of a Nation* had been shown in other cities, audiences had yelled and cheered and on one occasion had even shot up the screen in an attempt to save Flora Cameron from her African-American pursuer. Atlanta was no different. *The Atlanta Journal* reviewer wrote, "It swept the audience at the Atlanta Theater Monday night like a tidal wave. A youth in the gallery leaped to his feet and yelled and yelled. A little boy downstairs pounded the man's back in front of him and shrieked. The man did not know it. . . . Here a young girl kept dabbing at her eyes and there an old lady just sat and let the tears stream down her face. For *The Birth of a Nation* is an awakener of every feeling."

SIMMONS'S BUBBLE BURSTS

The Stone Mountain cross-burning and the emotions aroused by *The Birth of Nation* gave Simmons' Klan an auspicious start, but his bubble quickly burst in 1916. Jonathan B. Frost, one of the charter members and Simmons' partner in his Woodmen of the World insurance enterprise, embezzled the Klan of its accumulated funds and fled the state to form a counterfeit order. Simmons successfully sued Frost to retain sole rights to his Klan's use of the regalia and ritual, that he had had the foresight to copyright. Even so, the Klan's founder was left in financial trouble and his Klan in great disarray. Simmons, now the Imperial Wizard, mortgaged his home to hold the order together during the crisis.

In late 1918, the World War put the Klan back into the spotlight. Operating most noticeably in Alabama, the Klan rode against those suspected of being alien sympathizers, idlers, or slackers who were not doing their part to defeat the Germans. Klansmen also chased "immoral women" away from Army camps in the South and intervened to prevent wildcat strikes in Alabama cities. When an outside labor leader came to Mobile to try to organize a strike among stevedores and washwomen, he was mysteriously abducted by a white-sheeted platoon traveling in a squad of cars draped with white sheets. By 1919, Simmons was plagued by reports of increasing violence by Klan night riders, although there were two other Klan-like organizations in existence at the time. Simmons' betrayer, J. B. Frost, had emerged in Tennessee as Majestic Sovereign of the Columbian Union that despite its name, was a photostatic copy of Simmons' Klan. Frost's order had also spread into Virginia. Another pseudo-Klan was operating out of Charlotte, NC. The public saw little difference in these hate groups. Simmons' Klan continued to lose money, and its membership dwindled to some 3,000. The Ku Klux Klan might have died out completely, driving its Wizard into bankruptcy had not publicists Edward Young Clarke and Bessie Tyler come to its rescue— much to the harm of future generations. Prohibition had doomed the Klan's possessive function as a bottle club.

ENTER THE SOUTHERN PUBLICITY ASSOCIATION

Simmons, who had earlier shied away from publicity for fear that it would take the aura of mystery away from his secret order, had, in desper-

ation, placed a quarter-page ad in the *Atlanta Constitution* in an effort
to attract members. The ad featured a robed Klansman rearing his horse
under the words, "The Most Sublime Lineage in History" and extolling
the Klan "This order is not a mere social, fraternal organization
but it is the embodiment of a GREAT CAUSE that strongly appeals
to sober manhood." A professional fund-raiser and self-styled boot-
legger, J. Quincy Jett, saw the ad and wrote to the P. O. Box number
for information about this order. The Imperial Wizard visited Jett and
signed him up as a member. After Jett had heard Simmons give several
sermons, he became convinced "that the only thing that would save
America and the white people of the world, would be the Ku Klux
Klan."

Jett worked for his mother-in-law, Mrs. Elizabeth Tyler, and her partner,
Edward Young Clarke, in the Southern Publicity Association, which had
been started in 1917 to provide publicity for war causes. The firm had
successfully managed two campaigns for the Salvation Army, one for the
Red Cross, one for the Atlanta YMCA, and one for the Anti-Saloon
League. Jett reasoned that the fund-raising techniques used by Clarke and
Tyler could be applied just as easily to spreading the Klan and urged
Simmons to hire the publicists. The colonel was more easily persuaded than
Clarke who, as a journalist knew that the Klan had a reputation for being
anti-Catholic, anti-Semitic, and anti-African American. Though not par-
ticularly broadminded, Clarke's objections were purely pragmatic. Catholics and Jews had been among his clients, and many had helped in his fund
drives. He did not want to lose their support unless it was worth his while.
Bessie (as she was popularly known) Tyler later recalled, "We found that
Colonel Simmons was having a hard time getting along. He couldn't pay his
rent. The receipts were not sufficient to take care of his personal needs. He
was a minister and a clean living and thinking man, and he had his heart and
soul for the success of his Ku Klux Klan. After we investigated it from every
angle, we decided to go into it with Colonel Simmons and give it the impetus
that it could best get from publicity." A fateful decision for American
society!

Their price came high. The contract between Simmons and Clarke, dated
June 7, 1920, shows that out of every $10 initiation fee, Clarke and his
subordinates kept $8. Additionally, the Southern Publicity Association
received the other $2 for members added within 6 months to Klan chapters
his organization had initiated. Clarke was given the title Imperial Kleagle,
a general superintendent of the propagation department of the Klan. As a
woman, Bessie Tyler could not hold an official position within the Klan.
When first organized it was for White Christian males only. The Women's
KKK was founded in 1923 after Clarke and Tyler had been forced out of the
organization.

E. Y. CLARKE—ATLANTA'S P. T. BARNUM

Edward Young Clark's talent for promotion and publicity was inherited from his father, E. Y. Clarke, Sr., a prominent figure in 19th century Georgia journalism. Two years after the *Constitution* was founded in 1868, the elder Clarke, a former Confederate colonel, bought the newspaper and made himself managing editor. While he owned the newspaper in 1875, he led a widely publicized expedition into the Okeefenokee Swamp in South Georgia. These explorers, which included scientists, educators, and surveyors, were the first Caucasians to enter the swamp. In a few years, Clarke sold his interest in the *Constitution* and set about to promote the city of Atlanta in an effort "to speedily bring thousands to our population, and add millions to our capital and taxable values." The elder Clarke remained active in various journalistic ventures until his death in 1911.

The younger Clarke, born in Atlanta in 1877, at first aspired to the ministry. He and his new employer had this common bond. He was a Presbyterian and believed in foreordination, a belief that was reinforced when he escaped unscathed from an auto accident and attributed this to divine protection. According to one close associate, he often asserted that his later successes with the Klan had been predestined by the Almighty. Clarke eventually discarded the pulpit and along with his brother Francis, landed a job as a reporter on the *Constitution* in 1902. Because of his religious training (and perhaps due to his father's influence), he was soon made religious editor. Although E. Y. spent only 7 years with the paper, his brother, Francis, worked his way up to managing editor and retired in 1937. E. Y. Clarke's Klan work often proved embarrassing to Francis. There is evidence that he tended to give his brother the benefit of the doubt when the latter's Klan ties were revealed by the newspapers. Editor Clarke never attacked the Klan.

In his definitive history of the Klan, Wyn Wade *The Fiery Cross: The Ku Klux Klan in America* described Clarke as "A short, intense, long-faced man with bushy black hair and black-rimmed spectacles [who] had learned his public relations skills from journalism." Clarke has also been described as "a disciple of P. T. Barnum," a super salesman, and "a man of courage, vision, ideals, understanding, energy, and undying loyalty." Wade described Mrs. Tyler this way, "[She was] a gutsy woman in her mid-thirties who had married at fourteen, widowed at fifteen with a daughter. Chunky, buxom, and blowsy, she was an unusually independent woman for the South in the 1920s." Even a man who detested her was forced to call her an extraordinary woman. She was untaught but endowed with unusual intelligence and a keen insight into male behavior.

Clarke presents something of a paradox as I review his career. He was obviously a man of talent, boundless energy, and a keen sense of imagination, one who could have succeeded in many legitimate endeavors, especially public relations. Yet he often resorted to chicanery, fraud, and deceit to accomplish his goals, character flaws that ultimately landed him in prison. He ended his life as a fugitive from justice. Clarke quit his job as religious editor of the *Constitution* in 1909 and for the next 5 years, he was involved in several quick money schemes. Then he went "straight," taking a job with the Georgia Chamber of Commerce in 1914. His talents soon won him the reputation as "The Doctor of Sick Towns." Following in the footsteps of his father in city promotion, Clarke helped Georgia communities that had stagnated commercially. This was the era when civic boosterism was in full flower. The era of municipal reform was taking hold nationwide in the wake of Lincoln Steffans' muckraking expose, *The Shame of the Cities*. This was also the period of Woodrow Wilson's New Freedom reforms. The American City Bureau, founded by Harold and Edgar Buttenheim, publishers of *The American City* magazine, spearheaded the Chamber of Commerce movement that spread across the nation just prior to World War I. Clarke was an important figure in this movement.

His position with the Georgia Chamber of Commerce led to his selection as general manager of the Georgia Harvest Festival, a week-long event conceived by the Atlanta Presidents Club, an elite power group in Atlanta. In 1914, Georgia's agriculture had suffered heavy losses from drought, and when 1915 brought a bumper crop, the Atlanta club voted to sponsor a fair "in celebration of the return of prosperity in the harvest season." Clarke staged a memorable event replete with nearly a dozen parades, carnival rides, Wild West shows, circus stunts, three band concerts daily, open air vaudeville acts. Clarke had all of downtown Atlanta decorated with red, white, and blue bunting. The festival concluded with a spectacular Fighting of the Flames exhibition. At the conclusion, the *Atlanta Journal* called it "the most successful event Atlanta had ever staged" and praised its director "for the highly efficient way in which all events were handled."

The important consequence for our story is that the festival brought E. Y. Clarke and Bessie Tyler together. Far from a public relations professional, Tyler was allegedly the proprietress of a house of ill repute. In 1915, she was involved in a charity project, a Better Babies Movement, visiting tenements and counseling mothers on better hygiene for their children. The movement led to a "Better Babies Show," one of the highlights of the festival that brought her in contact with Clarke. A relationship developed. Sometime during the war, date uncertain, she combined her savings with Clarke's talents, and the Southern Publicity Association was born. Clarke and Tyler complemented each other very well. He was an idea man, a visionary, a schemer. She was a down-to-earth business woman, pragmatic, and ruthless. Although Clarke was married, they were sometime partners in bed as well as in business.

In her book *Women of the Klan*, Kathleen M. Blee quoted Edgar J. Fuller, a former secretary to Clarke, as saying Tyler's great strength was her power over men. Tyler, he argued, had amassed great influence with the KKK in part through her knowledge of the South but foremost through her intimate knowledge of men. He said, "Her experience in catering to [men's] appetites and vices had given her an insight into their frailties. She knew how to handle them all."

Typical of Clarke's imaginative mind was the stunt he created in support of an Anti-Saloon League fund-raising drive. Clarke hired an airplane — then a relatively new and risky mode of transportation — and Tyler flew over Atlanta dropping leaflets. This was probably the first use of this publicity technique, one that the Allies used extensively in World War I. Enactment of Prohibition stunted this fund drive, and it fell short of its goal. The pair got into trouble with another account for the Theodore Roosevelt Memorial Association. This client was so unhappy with the association's work that it sued Clarke and Tyler for over $1,000 it claimed that Clarke had embezzled and another $4,000 he had been unable to account for. The firm conducted fund drives for the Red Cross, the Salvation Army, and the Atlanta YMCA, all low-paying clients. Colonel Simmons offer to promote the Ku Klux Klan promised the duo the big money they both longed for.

THE PLAN FOR THE KLAN

In Wade's view, "To the keen-minded Clarke, the national temper suggested a market hungry for a hard boiled nativist movement, and he wanted to go after it in a big way." Before signing the contract with Simmons, Clarke said, "Colonel, it's going to take a lot of money to create an organizational force. We have no machinery of that nature, and I've got to find men. We'll have to spend a lot of time finding men, and this machinery must be constructed and it'll cost something." Clarke then persuaded Simmons to make the Southern Publicity Association the independent Propagation Department of the Klan that would keep 80% of all fees collected from Klansmen. Out of this 80% the Propagation Department would pay all its expenses including the wages and commissions of employees and fieldmen. Simmons agreed, and the contract was signed June 7, 1920.

By his constitution, Colonel Simmons was Imperial Wizard of the Klan, Emperor of the Invisible Empire, and administrative and mystical leader of his organization. His immediate subordinates, who composed the Imperial Kloncillium (national cabinet), included the Imperial Klaliff (vice-president), an office Clarke assumed in January 1921. Next in line were the state leaders, the Grand Dragons. As Imperial Kleagle, Clarke was the chief executive of the Propagation Department that he organized as a completely separate Klan with an independent hierarchy. Rather than let the Klan grow randomly outward from Georgia, Clarke developed a national plan for recruiting and organizing Klans throughout the nation.

Clarke's plan for the national Ku Klux Klan called for nine domains (regions) of several realms (states) each. The domains were to be ruled by Grand Goblins – the equivalent of regional sales managers. King Kleagles supervised the organizing in each state. Kleagles were the individual salesmen and recruiters who were to fan out and set up provisional Klans. In the days of the Klan's early growth most of the empire was provisional, which gave Clarke virtual control over the organization with Simmons left pretty much as a figurehead. When Simmons took an extended leave of absence in 1922, he appointed Clarke to serve as Imperial Wizard Pro Tem while retaining his posts as Imperial Kleagel and Imperial Klaliff. When Clarke explained this arrangement to a U.S. Senate Committee, one member commented, "You came pretty near to being the whole shooting match, didn't you?" Clarke replied that it had just "worked out that way." Simmons was no match for the wily Clarke in the power game.

KLAN FINDS FERTILE GROUND FOR ITS POISONOUS SEEDS

In his *The Klan in the City, 1915–1930*, Kenneth T. Jackson quoted Clarke as stating "there were only 10 to 15 Klans, and approximately a membership of 3,000" when he signed the contract with Simmons. Within 3 months, Clarke and Tyler had added 48,000 men to membership in the Klan. Clarke exulted, "In all my years of experience in organization work I have never seen anything equal to the clamor throughout the nation." On July 2, 1921, Clarke sent a memorandum to Simmons describing the Klan's growing pains:

> The headquarters of the domain chiefs are located in New York, Washington, Indianapolis, Denver, Dallas, Houston, and Los Angeles. In all these cities our investigators are working eighteen hours a day, and in most instances are three months behind in their list of applicants. . . . We are completely camouflaged in each of these places and it will be almost a miracle if we are located [i.e., discovered] in any city where headquarters have been established.

This memorandum reflects Clarke's effort to maintain Simmons's desired secrecy by working undercover. When an Atlanta photographer, Tracy Mathewson, heard about the Klan and approached Clarke and Tyler for a photograph, he was brusquely turned away. This resourceful journalist was not to be denied. For 25¢ a head he hired 20 men (all African-Americans) to drape themselves in sheets and hoods he had devised, based on his recollection of *The Birth of a Nation*; he lit a couple of crosses and took his pictures that he subsequently sold to newspapers in several cities, including *The New York Times* that used them in its Sunday rotogravure section. The photos brought the Klan its first nationwide exposure and led to an unplanned avalanche of publicity. In expressing her amazement at the sudden attention, Tyler told an interviewer that the Klan's original publicity was centered only in the South, "but the minute we said 'Klu Klux' editors from all over the country began pressing us for publicity." Clarke was quick to seize Mathewson's cue; he hired a photographer and had Klansmen pose for pictures atop Stone Mountain.

Clarke and Tyler had a fertile soil in the early 1920s in which to plant their poisonous seeds. Clarke, a man of shrewd insights, had sensed this in seeing the opportunity for big bucks in boosting the KKK. The immediate years after World War I were troubled and turbulent ones. Organized labor was making a vain attempt to unionize the coal fields and industrial plants. A glimpse of the lengths to which mine and plant owners went to break labor's efforts to organize war presented in the John Price Jones and Ivy Lee chapters. The Bolshevik Revolution in Russia had loosed a violent, unthinking Red Scare in the United States. Industrialists linked organized labor's efforts to organize unions to this Red Scare. They charged that American unionists were Communist (e.g., the reports from John Price Jones' firm to the West Virginia Coal Operators). Some in fact did use bombs and firearms to subvert management and to defend themselves against armed strikebreakers and police, unbridled emotion greatly magnified their threat to American institutions. In *The Fiery Cross*, Wyn Wade described this hysterical era:

> Teachers and professors who suggested anything positive about the Russian Revolution were fired. Editors, writers, and humanitarians from Oswald Garrison Villard to Jane Adams, were denounced as "Red" for any kind of criticism of United States policy. A Tennessee Senator suggested using Guam as a concentration camp for disloyal Americans. Taking advantage of Woodrow Wilson's illness and seclusion in the White House, . . . Attorney General A. Mitchell Palmer launched a strategic attack on the Red Menace. He created in the Department of Justice a General Intelligence Division . . . and put twenty-four-year old J. Edgar Hoover in charge of it. Hoover's legal talents were unremarkable, but as a former employee of the Library of Congress he brought to the GID a striking innovation — a card catalog. In a few months, Hoover had assembled a file of over 200,000 cards that identified American Reds, pinks, and suspected pinks. The GID quickly became the nerve center of the Justice Department, and in December, 1919, Palmer secured the deportation of 240 radical non-natives, including Emma Gold-

man. . . . The following month Palmer's network staged a series of raids, rounding up four thousand Reds in twenty-three states.

In his *J. Edgar Hoover The Man and His Secrets*, a lengthy biography, Curt Gentry said of Hoover's work as the newly appointed head of the General Intelligence Division (GID) on August 1, 1919, "Finding it just as easy to categorize people as he once did books—a simplification he would follow all his life—within three months he had amassed 150,000 names and by 1921 some 450,000. Moreover, they were cross-indexed by localities." His zeal for hunting Communists never flagged until he died in May 1972. His anti-Red zeal was shared by his boss, Attorney General Mitchell who asserted, "Like a prairie-fire the blaze of revolution was sweeping every institution of law and order. . . . It was eating its way into the homes of American workmen, its sharp tongues of revolutionary heat were licking at the altars of the churches, leaping into the belfry of the school bell, crawling into the sacred corners of American homes."

Hoover worked as a clerk in the Library of Congress for $4\frac{1}{4}$ years while studying law at George Washington University. Although he had a ROTC commission, he did not enlist in the Army but instead took a clerkship in the Department of Justice in July 1917. Two years later, he was promoted to attorney and then to head the GID—a job he would used to catapult himself into the headship of the FBI that he ruled with an iron hand until his death. In his Hoover biography, *Secrecy and Power*, Richard C. Powers wrote that Hoover's first months in the Justice Department put him in the middle of wartime hysteria over traitors, spies, and saboteurs, undoubtedly shaping the mind set that influenced his actions the rest of his career. Before the war ended, he moved to the Alien Enemy Bureau. Powers believed that Hoover's wartime experience in the Alien Enemy Bureau accustomed him to using administrative procedures as a substitute for the uncertainties and delays of the legal process. At the war's end, Hoover joined in Palmer's witch hunts, and thus began his long battle against what he perceived to be radicalism.

Powers wrote, "Early in 1919, Hoover along with the rest of the country was subjected to a barrage of hysterical warnings from pulpit, rostrum and editorial page that the institutions of government and property of America were under attack . . . and that the Red conspiracy was the cutting edge of the radical movement."

The national paranoia and the hysteria about the Red Menace that swept the nation in the 1920s and again the in the 1950s appears incredible to citizens in 1992. Yet it provided the climate of opinion that enabled the Klan to flourish in those years, years that were characterized by Red scares, Jazz Age immorality, bootlegging, and anxieties of Middle America that targeted African American, Roman Catholics, Jews, and foreigners in bigotry and worse. Also into this emotional mix must be fed the cynicism born of President Wilson's failure to gain the peace for which Americans fought and died. Growing lawlessness born of an effort to effect national Prohibition was another factor. Such was the emotion-charged political climate that Clarke, Tyler, and their minions could exploit and did.

THE NIGHT RIDERS RETURN

The Klan's rapid expansion in 1920 and 1921 was coupled with a revival of the night-riding tactics used by the original Klan. In October 1920, a massive night-riding campaign to force the closing of cotton ginneries (unless the price of cotton was raised) was attributed to the Klan. Masked riders clothed in white burned some of the gins and terrorized the African-American field hands. On October 21, the Klan released a statement to the press announcing a decree by Simmons commanding "every branch of the Knights of the Ku Klux Klan and all members of this organization . . . to use all influence within their power to suppress operations of so-called 'night riders' and to assist officers of the law in their apprehension." The release quoted Simmons as accusing the terrorists of bringing "odium" upon the Klan by clothing themselves in garments similar to those worn by Klansmen.

Simmons's decree apparently went unheeded. The next day, 1,000 men attired as Klansmen marched through the streets of Jacksonville, Florida, and another 500 paraded in Orlando as a warning to African Americans to stay away from the polls the next Tuesday. The tension created was as much partisan as racial. The marchers were Democrats, and in those days, African Americans voted Republican if they dared vote at all. On November 2, two prosperous African-Americans who had registered and paid their poll tax, attempted to vote in Ocoee, a suburb of Orlando. An ugly confrontation ensued and a mob formed. The terrorized African Americans fled and barricaded themselves in one of the pair's home. The mob followed and started breaking in the house when the African-Americans opened fire and killed two Whites. The Whites at first fell back, then regrouped and attacked the African Americans settlement setting it ablaze with kerosene. African Americans seeking to escape were shot. Two churches, a lodge hall, a school, and about 20 houses were burned. Orlando newspapers put the number of deaths at five. Simmons later told a crowd that "Florida killed 36 niggers" at Ocoee although he maintained that his Klan had no connection with the massacre.

To counter these attacks of lawlessness and to distinguish Simmons's Klan from the others that were springing up, Clarke and Tyler sought to establish a more definitive image for their Imperial Wizard. This was image building at its best. Simmons was an affable man and could speak with fervor but lacked that indefinable charisma. One of Clarke's first acts after taking over the Klan was to cancel all of Simmons' speaking engagements. One of Clarke's associates wrote in 1924, "Simmons possessed none of the qualities to lead a great movement or to effect a great organization of men."

Clarke decided to create a fictitious Simmons and sell him to the American people, according to Edgar I. Fuller in *The Visible of the Invisible Empire*. After some coaching and much speech writing, Clarke returned the Wizard to the public eye. The Southern Publicity Association arranged to have a *New York Herald* correspondent visit Atlanta for an article on the workings of the new Klan. Tyler, who had a talent for portraying sincerity, gave the *Herald* reporter a canned tour of the Klan's operations. He was taken in and returned to New York and wrote a series of articles that described the Klan as a benevolent and business-like fraternal order. According to a former King Kleagle, the articles were helpful in launching the Klan's drive in the East. Another Simmons interview, this with Angus Parkerson of the *Atlanta Journal*, portrayed the Imperial Wizard as a man of great spiritual purpose and soul and pictured the Klan as an upstanding law-and-order organizations. Simmons told Parkerson that the Klan did not burn cotton gins but rather guarded them to prevent destruction. He assured the reporter that wherever the Klan was strong, citizens need not fear crime. Within 2 weeks of these articles, Clarke and Tyler persuaded the producers of the *Fox News Weekly,* a theater newsreel, to portray the Klan favorably. Thus did the buildup of the Klan begin.

THE BIG BUILDUP HITS FULL STRIDE

In less than a year after he took charge of the Klan, Clarke had 1, 100 Kleagles in the field "making things hum all over America" in his words. Each week Kleagles had to send Clarke a report on the number of prospects canvassed, the total amount collected, the towns they had worked that week, and where they expected to work the following week. (Kleagles sold memberships for $10 a piece and kept $4 for themselves. The remaining amount was sent to the King Kleagle, who kept $1, and sent the $5 to his boss the Goblin. The Goblin kept 50¢ and sent $4.50 to Clarke and Tyler who kept $2.50 for themselves and supposedly deposited the remaining $2 in the Klan treasury.) In making their pitch, the Kleagles used the appeal most likely to work in a particular community. Wade said "In large cities, Kleagles invariably haunted showings of *The Birth of a Nation*, and this paid off well in Dallas, Richmond, Portland, New York, and Chicago."

If a place were afraid of labor unions, then the Kleagles stressed the Klan's position against alien-inspired strikers. If the community were dry, prospects were told that only the Klan had the courage to deal with bootleggers. If the city or town had a lot of new immigrants, prospects were told that the Klan stood for 100% Americanism. If a town or city, especially in the South, were fearful about African Americans asserting their rights, prospects were told that the Klan had long known how to deal with "niggers." In sum, Clarke directed his organizers to exploit every fear and every hatred they found in a community. Wade observes, "Never before had a single society gathered up so many hatreds or given vent to an inwardness so thoroughgoing." He termed it "very much a twentieth century success story." This all depends on how one defines success.

Clarke developed a literature for the Klan to appeal to this highly elastic nativism. An early Klan flyer proclaimed, "The Declaration of Independence is the foundation of our patriotic ideals. If you are a Native Born White, Gentile, Protestant, American citizen, eventually you will be a Klansman and proud of that title." He next perfected the machinery by which unorganized Klan initiates formally entered the Invisible Empire. The organizing Kleagle remained in charge until the community had been thoroughly milked for members. The initiates then applied for a charter and were granted the status of Klan or Klavern that then could elect an Exalted Cyclops to head it.

Wade continued:

> The impact of Clarke's program was quickly and strongly felt in the Southwest—Texas, Louisiana, Oklahoma, and Arkansas. It then fluttered about the Southeast and in the Northwest, surprisingly capturing Oregon. By the summer of 1921 it had crossed the Ohio River into the Midwest, the Potomac into the Northeast, and was creeping up the Atlantic seaboard. In less than fifteen months, Klan membership mushroomed from 4,000 to nearly 100,000, and initiates had spent over $1,500,000 in "klectokens" (the $10 fees donated for a membership, white robes, literature, and paraphernalia).

Wade estimated that of this total, Clarke and Tyler earned $212,000 in these 15 months. Even though he had been relegated to nothing more than a figurehead, Simmons reaped $170,000 in commissions for being little more than a publicity prop. For example, Clarke and Tyler had him pictured in all his royal robes falling to his knees in front of the Liberty Bell. He was also used to rouse the members with his oratory.

Clarke and Tyler got a big break when Protestantism's new "Social Gospel" brought a bitter backlash from Protestant fundamentalists. In the spring of 1922, Harry Emerson Fosdick, leading advocate of the Social Gospel, delivered a strong sermon, "Shall the Fundamentalists Win?" in

New York's First Presbyterian Church. He was quickly and roundly denounced by the Fundamentalists—a force not yet 2 years old—as a "scoundrel," "a hypocrite," and "seducer of the young." Imperial Kleagle Clarke was quick to capitalize on these aroused emotions.

Because of his early background in the ministry, Clarke had realized from the start the Klan's appeal to evangelical ministers. As Wade noted, "From his booster work for the Anti-Saloon League, Clarke knew that many fundamentalists shared several important characteristics: an intolerance for ways of life different from their own, a frustration with postwar change, and a passionate commitment to restoring things as they used to be." Even before Fosdick gave his provocative sermon, Clarke had instructed his army of Kleagles to approach Fundamentalist ministers to enlist their support of the Klan. Often these preachers were the first targets solicited in local communities. The Kleagles shared with the preachers their concerns about bootlegging, crime, and vice, portraying the Klan as the best force to deal with these ills. The clergymen were given free memberships. When Clarke's organizers began meeting a favorable response in many communities, he broadened this appeal to the national market. The Klan's books, tracts, magazines, flyers, and placards stressed the Christian message linking the goals of the Fundamentalists and the Klan.

One flyer, "The Klansman's Creed" vouched:

I believe in God and in the tenets of the Christian religion and that a godless nation cannot long prosper.
I believe that a church that is not grounded on the principles of morality and justice is a mockery to God and man.

The message fell upon receptive ears among the Fundamentalists.

THE KLAN GOES PUBLIC

As indicated earlier in this chapter, when the Southern Publicity Association first took over the Klan account, Clarke and Tyler kept external publicity at a minimum, preferring an undercover campaign for recruiting members. Secrecy was the watchword. For example, no "aliens" were ever permitted to gaze upon Klan rites that were usually conducted in the seclusion of woods. This all began to change in early 1921 because of increasing incidents of Klan brutality that was damaging the image Clarke and Tyler were trying to promote. For instance: A African American, J. C. Thomas, ran a small lunch grill in a predominately African-American section of Atlanta. In late 1920, he began receiving threatening letters telling him to leave town. He was not intimidated and continued to sell his hot dogs to his African American customers. In January 1921, five men abducted him and dragged him to a nearby amusement park. Thomas surprised them by whipping out a knife and stabbing one of them to death. The others fled. Thomas went to the police to report the abduction and was promptly arrested for murder. In the trial, he was acquitted and two of his abductors were indicted for attempted murder. Word quickly spread that this had been the work of the Klan. According to Tyler's son-in-law, J. Q. Jett, Clarke and Simmons both fled the state when the incident broke and did not return until Tyler "got it fixed up until there was no danger." The accused Klansmen were defended by the Imperial Konsul, William S. Coburn, and they were ultimately acquitted; the Klan was cleared of any official connection with the affair. Nonetheless, the Klan's "law and order" facade had been blackened.

Clarke and his associates staged a spectacular show in Birmingham, Alabama, on January 27, 1921, to dramatize their shift in publicity strategy. On that date, the Alabama Fair Grounds was knee-deep in water, mud, and slush, when a line of 500 Ku Klux Klan candidates, dressed in street clothes, marched in rows through the muck, surrounded by hundreds of hooded Klansmen whose white robes flowed to the ground to be stained by Alabama's red clay. Each Klansman held a red-and-white cross aloft while two great searchlights played upon them. Mounted Klansmen patrolled the outer perimeters of the gathering, keeping out all those who were not versed in the proper shibboleths and countersigns. As the 500 initiates marched to the base of the Imperial throne, the searchlights were extinguished. Behind the throne another thousand Klansmen assembled in the shape of a giant cross. Each lit a small cross that with the two tall blazing crosses beside the throne of the Imperial Wizard, provided the only illumination. The Wizard, resplendent in his royal purple satin robes, administered the oath to the initiates—exactly 55 years after General Nathan Bedford Forrest, leader of the original Klan, was initiated into the Invisible Empire.

After the initial interviews with Simmons that resulted in the favorable *New York Herald* series and the one with the *Atlanta Journal* in January 1921, the Klan began opening up its konklaves (meetings) to permit the public to catch a glimpse of klankraft in action. Mass initiations were often set in connection with a national holiday or Klan anniversary. From 1921 to 1925, barely a Flag Day or Independence Day passed without a major Klan konklave or klanvocation (state convention). The Birmingham konklave described previously was the first one to be opened to the public and press. Inasmuch as Imperial Wizard Simmons rarely appeared in public without Clarke's guiding hand, it may be assumed that Clarke staged the Birmingham show. Clarke was definitely on hand for subsequent similar initiations and rallies. When a mass initiation was held in Cincinnati on

June 17, 1921, 2,000 members were inducted with Clarke as the guest of honor. The pattern of these public initiations was quite similar – *pseudo events* long before historian Daniel Boorstin popularized the term.

Clarke and his aides did all they could to exaggerate the numbers joining the Klan in an effort to create a mass psychology to increase membership. The larger Klan gatherings were followed by news releases to local and national news media. For example, a Chicago Klan initiation was followed by a press release stating that 2,000 candidates had been "naturalized," that 6,000 automobiles had been used to bring the initiates from a radius of 200 miles, and so forth. As the Klan grew, so did the mass gatherings, each being billed as "the largest ever." One realm competed with the others for the largest numbers. Another technique developed by Clarke to create the impression of numbers was to have the Klansmen march in single file some 8 feet apart.

Fears of the Klan's growing strength and journalistic sensationalism of the 1920s tended to also inflate the Klan's numbers. For example, the national press reported attendance figures of 100,000 to 200,000 for a konklave in Kokomo, Indiana, on July 4, 1943. Although this was one of the largest konklaves ever held, the Klan's own estimate in its official publication, the *Imperial Knight-Hawk*, was only 50,000. Probably the largest Klan gathering was Klan Day at the Texas State Fair on October 24, 1923, when more than 200,000 persons attended the fair on that date. The first public Klan ceremonies were austere and mysterious, but as the rallies increased in size they became less supernatural in character. More and more Klansmen brought their families. Barbecues were held to feed the crowds. By 1923, the hours of mystifying ritual at the initiation came more and more to resemble a high school baccalaureate. Typical is this one sponsored in 1923 by the Pueblo Klan No. 6 of Colorado:

Song: "The Star Spangled Banner"
Invocation
Flag lowered: Fiery Cross lighted
Song: "Onward Christian Soldiers"
Naturalization ceremony
Song: "America"
Tableau
Address: By the Grand Dragon, Realm of Colorado
Inspirational address
Song: "Blest Be the Tie That Binds"
Benediction
Barbecue Supper

In the Midwest particularly, the giant rallies took on a festival atmosphere, featuring bands, drill teams, parades, prominent speakers (Imperial officers were a big draw), and even weddings (the bride was veiled, the groom was hooded). Far from being secret, these meetings were advertised and the general public invited to attend. For example, red-white-and-blue posters heralded the "Spring Festival and Entertainment" to be held at Pleasant Valley Park in Milwaukee County, Wisconsin, on Flag Day, 1924. The poster promised music, lectures, and refreshments. Adults were to be charged 25¢, children admitted free. A similar rally in San Antonio, Texas, included the added attractions of a rodeo and a cowboy contest. Though Clarke and Tyler had set the policy and pattern for these public displays, the local officers had the responsibility for staging and promoting these *pseudo-events*.

When the true nature of the Klan became more apparent as the result of increasing terror-promoting incidents, these rallies began to draw protests. Usually these were only vocal protestors, but these hecklers were usually outnumbered by Klan sergeants-at-arms or the local police. In Texas, an "alien" tried to break up a parade by crashing his car though a rope balustrade, injuring several Klansmen. Other Klansmen jerked him from his car and gave him a sound beating before the police could take him away. On a hot summer night in Steubenville, Ohio, a confrontation at a Klan rally even resulted in four persons being wounded by gunfire. A week later in Carnegie, Pennsylvania, a mob attempted to halt a group of nearly 20,000 Klansmen from marching. The battle lasted over an hour, covering four city blocks before Pittsburgh police arrived to quell the riot. The melee left one Klansman dead, 12 persons seriously wounded, and scores injured. For the most part, however, the Klan "monster rallies," celebrations, and parades were beneficial to local Klan units. By inviting the townsfolk and providing them with entertainment, the Klan sought to improve its community relations and provide merchants with an economic boost. The resultant publicity was nearly always favorable, thanks to the facilities arranged for the press.

Another community relations gimmick that the Klan started using in this public relations campaign was the church visitation. In April 1922, the *Literary Digest* commented, "Scarcely a Sunday passes without the publication of a Klan visit to a church somewhere, either to signify approval, sit decorously through a sermon, or present a donation." Although the format varied, the scenario for church visitations usually involved the sudden appearance of hooded Klansmen during a Sunday service. They would walk silently down the aisle to the pulpit, hand the minister an envelope, and then just as silently exit, leaving the congregation aghast or in some cases applauding. If the minister were sympathetic to the order and had been forewarned of the visit, he might arrange for the choir to break into a chorus of "Onward Christian Soldiers" as the Klansmen filed out of the church. Such visitations fell into common use after 1922 and helped to offset some of the hostile reports that were appearing in the national press with increasing frequency. In retrospect, it is disturbing to reflect on the support many Protestant churches gave this terroristic, hate-mongering order. The realistic term for these "donations" is *bribes*.

THE IMPERIAL KLOKARDS: THE KLAN'S
SPEAKERS BUREAU

In a day when radio was in its infancy and television not yet invented, the Klan developed a large speakers bureau program to carry its message to the faithful and to the prospective initiates. A speakers bureau is a common tool for organizations to convey their message to serve clubs, schools, chambers of commerce, dedications, and anniversaries — wherever a potential audience is to be found. Shortly after the Southern Publicity Association took over the propagation activities of the Klan, Clarke recruited a host of lecturers or Klokards in the Klan K terminology. The Klokards, like the Kleagles, also worked to recruit members. Many of each group had worked for Clarke and Tyler in their fund-raising campaigns. The Kleagles worked on a commission basis, but the lecturers were paid a salary. The speakers were dispatched to Klan ceremonies to fire up the esprit among Klansmen and organizers, to civic and fraternal meetings to attract potential members and sympathizers, and to political meetings to speak against anti-Klan candidates. Although the exact number of lecturers Clarke used in this way is not known, one Georgia newspaper disclosed that 40 such lecturers were utilized during the 1922 Georgia gubernatorial campaign. The speakers lectured with Chautauqua-style oratory to convey this underlying message:

1. Catholics, aliens, Jews, and Negroes are organized and are a threat to American institutions; it is necessary to fight these menaces to the American way of life.
2. Because these forces have so infiltrated or influenced all levels of government, the sole weapon against them is the Ku Klux Klan; therefore if you are a true American, join the Klan.
3. Morals in the United States are rapidly deteriorating; bootlegging, sexual vice, and gambling are rampant.
4. The sole weapon against such sin and degradation is a Protestant alliance through the Ku Klux Klan; therefore if you are on the side of God and the heavenly hosts, join the Klan.

The speakers were usually successful in gauging how far they could go with this message of hate and bigotry and sometimes stuck almost wholly to a star-spangled theme of 100% Americanism without attacking any specific group. Clarke coached them to vary their message according to the occasion. But occasionally they overshot the tolerance of their audience and its community. For example, on October 5, 1922, a Klan speaker, Dr. C. Lewis Fowler, a former president of the Klan-owned Lanier University in Atlanta, spoke in Milwaukee, Wisconsin, and his speech was so viciously anti-Catholic that it enraged and shocked the Milwaukee citizenry. (Milwaukee is the home of Marquette University, a Catholic institution.) The Klan's takeover of Lanier University is described later. Fowler later became editor of the anti-Catholic *American Standard*, the only pro-Klan paper published in New York City. After his Milwaukee speech, Fowler was denounced by every religious and social organization in the city.

Other paid lecturers often brought a backlash of community opinion by blatantly lying in their emotion-arousing efforts. J. Q. Nolan, a veteran politician who had lectured in Clarke's Anti-Saloon League drive, told a Hartsfield, Georgia, audience a wild tale about the Klan preventing a race riot in Atlanta after the governor and chief of police had been unable to handle the situation. A concerned minister informed the Atlanta Committee on Inter-Racial Relationships, which checked out the story with the official involved and found it to be "a fabrication out of whole cloth." The resultant publicity revealed that Nolan had made similar false statements in other Georgia cities. The Klan's inept response was to have its Klounsel, William S. Coburn, denounce the governor, the inter-racial committee, and the informant minister. Coburn called the incident "a planned and concerted attack and effort to discredit the organization in its fight for white supremacy."

Despite some of these outrageous attacks that backfired, the Klan continued to benefit by having seasoned speakers on its side, many recruited from the Protestant pulpit, which increased its identity with Fundamentalism. One was the Rev. Oscar W. Haywood, so popular a preacher in New York City that he was asked to join the staff of the wealthy Calvary Baptist Church as a General Evangelist. Haywood reportedly distributed Klan literature during worship services, and as a result, the church earned a reputation for being a "nest" of the Klan. Finally, dissident churchmen forced their pastor, Fundamentalist leader Dr. John Roach Straton, to dismiss Haywood. Perhaps the most popular of these Klokards was the Imperial Kludd (chaplain), Caleb A. Ridley, pastor of Atlanta's Central Baptist Church. Ridley generally drew a full house whether on the circuit or in his own church. The outspoken Ridley bragged about his Klan affiliation and thought the "melting pot" ideal a "bastard theory." In July 1921, Ridley lectured in Tulsa, Oklahoma, barely a month after a race riot had left 30 or more African-Americans dead. Ridley called the race riot "the best thing that ever happened to Tulsa." Such was the Protestant Fundamentalism of the 1920s in the South.

Available evidence suggests that E. Y. Clarke was himself a dynamic speaker. Addressing an Erie, Pennsylvania, audience on December 4, 1923, Clarke laid out his vision for the Klan:

> I am inclined to think, Klansmen, as I see it now, that we are going to have to reach out and spread the roster of this organization to every white man on the face of the globe. (Applause.) And when we do that I have a vision . . . that some day when the heads of all the national Ku Klux Klan bodies of the world meet together in the city of Washington or in the city of Atlanta, and when they must band together as were are bound to gather, representing the white men of the world, then you will have a League of Nations, the like of which the world has never seen. (Much applause.)

Thus was this message of white supremacy carried across the nation's pulpits and platforms by the Klan's large paid speakers bureau.

THE USE OF SYMBOLISM

From the dawn of civilization, from the star of David and the cross symbols have been used in persuasive efforts to arouse and motivate large audiences. Symbols are a facile way to instantly convey complex ideas and identify an organization with an ideology. The American flag is such a symbol; and the bitter debate that takes place in the United States when a small group burns it or defiles it to protest some public policy speaks to its potency as a symbol. Clarke, Tyler, and their associates knew the power of symbols and set about to create several potent ones. They knew, too, that symbols are most effective among the less educated members of a community, a prime target group for Klan membership. Clarke and his staff used these symbols with great effect in their recruiting campaigns:

1. The Bible .... The presence of God
2. The Cross .... Sacrifice and service
3. The Flag .... The Constitution and Bill of Rights
4. The Sword .... Law and Order
5. The Water .... Purity of life, Unity of purpose
6. The Robe .... The righteousness of Christ; the rewards of the hereafter
7. The Mask .... Unselfishness(with our mask we hide our individuality and sink ourselves into the great sea of klankraft.)

The symbol most identified with the Klan was, of course, the fiery cross. Simmons described its significance this way, "It carries the idea of illumination and sacrifice. It symbolizes a love that lights the way to the noblest service; it symbolizes a service that is impelled by a burning love. . . . The World's amelioration is proclaimed by the glowing cross." To millions of non-Klansmen, however, the sudden appearance of a fiery cross on a prominent hillside on the edge of town symbolized the Invisible Empire in their midst and, in time, became a symbol of everything they feared from the Klan. I know this from my own childhood experiences.

The preponderance of symbols and their effective employment augmented the esoteric appeal of the Klan and enhanced an exotic flavor that was popular in the 1920s. This was the age of Art Deco. All of the Klan's Imperial hocus-pocus and mysticism obviously had an appeal to the dirt farmers, shopkeepers, and blue-collar workers whose lives in the 1920s had seen little travel, less adventure, and nothing but hard work grubbing out a living. In his thesis, *Crystallizing Public Hatred*, Shotwell observed:

> The average male citizen of the twenties, whose daily existence had been about as exotic as cornbread and string beans, was suddenly declared an elite by these strange messages designating him as a real man. During the day he would sweep chicken droppings out of the hen houses or sell gingham to elderly spinsters; but at night, clothed in a flowing gown, his face concealed, he could ride on horseback, illuminated by a flaming cross. And all of it in the name of God, America and White Supremacy.

THE NEWSLETTER NETWORK

Samuel Adams and his imaginative band of revolutionaries, in their struggle to bring about the American Revolution, had demonstrated the power of letters in mobilizing public opinion. Newsletters are an effective means of interorganizational communication because they can supplement less frequently published house organs by providing a speedy, inexpensive communication with specifically targeted groups. The resourceful Clarke and his aides were quick to exploit the newsletter. During the early 1920s, nearly every officer in the Klan's chain of command, from Imperial Kleagle down to Exalted Cyclops, sent regular newsletters to his subjects. The *Weekly News-letter*, published by the Imperial Propagation Department, was sent to all Kleagles, with copies forwarded to each chapter's secretary and presiding officer. According to one of Clarke's assistants, the *Weekly News-Letter* conveyed news of "either some event that had been pulled off by Klansmen in some part of the country, or a speech or some happening that we thought would be of propagating interest to Klansmen and would assist them in propagating the Klan." Clarke more than once referred to the newsletters "as a clearing house for Klan activities everywhere." He requested the cyclops to send him "all items of news concerning his Klan and the activities of his Klansmen that would be suitable for publicity purposes." Clarke utilized newsworthy items in the *Weekly News-Letter* and in publicity releases. The newsletters, intended only for internal distribution, were often laced with falsehoods, nor were these letters subtle in regard to the Klan's political aspirations. Often the newspapers got hold of a newsletter and brought the Klan public embarrassment. One of these newsletter, datelined Norfolk, Virginia, June 10, 1921, and endorsed by Clarke, illustrates how the Klan made every effort to appear successful and powerful in the eyes of its members to build espirit de corps:

> We have just taken in the chief of police. . . . We had a hard time getting information regarding him, but when we found he was eligible we had no trouble enlisting him in our ranks, and when he was initiated you never saw a more pleased fellow, he radiated it, and when he learned that he would have our support in upholding the law, he was certainly pleased, especially with our military organization, which was offered him in case of trouble.

Clarke added a personal note to the Norfolk letter. "We call that mighty fine. The Norfolk Klan is working along the right line and deserves to be highly commended for the steps it has taken in the enforcement of law and preservation of order." Clarke had an infinite capacity to turn words on their heads. This letter was leaked to the press, and the Norfolk chief of police vehemently denied that he was a Klansman or that any weapons had been given to him by the Klan. For the most part the newsletters followed no uniform pattern and usually consisted of notices and general information on coming events. Among other things they encouraged church attendance, announced Klan bazaars, reminded members to pay their dues, and extended greetings from the Imperial officers.

THE KLAN'S EXTERNAL PUBLICITY

By the summer of 1921, Clark, Tyler, and their associates had made a great leap from Simmons's early policy of secrecy and no publicity to a full-blown public relations campaign. Clarke was one of the first publicists to employ paid advertising as a publicity tool. He was forced to this task because of the growing public criticism of the Klan and its hate-propagating tactics and deeds. That summer Clarke started to experiment with advertisements in the major dailies in New York, Chicago, Milwaukee, and other cities. He bought full-page or half-page ads. An ad that appeared in the *Chicago Tribune* of August 16, 1921, was typical of these ads designed to tell the Klan's side of the story. It featured a long letter from Simmons denouncing those who had been attacking the Klan, saying that they were "not pure

Americans at heart" and that the Klan would soon become "the greatest force in America to all men that this country shall forever be what its founders intended, THE LAND OF THE FREE AND THE BRAVE."

Clarke entered into contracts for the Klan advertising with Albert Lasker's Lord & Thomas Agency of Chicago and the Massengale Agency in New York City. Not so strangely, Lasker's willingness to take the Klan's money is not mentioned in John Gunther's favorable biography, *Taken at the Flood*. These agencies were unable to persuade some newspapers, to their credit, to run such ads—the *New York World* and the *Louisville Courier—Journal*, for example. The *World* specifically refused because of a letter from Simmons in August 1921 announcing that the Klan was planning to spend $100,000 for advertising but only in newspapers that "stood by" the Klan. The *World* properly saw this ploy as a bribe to get good publicity.

From June 15 to October 1, 1921, the Klan had spent only $13,431.29 for advertising. This money was taken from the Klan's general fund, not from Clarke's propagation fund that only spent $329.43 on advertising in this same period. Clarke, keeping his eye on the dollar through all this promotional-organization effort, was careful to keep as much of the 80% commission for the Southern Publicity Association as he could.

Clarke also utilized billboards in his ad campaign to reach the public. Anyone passing the corner of 28th and Ingersoll Streets in Des Moines, Iowa, in December 1922 would have seen a billboard with black-and-red lettering proclaiming:

STOP! When you speed you violate the law
Good citizens uphold the law
Knights of the Ku Klux Klan

In 1923, the Klan paid for several billboards that they changed weekly, boosting the Klan and its principles. Once again in these and similar billboards, these lawbreakers wrapped themselves in the unctuous garments of upholding the law.

Clarke also fully utilized his journalistic expertise, gained in 7 years on the *Constitution* and in subsequent promotional activities, to spread the message through the nation's press. Clarke knew the way to gain access to the news column was to make things easy for the press. He knew enough not to flood the newspaper with mimeographed releases, instead he chose to supply his news in boilerplate form so that his handout could go directly from the mailroom to the composing room without the editor having a chance to edit his copy. Boilerplate stereotype plates were still in common usage in the 1920s, especially on smaller dailies and weeklies.

Tipped to the photographic appeal of hooded Klansmen, especially those on horseback, by Tracy Mathewson's photos of his counterfeit Klansmen, Clarke made extensive use of photographs in getting public attention through the nation's press. The photos were often fed to newspapers through the Grand Goblins who, in turn, provided them to local newspapers. Most of these publicity shots were taken in 1920 showing garbed Klansmen stiffly posed among the pines of Stone Mountain, Georgia, feigning some portion of their ritual. One picture depicted E. Y. Clarke posing as a nonrobed initiate, kneeling before the sacred altar. At Clarke's left stands a Klansman holding a makeshift fiery cross, its flames fashioned from cardboard, on Clarke's right stands another Klansman. The flag and cardboard fiery cross provide the backdrop. The caption read: "Simmons is congratulating one of his cyclops after a noble achievement." Whatever the noble achievement, the Klansman in the picture is wearing the insignia of the Georgia grand dragon. A later, less circulated series of photos circa 1921–1922 shows Simmons at his desk. He is reading the Bible and the American flag is unfurled behind him. Pictures on his wall include a still photo from *The Birth of a Nation*, a large painting of a mounted Klansman, and a portrait of Mrs. Simmons. Clarke knew how to exploit his chosen symbols—this photograph was intended to identify the Imperial Wizard with God, country, purity of womanhood, and the Klan, all in one shot.

Undoubtedly, the most powerful pictorial appeal of all was supplied by the continuous showings of *The Birth of a Nation*. Unlike most motion pictures that have a theater life of a year or so, *The Birth of a Nation* was shown in motion picture theaters, large and small, for 5 years from 1915 to 1920. As late as 1924, 9 years after its initial release, local Klans were still supporting engagements of the film. In Chicago that year, a Klan-sponsored showing brought in crowds that surpassed house records for the Auditorium Theater. In Milwaukee, the local Klan reserved the Garrick Theater for the week of May 18, 1924, sold tickets, and kept 25% of the take. During these showings, Klansmen stood on the sidewalk in front of the theater and handed out circulars, tracts, and other propaganda before and after the show. One Klan official ordered his Kleagles to take full advantage of the now wrought-up viewers as they emerged from the theater: "When they see the picture, produce a membership form to sign. If they don't sign, then they aren't the type of men we want anyway."

In an effort to exploit the hysteria generated by *The Birth of a Nation*, the Klan produced its own film, *The Face at the Window*. The *Weekly News-Letter* of April 22, 1921, urged Klansmen to see the movie because "it strikingly depicts the serious working of those forces which are antagonistic to all the principles for which the Ku Klux Klan stand and which would tear down and scatter to the four winds those principles, ideals, and institutions inseparably associated with our Government." In the climax of *The Face at the Window*, the Klan rode to rescue and portrayed the triumph of order and decency by real Americans over alien influences. The "face" was intended to refer to "the face of Bolshevism at the window of the United States." This film depicted an attempted overthrow of the United States, with terrible atrocities, prevented at the last moment by members of the American Legion dressed in Klan-like garments. The Red Menace was one of the fear appeals ceaselessly exploited by Clarke and his propagandists. Later, Clarke planned a much more expensive motion picture, one to rival *The Birth of a Nation* at a cost of $400,000. He made an initial agreement with Wheeler Productions of New York City for the film, *Yesterday, To-Day, and Forever*, but the picture never materialized.

KLAN DEVELOPS ITS OWN PRESS

To augment and reinforce his use of other publicity channels, Clarke and Tyler started a newspaper, *The Searchlight*, the only Klan periodical directly sponsored by the Southern Publicity Association. It was sold at newsstands across the country in an effort to bolster the Klan's reputation and attract recruits. *The Searchlight* billed itself as "Not a Moulder but a Chronicler of Public Opinion." To give the new paper credibility, Clarke and Tyler sought and got the joint sponsorship of the Junior Order of United American Mechanics (JOUAM). This outfit was an offshoot of the older Order of United American Mechanics from which it split in 1885. JOUAM found its strength in latching on to whatever nativist movement predominated at the moment.

After a brief decline in the first part of the century, this oddball organization re-emerged in the second decade under a fervent Anglo-Saxon anti-immigrant banner, and by 1914, it had a membership of some 224,000. Historian John Higham wrote, "Indeed, the organization echoed almost every theme in the racial polyphony." Obviously the Klan and the JOUAM had close kinship in their fanning of nativist hatreds, and thus became joint sponsors of the newspaper, although the Klan would never admit its official connection with *The Searchlight*, ostensibly sponsored by JOUAM. The paper that bore the curious motto "Free Speech: Free Press: White Supremacy," sold for 5¢ a copy and was distributed as far west as Butte, Montana, where the *Butte Bulletin* described it as having "four divisions of propaganda." Most prominent are the anti-African-American and anti-Catholic divisions . . . it is also an illuminating example of the anti-Semitic rage which murdered Leo Frank, and imitates the rabid hatred to progressive thought characteristic of A. Mitchell Palmer and E. H. Gray.

The *Searchlight* perceived a loose conspiracy between Jews, Catholics, and Communists against Protestant Americans. According to Shotwell, "It accused the Jews of trying to create a race war . . . not to benefit blacks but to destroy the government." J. O. Wood, a member of the Atlanta City Council, edited the newspaper. "I am the original Ku Klux Klansman," Wood boasted at campaign rallies when he ran for the Georgia General Assembly in 1922, "and I am proud of it. I belong to everything anti-Catholic I know of." He was elected, running almost a thousand votes ahead of the 12-man field. *Searchlight's* associate editor, Carl F. Hutcheson, was Wood's law partner and a member of the Atlanta Board of Education. He created quite a row in 1921 when he wrote an editorial urging the Klan to take up arms against Catholics after newspapers had assailed Tyler's reputation. Less than a week later, Tyler sold her interests in the paper for $1,000.

Tyler left *Searchlight* declaring that she had lost money on it, even though the publication appeared to have substantial income from advertisers, including such prestigious names as Coca-Cola, Studebaker, Elgin Watch Company, and many local advertisers. J. W. Wood continued to edit the paper although its circulation declined because of factional infighting in the Klan in 1923 and 1924. (This is recounted later.) Wood kept the *Searchlight* alive until 1926 as a supportive organ in his race for the U. S. Senate. He was decisively defeated and the *Searchlight* was put out soon thereafter.

In January 1923, the Klan voted to establish an official publication, The *Imperial Night-Hawk*, "by the Klan for the Klan," to carry a weekly message from the Imperial Palace to every Klansman in the country. Unlike the *Searchlight*, it carried no advertisements and was not sold at newsstands. *The Imperial Night-Hawk* was not intended for public consumption and was produced in slick paper, magazine format. According to Shotwell, "*The Imperial Night-Hawk* flourished during the period of the Klan's largest rallies, celebrations, and initiations, and these provided the most colorful copy in what was otherwise a rather dull weekly." This publication featured weekly essays on topics such as "Jews Control Bolshevik Russia and Are Aiding Extension of Communism," "The Blood of White America Must be Kept Pure and Uncontaminated," and "Poorly Restricted Immigration is One of the Greatest Perils Confronting America." The *Imperial Night-Hawk* was first edited by Philip E. Fox, a former Dallas newspaper editor; later he was replaced by Milton Elrod, former editor of *The Fiery Cross*. Noting that there was a marked reduction in nativist content in the *Night-Hawk* after Elrod took over, Shotwell thought Elrod "might possibly have been the most sensitive public relations man to serve the Klan." Elrod later established a national Klan newspaper with regional editions.

Thus did publicists Clarke and Tyler pull out all the stops and use all known channels of public communication and internal communication to promote Klan membership and thus enrich themselves at the expense of the public weal. It was inevitable that their hate campaigns would produce a violent reaction. This was not long in coming.

AND ITS OWN UNIVERSITY

The Knights of the Ku Klux Klan announced on September 10, 1921, that the Klan had acquired Lanier University, a Baptist-related institution, located in the fashionable Druid Hills section of Atlanta, according to *The New York Times* of September 12 of that year. Colonel Simmons announced that he would become the institution's president and that Lanier henceforth would be devoted to the teaching of the principles of "one hundred percent Americanism." General Nathan Bedford Forrest, grandson of the founder of the original Klan, was appointed secretary and business manager of this educational front for the Klan. The Klan's announcement from its plush headquarters on Peachtree Street in Atlanta boasted that professors of the highest qualifications would be recruited to supplement the existing faculty and that a million dollars would be spent to expand and improve the Lanier campus. According to historian Thomas G. Dyer, "While the press and the general public greeted the project with some skepticism, no one challenged the Klan's declaration that it had only recently become an important part of the scene at Lanier. In truth, the Invisible Empire had wielded a powerful influence over the college's affairs since it first opened four years earlier."

Lanier had been founded by C. Lewis Fowler, an ambitious Southern Baptist minister–educator who promoted the notion that Atlanta and the South needed an "All Southern" university. Frustrated in his efforts to get a large gift from Asa Candler, the soft drink manufacturer, who had given Emory College a big boost with a $1 million gift, Fowler turned to the Klan for financial assistance. Although Fowler made no public announcement of a Klan connection with Lanier, his several steps left little doubt that the school was sympathetic to Klan principles. All the college's advertisements announced in bold print that Lanier was an "ALL SOUTHERN" university, launched by "the best Southern men." Although the editor of the *Christian Index*, Louie D. Newton, was expressing his fear that Fowler was fronting for the Klan, the local press, Atlanta's elite, and the Baptist establishment seemed unperturbed by this possibility. This fact again affirms the lack of protest of this burgeoning source of racism and bigotry by the so-called decent forces of society.

The Lanier presidency only added to the difficulties that were plaguing Simmons in the winter and spring of 1921–1922. According to Dyer, "Faced with the certainty that Lanier would not survive, challenged from within by a new cadre of Klan leaders who sought to depose him, the Imperial Wizard and President of Lanier took a six-months 'rest' from his duties. Because of the financial burden it had come to be, the Klan was ready to quit its Lanier connection." By 1922, Imperial Headquarters had put at least $77,000 into the college's operation, but this was a pittance against the heavy debts that

Fowler had run up. The Klan agreed to put the institution into bankruptcy, thus on August 7, 1922, bankruptcy proceedings were commenced in the federal district court of Atlanta. This bankruptcy marked the end of their "careers" in higher education for William J. Simmons and C. Lewis Fowler. Whereas Simmons was excommunicated from the Klan in 1923, Fowler won the support of the new Klan leadership and became one of the most widely traveled and best known Klan organizers.

THE *NEW YORK WORLD* EXPOSES THE KLAN

The *New York* World's exposé was triggered by a Henry Peck Fry of East Tennessee. Fry was attracted to the Klan because of the "high caliber" of the members he met and began working part time as a recruiter. Immediately after Fry was sworn in as a full-fledged Kleagle, he became suspicious. According to Shotwell, "The Kleagle's Pledge of Loyalty that he was required to sign as a promise of unswerving loyalty to a man named William Joseph Simmons, somehow seemed to contradict his other obligations. He was an Army reserve officer and this devotion to the monarch of an Invisible Empire made him uncomfortable. The full-page ads he saw in the Knoxville newspapers did nothing to allay his apprehensions. To the contrary, because his Masonic Order did not advertise. As reports of acts of violence by masked men continued, Fry became quite nervous about his Klan membership. The last straws were when one of his young friends advocated that the Klan "bust up a restaurant owned by Greeks as an object lesson that they are not wanted in Johnson City," and when local businessmen started withdrawing advertising from the Johnson City *Staff* when it berated the Klan, Fry, in Shotwell's words, "smelled a rat under the sheets."

In June 1921, Henry Peck Fry, ex-Kleagle ex-Klansman, gathered up all the documents, propaganda, and correspondence he had accrued and took them to New York City where he turned them over to Herbert Bayard Swope, executive editor of the *New York World*. Swope saw a blockbuster of a story in the Klan papers but wanted verification. He organized a team of reporters who spent July though August 1921 investigating the Klan under the direction of Rowland Thomas, novelist and short story writer. In all, some 30 reporters worked on the story. The *New York World's* exposé began on September 6, 1921, the eye of a hurricane that had been building for nearly a year. As noted earlier, *the World*, had run its first major Klan story on October 10, 1920, bringing the Klan its first national attention. The 3-week period from September 6 to September 28, 1921, was crowded with sensational stories, but the *World* gave its top play to the Klan with one devastating headline after another. The *World's* circulation jumped by

60,000. Other major newspapers—the *Boston Globe*, the *St. Louis Post-Dispatch*, the *Cleveland Plain Dealer*, the *Milwaukee Journal*, and others—picked up the series to give the exposé a national impact. The *World* implicated the Klan in more than 150 specified acts of terrorism, including murder, mutilation, and tarring and feathering. The articles portrayed Klansmen as law-defying vigilantes, hate mongers, or innocent ones. The newspaper printed some of the Klan's most viciously bigoted *Searchlight* passages, propaganda, and Klan news letters.

The most glaring fusillade, however, was fired at "The Big Three," Simmons, Clarke, and Tyler, who were depicted as vicious aggrandizers, feeding upon the fears and prejudices of a nation to enrich themselves. Clarke's first reaction was predictable—he threatened to sue the *World* for $10 million and said that he was engaged in notifying the 200 lawyers the Klan had contacted 2 days earlier. This proved an idle threat. Elizabeth Tyler, the Klan's mystery woman who had remained very much behind the scenes until the *World* made her a national celebrity, took the first constructive action after the *World* series broke. She went to New York, rented a suite in one of the city's poshest hotels, and opened it up to the press. When she arrived she told a *Times* reporter that she had come to New York to shop, that the Klan was the least of her worries. Nevertheless, she released statements to the press, granted interviews, and generally radiated goodwill and glowing propaganda for the Klan. She accused the newspapers of being "most unfair" and of printing "malicious and damaging statements" but thanked them for the publicity, adding that thousands of new applications were flooding the Imperial Palace. Tyler gave the press a complete breakdown of how the $10 donation distributed among the Kleagles and Goblins. The $4.50 that wound up in the offices of the Southern Publicity Association went mostly for "rent, clerk hire, stenographic expenses, the cost of literature, as well as the cost of Klan supplies furnished to each chapter." Tyler insisted that she was "just a business woman" and that the Southern Publicity Association was legitimate business with a high overhead and low-profit margin. Before she left New York, she had impressed even the *World* reporters with her apparent sincerity. She even softened her stand against the *World*, saying that it had been misled by its informants. Not long after Tyler returned to Atlanta, her *Searchlight* switched from weekly to daily publication to respond to the growing barrage of media attacks. Unlettered she may have been, but Bessie Tyler was a skillful publicist.

HEARST JOINS THE ATTACK

Soon Clarke and Tyler found themselves in the cross-fire of one of nation's historic and bitter circulation wars, that between the *World* and William

Randolph Hearst's New York *American*. "The Chief directed C. Anderson Wright, former chief of staff of the ill-fated Knights of the Air, to syndicate a series of twenty articles exposing the Klan." The *American* billed Wright as an "ex-Grand Goblin" though he never rose above the rank of Kleagle. Wright's revelations, superficial and exaggerated, suggested that he was not the "insider" he pretended to be. He mistakenly called the Southern Publicity Association the Imperial Palace. His main theme was that Tyler was the "real power behind the Klan" with a Rasputin-like hold over Simmons and Clarke, a rich irony for an organization of White males only. He later wrote a play, *Masked Men*, a drama denigrating the Klan and exalting Catholics, Jews, and African Americans. He also tried to capitalize on his anti-Klan series by organizing "Knights of the Tiger Eye" as an anti-Klan group. Both the play and Knights bombed. The *American* and the *World* were the only two New York City newspapers to expose the Klan. The good grey *Times* thought the *World* and *American* were "properly but somewhat excessively excited" about the Klan. In August 1922, the *Literary Digest* sent out over a hundred letters to newspaper editors in sections of the country where the Klan was strong and received hundreds of editorials in reply, not one favorable to the Klan. Even E. Y. Clarke was forced to admit that at least 80% of the daily newspapers were bitterly attacking the Klan. However, it should be noted that the Klan received little press opposition in its home realm of Georgia.

The *Atlanta Constitution* that years later under the courageous editorship of Ralph McGill attacked the Klan unceasingly was in Clarke's time most cautious in its treatment of the Klan. The Clarke family ties with the newspaper stretched back nearly 50 years, and the managing editor at the time was Francis Clarke, E. Y.'s brother. There is no evidence that the editor was a member of the Klan, but the fact remains the paper published no unfavorable stories in the early 1920s. The rival *Atlanta Journal* also stayed above the controversy because its editor, John S. Cohen, was fearful of triggering more anti-Semitism if he fought the Klan. The only Atlanta daily to criticize the Klan was Hearst's *Georgian*. Curiously, the *Georgian* carried the *World's* series of articles, not the *American's*.

In this context, it is important to understand that the Atlanta "Establishment" supported the Klan. By 1923, its members included Mayor Walter A. Sims, Sheriff Thomas I. Lowry, Governor Clifford Walker, U. S. Representative William D. Upshaw, and both United States Senators—Walter F. George and James L. Harris. A former *Atlanta Journal* reporter, Ward Greene, later observed, "There was also, to put it bluntly, the money. A new million-dollar industry within your gates is not be hooted at." Senator George resigned from the Klan in 1923 because he anticipated that he might be called as a witness in the case of a Texas Senator whose seat was being contested because he had been financed by the Klan.

THE BEGINNING OF THE END FOR CLARKE
AND TYLER

Clarke and Tyler's get-rich-quick scheme of building the Ku Klux Klan into a multimillion member national organization was dealt a stunning blow on September 19, 1921, when the *New York World* dropped a bomb that proved to be the beginning of the end for Clarke and Tyler and their Southern Publicity Association. On that date, the *World* revealed that on October 3, 1919, Clarke's wife May, her brother, and a policeman had discovered Clarke and Tyler sleeping together at Tyler's home. Mrs. Clarke had the pair arrested and hauled away in their pajamas to police court where they gave their names as "Jim Slaton and Mrs. Carroll." After spending a night in jail, Clarke and Tyler were tried under their real names and convicted of "disorderly conduct." Additional charges of possession of whiskey were dropped when Tyler's son-in-law, J. Q. Jett, who worked for the firm, stepped in and claimed possession of the liquor and paid the fine. May Clarke filed for divorce on October 18, 1919, charging that her husband had deserted her and their young son 3 years before. The divorce did not materialize when the Clarkes reached a settlement. With his new-found income, Clarke placated her with a new home, but the couple remained separated. This incident had gone unreported in Atlanta's papers.

Clarke tried mightily to suppress the story. When the September 21 *World* hit the Atlanta newsstands, Clarke frantically sent henchmen all over town buying up copies from vendors at 3¢ more than the 7¢ price. When this was unsuccessful, Clarke called a news conference. He confided to a *Georgian* reporter that he and Tyler had been living together in 1919. He claimed he was ill, and his partner had taken him in. Tyler, for her part, issued a statement to the press calling the entire story "a malicious lie." In part, her statement read, "Trying to injure an organization which stands primarily for the protection of womanhood by stooping so low as to unjustly attack the character of an innocent woman will not help their side. Shame on them, is all I have to say." Next Clarke stormed into the *Georgian's* news room to demand that editor print a complete retraction of its story. Clarke fell back on the hoary excuse that he had been misquoted and misinterpreted. The *Georgian* decided to check the story out and sent a reporter to the police records of October 3, 1919. The records were missing. The Solicitor General, John A. Boykin, a Klan member, promised a "vigorous investigation." None materialized. In this comedy of errors, publicists Clarke and Tyler violated the public relations fundamental that one does nothing to keep a bad story alive.

Exacerbated by their inept handling of it, this scandal began to erode their position in the Klan. A New Jersey Kleagle wired Simmons to fire Clarke and Tyler or else his "entire house" would fall down. When Tyler found this out, she fired the Kleagle without consulting either Clarke or Simmons. She was confident she had the power to throw "the scoundrel" out. The next day, Tyler asserted her independence by appearing before a closed meeting of the Klan. Constantly referring to the press as "the enemy" she declared, "[We] have what we consider authentic information that the enemy intends to stop at nothing to besmirch the names of the officials of the Ku Klux Klan. They are going to attack me personally from every angle." She dramatically offered her resignation that was unanimously rejected. However, on September 24, Clarke sent Simmons a long letter requesting that he accept his and Tyler's resignation to save her from "attacks by the enemy." Clarke did this without consulting Tyler, and she was furious. Two hours after Clarke leaked his letter to the press, she issued a statement damning her partner and erstwhile lover as "weak kneed" because he would not stand by his guns. Tyler saw her easy money going down the drain. Simmons did not accept the resignations.

While Clarke and Tyler were squabbling across the front pages, they apparently lost their grip on their own propaganda system. On September 28, an editorial in *Searchlight* entitled "American Patriots, Hark!" urged citizens to take up arms to defend Tyler's honor. In his editorial, Carl F. Hutcheson commanded Klansmen to "unleash your dogs of war and make these hounds of convict stripe pay penalty for the great injury done." He aimed his fire at Roman Catholics whom he charged "controlled the press of the nation."

The fiery editorial drew the attention of U. S. postal authorities, who threatened action under Section 480 of the postal laws and regulations providing penalties for inciting murder, arson, or assassination. Hutcheson wrote a weak retraction. The *World* properly pointed out that the Hutcheson editorial demonstrated that whoever was directing the Klan's publicity "had slipped a cog."

The closing days of the *World's* exposure brought more skeletons falling out of Clarke's closet. The paper revealed that Clarke had allegedly embezzled $1,108.59 while handling a fund drive for the Theodore Roosevelt Memorial Association. The association brought charges against the Southern Publicity Association, but Solicitor General Boykin never found time to press these charges either. Next an enterprising *Georgian* reporter dug further back in Clarke's past and found that he had been expelled from the First Congregational Methodist Church of Atlanta in 1910 for "lying, extortion, fraudulent and unjust dealings, improper handling of funds, false and malicious slander, inordinate ambition, hypocrisy, and treachery." Quite a bill of indictment! This was an outgrowth of Clarke's selling the church elders $150,000 worth of stock in the Congregational Methodist Publishing House that proved in 3 years, to be worth only $2\frac{1}{2}$¢ on the dollar. According to the *World*, Clarke formed a number of such phony corporations from 1907 to 1910, "all of which showed the same attempt to rear big promotions on small foundations." Clarke and Simmons had not only their character in common; both had been thrown out of their churches.

CLARKE AND TYLER BECOME DESPERATE

Feeling their money-making empire crumbling from within, Clarke and Tyler resorted to some desperate measures to create the illusion of "a grand conspiracy" against them. At about 10 p.m. on October 11, 1921, an Atlanta *Constitution* reporter got a phone call, "I just want to tell you that we got Mrs. Tyler tonight." The caller then hung up. The reporter called the police and found that they were investigating a shooting at Mrs. Tyler's home on Howell Mill Road. A gun had fired five shots through a window of her home, but she was unhurt. The paper quickly assumed that there had been an attempt to assassinate Mrs. Tyler. One of Clarke's former employees later averred that the shooting had been staged. Whether or not, there does appear to have been an effort on the part of the Big Three to gain support through sympathy. On the day after the incident, Clarke announced that gunmen from New York had been hired to kill officers of the Klan. As press criticism intensified, all three dramatized their various illnesses.

The real danger to the end of this lucrative account was coming from within the Klan, born of a resentment easy to understand. The press had made it clear that Clarke and Tyler were becoming quite wealthy through their arrangement with the Imperial Wizard. Records that Simmons had provided earlier to the House of Representatives showed that since he had turned over the Propagation Department to the Southern Publicity Association, they had received $225,568. Two days later, Clarke said he had pocketed only $16,000 of that sum. He claimed the remainder had gone for expenses. However, Clarke did not mention his income from his independent Klan-related endeavors. After the Southern Publicity Association joined forces with the Klan, the Klan regalia contract was turned over to the Gate City Manufacturing Company, newly established by C. B. and Lottie Davis, who were undoubtedly Clarke and Tyler. The Klan paid Gate City $4 for the robes and masks and sold them to Klansmen for $6.50, a two-way profit for Clarke and Tyler. ("Klansmen were forbidden to make their own robes.) Clarke also owned a realty company that specialized in land purchases for the Klan. Tyler's Searchlight Publishing Co. handled all the Klan's printing. Within a few months after the newspaper exposures brought a large wave of Klan applications and donations, the income of Clarke and Tyler rose by an estimated $40,000. Such a bubble would burst sooner or later.

THE THIEVES FALL OUT

Despite Clarke's continued efforts to divert attention from the widely publicized scandals involving him and Tyler by discrediting the critics, opinion was building in the Klan that Clarke and Tyler were hurting "the cause" by creating dissension in the ranks. This move was led by the four Grand Goblins of the Northeastern domain who went to Atlanta to confront Simmons with their demand that Clarke and Tyler had to be fired. Simmons caved in but then backed down. On December 21, 1921, the disgruntled Goblins took their case to the press. In the Propagation Department, the Goblins ranked second only to Clarke and Tyler. When the Goblins made public their demands, Simmons responded by firing their spokesman. He then quickly departed for a vacation, leaving Clarke in charge of the Klan. The remaining three protesters quit the Klan the next day.

A week later, Simmons announced that a committee of 13 had looked into the charges against Clarke and Tyler and had fully exonerated them. This whitewash, like many others over the next 11 months that came from the Imperial Palace over Simmons' name, was in all probability written by Clarke because Simmons was on leave. By mid-December the publicists were dealt another body blow when Z. R. Upchurch, who had worked with the Southern Publicity Association since well before the firm had taken on the Klan account, published an affidavit that the Klan proper was nearly bankrupt whereas the Propagation Department was accumulating great wealth. Upchurch then joined forces with the deposed Goblins and 169 other Klansmen to file a petition on December 21, 1921, for receivership of all property, funds, documents, and records of the Klan. On March 7, 1922, the petition was denied by the Fulton County Superior Court. A subsequent appeal to the State Supreme Court was unsuccessful. Clarke had won the first round.

In early 1922, Tyler announced that she was resigning because of the illness of her daughter, Mrs. J. Q. Jett. Apparently this was a diversionary tactic, because she continued to work in the Imperial Palace and collect her portion of the commissions. The tactic appeared to work momentarily because there were few disruptions over the next 6 months. In June, Simmons announced a prolonged leave of absence and made Clarke Imperial Wizard Pro Tem. Clarke found that there was too much administrative detail for him to handle, so he hired as his assistant Hiram W. Evans, a cut-rate dentist from Dallas, and turned over most of the propagation work to Tyler. To make a position for Evans, who had earlier gained fame in Texas as a Masonic leader, Clarke decided to force out the secretary, Louis D. Wade, a Bell Telephone executive. Wade fought back; he stormed into the courts to allege what other Klansmen has suspected for some time—that Clarke had "gained complete control" over Simmons. After Wade publicized his charges, other Klansmen added others. The collapse of Clarke's popularity was accelerated in the autumn of 1922 when he was indicted separately for violation of the Volstead Act and Section 215 of the postal code. The first arrest came in Muncie, Indiana, where he had gone to address a Klan rally, and police officers, acting on a tip, found a bottle of liquor in his luggage. He decried that he had been framed—as he probably had been.

The postal code violation, much more serious, was for using the mails to defraud. This grew out of charges for the four dissident Goblins that Clarke had a "rake-off" of bonds required of all high officials of the Klan. He had obtained a blanket bond contract with a surety company, then charged premiums that left him a profit. Although Clarke was never prosecuted for these two charges, the arrests prompted him to remove himself from the Klan's helm. Clarke's resignation may have been prompted by fear of future probes by the Department of Justice.

His enemies in the Klan continued to hound Clarke. In March 1923, someone's "investigators" turned over evidence to the Justice Department that led to Clarke's arrest for violation of the Mann (White Slave Traffic) Act. Clarke had persuaded a young lady from Houston, A Miss Laurel Martin, 22, to come to New Orleans where she registered in a hotel February 11, 1921, as Mrs. E. Y. Clarke. Five days after Clarke's arrest, the new Imperial Wizard Hiram Evans canceled his propagation contract for "the good of the order" and severed all Clarke's official connections with the Klan. Evans proclaimed that money incoming from propagation activities would "henceforth be turned back into the extension of the order." Clarke called his arrest "simply another effort to discredit me and, through discrediting me, damage the Knights of the Ku Klux Klan." Nevertheless, he pleaded guilty a year later and was fined $5,000.

Whatever romantic relations Tyler had with Clarke in the past, she remarried in late 1923 to Stephen Grow, an Atlanta film entrepreneur. Not long after the propagation contract was canceled and her Klan income cut off, Bessie Tyler Grow moved to California where she died in 1924. According to the Edgar I. Fuller in *The Visible of the Invisible Empire of the Maelstrom*, Tyler left Atlanta with $750,000.

Clarke made one final grandstand play to bolster his badly damaged public reputation. In late December 1923, he wrote a long letter to President Coolidge denouncing the Klan as a "cheap political machine." Clarke told the President that he was speaking for thousands of magnificent men in offering his assistance for "either forcing the lawless element out of the Klan" or else "stamping out . . . the menace the Ku Klux Klan had become." The White House rebuked Clarke for giving his letter to the press before it had reached the White House. Coolidge's spokesman observed, correctly, that the letter was written more for publicity than for consideration by the Chief Executive.

Trying to capitalize on the growing rift in the Klan between Hiram Evans and Colonel Simmons, Clarke made one final last-gasp effort to restore himself to power in the Klan. Less than a week after his letter to Coolidge, Clarke called for a "National Congress" of the Klan to meet in Atlanta on February 26, 1924, to consider methods of eliminating existing evils in the order. Evans took Clarke's threat seriously and struck a deal with Simmons, paying him $146,500 to abandon all his disruptive activities. Simmons bought the deal and never again meddled in Klan affairs. This crook too had enriched himself. Clarke held his national congress anyway, but only 150 of the "hundreds of thousands of magnificent men" showed up. Under Imperial Wizard Evans, the Klan reached a peak membership of an estimated 4 to 6 million. The Klan's descent from power after 1925 was almost as spectacular as the clandestine order's ascension. The membership dropped to some 2 million in 1926, plummeted to 350,000 by 1927, and sunk to a scattered 200,000 in 1928. Yet the small remnants active today continue to blight and divide American society, an ugly monument to the avarice and skill of two unprincipled publicists.

WOMEN'S KKK IS FORMED

The departure of Clarke and Tyler and the ensuing struggle for power between Evans and Simmons left the Klan in disarray but opened the way for the formation of the Women's Ku Klux Klan, a story told in an excellent history by Kathleen M. Blee, *Women of the Klan*. Evans and Simmons believed that the Klansmen were now ready to accept women, however grudgingly. Blee wrote, "Before women were admitted officially to the Klan, informal Klan auxiliaries and woman's patriotic societies provided an opportunity for many women to participate in Klan work." Tyler herself had been a member of Ladies of the Invisible Eye, a woman's organization with close ties to the KKK. In 1923, Evans induced the Imperial Kloncilium to establish the Women of the Ku Klux Klan (WKKK). In the asendency of the Klan in 1923 and 1924, Women of the Ku Klux Klan had chapters in 39 states and was especially strong in Indiana, where the Klan held sway over Indiana's politics. D. C. Stephenson, who eventually became Grand Dragon of the Klan, built the Klan into a powerhouse in that state where at that time 97% of the population was native born, White, and Protestant. For the women, according to Blee, "Belonging to the Klan became a complete way of life as they participated in youth groups, family picnics, floats in local parades, and exhibits at county fairs." This post-Tyler–Clarke development has no part in my story, added here as a footnote.

CLARKE TRIES TO BUILD ANOTHER KLAN

Having found riches in propagating hatred and bigotry, the greedy Clarke wouldn't give up. The 150 Klansmen who joined him in Atlanta on February 26, 1924, were persuaded to form the Knights of the Mystic Clan to avowedly oppose the Klan ruled by Hiram Evans. In July 1924, Clarke changed the name of the "Mystic Kingdom and took what he described as a broad approach." "The Kingdom would weld together the Protestant white people of the world into a universal movement for the furtherance of the Protestant faith and the preservation of racial integrity." Claiming a strength of 5,000, Clarke announced that the organization would build a $1 million maternity hospital in Atlanta and a $2 million narcotics sanitarium in Chicago. A conservatory of music was also in the pie-in-the-sky plans for the future.

As the Mystic Kingdom began to fade, Clarke saw in the Dayton, Tennessee, Scopes Trial a more specific cause around which to build his order. In early 1926, he formed the "Supreme Kingdom" to "drive out of the schools and colleges of the nation all proponents of evolution, atheism, or revolution." This charlatan publicist knew no bounds. In May 1924, Clarke announced a $5 million drive for funds. Clarke opened his new order to Jews and Catholics, banned the use of the hoods and masks, and charged no initiation fee. The membership fees went into a separate entity, the Organization Service Company, of which Clarke was president. His most recent female companion, Martha Mason, was the Kingdom's secretary. Later Clarke changed the name of his organization to Esskaye and surfaced next in Chicago in 1932 with grandiose plans to end the Great Depression. This get-rich-quick scheme soon brought him afoul of the Illinois securities laws. He evaded prosection by invalidating the phony contracts he had issued before the case was adjudicated. His escape was only temporary.

On May 4, 1934, E. Y. Clarke and Martha Mason Clarke were convicted in U.S. District Court on six of seven counts charging use of the mails to defraud in connection with Esskaye. On July 19, 1934, Clarke was sentenced to 5 years in the Atlanta Penitentiary and his wife 2 years in women's prison. Clarke at some point won parole from prison.

CLARKE ENDS LIFE AS FUGITIVE

The last known trace of Edward Young Clarke, flamboyant publicist and avaricious conniver, occurred on March 25, 1949. He apparently had violated his parole and was being escorted from New York to the Atlanta Penitentiary when he escaped from his parole supervisor at a Philadelphia train station. Clarke was 73 at the time. In a letter to me dated March 1,

1990, the Federal Bureau of Investigation confirmed this: "A search of the National Archives, Reidsville Georgia State Penitentiary, and the U. S. Penitentiary in Atlanta, Georgia has revealed no further information." Thus this sad chapter in public relations history ends in an aura of mystery.

The secret of the success of the Southern Publicity's Association's campaign, wrote historian John Higham, "lay essentially in the mood and circumstances of 1920." Whether this hate-mongering terroristic organization would have materialized in all its destructive, divisive results without the organizing and propaganda skills supplied by Edward Y. Clarke and Bessie Tyler can be only a matter of speculation. What did flow from their skills and efforts to enrich themselves remains forever a discredit to them and to the vocation of which they were a part. This is a dark side of public relations history.

A nagging "if" question remains: Although the nation's public climate in the early 1920's was ripe for exploitation of its fears and hatreds, would the KKK have become a national force for evil if these two unprincipled but shrewd publicists–promoters had not happened along in 1920?

NOTES ON SOURCES

This chapter relies heavily on the research of Lt. Col. John M. Shotwell, USMC, that he did for his master's thesis, *Crystallizing Public Hatred; Ku Klux Klan Public Relations in the Early 1920s,* written under my direction at the University of Wisconsin-Madison in 1974. Lt. Col. Shotwell used the archives of the State Historical Society of Wisconsin, of Emory University Library, and the Atlanta Historical Society, and other sources. My debt to Lt. Col. Shotwell is large indeed.

Another major source was Wyn Craig Wade's *The Fiery Cross: The Ku Klux Klan in America,* Simon & Schuster, 1987. The quotations from Wade's book are used with the permission of his agent, John Hawkins & Associates, Inc. Wade holds the copyright.

Other major sources included: Leonard Dinnerstein, *The Leo Frank Case,* The University of Georgia Press, Brown Thrasher Edition, 1987; Edgar I. Fuller, *The Visible of the Invisible Empire, or the Maelstrom*, Maelstrom Publishing Co., 1925; John Higham, *Strangers in the Land: Patterns of Nativism 1860–1925*, Rutgers University Press, 2nd ed., 1963; E. J. Kahn, Jr., *The World of Swope,* Simon and Schuster, 1965; Robert K. Murray, *Red Scare: A Study in National Hysteria,* University of Minnesota Press, 1955; Kathleen M. Blee, *Women of the Klan,* University of California Press, 1991; Richard K. Tucker, *The Dragon and the Cross, The Rise and Fall of the Ku Klux Klan in Middle America,* Archon Books, 1991; and Curt Gentry, *J. Edgar Hoover the Man and His Secrets,* Norton, 1991.

Extensive use was also made of Klan publications and its periodical press. An exhaustive bibliography of Klan literature was compiled by Lenwood G. Davis and Janet Sims-Ward, *The Ku Klux Klan, a Bibliography*, Greenwood Press, 1984. The account of the Klan's use of Lanier University as a front is based on Thomas G. Dyer's "The Klan on Campus: C. Lewis Fowler and Lanier University," *The South Atlantic Quarterly*, Autumn 1975. For a harrowing tale of latter day Klan violence against the Jews of Mississippi, read Jack Nelson's *Terror in the Night, The Klan's Campaign Against the Jews*, Simon & Schuster, 1993.

Chapter 15

John W. Hill: Builder of an Enduring Legacy

Like his fellow pioneer and longtime friend, Pendleton Dudley, John Wiley Hill was born and reared in agricultural America (the 1900 census was the nation's first to show more people employed in industry than in agriculture) and like Dudley, Hill built a successful career as a public relations counselor to corporate giants of industrial America. Unlike Dudley's agency that faded from the scene in the late 1980s, Hill's public relations firm, Hill and Knowlton, Inc., continues as one of the world's largest public relations firms. Of all the major firms started by the innovative band of men in the post World War I era, only one other still survives—Ketchum that Public Relations, Inc., which had its genesis when Carlton and George Ketchum opened a publicity office in Pittsburgh in 1919. The brothers split in 1923, Carlton going on to build a highly successful fund-raising firm and George an equally successful advertising and public relations agency.

John Hill's career reflects the growth of public relations from an uncertain shaky publicity vocation into the large and vital field of endeavor that today employs some 150,000 persons in the United States and exerts a powerful influence on American society and on international relations. When John Hill opened what he defined at the time as a "corporate publicity office", in 1927, he rented an office for $100 a month and paid for one tenth of the time of a secretary in a joint office arrangement. In July 1980, the Hill and Knowlton firm he built was sold to the J. Walter Thompson Group for $28 million. Reflecting the growing internationalization and merger of advertising and public relations firms, the J. Walter Thompson Group was brought by the England-based WPP Group for $585 million in 1987. If he were alive, John Hill would boggle at these numbers.

John W. Hill died Thursday, March 17, 1977, at his home in Manhattan after a brief illness. He was 86. Hill had relinquished active management of his now far-flung public relations empire in 1962. Although no longer active in client service, he continued as a member of the firm's policy committee until his death. Until his last illness. Hill kept a battery of secretaries busy and quite a few others at H&K by strenuously kibitzing the firm's major accounts. His kibitzing was taken seriously because although he was now only a minority stockholder, he remained the towering, dominant figure he had always been. In the 1970s he had moved the majority of his H&K stock into the John W. Hill Foundation. Thus, Hill's public relations career spanned a half-century — a momentous half-century of public relations. His career's longevity was second only to that of Edward L. Bernays and Pendelton Dudley.

John W. Hill was born on a farm near Shelbyville, Indiana, on November 26, 1890, the third of four sons of T. Wiley and Catherine (Jamison) Hill. He spent his early years on the farm where he developed a deep sentimental attachment for horses and farm life, a feeling he manifested until his death. In his latter years after he had achieved affluence, Hill was happiest when horseback riding or puttering about his farm at Towners, New York. The Hill papers in the Mass Communications History Center of the State Historical Society of Wisconsin are replete with instructions to his farmhands on the care and feeding of his horses, hay bills to be paid, and so forth. An avid horseman, Hill's most enjoyable vacations were on a dude ranch in the West.

Hill was often nostalgic about the "homeplace." In May 1957, he wrote a boyhood friend, General Daniel Wray De Prez, "Your description of the house gives me a nostalgic feeling and a desire to come out that way before too long. It was built by my grandfather, James Hill, during the Civil War days. Stones for the front porch and other uses were brought there by oxen teams from Flat Rock."

In a letter to Colonel George Hamel written November 18, 1965, John Hill recalled his family roots:

My grandfather migrated from Kentucky to Indiana and became a wealthy farmer, with a separate farm for each of his five children. My father, Wiley, the youngest, was the only one who went to college and he chose Wabash. He returned to the farm, but after his marriage he went to Wichita, Kansas, where he owned and operated a grain elevator. After some years this failed and he returned to Shelbyville. He was a first rate farmer but a poor business manager and died poor.

In his early youth, John Hill developed an urge to write. In his later years, he recalled that he had started a novel when he was about 10. He became an avid reader, too. In a letter to another boyhood friend, Hill recalled, "Your letter takes me back many years to my boyhood and the busy drugstore of Morrison and De Prez on Harrison Street. It was in this store that someone each day delivered the *Indianapolis News* — a great newspaper in its day and my steady diet for years. And my father always went there to get his paper and a handful of five-cent cigars before going around the corner to the livery stable for his horse and buggy to drive home." In an interview with your author, Hill couldn't recall any discernable family influence that led him into newspaper reporting and thence into public relations. Surely his avid reading of the daily of the *Indianapolis News* and of the Shelbyville dailies had an influence. Also an older brother, Joseph, preceded John into the newspaper field. At the time of his death in 1947, Joseph Hill was editor of the *Palm Beach Post-Times* in West Palm Beach, Florida. John Hill died 30 years later.

Following his graduation from Shelbyville High School, Hill was hired as a reporter for the Shelbyville *Republican* at a salary of $6 a week. After about a year he moved over to the competing *Shelbyville Democrat* for a slight increase in pay. Hill subsequently left the *Democrat* to take a job on the Akron, Ohio, *Press*, that he got through a reporter he had befriended. Hill worked in Akron the spring and summer of 1911. By this time he had come to realize that he needed more education if he were to continue in journalism. That fall he enrolled in Indiana University with the intention to major in English and journalism. After a year at Indiana, Hill, who had a first-rate mind, decided that he was not getting the education he needed. After a lot of brooding about it, Hill decided to leave the university and return to the big white farmhouse in Shelby County to devote himself to reading.

Everyman's Library became his university, and he obtained boxes of volumes ranging from the Greek philosophers, Plato and Socrates, down through the ages to Francis Bacon, Boswell's Johnson, Thomas Huxley, William Hazlett, Charles Lamb, and other famous writers. Although he returned to Indiana University for 1 more year, he continued to educate himself with intensive reading, sometimes for 15 hours a day, over a period of some 3 years. Hill wrote Colonel Hamel that this concentrated reading program instilled in him a love of reading that persisted through his adult life. Hill wrote Hamel that he believed that this reading, together with his early newspaper experience, formed the foundation on which he built his success in public relations. Hill quit Indiana University for good in 1912. Although he never earned a baccalaureate degree, Hill in his mature life developed a deep interest in higher education. In his later years, he made substantial contributions to Harvard and Boston Universities to support public relations and business education. Indiana University and Boston University awarded him honorary doctorates late in his life.

After leaving Indiana University, Hill's next newspaper job was as a reporter on the Akron, Ohio, *Beacon-Journal*, a newspaper owned by Congressman Charles Knight. Knight's son, John, later to lead the large newspaper chain, Knight-Ridder, was working as a cub reporter on the paper during school vacations.

While in Akron, Hill had an idea for a small daily newspaper, a tabloid, to be published in a large city. Convinced that such a newspaper offered a road to riches, Hill quit the *Beacon-Journal* and went to Chicago. Hill persuaded a young man, Gordon Ingalls, son of a wealthy widow, of the feasibility of his idea. Ingalls got the requisite financial backing from his mother. As a result, the *Chicago Daily Digest* was born in the spring of 1913. Hill handled all the editorial chores and Ingalls sold advertising. Hill later claimed that this was the first big city tabloid. The young publishers sold their newspapers to restaurants where they were distributed with the menus. Circulation income proved insufficient to pay publication costs, and Ingalls couldn't sell enough advertising to keep the tabloid afloat. Ingall's mother saw this and cut off her funds; this was the end of the *Chicago Daily Digest*. Six years later Capt. Joseph Patterson proved the validity of young Hill's idea with the New York *Daily News*.

This abortive venture did not discourage Hill from his ambition to be a publisher. He returned to Shelbyville and with a friend, Irwin Harrison, started another paper in the fall of 1913. This was a Sunday newspaper distributed free to every home in Shelbyville, the forerunner of the advertising shoppers that cover most neighborhoods today. Hill insisted to George Hamel that his new paper had far more editorial matter than today's shoppers. Again the paper appeared to prosper for a time but collapsed early in 1914 after the January clearance sales were over.

The short-lived newspaper led to an offer from the owners for Hill and Harrison to buy the *Shelbyville Republican*, where Hill had first worked as a reporter. Knowing the state of the combined fiances of the young men, the owners offered to let them pay for the paper out of profits. However, negotiations feel through when Hill and Harrison insisted on a weekly salary of $15 a week each. The owners refused to go above $10. Another big "if" of public relations history — Had the deal gone through would Hill have remained in Shelbyville and in time become a prosperous newspaper publisher?

Hill needed a job and returned to Akron where he was known from his earlier reporting and worked first for the *Akron Press* and then the *Akron Times*, neither of which exists today. In 1915, Hill moved to Cleveland, Ohio, where he got a job on the *Cleveland News*. Working as a general reporter, Hill's salary rose to $25 a week the second year. He said of this period, "I lived an exciting life on the newspaper, covering a variety of assignments from murder cases to politics. One of my beats was city hall.

My opposite number on the Cleveland *Press* was an exceedingly bright young Lithuanian, Otto Tolischus, who later became a noted correspondent of the *New York Times* and is today (1965) a member of the editorial board of that paper."

While Hill was with the *News*, which later combined with the *Press*, one of the cub reporters on the paper was a young man of 18, Louis B. Seltzer, who later went on to become the distinguished editor of the *Cleveland Press*. Writing in Hill's book, *The Making of a Public Relations Man*, Seltzer later had this to say of the young John Hill, "John was a rather reserved person, although he was and is one of my best friends. He was an excellent reporter, being thorough and resourceful. I believe that John's success has been due to his understanding of people, together with a gifted ability as a writer, which has enabled him to translate business problems into understandable terms." Indeed it was these talents that carried John Hill to the pinnacle of his new vocation.

In June 1916, the young reporter married Hildegarde Beck of Cleveland. She was the daughter of Johan Beck, a composer, who organized and first conducted the now world-famous Cleveland Symphony Orchestra in 1910. Hill and his wife separated in 1934 after he started commuting to New York. The marriage later ended in divorce. In 1917, Hill got an offer of $27.50 a week from the *Daily Metal Trade* and accepted the position of financial editor. This move ultimately led Hill to public relations. Hill recalled in an interview with your author, "When I went to work on the *Daily Metal Trade*, I feared that a job on a trade paper would be dull. But I was wrong."

In his new job, Hill was forced to study finance, business, and the steel industry. This was to play a big part in Hill's entry into and success in public relations. He found he was fascinated with business, its finances, and its operations. At the end of 3 years, he was not only writing a signed column for the *Daily Metal Trade* but also on nights and weekends, he prepared a syndicated monthly economic and business letter for about 40 banks from coast to coast. This led the ambitious Hill to propose to the officials of the Cleveland Trust Company that it would be profitable for them to publish a business newsletter covering the Cleveland area. The bank agreed to pay Hill $50 a month to prepare such a letter, and in January 1920, the first issue of the *Cleveland Trust Business Bulletin* was published. Hill boasted proudly in an interview in 1965 that the *Bulletin* was still being published in the same format. He termed this the "first faint brush with the field that I was later to enter."

Editing the *Bulletin* led Hill to another part-time job, that of writing a syndicated column for the Newspaper Enterprise Association (NEA), a feature service founded by E. W. Scripps and headquartered in Cleveland. After a year because of the 1921 depression, NEA discontinued the column.

The ambitious, workaholic Hill then went to the *Cleveland Plain Dealer* and sold its editors on carrying his column. Hill later reflected that this column served to keep his name before the Cleveland business community. He said, "This was to be of great value to me when I hung up my shingle later on." The Portland *Oregonian* and the Buffalo *Times* also published Hill's column. In his memoir, *The Making of a Public Relations Man*, Hill wrote of this turn of events:

> I was depressed by the loss of the column and began to wonder what I could do to salvage or replace it. I thought of Eric Hopwood, editor of the *Cleveland Plain Dealer*, who some years before had offered me a job as the economics editorial writer for his paper. I asked if he would like to take on my column, and he agreed. . . . I was able to show the gratitude I felt for Mr. Hopwood some twenty years later when, as public relations counsel for Republic Steel, I employed his young son, Henry Hopwood, as an assistant on the account

Hopwood later became public relations director at Republic.

Like Pendleton Dudley, Hill's interest in the possibility of a career in public relations was stimulated by Ivy Lee. Hill happened onto a copy of Lee's little book, *Publicity — Some of the Things It Is and Is Not*, published in 1926. Of Lee, Hill wrote George Hamel in a letter dated November 18, 1965, "He became known throughout the country for his work with his now most famous clients, and he served many other important companies before his death in 1934. Public relationships, he wrote, involved not simply 'saying' but 'doing' — not just talk but action. His book abounded with straight-from-the-shoulder talk to business that seemed to make sense. It kindled in me a determination to go into this kind of endeavor."

In an interview with your author on April 17, 1964, Hill reiterated this story saying "I don't remember how I happened upon this little book." In his view, Ivy Lee was unquestionably the "father of modern practice." Explaining his decision to enter this new and uncertain vocation, he recalled, "I was offered several bank and bond jobs, but I knew I didn't want to be a banker." Continuing his explanation of his decision to enter public relations, Hill said:

> I was editing the bank publication. I got news releases that came in terrible shape. Most of them were sloppily done. I knew from my work that there was a helluva lot of interesting news going on in business that would be of interest to the public if there was someone in the business organization to handle it. I mulled over the possibility of starting on my own public relations firm for three years. I confess I was thinking of it largely in terms of press relations for business.

In 1927, Hill was offered a $500 a month retainer fee to handle publicity for the Union Trust Company, the most powerful bank in Cleveland at that time. This was the catalyst that Hill had been waiting for although he realized that this fee would not be enough to support him on a full-time basis. He decided to gamble and accepted the offer with a provision that John Sherwin, the bank chairman, obtain some other clients for him. Sherwin called E. J. Kulas, president of Otis Steel Company, and told him to hire Hill. Thus began Hill's long and influential involvement in the steel industry as a counselor. Union Trust, a rival to Hill's longtime employer Cleveland Trust, sought Hill's help in publicizing its side of a dispute with officials of the Goodyear Tire & Rubber Co. That assignment and Kulas's call to Otis Steel Company started John Hill on his long, successful, and lucrative career as a giant in this fledgling field.

HILL OPENS PUBLIC RELATIONS OFFICE IN 1927

John Hill quit his job with the Penton Publishing Company in April 1927 and opened an office in Cleveland. "When I started, I paid $100 a month rent and one-tenth of a secretary's salary in a joint ten-office arrangement. I was in this combined office setup for 18 months." He told me, "I thought I was going into a 'corporate publicity'—the term 'public relations' was in scant use at that time." Not in his wildest dreams, could John Hill have dreamed this modest start would flower into the corporate giant, Hill and Knowlton, Inc. and be sold to J. Walter Thompson for $28 million in 1980 and after that be absorbed into a worldwide advertising—public relations conglomerate. Hill, now 36, had found his life's work. He never looked back.

Hill brought a wealth of valuable experience to his new venture. Though largely self-educated, he possessed a wide range of knowledge. He had already had more than 16 years of experience as a newspaper reporter and business editor. He had worked for six newspapers and published two others, short-lived though they were. He had spent 10 years working on *Daily Metal Trade* that schooled him in the industry that provided the foundation for building one of the largest public relations firms in the nation. He had gained a broad knowledge of economics and business through gathering information for his business column and his financial newsletter, that was still being published in 1965.

Of his first year in this new venture, Hill had this to say in his autobiography, *The Making of a Public Relations Man*:

> During that first year in my tiny office, I began to realize that my activities were destined to extend far beyond the important job of press relations. I was

getting into other forms of communication. My steel company client asked me to take over the job of editing an employee publication. This put me into many problems of labor relations and communication. I conferred at regular intervals with the president and members of his top management, all of whom took me into their confidence.

In addition, he arranged press conferences and did other chores for his two clients. He even began moving into counseling when he persuaded Kulas that it was wrong to publish earnings only when they were favorable. After a few months with his two clients, Hill began to get others. These included the Austin Company, construction engineers; Pickands Mather, an ore firm; Cyrus Eaton's Continental Shares; United Alloy Steel; Richman Brothers, clothiers; and Standard Oil of Ohio, a longtime user of public relations counsel. Hill recalled in our interview that despite the Stock Market Crash of 1929, his business remained good until the banks closed in 1933. After this, his clients either dropped Hill or insisted on reduced fees.

In March 1933, Hill's first client, the Union Trust Company, became a casualty of the Depression when it failed. One of those put out of work as a result was its director of advertising and publicity, Don Knowlton. Hill asked Knowlton to join him in a partnership and thus Hill and Knowlton, later to be identified as Hill and Knowlton of Cleveland was created. Don Knowlton never had a role in Hill and Knowlton, Inc., of New York. Hill later explained this partnership by saying he had worked closely with Knowlton before the failure of Union Trust and liked him. He considered Knowlton to be an able writer and for that reason thought he would make a useful partner.

When asked in an interview with your author on Friday, April 17, 1964, why Don Knowlton was not involved in the New York operation, Hill responded, "I hired him as a writer. I knew he couldn't contribute much here. Knowlton was given 100 shares of stock at $1 per share in Hill and Knowlton, Inc. This he sold in March, 1964, for $24,000."

HILL MOVES TO NEW YORK, FORMS NEW FIRM

As he had demonstrated in his formative years John Hill was a person of intelligence, judgment, and a gnawing ambition. As he found his metier in public relations, he began to think of opening an office in New York City because he reasoned, "Growing numbers of corporations were establishing their headquarters in Manhattan. It was clearly destined to be the center of the public relations business." His big break came in mid-November of 1933. Tom Girdler, president of Republic Steel, phoned Hill after a meeting of the board of the American Iron and Steel Institute (AISI), and told Hill that he was to call Walter S. Tower, executive secretary of the institute. Hill quickly phoned Tower and was instructed to come to New York for a conference 2 days hence. As Hill recorded in his memoir, "When I arrived in his office in the Empire State Building, Mr. Tower explained that the leaders of the steel industry were beset by many problems of public relations growing out of the Depression and political developments in Washington. . . . The outcome of the meeting was that my firm was retained and, after thirty years, it still is serving the Institute."

Hill recalled later in an interview, "My firm has lived through the thick of all troubles in the steel industry for three decades." Hill indicated to your author that the institute felt obliged to develop a public relations program because of the passage of Roosevelt's NRA Code that gave labor the right to organize and bargain collectively. In this, Tower and his associates were prescient — labor battles would plague the steel industry for the next three decades. Tower told Hill there was a need for press relations facility because the industry was having difficulties with the press and public as well as the Roosevelt's New Deal government. Hill took the position on a counseling basis, not as an individual. He moved to New York in November 1933, and took an office in the institute.

For many years the Cleveland office remained the headquarters of the firm. In the mid-1940s, the New York branch had grown to the point that Hill decided to establish a new and separate firm, Hill and Knowlton, Inc., and turned over nearly all his interest in the Cleveland firm to Don Knowlton. From then on the only connection between the two agencies was that Knowlton held 1500 shares of Hill and Knowlton, Inc., which at the time was valued at $8.78 a share. Inasmuch as Knowlton was given 100 shares in Hill and Knowlton, Inc., when it was incorporated, presumably for the use of his name, this would indicate that as H&K grew into the giant it became, there were several stock splits along the way.

In his 1964 interview with me, Hill said, "About this time business began to pick up in Cleveland so I commuted to New York City from Cleveland for three or four years. I then opened a separate office for Hill and Knowlton in New York City. I got my first account other than AISI from the Sterling Drug Co. but soon lost it because I could not adequately staff it. My next new account was that of the Lehigh Navigation Coal co." He recorded in his memoir that J. Handly Wright was his first employee, but soon left to accept a much better offer. Wright later became vice-president of public relations for the American Association of Railroads and a leader in the profession in his time.

Two key persons in building the successful Hill and Knowlton, Inc. were John G. Mapes and Bert Goss. Mapes, who had been public relations director of the American Society for Metals and before that an assistant editor of *Metal Progress*, applied to Hill for a job at the AISI in 1934 and was put to work on the spot. He became in Hill's words "a mainstay of our organization throughout the subsequent years." In 1943, when the firm was retained by the Aeronautical Chamber of Commerce, Hill needed "a responsible representative on the ground." He asked John Mapes to find such a person. He did—Bert Goss. Goss had earned a doctorate in economics at New York University, been business editor of *Newsweek*, and editor of the *Journal of Commerce*. After serving in Washington for 7 years, Goss was brought to New York and eventually took over the leadership of Hill and Knowlton, Inc. when John Hill started stepping down. Another influential person in the success of the firm was Richard W. Darrow, who joined it 1952, coming from the Glenn L. Martin Company (now Martin–Marietta) where he had been director of public relations. In time, Darrow succeeded Goss as president.

At first Hill and Knowlton of New York was formed as a partnership along the lines of that set up by Ivy Lee and T. J. Ross, but according to Hill, "this didn't last long. We decided to incorporate." Thus was Hill and Knowlton, Inc. born. As of 1967, Hill held 37% of the stock in the company, Darrow, now president, and Goss, now chairman and chief executive, and John G. Mapes, president of Group Attitudes, were the other major stockholders.

Although Hill made it clear there was little connection between the growing New York operation and his former Cleveland office, apparently the Cleveland office served as a base for an account executive for the American Iron and Steel Institute. On February 27, 1948, a release was issued by AISI announcing the appointment of Harry Lundin as AISI field representative with this paragraph: "Mr. Lundin has his office in the public relations firm of Hill and Knowlton of Cleveland. The Cleveland form has been separate from Hill and Knowlton, Inc. for several years. John W. Hill is president of hill and Knowlton of Cleveland. The two organizations are self contained but cooperate on matters of mutual interest." Apparently Republic Steel was one of these mutual interests. An indication that they were working together on this account is found in the Hill Papers when in 1947 Republic's ad agency forwarded a Hill and Knowlton Cleveland release, several ads, and a radio script at Don Knowlton's request. The New York office did issue an occasional news release for Republic but that was apparently its only involvement with John Hill's early client. Lundin succeeded Edgar S. Bowerfind in the Cleveland AISI in this post. Bowerfind resigned as the Cleveland AISI liaison post in December 1947 to become director of public relations for Republic Steel. Presumably this "office" arrangement lasted until 1964. In response to a query from William Ong, public relations director of U.S. Steel Corporation subsidiaries, Hill wrote on February 18, 1948:

For your information that [emergence of the two firms] came about when it
became necessary to set up a self-contained organization in New York in order
to handle our interests here. The Cleveland organization remained a partnership although my interest became minor [Hill's share earned $3,000 in 1957]
while in New York we incorporated. Don Knowlton's interests are mainly in
Cleveland, while mine are mainly in New York. This did not result from any
"falling out" between Don and me, as we have remained the closest of
personal friends. It was the result merely of business considerations. As you
probably know, the Cleveland Hill and Knowlton has no steel accounts
whatever and has stated a policy of accepting none. Of course our interest in
the steel industry is tied up in the institute.

Hill's letter to Ong of 1948 seemingly contradicts a letter he wrote to
Victor Emanuel of Avco on May 24, 1950, "I don't believe I ever told you
that Hill and Knowlton, Inc. (the New York firm, which is separate and
different from Hill and Knowlton of Cleveland) never served Republic Steel
except for distributing an occasional news release for them, which we still
do. The major Republic work was handled by the Cleveland firm, in which
I have only a small interest of about 5 percent." Continuing, Hill wrote
Emanuel, a major client:

Some years ago, as the Institute work expanded in magnitude, my connection
with Republic (through the Cleveland firm) became a possible source of
embarrassment both to Charlie White and me. We didn't discuss it, but it was
tacitly understood between us and after 1945 I virtually withdrew from the
Republic picture. This was the situation some years later Republic discontinued its relationship with the Cleveland firm. The New York firm was not
involved and the financial effect on me was almost nil. I don't believe you
were acquainted with these facts.

It appears then that the Cleveland firm lost the Republic account in
December 1947 when H&K staffer Edgar S. Bowerfind was named director
of public relations of Republic Steel.

Don Knowlton sold the firm in 1964 and then retired.

VICTOR EMANUEL—MAJOR CLIENT AND CLOSE FRIEND

In 1940, Victor Emanuel became John Hill's first major industrial client and
over time, they became close friends. Emanuel, born in Dayton, Ohio,
where he knew and was influenced by the Wright Brothers, first made his
fortune in the utility business in partnership with his father. Father and son
sold their utility to Samuel Insull's far-flung utility empire, and Victor

Emanuel, still in his late twenties, was worth $40,000,000. He spent the next several years in England living in luxury and riding to the hounds. But when the Great Depression began to shrink his fortune, he decided to return to the United States and rebuild it. His first move was to get control of the Aviation Corporation after a stiff proxy fight with E. L. Cord. At that time, Aviation Corporation was primarily a holding company with no management nor operating responsibilities. Emanuel retained John Hill in 1940 to prepare hisannual report and to provide him with personal advice.

When the Japanese bombed Pearl Harbor and the United States went to war, Emanuel bought control of Consolidated Aircraft from Reuben Fleet and merged it with Vultee Aircraft, a subsidiary of his holding company. Later he two companies were merged into Consolidated Vultee, that later became the Convair Division of General Dynamics.

In January 1942, Emanuel recruited Tom Girdler of Republic Steel to run these two companies and Girdler immediately took charge, working out of the San Diego office. Girdler's first act was to retain his trusted public relations counselor, John Hill. According to Hill, "Girdler wanted me to take over the work because we had been together for years." Hill's first unpleasant task was to meet with Steve Hannagan, whom Vultee had retained in 1941, and tell the skilled publicist that his contract with Vultee would not be renewed. But Hannagan's experience with the aircraft industry soon landed him a contract with the Ford Motor Co. to handle public relations at its Willow Run plant, that was making Consolidated's B-24 bombers for the Air Force.

As Hill recalled in his memoir, his task was to make Consolidated's B-24, the *Liberator*, more widely known. He wrote, "Emanuel and Girdler were irked by the fact that, whenever an effective bombing raid occurred, the credit all went to the Flying Fortress, even if Liberators had been the bombers in action." To meet this complaint of the clients, Hill staged a 4-day press conference, inviting newsmen from across the nation. The well-known newspapermen stayed in San Diego 4 days at the client's expense, and on the last day, a battery of Army and Navy censors were on hand to clear their stories. From that time on, recalled Hill, the *Liberator* was no longer a forgotten airplane.

Consolidated got another big burst of publicity when Victor Emanuel persuaded his friend, President Franklin D. Roosevelt, to visit the Consolidated plant at San Diego. Thousands of people lined his route to see the War President. He was driven through the aircraft plant, accompanied by an arch-foe in the Little Steel Strike, Tom Girdler, who explained the plant's operations and output on the drive through. Tour over, they said a stiff good-bye.

In recalling his early days on this job, Hill wrote, "When I went to San Diego on my first visit in January, 1942, Consolidated Vultee had 5,000 employees and one plant. Before the war was over, there were 100,000 employees in thirteen plants. . . . It was my job to staff and direct the public relations departments in the thirteen plants. At the peak of the operation, I had seventy people scattered over the map of America, and the job of supervising and directing these distant and diffused staffs was not easy." It was in the course of this work that John Hill discovered Kerryn King in Fort Worth. A few months later, Hill brought King to New York where he became a key executive until hired away by the Texas Company. At Texaco, King, a leader of public relations professionals in his time, had a successful career.

In 1947, Emanuel sold Consolidated to Floyd Odlum, thus ending Hill's association with Consolidated. Odlum turned to his longtime friend, Harry Bruno, a counselor who specialized in aviation promotion, for counsel. Foreseeing a collapse of the aviation industry at the war's end, Emanuel turned to making household appliances and running a broadcast business. He took his Consolidated money and bought radio station WLW and the Crosley Corporation from Powel Crosley, Jr. He also bought New Idea, Inc., a farm implement manufacturer, and later the Bendix Home Appliances, located in South Bend. Emanuel saw the pent-up demand for home appliances and farm equipment after the war and capitalized on it for a few years. Hill and his staff went from glamorizing *Liberator* bombers to promoting TV sets, farm implements, and washing machines. Emanuel consolidated these properties into the Avco Manufacturing Corporation, popularized under the name Avco. Hill and Knowlton were initially retained by Emanuel for counsel on financial relations in January 1947. In a memorandum of January 20, 1947, Hill urged Emanuel and his associates to change the name of Avco. Hill argued:

> The Corporation's name is a handicap under present conditions. Consideration should be given to changing the corporate name. Avco's name now identifies the Corporation with the aviation industry and any unfavorable developments in aviation must inevitably react upon it. But a more fundamental reason for change is the fact that the present name is a misnomer. Avco is regarded by many investors and potential investors as a holding company. Its transition to a manufacturing and operating organization could more easily be established in the public mind by adoption of a more appropriate name such as the Avco Manufacturing Corporation or the American Manufacturing Corporation.

The former was accepted by Emanuel.

The shift in emphasis from financial relations to sales promotion and employee relations on this account came in August 1947 when an agreement was reached to extend H&K's services to cover all the manufacturing divisions and products. Significantly, the extension was negotiated with Ray Cosgrove, vice-president for sales of Avco's Crosley division. The agreement called for the following arrangements:

> The field representative in Cincinnati [is] to visit and keep in touch with each of the Avco divisions, developing material for product and general publicity, etc. He will also consult and assist division managements on public relations matters affecting the divisions including community relations, employee communications, and plant publications. In general, this representative will serve as a liaison between the manufacturing divisions of Avco and the Hill and Knowlton general offices.

Paul Boxell was named account executive with oversight provided by Hill and John G. Mapes. The agreement was signed in late September. Boxell went to Cincinnati on October 1.

In December 1947, Hill concluded that after working on the account for 90 days, there was "urgent need for centralized responsibility and a clear cut line of authority"—a problem that plagues all public relations arrangements from time to time. He put this need in three categories:

1. Overall prestige building and policy, together with financial and stockholder relations;
2. Trade and product publicity for various divisions;
3. Employee and community relations and communications.

To meet this problem, Hill urged Avco to authorize H&K to appoint an executive who would remain at H&K but who would be the director of public relations for Avco Manufacturing. This is an accepted procedure in public relations. In this period, Carl Byoir & Associates was using the same procedure except that in Byoir's case its principal was based with the company, not in headquarters. At this time, Byoir was H&K's main competitor. Kerryn King was designated for this role.

The Avco account brought Hill and Knowlton to the world of product promotion—a far cry from battling union organizers in the steel industry or fighting drug legislation. A typical example of how H&K went at this new-found assignment is illustrated in the elaborate preparations for introduction of Crosley's 1951 model TV receivers in a time when TV was relatively new in America. The new TV would be unveiled at a large press conference in Chicago on August 10. Invitations went out to newspapers, press associations, magazine syndicates, and radio representatives in Chicago. Key TV contacts in New York were invited as guests of Crosley and H&K. Financial and women's editors in the nearby cities of Detroit, Milwaukee, St. Louis, and Cleveland were also invited. Plans called for the press showing to be conducted in adjoining suites that showed Crosley receivers in well-designed room settings—modern, traditional, and rumpus rooms.

In another promotion, Crosley announced its Second Giveaway in which $2,000,000 would be given away plus a $500,000 to charity. This giveaway was announced in an elaborate press conference in New York's Waldorf–Astoria. The Plan read:

> The entire ballroom will be utilized for exhibits arranged to give the guests a smash impression of hugeness. The products on exhibit will total approximately $200,000 in value at retail so that Mr. Blees may explain to the press that it would require more than ten ballrooms this size to hold all the products which Crosley and its dealers are giving away to the American public in the next 90 days. An effort will be made to obtain 500,000 silver dollars which will be displayed during the press conference to dramatize the huge charity donation organized by Crosely. Arrangements will be made with 10 or more outstanding charities to have representatives at the press conference to participate in this phase of the program—either photogenic Junior Leaguers active in each charity enterprise or name personalities identified with the charities, such as Walter Winchell or Gene Tunney, etc. Publicity of local winners will be handled by Ruder and Finn. National coverage by Hill and Knowlton. Dealer meetings in 38 cities will be handled by Crosley public relations department—interviews, releases, etc.

Other public relations activities for Avco provided by H&K included:

Press Relations. Preparing Mr. Emanuel for a 1956 interview with *Fortune* magazine:

> Bill Harris suggests that Mr. Emanuel make the following points to the *Fortune* people: (1) Disarm them at the outset with his candor in explaining why Avco has decided to go out of the appliance business. (2) Point out what is happening in the industry as a whole and how many other companies have been forced to the same decision. (3) Frankly discuss the losses the company has had to absorb during the past year or two in the appliance business, but show that over the years the company has not lost anything for the stockholders as a result of this transition. (4) Explain how the company happened to get into the appliance business. (5) After having discussed various questions by the *Fortune* people, Mr. Emanuel should turn the conversation away from this phase and call attention to the future of the company." The memo also urged full cooperation with the writer, Spencer, Klaw, and emphasis on the position the company is now in.

Preparation of the executives for key press interviews is a common task in public relations.

Community Relations.   H&K's executives constantly urged the Avco divisions to hold open houses for their employees and the community. To guide them, John Hill sent an Open House booklet H&K had prepared for the steel industry with this note: "The booklet is based on an actual Open House programs on which we have assisted more than fifteen steel companies in planning during the past year and the recommendations outlined have been tried and tested."

This reflects the synergy a counseling firm brings to clients.

Employee Relations.   A memo from John Hill to Eric O. Johnston of Avco's American Central Division:

> I have been thinking further about your December employee meetings. It seems to me that you could follow up the showing of the movie which is designed to build a better understanding and appreciation of our form of government, with some points such as those suggested in the attached. There may be a thought or two in this which you can use in your talks to employees, Eric. Someone has got to find some way to give the wage earner the facts of life or we are lost. Let me know if we can be of any help at anytime." [This memo, written November 22, 1948, reflects a time when industry was being racked by postwar strikes as labor sought to retain its wartime pay and resolution of grievances pent up during World War II. This was the period of the National Association of Manufacturers' ineffective "Free Enterprise" campaign.]

Avco Shifts to Shock Tubes.   By the mid-1950s Avco's appliance business was losing money, as was indicated in the November 1956 memo prepared for Emanuel's interview with *Fortune*. Emanuel was rescued by a fateful circumstance. Emanuel, a Cornell University trustee, at a Cornell gathering met Dr. Arthur Kantrowitz, a professor of aeronautical engineering. The scientist had perfected a so-called shock tube to simulate in a laboratory the same kinds of difficulties that would be encountered in the reentry of an ICBM missile. Victor Emanuel persuaded the professor to leave Cornell and join his firm.

Hill recorded, "It was discovered that Avco's work held help promise of capturing the public imagination. Announcement of this work generated wide interest in the press." Avco's management then decided to construct a large scientific laboratory in Wilmington, Massachusetts. Hill and Knowlton prepared a major public relations program for the dedication of this facility in May 1959. The program was built around a panel discussion, "Mankind and Space" moderated by Bob Considine and John Charles Daly, and the unveiling of the first ICBM reentry vehicle to be recovered after a flight through space. The program got national coverage in the press, on radio, and on TV. By the mid-1960s, Avco was participating in more than

30 missile and space programs and employing some 27,000 employees. Avco was also involved in adapting space technology to peacetime uses, for example, generating electricity through magnet of hydrodynamics. Avco had moved into the space age, leaving the sale of TV sets far behind, and H&K moved into the space age with it. John Hill, whom *The New York Times* once described as a "corporate confidant" was much more at home in dealing with major industries such as steel, aviation, and missiles than with product promotion.

But financial relations remained at the core of H&K's counseling to Emanuel and his corporations from 1960 until John Hill's retirement. This was because, as Hill wrote in a "Memorandum for Avco Manufacturing Corporation Sub-Committee on Financial and Stockholder relations," dated July 15, 1948:

> It is in the financial community in general upon which Avco, like all other publicly-owned corporations, must depend for financial support—that has not been reached with a broad and comprehensive story concerning the NEW Avco. Time alone will correct many of these problems and give Avco the stability and prestige to which it is entitled. The only substitute for time, and the only way to accelerate the aging process, is the adoption of an aggressive program which will act as a catalyst between the Corporation and the investing public.

Hill then outlined a program for financial relations for Avco in the years ahead. Only those items marked by an asterisk were then in effect:

*1. Annual report—increase distribution to financial community.
*2. Stockholder News letter—to 58,000 stockholders—and springboard for stories to financial press.
*3. Letter of New Stockholders.
*4. Corporate analysis—background memoranda.
*5. Institutional advertising—series for financial press.
 6. Product Advertising—to appear before/after institutional ads.
 7. Institutional booklet—background of corporation and its products.
 8. Direct mailings—monthly bulletin for financial community individuals.
*9. Financial publicity-personal contact with editors who serve the investing public.
*10. Corporate spokesman—high ranking corporate executive to handle inquiries that cannot be handled by public relations staff.
*11. Liaison—between PR counsel and financial information services.
*12. New York Press Show for financial and news editors.

Over these 25 years, John Hill and Victor Emanuel became close friends, and Hill became Emanuel's trusted counselor on personal matters as well as corporate ones. For example, in January 1958, Emanuel asked Hill for advice on how the American Jewish League Against Communism should celebrate its 10th birthday and asked if H&K would handle an anniversary dinner to raise money. Emanuel thought he could attract FBI Director J. Edgar Hoover as a drawing card. Hill responded, "There is a terrific problem in selling out enough tables. I think this would be true of a dinner for the 10th anniversary of the League, notwithstanding the powerful drawing power and great stature of J. Edgar Hoover. Further, the league has no large organization nor wide popular membership." Finally, Hill wrote in his letter of January 6, 1958;, "Knowing something of the demands on your time and the problems facing you, I would hesitate to recommend your taking on this added effort."

Like many rich industrialists, Emanuel became quite alarmed by the many groundless charges being hurled into the air by Senator Joseph McCarthy and his followers in the mid-1950s. Responding to a query from Emanuel, Hill wrote him on February 1, 1954:

While I am not aware that Communists in its employ has been to date a problem in any of the division of Avco, I believe it would be well worthwhile to investigate means of handling such an issue if it should become a problem. It is my recollection that the AFL unions have a constitutional provision against Communists enjoying membership in their organizations. Perhaps it would be possible for the industrial relations people to have a provision written into their contracts with the unions such as Stewart–Warner has arranged, under which it is not required to retain in its service any employee who is not eligible to membership in the union under its constitution. It is interesting to note in the *Business Week* article that the Steel Workers Union, which has representative rights at New Idea, is reported to be antagonistic toward anti-Communist policy on the part of the company. It might be well to have the industrial relations people explore the attitudes of the UAW (CIO) which is the union at both Lycoming plants, Fort Dodge and Connersville.

Hill and Emanuel, both ultra conservatives, were also united in support of Senator Robert P. Taft for the Republican nomination for President in 1952. Hill wrote Emanuel on February 7, 1952, to report on an organization meeting of Taft supporters the night before:

I think you will be interested in some of the highlights of our meeting in Washington last evening. The Senator [Taft] wants to set up a small public relations advisory committee which will advise with him and carry on specific projects.

For example, he wants suggestions as to the line to take as he goes into New Hampshire on a speaking tour. He is also worried about the adverse effect of the polls and the propaganda that he can't be elected.

There was consideration of the pros and cons of a National Citizens Committee headed by names. The consensus was that, while this could be helpful, perhaps a series of special Taft committees would serve the purpose equally well. This would include such groups as actors and writers, small business men, doctors, publishers, etc.

It was agreed that immediate steps would be taken to explore these possibilities. Morris Riskind has already promised to head up such a committee for actors and writers. I am going to ask Forrest Davis to work with this group for the one-quarter of his time which Hill and Knowlton, Inc., is paying for now. Jim Selvage of Selvage and Lee, Jim Ellis of the Kudner Advertising agency, and Franklyn Waltman of Sun Oil Company were present and took some follow-up assignments. Carl Byoir was not present but is to be a member of the small public relations committee.

I think this committee can have good results only if ways are found to give it continuing effort and a degree of coordination and I hope that this can be brought about.

Hill had been an admirer of Senator Taft for many years because they saw eye to eye on the need to curb what they viewed as organized labor's excesses. As far back as late 1947, Hill was working to put Taft in the White House. In a letter to William D. McAdams of November 26, 1947, Hill wrote, "What I have been thinking of is how to get the Senator and his views before more people in more parts of the country." To do this, Hill outlined a program to have a book of the Senator's recent speeches published, a series of movie-shorts made with one subject for each short, and distribute these to the Taft-for-President Committees. Hill was prescient in seeing the advent of TV as a major player in Presidential campaigns. He planned to make TV shots for distribution to the nation's burgeoning number of TV stations with "the obvious purpose to get people in hundreds of locations to see the Senator and hear his logical views through a medium far better than any other method except that of personal appearances."

As American political history unfolded, Hill was frustrated in his hopes of putting Taft in the White House. In 1956, believing that if you can't lick 'em, you join 'em, Hill worked to raise money for President Eisenhower's reelection among New York's major counseling firms. He and John Hay (Jock) Whitney staged a fund-raising benefit in H&K's office on September 24, 1956, for New York's major counselors.

Emanuel and John Hill had a long, close relationship that was profitable to both. Hill saw Emanuel as "a true gentleman from the old school."

He was genuinely courteous and took great joy in doing thoughtful things for others. Warm notes of thanks or of congratulations or of sympathy flowed endlessly from his office. . . . Emanuel was one of the first executives to recognize the value of public relations and the importance of taking public relations advisors into his confidence. He made this clear early in our relationship by inviting me to attend all meetings of the Board of Directors and this has continued down through the years.

Hill's first industrial client proved to be cooperative as well as profitable.

A CAMPAIGN TO INHIBIT SALE OF MARGARINE

In an address to his firm's annual staff conference in 1953, John W. Hill stressed the importance of the public relations function, "Public relations has two additional categories of usefulness for industry; in the presentation incident to a public controversy, and in defense and explanation of the system of competitive enterprise which gives it life and vitality." Much of Hill's career was spent in public controversies, starting with the Little Steel Strike in the 1930s. Hill's influential role in two major campaigns, one to prevent unionization of Little Steel and subsequent defenses of Steel and another on behalf of the tobacco industry in its effort to debunk and obfuscate the scientific evidence linking smoking to lung cancer and heart disease, are told in the next chapter. Hill and Knowlton's campaigns to inhibit the sale of oleomargarine on behalf of the dairy industry, to prevent passage of more effective drug legislation by the U.S. Congress, and to obtain Congressional action to free natural gas from federal price controls is described next. In fact, most of the public controversies that have surrounded the work of Hill and Knowlton have involved their representation of trade associations confronted with critical public relations problems.

As. T. A. Wise wrote in *Fortune*, "The kinds of problems it [H&K] is now dealing with may serve to explain a lot about p.r. these days — to explain, especially why it is such a prosperous and growing business. Indeed, the growth of government regulation, active consumerism, and litigation are key factors in the steady growth of public relations counseling."

The oleomargarine industry launched a drive early in 1948 to repeal the federal excise tax and other restrictions on the sale of oleomargarine (as it was generally called in this time) that had been imposed years earlier by the influence of the dairy industry on Congress. The campaign to remove the restrictions on margarine was being led by the public relations firm of James Selvage and Morris Lee. As Congressional support for repeal of the excise tax mounted, the butter and dairy industries turned to Hill and Knowlton in 1949 for help in fashioning a counterattack. As correspondence in the Hill Papers records, "Hill and Knowlton was retained by the dairy and butter industries in April, 1948, to suggest plans and assist in operations to meet the critical emergency then prevailing against gaining any success for the cause of butter." The clients in this legislative battle were the National Cooperative Milk Producers' Federation, the American Butter Institute, and the National Creameries Association. Charles W. Holman, former journalist, now secretary of the National Cooperative Milk Producers, coordinated the counterattack for the clients. Hill and Knowlton ultimately lost this battle, presumably because Selvage and Lee had the better cause.

However, it must be noted that the beneficial effects of margarine, particularly for heart patients, was not widely known in the late 1940s. It would perhaps be unfair to impose today's health knowledge on Hill and Knowlton and the butter industry of that time frame. The margarine case was based mainly on its lower cost and the unfairness of the restrictions. For example, at that time a housewife would have to spend several minutes coloring her margarine. Selvage and Lee pitched the battle as a struggle between the butter interests and consumers. Articles began to appear in national magazines such as *Better Homes and Gardens*, *Business Week*, *Harper's*, *Newsweek*, *Newspaper*, *Reader's Digest*, and *Time* pounding on this common theme. It was no coincidence that these articles began to appear or had a common theme. For oleo, it was "good PR."

The crisis for the dairy industry began to build in 1948 when the House of Representatives passed decisively Rep. Mendel Rivers' bill to repeal the federal excise tax on the sale of oleomargarine. Congressmen voted for oleo by a margin of 8 to 1 on the sole issue of taxes. The events of 1948 led Hill and Knowlton to speculate in its proposal to the dairy groups, dated June 1948: "Oleo supporters in the months ahead can be expected to stir up a great deal of resentment over the failure of the Senate to vote on the repeal bill in view of the House action and the two Senate votes. Accusations about the butter lobby will become more bitter and, in a public relations sense, the dairy industry's position will be worse than if it was the start of the session because of such resentments." The whiff of hard sell is apparent in this lengthy proposal. The stated objectives of the campaign were:

(1) To retain regulation of oleomargarine by showing the public that the interests of the consumer, as well as of agriculture, require such regulation; (2) To regain lost goodwill for the dairy and butter industries by bringing about a more complete understanding of the factors responsible for the high cost of butter and the current plight of the dairy industry; (3) To help generate support for long-term measures designed to build dairy cattle numbers, with emphasis on measures to correct conditions which would be aggravated by oleo tax repeal.

The Hill and Knowlton proposal then outlined these activities:

I. *State organization work* — "organize state-by-state campaign for safeguards against fraudulent substitution and imitations of butter and the regaining of lost goodwill. Any attempt to continue to center the fight for preservation of oleo margarine without a greater intensification on the work in the field will be simply a surrender of the battle to the oleo industry. Increased activities in Washington will merely furnish grist for those who are grinding out stories about the "butter lobby.' "

  A. *Advertising* (1) state's vital interest in the prosperity of the dairy industry — employment, farm income, etc.; (2) the importance and economic conditions in the community and in the state; (3) fraud and deception likely to occur if regulation is repealed.

  B. *Radio advertising* — provision of scripts and recordings.

  C. *Speaking program* — civic and luncheon clubs in states a full-time professional speaker to appear where needed.

  D. *Editorial conference* — state directors and their committees with the help of counsel, arrange for industry leaders to call on every important publisher and editor in the state.

  E. *Polling candidates* — interviews to be sure they understand the issues and to find out their point of view.

II. *Literature* and material for use in the State and National Campaigns.

III. *Educators and Research* — sponsor a research project at a leading university — "butter as the balance wheel and dairy industry's contribution to soil improvement through grasses and manure."

H&K's proposal recognized that "although prejudice against the dairy industry and butter in educational circles is almost overwhelming, a positive effort should be exerted to regain lost support among those influential leaders of public opinion." The proposal went on to outline a program of national activities, for example, editorial conferences in New York, Chicago, Los Angeles, and Washington, supported by motion slide film and speakers from national organizations, "Silver Dollar" days to show the economic importance of dairying, and so forth.

Hill & Knowlton also resorted to the use of Pinkerton detectives to determine if there were fraudulent products being marketed marked as butter. Russell Crenshaw, part of the employing butter lobby, wrote a memo to John G. Mapes on September 27, 1948, recommending that H&K consider hiring Pinkerton detectives to make a trial investigation of butter fraud in a test city, either Kentucky or Ohio. Subsequently, John G. Mapes, the account executive, signed a contract with the Pinkerton's National Detective Agency, Inc. on December 20, 1948, for a "Fact Finding Survey and Inventory Baltimore" at the rate of $20 a day for each operative assigned to the investigation. Records in the Hill Papers show only the results of an investigation in Indianapolis, Indiana. Of nine samples bought in grocery stores, there only two were found to be less than pure butter, one from Beatrice Foods Co. and one with no brand name was found to contain insect viscera and cinders. In another sampling, Pinkerton's Agency reported back to Mapes that "these additional tests have convinced the laboratory experts that samples are reprocessed butter, meeting in all cases the requirements as to butter fat content." In short, H&K found that there was no margarine fraud—at least in these markets. The Pinkerton contract is reproduced in Fig. 15.1

Seeing the handwriting on the wall in the public sentiment against taxes on oleo, the dairy and butter trade associations, presumably with the counsel of Hill and Knowlton, retreated in October 1948 from that position. That month, the three sponsors of the campaign issued a public statement announcing they favored the elimination of all taxes and license fees on oleo.

The crisis building for the dairy industry intensified when Rep. Mendel Rivers of South Carolina again introduced his bill to repeal the federal excise tax as Congress reconvened on January 3, 1949. President Truman, fresh from his surprise election in 1948, voiced support for the Rivers bill. Seeing Congressional support slipping from them, the dairy groups, reiterated their position that they would not oppose the lifting of the tax if the sale of colored oleo would continue to be barred in interstate commerce. The House ultimately passed the Rivers measure by a vote of 260 to 106. Two adverse votes on a companion bill were taken in the Senate in 1949, but final passage of the tax bill did not come until 1950. Meantime in 1949 and 1950, other states were moving to lift the restrictions on the sale of margarine, including its color—Connecticut, California, and New Hampshire among them. New York's legislature lifted the barrier to oleo's use in its state institutions. The crowning blow to the butter forces came when the voters of Ohio in a general election on November 8, 1949, voted by a large margin to free the sale of oleo, despite a large campaign fund of $100,000 that had been raised by the dairy industry. Hill and Knowlton was quite active in the Ohio campaign and another in Michigan.

In a letter to Graham Patterson, president *The Farm Journal*, John Hill said of the forthcoming Ohio vote:

> It has produced more reaction from dairy farmers than has been displayed in any state heretofore, with the possible exception of Michigan. It is constantly said by oleo repeal proponents that farmers are not really interested in butter markets. This is being disproved once and for all in the Buckeye state. . . . Considered by itself, as demonstrated in this campaign, it will prove to be a factor that must be taken into account by all members of the U.S. Senate who seeking reelection in 1950 and 1952.

Form 7 1-47 5m d.es **Ptd. in U.S.A.**

PINKERTON'S NATIONAL DETECTIVE AGENCY, INC.
(FOUNDED BY ALLAN PINKERTON 1850)

154 Nassau Street, New York, New York

CONFIRMATION

December 20,
Our 99th Year,
1948

Hill and Knowlton, Inc.
350 Fifth Avenue
New York, New York

Gentlemen: Attention: Mr. John G. Mapes

This letter is to confirm an understanding reached on December 20, 1948
between Mr. John G. Mapes, representing Hill and Knowlton, Inc.
and Asst. Supt. E. J. Payson   , representing Pinkerton's National
Detective Agency, Inc. It was agreed that the Agency shall furnish for the account
of Hill and Knowlton, Inc.   the following service:

> Fact Finding Survey and
> Inv. Baltimore

The rate for this service shall be $ 20.00 a day for each operative detailed,
plus expenses.

This rate contemplates an eight hour day for those engaged. If it should be
necessary or advisable to work beyond eight hours in any one day, the additional time
shall be charged at an hourly rate of $ 2.50

Agency bills shall be rendered monthly and/or at the conclusion of the work
and are payable upon presentation.

As your client is not known to the Agency in this matter, it is understood that
you will be responsible for the account and will pay same when due.

If the foregoing is in accordance with your understanding, please approve and
return the enclosed copy of this letter.

PINKERTON'S NATIONAL DETECTIVE AGENCY, Inc.

Peter C. Low
Superintendent.

(continued)

FIG. 15.1.

In this, Hill proved a poor political prophet.

Trying to persuade Patterson, a key influential in farm matters, Hill
continued: "There is new awareness in political circles that unfair competition from yellow oleo-margarine threatens a considerable increase in
Federal price support expenditures," but in effect he refuted that argument
by continuing, "Meanwhile, butter seems to be winning its battle for the

PINKERTON'S NATIONAL DETECTIVE AGENCY, INC.

(FOUNDED BY ALLAN PINKERTON 1850)

ROBERT A. PINKERTON, PRESIDENT
RALPH DUDLEY, VICE PRES. & GEN'L MGR.
ORBAN C. TURRELL, SECT. & TREASURER

EASTERN REGION
DANIEL T. GREEN, ASST. GEN'L MGR. NEW YORK
JOHN F. LARKIN, DIVISION MGR. NEW YORK
CHARLES E. McGINLEY, DIVISION MGR. CLEVELAND
PETER G. LOW, DIVISION MGR. PHILADELPHIA

154 Nassau St. New York 7, N. Y

October 26th 1949

Hill & Knowlton, Inc.
350 5th Avenue
New York City, N. Y.

Gentlemen: Attn: Mr. John G. Mapes

This letter is to confirm an understanding reached on October 21, 1949, between Mr. John G. Mapes, representing Hill & Knowlton, Inc., and the writer, representing Pinkerton's National Detective Agency, Inc. It was agreed that the Agency shall furnish for the account of Hill & Knowlton, Inc. the following service.

Investigation: Mrs. John Weinstein.

The rate for this service shall be $20.00 a day for each operative detailed, plus expenses.

This rate contemplates an eight hour day for those engaged. If it should be necessary or advisable to work beyond eight hours in any one day, the additional time shall be charged at an hourly rate of $2.50.

Agency bills shall be rendered monthly and/or at the conclusion of the work and are payable upon presentation.

You may terminate the employment of this Agency at any time upon due notice to the undersigned.

If the foregoing is in accordance with your understanding, please approve and return the enclosed copy of this letter.

Very truly yours,

PINKERTON'S NATIONAL DETECTIVE AGENCY, Inc.

Carbon returned

10/27/49

Superintendent.

OFFICES

ATLANTA
BALTIMORE
BOSTON
BUFFALO
CHICAGO

CINCINNATI
CLEVELAND
DALLAS
DENVER
DETROIT
HARTFORD

HOUSTON
KANSAS CITY
LOS ANGELES
MIAMI
NEW ORLEANS

NEW YORK
PHILADELPHIA
PITTSBURGH
PORTLAND, ORE.
PROVIDENCE
ST. LOUIS

ST. PAUL
SAN FRANCISCO
SEATTLE
TORONTO
WAUWATOSA WISC.

FIG. 15.1.

consumer dollar in the marketplace." Hill lamented the fact that yellow oleo sales had jumped from 2½ case million pounds in 1940 to almost 100 million pounds in 1948. And there was the nub of the issue in this legislative battle that the margarine forces finally won in 1950.

In its campaign to hinder the sale of oleo as a product fraudulently imitative of butter, Hill and Knowlton came up with some pretty screwy ideas. Bert Goss, then in charge of the H&K Washington office and heavily involved in this campaign, wrote Charles Holman, a key figure in the dairy industry, on February 11, 1949:

It occurs to some of us that you need a bill introduced into Congress to dramatize the phony food situation. Accordingly, we think careful consideration should be given to the introduction of a bill legalizing the sale and restaurant use of horse meat. What we have in mind is a bill that would provide that horse meat could be sold and served under conditions absolutely identical with those permitted oleo under the Pogue's (D, Texas) bill. Thus we think the bill should state that horse meat could be colored any shade of red desired, that it could use any appropriate preservative and any appropriate flavoring. . . . We think the introduction of such a bill and its subsequent reference to the House Committee on Agriculture would be one of dramatizing the situation.

Replying to Goss in a letter dated March 21, 1949, Holman sensibly responded, "I have checked the horse meat proposal and find that it would be subject to a point of order and by being ruled out by a point of order it would make our case ridiculous. Accordingly, as far as I'm concerned, it's out."

Later that year, Goss outlined a somewhat more rational approach to the firm's uphill battle against the sale of oleo in a memo to John G. Mapes and Russell Crenshaw:

For a long time I have been kicking around an idea for butter. This idea is a compromise which would be submitted to the client only if everything began to look awfully dark for the January test. It would certainly not be submitted until after the Ohio vote, and then only if the Ohio vote was completely discouraging. [Ohio voters voted in a referendum November 8, 1949, on a proposition to repeal the tax and other restrictions on the sale of oleo.]

Briefly, the idea would be for butter to say in effect, 'All right, oleo, has fought for the color yellow—let them have it.' But, at the same time, let butter have a distinctive shade of yellow. Then let us have a Federal statue forbidding oleo to ever, in anyway shape or form—either by squeeze bag, color bars, or otherwise—ever to have the right to imitate that shade.

From the viewpoint of the butter–oleo fight, the effect of such a compromise would be to throw the oleo strategy into the ash can. If they were given the right to use the historic yellow, they could never, with any conscience or grace whatsoever, ask for the right to imitate the new butter color.

Ultimately the dairy industry lost its battle to restrict and inhibit the sale of margarine and today yellow margarine and butter reside side by side in the supermarket dairy case. Concerned that the 1950 repeal of the federal excise tax and increasing state actions favorable to margarine would appear to be a public relations defeat for Hill and Knowlton, Vice-President John G. Mapes wrote Glenn Griswold, editor *Public Relations News*, a letter dated January 1950, to blunt the appearance of a Selvage and Lee victory. Hailing the effectiveness of H&K's campaign, Mapes asserted that "this bill [the Rivers bill that repealed the excise tax] truly provides protection for the dairy industry as much or more protection than the Gillette-Wiley [Senator Guy Gillette of Iowa and Senator Alexander Wiley of Wisconsin] backed by the dairy farmers." Mapes concluded in his letter to Griswold, "The protective amendments to the final bill passed by the Senate, as thus appraised by Senator Aiken, should certainly be taken into account in considering the far from one-sided outcome of the dairy–oleo controversy."
Mapes continued:

The first measure actively supported by the oleo industry to repeal the taxes — the Rivers bill — as passed by the House in the Spring of 1948, contained no protective provisions whatsoever against butter imitations. The case of the dairy farmers at that moment was generally considered to be quite hopeless. The bill which passed the Senate last week eliminated the dairy-sponsored prohibition against interstate shipment of oleo, but contained our important provisions for safeguarding dairy farmers and consumers against butter imitations.

Mapes was claiming these amendments as something of a win for Hill and Knowlton. The amendments provided that:

1. any restaurant serving yellow oleo must identify it to the patrons,
2. oleo manufacturers and distributors could not represent their product to be a dairy product,
3. manufacturers of yellow oleo would be required to mold all yellow oleo in triangular sections to make its identity readily distinguishable,
4. the Food and Drug Administration was directed to inspect the raw materials going into oleo for sanitary handling.

These provisions represented only a short term victory for the dairy industry as the public ultimately got its right to buy margarine without restrictions.

A CAMPAIGN TO DEFEAT REGULATION OF THE GAS INDUSTRY

Another major controversy involving Hill and Knowlton began in late 1954 when the firm was hired as counsel by the Natural Gas and Oil Resources Committee (NGORC) to fight government regulation of the price of natural gas. Writing in *Image Merchants*, Irwin Ross said of this account, "Hill and Knowlton, according to their lights, were acting in the public interest when defending the natural gas producers against the incubus of federal price regulation."

The NGORC public relations program was undertaken as a result of a Supreme Court decision in June 1954 that had placed all natural gas producers who sold gas for shipment in interstate commerce under control of the Federal Power Commission. Shocked by the Supreme Court's decision in the Phillips case, the oil and gas producers decided two steps were necessary—to take their case directly to the public in an expensive, full-scale public relations campaign and to start a drive for legislation that would free gas from federal price controls. The movers and shakers in the industry saw the need to keep the public relations and lobbying efforts distinctly separate because of federal tax and lobbying laws. M. J. Rathbone, then president of Standard Oil (New Jersey), proposed the organization of the Natural Gas and Oil Resources Committee to mount the public relations effort. An entirely separate organization, the General Gas Committee, initiated the lobbying effort. Shortly after the NGORC was set up, it chose General Baird H. Markham, who had earlier retired from a position in the American Petroleum Institute, to head the NGORC and he, in turn, turned to Hill and Knowlton for counsel. John Hill's firm was hired to plan and execute a national campaign.

In a letter of December 15, 1954, Hill wrote a confirming letter to General Markham informing him that a management committee composed of himself, Bert Goss, Ed Barrett, and Dick Darrow—H&K's top brass in 1954—would manage the campaign, with Barrett having the chief responsibility. Hill outlined plans for a staff coordination that would "ensure an orderly transition on the account," presumably a shift of primary direction to H&K from NGORC. A H&K vice-president, John H. O'Connell, was assigned as the account executive. At the height of the program, the campaign involved 18 full-time employees and the part-time services of another 15 to 20 employees, a massive effort no less.

The H&K strategists decided that the campaign's primary target would be opinion leaders—editors, business and professional men, club leaders, political leaders. Consumers and the general public would constitute a secondary target. The management group decided to launch a nationwide advertising campaign, using smaller ads to disguise the expense involved.

The ads were launched on behalf of the 5,000 producers of natural gas to deflect the Big Business label. A decision was made to mobilize the natural gas industry to assist in the campaign. Hill and Knowlton was provided with the assistance of industry personnel in preparation of all campaign material so that it would be factually correct.

An organization was set up within the industry that consisted of 15 regional chairmen as well as state chairmen in the 48 states and the District of Columbia. These chairmen directed the work of 2, 100 volunteer workers from all branches of the oil and gas industry. A 2-day indoctrination session to launch the campaign was held for the regional and state chairmen in New York in December 1954, at which time kits of material were distributed together with instructions for such activities as contacting editors, making and arranging for speeches before civic groups, and showing of films on TV stations and to live audiences.

In January 1955, Hill and Knowlton held a luncheon press conference in New York to explain the NGORC position to editors of trade publications, reporters from the wire services, and the financial editors of New York's dailies. Representatives of Hill and Knowlton visited editors of *Saturday Evening Post, Time, Newsweek, Business Week, and Collier's* to brief them on the gas cause. A vast assortment of speeches, press releases, and canned editorials were provided to volunteer workers by the public relations firm. In addition, a file was provided to every daily newspaper and thousands of weeklies containing a background pamphlet, canned editorials, feature stories, and short fillers.

In the early days of this propaganda blitz, a breakdown of press comments on the federal regulation of natural gas of January 14 showed editorials against—6, columns against—10, editorials for—4, columns for—4. In the trade press, there were 4 editorials against regulation, 3 for. Magazine articles tabulated 5 against, 1 for. At a later stage, as Hill recorded in his memoir, there were 1, 718 editorials published favorable to the NGORC position. During the same period, 513 unfavorable and 210 neutral editorials were published on this issue. The propaganda was paying off, or so it seemed.

In his account of this campaign, Irwin Ross wrote that by September 1955, midway in the campaign, Hill and Knowlton reported to the gas producers that it had done these things:

(1) The making of 6,300 speeches and showings of a film, "You, the People."

(2) Two hundred thirty showings of "You, the People" on TV stations. (This is a day when the number of TV stations was still small.)

(3) Four hundred seventy five radio speeches.

(4) Sixty television shows.

(5) Twenty four hundred contacts with local chambers of commerce.

(6) Adoption of favorable resolutions by 120 civic, municipal, and business organizations of 34 states.

(7) Distribution of 5,500,000 pieces of literature.

As these figures indicate, the campaign was intense. As Bert Goss told Irwin Ross, "Every time an editorial or statement appeared opposing our stand, we would arrange for an answer." These tactics appeared to be gaining the day for the gas producers. The House of Representatives passed a bill in 1955 exempting producers of natural gas from federal regulation.

Capitalizing on the success thus far of this massive effort to mold public opinion, Hill and Knowlton submitted a memorandum to NGORC for a "Long Range Program for Natural Gas Producers," dated July 21, 1955. The memo stated:

Experience with the educational program on natural gas and a review of the problems of gas producers, indicate the desirability of creating a permanent organization to deal with major and continuing problems peculiar to the gas production industry. The functions of such an organization or association would be chiefly concentrated on research, industry relations, and information–education activities on behalf of gas producers. It would not involve selection of a large staff organization. The organization would give clear and consistent voice to the viewpoint, policies and programs, carry on research activities, develop statistical and other factual data, cooperate with distributors and pipelines to increase the market for natural gas.

A *separate* organization of gas producers is recommended advisedly even though gas production is closely related with petroleum production. To have the job done by a division of the petroleum industry would (1) perpetuate the impression that gas production is dominated by "Big Oil," and (2) tend to make work on behalf of the gas production industry a very small tail on a very big dog.

Hill's memoir and the Hill Papers are silent as to whether this long range program was adopted. Presumably not.

The campaign was going swimmingly as the U.S. Senate prepared to take up the House-passed bill early in 1956 — and then the roof caved in. Senator Francis Case of South Dakota announced to the Senate that two lawyers representing an oil company (not a member of NGORC) had contributed $2,500 to his campaign in the apparent belief that this would cause him to vote for the gas bill. Case said he had planned to vote for the bill but would now oppose it. Nonetheless, the Senate passed the bill amidst the public uproar caused by Case's revelation—testimony to the strength of the H&K campaign. President Dwight D. Eisenhower vetoed the bill because of the controversy, saying that although he favored the bill, he could not sign it in face of a pending Senate investigation into Senator Case's charges.

A special star-studded Senate committee was appointed to investigate the matter—Senator John F. McClellan of Arkansas as chairman, Senators John F. Kennedy, Clinton P. Anderson, and Albert Gore of Tennessee on the Democratic side, and Republican Senators Thye, Purtell, and Goldwater for the minority side. John Hill recorded:

> This special committee and its staff subjected our public relations program to a searching investigation and devoted two full days of hearings to our program and the activities carried on. Attention naturally focused on the NGORC because of the well publicized scope of our activities and our rigid avoidance of all lobbying activities. . . . More important to us was the fact that the probe resulted in a complete clearance of our client, the NGORC, and of the Hill and Knowlton program carried out for NGORC.

At the end of the 2 days of hearings, Senator McClellan commented to reporters about the NGORC program, "In my opinion, and without the slightest suggestion that anything is wrong with it—the program it adopted might be calculated to have more influence on Congress than direct action." *The Washington Star* headlined the Senator's comments: "MCCLELLAN CALLS PUBLICITY BETTER THAN LOBBYING."

The committee found that the two lawyers who had contributed to Senator Case's campaign were not registered as lobbyists and that they represented an oil company that had not joined or supported either the industry's education or its legislative committees (NGORC or the General Gas Committee.) But the damage was done. One news event capturing the nation's headlines had undone all the effort and expense put into the NGROC campaign by Hill and Knowlton. The impact of the campaign led to Bert Goss's assertion to the committee that "if you give the people the facts, they will eventually operate on the basis of those facts, if you give it to them convincingly and effectively."

During the 17 months of this campaign, the NGROC paid Hill and Knowlton $1,687,706.30. Of this amount, $400,000 constituted retainer fees and staff charges. The balance was for out-of-pocket expenses. The advertising campaign, included in these figures, cost $800,000. For this expenditure, John Hill felt that "looking back over this effort, oil and gas producers can take considerable pride in the activity carried on." However, Edward Barrett who was the coordinator of this large-scale propaganda effort was more skeptical. In commenting on Hill's evaluation as written in *The Making of a Public Relations Man*, Barrett wrote in a memorandum to

Hill on July 13, 1962, statin, "I do not really believe this is a good example of a successful program, for I do not believe it really had any appreciable impact on public opinion. All that can fairly be said is that it probably accomplished a very, very small amount despite enormous obstacles. The real lessons, if stated, would injure many feelings."

However one may assess the effectiveness of the Hill and Knowlton campaign, the hard fact is that the natural gas industry did not free itself from federal price regulation until 1978, 24 years later. Again a major news event was more influential than a 6-months public relations campaign—a cold, severe New England winter that produced an acute shortage of natural gas provided the impetus for Congress to enact the Natural Gas Policy Act in 1978 that freed gas from federal price controls.

A CAMPAIGN TO THWART TOUGHER DRUG LAWS

Three years later, Hill and Knowlton again he hired by a trade association to affect Congressional legislation—this time to block passage of a bill, not promote its passage. And once again a dramatic news break blunted the effects of Hill and Knowlton's efforts. In 1959, H&K was retained by the Pharmaceutical Manufacturers Association (PMA) when the drug industry came under the informed and relentless attack of Senator Estes Kefauver of Tennessee, a U.S. Senator with national political aspirations. This proved to be another intense, controversial campaign but one decided more by a news break than public relations at the end of the day.

The issue of more effective regulation of drugs became public on December 7, 1959, when, after solid staff investigation, Senator Kefauver called the Subcommittee on Antitrust and Monopoly to order in the Senate Caucus Room. The first witness was Francis C. Brown, president of the Schering Corporation. The magnitude of the task H&K had taken on became apparent after the first day's hearings. That evening's *Washington Evening Star* headlined its story: "SENATORS FIND 1, 118% DRUG MARKUP." Next day's *The New York Times* headlined its story: "SENATE PANEL CITES MARKUPS ON DRUGS RANGING TO 7,079%." The *San Francisco Chronicle* ran a head: "MARKUPS ON DRUGS 7,000 PER CENT." That paper followed with an editorial stating, "There is virtual unanimity of lay opinion that drugs . . . are shamefully overpriced, and that opinion has received what looks like formidable cooperation in the current inquiry." Drugs, their efficacy, their cost, and their side affects were now on the public agenda. Hill and Knowlton and the PMA set out to prove, with some justification, that the Kefauver hearings were unfair to the drug industry. For example, Brown accused the subcommittee of being insulting, of trying to exert thought control, and of placing him at an unfair advantage, according to Richard Harris in *The Real Voice*, a definitive account of the hearings first published in *The New Yorker* and later as a book.

However, the industry recovered quickly and developed a sound, thorough, and consistent program coordinated by the Pharmaceutical Manufacturers Association. Although the exact role part played Hill and Knowlton in the preparation and execution of this program cannot be ascertained, it can be assumed that the firm, as counsel for the PMA, played a substantial role. Surprisingly, there are no records of this account in the client files of the John W. Hill Papers. The public relations story told by the industry was remarkably consistent both in the material published by the PMA and the individual drug companies. Presumably this story line was crafted by the PMA public relations staff in consultation with Hill and Knowlton's staff.

As reported by *Business Week* magazine, "The first thing the nation's pharmaceutical industry did a few months ago when Sen. Estes Kefauver launched his probe of drug prices was to put a PR man on the staff of its industry association (the PMA) and hire Hill and Knowlton, public relations counselors, at a fee of $5,000—plus a month to handle the industry's public relations during the hearing—and after."

The major points made in the public relations counterattack to the Kefauver charges were:

1. Emphasis on the extent and expense of drug research.
2. Downgrading high drug profits by pointing out the uncertainty of the industry and the fact that the profit picture of the drug companies often changed quickly.
3. The costs of research and product promotion were confined to the large companies. Therefore, small companies could often sell drugs for less.
4. The use of brand names in prescribing drugs was convenient and safe for doctors, and insured quality drugs for their patients.
5. Patenting and licensing provisions protecting drug firms were necessary as incentives for private research.
6. It was impossible to compare drug prices overseas with those in the United States.
7. The low cost of drugs to the government as compared to private citizens was defended.
8. The value of the detail man to doctors was emphasized.
9. Good works of the drug companies were publicized.
10. It was argued that restrictions on the drug industry would delay getting new drugs on the market. This could even cost the lives of sick people.

11. Doctors and drug employees were exhorted to write to their congressman opposing drug legislation.

This public relations story was widely disseminated through the usual channels — speeches, printed summaries of Congressional testimony, press conferences, internal publics through publications, booklets and brochures, and lobbying.

There is no evidence that H&K was involved in lobbying. According to *The New York Times*, when the battle finally concluded in 1963, an industry spokesman had estimated that the out-of-pocket costs to be met in refuting the Kefauver charges and campaign had come to $5 million. Over the 4-year period, Kefauver's committee had spent some $300,000.

However, Colonel George Hamel, after a thorough study of this controversy, concluded that the hearings did uncover abuses in the industry. He listed these:

1. Excessive profits on certain drugs.
2. Inadequate testing of new drugs due to eagerness to get them on the market.
3. Evidence of poor advertising practices to include failure to note the serious side effects of certain drugs.

As a result of these hearings, tighter regulatory legislation affecting the drug industry was drafted. The attack by the Kefauver Committee caught the industry by surprise and quickly forced it on the defensive.

The counterattack appeared to be effective — for a moment — as consideration of the drug regulation measure dragged on and on. Probably a weak bill or none at all would have passed the Congress had it not been for a shattering news event. (As in the campaign on behalf of the Natural Gas and Oil Resources Committee, a major news break rendered ineffective a long term public relations effort, no matter how well crafted.) On April 12, 1961, Senator Kefauver submitted his drug bill, designated S. 1552. The hearings on the bill were dragged out mainly through the influence of the conservatives in the drug industry and Senators Dirksen, Eastland, and Hruska. Harris wrote, "To a considerable extent, the legislative hearings covered ground that had been gone over earlier. The hearings finally came to a close on February 7, 1962, after some twenty-six months and 12, 885 pages of testimony. On July 19, a weakened version of the bill, a substitute authored by Senators Dirksen and Eastland, was voted out of committee." Harris recorded, "The general feeling in Washington now was that S. 1552. was dead for that session." Senator Hruska of Nebraska carried the ball for the PMA.

Then the thalidomide scandal broke. In April of that year, physicians in West Germany were frantically searching for the cause of an epidemic of the birth of deformed babies (phocomelia) in West Germany, Great Britain, Sweden, Italy, Switzerland, and other countries. The cause was finally traced to Contergen, a drug that women had taken during pregnancy. Contergen was a trade name for thalidomide. Chemie Grunenthal, a German drug firm, had sold the drug as a sleeping pill, a nonprescription medication. Deaths in Australia, Britain, and other countries were traced to Distaval, the British brand of thalidomide. Soon thereafter, Grunenthal and Distillers, Ltd., the British manufacturers, withdrew their thalidomide-based drugs from the market. The William S. Merrill Drug Company had an application pending with the Food and Drug Administration for its brand, Kevadon. Merrill had earlier received a marketing permit in Canada and left its Kevadon on the Canadian market for 3 months after the British and German firms had taken their brands off the market. Merrill's application had been held up in the FDA by the stubborn refusal of Dr. Frances O. Kelsey to approve its licensure. Merrill had filed its application on September 12, 1960. Morton Mintz published a story of Dr. Kelsey's refusal in the July 15 *Washington Post* under the headline: "HEROINE OF FDA KEEPS BAD DRUGS OFF THE MARKET." Harris said, "The press buildup accelerated on July 25th, when a Phoenix housewife, Mrs. Robert Finkbine, who was then pregnant, and who had been taking Distaval, bought in England by her husband, flew to Sweden for an abortion." Two days later, it was revealed by United Press International that Merrill had sent its Kevadon to 1,200 doctors for testing and that not all these pills had been recovered.

These news stories gave new life to the Kefauver version of drug legislation. The Senate took up the bill, as amended, on August 23, and immediately Senators Kefauver and Humphrey offered amendments restoring teeth to the bill. After long, heated debate, that evening a roll call vote was taken on the entire bill. It passed 78 to 0! The thalidomide scandal leaving hundreds of deformed babies in its wake had swiftly changed public opinion. Even so, the industry won elimination of patent restrictions from the bill and nearly prevented passage of the requirement for a conspicuous warning of possible ill effects on drug labels. Surely the PMA–H&K campaign had considerable effect and may have totally defeated this needed drug regulation had not the thalidomide story broken when it did.

The flavor of the PMA–H&K countercampaign can be seen in this passage from Harris's *The Real Voice*:

> At the start, it was a gentlemen's war by and large, although the right-wingers in the industry did at times resort to guerrilla tactics. Some sent doctors lavish, and distorted brochures urging them to write to their senators and represen-

tatives about the vicious attacks that Kefauver was making on the free-enterprise system, and assuring them that his bill would wipe out drug research. Others got their employees to send letters to key men on the subcommittee; a perusal of Senator Hart's mail, for instance, revealed scores of letters from constituents in Detroit—most of them identical. In addition, some drug firms set up training programs for several thousand detail men, designed to prepare them to give lectures around the country before audiences of P.T.A. groups, women's clubs, and fraternal organizations on the dire consequences to the health of the American people if the Kefauver bill became law.

These strongly resemble H&K tactics in other campaigns. This campaign, — like those crafted for the tobacco industry and the dairy industry in which health and moral issues have been of paramount importance, again raises the question of public relations practitioners' oft-proclaimed adherence to the public interest. Bert Goss replied obliquely to this point in an interview with Colonel George Hamel, "John Hill has never been involved in anything shady. There were threats several times that Hill and Knowlton would be pulled into the Kefauver investigation of the drug industry but nothing ever happened. The committee wouldn't have hesitated had they found anything wrong in Hill and Knowlton's operations."

Not being accused of improper public relations activity is far short of the question, "In opposing tighter drug regulation on behalf of the consumer, did Hill and Knowlton serve the public interest?" The philosophical rebuttal to that question is the practitioners' justifiable claim that every individual, every institution, every industry has a right to be heard in the public forum and that it is the public relations practitioner's duty to see that all causes are heard. Without the expertise of the public relations counsel, a cause's voice is likely to be lost in public clamor of today's public opinion marketplace.

In 1962, in the wake of the passage of the Kefauver drug bill, Hill and Knowlton started holding seminars for educators on behalf of the PMA. This forum, developed first for the steel industry in 1960, came as the result of the firm's questioning of a large number of economics professors and deans of business schools who told Hill and Knowlton's staff "they would benefit from hearing frank talk by business executives about their economic problems and their industry's point of view." The sponsor paid the expenses of the host institution and the participating educators. Hill wrote in his memoir, "The educators have told us that the seminars were valuable to them and that more should be held. . . . Industry executives, for their part, have been nearly unanimous in their opinion that the seminars provide effective means to two-way communication with an important group of opinion leaders." DuPont and International Harvester (now Navistar) pioneered this effort to establish two-way communication with the academic community.

As a result of these interviews with university deans and professors, Hill and Knowlton set up the first Steel Industry Economics Seminar for College Professors in Youngstown, Ohio, in November 1960. The first one's apparent success caused its continuation for several years. In 1962, the firm set up similar seminars for the Pharmaceutical Manufacturers and for the Aerospace Industries, also a H&K client. Hill recorded in his memoir, "I feel strongly that it would be to the benefit of all private enterprise, as well as our educational system, if more industries would undertake projects of this nature."

AN UGLY BOOK DEAL

In his later years, John Hill was honored for his efforts to make public relations an ethical profession by two universities, by professional associations, and generally by his peers. Responding to a query from Almo C. Conay of A. K. Masten & Company, Pittsburgh, asking if a way could be found to start "a movement without any apparent sponsorship from any source," Hill replied bluntly:

> For our part, we would never be identified with any movement for which the source was not open and above board for everybody to know. As you may know, some public relations firms — upon being retained by a client who does not want his name identified with the movement or objective sought — have set up paper organizations with high sounding names. In the name of the paper organization, publicity is used and activities of various sorts are carried on and, sometimes effective results are obtained.

> Our method is to operate in the daylight without the use of false whiskers. I think the best way to deal with these problems is to lay the cards on the table.

In 1965, 3 years after Hill had relinquished active management of his firm, Hill and Knowlton's reputation was badly stained when it chose to serve a client in the dark, not in the daylight. When H&K purchased Robinson–Hannagan Associates in 1955, it had acquired the lucrative Bahamas tourist account. For its publicizing of blue waters, cloudless skies, and white beaches, H&K received a fee of $600,000 and supervised a budget of $5 million, according to *Fortune* magazine. A staff of 35 persons worked on this account. During the 1960s, when the firm was publicizing the glories of the Bahamas as a tourist attraction, the gambling houses came under the control of gangster elements. According to *Fortune* of September 1, 1967, "While the links between the Bay Street Boys, the island politicians, and U.S. gangsters were widely rumored, there was no detailed evidence to support it."

Then Allan W. Witwer, a former reporter now in employ of the H&K on the Bahamian account, set about to expose the gamblers and gangsters. In April 1965, he quit his job and returned to the States with loads of confidential information. He wrote 7 chapters, 250 pages, of a proposed 29-chapter book, *The Ugly Bahamians*. In May 1965, Witwer tried to peddle his book to a publisher through the Ashley–Famous Agency and was turned down because the chapters were "atrociously written, motivated by spite, and unmarketable in the legitimate publishing world."

Then with an obvious motive, he took the chapters to Hill and Knowlton and not so subtly suggested that Sir Stafford Sands, Minister of Bahamian Tourism, might be interested to know about his proposed book. According to *Fortune*, "Bill Durbin, H&K's vice president for foreign accounts, read the book and hurried on down to Nassau." After perusing the chapters, Sir Stafford asked Durbin if the book would hurt the Bay Street establishment. Durbin assured him that it surely would be damaging. Then, according to a statement filed by H&K with the Department of Justice, with the approval of Sands, H&K attempted to find a publisher to buy the manuscript on behalf of a "nongovernment figure." H&K chose as a possible buyer, Exposition Press, a "subsidy" publishing firm headed by Edward Uhlan. Subsequently, Uhlan offered $10,000 to Witwer for his book, which Witwer indignantly rejected, shouting the book was worth $100,000. Exposition raised the bid to $30,000, but again Witwer balked.

The sale was finally consummated in a room in the Tuscany Hotel in which Witwer agreed to surrender all manuscripts, papers, and any other material connected with the book for a price of $53,050 paid by the Grand Bahamas Development Corp. It appears that Witwer didn't keep his bargain. Some copies of the book got into the hands of Lynden Pindling, the African-American candidate for Prime Minister who used the information in a blistering attack on the Bay Street Boys.

As *Fortune* concluded, "There are really two questions about H&K's conduct in this episode. The first is how such an informed, sophisticated organization could remain ignorant of what was happening on the is- land. . . . The second question is how could H&K become involved, even indirectly, in *The Ugly Bahamians Episode*." The firm could give *Fortune* no good answer. Published in the *Wall Street Journal* and other newspa- pers, the story damaged the firm's reputation. John Hill later acknowledged that the whole matter was unfortunate.

H&K'S OPERATING PHILOSOPHIES AND PROCEDURES

As John Hill's firm grew and matured in the 1950s, his papers reveal a maturing operating philosophy and firm procedures. Hill repeatedly vowed that H&K would not solicit accounts. On July 23, 1958, he wrote his Cleveland partner, Don Knowlton, who had written to urge Hill to solicit the account of the Lake Carriers Association that was promoting the Great Lakes Seaway, "This is one that I would stay a mile away from unless the steel industry's position were completely clarified and they expressed their interest in the situation." Hill then added, "Also, you know that we don't solicit an account no matter what the circumstances—so, all in all, H&K Inc. would not be interested in pursuing the matter."

Yet, just a year before on August 29, 1957, Hill wrote his former vice-president, Kerryn King, now vice-president of the Texas Company, a letter enclosing a memorandum puffing the value of a public relations counseling firm in what seemed an apparent effort to arm King with strong arguments for continuing retention of H&K by Texaco. Hill wrote his former colleague:

> While you obviously have a thorough and first-hand knowledge of the benefits derived by a corporation from having public relations counsel, we thought it might be helpful to have at hand for any future need a checklist, in writing, of some of these advantages. . . . In this connection, I think you will be interested in the enclosed . . . publications of Procter & Gamble [a H&K client] which includes a story, pictures and captions which outline the way Procter & Gamble teams up its public relations department and the staff of public relations counsel for greater effectiveness of operations.

Just what was behind this hard sell to King, long a valued associate, I could not ascertain. Here is the memorandum to King in full:

USEFUL OPERATIONAL ASSISTANCE
SUPPLIED BY PUBLIC RELATIONS COUNSEL

1. Availability of a trained and experienced reservoir of manpower for meeting emergency needs or special assignments, without the expense of keeping a tremendous staff employed directly year-round.

> (In the case of the Texas Company and its counsel, this means a staff of more than 200 is at hand to supplement the Public Relations Department's own efforts, as needed.)

2. Services of a full staff of experienced publicity placement people, including specialists in business and financial news; newspapers, press associations and feature syndicates; magazines, radio and television.

> (Because they are in frequent contact with the media on behalf of a variety of clients, these specialists can keep the Texas Company's Public Relations Department more closely advised of opportunities for placement of the Company's materials and information and provides advance notice of

significant or even unfavorable stories about which the Texas Company will want to take action.)

3. Access to a sizeable staff of successful writers with a broad range of special interests and abilities—book and magazine authors, speech writers and specialists in industrial and financial advertising, corporate finance and economics, educators and others.

4. Access to the services of the largest Washington and Los Angeles public relations staffs in the counseling field, as well as offices in other U.S. cities.

(In Washington service, for instance, Hill and Knowlton, Inc. can offer the services of seven staff members with 10 or more years experience, each, in Washington political reporting or public relations work.)

5. Assistance on scholarship plans and relations with schools and colleges through the largest Education Department in the public relations counseling field.

(Hill and Knowlton's Education Department is staffed by professional educators with many years of experience in high school and college teaching, school administration and state education department activities.)

6. Access to a variety of specialists in the broad range of public relations needs and interests including:

a. *International Public Relations*—on-the-spot service through a widespread network of foreign public relations offices staffed by experienced professionals who can provide, on short notice, counsel or operational assistance such as publicity placement. Hill and Knowlton network includes subsidiaries of associated firms in England, France, West Germany, The Netherlands, Belgium, Canada, Latin America, Australia and New Zealand.

b. *Community Relations*—a staff accustomed to on-the-spot counseling, the meeting of emergency needs and conducting clinics for plant or division personnel.

c. *Employee Communications*—specialists in all forms of employee communications, the public relations aspect of labor problems and employee recruitment; evaluation of the readability and effectiveness of internal and external publications, newspaper and magazine layout, advice on editorial content and approach.

d. *Art and Production*—development of attractive and effective art work and printing of brochures, annual reports, institutional advertisements and other types of publications and visual materials.

e. *Television and Motion Pictures*—qualified staff members well versed in the supervision of film or script production for television use, as well as the development of effective motion pictures—color or black and white—for general showings.

f. *Stockholder and Financial Relations* – a large number of staff members
well acquainted with the financial community and successful means of
communicating with it; prepared to assist in or handle the preparation of
Annual Reports, special materials for stockholders or analysts, financial
publicity and speeches or articles on corporate finance or economics.

In addition to the above specialized services, public relations counsel has
available as great a number of staff members with breadth and depth of
experience in all phases of public relations as any counseling firm in the
world. Through the combination of its own department and the staff of
public relations counsel, the Texas Company therefore has available to it
the largest possible staff of experienced public relations people qualified to
handle any type of public relations problem or assignment.

H&K ACQUIRE OTHER FIRMS ALONG THE WAY

Although Hill and Knowlton grew steadily to become the nation's largest
public relations firm by acquiring major new clients on the strength of its
performance on behalf of such clients as the American Iron and Steel
Institute, AVCO, and the Pharmaceutical Manufacturers' Association, it
also grew by acquisition of smaller firms. The first significant acquisition of
another firm came in December 1954, when H&K purchased the Edward W.
Barrett organization. Edward Barrett, later to leave Hill and Knowlton to
become dean of Columbia University's Graduate School of Journalism, had
formed his international consulting firm after serving 2 years, 1950–1952, as
Assistant Secretary of Public Affairs in the U.S. State Department. Before
that Barrett had a distinguished career in newspaper and magazine journalism. Through this purchase, the firm acquired two major accounts, the
government of Japan and the Suez Canal Company. The Suez account was
lost when Egypt seized control of the canal in 1956, which provoked an
international crisis at the time, a crisis that brought down Prime Minister
Anthony Eden's British government.

Barrett became an executive vice-president of Hill and Knowlton and
continued to play a major role in the firm, even after resigning in 1956 to
take the Columbia deanship. At that time, Barrett Associates, which had
continued to operate as a H&K subsidiary since 1954, was dissolved. In
leaving H&K, Barrett explained his reasons in a memorandum to Hill,
Goss, and Darrow:

> Although this change involves a financial comedown and less excitement, it
> also offers less tension and a challenge to address the shortcomings and
> potentialities of American journalism. The chance to bring about improve-
> ment in American journalism shouldn't be brushed aside. The full-time work

in the field may be tedious or even boring later. In addition, there is always the possibility of finding myself assisting causes with which I'm not sympathetic. I recognize that the position will have frustrations, but also possibilities remodelling the School, and undertaking new projects.

One worthwhile new project Dean Barrett took on was the founding of the *Columbia Journalism Review* which, continues to monitor the media's performance to this day. Ed Barrett's deal with Columbia University permitted him to spend 20% of his time on outside counseling. Thus, he continued to be closely involved with John Hill and the firm, particularly in promoting Hill & Knowlton International on which he served as a member of the board. He also had a large hand in *The Making of a Public Relations Man*.

Hill & Knowlton's second acquisition came when it bought Robinson-Hannagan (R–H) Associates for $200,000. After Steve Hannagan's death in 1953, William Robinson, longtime public relations executive with the *New York Herald-Tribune* before it ceased publication, bought the controlling interest in the Hannagan firm. After Robinson was tapped by his major client, Robert W. Woodruff, builder of the Coca-Cola empire, to be Coca-Cola's president, he sold the firm to Hill and Knowlton. At the time of the purchase of R–H in 1955, it was announced that it would continue to operate independently, but a year later the publicity firm was absorbed into Hill and Knowlton. The details of this transaction are told in chapter 10.

Of the major accounts acquired in the R–H deal, a major one was soon lost, and the other involved Hill and Knowlton in a shady book deal that stained its generally good reputation. Four years after Robinson sold the firm to take the top post at Coca-Cola, H&K lost that lucrative account. What part Robinson played in this decision is not known. Robert Woodruff, though now carrying only the title of chairman of the finance committee, still ruled his soft drink empire with a strong hand. Woodruff came to the conclusion, understandably, that H&K was too institutionalized and that it lacked the flair and style he had grown accustomed to with the flamboyant Steve Hannagan. In 1960, Woodruff was in the steam room of New York's Biltmore's baths with Bernard Gimbel when he was introduced to Tom Deegan, who was formerly public relations director for Robert R. Young's C&O railroad and other enterprises and now had his own firm. According to *Fortune*, "On the spot, standing in white towels and bathed in steam, Woodruff said he wanted Deegan's firm to handle Cocoa-Cola public relations." The news was a surprise to Deegan and a shock to Hill and Knowlton's top brass.

The other account acquired in the R–H deal that also brought a headache was that of the lucrative Bahamas –Nassau Development Board that promoted tourist traffic to Nassau and the Bahamian Island. It was a rich account but one that spelled trouble. The story of the Ugly Book Deal was told earlier.

It was understandable that Woodruff and his associates were struck by the sharp contrast between the personalities and methods of work of Steve Hannagan and John Hill. Hannagan was a loud-talking, brassy extrovert who enjoyed good times and good stunts. Hill, on the other hand, was a rather stoic business-like individual, sensible and cautious and far from flamboyant. Throughout his career, Hill viewed himself more as a businessman than as a publicist. It was the calm institutionalized atmosphere of H&K that took Woodruff aback. Woodruff, possessing both a keen sense of financial acumen and a flair for public relations, had built Coca-Cola into the giant it is with imaginative advertising and public relations.

Accounts acquired in the Robinson–Hannagan buyout with H&K retained for the next several years included Owens–Illinois Glass Company, Gillette Safety Razor Company, Cities Service Petroleum, American Potash and Chemical Corporation, and Boys' Republic.

In August 1967, H&K acquired a stock interest in Gardner, Jones, & Cowell, a Chicago firm with a staff of 30 and 16 clients. By this purchase, H&K acquired the accounts of Green Giant and Seco. The Chicago firm continued to operate under its own name but was largely owned by H&K and closely supervised by the H&K top executives.

The most satisfying acquisition came when Hill and Knowlton purchased Carl Byoir & Associates from the advertising firm of Foote, Cone, and Belding (FCB). The Byoir firm, in the 1950s and 1960s was number one in billings and thus the chief rival to Hill and Knowlton's aspiration to be number one. The Byoir firm was the first to be acquired by a major advertising agency—others followed as Young and Rubicam bought Burson–Marsteller, Inc., now the nation's largest counseling firm, and ultimately J. Walter Thompson purchased Hill and Knowlton, Inc.

At its zenith, Carl Byoir & Associates was charging an annual retainer fee of $50,000 to corporate clients and was counseling such major firms as RCA, Howard Hughes, Honeywell, B. F. Goodrich and others, 29 in all. FCB bought the Byoir firm in 1977, then headed by Robert Wood, president, and George Hammond, chairman. In March 1983, FCB made wholesale changes in the Byoir management, firing many of its veteran executives. From there on, the firm declined in accounts and prestige. In August 1986, Hill and Knowlton bought the firm, its assets, and its accounts and absorbed these into Hill and Knowlton, Inc. Thus, the firm built from 1930 on by Carl Byoir and Gerry Swinehart went into the Public Relations Pantheon. H&K revived the firm name in 1986 and operated it as a subsidiary under the leadership of John F. Budd, Jr., but it remained but a shadow of the once dominant firm of Carl Byoir & Associates. Budd left H&K in 1991. The story of the sad end of the Byoir agency is fully told in chapter 17.

NOTES ON SOURCES

A complete listing of the sources on which chapters 15 and 16 are based is at the end of chapter 16. The principal sources for the content of this chapter are the following.

The John W. Hill Papers, including client files, in the Mass Communications History Center of the State Historical Society of Wisconsin. Another primary source was Colonel George F. Hamel's master's thesis, written under my direction at the University of Wisconsin in 1966. Colonel Hamel's research included extensive interviews with Hill and other members of his firm, and considerable correspondence with Hill and with his peers in public relations.

I had several interviews with Mr. Hill and with his top aides of the time, Bert Goss, Richard Darrow, and William Durbin. Also relied on were Hill's two books, written with the help of key staff aides, *Corporate* Public Relations (Harper) and *The Making of a Public Relations Man* (McKay).

Other specific sources for this chapter include: Irwin Ross, *The Image Merchants*, Doubleday & Company, 1959. Quotations from this book are with Mr. Ross' permission. Richard Harris, *The Real Voice*, Macmillan, 1964. Harris tells the story of the drug industry's fight against stronger drug regulation and is quoted with permission.

United States Congress, Senate, *Oil and Gas Lobby Investigation*, Hearings before the Senate Special Committee to investigate political activities, lobbying activities. Washington: Government Printing Office, 1956.

The Bahamian book deal is told by T. A. Wise in, "Hill & Knowlton's World of Images," *Fortune*, September, 1, 1967. Also see: R. Oulahan and W. Lambert, "Scandal in the Bahamas, *Life*, Vol. 62, February 3, 1967.

Richard A. Ball and J. Robert Lilly, "The Menace of Margarine: The Rise and Fall of a Social Problem," *Social Problems* Vol. 29, June, 1982.

Chapter 16

John Hill's Two Major Battles: Steel and Tobacco – and the Person

John Wiley Hill's public relations practices and ethical standards were tested in his service to two major industries – steel and tobacco – and these are the primary focus of this chapter. The chapter concludes with Hill's professional views and an appraisal.

By accident of his Cleveland location, an early steel company client, and his friendship with Tom Girdler, president of Republic Steel and adamant foe of labor unions, John Hill became involved in the labor and legal battles of the steel industry from mid-November 1933 until the end of his active involvement in Hill and Knowlton, Inc. His counsel to the steel industry, primarily through the American Iron and Steel Institute, spanned three turbulent decades in that industry.

Hill became involved with the tobacco industry when the presidents of the six largest tobacco companies, frightened by the growing evidence linking cigarette smoking with lung cancer and heart disease, sought Hill's counsel on December 15, 1953. Although John Hill questioned the ethics of the tobacco industry's position, he accepted it as a client when, on the basis of his advice, the manufacturers agreed to underwrite the Tobacco Industry Research Committee (TIRC). This committee supplied research funds to scientists and doctors ostensibly to ascertain the "facts" in the raging controversy.

The TIRC in fact became a public relations front as Hill and Knowlton continued to present the industry's side in the smoking debate as evidence of the damaging effects of tobacco on a person's health mounted. Hill's firm lost its tobacco accounts with his retirement from active involvement in them.

In 1962–1963, the TIRC changed its name to the Tobacco Research Council (TRC). The TIRC/TRC retained Hill and Knowlton on a part-time basis through the 1960s. In 1969, Leonard Zahn, vice-president who worked on the account at H&K, left the firm to set up his own agency on Long Island. A short time later, he became public relations counsel for the Tobacco Research Council.

In 1958, John Hill helped the tobacco industry set up public relations lobbying for organization in Washington as the campaign against smoking intensified—the Tobacco Institute. Hill and Knowlton lost the Tobacco Institute account in 1968 when the institute hired William Kleopfer, Jr. as Vice President for Public Relations. Kleopfer, who had formerly been with the Pharmaceutical Manufacturers Association, a H&K client, retired in 1989 and was succeeded by Walker Merryman. Merryman wrote to me in a letter dated December 2, 1991, "Beginning in approximately 1980 and continuing through this year, we again began using Hill & Knowlton's services for some specific projects. We have had similar relationships with other agencies."

THE LITTLE STEEL STRIKE

As noted in the previous chapter, John Hill's retention as counsel to the American Iron and Steel Institute (AISI) led soon thereafter to his setting up a New York office as Hill and Knowlton, Inc., an agency independent of the one in Cleveland. The AISI had been organized earlier that year to deal with President Roosevelt's National Industry Recovery Act (NIRA) that required adoption of business codes for each industry.

When John Hill assumed his new duties with the American Iron and Steel Institute in mid-November 1933, it was stipulated that he attend all meetings of the Institute Board of Directors (a *sine qua non* for effective public relations counseling), and thus, he became enmeshed in all the Depression Era problems of that powerful industry. Hill later recalled, "The thirties were crucial years in which . . . the industry struggled to surmount the Depression, worked with the Federal Government to carry out the NIRA Code of Fair Competition, went through the throes of unionization of most of the industry by the CIO, and faced the uncertain demands posed by the outbreak of war in Europe." It is worth noting that in 1933 only four steel companies employed public relations directors—Jones & Laughlin, Bethlehem Steel, Armco, and National Steel. As the industry's battle to stave off unionization intensified, other companies set up public relations departments.

The National Industrial Recovery Act made it possible for labor unions to organize the nation's industries. Given this green light, John L. Lewis, longtime head of the United Mine Workers, organized the Congress of Industrial Organizations (CIO) and announced his intention to organize the steel industry. Steel had not had a strike since the abortive one in 1919 and had in the 1920s protected itself with company unions, termed *employee representation plans*. As the CIO's drive gained ground, the industry leaders of steel decided to make public their acceptance of employee representation. It was decided to run this statement in a full-page newspaper ad.

The task of writing the ad was assigned to Hill and his small public relations group. Hill then encountered a problem public relations counselors have had from the days of Ivy Lee to this day—the intervention of lawyers into public relations matters. Hill's copy was turned over to the industry's lawyers for review. The attorneys came up with a version of their own, and it was approved by the industry executives. Hill argued, "We believed the industry should say that its employees were free to choose whether or not to join a union but that no union should be permitted to use coercion and violence." Hill had both versions set in type and then appealed to Eugene Grace, president of Bethlehem Steel, to reverse the industry decision. Hill had found that "most lawyers of that day regarded public relations people as interlopers in the corporate arena." Many still do. Grace agreed to have a meeting about the ad at a Wall Street club with the result that a modified version of Hill's statement was agreed upon. This provides an interesting background on an ad that later figured importantly in a Senate investigation of the Little Steel Strike.

The ad's text on the points in the debate finally read:

> The Steel Industry believes in the principle of collective bargaining, and it is in effect throughout the industry. The overwhelming majority of the employees in the Steel Industry recently participated in annual elections under their own representation plans and elected their representatives for collective bargaining. The elections were conducted by the employees themselves by secret ballot. One of the purposes of the announced campaign is to overthrow those plans and the representatives so elected.

Many years later Hill wrote in a memorandum to Richard Darrow and Bert Goss, dated October 8, 1958, "This was thrashed out with Gov. [Nathan] Miller and Mr. Moore in the office of Mr. Grace and I was able to get some slight modification of language, but not nearly enough. The lawyers frankly stated that, if I had my way, the industry would have been unionized within 30 days."

John Hill had understood public opinion of the time better than the lawyers when he urged the industry to recognize the right to organize. He wrote, "The mood of the times made it clear . . . that industry would gain stronger support from the public and its employees by taking this position."

As Hill wrote in his autobiography, "Time and mounting political pressures were soon to bring a complete turnabout in management's attitudes toward collective bargaining."

The Steel Workers Organizing Committee (SWOC), financed by Lewis' CIO and led by Philip Murray, was begun in June 1936 and accepted by the steel workers with enthusiasm. The industry, hit hard by the Depression, proved to be a fertile ground for the organizers. By the end of 1936, enough steel workers had joined the SWOC that the union demanded recognition and collective bargaining by the industry. SWOC threatened a nationwide strike in steel if its demands were not met. The CIO made a big breakthrough when after lengthy negotiations, the United States Steel Corporation signed an agreement with the union on March 1, 1937. More than 100 independent companies followed suit by signing agreements with the union, and by May 1937, the SWOC had more than 300,000 members.[1]

TO THE PUBLIC AND EMPLOYEES IN STHE STEEL INDUSTRY

A campaign to unionize the employees of the Steel Industry has been announced. In order that the employees and the public may know the position of the Steel Industry, the Industry makes this statement through the American Iron and Steel Institute.

Persons and organizations not connected with the Industry have taken charge of the campaign.

There are many disturbing indications that the promoters of the campaign will employ coercion, and intimidation of the employees in the Industry and foment strikes.

The objective of the campaign is the "closed shop" which prohibits the employment of anyone who is not a union member. The Steel Industry will oppose any attempt to compel its employees to join a union or to pay tribute for the right to work.

No employee in the Steel Industry has to join any organization to get or hold a job. Employment in the Industry does not depend upon membership or nonmembership in any organization. Advancement depends on individual merit and effort. These are fundamental American principles to which the industry will steadfastly adhere.

The Steel Industry believes in the principles of collective bargaining, and it is in effect throughout the Industry.

---

[1]The text of the American Iron and Steel Institute advertisement was published in July 1936 on the heels of the formation of the Steel Workers Organizing Committee under the newly formed Congress of Industrial organizations. The ad was placed in 382 newspapers in 34 states and Washington, DC at a cost of $114,365.01.

The overwhelming majority of the employees in the Steel Industry recently participated in annual elections under their own representation plans and elected their representatives for collective bargaining. The elections were conducted by the employees themselves by secret ballot. One of the purposes of the announced campaign is to overthrow those plans and the representatives so elected.

The Steel Industry is recovering from six years of depression and huge losses, and the employees are now beginning to receive the benefits of increased operations. Any interruption of the forward movement will seriously injure the employees and their families and all businesses dependent upon the industry, and will endanger the welfare of the country.

The announced drive, with its accompanying agitation for industrial strife, threatens such interruption.

The Steel Industry will use its resources to the best of its ability to protect its employees and their families from intimidation, coercion and violence and to aid them in maintaining collective bargaining free from interference from any source.

Nonetheless, a group of companies known as Little Steel, influenced by the strong leadership of Tom Girdler, had determined that they would not sign bargaining agreements with the SWOC. These companies—Republic Steel, Youngstown Sheet and Tube, Inland Steel, Bethlehem Steel, and Jones and Laughlin Steel—were actually very large corporations, being "little" only in comparison with U.S. Steel. The heads of Little Steel companies were bitter with what they termed the capitulation of United States Steel because they were convinced that the CIO was bad for the companies, the employees, and the country, as Tom Girdler wrote in his autobiography, *Boot Straps*. Economic factors and a determined opposition to trade unionism were the main reasons in Little Steel's decision to have a showdown with the SWOC. Girdler emerged as the unofficial spokesman for the Little Steel companies and thus became a lightning rod for attacks by labor leaders and political leaders favoring union organization in industry.

Because of the way the basic industries, coal and steel, had run roughshod over efforts of employees to organize unions in the 1920s and with the advent of President Roosevelt's New Deal, public opinion in the 1930s was quite favorable to labor unions. As Thomas Geoghegan wrote in his *Which Side Are You On?*, "Playwrights, novelists, professors, artists, civil libertarians, and New Deal Democrats actively supported the great industrial organizing drives and strikes of that era. Union demands for justice on the job were perceived to be part of the larger fight for social and economic justice for all Americans. Many labor struggles were suffused with radicalism and romanticism that appealed to middle-class sympathizers." Hill took a more antagonistic view when he saw the looming Little Steel strikes as "a tough struggle because Communist agitators were everywhere in evidence around the steel plants." Hill met with Girdler and Charlie White at AISI in May 1937 to draw plans for defeating the strike. All three agreed that everything should be done to avoid violence, Hill later recounted. But violence was inevitable, given the uncompromising line taken by the steel companies under Girdler's leadership.

The Little Steel Strike was actually a series of strikes called against the individual companies and their plants rather than a simultaneous strike against all the companies. The SWOC called these shots for strategic and manpower reasons. Late in May, strikes were called against Republic, Youngstown Sheet and Tube, and Armco companies with a total of 75,000 workers. Ultimately 155,000 workers were involved in these strikes. These steel companies fought back successfully though their strong control of company towns, including the media, and succeeded in breaking the morale of the workers and handing the CIO its first defeat. By mid-July, the strikes were virtually ended. There were two exceptions to this situation. One was a strike against Bethlehem Steel called June 11 by local union members, against the instructions of the SWOC that did not want to strike Bethlehem because it knew it was in a weak position. This strike was a dismal failure because the company refused to deal with the union and utilized effective strikebreaking tactics. The Bethlehem plants were reopened on June 27. The reasons the Bethlehem strike failed were told in chapter 9, "John Price Jones Tries to Ride Two Horses." Jones was the chief public relations counsel for Bethlehem in that strike but was provided material assistance by James Selvage, vice-president for public relations of the National Association of Manufacturers (NAM). The NAM had retained Hill and Knowlton in February 1936 as outside counsel, and thus it may be presumed that Hill and his staff gave support to Bethlehem Steel through the NAM.

The other exception was Jones and Laughlin Steel Company, which was struck on June 12, a day after the abortive strike was called by the SWOC local against Bethlehem. Thirty-six hours after the strike began, Jones and Laughlin signed an agreement providing exclusive recognition of the union, provided a majority of the workers favored it. The SWOC won a lopsided 2-to-1 victory in the ensuing election conducted by the National Labor Relations Board (NLRB).

Because of Tom Girdler's bitter antiunion position and his leadership in the battle against the SWOC/CIO, it was inevitable that the feared violence would erupt at Republic plants. Hill saw Girdler, because of his leadership, "the target of labor and New Deal attacks," adding, "the most vicious of these centered about the Memorial Day riot at the Republic Chicago plant." At Republic's plant on the South side of Chicago on May 30, 1937, several hundred pickets marched on the plant but were halted by police when they attempted to conduct a demonstration outside the plant. Some missiles were thrown by the demonstrators, and suddenly the police opened fire on the union supporters. Ten demonstrators were killed and 100 were injured, as were 22 policemen. This became emotionalized by the union as "The Memorial Day Massacre." In another incident at the Warren, Ohio, plant, a large group of employees refused to walk off the job, and then pickets surrounded the plant and would not permit food deliveries to the workers inside. Girdler hired a group of airplane pilots to drop food into the plant.

The determination of Girdler and the other presidents to break the strike was quickly reflected in the failure of the governors of Ohio, Pennsylvania, Michigan, and Indiana—states all adversely affected by the strikes—to mediate a settlement. Next Miss Frances Perkins, Secretary of Labor, appointed a distinguished mediation board to make recommendations and act as arbitrators between the companies and the union. Members of this panel were Charles P. Taft of Cincinnati, Dean Lloyd K. Garrison of the University of Wisconsin in Law School, and Edward F. McGrady, an official of the Department of Labor. This board proposed that the companies sign an agreement with the union to become effective only if the union won a majority vote in an election supervised by the National Labor Relations Board. Should the union lose the election, the agreements were to be torn up, but in the meantime the strike would be ended. The Union accepted the agreement immediately, but the steel companies, predictably, refused to sign. Dismissing the proposal, Girdler said, "Since you can't mediate between right and wrong, they were allowing themselves to be used shamefully."

The Little Steel companies won the battle but ultimately lost the war in their last-ditch stand again unions and industrial government. Late in 1941, after hearings that cost Republic Steel and the government hundred of thousands of dollars, a check of union membership was ordered, and the majority of Republic's employees were found to be union members. Republic was ordered by the NLRB to negotiate a contract with the union, but even so it took nearly a year before a contract was finally signed in August 1942. The strike not only cost the lives and the injured in the Memorial Day Massacre, but the workers suffered hardships and harassments as well as losing money they could ill afford. The union spent $1,500,000 in its campaign to organize steel. Some indication of the cost of the companies is found in the fact that Republic's profits increased 2% during 1937 whereas U. S. Steel's profits increased 94% over 1936. Later costs of Republic included reinstatement of 7,000 employees with back pay of $2,000,000, as directed by the NLRB and $350,000 paid to settle suits against the company on behalf of strikers who were killed or injured. These costs do not include the money spent on public relations, on advertising, strikebreakers, detectives, and other means used to defeat the union.

The companies charged repeatedly that the CIO was Communist-dominated and irresponsible. As Jerold Auerbach wrote in his summation of the LaFollette hearings: "The fear of Communism was used to justify everything from the confiscation of union literature to the death of ten strikers at the hands of the Chicago police during the Little Steel trouble." This is reflected in John Hill's view of that bloody confrontation of police and strikers:

> The rioters, inflamed and urged on by their organizers, violently attacked a line of Chicago city police stationed well outside the plant. The police, in self-defense, started firing and killed three of the rioters. Seven others died in hospitals later. Of the ten dead, only one was a Republic employee. Of sixty-seven arrested, only fourteen were Republic employees. Twenty-eight policemen were injured. In no time, the Illinois State Committee of the Communist Party was showering Chicago with handbills shouting that "Old Czarist Russia had its bloody Sunday but it did not save the Czar. . . . Memorial Day, 1937, becomes for us a Memorial Day for the working class heroes who died for democracy in Chicago." The Communists demand the indictment of Girdler "for his conspiracy to violate the Wagner Labor Relations Law by force and violence."

The threat of the Red Menace had been used by the steel and coal companies in 1919 and 1920 to crush unionization of those industries, feeding upon the climate of fear that had been unleashed by Attorney General Mitchell and his young aide, J. Edgar Hoover, in their Communist witch hunts. These were described in chapter 14.

It was true that some Communists did hold positions of responsibility within the CIO. In my opinion, the following statement by Walter Galenson in his book, *The CIO Challenge to the AFL*, is a fair one:

> The steel companies in fighting the SWOC had been hammering away on the theme of Communist infiltration into the SWOC, and there seems to be little question that a number of Communists or Communist sympathizers had managed to gain positions on the SWOC payroll. However, the Communist party never got a strong foothold in the SWOC, and by 1939 the SWOC was openly fighting it, at a time when tolerance was the watchword in many other CIO unions.

Surely the policies of Tom Girdler, supported fully by the other Little Steel companies, with the exception of Jones and Laughlin, and by his public relations counselor, John Hill, offered no encouragement to responsible actions and stable industrial government if other industrial leaders were to follow their leadership. The facts and true nature of this epic labor–management struggle were laid bare in the investigation and hearings of Subcommittee of the U.S. Senate Committee on Education and Labor, held in the 77th Congress and chaired by Senator Robert M. LaFollette, Jr. of Wisconsin. Because Hill and Knowlton became a target of the investigation and a subject of the hearings, these are dealt with at some length. The evidence, along with Hill's account in his memoir, shows that Hill encouraged Girdler's antiunion stand rather than seeking to moderate it in the best interest of all parties affected. As earlier revealed in the Carl Byoir and Ivy Lee chapters, Congressional hearings lifted the veil of secrecy on the tactics, techniques, and rationale utilized by practitioners in their efforts to sway public opinion this way or that.

THE SENATE INVESTIGATES

The violence and strikebreaking tactics used to break the Little Steel strikes called by the SWOC provoked two Senate committee investigations—one by the Senate Post Office and Post Roads Committee and the second and more important one by a subcommittee of the Senate Committee on Education and Labor chaired by Senate Robert M. LaFollette of Wisconsin.

The first of these, by the Senate Committee on Post Offices and Post Roads, was held in June 1937 to investigate charges that the strikers had interfered with mail deliveries to the strike-bound plants. This one was notably mainly for the fact that it almost got John Hill fired from the AISI account—his firm's bread and butter. Hill had carefully prepared Tom Girdler's statement for the Senate committee and accompanied him in his appearance before that committee. According to Hill's memoirs, Girdler had been persuaded by friends to employ a Washington public relations counselor in addition to Hill for his Washington appearances. Following the Post Office Committee appearance, the Washington counselor urged Girdler to have a lunch and press conference for the Washington reporters covering the Capitol. John Hill advised against it, but a compromise was reached—Girdler would have an off-the-record lunch. In the meantime, Hill and the other Republic officials had returned to Cleveland because of the press of events there.

One of the newsmen present, violating the off-the-record agreement, broke a story stating that Girdler had strongly criticized those steel executives who had signed union agreements. Hill wrote, "When I saw Mr. Girdler the next morning he was shocked and angry that such a story had been printed. . . . As I expected some members of the Steel Institute Board

of Directors thought I had been responsible for the offending news story."
Subsequently, a special meeting of the AISI Executive Committee was
called to determine if Hill and Knowlton should be retained. The outcome
was a unanimous vote of confidence in Mr. Hill.

THE LAFOLLETTE HEARINGS

The second and more illuminating hearing was the one conducted by a
subcommittee of the Senate Committee on Education and Labor in 1938.
This became known in the press as The LaFollette Committee or the Civil
Liberties Committee. Understandably, John Hill later characterized this
committee's work as "totally unfair," buttressing his argument with this
statement, "Ten years later, in an article in *Collier's* magazine, LaFollette
acknowledged the unfairness of his hearings and declared that his staff in
the investigation had been dominated by Communist sympathizers." Quite
to the contrary, the *Collier's* article by the Senator consisted of a discussion
by LaFollette on the dangers of Communism. What LaFollette wrote was,
"I know from first-hand experience that Communist sympathizers have
infiltrated into committee staffs on Capitol Hill in Washington. A few years
ago, when I was chairman of the Senate Civil Liberties Committee, I was
forced to take measures in an effort to stamp out influences within my own
committee staff." This statement does not justify Hill's assertion.

But there is little doubt that the Committee was prounion in its conduct.
The committee concluded, "What gave the steel strike of 1937 its peculiar
bitterness was the companies were refusing to conform to a labor policy laid
down for all industries in the law of the land." The Wagner Act creating the
National Labor Relations Board and legalizing the right to organize and to
strike was upheld as Constitutional on April 12, 1937, by the U. S. Supreme
Court. In the Little Steel strikes, the unions faced what the committee
termed "a campaign of hostile propaganda." This propaganda campaign
was orchestrated by John Hill, first through Hill and Knowlton of
Cleveland, then through Hill and Knowlton, Inc. serving the AISI, Republic Steel, and Youngstown Sheet and Tube. The propaganda campaign
was generously supported by the National Association of Manufacturers
and its front, the National Industrial Council (NIC). In this period the
NAM became a client of Hill and Knowlton, Inc. The NAM and AISI
worked hand-in-glove in combatting organization of steel by the SWOC.
John Hill and Charles R. Hook of Armco Steel were the linchpins in this
cooperation.

REPUBLIC STEEL

John Hill was retained by Girdler's Republic Steel from November 1933
through January 1938, during which time Hill and Knowlton was paid $79,

336.89 for its services. The amount increased each year during this period, and in 1937 Hill and Knowlton received $51, 197.44 of the total. A prelude to the 1937 strikes came in 1935 at Republic's Berger plant in Canton, Ohio, which proved abortive to the union cause. Don Knowlton handled the publicity in that strike, but he was dissatisfied with the way the strike was treated in the press. The LaFollette Committee reported, "In light of the experience of the Berger plant (Canton, O.) strike of 1935, Republic Steel made no change in principle in labor policy, but in practice. . . . Republic began to employ to a very great extent the services of Hill and Knowlton as public relations counsel." Hill and Knowlton had been employed before the Berger strike but the statement of payments contains this notation: "Hill and Knowlton rendered no services in connection with industrial relations prior to June, 1935."

The committee found that "another novel phenomenon of the 'Little Steel' strike invited investigation. This was the flowering of organizations purporting to speak for the community—organizations which were accused by the labor unions of being inspired and dominated by the employers. These organizations had tremendous influence in the strike, an influence exerted so as to favor the employer." This was evidence in John Price Jones's role in breaking the ill-timed strike at Bethlehem Steel. Edgar S. Bowerfind, then an H&K executive and later public relations director of Republic, testified before the LaFollette Committee, "Members of the firm of H&K appeared during the course of the 1937 'Little Steel' strike in Youngstown, Canton, Warren, Massillion and Monroe. They aided in the formation of citizen committees and in the preparation of news releases and propaganda in all forms for the steel companies." These "citizens committee" efforts were strongly backed by the AISI and the National Association of Manufacturers. With the encouragement of John Hill, Republic greatly increased its contributions to these two organizations. During the period of 1933–1937, Republic gave $25,845.70 to the NAM and $219,812.35 to AISI.

Republic Steel maintained a strict, centralized control of press relations. The company policy was that press queries would not be answered by a local Republic plant manager. The inquiry would be referred to the central Youngstown office or to the Cleveland office of Hill and Knowlton. Hill and Knowlton prepared and released all news about Republic to the newspapers. Although this system had its advantages, it had its flaws in that it did not promote good press relations in the plant communities. Consequently, H&K proposed that the policies be modified to permit district managers to answer on their own questions about routine events not involving company policy. Hill and Knowlton suggested that these plant managers establish friendly relationships with local editors and reporters. Girdler bluntly rejected Hill's recommendation although Hill was a trusted adviser. His rejection of this sensible proposal simply reflected Girdler's intransigence in this struggle. Then Hill and Knowlton staffers were stationed at all strike locations to prepare and issue approved news releases. Hill personally assisted Girdler in the presentation of critical issues to the press, community, and Congressional committees when Girdler had to testify. Hill always accompanied Girdler when he testified on Capitol Hill. Girdler's view of such hearings was put succinctly in his autobiography, *Boot Straps*, "It has been my experience that a Congressional investigation is about as fair to its victim as the older and kindred institution, the Spanish Inquisition."

An indication of the extent of H&K's "hostile propaganda" activities for Republic can be seen in this summary:

1. Eighty thousand copies of a four-page letter on labor policies distributed to Republic employees.
2. One hundred sixteen thousand copies of a booklet, "The Real Issues," distributed to Republic employees and, in addition, as follows: 1,000 to colleges and universities; 8,000 to investment bankers and brokers; 650 to newspapers, and 360 to public libraries. This booklet explained the reasons for the refusal by steel companies to sign a contract with the CIO. It argued that the contract would be the first step toward later demands for the closed shop and the check off.
3. Twenty-two hundred reprints of an editorial from *Daily Metal Trade* were sent to 1,900 daily newspapers.
4. Twenty-one hundred copies of a booklet, "Who Is John L. Lewis?"
5. Twenty-nine thousand copies of Tom Girdler's statement before the Senate Committee on Post Offices and Post Roads.
6. Three thousand copies of a booklet, *What I Should Do To Maintain Democracy.*
7. Two thousand copies of an address by Tom Girdler before the Warren, Ohio, Chamber of Commerce.
8. Thirty-nine thousand copies of a pamphlet, "CIO Versus American Democracy."

In the long run, this barrage of propaganda proved unavailing against the strong tide of public opinion favoring unions and stable industrial governments in industry.

The only embarrassing moment for Hill during these hearings came when Senator LaFollette introduced into evidence a memorandum that had been written by a staff member to Republic Steel and had thus gotten in the committee's hands. Hill argued:

[It contained a] wholly innocent but unfortunately phrased sentence that would be twisted into meaning that the client was advised to use the "pressure" of advertising in connection with a hostile newspaper. Any such advice would have violated the principles and practices of our firm, but to Senator LaFollette, the memorandum was a juicy morsel. He read the document into the record with his unfavorable interpretation just before adjournment of the afternoon session and handed out mimeographed copies to the press. We were given no chance to clarify the memorandum nor refute his interpretation of it.

In fact, Hill and his associates were afforded a full opportunity to discuss this memorandum. The memorandum, written by Edgar S. Bowerfind, an H&K executive, had been sent to the manager of Republic's Birmingham, Alabama, plant, and the La Follette Committee had found it in Republic's files. Bowerfind had suggested that the newspaper publisher's friends be contacted in an organized way and requested to talk with the publisher about his unfriendly editorial policy toward Republic and its Birmingham plant. Bowerfind went on to say, "Some pressure might also be judiciously exerted through the advertisers in Birmingham." Wholly innocent!

It was the discovery of this memorandum that caused the committee to investigate Hill and Knowlton in detail. Hill and Knowlton files were thereafter subpoenaed and thoroughly searched, some of which were read into the record of the LaFollette hearings. Bowerfind testified that as a former newsman he was personally opposed to any attempt to apply pressures on a newspaper through its advertisers. He was at a loss to explain why he had written in this manner and stated that it must have been an aberration. John Hill and Don Knowlton both testified that their firm never advocated the use of pressure of advertising to influence a newspaper. Both Hill and Knowlton denied ever having seen the memorandum. The LaFollette Committee was unable to establish that any attempt was ever made to exert influence on the newspaper. Bowerfind continued to work for H&K until Republic established its own public relations department in 1948 and hired him.

YOUNGSTOWN SHEET AND TUBE

By contrast, Hill and Knowlton's activities for Youngstown Sheet and Tube during the strike period were focused mainly on counseling and product and institutional publicity. During the period 1933–1938, Youngstown paid H&K $130,598.95 of which $12,362.97 was paid in 1937. Youngstown Sheet and Tube had its own public relations department and prepared most of its own news releases, but H&K handled distribution of the releases for nonlocal media. Another service performed for this client was the preparation of the "Management" and "How's Business" pages for the company publication, *Bulletin*. But, according to the LaFollette Committee report:

The Youngstown Sheet & Tube Co. did not confine its activities to its own plants or even its own employees, but extended into the life of the community. In addition to its espionage activities and the subjection of employees to pressure, a campaign to mobilize public opinion was begun. Youngstown Sheet & Tube did not act alone in this drive. The exchange of espionage information was only a small part of its cooperation with other large industrial manufacturers. In 1936, during the drive of the Steel Workers Organizing Committee, the contributions of all the "Little Steel" companies to that association [NAM] rose sharply. That of Youngstown Sheet & Tube jumped from $2,500 in 1935 to $9,000 in 1936. The American Iron and Steel Institute endorsed the work of the National Association of Manufacturers and suggested that its company members lend support.

A Youngstown official, appearing before the committee, testified that the jump to $12,362 paid to Hill and Knowlton in 1936 included $1,500 for "a survey of labor problems." But Hill rebutted this in his testimony, saying "None of these payments cover any items included in the subpoena, as Hill and Knowlton were not engaged for labor relations work." Of the money paid H&K by Youngstown Sheet & Tube, Hill testified that $7,133.22 was paid to George E. Sokolsky, Hearst right-wing columnist, whom John Hill used in many instances to shill for conservative causes. In the hearings, Youngstown steel officials could not recall ever having seen any of Mr. Sokolsky's work on their behalf. This testimony flies in the face of the fact that Sokolsky was the principal speaker at a "civic progress" meeting in October 6,1936, silently sponsored by the Mahoning Valley Industrial Council. This meeting was accomplished through a committee composed principally of members of the so-called "John L. Lewis" committee of the council. This group selected the Youngstown Foreman's Club as the public sponsor. Kenneth M. Lloyd, secretary of the council, admitted that this civic progress meeting followed the formula laid down by the National Association of Manufacturers. The expenses for this meeting were paid for by an assessment against the council members.

All told, Hill and Knowlton paid Sokolsky more than $28,000 during the period June 1936 to February 1938. Sokolsky performed consultant services, drafted booklets or statements, made radio broadcasts and transcriptions, and gave lectures at similar meetings. Although much of Sokolsky's propagandizing was done for the American Iron and Steel institute, more than $14,000 of his fees were charged to Republic Steel and the $7,133.22 to Youngstown Sheet & Tube for the civic progress meeting.

The revelation of Sokolsky's employment by Hill and Knowlton during the LaFollette hearings evoked considerable comment in the press. *Time* magazine had this to say under the caption of "Self-Evident Subtlety," "And subtlest performer for Hill and Knowlton was George Ephraim Sokolsky, author, lecturer, industrial consultant. Some of Mr. Sokolsky's lecturing was done at 'civic progress meetings' arranged and paid for by local employers but publicly sponsored by 'neutral groups.' " Heywood Broun responded to a Sokolsky column praising Tom Girdler by writing, "In spite of Mr. Sokolsky's justification of dual columnist, I think it looks bad. Publishers should discourage it." Typical of Sokolsky's shilling was an article in the *Atlantic Monthly* of September 1937, "The C.I.O. Turns a Page" in which he preached the steel industry's point of view that the real issue in the strikes was the closed shop and check off. He also criticized the Wagner Act and the NLRB as useless instruments in the field of labor relations. Another column had high praise for Girdler's appearance before the Senate Post Office Committee. Sokolsky also wrote a booklet during this period in which he again espoused the steel industry view of the labor situation. This was widely distributed.Sokolsky was also in the pay of the National Association of Manufacturers, as he admitted in a column of December 20, 1937. He argued that he was retained as a "consultant." Shill is more accurate.

As illustrated by the civic progress meeting and the use of George Sokolsky as a propagandist, the steel companies, fully supported by the Hill public relations firms, commonly used fronts in their effort to build public opinion against the SWOC and unionization. Thus, the much criticized third party technique rears its ugly head in this situation. In Republic's and Youngstown Sheet & Tube's tactics there is a replay of those used successfully in breaking the ill-timed strike at Bethlehem Steel. To further illustrate, with the leadership of Ernest T. Weir, president of National Steel, and under the aegis of NAM, the National Industrial Information Committee (NIIC) was formed in 1935 to, as it proclaimed, "further better understanding of industry by the public." The 1935 NAM annual report stated that such committees "have been formed in the twenty major industrial states to facilitate developments of this N.A.M. campaign for dissemination of sound American doctrines to the public." The National Industrial Council, an NAM affiliate, was also reorganized in 1935 "in anticipation of the union drive," according to Kenneth M. Lloyd, secretary of the Mahoning Valley Industrial Council. The council was supporting Youngstown Sheet & Tube's efforts to build public opinion against the SWOC. The program of the National Industrial Council consisted of the circulation of "industrial information" furnished by the National Association of Manufacturers to employees, letters to stockholders, the sponsorship of civic meetings with speakers from the NAM, and the promotion of newspaper advertisements. All these techniques presented in the NAM "canned program" were faithfully followed by Lloyd and Youngstown Sheet & Tube.

Typical of the latter was the showing of a movies in the Youngstown plant touting employee representation plans. Also, the company's *Bulletin* of July 25, 1936, carried an article by a company vice-president that read in part:

> To Our Employees: Numerous oral and printed announcements have recently been made by certain labor organizations, stating it is their intention to unionize the employees of the steel industry. The real purpose of this campaign is of course to force the closed shop on the industry, thus compelling all employees to join and pay dues to the organization, and consequently be governed by its demands, whether they relate to the steel industry alone or as well to other industries which the leaders in this movement may control.

Youngstown Sheet & Tube also ordered 1,000 copies of a pamphlet from the NIIC entitled "Join the C.I.O. and Help Build a Soviet America," and managers were requested to "make distribution of these pamphlets to the supervisory force, including department superintendents and assistant and higher-ranking foremen." The LaFollette Committee found that "none of the high officials had read the pamphlet, and no independent investigation to ascertain the accuracy of the facts there presented was made."

To further reflect the tactics and tools of this antiunion campaign led by the AISI, the NAM, the NIC, and the NIIC and orchestrated in large measure by Hill and Selvage, in 1936 the Mahoning Valley Industrial Council set up a series of committees to carry out what it termed an "education" program. The first of these was the "John L. Lewis Committee," whose membership included officials of Youngstown Sheet & Tube, Republic, Carnegie–Illinois, Sharon Steel, and others. The aims of this group were explained in a letter from Lloyd to Frank E. Baggs, secretary of the Employees' Association at Portsmouth, Ohio. "Those of us who are interested in the steel industry are aware of the activity in our industry to organize it along industrial union lines. We are trying in Youngstown to do those things which will aid ourselves and the community in fighting this menace."

At the same time the council was sponsoring a series of advertisements captioned "Prosperity Dwells Where Harmony Reigns." This series of advertisements was prepared and sold by the McDonald–Cook agency of South Bend, Indiana, that recommended them for the purpose of "organizing a community against labor agitators before they get in their work." The council itself did not sign the ads, but various luncheon clubs and other civic group did. But the ads were paid for by industry when the Mahoning Valley Industrial Council levied a special assessment on members of the council of 25¢ per employee "for the purpose of defraying the cost to the Council for advertising and radio activity." In sum, in the conclusion of the

LaFollette Committee, "the community was . . . treated to an extensive campaign of propaganda in which the company never openly appeared."

The die-hard attitude of steel company officials against unionization, a policy that cost the company, the employees, and community dearly, was dramatically put by W. B. Gillies, a Youngstown vice-president, at a meeting of the Mahoning Coal Council when according to the testimony of Geoffrey E. Burke, a coal dealer present at the meeting, "He grew quite hot about it and told the group of coal dealers that the Sheet & Tube would spend, before they would deal with these people, every nickel of their resources, every cent of their resources, that it wouldn't be a matter of a year's strike, or six months strike, but it would be a matter of 7 or 8 years . . . that would result in ruining Youngstown as a business town."

In addition to direct methods of discouragement and indirect impediments through publicity and propaganda, the steel companies created other means of community pressure against the steel workers. Gillies, vice-president of Youngstown Sheet & Tube, brought pressure on the ministers of Youngstown at a meeting of the Ministers' Union to align them against the organizers. One minister at the dinner meeting took issue with Gillies and later several Youngstown Sheet & Tube members quit his church. Finally, the Rev. Orville C. Jones of the Plymouth Congregational Church in Youngstown was forced to resign the next year because of such pressures. Gillies also attempted to persuade the merchants of Youngstown to oppose the SWOC.

Understandably the LaFollette Committee concluded, in part:

> The company made no effort to comply with the spirit of section 7 (a) of the National Industrial Recovery Act. When the Wagner Act was passed, it was treated as a complete nullity until it had been upheld by the Supreme Court. Then a new form of company union was initiated under the benevolent eye of the company, although without its ostensible and active participation. Spies infiltrated the plants, and the professional services of the Railway Audit and Inspection Bureau were employed. The community was then treated to an extensive campaign of propaganda in which the company never appeared. Individuals were coerced and subjected to economic pressure to force them to cooperate with the company's policy of nonrecognition of outside unions.

The LaFollette Committee In its report, *Violations of Free Speech and Rights of Labor*, concluded this about John Hill's role in the antilabor campaign:

> A further collaboration of employer organizations was made possible through their common use of Hill & Knowlton as public relations counsel. The American Iron and Steel Institute retained the firm in November, 1933. . . .

The National Association of Manufacturers became a client . . . in February, 1936. Republic Steel Corporation and Youngstown Sheet & Tube Co. retained Hill & Knowlton. Through its employer organizations and steel company clients, Hill & Knowlton was able to carry out an integrated and far-flung program of opposition to section 7 (a) of the National Industrial Recovery Act, and later, to the Wagner National Labor Relations Act. The services of Mr. George Sokolsky were arranged entirely through Hill & Knowlton, who paid Mr. Sokolsky $28,599.47 between June 1936, and February, 1938. In addition [the firm] carried on a broad campaign to foster the growth of employee representations plans.

OTHER SERVICES

In another project, initiated by Hill, the firm was retained by Republic, Youngstown Sheet & Tube, Bethlehem, National, Inland, and American Rolling Mill (Armco) to make a comprehensive study of the problem of industrial relations. The purpose of the study was to gather facts useful to the companies in consideration of their industrial policies and what they professed as a furtherance of ideas for industrial peace. Each company agreed to pay $1,500 a month for the project, and Hill and Knowlton was paid about $74,000 from the time the project started until some of the firms dropped out in the spring of 1938. Until the project was reduced in scope in 1938, the companies received for this large fee only a weekly digest of news articles and editorials on all phases of labor matters.

WHAT OF THE ETHICS?

In the end, these die-hard and dubious means of trying to stem the inexorable tide of union organization in the 1930s failed. John Hill's role in this antiunion campaign was a major one, though not the dominant one. Although more moderate in his antilabor views than Tom Girdler, Hill, a stanch conservative, shared Girdler's basic attitudes. As Hill put it in his memoir, the issue was "basically identical in each case namely, the right of managements in a free economy to make decisions vitally affecting the welfare of their companies." Yet Hill recounted, "When I began my work for the steel industry in 1933, an old era was dying and a new one was dawning." Either John Hill did not accurately evaluate the changing public opinion climate in 1936–1937 or was unable to persuade the leaders of Little Steel that their tactics were doomed to defeat, especially after U. S. Steel recognized the SWOC in 1936. It is the responsibility of the public relations counselor to gauge the public climate through research and then relay its findings to management with the bark off. There is no evidence John Hill did this.

FOR LITTLE STEEL

As the LaFollette Committee concluded, Hill and the officials of the Little Steel companies were "committed to an antiquated concept of industrial absolutism."

Hill tended to minimize the counselor's responsibility for the client's policies and actions. In a letter dated November 24, 1964, to me, Hill wrote, "I think that some may have an exaggerated idea of the influence that counselors have in shaping corporate policies. The truth is that clients do often talk over policy matters with public relations counsel, but final decisions are made by the client and it is not seemly for the counselor to claim credit for good decisions or encourage anyone else to do so for him."

Though never enthusiastic about its efficacy, John Hill was a member of the Public Relations Society of America from its inception in 1948. The Society's Code of Ethics of this time read, "A member shall not make use of any individual or organization purporting to serve or represent some announced cause, or purporting to be independent or unbiased, but actually serving an undisclosed special or private interest of a member of his client or his employer."

As brought out earlier, the LaFollette Committee exposed the use of supposedly independent community associations in the steel plant communities that were heavily subsidized by the steel companies battling the SWOC. These associations' main effort was in conducting strong public relations campaigns for "labor stabilization." Most prominent among these were the Canton Development Corporation in Canton, Ohio, and the Mahoning Valley Industrial Council in Youngstown, Ohio. No evidence was produced in the hearings that Hill and Knowlton worked directly for these associations or front groups, but Hill and Knowlton personnel advised the associations on occasion and provided other kinds of support at the request of its steel company clients. For example, Bowerfind advised the Canton corporation on the procedure for conducting a "Silver Dollar Pay Day," one of the oldest public relations gimmicks in the book. In this commonly used stunt, a company pays its employees in silver dollars to demonstrate the worth of the company to local merchants. Also, noted earlier, H&K arranged for the Sokolsky speech at the Youngstown civic progress meeting in January 1937. The use of Sokolsky as a propagandist was sufficient to implicate Hill and Knowlton in practices that were considered then and are considered now to be unethical. This includes the use of fronts or third parties.

UPS AND DOWNS WITH STEEL

John Hill and his firm continued to be heavily involved with the steel industry and some individual companies for the next 25 years. The American Iron and Steel Institute continued to provide a solid financial base for Hill and Knowlton. This quarter century involved Hill and his staff in many confrontations with organized labor and the federal government. Space limitations do not permit detailed coverage of these years.

Year in and year out the H&K staff provided a wide array of routine public relations services to the industry. As Hill recalled, "One of the things to be done for American Iron and Steel Institute at the beginning of my work there was to get it established as a recognized source of trustworthy information about the steel industry." In mid-1934, Hill started a publication, *Steel Facts*. The first publication had a circulation of 5,000, and the circulation eventually passed the 200,000 mark. Immediately after World War II, Hill sold the institute board on starting a slick-paper magazine, *Steelways*, to dramatize the human and economic side of the industry. By the time of Hill's semiretirement, he could claim for *Steelways* "The highest readership of any industry magazine in the country."

In 1948, H&K established a community relations program for the industry setting up community relations offices in Chicago, Cleveland, Pittsburgh, and New York City. Their purpose was to help further the national public relations objectives of the institute through on the spot counsel to company members. In a "Ten Year Review of Steel Company Activities," Hill reported that "in nine major internal communications categories, company members have increased activities 189 percent. Prior to 1948 only 138 instances of such activities are known to have existed. Today this number has moved up to 399."

In addition to the multimillion dollar public relations effort of AISI, the individual steel companies were also greatly increasing their public relations budgets and efforts, especially in employee communication. A letter dated December 7, 1955, to Loet Velmans, then head of Hill and Knowlton International, gave the details of the U.S. Steel Company's public relations program:

> This company has the most extensive public relations organization. We know that USS spends something like $3,000,000 on a television program. . . . The public relations department of the corporation consists of 300 people located

in the New York headquarters and in various regional headquarters throughout the United States. They have an active speaking program for top officials who appear before important public groups. In addition, they run institutional advertising; distribute copies of pamphlets and speeches in large quantities; are active in communications to employees and stockholders and to various communities where plants are located. It is generally believed that, all in all, the Corporation spends between $5,000,000 and $6,000,000 on its public relations program.

[One of the paid speakers USS used in this program in the 1950s and 1960s was Harry Stuhldreher, quarterback of the famed Four Horsemen of Notre Dame and later football coach at the University of Wisconsin]

But $6 million does not necessarily buy an effective public relations program. In April 1962, when U.S. Steel led the way among several other companies in announcing price increases, the act broke what President John F. Kennedy thought was a tacit agreement that if labor held down its demands, there would be no price increase. A firestorm of criticism led by President Kennedy blindsided Roger M. Blough, U.S. Steel's chief executive officer, who admitted later that he was unprepared for such an angry reaction to the increase. Hill said, "The President's harsh words and the coercive moves against the steel men startled the entire business community." Blough had not consulted his vice-president for public relations, Phelps Adams, before making the move and was totally at sea when the waves of public criticism broke over him. The increases were rolled back by all the companies that had raised prices, giving President Kennedy a political victory although one tarnished by the massive government forces the President marshalled against the steel industry. John Hill had no involvement in this fiasco for steel. Hill explained to me, "In price matters each company is on its own."

But he was heavily involved in the industry's earlier confrontation with a President of the United States—this time President Harry S. Truman.

A SHOWDOWN BETWEEN STEEL AND
PRESIDENT TRUMAN

Though Hill and his firm were not involved in the 1962 Kennedy–Blough shootout, he was in the thick of the industry's first confrontation with a President of the United States—in the 1952 steel strike that President Harry Truman sought to end by seizing the nation's steel mills. Hill described this crisis as "the most extraordinary of all the controversies" he had been involved in over 3 decades. Hill was in the thick of this public battle. The night of April 8, 1952, he was conferring with "some thirty grim-faceted steel executives on the seventeenth floor of the Roosevelt Hotel in New York" as the clocked ticked away to midnight when the nation's steel workers were to go out on strike. In the midst of this tense atmosphere came word that President Truman would address the nation at 10:30 p.m. When he went on the air, the President made a strong attack on the steel industry executives and blamed them for "recklessly forcing a shutdown of the steel mills," and declared that "at midnight the government will take over the steel plants." Truman told the nation, "The Wage Board recommendations are less than the Union thought they ought to have . . . The fact of thematter is that the settlement proposed by the Board is fair to both parties and the public interest." His move stunned the assembled steel executives — and the nation.

As the Roosevelt Hotel conferees regrouped, they decided, with Hill's counsel, that they ought to seek network time to reply to the President the following night. Hill called the networks and was told they would have a decision by morning. They sent representatives to H&K's offices at 9:00 the next morning and agreed to give the industry time to reply to the President. Then Hill's staff next problem was finding "the right spokesman." "A name occurred to several of us simultaneously. It was Clarence Randall, the brilliant, articulate, and rapier-tongued president of Inland Steel." Hill put the idea before Ben Fairless, then president of U.S. Steel, who approved and agreed to try to persuade Randall to make the reply. Randall agreed, and Hill immediately offered writers to assist him in preparing the reply, but Randall waved them aside, because, as Hill wrote, "being lawyer-trained and skilled writer himself, he had no need for help." Randall made a stirring and straight-from-the-shoulder reply that won wide public support for the industry's position.

Randall told the radio and television audience that the President's "evil deed" had no precedent in history. The nation's media chimed in support of Randall and the steelmakers. *Newsweek* said, "Truman's talent for trouble gave the nation no rest." The *Washington Post* prophesied that the President's act would go down in history of the Presidency. Even in the Congress there were calls for President Truman's impeachment. John Hill and the steel companies clearly had won the battle in the public forum.

The next public relations move was to follow Randall's speech with a full-page newspaper ad in the nation's daily newspaper to set forth the significance of Trauman's unprecedented act in seizing the mills. Hill wrote the first draft over one weekend, talked over copy with Edward Ryerson, Ben Fairless, Irving Olds, chairman of U.S. Steel, and Carlisle MacDonald, assistant to Mr. Olds. Hill suggested a final paragraph urging citizens to write their congresspersons. The ad bore the headline: "A THREAT TO AMERICAN FREEDOM." The lead paragraph read, "Every man and woman who works, every citizen in America, has a stake in the great issues growing out of the seizure of the steel mills. If the President has the right to seize private property to enforce union demands, as has been done in steel, then both the right to property and the continuation of collective bargaining are in serious danger. Even the independence of the unions, themselves, will be in jeopardy."

This ad, run in 400 newspapers, brought an instant and wide response. The steel companies that had sponsored the ad began receiving hundreds of letters, most of which were copies of letters written to members of Congress or Senators. In a few days, Hill read a hard-hitting editorial in the *New York Mirror* strongly criticizing Truman's move. Hill immediately got the consent of the *Mirror* editor, Glenn Nevill, and the approval of Edward Ryerson and Ben Fairless to reproduce the editorial as a paid ad. It appeared in morning papers across the nation the next morning. This was an extraordinary effort in treating advertising as if it were news. It was no small feat to get a series of ads cleared, type set, and space reserved in the newspapers that were utilized.

The steel companies also moved quickly on the legal front, challenging the constitutionality of the President's action. On April 29, Judge David A. Pine of U.S. District Court ruled that there was "utter and complete lack of authoritative support" for the Presidential seizure of private property. Immediately Philip A. Murray, president of the United Steelworkers, ordered a strike even though the plants were under government control. The case went to the U.S. Court of Appeals that suspended Judge Pine's ruling pending a review of the case by the U.S. Supreme Court. On May 2, both the government and the steel companies asked the Supreme Court to take the case directly, and it agreed to do so. On June 2, the Court, by a 6 to 3 decision, ruled that the seizure was unconstitutional. President Truman immediately ordered his Secretary of Commerce to turn back the mills to their owners. Thirty-five minutes after the Supreme Court handed down its ruling, the steelworkers, who had been permitted to return to work by the Court of Appeals Decision, went out on strike. As the strike went into its 8th week, there was tremendous pressure mounting on both sides to settle it. Finally, President Truman brought Ben Fairless and Philip Murray to the White House on July 24 and locked them in a room with orders to settle the strike. Ben Fairless wrote in *Life* of August 4, 1952, "We were ushered into an outer office and left alone. Within 5 minutes Murray had accepted our compromise and the whole thing was settled." Out of their discussion came the idea of joint tours by the heads of the steel company and of the labor leaders to meet and talk with workers face to face.

Writing in his memoir of the public relations effort involved in this historic strike, John Hill, wrote:

All through virtually every scene in this long and tense melo-drama, public relations played an active role. Steel industry, public relations men and counsel were always close at hand during bargaining sessions. The industry's public relations men also worked around the clock to supply requests for information from the press, radio, and TV about all these administrative, legislative, and judicial procedures and the companies' viewpoints with regard to them. In fact, "around the clock" was a good description of the working schedules for steel industry public relations activities of our time.

Each of the steel companies loaned one or more of their public relations staff to Hill and Knowlton so the firm could meet this heavy workload. H&K also hired several specialists for the duration of the strike. Other strikes in the steel industry followed but none would equal the 1952 strike in "drama, excitement, and national interest," Hill opined.

As close as John Hill was to the leaders of the steel industry, he was not always fully appraised of their thinking and of their policies. This is a common complaint of public relations counselors, but given Hill's role in the industry for more than 30 years, it is a bit strange that he, too, encountered this problem. In a hair-down letter to Walter S. Tower, who first hired Hill for AISI and was now retired in Carmel, California, Hill wrote in a letter dated December 30, 1959, referring to the 1959 steel strike that lasted 116 days:

> Many people are saying that the companies have lost the public relations battle. I could write a book on that. It all depends on what you call "public relations." Actually the whole negotiation was a public relations contest, but not everyone realized that until it was too late, I fear. The public relations committee worked hard, but it was not privy to many of the vital events. For example, none of us knew about the eight points and *28* until they were on the table. I think it is generally recognized that the ground should have been prepared for this over many months. But of course we had nothing to do with that and God knows the policy makers were doing their best to work in the interests of the industry and the country. During these months I have often longed for the wise counsel of you and Ed Ryerson.

The reason for Hill's gloomy assessment can be seen in the verdict of A. H. Raskin, then a seasoned labor reporter for *The New York Times*, who wrote in a news analysis that the settlement "marked a rout for the major companies in what they considered a crusade to re-establish the lost prerogatives of management." Raskin quoted a "head of one of the biggest companies" as saying "We took a helluva licking." Roger Blough virtually admitted defeat when he said in a TV interview, "The agreement we must now live with is not what we tried so long and so hard to obtain." His public relations vice-president, Phelps Adams, tried to put a PR spin on the strike settlement when he said, "I wouldn't say we scored any touchdowns, but we did gain yardage." In a story in *Editor & Publisher* of January 16, 1960, a labor law authority, J. Mack Swigert, expressed the belief that "poor public relations and bad timing put the steel industry on the defensive and kept it from getting more than a compromise settlement." Swigert rubbed salt into Hill's wound when he credited the union "with conducting a whale of a publicity campaign."

In these battles for public opinion, public relations has its uses and its clout, but it is not as potent as counselors claim or as the public often fears. Events coupled with their interpretation are the prime movers of the tides of public opinion.

HEALTH AND MORALITY—TOBACCO'S COUNTER CAMPAIGN

Although first introduced to Europeans for its supposed medical value, tobacco has been strongly criticized for its deleterious effects since Sir Walter Raleigh brought it to the Virginia Colony in the 17th century. Today the tobacco industry is in the eye of a raging storm of controversy as evidence steadily mounts of tobacco's injurious effects on a person's health. Undoubtedly no Hill and Knowlton account has brought the firm John Hill founded as much criticism as its effort to defend a beleaguered tobacco industry. This continuing controversy raises moral issues far outweighing the economic concerns at issue in most public relations campaigns, for example, the steel industry. The stakes in this ongoing public relations battle are enormous. On one side of the ledger, is the health of more than 200 million teenagers and adults. On the other side, are the profits, even survival, of the tobacco industry in dependence on the 55.8 million addicted smokers of 1988. That year the Tobacco Institute boasted that these smokers represented a buying power of $1 trillion, arguing "they help fuel the engine of the largest economy on the globe." In the 1990s, America's tobacco companies began compensating for the shrinking domestic market by stepping up exports abroad with the help of the United States Government!

Throughout the first half of the 20th century, smokers and doctors largely ignored negative news about smoking because antitobacco claimants presented their finds more in moral than in scientific terms. But soon after World War II, a renewed interest in research, funded by the increase in money given to universities and hospitals in the postwar science boom, helped doctors accumulate enough medical evidence to alarm tobacco manufacturers, smokers, and doctors. A major study associating lung cancer with smoking appeared in an article by Ernest Wynder and Evarts

Graham in the *Journal of the American Medical Association* in 1950. Two other articles by Richard Doll and Bradford Hill were published in the *British Medical Journal* in 1950 and 1952 and one by Alton Ochsner all led to the conclusion that smoking was more than merely associated with cancer. Indeed, Ochsner opened his 1954 book, *Smoking and Cancer, A Doctor's Report* with the blockbuster sentence, "Smoking causes cancer." Other scientific reports linking smoking with lung cancer and other diseases were being released with increased frequency and were receiving wide publicity. The harmful effects of smoking was now on the public agenda.

The tobacco industry was face to face with a crisis, one affecting the future existence of the industry itself, thus one requiring action. It has been observed that the industry had four courses open to it in its response to this crisis:

1. The industry could have stopped the manufacture of cigarettes, a Utopian notion that got no consideration.
2. The charges could have been ignored, ostrich-like in the outmoded public relations notion that responding to attacks only fuels publicity of the original charge.
3. The industry could have taken the position that the cigarette–health link had not been fully established, but neither had it been disproved. Therefore, there was a strong burden of proof on the industry. In this course, the industry could urge caution to smokers and fund research to ascertain the true facts. This would have avoided controversy in favor of clarification and unbiased inquiry.
4. Finally, the industry could have treated those opposed as enemies of smoking and used public relations to reassure the public and provide rationalization to addicted smokers to continue their habit. In this course the serious question of public health could be turned into a controversy. In short, the industry could fight back and try to refute evidence opposed to its profits.

Perhaps the last straw that led to the tobacco industry to turn to Hill and Knowlton for help was when Dr. Ochsner spoke in New York City on December 8, 1953, and asserted that "the male population of the United States would be decimated if cigarette smoking increases as it has in the past unless some steps are taken to remove the cancer-producing factor from cigarettes." Cigarette stocks dropped 1 to 4 points after the meeting, and as *Business Week* noted, "fast paced events loosened up for the first time official tongues of the tobacco industry. E. A. Darr, president of R. J. Reynolds, was quick to respond there had been 'no real or substantial evidence showing cigarettes cause lung cancer.' " Such responses caused Senator Maurine Neuberger, whose late husband had died of lung cancer, to respond, "Ridicule and derision became deliberate defensive weapons in the hands of the tobacco industry public relations experts." Within days after the speech by Dr. Ochsner, six nervous company presidents turned to John Hill for help.

John R. Newsom, son of Earl Newsom and a partner in his father's firm at the time, wrote your author in a letter dated February 8, 1992, that the scared tobacco presidents first sought the respected Newsom's counsel and that he turned them down and referred them to Hill.

HILL AND KNOWLTON RETAINED, TIRC SET UP

In response to an urgent telegram from Paul M. Hahn, president of the American Tobacco Company, the presidents of six major companies met in New York City on December 10 and 11, 1953, to consider what action they could take to mute the evidence of the dangers of smoking. As executives do when faced with a public relations crisis, they agreed to confer with John W. Hill. These executives met twice, once on December 15 and again on December 29, with Hill and his key aides to discuss ways of developing a public relations response to the mounting evidence against smoking's ill effects. In the words of one Hill aide, "This is . . . the most challenging problem our organization has ever faced—and perhaps the most challenging problem that ever faced a great industry, one with annual sales of almost $5 billion and with economic roots that reach clear back to the farm."

After the December 15 meeting in which H&K was asked to do an intensive study of the problem and report back in 2 weeks, intensive research was begun: "Research directors and other representatives of leading companies have been interviewed and immediately all available material on the subject has been read, including newspaper and magazine articles, company statements and various reports of medical research organizations." One of the reasons for Hill and Knowlton's steady growth in the post-World War II years was its emphasis on research to determine a course of action. On December 22, 1953, H&K sent a recommendation to the six presidents stating:

> Because of the serious nature of the attacks on cigarettes and the vast publicity given them over the air and in the daily press and in magazines of the widest circulation, a hysteria of fear appears to be developing throughout the country. There is no evidence that this adverse publicity is abating or will soon abate. This publicity has given rise to a situation which makes it imperative for the cigarette makers to inform the public regarding the facts. . . . The following name is submitted for the Committee: *Cigarette Research and*

Information Committee. It is believed that the word "Research" is needed if the name is to give weight and added credence to the Committee's statements. However, the word cannot be used unless the industry is prepared to back it up with genuine joint research action and support. The research to be sponsored by the Committee would be of two kinds, namely (a) medical research to be financed jointly and (b) editorial and statistical in all phases of the cigarette problem to be carried on through public relations counsel.

The presidents agreed on this approach and decided that the committee would be headquartered in H&K's offices in the Empire State Building. Aides said John Hill made this a condition of accepting the account—that research be financed to ascertain the facts. Strangely, Hill's memoir, *The Making of a Public Relations Man*, published in 1963, stands silent on the tobacco account. H&K considered independent scientific research essential, though industry leaders had hoped to avoid this approach. The companies argued that they had conducted considerably more research in their own laboratories and had sponsored work at universities and hospitals that was not generally known. The tobacco presidents of the "Big Six" argued that what was needed was dissemination of information already gathered rather than conducting new research. Hill "strongly disagreed and emphatically warned the companies that they should probably expect to sponsor additional research," Goss wrote in a memo found in the John Hill Papers. Hill and Knowlton saw that by creating an independent committee and by publicizing each new grant they could generate positive publicity for the tobacco cause.

Although Hill and Knowlton had represented many large corporate clients—Avco Manufacturing, Texaco, Procter & Gamble, and Gillette—it had built a solid reputation serving trade associations—steel, aviation, and the drug industry. Hill who had a reputation as a "corporate confident," was then chairman of the firm he had founded and led to dominance in the agency field. Hill had always stressed that corporations should present supporting evidence, facts, to influence public opinion. Hill believed "different interpretation of the facts is possible, and each side is entitled to present its views, leaving it to the public to decide which to accept." Bert Goss, then H&K president, once told Congress, "We believe that if you give the people the facts they will eventually operate on the basis of those facts, if you give it to them convincingly and effectively." H&K's economic writer Edwin F. Dakin, saw the public relations problem "as one that revolves around the interpretation of facts," adding, "There is only one problem, confidence and how to establish it, public assurance, and how to create it." He wisely opined, "No resort to logic ever cured a panic." And panic was the word for the tobacco industry's leaders with its $5,000,000,000 business and large profit margins at stake.

The tobacco presidents finally agreed to the formation of the Tobacco Industry Research Committee and adopted a budget of $1.2 million for the year 1954. The presidents agreed that "the purposes and objectives of the Committee are to aid and assist research into tobacco use and health, and particularly into the alleged relationship between the use of tobacco and lung cancer, and to make available to the public factual information on this subject," adding, "It is the considered judgment of the Committee that its activities shall be confined to the purposes set forth above." The presidents were guarding against the appearance of any activity that might come under the ban of the Sherman Anti-Trust Act.

Hill and Knowlton rapidly put its hurriedly drafted program into action. The first step was to publish an advertisement on January 4, 1954, in 448 daily newspapers across the nation. This advertisement, "A Frank Statement to the Public by the Makers of Cigarettes," contained the following points that even today expresses fairly well the industry's public relations position:

1. The reports that cigarettes cause lung cancer, while not conclusive, should not be "disregarded or lightly dismissed."
2. Eminent doctors and research scientists have publicly questioned the significance of the experiments already conducted.
    a. Medical research indicates many possible causes of lung cancer.
    b. There is no agreement among authorities as to the cause of lung cancer.
    c. There is no proof that cigarette smoking is one of the causes.
    d. The validity of the statistics cited in the reports which have been released have been questioned by noted authorities.
3. The tobacco industry accepts an interest in peoples' health as a "basic responsibility, paramount to every other consideration in our business."
4. The manufacturers do not believe their products are injurious to health.
5. The manufacturers always have and always will cooperate on safeguarding public health.
6. Tobacco has offered solace, relaxation, and enjoyment to mankind for more than 300 years. During that time it has been held responsible for practically every disease of the human body. One by one the charges have been abandoned for lack of evidence.
7. The fact that cigarette smoking is *even suspected* as the cause of serious diseases is a matter of deep concern to the industry.
8. What will industry do about it:
    a. It will give aid and assistance to the research effort into all phases of tobacco use and health.

    b. It has formed a joint industry group, the Tobacco Industry
       Research Committee.
    c. The research activities will be supervised by prominent scien-
       tists.

The statement was signed by the heads of the major tobacco companies who
belonged to the TIRC.

How much influence did John Hill have on the establishment of the
Tobacco Industry Research Committee and on the formulation of this
public relations defense? When directly asked this question in 1966 by Col.
George Hamel, who was then writing his masters's thesis at the University
of Wisconsin on Hill's career, Hill wrote Hamel, "I decline to comment on
this matter on the basis that this is an active, highly sensitive account." That
may explain Hill's omission of the account in his memoir. Publicly, the firm
was given credit for a highly influential role in the cigarette companies'
adoption of a public relations campaign. Senator Maurene Neuberger wrote
in her book, *Smoke Screen*, "Cool heads among the public relations-wise
labored and brought forth a counter-offensive weapon with which to slay
the smoking and health dragons: the Tobacco Industry Research Committee. The creation of the TIRC, the brain child of the resourceful public
relations firm of Hill and Knowlton, was a stroke of ingenuity." In an
article on the state of public relations in 1960, *Business Week*, commented,
"Probably one of PR's best finger-in-the-dike jobs was during the tobacco-
lung cancer scare when the tobacco industry brought in Hill and Knowlton.
H&K helped set up the Tobacco Industry Research Committee, run by
prominent scientists had based on the premise that 'there is no conclusive
proof that cigarettes cause cancer, but that the industry has an obligation to
get the full facts." H&K Staffer, E. C. K. Reed wrote Hill "Both the
statement and the preliminary program strike me as about as sound as
anything we have ever put out."

To lend credibility to its program, the TIRC hired Dr. Clarence Little as
director. Dr. Little brought impressive credentials if not much competence
to the job. He had been president of the University of Maine and of the
University of Michigan. More importantly, and ironically, from 1929 to
1945 he had served as managing director of the American Society for the
Control of Cancer, which later became the powerful foe of cigarette
smoking, the American Cancer Society. In those years, Dr. Little had done
little to arouse the public to the dangers of cancer or to muster much
research into cancer's causes. Another irony: He was forced out of his
position in the cancer society by the indomitable Mary Lasker, widow of
Albert Lasker, who had played a major role in the 1920s campaign to get
women to smoke. Lasker's agency, Lord & Thomas, was aided in this
campaign for the American Tobacco Company by public relations pioneers,

Edward L. Bernays and Ivy Lee. At Mrs. Lasker's insistence, Lasker's successor agency, Foote, Cone, and Belding, was brought into her campaign to strengthen the cancer society and educate the public about the danger signs of cancer. Mrs. Lasker moved in on the society in 1944 and put it on the road to its large resources and powerful educational efforts of today. Scientists were greatly perturbed that Dr. little would lend his name and credibility to the tobacco companies. What Little's motivation in going over to "the other side" is an unknowable.

The research funds of TIRC were administered by a scientific advisory board composed of eight independent scientists or doctors and Dr. Little. The funds were provided by contributions from the cigarette companies based on sales. By the mid-1960s several million dollars had been contributed and distributed. For example, $800,000 was allotted for research in 1963. A cynic would observe that this amount was equal to only one half of 1% of the industry's advertising expenditures that encouraged people to smoke.

The *Wall Street Journal* story of June 16, 1954, breaking the news of Dr. Little's appointment, described him as a "husky, suntanned man of 66" who "toyed with a pipe during a press conference yesterday and said he avoided smoking cigarettes because, as they burned, they threatened to singe his mustache." The story quoted Little as praising "the tobacco industry for its willingness to finance and permit free investigation of all phases of the relationship between smoking and cancer." He asserted that if research did discover a direct relationship "the next job tackled will be to determine how to eliminate the danger from tobacco." In this period, the *Wall Street Journal* accepted industry information uncritically.

In fact, most newspapers reported the formation of the Tobacco Industry Research Committee favorably. A memo prepared by H&K on a breakdown of editorial opinion showed only 9% of the newspapers expressing opinions on TIRC were unfavorable, predicting biased research, whereas 65% were favorable without reservation. "Newspaper reaction throughout the country to the announcement of the Tobacco Industry Research Committee was nearly 13 to 1 in favor of the Tobacco Industry's action," the report concluded, "News handling of the announcement story was nearly 100 percent favorable. yet, in contrast, 73 articles indicated a belief that a conclusive proof linking smoking to lung cancer already existed.

One of the initial recommendations in the H&K proposal was to conduct a public opinion poll on this issue, a standard procedure in most public relations programs. E. C. K. Reed persuaded Hill that this would be a mistake. "Any widespread public opinion poll would seem to come under the heading of fanning the flames. I don't think you will find out anything anyway except that people are concerned about smoking and would like to see it given a clean bill of health by the medical profession."

Dr. Little was quick to enter the fray. *The New York Times* published a story June 22, 1954, headlined, "CIGARETTES FOUND TO RAISE DEATH RATE IN MEN 50 TO 70," reporting a study by Drs. E. Cyler Hammond and Daniel Horn that had been sponsored by the American Cancer Society, which by now was in full cry against the dangers of smoking. Their paper was given at a medical meeting in San Francisco. The article stated, "Cigarette smokers from 50 to 70 years of age have a higher death rate, from all diseases, as much as 75 percent higher than that of non-smokers." The next day *The Times* printed a second story, this one based on a statement by Dr. Little, who had been appointed just the week before, in which he characterized the Hammond–Horn study as "preliminary" and said it was only "a statistical examination of the last two and one half years." *The Times* reported that American Tobacco and P. Lorillard had "referred questioners to Dr. Little's report." Thus, it became evident that under H&K guidance, the tobacco industry was now speaking with one voice on this issue.

Hill and Knowlton's strategy at the outset was not to seek publicity that might fan the flames of the burning crisis but to influence stories already in the works. Bert Goss instructed his staff to remember "we are not interested in stimulating or encouraging the publication of any articles or news stories on the subject of tobacco and cancer or the work of the Committee." Instead, he wrote in a staff memo, Hill and Knowlton's "sole interest is in knowing what is being written and in getting our side of the story over if an article is scheduled for publication." The agency monitored medical and scientific journals and conferences, and although they did not actively try to counter attack by sending protobacco doctors to medical meetings, staff members did gather information into a compendium that was sent to doctors across the United States. The strategy was to avoid case-by-case responses to new charges and direct debate with scientists, the agency responded mostly through the popular press.

Initially this strategy appeared to pay off. For example, *The New York Times* coverage of the massive American Cancer Society study, the first report that followed the creation of the TIRC, tended to be balanced, quoting doctors on both sides of the issue in the first story and then seeking TIRC's response the next day. Despite the generally positive reception TIRC had received in the press, by September 9, 1954, the staff at Hill and Knowlton considered science writers an "obstacle" to their program, asserting that "an influential section of science writers" completely prejudiced against cigarettes were able "to color and slant stories in magazines and the daily press," according to a memo in the John Hill Papers.

To counteract this presumed bias, the PR firm set up meetings in August and September 1954 for Dr. Little and the chairman of the TIRC with a host of publishers, editors, and science writers from major publishing groups, including Arthur Hays Sulzberger of *The New York Times*, William Randolph Hearst, Jr., Jack Howard of Scripps–Howard, and Roy Larsen of the Luce publications. Nonetheless, stories continued to appear that were critical of the industry. One student of this campaign, Karen Miller, wrote that "skepticism by the journalists toward the Tobacco Industry Research Committee is striking because American beliefs about science and medicine overall were very optimistic during the 1950s." Despite journalists' doubts, TIRC statements continued to appear frequently in the press. Journalists who may have distrusted committee reports were constrained from reporting their suspicions by adherence to the journalistic tradition of *objectivity*, which means the reporter must get "both sides of the story." Another problem was the journalists' necessary reliance upon official sources because they were not scientists or doctors. Science writing was still maturing in this period.

The Raleigh News and Observer reported on January 1, 1954, that "the Justice Department has informed cigarette manufacturers that they cannot legally act in concert to combat medical claims that cigarette smoking may cause lung cancer" and that contributions to medical research would have to be made by individual companies. The TIRC got around the Justice Department's advice by creating an "independent" organization that had its own public relations agenda separate from the campaigns the companies sponsored. In reality, public relations, not research, was the agenda of TIRC. In all this, Hill and Knowlton kept a low profile because if TIRC were to have credibility, the public must be shielded from the fact that public relations professionals were writing TIRC's well-organized reports.

Over time, John Hill stoutly asserted that paper groups established by a client to promote a cause under the guise of being independent should be eliminated from the public relations profession. "The right of free speech also carries the obligation that the source of it will be open for all to see," he wrote. "It is not the work of public relations—let it always be emphasized—to outsmart the American public by helping management build profits." But in fact TIRC was essentially a front for the public relations work of the industry, created to blunt the growing threat to the cigarette makers' enormous profits.

True, the Tobacco Industry Research Committee was clearly identified with its sponsors, but its true nature as a public relations effort was not. The issue here was and is not the right of tobacco companies to put forth their views, but rather, in the opinion of Joel B. Cohen, director of the Center for Consumer Research at the University of Florida, "denying the public an adequate understanding of the consequences of smoking." That the companies were being less than honest in their efforts to abfuscate the dangers of smoking was brought to light through the discovery process in a landmark lawsuit brought against three cigarette companies in the 1980s by

Rose Cipollone of Little Ferry, NJ, who was then dying of lung cancer as a result of her smoking for more than 40 years. The documents uncovered in the discovery process showed that these cigarette companies were aware of smoking's link to cancer as early as 1946. Relying on these documents, Richard Daynard, head of the Tobacco Products Liability Project, a national organization involved in litigation against tobacco companies, asserted, "The public should understand that the cigarette companies knew before the surgeon general that smoking caused cancer and that nicotine was an addictive substance."

TIRC's research strategy was outlined by Dr. Little in a press release issued July 28, 1954. The release quoted Little as saying:

> In order to find conclusive facts concerning questions that have been raised about tobacco use and health, the Scientific Advisory Board has adopted a three-fold policy which will direct funds into research on:
>
> 1. Study of the physical and chemical composition of tobacco and accompanying products.
> 2. Study of tissue changes in humans and animals under various conditions.
> 3. Study of smoking and other tobacco habits and of the emotional and physical makeup of smokers.

Little argued that "research to date has not succeeded in pinning down any single cause of cancer." This became the common theme in TIRC's effort to knock down the growing evidence of tobacco's ill effects on health.

By the time Dr. Little had been appointed in June, TIRC had already conducted a significant public relations project. In its first 6 months, the committee had issued 11 press releases, built a library of information on the scientific case against smoking, assisted at least two dozen press and broadcast reporters with stories and editorials, published several brochures, monitored press coverage of the committee, established personal contacts with doctors, medical organizations, and science writers, and built mailing lists.

Evidence that TIRC's purpose went beyond funding research to get the "facts" about the dangers of smoking is found in a memo by Carl Thompson dated August 25, 1954, outlining a Congressional Information Program. He wrote:

> Some members of Congress have expressed direct interest in the Tobacco Industry Research Program. Congressmen from at least sixteen states should be kept informed on activities. . . . A Congressional Information Program should be tailored especially for members of Congress from these states to: 1. Furnish basic information concerning the Tobacco Industry Research Com-

mittee's objectives and functions on a continuing basis. 2. To seek advice from
these Congressmen from time to time on matters relating to general public
relations in their states as well as possible developments in legislative matters
3. To maintain liaison with a core of Congressmen who care about the
tobacco problem.

He also recommended that a Congressional Information packet be put
together to include origin/purposes/function of TIRC, members of the
Scientific Advisory Board, research policy, the booklets, "Editorial Comment on Tobacco and Health," "A Scientific Perspective on the Cigarette
Industry," and a discussion of research grants to date.

Hill's strategy for TIRC is set out in a "PR Report to the TIRC," dated
November 3, 1955:

> The subject of smoking and health is still very much alive, but in 22 months
> since the Tobacco Industry Research Institute was formed, public reactions
> has changed.

> New attacks continue to rise but they appear to be creating less heat and
> hysteria. They are still considered newsworthy but the press is less inclined to
> treat them sensationally.

> It has been TIRC's public relations policy to avoid stimulating new or
> additional public attention on the subject and at the same time to take steps
> that would help the public maintain a balanced view of the situation. The
> policy has protected the dignified and objective position of the Scientific
> Advisory Board by refraining from any move or action that would seem to
> involve the research program in any controversy.

> When critics have exceeded the proved facts, TIRC's statements have sought
> to minimize unwarranted public hysteria and alarm. This has been done by
> pointing out that statistical data do not provide the answers and that much
> more research is needed before the cause or causes of the diseases involved in
> the charge are known. Public statements have been issued only about attacks
> considered significant in their impact.

It should be noted that public relations agencies tend to put their efforts in
the most favorable terms possible when reporting to clients.

Instead of seeking publicity on the issue, H&K followed the dictum of
John Hill and Bert Goss not "to fan the flames of the controversy." Their
tactic was to make certain reporters consulted them before publishing
articles on smoking. To this end they provided background memoranda on
the TIRC and on research positive to smoking, and they met with science
writers and editors to explain there was more than one side to the smoking
story. When unfavorable stories did appear, they dealt with the source but
did not issue a countering statement. For example, H&K sent a report to

T. V. Hartnett, chairperson of TIRC, claiming "one negatively aimed program (WNBT) which was being scheduled on the cigarette controversy was postponed after a discussion of TIRC facts."

When *Newsweek's* Periscope published a "rumor" unfavorable to cigarettes, Bert Goss called the editor, "I informed Roberts that our checks with the insurance companies indicated there was absolutely no basis for their report. I told him that I realized that the Periscope people would not want to tell us the source of their story nor would they be particularly anxious to publish a retraction. I did emphasize our hope that the rumor would not crop up in another future story *Newsweek* did." This tactic paid off. John Hill wrote Hartnett, a tobacco company president, on December 1, 1954, "Art Hall, director of public relations of Alcoa [the sponsor] told me that Ed Murrow and Fred Friendly would keep him in the know when the tobacco program would air. He said Mr. Friendly had told him they had done their best to make the program a balanced one, but that due to the superior presentation by the tobacco people, he [Friendly] believed that if anyone gets a break in the program it would be the tobacco industry." Murrow, a chain smoker who ultimately died of lung cancer, did two CBS documentaries on "Cigarettes and Cancer."

H&K's tactic of dealing with unfavorable stories on a case-by-case basis was described by Senator Maurene Neuberger like "a tail of a kite, no story about the risk of smoking goes anywhere without a tobacco industry rebuttal trailing long behind."

The careful methodology of the Hill firm is revealed in this memorandum from Carl Thompson to T. K. Hartnett, dated August 17, 1954:

> We have built a cross indexed file of medical and scientific papers from 2,500 medical journals, with most pertinent obtained in full; special files of all pertinent press clippings; a cross indexed file on medical opinions as noted from press, radio and other popular media; full texts of speeches, announcements and panel discussions which were germane and available; files drawn from documents of the U.S. Health, Education and Welfare, Internal revenue, Agriculture Departments, the U.S. and other official bodies.

This well before the day of computer databases!

Like the tobacco industry, scientists need the media to disseminate their findings. A few like Ochsner wrote books, but most depended on delivery of papers at medical or scientific meetings. There reporters were constrained to present balanced stories and often took countering statements from the TIRC without questioning their accuracy. The tobacco Industry had a big edge with its money to purchase the services of professional public relations and advertising agencies. The formation of the TIRC meant that the public relations professionals could coordinate the statements of the tobacco companies into complete, well-organized reports, whereas scientists, in the opinion of Karen Miller "could only patiently wait for their theories to be confirmed." as they release their findings piecemeal.

In entering this fray, Hill and Knowlton considered different responses to the scientists who were promoting the antismoking message. "We must early decide our own attitude toward the findings of men like Wynder, Rhoads, Ochsner, et al.," a staff member wrote. "We have a choice of (a) smearing and belittling them, (b) trying to overwhelm them with mass publication of the opposed viewpoints of other specialists, (c) debating them in the public arena, or (d) we can determine to raise the issue far above them, so that they are hardly even mentioned and then we can make our real case."

Ultimately, H&K chose a combination of these approaches. H&K emphasized several messages in their efforts to contain the damage of the health scare through the popular press. First, they argued the case against tobacco had not been proven. Animal experimentation might be useful, but who could be sure mouse skin was comparable to human lung tissue? Furthermore, painting the skin of mice was not the same as inhaling into human lungs. Other data collected by anticigarette scientists could be dismissed as hogwash. Industry arguments, at least to one writer, appeared "both effective and to some extent well founded." The industry also consistently used the argument that the charges all came from a small group of doctors who were either puritanical zealots or publicity seekers. Typically, E. A. Darr, president of R. J. Reynolds, said in 1953, "One of the best ways of getting publicity is for a doctor to make some startling claim relative to people's health, regardless of whether such statement is fact or theory." Also, as long as some nonsmokers got cancer and other lifelong smokers did not, the tobacco industry could and did argue that smoking was not the only cause of lung cancer. Another response to the growing evidence against cigarettes was that the tobacco industry introduced filtered cigarettes. Filters appeared to offer some protection for worried smokers. In 1950, filter cigarettes held less than 1% of the market; by 1986, 94% of all cigarettes sold in the United States were filter tipped. Scientists and doctors argued that misleading cigarette advertising caused smokers to believe that filters could protect them from cancer. During the mid-1950s, cigarette advertising on which the companies spent millions sought to minimize worries over smoking and health. Hill and Knowlton constantly advised the tobacco companies that no one should seek a competitive advantage "by inferring to its public that its product is less risky than others." Although no campaign was blatant, many continued to imply that their brands were safer than others. An H&K staffer, in a memo to Hill on "Obstacles Facing Progress of TIRC," wrote, "The impression in the public mind and implanted and aggressively cultivated over the years by much cigarette advertising is that cigarette smoking in some way is bad for the health."

In another staff memo, J. J. Daniels of H&K wrote that "the public is probably irritated by existing cigarette advertising as witness the ridicule resulting from claims and counterclaims of the various manufacturers. This attitude will have some bearing on the activities to be undertaken." Privately, Hill and other members of his staff placed the blame for some of the industry's problems on its own advertising. Agency employees concluded that one of the obstacles facing TIRC included the "impression in the public mind implanted and aggressively cultivated over the years by much cigarette advertising that cigarette smoking is in some way bad for the health." Another staff member, E. C. K. Read, remarked to Hill, "While it may be a delicate area for us, we should be emphatic about individual company advertising." But Hill and Knowlton did not intervene in tobacco advertising because tobacco executives told Hill that advertising was one activity "that might very clearly fall within the purview of the Anti-Trust Act." Despite Hill's concern, the tobacco industry continued its negative advertising practices. Typical was Old Gold's oft-repeated claim: "Not a cough in a carload."

To balance the record, it should be noted that many of the industry's advertisements were not countenanced by Hill and his associates. For example, a staff member questioned an R. J. Reynolds survey claiming "more doctors use Camels than any other cigarette." Persons reading this ad did not know, as a H&K staff member wrote in an internal memorandum, that "interviewers had placed in the doctors' hotel rooms on their arrival (at a medical conference) cartons of Camel cigarettes." H&K's executive worried that this kind of scam was "not the most effective way to build cordial relations with a group whose support is almost required." J. J. Daniels concluded in his memo to Hill, "My understanding from outside sources that the claim is not a valid one." He then went on to argue, "In any consideration of the public relations approach to such a problem, basic facts are required. In this particular case, serious charges and/or implications have been levelled against cigarettes by professional men who apparently have stature and reputations in their fields."

Despite the growing doubts of some of his staff, several of whom urged caution against any industry health claim, Hill thought that H&K's program was ethical. He argued, "The mind of the college professor as well as the unschooled crop picker is inclined to select and retain the facts it wants to retain—those facts that confirm established prejudices or leanings." Although Hill had a large economic stake in the tobacco industry, he apparently rationalized that by presenting the "facts" of independent studies and by asking manufacturers to stop production if researchers ever isolated a cancer-producing agent; he was not responsible for other people's decisions. In his only public comment on TIRC, Hill wrote in 1957 that the committee put industry in the position to "draw some public attention to other sides of the question." "The normal American sense of fair play," he concluded, "let people decide; despite sensational charges, the truth is not yet known and the industry itself is doing what it can to speed the availability of true and reliable answers." Yet Hill and Knowlton's work continued to obfuscate the issue to the benefit of the tobacco companies— and knowingly so. Richard Darrow, H&K vice-president, was given a memo from the Mediametric Institute dated July 22, 1954, reporting a survey of doctors that concluded that heavy smoking (i. e., 30 cigarettes plus a day) had a 91.8% harmful effect on the heart.

It is the basic rationale of public relations that in a free society every individual, every institution, every industry, every cause has the right to be heard in the public forum. A corollary of this principle is that to be heard in today's public arena one must have the expertise of a public relations professional. This fundamental right was upheld by the U.S. Supreme Court in the Noerr (the Pennsylvania Truckers) v. Eastern Railroad Presidents Conference when it held in an opinion written by Justice Hugo Black that antitrust laws do not bar corporations from joining with public relations counsel in a "no holds barred" campaign to affect legislation. (This case that involved Carl Byoir & Associates is discussed in chapter 18). Raising this commonly used defense, Hill wrote, "When an industry is, in effect, accused of mass murder, it is naturally agonizing to it when few voices are lifted in its defense before the bar of public opinion." Nonetheless, Hill seems to have had some qualms about this account. In a letter to a British counselor, Campbell Johnson, Hill wrote on June 25, 1956, congratulating Johnson on his retention as counsel by the British tobacco industry, saying, "I feel the course of events is a tribute to the soundness of the policies of TIRC, as I do that your folks were inclined to look down their noses at what we were doing and, I am sure, aghast at the idea of Hill and Knowlton, Inc. as public relations counsel."

TIRC AND H&K SPLIT; TOBACCO RESEARCH COUNCIL REPLACES TIRC

With the formation of the Tobacco Institute—to be detailed next—the cigarette manufacturers shifted much of their public relations effort and expenditure to the nation's capital. In 1963 the Tobacco Industry Research Committee changed its name to the Tobacco Research Council (TRC) Coincident with this shift, Hill and Knowlton, Inc. took a much diminished role in the new organization. Loet Velmans, president of Hill and Knowlton, Inc. from 1978 to 1986, asserted that H&K dropped the tobacco industry as a client at this time. "We couldn't do anything for them because they wouldn't take our advice—to research what smoking would do you to you and to invest in cancer research. It was useless to represent them."

Leonard Zahn, and H&K vice-president who worked on the TIRC account, told me in 1992 that the Tobacco Research Council retained H&K on a part-time basis through most of the 1960s. Zahn left H&K in 1969 to set up his own agency and was soon thereafter retained by the Tobacco Research Council. Walker Merryman of the Tobacco Institute wrote your author that after the institute was well along, it dropped Hill and Knowlton, Inc. as counselors but did retain the firm from time to time on a project basis.

These changes coincided with John Hill's stepping down as his firm's chief executive officer in 1962. The fact remains that for the last decade of his active career he fought the tobacco wars on behalf of the cigarette industry.

Since its founding in late 1953 at the recommendation of Hill, TIRC and the council have spent $185 million in administration, public relations, and in research grants as of 1991, according to Zahn. The TRC budget for 1990 totaled $18 million. Despite the change in name from Tobacco Industry Research Committee to the Tobacco Research Council the defensive approach changed little from the time when the American Cancer Society asserted, "TIRC is fighting a delaying action to mislead the public into believing that no change in smoking habits is indicated from existing statistical and pathological evidence nor will be until 'direct experimental evidence' is at hand."

TIRC AND TRC SEEN AS FRONTS BY THEIR SPONSORS

The gullibility of the media for the public relations handout and front was demonstrated anew when in 1992 when a U.S. Federal Judge, H. Lee Sarokin, ruled in effect on February 6 of that year that according to *The New York Times*, "The tobacco industry's chief research arm for 40 years described its own mission as a 'front' and a 'shield' against potentially harmful Congressional hearings, lawsuits, or scientific research about the health risks of smoking." Judge Sarokin was quoting from secret industry memorandum for the first time. *The Times* account continued:

> The judge . . . "said that a jury might reasonably assume that the industry's decades-old vow to disclose its research findings were nothing but a public relations ploy—a fraud—to deflect the growing evidence against the industry, to encourage smokers to continue and nonsmokers to begin, and to reassure

the public that the adverse information would be disclosed. Despite some
rising pretenders, the tobacco industry may be the king of concealment and
misinformation," Judge Sarokin said in ruling to permit the documents' use in
a lawsuit on behalf of a New Jersey man who died of lung cancer in 1982 after
a lifetime of heavy smoking. He based his ruling on a review of small fraction
of the 1,500 documents at issue and said that the documents would not be
released until a special master he appoints reviews the entire file.

Speaking for the industry, William Alinder, a lawyer, who represented
Philip Morris Companies and Lorillard, two of the defendants in the
lawsuit said, "We do not agree with the inferences Judge Sarokin had drawn
from the documents he reviewed." The documents came from the files of
the Tobacco Industry Research Committee and its successor organization,
the Tobacco Research Council. The attorneys for the five tobacco companies argued against releasing the files, saying it would be a violation of the
attorney–client privilege. Judge Sarokin countered that the documents he
reviewed presented sufficient "evidence of fraud in connection with the
public assurances" that the attorney–client privilege does not apply. One
internal document in TIRC files that the judge quoted said the committee
was set up as a "shield." In referring to a document from the TRC files, the
judge quoted a memorandum as stating, "On these projects TRC acted as a
front." The memo quoted by Judge Sarokin also stated, "It is extremely
important that the industry continue to spend their dollars on research to
show that we don't agree that the case against smoking is closed."

Once again public relations counselors have been caught in constructing
a front to deceive the public.

TOBACCO INSTITUTE FORMED

As John Hill wrote his friend Campbell Johnson in 1956, "This whole
matter, instead of abating, seems to be getting hotter here and abroad—all
without any real evidence having been adduced that cigarettes are the *cause*
of anything." Indeed, after the TIRC was formed in 1954, the flames of
controversy continued to "get hotter." To intensify its effort to becloud and
obfuscate the steadily mounting evidence of the dangers of smoking, the
tobacco industry decided to separate its public relations and lobbying
efforts from the TIRC by organizing the Tobacco Institute in 1958. The
institute was organized by the 12 leading tobacco companies, including
Liggett & Myers that had refused to support the TIRC.

Hill and Knowlton, Inc. was instrumental in organizing the institute and
was immediately hired as public relations counsel. H&K issued a news
release January 30, 1958, announcing the new institute and stating, "The

principal purposes of the newly formed Tobacco Institute, Inc. are to provide a better public understanding of the tobacco industry and its place in the national economy and to compile and disseminate information relating to the industry and to the use of tobacco products. The Tobacco Institute will not be concerned with any aspect of the marketing or sale of tobacco or with the commercial activities of its member companies." James P. Richards, a former Congressman from South Carolina, was appointed president. The announcement made it clear that this new institute was "separate and distinct from the Tobacco Industry Research Committee, which is supporting a program of scientific research into the subject of tobacco use and health."

The Tobacco Institute emerged over the next 3 decades as one of Washington's most powerful public relations and lobbying organizations. By 1990, the institute was spending an estimated $20 million a year to combat and becloud the growing evidence of the dangers of smoking. The "tobacco wars" continued into the 1990s with the Tobacco Institute on one side and the Surgeon General of the United States, the National Cancer Institute, the American Cancer Society, the American Heart Association, and the American Lung Association on the other. In December, 1988, these wars were described in the *Public Relations Journal* as one of the most dramatic examples ever of huge public relations powers squaring off and fighting to the bitter end." A retired vice-president of the Institute was quoted as saying, "I don't think it's going to end. These things tend to wax and wane. I don't think there is going to be any really resolution." The fact was that by 1992, restrictions against smoking were becoming universal and cigarette sales, except among teenagers, were steadily declining in the United States.

Even as the institute was being organized, efforts of the antismoking forces to curb the sales and require warning labels of the dangers of smoking were on the rise. Labeling legislation was under consideration in Massachusetts, New York, and "one of the Carolinas." Joe Cullman of the institute appealed to Hill to jump into the battle to oppose such legislation because "the Institute formed to do this job is not yet ready to function," asking Hill if H&K "would be in a position to take on this coordinating job." Hill said H&K would take on the coordinating job and quickly set up an executive committee to "develop a plan for opposing the legislation, select people to appear at the hearings, and develop the line of opposition argument." Hill's memo added that it had been arranged for a Dr. Hammer to appear, who would point out "how it would be impossible for any company to label the precise extent of tar and nicotine contained in cigarettes because the amount varies."

In the early 1960s, as John Hill was relinquishing leadership at H&K, the tobacco industry was engaged in a desperate battle to keep the government from requiring warning labels on each package of cigarettes and in all tobacco advertising, but to no avail. In 1965, Congress passed the Federal Cigarette Labelling and Advertising Act authorizing the Surgeon General to require such labels on packages and in all advertising. (The Tobacco Institute earlier had given up TV advertising after the Federal Communications Commission had required the networks and stations to match each cigarette ad with one warning against the dangers of smoking.) Since 1985, the manufacturers have been required to print four warnings on a rotating basis.

It is indeed a grim irony that when the cigarette companies were faced with Mrs. Cipollone's landmark lawsuit, the companies were quick to use the warning labels as a defense. Mrs. Cipollone died in 1984, but her husband, aided by antitobacco forces, continued the lawsuit. The jury's verdict came down July 13, 1988, and found that the three companies whose brands Mrs. Cipollone had smoked—Philip Morris, the Liggett Group, and P. Lorillard—had not conspired to misrepresent the dangers of smoking. But the jury, in a precedent-setting verdict, awarded damages of $400,000 to her husband, Antonio Cipollone. The jury held that the Liggett Group had breached a health warranty by its 1950s ad describing cigarettes as "just what the doctor ordered." The companies appealed the verdict to the U.S. Court of Appeals, Third Circuit, where the award was set aside.

The Appeals Court ruled that once the Federal labeling law took effect January 1, 1986, all lawsuits seeking damages for smoking after that date were preempted to the extent that they were based on allegations of misleading advertising. The case was carried to the U.S. Supreme Court and argued October 8, 1991, with a ruling expected in July 1992. Thus, the law the tobacco companies fought so hard to prevent turned out to be their protection. For document of this case see p. 523.

Hill and Knowlton was not involved in the lawsuit but nonetheless, according to *PR Week*, "Public relations firms representing cigarette companies came under fire . . . from a witness who charged that they share some responsibility for deaths and health problems resulting from smoking." The plaintiff's case was based largely on the public relations and advertising campaigns of the tobacco industry before 1966, the first year of the warning labels. And justifiably so to the extent TIRC and later the Tobacco Institute sought to nullify the warnings that were coming in increasing volume from reputable scientists and doctors.

A 1972 memo obtained by Cipollone's attorneys provides a candid insight into the Tobacco Institute's strategy as it evolved over the years. In it, an institute vice-president described "a brilliantly conceived and executed plan" that has served the industry well for 20 years. It speaks of using litigation, politics, and public opinion aimed at "creating doubt about the health charge without actually denying it; advocating the public's right to smoke without actually urging them to take up the practice and encouraging objective scientific research as the only way to solve the question of the health hazard." In the 1990s, the institute had a budget of more than $20 million and 120 professional public relations persons organized into one of the "most formidable public relations/lobbying machines in history," in the view of the *Public Relations Journal*. Hill and Knowlton was a vital cog in that machine.

In 1968, revealing the Tobacco Institute's tactic of buying ghosted stories and then planting them in offbeat publications, the Federal Trade Commission (FTC) exposed the institute's role in placing stories in *True* and the *National Enquirer*. The latter's headline filled the front page with a bold declaration that "CIGARETTE CANCER LINK IS THE BUNK"—a headline viewed by millions of shoppers at the supermarket checkout counters and read by millions more. Ads in the daily press encouraged readership of the *True* article. The institute mailed hundreds of thousands of reprints of the *True* article to doctors, educators, researchers, and members of Congress with an "editor's note" attachment rather than exposing the institute's dirty hand. The American Medical Association mailing list was obtained by the institute with the pretense that it was for a circulation campaign for *True*. Both articles were written by the same author who was then hired by Hill and Knowlton. In its annual report of 1968, the FTC concluded, "These are not the acts of an industry either confident of its facts nor solicitous of its reputation."

Though John Hill had long since passed from such earthly battles, the fact remains that he was the guiding force in the formation of the Tobacco Industry Research Committee and later the Tobacco Institute. Thus, Hill must bear responsibility for that "brilliantly conceived and executed plan" that has served the selfish interests of the tobacco industry at the expense of millions of American's good health. Hill actively managed the firm he built into the world's largest agency until he relinquished his position as chairman and chief executive office in 1962, somewhat against his will. He tried to keep his hand in as a member of the firm's policy committee until his death. In assessing John Hill's considerable and imaginative efforts to becloud and confuse the facts about the dangers of smoking, it seems pertinent to again quote what Hill wrote to his friend Almo C. Casey on November 8, 1955: "For our part, we would never be identified with any movement for which the course was not open and above board for everybody to know. As you may know, some public relations firms—upon being retained by a client who does not want his name identified with the movement or the objective sought—have set up paper organizations with high sounding names. In the name of the paper organization, publicity is issued and activities of various sorts are carried on." True the Tobacco Industry Research Committee was clearly identified with the tobacco industry, but its true nature as a public relations front was not. The issue here was and is not the right of the tobacco companies to put forth their views, but rather, "denying the public an adequate understanding of the consequences of smoking."

In *The Consumers Union Report on Smoking and the Public Interest*, the Consumers Union made this evaluation of the TIRC's public relations campaign in 1963, the year after Hill had retired from active involvement in H&K accounts:

> The case the TIRC has lacked is the ability to disprove the health charges or even come up with a defense acceptable to a significant part of the scientific community. Under these circumstances, the TIRC's response has been somewhat monotonous. The TIRC, and, by extension, the tobacco industry, has two principal spokesmen: Timothy V. Hartnett, chairman of the Committee and retired president of the Brown and Williamson Tobacco Corp., and Dr. Clarence Cook Little, the TIRC's scientific director. Whenever a new finding implicating cigarettes has been announced, Mr. Hartnett or Dr. Little has come forth to deny that it is true or new or meaningful.

Irving Rimer, retired vice-president of the American Cancer Society, was quoted in the Consumers Union report as saying, "Hill and Knowlton has done a professional job for the tobacco industry. No one could question the ethics of their method of operation. They have conducted a smart, clever campaign of constant denials and attempted diversion, such as point the finger at air pollution as the real villain in lung cancer. The campaign was firmed up early in the controversy and hasn't changed." Evidence of this is a pamphlet entitled "The Cigarette Controversy: Why More Research Is Needed," which was distributed by the Tobacco Institute in the early 1990s as the latest word on the subject. This is a compilation of testimony by medical authorities before various Congressional Committees in 1982 and 1983. Walker Merryman, vice-president of the institute, wrote to me on October 10, 1991, "There have been no new developments since then which would warrant an additional publication."

Dr. Karen Miller, who is at work on a biography of John W. Hill, reached this conclusion in her evaluation of his role in the tobacco–health public relations battle:

> John Hill created a carefully-calculated, well-executed, and apparently effective program. The TIRC campaign aimed to discredit anti-cigarette scientists, present findings to conflict with the growing evidence against smoking, and bombard the public with messages intended to persuade people that cigarette manufacturers were working for the public interest. Committee advertising said, "We care about your health, American smoker. . . . The Tobacco Industry Research Committee was not formed to answer medical questions; created by Hill and Knowlton, headquartered in its Empire State Office Building Offices, it marketed confidence. If cigarette consumption levels provide an indication, Hill and Knowlton succeeded.

During his long career from 1927 until his quasi-retirement in 1962, John Hill developed a reputation as a staunch conservative, a shrewd business-man, and as an ethical practitioner. Hill worried about public relations having a reputation for being unethical and openly acknowledged that the profession was blighted with quacks: "Not all the uses of the power of public relations are honest and legitimate." But he defended it saying "the public relations counseling field is comprised largely of practitioners with sound ethical standards." John Hill had a deep abiding concern for his profession. This was demonstrated in his effort learn from other counselors and in his effort to form an elite group of counselors who would enforce high standards. And his insatiable desire to learn the ways and means of public relations by learning from others is reflected in his starting The Wisemen.

HILL'S EFFORT TO FORM A COUNSELORS GROUP FAILS

As he neared retirement from active direction of his firm and as he saw the proliferation of new agencies, John Hill became convinced of the need for an organization of the prestigious counselors to, as he put it, "to separate the sheep form the goats." As he wrote counselor Earl Newsom on January 19, 1959, "I realize there have been a number of motions made in this direction at various times in the past and that nothing has come of them." But as he told me in 1964, "I long worked for a PR counselors association so that we could establish higher standards, but I finally threw in the sponge on this one. We could never resolve the tough questions of who should be members, and who shouldn't."

Hill first outlined in detail his proposal for such an organization in a memorandum dated January 23, 1957, to his colleagues Bert Goss, Richard Darrow, and John Mapes. He prefaced his proposal by saying, "I am having a meeting Wednesday night with Messrs. [T. J.] Ross, [Pendleton] Dudley, [Gerry] Swinehart, and [James] Salvage to discuss the question of forming an organization of public relations counseling firms." Then he made clear that the first question in his mind was "whether this would be a good thing for the profession." To support his belief that it would, he argued these points:

1. It would provide a focal point for discussing mutual problems
2. It would provide the means for doing a public relations job for the counseling profession.
3. It would encourage the lifting of standards of performance in counseling.

4. Under *rigid* auspices, it would head off the formation of such a group under the *wrong* auspices to the disadvantage of leading firms.

Hill's primary concern in advocating such an organization was its possible illegality as a violation of the Sherman Anti-Trust Act. "It is necessary to ascertain whether it would be legally possible to pick and choose new members according to criteria to be established." With reference to suggested criteria, Hill thought it would not be desirable to have subsidiaries of advertising companies as members. Little did Hill foresee the day when his firm and other major firms would be bought by major advertising agencies, and thus become, subsidiaries themselves. Hill's suggested criteria were: (a) number of employees, (b) kind and scope of service, (c) years in business, (d) independence of operation, and (e) professional ethics subject to the appraisal of the association.

Apparently at the Wednesday, January 30 meeting at the top executives of Pendleton Dudley & Associates, T. J. Ross & Associates, Carl Byoir & Associates, and Selvage and Lee, there was, in Hill's opinion, "A crystallization of opinion on the advisability of forming a public relations counselors organization" that required moving on to the basic question of arriving at an agreement on the other questions arising out of it. In a memo addressed to Pendleton Dudley, George Hammond [Carl Byoir & Associates] T. J. Ross, and James Selvage, in Hill's mind these questions were:

1. To promote or encourage wider acceptance and adherence to higher ethics or professional standards by firms engaged in the practice of public relations.
2. To help bring about a better understanding and recognition on the part of business of the role of public relations counsel and the contribution they can make.
3. To provide a focal point for discussion of problems of mutual concern, and by the exchange of information relating to matters of mutual interest.
4. To encourage—to the extent that it may be feasible—a business-like operation of public relations firms, and a reasonable respect for the overhead of business.
5. To develop suggestions helpful to young people desirous of preparing themselves for careers in public relations.

On the latter point, it is to John Hill's great credit that he was among the few leaders in the field in his time who did much to encourage and support public relations education, as exemplified in his provision of internships for students and teachers and his gifts to Harvard and Boston Universities to support such educational efforts.

Based on the correspondence in the Hill Papers, little of consequence flowed from these initial efforts in 1957 for the next 2 years. In a letter to Earl Newsom, T. J. Ross, Verne Burnett, James Selvage, Gerry Swinehart, Pendleton Dudley, and Stanley Baar, Hill invited these leading counselors to have dinner with him at his apartment, 290 Park Avenue, on Wednesday, March 4, 1959, to discuss, among other topics, "the feasibility of setting up a formal or informal counselors' group." It was in this invitation, dated January 19, 1959, that Hill admitted that such previous efforts had failed, but then wrote, "However, I know a number of counselors now feel that events have moved to a point where some formal or informal group might serve a useful purpose."

Subsequently Earl Newsom wrote Hill that "it is not only in our self interest to start thinking about organizing executives, but a duty we face if we are to continue to gain in public confidence."

Newsom, in his letter, warned against appearing to set up a "snobbish clique," to which Hill replied in a letter dated March 30, 1959, "Neither do I presume to set myself above others in the field. At the same time, I know that there are some who simply would not qualify as members of a group established to maintain a standards of ethics in the conduct of their business." The problem Hill repeated, "is how to separate the sheep from the goats." Hill's reply was copied to Ross, Burnett, Dudley, Hammond, Baar, and Salvage.

In his reply to Newsom and the others he had involved in this exploration, Hill reported, "I have been informed by the head of a small firm that a group of his compatriots is planning to form a counseling association, provided the larger firms in the business decide not to take the lead in doing so." Apparently, "neither did so" as the Public Relations Society of America moved in to take the ball out of the Hill group's court.

In July 1959, Hill wrote his good friend, Tommy Ross, asking, "Have you looked over the questionnaire sent out to PRSA counselor members by the Counselors Survey Committee under date of June 30?" He added, "Where does this put our recent discussions?" Hill made it clear in his letter to Ross that he "would not like to see this ball in the hands of PRSA, but I see no way to take it from them. If we move ahead fast enough perhaps we could." A group of counselors within PRSA did take the ball from Hill, Ross, and the other counselor giants of the day and run with it. As Hill reflected in talking to me, his effort foundered in the difficulty of selecting members for what he envisioned as an elite group. The group spearheaded by Robert Wolcott, a West Coast counselor, had no such problem—it would open their membership to all counselors who were members of PRSA.

What today is the Counselors Academy of PRSA began in the late 1950s with much the same reasoning as Hill and his group had in mind—that it would be useful for counselors to get together, exchange ideas and information, and in "the process, upgrade the practice of public relations counseling." The genesis of the Counselors Academy was planted with the formation of a Counselors Committee following the 1958 PRSA Conference in New York City. Its purpose, as described in a committee report of April 14, 1959, "was to obtain the collective views of counselor members of PRSA on a number of matters of special interest to these practitioners."

Members of the original committee were Wolcott, Stephan Fitzgerald, Dale O'Brien, Robert Hillard, William M. Smolkin, Ayres Compton, and Burns W. Lee, counselors representing all section of the country. Under the committee's auspices, a questionnaire was sent in the summer of 1959 to all counselors in PRSA (the one to which Hill had referred). Reporting to the PRSA Board on September 12 of that year, Wolcott outline these findings:

1. By a slight majority those responding voted against the idea of a special section for counselors.
2. Those responding were split down the middle on the question of licensing.
3. A majority of counselors do not frown on competitive bidding.
4. Most of those responding thought it would be permissible to handle competitive accounts, but only if each client knew of the arrangement.
5. Approximately a two to one majority favored the payment of finder fees.
6. There is a great desire on the part of counselors to obtain and exchange information re their specific types of practice.
7. Most counselors are disturbed about the lack of a definite description of their type of business, and most felt there should be a . . . screening procedure to qualify a counselor for membership in PRSA.
8. Most responders believe there should be no restrictions on the scope nor the dollar investment in new business presentations.

To accommodate the desire expressed by half of the some 800 queried for a counselors section, in 1959, the PRSA Board amended its bylaws to permit the formation of special interest sections and the counselors group meetings were, for the first time, a formal part of the annual conference program. According to Robert Wolcott's, *First Thirty Years: An Informal History of the Counselors Academy*, "With the way thus paved, the Counselors Committee went to work. A survey mailing drew a large, favorable response. However, this initial sounding drew critical reaction from some of the renowned leaders of the counseling business, who wondered why such a formal group was necessary. Thanks to the missionary work of George Hammond of the Carl Byoir agency those negative and potentially damaging reactions were turned around."

It may be presumed that those "negative reactions" came from the giants, John Hill, T. J. Ross, Earl Newsom, and Pendleton Dudley who had been frustrated in their efforts. Interestingly, George Hammond had taken part in the discussion of the Hill group.

In the spring of 1960, the petition mailing that was to launch this new section drew some 400 signatures . . . and among them were some onetime nay-sayers." Presumably in the "naysayers" was Bert Goss, John Hill's right-hand man at Hill and Knowlton. At the meeting of the PRSA board in Washington, DC, on September 29, 1960, it was Bert Goss who moved "that it be the consensus of the Board that this proposed plan for establishment and operation of the PRSA Counsels Section is in order for presentation to the counsels at the section meeting November 2." Public relations practitioners are pragmatists, if nothing else, and Goss decided, with Hill's approval to be sure, that if you can't lick 'em, you join 'em.

On November 6, 1960, at the Conrad Hilton Hotel in Chicago, the Counselors Section (now Academy) was born. As Wolcott recalled, "It was the fruition of several years of hard work by the Counselors Committee, chaired by Wolcott of Los Angeles, George Hammond and Ralph Major of New York City, Felton Goodman of Atlanta, Burns Lee of Los Angeles, Ron Goodman of Chicago, Paul Eden of Cleveland, and Paul Cain of Dallas."

The validity of Hill's and Wolcott's vision, however they differed in concepts, is demonstrated in the fact that by 1990, its 30th year, the Counselors Academy has 1, 200 members and an annual budget of more than $300,000. It sponsors 8 to 10 seminars annually and has published dozens of studies and monographs. In more recent years, it has donned the role of advocate to lobby on behalf of public relations counselors.

As Hill's letter of July 8, 1959, to Ross indicates, this pioneer took a skeptical view of the Public Relations Society and its ability to promote professionalism and the profession, or the business, as Hill more commonly referred to his field. This was also reflected in a letter dated September 13, 1959, to Dan J. Forrestal of the Monsanto Chemical Co. and newly elected president of the society. Hill wrote to decline Forrestal's request that Hill serve as chairman of the society's Public Service Committee for the coming year. Hill declined for this reason, among other reasons:

> The public relations industry—or profession—is not ready to tackle the job which the Committee involves, and do the job properly. There just aren't enough public relations firms with enough surplus manpower to enable them

to devote much time to such non-productive projects. . . . It is my feeling that the sum total of all the work that public relations profession can do, at this stage, anyway, would look pitiable in comparison with the efforts of the Advertising Council—and I do not see how this possibly could reflect the credit upon the public relations that we are all hoping for.

Please note that in this reply to Dan Forrestal, Hill variously refers to his field as an industry, as a profession, and as a business. Little wonder the semantics of this field remain fuzzy.

John Hill joined the Public Relations Society of America in 1948 when it was organized in the merger of the American Public Relations Counsel on the West Coast and the National Association of Public Relations, based primarily in New York City. Although Hill told your author that the influence of PRSA had been on the "plus side," it was apparent he did not think PRSA in his time was effective in establishing standards of competence and ethics for public relations practice. This is reflected in his correspondence and memoranda in pursing the goal of an select group of counselors. Foresightedly he told Col. George Hamel in an interview, "It is difficult to enforce codes. You can't legislate ethical practices into public relations. Neither is licensing of public relations practitioners a practical or feasible alternative." This problem confronts the practice to this day.

THE WISEMEN

John W. Hill was instrumental in organizing an elite group of counselors known as The Wisemen that endures to this day as a lively forum for discussion of social, economic, and political trends and a force of unknown dimension in the professionalization of public relations.

The name, The Wisemen, grew out of an early occasion when member John Long, public relations director of Bethlehem Steel, invited the group to Bethlehem and transported them there in two company planes. During the "happy hour" at the next meeting, the question of a name for this exclusive group came up, and Verne Burnett said, "Since we have made our pilgrimage to Bethlehem, how about 'The Wisemen.' " It struck a popular chord.

The idea for such a dinner meeting for professional give-and-take was born in Edward L. Bernays' active mind. In January 1938, Bernays hosted a dinner and included Hill, then new to New York PR circles. Others invited were Dr. Claude Robinson, the pollster, Paul Garrett of General Motors, Merle Crowell, Frank E. Mason, a veteran newsman who had gone into public relations, Prof. James H. Rogers of Yale, Sociologist Robert Lynd; Lyman Bryson, Joseph D. McGoldrick, and Clyde Raymond Miller. Main topic of the evening was a debate between Bernays and Miller on their differing views of propaganda. Bernays envisioned this as a regular forum for the exchange of ideas.

Typically, Bernays' insatiable lust for publicity killed his plan, just as his eagerness for publicity had doomed the first effort of New York counselors to organize a few years earlier. It was painful to Hill and the other giant figures at that dinner to read in *Time* magazine of January 24, 1938, "Around a dinner table in Manhattan frequently gather some 20 of the ace propagandists in the United States. This unpublicized, high powered group calls itself the Council on Public Opinion. The chairman is Edward L. Bernays, the Nation's No. 1 publicist. . . . Back and forth across the council table flies weighty talk of big U.S. problems about which the public forms opinions."

In the excessive hyperbole that characterized *Time* in its early years, it editorialized, "This small group might be the seat of a sinister super-government were it not that no two members of the Council on Public Opinion completely agree on anything very important."

The idea of men of the stature of Dr. Robinson, Hill, Mason, and others at the dinner in Hill's words, "sitting at the feet of the master to learn public relations" was more than these men could stomach. Hill told me on April 17, 1964, that out of this session did come on reward, a lifelong friendship with "Robbie" Robinson, whom he had met there for the first time. Hill also thought that these meetings were interesting and a good idea because "it gave people a chance to know others in fields of common interest." John Hill was relatively new in New York and among other reasons, sought to broaden his friendships with other counselors. With these thoughts in mind, Hill issued an invitation to come to dinner at his apartment in Manhattan on the night of November 18, 1938.

In notes he prepared for the 20th anniversary dinner held November 21, 1958, Hill recalled:

> The idea had occurred to me sometime previously and I talked it over one evening with my friends, Jim Selvage and Bronson Batchelor. They approved and together we developed a list of about fifteen names. All those whom I invited were people active in public relations or in the field of public opinion, with two exceptions. One was my friend Allen Billingsley, an advertising man, and the other was George Sokolsky, a columnist. At the end of the dinner the consensus was that the dinner should be repeated monthly. There was to be no organization, no officers, no formulation of any kind. Hosts were to rotate. Someone factiously dubbed the group The Wisemen and this has stuck. This was the start of one of the most unique groups in the country. . . . As the years rolled on, the group has been kept alive and redblooded by the addition of new members. Now there are forty members.

Until his death, Pendleton Dudley was the only officer — " keeper of the great seal, shepherd, and grand master all in one."

In his letter of invitation for the 20th anniversary dinner, Hill wrote, "On November 18, 1938, Roosevelt was in his second term, Hitler was riding high in Germany, the police were fighting Reds in Paris, the CIO was trying to organize Ford, the British Empire was still intact, World War II was year away, 'You Can't Take It With You' was as the hit on Broadway—and on that evening the first meeting of the Wisemen was held."

Little did John Hill know that World War II, brought on by Hitler, would involve The Wisemen in highly secretive counseling to the Manhattan Project that was successfully developing the atomic bomb—a weapon of terror that brought the war to an abrupt end in August 1945. This hitherto unknown story unfolded this way according to the informal history of The Wisemen's early years written by veteran counselor James W. Irwin, one of The Group's early members. Irwin's history, included in his papers in the State Historical Society of Wisconsin, was written March 10, 1978.

Major General Leslie Groves, newly appointed chief of the Manhattan Project that developed the A-bomb, sought the counsel of DeWitt Wallace, founder of *Reader's Digest*, on how he could handle the public relations aspect of this highly secretive undertaking. Mr. Wallace asked for permission to consult his longtime friend and counselor, Pendleton Dudley. DeWitt Wallace had founded the *Reader's Digest* in the early 1920s in the basement of a Greenwich Village speakeasy but then in 1922 Wallace and his bride Lila Acheson set up housekeeping and magazine operations in what their biographer described as a garage apartment rented to them by Pendleton Dudley. In our many conversations Dudley always referred to it as his pony born. Presumably it had been converted. This association proved to be a lucky strike for Publicist Dudley. (The Wallaces moved their burgeoning empire from Pleasantville to north of Chappaqua in 1939 but kept the Pleasantville address.) Pen Dudley suggested to DeWitt Wallace that General Groves meet with "the group I meet with every month and ask for help." General Groves accepted the recommendation, obtained a list of The Wisemen members and got permission from the Secretary of the Army to meet with them, and these members were cleared by Military Intelligence and the FBI. According to Irwin, "Groves was surprised at how many of us already had a 'Q Clearance' Groves met with the members at the University Club. "When we arrived at our drinking room we found Pen at the door with two sharp looking men flanking him. Pen and Chet Lang identified us individually to the men, who were from G-2. The rooms on each side of our dinner room had been blocked off."

Irwin's account continued:

Groves briefed us on the atomic development, described Oak Ridge, Clinton Engineering, Hanford and Savannah River to us. Mentioned rather casually that GE, DuPont, Monsanto, Union Carbide were playing important parts in the project, and asked our advice on how to handle public relations wise the first tests at the Flats in New Mexico. It was a almost unanimous, I believe, that the War Department retain for such a sensitive assignment either Ivy Lee–T. J. Ross or Hill and Knowlton. John [Hill] suggested that it was a perfect assignment for Tommy and Tommy took it in on at no fee. We also suggested that the War Department borrow one of the outstanding journalists in the United States to be tied into the tests, and on to then hoped-for forays over Japan. It was almost unanimous by those of us who had dealings with the science press that Bill Lawrence of the *New York Times* be tagged.

In Irwin's words, "Bill Lawrence not only was an eye witness at Sands and on to the bombing runs, but proved an extraordinary pool reporter feeding the information to the group the Army had assembled in Manila, to get his playbacks."

Irwin's bosses were astounded when he returned to Monsanto in St. Louis to tell them that General Groves had told him that Monsanto had designed, built, and was operating Oak Ridge. General Groves's office vouched that Irwin had security clearance and from then on he was included in the tight group of Monsanto officials dealing with the A-bomb. Irwin concluded his account with this, "I cite this particular dinner only because it shows the esteem and trust we enjoyed in the forties."

John Hill was justly proud of The Wisemen, writing in remarks prepared for the 20th anniversary meeting in 1958, "Over the years, men working together in the same field have been brought together on intimate terms, and friendships have been cemented that could have happened in no other way." Yet all did not always go smoothly for The Wisemen or The Group, as it is sometimes called. In the 1950s, James Selvage, who had cut his public relations teeth working for the National Manufacturers Association in the turbulent strike breaking 1930's, accused Hill and Pen Dudley of dominating The Group and of perpetuating their control of its membership. One year, Bert Goss, Kerryn King, formerly an H&K executive and later vice-president of the Texas Company, and George Anderson of Dudley-Anderson-Yutzy were proposed for membership at the same time. As Hill told me, Selvage blackballed Kerryn King in protest. King, who emerged as a strong leader of the profession in the 1960s, later was admitted.

In his 20th anniversary remarks, Hill concluded, "Since that evening [1938] the World has fallen apart, but The Group has held together." And it holds together today. Another enduring legacy John Hill left the vocation he helped pioneer and shape.

THE PRACTITIONER AND THE PERSON—AN ASSESSMENT

Until near his death at age 86, John Wiley Hill was a person with tireless energy, driven to succeed, and restless mind looking for new worlds to conquer. He was a tall, ruggedly handsome man blessed with good health, a rugged individualist born of born of his heritage as an Indiana farm boy. Hill had a capacious mind and an eagerness to learn that motivated him from the days of his retreat from Indiana University until the end of his highly successful career, one that brought him to the top in public relations and provided him with an affluence he dared not dream of when growing up as the son of "a good farmer but poor businessman." John Hill was basically a quiet, reflective person, a long way from the stereotypical public relations extrovert. Hill was essentially a private person. At age 75 when most persons have retired, Hill was active as head of Hill and Knowlton, Inc. and Hill and Knowlton, International, the dominant public relations agency in the world in those years. As Kerryn King, a Hill protege who later became vice-president of Texaco, observed at that time, "Even today, at 75, he has tremendous energy, and when the chips are down can carry his end of the load as well as any man in his organization." Although quiet and soft spoken, this demeanor could be quite deceptive as many of his staff and opponents discovered over time.

The courage and vision that enable John Hill to build the nation's largest public relations agency was demonstrated anew when in September 1956, Hill boldly entered the international arena with the formation of Hill and Knowlton, International. Chairman Hill announced that the new firm would have headquarters in The Hague, Netherlands, and offices in Dusseldorf, Germany, and would include the facilities of experienced nationals in Great Britain, France, Belgium, Holland, Sweden, Australia, New Zealand, Canada, Mexico, and Latin America. Hill chose an ally from the steel battles, J. Carlisle MacDonald, as director of the new firm and its senior consultant in Europe with offices in Paris. This was a bold, pioneering move on Hill's part, one that lost money its first several years but eventually became profitable.

HIS PERSONAL LIFE

Typical of his reserve, Hill was reluctant to discuss his private life with me. He made it evident that his first marriage, which had ended in divorce, was an unhappy one. After starting to work for AISI and commuting to and from New York and in the war years, Hill was much too busy for much social life. In those days, he was almost totally preoccupied with his work for the steel industry and the aviation industry during World War II. In 1948, John Hill married an actress, Elena Karam of New York. Mrs. Hill had a daughter, Alexandria, by a previous marriage. Hill adopted her and gave her his name. He also had a son, John Wiley, who was has adopted in 1956. Neither child survived him; only his widow and two granddaughters survived. By all evidence this marriage was a happy one. In his last 20 years, Mrs. Hill was able to persuade the tycoon to take more pleasure trips and vacations in the United States, usually on a dude ranch in the West. He enjoyed his weekends at his farm at Towners, New York, horseback riding — his favorite recreation.

THE AUTHOR AND SPOKESMAN

To promote a clearer understanding of this still fuzzily defined vocation and to promote his firm, Hill was a prolific author and public speaker. As a result, he became a leading spokesman of the field in the post World War II years, much akin to the role Ivy Lee had occupied prior to his death in 1934. Hill was the author of record of two books, *Corporate Public Relations* and *The Making of a Public Relations Man*. Both books had considerable input from his H&K staff. *Corporate Public Relations* was conceived, in Hill's words, as "a small anniversary book setting forth H&K's philosophy on public relations, together with other points directed to businessmen, [that] would be of service to the profession and of value to H&K as an organization." The book was to commemorate the founding of Hill's one-man firm in Cleveland in 1927. In a memo addressed to Bert Goss, Richard Darrow, John G. Mapes, and Edward Barrett, Hill wrote on January 1, 1957, "Robbie [Dr. Claude Robinson] thinks that some of the old-timers in public relations itself as well as businessmen ought to be interviewed. He is to formulate some recommendations as to the nature and extent of research that his group might carry out and give us an estimate of the cost. It was agreed that we would develop a list of points to be covered in the book."

Hill's memo made it clear that "the book should start out by explaining that at age 30 Hill and Knowlton, Inc. had spanned the era of the development of professional public relations" and "would make it clear where PR stood 30 years ago and now."

A memo to Hill from Ed Barrett, dated May 23, 1957, makes it clear that Barrett was overseeing the writing of the anniversary book: "Please note the attached memorandum to Ed Dakin [an H&K staffer]. As you can see, I am asking him to check dates, figures, and other statements. Also to be sure that any quotations from published works . . . are cleared . . . I have asked Paul Bozell to write a draft of a 200–300 word outline of the scope and purposes of the book as requested by the publisher." This and other internal memoranda make it clear that *Corporate Public Relations* was corporate effort, not Hill's alone. Hill was a lucid writer but simply did not have time as head of a flourishing enterprise to write the book. In a letter to Ordway Tead, editor at Harper & Brothers, the publishers, Hill acknowledged "the good work of Ed Dakin and Dean Barrett."

His memoir, *The Making of a Public Relations Man*, was similarly a product of Hill's guidance and of staff assistance. Because of this committee effort, his autobiography, like the anniversary book, was somewhat colorless. These should be viewed as promotional books for H&K, not the memoirs of a man safe in the sanctuary of retirement and secure in his place in public relations history. The same procedure was followed: An initial draft is made by a staff member that is then reworked by Hill into his own style contributing his own philosophy. Next, the manuscript is carefully checked by senior staffers with each word carefully weighed. In cases where individuals were mentioned, the copy was checked with the persons concerned to insure that they have no objection.[2] Consequently, in the view of biographer Col. George Hamel, "His . . . is probably one of the few memoirs where a fuzzy picture of the author emerges. He remains indistinct, appearing more as a corporate entity than as an individual." The book is a compound of Hill's accounts and an uncritical collection of polemical platitudes. The book was published jointly by David McKay Co. and Robert B. Luce, Inc., in 1963.

Hill also furthered the education of businessmen as to the importance of public relations and promoted his firm through frequent speeches that were then published and widely circulated. Typical was his speech, "The Role of Public Relations in Industry," a talk given at the H&K annual staff conference in New York City on October 30, 1953, in which he outlined his public relations philosophy.

HIS PUBLIC RELATIONS PHILOSOPHY

In that speech, Hill philosophied:

> To understand the full meaning of corporate public relations . . ., it is necessary to envision the operation as a whole. Many people even now think of public relations merely as press relations or publicity. . . . Public relations is composed of various elements, of which publicity is only one. . . . From this it is obvious that the public relations of a company is not in the exclusive custody of the public relations department. Public relations thinking should permeate all echelons of management. To top management alone belongs the

---

[2]A latter-day successor to John Hill, Robert L. Dilenschneider lost his job as president and CEO of Hill and Knowlton, Inc. in September 1991 because he lacked John Hill's prudence. His book *Power and Influence*, published in 1989, bruised many individuals and lost at least two major accounts for H&K. In the view of *Time*, "the more powerful he became, the more he believed in his own greatness." How unlike Hill, a modest man to the end. For a look at the post-John Hill Hill & Knowlton, Inc. see: Jeffrey Goodell, "What Hill and Knowlton Can Do for You (And What It Can't Do For Itself," *New York Times Magazine*, September 9, 1990.

responsibility for public relations policy decisions. This responsibility cannot be delegated to public relations practitioners. It is their function to give advice and counsel, to coordinate public relations activity, and to implement and carry out policy.

This excerpt from a letter from Jack Bail written to Hill on August 29, 1958, reflects Hill's approach to the problems of public relations:

> You and I were having a quick lunch at Longchamps and I asked you if you had any fatherly advice to give me as I departed to run the office in Washington. You pondered this for a moment and then replied that the only practical advice you could pass along was to try to get our clients to tell the truth about things when they had something constructive to say to the public about their company's affairs. And, if on the other hand, they didn't have something constructive to say, to try to get them to keep their mouths shut.

[Hill's approach is also reflected in his most commonly used definition of public relations, "The management function which gives the same organized and careful attention to the asset of good will as is given to any other major asset of the business]. From day one, Hill recognized that "Public opinion, confused, obscure, and unpredictable as it may often seem, is the ultimate ruling force in the free world." He said, "Public relations plays a vital and active role in correcting, in focusing, and in organizing public opinion." Hill often astutely observed that "the public opinion we deal with never stands still, is never viewable in present as the same entity as it was in some past." John Hill never got hung up by the word *propaganda* as many practitioners do. "Any program of public relations involves the use of propaganda techniques. To many people the word 'propaganda' has a bad odor. But there is nothing wrong with propaganda. It is education. It is the diffusion of knowledge. It is only when it is misused that it becomes odious. Propaganda basically is merely the art of persuasion."

A POLITICAL CONSERVATIVE

Equally influential in his life and in his counseling were John Hill's conservative political views, strongly held and readily evident in all his speeches and letters. His writing was liberally sprinkled with terms such as *free-handed government spending* and *bureaucratic authority*. The Hill Papers reveal Hill's considerable activity in support of conservative Republican candidates such as former President Herbert Hoover, Senator Robert A. Taft, and retired Army Lt. Gen. Albert C. Wedemeyer. Hill was a member of a public relations advisory group for Senator Taft in his

campaign for the Presidential nomination in 1948 and again worked for
Taft's nomination in 1952. Hill's use of the rightwing columnist George
Sokolsky as a paid propagandist for the Little Steel companies in 1937 and
for other clients also reflects his ultra conservatism. He regarded Sokolsky
as a close friend.

His strong antilabor views were plainly evident in his work for AISI and
Little Steel. After the 1950 elections, Hill wrote his friend Victor Emanuel
to gloat, "Labor's prestige as an election-determining factor is smashed.
Labor was putting all on the defeat of [Senator Robert P.] Taft and lost not
only in this effort but such key supporters as Lucas, Thomas, and Myers.
It means all moves to weaken the Taft–Hartley Act are obviously dead for
years ahead."

The intensity of Hill's right wing views are shown in a letter dated
January 24, 1958, to J. B. Matthews, notorious Communist-hunter:

Dear J. B.:

I am deeply grateful to you for sending me the "Joe McCarthy Memorial
Book." He truly was a man of destiny, and he performed a great and
unforgettable service for his country.

This accolade was for one of the most dangerous and discredited
politicians of this century, whose legacy is an ugly political adjective in our
dictionaries!

In November 1951, John Hill held a dinner party at his Manhattan home
as a welcome for newly retired General Wedemeyer. Guests included former
President Hoover, George Sokolksy, Victor Emanuel, Cloud Wampler,
president of Carrier Corporation, and H. M. Horner, president United
Aircraft. The purpose of the dinner was to discuss the 1952 Presidential
campaign and the future of *Freeman*, a conservative magazine. Hill was on
the board of directors of *Freeman*, a magazine that was never able to pay
its way and expired in 1954. In 1956, Hill served under John Hay Whitney's
chairmanship to raise money for President Eisenhower's reelection campaign.

Conservative thought he was, John Hill was shrewd enough to court and
win friends in the Democratic party. Among these were George E. Allen, a
courtier to presidents—a Democrat during the Truman years and a Republican in the Eisenhower years—and Democratic Representatives Richard
Bolling of Missouri and Chet Holified of California. Of this he wrote
Emanuel on May 29, 1958, "Incidentally, I have been making a little
headway recently in developing some close personal friendships with a
number of important people on the Hill. One of these is Congressman
Richard Bolling, who I am told . . . is being groomed by the Democratic

leadership for Speaker in the next few years. One of the others is Congressman Chet Holifield, a member of the Joint Committee on Atomic Energy."

It is a bit paradoxical that Hill's strong and sincere political philosophy has an almost bitter antigovernment stance when it is the very philosophy of government that he opposed so vehemently that made possible his success. As Irwin Ross wrote in *The Image Merchants*, "Ironically, public relations owes both its establishment and vast expansion to two great surges of social reform—the era of the muckrakers and the era of the New Deal. PR was the businessman's answer to his detractors." In fact, it was President Franklin Roosevelt's early New Deal measure, the National Industrial Recovery Act, that caused the American Iron and Steel Institute to hire John Hill and thus put him on the road to success as a national and international public relations counselor.

THE PHILANTHROPIST

In 1957, Hill, now a wealthy man, established the John W. Hill Foundation that he supported by turning over more and more shares of H&K stock to the point where he ultimately gave up control of the firm. Its charitable activities have been largely confined to education because Hill, a largely self-educated man, valued education and saw the need for a successful counselor to be a broadly educated person. Starting in 1956, Hill and Knowlton sponsored an internship in public relations in conjunction with Boston University. In 1958, the Hill Foundation established a doctoral fellowship in public relations at the Harvard Graduate School of Business, one worth $5,000. Earlier Hill had established a professional chair in "Economic Communications" at Boston University in 1950. Hill and Knowlton agreed to pay $7,000 a year and AISI, at Hill's urging, would pay another $10,000 for research in connection with the program. However, once a candidate was selected to occupy this chair, it became obvious that he was more an employee of H &K than an independent scholar. The professor was required to submit regular progress reports to Hill and was constantly prodded to produce results. Hill obviously didn't understand the traditions of academic freedom. The first occupant quit after 1 year, and the fiasco was terminated in 1953. The Hill Papers clearly indicate that the project was equally frustrating to Hill and to Boston University. Similarly, the foundation scholarships didn't last much beyond Hill's retirement from the agency. Hill was awarded an honorary degree by Boston University in 1951 and also served on the Board of Visitors of its School of Public Communication.

John Hill was earnest in his efforts to support public relations education even though he was untutored in the mores of academe. It was to further public relations research that motivated Hill to give his papers to the Mass Communications History Center of the State Historical Society of Wisconsin.

AS SEEN BY HIS PEERS AND HIS CRITICS

Whether his services to Little Steel, to the pharmaceutical industry, and particularly to the tobacco industry served the public interest or not, John Hill saw himself as a man of integrity and preached its gospel. In a memorandum dated December 3, 1958, in the Hill Papers, he wrote:

> The key word in the answer to this question is *integrity*. People either have integrity or they do not. Any public relations counsel with integrity will not accept a client whose policies and objectives, according to the lights of the counsel, are opposed to the public interest.

> Should an existing client company adopt policies which the counsel believes are not in the public interest, he would advise against such policies — and, if he has integrity, be prepared to resign the account in case the client persisted.

Apparently Hill did act on this precept, although there is no record in the Hill Papers of his resigning an account for this reason. Yet his long time associate, the late Dean Edward W. Barret, wrote in *The Making of a Public Relations Man*, "I have seen John Hill decline an exceedingly lucrative new account because the would-be client impressed him as wanting to shade the truth in dealing with the public." Also Robert Gray, a Washington lobbyist who later joined H&K, told an interviewer in 1965, "You could start a pretty lucrative public relations practice with the accounts Hill has refused just since I joined Hill and Knowlton in 1961."

In a letter to Colonel Hamel, dated November 5, 1965, T. J. Ross, said, "I have the highest regard for Mr. Hill and I think the public relations business is better for his being in it." George Hammond, then chairman of Carl Byoir & Associates and long H&K's leading competitor, wrote Hamel. "John has always approached public relations from the standpoint of sound counseling to be sure that sound policies underlie the program. . . . The general high standard to which he adheres are . . . a major factor in his success." William Ruder, formerly chairman of Ruder & Finn, Inc., wrote Hamel, "I think his personal qualities of dignity and courage are important contributing factors. As industry saw the PR field through his person, they learned to respect it." His close friend and longtime pioneer, Pendleton Dudley, told me more than once, "He was the first among the independents to comprehend the scope of a public relations operation and to set up an organization of diverse experience and talents adequate for doing an effective job."

Clearly John Hill had the intelligence, the vision, the industry, and management talent to build an ongoing legacy in Hill and Knowlton, Inc. and Hill and Knowlton, International that stands today as a monument to his talents and his perseverance. But did he in the service to some clients serve "the public interest" he so often proclaimed as his guiding star?

For an opposite view, consider this indictment by Walter Goodman, then with the *New York Herald–Tribune*, in a review of Hill's autobiography, *The Making of a Public Relations Man*, on November 10, 1963:

> John W. Hill, founder and chairman of the board of Hill and Knowlton, one of the nation's more notorious — oops, prominent PR firms, comes to scotch the slander that public relations men do not believe in every cause they undertake. Among the clients he discusses with unrelenting reverence are the steel industry, which he has been serving since the thirties when he stood at the bulwarks with Republic Steel's Tom Girdler to prevent "Communist agitators" from unionizing the companies; the aircraft industry, which he helped win the war by making sure newspapermen reported that the bombs were being dropped from B-24s; and the natural gas industry, which he advised in his gaseous campaign against F.P.C. regulation in 1955.
>
> Among the clients whose problems, regrettably, are missing from these pages are the drug manufacturers whom Mr. Hill has been defending against charges of overpricing, overpromoting, and under-testing, and the cigarette manufacturers, whom he has been defending against the charge of abetting lung cancer.
>
> Mr. Hill believes in all these causes because he believes in big business. He believes the profit motive is the true star to national virtue, that welfare programs are debilitating handouts, and that the greatest threats we face today come form socialist visionaries, vote-happy politicians, and monopolistic labor unions.
>
> His book gives away about as many secrets as a Tobacco Industry Research Council [*sic*] press release. On the evidence of these memoirs, he has never met a moneyed man he didn't like.

As a result, John Hill's oft-stated precepts and his practices for some clients did not match.

NOTES ON SOURCES FOR CHAPTERS 15 AND 16

These two chapters chronicling the career of John W. Hill are based primarily on Hill's personal papers and client files in the John W. Hill

Papers in the Mass Communications History Center of the State Historical Society of Wisconsin. Another primary source was Colonel George F. Hamel's master's thesis, *John W. Hill, Public Relations Pioneer*, written under my direction at the University of Wisconsin in 1966. Colonel Hamel's research included extensive interviews with Mr. Hill and other members of the firm and considerable correspondence with Mr. Hill and his peers.

I had several interviews with Mr. Hill, the most extensive of which was held on April 17, 1964, and with his colleagues Bert Goss, Richard Darrow, and William Durbin.

The quotes from my former research assistant, Dr. Karen Miller, are from two of her several papers about Mr. Hill. One is entitled "Marketing Confidence: The Ethics of the Tobacco Industry," written in November, 1990, for the *Journal of American History;* the other, "Two Sides of the Story: Scientists, the Tobacco Industry, and Press Coverage," presented at the convention of the Association of Education for Journalism and Mass Communications, 1991.

Hill's two books written with the help of his key staff people, *Corporate Public Relations* (Harper) and *The Making of the a Public Relations Man* (McKay) plus a collection of speeches provided insight on his concepts and practice of public relations. The firm also published a collection of speeches by its executives including one by Mr. Hill, *The Future of Public Relations.*

His obituary, "John W. Hill Dies; Led Hill and Knowlton," was carried in *The New York Times*, March 18, 1977, IV, 16:1. A longer version is in a press release issued by his firm March 17, 1977.

Chapter 15 and chapter 16 also utilized a large number of books and periodicals relating to Mr. Hill, his firm, or to public practice of his time.

Books

Allen, George E. *Presidents Who Have Known Me*, Simon & Schuster, 1960; Barbour, Robert L. *PR Blue Book, 1964*, PR Publishing Co., Inc., 1963; Boone, Julian, *Industrial Advertising Handbook*, McGraw-Hill Book Co., Inc., 1953; Brooks, Robert R. R. *Unions of Their Own Choosing*, Yale University Press, 1939; *Ibid.*, *As Steel Goes: Unionism in a Basic Industry*, Yale University Press, 1940; Broughton, Averell, *Careers in Public Relations—The New Profession*, E. P. Dutton & Co., 1943; Burtt, Everett Johnson, *Labor Markets, Unions, and Government Policies*, St. Martin's Press, 1963; Consumers Union, *The Consumers Union Report on Smoking and the Public Interest*, Consumers Union, 1963; Cronon, E. David, *Labor and the New Deal*, Rand McNally and Co., 1963; Dulles, Foster Rhea, *Labor in America*, Thomas Y. Crowell Co., 1955; Galenson, Walter, *The CIO Challenge to the AFL*, Harvard University Press, 1960; Girdler, Tom

M, *Boot Straps*, Charles Scribner's Sons, 1943; Harris, Herbert, *Labor's Civil War*, Alfred A. Knopf, 1940; Harris, Richard, *The Real Voice*, Macmillan, 1964; Kefauver, Estes, *In a Few Hands*, Pantheon, 1965; Lens, Sidney, *Working Men: The Story of Labor*, G. P. Putnam's Sons, 1960; Neuberger, Senator Maurine B., *Smoke Screen: Tobacco and the Public Welfare*, Prentice-Hall, Inc., 1963; Peters, Raymond W., *Communications Within Industry*, Harper and Brothers, 1950; Pimlott, J. A. R., *Public Relations and American Democracy*, Princeton University Press, 1951; Ross, Irwin. *The Image Merchants*, Doubleday and Co., 1959; Shannon, David A., *Twentieth Century America*, Rand McNally and Co., 1963; Solkolsky, George E., *The American Way of Life*, Farrar and Rinehart, Inc., 1939; *Ibid.*, *The Labor Crisis in the United States*, John Wiley & Sons, Inc., 1938; Stephenson, Howard, *Handbook of Public Relations*, New York: McGraw-Hill Book Co., Inc., 1960; Wright, Milton, *Public Relations for Business*, McGraw-Hill Book Co., Inc., 1939.

For effects of smoking on a person's health, see: Elizabeth M. Whelan, *A Smoking Gun: How the Tobacco Industry Gets Away With Murder*, George F. Stickley, 1984; John Harvey Kellogg, *Tobaccoism, Or How Tobacco Kills*, 2nd. ed., Modern Medicine Publishing Co., 1929.

Periodicals

"A New King Pin for the PR Business," *Business Week*, *1355*, 114, August 20, 1955; Auerbach, Jerold S., "The LaFollette Committee: Labor and Civil Liberties in the New Deal," *The Journal of American History*, *51*, 435-459, December 1964; Barrett, Edward W., "Business of Building Good Will" (review of *Corporate Public Relations*), *Saturday Review*, *41*, 21, 55, Jan. 18, 1958; Bart, Peter, Review of *The Making of a Public Relations Man*, *The New York Times Book Review*, *58*, Nov. 10, 1963; Blumenthal, Frank H., "Anti-Union Publicity in the Johnstown Strike," *Public Opinion Quarterly*, *3*, 676-682, October 1939; Brayman, Harold. Review of *Corporate Public Relations*, *Public Relations Journal*, *14* 21-22, February 1959; Broun, Heywood, "L'Affairs Sokolsky", *"New Republic*, *95* 360-361, Aug. 3, 1938; Goodman, Walter, review of *The Making of a Public Relations Man*, *New York Herald-Tribune Book Week*, Nov. 10, 1963; LaFollette, Robert M., Jr., "Turn the Light on Communism," *Collier's*, *119*, 22, Feb. 8, 1947; Lewis, David L. "International Networks: PR's New Golden Age," *PR*, *2* 13-23, October 1957; McIntyre, Robert B. "European Press Many Things to H & K Executives," *Editor & Publisher*, *96*, 20, 46, March 23, 1963; Pomer, Gerald, "The Public Relations of Organized Labor," *Public Opinion Quarterly*, *23*, 483-494, October 1959; "Public Relations Today," *Business Week*, *1609*, 3-16, July 2, 1960; Reef, Arthur, "International PR for American Companies Abroad," *PR*, *5*, 1, 7-22, January 1960; Review of *The Making of a Public Relations Man, Saturday Review, 47*, 83, Jan. 11, 1964; "Smoking and News: Coverage of a Decade of Controversy," *Columbia Journalism Review, 2*, 6–12, Summer 1965; Sokolsky, George E., "The C. I. O. Turns a Page," *The Atlantic Monthly, 160*, 309–317, September 1937; Stratton, Samuel S., "Public Relations in Steel," *Public Opinion Quarterly, 1*, 107–111, April 1937; Walker, S. H. and Paul Sklar. "Business Finds Its Voice," *Harper's Magazine, 176*, 113–123, January 1938; Richard W. Pollay, "Propaganda, Puffing and the Public Interest," *Public Relations Review*, Vol. XVI, Fall 1990 (he tells the *True Magazine* story).

An update on the Tobacco Wars: A Study in Public Relations Ethics," by me is in *The Corporate Public Relations Journal* (Northwestern University) Vol. 3, 1992–93. Also see for late developments, Joe Cosco, "The Tobacco Wars," *Public Relations Journal*, Vol. 44, December, 1988.

The quotes of Judge Lee Sarokin can be found in *The New York Times* of February 7, 1992, and *The Washington Post*, February 8, 1992, under the headline, "Federal Judge Orders Council for Tobacco Research to Open Internal Files.

John Hill's letter decrying false fronts written to his friend Almo Coney, Pittsburgh, is dated November 8, 1965—long after his involvement in the TIRC account.

Publications Of the Government and Other Organizations

American Iron and Steel Institute, *Communication Countdown*, pamphlet; Chamber of Commerce of the United States of America, *Communists Within the Labor Movement*, Washington, DC, 1947; Hill and Knowlton, Inc., *Can We Afford Ignorance?* pamphlet; _____ . *Education and Industry Cooperate*, 1952, pamphlet; _____ . *Your Guide to Written Communications*. Pamphlet Hill, John W., *The Whipping Boy Fights Back, Hill and Knowlton, Inc., 1950, Pamphlet;* _____ . *The Role of Public Relations in Industry*. Hill and Knowlton, Inc., 1953, pamphlet; National Council of the Churches of Christ in the USA, *In Search of Maturity in Industrial Relations*, 1960, pamphlet; Prentice-Hall Executive Report, *Inside Public Relations*, Englewood Cliffs, NJ, 1963; United States Congress, Senate, *Oil and Gas Lobby Investigation*, hearings before the Special Committee to investigate political activities, lobbying, and campaign contributions, Washington: Government Printing Office, 1956; United States Congress, Senate, Committee on Post Offices and Post Roads, *Deliver and Non-Delivery of Mail in Industrial Strife Areas*, Hearings, 75th Congress, June 11–24, 1937, Washington: Government Printing Office; United States, Congress, Senate, Committee on Education and Labor, *Violations of Free*

Speech and Rights of Labor, Hearing before Subcommittee, 76th Congress, 1939-1940, Vols. 103-109, Washington: Government Printing Office; United States Congress, Senate Committee on Education and Labor, *Violations of Free Speech and Rights of Labor*, Report 151, 77th Congress, Washington: Government Printing Office, 1941; United Steelworkers of America, *The Foreign Competition Hoax*, Pamphlet; _____ , *The 1959 Steel Strike*, pamphlet.

The U.S. Supreme Court, in a 100-page decision, ruled on June 24, 1992, that smoking victims could sue cigarette makers in state courts but the tobacco companies saw this as a victory because the Court prempted lawsuits from 1966, the date of the warning labels. On November 5, the law firm representing the Cipollones dropped the case as too expensive to pursue. This case ends.

Part III

The Depression And The Years Beyond

The catastrophic Stock Market Crash of 1929 and the ensuing Depression threw Americans and their values into a tailspin as clouds of doom and gloom settled across the land. No aspect of American society was left untouched, unchanged—including the newly enlarged public relations vocation.

President Herbert Hoover, who learned the value of public relations in his World War 1 assignments, had used this weapon to the hilt to propel himself into the Presidency in 1929. The power of publicity was demonstrated anew when Democratic Party Publicist Charles Michelson hung the Depression around Hoover's political neck and made him easy to defeat by Franklin D. Roosevelt, a consummate practitioner of the art under the tutelage of Louis McHenry Howe, who had served FDR since 1912. Michelson, who had headed the Washington bureau of the *New York World* for 12 years, was hired by Democratic Party Chairman John J. Raskob to blast President Hoover and revive the Democratic Party spirits that had been devastated in the 1928 Presidential election. In his *Crisis of the Old Order* Arthur Schlesinger, Jr., wrote of Michelson:

> A hard-bitten cynic with a wintry, satanic smile and a dry humor, who had seen everything and lost all illusions, he brought a new professionalism to political publicity. While [Jouett] Shouse toured the country making speeches, Michelson turned out an uninterrupted stream of interviews, statements, and speeches in Washington. These releases—over 500 in the first two years—signed indifferently by leading Democrats in the House and Senate—poured ridicule on the Hoover administration.

Thus, President Hoover, who was the first President to create the office of White House Press Secretary in 1929, was hoisted by his own petard. To keep the influence of Michelson in perspective, it should be emphasized that it was Hoover's weak response to the Depression that created the image in the first place. Michelson shrewdly exploited it. Michelson modestly wrote in his memoirs, *The Ghost Talks*, that "good luck and good management must be accorded equal responsibility for the rise of Franklin Roosevelt FDR. During every phase of this advent to eminence his fairy godmother was on the job." That fairy godmother was Louis McHenry Howe, an unlikely description for this humorless, grumpy, disheveled little man, usually seen with a cigarette in his mouth and ashes all over his vest. But he was brilliant, and he could tell Roosevelt "No" and make it stick. So much for the glad handling stereotype of the Public Relations Man in a Grey Flannel Suit!

These years brought another boom in the number of public relations practitioners and agencies. Under the leadership of Franklin D. Roosevelt and his public relations mentor, Howe, government greatly increased in size and scope as FDR moved to avert financial collapse in the nation. This called for many new action agencies that had to be promoted to be understood and utilized. FDR combined strong leadership with consummate public relations skills to harness the forces of protest into an effective political coalition. Howe, today a name little known, ably directed FDR's political fortunes from 1912 when he managed Roosevelt's State Senate campaign until his death in 1936. Howe was the first to introduce feedback devices in the White House, a technique carried to a fine art by his successors.

The year 1933 brought the nation's first political campaign management team, Clem Whitaker and Leone Baxter, when they were hired to promote a California referendum, the Central Valley Water Project. Out of that campaign, came a business partnership, later sealed by marriage, and an innovative campaign organization that brought a sea change to American politics – The New Politics. Whitaker's and Baxter's methods of campaign management brought today's political consultants and handlers who dominate the political process with their use of the mighty instrument of television. Their story is told in chapter 19.

The Stock Market Crash of 1929 and the ensuing Great Depression virtually destroyed Big Business's credibility. The "Permanent Prosperity" had proved illusory. Business, as it got up off the floor, realized that it had to resell its worth to the public and to justify its role in society. As Bernays recalled, "Many leaders in and out of business stressed the importance of sound public relations. They took up the cry first uttered in 1923 and urged business to modify its attitudes and actions to conform to public demands." AT&T led the way in corporate public relations in 1927 when it hired Arthur

W. Page as vice president for public relations, the first such title in American business. Arthur Page built AT&T's sophisticated corporate program that set the pace for other corporations over the next 20 years. In 1947, he retired from AT&T and set up shop as a consultant. Arthur W. Page and Louis Howe were two of the prime architects of today's public relations structure. Another prime builder of today's profession was Paul Garrett, a *New York Post* business reporter, hired by Alfred Sloan in 1931 to initiate a public relations program for General Motors. With Sloan's support, Garrett brought GM to the forefront in public relations and in public esteem. After his retirement in 1957, he counseled the newly founded Xerox Corporation. This period also brought a prime public relations tool — the public opinion poll. Both the Roper and Gallup Polls made their debut in the 1936 Presidential election, one that saw the *Literary Digest's* straw poll die a deserved death.

In the depth of the Depression, somewhat by accident, Carl Byoir organized his firm, Carl Byoir & Associates, an agency that dominated the counseling business in the immediate post-World War 11 years. Byoir had gone to Cuba in 1929 in search of relief from a painful, nagging sinus problem. There restless, energetic Byoir soon bought two American-language newspapers, and to make them profitable, he sought a way to increase tourism in Cuba. This led to a contract with the Cuban government and the start of his firm in 1930, the beginning of a rags-to-riches Horatio Alger epic. Byoir's saga is told in chapters 17 and 18.

Five years later, Earl Newsom, who had gained his public relations baptism with the *Literary Digest* and the Oil Heating Institute, opened his public relations office, The Earl Newsom Company. Newsom developed as a breed apart among public relations counselors. In time he became a trusted counselor to the corporate giants of America — Standard Oil (New Jersey), International Paper Co., Henry Ford 11 and the Ford Motor Company, Campbell Soup Co., General Motors, and other large companies, and to John D. Rockefeller III. Newsom emphasized counseling and editorial services, eschewing becoming a large service agency in the manner of Hill and Knowlton, Inc. and Burson–Marsteller, Inc. Newsom's exciting, influential career is told in chapters 20, 21, and 22.

WORLD WAR II, 1941-1945

World War II, which came for America on December 7, 1941, when the Japanese bombed Pearl Harbor, found the government's central public relations machinery in great disarray. Three information agencies overlapped and were constantly warring for dominance. This situation existed because FDR was afraid that if he created a strong central agency he would be accused of propagandizing for America's entry into the war, then raging in Europe. Also, remember Louis McHenry Howe was no longer at his side.

But urgency of American entry into the war caused Roosevelt to create, by Executive Order, the Office of War Information. Elmer Davis, a newscaster and columnist, was appointed director. Davis never effectively brought the warring forces under firm control, nor did he match Creel's and Byoir's brilliant efforts: OWI became in a sense the predecessor agency of today's worldwide U.S. Information Agency, the nation's public relations agency. The armed services which had only skeleton public information forces prior to the war, developed massive public information and public relations program. And in so doing trained some 100,000 persons in the techniques of this new craft. These ex-military Public Information Officers (PIOS) played a major role in the public relations boom that came after the war's end in 1945. The war also brought paid public relations advertising to the fore as a major means of public communication. Formation of the War Advertising Council in 1942 played a major role in promoting the sale of war bonds, combatting absenteeism, promoting support of rationing, and so forth.

POSTWAR BOOM II

The pattern of expansion of public relations that followed World War I was repeated on a much larger scale after World War 11. As Harold Burson noted, "After World War 11, public relations firms and corporate public relations departments began to proliferate in the American business landscape." The same was true for governments with new postwar problems and universities with pent up needs for funds. Much of the impetus came from the same 100,000 public information officers who learned their calling with U.S. military units around the world. The government's mobilization of public opinion did much to advance the understanding of the need for public relations.

With the war's end, many military public information officers took their newly gained experience to the private sector, for example, Farley Manning, John Moynahan, Milburn McCarthy, Steve Fitzgerald, and Harold Burson. A new generation of public relations firms were born in this period— Burson—Marsteller, Ruder & Finn, and Daniel J. Edelman. The 1945–1965 years were highlighted by a number of developments. There was a steady growth in the numbers of programs and practitioners in business, trade associations, government bureaus, and colleges. Established publicity programs were forced to move to a more mature two-way concept of public relations. The number of agencies greatly increased. A tremendous increase in the number of books, articles, and journals came with the growth in number of practitioners. There was the organization of new professional associations, including establishment of the Public Relations Society of America, born in 1948 out of the merger of the New York-based National Association of Public Relations Counsels and the West Coast-based American Council on Public Relations that had been founded earlier by another pioneer, Rex Harlow. Public Relations education in the nation's colleges and universities spread rapidly. In 1946, there were only 26 institutions offering public relations instruction, by 1964, some 300 had courses in the subject, and 14 offered bachelor degrees in public relations, another 29 had sequences, most of which were accredited by the American Council on Education in Journalism and Mass Communications.

The Public Relations News (1944), the PR Reporter (1958), and the Public Relations Journal chronicled and promoted this wide expansion of the practice. Rex Harlow started the Public Relations Journal in 1945 as the publication of the council, later to be merged into PRSA. The Washington DC-based American Public Relations was merged into PRSA in 1961, and its PR Quarterly was taken over by its then editor Howard Penn Hudson.

This period also brought the introduction of the paid publicity wire, an innovation of Herbert Muschel in 1954. An international network of these publicity wires and fax machines now give public relations offices instant access to newsrooms around the world. These wires, in effect, constitute another major worldwide news service, only in this case the sponsor not the news organization foots the bill. and motorboating, or in the more socially responsible business leadership that emerged after World War 11. Generally the public moves along unaware of the influence of the practitioner.

NOTES ON SOURCES

To understand the context of public relations' history in the Depression era and beyond, we suggest the books and articles that follow.

Arthur M. Schlesinger, The Age of Roosevelt, Houghton-Mifflin Co., 1957, especially The Crisis of the Old Order, the first volume in this history of the New Deal; David A. Shannon, The Great Depression, Prentice-Hall, Inc., 1960; Charles Michelson, The Ghost Talks, G. P. Putnam's Sons, 1944, memoirs of Democratic publicist; Arthur B. Rollins, Jr., Roosevelt and Howe, Knopf, 1962, biography of Louis McHenry Howe, who served as FDR's mentor from 1912 until his death in 1936; Allen M. Winkler, The Politics of Propaganda; The Office of War Information 1942–45, Yale University Press, 1978; Elmer Davis, "The Office of War Information, 13 June 1942–13 September, 1945, Report to the President," in Journalism

Monographs, edited by Ronald T. Farrar, No. 7, August 1968, Association for Education in Journalism; L. L. L. Golden, *Only By Public Consent: American Corporations' Search for Favorable Opinion,* Hawthorn Books, 1968 gives brief history of public relations programs at A. T. & T., General Motors, Du Pont, and Standard Oil [New Jersey].

Chapter 17

Carl Byoir: The Little Giant of Public Relations

When Carl Byoir, one of the towering giants who built today's highly successful public relations business, died on February 3, 1957, the public relations agency he had founded in 1930 was at the top of heap with 25 major industrial and trade association clients. Five years earlier, *The Reporter* had described Byoir as "undoubtedly the most successful public relations counsel now in business." Yet 30 years later, the firm was dead, killed by its longtime archrival, Hill & Knowlton, Inc. H&K had purchased the Byoir firm from Foote, Cone, and Belding, a major advertising agency. Foote, Cone, and Belding, successor firm to pioneer Albert Lasker's Lord & Thomas, had bought the Byoir agency from Chairman George Hammond, President Robert Wood, and other shareholders in 1978 but had been unsuccessful in managing this public relations agency.

Although Carl Byoir was a major architect and builder of the public relations counseling profession, he had difficulty in defining the function as late as 1950. That year he told the National Industrial Conference Board, "If you were to ask me to define public relations I confess that I would be at some difficulty because public relations is not like the learned professions. . . . We in public relations are self-baptized." Ironically, The New York Times headlined his death: "CARL BYOIR DEAD: PUBLICIST WAS 68."

The rise and fall of the agency that Carl Byoir's talent, drive, and innovative ways had built demonstrates that in the highly personal field of public relations an agency is often but the lengthened shadow of a person.

Carl Byoir's "self-baptism" in public relations was a meteoric career starting as a newspaper reporter at age 15 that provided the broad range of experience that enabled him to star at a highly successful counseling agency in the depths of the Great Depression. Byoir's rise to success from a humble boyhood as the son of immigrant Polish parents to riches and power in the world of industry and politics is the fabled Horatio Alger story, "From Rags to Riches," doubled in spades.

Carl Byoir was born in Des Moines, Iowa, on June 24, 1888, the last of six children born to Benjamin and Minna Gunyon Byoir, who had come to America from their native Poland in 1875. His parents often told him of the cruel conditions under which they lived in Russian-occupied Kinishin, Poland. The Byoir family was always short of money. The father had been a cabinet maker in Poland but did not follow that trade in Iowa. He tried several ways of earning a living but was not successful at any. As soon as they were old enough, the Byoir children were expected to get part-time jobs, and the mother took in roomers in an already crowded household to make ends meet. One Christmas, the family had 11¢ in hard cash.

His parents' pride to their adopted America and their joy in its freedom, in sharp contrast to the land from which they had fled, was conveyed to their children in many ways. From them, young Byoir learned a love of country that made later political attacks on his lack of patriotism especially bitter. In adult life, Byoir served his nation loyally in many ways.

Gifted with a brilliant mind, young Byoir could read at the age of 4 and became in his words, "an omnivorous read," one fascinated with words. In his Des Moines school days, Byoir was active in forensics, debating, school plays, and played high school basketball despite his slight build and height. Byoir reached 5 feet 7 inches in height as an adult. Though small in stature, he stood tall as a leader of men.

To earn his share of the family's support, Byoir, when a sophomore in high school, got a part-time job at the *Iowa State Register* filing cuts in the newspaper's morgue. In his senior year, he became a full-fledged reporter, working after school for $25 a week. He also became a stringer for the *Minneapolis Tribune*, which later became one of the first clients to his newly founded public relations firm. The ambitious, energetic young Byoir also found part-time jobs as a clerk in the Iowa legislature and as a scorekeeper in the Western Baseball League.

Byoir's ability to write and to get news did not go unnoticed. Immediately upon his graduation from high school, Byoir was offered and accepted a job as city editor of the *Waterloo Times–Tribune*. Three days after Byoir was on the job, the managing editor died of a heart attack, and the youthful Byoir took over that post at a salary of $60 per week. This was a large salary for one of 17 years in 1905. The young Byoir met the challenge of the larger job from June 1905 until September 1906. Then a friend and fate intervened.

In his high school debate team, Byoir had formed a lasting friendship with classmate Walter Stewart. Stewart persuaded Byoir to give up his job so that they could enroll together as freshmen at Iowa State University in Iowa City. Byoir finally agreed to this, somewhat reluctantly. Mr. Wilbur Marsh, who owned the *Times-Tribune*, had become so impressed with the young editor's drive and determination to succeed that he offered to finance Carl's education at Iowa. "My best thanks," said Byoir, "but that would leave me in debt after graduation. All I need to make expenses is a typewriter." He got the typewriter as a going-away gift from Mr. Marsh. At the university, Byoir proved he was right.

Byoir knew that he would have to earn his expenses at Iowa, so, before leaving the *Times-Tribune*, he had arranged to become a stringer for several Iowa newspapers. Also, when he arrived on the campus, Byoir got similar jobs with Chicago and Minneapolis papers.

Understandable, this heavy load of reporting for several papers took its toll on Byoir's grades. In later years, he recalled, "I cannot look back upon my first three years at Iowa City with any especial pride so far as my scholastic standing was concerned. I got through but that was about all." But in his reporting, Byoir learned a valuable lesson he applied the rest of his life. He came to realize that well-written, factual newsworthy stories would be published, but that poorly written, superficial news was either discarded or condensed by editing, that cost him money as he was paid by the column inch. This lesson he learned as a part-time correspondent was reflected in the high journalistic standard he set for publicity releases when he established his public relations firm 25 years later.

In his quest for money, Byoir learned another valuable lesson that stood him in good stead in later years—that of winning support for a group's decision. Byoir later recalled:

In looking about for ways to make money, I discovered fairly early in my freshman year that though there were many offices to which an undergraduate could be elected by his fellows, there was only one that offered economic opportunities. Each year the junior class got out an annual publication called the *Hawkeye* which, when it was properly handled, was apt to be reasonably profitable. . . . The general manager who would ultimately be selected by my class, of course, would not be chosen until the end of the sophomore year, and would be in office throughout the junior year. That was a long way off, but I decided that was the job I especially wanted. With that idea in mind, I began to lay my plans.

Byoir orchestrated a campaign that brought him election as manager of the *Hawkeye*. He systematically tackled the task of producing a profitable yearbook. Reflective of his later approach to a public relations problem, Byoir made a thorough analysis of the previous yearbooks and the way they were handled. He found there had never been a properly organized circulation effort, that advertising had been sold as one-quarter page "complimentary cards," and that the *Hawkeye* had not had an organized solicitation of advertisers. He recruited and organized a staff to increase the circulation and advertising of the *Hawkeye* with the result that he netted $2,100 for his managership, three times what his immediate predecessor had earned. But he gained more than $2,100 from this experience.

Byoir saw an opportunity to cash in on his successful formula for a profitable college annual. He wrote a manual of instructions for "inexperienced annual managers" that he planned to sell along with a printing contract on a commission basis. He sold the idea to James M. Pierce, publisher of the farmer's magazine, *The Homestead* that had a backup press and engraving facilities. Byoir spent the summer of 1909 traveling the country to sell his package deal. That summer he earned $9,500 by selling the package to 36 colleges and universities, including Yale, the University of Texas, and the University of Washington. This new-found wealth enabled Byoir to devote full time to his studies in his senior year, and he made all A's that year. He also earned another $1,300 by publishing a new college humor magazine, the *Haw-Haw Hawkeye*, modeled after the *Harvard Crimson*. This was another learning experience that proved helpful in his magazine career. The success of these enterprises enabled Byoir to pay off all college debts and leave Iowa with his degree and $6,500 in the bank.

But all was not beer and skittles for young Byoir at the University of Iowa. As he had as a child, he once again met the ugly face of anti-Semitism. His close friend Walter Stewart was pledged to a fraternity. Byoir was not—the victim of an unwritten rule that barred persons of Jewish blood from membership. Nonetheless, he and Stewart remained close friends for life. Some 30 years later, when under attack for his firm having provided service to the German Railroad Tourist Board under Hitler, Byoir told a Congressional committee:

> I think I can speak . . . as an expert . . . on this Jewish question. I have lived with it for forty-six years. My boyhood was embittered by it. You know there is no cruelty like the unconscious cruelty of children. For any difference in race or religion, or social or financial status of the parents, you are barred from childish games, you are called by foul and belittling names and obscene names. In college, twenty-five years ago, my best friends literally wept over the fact that their college fraternity had a national unwritten rule that no one of Jewish race or blood could be a member.

There is little in the record of Byoir's life to suggest that he was deeply embittered by these experiences, but there are suggestions it made him cautious in his relationships with non-Jewish organizations. Unlike many in his generation, Byoir never become a joiner. At the time of his death, he was a member only of the Advertising Club of New York and the Army and Navy Club of Washington, DC. Friends recall Byoir never pushed for social recognition in nonbusiness environments.

After graduation from Iowa, Carl Byoir and his friend, Walter Stewart, decided to study law, applied to the Columbia Law School, and were accepted. They were off in the fall for New York City and law school. (Walter Stewart was the only close, intimate friend Byoir developed over his lifetime. Upon their graduation in 1912, Stewart returned to Des Moines to build a prosperous law firm. In 1951, he arranged for Byoir to address the annual meeting of the Iowa Bar Association. Theirs was a special relationship until Byoir's death.) Byoir's first year at Columbia was a fairly placid one for this dynamic young man. Byoir later recalled that his study of law caused him to acquire the habit of "exact thinking." His law studies also reinforced his penchant for preciseness in use of the language.

On the long train ride from Des Moines to New York City in the fall of 1911, Byoir happened to read an article in *McClure's Magazine* describing Dr. Maria Montessori's method of teaching kindergartners, which he saw as a refreshing contrast to his early schooling. Byoir's entrepenurial lights flashed. He thought this Italian educator's methods would be highly appealing to American mothers and teachers. To him it was a new opportunity to make money. One of his longtime associates, John F. Budd, Jr., recalled that "Byoir was always more the entreprenuer than the public relations counselor." Byoir was not long in putting his cash on hand to work. He learned that Dr. Montessori was represented by the law firm, White and Case, and he persuaded attorney Robert Walker of that firm to give him exclusive sales rights for the system in the United States.

Young Byoir invested $6,000 and set up a corporation, The House of Childhood, to direct this sales effort. He went to Italy to confer with Dr. Montessori and acquire a set of the physical equipment required for her methodology. In the process of this expedition, Byoir missed several weeks of law classes, but these he was able to make up using the research and class notes of his chum Walter Stewart. Thanks to his quick mind, he was able to pass his exams and graduate in 1910. Upon graduation, Byoir passed up a $15 a week clerkship in a New York law firm to pursue his new business. He set out to promote the Montessori kindergarten system by planting articles in magazines and going on a lecture tour. By the fall of 1912, Byoir had an office in New York, two thick books of orders, a storehouse full of newly manufactured Montessori equipment, and manuals of instructions. After a busy year as salesman and promoter, Byoir sold his 80% interest in The House of Childhood to his former employer, James M. Pierce of the Iowa *Homestead*. His year of promotion had netted him $63,000 and convinced him that his future lay in business, not in law. The money-making bug born of necessity in Byoir when he was a child never left him. In introducing the Montessori methods of teaching young children in the United States, Carl Byoir left his mark on American education.

His next move was into the world of magazines to provide another serendipitous experience that molded the masterful public relations counselor of his later years. About the time he sold his interest in The House of Childhood, Byoir met Morgan Shepherd who approached Byoir with an idea for a magazine for preschool children. They collaborated on the idea of a magazine designed for young readers but aimed at their parents, who could use the magazine to satisfy a child's insatiable demand to "tell me a story." Shepherd, using the pseudonym of John Martin, was writing a successful children's page in the *Ladies Home Journal*. Thus was born *John Martin's Book*. It was a well-edited, hard-to-tear publication designed to attract children and their parents. It had an initial circulation of 15,000, but Byoir sold the advertising at $125 per page, more than its popular competitor, *St. Nicholas*, charged. Shepherd thought Byoir's advertising copy was too "hard sell," and this difference led Byoir to sell out early in 1914 with a $33,000 profit.

His experience with *John Martin's Book* made him realize that he needed much more knowledge of the circulation and advertising techniques of magazine publishing before he could launch another publication. This inspired him to seek an apprenticeship in the Hearst magazine empire — then a powerful one. He sought a job with George van Utassy, general manager of Hearst magazines. Told there was no opening, Byoir said that he was willing to work for $50 a week if a van Utassy would move him around as an apprentice. He was hired on that basis and was first given an assignment in advertising sales. Again, young Byoir showed the great acumen and talent he possessed as a master salesman. After 3 months, he was selling more ad space in the *Hearst Magazine* than the other seven experienced salesmen. He was soon shifted to promotion manager and given a $10 raise. Here again the future public relations man demonstrated sure grasp of influencing opinion. Byoir's last assignment with the Hearst organization was in circulation for *Cosmopolitan magazine* that was losing newsstand circulation. Once more he demonstrated the importance of fact-finding before coming up with a solution to a problem. He spent 6 weeks interviewing newsstand dealers from New York to San Francisco. He concluded the trend could be reversed if the dealers were given more incentives, so he set up a series of prizes. Byoir's plan worked and within 3 months the *Cosmopolitan* circulation had bounced back from 790,000 to 1,060,000. This won Byoir a promotion to circulation manager of all Hearst magazines. Byoir stayed with Hearst until 1917 when he was drafted to serve his nation in World War I as an official of the newly created

Committee on Public Information, the Creel Committee as it came to be nationally known.

In his uncompleted autobiography, Byoir later reflected that his Hearst experience had taught him:

1. Tenacity and determination on the part of a salesman is not a substitute for imagination and knowledge based on careful analysis;
2. There is no essential difference between personal salesmanship and salesmanship in print;
3. It is often easier to sell a big package than a little one;
4. Never make a sales presentation unless you have personally studied the problem in detail, but make your presentation short; and
5. A successful salesman is an attention getter.

Applying these lessons brought the 28-year-old Byoir attention in the industry as "a comer."

BYOIR AND THE CREEL COMMITTEE

The new vocation of public relations had emerged in the years 1900–1917 largely as a defensive measure on the part of Big Business that turned to newspapermen to defend itself from the attacks of the muckrakers and the regulatory programs of Presidents Theodore Roosevelt and Woodrow Wilson, both of whom sought and got unprecedented laws to curb the public abuses of the railroads, meat packers, banks, and industries. Many of these defensive public relations efforts were unavailing. It remained for World War I and George Creel's Committee on Public Information to demonstrate the awesome power of a brilliantly led, highly organized campaign of propaganda to mold and motivate public opinion. Carl Byoir played a key role in the success of the Creel Committee.

When America entered World War I in April 1917, public opinion was sharply divided over President Wilson's decision to go to war against the Central Powers. Soon after Congress declared war, President Wilson, acting on the advice of Josephus Daniels, newspaper publisher and Secretary of the Navy, created the Committee on Public Information to mobilize public support of the war at home and sell America's peace aims abroad. It was also responsible for news censorship.

The committee, composed of the Secretaries of War, Navy, and State, met only a few times because George Creel, a fiery, crusading journalist, chose to organize and run the committee his way. Creel had suggested the need for such an agency to Daniels. It was a confused, unprepared nation that President Wilson led into World War I. Historian Arthur Link wrote, "The American people entered the First World War not knowing what the struggle was about or the objectives for which their new friends and enemies were fighting." George Creel and Carl Byoir changed this with a dramatic, powerful propaganda campaign at home and abroad.

Creel started from scratch. He had no precedents and no organization at the outset. Yet, in the words of Mock and Larson in *Words That Won the War*, "Mr. Creel assembled as brilliant and talented group of journalists, scholars, press agents, editors, artists and other manipulators of the symbols of public opinion as America had ever united for a single purpose." It was Carl Byoir, not yet 29 years old, who provided the glue to hold this organization of improvisation together and provide the direction to make it effective. George Creel was busy recruiting staff, on the road making speeches, and serving as public relations adviser to the President. Creel later described his task as "Putting the Committee together was like asking Babylonians to build a threshing machine."

Quite early Creel recruited a team of scholars, headed by Dr. Guy Stanton Ford, to write a series of red-white-and-blue pamphlets to persuade the nation of the justness of its cause. Soon a logjam in the Government Printing Office was blocking the printing and distribution of these pamphlets. At the suggestion of Edgar Sission, CPI associate chairman, Creel turned to Carl Byoir for help. Sisson had been editor of the *Cosmopolitan*. Byoir left his job with Hearst and reported for duty at the CPI in June 1917.

Byoir soon solved the pamphlet printing problem. He knew that New York catalog printers had idle presses between spring and fall catalogs and quickly signed contracts with a few of them that saved the government 40% of the cost. Creel was so impressed with the rapidity of Byoir's solution, he asked him to stay on as an associate chairman. The young Byoir quickly assumed "a great deal of the executive administration and the business end . . . of the various divisions," he told a Congressional committee in 1918. In July 1918, Creel wrote Byoir's draft board asking that he be deferred because he was "indispensable" to the nation's war effort. Creel wrote in 1920, "Mr. Byoir had, like Mr. Sisson, 'grown up' with the Committee. Sacrificing his own business interests to serve, he soon came to be known among us as 'the multiple director,' for I used his organizing ability in division after division . . . and whether the activity was domestic or foreign, he showed equal skill in giving it efficiency, force, and direction."

Among other duties, Byoir was involved in organizing and directing CPI propaganda to various European ethnic groups living in the States. The committee records show that he was active in promoting and creating new social and political clubs among the foreign-language speaking citizens in

America's large cities. In later years, Byoir made a great point of this propaganda work and was particularly proud of creating the League of Oppressed Nations to sap morale behind the Central Powers' lines.

Byoir was one of the innovators of the staged event, today a common technique in public relations to attract the public interest. He arranged for President Wilson to speak at hallowed Mt. Vernon on July 4, 1918, to the League of Oppressed Nations. Byoir arranged for 33 ethnic groups to make the pilgrimage to Mt. Vernon, all expenses paid, to hear Wilson enunciate the right of European minorities to live under governments of their own choosing. On this same date, Byoir arranged for the proclamation of Czech Declaration of Independence by Thomas Masaryk at Independence Hall in Philadelphia. Byoir also got Masaryk to serve as chairman of the League of Oppressed Nations. While President Wilson and Chairman Masaryk were speaking at these national shrines, Byoir staged loyalty demonstrations in over 800 cities in the United States.

In his work with the foreign born in the United States and his propaganda operations among the minority groups in Europe, Byoir developed the *third party technique* that he later used in his public relations work, a strategy that brought him widespread criticism and lawsuits. This third party or false front ploy was fully acceptable to the President and Byoir's peers in fighting a war but proved less acceptable on the domestic political front, as Byoir ultimately learned.

Creel and Byoir had faced an enormous task at the outbreak of war, one for which there were no precedents, no blueprints. Their demonstration of propaganda was to have a profound effect on American culture and on the future of public relations. Creel, Byoir, and their associates, led by President Wilson, had been so successful in building fervent hopes for "a world made safe for democracy" at home and in Europe that when these hope were crushed in the wake of the Treaty of Versailles, their work led to the corrosion of the word *propaganda*, now used as a derogatory, pejorative term. Consequently its use was dropped in the worlds of advertising, public relations, and politics. In the immediate postwar years, men who had gained experience under Creel and had observed the efficiency of the propaganda campaigns for Prohibition and Women's Suffrage that came to successful fruition in 1920 carried this knowledge back into civilian life.

One of the ethnic groups Byoir had organized was the Lithuanian National Council of the United States by merging voluntary associations of Catholic and Protestant Lithuanians in the United States. The tiny Baltic nation, freed from German occupation at the time of the Russian Revolution, declared its independence on February 16, 1918. Soon the Lithuanian National Council engaged Carl Byoir at a fee of $25,000 to win public support for U.S. recognition of this newly declared independence. Byoir then hired Edward L. Bernays at a salary of $150 a week to produce and place the publicity to gain this objective. This is the only time these two giants of public relations counseling worked together.

Byoir and Bernays waged a successful campaign, using techniques that had been developed in the Creel Committee. They spread their message through chosen spokesmen in the nation's large cities and newspapers of the nation. They were successful in eliciting editorials and telegrams to U. S. Senators in support of the Lithuanian cause. The Senate in 1919 duly recognized Lithuania as an independent nation, but formal U.S. recognition did not come until July 1922.

Byoir, who took no pay for his part in the campaign, was given a unique square watch by the Council as a token of its appreciation. According to one biographer, Colonel Robert Bennett, "Carl Byoir seems to have been unimpressed by the joining of the Byoir–Bernays public relations team." Byoir recalled, "After the war . . . Eddie Bernays and I started a little (public relations) business — it was so little that . . . I decided to go into something more profitable."

Byoir, who had felt the sting of poverty and anti-Semitism in his early years and who later in life made millions in public relations, did not see the potential in the fledgling vocation that existed after the World War as did such pioneers as Bernays, Harry Bruno, Ivy Lee, and John Price Jones.

IN THE SHADOWY WORLD OF PATENT MEDICINES

The war's end and the rapid dismantling of the Creel Committee found Carl Byoir broke. He had served his nation for a $1 a year! In one of his rare mistakes of judgment, Byoir did not see a lucrative field in public relations and was hungry for big bucks. He set up a motion picture company and went into an import–export business with Emanual Voska to exploit what they saw as money-making opportunities in the war-devastated nations of Europe. Byoir had come to know Voska, who was Masaryk's main propaganda contact in the United States during the war. The motion picture company produced only one film that netted Byoir $7,000. For a time, the Byoir–Voska partnership made fabulous profits but then started losing thousands of dollars every day when the foreign exchange market collapsed due to the uncontrolled currency inflation in postwar Europe. Through Masaryk's influence, Byoir sold American leaf tobacco to Czechoslovakia and recouped a large share of their losses. Nonetheless, Byoir was compelled to shut down the business and came out with personal debts of $120,000. Byoir refused to take the escape route of bankruptcy but was determined to pay of these debts. This led him to the shadowy world of patent medicines and its large profit margins.

Byoir first sought an advertising job with E. Virgil Neal, president of a firm selling spurious nostrum, Nuxated Iron. Neal was a well-known medicine man who on occasion used the pseudonym X LaMotte Sage, A.M., Ph.D., LL.D. Neal told Byoir he had no openings. As he had done before when rebuffed in seeking employment, Byoir proposed to Neal that if given sales rights to Nuxated Iron in several cities, he would demonstrate a sales increase and would take no pay. Using fact-finding and a personalized sales approach, Byoir increased sales in his territory at such a fast clip that Neal made him vice-president and general manager. Byoir was again proved to be a master psychologist and super salesman. His talents ultimately brought him a substantial interest in the firm. Nuxated Iron, which sold for $1 a bottle, was touted as a valuable blood and nerve force with tissue building properties,"

After analyzing the patent medicine, the American Medical Association said it contained "a practically negligible amount of nux vomica and less than four cents worth of medicinal iron." Byoir stayed with Nuxated Iron until he had made enough money to pay off his import–export debts and then sold his interest in the company. The date of this sale is not clear.

Byoir next went into business with Julius and Louis Tuvin, who peddled such preparations as Seedol ("Natural Seed Bowel Tonic Works Wonders"); Kelpamalt, a weight builder; and Viaderma, a rub-on reducing compound dismissed by the AMA as "*a humbug per se.*" All these dubious products brought Byoir and his partners before the Federal Trade Commission (FTC) for using unfair methods of business competition in interstate commerce. The FTC found, for example, that the pitch for Viaderma was misleading and deceiving the public. The partners were ordered to cease and desist such claims. The FTC also found that Kelpamalt's claims for weight building were "erroneous, misleading, and deceptive." This brought another cease and desist order.

Carl Byoir also became a major stockholder of Bymart, a firm that manufactured and sold Blondex hair tonics, dyes, and shampoos. To promote Blondex, Byoir did much to glamorize platinum blondes and the sexiness of blonde hair for women. Once more, the Federal Trade Commission found some of the Blondex advertising extravagant, and its producers were ordered to cease and desist from claiming among other things, that Blondex Hair Tonic would check falling hair or stimulate the growth of new hair.

In 1928, Byoir discontinued his participation in the management of these proprietary firms because of poor health. Byoir had come down with a severe sinus condition that threatened to blind him. His doctors advised him to move to Arizona, thinking the hot desert climate would cure his affected sinuses. Byoir found little relief in Arizona and later in 1928, moved to Cuba hoping to find relief there. This led, ultimately, to founding his public relations firm that brought him fame and the millions he tirelessly sought.

This patent medicine period in Byoir's career, even though entered into for its quick bucks to pay off his debtors, represents the low point in Byoir's varied and successful career. To be fair, he engaged in these hard-sell, overblown sales pitches in the era of the Roaring Twenties, the era of the flapper, bathtub gin, speakeasy, when Albert Lasker, Ivy Lee, and Edward L. Bernays were persuading women to smoke to double the market for cigarettes. During the 1920s, the Federal Trade Commission issued several cease and desist orders on products similar to those being peddled by Byoir. Also, it should be noted that Byoir was a defendant in only one of these FTC cases — that of Viaderma. The FTC complaint in this case was not filed until August 31, 1929, and the cease and desist order was not issued until April 6, 1931 — both coming long after Byoir had quit his patent medicine shilling. Yet given his talents and his share in these companies, he must remain fully accountable for their shady practices.

CARL BYOIR & ASSOCIATES IS BORN

Within weeks after his arrival in Cuba, Byoir found that its climate had cleared his sinus infections and once again he was full of bounce, eager to work and make a living. For an interim of nearly a year, he bought and operated a bakery, but this got to be a boring business for him. Thus, he returned to his first love, journalism, by leasing two small, struggling English-language newspapers: the *Havana Post*, a morning newspaper, and the *Havana Telegram*, an evening paper. These papers were owned by Raphael R. Govin, publisher of Havana's largest paper, *El Mundo*. Byoir's research found that his papers were read only by English-speaking residents and American tourists. Also he found that increasing advertising sales would be difficult without larger circulations. He struck upon the idea that the only way to make these papers profitable would be to increase the flow of American tourists to Cuba.

In this period, Cuba was under iron grip of its dictator, President Gerardo Machado, who had seized power in 1928. After several rebuffs, Byoir finally got an audience with the dictator in which he sought to persuade Machado to hire him to promote American tourist traffic to Cuba. Machado was not persuaded at first, but again Byoir came up with the kind of proposition that had gained his way with Hearst magazines and with Virgil Neal: "All right," Byoir said, "I'll make you a sporting proposition, Mr. President. If I spend my money promoting the . . . [American] tourist traffic for a year, and show marked increase in it, Cuba will be the largest beneficiary. . . . Then will you sign a five-year contract with me at $60,000 a year to promote tourist traffic to Cuba?" Machado saw he had little to lose and much to gain and agreed to Byoir's proposition.

Thus began an association that later cast more shadows across Byoir's reputation.

The energetic, imaginative Byoir set about to mount a promotional effort to accomplish his objective and decided to spend up to $50,000 of his own money to make certain that the publicity campaign would be a success. First, Byoir phoned his friend Stuart Hall, an advertising executive in Miami, to ask for a recommendation for a person to help in this campaign. Fortunately for the future of the Byoir firm, Hall recommended Gerry Swinehart, then publicity manager for West Palm Beach, Florida. Byoir got in touch with Swinehart, offered him a job, and Swinehart, who would play a major role in building Carl Byoir & Associates (CB&A), reported for duty in Havana on March 1, 1930.

Byoir first asked Swinehart to draw up a detailed promotion program together with the estimated cost for its implementation. Swinehart recommended a number of projects, urged that more staff be hired and a New York office be opened, and put the cost at $25,000. Byoir accepted the plan but doubled the budget to $50,000. Byoir next hired Charles Canny, a newspaper reporter, to work with Swinehart. To man the New York office Byoir persuaded a person he knew, Carl C. Dickey, to join the embryonic firm as a junior partner. Dickey had been on the staff of the magazine *Outlook*, but like many journalists he was, in his words, "pushed into public relations by the Depression so I went to Wall Street where business nested." When Byoir called Dickey, he was account executive on the Pan-American Airways account for the Doremus & Co. advertising agency. Dickey told me on February 29, 1960, that a few hours after he had accepted Byoir's offer, he was given a chance to become public relations director of the Panagra Airline.

At Byoir's direction, Dickey rented office space at 10 East 40th Street, where the Byoir firm would prosper and grow. The New York office first had the name *Havana Post* on its door but this was later changed, at Dickey's direction, to Carl Byoir & Associates. Like Byoir and Swinehart, Dickey had newspaper experience and with Byoir directing the broad strategy, all three pitched into popularize Cuba as America's vacation land. The campaign stressed Cuba's proximity to America's ports, its low prices for hotels and food, its entertainment, its music, and its balmy climate. Byoir used all communications media and channels to reach his target audiences. In a memorandum to his staff in 1933 Byoir wrote, "That was the beginning of Carl Byoir & Associates. To wind up that story, we increased the Cuban tourist business in a single year from 80,000 to 165,000 persons. The Cuban Government woke up one morning and found they were taking in roughly $125,000 more in ticket taxes on the tourist business than they had before."

Early in 1931, Byoir reminded President Machado of the proposition he had made the year before. Keeping his word, the dictator signed a 5-year tourist promotion contact with CB&A at $60,000 a year. The contract remained in force until Machado was overthrown in August 1933. Byoir's longtime secretary, Elsie Simon who joined the firm in the fall of 1932, recalled that "we didn't have the Cuban account at that time." Gerry Swinehart's memory on this point was more certain, "It's for damn sure when Batista chased Machado out of the country."

Understandably, the Cuban account brought Byoir much vehement criticism, including the publication by *Editor & Publisher* of a faked version of Byoir's contract with the Cuban dictator. Carl Dickey responded to *Editor & Publisher*, "The alleged propaganda proposal . . . has been floating around for weeks. Various changes have been made from time to time in the forged comment." Carlton Beals, the historian, was quite caustic of Byoir, claiming without supporting evidence, that Byoir and Ivy Lee "were beating the drums of publicity" for American sugar traders to close a deal with Machado. Byoir later recalled that Ivy Lee was active in Cuban public relations at that time. The evidence generally indicates that Byoir was apolitical and dealt with Machando as a way of salvaging his investment in the Havana newspapers. His alternative would have been to give up and return to America broke.

Despite the fact that Byoir later recalled, "I had no thought of going back into public relations or [of] building the Cuban public relations venture into a full-time . . . business," through a set of coincidences, Byoir and his associates found themselves with tourist and other publicity accounts that kept the doors open in the early years.

Their prowess in tourist promotion for Cuba soon brought them the Province of Quebec account for tourist promotion that Swinehart handled. Other early accounts included the Trotting Club of America to promote the Hambletonian for trotting horses. Byoir's reputation for tourist promotion also brought an account that cast another dark shadow across his reputation. A chance meeting in Cuba with Clement Melville Keys brought the agency its first industrial account, the type of client that carried Byoir to the front ranks of U. S. agencies in 20 years.

Keys was one of the pioneers of American aviation. A millionaire and former editor of the *Wall Street Journal*, Keys was a power in New York financial circles and chairman of North American Aviation—the man who, in Byoir's words, "really put commercial aviation on the map." In their conversation aboard a Cuban train, Byoirs later recalled, "Keys said, 'Well, as long as you are back in public relations, how would you like to represent North American?' " This in Byoir's view was the event that made it possible for his firm to move into big-time, professional public relations—not an easy feat in a nation gripped in the economic paralysis of the Great Depression. The Keys account provided the bridge to take the agency from the simpler functions of tourist promotion and publicity into the broader field of counseling.

Byoir realized that the firm's growing list of accounts, including Key's North American Aviation, required his personal direction, so he and Gerry Swinehart returned to New York and took up quarters at 10 East 40th Street in 1932. Charles Canny remained in Cuba to work on the Cuban account. Byoir added his brother-in-law, Vincent Lancaster, to the staff to serve as secretary and treasurer. At first Byoir, Swinehart, and Dickey hired only part-timers on a spot basis to support specific publicity projects. But in the next 2 years, two persons who played a major role in the success of the Byoir agency were hired — Jane Buck who was hired in 1931 and George Hammond who was hired in 1932. Jane Buck was among the first women to be successful in public relations and was a stalwart member of the Byoir team until she retired.

George Hammond, in time served as president and finally as chairman of the Byoir agency, was a native of Brooklyn who started covering sports for the *New York Sun* while still in high school. Encouraged by the *Sun* sports editor, Hammond sought and got a Pulitzer scholarship to attend Columbia University. He was hired by the *Sun* full time after doing a publicity stint for the Biltmore Havana Hotel in 1930. Later in Havana, he was doing a column for the Byoir newspapers. In 1932, when Byoir was asked to develop a sports program for Henry L. Doherty's hotels, he recruited Hammond for the task. Hammond retired as chairman of the agency in 1978 when Carl Byoir and Associates was sold to Foote, Cone, and Belding. All these except Lancaster had had newspaper experience, which became a firm requirement for employment at Byoir, which in time would operate one of the toughest copy desks in journalism.

For example, to handle the North American account, Byoir hired Howard Mingos, an aviation writer, to prepare publicity booklets to promote aviation, commercial air travel, and public support for the growing Air Corps of the U. S. Army. Carl Dickey told me that it was Byoir who came up with the idea of the air stewardess to glamorize air travel — not an easy idea to sell to an uninitiated public. This claim is not documented.

The pioneer members of the agency recalled these clients: John Hay Whitney's *Outlook* magazine, Household Finance Corporation, McFadden's Penny Restaurants, the *Minneapolis Tribune*, and David Stern's *Philadelphia Record*. Another early client, again a tourist promotion account, was N. B. T. Roney's Roney Plaza Hotel and the Miami Biltmore Hotel, owned by Henry L. Doherty but managed by Roney. Byoir's work with Doherty led him into the national spotlight in 1933 as the organizer of the President's Birthday Balls to pay off the debts on FDR's Warm Springs Foundation and to raise money for polio research.

Before turning to that saga, I should set forth the basic rules Byoir set down to guide the conduct of his new public relations firm:

1. New accounts would not be directly solicited. This did not mean that the firm would not respond to queries. If a client approached CB&A, detailed promotion programs tailored to the client's particular needs would be provided.
2. CB&A would charge each client a minimum yearly fee of $36,000 plus the actual expenses in implementing the programs and plans approved by the client.

This was the highest fee then being charged a PR agency and created much talk in the advertising and public relations circle. Byoir was convinced that only a high fee would reflect high quality of counsel and service. This is how he got the Henry L. Doherty account.

The wealthy Doherty, who had acquired a fortune of a half billion dollars, more or less, in the utilities and petroleum business, had bought the Roney Plaza. In the summer of 1932, Doherty sent a telegram to all the agencies listed in the New York telephone directory inviting bids to promote his Florida properties that also included golf clubs, fishing clubs, and vast real estate holdings. The wire specified that all bids should be submitted in writing. Byoir ignored this stipulation and got an appointment with Doherty personally. The interview took place in Miami.

Byoir's first question was, "How much did the Miami Biltmore, a $10,000,000 property, spend on advertising last year?" Doherty answered, "Six thousand dollars." Byoir quickly replied: "We'll spend $254,000 next year and start the season by filling the hotel with free guests the first week." Doherty was taken aback. The always persuasive Byoir not only got Doherty to sign a publicity contract but also came away with a contract to manage the Florida properties at a salary of $50,000 a year with the stipulation that Byoir need devote only 50% of his time to this task. Once more Byoir proved he knew how to boom a business. Prior to the time Byoir took over the Miami Biltmore's management, its season was 60 days long and in those 2 months housed roughly 650 guests. Two years later, Byoir had extended the season to 9 months and attracted 12,000 guests. The golf tournaments, water shows that Billy Rose later copied, and countless other promotions soon put the Doherty properties on a profitable basis. Byoir's shrewd sense of mass psychology that he had first learned in World War I again paid dividends.

BYOIR FINDS PUBLICITY CAN'T SOLVE
EVERY PROBLEM

As the Depression year of 1932 continued to paralyze the nation's economy, the perceptive Byoir saw that it might take down his young agency. That year C. M. Keys had lost control of North American Aviation, and the new management had notified Byoir that his contract would be renewed in 1933. Byoir became increasingly frustrated as he saw that President Hoover's efforts to restart the nation's economic engine had come to naught. He got an appointment with the President, as a public service and at no cost to the government, to direct a "War Against the Depression." Hoover reluctantly agreed to Byoir's plan so long as no government funds or support were involved. With President Hoover's endorsement, Byoir sought the participation of several national organizations to lend credibility to the campaign. He won the endorsement of the American Federation of Labor, the Association of National Advertisers, the American Legion, and the American Legion Auxiliary, all of which nominated representatives to serve on the war's national committee.

Byoir established the war headquarters at the Hotel Biltmore and announced to the media that President Hoover, as Commander-in-Chief, had ordered the national committee to find 1 million jobs for the nation's unemployed. Byoir later recalled, "After the Hoover Administration had failed in their [sic] attack on the employment problem, a group of public spirited citizens decided that they would organize the people of the country to seek employment for a million of the unemployed. These [public spirited] citizens had no funds and no power of government. Nevertheless they went ahead."

The war effort attracted much national attention at first but quickly floundered. Byoir's nationwide publicity effort was doomed to failure, demonstrating that publicity alone could not solve the deep economic woes of the United States. Within 2 months, Byoir and his fellow committeemen quietly closed shop and abandoned their impossible task. This is one of a very few instances in which Byoir's sense of public opinion proved wrong, terribly wrong. Clearly this was a move born of desperation and frustration with the mounting effects of the Great Depression on the nation and on CB&A

THE GERMAN TOURIST ACCOUNT: ANOTHER BLACK
EYE FOR BYOIR

Contrary to Carl Byoir's early decision that his firm would not solicit new accounts, Carl Dickey, his junior partner, told me in interviews on March 17 and 18, 1959, that "we were scratching for every account we could get.

We sought mostly tourist accounts because this was the way the firm got started and the kind of promotion all of us knew." They were soliciting travel accounts from Italy, Germany, and Austria. The law firm of Katz & Sommerich was the attorney for Byoir and also for the German Counsul before Hitler. The Byoir firm had been working on getting the account of the German Wine Development Board. "We finally got the account of the German Railroads Tourist Bureau to promote travel to Germany," Dickey recounted. This brought another black eye to the young agency.

Carl Dickey negotiated a contract with the German Railroads Tourist Bureau with the help of the notorious Nazi sympathizer, George Sylvester Viereck, and it was signed October 1, 1933 — just 8 months after Adolf Hitler had seized power in Germany. There is no evidence available to suggest that Dickey acted without Byoir's approval in landing this account. The unhappy consequences of this service to a German agency led to a split between Byoir and Dickey in 1935.

Dickey later joined T. J. Ross & Associates, successor firm to Ivy Lee and T. J. Ross. The Ross firm was still reeling from the blows of Ivy Lee's counseling I. G. Farben after Hitler came to power. (That was dealt with in an earlier chapter.) It was revealed in 1934 before a Congressional committee that Viereck, then busily engaged in trying to sell Der Fuehrer to the American people, had recommended Byoir to an official in the German Propaganda Ministry and in return for his good offices, had been put on Byoir's payroll at $1, 750 a month and provided an office. During World War II, Viereck was convicted of violating the Foreign Agent Registration Act and sent to prison. He was paroled in 1947 and died March 18, 1962.

Dickey later insisted that the CB&A contract with the German Railroads Tourist Bureau called for the promotion of travel, and in line with that, they worked with German railroads, steamship companies, and hotels. According to Lore Ludwig, writing in *The Nation* of November 29, 1933:

> The [German Propaganda Ministry] endeavors to sell Hitlerism to the somewhat skeptical public . . . are more extensive than ever. Approximately three months [*sic*] ago it arranged with Carl Byoir & Associates . . . for the distribution of informative material on the "New Germany." Under terms of this contract, George Sylvester Viereck went to Germany with Carl C. Dickey, one of the "associates," to look around and interview Hitler, Goering, Goebbels . . . and most of the other Nazi dignitaries; these absolutely unbiased and objective impressions will be served up to Americans in a series of widely syndicated articles in the near future.

Subsequent to the Viereck–Dickey trip to Germany, the October 1 contract was modified and the stipend increased to $6,000 per month for 18 months. In return, Byoir opened an office in Berlin at a cost of $1,000 in salary and expenses. A Mr. Hamlin, the Byoir agent in Berlin, wrote stories and acquired pictures for the Byoir-produced publication, the *German–American Economic Bulletin*.

This bulletin was published bimonthly and was sent to a mailing list of 3,000 to 5,000, mainly newspapers. An informal committee of several German businesses was formed to sponsor it. Its objective was to get the press to reprint articles or to use them as reference material so that German issues would be put in "perspective." Another service Dickey provided the tourist bureau was periodic surveys of editorial comment on Germany in U.S. newspapers. These compilations were translated and forwarded to the German Railroads Tourist Bureau.

On Tuesday, June 5, 1934, Carl Dickey was called to testify before a special House committee, chaired by Rep. John W. McCormack of Massachusetts, who later served as Speaker of the House. Rep. Samuel Dickstein was vice-chairman. Byoir, in this period was busy with managing the Doherty properties in Florida and the President's Birthday Ball of 1934 that he directed. When Dickey was summoned to testify, Byoir was in Europe on what his loyal secretary, Elsie Simon, termed "a long overdue and well deserved vacation."

Dickey told the House committee that he and Byoir were engaging solely in tourist promotion, not propaganda. Dickey admitted, however, that he had collected $4,000 in cash from the German Consul General in New York for help in getting out press releases intended "to create a better feeling here, as the result of the anti-Semitism campaign [in Germany.]" The head of the German Railroad Tourist Information Bureau, located in New York City, testified that he had decided to enter into the Byoir contract without approval of his superiors in Germany.

The McCormack Committee found that "several American firms and American citizens as individuals had sold their services for express propaganda purposes, making their contracts with the accepting compensation from foreign business firms. The firms in question were Carl Byoir & Associates and Ivy Lee–T.J. Ross. The committee finds that the services rendered by the Carl Byoir & Associates were largely of a propaganda nature." Dickey had not informed Byoir of his subpoena to appear before the House committee, and Byoir first learned of it from an Associated Press reporter in a London hotel. Byoir was furious and immediately called his office and asked to be informed on Dickey's testimony. Miss Simon later recalled that "Mr. Byoir was absolutely stunned and surprised by the investigation and the newspaper reaction to it." Once again his shrewd sense of public opinion left him in a moment of fury. He was angry that Dickey had not informed him or cleared his testimony with Byoir in advance. This led ultimately to a dissolution of their partnership early in 1935. In a March 10, 1959 interview with me, Carl Dickey confirmed the secretary's recollection and admitted their breakup came over disagreements about the German account. He also said that Byoir "felt he [Dickey] had too big a piece of the business." Yet Dickey insisted in this interview that his parting with Byoir was "amicable."

The German tourist account did much damage to Byoir and his firm in its early years. The account caused adverse publicity for CB&A: It was a source of public and personal embarrassment for Carl Byoir in 1934–1935 and again in 1940 when he was attacked by a bitter political foe, Rep. Wright Patman, and by the departure of Carl Dickey.

Byoir was especially vulnerable for this work for Germany because he was a Jew, and Hitler's savagery toward Jews was already plainly evident when CB&A signed this contract. This fact was widely noted at the time. Five years later, Rep. Wright Patman of Texas, a bitter foe of Byoir for his representation of the A&P supermarket chain, made a vicious, unjustified attack on Byoir on the floor of the House of Representatives, asserting Byoir was "the man who rode Hitler's first Trojan Horse into the United States" and accused him of trying to "infiltrate spies into this country's big business." In 1958, writing in his *The Image Makers*, Irwin Ross commented, "That same year [1934] Byoir picked up the German Tourist information Office, an account he got through the good offices of George Sylvester Viereck, a well-known Nazi sympathizer. Byoir was a Jew and there seemed a certain piquancy, widely noted in the trade, in his employment by the Nazis." His longtime associate, George Hammond, in discussions with your author, said in defense of the German contract that at that time the official governmental policy of the United States was to encourage international trade and commerce with Germany. Hammond recalled that Byoir always insisted that at the time when CB&A first undertook tourist promotion, only a few people in this country had any conception of the evils that would be inflicted on mankind by Hitler and the Nazis.

Byoir's own defense of the German tourist contract came in February 1935, during a nonpublic, no-record session of the McCormack–Dickstein Committee that substantiates Hammond's recollections:

> You may disagree with me but it was my sincere conviction, out of the experience I have had, that by placing myself in the position of Public Relations Advisor to German business interests in this country that I could persuade these interests to carry the message to their government that American good will could never be won so long as the German Government pursued this policy of violent anti-Semitism. I believed that the influence of the representatives of the German railroads, of the German hotels, of the German spas, and the German steamship lines would in large measure influence the policy of their government and that gradually the oppressive measures [of Hitler] might be relaxed. . . . Now gentlemen, I have had very little to do personally with the active work on this . . . account but I am head

of the organization, responsible for all that it does and, I do not here seek to evade that responsibility. . . . I confess that I was a little bewildered and a good deal staggered [by the public outrage against Byoir].

CB&A'S LAST FOREIGN ACCOUNT—ANOTHER LOSER

In 1938, the Chinese government of Chiang Kai-Shek retained the Byoir agency to raise funds to alleviate starvation in China. This, too, turned out to be a loser for the agency. By organizing Bowl of Rice dinners for Chinese relief in scores of American cities, Byoir in a single night, netted $175,000 for China. This account ended when the Chinese government claimed it couldn't pay its bills because of lack of funds. Byoir, who had financed several other campaigns for China besides the Bowl of Rice dinners out of his own pocket, was $104,000 in the hole. The Chinese Ambassador called to apologize and promised to pay when the war was over. "That's very kind—but a little inconvenient," Byoir replied drily. Until Chiang was forced to flee to Formosa, a bill for $104,000 arrived monthly in Chungking from the Byoir firm. This account also involved another lawsuit for Byoir— this time the agency was the plaintiff. Byoir's complaint charged that CB&A had rendered service to the Chinese government to the extent of $83, 9056.49 and thereafter the Chinese Government sent its general counsel in New York $22,000 to pay on its account, but that the defendant, Teune-Chi Yu, converted and appropriated the money. The litigation that went to the U.S. Court of Appeals, Second Circuit, on June 10, 1940, was unsuccessful. This account was small potatoes in the long history of the Byoir firm, but it led to a decision by then President Gerry Swinehart that "we'll never take another foreign client as long as I am president of this firm." As a consequence, CB&A was late in getting into international public relations.

Byoir's next big accomplishment on behalf of charity did much to dissipate the clouds left by the German tourist account—the raising of more than $4 million to launch the effort to eradicate the scourge of polio from this land.

ACKNOWLEDGMENT

Much of the documentation upon this chapter is based on a master's thesis written by Col. Robert J. Bennett under my direction at the University of Wisconsin-Madison in 1968. Colonel Bennett was given access to the file of Byoir's papers, including his unfinished autobiography. Since then the papers have been withdrawn from public access. Their location is unknown. Thus, I owe a tremendous debt to Colonel Bennett for preserving this important chapter of public relations' history. He deserves full credit for his contribution.

NOTES ON SOURCES

As indicated in the acknowledgement, this chapter and the one to follow is based in large measure on Colonel Robert J. Bennett's master's thesis, *Carl Byoir: Public Relations Pioneer,* written under my direction at the University of Wisoonsin-Madison in 1968. Bennett's thesis, as indicated, was based on access to the Carl Byoir Papers, no longer acessible to the public. His work has been supplemented by my extensive interviews with the key persons in building the successful Byoir agency: Gerry Swinehart, Jane Buck, George Hammond, Robert Wood, and Elsie Simon, Byoir's longtime secretary.

A complete listing of sources can be found at the end of chapter 18. Specific sources used in this chapter include the following.

Congressional Record, House 64th Congress, 1st Session, Vol. 79, Part 3, Washington, DC: Government Printing Office, 1935; George Creel, *How We Advertised America,* Harper & Brothers, 1920; George Creel, *Rebel at Large,* G. P. Putnam's Sons, 1947; Josephus Daniels, *The Wilson Era,* University of North Carolina Press, 1946; James Mock and Cedric Larson, *Words That Won the War,* Princeton University Press, 1939; Irwin Ross, *The Image Merchants,* Doubleday & Company, 1959; Edward L. Bernays, *Biography of An Idea,* Simon and Schuster, 1965; Thomas G. Masaryk, *The Making of a State,* Frederick A. Stokes, Company, 1927; *Federal Trade Commission Decisions,* Vol. 15, Washington, DC: Government Printing Office, 1933; *Federal Trade Commission Decisions,* Vol. 37, Washington, DC, 1936. Carlton Beals, *The Crime of Cuba,* J. B. Lippincott, 1933; Frederick Lewis Allen, *Only Yesterday: An Informal History of the 1920s,* Harper & Row, 1954; and the article, "Nazi Politics in America," by Lore Ludwig, *The Nation,* Vol. 137, November 29, 1933.

My interview with Carl Dickey was held in the T. J. Ross offices on March 10, 1959.

Chapter 18

Carl Byoir: Years of Success and Storm

BYOIR SETS PATTERN FOR TODAY'S MAJOR HEALTH DRIVES

A rare combination of personalities and events converged at precisely the right moment in history to launch the successful crusade against crippling poliomyelitis. But more than prevention of polio was found in the process. Successful nationwide fund-raising patterns were developed that have been utilized by those battling cancer, heart disease, muscular dystrophy, and a host of other still unconquered diseases. High-pressure publicity and skilled organization methods are used to get millions of volunteers to solicit gifts from as many as 80 million Americans in a single drive. A blending of the talents and energies of shrewd, persuasive Carl Byoir, doughty, tough-minded Henry L. Doherty, super salesman Keith Morgan, and last but far from least, bold, thick-skinned Basil O'Connor in exploiting the magic name of Franklin D. Roosevelt built a National Foundation for Infantile Paralysis that "stood beyond all challenge as the most successful voluntary health organization on earth."

On a hot August day in 1921 on Campbello Island, New Brunswick, a happy, healthy Franklin Delano Roosevelt was vacationing with his family. The 39-year-old former Assistant Secretary of the Navy had left a steaming, humid Washington, DC, in July, not knowing that he carried with him the deadly virus of polio. FDR had been shunted to the political sidelines by the defeat of the Democratic presidential ticket of James. M. Cox and FDR in the 1920 election. Roosevelt was stricken with infantile paralysis, as polio was called in those days; he escaped death by a narrow margin. He was

553

never to walk again yet he was destined to lead his nation through some of its most perilous hours and to be the only man ever elected President of the United States for four terms. In the long, vexing struggle to regain his health and to make his political comeback, Roosevelt had, in the words of Frances Perkins, "the intelligent support of Mrs. Roosevelt and Louis Howe, his faithful aide of Navy Department days." Years earlier, Louis McHenry Howe had made up his mind to guide FDR to the Presidency of the United States, and he succeeded.

In mid-1924, philanthropist George Foster Peabody had acquired control of the Warm Springs, GA, resort hotel then "in genteel ruin." He sensed the spa's possibilities as a recuperation center for the crippled victims of infantile paralysis. Peabody, described as "a man of great caution and persistence, in some ways philanthropic," instructed his manager, "I know a man named Roosevelt who just last month made quite a speech in Madison Square Garden." Roosevelt accepted Peabody's invitation and became enthralled with Warm Springs, its curative powers, and friendly Georgian people. In 1926 after prolonged negotiations, FDR bought the property—springs, hotel, cottages, and 1,200 acres of land for $195,000. He took out a mortgage to cover the purchase.

When Roosevelt was elected Governor of New York in 1928 he realized he would not have the time to raise funds and guide the program at Warm Springs so he airily turned it over to his trusted friend and law partner, O'Connor, with the terse command, "You'll have to run Warm Springs now."

Hard pressed for money to repair and rehabilitate the rundown resort, O'Connor turned to Keith Morgan, a million-dollar-a-year insurance salesman, as the money raiser. Morgan's interest in Warm Springs had been enlisted through his friendship with one of the first patients, Arthur Carpenter. Carpenter, at the time advertising manager of *Parents' Magazine*, first went to Warm Springs in the spring of 1928, and a few weeks later Keith Morgan went down to visit him. There Morgan met FDR and was captivated by the man's personality and courage. After chatting for a while with Morgan, FDR said, "Carpenter tells me you can sell anything. How about selling this place to a lot of wealthy people who've never heard of it?" And this Morgan was to spend much of his next 30 years doing because that summer O'Connor followed up FDR's suggestion and drafted Morgan "for the duration."

By the time Roosevelt was elected President in 1932, the Warm Springs Foundation was nearly bankrupt. The bills were piling up. Just as O'Connor and Morgan had begun in 1929 to raise money to put Warm Springs on a sound financial base, the stock market crashed and the Depression set in. Yet the bills piled up. Suppliers were demanding their money, and hundreds of polio victims were begging to come to Warm

Springs. O'Connor recalled wryly that "Warm Springs could not pay for its pots and pans." He called a meeting of the trustees, who voted to authorize a public campaign. It became apparent that a new approach and a nationwide effort would have to be made if Warm Springs was to become a reality, not just FDR's personal dream. Whose idea it was has been lost in dimmed memories, but Keith Morgan decided to put the problem before Carl Byoir. Out of Morgan's call on Byoir at the latter's office came the President's Birthday Balls, the March of Dimes, the National Foundation for Infantile Paralysis, and finally, victory over the disease itself. It was perhaps fortunate that Morgan turned to a public relations man, not a professional fund-raiser.

CARL BYOIR AND HENRY L. DOHERTY ENLIST

As mentioned earlier, Henry L. Doherty was one of Carl Byoir's early clients and also his employer. Doherty, like Byoir, epitomized the Horatio Alger rags-to-riches saga. Born in Columbus, Ohio, of poor parents he quit school at the age of 12 and went to work as an office boy in the local utility. A bold, buccaneering utility tycoon and financial manipulator, he gained his wealth, as did the other utility barons of the pre-New Deal era, by exploiting the nation's resources, by financial rigging, and through municipal franchises granting monopoly of service without adequate rate fixing.

Keith Morgan put his case to Byoir bluntly, explaining that he knew that Byoir represented Doherty and that Doherty ought to be interested in helping Warm Springs. "Why?" asked Byoir. "He has a public reputation as a pirate of finance. Aside from the annoyance, it must get in his way," Morgan replied. Byoir readily saw the possibilities of refurbishing the oil magnate's reputation. He told Morgan, "The colonel is at the Shoreham in Washington. I'll phone him, but you'll have to go down and talk to him yourself." In that Washington hotel, Morgan found "the remarkable Doherty in a big bare top-floor suite, clad only in red woolen underwear which he claimed was the most sensible attire." In response to Morgan's plea for help, Doherty bluntly asked, "Why should I?" "Because it might get an old pirate like you into heaven," Morgan answered. Doherty first glared, then laughed and said, "Who's the head of your organization? Byoir says you're a good outfit. I'll talk to the head man." And with that Doherty and Morgan were off to the White House to see President Roosevelt. The next move was to invite Carl Byoir and Doherty to Warm Springs for the traditional Thanksgiving celebration to discuss specific ways and means of raising money. Doherty liked what he saw, and Byoir was enthusiastic.

Doherty suggested that some sort of fund-raising celebration be planned, and he volunteered to underwrite the publicity and administrative costs. "I'll put up a hundred and fifty thousand, maybe a little more, to finance a practical program for raising some really important money." Those conferring agreed that the appeal must be nationwide and that it should be a quick drive. Doherty barked, "Give 'em one event that will stir them up, make them contribute, and then go home to bed." Byoir spoke up, "I like the idea of a party, of people dancing." This idea was later cast into a memorable slogan, "Dance so that a child may walk," by Columnist Walter Winchell. "When could we hold it?" someone asked. "The President's birthday," Byoir responded. "What an idea!" he added as the possibilities paraded across his imaginative mind. Morgan telephoned for Roosevelt's permission. "If my birthday will be of any help, take it." He, too, saw the possibilities of getting big money for the project nearest his heart, even if it meant dealing with one of the "money-changers" he was then publicly excoriating.

Byoir later confided to his associates that "F.D.R. is scared about what the public reaction might be to this fund-raising effort because of the bonds outstanding against Warm Springs." The subterranean charge that FDR was using the money raised for Warm Springs to pay off his personal debts incurred in starting the Foundation, continued to circulate for years. This bothered him considerably.

Thus, it was understandable that those around Roosevelt were a bit apprehensive about the public's reaction to use of the Presidency in a fund-raising venture, however noble the cause, especially Marvin McIntyre, one of his press secretaries. McIntyre and Byoir had become friends in World War I when McIntyre was serving as FDR's press secretary in the Navy Department and Byoir was associate chairman of the Committee on Public Information. McIntyre is reputed to have told Byoir, "Carl, for God's sake keep this business away from the White House." Whatever the fears of FDR and his coterie, the decision was made to use a celebration of the President's birthday to raise money to fight infantile paralysis.

Doherty was made chairman of the National Committee for Celebration of the President's Birthday and contributed $25,000 to underwrite the costs of organizing and promoting the affair. Byoir and Keith Morgan presented their idea to the American people, Byoir directing the promotion and Morgan handling the housekeeping. O'Connor joyously looked forward to an end of Warm Springs' hand-to-mouth, debt-ridden existence. FDR watched from the White House with deep satisfaction but was careful to take no visible role in the fund-raising campaign. He did, year after year, go on the national radio hookup to address all of the Birthday Balls across the country. The drive was launched by a resourceful trio: the shrewd, not always scrupulous Doherty; the imaginative, energetic promoter Byoir; the intelligent, egotistical O'Connor. These three men, who had fought their way to success from poverty and were not accustomed to failure or halfway measures, began the crusade to conquer polio.

THE PRESIDENT'S BIRTHDAY PARTY

In baseball parlance, Carl Byoir was a "take charge guy"—imaginative, tireless, and persuasive. Once the decision was made in early December to celebrate the President's birthday on January 30, 1934, Byoir became general director. Doherty, who was taking the public bows, persuaded the Waldorf–Astoria Hotel to provide free space for the committee headquarters. In mid-December, Byoir moved out of his own firm to set up shop at the Waldorf and quickly assembled a staff. He recruited his close friend, J. Stephen (Steve) Flynn, to be executive secretary and serve as Byoir's alter ego in campaign direction. His able personal secretary, Mrs. Elsie Simon Sobotka, worked for these two men day and night, taking calls, making appointments, arranging trip schedules, and straightening out one minor mix-up after another.

Byoir used his own staff to provide the publicity. Most of the promotion came from the typewriters of Gerry Swinehart and Jane Buck with frequent assistance from Carl Dickey, Howard Swain, and Alden Calkins. George Hammond, now president of the Byoir firm, recalled that he stayed at the firm and "kept the store." Byoir made no charge for his day-and-night services. In fact, he spent about $2,000 out of his own pocket in organizing the celebration.

Byoir's associates confirmed later that his only remuneration for this night-and-day effort was the Doherty annual retainer fee. Keith Morgan served as committee treasurer and lent a helpful hand in many ways. Committee workers recalled Morgan as "a great organizer."

January 30 was only 6 weeks away. Byoir had envisioned a birthday ball in every American community "to stamp out infantile paralysis." Most people's thoughts were centered on Christmas. How could so many events be organized in so many cities and towns in so little time and in the absence of a functioning national organization? He and his public relations aides decided to get newspaper editors involved. Wires were sent to one newspaper in each city and town, asking the editor to nominate a chairman to organize a Birthday Ball in honor of President Roosevelt. Where the editor failed to respond, Byoir turned to the local Democratic party chainman or the Roosevelt-appointed postmaster. There was no time to observe nonpartisan niceties if a successful event was to be planned and promoted.

"Byoir swamped the nation's press and radio with publicity material. Democrats, especially postmasters and collectors of Internal Revenue, rallied to organize local balls. We couldn't wait to find out where the Republicans were," explained a member of the national committee. Byoir got Wiley Post, the one-eyed around-the-world flier, to fly him across the country to create publicity and to arouse the local committees. He persuaded Howard Chandler Christy to create a poster to publicize the event and as a cover for a fund-raising book published by the committee. Pictures of crippled children filled the nation's newspapers. Radio personalities tried to outdo one another in promoting the event. Walter Winchell, gossip columnist and broadcaster, presented a potent appeal that was used repeatedly for Birthday balls and March of Dimes to come.

The idea of celebrating the President's birthday to raise money for polio victims quickly stirred national enthusiasm. In those days, FDR was seen as the courageous leader who had overcome a great handicap and was now leading the nation out of its slough of despondency. Byoir, the public relations man, knew that the timing was right. FDR was now the nation's hero, not yet "That Man in the White House," to be revered and reviled with equal vehemence.

An editorialist for *The New York Times* accurately reflected public opinion when he wrote, "We have seen the fact that he [Roosevelt] has appeared to the country to be a spirited and gallant commander-in-chief in a time of national crisis. Not to give him loyal and almost unquestioning support has been all through regarded as something next door to treason." Here was double-barreled appeal hard for people to resist. As Carter said, "The 1934 balls transcended their original purpose and became a national celebration of the fresh hope that Americans felt for their country, as well as an honor to Roosevelt and an occasion to 'dance so that others may walk.' "

There is no sure count as to exactly how many events were held. The common estimate in the press was that some 6,000 events were staged in 3,600 communities. Birthday Ball attendance ranged from 10,000 persons crowding a mammoth ball in Philadelphia to one attracting 15 couples in a small Illinois town.

When all the receipts had been collected and all the bills paid, the Doherty Committee had raised the more than $1 million Byoir predicted. On May 9, 1934, a presentation ceremony was held in the East Room of the White House. A proud Byoir presided. (He was still so little known then that *The New York Times* spelled his name Byers.) Mr. Doherty was unable to be present because of illness. Byoir introduced Rear Admiral Gary T. Grayson who presented the yard-long, 18-inch wide parchment check for $1,003,030.08 to Roosevelt as president of the Warm Springs Foundation. FDR in turn handed the check to O'Connor and quipped, "I am going to appoint all of you a committee to watch Doc O'Connor." A jubilant FDR grinned and turning to Byoir said, "Carl, I'll bet you a good tie that you can't top this figure next year," thus making it clear that he hoped that this fund-raising plan would be used again. Byoir took the bet and a new and powerful pattern of nationwide fund raising was put on a permanent basis.

The 1935 Birthday Ball for the President represented another crowning achievement for the hard-driving Byoir and his able, energetic crew. In 1935, the Birthday Ball was repeated with even more flourish. Byoir won his bet with the President by raising more than $1 million in gross receipts and the tie, with the initials FDR woven into it, became a prized possession. The mass media were saturated with publicity urging support of the President and the battle against polio. Byoir again took command as general director and did the work while his client, Henry L. Doherty, took the public bows.

Byoir's firm again provided the publicity support. The nation was told by press, radio, poster, town assembly, newsreel, telegram, telephone, and letter that President Roosevelt "has given his 53rd birthday to the cause of Infantile Paralysis which means the present welfare and future safety of American children." This time, to spur broader local support, the Birthday Ball Committee announced that 70% of the receipts would stay in the community where they were raised and 30% would go to the newly organized Commission on Infantile Paralysis Research, also headed by Colonel Doherty. None of the money would go to Warm Springs Foundation this time. The decision to share the funds with the community and to start support of research was attributed to the President in the Birthday Ball releases.

Day and night for 2 months, Byoir, Gerry Swinehart, Jane Buck, George Hammond, and others of his staff publicized the President's Birthday Ball. Newspaper publishers across the nation were again asked to foster affairs for their cities and towns and to encourage more community participation. Placards were placed in the nation's show windows, in the New York subways, and on motorbuses. Howard Chandler Christy again painted a campaign poster. Radio personalities were encouraged to repeat the appeal again and again, and they did. Newsreels reached movie audiences with publicity messages weeks before the celebration. Everywhere people turned, they were reminded that they should "dance so that a child may someday walk." Big city hotels and country schools furnished ballrooms. Even country barns were dusted out and used for square dances. There was no end to the ideas dreamed up at the local level to gather crowds and raise money to fight polio.

When all the celebrations had ended and the expenses had been paid, only something like $750,856, according to Keith Morgan, had been realized in the 1935 Roosevelt birthday parties. Total receipts were not announced until November 19, when Colonel Doherty notified President Roosevelt at a White House luncheon that a gross total of $1,071,000 had been raised. FDR presented Byoir with the victory tie at this luncheon. Byoir, Doherty,

Morgan, and O'Connor went ahead with plans for a third fund-raising celebration on January 30, 1936. Doherty made the official announcement on December 3 and again appointed Byoir as general director, Morgan as committee treasurer, and Steve Flynn as executive secretary. The same organization went at the task with the same basic plan, including a split of receipts with the local communities, exploiting the same publicity patterns of appeals to help crippled children and demonstrate support of the President. The biggest innovation in the 1936 Birthday Ball celebrations came from George Allen, who brought the magic of Hollywood to them. "This movie star thing grew like wildfire."

To promote the 1936 Birthday Ball celebration, in the year that Roosevelt was up for reelection, Byoir and his staff asked Howard Chandler Christy to paint his third official poster for the programs, billboards, and placards; got the advertising agencies and major advertisers to contribute ads and space to publish them; announced the balls over every radio station and through every major program; issued reams of copy for press and periodical; developed new sequences for the newsreels; and publicized harder if perhaps more routinely. Colonel Doherty repeatedly pleaded, through Byoir's publicity, that "only nation-wide generosity can remedy the plight of the nation's 300,000 infantile paralysis victims" and repeatedly reminded Americans that "from the scourge of 1935 . . . this dread disease added approximately 10,000 victims to its rolls." One of the reasons that it was relatively easy to dramatize the threat of polio was the fact that it was an epidemic disease and, unlike heart disease or cancer, periodically dominated the nation's front pages.

One new promotional idea was introduced to give support to the 1936 balls — that of sponsored advertising. This was in the days before institutional advertising for public relations purposes had become as widespread as it did in World War II and thereafter. To promote the idea, Byoir and his staff put out the *Bulletin* in newspaper format with promotional ads of varying sizes that enterprising advertising salesmen could sell to local merchants and other business firms. The 14-page promotional newspaper, distributed to local committees, advertisers, and advertising agencies, also carried news stories and news pictures that could be and were utilized in local publicity campaigns. The *Bulletin* was produced by the William H. Rankin Co., which also produced the annual *Birthday Magazine*, another money raiser. A review of the 1936 publicity effort indicated that some 10 million lines of advertising costing $1 million had been contributed by commercial advertisers to promote the sale of Birthday Ball tickets. Byoir asserted that this was the first fund-raising effort to receive the benefit of sponsoring advertising, an invalid claim. But it was certainly the most intensive use of paid advertising for fund-raising up to that time.

Yet, despite the million dollars worth of advertising and the millions of dollars worth of free publicity that Byoir's staff obtained, the 1936 Birthday Ball was less successful than the first two. News reports, obviously stemming from the Doherty Committee, put the gross receipts at $1.5 million a few days after the party. Doherty later said the gross receipts totaled $750,000. In 1937, Keith Morgan said the 1936 receipts were $572,756. Again the receipts were shared, with 70% staying in the community where it was raised and 30% going to research. This fact made accurate accounting of amounts collected difficult.

Doubts about the declining popularity of President Roosevelt and the waning power of the President's Birthday Ball as a money raiser were convincingly dissipated by FDR's overwhelming reelection in November 1936 when he carried every state except two. In the wake of this sweeping triumph at the polls, Colonels Doherty and Byoir and Warm Springs Foundation officials O'Connor and Morgan began to make plans for the 1937 Birthday Ball.

Carl Byoir again took charge of the fund-raising promotion as executive director. His firm sent out reams of publicity copy and placed scores of plugs with columnists and radio personalities. Again Howard Chandler Christy contributed an official poster and program cover. Once more the people were told, "The proceeds of all these entertainments—every cent of them—go to carry on the fight against infantile paralysis. Seventy percent remains in the community which raises it, to support local hospitals that treat the disease and its after effects. The remaining thirty percent goes to Warm Springs Foundation in Georgia where so much is being learned about the treatment for disabled victims. A great deal of money is needed." This time the Byoir staff estimated that some 6,000 events drawing 5 million persons were held across the nation and even on the foreign soil of Bermuda. In 1937, $1 million was raised in gross receipts.

In a statement issued September 14, 1937, Chairman Doherty said that a gross of $1,000,779 had been realized in the 1937 celebrations. Of this amount, $325,000 had been sent to the National Committee from 3,591 communities and another $15,000 was expected before the books were closed. Doherty reported that Western Union and Postal Telegraph had, between them, raised $80,106.19 from the birthday greeting messages sent to President Roosevelt. The colonel explained that he had given $50,000 to underwrite the expenses of the 1937 birthday party. This presumably is the same $50,000 he announced as a gift to the National Committee on January 30, when he wrote President Roosevelt that "I want to support your own leadership in raising both flood and paralysis relief funds." The 1937 polio fund-raising came in the midst of the tragic floods in the Ohio and Mississippi River valleys. The Red Cross was appealing for flood relief money at the same time that Byoir was appealing for money to battle polio. The Doherty gift, duly publicized by Byoir, was apparently an effort to prod people to give to both causes and make them appear noncompetitive.

Although the Birthday Balls had once more grossed more than $1 million, there continued to be a rumble of criticism, both within and without the foundation. Dr. Michael Hoke, surgeon-in-chief at Warm Springs, was deeply pained by the emotional appeals Byoir and his aides used to promote the polio crusade. Dr. Hoke was angry that the medical methods used at his institution had been publicized, dismayed that patients had been interviewed on the radio, horrified that polio sufferers throughout the country had been misled to think that they could come to Warm Springs, where there was no room for them, and be cured, which was impossible." Other physicians were unhappy about the high hopes raised by the Byoir-directed campaigns. Republican editors continuing to carp at the idea of linking a political leader with a philanthropic appeal made it clear that another plan was needed.

At this point, Carl Byoir resigned. His associates give two reasons: first, his break with Roosevelt over the President's effort to "pack" the Supreme Court early in 1937 and second, what he considered Roosevelt's ingratitude to Doherty in refusing to name him a trustee of the about-to-be-formed National Foundation for Infantile Paralysis. Byoir had been an enthusiastic political supporter of Roosevelt from 1930 on.

In 1936, Byoir raised large sums for the Democratic National Committee with his Roosevelt nominators plan whereby a person could join in the nomination of Roosevelt by signing a nomination certificate and contributing a minimum of $1. As part of this fund-raising campaign, Byoir staged Nominator Rallies across the nation to coincide with Roosevelt's ringing acceptance speech in Franklin Field on June 27, 1936, the speech in which he introduced the stinging epithet "economic royalist." And certainly one of these was Doherty. In appreciation of Byoir's efforts, Roosevelt wrote him this letter under the date of July 10, 1936:

Dear Carl:

I am just off to start my cruise but I do want to send you this line to tell you how much I appreciate all that you did in organizing the "Roosevelt Nominators." I know what a tremendous amount of hard work this entailed, and I hope much that you are going to get a little holiday yourself. My thanks to you and my very best wishes. I hope I shall see you soon.

Byoir ultimately became a Republican and, at different times, a vigorous supporter of Senator Robert A. Taft and Governor Thomas E. Dewey for the Presidency.

Surely another factor in Byoir's decision to retire from Birthday Ball campaigning was the fact that the pattern had become routine, and the task had lost its challenge. In the estimate of his associates, Byoir was primarily an idea man and an organizer; once a challenge had been met and solved Byoir, tended to lose interest in it. He was not a detail man and needed the fresh stimulation of new tasks to keep going at his fast pace.

No one can surely ascribe the motives that move men, but it appears that Doherty and Byoir got the deep satisfaction that comes from promoting a worthwhile cause and much favorable personal publicity for their efforts, but nothing more from a canny Franklin D. Roosevelt. In his final appearance as executive director of the Birthday Balls, Byoir told the 1937 nationwide radio audience and the celebrants, "You are the painters of rainbows in lives clouded by pain and sickness and lost hope." The real painter of the brilliant hues in those rainbows of hope had been Carl Byoir. As the key force in raising more than $4 million that underwrote the beginnings of research that ultimately eliminated the scourge of polio, Carl Byoir left another large mark on his nation.

BYOIR MOVES INTO THE BIG LEAGUES — AND MORE LITIGATION

Carl Byoir's successful management of the Henry L. Doherty Florida properties and his "glorious success" in raising millions to fight polio appeared to effectively dissipate the clouds of the German tourist account and build a reputation for CB&A that it was a "no-nonsense, can do outfit." Typical of the way big industrial accounts started coming to the agency is that of Libby–Owens–Ford (LOF). John D. Biggers, then president of LOF, first met Byoir in 1936 in Miami when the former was working on an FDR-sponsored commission for census of the unemployed. Biggers later recalled that he was greatly impressed with Byoir's "obvious confidence and competence in handling this presidential press detail." Biggers was particularly impressed with his easy access to Steve Early and Marvin McIntyre, FDR's press secretaries, with whom Byoir had worked in World War I. The synergy of contacts! These impressions led Biggers to engage the Byoir firm as LOF's "outside" public relations counsel in 1938 at the annual fee of $36,000—then the highest figure among PR agencies. In the view of Biggers and other clients obtained in the late 1930s, Byoir, had established through performance that his public relations concepts had practicality when applied to the problems facing Big Business, still very much in the public doghouse as the Depression endured.

After Carl Dickey's departure, Byoir reorganized his firm in 1936. Byoir took the positions of chairman and president in name as well as in fact. Gerry Swinehart was named general manager and given commensurate authority. George Hammond and Jane Buck, early staff members of the firm, remembered that Swinehart, a hard driving, talented, no-nonsense executive, brought a new atmosphere to CB&A. Byoir's secretary, Elsie Simon, recalled that "Mr. Byoir always felt that Mr. Swinehart provided the perfect complement to his own managerial interests. Byoir was not a detail person, Swinehart was." In 1936, stung by the German tourist experience, the firm turned to corporate counseling and industrial public relations. In 1936, CB&A was retained by B. F. Goodrich to win stockholder approval of a reorganization plan. Goodrich remained as a major Byoir account into the 1970s. Other clients landed by CB&A in this period included Freeport Sulphur Company of Louisiana; Schenley Industries, liquor distillers; and Chrysler cars. Dickey thought that Byoir's work in introducing Chrysler's Airflow design had made *streamlining* a common word in our language. Also, this period brought the Great Atlantic and Pacific Tea Co. (A&P) into the Byoir portfolio, an account that demonstrated the gathering power of public relations-and brought Byoir more painful litigation.

It was Byoir's work for the Freeport Sulphur Company that brought the A&P account. The Freeport firm had large sulphur deposits in Louisiana and Texas. In 1936, the Louisiana legislature raised the sulphur severance tax from $.60 to $2.00 per ton. Freeport Sulphur feared that this might bring a similar increase in Texas. Freeport Sulphur was the only such firm in Louisiana, thus any effort to repeal or reduce this tax increase would appear to benefit only one private company. Byoir's research found that the tax increase had widespread political support.

Carl Byoir's executives chose to use the third party technique in this campaign, one that faced long odds for its defeat. Byoir recalled in his unfinished autobiography, "We planned a campaign to show that the tax was not merely against the company but against the interests of the whole economy of the state. It was not merely a publicity campaign. It was a campaign of organizing those groups in the state which represented large segments of [Louisiana] public opinion; permitting them to take a stand against the tax and permitting . . . [CB&A] to publicize their positions."

Byoir's persuasion efforts were focused on women's groups, labor groups, businessmen's trade and commercial associations, suppliers' groups—in fact any group that the Byoir people could persuade to oppose the tax. Louisiana legislators started hearing from opinion leaders that they had made a mistake. They got the message. The legislature rescinded the earlier legislation and replaced it with a $1.03 tax, the same as that of neighboring Texas. This amazing reversal did not go unnoticed in business circles. Successful use of the third party technique that Byoir had developed in the Creel Committee continued to be a part of the CB&A repertoire—one that brought criticism and litigation.

In the volatile political atmosphere of the Depression when all basic institution were under attack, a movement emerged to tax chain stores as governments desperately sought new revenues for their depleted treasuries. This movement gained political momentum as a way of saving the friendly neighborhood grocer—the one who would deliver your groceries and extend credit to customers hard hit by the Depression. Among the exploiters of this movement was a Louisiana broadcaster, "Old Man" Henderson, who went about the country organizing boycotts of chain stores. In 1933, at the depth of the Depression, only two states had antichain store taxes. In 1936, the brothers John and George Hartford, sole owners of A&P, took this position on such taxes, "If the people of the United States like our stores so little that they are willing to tax us out of business, that is their affair. We will shut up our shop."

In 1936, Rep. Wright Patman of Texas and Senator Joseph E. Robinson of Arkansas introduced into Congress a bill to amend the Clayton Anti-Trust Act that took dead aim at the large-scale buying practices of the chain stores and large mail order houses. *Business Week* reported that Patman had "heard the cry of the little wholesale jobbers and grocery brokers for protection against the [unfair competition of the chain stores.]" By 1938, 22 states had antichain store taxes on their books. The Hartford brothers changed their minds—emphatically so—and came to realize that they must fight "fire with fire" and retained Carl Byoir & Associates on October 1, 1937, to campaign for repeal or modification of antichain store taxes as Byoir had done so successfully for the Freeport Sulphur Company.

Byoir's first task was to obtain defeat of an antichain store tax then pending in the State Legislature of New York. This bill, if passed, would cost A&P $2 million, $1,000 per store for its 2,000 stores in the Empire State.

Byoir did such a successful job that this bill never got out of committee. Once more he used his technique of organizing third party groups to oppose the legislation. In a speech to the Association of Advertising Men on November 10, 1938, Byoir advised:

> "Now the most you can do is get out material . . . for organizations simply giving them the fact story of their interests in the chain store. . . . We [in CB&A] think that the far-sighted thing is to examine the other man's interest [to find where it coincides with your client's interest]. We made no appeal for the chain stores as such. We say to the farmer, "This is part of your market machinery. If it serves you, keep it." . . . We say to the farmer, "Here is the question; study it. If we are wrong, be against us."

This victory brought a solid relationship between the Byoir firm and the Hartford brothers. Gerry Swinehart once told me, "This was a sweetheart of an account. You dealt directly with the brothers without any go-betweens or lawyers. Once they oked an ad, that was it."

The Byoir firm's next step was to undertake a nationwide fact-finding search for data on taxes levied against food supermarkets, either direct or indirect taxes. CB&A also undertook consumer polls to gauge opinion among A&P customers. This was in a year when the public opinion poll, first introduced in the 1936 Presidential election, was a rarely used technique by PR agencies. The polls found a strange paradox: A&P's customers liked the stores because of their low prices and good quality but at the same time favored higher taxes on the chains. This dictated a campaign to make the grocery shopper aware that higher taxes would inevitably be reflected in higher food costs. Confronted with this data, the Hartford brothers retained CB&A for another year and accepted an increase in retainer fee to $75,000—the highest known fee among PR firms.

Using the data gathered in the tax surveys and opinion polls, CB&A launched a large-scale campaign to inform selected segments of the public that these taxes were unfair to their interests as well as to the interests of the A&P. Byoir saw to it that these data got to consumer groups across the nation. The "hidden tax" was used in New York by a group called the Consumer's Tax Committee, headed by Mrs. William Sporburg. In an emotion-rousing presentation to women's groups, Mrs. Sporburg proclaimed that there were "53 taxes on the daily loaf of bread that everyone must buy, 57 taxes on every quart of milk." That Byoir was the source of this statement was revealed in the July 1939 *Public Opinion Quarterly*. In May 1938, a Byoir agent inspired a tax rebellion among the students attending Rensselaer Polytechnic Institute in Troy, NY.

In addition to these third party techniques, the Byoir was the first agency to utilize the power of newspaper advertising in a public relations campaign. At Byoir's urging, the Hartford brothers published a personally signed newspaper ad that set forth in strong language their plan and their reason for opposing the Patman antichain store tax. The ad first appeared in 26 newspapers in New York state on September 15, 1938, and on the basis of favorable reactions the ad was published nationwide on October 6. Headed "A STATEMENT OF PUBLIC POLICY BY THE GREAT ATLANTIC AND PACIFIC TEA COMPANY," the ad was five columns wide, 15 inches deep. This ad marked the complete reversal of the Hartfords' 1933 threat "to shut up shop." In his 1950 speech to the Advertising Men's Association quoted earlier, Byoir said of this innovative technique:

My own first use . . . of extensive newspaper advertising as a dynamic force to obtain a definite and specific objective rather than the building of general good will, was in the case of the Patman chain store tax. . . . We made a survey in Utica, New York, and found that 58 percent of the customers of the chain stores thought that the chain stores should be specifically taxed. . . . The public relations problem was intensified because we were dealing with legislation . . . Actually, while that ad ran in papers of some 40 million total circulation [at a cost of $280,000], it was intended to be read by the legislators [in various states] and by members of Congress "over the shoulders of the public."

Thus, Carl Byoir and his lieutenants brought the public relations ad to counseling. Such advertising now is a major tool and cost in public affairs issues.

In the ad, the Hartford brothers took this tack, "We have arrived at the decision that we would be doing less than our full duty if we failed to oppose, by every fair means, legislation proposed by the Honorable Wright Patman." The advertisement also explained the ret ention of the Byoir firm, "Since the task we have set before us is one involving the widest dissemination of complete information to all of the American people, and since this is a profession in which we are not expert, we have engaged Carl Byoir & Associates, public relations counsel, to do this work." *Printer's Ink* in its issue of October 13, 1938, observed, "Clearly, this is a new approach. It embodies the first complete and public statement of the public relations method of a business organization of major importance." Thus, the ad did more than serve A&P's cause, it brought attention to a still emerging business – public relations counseling.

With this A&P policy statement, Byoir and his associates set out to turn the tide of public opinion in favor of chain stores in general and the A&P in particular. Byoir organized Business Organization, Inc. in separate offices at 10 East 40th Street, to handle the organization of consumer groups against the taxes and antichain store legislation and to continue the consumer research. He directed that the A&P financially aid an organization in Trenton, NJ, The Emergency Consumer's Tax Council that represented women shoppers in more than 100 communities. In May 1959, *The New York Times* reported the statement of a Dr. R. W. Ayers that the A&P was financially assisting the National Consumer's Tax Commission that had 4,000 subsidiary chapters across the nation.

On July 7, 1939, *The Times* published information provided in a release from Byoir that during the first half of 1939, legislators in 26 states either killed or adjourned without taking action on proposed antichain store tax bills; chain store tax levies had been held unconstitutional in Kentucky, Pennsylvania, and New Jersey. Repeal of antichain store taxes was being pushed in Michigan, Texas, and Wisconsin; 34 states had considered and rejected more than 60 chain store tax proposals; not one new state had been added to the antichain store tax roster. The Byoir release trumpeted a complete shift in the legislative trend, proclaiming a great public relations victory.

The victory was made complete when the bill of Rep. Wright Patman was defeated in the Congress. Hearings on the Patman bill began in March 1940 and concluded May 11, during which a powerful array of opponents mobilized by CB&A testified against the bill. The Congressional subcommittee that had conducted the hearings voted on June 19, 1940 to reject Patman's proposal. This brought the vitriolic denunciation of Byoir by Patman on the House floor, mentioned earlier.

Byoir was denounced as a Nazi sympathizer and propagandist and as a "front man for Big Business." Speaking on the House floor where he was immune to libel suits, the Texas congressman demanded that Byoir be investigated by the House Un-American Activities Committee and by the Department of Justice. Patman charged that Byoir's "front" activities were probably illegal because he was a lieutenant colonel in the Army Reserve. Byoir vigorously denied Patman's "espionage" charge and asked for a full investigation to clear his name. He also wrote a letter of protest on June 3, 1940, to his Commander-in-Chief, President Roosevelt, whose friendship and gratitude he had earned in directing the President's Birthday Balls. Byoir was investigated by the Federal Bureau of Investigation as the result of Patman's charges, obviously born of malice, and cleared of any wrongdoing by the U.S. Department of Justice on July 17, 1940. The press generally came to Byoir's defense. The New York Herald–Tribune editorialized under a head, "AN UN-AMERICAN EPISODE," that "the Department of Justice is to be congratulated on its prompt and incisive action in investigating and scotching the baseless charges of un-American activities against Mr. Carl Byoir." It lamented the "needless hysteria in the nation." Byoir and his associates always had strong, cordial working relationships with journalists. Byoir also went through two investigations by the notorious Dies Committee before he was done with Wright Patman's charges. The 1933 German tourist account carried a long shadow indeed.

But Byoir was not done with the fallout from CB&A's successful campaign for A&P.

A SIMILAR CAMPAIGN WINS IN CALIFORNIA

A similar and equally successful campaign against a chain store tax was waged in 1936 in California under the direction of Don Francisco, then executive vice-president of Lord & Thomas. The California Chain Stores Association retained Lord & Thomas to defeat Proposition 22 that would put a $500 tax per store on all stores in a chain above nine. In all probability, Francisco was retained for this referendum because just 2 years earlier, he had helped in a successful campaign to defeat Upton Sinclair, the muckraking journalist, for governor of California. The referendum was to be voted on in the general election of November 3, 1936. The campaign between the independents and the chains was a spirited and expensive one, again illustrating why California's system of reliance on referenda for making laws provided a fertile breeding ground for the emergence of the political publicist.

Francisco explained the popularity of such a tax in a speech to the Safeway Division managers in San Francisco on November 30, 1936—after the election—this way:

> Why were the chains vulnerable? The principal reason was that they suffered from the current antagonism to all big business. After the election, a survey was made in an effort to determine why people voted for or against the chain store tax. Among those voting in favor of the tax, 43 percent gave reasons that might be summarized as "against big business" and 27 percent gave reasons that might be summarized as "soak the rich." The chains were rowing against strong tides.

But row successfully they did. Francisco and his staff developed the slogan "22 is a Tax on You" and chose to disregard their opponents' charges and instead to launched a counterattack that was "so vigorous that our opponents were put on the defensive." He made it a rule to never attack the independent merchants. Like Byoir, Francisco set out to build a coalition of supporters who had a common interest with the chains—employees, farmers, renters of store properties, and so forth. Francisco and Byoir pioneered today's common public relations strategy of coalition building. Francisco said in his Safeway speech, "We concentrated to develop these 'naturals' to the utmost as the nucleus of our army of 'No' voters, realizing that there were other groups where a majority would be against us and could not be converted in a one year campaign."

Even in this early day of public relations, Francisco recognized the importance of research. "One of our first tasks was to build a library containing all the pertinent data on chain stores and chain stores taxes. It was important that our facts and figures be accurate and beyond dispute. We published a handbook for our workers and chain store members containing all the facts and arguments that might be demanded during the campaign." Like Byoir's A&P campaign, the Lord & Thomas campaign, understandably, placed heavy reliance on newspaper and radio advertising. For radio, it developed the "California's Hour," "an obvious natural for our purpose so we made it the official voice of California's chain stores. Each week we saluted one California city or county, delivering a tribute to that community. . . . During the year we ran three essay contests in connection with California's Hour." The newspaper advertising hammered away at the chains' slogan, "22 is a Tax on You." In the last 2 months, all stops were pulled out and all media used from billboards to streetcar cards to bumper stickers. The chain store tax lost in 57 out of California's 58 counties.

Francisco concluded in his Safeway speech that by this campaign, "the chain stores of California not only defeated the . . . tax, but they improved their relations with their employees, farmers, and customers, and made themselves better understood and increased their sales." He saw this as the lesson of this campaign against Proposition 22: "Business can protect itself by first demonstrating and telling how it serves America, and then by showing how unfair legislation handicaps its ability to render that service."

Don Francisco was later promoted to the presidency of Lord & Thomas, leaving it when the agency was sold to Foote, Cone, and Belding to become vice-president of the J. Walter Thompson agency. He died October 25, 1973, at the age of 84.

Did Byoir know of and study the California campaign? There is no evidence that he and Gerry Swinehart copied from the Lord & Thomas work. George Hammond, who had joined Byoir a few years earlier, told me, "Not to my knowledge," when questioned on this point.

THE A&P LITIGATION

The Byoir campaign to turn the tide against state and national antichain store tax proved to be only a "battle," not the "war." The campaign and its use of the third party technique was put on trial by the U.S. Department of Justice. On November 25, 1942, a Federal Grand Jury in the U.S. District Court of Dallas, Texas, returned an indictment of the A&P, 12 of its subsidiary companies, its corporate officers, Carl Byoir, and the corporate firm, Business Organizations, Inc. The indictment charged violations of the Sherman Anti-Trust Act. The government alleged that A&P had suppressed competition from independent grocers through price wars, had consorted with manufacturers and other chain stores to fix prices, and had obtained discriminatory buying preference over competitors. This indictment also alleged that a public relations practitioner and his corporate research and analysis unit, Business Organization, Inc., had also violated the Sherman Anti-Trust Act. To indict the public relations counsel for his services to a client was the first such legal action known. The defendants promptly submitted a general demurrer, and Carl Byoir's petition asked that the government specify how his conduct of public relations violated the Sherman Act. On February 13, 1943, Judge William E. Atwell sustained the demurrers and quashed the indictments against all defendants. The Justice Department appealed the judge's decision to the Fifth U. S. Circuit Court of Appeals, New Orleans. The judicial panel reversed the dismissal of the A&P indictments but approved dismissal of the indictments against Byoir and Business Organization, Inc. In a landmark for public relations counseling, the court ruled, "The only factual allegation in the indictment even inferentially connecting these defendants with the other defendants is that 'said defendants' are public relations counsel for the A&P group. No facts are alleged to show that they committed any act, overt or otherwise, or that they dealt in food products."

Thus began the long debate, still in progress, in American courts and professional journals as to what responsibility the public relations counselor has for the behavior of his or her clients. Unlike the established precedents of law where the lawyer is regarded only as a counselor and pleader of the cause, not a coconspirator.

The Department of Justice, given Judge Atwell's earlier ruling, requested a *nolle prosequi* (equivalent to dismissal) in the Dallas Federal Court and filed an information (the equivalent of an indictment not requiring the presentation of evidence to a Grand Jury) in the U.S. District Court of Danville, Illinois. *Business Week* editorialized, "The trust busters had decided that Dallas was no place to try A&P." Carl Byoir and Business Organization, Inc. were again included in the criminal charges. This time, the Department of Justice was more specific in its charges against A&P and Byoir. Byoir and his subsidiary were specifically charged with assisting A&P in dominating fruit and vegetable growers and shippers by organizing "cooperative shipper and grower associations" and thereby increasing A&P's economic power in produce markets.

The trial of A&P and its codefendants began on April 16, 1945 — $2\frac{1}{2}$ years subsequent to the indictments in Dallas. The trial, which lasted 89 court days, was heard by Judge Walter C. Lindley without a jury. When the trial ended, the court had accumulated some 50,000 pages of testimony and exhibits. September 21, 1946, Judge Lindley found all but three lesser A&P officials guilty of certain criminal misdemeanors. Also, the defendants were found not guilty of a number of the allegations. In the matter of the use of false fronts, the judge's verdict was a bit cloudy. He ruled that Byoir and the A&P had not made clear to the public the full extent of A&P's support of third party groups but that had no relation as to whether the defendants had violated Section 1 and 2 of the Sherman Anti-Trust Act. For what he deemed violations of the Sherman Act, Judge Lindley fined A&P $175,000 and Byoir $5,000. The judge's Byoir opinion, which had serious implications for all public relations counselors, read in part:

> It is probably true that many actions of the defendants of which the government complains, standing alone, are devoid of wrongful character, but when the fabric woven from them is considered as whole and it appears contaminated by a single tainted thread running throughout the completed texture, the whole becomes a tainted product and all partaking in its creation,

having voluntarily contributed to the structure, are charged with responsibility for the fabrication.

Judge Lindley's opinion indicates that A&P and CB&A did operate, on some occasions, through spokesmen or groups that did not identify their connection with A&P and Carl Byoir. Whether A&P and Byoir invoked such concealment through overt deceit is not at all plain in the opinion. It did not argue that A&P or Carl Byoir deliberately conceived and directed a deceitful effort to delude the public.

The judge's final sentence read, "What, if anything, those activities [on the part of CB&A] have to do with innocence or guilt is another question." Thus, the legality of the use of the third party technique, then and now still common in public affairs campaigns by business, government, political candidates, and public relations professionals, was left unresolved.

All defendants found guilty by Judge Lindley appealed his decision to U.S. Court of Appeals Seventh Circuit in Chicago. Judge Sherman Minton, later appointed to the U.S. Supreme Court, handed down the opinion of the three-judge panel. He noted that all defendants had been convicted in the lower court "of conspiracy to restrain and to monopolize trade, in violation of Sections 1 and 2 of the Sherman Act." Minton's opinion did not discuss false fronts in specific terms, thus leaving this technique's legality unresolved. The Seventh Circuit court affirmed the findings of Judge Lindley and conviction of all defendants, corporate and otherwise, on February 24, 1949.

The criminal proceedings were not the end of the A&P litigation. Getting a drop on the defendants, Attorney General J. Howard McGrath issued a lengthy press release on September 15, 1949, "to announce the filing of a civil antitrust suit against the A&P food chain." The suit was to break up the A&P food chain and force a separation of its buying and selling from its manufacturing and processing business. The Department of Justice's action followed logically from Judge Lindley's earlier opinion. Byoir and Business Organizations, Inc. were not charged in this lawsuit. Five days after the filing, CB&A launched a massive paid advertising campaign to explain A&P's side of the case. The ads asked 2,000 daily and weekly newspaper readers in these headlines: "DO YOU WANT TO PUT YOUR A&P OUT OF BUSINESS?" and "DO YOU WANT HIGHER PRICES?"

The full campaign argued that if the government's civil suit succeeded, A&P, as its customers knew it, would be put out of business. Byoir stressed the message in these words, "Why Do They Want to Put A&P Out of Business? They say . . . and these are the anti-trust lawyers' own words . . . that we have 'regularly under-sold competing retailers.' To this charge we plead guilty." Such ads continued on a weekly basis. Justice Department lawyers denounced the ads as "propaganda" and warned that A&P and Byoir were risking contempt of court action. Byoir never denied that in fulfilling the role of public relations counselor it is often necessary to act as a *propagandist*. He never saw any need to dodge the term as many public relations persons did then and do now. As he told a Congressional committee on one occasion *propaganda* is a very large word. Understandably, when Carl Byoir first used it in support of World War I, it was a patriotic word. But by the 1930s, it had become a corroded and pejorative word.

The A&P civil suit hung in limbo from 1949 until 1954 in a New York Southern District U.S. Court. The government made no effort to bring it to trial. The newspaper ads, newspaper editorial support, letters, resolutions of organized groups, and other expressions of public opinion made it clear that CB&A had won the public opinion battle if not the legal battle. On January 19, 1954, 11 years after the original indictments in Dallas, Department of Justice lawyers agreed to a consent decree offered by A&P that left A&P in essentially the same market position it had held when the litigation started 15 years earlier. An economist, Morris Adelman of MIT, termed the consent decree "a sweeping victory for the defense." *Business Week* reported, "The government's famous anti-trust suit against the Great Atlantic & Pacific Tea Co., begun with fanfare back in 1949, ended this week without any fireworks, a consent decree that didn't do too much damage to the huge retaining chain."

It had also been a triumphant public relations victory for the Carl Byoir organization, one that brought it new clients and new prestige. In a landmark article, "Business is Still in Trouble," in May 1949, *Fortune* gave this accolade to Byoir's work for A&P, "The chain grocery stores are the epitome of good business public relations – i.e. good performance that's understood and appreciated [by the public]."

But the publicity of the litigation and Byoir's conviction of a misdemeanor, like the German tourist account before, continued to cast a long shadow of unfavorable publicity over Byoir until his death. Terming the Byoir-authored campaign *psychological warfare,* J. Begeman wrote in the November 14, 1949, *The New Republic:*

> The A&P has poured $5 million into its campaign, running full-page ads in daily newspapers across the nation and in most of the most important weeklies. Copies of these ads are blown up to poster size and put in the A&P stores and in grocery bags. . . . Virtually all of the newspapers in the Scripps-Howard, Hearst, and Gannett chains followed up the ads with editorials in support of A&P. . . . But when Attorney General J. Howard McGrath and his assistant, Herbert A. Bergson, criticized . . . the campaign, few newspapers gave them more than one paragraph.

Then Begeman criticized Byoir for "A typical deception found in the A&P ad which reads 'They say . . . and these are the anti-trust lawyers own words . . . that "we have regularly undersold competing retailers' " "and then Begeman noted that these words had been taken totally out of context from the government's charge.

Writing in *The Reporter* magazine of June 10, 1952, Spencer Klaw reviewed the testimony from the Danville trial in a negative light. He gave this example of Byoir's creation and use of a front group:

> The most imposing of these was the National Consumers Tax Commission, ostensibly organized to study "hidden taxes" — among them of course, taxes on chain stores. At one point N.C.T.C. claimed 650,000 members, divided into 6,000 study groups. The degree of independence it enjoyed is indicated by the fact that the A&P had laid out a total of $411,323.69 for the N.C.T.C. while contributions from all other sources added up to only $2200. 'The organization was in effect, a creation of the defendants.'

Klaw's piece, which also recounted the German tourist account, was typical of the continuing unfavorable publicity Byoir got from his work for the A&P.

Gerry Swinehart issued a memorandum to the Byoir staff on January 4, 1945, to review Byoir's testimony in the Danville trial that "threw a bright, clear light on some of the outstanding phases of our philosophy." The memo quoted Byoir as stating, "Our concept of public relations is that it is an advisory service on all those questions of policy in the client company that involve the making of good or ill will with the public, or relations with labor and labor organizations, with their suppliers, with their customers, and in the case of corporate enterprises, with their owners, the stockholders." In another place, Byoir testified "that Carl Byoir & Associates was primarily an advisory organization on public relations programs, a specialized machinery for use of publicity as a tool of business relations." Still in another place, he elaborated, "We had a highly specialized service because we believed that when a company had right policies, they ought to let the public know about them, and we had built machinery for that purpose."

An irony in the long litigation is one that public relations practitioners can best appreciate. Byoir, Swinehart, and Al McMillan, a vice-president who worked on the account, had the ideal relationship with the Hartford Brothers and Ralph Burger, president of A&P, a relationship that was open, candid, and mutually respectful. Yet in the trials, Byoir had to testify that he did not make nor influence A&P policy.

THE RAILROAD–TRUCKERS BRAWL

A bitter public opinion battle, termed by *Fortune* as "The Railroad-Truckers Brawl," between the Pennsylvania truckers, served by David

Charnay's Allied Public Relations Associates, and the Eastern Railroads, served by the Byoir firm, brought more litigation and unfavorable public attention to Byoir and his firm. But it also brought freedom for what Justice Hugo Black termed "no holds barred" public relations battles.

Carl Byoir was not in the forefront of this campaign as he had been in the A&P fight against antichain legislation. The Eastern Railroads account came to CB&A after Byoir had relinquished day-to-day management to Gerry Swinehart. He testified in the pretrial hearing in U. S. Federal District Court that he was now active in only three accounts, A&P, Libbey–Owens–Ford Glass Co., and RCA–NBC. "I prefer to let men who got the accounts work on them."

After World War II, the trucking industry grew rapidly, raising trucks' share of ton-miles of freight hauled from about 4% to 12%. This increased affluence of the industry led to increased political influence that the trucking associations began using to get state legislation to permit larger and larger trucks on their highways. This inevitably led to lobbying and public relations battles with the railroads. In 1949–1950, the Pennsylvania Motor Truck Association (PMTA) was strong enough to get the Pennsylvania House of Representatives to raise truck weight limitations from 45,000 pounds to 60,000 pounds, but the PMTA could not muster enough votes to push the bill through the Senate.

This partial legislative success convinced the Eastern Railroads Presidents Conference (ERPC) that it needed public relations counsel to cope with the growing power of the trucking associations. In May 1949, the ERPC asked several public relations firms to make presentations for such a campaign. Several firms, including Hill and Knowlton, Inc., did so. The Byoir presentation, which stressed its success in the Freeport Sulphur and A&P campaigns, won the account. Byoir was granted a $75,000 retainer fee and a budget of $300,000 for expenses. These figures were later the source of critical comment for spending such sums to "influence" legislators. The ERPC spokesman, David Mackie, retorted, "That [amount] is picayunish for a $40 billion industry."

Although this chapter focuses on the Byoir firm and the volumes of unfavorable publicity the brawl produced, to put matters in perspective it should be recorded that Byoir executives worked hand-in-glove with Thomas J. Deegan, public relations vice-president for the Eastern Railroads Presidents Conference, and T. J. Ross of T. J. Ross & Associates, who was outside counsel for the ERPC. In effect this was a joint effort spearheaded by three public relations stalwarts of the post-World War II period.

The CB&A campaign plan in support of the railroads read in part:

> The public is only a collective name for countless groups of people, many of whom have bonds of common interest. In terms of our objectives, our

subsidiary goals include informing, organizing and activating as many legitimate, strong and politically aggressive groups as already exist, or that can be brought into existence for their own self-interest. . . . The public and its separate parts must be informed by a purposeful barrage of continuing publicity.

This represents a classic expression of Carl Byoir's third party technique. Kalman Druck, who was with the Byoir firm from 1939 to 1957, insisted on numerous occasions that in that time he never heard Byoir suggest that he created a false front as a public relations strategy. Druck said, "Carl Byoir's purpose was always to form 'common fronts,' or make 'common cause' with interests coincident with those of his client."

Reynolds Girdler, the ERPC account executive, wrote a later memorandum that a became the focus of much of the testimony in the ensuing litigation. It read in part:

Specifically, we must write all publicity in terms of the self-interest of certain groups. This publicity must be aimed at Motor Groups, Real Estate Boards, and individual owners, Economy Groups, Service Clubs, Safety Groups, City and County Officials, Rural Road Improvement Groups and others who have something to gain if the burden of financing the highways can be transferred from the individual citizen and the individual motorist to those who alone profit by it — the heavy trucks.

And then he added two sentences that became the source of much embarrassment, "You can see from the foregoing that this is an account utterly unlike the conventional one. Here we do not have a client for attribution."

The Pennsylvania truckers resumed their effort to raise the weight limit on trucks to 60,000 pounds in the 1951 session of the Pennsylvania legislature and this time appeared headed for success. The ERPC lobbyist, William A. Reiter, sensed this and pleaded with the ERPC for help in this battle. The Byoir firm was summoned to mount a counteroffensive. Even though it got into the fray late, CB&A made an impressive showing. It again used public relations advertising as a major weapon. One ad showed a large truck with the face of a greedy pig, with the message: "YOU CAN'T SATISFY A ROAD HOG!" — signed by the Pennsylvania State Association of Township Supervisors, H. A. Thomson, Secretary. CB&A also used its magazine department to generate antitruck data that it fed to freelancers and thus got antitruck articles published in such publications as *Country Gentlemen* and the *Literary Digest*. All in all, a drum-fire of opposition began to appear in newspapers, magazines, and radio broadcasts in Pennsylvania. But in spite of this barrage, the bill was passed by the legislature and sent to Governor John S. Fine for his signature.

The governor had not taken a position on the bill, so he became the target from both sides. He scheduled a public hearing on the bill. CB&A marshaled a strong appearance from representatives of organizations opposed to the bill. Further the Byoir firm presented to the governor an advance copy of the findings of the Maryland State Road Commission's test of the effects of various truck axles on highways. It was later charged unfairly in court that the firm got these results by bribing a Maryland road official. In the end, Governor Fine vetoed the truck bill because he indicated that he believed that the Pennsylvania Legislature would not have passed the bill had they known about the data from the Maryland Road Test. The Pennsylvania truckers were dumbfounded and outraged at this outcome. So the association, too, decided to fight fire with fire and engaged the Charnay public relations agency, which went to work presenting the truckers' case, using most of the same tactics and techniques that the Byoir firm employed.

Then came a fateful turn in this brawl. Miss Sonya Saroyan, who had been secretary to Reynolds Girdler, the CB&A account executive in charge of the railroads' campaign, left the Byoir firm in 1951 under circumstances still in dispute. Byoir officials asserted that she was fired; she maintained that she quit because she didn't get a promised promotion. Whatever the reason, she compiled a complete file of copies of the interoffice memos, letters, reports, directives, and so forth and carried this incriminating file to the American Trucking Association in Washington, DC. Whether she did this for pure spite or for money probably will never be known. There the file stayed until a David Charnay executive, Henry Paynter, contacted Miss Saroyan in May 1952. She agreed to the file's release to the Charnay firm.

After examining this Byoir file, the directors of the Pennsylvania Motor Truck Association quickly seized upon this trove as evidence they needed to file a lawsuit against the Eastern Railroads Presidents Conference and Carl Byoir & Associates, charging both with violations of the Sherman Anti-Trust Act and the Clayton Act. The PMTA sought $250 million in damages. The complaint alleged that ERPC and CB&A entered into an illegal conspiracy in May 1949, whose purpose was to eliminate the PMTA and others as competitors of the railroads in the long-haul freight business and to create a monopoly on freight hauling in interstate commerce.

The defendants countered with a denial of any conspiracy against the truckers. They asserted that the truckers, while competing with the railroads, enjoyed huge public subsidies through free use of public highways; that the truckers habitually exceeded load limits set by law; that fines for violating load limits had not deterred the truckers from continuing to overload their trucks, and that the ERPC and CB&A goals were attaining legislative measures and that such efforts involved the right of free speech and right to petition guaranteed by the U.S. Constitution.

The PMTA got a heavy play in the press because of the "femme fatale" angle, and its lawyers boasted to the media that they expected to prove with the Saroyan "evidence" that ERPC and CB&A had used "dishonest means to achieve illegal ends." The first consequence of the suit was that the Philadelphia District Court granted PMTA an injunction that the Byoir firm cease forthwith its public relations campaign on behalf of the railroads.

The pretrial hearings opened in early 1953. Because of the inside public relations angle of the Saroyan file, the reporters turned out volumes of "good" copy, all adverse to the Byoir firm and to public relations. Carl Byoir was scheduled to appear as a pretrial witness on May 8, 1953. Prior to appearing, Byoir held a long and emotional staff conference. He visibly showed his distress of the adverse effects on the staff's morale caused by the "sensational" reporting of the hearings. Byoir spoke without interruption for nearly 2 hours. After reviewing the history of public relations, how his firm had become a part of it, and the concepts on which he based his philosophy of public relations, Byoir said:

> I do want you to know [because your being here means that you have chosen public relations as a career] that nothing takes the place of good will and sincerity and integrity when you are in a good will business. And that brings me to the railroad suit. . . . I want you to know that because my name is on the door I catch all the dead dogs and cats. If anybody here does anything wrong, my shoulders have to be broad enough to hold it up. Now a mistake can be a mistake in judgment — it can be a mechanical mistake . . . and it's no use for me to say to the client, "Well, I was out of town because he employed Carl Byoir & Associates. I'm not too critical of any mistake that anybody makes if it is in good faith. If it is made in bad faith you ought to be in some other business. . . . [You are probably asking yourselves] if we lose this suit will we be out of jobs here? . . . So I say to you what I said before [the A&P lawsuit], we will emerge with more business, more stature, more reputation, more character, if we learn the lessons that go with these things, than we've ever had in all our history.

Byoir's optimistic prediction would come true but only after a prolonged painful legal battle through three courts and some 4 years after his death.

Thus began the trial of Noerr Motor Freight, Inc. et al. v. Eastern Railroad Presidents Conference et al. on October 1, 1956, before District Court Judge Thomas J. Clary. As in the A&P trial, both sides waived the right to a jury trial. The court recessed on January 25, 1957, after a complex trial involving some 100 lawyers, and hundreds of witnesses that produced a trial transcript of more than 6,000 pages. Months later, Judge Clary issued his decision, ruling on October 10, 1957, in favor of the plaintiffs and against the defendants. Judge Clary wrote, "The court has found as a fact that the railroads and Byoir [this referred to the firm, not Mr. Byoir, who was not a defendant] entered into a conspiracy in unreasonable restraint of trade, the nature and purpose of which was to injure the truckers in their competitive position in the long-haul freight industry in the northeastern section of the United States. This, of course, involves interstate commerce."

The Clary decision, like the trial, had focused on the role and propriety of public relations as no previous litigation had done. Judge Clary made it clear that his ruling was "no attack upon public relations or the achievement of legislative goals through publications, speeches, press releases, or the alignment of friends to seek to accomplish a valid legislative purpose." But then he wrote:

> Public relations techniques are closely interwoven with every facet of this case. The chief device used by the railroads, and to a lesser extent by the plaintiffs . . . is one long known to political experts as "The Big Lie." This technique, as it appears from the evidence in this case, has been virtually adapted in toto by certain public relations firms under the less insidious and more palatable third-party technique. Its sole means and its effectiveness is to take a dramatic fragment of the truth and by emphasis and repetition distort it into falsehood. That was the technique employed almost without exception. . . . by [CB&A] and the railroads throughout the campaign.

Judge Clary then proceeded to establish CB&A's third party technique by quoting from the "Saroyan Papers." Judge Clary did clear the Byoir firm of the bribery accusation in connection with its obtaining the Maryland Road Test results.

The Eastern Railroads and the Byoir firm promptly appealed Clary's decision to the Third U.S. Circuit Court of Appeals. On December 10, 1959, that Court upheld Judge Clary's decision by a 2-to-1 vote. In his dissenting opinion, Chief Justice Biggs admitted to some moral qualms about the public relations practices involved in this case but pointed out that if Judge Clary's decision were permitted to stand, then basic U.S. Constitutional rights would be circumscribed: the First Amendment would be unduly limited and partially destroyed; rights under the Tenth Amendment would be "endangered, and in the future there might be instances of both criminal and civil sanctions or punishments imposed upon persons seeking the enactment of laws of Congress or by the legislatures of the states.

John W. Hill, responding to a suggestion from his Cleveland partner, Don Knowlton, that Hill and Knowlton seek the railroad account in wake of Judge Clary's decision, wrote in a letter dated November 27, 1957, "My own opinion is that it is extremely unlikely that the railroad group would drop the Carl Byoir organization very soon, as this would be a confession on their part that they agree with the adverse decision." Hill continued, "I had lunch last week with Gerry Swinehart, who is chairman of Carl Byoir, and he said they estimate the cost will run from $1,000,000 to $1,500,00. Byoir, according to the court decision, must pay 20 percent of these costs and the railroads are prevented from reimbursing Byoir for such payment." Hill concluded his letter, "Moreover, we would not under any circumstances make any move in the direction suggested by Mr. [Talbot] Harding."

Encouraged by Judge Bigg's dissent, the ERPC and Byoir firm further appealed the Clary decision to the U.S. Supreme Court. On February 20, 1961, in a landmark ruling for the practice of public relations, the Supreme Court unanimously reversed Judge Clary's decision and restored the parties at the bar to their respective status quo ante trial conditions. Justice Hugo Black, staunch defender of the First Amendment, wrote the historic decision:

> No violation of the Sherman Act can be predicated upon mere attempts to influence the passage or enforcement of laws. . . . The Sherman Act does not prohibit two or more parties from associating together in an attempt to persuade Legislative or executive to take a particular action with respect to a law that would produce a restraint or a monopoly. . . . It is not illegal for people to seek action on laws in hope that they may bring about an advantage to themselves and a disadvantage to their competitors. . . . Since it is undisputed that the truckers were as guilty as the railroads of the use of the [third party] technique, this factor could not in any sense been controlling of the holding against the railroads. . . . In this particular instance, each group appears to have utilized all the political powers that it could muster in an attempt to bring about passage of laws that would help it or injure the other. But the contest itself appears to have been conducted along lines normally accepted in our political system.

Finally, Justice Black issued what might be called a "Magna Carta" for such public affairs campaigns in reversing the lower courts:

> In doing so, we have restored what appears to be the true nature of the case— a "no holds barred fight" between two industries, both of which are seeking control of a profitable source of income. Inherent in such fights, which are commonplace in the halls of legislative bodies, is the possibility, and in many instances, the probability, that one group or the other will get hurt by the arguments that are made. . . . Deception, reprehensible as it is, can be of no consequence so far as the Sherman Act is concerned.

A columnist for *Advertising Age* wrote in its March 6, 1961, issue: "The decision makes it safe for lobbyists, and for public relations experts who work for them, to operate without fear of costly legal reprisals."

Understandably, the long litigation and the decisions rendered by the courts fueled strong debate on the third party technique—a debate that continues. In his pretrial testimony, Byoir insisted that any public relations emissary must approach any element of the public openly, stating, "If deception is involved [in any public relations technique], it's no good." Gerry Swinehart said, after the case was over, "It's done all the time in politics. To my dying day I will maintain that we didn't do anything illegal." David Mackie, president of the ERPC, testified, "The Byoir people went out and told the story to the public. . . . All of the organizations, all of the allies, that we obtained from the public knew who Byoir was, knew whom they [sic] worked for. All that Byoir did was to help in gathering together of factual, basic underlying data and then take these data to these segments of the people." Robert Bendiner wrote an article for *The Reporter* of August 1955, providing a detailed account of the pretrial testimony. Entitled "The Engineering of Social Consent," Bendiner laid out chapter and verse the "third party or front technique." Responding to Bendiner's article, Harry Paynter, a Charnay executive who had located Miss Saroyan and her "papers," wrote the editor:

> I am quite pleased that your documentation reflects the case built up, under my direction, against the Byoir type of public-relations propaganda. The important ethical question lies in the sentence Mr. Bendiner italicized: "Here we do not have a client for attribution." In fairness to Messrs. Byoir, T. J. Ross, and Tom Deegan, who shared responsibility for the campaign . . . none of the techniques was new. Most of them had been used for a century or more by finance and industry through lobbying and promotional-publicity campaigns.

And they will continue to be used in political and economic struggles in the 21st century.

CARL BYOIR: A SUMMING UP

When the Supreme Court decision came down exonerating his firm of conspiracy charges under the Sherman Act, Carl Byoir had been dead 4 years. Yet his firm, under the leadership of Gerry Swinehart and George Hammond, who had been with him from the genesis, was continuing to serve a large list of clients. As Byoir had predicted in his emotional talk to his dispirited staff at the outset of the truckers' lawsuit, the Byoir firm had emerged stronger than it was before the lawsuit. Byoir died on February 3, 1957, after a painful 2-year illness with an inoperable cancer. After his pretrial testimony, Byoir had no further involvement in the truckers case and no involvement in the work of his firm after the latter part of 1953. At his death, the firm he had founded in 1930 to promote tourism for Cuba, though no longer the No. 1 firm, was on everyone's list as one of the premier agencies. In 1960, a *Printer's Ink* survey of New York public relations executives placed CB&A fifth, ranked behind Hill and Knowlton, Inc., Ivy Lee and T. J. Ross, Selvage and Lee, Inc., and Dudley–Anderson–Yutzy. In another *Printer's Ink* survey, this one of newspaper editors in New York, CB&A ranked fourth in the esteem of the print media. In sum, Carl Byoir's intellect, driving energy, and knowledge of the psychology of public opinion had built a strong, profitable, and innovative public relations agency. In the practice of public relations, he was a genius. In many of his business ventures, he was less successful.

Like many of his contemporaries, including Ivy Lee, he had difficulty in precisely defining the function, but he knew its fundamentals well — research a problem before planning a course of action, target segmented publics with an interest common to your client for an intensive communications program, and above all else, that ultimate success depends on the client serving the public interest. Byoir frequently proclaimed on public platforms — he was in great demand as a speaker — that public relations practitioners could do nothing for the "Bourbon employer." Byoir recognized that his and other public relations agencies had an obligation to train bright youth persons for this field. Some of Carl Byoir alumni who went on to found or join other firms included: Edward Gottlieb, chairman of E. Gottlieb and Associates; John Doherty, president of Doherty Associates; William Gaskill, president and later owner of T. J. Ross & Associates; Gordon M. Sears, vice-president of T. J. Ross and Associates; Oscar M. Beveridge, president of Beveridge, Penney, & Bennett, Inc., and several others. Thus, Byoir spread the gospel of effective public relations by precept and by example.

As indicated earlier, Carl Byoir was not a joiner and did not have a strong collegial relationship with other leading executives in the emerging public relations profession. For example, he was not a member of The Wisemen, an informal group led by John W. Hill, Pendleton Dudley, T. J. Ross, and other movers and shakers in New York public relations circles. Five contemporaries of Byoir had these revealing comments:

John W. Hill: Carl Byoir was one of the pioneer "great salesmen" of public relations. I didn't know Byoir personally in any sort of close way but I think he conceived some public relations techniques that were very successful. . . . He had some ideas that were original in their approach.

William H. Baldwin: Although Carl Byoir was a contemporary there never was situation where we came together on either the same or on opposite sides. My sole personal contact with him was one evening when ten or a dozen of us met at dinner to explore what we could do to advance public relations counseling.

Earl Newsom: I did not know Carl Byoir well enough to be able to make an informed judgment about him. I am ashamed to say that I saw him infrequently. I recognized him as a vigorous and creative publicity man. I admired the way in which he carefully built a strong firm.

T. J. Ross: Carl Byoir had genius and toughness and resourcefulness. He founded and built his firm during an era which put to use his constructive qualities. And it was these qualities which helped him to participate and contribute constructively to some of the historic problems and events of his time, starting with World War I and up until the time of his death.

Kal Druck: I was with CB&A from 1939 until 1959. Carl Byoir made CB&A into one of the greatest affirmative publicity organization in the world. His purpose was always apparent to me in every contract I had with him and that purpose was to affirmatively plan, based on a thorough comprehensive analysis of the client's business and problem areas, a public relations program that would achieve maximum public exposure of ideas. . . . As a public relations strategist I don't think Byoir had a peer in the field. [Druck's admiring comments were echoed by every member of the Byoir organization when interviewed in 1968 by Col. Robert J. Bennett for his master's thesis.]

Peter Earle, who worked for CB&A from 1965 to 1968, viewed the "Byoir magic" this way in *PR Week*, November 21–27, 1988:

"Kentucky Windage," speed, timing and decisive action were Mr. Byoir's hallmarks until his death. Our founder could hold up a finger and feel the direction of the slightest zephyr, then fan it into a whirlwind for the benefit of a vacillating client. He had charm, confidence in what he urged upon the mighty, and intestinal fortitude and finesse before the editors who shaped public opinion and images. He needed no committees and often no research. . . . If you wanted something to happen fast, you saw Carl Byoir.

The life of Carl Byoir has been writ. It is the American Horatio Alger writ large. Clearly he was a masterful leader of men, a person of great vision and imagination, of unlimited energy and a driving ambition to succeed in everything he undertook, from his youthful reporting days in Des Moines to his counseling of some of the nation's major corporations. Carl Byoir's career forcefully illustrates a fact of American democratic society that generally goes unstated and unnoticed: the pervasive impact of public relations on the life, culture, philanthropy, politics, and economics of American society.

Ponder, for instance, the introduction of the Montessori schools across this land and their impact on educational methods. Or ponder the profound contribution Byoir made to America's victory in World War I as the major stabilizing force in the Committee on Public Information, whose work not only helped rally the nation and the world to President Wilson's crusade to make the "world safe for democracy" but also had a profound impact on the shape and growth of government public relations. Add to this monument of accomplishment, his starting the fund-raising ball rolling to raise the money for the research that in 20 short years lifted the scourge of polio from the hearts of parents around the world by staging the four President's Birthday Balls that raised more than $4 million and paved the way for the March of Dimes. More than eliminating polio, Byoir's innovative and flamboyant ways of promoting the Birthday Balls gave impetus to today's large-scale fund drives in the health field. Complete this equation with his contribution to public relations by establishing a successful agency in the depth of the Great Depression and guiding it to the top of the nation's agencies with his brilliance and unbounded energy. Carl Byoir truly was the Little Giant of American public relations.

Some 6 years after Carl Byoir's death, Gerry Swinehart, his able, dynamic, and affable right-hand man became seriously ill, which resulted in his stepping down from active management of CB&A to chairman of the executive committee. George Hammond, who was also in at the beginning, moved up to chairman of the board, and Robert J. Wood was elected president in October 1963. Gerry Swinehart died at age 63 of cancer on October 31 the following year. Early in the 1970s, Hammond and Wood began to have talks with several large advertising agencies but these, in Wood's word "never went anywhere." Then in late 1977, Arthur Schultz, president and CEO of Foote, Cone, & Belding—the successor agency to Albert Lasker's pioneering Lord & Thomas—persuaded Hammond and Wood that there "were going to be more and more marriages of advertising and public relations agencies because the market demanded them." At this time Byoir was the third largest public relations agency in the country with a substantial list of longtime clients. After many meetings and protracted negotiations, Hammond and Wood agreed to let Foote, Cone, & Belding acquire CB&A. The engagement was announced in April 1978, and the marriage consummated on August 1 of that year. This was the beginning of the end of the original Carl Byoir agency.

The contracting parties had a clear agreement, according to Hammond and Wood, that CB&A would be given autonomy and Foote, Cone, & Belding would "get back to what they did best, advertising." In a bitter concluding chapter to his book, *Confessions of a PR Man*, Robert Wood asserted:

> Unfortunately the arrangement didn't last. After letting the Byoir staff run its own show for a while, the Foote, Cone people, for reasons of their own, began to play a more and more active role in our affairs. Byoir staffers found themselves reporting to managers who . . . knew nothing about public relations. Understandably, frictions developed. The climax came early in

March, 1983, when the Foote, Cone management abruptly fired twelve Byoir staff people, including two executive vice presidents."

This explosion at CB&A attracted wide notice in the daily and business press. Jack O'Dwyer, publisher of a public relations newsletter, termed the day "Bloody Friday.' O'Dwyer commented that there was no doubt in his mind that the Foote, Cone group had mismanaged Byoir. He saw as FCB's mistake the "bringing in two PR executives in their early 40s as the new leadership." Hammond and Wood were replaced after decades of experience, working closely with their major industrial clients.

As these upheavals were taking place the once-proud Byoir staff began to scatter or become demoralized, and clients began to cancel their contracts. In a short span of time, CB&A lost these clients: Hughes Aircraft, a client of 40 years; Hallmark, 37 years; RCA, 34 years; CIT Financial, 33 years; and Borg Warner, 20 years. Consequently, the Foote, Cone, & Belding sold Carl Byoir & Associates, or in Wood's words "what was left of it," to Hill & Knowlton, Inc. for a reported $12 million. Hill & Knowlton, long one of the two chief competitors to Byoir, simply absorbed the agency, and the Carl Byoir & Associates founded in 1930 passed into public relations counseling history. Peter Earle, now with the reborn Carl Byoir firm holds the opinion that the veteran Byoir's leadership failure to change with the changing demands of public relations was the source of CB&A's demise. He wrote, "The closeness which he [Carl Byoir] and his immediate successors held the reins, and the very system he created to make it happen, in large part explain why Carl Byoir 'lost it' as the times, the leadership, and ownership continued to change."

Hill and Knowlton Inc. in 1988 revived the firm name, Carl Byoir & Associates, with a new mission and new structure under the leadership of a veteran Byoir executive, John F. Budd, Jr., who had earlier left Byoir to head Emhart's public relations. According to Earle, "The new Carl Byoir internal philosophy of human resource management will be to encourage broad thinking, employ and develop people with a full set of credentials, and seek diverse leadership with different, not similar, skills which are mutually respected and interwoven." John F. Budd left the Byoir "shell" in 1971. The success of this formula must be left to future historians.

NOTES ON SOURCES FOR CHAPTERS 17 AND 18

As indicated in the acknowledgment in chapter 17, these two chapters relied heavily on the master's thesis of Colonel Robert J. Bennett, written at the University of Wisconsin-Madison in 1968 under my direction, *Carl Byoir: Public Relations Pioneer*. This reliance was made essential because since

Colonel Bennett was given access to the Carl Byoir papers, these papers have been lost to public access. The collection Colonel Bennett used in his thesis included a partial autobiography (draft typescript), official biographical and career summaries prepared for newspapers and magazines, Byoir's many speeches, personal comments at staff conferences, memoranda written by Byoir, correspondence, and a personal collection of news clippings. Bennett's thorough research at least preserves the essence of these documents for future scholars.

These chapters also reflect friendships, numerous interviews, and extensive correspondence I have had with key Carl Byoir executives — Gerry Swinehart, George Hammond, Elsie Simon, his longtime secretary, Jane Buck, and others in the once dominant public relations agency in the nation.

The Birthday Balls saga is based on that chapter in my volume, *Fund Raising in the United States: Its Role in America's Philanthropy*, first published by the Rutgers University Press in 1965 and republished by Transaction Press in 1990. This chapter was thoroughly vetted by the Byoir executives involved in those campaigns.

These two chapters are also based on extensive documentation in books, journals, court proceedings, and Congressional hearings. This documentation includes:

Books

Morris A. Adelman, *A&P: A Study in Price-Cost behavior and Public Policy*, Harvard University Press, 1959; Frederick Lewis Allen, *Only Yesterday: An Informal History of the Nineteen-Twenties*, Harper & Row, 1964; Carlton Beals, *The Crime of Cuba*, J. B. Lippencott, 1933; Edward L. Bernays, *Biography of an Idea*, Simon & Schuster, 1965; George Creel, *How We Advertised America*, Harper & Brothers, 1920; George Creel, *Rebel at Large*, G. P. Putnam's Sons, 1947; Josephus Daniels, *The Wilson Era*, University of North Carolina Press, 1946; Andrew Hacker, "Pressure Politics in Pennsylvania: The Truckers versus the Railroads," *The Uses of Power*, Alan F. Westin, ed., Harcourt, Brace and World, 1962; Thomas G. Masaryk, *The Making of a State*, Frederick A. Stokes Co., 1927; Herbert L. Mathews, *The Cuban Story*, Braziller, Inc., 1961; James Mock and Cedric Larson, *Words That Won the War*, Princeton University Press, 1939; Irwin Ross, *The Image Merchants*, Doubleday & Co., 1959; Richard Carter, *The Gentle Legions*, Doubleday & Company, 1961; Henry Ladd Smith, *Airways: The History of Commercial Aviation*, Knopf, 1942; James Harvey Young, *The Medical Messiahs: A Social History of Health Quackery*, Princeton University Press, 1967, Robert J. Wood, *Confessions of a*

PR Man, New American Library (NAL), 1988; Turnley Walker, *Roosevelt and the Warm Springs Story*, Wyn, 1953.

Periodicals

"A&P Case Ends", *Business Week*, January 23, 1954; "A Case Study— Concluded," *The Reporter*, Vol. 5, October 31, 1957; Morris A. Adelman, "The Great A&P Muddle," *Fortune*, Vol. 42, December 1949; "Ads Win Wide Support for A&P," *The American Press*, Vol. 68, March 1950; John Williams Andrews, "U. S. vs A&P: The Battle of Titans," *Harper's*, Vol. 201, September 1950; Robert Bendiner, "The Engineering of Social Consent," *The Reporter*, Vol. 13, August 11, 1955; "Business is Still in Trouble," *Fortune*, Vol. 13, May 1949; Carl Byoir, Joseph C. O'Mahoney, and Theodore Granik, "Is the A&P Suit in the Public Interest?" *American Forum of the Air*, Vol 13, January 22, 1950; "Byoir Relates His Career in Anti-Trust Case," *Editor & Publisher*, Vol. 86, May 16, 1953; Spencer Klaw, "Carl Byoir: Opinion Engineering in the Big Time," *The Reporter*, Vol. 6, June 10, 1952; Lore Ludwig, "Nazi Politics in America," *The Nation*, Vol. 137, November 29, 1933; "Medicine Makers Clean House," *Business Week*, May 16, 1930; "Miami Appoints Byoir," *Editor & Publisher*, Vol. 63, November 29, 1930; "Public Relations on Trial," *Tide 27 May 5, 1956; "The Railroad–Trucker Brawl,"* *Fortune*, Vol. 47, June 1953; "Who is Carl Byoir?" *Automotive News,* November 28, 1949; S. H. Walker and Julia Riera, "Now Comes a New Brand of Public Relations: A&P Points the Way," *Printer's Ink*, Vol. 185, October 13, 1938; Talks by Gerry Swinehart: "You Are In Public Relations," given at Chicago Industrial Editors Association, February, 1948; "What Is This Thing Called Public Relations," given to Southern Gas Association, April 29, 1952; "Gerry Swinehart Dead at 63; Led Public Relations Agency," *The New York Times*, November 1, 1966; "Carl Byoir: A Portrait," *Fortune*, Volume 47, June, 1953. (Sidebar to Railroad-Trucker Brawl," op. cit. Scott M. Cutlip, "Lithuania's First Independence Battle: A PR Footnote," *Public Relations Review*, Vol. 16, No. 4, 1990.

Government Publications

United States Congress

Congressional Record, Senate, 56th Congress, 2nd Session, Vol. 56, Part 5, Washington, G.P.O., 1919; *Congressional Record*, House, 64th Congress, 1st Session, Vol. 79, Part 3, Washington, G.P.O., 1935; *Congressional Record*, House, 76th Congress, 3rd Session, Vol. 86, Part 16, Washington, G.P.O., 1940; *Congressional Record*, House, 76th, Congress,

3rd Session, Vol. 86, Part 17, Washington, G.P.O., 1940; *Report of Hearings on 1919 Sundry Civil Bill*, House, 65th Congress, 2nd Session, Vol. 2, Part 3, Washington, G.P.O., 1919, *Report No. 75 of Hearings, Special House Committee on Un-American Activities*, House, 73rd Congress, 2nd Session, Vol. 99, Part 3, Washington, G.P.O., 1934, *Report No. 1533 of Hearings, Special House Committee on Un-American Activities*, House, 74th Congress, 1st Session, Vol. 99, Part 3, Washington, G.P.O., 1935, *Report of Hearings, Special House Committee on Un-American Activities*, House, 77th Congress, 1st Session, Vol. 51, Part 14, Washington, G.P.O., 1941.

United States Federal Courts

Supreme Court Reporter, Vol. 81, St. Paul: West Publishing Co., 1961; *Federal Reporter* (Second Series), Vol. 137F, 2nd. St. Paul: West Publishing Co., 1943, *Federal Reporter* (Second Series), Vol. 147F, 2nd. St. Paul: West Publishing Co., 1945, *Federal Reporter* (Second Series), Vol. 173F, 2nd. St. Paul: West, Publishing Co., 1949, *Federal Reporter* (Second Series), Vol. 273F, 2nd. St. Paul: West Publishing Co., 1960, *Federal Supplement*, Vol. 58, St. Paul: West Publishing Co., 1945, *Federal Supplement*, Vol. 67, St. Paul: West Publishing Co., 1958, *Federal Supplement*, Vol. 155, St. Paul: West Publishing Co., 1958.

United States Federal Trade Commission

The Federal Trade Commission, during the 1920's, issued several cease and desist orders on products similar to those peddled by Carl Byoir. For example, Stipulation No. 101 of the FTC for March 31, 1926, ordered that a firm stop falsely advertising certain bath salts as having the property of reducing obesity. See *Federal Trade Commission Decisions,* Vol. 10, Nov. 28, 1925–Nov. 4, 1926. Such were the ethics of making money in the 1920s.

For decisions affecting Byoir's products, see *Federal Trade Commission Decisions*, Vol. 15, and *Federal Trade Commission Decisions*, Vol. 37, Washington, DC: Government Printing Office, 1933 and 1936 respectively.

Chapter 19

Whitaker & Baxter: Architects of the New Politics

The political propagandist/publicist has played a vital role in the nation's politics since the first party system was formed in the late 1790s. The second party system, born in the Jacksonian Revolution of the 1820s and 1830s, brought an enhanced role for the political propagandist and the first White House public relations adviser. The third party system, that was born of the divisive issue of slavery on the eve of the Civil War and dominated by the Republican and Democratic parties, has governed American political elections until recent times when the influence of the party in campaigns has been lessened by the emergence of the political campaign specialist, a burgeoning field of public relations practice.

Today's *political campaign specialist or consultant*, the more commonly used term, can be an independent consultant, for example, James Carville, who managed Senator Harris Wofford's upset victory in the 1991 Pennsylvania Senate race and went on in 1992 as consultant to President Bill Clinton's successful Presidential campaign; a public relations firm for example, Spencer and Roberts of California that managed all of President Reagan's campaigns; a standard public relations agency, for example, McDonald–Davis of Milwaukee; or an advertising agency, for example, Batten, Barton, Durstine, & Osborne, which directed the public relations and advertising strategy of President Eisenhower's 1952 campaign. These consultants or agencies who manage candidate or party campaigns employ an array of subspecialists: pollsters who measure the changing political climate, TV and video producers who prepare the all-important TV commercials, advertising agencies, and mailing firms with their computerized mailing lists to solicit political or financial support. This array of modern technicians is utilized by both political candidates for national and state office and by the two major political parties, national and state.

The political campaign specialist has greatly weakened the major parties' organizational control in the selection of candidates and in the control of national, state, and local campaigns. The trend has made the elected officeholders less beholden to their political party and thus more independent of party discipline that once characterized the Congress and state legislatures. Nonetheless, the two major parties, Republican and Democratic, still play a major role in fund-raising and in campaign support at the national and state levels. The emergence of the political public relations specialist to manage political campaigns is only one factor in the decline of the major parties in the American political process. This decline began with the progressive reforms of the first part of this century and proceeded unevenly across the nation. These reforms began in California, long a trend-setting state, and there gave birth to the first agency specializing in campaign management. American politics—the rise of special interest groups with their large financial contributions and the decline of party control in the selection and election of candidates—has provided a special kind of opportunity for the professional public relations campaign specialist.

Even so, in Great Britain and on the European continent where the political party remains dominant in the political process, the parties and candidates use the campaign consultant or specialist. The parties in those nations use these specialists because there, as in the United States, television has become a controlling factor in elections.

This chapter tells the significant story of Clem Whitaker and Leone Baxter who effected a sea change in American politics by paving the way for today's campaign specialist who uses modern technology to strongly influence the political process. These carpetbagger consultants or political management firms are now an essential part of the national and state elections. Their consequence in the political system is profound. Each chapter of this book has brought to light the significant impact public relations counselors have had on American society, an impact that generally goes unnoticed by the public. None have had a more profound influence on American society than Clem Whitaker and Leone Baxter.

First a bit of political history to put the changes wrought by Whitaker and Baxter (W&B) in perspective. In the increasingly bitter conflict between Alexander Hamilton and Thomas Jefferson, both inside Washington's cabinet and in the press, were planted the seeds of America's two-party political system—a development that the framers of the Constitution had feared and had not foreseen its necessity. By 1792, the conflict between the ideas and economic interest in these Founding Fathers began to crystallize in the form of political parties. Publicity has long been the meat and drink of politics – in fact from the beginning.

Virginia's John Beckley must rank as the first in a long line of political publicists who have made the American political system work. Beckley was instrumental in prodding Thomas Jefferson into the leadership of the Republicans and was an energetic and resourceful propagandist for Jefferson's ideas. He was more – he was Jefferson's eyes and ears, collecting political intelligence, gossip, and rough measures of public opinion. Beckley was Jefferson's campaign manager for the key state of Pennsylvania in the 1796 election. Noble E. Cunningham wrote of this effort, "His publicity campaign to familiarize the voters with the Republican ticket is probably not equalled in any election of the 1790s. Tickets were scattered across the state by the thousands and political handbills were sent out from Philadelphia in bundles." A "skillful electioneer," Beckley took the lead in utilizing publicity as a means of winning elections in a time when it was not considered proper to openly seek office. Beckley played a major role in the 1800 Presidential election that Joseph Charles, in his *The Origins of American Party System*, described as "one of the bitterest and most momentous elections which the country has ever seen." Charles concluded with these words, "A party becomes an entity like a nation, and, as with a nation, the question of its own survival is likely to be paramount."

But the Federalist and Republican parties did not survive. In his *The Second American Party System*, Richard P. McCormick wrote, "The first American party system, which had its origins late in Washington's presidency, entered upon a stage of arrested development after 1800, and by 1820 had all but disintegrated." This disintegration came about in the Era of Good Feeling in the presidencies of James Madison and James Monroe. McCormick continued, "In 1824, essentially as a result of the revival of the contest for the presidency, there began a new era of party formation. . . . By 1840, when the new parties had attained an equilibrium of forces nationally, politics in every state was conducted on a two-party basis."

The first clear beginnings of the Presidential campaign and of the Presidential press secretary's function came in the Era of Andrew Jackson and in the work of Amos Kendall. This era of the late 1820s and early 1830s brought a shift of power from the Virginia aristocracy to the growing populations of the expanding Western frontier; a shift stimulated by the spread of public schools and growth of newspapers. The literate public was greatly enlarged and its political interests stimulated by a strident party press as a new generation pushed to the fore. As people gained political power, it became necessary to campaign for their support. The leader of "The New Democracy" was war hero and frontiersman, Andrew Jackson. Jackson gave renewed life to the American political party system, nourished it with the spoils system, and brought power and glamour to the Presidency. In all this, he had the off-stage counsel and public relations assistance from the nation's first full-time Presidential public relations aide, Amos Kendall, although the title of White House Press Secretary did not originate until Herbert Hoover's Presidency in 1929.

Andrew Jackson's campaign for the Presidency in 1828 against incumbent John Quincy Adams who had defeated him in 1824, opened with a flourish that would do a modern day campaign consultant proud. It was built around a celebration of the Battle of New Orleans from which Jackson had emerged as the nation's hero. The campaign centered on Old Hickory the Hero, and there was little discussion of issues. Arthur Schlesinger, Jr. wrote in his *Age of Jackson*, "Hardly an issue of policy figured in the canvass." Amos Kendall, a New Englander who had been educated at Groton and Dartmouth College, migrated to Kentucky and there became a newspaper editor. As editor of the *Western Argus of Kentucky*, published in Frankfort, Kendall, long a foe of the Bank of the United States, became heavily involved in Jackson's campaign to carry Kentucky. Influenced by Kendall, the Jacksonians made it appear as a contest between the rich and the poor, the plowholders versus the bondholders, thus establishing a basic theme that has threaded its way through most subsequent Presidential campaigns. Robert Remini said that "by linking organization and ballyhoo of entertainment behind an appealing candidate who supposedly represented the common man, politicians were able . . . to stir the people from their lethargy to a fleeting interest in national politics." The campaign that brought the nation its second political party system was a lively and bitter one, a prototype of Presidential campaigns to come late in the 19th century.

The role played by Kendall in the Jackson Administration can be compared with that performed by the large public relations staff that serves today's President. Kendall worked at the top policy-making level and was always closely consulted on major issues while they were being shaped. He devised much of Jackson's strategy, wrote most of his speeches, drafted his messages to Congress (many were in Kendall's handwriting), prepared reports, and answered letters. Kendall organized and developed the administration's official mouthpiece, *The Globe*, and issued countless press releases. Kendall possessed a keen mind and demonstrated an extraordinary ability to communicate complex ideas in the plain language of the frontier. Jackson's biographer, Remini, believed that Jackson's "larger than life personality and equally heroic convictions and prejudices changed the Presidency and the character of American political parties." Remini concluded that Jackson changed the republican character of the political system by "insisting on greater representation of the people." In this significant change in American politics, Amos Kendall was a strong influence.

The two new political parties—the Democrats and the Whigs—were balanced and competitive in every region of the nation from 1840 to 1852 when the Whig party broke apart over the slavery issue. McCormick holds that the second party system was contrived because it ignored regional interests and feelings. The Republican Party was born in 1856 to confront the Democrats on the slavery issue. McCormick concluded, "The second party system brought into general acceptance a new campaign style that was popular and dramatic."

The pattern of Presidential campaigns that was to prevail until the 1950s and the Age of Television and the campaign consultant had its origins in the last two decades of the 19th century. The political campaign methods fashioned by Amos Kendall in the 1820s and 1830s had remained little changed with the rise of democracy and enlargement of the voting franchise until 1880. The Republican Party, which had dominated the nation's politics since the Civil War, got a rude jolt in the Hayes–Tilden squeaker of 1876. Republican leaders were forced to realize that they could no longer take victory for granted by waving "The Bloody Shirt." Democrats were inspired to increased effort by their near success. More systematic efforts to carry the party message to the growing number of voters were developed in time for the 1880 Presidential campaign.

This period of American politics saw the emergence of another political public relations pioneer, George F. Parker, a former Indiana newspaperman, who served as President Grover Cleveland's public relations adviser in his three campaigns for the Presidency. It was Parker who hired young Ivy Lee as his assistant in the 1904 Democratic campaign of Judge Alton B. Parker. Parker and Lee opened the nation's third public relations agency.

The 1896 dramatic, hard-fought campaign between Conservative William McKinley and Populist William Jennings Bryan brought a stepped up emphasis on publicity, campaign management, and appeals to special groups and interests, with special emphasis on appeals to the new immigrants then pouring into the United States. Reflecting the shift of the nation's population, both parties moved their campaign headquarters to Chicago to pour out news releases, pamphlets, and other propaganda in unprecedented quantities. Both campaigns were directed by the political party officials.

By the turn of the century, a writer for *Munsey's Magazine*, Luther B. Little, observed, "Expert and experienced political managers give their closest attention to this [campaign literature] detail. Men who are learned in regard to the issues at stake, and who possess that requisite of the successful politician which might be termed a knowledge of applied psychology, hold the blue pencil. Paragraphs, sentences, and words are weighted with reference to their effect on the mind of the reader."

In the 1896 campaign the large-scale publicity bureau and the campaign train became a part of national election campaigns in a nation whose electorate now stretched 3,000 miles across the continent. This pattern prevailed, save for the modification brought by radio broadcasting in 1928, until the 1950s with one exception — California.

HIRAM JOHNSON SOWS THE SEED OF CHANGE

The political party machine that had been built up over the years of the late 19th and early 20th centuries was wiped out in the first decade of the 20th century in California by its Progressive Republican Governor Hiram Johnson. In *Breach of Faith*, Theodore White summed up Johnson's reforms this way, "Leading a revolt of moralistic, church-going, Midwestern transplants to California, Hiram Johnson purged the state of railway control; his revolt wiped out political patronage more completely than anywhere else in the Union, forbade party nominating conventions, fumigated every cranny of conventional party politics."

Governor Johnson's reforms included a direct primary, the initiative, referendum, and recall as well as civil service regulations and woman's suffrage. In his biography of Richard Nixon, Roger Morris observed, "Swept away in the debris were also the discipline and organizational cohesion of both the Republican and Democratic parties, and Hiram Johnson's hopeful reforms were to have an unexpected sequel." He explained:

> As the traditional party structures collapsed, the old graft and control simply seeped into new channels. Intended as tools of popular participation in government, the new and exploitable levers of petition politics allowed well-financed special interest groups and other disciplined factions — those with the price of a public relations firm, the quarter-a-signature petitions, the budget for advertising — to seize the legislative agenda or punish a foe. The press and other purveyors of image would come to replace the old party bosses as the brokers of the new power. Throughout the state . . . politics passed from a program of conviction to manipulation of the shifting crowd. What emerged was California's then still unique political feudalism and feats, campaigns formed around personalities, with issues, ideology, and party accountability increasingly blurred.

Other states, including Wisconsin, also adopted antiparty organizational legislation early in this century. California's legislation was in some important respects more extreme despite the state's retention of the closed primary. The mix, mobility, and unrooted nature of California's booming population contributed to making it a favorable climate for the emergence of the campaign management specialist. Incidentally, the flood of immigrants to California in the early part of this century was being promoted by publicity campaigns. Hamilton Wright I was one of these California drumbeaters. His work was described in chapter 4.

WHITAKER & BAXTER EMERGE TO PIONEER THE NEW POLITICS

California has repeatedly demonstrated that it is the nation's most innovative state. From its unique political system created by the reforms of Governor Johnson (later a United States Senator) came the pioneers Clem Whitaker and Leone Baxter to develop campaign management as a specialty in the public relations spectrum. They set the pattern for the dominance of the political campaign specialist financed by a wide array of special interests (Political Action Committees (the (PACs) for example) and the resultant diminution of the party's influence in the American political process. The California pattern is unique no longer.

In his *The Political Persuaders*, Dan Nimmo saw campaign management as "a direct descendent of the public relations industry that matured in this country after the 1920s." The demand for public relations expertise in California politics was created not only by the need of political candidates who had to run without political party support but also by the need for voters to decide complex issues in the growing number of propositions on each election ballot. Into this vacuum moved Clem Whitaker and Leone Baxter. From their innovations emerged the New Politics in the 1960s. The elements of the New Politics as defined by James M. Perry, a *Wall Street Journal* reporter are: "There are two essential ingredients of the new politics. One is that appeals should be made directly to the voters through the mass media. The other is that the techniques used to make the appeals — polling, computers, television, direct mail — should be sophisticated and scientific." Perry recognized Whitaker and his wife, Leone Baxter, as the founders of the New Politics.

Clem Whitaker was born on May 1, 1899, in Tempe, Arizona, the son of William C. Whitaker and Martha Hays Whitaker. His father was a Baptist minister. He was reared in Sacramento, California. Like most of the pioneers of public relations, Clem Whitaker entered the field after a thorough grounding in journalism. His mother persuaded the *Willits News* of Willits, California, to give him a job as a reporter when he was only 13. At age 17, Whitaker took a year out to attend the University of California at Davis, then returned to newspaper work, this time on *The Sacramento Union* where he became city editor after covering the state legislature for one session. In 1921, he left the newspaper to establish a Capitol News Bureau, a press service for some 80 small-town dailies and weeklies that could not afford a Capitol correspondent. Whitaker's youthful start in journalism matches that of pioneers Carl Byoir, Steve Hannagan, and John W. Hill. A year after opening his news syndicate, Whitaker married Harriet E. Reynolds and to them were born four children, Clem, Milton, and Patricia, and a fourth child who predeceased him. He and his first wife were divorced in 1935, 2 years after he had formed a public relations partnership with Leone Baxter.

During his years of managing his news bureau, Whitaker often worked on the side as a lobbyist, an experience that stood him in good stead when he went into campaign management. Stanley Kelley recorded in his *Professional Public Relations and Political Power*, "As a lobbyist, he worked on one occasion for legislation to create a Board of Barber Examiners and succeeded in getting his bill passed by presenting his case not to the legislators themselves but to their principal supporters in their home districts." This lesson he learned well — one that Ivy Lee had taught in the early days of public relations — and used repeatedly in the days ahead.

In another instance, he took on unsuccessfully a statewide campaign to abolish capital punishment. Fremont Older, publisher of the San Francisco *Call-Bulletin*, put Whitaker in touch with Noel Sullivan, a wealthy San Francisco patron of the arts and other causes, who was willing to support the campaign to abolish capital punishment. With the full backing of the Hearst press, Whitaker put on a campaign that attracted national attention. During the debate in the State Senate, Clem sat next to his crony, Senator John B. McColl, and told him what to say from time to time during the debate. Carey McWilliams thought that the measure might have passed except for "(1) the lobbying activities of his comely assistant, Frances Vickers, became so blatant that they drew the fire of the opposition and (2) a particularly atrocious murder in San Diego on the eve of the final roll call." In this decade or so of political reporting and lobbying the legislators' home districts, Whitaker developed into an effective speaker and shrewd political strategist. A tall, slender man with a craggy face and white hair and the mien of a minister, he was quite an impressive figure.

Whitaker met Leone Baxter, then a beautiful young widow 26 years old with sparkling green eyes and deep auburn hair, who was manager of the Redding, California, Chamber of Commerce in 1933. Before that she had been a newspaper reporter. They met in Sacramento at a meeting of proponents of the passage of a referendum in support of the Central Valley Project (CVP). Whitaker was immediately attracted to Ms. Baxter, and out of this came a political and marriage partnership that lasted until his death on November 3, 1961. Whitaker, who had long suffered from asthma, died of respiratory ailments at the University of California Medical Center. Ms. Baxter was something of an expert in publicity and was a prime mover in the Central Valley Project that had been enacted by the California legislature as largely a flood-control, irrigation, and salinity-control development for northern California. The CVP had the backing of the state's political leaders, but because the act permitted public agencies to purchase the project's power, the private utilities, led by Pacific Gas & Electric (PG&E), brought it to referendum to defeat it.

As a result of this meeting, Whitaker and Baxter were asked to organize a campaign to defeat the utility referendum. They were provided a modest budget of $40,000. They actually spent $39,000 to saturate small town and weekly newspapers with appeals to California's farmers and to use radio, which up to this time had been little used in political campaigns. Their campaign was successful, winning by 33,000 votes. Whitaker and Baxter, with their knowledge of California, knew that voters in southern California would automatically oppose any project that would benefit northern California, so they concentrated on building big pluralities in the rural counties that would benefit. They carried Kern County 25-1, Contra Costa 30-1. The revenue bonds were authorized but never issued.

Their victory took on an ironic twist. The astonished and angered PG&E executives promptly hired the team on a $100,000 retainer, an account they kept until they semiretired in 1959, because of Whitaker's failing health, and formed Whitaker & Baxter International. With the PG&E retainer in hand and the success of their CVP campaign to give them confidence, they formed a professional partnership as Campaigns, Inc.—a decision that would reverberate down through the nation's political history. A footnote on the CVP campaign: When a attempt was made to unfreeze the authorization for the bonds and issue them in 1938, PG&E launched a successful opposition initiative campaign—successfully managed by Whitaker and Baxter. Later in an address to the 1949 Conference of the Public Relations Society Leone Baxter observed:

"When the firm of Whitaker and Baxter was organized nearly 20 years ago [sic], the business of directing in ethical business-like fashion, campaigns for candidates, and campaigns for and against public issues, was virtually non-existent. In our part of the country such matters generally were the natural province of broken down politicians and alcoholic camp followers. We were enchanted by the broad horizon—the absolute absence of competition—and frankly by the pride of helping create a new profession.

And create a new profession they did—today's campaign consultant who dominates every important political race in this country from President to mayor is their legacy. In Carey McWilliams's view, their decision "ushered in a new era in American politics—government by public relations."

Looking back 20 years later, McWilliams, writing in *The Nation*, commented:

"Whitaker and Baxter were enchanted to discover twenty years ago that they had hit upon a business in which there was absolutely no competition. Professional campaign management was unknown. Campaigns were seldom planned and never budgeted. Whitaker and Baxter insist that politics is merchandising men and measures, but they explain that, unlike sales campaigns, political campaigns are carried on under combat conditions, there is a definite opposition, a limited time, and the outcome is decisive.

In his *Breach of Faith*, Theodore White observed, "The technique for running a campaign divorced from a political party would probably have been inevitably developed by someone in the past forty years. Its apotheosis was to be reached in 1972 Richard Nixon's CREEP Committee for the Re-Election of the President. But almost certainly it had to be invented in California." And it was.

Clem Whitaker was absorbed by politics and would talk politics endlessly. He thought, "Most Americans love a contest; he [the voter] likes a good, hot battle with no punches pulled." Consequently Whitaker thought it essential to put on a good fight. He also saw the value of entertainment in political campaigns — a value demonstrated as early at the 1828 Jackson campaign. He saw the pulling power of the simplistic slogan. A vintage quote: "It was Patrick Henry who said, 'Give me liberty or give me death!' That's what I call laying it on with a ladle." Whitaker early understood that it is dynamic sloganeering that molds public opinion and wins campaigns. Whitaker possessed a genius for long-range planning and laying out the basic strategy for a campaign. As *Time* observed:

Leone defers to his political judgment. Leone is a talented writer, a minter of bright ideas and more the day-to-day executive. Throughout the life of Whitaker and Baxter, they alternated as president, switching jobs every year. They seldom used the pronoun I, it was always "we." They would usually answer telephone calls on two extensions. They divided the profits of Campaigns, Inc. evenly. Their political campaigns were planned in seclusion, usually at an oceanside resort.

In forming Campaigns, Inc., as a corporation, Whitaker and Baxter became in *Time's* view, "the acknowledged originals in the field of political public relations." In 1955, *Time* described them as "the world's only permanent specialists in the field." This was on the eve of the New Politics. In 1938, they made it a full-time partnership by getting married and settling down in a rambling Marin County home of large dimensions. After signing up with PG&E, the team was accused by its critics of selling out to private interests. Clem Whitaker stoutly denied this, explaining, "The Central Valley Project was not conceived as a power project, but it began to turn into one when the Federal Government stepped in. We were against that but not the original purpose of C.V.P." The partners insisted from the beginning that they would refuse to handle a campaign unless they believed in it. Whitaker said more than once: "There is too much personal breakage in this business to do it any other way. You give too much of yourself during a campaign." Yet their next successful campaign, one to defeat the Muckraker Upton Sinclair for governor of California in 1934, later brought rueful regrets to the partners.

THE CAMPAIGN TO SMEAR SINCLAIR

Upton Sinclair, longtime muckraking socialist writer, captured the Democratic nomination for governor of California in 1934, and set alarm bells off in the homes of the rich and well-to-do. They were alarmed by his program, End Poverty in California (EPIC) — of which there was a great deal in that Depression year. The Republican state chairman was the motion picture mogul, Louis B. Mayer. He early retained the Lord & Thomas advertising agency to mount a campaign, in Arthur Schlesinger, Jr.'s words, "to discredit and destroy Upton Sinclair as expediently and as permanently as possible." A group of movie producers raised $500,000 partly by assessing directors and stars one day's salary. Mayer induced Hollywood studios to turn out fake newsreels in which substantial community leaders and gentle old widows played by bit actors would declare for the Republican candidate, Frank Merriam, whereas bearded figures with heavy Russian accents explained why they were voting for Sinclair. Yet by September, Sinclair appeared to be running ahead, so Whitaker and Baxter were brought into the campaign for its last 2 months.

Under the chairmanship of Mayer, the Republicans had already determined that the traditional political party apparatus would be inadequate to reelect Governor Merriam. Mayer put the campaign in the hands of Don Francisco, head of Albert Lasker's Lord and Thomas West Coast office. Francisco, a young horticulturist who had brilliantly promoted Sunkist oranges and orange drink, was hired by Lasker in 1921 and made director of California operations 3 years later. Francisco and his associate, Don Belding, took charge of the smear-Sinclair drive in southern California. In his definitive account of this campaign, *The Campaign of the Century*, Greg Mitchell said, "This was an unprecedented step based on fear and desperation."

Earlier Whitaker and Baxter had decided to sit out the 1934 gubnertorial campaign because they regarded Merriam as "an incompetent fool" and because Upton Sinclair was a close friend of the Whitaker family. They decided, instead, to concentrate on electing George Hatfield lieutenant governor. (At that time the governor and lieutenant governor were elected separately in California.) The Republicans had offered the firm $5,000 to help with the Merriam campaign in northern California, but they had refused.

Yet by September, Sinclair appeared to be running ahead, so Whitaker and Baxter reconsidered and were brought in to the campaign for its last 2 months. They were hired by a front, the California League Against Sinclairism (CLAS), a group that was heavily financed by big money interests. Mitchell wrote, "Officially, Whitaker served as CLAS' publicist, but he was that and so much more. As a free-lance political strategist, Clem was literally one of a kind."

In his profile of the couple, Irwin Ross quoted them as saying, "We felt we had to do a fast job, we had to make a drastic change in public opinion." Their strategy was the ultimate in what might be called the diversionary technique—shifting attention from Sinclair's program to his personal foibles. In a harsher age, it has become known as a smear job. Whitaker admitted later, that "Upton was beaten because he had written books." In taking on this campaign, the pair secluded themselves to thoroughly research Sinclair's writings to cull out a series of damaging quotations.* After this they hired an artist, Bill LeNoire, to draw a series of 30 cartoons illustrating "the blot of Sinclairism"—generally a blob of ink "flung against some typical scene of American felicity." Typical was one showing a bride and groom emerging from a church who are assailed by a Sinclair comment that in a capitalist society the institution of marriage has the qualities of "marriage plus prostitution." Another cartoon showed a picture of a madonna and a child defiled by Sinclair's quote, "Of a score of religions in the world . . . each is a mighty fortress of graft." These cartoons were matted and placed in California newspapers. Irwin Ross estimated that "at least a thousand appeared in print." Thousands of pamphlets were distributed using the same themes. Whitaker later admitted "Sure, the quotations were irrelevant." Sinclair was easily defeated by Merriam, a staunch conservative whom they were able to portray as a liberal. Merriam reluctantly endorsed the Townsend Plan. A Dr. Francis Townsend had come up with a quack scheme to lick the Depression by giving every family "Thirty Dollars Every Thursday." Both Sinclair's EPIC Plan and the Townsend Plan were quick fixes to silence the pains and protests of the Great Depression. The situation was particularly acute in California because thousands of jobless Americans had been lured there under false pretenses from California's growers. The misery of these unemployed "Okies" was vividly portrayed in John Steinbeck's *Grapes of Wrath*. In the final days of the campaign, Sinclair's campaign fell apart under Whitaker and Baxter's bludgeoning through their cartoons, pamphlets, and sloganeering.

Many years later, Leone Baxter said, "We had one objective: to keep him

---

*Many of these quotations were spoken by characters in Sinclair's novels.

from becoming Governor. But because he was a good man, we were sorry we had to do it that way." "That way" included the theme "Out of his own mouth, he shall be judged." Where Sinclair's writings did not suffice to damn him, Schlesinger asserted that "his opponents had no scruple about fabrication and forgery. Thus, he was freely confused with Sinclair Lewis and denounced for having written *Elmer Gantry*. Fliers were circulated endorsing Sinclair signed by the 'Young Communist League, Vladimir Kosloff, Secy.' though no such person or organization existed." The "Willie Horton" technique is not as new as currently thought. In *The Politics of Upheaval*, Schlesinger saw the long-term significance of the smear Sinclair campaign:

> Sinclair got licked all right. But the manner of his licking reshaped California politics for a generation. The Republican success marked a new advance in the art of public relations, in which advertising men believed they could sell or destroy political candidates as they sold one brand of soap and defamed its competitor. Humdingery and dynamite dominated California politics from then on. In another twenty years, the techniques of manipulation, employed so crudely in 1934, would spread east, achieve a new refinement, and begin to dominate the politics of a nation.

An ironic footnote on the anti-Sinclair campaign: Upton Sinclair was a close friend of the Whitaker family, especially Clem's uncle, Robert Whitaker, a Baptist minister and socialist who served for a time as field secretary of the American Civil Liberties Union. Whitaker later admitted that his uncle and a few other family members quit speaking to him as the result of this campaign.

The historic significance of the Upton Sinclair race and the role of the campaign specialists in it is summed up by Mitchell in his book-length account of that campaign, *The Campaign of the Century*:

> The prospect of a socialist governing the nation's most volatile state sparked nothing less than a revolution in American politics. With an assist from Hollywood, Sinclair's opponents virtually invented the modern media campaign. It marked a stunning advance in the art of public relations. The 1934 governor's race in California showed candidates the way from the smoke-filled room to Madison Avenue. Media experts, making use of film, radio, direct mail, opinion polls, and national fund-raising, devised the most astonishing (and virtually clever) smear campaign ever directed against a major candidate. . . . The political innovation that produced the strongest impact, both in the 1934 race and long afterward, was the manipulation of moving pictures.

This innovation presaged the dominance of television in today's political campaigns.

W&B'S PHILOSOPHY AND PROCEDURES

Clem Whitaker frequently quoted Abraham Lincoln's classic statement, "Public sentiment is everything." He saw Lincoln not only as a great president but also as "one of the most astute politicians and as one of the finest public relations men of all times." Carey McWilliams was a bit dismayed by the partners' deep faith in the wisdom of public opinion: "Strange as it may seem, these political hucksters have a robust faith in public sentiment. They believe that the intelligent conduct of political public relations has undermined blind party regularity and encouraged independent voting. Both members of the firm are confident of their ability, given a good issue and reasonably adequate funds, to defeat the strongest boss-directed machine." In those thoughts lay the beginning of the end of the dominance of the political party.

Both Whitaker and Baxter placed great emphasis on the importance of words and slogans. Whitaker wrote in 1946, "Words still mold the minds of men — and still direct the ebb and flow of their emotions. Vigorous, fighting English. . . . colorful persuasive language . . . words that play tunes on the senses and paint pictures on men's minds. These are the best campaign tools, as they have been through the course of history." In their planning, they searched for the simplistic slogan and the right word. A typical example was the word *squandermania* that Leone once came up with. They were also adept at creating symbols. When San Francisco Mayor Roger Lapham was threatened by petition for his recall, Whitaker & Baxter saved his job with a brilliant campaign against "The Faceless Man." The "Man" was the creation of Leone — a drawing of an evil looking politician with no face that she doodled on a luncheon table cloth and then splashed on billboards all over San Francisco. As *Time* observed, "It had, like most Whitaker & Baxter campaigns, a certain basic logic. In the very nature of most recall fights, the challenged official must expose his record to attack, but there is no opponent to take the counterpunches."

Writing in the *Public Relations Journal* of July 1946, Whitaker looked back to the beginning:

> Managing a campaign is no longer a hit-or-miss business, directed by broken-down politicians. It is rapidly emerging from its swaddling clothes to become a mature, well-managed business *founded on sound public relations principles* [italics added], and using every technique of modern advertising. When my partner and I first went into the campaign business, there were hundred dollar bills floating around campaign headquarters like pennies raining down from heaven. But that condition was one of the circumstances which had kept politics in the realm of the racket — and it is one of the conditions that we set about to cure in a hurry. Today there isn't a dollar spent in any campaign conducted by our office that isn't reported in a check-by-check accounting — and we have a pardonable pride in that accomplishment.

Whitaker declared that their firm had made an important contribution to lifting the level of California politics, asserting, "California votes are not bought and sold; bosses will never be a problem because machines could never stand the light of a hard-hitting modern public relations and advertising campaign."

In a somewhat platitudinous statement, Whitaker said, "Fundamentals in a successful campaign are a good candidate and good issues." In the *Journal* article he amplified this thought, "The best man isn't necessarily the best candidate, unfortunately. One of the best governors that California has had in the past twenty-five years was one of the poorest politicians. And, conversely, one of the best candidates I have ever known didn't turn out so well as a governor."

One of the reasons Whitaker and Baxter were so successful in their nearly 30 years of campaign management was that they were selective in the candidates or issues they accepted. Staunch Republicans, Whitaker and Baxter managed only one campaign for a Democrat, that of George Hatfield, candidate for lieutenant governor in the 1934 California general election. Hatfield won at the same time Republican Frank Merriam was defeating Upton Sinclair. Both Whitaker and Baxter repeatedly insisted that political public relations "requires idealism and realism." Whitaker wrote, "There is a somewhat simple creed that determines the campaigns we accept or reject. It's simply this: you can't work your heart out for a man you don't believe in, and there's no sense working your heart out for a man who isn't electable. If our batting average has been fairly good throughout the years, I think it's mainly because we never enter a campaign where we can't put everything we have into winning." They held that "you can't wage a defensive campaign and win." And win they did. By the mid-1950s, they had won 90% of the 75 campaigns managed up to that time.

Whitaker and Baxter would also drop the account of a candidate who would not follow their advice. At least they did so in one instance. The pair had successfully managed Goodwin Knight's campaign for governor of California in 1954. Whitaker and Baxter insisted on total control of a campaign. In *The New Politics*, James Perry cited this memo for the Knight campaign as an example: "The Campaign will concentrate on a few major issues which will be outlined in the Campaign literature, in the Speakers Manual, and throughout campaign materials. With such a brief working period as that which lies ahead, you will recognize that we must *stick closely to the main issues outlined*, and leave out many of the secondary and less important issues, however interesting they are."

Early in 1955 Governor Knight announced that he would be a "nominal" candidate for the Republican presidential nomination if President Eisenhower would choose not to be a candidate because of his health. Knight was seeking to have the powerful 70-person California delegation pledged to the President if he were a candidate and to himself if Eisenhower were not a

candidate. This was a ploy to head off Vice President Richard Nixon by
gaining control of the delegation. Again, the Governor retained Whitaker
and Baxter for this political effort.

Despite their long association with Governor Knight, they made their
insistence on being in total charge of a campaign when in 1958 they were
managing Knight's campaign for the United States Senate. That year
Knight, who had a served as lieutenant governor before being elected
governor, was running for the United States Senate. The firm dropped
Knight after the primary because he would not stick to their plan and
insisted on attacking his running mate, Senator William Knowland, then a
candidate for Governor of California, rather than aiming his fire at the
Democratic candidates. Irwin Ross observed of this decision to drop
Knight, "Not many press agents, one can assume, feel sufficiently secure to
fire a Governor. Whitaker and Baxter, however, have an exuberant respect
for their own political wisdom—and they hate a loser." Knight lost badly!

Clem Whitaker understood the political apathy of the average citizen.
"The average American, when he isn't at work, wants to enjoy his leisure.
He resents your trying to put him to work on something in which *you* are
interested. He doesn't want to be educated; he doesn't want to have his mind
improved; he doesn't even want to work—consciously—at being a good
citizen." The couple held that one arouses the voter's interest in a campaign
by providing a good fight and entertainment. Whitaker saw his hero,
Patrick Henry, not only as a great patriot but "as a great campaigner." (He
thought this even though Henry lost in his campaign to defeat Virginia's
ratification of the U.S. Constitution!) Whitaker asserted that even in these
modern times, Henry's kind of sloganeering builds public sentiment and
wins campaigns. W&B proved this repeatedly in winning or defeating
complex proposition proposals on the California ballot. Bluntly put, the
pair saw themselves as salesmen with a product to sell. Whitaker, speaking
to the Los Angeles chapter of the Public Relations Society on July 13, 1948,
said, "We do our utmost in every campaign to get a dollar's value for every
dollar spent, just as we would if we were merchandising commodities,
instead of selling men and measures. . . . We use campaign funds not to
dispense favors, but to mould public sentiment."

W&B'S BASIC PRINCIPLES

Leone Baxter saw the innovative firm's forte as "building specific public
opinion on highly-contested issues." Continuing in a speech she gave at the
1949 PRSA Conference she said:

> We had established for our course a set of 50 sound procedures designed to
> create a healthy new profession, and to keep it that way. Through years of

testing every conceivable type of campaign concerned with creating public opinion, we have found no occasion to change the rules. They remain the foundation of all our campaigns, whether our objective is to help elect a governor or write an new law; raise teacher's salaries in our state, or try to stop socialized medicine nationally.

Then Miss Baxter proceeded to list ten of these procedures and discuss their specific application:

1. *Fresh Air in the Finance Department.* Any committee, industry, etc. has the right to tell its story, but also has an obligation to report its expenditures accurately to the proper authorities.

2. *Convictions Are Important.* For us, its basis concerns certain fundamentals that we personally believe in — individual initiative and personal responsibility; the free operations of our economic society; reasonable freedom from government control and directive. Our rule simply means that we wouldn't run a campaign whose objectives run counter to ours.

3. *Don't Underestimate Your Opposition.* In preparing our Plan of Campaign for our current job last January, we spent just as much time projecting the probable mores of the advocates of Compulsory Health Insurance as our own campaign against it. . . . We produced our own campaign only after writing out what seemed to use a reasonable plan of campaign for our opposition.

4. *Don't Underestimate the Man on the Street.* It has been our experience that the Man on Main Street will render a pretty fair decision if he is given a fair chance — a chance to hear both sides of the argument.

5. *Mobilize Your Natural Allies and 6. The Soundest Approach is the Grass Roots Approach.* A brief case history: In January compulsory health insurance bills were pending in the Congress and had been labelled "must" legislation by the President. The nation had not heard the doctors' story. We took our story to the people through the media and organizations across the country. In January this year, the doctors stood alone in their opposition to Government medicine. But by November the threat of such legislation was long past.

6. *Stick to the Facts.* Most people don't like to be fooled. Without qualification, I will say that because the greatest help the doctors have had in their current campaign is the Federal Security Agency's own treatise titled "A Ten Year Plan for the Nation's Health." The "Ten Year Plan" was sent out broadly to immense numbers of people. However, we exposed the treatise as a propaganda effort based on garbled facts and juggled figures.

7. *You Can't Beat Something With Nothing.* Ordinarily, a negative, wholly attacking campaign isn't sound and is fair neither to the client nor to the public.

8. *The Masses Are Individuals*. Classifying people too categorically is dangerous. Nobody likes it. I like to be a good public relations man [*sic*]. If I were to find myself one day stuffed into a pigeon hole, to the exclusion of other perhaps more feminine classifications, I'd not enjoy the seclusion at all. A Democrat may be a farmer, a truck driver, a salesman, teacher, even a Dixiecrat.

9. *More Americans Like Corn Than Caviar*. From time to time sophisticated observers prod us more or less gently for a certain obvious domesticated approach we often use to the public. The observers are right. We wave the flag and we mean it. We talk in simple language because we intend to be understood.

The partners' *modus operandi* was that every campaign should have a dominant, arresting theme. Whitaker explained, "The theme should have simplicity and clarity. Most importantly, it must high-point the major issues of the campaign with great brevity—in language that paints a picture understandable to people in all circumstances." Sometimes they used an oversimplification, for example, "socialized medicine." They demonstrated repeatedly the power of the simplistic slogan.

A WINNING SLOGAN: "POLITICAL MEDICINE IS BAD MEDICINE"

The power of the simplistic slogan in politics was demonstrated in the Whitaker & Baxter campaign to defeat Governor Earl Warren's proposal for a state health insurance plan, which he presented to the California legislature in January 1945. Political writers at the time saw Warren's motive as thinking he should sponsor at least one piece of social legislation as he approached his reelection campaign in 1946. Carey McWilliams thought "this was an excellent choice. It would offend only the doctors, a limited professional group with little political influence, and a notoriously inept sense of public relations." But the state's doctors had the wisdom to retain Whitaker & Baxter.

After working out their campaign plan in seclusion, the firm, ignoring legislators in Sacramento, went directly to the people with the campaign that "Political Medicine is Bad Medicine." As described by McWilliams:

The main prongs of the attack were (1) a campaign for endorsements, not because endorsements are important *per se* but because they are a means by which sentiment is organized—within three months more than a hundred powerful state-wide organizations were corralled; (2) a speech-making campaign in which 9,000 doctors were first inflamed with Whitaker's rhetoric and then sent out "to do a job," heavily laden with Whitaker and Baxter speeches couched in "fighting prose"; (3) an intensive, lobbying campaign in which doctors in each of California's eighty assembly and forty senatorial districts were told to approach the principal backers of their legislators. Whitaker and Baxter insisted that if the legislators' principal backers are thoroughly lobbied, the legislator will have to deliver; (4) an equally intensive lobbying of "thought leaders" including the presidents of 400 service clubs, 280 officers of veterans' organizations, 500 officers of women's clubs, lodges, and civic organizations, 200 insurance executives and almost every city, county, and state official. Incidentally, one of the keys to the influence of Whitaker and Baxter is the enormous quantity of political favors that the firm had accumulated from previous campaigns. Also, they heavily used newspaper advertising, clipsheets, and news releases in the successful campaign to kill Governor Warren's proposal in the legislature.

They also countered the governor's measure by promoting voluntary health insurance and proclaimed a Voluntary Health Insurance Week. The campaign firm claimed that consequently 2,500,000 Californians were enrolled in voluntary health insurance plans—"more than Warren promised to care for with his plan." Critics thought these numbers were exaggerated, but as Carey McWilliams, wrote, "This crude realism should not be permitted to minimize the accomplishment of Whitaker and Baxter in which doctors, originally cast as special interest heavies, emerge as crusaders for the people's health. This is expert political management, this is government by Whitaker and Baxter." This successful campaign for the doctors of California brought the firm the account of the American Medical Association in its effort to defeat President Harry Truman's national health insurance plan, proposed in 1948. Again the firm was successful, gaining national attention for them and their methods. The AMA campaign is described later.

FIRM SETS UP SUBSIDIARIES TO MAINTAIN CONTROL, INCREASE PROFITS

Once the firm was on a sound financial footing, the partners decided to set up an advertising agency, Whitaker and Baxter Advertising that continues to this day under the management of Clem's son, Clem Jr., with offices in the Flood Building in San Francisco. Because advertising was a major tool in W&B campaigns, the partners insisted on controlling the copy to insure its conformity with the campaign themes and to place their own advertising. The subsidiary received the standard 15% commission an accredited ad agency gets from the media in which advertisements are placed. The late CBS media critic, Don Hollenbeck, once criticized the couple by asserting their advertising schedules were "an improper attempt to influence editorial opinion." The fact was that they sent their ads to every newspaper whether it was supporting or opposing a campaign. This advertising revenue augmented their campaign fees that in the 1940s and 1950s ranged from $25,000 to $75,000 plus all campaign expenses. However, they collected the 15% commission on advertising they placed only from the daily newspapers. Advertisements placed in rural papers were typically accompanied by a check and a letter noting that the commission had not been charged. In this way the firm built goodwill among the rural weekly owners in the state.

Also to increase their revenues and to enhance their publicity output, Whitaker and Baxter started a printed one-page clipsheet, the California Feature Service (CFS), in which sponsors paid to have stories included that was sent to all California newspapers. The clipsheet is a standard tool of public relations. Usually they inserted one or two of their own clients' releases. Much of its content was without an obvious partisan slant. Stanley Kelley told of one California editor who played a game with his staff each week when the CFS clipsheet arrived. They called the game "Where's the Plug?" The object was to be the first to discover the hidden propaganda in a seemingly innocuous story or editorial. The State Farm Bureau of California was a client. In the May 11, 1953, clipsheet was an editorial entitled "The Farm Bureau Aids CARE." The suggested editorial began, "California farmers, under the leadership of the California Farm Bureau Federation, are currently conducting a unique experience in good will," and ends with this clincher, "The Farm Bureau is to be congratulated for instituting a program of simple self-help from individuals to individuals which would well prove to be of more lasting value than many of the grandiose, tax-supported schemes fathered during the post-war years in Washington." "Schemes" was a pejorative word the couple used with great frequency. The CFS clipsheet was the work of Clem Jr., James Dorais, and Will Davidson.

Normally on a year-round basis, the W&B staff totaled not more than 15 persons but would be expanded to 50 or so when they took on a statewide campaign. Their year-round business included major business clients such as PG&E, Pacific Telephone and Telegraph, Standard Oil of California, and others. In the late 1950s, Irwin Ross put their annual income at $250,000. This does not count the millions paid out in expenses for their campaigns. It was not unusual for a state campaign to cost $500,000 in those days. Two decades later, millions were spent on both sides of a hotlycontested proposition. For example in the late 1940s and early 1950s, the firm conducted three campaigns sponsored by the California Teachers Association to raise teachers' salaries—which they did, from $77 million to $400 million annually. These campaigns cost the Teachers Association $772,000 all told.

Some years after forming Campaigns, Inc., Whitaker and Baxter brought Whitaker's son, Clem, Jr. and James J. Dorais in as junior partners. These four plus some half dozen or so professional employees formed the core staff. In 1959, when Clem, Sr.'s health began to plague him, he and his wife sold the firm, Campaigns, Inc., and its allied advertising agency to Whitaker's son Clem, Jr., James Dorais, and Newton Stearns. Whitaker and Baxter then established themselves in a plush penthouse atop the Fairmont Hotel as Whitaker & Baxter International. After Whitaker's death in 1961, Leone Baxter continued to be active in Whitaker & Baxter International until she eased into retirement in the early 1980s. Clem, Jr. wrote to me on October 31, 1991, "Years ago when I assumed management of Whitaker & Baxter we phased out of the campaign management business. Our last candidate campaign was the election of Senator Robert Griffin over Governor Mennen 'Soapy' Williams in Michigan in 1966. We ceased ballot issue campaigns in 1973." Today Whitaker & Baxter is a consulting firm in the area of public affairs basically representing energy clients. It maintains offices in San Francisco and Washington, DC, thus now is in the flourishing business of public affairs lobbying.

The son's decision to abandon campaign management and go into lobbying has an ironic twist to it. Kelley quoted Whitaker Senior as saying, "Lobbying is inconclusive: the actions of one legislature are not binding on the next; and the favors done during one session need not be acknowledged at the succeeding one." Speaking before the Southern Public Relations Conference at Tulane University in May 1951, Leone Baxter asserted:

Our conception of practical politics is that if you have a sound enough case to convince the folks back home, you don't have to buttonhole the senator. He will hear from home, and he is prone to respect very highly the opinions he gets from that quarter. Our method is not the easy way, particularly when the time is short. It takes an army of volunteers, and it is costly in time and energy. But it is sound. It is realistic. It is lasting.

Apparently the son differed from his father on another matter—that of campaign disclosure. Early in 1966, Senator Everett Dirksen of Illinois announced the formation of the Committee for Government by the People that would permit states to apportion one house of their legislature by factors other than population. Whitaker and Baxter was retained to promote adoption of the measure. Senators Joseph Tydings of Maryland and William Proxmire of Wisconsin told the Senate on March 6, 1966, that the campaign firm had refused to disclose how much was being spent on this campaign and who was providing the money for it.

In Theodore White's opinion:

From 1933 to 1959 [when California abolished cross-filing in an attempt to give some coherence to party politics] Whitaker and Baxter were to California politics what Tammany had once been to New York politics. Managing sixty campaigns and referenda in the fifteen years prior to 1957, they had won fifty-five of them. Their clients were of such eminence as Earl Warren, William Knowland, Thomas Kuchel, Richard Nixon, and Goodwin Knight. Their fee for rounding up enough signatures to put a referendum on the ballot was at least $120,000.

The late "Teddy" White, whose books on the presidential elections of the 1960s and 1970s had great impact on political reporting, believed that "Whitaker and Baxter were themselves sublimely uninterested in any substantive issues. Their ethics were those of a skilled lawyer who does his best to win a case. They would, for their fee, deliver a tailor-made campaign for anybody or any cause; and they usually won." As indicated earlier, Clem Whitaker stoutly denied that this was so.

TYPICAL CAMPAIGNS

The partners always proceeded on the basis that each campaign had to have a basic theme expressed in a simplistic slogan. They also believed that a campaign must have an inner rhythm, a pace, a timing that would capture the attention of the news system, both print and electronic. Another basic was to mobilize natural allies. This term in plain English meant, according to Kelley, "(1) those who have a direct financial interest in the outcome; (2) those who ideological affinities should lead them to sympathize with the campaign's objectives, and (3) those whose relationship to the client gives the client some financial or psychological hold over them." For example, in a campaign for a school building program, Whitaker and Baxter gained the support of organized architects, building suppliers, consulting engineers, electrical contractors, painters, plasterers—all of whom would profit from the construction of new school buildings.

Once the partners had decided on the theme of the campaign and had developed the marketing plan for it, Whitaker and Baxter used intensively the standard tools of a campaign—speeches, news stories, printed pamphlets, radio spots, and after the mid-1950s, TV spots. Irwin Ross provided these examples: In 1950 California voters were presented with a scheme to pay old age pensions out of the proceeds of legalized gambling. Whitaker and Baxter were hired to defeat what was a flawed scheme. They pitched their entire campaign on the theme, "Keep the Crime Syndicates Out!"— even though nobody had advocated letting the crime syndicates in. In 1958, there was a proposition on the California ballot to increase a state revenue with a series of new taxes. Whitaker and Baxter, hired to defeat the proposal, came up with the label, the Monkey Wrench Tax Bill. In their newspaper ads they warned voters that if the Monkey Wrench Tax Bill were passed, the state would have to impose new taxes on real estate, food, and gasoline in order to raise the needed revenues. But, as Ross pointed out, "Their highly effective TV spots eliminated the argument and merely demanded, 'Do you want to pay a state property tax on your home?' Loud voice in the background: 'No!' Announcer: 'Then vote No on Proposition 17 — the Monkey Wrench Tax Bill.' The unwary listener could hardly have gathered that Proposition 17 was not in itself a real estate tax. In 1948, there was a proposition on the ballot to repeal the full-crew law on trains, a law opposed by the railroads but favored by railroad unions: W&B was retained by the railroads to pass it. This time they came up with a campaign song, "I've Been Loafing on the Railroad," sung to the popular sing-along tune of long ago. It was sung at meetings, on radio spots, and provided the caption for a widely distributed cartoon of a railroad employee lolling in a bed atop a freight car. This visual was also plastered on billboards all around the state.

In preparation for a candidate campaign, the partners and their staffs prepared exhaustive dossiers on their candidate and the opponent. In some instances these dossiers ran to a million words. From these lengthy resumes prepared by assistants, summaries were prepared for Whitaker and Baxter. In a typical campaign in 1948, Whitaker & Baxter distributed 10 million pamphlets and leaflets, 4.5 million postcards, 50,000 letters to influential voters placed 70,000 inches of advertising through its advertising subsidiary, and contracted for 3,000 radio spots and twelve 15-minute radio programs. It put up 1,000 highway billboards and 20,000 smaller posters; it prepared slides and trailers for showing in 160 theaters. This campaign, said Kelley, "was no more than average Whitaker and Baxter." Understandably, it was successful. Few opponents could match such an outpouring of political propaganda. Despite this massive dissemination of propaganda in each campaign, the managers were sticklers for every piece they produced. They were perfectionists. During the 1954 gubernatorial campaign, the kept "Goodie" Knight wilting under the klieg lights and camera for a full day before they were satisfied with four 60-second TV spots.

Irwin Ross recounted an example of the partners' resourcefulness. Early in 1958, they were retained by the Port of San Francisco to win a referendum in support of a $50 million bond issue to improve that port. Although it was a justifiable expenditure, the measure, they conceded, would have little support beyond San Francisco — particularly in a hostile southern California. Even though the bonds would be repaid out of revenues and thus cost the taxpayers nothing, this was a difficult proposition to sell to 6 million voters. Whitaker had observed more than once, "The more you have to explain, the more difficult it is to win support."

One morning at breakfast Leone read a newspaper story about another bond proposal—a $10 million issue to expand small boat harbors throughout California. It would also be self-liquidating. Whitaker and Baxter suddenly saw a way to enhance the appeal of the San Francisco Part issue—merging the bond proposals into one. They mobilized their supporters in Sacramento and got a new bill passed. Then they set out, successfully, to sell California voters on approving bond issues to improve California's harbors from Oregon to Mexico. Then the floodgates opened with supporting handbills, pamphlets, newspaper and radio advertising, and TV spots. Savoring his victory, Whitaker said, "A good example of how you can win a campaign in the board room—long before it starts."

Thus, from 1933 until 1959, this attractive and able team were involved centrally in California politics. Kelley concluded, "By some, Whitaker is rated as the state's closest approximation to a boss. Others note that Whitaker and Baxter campaigns have almost always been well financed, have mostly received overwhelming press support, and that their candidates, men like Governors Warren and Knight, have often been canny politicians in their own right." A basic factor that cannot be overlooked in their success: the peculiar characteristics of the California political system— weak state organizations, direct legislation, a growing population of immigrants, and legislation by referendum.

This section concludes with a listing of the measures that Whitaker and Baxter got passed or defeated: The defeat of the Garrison Revenue Bond Act of 1938; the defeat of the Ham'n Eggs pension plan in 1939; increasing aid to state schools in 1946, 1948, and 1952 to increase teachers' salaries; the defeat of legislative reapportionment in 1948; the repeal of the full-crew law in 1948; the killing of Governor Warren's health insurance proposal in 1945; and the passage of the state Employees' Retirement System Act. By 1956, they had won 90% of 75 campaigns—a high batting average in any political system! Demonstrably Whitaker and Baxter had moved political propaganda and campaign management from an auxiliary weapon to that of a central one.

WHITAKER AND BAXTER PROVE THAT THEIR METHODS WORK IN THE NATIONAL ARENA

Whitaker and Baxter took their highly polished campaign plan into the arena of national politics and proved that what worked in California would work nationwide and thus gave the campaign specialist movement new impetus and new recognition. In 1949, they took on a national campaign for the American Medical Association (AMA) to defeat President Harry Truman's plan for national health insurance—a plan these seasoned campaigners promptly dubbed with the opprobrium "socialized medicine." The

American Medical Association became panicky with the surprise reelection of President Truman in 1948 that gave his health insurance plan new life. Clem Whitaker was invited to the National Medical Public Relations Conference in St. Louis on November 27, 1948—the month of Truman's reelection. Quite impressed with Whitaker's presentation, the AMA formed a National Education Committee and named Leone Baxter general manager. Whitaker was to be director of the national campaign. These plans were ratified at the annual convention of the AMA held in Chicago in early December. At this convention, the AMA officers announced imposition of a $25 "voluntary fee" for its 140,000 doctor members to sponsor a nationwide plan of education to alert and arouse the public against the threat of socialized medicine. On December 16, 1948, Major General George F. Lull, general manager of the AMA, announced that Whitaker and Baxter had been retained to direct the campaign. Over the next $3\frac{1}{2}$ years, Whitaker and Baxter spent nearly $5,000,000 to thoroughly quash the Truman proposal. They were paid $100,000 a year for their campaign direction.

Some Background

Plans for a national health insurance program date from the Franklin Roosevelt New Deal. In 1946, it was promoted by a Committee for the Nation's Health, whose membership included Eleanor Roosevelt, Phillip Murray of the CIO, and William Green of the AF of L. The proposal was endorsed by the American Federation of Labor, the Americans for Democratic Action, the American Veterans Committee (which had a short life), the CIO, the NAACP, and the National Farmers Union, among others. In May 1948, President Truman—undoubtedly looking forward to the November election—convened a National Health Assembly that was attended by 800 professional and community leaders. Federal Security Administrator Oscar Ewing presented a report prepared for the President, "The Nation's Health: A Ten-Year Program." This outlined a plan for federally sponsored health insurance. Government health insurance, then an anathema to doctors, had been consistently opposed by organized medicine. The AMA sponsored a National Physicians Committee that spent about $1 million between 1946 and 1948 to combat the growing support for such a program. The Whitaker and Baxter massive propaganda and advertising campaign buried the issue in the early 1950s. It would not be raised again nationally until President Lyndon Johnson pushed through Congress his proposals for Medicare and Medicaid. A campaign for national health insurance for the some 35 million Americans without health insurance reemerged in the early 1990s as a "hot button" political issue. Senator Harris Wofford of

Pennsylvania exploited the issue to win his Senate seat in 1991. President Clinton used the issue to win the Presidency in 1992.

The Campaign

Their research done and their campaign plan formulated, the partners moved to Chicago in February and opened the National Education Campaign headquarters with a staff of 37 persons. The Whitaker and Baxter team reported to a coordinating committee headed by Dr. Elmer Henderson, president of the AMA, and that committee reported to the House of Delegates. The basic plan was that the professionals would develop the themes, prepare the literature, and then state and local societies would distribute it – mainly through the doctors' offices. Their basic approach was to damn the Truman plan as socialized medicine in much the manner they killed Governor Earl Warren's health insurance plan in 1945 in California.

On the positive side, the campaign claimed that the United States had the highest standards of medical care in the world. The campaign literature admitted that there were many health problems facing the nation but argued that these would not be solved by national health insurance. They also used the bugaboo of socialized medicine as practiced in England – "government medicine would mean assembly-line service, bringing personal hardships, patients assigned to doctors, doctors to patients, and destruction of the privacy of medical records." To blunt the force of the support for national health insurance, the AMA did give way and give doctors permission to join voluntary health plans. This made the issue compulsory versus voluntary or socialized medicine versus voluntary. In their later advertising campaigns, the specialists use two-thirds of their budget to promote voluntary plans, "The Voluntary Way is the American Way," and one-third to denounce socialized medicine and Oscar Ewing, who became their "bad guy."

Their strategy set and their staff in place, the partners went full bore with their campaign of propaganda, advertising, and enlistment of national support. Their campaign had four main parts: (a) a drive for endorsement of the AMA stand by lay national, state, and local organizations; (b) a publicity campaign; (c) a speakers' bureau; and (d) preparation and distribution of pamphlets and posters. For example, they distributed Sir Luke Fildes' painting of a doctor at a sick child's bedside, with the caption, "Keep Politics Out of This Picture," to some 70,273 doctors to put up in their offices. This was only the beginning!

According to Frank Campion in *The AMA and Health Policy Since 1940*, Whitaker and Baxter reported to the AMA House of Delegates in June 1949 that they had contacted 12,000 trade associations, 2,700 chambers of commerce, 500 civic clubs, 120 advertising clubs, 1,500 Kiwanis clubs, 4,500 Lions clubs, 2,300 Rotary clubs, 1,300 Carnegie libraries, 900 college libraries, 8,000 public libraries, 14,000 school principals/superintendents, 9,000 YMCA city associations, 200 YWCA city associations, and 130,000 dentists/druggists. These contacts were made on the basis of information supplied by state and county medical societies. These societies were directed by AMA headquarters to compile lists of civic, business, farm, fraternal, political, and patriotic organizations. Whitaker and Baxter then sent form resolutions, speeches, and lists of groups holding conventions with dates and the contact person to the medical societies across the nation. W&B dispatched professional organizers to such meetings and conventions to ask those assembled to distribute literature, contribute speakers, and help obtain other endorsements. By the end of 1949, Whitaker and Baxter claimed that they had obtained 1,829 endorsements of the AMA campaign, and by end of the campaign they claimed a total of 8,000 such endorsements.

The campaign staff steadily ground out news releases and feature articles on the substance of the campaign plus a steady flow of endorsement stories to build a picture of strong public opinion support for the AMA's position. The partners also spent a lot of time persuading doctors with known contacts in the media to use these contacts to further the cause. A cascade of pamphlets began streaming from the campaign headquarters and in the $3\frac{1}{2}$ year campaign, a total of $1,351,000 was spent on printing. This literature was distributed through doctors' offices and by direct mail. In the first year of the campaign, nearly 55 million pieces had been distributed in this fashion. The prodigious expenditure and output of the campaign was unprecedented for one organization.

THE PARTNERS FIRE THE "BIG BERTHA"—ADVERTISING

Whitaker and Baxter waited until the fall of 1950—just prior to the off-year Congressional elections—to fire the "Big Bertha" gun of their campaign to kill the Truman health insurance plan. In late August, the partners announced that the AMA would launch a $1,110,000 advertising program for October. In the week of October 8, they published large ads in 11,000 newspapers in the 48 states as well as Alaska, the District of Columbia, and Hawaii. $560,000 was spent on newspapers and $250,000 on magazines. The more than million dollar campaign was underwritten by some 144, 500 doctors through their extra assessments by the AMA; an assessment to which a minority of doctors vehemently objected.

Whitaker and Baxter boasted:

This, without a doubt, is the broadest coverage newspaper advertisement of the year, judged from the standpoint of the number of newspaper included in the schedule. This ad campaign was handled by the Lockwood–Shackleford Company in Chicago, not by the W&B ad subsidiary. The ad was 70 inches, 5 columns by 14 inches in black and white. Full page ads were also scheduled in the Sunday supplements, national magazines, and business, professional, and trade publications. The artillery of radio was wheeled into action the second and third weeks of October with more than 1,000 stations carrying paid ads as the medical tom toms carried on their steady beat.

Whitaker and Baxter told *Editor & Publisher*:

> This is a grass roots campaign. Wherever there is a newspaper there are doctors — and the doctors' patients. The AMA advertising program is designed to blanket every area of medical practice. Consequently, the schedule calls for the use of advertising space in all the newspapers in America. There will be some duplication of circulation, but the added impact of that duplication is desired, so that medicine's story is hammered home by repetition."

Not content with this nationwide blast against national health insurance, the firm next wheeled onto the firing line their natural allies. Whitaker and Baxter sent newspapers an advertising kit outlining 20 or more profitable tie-ins at the local level — drug stores, manufacturers, insurance companies, local health plans, and hospitals. Local Blue Cross and Blue Shield plans were provided with material to use as part of their own institutional programs to coincide with AMA's advertising campaign, Lawrence Wells, public relations director of Blue Cross and Blue Shield, told *Editor & Publisher*. On top of all this, Dr. Elmer Henderson, president of the AMA, and Dr. Louis Bauer, chairman of the board of trustees, wrote letters to 25,000 persons explaining to them the objects of the campaign and giving reasons why the AMA effort should be supported. Another letter from the officers was sent to 7,000 members of the National Retail Dry Goods Association urging retailers at the local level join in the campaign.

As Stanley Kelley pointed out in his *Professional Public Relations and Political Power*, this was part of the Whitaker and Baxter basic strategy — "to effect a maximum of reiteration from as many independent sources as possible. For themselves and their headquarters, they reserved the task of producing all basic campaign literature and materials: posters, pamphlets, leaflets, reprints, form resolutions, form speeches, cartoons and mats, and all publicity adaptable for local use." Whitaker and Baxter recognized the social role of the family doctor in community life and exploited it.

Illustrative of the political power the campaigners harnessed to bring medical costs from the periphery of political issues to the nation's agenda in the waning days of the Truman Administration, was the tie-in of the AMA with the National Association of Insurance Agents, a natural ally in the W&B lexicon. This association had 20,000 independents agencies of the country, reaching into every city, town, and hamlet. The association was persuaded to set up displays at the state conventions and place posters in agents' offices similar to those already gracing doctors' reception rooms. Others marshaled for the campaign included the Provident Mutual Life of Philadelphia, Bankers' Life and Casualty Company of America, and the International Association of Accident and Health Underwriters. The latter set up a speakers bureau and lined up 1,500 speakers to carry the message to the provinces. The *New Republic* asserted in its issue of December 12, 1949, that the cost of these supplementary campaigns "will run into the millions—enough to provide adequate medical care for a lot of people."

Whitaker and Baxter were great believers in swamping their clients with figures showing their success. The firm had the tie-in campaigns checked by the Advertising Checking Bureau, Inc., the Western Newspaper Union suppliers of boiler plates to newspapers, the National Editorial Association, and by IBM. These agencies reported that 65,246 individual advertisers had participated in this blockbuster advertising campaign and in so doing had spent $2,019,849 in addition to the AMA's expenditure of more than $1 million. The national had never witnessed such an intensive and expensive propaganda campaign in its history. More than $3 million!

SPEAK ONLY WITH ONE VOICE!

A basic public relations principle is that an institution must speak only with one voice if its message is to have clarity. Whitaker and Baxter enforced this principle on all their clients. Dr. Morris Fishbein, editor of the *Journal of the American Medical Association* (JAMA) had long been the AMA's public voice and over the years had accumulated many critics. He was fired from his post at the 98th annual meeting of the AMA in Atlantic City in June 1949. In Dr. Elmer Henderson's announcement, the first paragraph read, "The Board of Trustees recognized that the public has come to believe that the editor [Fishbein] is the spokesman of the association." The announcement made clear that henceforth Whitaker and Baxter would be the AMA spokespersons. The *Commonwealth* of October 23, 1949, put it harshly, "The AMA which has long suffered from a malignant disorder of its public relations, often complicated by the growth of Dr. Fishbein, has now put its convalescence in the hands of two experienced California public relations professionals."

CONSEQUENCES OF THIS MASSIVE CAMPAIGN

What were and are the consequences of this massive, unprecedented campaign to put medical care and health cost on the national agenda for a span of 3 years? Writing in the *Public Relations Journal* in January, 1950, Clem Whitaker claimed:

> The controversy served good purpose because sharpened interest helped bring the issue under scrutiny; it is to AMA's credit that it didn't turn away from the battle but faced it head on. Our strategy was to use the controversy to capture, not stifle, public interest; win the controversy by winning the public support. The underlying reason for this strategy was that American medicine already had reached the basic decision that on the principle of compulsory health insurance there could be no compromise, there could be no appeasement.

This campaign squared perfectly with the couple's right-wing views. Whitaker continued:

> The goal most of us have is to keep our clients out of controversy. Under normal conditions, that is a worthy objective. But these are not normal times – and there are circumstances under which it is both bad public relations and moral cowardice to keep out clients out of controversy. To avoid socialism, we need more than passive public acceptance of our social and economic system – we need complete confidence and militant support. Our profession has to prove that it is a dynamic force in our American economy, rather than just a low horse-power auxiliary engine. . . . We have to provide real leadership in the economic civil war which is ahead of us.

This assertion gives weight to Frank Campion's view:

> Whitaker and Baxter had no gift of humor, little appreciation for subtlety. As a matter of professional conviction, they dealt in hammer blows, repeated hammer blows. Hard-sell marked their ads, the pamphlets they prepared, the speeches they wrote. They simplified the issues; they emotionalized them, often they exaggerated and overstated them. They liked to claim that government health insurance constituted a first step toward totalitarianism. They did not hesitate to decorate their pamphlets with pealing Liberty Bells, to wrap their arguments in the flag, to threaten President Truman was going to bring the unpleasantness of the Army's "sick call" to the whole population and put a politician "between you and your doctor."

Yet Campion said that their claims and exaggerations did not go beyond the bounds of acceptable political hyperbole. But close!

President Truman and the other advocates of national health insurance were hopelessly outgunned and outspent by the AMA, and no strong movement developed in Congress to pass such legislation in this period. The Committee for the Nation's Health could not match the AMA's vast resources. The committee was able to raise and spend only $104,000 in 1949. It distributed some pamphlets and condensed reports to the liberal press and especially to the labor press. Even though vilified by the Whitaker and Baxter campaign, President Truman never gave strong support to the Ewing proposal. He confined his public utterances on health largely to formal communications to the Congress, including the 1949 State of the Union message, the 1949 Budget message, and a special message to the Congress on the nation's health needs on April 22, 1949. Truman responded somewhat cursorily to reporters' questions on this topic at his press conferences. He even pulled in the reins on his Secretary of Federal Security, Oscar Ewing, who with Senator James Murray of Montana, were the chief proponents. At one point the President reminded the zealous Ewing that "legislative policy had to conform to still to be determined budget policy," adding, "Extreme caution must be exercised in making public statements about the speed at which we can move toward our goals. . . . I count on you to prevent any premature announcements until we are in a position to know which things must be done first and how rapidly they can be done." On February 27, 1949, *The New York Times* correspondent wrote that most members of Congress "are in the middle and say frankly that they do not know which way they will jump when the time of decision finally arrives." Little wonder the tidal waves of the Whitaker and Baxter AMA campaign quickly engulfed the few white caps whipped up by the Ewing public relations department and the Committee on the Nation's Health.

Furthermore, a Truman Administration political blunder played into the hands of the AMA public relations campaign that government health insurance posed the threat of government totalitarianism. In the fall of 1949, U.S. Attorney General J. Howard McGrath notified the AMA that in the light of an investigation by the Department of Justice of alleged violations of the Anti-Trust laws, that AMA's records must be made available for examination by FBI agents of any files requested. He announced that files of 14 county/state medical societies were also under investigation. Beginning in October 1949 and extending into April 1950, peak months in the AMA's campaign against the administration's proposal. FBI agents combed through the AMA, pulling documents from files and selecting some 14,000 items for microfilming. Because nothing ever came of this investigation of the AMA, it has to be put down as an effort to intimidate and slow down the National Education Campaign. It didn't. In January 1952, as he entered the last year of his Presidency, Truman started backing away on this issue when he announced the appointment of a Commission on the Health Needs of the Nation. *The Nation* saw this as "in one sense a confession of failure, since it means that he has abandoned hope of early passage by Congress of his national health insurance bill. However, the move shows that Mr. Truman was not prepared to surrender to the

AMA, whose expensive and unprincipled propaganda against "socialized medicine" has been a prime factor in blocking action for a national health service." Mr. Truman announced that this committee would hold hearings in six major cities and present its report to him in December, just before he would leave office. The AMA blasted the appointment of the committee as a political move but only after a heated debate and divided vote. The president of the AMA was invited to serve on the committee but refused. The committee report declared that access to health services was were a basic human right, and urged greater public interest in health services to cut abuses. It also called for expanded community health services. There was no clear call for national health insurance. This was an idea whose time had not come. It had been killed aborning by the sledgehammer blows that only a Whitaker and Baxter team, given unlimited resources, could administer. Surely this was a case of propaganda overkill!

President Truman, now a lame duck, threw in the sponge in a speech to the American Hospital Association in Philadelphia on September 22, 1952, in which he praised the work of his health committee and urged withholding judgment until it had completed its work. Shortly after the President's hospital association speech, the AMA announced an end to Whitaker and Baxter's National Education Campaign. A few days later when the President was asked at a news conference what he thought about this development, Truman claimed that his recent health speech had caused the AMA to admit that it was wrong and to disband its propaganda effort! In fact, the AMA's campaign against national health insurance had lost much of its intensity since the 1950 Congressional elections. When the campaign staff folded their tent, it had cost a total of $4,678,000 and of this amount $775,000 went to pay the campaign firm and its staff. A new benchmark in the history of public relations!

THE POLITICAL FALLOUT

It is risky to isolate any one factor as having influenced the outcome of a political election. There are always a myriad of factors influencing voters. But it is probable that AMA's massive political campaign brought the defeat of the two leading proponents of health insurance in the Senate — Senator James Murray of Montana who sponsored the bill and Senator Claude Pepper of Florida. In five senatorial contests in which the doctors were politically active, each decided by less than 5% of the vote, four incumbents opposed by the AMA were defeated and in only one case did a doctor-supported incumbent lose. Columnist Drew Pearson reported that "Democrats privately concede that they lost Senator Elbert Thomas of Utah, Representative Eugene O'Sullivan in Nebraska and Representative Andrew

Biemiller in Wisconsin largely as a result of the doctor-to-patient propaganda." In Biemiller's case, he was from a Milwaukee district that historically swung back and forth from Presidential to off-year elections.

Earlier in the Florida Democratic primary on May 2, U.S. Senator Claude Pepper was defeated by Rep. George Smathers because of the concerted opposition of the medical profession. *United Mine Workers Journal* had this to say of Senator Pepper's defeat, "In 44 years of covering political campaigns in the nation and many states, your editor has never witnessed such effective and productive quiet solicitation of votes as demonstrated by Florida doctors, druggists, hospital staffs, insurance companies and pharmaceutical representatives, aided and abetted by other professional men." Whitaker and Baxter had unquestionably energized the nation's doctors as a political force—at least for the time being.

More seriously for the nation, the issue of national health insurance was driven from the public agenda for some 40 years as the result of the National Education Campaign, financed by the AMA and planned and directed by Clem Whitaker and Leone Baxter[1]. Once again as shown throughout this volume, the profound impact on American society by the public relations practitioner operating from the wings of the public stage is demonstrated. Moreover, by developing their campaign strategies and tactics to win a majority of their political battles, this husband-and-wife team created today's army of campaign consultants.

CAMPAIGN MANAGEMENT BECOMES A BUSINESS—AND A FORCE IN POLITICS

Whitaker and Baxter's spectacular demonstration of the power of propaganda to put an issue on the national political agenda and mobilize public opinion behind it was certain to arouse imitation by those in public relations looking for new accounts and to be employed by politicians seeking to win office or defeat political issues. It did. Today the campaign consultant is a prominent figure on the American political scene. Clem Whitaker and Leone Baxter not only became a decisive factor in politics, but they also spawned a whole new "profession" as its practitioners choose to term it. They were on the cutting edge the change in the way public opinion is motivated and moves on legislative issues and political campaigns. The respected University of Chicago political scientist, Charles F. Merriam, asserted in a report to President Herbert Hoover in 1933, "The older system

---

[1]Universal health insurance coverage for all citizens did not again emerge as a national political issue until the 1992 Presidential election and carried over into the 1993 Congress as a major issue.

consisted chiefly of lobbying, personal interviews with governmental representatives, social influence, campaign contributions and assistance, and sometimes money payments direct and indirect." He saw as the hallmarks of new lobby "the employment of professional press agents, public relations counsels, and propagandists who would organize educational campaigns on an elaborate scale."

Given the fertile soil California provided with its legislation by referendum and weak party system, little wonder the first firms would originate in that state. Don Francisco, at that time vice-president in charge of Lord & Thomas' West Coast operations, was the first person to wage campaigns alongside Whitaker and Baxter. As mentioned earlier, he had been retained by Louis B. Mayer to help defeat Upton Sinclair for the governorship of California in the shameful 1934 campaign. (Lord & Thomas was the advertising agency headed by Albert Lasker, often termed the "father of American Advertising.") Apparently unimpressed by Francisco's efforts, an apprehensive Mayer brought Whitaker and Baxter into the fray its last 2 months.

As discussed in chapter 18, in the Depression a movement emerged to tax chain stores as governments desperately sought new revenues and the neighborhood grocer demanded protection from the chain store supermarket. In 1936, California, always a front runner in such matters, put an initiative on the ballot to pass a heavily graduated chain store tax. Safeway and other major chains retained Lord & Thomas to defeat this measure. Don Francisco successfully mounted a campaign that brought the initiative's defeat.

Yet the dominance of Whitaker and Baxter was so great and their political network so strong that they kept strong competitors from emerging to challenge them until after Whitaker's death in 1961. The first one to emerge was Spencer & Roberts, formed by Stuart Spencer and William Roberts in the early 1960s, a firm that in time became as well known as Whitaker and Baxter because of their close association with President Ronald Reagan. The pair first gained national recognition when they managed Governor Nelson Rockefeller's presidential campaign in California in 1964. Though Rockefeller lost to Barry Goldwater, the close margin brought praise for the campaign Spencer & Roberts had waged. That same year, they successfully managed Thomas H. Kuchel's campaign for the U.S. Senate. They even helped elect a fellow public relations practitioner, John Rousselot, to Congress. They cut their relationship with him when he became president of the John Birch Society. Spencer & Roberts gained increased recognition when they guided Ronald Reagan to the governorship of California in 1966. Reagan, a political novice, knew he had to have professional help and sought them out. James M. Perry asserted that "Spencer and Roberts are professionals." Stu Spencer was involved in every subsequent Reagan campaign, including his three for the Presidency. Perry thought their work "combines elements of old fashioned politics and the new methodology, a bridge between what has been and what will be."

Roberts entered politics as the executive director of the Los Angeles County Republican Central Committee, heading a staff of 25 and spending a budget of $1 million. Spencer got his introduction to politics as director of recreation for the City of Los Angeles. He then became a precinct director under Roberts. Perry wrote, "The firm is in fact more than two men; an important partner has been Fred J. Haffner, who worked out of San Francisco in 1967." Spencer and Roberts worked only for Republicans — but Republicans of a conservative ideology. To provide year-round income, the firm worked out affiliations with other firms that had industrial accounts.

Two staffers who mastered the art of political campaign management working for Whitaker and Baxter left them to form their own campaign consultancies — Herbert Baus and Harry Lerner. Baus later formed a partnership with William A. Ross. Baus opened an office in San Francisco in 1950 after quitting Whitaker and Baxter in Chicago because he disagreed with their tactics in the AMA campaign. Baus, a veteran publicist and author of an early book on *Publicity: How to Plan, Produce and Place It*, like his mentors, had extensive newspaper experience before going into political public relations. This experience Stu Spencer and Bill Roberts lacked. This weakness showed up in their early campaigns. After the 1964 Republican primary, a Rockefeller staffer confided, "Spencer–Roberts' weakness is their inability to put together a total campaign and sell it to the voters. They don't understand the mass media." But they learned as they demonstrated when they put together the campaign that enabled Ronald Reagan to beat Governor Edmund "Pat" Brown by 1 million votes.

Lerner set up shop in San Francisco, Whitaker and Baxter's home turf. In 1956, Alumnus Lerner dealt the partners their stiffest defeat on an initiative measure, one to unitize California's oil fields and thereby lift oil production. Whitaker and Baxter, retained by the oil companies to get the measure passed, campaigned for it as a conservation measure. Lerner, retained by the independent oil companies, attacked the measure as one to protect the monopolies of the big oil companies. In the kind of slashing attack taught him by his former mentors, Lerner developed two symbols of the "oil monopoly," a hog wallowing in oil, and a whale swallowing up the independents — both splashed on billboards across the state. Ross thought Lerner's printed copy and TV spots were equally rough as the billboards. The independents won easily, 3,950,532 votes to 1,208,752 votes. As competitors began to emerge in California, Campaign, Inc.'s batting average began to slip. A notable defeat came when Clem Whitaker, Jr. and

Leone Baxter were hired, belatedly, to manage child movie star Shirley Temple Black's campaign for Congress in a 1967 special election. This was an "ill-starred" campaign in Dan Nimmo's opinion.

Other competitors began to spring up as a new and lucrative specialty of public relations practice became more in demand. One was a short-lived Public Relations Center, Inc., operated by Hal Evry, who specialized in getting unknowns elected to office. He never managed a campaign of consequence. Two former Kennedy associates set up U.S. R&D in the mid-1960s but had not won a major campaign by 1967. They managed the unsuccessful campaign of Detroit Mayor Jerome P. Cavannaugh against Governor Mennen "Soapy" Williams in the 1966 Democratic primary. Williams won but then was defeated by Senator Robert Griffin, whose campaign was managed by Clem Whitaker, Jr. This signaled the growing nationwide involvement of this new breed.

Another to enter the field in 1966 was Joseph Napolitan. And he entered it with a bang. State Senator Robert P. Casey of Lackawana County, Pennsylvania (now Governor of Pennsylvania) was odds-on favorite to win the Democratic gubernatorial nomination of 1966 when he was beaten by a political novice and unknown millionaire, Milton Shapp. Never before had the official Democratic candidate for governor been beaten in the primary. Napolitan managed Shapp's expensive and effective campaign. Casey explained the lesson he learned—painfully, "You have to do what Shapp did. You have to use the new sophisticated techniques, the polling, the television, the heavy staffing, and the direct mail. You can't rely any more on political organizations. They don't work any more." Casey was not only sounding the beginning of the end of the dominance of political organizations but the beginning of the New Politics, dominated by the campaign consultant who works nationally and state by state to influence politics by defining issues and portraying personalities as they pragmatically see fit.

TV PROVIDES THE NEW CONSULTANT A POWERFUL NEW WEAPON

The historic 1896 William McKinley–William Jennings Bryan Presidential contest shaped the outlines of Presidential campaigns from that day until 1948 when the contest between President Harry S. Truman and Governor Thomas E. Dewey marked the last of such campaigns. These candidates relied on strong national and state party organizations and carried their message to the voters in nationwide speaking tours on campaign trains. Then in the late 1940s, television began developing as a new and powerful communication medium. TV was first effectively used in a Presidential campaign in 1952 when General Dwight D. Eisenhower's campaign staff developed for him a series of hard-hitting, simplistic 20-second TV spots and tailored his 20-minute TV addresses to the requirements of the new medium, whose power was not yet fully appreciated.

The large advertising agency, Batten, Barton, Durstine, & Osborn (BBD&O), was in charge of General Eisenhower's campaign. They had been using TV advertising enough to know its requirements. Though they had to buy a half-hour's time, this agency decided no speech could be more than 20 minutes long and was planned in three acts: (a) Arrival of the war hero, (b) a speech created by their speech writers, and (c) departure of the hero. Much attention was given to create drama and to the use and placement of cameras. In 1948, this same agency had proposed to Governor Dewey that a TV spot barrage he prepared but the governor chose to campaign the old-fashioned way—and lost. Ike's TV spots were written by a campaign volunteer—Rosser Reeves of the Ted Bates advertising agency. Reeves' formula called for a question posed by an "citizen" and a response by Ike. These were simplistic in the mode of the banging anvil in a person's head Reeves had used to sell Anacin. A typical one went like this:

ANNOUNCER: Eisenhower answers the nation!
CITIZEN: What about the cost of living, General?
IKE: My wife, Mamie, worries about the same thing. I tell her it's our job to change that on November fourth!

The citizens were filmed in various parts of the country to represent "typical" voters. Eisenhower filmed the answers for all 50 spots in 1 day in a Manhattan studio that specialized in TV commercials. The spots were run during the last 2 weeks of the campaign at a cost of $1.5 million. These spots undoubtedly made more decisive what was already probable—an Eisenhower victory.

Adlai Stevenson's campaign staff learned of these spots when they were in production, but the governor decided that he would not emulate Eisenhower. Stevenson insisted on waging a radio campaign when the age of radio was rapidly waning. Erik Barnouw observed, "As the television campaign progressed, his brilliance tended to become a liability. He came under criticism for his tea-cup words and his verbal brilliance by the rank and file voters."

An even more powerful demonstration of the power of TV came with Vice President Richard Nixon's famous "Checkers" speech by which he saved his place on the 1952 Republican ticket. On September 18—in the midst of the 1952 campaign—Peter Edson of the NEA feature service broke the story of the Nixon Fund: "Republican Vice Presidential candidate Richard M. Nixon has been receiving an extra expense allowance from between fifty and one hundred and fifty well-to-do southern California

political angels since he entered U.S. Senate in 1951." An angered Eisenhower declared that a candidate on his ticket must be "as clean as a hound's
tooth." A movement developed, led by Governor Dewey, to drop Nixon
from the ticket. Advised by Murray Chotiner, one of the new breed of
consultants, and others, Nixon chose to take his case to the people utilizing
the new medium of TV. His emotional speech brought a deluge of calls and
telegrams to the National Committee to keep him on the ticket. The rest, as
they say, is history. But in his 1960 debates with Senator John F. Kennedy,
Nixon was severely hurt by TV. The awesome power of this new medium
was becoming clear to politicians and consultants alike.

Herbert Alexander, director of the Citizens Research Foundation and an
authority on campaign expenditures, summed up broadcasting's effects on
politics between 1952 and 1960:

> With the advent of television, campaign itineraries and speeches were timed
> for prime viewing hours to get maximum audiences. National nominating
> conventions were scheduled with a view to providing maximum exposure to
> the American people while putting the party in the best possible light. . . .
> Candidates are sometimes chosen because they have appealing personalities,
> smiling families and good television presence. When the candidates are
> nominated on personal factors, the parties tend to be downgraded and
> become less important. The candidate is not necessarily a party personage, but
> a popular figure in his own right.

THE NEW POLITICS COMES IN FULL BLOOM IN 1968

It is difficult to establish a milepost on an evolving continuum, but most
political pundits agree that the 1968 Presidential election between former
Vice President Richard Nixon and Vice President Hubert H. Humphrey
brought the New Politics into full flower. In *The New Politics*, James M.
Perry saw that as the year business and industrial technology took over in
politics: "This new technology is already at work in politics, though most
people, politicians among them, have chosen to overlook it."

Joseph Napolitan, the consultant who took on and defeated the Pennsylvania Democratic organization to nominate the unknown Milton Shapp
for governor in 1966, was chosen to map and implement the strategy for
Vice President Hubert Humphrey in the 1968 presidential campaign.
(Napolitan founded the American Association of Political Consultants and
later co-founded the International Association of Political Consultants.) He
was brought into the Humphrey campaign after the Democrats' stormy
nominating convention in Chicago when Humphrey, who had led Nixon in
the polls in the spring and early summer, was now well behind because of

the Chicago convention debacle. Napolitan was persuaded to join the Humphrey campaign by the late Lawrence O'Brien, who was Humphrey's campaign chairman. Napolitan told the story of this campaign in *The Election Game and How to Win It*. On Labor Day when the national campaigns normally begin, Napolitan presented a memorandum to Larry O'Brien that he had drafted on a yellow legal pad while waiting for the candidate to arrive at his plane — a late start indeed. He faced "the three big problems of the Humphrey campaign" — (a) time, (b) money, and (c) the candidate's positions. Yet, despite the debacle of the Democrats' nominating convention, Humphrey, using Napolitan's media campaign plan, came within 250,000 votes of defeating Nixon. The Humphrey campaign was loose and sometimes chaotic.

On the other hand, Nixon's campaign was tightly controlled and orchestrated by his campaign consultants and advertising agency. Writing in *The New Yorker*, the late Richard Rovere said Nixon had an advertising man's approach to his work, "acting as if he believed policies were the products to be sold to the public — this one today, that one tomorrow, depending on the discounts and state of the market." It was no coincidence that the campaign manager and later chief of staff in the White House was H. R. Haldeman, an advertising executive. Ronald Ziegler, campaign press secretary and later White House press secretary, was also from the same ad agency where he was a subordinate of Haldeman. Herbert Klein, who had formerly served Vice President Nixon as press secretary and who had standing with the news media, was pushed to the outer edges of the campaign and of the White House. This advertising approach to the campaign and later the Presidency would prove flawed in the White House.

Harry Treleaven was Nixon's chief campaign consultant; he was then with the Fuller, Smith, and Ross advertising agency. But, as Joe McGinniss wrote in *The Selling of a President 1968*, "The agency was incidental to the campaign." Treleavan cut his eye-teeth on political campaigning when he handled a then little-known George Bush's campaign for Congress in Texas in 1966. When Treleaven took charge of that campaign, Bush was trailing his opponent, Frank Briscoe, in the polls but then won in a district that had never elected a Republican before. At that time Treleaven was on leave from the J. Walter Thompson agency.

Treleaven set down the theme of Nixon's campaign before the primaries in these words, "There's an uneasiness in the land. A feeling that things aren't right. That we're moving in the wrong direction. That none of the solutions to our problems are working. That we're not being told the truth about what's going on. The trouble is in Washington. Fix that and we're on our way to fixing everything. Step one: Move LBJ out and a Republican president in."

The typically hypocritical Nixon declared at the start of the fall campaign, "I am not going to barricade myself into a television studio and make this an antiseptic campaign." But that is exactly what he did in the view of McGinniss, who was permitted to sit in on the Nixon campaign start to finish. The center-piece of Nixon's campaign was 10 programs, filmed from Massachusetts to Texas, that made him appear to be meeting with people and answering their questions. Treleaven and Frank Shakespeare, a TV executive, developed the "show." For 1 hour, Nixon sat in a group of people to answer their questions. It was filmed live to provide suspense and there was a studio audience primed to cheer on cue. McGinniss wrote, "The cheers made it seem to home viewers that enthusiasm for his candidacy was all but uncontrollable; and there would be an effort to achieve a conversational tone that would penetrate Nixon's stuffiness." McGinniss added, "One of the valuable things about this idea, from a political standpoint, was that each show would be seen only by the people who lived in that particular state or region. . . . Nixon would get through the campaign with a dozen or so carefully worded responses that would cover all the problems of America in 1968." Roger Ailes made his debut on the national political stage when he was hired to produce these 1-hour programs. Ailes, who was instrumental in George Bush's election as President in 1988, is one of today's tough breed of consultants. Thus did Nixon use television to win the election and to keep himself insulated from the press he hated so and had blamed for his loss to John F. Kennedy in 1960. Yet Nixon said in a TV spot for the Oregon primary, "And I for one rejected the advice of the public relations experts who say that I've got to sit by the hour and watch myself." But that's exactly what he did.

But 1968 was only the beginning of the dominance of television and the campaign consultant who uses it so effectively. Robert L. Bower's research found that "between 1960 and 1970 television took a significant leap in the public's view as giving the clearest understanding of national elections." And this was done in 9-second spots.

Unfortunately for the Nixon Presidency and the nation, the winning candidate carried these successful strategies into the White House in 1969. Kevin Phillips, an astute political observer who once worked on Nixon's staff, wrote in his book, *Mediacracy*, that this "mediacracy" reached its nadir in the Nixon Administration: "Nixon's chief aides were merchandising men and technicians" and that "the White House planning leaned toward advertising manageralism, espionage, surveillance, and kindred tools of the communication age, rather than philosophy, program formulation, or grass-roots party commitment." Phillips echoed James Perry's belief that it is "industrial and business technology" that has taken over American politics. And, to some degree, government!

The profound impact on government is evidenced in the millions upon millions of dollars that candidates must raise to finance this new technology of politics. Incumbents and their opponents, to a less degree, raise this money from special interest groups, symbolized by the PACS. Every industry, every profession, every service organization has a profound stake in legislation passed or defeated in the Congress and in the state legislatures. These special interest groups feel compelled to supply the dollars to candidates from the White House to the Court House to advance or defend their being. The New Politics has exponentially raised the ante of campaign costs, posing a problem American democracy has yet to solve.

IMPLICATIONS OF THE CAMPAIGN CONSULTANCY

Stanley Kelley astutely saw that "with these developments, the activities of the public relations man have become a significant influence in processes crucial to democratic government. . . . It is into this fundamental relationship between the politician and electorate, between those who seek power and those who bestow authority, that the public relations man inserts himself, seeking to guide the action of the politician toward the people and the people toward the politician." Joseph Napolitan, one the pioneers in this new craft, sees the political consultant as a specialist in political communication. Writing in *The Election Game and How to Win it*, Napolitan left no doubt as who is in charge of a campaign. "A manager . . . is a full-time worker who should have day-to-day control and decision-making authority in a campaign, subject only to the veto power of the candidate. He should also have complete control over the expenditure of campaign funds." These are the principles first laid down by Clem Whitaker and Leone Baxter. Napolitan said there are only three steps to winning any election: "First, define the message the candidate is to communicate to the voters; Second, select the vehicles of communication; Third, implement the communication process." Again these are overtones from Campaigns, Inc.

The New Politics, with campaigns directed by campaign consultants and based on issues as defined by intensive polling, arrived in the 1960s — signaled by the Nixon–Humphrey Presidential campaign. In Dan Nimmo's opinion:

> By the 1960s campaign management had become a nationwide service industry that reached all political levels. Initially Republican candidates took greater advantage of professional management, perhaps because of the traditional Republican ties to business firms and public relations. But professional personnel have served both major parties in presidential elections since 1952; congressional campaigns also attract professionals. . . . Finally, a popular referenda throughout the nation increasingly are conducted under the direction of management firms.

What are the implications of this profound change in the political process initiated by Whitaker and Baxter? In a chapter in *The Political Image Merchants*, Lawrence F. O'Brien observed in 1971:

> Never before has it been possible to reach the voters so directly and with such frequency, whether through television and radio or such devices as computer letter. Never before have we known so much about voters—their opinions, motivations, hopes and fears—as well as their addresses and phone numbers accurately listed by computer. If one considers no more than the impact of these technologies, we find certain profound changes in the nature of the democratic decision. . . . More than this, the new technologies have made it possible for candidates to operate successfully outside the party structure.

This emphasizes one of the profound implications of the changes put in motion by Whitaker and Baxter in the 1930s—the weakening of the role and influence of the political party in American government. Long ago the authority on political parties, E. E. Schattschneider, asserted that modern democracy would be unthinkable save in terms of political parties. This notion is now questionable. In *The Decline of American Political Parties 1952-1980*, Martin P. Wattenberg wrote, "The decline of public affection for the parties . . . is due to an increasing sense that the parties just no longer matter much in the governmental process. It is increasingly difficult for Americans to see the relevance of political parties in this candidate-centered age of mass media."

Agreeing with this conclusion are Harold Mendelsohn and Irving Crespi in *Polls, Television, and The New Politics*, "It is important to note that 1968 represents a point in time when the efficiency of both political attitude-polling and the utilization of television appear to have reached a zenith, even though the ultimate potential of both have yet to be realized." They concluded, "They [polls and TV] are making fundamental changes in the national selection conventions and they are making fundamental changes in the traditional national party structures and function." But these changes have brought disquiet to politicians and concern to voters. A Twentieth Century Fund study, published in 1976, of the American voter found, "Today the electorate is more politically aroused, more detached from political parties than at any time in the past forty years, and deeply dissatisfied with the political process." This dissatisfaction is confirmed in the declining percentage of eligible voters participating in state and federal elections. The noted political scientist, James McGregor Burns, offered another view, "The main reason so many concerned people are alien to the political process . . . is that politics to them is dominated by old and sterile issues and appears unable to grapple with two cardinal problems of the late 20th Century civilization . . ., the life style of urban man and the need for fresh and creative ventures in foreign policy."

In his book *The Permanent Campaign*, Sidney Blumenthal agreed with this author, "The rise of the consultants has paralleled the decline of the parties. It represents a new stage in American political history as significant as the growth of political parties. The parties were superseded by the consultants. With the decline of parties, the candidates must wage their own campaigns." Blumenthal postulated that the "permanent cure" for this new stage of politics is "the permanent campaign." This he defined as combining "image making with strategic calculation," adding, "It is the engineering of consent with a vengeance." And that's what Whitaker and Baxter did—in spades.

Leon D. Epstein, a noted student of political parties for some 40 years, is not ready to write their obituary. In his seminal work, *Political parties in the American Mold*, he held, "It should be apparent from the record of the last decade, today's institutionalized Republican and Democratic parties have developed significant organizational roles within the candidate-centered pattern. Thus they survive and even moderately prosper in a society evidently unreceptive to much stronger parties and yet unready, and probably unable, to abandon parties altogether."

The 21st century will define the ultimate pattern of politics, a pattern that will undoubtedly be heavily influenced by the political consultancy first introduced by Clem Whitaker and Leone Baxter, who were the first to bill themselves as professional campaign managers.

Theodore White, great journalist and chronicler of Presidential campaigns, paid Whitaker and Baxter the ultimate tribute in 1982, "Clem Whitaker and Leone Baxter are now gone. But their kind of politics—professional image-making has not only persisted but thrived; and, in thriving, swept East where a politics industry has grown up—a gathering of professionals who merchandise control of voter reactions." A nagging, persistent question remains: Do these image-makers serve well the democratic process?

NOTES ON SOURCES

This chapter, unlike those that preceded it, had to be based primarily on secondary sources. Clem Whitaker, Jr. deposited the papers of his father and Leone Baxter to the State Archives in the Bancroft Library at the University of California. These papers were being processed and catalogued when this book was in preparation and thus were unavailable to me.

Books

James David Barber, *The Pulse of Politics*, Norton, 1980; Erik Barnouw, *Tube of Plenty, The Evolution of Television*, Oxford University Press,

1975; Herbert M. Baus and William B. Ross, *Politics Battle Plan*, Macmillan, 1968; Sidney Blumenthal, *The Permanent Campaign*, Beacon Press, 1980; Robert T. Bower, *Television and the Public*, Holt, Rinehart, Winston, 1973; Frank D. Campion, *The AMA and U.S. Public Health Policy*, Chicago Review Press, 1984; Edwin Diamond, *The Tin Kazoo, Television, Politics and the News*, The MIT Press, 1975; Leon D. Epstein, *Political Parties in the American Mold*, The University of Wisconsin Press, 1986; Ray E. Hiebert, ed., *The Political Image Merchants*, Acropolis Press, 1971; Stanley Kelley, *Professional Public Relations and Political Power*, The John Hopkins Press, 1956; Harold Mendelsohn and Irving Crespi, *Polls, Television and The New Politics*, Chandler, 1970; John A. Maltese, *Spin Control*, University of North Carolina Press, 1992; Greg Mitchell, *The Campaign of the Century, Upton Sinclair's Race for Governor of California and the Birth of Media Politics*, Random House, 1992; Roger Morris, *Richard Milhous Nixon*, Henry Holt, 1990; James M. Perry, *The New Politics*, Clarkson N. Potter, 1968; Kevin P. Phillips, *Mediacracy*, Doubleday & Company, 1975; Monte M. Poen, *Harry Truman Versus The Medical Lobby: The Genesis of Medicare*, University of Missouri Press, 1979.

David B. Truman, *The Governmental Process Political Interests and Public Opinion*, Knopf, 1951; Joe McGinniss, *The Selling of the President, 1968*, Trident Press, 1970; Richard P. McCormick, *The Second American Party System*, University of North Carolina Press, 1966; Dan Nimmo, *The Political Persuaders*, Prentice-Hall, Inc. 1970; Joseph Napolitan, *The Election Game and How to Win It*, Doubleday & Company, 1972; Irwin Ross, *The Image Merchants*, Doubleday & Company, 1959; Martin P. Wattenberg, *The Decline of American Political Parties 1952-1980*, Harvard University Press, 1984; Theodore H. White, *Breach of Faith: The Fall of Richard Nixon*, Atheneum, 1975. Joseph Charles, *The Origins of the American Party System*, Harper Torchbooks, 1956.

Periodicals

"The AMA and Health Insurance," *The Commonwealth*, October 23, 1949; Leone Baxter's 1949 address to the Public Relations Society was reprinted in *The Public Relations Journal* of January 1950; Jean Begeman, "The Crude Big Lie," *New Republic*, October 2, 1950; George A. Brandenberg, "AMA's $1, 110,000 Ad Program," *Editor & Publisher*, August 26, 1950; Carey McWilliams, a series of three articles in *The Nation*, entitled "Government by Whitaker and Baxter," April 14, April 21, and May 5, 1951; Elmer Henderson, "Here's Health the Voluntary Way," *Reader's Digest*, May 1950; "Mr. Truman Versus A.M.A.," *The Nation*, January 12, 1952; "Propaganda Clinic," *The New Republic*, December 12, 1949; "The Doctors

Gird for Battle," *Newsweek*, June 20, 1949; "The Partners," (a profile of Whitaker and Baxter) *Time*, December 26, 1955.

Permissions

Permissions to quote from Greg Mitchell's *Campaign of the Century* was graciously granted by Random House, Inc. which holds the copyright. Permission to quote extensively from Carey McWilliams three articles in *The Nation* magazine of 1951 was granted by The Nation Company, Inc. Permission to quote from Irwin Ross' *The Image Merchants* was granted by him, the holder of the copyright. Permission to quote from Roger Morris' *Richard Milhous Nixon* was granted by the Henry Holt and Company, Inc.

Chapter 20

Earl Newsom: Counselor to Corporate Giants

Edwin Earl Newsom was born in Wellman, Iowa, on December 13, 1897, the fourth of six children of Reverend John Edward and Emma Day Newsom. He grew up in the rolling, fertile countryside of early 20th century Iowa, where his father, a Methodist preacher, served the congregations of several southeastern Iowa towns. The Newsom family was a family of teachers, ministers, and musicians—a family that stimulated a lifelong intellectual curiosity and principled values in the future counselor. Newsom, like five of his pioneer peers who helped create and build the profession of public relations, was a product of the Midwest and agricultural America that would be overtaken by industrial America at the turn of the century. Like George Parker, Pendleton Dudley, Carl Byoir, Steve Hannagan, and John Wiley Hill, Newsom, in time, became an influential adviser to corporate giants as they coped with the complex problems of the Depression, World War II, and the turbulent postwar industrial era.

Earl Newsom, the name he used in his career, died April 11, 1973, in the Sharon, Connecticut, hospital at the age of 75, recognized by *The New York Times* as "one of the most influential public relations counselors in private industry." Indeed he was that. In time through his major corporate clients and their legal advisers, Newsom became an influential person in what came to be known, not always popularly, as the "Eastern Establishment." Newsom had lived a productive and vigorous life, although he had been plagued by a number of chronic health problems, though none serious. In the 1930s, he lost an eye to glaucoma and from time to time suffered attacks of colitis. These problems did not slow him down professionally or keep him from his favorite pastime—after reading, perhaps—golf. Newsom was a heavy smoker until he quit cold turkey in 1970 when his lungs started giving out. Newsom died after a 6-week battle with a brain tumor; the swiftness of his passing caught his family and friends by surprise.

Earl Newsom began in his teens to develop a talent for persuasion when, with his two older brothers, he formed the Newsom Brothers Piano Company, a piano-selling enterprise that was profitable enough to send the Newsom brothers and their sister to college. Possessing a keen mind and insatiable thirst for knowledge, Newsom went to Oberlin College where he later served as a trustee. Newsom interrupted his studies at Oberlin to serve as a naval aviator in World War I. Regarded as a good student, Newsom graduated in 1921. Unlike most of his peers who came from journalism into public relations, Newsom found his way through the academic route. After his graduation from Oberlin, he taught English for 2 years at Western Reserve Academy. At Oberlin began what Newsom, late in life, termed his "endless search for mastery in the use of that thrilling phenomenon, the English sentence." Newsom recalled in an interview, "I was courting an Oberlin undergraduate, Lois Ruth Rinehart, and I thought teaching would enable me to get married." Miss Rinehart and Newsom were married on June 14, 1923. They had a strong marriage and bore two children, John, who later joined his father's firm, and a daughter, Barbara. Newsom had enjoyed teaching English at Western Reserve Academy in Hudson, Ohio, and with the encouragement of his new bride, he decided to pursue a PhD in English at Columbia University that fall. To support himself and his wife, he took a job teaching English and math at the McBurney School for Boys in New York City. With the arrival of their first child, John, Newsom was pressed to take a more lucrative teaching job, this one as head of the English department at Memorial High School in Pelham, New York, a Manhattan suburb where the Newsoms made their home for many years.

BECOMES INTERESTED IN PUBLIC OPINION

As indicated earlier, the spectacular demonstrations of the power of public opinion, when organized and stimulated by communication in the second decade of the 20th century, focused the attention of many scholars on this process. The years from 1910 to 1920 had seen the successful campaigns for women's suffrage, for national Prohibition, the powerful effects of the Creel Committee, and the Liberty Bond and Red Cross drives in World War I. Walter Lippmann's *Public Opinion*, published in 1922, and Edward L. Bernays' *Crystallizing Public Opinion*, published in 1923, that applied what was known of the public opinion process to public relations were great stimulants to the study of this power. Surely a mind as alert as Newsom's would focus on this discussion. His son, John, recalled that his father was a voracious reader all his life. "He became especially fond of biography, and would often refer in conversation to his current reading—usually applying to the matter at hand some aspect of someone's life or thought."

In this period he picked up a book by Gustav LeBon, a French sociologist, entitled *The Crowd—A Study of the Public Mind*. This book, first published in France in 1898, was later translated and published in the United States in the 1920s when the study of public opinion became a hot scholarly and business topic. LeBon was the first to explore why public opinion behaves as it does. He advanced the idea that "crowd" opinion is not the sum total of attitudes of each individual in it but a different phenomenon. The "crowd mind," according to LeBon, had singleness of purpose; its thinking was primarily emotional. These theories impressed Newsom, and he then read Everett Dean Martin's *The Behavior of Crowds* and William Trotter's *The Instincts of the Herd in Peace and War*. Martin, who was quoted extensively in Bernays' book, believed that the crowd was psychotic in nature. Newsom remembered being driven, for example, by a desire to kill or a need for self-punishment.

As Robert Frost wrote, life is a matter of roads taken or not taken. In 1925, the father of one of Newsom's students in Pelham, Richard Walsh, offered him a job at *Literary Digest* in its promotion department. Newsom gave up his aspirations for a PhD and took the road that would lead him to public relations. He was 27 and the time—1925—was significant because the fields of advertising and market research were booming in the "permanent prosperity" of the 1920s. New market theories were evolving. At the *Digest*, ad campaigns were being based on the rising status of telephone families, then put under 10,000,000. (This reliance on telephone owners for its Presidential straw polls brought the demise of the *Digest* after its 1936 Presidential poll fiasco.)

His work at the *Digest* led Newsom back to a restudy of LeBon. In a speech on "Corporate Ethics" at Boston University on March 13, 1948, 23 years later Newsom quoted this passage from LeBon:

> On whatever lines the societies of the future are organized, they will have to count with a new power—with the last surviving sovereign force of modern times, the power of crowds. . . . while all our ancient beliefs are tottering, while the old pillars of society are giving way one by one, the power of the crowd is the only force that nothing menaces, of which prestige is continually on the increase. The age we are about to enter will in truth be the era of the crowds.

Newsom took LeBon to heart. But he added an essential dimension—the American experiment. In that same speech, Newsom said:

> But LeBon seems to me to have underestimated an underlying significance in the experiment started in America in 1776. The founders of our country came

here to get away from the frustration of a society of classes. No one was more aware than they, I think, of the human tendency to join crowds, to think as a crowd man, to act as crowds. But the idea that the crowd, since it involved emotions, was merely an example of the natural mental inferiority of the common people, and a proof of their general unfitness for self-government, was completely repugnant to these founders of a new republican form of government.

Newsom stoutly declared, "Nowhere in the world today is the sovereign power of public opinion so much in evidence as in the United States." Newsom spent the rest of his career dealing with this "sovereign power" on behalf of employers and clients.

Newsom left the *Literary Digest* in 1927 to take a job with the Oil Heating Institute at twice the salary he was making at the *Digest*. Newsom was recruited to map and launch a campaign to persuade American home owners that oil furnaces were a safer, cleaner way to heat their homes than the traditional coal furnace. Newsom's research found that there were fears of oil furnaces that held back home owners converting to oil heat. In fact, there were still some bugs in the early oil furnaces, and there had been some explosions. His was a complex task, made so by these fears and by the always difficult public relations task of getting people to accept change. Resistance to change is one of the strongest laws of human nature.

Newsom found that some coalmen were publicizing the oil burner fires. He collected statistics on coal furnace fires and went over to the coal trade association and told them that he would sent out monthly releases on these coal furnace fires unless they stopped their tactic. They stopped. Newsom persuaded the oil industry to change its terminology from oil burners to oil heaters. He then developed a publicity campaign for home and builders magazines on using the cellar space made available by taking out the coal furnace for playroom, workshops, and store rooms. The "basement playroom" were a success. The oil furnaces improved, too, thus a basic change in home heating came to be accepted. Today's "rec room" is a Newsom legacy.

ANOTHER ROAD TAKEN

In 1931, Newsom's Pelham neighbor, Richard Walsh, offered him another road to take. One night the Walshes invited the Newsoms to dinner, and Walsh offered him "whatever you are making now and stock" to come with his John Day Publishing Co. Walsh said his firm was publishing fine books, but he had a genius for losing money. As *Printer's Ink* observed, "Newsom's bookish interests were strong and he went." In 1931, a manuscript by a young missionary from China came in. Newsom thought it wouldn't sell but urged buying it for a small printing. Next year, the same missionary, Pearl Buck, sent another manuscript. Walsh, over Newsom's objections, changed the title to *The Good Earth*. Its success put the Day company on a solid financial footing. As a footnote to this book's success, Pearl Buck came to the United States to promote the book, she and Walsh fell in love, divorced their mates, and married.

For reasons he never revealed publicly, Newsom became dissatisfied with his job at Day Publishing. *Printer's Ink* speculated, "Possibly he didn't know the reasons. He thought perhaps he should go back to campus life. He had begun to have confidence that what he wanted to do it on his own." Newsom did say of this move, "It isn't easy to explain why you make decisions. It wasn't money. I haven't made a lot, never have, never will." He gave his stock to Walsh and left. For a period, he directed public relations and sales for an investment house.

Then in 1933, he became a partner of architect Norman Bel Geddes, and they got along very well. It was in this period that Bel Geddes and his close friend, Paul Garrett, director of public relations at General Motors, were in the process of making public relations and social history with their development of GM's futurama exhibit at the 1934 New York's World Fair. (Newsom later became GM's outside counselor in GM's "Safety–Nader" crisis) But here too Newsom became dissatisfied and left after 2 years. Bel Geddes said at the time, "Newsom was looking for something and unfortunately we couldn't give it to him." What appears to be stirring in his search for that "something" was to have his own business. Newsom had met and come to admire Fred Palmer at the Oil Heating Institute and decided that he wanted to go into a counseling business with Palmer. In 1935, Palmer was in a public relationship with J. Handley Wright. Newsom talked to them and the outcome was a new partnership, Newsom, Palmer, & Wright, a partnership that lasted briefly.

Newsom and Palmer's ideas on public relations didn't square with those of Wright. Newsom bought him out. Wright then worked briefly for John Hill's new New York agency, and later became vice-president for public relations of the American Association of Railroads. Then Newsom and Palmer retitled their firm Newsom and Palmer. In a year or so, Palmer decided to strike out on his own and bought a weekly newspaper in New Jersey. When he left, Newsom renamed his firm Earl Newsom & Company (ENCO). In a couple of years, Palmer decided to return to ENCO, as it was known internally, and became a valued partner until he and Newsom retired at about the same time in 1966. In a letter to me dated March 27, 1992, John R. Newsom commented, "Palmer and Newsom were there from beginning to end with a small break in the later 1930's, and without Palmer's writing and design skills, combined with his blunt, tough-minded powers of analysis and his essential sympathy with the American corporation, Earl Newsom & Co. would not have succeeded nearly as well. Fred was crucial."

Business did not come quickly to the new firm. It was 4 months before Newsom got a call from Fred Corey of the Atlantic Refining Co. in Philadelphia. He explained that he had a problem and wanted Newsom's counsel. Atlantic Refining had developed what it thought was a superior lubricating oil and was puzzled how to dramatize its discovery to the trade. Newsom's solution was to run a test, using six automobiles that were driven 24 hours a day until each had run 100,000 miles. As Ross wrote, "Newsom publicized the results throughout the land." This success brought his next product publicity account. A member of the Atlantic Refining board had a heavy investment in tea, and he was impressed with Newsom's work on the oil test. Irwin Ross recorded:

> The tea people were concerned that consumption in the United States was far less than in Britain. To discover the cause, Newsom, ever the believer in opinion research, retained Elmo Roper to conduct a survey. Roper conclusively proved that tea was regarded by Americans as (a) a sissy drink, and (b) a foreign drink. Newsom thereupon devoted himself for several years to correcting that impression—a deluging the media with the glories of tea. Tea consumption rose.

The Tea Bureau proved not only lucrative—in a time when Newsom needed income—but also proved stimulating as well. The Tea Bureau was headed by Gervas Huxley of the distinguished English Huxley family, and his wife, Elspeth Huxley, was a successful novelist. Her *The Plane Trees of Thika*, based on her childhood in Kenya, became a Masterpiece Theater Production. And this connection led to Newsom's retention by the International Wool Secretariat, headed by Ian Clunies-Ross, who was highly regarded in his native Australia. To promote wool against the emerging synthetics of the 1930s, Newsom stressed a campaign of "Wool the Genuine Product," but in time this was a losing battle for the wool growers.

This early phase of the Newsom company, one of product promotion, ended with one more account, the wallpaper industry. As his reputation grew, Newsom became more and more a corporate counselor. As one confidant told me, "He began to find that in trade association accounts you had to contend with the lowest common denominator." Of this period, Newsom later recalled, in a speech titled "Our Common Interest," to the New York Chapter of the Public Relations Society, on November 19, 1958:

> When I first came to New York to work thirty-five years ago [1923] alert businessmen were becoming increasingly aware that mass production had little value without mass distribution. Bright and ambitious minds were

tackling the problem of how to establish and maintain new markets. I watched the early growth of our great modern advertising business and was for a while part of it. Fed by advertising revenues, the circulation of newspapers and magazines expanded rapidly, opening up new markets. A new technical miracle, called radio and much later television, grew strong from revenues provided by manufacturers and distributors who simply had to have huge markets to absorb their mass-production output.

The result of this was that a need developed for capitalizing on the news potential of products and services, and people rose up to fill this need. They properly called their job product publicity. It was a job that required ever-expanding knowledge of the market and the most effective way of attracting people in these markets to the new things available at prices they could afford.

It was these forces that started Earl Newsom's telephone ringing in the mid-1930s and gave rise to the burgeoning public relations vocation in the post-World War II, and Newsom turned to counseling some of America's corporate giants. His first wartime account was with the American Loco-motive Co. Then, as Ross noted, "came the gilt-edged account which established his status – Standard Oil (New Jersey) – later to be known as Exxon."

As it did for Ivy Lee when he was retained by the John D. Rockefellers, Earl Newsom's role as counselor to the mighty Standard Oil Company (New Jersey) (SONJ) brought him prestige as a counselor and a solid financial base from which to enlarge his staff, one that would be required as other corporate giants, caught up in the turbulent changes and demands that followed the end of World War II, would seek Newsom's counsel. When he took over the ailing Ford Motor Company from his grandfather in 1945, young Henry Ford was quick to seek Newsom's counsel. That same year, John H. Hineman, then president of International Paper Company (IP) and a neighbor of Newsom in Pelham, sought his advice on restyling IP's annual report. From this initial request flowed another major account. In time, John D. Rockefeller III sought Newsom's counsel for his Colonial Williamsburg project and his other interests. Other major corporations were not far behind.

Earl Newsom's vision for his agency was quite different from that of his major competitors. He saw his role as that of a counselor, not as an agent for a client. Dealing with the powerful mass media is a large part of the task in most public relations agencies. Newsom did not issue press releases for clients or deal with the press in a public relations capacity. Because of these differences, the Newsom firm came to occupy a special niche in the development of institutional and corporate communications in the United

States. Because his work relied so heavily on him, Fred Palmer, and their talented associates, the major Newsom influence was short-lived as the history of public relations goes. This was due partly to the passage of time and partly to the eclipse of the Newsom philosophy for an enlightened and socially responsible performance as the only sound base for favorable public relationship. That common phrase of his day ultimately gave way to expedient fix-it media relations activities. Earl Newsom would have been wholly out of place in Corporate Greed Decade of the 1980s!

In a few short years, the Newsom firm developed four main services to justify its high fees and to supplement its customary role in helping clients deal with sudden and usually short-lived public relations crises. The first of these was to plan a communications and public relations program for the client along with an internal organization, if one was not in place to carry it out. Newsom often claimed, in this respect, that his firm was inevitably working itself out of a job.

Given Newsom's superb command of the English language, it was logical that the nub of these services was editorial: the writing, editing, and publication, where warranted, of corporate materials. These included speeches, annual reports, booklets, position papers, statements for Congressional hearings, and backgrounders. Ability to write was essential to make it at ENCO. Third was helping clients build public relations departments where none existed. This was done for Jersey, Ford, International Paper, and other corporate clients. As John R. Newsom observed, "The company was, in effect, an executive search firm specializing in recruitment and screening of candidates for all the functions in its client departments, from the top down. In fact many clients and non-clients would, in time, tap Newsom staffers for public relations positions." Partner Richard Aszling who went to General Foods as vice-president was an example of the latter.

The fourth service was research. Earl Newsom was among the first of the counselors of his time to see the importance of research as the basis of public relations planning and action. He was one of Elmo Roper's first clients, and in time, they became very close friends. He also used James S. Twohey Associates of Washington, DC, for studies on labor matters and the Link Audit, conducted every May and November, by the American Psychological Association to measure long-term trends in public opinion. He also built a strong in-house research capacity. In the 1940s, the primary person was Jack Slaughter, an economics researcher and statistician who had been with the National Industrial Conference Board. When Slaughter moved to the wool account, Newsom hired Lilian Rixey, a former *Time-Life* researcher. Associates described her at the time as "resourceful, accurate, clear-minded." Another researcher hired was Mireille Gerould, a *Fortune* researcher. These researchers gathered data on prospective clients, current issues, critics of clients, and present and future threats to clients—looking for client clouds out there on the horizon when they were small enough to disperse.

These research services were bulwarked by the long-term relationship between the Newsom company and Arthur Newmyer Associates in Washington, DC. Newmyer and his sons were invaluable in helping Newsom and his clients understand the developing relations between business and government, how to react to Congressional queries or attacks, and what to say and when in response to these attacks or in testimony before Congressional committees. The Newsom–Newmyer relationship developed in the early 1940s with the Standard Oil (New Jersey) account and continued through the Ford account and others. Newsom and Newmyer shared clients, and Newsom was a Newmyer client as well. According to Craig Lewis, a member of the Newsom firm in its later years, Arthur Newmyer, Sr. first came to Newsom for guidance when he decided to go into the counseling business in Washington.

As business expanded in 1945, Newsom and Palmer moved to strengthen their staff. Hired that year was W. H. "Ping" Ferry who was made a partner. (Because he was widely known as Ping that name is used in this volume.) Ferry was truly a *rara avis* as corporate counsels go—he was a liberal or more, a person of strong views. Newsom, an intellectual in his own right, sought out intellectuals. Ping Ferry was born in Detroit on December 17, 1910, the son of Hugh Ferry, later president of the Packard Motor Company. Ping Ferry graduated from Dartmouth College in 1932 and then spent 2 years teaching Latin and coaching at Choate, the well-known prep school. From 1933 to until 1941, save for a year spent at Eastern Airlines in publicity, he worked as a reporter on Detroit newspapers. In 1944, the very unconventional Ferry shocked his family and Grosse Point friends by taking a job with the CIO Political Action Committee in the 1944 Presidential campaign. Ferry brought to the Newsom firm a knowledge of labor and wide contacts with labor leaders, an asset that served the firm in good stead in counseling the Ford Motor Company during its difficult postwar labor negotiations with the United Auto Workers (UAW). Victor Navasky wrote a laudatory article in the *Atlantic Magazine* of July 1966, about Ferry headed "The Happy Heretic." He was that.

Other postwar recruits included Stephen Fitzgerald, a former *Baltimore Sun* reporter; Nieman Fellow, who later quit Newsom to form his own agency in 1950, and Martin Quigley who was a man of a varied background—construction laborer, semipro baseball player, University of Minnesota graduate, and veteran newspaperman. Quigley left with Fitzgerald and later came back into Newsom's orbit as public information officer of the Ford Foundation in April 1951. Another recruit was John Moynahan, a former newspaperman who had served to colonel in the U. S. Air Force from 1942 to 1945 as information officer for the secret Manhattan Project that produced the atom bomb. Moynahan left in 1948 to set up his own agency. Such was the talent that came to Newsom and continued to pass through his revolving door. Some of these stayed in Newsom's orbit, others did not.

Two other intellectuals who were brought in as partners and lent great strength to Newsom's counseling were Arthur B. Tourtellot and William A. Lydgate. Tourtellot, a native of Providence, RI, attended Harvard College from 1931 to 1935 and then turned to writing. In the next several years, he wrote six books, then in 1952, joined the *March of Time* production team and for 1 year served as producer of *March of Time*. At the end of 1952, he accepted a position with Newsom and a year later was made a partner. Tourtellot, who worked on the CBS account from 1957 on, left the year after Newsom's retirement in 1967 to become executive vice-president of CBS, dealing a rough blow to those who were trying to keep the company going. William A. Lydgate was an alumnus of Gallup's organization, an expert on public opinion, and author of *What America Thinks*. Lydgate remained with the Newsom company after its business was combined with Adams & Rinehart, Inc. in 1983. Lydgate retired in mid-1992 and moved to Maine.

In 1958, these five partners — Newsom, Palmer, Tourtellot, Lydgate, and Aszling — were working with every Newsom client. At its peak Newsom never employed more than 23 persons.

In 1958 when Aszling left for General Foods, Newsom persuaded his son, John to rejoin him in the firm. John, popularly known as Jack, had served in the Navy in World War II, then graduated from Oberlin College, a replay of his father's college years. He worked for Eastern Airlines briefly upon graduation, then joined his father's firm for 2 years. In 1950, he moved to the Kenyon Eckhardt Advertising Agency, then back to the Newsom Company for the years 1953–1956. In 1956, he took a position with the U.S. Information Agency where he worked until persuaded to rejoin his father's firm. In 1970, he left ENCO to work as a foundation grant-maker and as a consultant to nonprofit and public service groups.

Other early staff associates at Newsom's firm included A. K. Mills, popularly known as Kay, who later was shifted to Ford Motor Company's International Division when Newsom acquired the Ford account in 1945, Lynn Mahan, and Theodore Swanson. Swanson left Newsom to set up his own agency and was later joined by Mahan. Swanson and Mahan acquired the account of the Netherlands government when the Dutch were trying to maintain control of their interests in Indonesia. Mahan took a planeload of reporters to Indonesia so that they could observe what was happening there. Enroute home the plane crashed in India and all were killed, including Bert Hulen of *The New York Times*.

The Newsom agency, operating by its own pattern, did not have accounts nor account executives like other agencies. The partners and staff associates worked on the problems of many clients. Newsom believed that many minds were better than one when attacking a problem or devising a project – another indication that Earl Newsom was a breed apart.

Newsom's main tenet followed that of Ivy Lee – to earn a good reputation a client's conduct must merit such a reputation. Typical of Newsom's approach to public relations was the "preamble" of a policy memo he prepared for the Reynolds Metals Company shortly after taking it as a client: "We believe that a company's reputation is of major importance to its welfare, stability and growth. Companies, like individuals, earn their reputation by what they do, how they do it, and how effectively they communicate with others . . . Therefore our company must conduct itself in such a way as to deserve a good reputation and must win the understanding that is required to establish that reputation in the minds of men."

FIRST MAJOR CORPORATE CLIENT – SONJ

The crunch of events in the Great Depression and World War II that had brought widespread criticism and adverse legislation to America's Big Business brought a concomitant change in the public relations of the more far-sighted corporate executives – an acceptance, however grudging, that with their tremendous power over the lives of American citizens must come a sense of social responsibility. Earl Newsom saw this, as he reflected in a 1958 speech:

> Over the past twenty-five years many circumstances have combined to give public opinion a special modern importance. We see it as a growing need for institutional acceptance. I believe it has been established that the attitudes of large numbers of people – their ideas, the pictures they have in their heads – can have a powerful effect, for good or for ill, on the ability of leadership of any human institution to do what it is supposed to do. This is true not only for business enterprises, but for nonprofit institutions organized for education, philanthropy, or other projects in the public welfare. . . . Thus those in positions of leadership and authority, however limited, have come to the necessity of meeting a new challenge. We have had to recognize that large numbers of people believe they have a right to a voice in the conduct of any affair which touches their interest.

As *Printer's Ink* observed, "Some corporations that called Newsom had come to the end of a long history of corporate error and backwardness and had to change or go under." The first of these was Standard Oil Company (New Jersey) (SONJ), a major holding company and the world's third largest corporation. Standard Oil (New Jersey) had been under public criticism and suspicion since the rise of Hitler and the Nazis to power in Germany in 1933 because of its association with I. G. Farben. The reader will recall that in chapter 6, Ivy Lee's agreement to serve as counsel to the I. G. Farben chemical complex and through it to the Nazi Government had dealt Lee's reputation a devastating blow on the eve of his death. Lee's association with I. G. Farben started when in 1929 he accepted as a client I. G., the American holding company of the German firm. I. G. was connected to Standard Oil (New Jersey), and Walter Teagle, then president of Jersey, served on the board of the U. S. Farben board. In May 1934, the German Farben firm, concerned about the rising anti-German sentiment in the United States, sought Lee's counsel, and he accepted. This, in turn, led to a embarrassing Congressional hearing that Lee's colleagues felt caused his early death.

SONJ found itself in the vortex of a public relations storm in 1942 in the midst of World War II when it was accused by Senator Harry S. Truman of nothing less than "treason." Senator Truman reported the following to the United States Senate:

> Standard Oil had agreed with the German I. G. Farben company that in return for Farben giving Standard Oil a monopoly in the oil industry, Standard Oil would give the Farben Company complete control of patents in the chemical field, including rubber. Thus, when certain rubber manufacturers made overtures to Standard Oil Company for licenses to produce synthetic rubber, they were either refused or offered licenses on very unfavorable terms. . . . Needless to say, I. G. Farben's position was dictated by the German Government.

Nonetheless, Truman's Committee concluded that there was "no unpatriotic motive involved", it was only Big Business playing the game according to the rules.

Before the United States entered the war, SONJ had paid the Nazi-controlled I. G. Farben $35 million in an exchange of patents. On March 25, 1942, SONJ settled an antitrust suit brought by the U.S. Government accusing the company of conspiring to create a monopoly on the manufacture of synthetic rubber when its officers pleaded *nolo contendere*, were fined $5,000 each, and dedicated the rubber patents to the public domain. The next day, Assistant Attorney General Thurman Arnold, appearing before Senator Truman's Defense Investigating Committee, charged that SONJ had revealed its butyl rubber-making process to I. G. Farben in their exchange of patents but refused to reveal it to the American government and that this was the cause of the nation's critical rubber shortage in time of war. Senator Truman declared this as "treason." In this crisis, the company expected repercussions, too, when other international oil agreements were published. (In July 1944, SONJ brought suit against the U. S. Alien Property Custodian for release to it of the patents it had obtained from I. G. Farben.)

As corporate executives do when caught in the crossfire of a crisis, Jersey's top officials turned to Earl Newsom for help. This account set Newsom on his way to the top as confidential counselor to some of America's largest corporations. When Newsom took on SONJ as a client, he did not rush for the fire extinguisher but soberly took a long-range approach. Newsom, a shrewd student of the public opinion process and a strong believer in the importance of research into its specifics, first set out, through a series of surveys, to determine what people actually thought of SONJ and how they got their opinions.

Yet Newsom knew that he had to clear the air before a positive public relations program could be undertaken. In *The Image Merchants* Ross wrote:

His first move was to "get all the facts" on the I. G. Farben agreement and get them out to the public. A long and cleverly written presentation—which argued among other things, that the German patents were of great help to our war effort—was drawn up for President William Farish, who returned to Washington for another bout of testimony. He was on the stand for three days, but when he stepped down, Standard was off the hook. His statement was then printed and widely distributed to stockholders.

Earl Newsom's next move was to set about drawing up a positive public relations program for Jersey and developing an internal department to implement it.

In a memorandum dated May 14, 1942, addressed to vice-president R. T. Haslam of SONJ, Newsom made these points:

1. I have a growing feeling that the machinery for a modern corporation's contacts with the Public Mind has traditionally been hopelessly minimized in Standard's set-up.
2. The organization of Standard Oil to meet any onslaught of public attack now—and to serve as a constructive force in the future—has to be organized, departmentalized, comprehensive and patterned to operate like a well-oiled machine.
3. It has first got to have a means of discovering public attitudes—those of a big, broad general nature which influence basic ideas and those of particular application to the company or its products or its officials or its policies. This must not be a casual thing but a permanent area of the service. . . . Out of such a department could flow weekly memos on general public opinion trends; daily reports on Standard Oil in the news . . . based on examination

of clippings; and a special type of report: Adverse Comments and institutions. All reports should go to policy making officials but also to selected officers whose duty it is to report immediately the facts of the case whenever there is Adverse Comment or Insinuation.

4. Within such a Public Relations Office there is room for a variety of specialists—and they should be there. Financial News should be handled by a specialist. Marketing publicity should be handled by a specialist. . . . Such a staff of specialists would work within the company much as a press service— AP or UP operates.

5. Under supervision of the Public Relations Office should come all company publications. From the office should come a program of instructions, rules and education for company officials on public relations so that in due time the public relations of the company would be on an operating basis as well thought out as the company's manufacturing, sales, research, etc.

6. The first step is for the company to get and organize its manpower for the basic job.

In what became a pattern of Newsom's *modus operandi*, he set up a committee of his top people to design and implement a public relations program for the troubled client. The SONJ Committee included partners Fred Palmer and Ping Ferry and staffer Jack Slaughter. Stewart Schackne, another staffer, also worked on the account as it grew and later moved to SONJ in public relations in 1954. Under Newsom's careful tutelege, the agency and George Freyermuth, then in sales engineering at Jersey, set about to create the new SONJ public relations department. Freyermuth, who had a master's degree from MIT, became manager of the new department in 1944 and served in that capacity until 1959. After 3 years in a public relations partnership, Freyermuth joined Hill and Knowlton, Inc. in 1963. Schackne took over the department when Freyermuth left. Newsom began meeting with SONJ's top officials to educate them in the ways of public opinion and the "good citizen" role of modern corporations.

In a memorandum dated October 7, 1942, to set the stage for one of these early educational sessions with top SONJ management, Newsom made these points:

1. The Company is a holding company and thus the name Standard Oil of New Jersey is not closely associated in the public consciousness with the trade names of products marketed by companies of the Jersey group.

2. Unlike many companies whose public relations problem is chiefly that of filling a void—SONJ faces an already established attitude of disfavor and distrust on the part of many people. The problem is not simply one of painting a picture and, at the same time, erasing a picture already made.

This latter picture has two principal sources:

a. The "trust busting" campaign of the early years of the century, the memory of which has established certain associations with the name "Standard Oil."

b. The Truman Committee and the Thurman Arnold attacks upon the Company.

3. The size of Standard Oil Company (N.J.) makes it especially susceptible to attack. Although not inevitably, the company, as the third largest corporation in the world, is likely to be singled out by critics of an economic society in which it is eminent.

4. As the largest unit by far in its industry, the company has the most to lose from developments damaging to the industry as a whole. Conversely, it has much to gain from the general welfare of the industry. . . . Its public relations acts should be aimed not alone at promoting a favorable attitudes toward itself but also at the broader objective of achieving a respect and support for the petroleum industry. Therefore, the company should use its opportunities for leadership in ways which will benefit the industry as a whole.

In a supporting 15-page memo, Newsom and his staff outlined the target publics for SONJ's new public relations program and provided specific ways to reach these influential publics: "(1) The executives of affiliated and subsidiary companies; (2) The Federal Government labeled "Washington" (3) Stockholders; (4) Employees; (5) The Oil Industry; (6) Professional Groups—educators, scientists, engineers, etc.; (7) Communities in which affiliated or subsidiary companies operate; (8) General Public."

ATTACKS AND DISTRUST CONTINUE

As the full-scale public relations program for Jersey was being organized and manned, the attacks breeding distrust of the oil giant did not let up. In June 1943, Senator Harley M. Kilgore, who chaired a Senate subcommittee on military affairs, charged in a radio broadcast that SONJ, due to its connections with I. G. Farben, held up the starting of a toluol program. Toluol is a chemical ingredient used in making explosives. The Newsom firm drafted a letter of rebuttal for the company with a memorandum of the facts attached. The letter read, in part, "Such matters have apparently become so clouded by the prejudiced distortion that even sincere, public-spirited men like yourself—and through your public statements thousands of others who respect your judgment—are mislead." Then the letter stated a public relations truism: "Dramatic untruth seems always to travel faster than truth." SONJ insisted that it had told the U. S. Army in 1933 of the possibility of producing toluol from oil and that by 1935 the first small samples had proved satisfactory. The bottom line of the Newsom letter was:

"What is more important, the public interest in wartime suffers — and public confidence in the democratic system of individual opportunity becomes endangered."

The drafting of statements for corporate officials to use before Congressional committees became a standard and important part of the Newsom service to corporate clients. In 1943, Senator Kilgore introduced legislation to curb the power of monopolies as an outgrowth of his committee's hearings in the previous year. Two such statements were drafted by Stewart Schackne who was working on the SONJ account; one was entitled "'Big' Business and 'Little' Business," the other "Standard Oil Company (N.J.) and Patents." Such hearings made it hard for SONJ to get off the defensive as Newsom moved the company into a more mature and positive public relations posture.

This was reflected in a February 1945 memo drafted by the Newsom staff, based on its continuing public opinion research, and sent to SONJ officials including presumably George Freyermuth:

Standard Oil Company (New Jersey) has these basic public relations problems —

1. The people of this country distrust something they think of as "Standard Oil."

2. Almost two-thirds of the people of this country think that all Standard Oil Companies are one and the same, and are, therefore, the thing they think of as "Standard Oil."

The memo presented the situation to Standard officials with the bark off. It read in part:

The word "distrust" has been used advisedly. People consider "Standard Oil" a cold-blooded, selfish, greedy enterprise without moral sense. They think of it as a "monopoly" — which in their vocabulary is a bad thing. Even where they speak in an unfavorable way of products or services, they are reflecting an underlying prejudice against "Standard Oil" rather than a bad experience with goods or services. . . . This view is supported by much internal evidence in public opinion surveys made for the company.

No attempt to solve the first basic public relations problem of Standard Oil Company (New Jersey) can be successful which does not have the effect of letting the American people discover that the company is a *morally good* enterprise with admirable principles, a strong sense of citizenship, a warm respect for human beings, a sharp awareness of social responsibility, in short *heart*

To gain the confidence of the American people, the company must disclose, by a great variety of means, by speech and action, what it is *doing and thinking in the fields of human relations* (not what it did or thought yesterday). The company must make friends with the American people and help them develop a close acquaintance with Jersey, so that they will have every opportunity to discover the true character of the company.

Finally, the Newsom memo concluded:

1. To take leadership in developing, by Jersey's own activities, a new and good reputation for the thing people think of as "Standard Oil."
2. To encourage, by good example of Jersey's own activities, similar sound activities on the part of other Standard Oil companies unrelated to Jersey.

PUBLIC RELATIONS PROGRAM TAKES SHAPE

The new Public Relations department, guided by the Newsom staff, set about to develop "Jersey's own activities" to demonstrate that the corporate giant had a "heart" and possessed a sense of social responsibility. For example:

1. Authorized a series of distinguished studies of individual or subsidiary companies to demonstrate their contributions to the industry and to the Jersey group. Also, authorized a series of management studies instituted by SONJ to the benefit of the subsidiaries.
2. Started distributing reprints, attractively printed, of Jersey's director's speeches for distribution to influentials—business leaders, political office-holders, university professors, etc.
3. In an effort to publicize SONJ's contribution to the war effort and to offset earlier ugly and true accusations, a series of brochures were prepared. The first one was on toluol, for which the company had been castigated. Others covered high octane gasoline, synthetic rubber, etc. A business historian, Charles S. Popple, was commissioned late in '45 to put the company's war contributions in book form. His history covering the years 1938–1945 was published by the company in 1952.
4. The scholar in Earl Newsom realized that a modern, comprehensive history of Standard Oil was needed in the nation's public and college libraries because for too long historians and school textbook writers had relied on Ida Tarbell's muckraking two-volume history published early in this century for their histories of Standard Oil. Newsom persuaded the company to sponsor a Business History Foundation, incorporated in New York, and headed initially by N. S. B. Gras, distinguished Harvard business historian, to write a three-volume history of Standard Oil and latterly of Standard Oil of (New Jersey). The Foundation was given a grant of $500,000 and a firm promise of free and total access to the company's records. Professor Gras organized the project in its early stages and then Henrietta Larson took over. The first

volume, covering the years from Standard's birth in 1882 to its breakup by judicial decrees in 1911, was written by George Sweet Gibb and Evelyn H. Knowlton. The second volume, covering the period of 1911–1927, was written by Ms. Larson and Evelyn H. Knowlton. The final volume, 1927–1950 was authored by Professor Ralph Hidy and his wife, Muriel Hidy. All authors vouched that they were given free access and full cooperation with no strings attached on this monumental project.

5. To change the format and circulation of the company house organ, *The Lamp*, the publication was overhauled to become a prestigious representation of the company to its stockholders, members of the Congress, university professors, and other opinion makers. This attractive magazine marked by informative articles and great photography became a center piece in presenting the new "image" of Jersey. Stockholders also were provided financial information in quarterly reports. Company magazines were developed for the parent company and its affiliates to provide employees with news that affected them. *The Lamp* continued to be sent to employees.

6. Realizing that motion pictures are the most effective medium of education, a large share of the public relations budget starting in 1945 was put in films. Motion pictures developed for the employees of the company and its affiliates included *Oil Is Blood, Power and Octane*, and *The Battle for Oil*. Out of this project came one of the great motion pictures of the postwar era— Robert Flaherty's *Louisiana Story*. SONJ spent $258,000 to subsidize the film by this great documentary film director. Its wide distribution and high praise by film critics amply rewarded the company.

7. Newsom's interest in the arts, first nurtured in his family, led to SONJ subsidizing artists to paint oil industry subjects and a collection of documentary stills by leading photographers. It then provided these stills free to editors, circularizing them through a periodical called *Photo Memo*, which also was sent to teachers, librarians, and other opinion leaders. The Newsom program also suggested, "As the program of building a pictorial record— photographic and fine arts—of our company's activities is developed, interesting exhibits can be made available for display to employee groups in various parts of the country." The paintings of the artists were also featured in *The Lamp*, a handsome four-color magazine.

8. Efforts were made to reach educators from public schools to universities. Newsom recommended that booklets and reprints (such as Molecular Magic at Baton Rouge) should be prepared and especially adapted for use by science teachers in classroom work and distributed to a national list.

Stuart Schackne, who had been trained in the Newsom Company and was moved in to replace George Freyermuth in 1959, initiated the Jersey Roundtable. Although started in a somewhat different form, the Roundtable became a vehicle for Jersey's full-time directors and university professors to exchange viewpoints and criticisms. Until it was discontinued in the late 1960s, each year 25 university professors were selected from across the academic spectrum and various types of institutions to come to New York for $2\frac{1}{2}$ days as guests of Jersey. For this period, the directors, who managed Jersey unlike directors of most corporations, sat around the table for a free-wheeling, no-holds-barred discussion of the oil industry and Big Business in general. Your author attended the 1956 Roundtable and found it an illuminating exercise. SONJ's public relations department also prepared pamphlets on Standard's school systems and other educational activities in foreign countries and its program of providing scholarships to sons and daughters of employees in its South American subsidiaries. A program to provide conducted tours of its refinery and laboratory facilities for local science teachers was instituted.

Looking ahead to the end of World War II, Standard Oil (New Jersey), at Newsom's recommendation and with his staff's collaboration, SONJ published a series of three ads in New Jersey and in all states in which it had subsidiaries aimed at the returning GI Joes. The first 1,000 line as was headed, "HE'S STILL OUR GI JOE," labeled as the first in a series of ads on postwar opportunities. The ad addressed the concern of soldiers and sailors and their loved ones, "The question of post-war jobs — especially for returning veterans — is a big one and live one. It will get more so as the war comes nearer its end." The second one placed in July 1944 was headed, "OUR POST-WAR PLAN TO HELP SMALL BUSINESS." This outline the Esso Marketers Business Assistance Plan.

By 1963, there had been a complete change of management of Standard Oil since Newsom had come on board in 1942, and the question was apparently raised anew as to the use and necessity of institutional advertising. A memorandum dated October 28, 1963, and addressed to Robert H. Scholl responded to the Executive Committee's request for an assessment of the company's uses of institutional advertising. Apparently SONJ's officers were concerned about the approximately $7.5 million Jersey had spent in the past 4 years for institutional advertising — approximately $3.2 million in magazines and $4.3 million in television. Newsom's memo argued, "When one considers the huge budgets spent in this country by corporations in an attempt to bring public attention to their interests — nearly $13 billion last year — and nearly $50 billion during the four-year period, Jersey has certainly done extraordinarily well to achieve the good results it has achieved from its thrifty, limited expenditures." Seven and a half million dollars "thrifty"!

Newsom's memorandum concluded with these recommendations:

> It is our feeling that Jersey must use every useful means to accomplish its basic purpose to cultivate public understanding and confidence. This is a major purpose of the enterprise. It is essential to its profit objectives.
>
> To this end it must with great skill and effectiveness use the advantages of institutional advertising — not as a substitute for something else or as an

adequate answer by itself, but because the need is great enough to justify many means.

We think institutional advertising is a valuable instrument and its use should be continued and expanded.

These thoughtful and imaginative programs were supplemented by the standard techniques and tools of providing news releases and responding to queries for the news media, encouraging more speaking engagements and interviews with Jersey's top officials, and placing articles in trade, business, and general magazines to portray the more open, more responsive SONJ. Publicity per se was restrained. For example from December 1, 1944, to November 1, 1945, the Public Relations Department issued only 89 releases and almost a third of these involved appointments or deaths. Newsom and his associates relied on more substantive means of recasting Jersey's unfavorable reputation. The key was that Newsom, described by a former partner, Ping Ferry, as a "corporate charmer," had persuaded the company to go public and open its operations for public scrutiny. One may assume, for example, that it was no easy task to persuade Jersey's top brass that this giant and once highly secretive corporation should freely open its records to the historians. The rebuilding of Jersey's reputation was under way.

NEWSOM CHARTS ROAD TO REDEMPTION

The strategy of Newsom and his associates and the Freyermuth staff in this redemption of Jersey's unfavorable reputation is reflected in the public relations "Objectives Sought in 1945":

1. Correcting the false impressions left by the Truman and Bone Committee charges. Adequate refutation has not yet been achieved.
2. Combatting the belief that Standard Oil is a monopoly, has selfish interests. The public misconceptions in this connection are great.
3. Establishing a greater knowledge of the company's labor relations policies and record. The public thinks the company pays poor wages and has bad labor policies.
4. Promoting a better understanding of Jersey's management as to personalities, philosophy, and corporate functioning.
5. Presenting Jersey's part in the war effort. This may be the last year to tell effectively the Company's great part in the war effort.
6. Establishing the awareness by the Company of problems of national interest.
7. Improving the public understanding of the nature and operation of the oil business, particularly of the Jersey Company. General knowledge about the oil business is lacking.

8. Developing character for the Jersey company. The public must learn that the Jersey Company has a heart as well as brain. Its business principles and policies . . . must be brought out.

EFFORT TO DECENTRALIZE JERSEY'S PROGRAM FAILS

After 5 years of counseling SONJ on its public relations strategies and tactics, Ping Ferry wrote a memorandum on December 2, 1947, to Newsom suggesting a decentralization of the public relations program, a move that would, in Ferry's opinion, save half of the $1, 964, 400 SONJ was currently spending on its public relations program. After pointing out that the parent company's role to its affiliates and subsidiaries was that of policy making and advisory, with the exception of Maritime operations, Ferry proposed:

Revision of the Jersey PR program, it seems to me, should fall in line with these considerations. That is:

1. Its function should be to serve the parent company as a means for communicating policy decisions and news.
2. Its function should be to serve affiliates as a sort of counsel in PR matters.

Such an approach would obviously cut out a lot of present bureau setup of the Jersey PR department. Some of this load would be transferred to operating companies. Some would be eliminated entirely. . . . Under this approach, the Jersey PR department would consist of a small corps of PR experts. Many specialized operations, such as layout men, artists, etc. would be transferred to affiliates or dropped in favor of retaining such assistance on call. The elaborate photographic setup would be attended to in the same way, and only a small nucleus of the present news setup would be retained.

Predictably, when an entrenched bureaucracy is threatened, nothing happens. In a telephone interview on January 29, 1992, Ferry told me, "Nothing came of my proposal. All it did was to set off a helluva row." So much for decentralization of the large setup SONJ had created under Newsom's guidance.

TO LOBBY OR NOT TO LOBBY

Jersey's subsidiary, the Creole Petroleum Company of Venezuela, apparently requested the parent company in late 1953 to set up a Washington lobbying office to represent it in the International Oil Cartel probe that brought another government crisis to SONJ and its overseas affiliates. George Freyermuth of SONJ sought Newsom's advice on how to respond to this request. Indicative of the way the Newsom firm handled such matters, Newsom requested the opinions of Ping Ferry and Arthur Tourtellot, another key member of Newsom's staff. Ferry wrote in a memorandum of November 23, 1953, to Newsom:

> It is too easy to say yes off hand. My first reaction was to do so, but on thinking about it further I do not believe it is a very good idea. The object is to better relations with Congress. Are present relations poor? . . . I have the impression that Jersey has been well served by its policies with regard to Washington. These are the policies of candor, openness, nothing under the table.

> If Creole is under such pressure, it ought to be able to provide the Venezuelan Government with something better than assurance it has hired a lobbyist.

Tourtellot's advice was similar:

> The important question here seems to me to be what Creole and Jersey can expect to achieve through lobbying which they cannot otherwise achieve by appearances before Congressional committees, public statements, and informal meetings with legislators and newspaper men. . . . Lobbying American by private companies is, both by historical verdict and popular understanding, a suspect and not completely clean activity. . . . The simple truth of the matter is that lobbying in this country has never been associated in the public mind with good citizenship.

Consequently, Newsom wrote Freyermuth on November 25, 1953, incorporating the thoughts of Ferry and Tourtellot, advising against retention of a Creole–Jersey lobbyist in Washington, "Our feeling is that such action would be regarded as a reversion to the kind of doubtful practices that Ida Tarbell and Ray Stannard Baker wrote about so damagingly. We believe the company might well regret such a decision"

Much earlier in the service of the Jersey account, Newsom had established an outpost in Washington when his firm and SONJ had retained Arthur Newmyer & Associates. Newmyer became a valued counselor to Newsom and to the SONJ executives on their Washington problems. For example, at Freyermuth's request, he prepared an outline of suggested testimony on the hearings on oil imports before the House Ways and Means Committee in April 1953. The Newmyers did not lobby.

ANOTHER CRISIS FLARES

Despite the steady flow of constructive public relations actions and activities charted by the Newsom Committee for SONJ—Earl Newsom,

Fred Palmer, Ping Ferry, Arthur Tourtellot — another crisis with the federal government erupted to reinforce the public distrust that Newsom had set out to erase from 1942 on. In July 1952, a Federal Trade Commission report, apparently leaked to the press, charged Jersey Standard with being part of a "giant international oil cartel." This FTC probe ultimately resulted in a Federal Grand Jury's indictment of Jersey Standard and its three domestic affiliated companies — Humble, Carter, and Esso Standard — along with 25 other oil companies for an alleged conspiracy to fix prices of crude oil and gasoline in the United States. The indictments were handed down on May 29, 1958 — which indicates the length such a crisis can go unresolved.

This put a heavy burden on the Newsom staff over these years. From the first leaking of the forthcoming FTC report, the Jersey company, on the Newsom team's advice, took a positive posture rather than a defensive one. The team decided, "I think we are right in our belief than Jersey should not try its case in the press and in other public statements." Apparently Jersey and the other oil companies decided not to try the case in court. It was apparently settled out of court because there is no decision of record in the U.S. District Court of Northern Virginia.

After several days of internal discussion and debate, the Jersey team in Newsom's agency came up with these objectives for its public relations strategy to deal with this long-term crisis:

The objectives of the Jersey company in the current crisis include the following:

1. Obtaining a clean bill of health on the cartel charges.
2. Establishing to the people of the U. S. and the free world that Jersey has not profiteered on oil for defense.
3. Dramatizing the need for public understanding of the difference between rules of conduct for business and industry in the U.S. and the rules abroad.
4. Initiating steps to obtain a clear and definitive policy for American companies doing business abroad.
5. Maintaining (and enhancing) Jersey's good reputation within the oil industry and as a leader in American and world trade.
6. Forestalling restrictive, punitive, or discriminatory legislation.
7. Keeping Jersey stockholders and employees aware that the company continues to have their interests in mind.
8. Reiterating Jersey's belief in free access, free competition, free markets.

The leaking of the forthcoming FTC report initiated a long-term crisis that partially deflected the Newsom/SONJ comprehensive campaign — as crises do. The first task was to draft a letter to Standard Oil stockholders, who were told, "This F.T.C. report has not been available to us. We have no way of knowing what charges or statements, if any, have been made in this report about this company, or the basis on which they have been made." The FTC Report on Petroleum that was the springboard for submitting international oil operations to a Grand Jury investigation was published in August 1952 by the U.S. Senate Small Business Committee. The Newsom committee for the SONJ account decided to put the company in a positive posture, not a defensive one. Arthur Tourtellot recommended:

1. *Positivism*—i.e., Jersey should be concerned with a campaign of information, rather than one of defense.
2. *Confidence*—in the rightness of its actions and policies in its foreign operations as both sound business practice and thoughtful public conduct. This confidence should also, so far as the public goes, assume that it will win its case.
3. *Avoidance of political attack*—it ought to be remembered that a Justice Department action is on behalf of the people of the United States and nothing can be accomplished by reading evil motives into such actions even if they exist.
4. *Identification of Jersey's purposes and actions with the public interest.*

The Newsom staff was not prone to shoot from the hip as too many CEOs and their public relations counselors sometimes do. Over the next 6 years, Newsom and his staff were kept busy preparing public statements, letters to stockholders, and press releases outlining the company's position in this litigation.

Then in April 1953, another PR crisis arose when legislation was introduced in the Congress to restrict the importing of oil into the United States. This necessitated the preparation and release of a lengthy statement from the company arguing, "Restrictions on imports of oil into the United States, which has been urged upon Congress, would injure fuel consumers, jeopardize military fuel supplies, and would run counter to our country's efforts to help friendly nations toward greater economic strength through freer world trade." The statement was a digest of a study that had been made by the company.

Typical of the ghostwriting a counselor performs for clients was the credo of Frank W. Abrams, who had just retired as chairman of the board of Standard Oil, that was drafted by Newsom and his staff for publication in the *Saturday Review* that month. Apparently Abrams had sent Newsom a rough draft of his credo. On December 7, 1953, Newsom wrote Abrams, "Ping and Fred and I have all had a hand in this, so if you do not like it, there is no particular individual whom you can blame. Actually, it was a most fascinating experience for us. It seems to us important, because it is the kind of thing that is most apt to be picked up and used widely."

So went the Newsom work for Standard Oil (New Jersey), now Exxon, until his retirement.

CBS SEEKS NEWSOM'S COUNSEL IN TIME OF TURBULENCE

The end of Newsom's relationship with Henry Ford II and the Ford Motor Company and Foundation in 1957 made room for his company to accept another corporate giant as a client — William S. Paley's Columbia Broadcasting System. Newsom held to a firm policy of accepting no more clients than to whom he and his partners could devote full attention. The Newsom Papers indicate that his company was retained by CBS in mid-1957. Whether this was the reason for turning to Newsom or not, at the time there was a great inner turbulence in the top echelons of CBS. There was a growing split between CBS' longtime star, Edward R. Murrow, on one side and Paley and Frank Stanton, CBS president, on the other. Later on Paley and Stanton broke their long time close relationship with Stanton being forced out of CBS, as Murrow had been earlier. Out of this CBS relationship came a strengthened bond of personal friendship between Newsom and Frank Stanton; Stanton gave the eulogy at Newsom's service.

Interestingly because the News Division was in the "eye" of CBS's internal storm — a storm resulting from the winds of criticism born of several Murrow *See it Now* programs and the Quiz Show Scandal — Newsom's Papers indicate that its first task for the network was the "CBS News Project." An interesting footnote to CBS' history: This was the main thrust of Edward L. Bernays' counsel when he was retained by young Bill Paley, who had been given the infant network by his father in 1929. Readers will recall that Bernays, too, had an influential impact on CBS taking the news leadership among the three networks. Bernays stressed the importance of news broadcasts when Paley was uncertain about them. Bernays also, inadvertently, had a historic impact when he got his associate, Edward Klauber, a job with CBS because he and Klauber couldn't get along.

Klauber soon became Paley's second-in-command, and he took the lead in building a strong corps of radio news correspondents. Alexander Kendrick, a former CBS correspondent, told in his biography of Murrow, *Prime Time, the Life of Edward R. Murrow,* that it was Klauber who in 1935 hired Murrow as CBS "director of talks." This historic decision led to CBS's dominance in broadcast news for decades. Kendrick wrote, "At the same time that Murrow joined the CBS network, so did another young man from Ohio State University. He was Frank Stanton."

Stanton, later to become president of CBS, also played a major role in building CBS as a news leader. With the passage of time, Murrow and Stanton, long close friends as well as team associates split in a situation in which Earl Newsom was involved as a mediator. This trio pioneered radio and TV news with innovations that others had to follow. At Klauber's memorial service at Freedom House, New York City, in 1954, Murrow said of Klauber, "I do not know whether he believed in the essential goodness or badness of men. I do know that he believed passionately that the communication of information, unslanted, untarnished and undistorted, was the only means by which mankind would progress." Murrow regarded Klauber as the "father of radio news."

From the start—1929—William Paley had placed great importance on public relations for himself and for CBS as well in the promotion of the network programming and personalities. In their work with CBS' officials, Newsom and his partners worked closely with E. Kidder Meade, a former staff associate at the Newsom firm. Newsom circulated a memo to his staff saying that Frank Stanton was looking for a PR man to put on the CBS staff and did the staff have any suggestions. When Meade read the memo, he marched into Newsom's office and said he would like the job. Newsom, somewhat taken aback, arranged for Meade to interview Stanton. Stanton was impressed with Meade and hired him. After World War II, in which he had lost a foot, Meade had taken a public relations job at Colonial Williamsburg—another Newsom client, part of his counsel to John D. Rockefeller III in this period.

In her first-rate biography of Paley, *In All His Glory*, Sally Bedell Smith said of Paley's outside counsel and Kidder Meade, "They managed to smother all evidence of Paley's peccadilloes and fan his legend. Press interviews were taperecorded by CBS and the transcripts carefully edited before being sent out to reporters. The publicity men not only wrote Paley's speeches, statements, and letters; they on occasion drafted people from outside the company to promote the Paley cause." Ms. Smith then gave this example:

> Paley had given a speech at Syracuse University calling for the elimination of the Fairness Doctrine. The speech had been Paley's first major address in six years, and when a letter highly critical of Paley's position ran in the *Times* the following week, the publicity engines at CBS went into overdrive. At first the publicity men drafted an indignant reply to be signed by Arthur Taylor [then president of CBS]. When the law department vetoed the idea, public relations aide Leonard Spinrad wrote the "letter for the signature of someone outside CBS." The letter to the *Times*, with some minor corrections, was signed by David Manning White, then a professor of journalism at Boston University, on July 31. The *Times*, did not run the letter.

In the period of Newsom's counsel to Paley and CBS, the Arthur Newmyer Associates managed by the founder's sons, were also counseling the corporate giant. In this, as in all other cases, the Newsom Company and the Newmyers worked hand-in-glove.

Although there is nothing in the Newsom Papers to indicate such,

William Paley was undoubtedly the most egotistical, publicity-hungry, and temperamental client Earl Newsom had to deal with in his three decades of counseling. *The New York Times* review of Ms. Smith's 600-page biography said this of Paley, "If ever there were a man to confirm Lord Acton's maxim that no great men are good men surely it was William S. Paley. . . . Her superb and thorough reporting uncovered all the unpleasantness along with the greatness."

In his review of Ms. Smith's book for *The Times Book Review* Christopher Buckley summarized the portrait Ms. Smith painted of Williams S. Paley, warts and all: "The William S. Paley that emerges . . . is a toweringly small man; insecure, petty, jealous, ungrateful, snobbish, ashamed of his own Jewishness nearly to the point of anti-Semitism; a philanderer who cheated on his rather good wife as she lay dying, a tyrannical father . . . a pathological liar; abusive, resentful, cruel, neurotic, hypochondriac, self-absorbed and greedy." Such was the portrait of a client Newsom was to present to the public as a broadcast statesman and pioneer.

Fortunately for Newsom, Arthur Tourtellot, and other members of the Newsom Company team, most of their dealings were with Frank Stanton, CBS president, not with Paley. Newsom and Stanton had developed a friendship since 1941 when Newsom was engaged as counsel to the National Association of Broadcasters (NAB), then in a bitter battle with James C. Petrillo and the American Society of Composers, Authors and Publishers (ASCAP) over royalty payments for songs broadcast over the air. Stanton at that time was vice-president for research at CBS, thus was especially helpful to Newsom in this period. The NAB had been organized by the pioneer broadcasters in 1923 in order to present a solid front to ASCAP over this same issue. When NAB's negotiations with ASCAP broke down in 1941, the broadcasters formed Broadcast Music Incorporated (BMI) as a competitor to ASCAP and brought in Earl Newsom to help them present their side of the story to the public. BMI's plan was to recruit young composers and play music in the public domain. For months and months the music of Stephen Foster filled the airwaves.

A PROGRAM TO STRENGTHEN CBS NEWS

The Newsom staff early in January 1959 rewrote a first draft of Kidder Meade's memo to outline "A Program to Strengthen CBS News." This memo involved "CBS's own" philosophy of its news function, the presentation of its news program, and the promotion of its news department." These three elements are inseparable," the memo continued, "for certainly a major determinant of the degree of importance that the public attaches to

CBS News is the importance that CBS appears to attach to it." Then the memo defined the news function for CBS:

> CBS News regards the broadcast media as a unique opportunity to bring to the American people as close as possible to the actual scenes of the events of their time and into the presence of significant individuals and ideas. . . .
>
> To this end, CBS News sees as its central purpose the provision of a radio and television service ranging over the entire field of current affairs, in every field. This service involves both reporting and interpreting the news with broadcasting in the role of a guide.

The 11-page memorandum concluded with this CONFIDENTIAL note:

> It is strongly recommended that Sig Mickelson be appointed President of CBS News, bringing his title to the level of the other division leads.
>
> An announcement of his appointment, coupled with a statement of the CBS News philosophy and the first announcement of a week-night television network news special, would forcefully proclaim to network critics CBS's continuing and active belief in the vital function of news and public affairs, and its intention of implementing this belief in the most powerful and effective ways to command.

Sig Mickelson, who had joined CBS News in 1943 and had become chief of CBS News in 1954, was elevated to the title of President of CBS News shortly after this memorandum was submitted to CBS management. He served in this capacity until 1961 when he left CBS to become vice-president of Time–Life Broadcasting, Inc. In 1970, he retired from Time–Life to teach journalism, first at Northwestern University and later at San Diego State University. That such a memorandum defining the CBS News function was written in the offices of the Newsom company, rather than by CBS management, provides validity to the oft-stated view that Earl Newsom was more a management consultant than a public relations counselor.

Early in 1959, the Newsom staff prepared the "1958 Annual Review of CBS News" marking the first full year of CBS News as a division of CBS. The report boasted that in 1959 the news division had expanded its scope of operations, created new program forms, and advanced the maturity of television and radio as a medium of news, information, and public service. "CBS News presented a service that ranged over all aspects of world and national events; the issues, trends and ideas of the day and the fields of the arts, sciences, humanities, religion, politics, and sports." The report was obviously designed for wide dissemination to answer a growing chorus of critics.

IN THE MIDDLE OF THE PALEY-MURROW BREAKUP

A series of controversial programs by Edward R. Murrow on his lively, but controversial *See It Now* television program, produced by his friend and colleague, Fred Friendly, not only created a series of public headaches for CBS and its public relations counselors but in the end, led to a break between William Paley and Frank Stanton on one side, Murrow on the other, with Earl Newsom in the middle. The denouement of the Murrow's long and distinguished broadcasting career goes something like this:

Murrow made his television debut with a new program, *See It Now*, adapted from his radio program, *Hear It Now*, on Sunday, November 18, 1951. Sally Bedell Smith wrote, "For the first time the continental sweep, dramatic power and sheer magic of television were displayed in the simplest and most striking way." In time, in this era of McCarthysim, by fearlessly examining wrongs in society, the program became controversial and posed a problem for Paley and Stanton. Nonetheless, the program endured 7 years and died for lack of advertiser support and management courage. Murrow's program exposing Senator Joseph McCarthy for what he was—a reckless demagogue—and defending Dr. J. Robert Oppenheimer, father of the atomic bomb whose security clearance had been revoked by President Eisenhower, brought the pack of right-wing critics on in full cry.

After the McCarthy program, Murrow was a victim of an entire issue of *Counter-Attack*, the weekly blacklist put out by *Red Channels*. Increasingly Murrow became discouraged by these stinging criticisms and even more by CBS's submission to it. Ironically for Murrow, a chain smoker who ultimately died of lung cancer, he was the first to air programs on *See It Now* linking lung cancer to smoking, long before the historic Surgeon General's Report. Even more ironically, on the same night *See It Now* made its last broadcast, *The $64,000 Question* made its debut. This program, too, played a role in the Murrow–CBS breakup. Watching from the control room, Murrow was aghast to hear Frank Stanton introduce the new quiz show, later to be exposed as rigged, as "a program in which a large part of the audience is interested by that very fact . . . in the public interest." Your author concurs with Sally Bedell Smith, "If *See It Now*, signified television at its best, the quiz show represented the worst of the new medium."

A year after Newsom took CBS as a client, the networks hit rock-bottom in public opinion with the exposure that the popular quiz show had been rigged. The networks ignored the first warnings of this ticking bomb when *Time*, in April 1957, reported that Herbert Stempel had told NBC officials that his opponent, Charles Van Doren, had been fed questions in advance and that the producer of the show had told Stempel to give wrong answers. The producers, outside independents, denied the charges to NBC. In August 1959, 3 months after Paley had canceled *See It Now*, the quiz show scandal blew wide open when Edward Hilgemeier, a stand-by contestant on CBS' *Dotto* revealed that one of the contestants had been coached. Then Stempel went public with his accusations of fraud on NBC's *Twenty-One* that had been reported 5 months earlier in *Time*. Frank Stanton immediately ordered an investigation and took *Dotto* off the air. Next the Manhattan District Attorney and the House of Representatives started investigations of their own. In the middle of this crisis, Edward R. Murrow, fed up with Paley's and Stanton's timidity and the crass commercialism of broadcasting, threw his bomb—a sensational speech to the Radio and Television News Directors meeting in Chicago on October 15, 1958.

In this speech that he had carefully kept to himself and not cleared with his superiors, Murrow lambasted the networks for squandering their "powerful instrument of communication." He minced no words. Kendrick wrote of this, "Future historians, he said, would find in the film records of television 'evidence of decadence, escapism, and insulation from the realities of the world in which we live." Kendrick continued, "Television's timidity toward controversy, he thought, went hand in hand with its [TV's] lack of self confidence." Murrow said, "Each time they yield to a voice from Washington, or any political pressure, each time they eliminate something that might offend some section of the community, they are creating their own body of precedent and tradition."

Stanton and Paley were furious with the speech, knowing they were its main targets. Paley never discussed the speech with Murrow, but he told Stanton in anger, "He's fouling his own nest." Murrow asked for and got a sabbatical leave as of July 1, 1959, to be spent in Europe. Incidentally, the five full-length news shows that the Newsom staff had bragged about in CBS' 1958 free report were seen by many as a result of Murrow's scathing speech. Bill Paley and Murrow never had a serious conversation after the Chicago speech. Paley chose to freeze Murrow out rather than fire him.

The juxtaposition of these two events shattering the reputation of the networks, CBS in particular, brought much work and delicate counseling to Newsom and his partners. Newsom's first task was to a draft a *mea culpa* speech for President Frank Stanton to be delivered to the Radio and Television Directors on October 16 in New Orleans—just a year after Murrow had delivered his jeremiad to this group. The Newsom team's next task was to write a confidential draft of a memorandum implementing Dr. Stanton's announcement in New Orleans that the quiz shows involving large sums of money would be banned by CBS and promised other reforms to eliminate deceptions then common to broadcasting. The Newsom-drafted memo was "the first implementation of the general policy announced by Dr. Stanton." The bedrock policy: "The very nature of television requires its broadcasts be exactly what they purport to be." The memo drafted for TV President James Aubrey's signature set out these operating rules:

1. *Quiz Shows*. Recent disclosures have proved the impossibility of po-
licing adequately the honesty of these shows . . . Accordingly, CBS will
broadcast no quiz programs as presently conceived in which high money
prizes, lavish merchandise gifts, or other stages are offered the contestants.

2. *Panel Shows*. In these shows the prizes to the guest contestants are
usually moderate or low . . . producers of all such programs are being
informed that the practice of "feeding" lines to contestants must be
announced.

3. *Live, Recorded or Dubbed Performances*. If a performance or any part
of it, is in any way recorded—whether on film or on video-tape—that fact
shall be disclosed.

4. *Interviews—and Spontaneity Generally*. Any program in which spontaneity would or might be assumed and in which complete spontaneity is not the
fact, must be adequately described.

5. *Artificial Laughter and Applause*. It is traditional in broadcasting . . .
that radio audience applause is cued with false cards. . . . We agree that this
practice is a form of misrepresentation. To continue to foster it is not
consistent with our determination to make our programs exactly what they
purpose to be.

CBS, through its public relations office, proudly publicized these new
rules. Jack Gould, television critic for *The New York Times*, called Stanton
for details. The CBS president, according to Ms. Smith, said, "Devices like
canned laughter and phony studio applause would have to go, as well as any
rehearsing on news and public affairs programs." Gould then asked,
"Would this apply to Murrow's *Person to Person?*" Stanton replied "Yes."
Ms. Smith continued:

The next day, Murrow's office in New York read him Gould's follow-up in the
Times over the telephone to London, and Murrow hit the roof. He gave an
interview to United Press in London denying any impropriety on "Person to
Person," and dismissing Stanton as ignorant of radio and television production techniques. Murrow's attack made page one of *The New York Times*. It
also shattered a promising truce between Stanton and Murrow that had been
reached only four months earlier over a bottle of Scotch, on the eve of
Murrow's departure for his sabbatical.

Understandably, Paley and Stanton were furious that Murrow, in their
view had again washed dirty CBS linen in public. Paley wrote an angry
letter to Murrow with the clear implication that he should resign from CBS.
Stanton persuaded him not to send the letter. Stanton, too, wrote Murrow
a letter stressing the importance of corporate unity. Nor did Stanton send
his letter. Earl Newsom was clearly involved in these heated discussions.
Perhaps it was his idea to send Ralph Colin, a lawyer for CBS, to London
to persuade Murrow to issue a mollifying statement. Ms. Smith wrote,

"After hours of discussion, Murrow and Colin agreed on a statement that fell short of an outright apology. Murrow reaffirmed the integrity of his show, but conceded that he had reacted too harshly, without benefit of all the facts, and endorsed the new CBS policies."

Colin returned to New York to present the statement to Paley and Stanton. They were unhappy; they wanted an outright apology. Again, perhaps with Newsom's advice, Stanton called Murrow in London with Paley, Colin, and Newsom in the room. Paley refused to talk to Murrow. In fact, he would have no further communication with Murrow during the latter's sabbatical. Paley did have some misgiving about Stanton's handling of this difficult situation and disapproved of Stanton including *Person to Person* in his interview with Jack Gould. But he felt he had no choice but to back his president. Nonetheless, at the insistence of Jack Benny, Paley overruled Stanton on the canned laughter policy. These events were the beginning of the end of Murrow's position with CBS.

THE HOUSE HEARINGS

The next task to deal with in the Quiz Show Scandal for the Newsom partners was to prepare the statement of Thomas K. Fisher, vice-president and general attorney of the CBS Television Network, to present to the House of Representatives Subcommittee on Legislative Oversight on October 9, 1959. Right off, Fisher admitted, "It is clear that there were behind the scenes, improper practices of one sort or another in a number of the quiz shows created and managed by the independent producers and broadcast by the networks—some of them over the CBS Television Network. As a result, millions of Americans were deceived. So were we." Fisher added, "This deception of the television audience in this country strikes at the integrity of the networks, as well as that of the independent producers who created the shows." Fisher's testimony then gave an account of CBS's investigation.

A memorandum of November 2, from Newmyer Associates to E. Kidder Meade and Earl Newsom reported, "Before an overflow audience this morning, Charles Van Doren told the House Oversight (Harris) Subcommittee the full story of his involvement in the television quiz-fix scandals." More importantly, Newmyer reported, "Neither Subcommittee members nor witnesses showed any strong interest in criticizing the networks, and comment on the network role in the quiz scandals occurred in only a few, isolated cases."

Next Newsom task was to draft a statement for Frank Stanton who appeared before the House committee on November 6. Stanton vowed that "I was completely unaware until August 8, 1958, of any irregularity in quiz shows on our Network. When gossip about quiz shows in general came to my attention, I was assured by our Television Network people that these shows were completely above criticism of any kind. With the benefit of hindsight, it is now clear that I should have gone further." Stanton told the committee, "This has been a bitter pill for us to swallow." Indeed it was.

THE LATER YEARS WITH CBS

In all probability in response to Newsom's counsel, Frank Stanton in a speech (drafted by Arthur Tourtellot) to the Academy of Television Arts and Sciences in New York City on December 3, 1959, declared:

> I can report to you today that CBS authorized some months ago the development of a survey and detailed analysis of what people *want* from television. The study—now in the field in its preliminary stages—is being conducted by an outside organization under the direction of some of the country's leading social scientists. . . . I do not mean to suggest that in this one action we will find the whole answer to this problem. But we are entitled to hope that from it we can, step by step, evolve measuring devices that will keep us far more closely in touch with what the American people want in program content and program balance on the CBS Television Network.

A trade-mark Newsome touch!

For the nest several years until Earl Newsom's semiretirement from his company, his counsel consisted of advice on public policy matters, on the continued polishing of William Paley's public image, and writing speeches for Paley, Stanton, and other top officials—a Newsom specialty. These years were not as hectic as the first ones with the Quiz Show Scandal and the Murrow bombshell, though the growing strains between Paley and Murrow and between Paley and Stanton required moving carefully to avoid land mines in the Black Rock.

In a time when he was sending conflicting signals about his retirement, in 1965 Paley directed E. Kidder Meade to orchestrate a campaign to burnish the Paley image. This renewed publicity effort for Paley produced a 7-part series on Paley in May by Bob Considine in the *New York Journal-American*, a series entitled "Live from New York—This is TV's Bill Paley." The series was given a big spread in the Hearst paper and included such high praise as: "Paley has kept his equilibrium throughout this unprecedented period of ruckus in the annals of the slickest and most successful operation of its kind in the world." Many, including the *Gallagher Report*, took note of Paley's image-making campaign—one he apparently needed as he neared a retirement he dreaded. Paley was then 64; some years before Stanton had set a mandatory retirement age of 65 for CBS officials. Paley held Stanton to the mandatory retirement age but ignored it for himself.

In his effort to further hype his image, Paley raised the question with Arthur B. Tourtellot, who was heavily involved in the CBS account, of his (Paley's) becoming involved in some public service activity. John R. Newsom, then an executive with the Fund for the City of New York, wrote a memo to Tourtellot, with copies to Fred Palmer and William Lydgate, suggesting:

> You mentioned that he is especially interested in education and the arts, and you also noted that he already serves as a trustee or director of Columbia University, the Presbyterian Medical Center, and the Museum of Modern Art. As an alternative to his seeking out some other educational or artistic enterprise, we discussed the possibility of Mr. Paley's becoming concerned in some appropriate way with efforts to solve New York City's problems. These are times when the quality of urban life is commanding the critical attention of more and more thoughtful people, and there is every evidence that this will be the case for a long time. . . . New York City in many ways presents unique opportunities for anyone of Mr. Paley's stature to assume some private leadership in dealing with the city's problems.

The CBS Foundation later put together a major grant program focused on the problems of New York City.

Whether it was arranged or not, Sigma Delta Chi, the professional journalism society, on November 30, 1966, designated CBS News Headquarters as an Historic Site in Journalism and paid respects to the achievements of CBS News, Murrow, and Paley. Paley responded, "To me, as one intimately associated with the trials and tribulations and failures and triumphs of CBS News, for nearly 40 years, this tribute evokes a profound sense of history — history so bursting with drama and excitement that I feel greatly privileged to have had a share in it." Paley had the grace to acknowledge Edward R. Murrow's contribution, because Murrow was also being honored by the society. Paley said, "Broadcast journalism was scarcely ten years old when Murrow came to it. When he left it, less than twenty-five years later, it had been advanced all out of proportion to the passage of the years. Ed Murrow was not only one of its great architects he was — and remains — one of its chief inspirations." (Murrow found a graceful exit from his troubled situation at CBS when President-elect John F. Kennedy offered him the directorship of the United States Information Agency late in 1960.)

The issue of Pay TV was another problem that occupied a great deal of Earl Newsom's and Arthur Tourtellot's time in their work for CBS. CBS flatly opposed Pay TV — naturally. In a program to deal with this issue, the Newsom partners asserted:

> If pay television should crowd free television off the airwaves, it is the American people—not the broadcasting stations—who will suffer. This the core of CBS's position. CBS believes it therefore has a duty to do everything it can properly do to inform the American people and their leaders on the issues involved, and the essential gravity of those issues.
>
> Time is an important factor. The FCC has delayed until March 1 the date when applications for a test of pay television can be made. This leaves four months for public opinion to make itself felt before Congress and elsewhere.
>
> Many of the things that CBS can best do in a program of public information cannot be stipulated at this time as specific items in a projected program. They will flow naturally from the situation as it develops.

Pay television did come to viewers with the advent of cable broadcasting.

Newsom and CBS commissioned a Gallup Poll to measure public opinion on the issue of Pay TV and found that 72% of the people were aware of the issue. Of these persons, 7% were for Pay TV, 55% against, and 10% undecided. Those who favored Pay TV thought it would bring better quality shows. Those against it said it would cause too much expense for many people.

TOURTELLOT TO CBS

When Earl Newsom retired in 1966 from active participation in his company, his longtime friend and partner, Fred L. Palmer, also retired. The remaining partners, Arthur B. Tourtellot, William A. Lydgate, and John R. Newsom, organized the agency as a corporation with Tourtellot as chairman and Lydgate as president and CEO. Shortly after Earl Newsom retired, CBS came after Tourtellot with an attractive offer—"a lot of money" in the words of J. R. Newsom—and Tourtellot accepted. He became executive vice-president at CBS and served in that capacity until 1977 when failing health forced him to step down to the presidency of the William S. Paley Foundation. Tourtellot died in October of that year. Tourtellot and Paley had developed a close relationship. Tourtellot took over the speech-writing chore formerly provided by the Newsom staff. To the disgruntlement of some board members of the Museum of Modern Art (MOMA) when Paley took over the presidency of the MOMA, he often used Tourtellot as his proxy. It was Tourtellot's idea that eventuated in Paley's creating the Museum of Broadcasting, created for the public, that opened its doors in 1971.

OTHER MAJOR NEWSOM CLIENTS

In 1945, a Pelham neighbor of Newsom John H. Hinman, then president of the International Paper Company, asked Newsom for advice on restyling the company's annual report. The Newsom staff handled the entire production of the report, much to Hinman's satisfaction. Hinman thought that because his company did not sell directly to consumers that International Paper did not need a public relations department. Newsom set out to persuade Hinman otherwise. In a cogently persuasive memorandum of July 11, 1945, Newsom argued, "In its woodland operations the opinions that various groups of people—the people of Canada, Government, employees, inhabitants of the towns in which it operates—have of International Paper and its operations are important to the company's success. These opinions or attitudes which people have toward the company make up a sort of *climate* in which the woodlands operations are carried on day to day."

Newsom's memo continued: There are two characteristics of this "climate" which now seem to require attention and a program of action:

> The attitude of the people of Canada toward the function of the International Paper Company—and the whole paper industry—is based upon misunderstanding and colored by prejudice. . . . There is noteworthy evidence that the people of Canada have this general attitude toward . . . the Company and the business in which it is engaged. The woodlands of Canada make up one of our great natural resources. These resources are being exploited by Canadian International Paper (and other paper companies).

Newsom then set forth a program to solve this problem starting with typically, a reliable public opinion survey that would document qualitatively and quantitatively the existence of this prejudice in the minds of the people of Canada. This would be followed, if Newsom's plan was accepted, by a restatement of company policy and the organization of a Public Information Department that would implement a program of activities to communicate with the people of Canada in a continuous "report."

Newsom's plan was not immediately accepted by Hinman and his fellow executives, but when the company began laying plans to celebrate the company's 50th anniversary, they came back to Newsom and accepted his recommendation to set up a public relations department. The Newsom company handled the celebration in 1948 and later guided the new public relations department in a policy of emphasizing the company's role in conservation of forest lands. A series of speeches were written for the company officials discussing forestry. The company started putting out educational comic books for children, pamphlets on forestry, and impressive annual reports. At Newsom's urging, International Paper opened its privately owned forest lands to public hunting, fishing, and picnicking. IP's turnaround in public opinion had begun. For example, a public opinion survey taken in Three Rivers, Quebec, in September 1956 found that Canadian International Paper Co. (CIP) was the best known and most highly regarded company in that city. In 1955, the company set up a Public Relations Committee to involve more top executives in the public relations program. Fred L. Palmer, Newsom partner, wrote Vernon Johnson, CIP vice-president and general manager, on December 2, 1955, "I would suppose one of your objectives in having a public relations committee might be to help bring a variety of your executives into direct contact with public relations problems, opportunities and decisions." The Newsom partners had taught still another corporate giant the importance and the ways of public relations.

COUNSEL TO JOHN D. ROCKEFELLER III

In mid-1948, John D. Rockefeller III sought Earl Newsom's counsel on some questions about Colonial Williamsburg that were troubling him. After his father's death, Rockefeller had continued to financially support this historic American site. Out of this relationship came a close, continuing relationship with Rockefeller until Newsom's retirement. These assignments covered the wide range of Mr. Rockefeller's myriad of interests, including the Rockefeller Foundation.

At a conference in June 1948, Mr. Rockefeller asked Newsom to study two questions that were concerning the philanthropist: "1. To come to a clearer understanding and expression of the significance of Colonial Williamsburg; 2. To arrive at some concrete suggestions which could be the first step in a continuing program toward those objectives." In a memorandum dated August 30, Newsom wrote, in part, "We have become most conscious that Colonial Williamsburg has a good many meanings—depending on the direction from which you approach—and that our first decision as a group should be to determine what present day purpose we want a reborn and living Colonial Williamsburg to serve *within its traditions and because of its significance.*" Newsom, in conclusion, suggested a study be made on these questions by members of the site's staff because Newsom thought "it would be a grave mistake for our organization to 'blueprint' a program of action and hand it over to the Williamsburg staff to be carried out."

Rockefeller implemented this suggestion at the end of 1949. In a talk to the Colonial Williamsburg staff on December 9, 1949, the philanthropist admitted, "I want to make an admission and it may be a pretty serious admission in the eyes of some of you. I want to tell you that I am not altogether certain of what the basic significance of Williamsburg really is. Many of us have talked this question over for a long while. Often we felt that we were moving in direction of an answer. But the plain fact is that we have moved very slowly, for many good reasons." Then he announced that two staff members, Mr. Burbank and Mr. Goodbody, members of the resident public relations staff, were being detached from their regular duties for an indefinite period of time to define or more accurately redefine the purpose and significance of the famous Virginia recreated village. Then Rockefeller added, "Since I have been largely responsible for initiating this inquiry, I want to assume personal responsibility for the undertaking in every aspect — administratively, financially, and otherwise." He also assured the staff that steps would be taken to continue the normal operations of public relations and publications. The report of the two Williamsburg staffers was not in the Newsom Papers.

In 1951, the Newsom organization prepared an attractive, illustrated report, "Colonial Williamsburg, The First Twenty-Five Years," because the year 1951 marked the close of 25 years of planning and rebuilding of Virginia's 18th-century capital. The report "looked back over a period during which an estimated six million visitors had come to Williamsburg from every state in the United States and many foreign countries to see the Restoration . . . and subject themselves to the experience of stepping out of the present into another historic period of time." John D. Rockefeller, Jr., who financed the restoration until his death, said at the time of the initiation of the project, "The restoration of Williamsburg offered an opportunity to restore a complete area and free it entirely from alien or inharmonious surroundings, as well as preserve the beauty and charm of the old buildings and gardens of the city and its historic significance." Publication of the report brought widespread acclaim and expression of gratitude to Rockefeller III.

The preparation of speeches — long a hallmark of Newsom's firm — for Mr. Rockefeller was another service provided him. For example, the Newsom staff undertook a long study of the explosion of the world's population and then wove this information into a speech for Rockefeller given on November 8, 1965, to the New York Economic Club. This had been a continuing concern of John D. III and the Rockefeller Foundation because in his view "there will be no lasting peace or security in the world until hunger and want can be eliminated."

Early in 1963, Newsom's staff assisted the foundation by preparing a condensed "Chronological Biography of the Rockefeller Foundation" to provide background to reporters and legislators at a time when Representative Wright Patman was attacking philanthropic foundations. The report included a chart showing that the Rockefeller Foundation had from its inception in 1913 to 1956 dispensed more than one half billion dollars to charitable causes. The Newsom staff next prepared a statement for Dr. J. George Harrar, president of the foundation, for release on January 6, 1963, to reply to Rep. Patman's charges. President Harrar declared, "Mr. Patman's reports have tended to put the whole idea of private philanthropy under a cloud. They are sharply critical of voluntary efforts of dedicated and free men of goodwill who, in organizing themselves toward the advancement of human welfare, have made contributions of incalculable value."

These are mere snapshots of the long and close relationship Mr. Newsom and Mr. Rockefeller shared for nearly 20 years. For example, Newsom was heavily involved in the planning and publicizing of Rockefeller Brothers Jackson Hole, Wyoming, project and in the building of Lincoln Center.

ADVISOR TO PRESIDENTS

Understandably this "counselor to corporate giants" was a Republican and provided counsel to several important Republican leaders—President Dwight D. Eisenhower, Governor Thomas E. Dewey, and Vice President Richard Nixon. His advice was also sought by President John Kennedy. Newsom supported Governor Thomas Dewey's losing campaign against President Harry Truman in 1948. Dewey wrote Newsom on December 16, 1948, "Both personally and on behalf of the Republican Party, I want to tell you how deeply grateful I am for the fine and generous support you gave to me and the party during the campaign. Today, more than ever before, all of us who believe in the Republican Party have a tremendous responsibility to strengthen it"

Newsom counseled Eisenhower in his presidency at Columbia University, provided him polling information when he was Commander of the NATO forces, and in his White House years. As President of Columbia, Eisenhower wrote Newsom on March 9, 1950, "I am still turning over in my mind many of the items of information you gave me yesterday afternoon, to say nothing of the elements of advice regarding my personal situation and problems. . . . This morning I asked my assistant, Mr. [Kevin] McCann, to try to arrange a meeting with you. But I assure you that we will try to be considerate in our demands upon your time." In the 1956 Presidential campaign, Kevin McCann of Eisenhower's White House Staff asked Newsom for a suggested short speech on a special occasion—such as Columbus Day. Newsom wrote, "It is difficult to try to be helpful, if only because I am so far away from pressures of political expediency that are being used on all of you." Newsom urged that Eisenhower not get involved in a "materialistic brawl" but instead be true to himself. "People in all walks of life sense that he is a dedicated person, with no other ambition than to serve his country. They trust him." With the letter, Newsom sent a suggested short statement for Ike to use. In May 1958, the President wrote Newsom urging his support for Ike's "all out effort to secure legislation under which the Defense Department may be organized to meet modern security requirements with maximum efficiency and minimum cost."

The day before leaving the Vice Presidency in January 1961, Vice President Richard Nixon wrote to say "how deeply grateful I am for all that you did in behalf of our cause during the 1960 campaign. Losing the election was naturally a keen personal disappointment to Pat and me, but we shall always be proud of the fact that we had such a dedicated group of men and women on our team."

More important to Newsom in the 1950s and 1960s than any political activity was his participation in the Free Europe Committee and its operations, including Radio Free Europe. He raised very large sums of money among his clients and others for these operations through the Crusade for Freedom. He served on the board of the Committee for Free Europe from 1958 to 1968. Sadly, Newsom didn't live to witness the collapse of Communism and triumph of the democratic idea in which he believed so strongly and for which he worked so hard. President Kennedy, soon after taking office, called Newsom to the White House to "confer on future funding and administration of Radio Free Europe." President Kennedy wrote him on March 10 thanking him for his coming to Washington, adding, "I would like to reiterate the appreciation of the government for your sustained interest in this informational program. Your help has been indispensable to Radio Free Europe."

Given his growing reputation as a counselor, it was inevitable that he would get more demands of *pro bono* work than he could accommodate. For example, he felt it necessary to turn down an invitation to go on the board of the Cranbury School, a school designed to remedy the unequal opportunities for education among African-American children. Although sympathetic with the work of this school, Newsom said "I am heavily involved in other projects in this same area and, for the past several years, have been giving more time than I can afford toward bolstering our educational system." He added that he had "some doubts about the concept of the Cranbury School. It seems to me to look backward, not forward." Newsom did not think "establishment of a new school for underprivileged youngsters to be a fruitful approach to this problem."

Yet, despite his pressure-cooker schedule, Newsom was never too busy to see a young person aspiring to a career in public relations or a scholar seeking information. Typical of many letters found in the Newsom Papers is this one to William Griswold of Belmont, Massachusetts, to whom he wrote, "Do, please, write me and tell me what your conversations here in New York have done to clarify your immediate objectives, so that I can put in a helpful oar to those ends." Newsom's lifelong love affair with the English language also shows through in this letter, "You said that you liked writing. If you really do, you are already the slave of a lifetime crusade—

the endless search for mastery in the use of that thrilling phenomenon, the English sentence." Newsom also sent along to Griswold a copy of the old reliable of writers, Strunk and White's *Elements of Style* with a note, "I hope that you will be as much stimulated by it as I was, and I am years ahead of you in the endless search."

NEWSOM FIRM CARRIES ON ANOTHER 17 YEARS

The Newsom firm, reorganized as a corporation, carried forward for 17 years after Newsom's retirement under the leadership of William Lydgate, Craig Lewis, and Vincent Duffy. In 1983 – 48 years from the time the firm was founded – the Newsom partners merged with Adams & Rinehart. Meantime, Lydgate continued his executive search work under the Newsom firm name that operated as a division of Adams & Rinehart until 1986. In time, Lewis became manager of Ogilvy Public Relations' North American Operations. Ogilvy and Adams & Rinehart operated separately until 1992 when they were brought together as one firm. At this time Lydgate retired and moved to Maine. Lewis was a senior counselor based in Los Angeles. Duffy was managing director in charge of a major New York client group.

In commenting on the changes in public relations counseling that took place from the time of Newsom's retirement until the 1980s, Craig Lewis wrote to me in September 1992:

> For more than twenty years, the Earl Newsom firm was preeminent in its role as an institutional and corporate counselor, with Earl as the focus of its achievements but with important contributions from Fred Palmer and others. . . . Those of us running the firm over the next two decades tried to continue the tradition of counseling, but with a sharper focus on the specific services increasingly being demanded by clients. Ultimately we, and the few others like us, failed, and I believe that it was because, ironically, that industry finally took public relations seriously and organized for it on a broad scale.

> During the seventies, the Federal government went heavily into a new phase of regulation with the creation of the Environmental Protection Agency, the Occupational Health and Safety Administration and other agencies that suddenly began having a very marked effect on the corporate bottom line. . . . Realizing the importance of these matters, and reacting as it would to any other impact, industry got organized in a hurry. That meant creating or beefing up public relations and public affairs organizations and installing their own people in Washington in place of retained lobbyists. . . .

> There were two effects on counseling firms. One was that senior corporate public relations executives felt that they should advise their managements

exclusively. . . . The second was that those huge staffs needed work to keep them busy, so very few editorial, research, or other assignments were given to outsiders. Agencies tended to be assigned big national projects on behalf of trade associations or other coalitions.

EARL NEWSOM THE PERSON

In person Earl Newsom impressed one as a breed apart from his contemporaries in public relations. I interviewed Newsom in his office above the humming activity in the offices below on January 25, 1963. Mr. Newsom was tall, taut in manner, expressive in his carefully phrased answers to questions. Then 65 years old, he still moved with the agility of a younger man, propelling himself around in his arm chair as he talked, pausing only occasionally to pull another Kent cigarette from the brass box on his semicircular desk. Much was made by writers in his time of Newsom's resemblance to Abraham Lincoln. It was true that Newsom with his height, his dark complexion, and his craggy face did bear a resemblance to Abraham Lincoln. This association gained strength because Newsom kept a portrait of Lincoln on the wall behind his desk – one of Lincoln without the beard – and because of his constant quotation of Lincoln. In dealing with clients, Newsom frequently quoted Lincoln's belief that you can't fool all the people all the time.

The story of the Lincoln portrait is this: When Newsom opened his office in 1935 he could not afford an interior decorator, and he found a portrait of Washington that he put in his hallway and one of Lincoln that he put behind his desk. According to *Printer's Ink*, "Years later when Walter Teague decorated the Newsom's offices he searched for oil paintings 'suitable' for Newsom's fancy wall. He tried ships, still-life . . . nothing seemed right." Finally Newsom put the Washington and Lincoln portraits back in their original place. He said of this, "We just put the founding fathers back in their places and that's where they've been ever since." Newsom and Lincoln had more than a resemblance in common – both were eloquent writers. President Lincoln surely was the greatest writer to ever occupy the White House. Newsom's main forte was in counseling managements and in writing their effective public utterances.

To get to Newsom's office, one had to climb a circular staircase to the second floor of his offices. Four corner offices were occupied by the partners. In Newsom's office there was the feeling of being in a professor's ivory tower. In our interview, his wide range of scholarly interests, humor, and charm came through. His intellectual background was one of his strengths, yet he told me that he knew that one Standard Oil executive had criticized him for his "professorial manner." His bleached oak and gold furnishings gave off the aura of strength and stability.

Newsom outlined his thoughts on research as the base for sound public relations planning in a letter dated April 13, 1956, to Professor Alfred McClung Lee, noted sociologist and public relations scholar:

> We here regard special research in motivation, group processes, and public opinion as very important to public relations planning. In our public relations work we deal with the opinions, attitudes, prejudices and actions of people, and the more we know about what affects those processes the better we can do our job. At the same time, we are not always able to approach the public relations of our clients armed with such research. We find that the pressures of time or the unique circumstances of a situation or our failure to learn of and apply appropriate research findings — or combinations of these factors — often leave us in that old, familiar posture of approaching public relations problems with nothing but our experience, our general knowledge, and our energies to help us. In some cases we find it necessary to conduct research before making final decisions or recommending action, and we have always found this extremely helpful.

Newsom also wrote Professor Lee, in appraising the state of public relations in the mid-1950s:

> It strikes me that we are able to proceed more systematically in our work. The techniques of appraising situations, establishing programs, organizing for the future and the like seem to come more easily — and that unquestionably comes, in part at least, from our lengthening experience. . . . Our function seems now to be more widely recognized and understood than ever before. We are not struggling against ignorance and suspicion of our motives, nor are we as puzzled ourselves as we used to be about our place in society.

In its interview with Newsom in roughly in this time frame, *Printer's Ink* probably put its reportorial finger on Newsom's great strength: "Earl Newsom is a superb persuader. His mind works with trigger speed. He can take apart a complicated question and analyze instantaneously why it will or won't work, and can turn out creative ideas as unendingly as the salt machine on the bottom of the ocean. When he speaks he has a winning humor. He flashes into brilliant smiles to punctuate points, can break up abstract philosophical ideas with observations workers remember for years."

Newsom's abilities as a persuader played a key role in his success. This quality was most eloquently described by Frank Stanton, former president of CBS whose friendship with Newsom went back to the early 1940s, in his eulogy at Newsom's memorial service: "One of the great persuaders of this century, he used that vast gift never to diminish people or institutions but always to make them better than he found them." Stanton continued, "His limitless curiosity led Earl away from traditional callings and into one of the newest professions. In achieving outstanding status in it, he brought the zeal of the preacher's son, the passion to instruct of the teacher that he was in his young years, and the powers of advocacy comparable only to the talents of the artist, sensing the right time, the right occasion, the right word."

Printer's Ink asserted almost everyone he's worked with speaks of Newsom in laudatory terms. Not quite everyone. As late as 1992, his onetime partner, Ping Ferry, was still out of sorts over what he believed was Newsom's failure to see the potentialities of the Ford Foundation and his interference in its affairs. This view was shared by Dr. Robert M. Hutchins — fellow Oberlin alumnus — an executive in the foundation in its early years and by Martin Quigley, the former staffer who left the firm in 1950. Though eased out as public information officer of the foundation by Newsom, Quigley, unlike Ferry, has only the highest praise for Newsom. He still refers to him as "my great teacher."

Hewing to the role he chose for himself, Newsom took no more clients that he could serve personally with the assistance of his partners. He told me that his clients followed a "client curve" that" . . . starts with nothing, builds up to a high curve, then levels off at a low line as the client learns to handle his problems." This was certainly true when Henry Ford II felt he had reached the point he could handle "his problems."

Asked about fees, Newsom would deal only in generalities. In a interview on February 18, 1992, his son John told me that major clients paid a $3,000 a month retainer, some smaller clients $2,000 a month, and that partners and associates, except Newsom, billed their time at $55 an hour to cover their time and the office overhead. At the end of the year there was a profit sharing among the partners. As he had vowed earlier, Earl Newsom was not money hungry; he was content to earn enough to give him and his family a comfortable, enjoyable life and, at the end, left a very modest estate. This reflected the values he learned in his youth in the parsonages of Iowa.

DOUBTS ABOUT PRSA

An indication that Earl Newsom saw himself as one apart from the growing numbers of public relations practitioners in the 1950s was his initial refusal to join the Public Relations Society of America despite a number of entreaties to do so. In late October 1951, Rex Harlow, one of the cofounders of the 3-year old professional association, wrote Newsom urging him to join PRSA. Newsom replied in a letter dated November 13, "I have given considerable thought for sometime now to this question of membership in the Public Relations Society of America. . . . I do not feel I can undertake to join the organization at this time. It has always been my firm conviction that when an individual makes a commitment . . . to an outside organization, that with it should go a sincere desire to participate in its affairs to a significantly measurable extent."

In his reply, Newsom was reflecting the considered judgment of three of his staffers, Ted Swanson, Charles Moore, and Ping Ferry:

> It is our considered decision that you should *not* join the Public Relations Society of America for the following reasons:
>
> 1. The Society is not a first-rate representative of professional competence in the public relations field.
> 2. EN and EN & Co. have nothing to gain by joining PRSA.
> 3. From the professional standpoint, it is not necessary to gain membership in the Society.

Apparently somewhere along the line in the next 4 years Newsom had a change of heart because in May 1955, he was elected to active membership in the society. Carbon copies of Executive Vice-President Robert Bliss's letter of welcome to Newsom to PRSA membership went to George H. Freyermuth, Dudley Parsons, Thomas J. Ross, Kalman B. Druck, Bates Raney, and William Ruder. It is fair to speculate that Freyermuth of Standard Oil of New Jersey and T. J. Ross were persuasive in changing Newsom's decision. His son said that he joined because he didn't want to appear "snobbish" to his fellow practitioners.

Newsom's modesty about his command of public relations is reflected in a letter written May 2, 1962, to L. L. L. Golden, longtime columnist on public relations for the *Saturday Review*. Apparently declining an invitation to speak, Newsom wrote Lou Golden, "I avoid making speeches about public relations — if only because, in a field where all of us are still learning, it is difficult to be certain of the truth." In this letter, Newsom admitted that he was probably among the first to use the phrase *public image* in a 1946 talk to the staff and officers of the Standard Oil Company. Like many others, he came to detest the use of "image" instead of reputation in trade talk. As the salty Bernard DeVoto once wrote, "Americans don't just fall in love with a cliche, they hug it to death." Newsom reiterated to Golden his basic premise that "the general view is that no institution can prosper in this increasingly political world without the confidence of large numbers of people."

It was this basic conviction that caused Earl Newsom to turn down many lucrative accounts — for example, the tobacco industry. His son, John R. Newsom, wrote to me in a letter dated February 8, 1992, that "I was there at the time" when the leaders of the tobacco industry, then in a state of panic because of the first evidence that smoking caused lung cancer, approached Newsom in early December 1953. Turned down by Newsom, the tobacco presidents next approached John W. Hill, who took the account. (This story is told in chapter 16.) The elder Newsom's judgment was confirmed nearly 40 years later when it was revealed in Federal District Court, according to *The New York Times* of February 8, 1992, that "the tobacco industry's chief research arm for 40 years described its own mission as a "front' and as a 'shield' against potentially harmful Congressional hearings." Judge H. Lee Sarokin said that "a jury might reasonably assume that the industry's decades old vow to disclose its research findings were nothing but a public relations ploy." "Ploy" was not in Earl Newsom's vocabulary.

Unlike many counselors over the decades since public relations emerged as a vocation — from Edward L. Bernays to Robert L. Dilenschneider — Earl Newsom would not violate client confidences in "kiss and tell" articles or books. In 1954, Thomas J. Deegan, at that time vice-president for public relations of the New York Central Railroad, asked Newsom to join "in the proposed symposium to be published by Simon & Schuster." Newsom declined for this reason:

> If I were to report what we here might consider an excellent story of how a client solved an important public relations problem, the mere fact of my reporting for the acts of management that provided the key to the happy solution; that we, not the client, were 'the bright boys' — the heroes of the situation. . . . Finally, I do not think we have the right to speak for any client or to seem to be putting it in the position of patting itself on the back.

Counselor Earl Newsom left this legacy to oncoming generations of public relations practitioners:

> I suggest that sober self-examination at this point requires that we come to an understanding of ourselves and what it is we really want to accomplish. This is not a problem that can be resolved by our Society or any committees thereof. It is purely a personal matter. Each of us lives but once, and each of us wants to spend his life constructively. . . . I am as certain as can be that if each one of us established the highest of standards for his own conduct, we shall eventually earn the status of profession.

With his intellect and his integrity, Earl Newsom did more than his part in earning recognition for public relations as essential calling in American society.

A revealing insight to Earl Newsom as a person, as a friend, is found in an Oberlin College classmate's remarks at Earl Newsom's Memorial Service held April 14, 1973. Richard A. Kimball, his classmate and a neighbor in Salisbury, said:

We also gratefully recall his happiness in his home with family and friends, in the humorous tale well told, the singing of close harmony, the unhurried talk, the sharing of thoughts and convictions and, in recent years, the joy in working on his place in the serenity of our village. We remember, too, the solid quality of his help in any moment of trouble, his giving himself and anything he had when there was need. Such was his modesty that in many cases only the beneficiaries ever knew of his understanding kindness.

The character of Earl Newsom, personal and professional, was eloquently expressed by Stanton, who knew Newsom as a counselor as a friend:

Earl Newsom was, in character, enormously courageous in temperament, boundlessly optimistic; in intellect, endlessly inquiring. Indomitable courage marked his whole life, personal and professional. . . . Professionally, the unique distinction he achieved in his field was due, in great measure, to his courage for the righteousness, his refusal to court approval by the ambivalent view or the soft word, and his insistence on absolute candor between himself and his clients. In temperament, Earl always took the affirmative path. He was an optimist in the true sense of the belief that, for all their follies and limitations, human institutions, once their problems are honestly faced, can be made to work, can be improved upon, and can enlarge and enrich human life.

Such was the character and counsel of Earl Newsom — counselor to the corporate giants of his time. A list of Newsom's clients follows in Table 20.1:

TABLE 20.1
Major Clients of the Earl Newsom Company

American Locomotive Co.	International Wool Secretariat
American Heritage Foundation	Investment Company Institute
American Institute of Accountants	Kennecott Copper Co.
Atoms for Peace Award (Ford Motor Co.)	Macy's Department Store
Barwick Industries	Martin Marietta Corporation
Broadcast Music, Inc.	Merrill Lynch
Bunker–Ramo Corporation	National Lead Institute
Campbell Soup Company	New York University
Colonial Williamsburg	Price Waterhouse Corp.
Columbia Broadcasting System	Pittsburgh Plate Glass
Eli Lilly Co.	Reynolds Metal Co.
Ford Motor Company	John D. Rockefeller III
Ford Foundation	The Tea Bureau, Inc.
General Motors Corporation	Trans-World Airlines
General Precision Equipment Co.	The New York Stock Exchange
Glass Container Association	The Wallpaper Institute
International Paper Co.	Worthington Corporation
Lincoln Center for the Performing Arts	Arthur Young Company

NOTES ON SOURCES

The primary source of information for this chapter was the Earl Newsom Papers, on deposit in the Mass Communication History Center of the State Historical Society of Wisconsin, Madison. Mr. Newsom's papers were deposited there by the last partners in the firm—Craig Lewis, now vice-chairman of North American Operations for Ogilvy & Mather Public Relations, Vincent Duffy, and John R. "Jack" Newsom, Earl's son and a former partner. The papers were deposited with a time seal of 1998. However, Messrs. Lewis, Duffy, and Newsom kindly granted me access to Newsom's papers with a 1966 cutoff date with the understanding that Mr. Lewis would review the manuscript to protect former clients confidentiality. Such a review was made by Mr. Lewis. The bare bones of the Newsom Papers have been fleshed out for me by his son, popularly known as Jack, who has given much time and effort to my book. This had been done through letters, numerous phone conversations, and by a personal visit to Athens. My debt to him and to Craig Lewis is large indeed. Another person to whom I owe a large debt is John E. Sattler, whom Mr. Newsom hired in 1946 to head the Ford Motor Company public relations office in New York city, a post Sattler held until he retired. His voluminous recollections of those years have been most helpful in this chapter and the next one dealing with the Ford account. Sattler, blessed be, has a capacious memory. W. H. "Ping" Ferry and Martin Quigley also were quite helpful with their recollections, provided in notes and in phone conversations.

Among the helpful secondary sources was the booklet of Newsom's memorial service, an interview with *Printer's Ink* entitled "PR Counselor Earl Newsom: Management Is Happier When It's a 'Good Citizen,'" "February 14, 1958; books by Sally Bedell Smith, *In All His Glory, The Life of William S. Paley*, Simon & Schuster, 1990; Alexander Kendrick, *Prime Time, the Life of Edward R. Murrow*, Little, Brown, 1969; and Erik Barnouw, *The Image Empire, a History of Broadcasting in the United States from 1953*, Oxford University Press, 1970.

My extensive interview with Mr. Newsom on January 21, 1963, was helpful to my assessment of the person. Extensive use was made of his speeches and articles in the public domain.

The quotation from Sally Bedell Smith's *In All His Glory* are used with permission of Simon & Schuster. Mrs. Smith holds the copyright to her work. The quotations from Irwin Ross' *The Image Merchants* are used with the author's permission. He holds the copyright. Judge H. Lee Sarokin's statements, quoted at length in chapter 16, are found in *The New York Times*, of February 7, 1992.

Chapter 21

Earl Newsom and the Auto Giants: Ford and GM

SECTION 1: THE FORD MOTOR COMPANY AND YOUNG HENRY

When Edsel Ford, who held the somewhat empty title of president of the Ford Motor Company, died in May 1943, the two top contenders to replace him were Harry Bennett, Henry Ford's longtime right-hand man and union buster, and Charles E. Sorensen, vice-president in charge in manufacturing. Bennett, whom old Henry admired, was the founder's choice. Learning this, Mrs. Edsel Ford, who despised Bennett, moved with Mrs. Henry Ford's help to make her 25-year-old son, Henry II, the new president. On June 8, 1943, less than a month after Edsel's death, Bennett had maneuvered himself into being appointed Sorensen's "assistant for administrative problems." But Mrs. Edsel Ford carried the day, and her eldest son was made president of the giant corporation. He assumed the presidency in September 1945. The company that young Henry took over was not dying in the opinion of Ford executive, Jack Davis, "it was already dead and *rigor mortis* was setting in."

Young Ford came to this awesome task with no public reputation. He had lived the life of a rich playboy who enjoyed parties more than books. He had attended the Detroit University School and then gone to Hotchkiss, an East Coast boarding school that prepares students for Yale. He had been dismissed from Yale University because he had left the bill for a term paper in the paper when he submitted it to his professor. Henry II later scornfully denied that he was stupid enough to leave the bill of a local cramming agency in the paper. He admitted that he was not much of a student, in prep school or at Yale. He enjoyed more tootling down to New York City for a weekend and a good time. As an overweight and cocky youth, he had acquired the nickname "Lard Ass." One biographer appraised his early years as "indolent." But as a youth and in adulthood, Henry II had a happy outlook yet was blunt spoken.

When his father died in 1943, young Henry, then an ensign in the Navy training at the great Lakes Naval Station, was brought back to take a position in the management of the company, then under heavy criticism for its failures to meet announced war production goals. He was ill-prepared for the mantle of leadership about to be thrust upon him. But he set about in earnest to gain a grip on the situation confronting the auto giant. Later in reminiscing with John Bugas, an ex-FBI agent who became head of Ford's industrial relations, Bugas asked Ford, "Henry, why did you bother? You didn't have to do it. Why didn't you just go out and play." With steely vehemence Henry II replied, "My grandfather killed my father in my mind. . . . I remember my father."

Young Ford quickly assessed the mess his grandfather had made of the company in later years. When Henry II assumed the presidency, Ford was losing money—big money—millions a month. He could not get accurate figures because of the company's antiquated bookkeeping. Ford had no cost accounting system. Every other auto company, including GM, was losing money in 1945–1946. But Ford did have one great asset: the lustre of the Ford name. Also the firm was suffering from a rigidified management, dominated by the heavy hand of Harry Bennett: a management that was ill-equipped to deal with wartime production and the postwar problems of production retooling, finance, and a strong UAW. Henry II knew that he had inherited a company with a sagging reputation. David L. Lewis wrote, "Henry II recognized that his personal public relations would influence the company's future and that when he became president public awareness of him was limited." Consequently, public attitudes toward him had not crystallized as they had hardened years before toward his grandfather, both positive and negative. Because he was "keenly aware of the importance of public attitudes toward himself and the company," he quickly sought public relations counsel. He turned to Elmo Roper, who was not only a business associate of Earl Newsom, but also a very close friend who recommended Newsom. According to Lewis, "Steve Hannagan, had been scuttled by Bennett two years earlier, the New Yorker was reluctant to advise Edsel's son while Henry II lacked complete power; he pleaded too full a schedule. Shortly after young Henry became president, however, Newsom agreed to work with him."

Roper recalled that this decision brought him a sense of relief, "I walked Henry over to Newsom's office to cement the relationship."

Newsom later recalled in his interview with your author that when he first conferred with young Ford, "he warned me that we would have two strikes against us before we started. In the first place, you come from New York, and everybody in Detroit is apt to distrust anybody from New York. In the second place, you are looked upon as experts, and businessmen in Detroit think that experts do not know what they are talking about – particularly experts from New York."

Undoubtedly Newsom's reassurance came from the fact that one of young Henry's first acts was to depose the notorious Bennett, his grandfather's amanuensis and his father's archenemy. In *Ford the Men and the Machine*, Lacey referred to Newsom as "a smooth publicity man from New York." This statement is far wide of the mark: Newsom was a counselor, not a publicist, who concentrated on policy utterances and guidance of corporate behavior that would win public favor. One former associate, Martin Quigley, described Newsom "as more a management consultant than a public relations man." With a shake of hands in Newsom's office in Roper's presence, Newsom and his staff set about to create a favorable reputation for Ford as one of the new generation of industrial statesmen in America. Newsom's deft hand would guide Henry II and the company through a difficult time of transition with his counsel and by building a strong Ford Motor Company public relations department.

Carefully Crafted Events Create a Statesman

Henry Ford II preferred to deal only with Newsom, but for assistance on "servicing" this important assignment, Newsom used Stephen Fitzgerald, Lynn Mahan, and primarily Ping Ferry. Their liaison was mostly with top Ford officers and Charles Carll, then head of the News Bureau, who had been hired by Steve Hannagan in 1942. (Fitzgerald, handsome and urbane and former Niemann Fellow, left Newsom in 1950 to set up his own agency. Mahan also left Newsom to join Ted Swanson, another Newsom staffer, in a public relations firm. Monhan later died in a plane crash in India.) Newsom's chief partner, Fred L. Palmer, was also heavily involved in the Ford account.

Ferry was the main liaison on the account. The son of a onetime president of the Packard Motor Company, Ferry knew the industry and the Detroit milieu. In fact, Ferry saw himself as something of an equal to Ford and would talk to him bluntly. "This did not always sit well with Ford," according to a member of the Ford PR staff. This staffer wrote to me, "Henry Ford II was a complex guy. In truth, he never really let anyone get too close to him, though there were some who thought they did – to their regret. He never forgot who he was, never no matter where he was, and he delighted in keeping people off balance. On several occasions he said to me 'You've got to jack people up or they begin to take things for granted.' He meant it and did it." Because of his work for the CIO Political Action Committee to reelect President Roosevelt in 1944, Ferry was sometimes referred to behind his back by some Ford executives as "Pink" Ferry.

The first important issue on which Newsom and Ford collaborated was labor relations. Henry Ford II had already gained some reputation as being friendly to labor by his firing of Bennett and even before assuming the presidency, by repeatedly saying that good labor relations would be one of his objectives. Lewis wrote, "Henry's friendly attitude toward labor unions spawned rumors that he was going to make concessions to the UAW whose birth his grandfather had so bitterly fought." Then on November 15 a letter crafted by Newsom and his staff delivered a "sock on the jaw" to the UAW. This 4-page letter was written in response to a union demand that all auto makers raise wages by 30%. Written by the Newsom staff and polished by Newsom "with the attentive care that a poet might lavish on a sonnett," the letter bluntly stated that Ford would not discuss wage demands until the UAW had agreed to give the company "the same degree of security that we have given to the union." The first page of this letter, that made front page news in the nation's press follows:

Efficient mass production can be reached only if production is uninterrupted and all employees work at high efficiency.

Since July, 1941, when the Ford Motor Company first signed a contract with the UAW-CIO, the Company's experience both as to continuous production and productive efficiency of its employees has not been good.

A total of 773 work stoppages have occurred. The productive efficiency of employees throughout the Company's plants has decreased over-all 34.8 percent.

The material presented here documents these statements. A further four-month recapitulation of work stoppages has been taken verbatim from Company records and appears in this report to illustrate their variety and extent. The four-month period covers May–August, inclusive, 1945, and may be regarded as typical.

This material is made available now for public inspection to show why the Company is firm in its insistence that it be provided with *Company Security.*

As a major step toward achieving Company Security, the Company has proposed that the UAW–CIO provide it with contractual guarantees which will effectively minimize stoppages and at the same time work toward increased productive efficiency on the part of its members.

The proposal accompanying the letter called for the union paying $5 per day for each employee engaging in an unauthorized strike. James Twohey, whose research reports Newsom relied upon, reported in a letter of December 5 to Newsom, "Nine percent approvingly note the Ford Company proposal that the union pay $5 a day for each employee engaging in an unauthorized strike. This latter proposal is held to be common sense, logical plan to make unions more responsible though there is apparently little belief that union authority over its members is great enough to permit such an arrangement." Twohey added, "The volume is not particularly large, . . . There may be also some feeling that it is too perfect, too reasonable in the sense that it is too far ahead of its time. Again, reaction suggests the possibility that the press may have viewed it as too obviously a tactical move."

The candid, cogent letter brought a quick retort from Dick Leonard, director of UAW's Ford department, "There is a very simple way to avoid work stoppages. That is to stop provoking them." The UAW reply lacked conviction in view of young Henry's firing of Harry Bennett and letting 1,000 Ford employees go in a spring housecleaning. The Newsom-crafted letter put Henry II in a strikingly different mold from the other auto executives. This became much clearer in the next staged event in Newsom's campaign to portray young Ford as an industrial statesman.

Earl Newsom played an influential role in shaping Ford's labor policies over the next several years, years that were pivotal in shaping the nation's postwar labor–industry relations. In this period, Newsom was the only outsider to sit in the inner councils of Ford management.

The Speech

The second major news event that projected Henry Ford II into the national spotlight as a new breed of industrial leader was the speech he made in his first public appearance as head of the Ford Motor Company. That speech made clear that he was setting himself apart from others leaders of the automobile industry, many of whom, in Lacey's opinion, "were still fighting the battles of the 30s." Ford was scheduled to address some 4,000 members and guests of the Society of Automotive Engineers on January 9, 1946, the influentials of the industry. Newsom sensed the importance of this opportunity, and he and his staff fine-tuned the speech that went through 12 versions in the Newsom office. Then it was endlessly revised by Ford and his staff in Detroit. Ford practiced reading it before his advisers, and if he stumbled on a word, out it came. On his way to catch a train to Detroit for the occasion, Newsom ran into Mrs. Ford on the street. He asked, "Are you going to Detroit for the speech?" "I scarcely need to," Mrs. Ford replied, "he kept me up nearly all night reading it aloud. He practically knows it by heart." With the Newsom touch, it was a conciliatory and constructive speech entitled "The Challenge of Human Engineering."

Today his words may sound like platitudes but in the strike-charged atmosphere of postwar Detroit, they appealed to the audience as radical and inspiring. Ford declared:

> Men who in their private lives would not think of entering into a brawl on the street have over the years found themselves blasting each other in the public press by colorful name- calling. . . . There is no reason why a grievance case should not be handled with the same dispatch as a claim for insurance benefits. There is no reason why a union contract would not be written and agreed upon with the same efficiency and good temper that marks the negotiation of a commercial contract between two companies.

Ford made it clear, "that labor unions are here to stay" and that he had no desire to turn back the clock.

Lewis concurred that "the address itself was timed perfectly. At a time when both labor and management had qualms about government intervention in labor negotiations . . . it called for a unified attack by labor and capital on common problems." "If we cannot succeed by cooperation, it doesn't seem likely that we can succeed by the exercise of force. We cannot expect legislation to solve our problems," Ford concluded.

The speech was heavily publicized coast to coast. Ford was shown in newsreels in the nation's theaters, virtually every newspaper front-paged the speech. Widespread editorial comment was most favorable — editorials headed "HORSE SENSE," "COMMON SENSE," "INDUSTRIAL STATESMAN," and others offered high praise. Henry II saw his prestige reach new heights.

In this same period, Ping Ferry was busy working the press to generate stories accentuating the emerging public portrait of Henry II. In a memo to Charles E. Carll, then head of the Ford News Bureau, Ferry reported that he had:

(a) Provided information to a *New York Times* writer, Walter Ruch, on the Ford investment plan on an exclusive basis for a "Sunday story";

(b) Discussed with Martin Hayden of the *Detroit News*, the question of supervisory morale at the Ford plants. Martin is very willing to use all the company material but he said emphatically that his desk will insist on at least a 15-minute interview with John Bugas [in charge of labor relations];

(c) Dan Anderson of the *New York Sun* is very interested in a story on the general "youth and age" management of the Ford Motor Company;

(d) I tried out Luke Carroll tentatively on a historical story which would revolve around a notion of what the Ford Motor Company has meant to

Detroit. . . . I am sure that he will do a good Sunday story if the material is culled for him.

Reprise in San Francisco

Young Ford next made national headlines and won widespread acclaim from business leaders by taking on the federal government's Office of Price Administration (OPA). In November 1945, the OPA fixed factory and retail prices for most 1946 cars—cars for which a starved market was hungry. The OPA's decision dismayed and alarmed car manufacturers because no auto maker could make a profit until production reached prewar levels, something not in the cards in 1945 or 1946. Henry II's first impulse was to launch a nationwide campaign against the OPA, but with Newsom's counsel, he issued a mild statement of protest, saying that "the prices do not properly reflect the changed economic circumstances in which a motorcar manufacturer must operate today." But after 2½ months of losing $300 on each car made, Ford telegraphed John W. Snyder, director of War Mobilization and Reconversion, protesting the inequity of the OPA order. David Lewis described this as "the third of the six statements which had an important bearing on his postwar relations."

Next on February 8, 1946, in San Francisco young Ford took his case to the people in his second major speech, this one delivered before the prestigious Commonwealth Club before an audience of 1, 600 persons. In a speech crafted by the Newsom staff, Ford gave a detailed comparison of his firm's manufacturing costs with the prices allowed by the OPA. He pledged that although the firm was losing $300, a car it would continue to produce to meet the pent-up demands for new cars. He received a standing ovation from the business-oriented audience. Again the speech was widely publicized and brought much laudatory editorial comment. He was applauded for "common sense," "sensible views," "sound judgment." The *Keokuk* (Iowa) *Gazette* wrote, "We believe with Henry Ford II that work can be a cure for the ills of the world."

Ford kept up his campaign against OPA price controls with a press conference in Los Angeles on February 14, one for which he was carefully prepared by the Newsom staff. His third attack on OPA within 3 weeks brought a bitter counterattack from OPA Administrator Chester Bowles. Bowles asserted, "The auto executive has allied himself with a few selfish groups which have worked continuously to undermine the American people's bulwark against economic disaster." On February 19, Bowles continued his attack on Ford before the House Banking and Currency Committee. Bowles conceded that Ford was losing $300 on each car built but said the problem was Ford's lack of production. David Lewis reported the next development:

Henry Ford II was in Los Angeles On February 19, the day Bowles testified. That same day an alarmed Newsom—who had drafted the Commonwealth speech—and Dearborn executives conferred on the crisis. Newsom reasons that Henry II, having taken the stand on the removal of price controls, had to defend his position; that the response to Bowles' counter-attacks could cause "a great many people to gain or lose confidence" in Henry II; and that "the newspaper boys would take Mr. Ford's part" The consultant recommended that a Dearborn executive officially rebut Bowles and draw the firm away from Mr. Ford, the rebuttal to be followed by preparation of a "very good factual presentation" which Newsom hoped could be discussed in private conference with OPA: This recommendation was telephoned to Henry II.

In this instance young Henry chose to reject Newsom's counsel and instead to meet Bowles head-on. On that evening, February 19, Ford sent a long telegram to Chairman Spence of the House Banking and Currency Committee charging that Bowles' testimony did not reflect all the facts. He telegraphed Spence that the OPA head had not made it clear that "manufacturers who supply our suppliers do have price ceilings," and "that parts made for trucks and all automotive replacement parts are subject to price ceilings." He accused Bowles of "hitting below the belt." Two days later after writing Spence, Ford sent a "blistering" telegram to Bowles in what was the last and sixth statement that went into the creating the public reputation of Henry II as a new industrial leader and spokesman. The telegrams to Spence and to Bowles were issued as news releases by the Ford Motor Company. The Newsom Papers do not indicate whether Newsom had a hand in these replies or not. Presumably he did. The battle between Young Henry and Bowles raged across the nation's front pages for weeks. Most publications found Ford "convincing."

A subsequent survey among organized labor members indicated that Ford may have been wise to accept Newsom's counsel to avoid a head-on collision with Chester Bowles. In a report to Newsom date February 5, 1946, James S. Twohey wrote:

> There was some scattered comment revolving about young Ford. It totalled 4% of the general labor comment and was thus of relatively small volume. Half of this discussion lauded young Ford for his statesmanship in labor disputes, his recent speech in Detroit, etc. The other half focused on his proposal to government officials for prompt removal of government price controls in order to settle management and labor disputes. All of the comment made on this latter proposal so far disapproves Ford's stand, holding removal of price controls is no solution and that prices would skyrocket.

Twohey then added, "This is the first time since young Ford has been in the public eye that he has received measurable unfavorable comment. . . . In so far as the analysis of press opinion is concerned, it can be said that all of his prior announcements were keyed with remarkable exactitude into the underlying trend of press thought."

Erasing the Antisemitism Stain

One of the unfortunate legacies Henry Ford II inherited from his grandfather was Henry Ford's blatant, notorious anti-Semitism. His long-standing hatred of Jews had cost the company dearly in business over the years. As a memo from Helen Winselman to Ping Ferry, dated July 14, 1948, suggests, "Historically, the personality of Henry Ford has overshadowed the actions of his company. In a series of depth interviews conducted by Elmo Roper in 1945, at least half of the business and professional thought leaders interviewed referred to Mr. Ford personally." In that survey, Roper concluded, "It is obvious that his activities and his influence on the policies of the Ford Motor Company are in the back of the minds of a good many respondents who do not actually mention his name." Roper, who started polling for the company in 1942, said the results "emphasized this strong tendency on the part of the public to associate personalities with the Ford Motor Company." Thus, there was a dollars and cents need for Earl Newsom to erase the stigma of anti-Semitism from the Ford name. He moved obliquely to do this. First a bit of background.

From 1919 to 1927 Henry Ford published a weekly magazine, the *Dearborn Independent*. During much of this time the newspaper had a circulation of some 250,000, and from 1923 to 1927 it topped the one half million mark. The *Dearborn Independent*, edited by William J. Cameron, who became nationally known as a spokesman for Ford, was publicizing Ford's views — especially his anti-Semitism. David Lewis thought Ford's attitudes toward Jews were shaped by his boyhood influences, attitudes that persuaded Ford that Jews were plotting "to destroy Christian civilization." The *Independent* even revived that hoary forgery, *The Protocols of the Wise Men of Zion*, which argued that the Jews were striving for world domination. At first, Cameron, who had replaced E. G. Pipp as editor, was disgusted with this blatant campaign of bigotry, but he eventually came to accept much of this anti-Semitic material. He wrote what Ford believed.

Sometime after taking command of the company, Henry Ford II stressed the importance of public relations saying, "We believe that we can sell more cars to our friends than to our enemies." Young Henry was painfully aware of his grandfather's bigotry, the blot it had brought to the family name, and the damage it had done to the sales of Ford vehicles.

Even before retaining Earl Newsom as his public relations counsel, young Henry had tackled the problem of the stain of anti-Semitism on the Ford name. In 1944, Ford retained a Jewish friend, Alfred A. May, to advise the firm on its relations with the Jewish community. For the next 3 decades, May had an important part in many of Ford's decisions affecting Jews. According to David L. Lewis, these included, "lending courtesy cars to Jewish organizations, advertising in Jewish newspapers and banquet programs, and framing a reply to charges that the company underemploys Jews. . . . Most of May's work has been behind the scenes."

Erasing or at least softening over time the Ford reputation for anti-Semitism was one of the first problems Earl Newsom and his staff tackled. In a memo of December 8, 1945, from Ping Ferry to Newsom, Ferry appraised the program "May is working on for Ford." Ferry wrote, "He has in mind something spectacular to throw his efforts in sharp focus. Specifically, he is considering a recommendation that Ford finance, supply and equip a mercy ship for Europe, designed for displaced persons generally, and for Jews in particular. I urged that he go no further until we had a chance to examine such a large-scale proposal from all angles." As will be seen in a moment, such an obvious effort to win the acclaim of Jews ran counter to the strategy ultimately adopted by the Newsom staff.

For example, May had written a "Memorandum for Ford Dealers" under the date of November 19, 1945, refuting the long-circulated charges against Henry Ford and the company. The last paragraph of the proposed memo read, "It is the desire of Mr. Henry Ford and Mr. Henry Ford II to advise all persons connected with the Ford Motor Company, as well as the public in general, that any of the forementioned statements attributed to him (Henry Ford) are false and misleading and are unauthorized and not sanctioned by either the Ford Motor Company or Mr. Henry Ford or Mr. Henry Ford II."

Ferry rightly stopped circulation of this memorandum because the public record of Henry Ford's anti-Semitism was writ large in the pages of the *Dearborn Independent* and in his private utterances. Ferry reported to Newsom "He [May] did not seem hurt when I turned down his proposed letter to dealers."

On January 16, 1946, Stephen E. Fitzgerald addressed a strategy memo to Newsom headed, "Alleged Anti-Semitism at Ford" The memo stated:

Fred [Palmer], Ping [Ferry] and I have generally agreed on the following:

1. We don't want anything like a "campaign" or a "program" on this.
2. We do want a general memorandum, analyzing the subject as it affects Ford. Such a memorandum is attached.
3. This memorandum should suggest a basic formula for handling problems as they arise in this field, and for seizing opportunities.
4. It can also indicate the kind of thing that should not be done and the kind of thing that can be done.
5. Key to what is done should be: Is it in character?

6. We believe that the whole subject should be discussed by you at a meeting which includes Ford, Bugas, Davis, Alfred May, and Carll. Out of this would grow a more unified understanding of the problem and a better understanding as to how it should be approached.
7. One result of this meeting should be a clear understanding that as actions are considered, they must be carefully checked against the formula.

The Fitzgerald memo was accompanied by a 7-page "outline of the situation" based on the fact that "Many people think that the Ford Motor Company is anti-Semitic." The suggested approach to the problem: "This opinion can probably be reduced in extent and in intensity, over a relatively long period of time, as company actions, and actions of company executives, make it plain that Ford is not anti-Semitic." This approach reflects Newsom principles that there are no quick fixes for long-standing problems and that actions taken must be in keeping with the character of the personalities and organization. The Fitzgerald group did not "suggest anything approaching a campaign or a program" to combat this hostile opinion.

The Newsom staff felt it necessary to confront this problem facing the company and Henry Ford II because of two Elmo Roper polls. A Roper Poll of October 1944 found, "Jews as a whole, probably because of a belief that Mr. Ford is anti-Semitic, are reluctant to credit the Ford Motor Company with outstanding virtue in *any* respect. In fact, the response of Jews to our questions is rather dramatic proof how, by alienating any group of people in *one* respect important to them, a company can so alienate that group as to reduce its standing among that group in *every* particular." In October 1945, Roper made a survey of Jewish, Protestant, and Catholic attitudes toward the Ford Motor Company and predictably found that it rated lowest among Jews. An excerpt from this poll report is shown in Table 21.1:

TABLE 21.1

	Protestant	Catholic	Jewish
Favorable attitude toward Ford	76.2%	74.9%	57.2%
Unfavorable attitude toward Ford	6.1%	5.6%	22.4%
Most admired and respected business executive:			
Henry Ford II	2.8%	2.4%	.6%
Henry Ford	1.9%	2.6%	—
Ford	1.9%	2.1%	—
Total Ford	6.6%	7.1%	.6%
Would use Ford Motor Company as model for their general conduct:			
	15.1%	13.3%	12.3%

Earl Newsom followed these discussions and plans with a "Personal and Confidential" memo to Henry Ford II dated November 14, 1946, reporting, "We took advantage of a staff luncheon yesterday, at which Allen Merrell was our guest, to re-examine the question of Ford policy and procedures involved in the charges of anti-Semitism occasionally laid against the company." Newsom reminded Ford of the January memorandum and reported a staff consensus that its basic policies be continued:

(a) That the company continue its attitude that anti-Semitism was *not* a distinct and pressing problem.

(b) That the company make no statement nor take any action which could be construed as deliberately attempting to win the friendship of Jews.

(c) That the company avail itself of all *usual* opportunities to show that it is not anti-Semitic.

(d) That no formal "program" for combatting anti-Semitism be adopted.

The Newsom staff also reached agreement on procedures to follow this matter: "That administration of all matters in this field become a function of your office. (This recommendation recognizes the highly personal nature of whatever problem exists.)"

Even though the idea of a "program" to deal with this problem was ruled out, Henry Ford II, with Newsom's and May's counsel, began to move obliquely to build a reputation as a friend of American Jewry. All evidence suggests that these moves were not "public relations gimmicks" but born of sincerity and conviction on young Henry's part.

In 1946, young Henry addressed the Community Committee of New York on behalf of the United Jewish Appeal. One of Henry's next moves was to become a strong supporter of the National Conference of Christians and Jews (NCCJ). For his financial support and participation in this organization, Henry Ford II was honored at a banquet at the Waldorf-Astoria in New York City on November 18, 1948. In a speech drafted for him by the Newsom staff, Ford made these points:

1. The first requirement of good human relations is a desire to achieve good relations.
2. The second requirement of good human relations, as I see it, is discovery of great areas of agreement.
3. The third requirement of good human relations, in my opinion, is religion — arguing that "unless men believe in their essential brotherhood — in the fatherhood of God — it is difficult, in my opinion for them to achieve the necessary humility and respect for one another as members of the same human race.

In 1950, Ford served as finance chairman of the Brotherhood Week Newspaper Committee headed by Oveta Culp Hobby, then publisher of *The Houston Post*. In a statement prepared by Newsom's staff to be incorporated in a publicity release from Hobby's committee, Ford stated, "On February 18, 1951, we begin the annual celebration of Brotherhood Week. This year . . . Brotherhood Week will be extended to all the Free Nations of the World. . . . This annual event is sponsored by the National Conference of Christians and Jews, and is but one week in this 52-week program of education for democracy—a program designed to free the world of bigotry and prejudice."

In 1951, while Henry II was serving as chairman of the National Conference of Christians and Jews' first national special gifts campaign, the Ford Motor Company made a gift of $1 million to the conference for a national headquarters building in New York. That same year, he was awarded an American's Democratic Legacy Award by the Anti-Defamation League, the civil rights arm of B'nai B'rith "for distinguished contributions to the American heritage of freedom." The not-so-subtle campaign fashioned by the Newsom staff was working. Events, substantial gifts, and awards are worth a ton of pious statements.

Ultimately the largess of the Ford Foundation was brought into play to provide philanthropy for such organizations. On April 20, 1952, young Benson Ford accepted an award from the Jewish Theological Seminary of America on behalf of the Ford Foundation. In thanking Rabbi Finkelstein for the honor, Ford said, "There is nothing that touches the interests of all of us more than this vital and fundamental idea of human brotherhood. Certainly there is nothing in which the Foundation is more actively interested." Could this be an example of Newsom using the newly formed Ford Foundation to advance Henry II's and the company's interests? This accusation was ultimately made against Newsom by Foundation Executive Robert Hutchins, Ping Ferry, and Martin Quigley.

Found in the Newsom Papers was a "Memorandum on a Proposed Foundation of Human Relations," proposed to the Ford Company and family by the American Jewish Committee, dated March 27, 1947. The memorandum urged, "The Ford Motor Company and the Ford family would perform an act of outstanding public service if they devoted some of their resources, their vision, and their 'know how' to the solution of the problem of creating better human relations—perhaps the most single critical problem in this critical era." Whether such support materialized or not is not known. At least it suggests that the Ford family was now receptive to such appeals from Jewish organizations.

But this ugliest of charges would not go away. Al May called Ping Ferry the morning of November 1, 1946, to report that the notorious bigot and rabble-rouser, Gerald L. K. Smith, had recently made a mailing of some

12,000 letters in the Detroit area announcing the republication of *The International Jew and the Protocols of Zion.*. May told Ferry, "The letters also set forth Mr. Henry Ford's original publication of these documents and explained that while Mr. Ford had apologized at one time for his part in the affair, the apology was directed to the act of publication, and was not intended as a renunciation of his belief in these documents." May also told Ferry, "A large number of protests and queries had been received by Ford regarding this letter." May said he had prepared a reply to this old charge, but Ferry asked him not to issue it until "we could talk it over," probably next week. There is no evidence in the Newsom Papers that a reply to this blast from Smith was issued.

Henry's brother, Benson, vice-president and general manager of Lincoln--Mercury, also became involved in this campaign to promote tolerance and thus erase the stain on the family name put there by his grandfather. In the Newsom Papers, there is a lengthy speech prepared for Benson Ford to deliver before the Florida chapter of the National Conference of Christians and Jews on March 10, 1953. That year Benson Ford was serving as cochairman of the NCCJ. The theme of Benson's address that night was "the growing surge of anti-Semitism in Russia and its satellite countries. In Communist language, it is called a 'purge,' not a 'pogram' — although the very word 'pogram' had its origin in Russia." Ford correctly saw that for that period of history, these purges were the beginning of a vicious attempt to eliminate all religion in those countries.

The Ford brothers didn't just give money and make speeches. Their actions undergirded this effort to paint a new picture of the Fords. In *Ford the Men and the Machine*, Robert Lacey wrote, "But Henry Ford's crusade against prejudice extended well beyond cheque writing — and also beyond the battles of black and white. In the mid-60s he had been one of the moving spirits in a campaign to get his friend Max Fisher and two other prominent Jewish businessmen elected to the venerable Detroit Club, which had previously blackballed all Jews." Lacey added, "Max Fisher has got closer to Henry Ford II than have many men, and he is generous in his praise of his friend's strengths — which he has seen few others have. "Henry honestly does things from the heart. There's lot of feeling deep inside him," Fisher averred.

The sincerity of young Ford's convictions on the brotherhood of man were put to the test in 1966 when he announced plans to let a Jewish entrepreneur assemble Ford trucks and tractors in Israel. The Arab League threatened a boycott of the Ford company, but Ford went ahead with the plan. "nobody's going to tell me what to do," Ford told his friend Fisher. The upshot was that all Ford cars and Ford trucks were banned from the Arab market for nearly 20 years. Lacey concluded of this aspect of young Henry's personality:

The war against racial injustice has brought out the finer side of this complex man. Henry Ford II's record on race has proved energetic and courageous, for he seems to have sensed how the particular era of urban decay and racial disharmony in which he found himself living did not get that way by accident. Its tragedy stemmed from the same genius, drive and wickedness that had made his own family so rich and famous. If ever the sins of the fathers were dramatically visited upon a community, it was upon downtown Detroit in the late 1960s, and, contemplating the devastation, the grandson of the great carmaker saw his destiny for a season in doing what he could to redeem them.

Young Ford also became heavily involved in the work of the National Urban League through a friendship he developed with Whitney Young, Jr. when they were on a 1966 fact-finding tour of eastern Europe. Young, the director of the National Urban League, recalled receiving a handwritten note from Ford and a check for $100,000 one Christmas.

Henry Ford II's complex and two-sided personality showed up on that Eastern Europe fact-finding tour that had been arranged by *Time–Life*. The *Time–Life* colleague who guided the tour later confided to a colleague, "I don't understand him. At the meetings he was one of the best participants — serious, well-informed, sensitive. He was very impressive. Then afterwards he was like another person — 'where's the booze?' 'Where's the pussy?' That sort of thing."

It was the assignment of Earl Newsom, Ping Ferry, and their colleagues to keep Ford's good qualities in the news, to do damage control when his drinking and womanizing made news. Not an easy assignment. It must be remembered that in publicizing Ford's dedication to tolerance and racial equality, Newsom and his staff were building on the requisite base of sound public relations — performance that serves the public interest.

The Buildup Continues

With the public reputation of Henry Ford II established under Newsom's tutelage in his first year as president of the company — a reputation as a strong, decisive, and progressive industrial leader representing a new generation in American business — the Newsom staff continued to focus a favorable spotlight on the Ford president. Typical of the press buildup Newsom's staff promoted in the press and in magazines is an article published in *Collier's* magazine of November 15, 1947, entitled "Revolution on the Rouge." Written by Andre' Fontaine, it lauds young Ford and contrasts him with his grandfather. Fontaine wrote of the founder, "Henry Ford was the father of the assembly line; his genius with machines led American industry into an era of undreamed production . . . In doing so, they said, he completely forgot the human beings who powered that production."

By contrast, the article continues:

Henry Ford II – 30 year-old grandson of the late genius, has embarked on the job of correcting this imbalance between men and machines. If his grandfather made robots out of men, young Henry seems determined to make men out of robots. Whereas old Henry had a passion for and an instinctive understanding of machines and little facility with people, young Henry has a primary interest and instinctive understanding of human beings, with no more than a layman's indulgence of machines.

Fontaine continued:

"In his two years as president of the multimillion dollar Ford Motor Company, this chubby-cheeked amicable young man has turned the old company topsy-turvy, and the basic drive has powered the revolution in his new idea of human relations." Edward Cushman, director of the Wayne State University Institute of Labor Relations, expressed the thought: "If Ford succeeds in revamping human relations in his own firm, he may well lead the rest of the industry and perhaps the nation into a solution of the basic economic problem in this country."

Pretty heady stuff! Just how the Newsom staff maneuvered young Henry Ford to be the speaker at the prestigious Gridiron Club's 1949 dinner was not discerned, but it did. This event is the highlight of the year in the nation's capital with invitations to attend highly prized. The Newsom staff crafted a speech for the occasion on the night of December 10, 1949, but one uncharacteristically heavy for a light and satirical occasion. Thanking his audience of political correspondents, political leaders, and business leaders headed by Vice President Allen Barkely for this honor, he opened, "I know it is an honor you customarily reserve for somebody more important than a young fellow from Detroit trying to make and sell cars, trucks – and tractors." On a light note, he twitted newly married Vice President Barkely about the fact that his bride was driving an Oldsmobile while the President's wife rides in a Lincoln. The important fact was that he had been chosen to speak to the Gridiron Club and its politically powerful audience. More evidence that he had achieved the Newsom goal of "industrial statesman."

The Newsom staff also promoted national magazine publicity for Ford executives. In early 1951, Newsom's writers drafted a statement for Ernest R. Beech, then executive vice-president of the Ford Motor Co., entitled "America's Secret Weapon." The statement prepared for Breech, read in part, "Make no mistake about it: the American system is a rough system. Competition is a very hard nursery; and the children who survive that nursery have to be tough-minded and quick-witted. But out of this run-for-your-life school of blows and hard knocks we have developed a secret weapon, a weapon that may save our lives in the next decade . . . The name of this weapon is management."

The article was placed in *Look* magazine, published March 27, 1951, under the title, "Management Is America's Secret Weapon." Another tessera in the mosaic of a now progressive Ford Motor Company!

Crusade for Freedom

To burnish his emerging stature as industrial statesmen of the new generation, Henry Ford II took a position of leadership in the 1951 Crusade for Freedom, kicking off the 1951 drive with a public demonstration on August 28 on the steps of Detroit's City Hall. A Newsom memo, written by John Slaughter, stated:

> In assuming a position of leadership with the drive, Henry Ford II identified himself with an organization making an imaginative, constructive and dramatic effort to fight Communism. Uses of Ford–Lincoln–Mercury dealerships throughout the United States as focal points for Crusade collections magnified this identity. The result of this association cannot, of course, be fully gauged; however, it is obvious that public awareness of Mr. Ford's and the Ford Motor Company's role in the fight on Communism has been firmly established.

Portrayal of Henry Ford II as a foe of Communism fit well into the current climate of public opinion being fired to white-hot heat by Senator Joseph McCarthy and his fellow witch hunters. The Detroit kickoff headed by Ford raised $60,000 in that city. As of October 24, the receipts totaled $70,000 represented 60% of the Michigan quota in the national drive. The public relations staff saw to it that extensive newspaper coverage was obtained throughout the campaign. The Slaughter memo stated, "Hundreds of inches of space (including pictures) appeared in the three Detroit newspaper."

Subsequently, in a letter drafted for young Henry's signature, dated November 26, 1951, Ford, responding to a letter from General Lucius Clay, national chairman of the Crusade for Freedom, raised the question whether or not the Crusade for Freedom should become a permanent organization. HF II thought not. Ford's letter read in part, "I agree with you that in some way or another the American people ought to be kept aware of the activities of the Crusade for Freedom and ought to be given an opportunity to participate in its support. I question, however, the advisability of attempting to achieve this by changing the Crusade for Freedom drives into a permanent organization with year-round duties." Ford's letter added, "It has been my observation that when a voluntary organization, founded to give the American people outlet for their feelings and instincts to help, has been successful, there is a persistent tendency to perpetuate the organization. When this instinct is followed, the organization – as well as the motive behind it – tends to become routine and to deteriorate."

The proposed letter was carried to Ford by Charles Moore, who a year later, became his director of public relations.

"The American Road" Celebration

The deft public relations touch of the Newsom staff, working in conjunction with the newly energized Ford public relations staff, is apparent in the approach it took to celebrating the 50th anniversary of the Ford Motor Company in 1953. In a memo for Newsom, Ferry, and Charles Moore, dated February 7, 1951, Fred L. Palmer wrote:

> As we talked about the Ford Motor Company and the original Henry Ford and Henry Ford II, it seemed to me that there was another partner in the enterprise who made the whole thing possible – that thing we call the United States of America. Henry Ford was an American success story. The Ford Motor Company is an American result. Henry Ford II, on the 50th anniversary of the establishment of the Ford Motor Company, has a considerable reason for being grateful not only to his grandfather but to his country. He might easily come to the conclusion that this was not an occasion to brag nor for the company to talk about itself or about Henry Ford, the elder, but to pay some kind of tribute to that silent partner who means so much to so many but is so difficult to describe to ourselves or others.

And this was the approach taken, celebrating 50 years of "The American Road." The centerpiece of this theme was the production of an outstanding film, *The American Road*, estimated at the start to cost $250,000. The film was planned to "make a classic statement" of the American enterprise system. Tracing the 50-year growth of America from mudroads to paved turnpikes, the film premiered in September 1953 to critical and public acclaim. Beginning with the opening of the horseless carriage age, the film, made largely from priceless original footage, told how transportation had influenced American life, business, health, and recreation.

J. R. (Jack) Davis, Ford vice-president and 50th anniversary chairman, explained the theme of the film, "In planning our 50th anniversary, we considered many programs for the celebration in which we hoped the whole nation would play a part. We felt a motion picture would best tell Americans the story of how far we all have come in the last 50 years." The script was written by Joseph M. March and actor Raymond Massay narrated the story.

The producers of *The American Road* had a rich lode of film to draw upon for their production because Henry Ford, in his hustling, promotion-minded days, was the first industrialist to exploit the communicative power of the motion picture. Intrigued with the new invention, the motion picture camera, Ford in September 1913, bought one and began recording the assembly line method of production in his plant. Ford was the only company to have a motion picture unit until 1916 when General Electric established a similar program. Ford spared no expense in staffing and equipping his Motion Picture Production Unit in 1914. Ford made films mostly for sales promotion but in the process built a rich store of footage on the development of the automobile in the United States. In the depth of the Depression, Henry Ford abolished his film unit, and it was not reestablished until 1952 in order to produce *The American Road*.

The joint public relations staffs of Ford and the Newsom agency also produced an 50th anniversary book telling essentially the same story for distribution to libraries, schools, and colleges. This book carried a foreword from Henry Ford II written by the Newsom staff and reflecting its approach to this anniversary celebration — a standard feature in all public relations programs:

> When we began to consider what we should do during 1953 to celebrate the fiftieth anniversary of the founding of the Ford Motor Company, a great many projects were discussed — among them an anniversary book. The more we talked about this proposal, the more we came to appreciate that the growth and achievements of the Ford Motor Company have been made possible by the kind of world we live in, by American democracy, and the economic opportunity to seek change and progress freely. . . . It seemed to us that we would like during our 50th anniversary year to pay tribute to the United States of America.

It should be noted that this public relations stroking of America was taking place in the midst of the Korean War; Newsom and his associates were always keenly attuned to the fact that the context in which a message is received largely governs its interpretation.

To evoke the nostalgia of the nation's first half century, the company, with Newsom's guidance, published a Norman Rockwell calendar. Ford's ad agency, J. Walter Thompson Company, produced a 2 hour television show, again carrying the American Road theme in tribute to the United States. An anniversary insignia was developed for all 1953 automobiles. A stream of anniversary news releases were sent to the nation's press. A typical lead read, "The Model T Ford, heroine of a thousand journeys, butt of uncounted jokes and the most famous automobile ever built, first chugged into history on October 1, 1908." A newsreel movie, also adaptable for TV, was produced. Also steps were begun to establish the Ford Archives at Dearborn. A staff member of Arthur Newmyer's Washington agency initiated this in discussions with Dr. Way C. Grover, United States Archivist, and Dr. Herman Kahn, director of the Franklin D. Roosevelt Library at Hyde Park. Both offered their advisory services for this project. Thus this anniversary celebration had the Newsom touch of class.

Ford Promotes Auto Safety

In the mid-1950s, the Ford Motor Company, with Newsom's counsel and with great fanfare, publicly acknowledged the motoring public's growing concern with the lack of safety features in America's automobiles. This public relations campaign backfired 15 years later with the Ford Pinto. The apparent genesis of the Ford safety campaign is found in a memo from Mr. Crider to William Lydgate, then a partner in the Newsom Company. In a memo dated June 28, 1955, Crider wrote:

> Your idea of a Ford safety car is one of the best I've heard in a long time . . . For Ford to do this would not only be admirable from the point of view of demonstrating the company's interest in public safety, but might very well spearhead a long neglected sales appeal with epidemic attractions for the car-buying public. Why the industry has only dabbled with this instead of hitting it hard is something I could never really understand. No company in the industry has really tested the sales appeal of a serious effort to build a death-proof car.

The Newsom-directed campaign to identify the Ford company with car safety was launched with Ford's National Safety Forum and Crash Demonstration at Dearborn, Michigan, on September 7 and 8. The forum was attended by engineers, researchers, state police officers, and other traffic safety specialists from all parts of the country to exchange information and discuss research progress. Henry Ford II used the occasion to announce that his company was giving a grant of $200,000 to the Cornell University Medical College to help expand the institution's automobile crash injury research program. The grant was to cover a 2-year period. Ford said, "The purpose of our financial contribution is to enable Cornell to substantially increase their testing sample and to expand their vital fact-finding activities of surveying, analyzing, and recording data concerning injuries resulting from highway accidents."

In late November of that year, the Ford company released a new documentary motion picture tracing the history of the company's automobile crash research program for general distribution. The film was made available to the public, schools, and organizations. The 25-minute sound movie, *Crash and Live*, was also accompanied by a 10-minute companion movie, *Crash Research*. The latter showed actual laboratory experiments that led to the development of instrument panel crash padding, safety door latches, and deep-center steering wheel. (At that time Ford maintained film libraries in New York and Oakland, California, as well as at Dearborn to facilitate its film distribution.)

That the public relations aspects of this new stress on auto safety by Ford were uppermost in the minds of the Newsom staff is reflected in this staff memo dated August 19, 1955 addressed to Newsom and Lydgate:

> In all probability Ford knows all about the radar-protected car described in the attached column by my friend, Fred Othman. But since we are talking about public relations, and even sales promotion value of safety pioneering by Ford, I thought we should not overlook this.
>
> There has been a lot of talk about safety belts, but the practice of using them has to start somewhere. Why doesn't Ford suggest to fleet owners of Ford taxicabs that their drivers use these belts? . . . Use of the belts by all cab drivers might even help to lower insurance rates since the drivers are probably the riders most likely to suffer death or the worst injuries in accidents.

Automobile safety was very much on the public agenda in the mid-1950s. A scan of the *Reader's Guide to Periodical Literature* makes this plain. A typical entry is "Let's Build Safer Automobiles," in *Today's Health* for July 1955. In this same period, the influential *Harper's Magazine* came out with a futuristic cover showing a death-dealing automobile with its pointed fins fore and aft to publicize an article on the need for a safer car.

To further link Ford and auto safety in the public mind, the Ford News Department issued a release for January 23, 1956, to publicize a speech by Benson Ford, vice-president of the company, calling upon the medical profession to step up its contributions to driver safety. Speaking to the 16th Annual Congress on Industrial Health in Detroit, young Ford said, "Ford and other auto manufacturers already have done much to make motor vehicles safer and to lessen the severity of highway accidents." Benson Ford assured his audience that the Ford Motor Company was "interested in all of the things that go to make for safer driving."

This Ford campaign to link it with safer cars backfired loudly with its marketing of the unsafe Pinto in 1971. Lee Iacocco, now the president of Ford Motor Co., had brought out the subcompact Pinto to sell for less than $2,000 at the end of 1970. Lacey told the story:

> But soon after the new car's launch, one day in May, 1972, Mrs. Lila Gray, a California housewife and mother, pulled out onto a highway near Santa Ana in her brand-new Pinto only to have the engine stall. . . . Coming up

from behind her, another car, also a Ford, . . . rear ended the Pinto, causing serious damage. The fuel tank of the Pinto, sandwiched between the rear bumper and the axle was ruptured. . . . The gasoline tank exploded and Lila Gray died a horrible death a few hours later. . . . Her less fortunate passenger, Richard Grimshaw, thirteen, lingered on, scarred inhumanely.

Grimshaw, who spent the next several years undergoing skin grafts and surgery, sued Ford Motor Company and after a long court battle won $3.5 millon compensatory damages and $3,000,000 in punitive damages because Ford had "thrifted" on its placement of the Pinto fuel tank. Ford appealed the verdict but lost and ultimately paid the unfortunate Grimshaw some $6.5 million with interest. By the end of the Pinto's life, Ford had made it a reasonably safe car. But the damage had been done, magnified by General Motors' disastrous Corvair in the mid-1960s. (The General Motors–Corvair–Ralph Nader story that also required Earl Newsom's counsel is told later.)

Thus, the Ford Safety Campaign worse than failed when the aroused expectations were dashed by the accident-prone Pinto that was making front-page news in the early 1970s. As is told in the next section, the Ford safety campaign brought derision in General Motors' management suite, an attitude for which GM would soon pay dearly.

Newsom, Ferry Play Key Role In Labor Negotiations

Much of Newsom's time and thought and that of his partners, especially Ping Ferry, were spent on Ford's relations with the CIO–UAW in the troublesome and turbulent years 1945–1950 as labor and management adjusted to the post World War II era of industrial relations. Newsom's and Ferry's memos indicate a constructive influence on Ford's labor policies in this period. The 1949 Ford–UAW contract negotiations illustrate this influence. As the 1949 contract talks loomed, Ferry wrote Newsom in a memo dated February 21, 1949, "The major problem is that Reuther and UAW have for several months conducted a campaign, both Union and public, to establish pension plans as the only major demand to be made of the auto industry this year. As far as Ford is concerned, the campaign has emphasized the Company's willingness in 1947 to set up a pension plan. A definite impression has been left that there is no longer a question of *whether* Ford will agree to such a plan." To create a favorable climate for the UAW in the forthcoming negotiations with Ford, Walter Reuther had indeed launched a public relations campaign creating the impression among Ford workers that Ford intended to offer a pension plan that would give employees $100 a month when they retired.

Newsom was asked to attend an inner council meeting on February 24 for a discussion on how to counter this "false impression." He wrote in his private journal, "General feeling was that this 'loose talk' should be stopped by a countering letter to employees." At Newsom's suggestion, the meeting broke up so that he and Ping Ferry could fashion some "instrument" for meeting the situation. Newsom and Ferry went to Dearborn Inn, had two typewriters brought to their room, and went to work. "Balance of the day spent in discussion and drafting and redrafting of a letter to Walter Reuther." Newsom and Ferry asked William Gossett to have dinner with them that evening to go over their proposed draft. Gossett, Newsom wrote, liked the general pattern of the letter.

The next morning, February 25, the letter was presented to the Ford Executive Committee; in the discussion that followed "opinions on letter mixed." By 1:00 general agreement was reached on the revised draft. Newsom got the committee to agree that no action would be taken "until all had had a chance to give a fresh look at our handiwork over the weekend."

Even with this public rebuttal to Reuther, the pension issues would not go away. By March 8, after reading the public opinion climate and watching other negotiations in progress such as those of the CIO and U.S. Steel, Ferry swung to a position favoring pensions for Ford workers. In a memo of March 8, 1949, to Newsom, Ferry wrote, presumably after a thorough discussion among the partners:

> All of us are agreed that Ford has got to discuss and arrive at a pension plan or present a suitable alternative. At Dearborn they say there is still another alternative — strike. This point of view seems to say that a strike would have a fine, purgative effect, and that after the strike the demand for pensions would somehow be eliminated. So there is a pension plan or a suitable alternative. Here is another one, and one which you might want to bring up if you go to Dearborn Friday.

Newsom reflected this consensus when he participated in a meeting on March II at Ford with the Industrial Relations Advisory Committee to arrive at a policy for the forthcoming labor negotiations with the UAW. Present were John Bugas, vice-president for industrial relations, Professor Sumner Slichter, distinguished Harvard economist, Ted Yntema, vice-president for finance, Charles Carll, public relations manager, and "10 or 12 members of industrial relations department — also Ray Sullivan of Manufacturing Division and Bob McNamara, Comptroller." The group adjourned for lunch and reconvened at 2:30 in the afternoon. When the meeting reached a lull, Newsom "injected myself" with the following statement:

> 1. International Union had gone so far in its instructions to locals and its public statements that it was quite apparent Ford would face a strike if no

pension or welfare plan were forthcoming. Publicly admitted that Ford is on the spot and that the Union's intention is to make major issue of pension with Ford and so establish an industry pattern.

2. In my opinion some sort of pension plan at Ford is inevitable. The only questions are when, what time, what kind of a plan and who was going to pay for it. With major oil companies, G. E., Eastman and a host of other corporations having established such plans, automotive industry will inevitably follow.

3. Failure to have a plan at this time is already costing Ford Motor Company large sums. A strike — costly in itself — will only postpone the issue and increase future cost of the plan.

Professor Slichter and Comptroller McNamara both agreed that a pension plan for Ford workers was inevitable. The major obstacle in the company to the ideas was Ernest Breech in whom Newsom saw "a tenseness in determination to sacrifice other considerations to need for profit for company," a concern Newsom conveyed to Henry Ford II on March 24. Lacey observed, "Figures were Ernie Breech's long suit. His specialty was then the little known science of cost analysis."

By April, Ferry was urging Ford policy makers to have a candidate of its own to defeat the pension demand — his candidate being "job security." Excerpts from his memo of April 24, headed FORD PLAN, suggests promoting Ford's "candidate":

A. The real interest of the worker is not old age security, but job security today.

B. Old age security is beginning at the wrong end of the problem.

C. If we spend all our money on retirement security tomorrow, we can't meet job security today.

F. Job security will appeal to all but the old men in the Company.

I. The immediate objective of Ford should be a delay on any pension plan until the current job security questions can be successfully investigated.

More than anything else, Ford is seeking the least expensive way out of a real dilemma. As far as I can see, there is almost no likelihood that Ford can escape a pension plan — it is only a question of when and how much.

Leadership on this issue presently rests in the hand of Reuther and the UAW. It would be most advantageous to get that leadership back in the hands of the industry — Ford particularly.

The industrial Relations Advisory Committee, including key members of the Industrial Relations staff, Dr. Sumner Slichter, Allan Merrell, William Ford, Ping Ferry, and Newsom met again on April 15, 1949, to thrash out the pension issue. At the end of the afternoon, Newsom reiterated his position that "a strike is inevitable unless the Company decides to face the pension issue with some solution satisfactory to the Union." Newsom firmly believed that "more social security for employees in the United States is inevitable" though he would prefer "to see a greatly enlarged government security plan rather than plans sponsored by individual companies." He strongly agreed with Slichter that "no question of socialism is involved." In Newsom's presence, Breech had many times expressed the fear that "the UAW is taking us down the road to socialism."

The showdown in the company on this issue came at a meeting of the Ford Policy Committee with Breech presiding on April 26. Henry Ford II and other top officials were there. Ford expressed general agreement with Breech's position saying the company "has been an easy mark of the Union since the war by substantially meeting all demands of the Union." John Bugas took issue with this position, disagreeing that "we ought not to offer any kind of pension plan until we are prepared with a 'completely adequate' one." According to his journal of this date, Newsom again expressed the opinion that members of the Advisory Committee had unanimously arrived at an opinion which was that the Company would be better off not only in 1949 but in the long run by avoiding a costly strike and offering a pension plan for its workers." This meeting broke up without a decision.

When these negotiations were in progress in July 1949, Earl Newsom in a memo to Ping Ferry dated July 7 wrote:

> This morning's news regarding the stalemate in the United States Steel negotiations . . . tends to substantiate our theory that the CIO is giving Ford a base on balls in order to get at United States Steel on the pension pitch.
>
> The danger is that the people at Ford will be lulled into a false sense of security. This is all right if they tend to follow whatever pattern is set at steel. On the other hand, it is all wrong if Ford management is determined to carry through its policy — to hold the line of labor cost and reduce all other costs as it can in order to get into a better competitive situation. I come back with new interest in the strategic situation as you and I saw it in Detroit last Tuesday morning.

Still Newsom, unlike Ferry, who was prolabor and who had formerly worked for the CIO, wasn't yet ready to concede on the pension issue. As he saw the situation in early July:

1. Employees, having just gone through a strike, are apathetic over the idea of pensions, which the Union is half-heartedly trying to maintain as the "Issue." This, on top of the fact that it would be difficult, under the best circumstances, to mount a strike over "pensions."

2. Union leadership itself is confused at the moment and somewhat frustrated.
3. We, on the other hand, are quite clear in our objective. We have a program. Our goal in the sharp reversal of economic trends is to provide steady jobs for as many employees as we can over the period ahead.
4. We must somehow have a continuing program for keeping our ideas and our plan before the attention of the negotiators and the employees.

A 1949 Ford UAW contract was agreed upon September 28, 1949, that did not provide for pensions for retired Ford workers. But because of rising inflation in the United States, the union demanded that negotiations be reopened in 1950. This brought a pension plan that had to be worked out over several months. As Ford's 1949 release stated "Development of a pension plan involves the solution of highly technical problems."

As often happens in these situations, events developed to force Ford to accept a pension plan for its employees. The Ford Motor Company News Bureau in Dearborn issued a statement for release on September 20, 1949:

On September 20, 1949, the President's Fact Finding Board investigating the labor dispute in the steel industry placed its report and recommendations before the President. While the report does not apply to the automobile industry, we nevertheless spent the next several days reviewing our situation . . . in the light of the Board's recommendations, and their inescapable national effect whether we agree with them or not. As a result, we told Mr. Reuther and his associates on last Thursday, September 15th, that we were prepared to discuss a pension plan for our employees. Negotiations toward such a plan began immediately and have consumed most of our time since then."

The climax in this public relations–labor relations struggle came on September 8, 1950 with the announcement that the UAW–CIO had reached a new agreement with the Ford Motor Company providing immediate economic gains equivalent to 19.4¢ per hour and a guaranteed $125 a month pension for all eligible workers. Ford issued a press release on September 3 announcing, "Ford Motor Company reached a new agreement with UAW–CIO on wages, pensions, insurance and other economic matters. Today's agreement, which runs until June 1, 1955, continues without change all non-economic provisions agreed to by Ford and the union in its contract of September 28, 1949."

The wisdom of Earl Newsom's counsel was demonstrated in 1950 when the Chrysler Corporation refused to grant its workers the pension Ford had agreed to. The ensuing strike cost Chrysler over $5 billion in lost production and provided Ford a chance to pass Chrysler in sales and take the Number 2 position in the auto industry.

David Lewis observed in *The Public Image of Henry Ford* "The new administration's concern with human relations and, more importantly, its fair treatment of employees and honest dealings with the union, sharply reduced the savage tensions which marked labor–management relations of the Bennett era." By mid-1947, *Fortune* magazine said, "There was general agreement that Ford was doing a labor relations job second to none in the tense Detroit area." For this turnaround the publicly unseen influence of Earl Newsom and Ping Ferry deserve much of the credit.

An insight to Earl Newsom's counseling philosophy can be seen when he was asked his opinion by Henry Ford and Ernest Breech of a plan to give top corporate officers "management shares" to enable these executives to make capital gains. Newsom was asked to meet with William T. Gossett, whom Ford had brought from Bendix, to create a strong legal department. Gossett wanted Newsom's opinion on the public relations aspect of such a plan. In his private journal of February 10, 1949, Newsom wrote:

> 1. Considered by itself plan is fairly normal and supportable as good business practice.
> 2. Must however be considered in light of (a) forthcoming labor negotiations; (b) Dearborn Motors [which had been created to handle tractor distribution]; (c) Ford Ferguson suit [a suit brought by Harry Ferguson, an Irish tractor and farm implement manufacturer with whom Henry Ford had formed a partnership in the 1930s]. If matter were to become known reputation of company and those participating in plan would be in jeopardy. Public attention would be focussed on it by labor, and matter would be picked up as confirming conspiracy pattern of Dearborn Motors as conceived by Ferguson.

Then Newsom added this in his private journal, "Where reputation is involved I insist upon counselling perfection, because lost-reputation can never be regained. Therefore firmly against the plan."

The plan was shelved for the time being but was ultimately adopted when in Lacey's words, "a more elegant solution was worked out" with the result that the 67 top executives became millionaires.

Newmyer Firm Also Involved In 1949 Negotiations

The Washington public affairs/lobbying firm of Newmyer Associates was also highly influential in Ford's public relations in this period, particularly in matters of Congressional legislation and hearings. Earl Newsom had almost from the start relied on Arthur Newmyer for guidance on "Washington problems" and had persuaded Standard Oil (New Jersey), Ford, and other major clients to retain the Newmyers. Earl Newsom was also a client of Newmyer. For reasons not explained either in the Newsom Papers or in

Earl Newsom's private journal, the Ford executives and Newsom chose to release the letter he and Ping Ferry had drafted in Detroit in late February through the Newmyer firm on its letterhead. The open letter, dated March 2, addressed to Walter Reuther and publicly released was a prelude to the contract negotiations slated to start in May or June between the UAW and Ford. The carefully drafted letter was intended to set the tone and the ground rules for the forthcoming bargaining. The letter was signed by John S. Bugas, Ford vice-president and director of industrial relations and Henry Ford II's closest confidant in the company. Reuther responded in a letter dated the same day hotly declaring, "Since your letter was used as a press release, it is quite apparent that it was written not in an effort to resolve the problems that confront the Ford workers, but rather as a publicity handout to confuse the real issues in the coming negotiations." Reuther added, "Despite the fact that your letter received nation-wide press and radio coverage, we are not releasing our reply to the press or the radio." This indicates that the Newmyers as well as the Newsom partners were heavily involved in counseling HF II and Bugas in these troublesome and turbulent times between management and the unions.

The Newmyers, especially son Jim, developed a close relationship with Henry Ford II that continued long after Newsom was dropped by the Ford Motor Company in 1957. The closeness of the Newmyer relationship with Henry Ford II was shown when Henry Ford II married his second wife, Cristina Vettore Austin, on February 19, 1965, a year after his first wife had obtained an Idaho divorce. Jim Newmyer made all the arrangements so that the couple could be wed quietly and privately in Washington, DC, and he served as Henry's best man.

Building An Internal Public Relations Department Troublesome

In the early years of Henry Ford II's administration, he, Ernest Breech, and other top executives, while highly pleased with Earl Newsom's Company, had difficulty in building an internal public relations department that suited them. They had inherited Charles Carll, a former Indianapolis newsman, who had been brought in by Steve Hannagan in 1942. He first headed a News Bureau, and after Newsom's retention, he was named to head a public relations department. He didn't last because in the words of a colleague, "The pressure was really too much for him." Charley Carll got along well with Ford, but his relations with Breech were a bit rocky, made so in part by an abrasive subordinate. Carll was eased out early in 1946 with a dealership in La Jolla, California. William Kennedy, then head of the Ford publications department, was tapped as Carll's successor but served only a few months. He was too laid back to suit top management and, in the words of a colleague, "He really didn't want the job."

Late in 1946, Ford's management turned to James W. Irwin, veteran newsman and former director of public relations at Monsanto Chemical Co., to come in and organize a full-scale public relations operation. Presumably, Irwin was hired on Earl Newsom's recommendation. Irwin demanded that he be placed on the policy level as assistant to the president and director of public relations. Irwin was the only Ford employee other than Executive Vice-President Ernie Breech who reported directly to Ford. One of his first acts was to change the name of the Ford News Bureau to Press and Radio Relations Section. (It was changed back after he left Ford.)

In a letter dated October 10, 1946, addressed to Breech, Irwin outlined his plans for an enlarged internal public relations program. Irwin wrote that as he saw it, "Ford Motor Company has two major advantages over the other two members of the Big Three insofar as public relations is concerned: (1) a new and strong personality who is and will continue to be a public relations asset, and who is backed up by several other strong personalities who can be made public relations assets; (2) a hard-hitting, fast-thinking organization that will find it possible to move quickly in the seizure of public relations opportunities." Irwin recognized that GM had an advantage in the minds of many for its leadership in research and styling and Chrysler "which stands out in recognition by opinion molders for its engineering achievements."

Irwin wrote Breech: "I believe strongly that whoever is chosen to organize and direct Ford's public relations should be of policy committee stature and officer of the company on a par with other offices who head departments." As indicated this condition was met by Ford, and Irwin's appointment was announced early in February 1947. The announcement stated that Irwin would continue his own public relations firm in Manhattan but would hire someone to run it in his absence. The announcement also made clear that Earl Newsom would remain as outside counsel.

One of the first tasks Irwin set for himself was to build an understanding of public relations and its importance to sales from top management to the Ford dealers. He prepared an elaborate slide show, "The Ford Motor Company Public Relations Program" that was used throughout the organization. Under Irwin, in the words of *Printer's Ink*, "Ford Motor Co. is making a bold, all-out bid for leadership with a tradition-smashing integrated PR, advertising, and sales approach." Irwin told *Printer's Ink:* "All key management personnel should be sincerely public relations-minded. The public, customers, and employees can quickly spot phoney efforts and thinking. And when that happens, product quality and sales are inevitably affected." Irwin argued with management that a competent advertising agency and public relations personnel must work together from the outset in this integrated approach to boosting car and truck sales. Speaking to Princeton University's 15th industrial Relations Conference in September 1947, Irwin said a "good business philosophy" should "include a recognition of certain responsibilities to the customer, the national economy, the stockholder, and the employee". He quoted Henry Ford II as saying, "Informed employees are more productive, certainly, than uninformed employees."

Unlike Carll or Kennedy, Irwin was quite assertive and felt and talked very much like a top management person. For whatever reason, Irwin was eased out in 1952 and given a bus distributorship in Ohio that he later sold and then returned to Chicago where he opened a counseling office.

In 1952, Charley Moore, who had joined Ferry in working on the Ford account as Ferry was spending more and more time with Ford Foundation matters, was named public relations director at Ford. He measured up to top management's expectations. Moore persuaded fellow Newsom staffer, Sydney "Bill" Morrell, to join him at Ford, telling Morrell, "We'll make a piss pot full of money."

Moore set about to build a strong staff in Dearborn, including speech writing capability that Newsom regarded as his responsibility and forte. This did not become a problem for the next 2 years when Moore was given leave from Ford to serve on the White House staff as a special consultant to President Eisenhower. A member of the enlarged Ford Public Relations staff wrote your author:

When Charlie Moore became a Ford employee in March, 1952, it was understood by interested persons in top management and on the PR staff that Earl Newsom's counseling function would within a few years be terminated and there would be total reliance on in-house services. It was necessary only that Charlie demonstrate strong competence — the ability to provide a quality of performance equal to anything that Earl might provide.

If Newsom assumed that there would be brighter days ahead for him at Ford with Charlie heading the PR staff, he quickly found the well starting to go dry. Charlie worked hard to gain the confidence of Breech, Bugas, Gossett et al and he succeeded to a great extent despite himself being an ex-Newsom partner. Ping and to some extent Earl himself had pushed HF II and others in management to adopt a more liberal posture than they were ready for. . . . Even Henry at times became alienated at some of Earl's proposals.

One of these Ford top public relations officers wrote your author, "During the Carll, Kennedy and Irwin years, Ford's public relations were pretty much run out of Newsom's office and Ford's New York public relations office, headed by John E. Sattler." Sattler had been recommended to Newsom in 1946 by Stephen Fitzgerald, and on Newsom's recommendation, Sattler was hired by Henry Ford II. Sattler headed the New York Ford office until he retired in 1980.

The mutually profitable 12-year relationship between Henry Ford II and Earl Newsom ended in late 1957 for a number of complex reasons, not all of which are verifiable. The Newsom Papers are silent on the end of the firm's account with the Ford Motor Company. The three principals involved—Earl Newsom, Henry Ford II, and Charles F. Moore, Jr.—are deceased. This account is based on the recollections of two key members of the Ford Company public relations staff who observed this parting of the ways of Ford and Newsom.

Perhaps the story begins when Earl Newsom took Charles E. Moore, Jr. in as a partner. Newsom partner Ping Ferry introduced Moore, a fellow Dartmouth alumnus, to Newsom in 1948 and urged that he be hired for the Newsom staff. Much to Ferry's amazement, Moore emerged from the interview as a partner. A colleague described Moore as "a politician and a charmer." Prior to joining the Newsom firm, Moore had been a journalist with the *Boston Herald-Traveler,*, *Boston Globe, Washington Post,* and *Nation's Business.* From 1946 to 1948, he was executive assistant to Governor Robert Bradford of Massachusettes. Moore, along with Ferry, worked on the Ford account after joining Newsom.

The evidence suggests that Moore encouraged terminating the Newsom relationship but tried to do it in such a way as not to appear disloyal to the man who had put him in the Ford job. One member of the staff recalled Moore repeating to management more than once, "Why buy milk when you've got a cow in Detroit?" that the staffer termed "a helluva crude way to put it." Also Moore and Newsom differed on the speech writing assignments: Moore wanted them prepared in Dearborn. Newsom wanted to keep his hand in how HFII presented himself and his company's policies publicly.

Two more substantial reasons appear to have been at work in ending this 12-year relationship. By 1957, Henry Ford had developed great self-confidence in his ability to manage the giant company and had also gained confidence in Moore's ability to serve Ford management capably. He pushed Moore to terminate the Newsom relationship amicably as soon as feasible. He was not unappreciative of the great job Newsom had done for him in building him into a respected industrial statesman, in erasing the anti-Semite stigma from the Ford name, and in encouraging a constructive bargaining position in labor relations. Another Ford public relations staffer of the time is less gentle. "Charley just didn't like having Earl Newsom looking over his shoulder."

Professor David L. Lewis said flatly that "Charley did see to it that Newsom was terminated."

Another valid reason for the Ford move was the recession of 1957 that had a strong effect on Ford management. This recession hurt the entire industry because it signaled the end of the long postwar market in which all manufacturers became rich. HF II was in a cost-cutting mood, said a staffer, and saw the Newsom billings as one way to cut. For a complex of reasons, then, this lucrative Newsom account was lost.

This is an oft-repeated pattern in the development of a corporate public relations program. A crisis occurs, an outside counselor is called in, and over time the counselor guides the corporation in building a strong in-house staff that is capable of handling the organization's public relations. Newsom did this with Standard Oil of New Jersey as he did with Ford.

Moore was elevated to a vice-presidency in 1955, a post he held until his retirement in 1963. Upon retiring, Moore moved back to his native Massachusetts where he died on November 11, 1980. He was succeeded as vice-president of public relations at Ford by Theodore F. Mecke, Jr., whom Moore had groomed for the job.

SECTION 2: GM TURNS TO NEWSOM IN SAFETY CRISIS

In the mid-1960s, the mighty General Motors Corporation, buffeted by lawsuits and Ralph Nader's criticism that its Corvair car was unsafe and threatened by state and federal auto safety legislation, sought Earl Newsom's counsel to guide it through that crisis. Newsom's relationship with General Motors was a troubled one that lasted less than 2 years. When Newsom resigned the GM account in 1967, there were bruised feelings on both sides.

The 1960 through 1963 Corvair, a Chevrolet product, was an innovative rear-engine vehicle. It burst into the nation's headlines on May 16, 1960, when a 16-year-old driver, Don Wells Lyford, was killed on his way to Carmel, California, because his car went out of control, crossed the center line of a two-lane highway, and crashed into an on coming car. General Motors and two Chevrolet dealers were sued by Lyford family for large damages. The accident was repeatedly cited by critics of the Corvair, led by Ralph Nader, then emerging as a national spokesman for public interest causes. He later documented this and other charges in a best-selling book, *Unsafe at Any Speed,* in 1965.

The Lyford case ended July 29, 1966, when Judge Bernard S. Jefferson of the Los Angeles County Superior Court ruled: "It is the court's conclusion that the Corvair automobile of the 1960 through 1963 variety is not defectively designed nor a defective product; that no negligence was involved in the manufacturer's adoption of the Corvair design . . . that the cause of the May 16, 1960, accident . . . was due solely to the actions of said deceased and not to the design or any handling characteristics of the Corvair."

By June 1964, the Los Angeles law firm that brought the Lyford lawsuit had filed 22 suits against GM relating to accidents in which a Corvair was involved. In June of that year, a suit filed in Santa Barbara, California, *Rose Pierini V. Washburn Chevrolet and General Motors Corporation* was settled out of court by the defendants and their insurers when it was revealed that a student employee in the dealership had just rotated the tires on this Corvair and had put 25 pounds of air in one front tire, 14 to 17 pounds in the other. The wire services picked up the settlement story and carried it nationwide. Twenty four more lawsuits were brought against GM and its dealers as a result of the Pierini settlement. Yet the third case tried, *Collins V. General Motors Corporation,* was heard in the Superior Court of San Jose, California, and ended in a verdict for GM.

In GM's eyes the Corvair was vindicated of the repeated charges leveled by Nader and other critics when it won two Corvair lawsuits and when the National Highway Traffic Safety Board issued a press release clearing the Corvair of all charges after a year of vigorous testing of the automobile. Nonetheless, Nader's charges and continuing news headlines had developed a hostile public opinion climate for General Motors. Clearly GM's reputation had been sullied, and auto safety was now on the public agenda – a fact that politicians were quick to exploit.

The flood of publicity and unfavorable editorial comments generated by the Corvair controversy led to the introduction of a National Automobile Safety bill by Senator Abraham Ribicoff of Connecticut in mid-1965. Growing public concern about GM's cars was further reflected in February 1, 1966, when Senator Roger Craig introduced a bill in the Michigan legislature to ban Volkswagens and the Corvair, 1960 through 1963 models, from Michigan's highways. This, too, was grist for Nader's mill.

When the Corvair storm broke over General Motors in 1960, Frederic G. Donner, chairman of the GM board, decided that it should be handled by GM's legal counsel and ruled out any involvement of Anthony G. De Lorenzo, GM vice-president for public relations since 1956, and his staff. Adhering to the Canons of Professional Ethics of the American Bar Association, the GM legal counsel ruled out any comment from his staff or the public relations staff, thus leaving General Motors mute in the face of the rolling tides of criticism.

A GM officer explained this policy this way, "In keeping with both the letter and spirit of these canons, it has been a General Motors policy of long standing that it will not make any public statements directly to news media or indirectly at any public hearings relating to matters that are in litigation." This lack of response to the chorus of criticism of GM alleging indifference to safety left the public with the impression that GM didn't give a damn. De

Lorenzo was excluded from all matters involving the Corvair. This situation often occurs in corporations where legal considerations are given more weight than public relations considerations. Recent examples are Exxon's stony silence in the *Valdez* disaster in Prince William Sound and Dow--Corning's long silence about the dangers of silicone breast implants.

It was difficult if not impossible for De Lorenzo or any other top official to take issue with Donner's position that the Corvair–Nader problem was a legal problem. In an article in the August 1966 issue of *Fortune,* describing Donner's authoritarian ways, Dan Cordtz wrote, "Others say that he does not get enough 'feedback' from those who report to him. Donner is a forceful man, with an intelligence livelier than of most of those around him, and very much the boss at General Motors. Even among the higher executives, there is reluctance to tell Donner anything than what they think he wants to hear." Prof. David L. Lewis, author of the history of public relations at Ford which he was not permitted to publish as long as he was employed at GM), who spent 7 years in GM's public relations department, said, "The critical views of the academic world are scorned at GM." Because of this awe-struck atmosphere at GM, it was Cordtz's opinion that "the company's well-organized public relations staff has trouble performing one of its important functions: interpreting subtleties of the outside world to management. Instead, its considerable energies are employed to a dispro-portionate degree in interpreting management to the world." Once when your author pressed De Lorenzo, a longtime friend, on this point he replied, "Scott, it is my job to tell the GM story, not to manage the company."

Cordtz and other journalists at the time pictured Donner as a high executive heavily insulated in his ivory tower, thus one insensitive to the issue of auto safety. De Lorenzo, his longtime public relations chief, vigorously disputed this. In a letter dated March 20, 1992, to me he asserted, "Fred Donner . . . had a wide-ranging mind and keen under-standing of people and business issues. He read widely on business and non-business issues . . . He made it his business to understand problems in our industry . . . He was not insulated" De Lorenzo continued, "As to GM's 'insulin' respected organizations kept GM management current on public issues."

Nevertheless, Dan Cordtz thought Donner was insensitive to the safety issue. He wrote in the *Fortune* article, "A favorite crack making the rounds at GM was: McNamara is selling safety, but Chevy is selling cars." This was a reference to the fact that when Robert S. McNamara became president of the Ford division in 1955 he was impressed with the auto safety studies that Cornell University had been conducting from 1955 through 1957. These studies were heavily financed by Ford and Chrysler; GM wouldn't con-tribute to them. McNamara stressed safety in the design of the 1956 Fords, touting their Lifeguard Design. When McNamara moved on in January

1961 to become Secretary of Defense, the Ford advertising and public relations emphasis on car safety was quietly shelved. Ford's early interest in and support of safety research was described in section 1.

This was the climate in which Frederic Donner turned to Earl Newsom for counsel. He and Newsom had been friends for many years and were members of the same golf club. The Newsom Papers suggest that the Newsom company was retained by GM in April 1965. Out of Newsom's first meeting with Donner and James F. Roche, president, came a memo suggesting these ideas for GM's consideration and development:

1. It is proposed that GM make direct contact with leading representatives from the undergraduate student generation in America, and that this contact be in the form of annual seminars where a dialogue can be opened which will enable an exchange of views.

2. We agreed that GM should find ways to take initiative in the reduction of air pollution due to automotive gases.

3. We agreed that GM should invite a distinguished guest to meet with the Board of Directors each month for a general discussion of current social, political, or economic issues.

4. It is suggested that Mr. Donner host a number of small "advisory" dinner meetings in New York on specific problem areas.

5. We think it would be advantageous for Mr. Donner to address a letter to President Johnson reviewing in some detail GM's policies and practices with regard to investment abroad.

6. Among the many crucial problems shared by the major urban centers of the world is the problem of traffic congestion. As public concern focuses more and more on this difficult problem . . . it would seem highly appropriate for the country's leading manufacturer of transportation vehicles to show evidence of concern.

7. In its search for new Board members GM should concentrate on finding broad-gauged individuals who will bring to the Board a keen perception and understanding of social and political movements here and abroad.

8. It was also agreed that a major problem of GM is to find and promote top individuals into top management within the company who are equipped to make judgments in broad areas involved in public opinion, even if this means reaching down the ranks and promoting without regard to seniority.

9. Finally, we agreed to look into the question of some kind of executive reading program for GM, to encourage men who are in top positions of responsibility to read broadly in the fields of history, politics, biography.

Clearly the thrust of these recommendations was to open up what the Newsom partners and others saw as a closed management of engineers and accountants. Chairman Donner had risen through the accountancy route, President James Roche rose up the engineering chain. Both fields provide a narrow, technical education, one little suited to dealing the storms of public opinion. De Lorenzo wrote of the Newsom memo, "This was not a fresh approach from an outsider, but an issue that was agonized over in GM long before Newsom joined us." The GM vice-president saw the Newsom staff as "naive" in matters of auto safety.

Worse was that De Lorenzo's saw Newsom and his staff as "the enemy." Professor David L. Lewis, then a member of De Lorenzo's staff, wrote me in a letter dated May 7, 1992:

> I can well understand why the Newsom–GM relationship was unsatisfactory from the standpoint of the Newsom organization. I was a member of GM's public relations staff when Newsom was retained. Chairman Fred Donner was dissatisfied with Tony De Lorenzo, an appointee of Harlow H. Curtice, and brought Newsom in to look overy Tony's shoulder and to improve GM's public relations policies. Tony resented the intrusion.
>
> Tony assigned me to introduce Fred Palmer (on his first working visit to the GM Building) to public relations and other personnel, and "to acquaint" Fred with the corporation's public relations program and policies. In giving me this assignment, Tony said, "Don't tell him a damn thing. We don't want Newsom stealing our ideas."

Lewis wrote that he was dumbfounded by De Lorenzo's attitude. Being a good soldier, Lewis followed De Lorenzo's instructions and did not acquaint Palmer with the PR staff's innermost thinking. Finally, after a good deal of soul searching, Lewis did tell Palmer that he was "not revealing as much to him as he'd like to." Palmer sensed trouble from this remark. Thus, the Newsom–GM relationship was doomed from the start and was consequently a short-lived one.

Donner's "safety chicken" came home to roost in August 1965 when he and Roche testified before Senator Ribicoff's Traffic Safety Subcommittee. News stories of their appearance and testimony caused Newsom partner Fred Palmer to conclude, "General Motors and the auto industry were clobbered." In a memo dated August 6 to Newsom Palmer, wrote: "The clear impression was left that the automobile industry was "buckling under pressure from Uncle Sam." Typical was a story in the *Los Angeles Herald-Examiner,* "Members of the Senate Traffic Safety Subcommittee received with chilly skepticism yesterday a report by the nation's leading auto manufacturer on what it had done to guard the safety of automobiles."

The story of the hearings fiasco goes something like this as related to me by a former GM official. GM's public relations staff recommended sending Harry Barr, vice-president for engineering, to testify in an effort to low-key the hearing. Legal Counsel Theodore Sorensen recommended instead that President Roche and Chairman Donner testify. Their appearance brought Senator Robert Kennedy to the hearings; he was the chief advocate of the safety legislation. "The story around GM was that Kennedy wasn't going to attend the session, until he learned that Roche and Donner would testify.". So, in the opinion of this former GM official, "GM brought out its 'big guns' and, in so doing, precipitated a battle with U.S. Senators that GM couldn't win under any circumstances." GM presumably had retained Sorenson as counsel because of his close friendship with Senators Ribicoff and Kennedy. This, as things turned out, was a miscalculation.

In the news stories following the July 13 hearing, Donner was widely quoted as saying, "If we were to force on people things they were not prepared to buy, we would face a customer revolution." As Palmer observed in his memo, "However true this may be, it is not the kind of statement that would persuade people that much progress toward safety was likely to come from GM." Donner announced to the committee that GM had made a grant to MIT of $1 million to conduct research on ways of making cars safer. Senator Robert Kennedy termed this sum "inadequate." In De Lorenzo's Opinion, Donner would have been a more effective witness had he stressed that GM at that time was spending millions on safety, safety research, and testing of all components of its cars.

In appraising the appearance of Donner and James Roche before the committee, Palmer wrote, "Neither Donner nor Roche photographed well. They do not look like warmhearted, generous men. The photo showing them with their heads together conferring on some point made them look like a couple of defendants." Palmer thought Ribicoff's question, "Should the industry always be lagging behind waiting to be told what to do?" was a fair question. Palmer concluded his memo of August 6, 1965, with these recommendations:

1. Donner and Roche should not have gone together. Attention should be concentrated on a single spokesman.
2. Their principal point should not have been that car safety cannot be achieved because people won't buy it.
3. General Motors should always appear with constructive suggestions and not reasons why something cannot be done.
4. Neither Donner nor Roche gives the appearance in a photograph of being warmhearted. Roche looks slightly lugubrious. This makes it all the more important that their words should be warmhearted, positive, cordial, and constructive.

Finally, Palmer wrote Newsom, "It may be argued that the 'clobbering' that took place revealed the inadequacy of General Motors program in the safety field."

The reverberations of Frederic Donner's "clobbering" before the Senate Subcommittee led to an internal discussion among the Newsom partners as to how the firm could help General Motors deal with two problems:

First: How can we develop a more useful working relationship with General Motors?

Second: How should the American people be made aware of the company's active concern for highway safety?

In a memo dated November 18, 1965, from Fred Palmer and William Lydgate to Newsom, they suggested:

> It seems to us that the useful contribution Earl Newsom & Company can make to General Motors lies almost entirely in speaking with the voice of an outsider. We have said from the beginning that the public relations department and staff of the company has great professional competence. It has in our opinion only one problem—its internal character. This put very heavy pressure upon it to be an advocate of management views. Its advice may not be so well received as if it came from an independent source. We see our function then as aides to the public relations director in counselling management—primarily the Chairman and the President—not as an operating staff. . . . There is one difficulty to face. We cannot think intelligently in a vacuum. We must think in relation to specific fields of corporate activity. We need the stimulation of an active and continued awareness of the concerns of management and the corporation.

In another paragraph, Palmer and Lydgate wrote, "We agreed to make some specific suggestions to Tony [De Lorenzo] on how General Motors should report to the American people having in mind particularly its concern for motoring safety." These thoughts were implemented in a letter to Vice-President De Lorenzo dated November 22,—written after a luncheon that included De Lorenzo, Roche, and Donner from GM and Newsom, Palmer, and Lydgate from the Newsom staff. Lydgate's letter told De Lorenzo:

> We are all agreed that we ought to get General Motors off the defensive in matters of public policy. This means that the corporation should not talk safety when challenged or against a background of public inquiry. We must find good ways to talk safety continually. We must reveal the facts of General Motors' leadership. There is some urgency in this because General Motors is first—for example in its collision sled—and Ford has already made a move to catch up. . . . We need to use every good technique for turning the spotlight on the corporation's constructive and significant safety research.

This letter stung De Lorenzo, who had been stressing GM's safety programs for some years in his public relations program. He fired back a letter on November 22 to Lydgate asserting:

> Activities in the safety area have been a part of our over-all public relations
> program for many years. We do not feel that these activities have been
> "defensive" in nature; on the contrary;, we have been employing many
> effective ways to talk safety continually. However, we recognize, as you do,
> the need for a stepped-up, positive continuing effort, and we are expanding
> and intensifying our public relations safety program. . . . you will recognize
> that some elements in this program are similar to the suggestions in your
> letter.

De Lorenzo then proceeded to outline the several public relations activities
to demonstrate GM's concern for auto safety. Then in a 4-page single
spaced letter, the GM vice-president outlined a comprehensive program in
automobile safety. He concluded, "I hope this brief outline of some of our
activities and thinking in the field of safety public relations will demonstrate
the top priority which we have given this subject." This exchange illustrates
the conflicts that often arise between an outside counselor and the in-house
public relations staff. This one was sour from day one.

The Newsom partners involved in the GM account sensed that De
Lorenzo and his staff were sensitive and irritated by the implication from
the Newsom staff that GM's public relations program was not doing its job.
This led to a memo of December 6, 1965, from Palmer to Newsom and
Lydgate entitled "Helping General Motors." Palmer's impressions as to how
the firm could help GM were these:

> Mr. Donner has found it stimulating and useful to discuss problems with
> EN-often but not always PR problems. This was a relationship between two
> people the he wanted to formalize. This led to a larger relationship involving
> our firm and the public relations department of General Motors.

> There does not seem to be any doubt that this personal relationship is a useful
> service which the chairman of the board would like to have available to them.
> EN believes that Mr. Roche shares Mr. Donner's feelings in this matter.

> Obviously, to the extent that EN can wisely influence the public relations
> thinking of the corporation through its top executives, he can help General
> Motors.

Thinking of Newsom's forthcoming retirement from active direction of
the firm, Palmer pointed out, "Whether anyone can share this responsibility
with EN, now or at any time, remains to be seen and its a question that need
not be decided now. But if the firm is to have a relationship with the top
management of General Motors, it must be established by EN and a way
must be found to create some kind of succession." The Palmer memo
addressed the difficulties in the relationship with GM's public relations
department. "After nine months of experiences I would conclude that we

cannot make a larger contribution to General Motors, except by way of top management. The public relations department, even with the best will in the world, cannot help but feel that Earl Newsom & Company is a source of danger. In a highly competitive world they are not anxious to have good ideas coming from some 'competitive' source."

Then Palmer put his sensitive finger on a problem that has long plagued the management of General Motors, even into the 1990s, and that is the insulated world in which its narrowly educated executives—engineers and accountants for the most part—live and think. Palmer wrote:

> One of the problems of the corporation is the danger that its public relations thinking and its public relations organization will become parochial, intro-spective, and promotion minded so that it will take too narrow a view of situations. Earl Newsom & Company can help the corporation, I believe, only as it is able to bring to public relations problems the competition of an outside point of view. It cannot do this if it works for and is subservient to the public relations department unless the director feels the need very strongly, and in fact instigates the relationship, which was not the case in this instance. I certainly do not feel that we or anyone else should try to work at cross purposes with the public relations department of General Motors. But we certainly should bring to it the competition of a more detached viewpoint and the ideas which may flow from it.

De Lorenzo had this response to the Palmer memo and the Newsom's agency's role in GM's public relations, "First of all, General Motors has been the foremost leader of safety in our industry since the mid-1920s. Neither Earl Newsom or his organization had anything to do with making GM more sensitive to safety." Then De Lorenzo cited a common source of difficulty between an outside counsel and an internal public relations department when he asserted, "Magnifying corporate problems is advanta-geous to outside consultants since they can 'solve' greater problems than actually exist. This tendency is apparent in the Newsom memo you cited." A former GM public relations staffer, in commenting on this, had this to say:

> Retaining an outside, independent viewpoint is highly desirable, particularly in times of crisis. But counselors need to understand the rules of the game and the environment in which it will be played. The greatest disadvantage of outside counselors is that they don't know the company, its built-in biases and its blind spots, or where the political power lies. In desiring to work directly with the CEO . . . they can alienate the PR staff and dilute the value of its counsel in terms of durable changes in the thinking of the staff. . . . From my base of knowledge, this is what the Newsom company did.

Again thinking of Earl Newsom's prospective retirement from active direction of his firm, Palmer wrote:

If we are going to build a broad foundation for our relationship with the corporation, I think we have got to provide machinery through which at least two members of our organization devote a great deal of time in Detroit. It seems to me WAL [Lydgate] is ideally equipped for this responsibility but he certainly will require a great deal of help. I see no other way for us to be sufficiently close to what is going on in GM. It seems to me that the service Earl Newsom & Company can perform is well worth the substantial cost.

De Lorenzo, for his part, was keenly sensitive to the mounting public concern for auto safety and continued to place strong emphasis on this topic in GM's ongoing public relations program. In an undated memorandum — found in the Newsom Papers — to Edward N. Cole, GM's executive vice-president, De Lorenzo provided a summary of the PR Department's "Highway Safety Public Relations." De Lorenzo stressed:

General Motors and the rest of the automobile industry are the targets of a disturbing, rapidly growing and often fact-distorting campaign to indict motor vehicle design as the major contributor to traffic deaths and injuries. Obviously this presents us with a challenge to take every opportunity to tell our side of the safety story. We should (1) let the public know what we have done and are doing to make our products even safer than they have been; (2)improve public understanding of the automobile's relatively minor role as a cause of accidents; (3) both inform the public of our continuing support of objective efforts to improve highway safety, and encourage the public to support these efforts which put their emphasis on the real causes of traffic deaths and injuries.

Among the PR projects undertaken by GM was the first annual General Motors Public Relations Safety Conference held in Detroit on January 6, 1966, an extensive pattern of newspaper and magazine publicity, preparation of film clips for TV, preparation of a documentary film, a campaign of advertising stressing the issue of car safety, and preparation of a safety booklet for wide distribution.

In January 1966, the Newsom staff prepared a long, persuasive letter for President James M. Roche to Senator Abraham Ribicoff in which GM now took the position of supporting the Senator's automobile safety legislation. Roche's concluding paragraph stated, "We believe that this bill, as introduced in the last session of Congress, promises to help with several of the problems outlined above, and for this reason we support it. We would hope, however, that you will accept suggestions for revising or strengthening it." The opening paragraph drafted for Roche stated, "Since last summer [the time of the "clobbering" before Ribicoff's subcommittee] we have been engaged in a thorough and detailed review of our policies and practices with respect to automobile safety so as to be quite sure that we are doing everything within our power to make automobile driving in America as safe as it can be." The letter then went on to summarize the plans that had grown out of this review. It can be safely speculated, I think, that Earl Newsom's counsel had turned GM from its strong opposition to auto safety legislation to support of it. This would be characteristic of the Newsom approach to such problems.

More Disagreement Between GM Public Relations And Newsom

In an effort to get a first hand look at GM's safety activities and to talk with GM officials about automotive safety, Earl and John Newsom and William Lydgate spent January 24 and 25, 1966, in Detroit. A resulting Newsom memo of February 10 described the trip as "an instructive and rewarding experience." John Newsom had drafted a memo on February 8 that was edited by his father and Lydgate to represent the findings of their trip. John Newsom wrote to me, "They kept telling us how much they were doing about auto safety, and we went out to see for ourselves." Then Newsom sent a carefully drafted memo to De Lorenzo, "a private report from us on our present impressions."

The Newsom staff reached these conclusions on the basis of this visit:

1. We still feel that the public heat that has been generated over the question of automotive safety reflects a genuine concern on the part of responsible leaders and institutions over highway death and injury rates.

2. Specifically on the matter of semantics, "safety" has not meant the same thing to all people.

3. With regard to posture, as the critics have turned their charges into a sweeping indictment of the industry, the rather angry and defensive reaction of the companies has tended to leave the impression that there is something to the indictment.

4. It appears to us that General Motors has been vulnerable to criticism in the following respects:

a. The interior design of cars has not gone forward with accidents primarily in mind.

b. The exterior of the cars has not had in mind the possibility of pedestrian impact.

c. Almost all of the specific devices on the GSA (General Services Administration) list are being planned for standard or optional inclusion in GM automobiles.

d. The formal rebuttal to the Nader charges has been kept confidential, and outsiders must carry the impression that Nader was at least partly right.

e. According to one of GM's research leaders, General Motors "already knows more than it is using", in the field of safety.

f. The contrast between the vast and highly impressive facilities for strength and stability testing of production items on the one hand, and on the other GM's programs for carrying out design research for safety (a remote facility with a lone engineer at work), is startling. [GM officials stoutly denied this assertion.]

5. With these specific findings in mind, there is no doubt that the entire situation is complicated politically by the great size and wealth of General Motors—particularly as this has been evidenced again recently by the formidable earnings announcement.

6. Indications thus now are that this will continue to be a problem for General Motors until positive action is taken. Failure to engage in direct public discussions which give evidence of a desire to move forward toward new achievements in highway safety will seem to be confirmation of the suspicion that the public interest can be protected only by the government.

This frank, hard hitting appraisal of GM's public relations problems concluded with specific possibilities for action and for helping General Motors to take initiative on safety instead of staying on the defensive.

Predictably, this appraisal of GM's problems with the public—accurate in my view—raised the hackles in GM's top echelons. Reaction was swift in coming. A memo written by John R. Newsom to his father and William Lydgate, dated February 16, 1966, reported:

Tony De Lorenzo has just called to say that he received our memo last Saturday, read it on Sunday, and had others of his staff read it on Monday. He has been too busy until now to call back to set the luncheon date we talked about last week.

He says that he and his management disagree with most of the points in our memo and he questions whether it would be worthwhile talking the matter over at lunch. He said they feel there are three factors involved in auto safety—the car, the road, and the driver—and that we seem to feel there is only one, the car. I told him this was not at all the case, but that we felt the automotive industry has a problem connected with the safety of the car and we are trying to devise ways to help the Company with its problem. I said that it was interesting that we disagreed on solutions. . . . He said that they are not about to support any law patterned on the Scandinavian model making it illegal for drinking person to drive . . . I did not explore with him on the telephone the inconsistency in his position with respect to (a) the view that the driver is at fault, not the car; and (b) the Company should not advocate measures to limit driver error, as with legislation on drinking.

I think we should discuss this situation among ourselves. I don't think we are ever going to get anywhere with De Lorenzo, and I have doubts whether we are going to get anywhere with Mr. Roche. Maybe the time has come to revert to nice, quiet conversations between EN and Donner.

Gumshoeing Nader—A New Crisis

Into the growing strains of the relationship of the Newsom firm and De Lorenzo's public relations a new bombshell dropped when *The New York Times* broke the story on March 6, 1966, that Ralph Nader had been being shadowed by detectives hired by General Motors and was being harassed by phone calls. General Motors issued a statement on March 9 admitting that it had ordered an investigation of Nader and His activities. In a memo addressed to his father and to William Lydgate, dated march 25, John Newsom assessed the damage that had been done to General Motors by this undercover investigation:

> 1. It appears that persons acting in behalf of General Motors, and with the company's authority, are quite prepared to take actions which are surprisingly thoughtless and disregardful of the interests of individuals. There is a strong hint of the organizational arrogance one expects in an authoritarian state, which is sharply out of phase with the atmosphere of our society where individual rights are protected with ferocity. There is a vivid impression of agents of a mammoth organization hounding an individual.
> 2. Added to this is the impression that this company is not only resisting but is actively trying to suppress legitimate questions which are being raised by zealous but otherwise blameless citizens over whether the company is serving the public interest as it goes about its business.

The crisis created by GM's legal counsel blunder in dealing with the Nader/safety problem necessitated a meeting between President James. M. Roche and the Newsom advisers. In preparation for a luncheon meeting the following Tuesday, John Newsom prepared a memorandum dated March 29 for discussion prior to the meeting with Roche. Newsom was frank to state, "There is no question in our minds that General Motors has been seriously damaged by the entire Nader affair. The company's public position has been dealt a severe blow." He also felt that Mr. Roche had done much to mitigate the damage by pledging to Senator Ribicoff that "new regulations must be promulaged within the company which will make it impossible for any Nader episode ever to take place again." Other suggestions Newsom presented to his father for presentation to Roche included:

> 2. The widespread public impression that members of top management of General Motors do not know what is going in the company . . . must be corrected.
> 3. A policy statement seems to us to be indicated in which Mr. Roche declares it to be company policy that the size, wealth and influence of General Motors are under no circumstances to be used by an employee of the company

to intimidate, harass, and otherwise push around anyone outside the company. [Earl Newsom wrote in a marginal note, "I don't like this.]

4. New regulations should also be issued, we think regarding the release of statements in response to accusations against the company. One of the devastating impressions created in the recent hearing was that the March 9 statement of General Motors actively sought to mislead the public." [As noted earlier, Vice-President De Lorenzo's hands had been tied by Donner at the outset of the Corvair–Nader crisis by placing all responsibility for handling these charges and lawsuits with GM's Legal Counsel.]

John Newsom followed up the luncheon meeting with President Roche with these reactions in a memorandum dated April 12, 1966, addressed to his father, Lydgate, Palmer, and Arthur Tourtellot, headed "Ideas for General Motors." Newsom wrote:

Unquestionably, Mr. Roche is an extremely nice, agreeable, friendly man who seems willing to take plenty of time to talk with us about GM's public relations problems. But I thought his reactions were pretty much as they have been since last fall—negative, both with regard to any proposals for significant action and regarding any shifts in company attitudes which might indicate that they have learned from their recent experiences. . . . This suggests to me that the basic climate at General Motors is essentially unchanged, and that any hope for stirring movement in our area is still quite limited.

John Newsom had reached the same conclusion that Dan Cordtz had in his *Fortune* article—that GM's top officers were sheltered and closed minded, a common failing of corporate officers once they reach the peak of the organizational pyramid.

Newsom's memo continued with these points:

3. There is an impression that top management doesn't know what's going on in the corporation and has relatively little control over actions taken in the corporation's behalf.

4. Related to this is the impression that large size may breed a sense of irresponsibility and unaccountability on the part of down-the-line corporate officers and agents.

5. Also, there is an impression that the corporation is so insulated from the concerns of people, and of their elected representatives, that it is unable to act in ways which are constant with the public interest.

6. An Impression from the hearing record—although it is one which may have escaped the public—is that GM is quite prepared to issue misleading and even factually inaccurate public statements. The company seems guilty of dissembling.

Newsom's concluding judgment was that "the damage to its public reputation—and perhaps even to American business—can not be underestimated."

He then proposed for a staff discussion these possibilities:

1. Disciplinary action inside the company must be taken the next week which will indicate publicly what the company's management recognizes and is prepared to act to correct the serious deficiencies in its performance;
2. Orders should be issued from the top making it mandatory to report to top management whenever any action is contemplated which might involve the corporation in conflict with an individual outside the company;
3. The company might arrange to survey attitudes toward General Motors among the adult population. . . . The aim of this would be to try to make clear to management just what the public attitudes in this country really are toward large corporations and toward this large corporation in particular.

This was a candid and sensible summation of the damage inflicted on GM by actions emanating from its legal offices. The damages were writ large in an editorial in the probusiness *Wall Street Journal* of March 25, "GM's Snooping Boosts Prospect of Safety Law." In fact spying on and harassing Ralph Nader did in fact crystallize public opinion that brought enactment of Ribicoff's automobile safety legislation—the very thing GM had set out to block or at least modify. This once more proved the truism that events, not press releases, move public opinion. General Motors President James Roche tried to lessen the damage with a statement to Ribicoff's subcommittee in effect apologizing for this unwarranted investigation and harassment. General Motors that had once branded Nader a "wild eyed critic," now saw him as "an eminently responsible and respectable citizen."

This decision on Roche's part to apologize to the committee and Nader did not come easily or readily. William Lydgate, a Newsom partner involved with the GM account, recalled in a letter to me dated June 15, 1992:

I vividly remember accompanying Earl to a dinner meeting with Roche and some of his staff, including De Lorenzo at the Detroit Athletic Club. It was a meeting that lasted well past midnight. The issue was how to make amends for GM's surreptitious investigation of Nader. Earl stated at dinner that there was just one thing to do—Roche had to go before the Ribicoff Committee and personally apologize to Nader.

While Roche sat silent and uncommunicative, most of his colleagues, including Tony, argued against such an appearance. Earl laid out all the reasons why he thought that anything less than such a dramatic move would fail to satisfy hostile public opinion. The argument went on and on, Roche listening intently but not commenting. Finally, well after midnight, Roche abruptly said, "Earl's right, I'll do it." He did, and won a great deal of praise for his forthrightness.

This again demonstrates Newsom's gifts of persuasion and his influence with corporate executives at the highest level.

CBS Broadcast Scores a Hit on GM

The Nader-Safety issue simply would not go away for General Motors. On May 13, 1966, CBS-TV network carried a damaging program, "Crash Project: The Search for a Safer Car," that drew a hot response from James M. Roche, GM president. In a letter to Dr. Frank Stanton, president of CBS, dated may 18, Roche wrote: "Progress in traffic safety requires informed and intelligent public support. In my opinion, the chances of developing that kind of support were damaged seriously by a program which could only have confused and prejudiced millions of viewers." Roche's letter continued:

> The program was limited to a single element of the traffic safety problem—the car. . . . The inclusion of a portion of the Congressional hearing dealing with Ralph Nader, which commentator [Charles] Kuralt acknowledged "had nothing to do with safety," was entirely unjustified if the intent of the program was to present an objective report on highway safety, or even on one aspect of it.

> The program was essentially a one-sided, distorted report on a subject of the greatest importance. As such, in my opinion, it was a grave disservice to the public.

President Frank Stanton of CBS replied to Roche in a letter dated May 26, 1966, asserting:

> We have considered most carefully your letter and the appended comments. We have reviewed our broadcast in the light of your letter and comments, and I must report, with all respect, we cannot agree with you. . . . And I take comfort with this statement by Cynthia Lowery, of the Associated Press, in her review of the broadcast: "It summarized the controversy on automobile safety in a lively and fair manner, covering both sides. It left the answer to the questions it raised to viewers of the program."

This dispute brought two Newsom clients, GM and CBS, into a head-on collision. Who wrote the letters engendered by this dispute can be only a matter of conjecture.

Roche's lack of receptiveness of the Newsom staff's recommendations for changes in GM's public relations posture caused John Newsom to renew his suggestion that the company undertake an intensive survey of opinion in the United States today, with the aim of seeing whether it might not bring its policies and communications more in line with prevailing attitudes. John Newsom's memo of April 12 once more revealed the differences in public relations thinking between the Newsom staff and De Lorenzo's staff. John Newsom wrote, "I do not believe that GM should engage now in more propaganda regarding safety—not because it isn't a good thing to do . . . but because it won't be done right. As long as material is written in Detroit I think it will sound as it always has, and will be out of touch with the people." As for the Corvair problem that Roche said must now be dealt with, John Newsom suggested a demonstration of the Corvair's roadability at the GM Proving Grounds with Corvair dealers and the press invited to attend. He also suggested a simplified, illustrated booklet to be mailed to Corvair owners. "If it were really well done, and not heavy-handed, as most of their stuff has been, it would convince readers that the automobile is safe and is being subjected to an unfair and misinformed campaign."

Earl Newsom and his associates spent the next several weeks appraising General Motors' public relations situation and in formulating recommendations to move GM out of its crisis situation. Earl Newsom wrote President Roche in early June 1966, emphasizing his firm's value in presenting "an outside, and presumably objective point of view." He continued, "We recognize that any such help may be important, since the direction of American opinion—particularly the opinions of people in positions of leadership or influence—can make a significant difference in the scope of the Company's freedom to operate." He enclosed the 18-page "Summary Appraisal and a Look Ahead" as prelude before "we want to get together as soon as it is practicable with you and Fred [Donner] to discuss possibilities for action as General Motors moves forward now from the troublesome period of the last several months." What results flowed from this meeting of the Newsom and GM top brass is not indicated in the Newsom Papers.

Moving on at GM

In moving on a positive public relations effort, Fred L. Palmer, in a memo to Earl Newsom and William Lydgate dated April 5, 1965, said the Newsom staff ought to urge General Motors to get out ahead in dealing with the "smog" problem, that is, the air pollution caused by cars. He cited an article by David R. Jones in that day's *The New York Times* about a little-noticed controversy "raging throughout the United States." The question is pitting the automobile industry against federal, state, and local authorities." Palmer suggested General Motors should take this position in the hearings of the Senate Public Works Committee's Subcommittee on Air and Water Pollution, slated to begin the next day:

1. 1The automobile is not alone responsible for smog conditions but it is unquestionably a contributor in many areas and, in any event, it is a long term problem which we should tackle now.
2. The basic problem is that the individual car owner does not obtain a personal benefit from investing in a device to prevent air pollution.
3. Any workable solution must require all companies to participate. If only one installs air purifiers, it would be at a cost disadvantage in competition with other companies.
4. The cost of a purifying device is too great to be absorbed by any one company.
5. We do not oppose legislation which will require installation of air purifying devices on all new cars beginning (date). This does not solve the problem of used cars, but it is a start.

This was the thrust of Palmer's 9-point suggestion for GM's position on this controversial issue just then coming to the nation's public agenda.

The issue of growing air pollution caused by auto exhaust fumes had been raised by President Lyndon Johnson in a special message to Congress in early February. In line with the Newsom counsel, Vice-president Hafstad of General Motors testified before the Senate subcommittee on April 7 and took a constructive stance, testifying that smog control is a major target of GM's product improvement efforts.

The final items relating to General Motors is the Earl Newsom Papers area series of discussion memoranda prepared for Chairman Donner and President Roche. These memoranda, clipped together, were dated June 6, 1966. The memoranda covered these topics: "A Contribution to Clean Air Management," "Broadening the Base of Management Interests," "Traffic Studies Center," "The General Motors Building," "General Motors and Undergraduate Students," and "Re-Examining The Role Of The Corporation."

The memorandum on the General Motors Building referred to the storm of protest against GM's new corporate headquarters building being built in New York City. The memo stated in part, "A good many New Yorkers may be left with an impression that the corporation—thought of as a Detroit enterprise—is revealing bad character in putting up a great building in one of the loveliest sections of New York without any feeling of community responsibility."

The other memoranda were obviously addressed to the public relations' weaknesses of GM that had been revealed from the 1960 Corvair accident near Carmel to Ralph Nader's *Unsafe At Any Speed* to its legal counsel spying on and harassing young Nader, a lawyer who has devoted his life to fighting for what he defined as the public interest—and as millions of his followers do.

This saga illustrates anew that the policies and behavior of an organization are the prime determinants of its public standing, not its public relations efforts save as those efforts provide the public with a favorable and accurate interpretation of the organization—its people, its policies, its performance. The Automobile Safety Act stands as something of a monument to GM's blunders on the safety issue.

Newsom Throws in the Sponge

Given Frederick Donner's and James Roche's lack of flexibility on safety and other matters and Anthony De Lorenzo's fierce opposition to the counsel of Newsom and his partners, it was inevitable that Newsom would resign the account in 1967. This represents Newsom's sole setback in a long string of corporate victories over his 30-year career. The reasons for the failure to turn GM around in public opinion were outlined in a July 31, 1967, memo to Earl Newsom from John R. Newsom, entitled "The GM Situation." The son wrote his father:

> We have found considerable evidence that GM tends to make trouble for itself with public opinion by following certain policies and practices.
>
> 1. Compared to our experience with other major corporations, GM is intensely secretive. The company seems to have developed over its lifetime the idea that almost any information can be related by the competition to product improvement, and fear of suffering competitive losses has resulted in what can only be called an extremely guarded posture at GM.
> 2. The quality of materials coming out of GM's public relations department is surprisingly low.
> 3. There is no strong voice within the company arguing for first-rate public relations programs.
> 4. GM's public relations output seems to be mostly promotion-oriented and is not sensitive to the public atmosphere in which the company is trying to communicate.
> 5. There is an instinct within the company to turn over to the Automobile Manufacturers Association any matter which has potential for political attention.

Newsom continued his insightful memo by asking the question "What Needs to be Done?" and suggesting GM's "ailments" could be corrected by:

> *First,* there should be a much more aggressive interest in the company's public position on the part of top management.
>
> *Second,* there is no question in our minds that the public relations function at GM requires a more aggressive and professionally competent leadership. Present leadership is loyal, energetic, resourceful and shrewd. What is needed are qualities of openness, objectivity, representation of outside points of view.

Newsom concluded his memo by saying, "All of this suggests that our relationship, if it is to be successful, cannot be primarily with the public relations staff under Tony. There are too many fears and resentments for them to overcome." Why Frederick Donner permitted De Lorenzo to undercut Newsom's counsel is an unanswered question.

Thus for the first time in history, ENCO threw in the sponge when it encountered an unresponsive top management and an entrenched, defensive public relations staff opposed to it.[1]

In the memorable words of Yoga Berra, "It's *deja vu* all over again." In the early 1990s, General motors, already besieged by a series of financial, managerial, and public relations setbacks, once again found itself in a reprise of attacks on the safety of one of its vehicles. GM's deteriorating public reputation in the late 1980s and early 1990s coincided with GM's downgrading its public relations staff in 1990. That year GM moved public relations from the vice-presidential level to that of a director of communications under the marketing staff. Whether this downsizing of the Public Relations function played a part in GM's weakened public reputation of this period can be only a matter of speculation. After a series of public relations blunders, GM reversed itself in 1992 and named Bruce G. MacDonald as vice-president of an independent communications staff with direct access to top management.

MacDonald found GM once again on the firing line on the issue of the safety of its full-size GMC pickup truck. This time GM responded more decisively and effectively than it did in the Nader crisis under Frederick Donner's leadership. Criticism and lawsuits mounted in the early 1990s with the allegations that the pickup truck from 1973 to 1987 models were "rolling firebombs" with exploding gasoline tanks. The criticism and lawsuits were directed at the "side saddle" gas tanks mounted outside the truck chassis, thus lacking the protection of the chassis frame. In this period, plaintiffs' lawyers claimed that GM settled a number of damage cases outside of court, and GM won three jury cases.

Then it was hit with a blockbuster lawsuit in an Atlanta, Georgia, court when the parents of a Snellville, Georgia, 17-year-old Shannon Moseley, who was killed when his 1985 GMC pickup was blindsided by a drunken driver, refused to settle out of court. Testimony indicated that young Moseley died from the flames that quickly enveloped his truck after the crash. The Georgia jury awarded the parents $105 million in collective damages. This record settlement made the nation's headlines and TV shows over the weekend, giving GM another safety blackeye.

---

[1]Anthony G, DeLorenzo died May 15, 1993 of a heart attack in Pontiac, Michigan. After his retirement from GM in 1979, Mr. De Lorenzo worked as a public relations consultant in association with Hill & Knowlton, Inc.

GM had been socked another bruising blow when NBC months earlier had aired an "investigation" into these alleged fire hazards in the GMC pickups. NBC's producers had rigged this investigation by fitting the test truck with toy rocket engines to make certain that truck would burst into flames upon impact.

In a quick and adroit move to take the Georgia jury award off the front pages, General Motors filed a multimillion dollar defamation against the General Electric-owned National Broadcasting Company. Now it was NBC in particular and television news in general that was suffering a blackeye. Caught in the act of faking news, NBC quickly capitulated by having *Dateline* anchors, Jane Pauley and Stone Phillips, read a 4-minute complete apology on their show the next night. Claiming vindication of these charges against its truck, GM then dropped its lawsuit against NBC. It had made its point. In *Newsweek's* words, the rigged demonstration "put a dent in NBC's distinguished journalist tradition." And perhaps it helped restore GM's. Nonetheless, the safety questions, pending lawsuits, and a possible recall by the National Highway Traffic Safety Board—the body created by law as a fallout from GM's blunders in the 1960s—remained to confront General Motors.

NOTES ON SOURCES

Again the Earl Newsom Papers provided the primary source for this chapter. The papers were greatly augmented by Earl Newsom's private journals from the Ford years, provided to us by John R. "Jack" Newsom, his son and former partner. The Ford section was also strengthened by the information and insights provided by two former key public relations officials at Ford—John E. Sattler, head of Ford Motor Company's New York office from 1946 until his retirement in 1980, and by the late Paul Burns, longtime deputy director of public relations at Ford. In additional to providing information, both Sattler and Burns read the Ford section and made helpful corrections and comments. The first draft of the General Motors section was submitted to Anthony De Lorenzo, longtime vice-president of public relations at GM, to afford him an opportunity to present his side of the case in his conflict with the Newsom Company. Professor David L. Lewis offered an inside view of the De lorenzo–Newsom conflict with a letter to me.

Again, the books by David L. Lewis, *The Public Image of Henry Ford,* and by Robert Lacey, *Ford the Men and the Machine,* Little, Brown, and Company, were useful in filling in the context of the Newsom materials. Two substantial magazine articles provided illumination on both Ford and GM public relations: Andre' Fontaine's "Revolution on the Rouge" published in *Collier's,* November 15, 1947; and Dan L. Cordtz, "The Face in the Rear View Mirror," published in *Fortune,* August 1966.

Professor Lewis, who teaches business history at The University of Michigan, offered valuable insights on this chapter out of his study of the Ford Motor Company's public relations and his 7 years in GM's public relations department. His *The Public Image of Henry Ford* is quoted with the permission of the Wayne State University Press.

Robert Lacey's book, *From Ford: The men and the Machine*, is copyrighted by Mr. Lacey and quoted by permission of Little, Brown, and Co., 1986.

Also useful was a long memorandum on the De Lorenzo–Newsom conflict by a General Motors staff member who chose to remain anonymous.

For this chapter, I was helped not only by John E. Sattler's response to my questions but by an advanced look at his memoirs, *Fifty Years Ahead of the News, A Lifetime of Public Relations Experience* before its publication.

Also used for this chapter was the James W. Irwin Papers in the Mass Communications History Center of the State Historical Society of Wisconsin. Scholars will find this a rather thin collection.

Chapter 22

Earl Newsom and the Ford Foundation

The Ford Foundation was created initially on January 25, 1936, when Edsel Ford, son of the founder and then president of the Ford Motor Company, set aside a block of stock to create a foundation for "scientific, educational, and charitable purposes." Thomas C. Reeves, in his history, *Freedom and the Foundation: The Fund for the Republic in the Era of McCarthyism*, suggested that an influential factor in setting up the foundation was the Tax Revenue Act of 1935 that greatly increased U.S. excess profits and inheritance taxes. Reeves asserted that this was the New Deal's way of outflanking Senator Huey Long's cry to "redistribute the wealth." Upon the death of Henry Ford's son, Edsel, the nonvoting Ford Motor Company stock willed to the foundation brought its assets to nearly one half billion dollars, making it the wealthiest foundation in the world. It became in a short time a source of large-scale philanthropy and of great controversy that hurt the Ford Motor Company and posed serious public relations problems for counselor Earl Newsom. With Henry Ford's death in 1947 and settlement of his estate in 1948, young Henry Ford II took control of the foundation as chairman of its board. Of him, Reeves wrote, "Well-meaning, earnest, thirty-one year old Ford, as might be expected of one of America's richest and most powerful men, issued the Foundation's significant pronouncements, posed for publicity pictures, and selected those responsible for planning and administering expenditures. One close associate later recalled that Henry II 'expressed an opinion on every project that was advanced.' "

Because he wanted to be deeply involved and saw a linkage between the foundation's activities and the reputation of the Ford Motor Company—

quite prophetically as things turned out—he asked his trusted counselor, Earl Newsom, to also serve as counselor to the foundation. This assignment involved Newsom heavily in the affairs of the foundation—too heavily in the opinion of a key official, Dr. Robert M. Hutchins, and in the opinion of two Newsom's former associates, Ping Ferry and Martin Quigley. Ferry, who had been working with the Ford company, especially in labor matters, and the Ford family, also became heavily involved in the foundation's beginnings. Ferry and Newsom split in 1954 when Ferry resigned his partnership to become assistant to Dr. Hutchins. Their parting came with what Ferry's termed a "scolding" by Newsom. Sources close to Newsom indicated at the time that their parting was one of mutual interest as the Ford Company's labor relations, in which Ferry was most helpful to Ford, had settled into a calmer time and Ferry's interest in the foundation and its offspring, The Fund for the Republic, had mounted. Quigley had left the Newsom firm in 1950 but resumed his relationship with Newsom in 1951 when Ferry recruited him to become the foundation's public information officer in 1951.

Earl Newsom was quite sensitive to this possible conflict of interest between the company and the foundation and thought about it a great deal before accepting this additional assignment from Henry II. Newsom wrote in his private journal of July 18, 1949:

> We [Newsom and Henry Ford II] discussed propriety of our being retained as a firm by Ford Foundation. I told him that we might face an ethical conflict in the future because the Trustees of the Foundation in fulfilling their public trust might find themselves pitted against Ford management. On the other hand, the public reputation of the Ford Foundation was so closely linked to its own reputation and that of Ford Motor Company that I was extremely reluctant to have his public relations policies in the hands of anybody but ourselves. At the moment my feeling was that we would take the risks of possible future conflict because of the importance of the latter point. I told him, however, that I would like to reserve decision until I had had a chance to examine legal opinion on possible conflict between the two institutions which had been made available to [William T.] Gossett, and which he promised to send me.

In time Newsom and his partner, Arthur Tourtellot, put pressure on the Foundation executives to push Quigley out because they thought he wasn't doing a good job. This led to a bitter break between these two. Unlike Ferry who still bears an ill feeling toward Newsom, Quigley has only affectionate regard for his memory.

Asserting his leadership early, Henry Ford II in the fall of 1948 selected a young San Francisco attorney, H. Rowan Gaither, to chair a blue-ribbon committee to write a charter for the foundation. A year later, Gaither's committee presented Ford with a 125-page report outlining areas for support. This study was undertaken in the rising wave of Red baiting and witch hunting in the late 1940s and early 1950s. Among the philanthropic objectives, the Gaither Committee suggested support "directed to the elimination of restrictions on freedom of thought, inquiry, and expression to the United States." This in the time of the House Un-American Activities Committee [HUAC] that Richard Nixon rode to the U.S. Senate and then to the Vice Presidency, Senator Joseph McCarthy's reckless and groundless accusations against officials in the State Department, the McCarren Internal Security Act, and President Truman's loyalty program for Federal employees. In this volatile, accusatory climate, the foundation, Henry Ford II, and Newsom found public relations pitfalls all across the landscape.

To get the Ford Foundation off to a favorable start in public opinion, the Newsom staff prepared a detailed public relations plan for the announcement of the president of the foundation and for the release of the Gaither Report. The plan called for the announcement of the new president on Monday, October 2 or earlier because "it does not seem to us possible to make any announcement regarding the program of the Foundation without first announcing the president." And to get maximum publicity for the Gaither Report that the Newsom staff regarded as "the most significant and important information which the Foundation has been able to release since it was established," this plan called for release of the Gaither Report on Friday, October 6 "in order to give editors and writers time to study the report." The report was to be sent to newspapers, news magazines, and radio stations on that Friday with a press conference to be held Monday, October 9 at 3:30 p.m. It was to be held at the University Club "in view of the educational nature of the Foundation's activities."

For reasons undiscernible, this plan was not implemented. The aims of the Ford Foundation, as spelled out in detail in the Gaither Report were made public on September 26, according to *The New York Times* of September 27. The selection of Paul G. Hoffman, former president of the Studebaker Corporation and currently chief administrator of the European Recovery Plan, to become president was not announced by Henry Ford II until November 6, 1950, with the appointment to become effective January 1, 1951. Young Ford stoutly asserted that the foundation "could not have found a better person in the world"—a judgment he later regretted and recanted. Young Ford assured Hoffman of his firm support, even if certain projects bring "adverse publicity." Before accepting Ford's offer, Hoffman had made two conditions that Ford agreed to but that were not made public in the announcement. One was that the headquarters would be located in Pasadena, California, where Hoffman made his home because of his wife's health, and, two, that he be permitted to choose his associate directors. Hoffman quickly chose the well-known and controversial educator, Dr. Robert Maynard Hutchins, to be his top associate director.

In his excellent biography of Robert M. Hutchins, *Unseasonable Truths*, Harry S. Ashmore wrote:

> At first, Newsom and his associates saw the Ford Foundation as a prime asset in their campaign to refurbish the company's image. The announcement of Paul Hoffman's appointment as head of the newly enriched philanthropy had met with general approbation in the media, as had the Foundation's initial programs of overseas aid and its bold new approach to education. But the McCarthy era was dawning and the Foundation also had a commitment to support work in the field of Civil liberties and civil rights. It was not long before a covey of right-wing commentators began charging that using the fruits of capitalism to further such a cause was Un-American.

POINTS ON FOUNDATION'S PUBLIC RELATIONS POLICY

To provide a working public relations policy for the foundation, Sidney Olson of the Newsom staff was asked to prepare a memorandum outlining what should be done to insure the foundation's public support. In a memo dated October 4, 1950, addressed to Newsom, Fred Palmer, Ping Ferry, and Charles Moore, Olson wrote:

> The extraordinary reception by the press and public of the Ford Foundation Trustee's Report brings with it public responsibilities of extraordinary dimensions. The very first problem is to become fully aware of the size and shape of those responsibilities. Most editorials thus far might well have borne the subtitle: "Great Expectations." . . . [This] reaction to the announcement means certain things. . . .
>
> First, that the Ford Foundation begins its active career in philanthropy in circumstances completely unlike those attending the birth of all previous foundations. . . .
>
> Seen in this light, the administration of the Foundation program might well re-examine, for example, the manner of its announcements. It seems obvious that its entire information program should be fitted to its own needs, the needs of its own program, rather than to any set of rules of conduct for older foundations. . . . From such arguments it follows that the Foundation should seriously reconsider the recommendation by the study committee that the grants should be announced only by the recipients. . . . Only by a very full information program by the Foundation can the Foundation hope to justify the great expectations aroused and it is obviously important not to let down

these expectations. By announcing its grants, it can show that these are actually parts of a great whole. . . .

The new path is not difficult; it presents problems not of gravity but of mere delicacy and tact. . . . There are even larger reasons, outside the immediate needs and problems of the Foundation itself, for a policy of full information.

Olson and his colleagues soon found to their dismay and pain that "the new path" would be most difficult.

HOFFMAN AND HUTCHINS SET UP SHOP

In setting up shop in Pasadena, Hoffman chose Dr. Hutchins as his top aide; others were Chester A. Davis, an old friend, to handle budget and administrative matters, and H. Rowan Gaither as third associate director — no doubt at the insistence of Henry Ford II, who was determined to keep a hand in the making of foundation policy. For instance, HF II saw to it that the Ford Motor Company public relations office that included a standby suite for him was located in the same building with the foundation's original offices — the Lamston Building at the corner of 51st Street and Madison Avenue.

The attacks on the Ford Foundation from the right-wingers were not long in coming as the foundation began its full-scale operations in 1951. The *Chicago Daily Tribune* started the assault with the headline: "LEFTIST SLANT BEGINS TO SHOW IN FORD TRUST." This attacked centered on Hoffman, who had been director of the European Recovery Program of the U.S. government as the man "who had given away ten billion dollars to foreign countries." Hearst columnists George Sokolsky, Westbrook Pegler, and Fulton Lewis, Jr. quickly joined the chorus. Pegler defined Hoffman "as a hoax without rival in the history of mankind." A right-wing hate group, Constitutional Educational League, began selling 5¢-pamphlets linking the Ford Motor Company with Communism. Others called for boycotts of Ford products. According to Reeves, "Letters from dealers, customers, cranks and others were being received by the sales-conscious Ford Motor Company officials complaining about the transmission of American dollars to foreign 'socialists' and 'Communists.' As early as January, 1952, Ford showed some of this mail to Ping Ferry expressing 'deep concern.'

Thus, Ferry soon found himself in the role of damage control officer. There was no question — the reputation of the Ford Motor Company and that of the foundation were inextricably linked in the public's mind. Thus, Newsom, Ferry, and their associates had a valid concern about the impact of the foundation's actions. Harry Ashmore wrote in *Unseasonable Truths*, "Ferry's initial problem was to allay Henry II's apprehensions about the Foundation's free-wheeling operations, and the only practicable means was to try to put a respectable gloss on the positions taken by Hoffman and Hutchins, so as to minimize controversy. Protecting and improving the Ford family and corporate image, after all, was what the Newsom company was paid to do." In this clamorous time, Westbrook Pegler told Ferry's father, "If I had a son like yours, I'd shoot him."

The feelings of Dr. Hutchins, Ferry, and Quigley that Henry Ford II and Earl Newsom were too concerned with the actions of the foundation and its offspring, The Fund for the Republic, and their impact on the public relationships of the Ford Motor Company must be placed alongside the hard fact that the company and its officials from the top to dealers were being bombarded with criticisms born of the right-wingers' unceasing attacks. In its early years, the foundation was spending the profits made on the Ford Motor Company stock, thus Ford people felt that they had a right to say in what the Foundation was doing. The public made little effort to separate the company and foundation in their mind. Ultimately, the Ford Foundation put the stock on the market and sold it for its $630 million endowment.

MARTIN QUIGLEY JOINS THE FOUNDATION

Martin Quigley who had left the Newsom firm along with Stephen Fitzgerald when Fitzgerald quit to set up his own public relations firm in 1950 came back "into Earl's orbit" later that year when Ping Ferry asked him to become public information officer for the foundation. Dissatisfied that Fitzgerald had not given him a partnership in his new firm, Quigley accepted. He and Hutchins hit it off right away. Ashmore wrote, "The peripatetic Hoffman was away from Pasadena and Hutchins' irreverent humor more or less set the tone at Tureck House [then foundation headquarters]. Quigley's talent for satiric verse matched Hutchins' and his work on the annual report for 1952 promoted the creation of 'Philanthropic Stew,' a poem that cited most of the Foundation's major projects in the jargon the newly-fledged 'philanthropoids' seemed unable to avoid." Ashmore continued, "Despite the fun and games, a great deal was accomplished."

Early on confusion developed as to who and which office—foundation headquarters in New York or Pasadena or the Newsom office—would release foundation news. On May 8, 1951, Russell M. Hart, on the Ford News Bureau staff, wrote a letter to Leggett Brown, manager of the bureau, laying out an agenda for a Ford regional public relations staff meeting on May 22–23 and included this item:

> 10. *Ford Foundation*. The Ford Foundation has become even more complicated recently so we think a rather thorough discussion on how we should handle future inquiries would be helpful. The situation is a little confusing right now because we have found that although we understand quite well that we should forward all inquiries for information, funds, etc. to the New York office of the Ford Foundation, some of the people in that office are not aware that we should do so. For example, Miss Kay Smalleried, an associate in the New York office, recently suggested that our office answer some of the inquiries about the Foundation. . . . She later called us, after checking with the Newsom people, and told us that we should forward all inquiries to the New York office, regardless of nature.

Hart added, "For our own protection, perhaps a better clarification of the whole relationship should be made."

This situation was complicated by Henry Ford II's continued involvement in and concerns about the foundation's courses. Ashmore wrote:

> Henry II always insisted that his concerns were with the Foundation's management style, not with the ideology of its most conspicuous executives. He complained about Hoffman's frequent absences from Pasadena and the influence this conferred on Hutchins, whose two Education-oriented funds were now receiving more than half the allocated money. . . . Ford said "I guess we gave it to him because he was the fastest talker. But I didn't like the idea of being a rubber stamp for his ideas."

Earl Newsom's and Ping Ferry's task of mediation between the foundation and Ford in order to promote a favorable reputation for both the foundation and the company was made more difficult when Mr. and Mrs. Henry Ford visited Pasadena. Ferry thought much of the friction between Ford and Hutchins could be traced to Mrs. Ford's concerns. Ashmore wrote, "Traveling to Pasadena with the Fords for one of their first state visits, he found Anne was being taken in by the anti-Hutchins propaganda that was appearing in the right-wing press. He assured her that when she got to know him she would be satisfied that the suggestion that he held pro-Communist views was absurd." At a cocktail reception Hutchins made matters much worse. In his book, *Ford: The Men and Machines*, Lacey recounted this conversation:

> "How nice," she said, flashing her brightest smile, "to meet someone who knows something about education. Henry certainly doesn't." She was very hopeful, she said, that thanks to the presence of Hutchins at the Foundation,

"we'll get some attention to the thing that I am interested in . . . the problems of Catholic education, mainly in the city of Detroit." Hutchins would later recount, with glee, that he told her, "education should be left to educators." For good measure, he gave Mrs. Ford, a devout Catholic, a lecture on birth control.

A former public relations staffer told me that she then left the room in tears. Ferry remembered that this was the "kiss of death for Bob and Paul." Martin Quigley quickly recognized that Anne Ford's hostility toward Hutchins and her powerful influence over her husband would be a major source of trouble for the foundation staff.

Troubles continued to pile up for Ford and the foundation and their public relations officials caught in the well-known middle. On April 4, 1952, the Republican-dominated House of Representatives in the 82nd Congress created a 7-man committee and authorized it to spend $75,000 to investigate possible un-American activities of foundations. At Newsom's counsel, a public opinion survey on the attitude of Congress toward the foundation was made. This survey found that the hostility to Ford was centered in the Republican Old Guard and that a few congressmen feared the financing of integrationist groups and that criticisms were not aimed at Ford himself but rather at "internationalism" and the unorthodox views of Hutchins and two other foundation employees.

Henry Ford II, Hoffman, and Hutchins were summoned by Committee Chairman Eugene "Goober" Cox of Georgia to explain why the foundation should not be considered subversive. All three came off well. Ping Ferry accompanied Hutchins to the hearing and counseled him not to get bogged down in specifics but to "take them to the mountaintop." Hutchins did. In his oral history held in the foundation's archives, Ferry recalled, "He did take them up the mountain, so much so that Murray Marder of the *Washington Post* was in tears when he finished. It was that effective. And Cox came down afterward and invited Hutchins to go on a turkey shoot with him. He said, 'Ah really don't like anything I've heard about you, Doctor Hutchins, but you're a marvelous man.' "

Cox's Committee gave the foundation a clean bill of health.

Paul Hoffman was eased out of the foundation presidency in February 1953 for ostensible reason that the board had decided to relocate the foundation headquarters in New York, and Hoffman couldn't leave Pasadena because of his wife's health. As Ashmore wrote, "The announcement made by Henry Ford II on February 4, 1953, was designed to save face all around but it had a palpable hollow ring." Hutchins continued to occupy the now nearly empty Tuerck House as an associate director with nothing to direct. Isolated and no longer an effective voice in the foundation's affairs, it became even more lonely for him in April when his fellow bard was put out of his job by the Newsom partners.

QUIGLEY FORCED OUT

The precursor of Quigley's ouster can be found in a memorandum to Newsom dated February 10, 1953, from Arthur Tourtellot entitled. "The Present Situation at the Ford Foundation, based on our conversation of February 9." Tourtellot concluded:

1. Organization

The chief deficiency in the Ford Foundation is organizational. It is a half-billion dollar corporation with no clear line of authority or responsibility in keeping its own house in order or organizing its own affairs. It has only a very loose and *ex tempore* divisional structure. It has no smoothly flowing internal communication system. . . . There are insufficient and divergent operational methods. . . .

3. Public Relations

The chief public relations function of a foundation is to provide the public with full, precise and up-to-date information on what it is doing with quasi-public funds. Its program should consist in both originating material so that it does not conflict in timing or emphasis or content with other material it originates and in responding fully to the queries of the press or the public without procrastination, circuitous routing or weaseling.

The Foundation has two problems here: the first is to have a policy, and a more adequate system of internal reporting, for the purpose of sending out more information; the second is to have sufficiently orderly channels to keep a central information office abreast of what is going on in order to answer the ordinary request for information. . . . The information office now gets what it can on an *ad hoc* demand basis as matters come up. . . . This situations is, I think, a powder keg, capable of exploding at any time that a responsible newspaperman asks the wrong question. . . . The public relations of the Foundation have been thus far relatively good because of the immense prestige of being the largest supporter of good works and because of the general loftiness of its aims. But the Foundation's public relations are headed for certain trouble if, as its operations multiply, it is not better supported by a disciplined internal organization that knows exactly what is being done, who is doing it, how far it has progressed and what it's all about. . . .

The major hurdle in improving the organizational efficiency of the Foundation is cleared with the decision to close Pasadena. Nevertheless, the organization is still held together by paper clips and Scotch tape.

This blistering memo was undoubtedly conveyed in essence to H. Rowan Gaither, now president and CEO of the Ford Foundation, put there by Henry Ford II. The next step was to ease Martin Quigley out of his job as public information officer and replace him with a person more qualified in the eyes of Newsom and Tourtellot. Perhaps Quigley's closeness to the now-isolated Hutchins was a factor in this maneuvering. Newsom broke the news to Quigley early in April, prompting this response in a personal memo to Newsom, dated April 24, 1953:

Dear Earl

During our last conversation, just two weeks ago, you told me that you were recommending that I be superseded as Information Officer. You gave me to understand that Rowan was accepting your recommendation and that Wally [Nielsen] had been selected as my successor. As a result I wrote out my resignation and handed it to Rowan, as I told you I was going to. In view of our conversation, I was surprised and heartened when Rowan asked me not to resign and expressed the hope that I would continue as Information Officer. I summarized my understanding of my conversation with him and those I subsequently had with Mac [George McBundy] and Wally in a letter I wrote Rowan on April 16.

I am familiar with the fact that you have since once again told Rowan and Wally that it would be a mistake to permit me to continue in my present position. I think you should know, too, that a friend of mine has reported to me that the word is going around our gossipy trade in New York that "Quigley has done a lousy job, and Earl is getting rid of him." This hurts me personally and professionally, of course, and I should think that it might add to the pain you told me you have already suffered over the fact that some people think you were the hatchet man in a couple of other cases. . . .

Newsom replied coldly in a letter dated April 27, "Dear Quig: There is no excuse for your writing to me such a letter as yours of April 24. Earl."

After the earlier conversation with Newsom in which Quigley was told that he was being superseded as information officer of the foundation, Quigley wrote Gaither on April 16:

In order to prevent further misunderstanding, I should like to write down what I learned from our conversation Friday. It is that Earl misunderstood your intentions and that he was not authorized to tell me that I had been demoted and to suggest that my resignation was expected unless I was willing to continue in an inferior capacity. My understanding is that you would like to have me continue in my present position with my present authority. . . . Even if my understanding about these matters is the same as yours, the fact that Earl has said that he did not recommend me for the job makes me doubt that it would be wise to remain. I think I might feel uneasy, and I should not want you to have to defend your confidence in me to anyone.

In a letter of May 1, to his former boss and friend, Robert Hutchins, Quigley confided, "Up to this point, Rowan has given me no indication that he had received my letter to him or the copy of my letter to Earl. I had interpreted this silence as wrathful displeasure, which was okay with me. But no, not at all. He was most friendly, and seemed, I thought, a little admiring." Nonetheless, Quigley saw only trouble ahead and resigned as of June 1. He accepted the offer of a partnership in Fleishman–Hillard, a St. Louis public relations agency. In his May 1 letter to Hutchins, whom he addressed as "Bold Robert," Quigley expressed this view of Newsom's involvement in the foundation:

> In all this, I was aware that he was impressed by my definition of the Information Office in my letter to him, in which I had pointed out that it was not its function to advise on what effect accurate information about programs and personnel might have on public opinion. Actually Earl's troubles and his malignancy[1] were caused by his belief that he could transfer the "behavioralist" concept that works well in industry—to be thought of as a nice guy, you have to act like one (though not necessarily be one)—to the Foundation. Once he was involved in what the Foundation should do, he became a menace to the very existence of the Foundation, and I think that Rowan now understands this. Although I took another shot at Earl on the Fund for the Republic thing this week, I do not intend to pick any fights with him.

Exit Quigley.

Quigley was replaced as public information officer by Porter McKeever, an experienced diplomat and public affairs officer. McKeever was, in all probability, the choice of Henry Ford II who came to know McKeever when he was serving as director of information for the U.S. Mission to the United Nations, on which Ford served for a term. McKeever later left the foundation to serve in a similar capacity for the Council for Economic Development. McKeever, who had a distinguished career and was the author of a biography of Adlai Stevenson on whose campaign staff he served in 1952, died March 3, 1992.

To back up for a moment, in August 1951, Dr. Hutchins had pushed Area II from the Gaither Report charting a course for the foundation onto the agenda with a study report innocuously titled "The Strengthening of Democracy" and proposed creation of a Fund for Democratic Freedoms. The liberal Ferry became an enthusiastic supporter of the proposal because of his sympathy for mistreated minorities. Ferry drew up an unrequested

---

[1]Newsom did not have cancer at this time. Quigley was using the word as a metaphor.

memorandum that he distributed in mid-September to HF II and others to bolster support for what became the Fund for the Republic and to head off fear of controversy:

> Such a policy is not a conflict with the real interest of the Ford Motor Company, although it may sometimes prove irritating to some of its officials, and may embarrass, temporarily, members of the Ford family. In the long run it will bring more credit to the Ford name than the easy and innocuous course of making impressive contributions to established activities or undertaking programs that cannot arouse suspicion or opposition. Here it should be remembered that the reputation of the Ford Motor Company largely centers around Henry Ford's lifelong preoccupation with experimenting and pioneering ventures.

In his history of the fund, Reeves wrote that "Ford and the trustees at least appeared affable in the face of this call to arms and seemed to have a guarded interest in undertaking such bold responsibilities." That October Hoffman presented the proposal to the foundation board that voted an initial grant of $1 million to establish the Fund for the Republic. Reliable sources indicated that the idea of the separate fund was initiated by Ferry and enthusiastically endorsed by Hutchins, not the other way round.

FORD DEFENDS FOUNDATION TO HIS MANAGEMENT

Because of the increasing flak being fired at the foundation and the newly formed Fund for the Republic, Newsom and his partners counseled Ford that it would be wise for him to explain the foundation's purposes and policies to the Ford Company management, which was increasingly concerned about what effect this critical drumbeat was having on the sale of Ford products. The meeting was held March 4, 1954, and followed a script prepared by the Newsom staff. The script called for a 5-minute introduction by Mr. Ford, who then would introduce Gaither as the one who presided over the study committee and "who is now President and Director of the Foundation." Ford told his executives:

> Since the Foundation is a public trust, I believe an understanding of it is important to men and women everywhere. With equal conviction, I believe that we members of the Ford Motor Company's management have a special interest in learning about the Foundation. In the final analysis, the results of our efforts — the profits we make — now provide the Foundation with most of the funds it invests in human progress. . . .

Today we have thousands of foundations in this country. But only about seventy of them have assets of ten million dollars or more and, of these, the Ford Foundation is the biggest. Besides its size, the Ford Foundation is unique in two other important aspects: its aim and its scope. It is here that the Foundation's activities have been misrepresented from time to time. . . .

I know—and I am sure that you do—that there has been so criticism of the Foundation. Much of it is unwarranted; some of it has been malicious. For instance, here is the voice of a Soviet spokesman. . . .

The Soviet spokesman, Georgi Sakskin, was criticizing the foundation for its support of projects "in the explosive Middle East, in India, in Southeast Asia, the Far East, in Western Europe." Pointing to a world map, Ford said, "as you can see, our overseas program forms a ring of democratic efforts along the sensitive border of the Soviet Iron Curtain. There is good reason for Russia to be sore." Ford did not mention the heavy flood of domestic criticisms. He defended the foundation's policy of finding and attacking "the basic causes of human problems rather than attempt to relieve the disastrous consequences of those problems." Gaither then outlined the five areas of the foundation's present activities.

NEWSOM'S 1954 ASSESSMENT

In a memorandum dated December 3, 1954, addressed to President and Director Gaither Earl Newsom assessed the foundation's public relations after its first 5 years since acquiring major resources. Newsom wrote:

The Foundation was widely publicized in 1950 as the most massive philanthropy in the history of this country. It linked a name already familiar to every community in the land with an unprecedented promise of good works. . . .

After five years, there can be no doubt that the Ford Foundation has failed to make an impact anywhere near commensurate with the great resources or the giant interest that its enlargement provoked in 1950. It has failed to penetrate to the American people, to average communities across the country. It is at best a great, unknown organization operating in the clouds, at worst a conglomeration of wordy dreamers. What are the reasons for this lack of general confidence and support? They must grow from the things the Foundation does—from its program. . . . Many of the projects have seemed nebulous, or highly theoretical, or even hair-splittingly academic.

It is too late for the Foundation to go back and to do it the other way—that is, first to get known to the people with a program readily comprehended by them and then move on to more remote and highly specialized things. But it is not too late to recognize that the Foundation is in fact a mystery to most Americans, and to bring its program into balance.

The Foundation can do this logically enough. It has reached a phase in its early history that is hospitable to a shift in emphasis. It has established and set free the Fund for the Republic to take the major role in Area II, and it could withdraw from that field for some years.

Newsom concluded that "the Foundation never gained the strong public confidence that it must have to be effective," then asserted, "The Foundation can rectify this situation by studying human needs from below and coming up with a program that bears immediate fruit in thousands of communities."

Undoubtedly memos such as this from Newsom led Dr. Hutchins, Ping Ferry, and Martin Quigley to their conclusion that he had a limited vision of what the Foundation could accomplish and was overly concerned about its reputation and troubles impacting on the Ford Motor Company.

Little wonder that many persons inside and outside the foundation thought Newsom's influence was behind funding the Fund for the Republic with a terminal grant to get the controversial project that were bringing the criticism to the foundation, the fund, and the Ford company out of the foundation and thus disassociated with the Ford name. The evidence indicated that the fund was the creation of Robert Hutchins and Ping Ferry for nobler reasons. Hutchins later told associates at the fund, "W. H. Ferry and I worked out the plans for the Fund for the Republic." In commenting on the separation from the foundation, Hutchins wryly observed, "The Fund was not only wholly independent of the Foundation, it was wholly disowned." Ashmore thought that many of Hoffman's critics saw this, with malice aforethought, as giving the chairman his "severance pay." This was nonsense because the chairmanship was a nonsalaried position. Hutchins did need the salary the new job paid.

THE FUND FOR THE REPUBLIC: EXIT FERRY

The Fund for the Republic was chartered in the State of New York as an educational corporation "to defend and advance the principles of the Declaration of Independence and the Constitution." The fund was incorporated in 1952 and began operations in 1953. The fund's first president was Senator Clifford P. Case of New Jersey, who resigned in 1954 to run for the U.S. Senate. Hoffman and Hutchins, now out of the foundation, took over as chairman of the board of directors and president respectively. The Fund for the Republic was established as an autonomous body with its own board of directors.

In January 1953, the planning committee of the fund agreed on these as the primary concerns of the fund's grants. These were listed in order of importance:

1. The size, nature and location of the international Communist menace.
2. Restrictions upon academic freedom.
3. Due process and equal protection of the laws.
4. The protection of the rights of minorities.
5. Censorship, boycotting and blacklisting activities by private groups.
6. The principle of guilt by association.

In February 1954, with Henry Ford's approval, the foundation made a terminal grant of $15 million to the Fund for the Republic and in effect totally disassociating it from the Ford Foundation and the Ford name.

This charter, when implemented, was bound to bring public relations storms aplenty. The Fund for the Republic was in historian Eric Goldman's words, "born in a time of vast impatience, a turbulent bitterness, a rancor akin to revolt . . . a strange rebelliousness, quite without parallel in the history of the United States." In fact, it was this emotion-charged public climate that gave rise to the need for such a program.

Hutchins, in accepting the presidency of the fund, agreed that the fund's headquarters should remain in New York City but stipulated that he would maintain his residence in Pasadena. Ashmore wrote, "To make this arrangement work he had to have a deputy to run the day-to-day operation at the main office, one who shared his views and had the moral stamina to take the heat that was bound to come. His choice was Ping Ferry, who had become a wholehearted convert to the cause and had openly sided with Hutchins in his standoff with the Foundation, with the result that he, like Quigley, was at odds with Earl Newsom." In a diary for his children and grandchildren, Ferry wrote, "EN & Co. split also, decided to join RMH and Fund as Executive Vice President, hurt by ungracious farewell from Newsom. Stormy passage begins."

Ferry's terse "stormy passage begins" was prophetic. He knew what he was getting into. He inevitably became the point man for all those on the Right whom he identified as natural enemies of the fund's objectives. Again to quote from Ferry's oral history, "The American Legion, the House Un-American Activities Committee and McCarthy, the Hearst papers, and [Westbrook] Pegler and Fulton Lewis, Jr. . . . they were all ranged up there on the horizon waiting for us to come out."

Ferry's liberal beliefs, his combative nature, his deep devotion to civil liberties coupled with his growing irritation with Newsom's "meddling" in foundation affairs led Ferry to accept the fund vice-presidency at half the partner share amounting to perhaps as much as $75,000 he was drawing each year from the Newsom firm. He reported for duty at the fund's New York headquarters on July 1, 1954. Newsom's records indicate that his salary figure was not that high.

FRANK KELLY NAMED VICE PRESIDENT FOR PUBLIC RELATIONS

The fund board set up a Temporary Committee on Information to conduct a search for a public relations vicepresident. The committee was chaired by pollster Elmo Roper, a board member. It quickly zeroed in on Frank K. Kelly, then a staff member at the Stephen Fitzgerald agency. Ashmore wrote, "Hutchins treated journalists with a cool detachment relieved by flashes of mordant wit, which alienated as many as it charmed, and Ferry often became truculent when crossed. Kelly, a rotund, effusive, sentimental Irishman, enveloped reporters in a bubble-bath of flattering attention." Kelly had started his career as a reporter on his hometown paper, The *Kansas City Star*, and then joined the Associated Press in New York. He was one of the first Nieman Fellows at Harvard—as was Fitzgerald. Kelly had also served as an aide to Senator Scott Lucas, the Democratic leader of the Senate, and had also written speeches for President Harry Truman, thus, he had good Washington connections.

In his memoirs, *Court of Reason*, Kelly recounted:

> My first meeting with him [Hutchins] had been in December, 1955, when he had come to the offices of Stephen Fitzgerald & Co. at 575 Madison Avenue in New York. He had outlined the Fund's problems frankly and had told Fitzgerald and me what he had planned to recommend to the board. He told us that he expected new assaults when the reports on blacklisting, the testimony of ex-communist witnesses, postal censorship and fear in education were made public. . . . Hutchins reiterated . . . what he had said to the board. "If we operate in terms of tomorrow's headlines we will be permitting the Fund's enemies to manage it."

Then Kelly added, "When Hutchins telephoned me in January, 1956, to tell me that he had recommended the use of the Fitzgerald Company as consulting agency and my election as an officer of the Fund, I was filled with a mixture of joy and trepidation. I was pleased to be associated with Hutchins. . . . But I was concerned from the beginning about my relationship with W. H. Ferry."

Ashmore agreed with Kelly that he was more an appointment of the board than of Hutchins and Ferry. Ashmore said there was no doubt that Kelly was the board's man. Kelly said, "I realized that . . . I had been brought into the picture because there were some members of the board who wanted a public information officer who could keep Hutchins and Ferry from engaging in imprudent action."

On President Hutchins's recommendation, the board approved the appointment of Frank Kelly at a meeting on March 12, 1956. On March 22, Hutchins proposed a reorganization of the fund's New York Office; Frank Kelly was put in complete command of the fund's preparation and distribution of information. Also the board appropriated money to further the preparation of a full-scale public relations program under the direction of a new staff member, James Real. A bimonthly bulletin was discussed and approved in principle. The Stephen Fitzgerald firm was retained on a month-to-month basis as the outside consultant.

After his first session with the full board, Kelly wrote in his memoirs:

> After the meeting several of the directors asked me to send frequent communications to the board. [Dean Erwin N.] Griswold told me that he would expect to hear from me on all major issues that arose.

> I promised the directors that I would keep in close contact with all of them. I did not agree to make private communications to any of them. I did not regard myself as an agent for the members of the board who sought to remove Hutchins and Ferry.

As an example of members of the board looking to Kelly to keep Hutchins and Ferry from engaging in "imprudent actions," Board Chairman Paul Hoffman privately asked Kelly if he would persuade Hutchins to recant his statement that there were circumstances under which he would hire a Communist. This statement had provided more fuel for the enemies of Hutchins and the fund to pour on the fire of protest. In his book, Kelly recalled that when he told Hutchins this, Hutchins took him to dinner at the Yale Club, and after dinner Kelly made the request. Hutchins replied, "I won't recant." Inside Kelly was happy that Hutchins had stood his ground

QUESTIONS ON THE FOUNDATION-FUND RELATIONSHIP

At the height of the attacks on the Fund for the Republic in mid-1955, Arthur Tourtellot in a memo dated September 10, 1955, with copies to Newsom, Palmer, Lydgate, and John Newsom, raised the question of what the foundation's relationship should be to the troubled fund. Tourtellot had been asked to chair a committee "to recommend for consideration of the Trustees' Committee a suitable action for the Foundation to take with regard to the present program and operations of the Fund." The committee's charter did not include "action for the Ford Company to take in its own interest or for the Fund for the Republic to take in its own interest." First Tourtellot reviewed the attacks on the fund:

> During the last month the Fund for the Republic appears to be the focus of considerable critical attention, including some repeated attacks that have the appearance of a campaign, specifically, Fulton Lewis, Jr., David Lawrence and the American Legion. The attacks thus far have been against the program of the Fund, the Board and management of the Fund and the purposes of the Fund. The attacks are not new, but follow pretty closely of those in the spring of 1953 when the American Legion's bi-monthly newsletter opened fire on the Fund. . . .

> We have all agreed that the Foundation cannot possibly dismiss the Fund as of no concern to it. We are seeking an honorable and realistic attitude for the Foundation to adopt with regard to the Fund. . . . I believe that the Foundation must be able to produce a record that it has followed closely the Fund's activities and that it has assumed the same moral responsibility for the Fund that it assumed in the formal answer to the Reece committee dated July 16, 1954.

Tourtellot's committee suggested that the chairman of the foundation board appoint two members of the board to meet with the board of directors of the fund. He wrote:

> It seems to me that the posture of these committee members would be that the Foundation has, from time to time in the past, reviewed the activities of its subsidiary funds in order to determine whether the Foundation is fully realizing its opportunities in a given area. This meeting should result in a report to the Foundation Board on two points:

> 1. What are the practices of the Fund's Board with regard to the approval of grants, and
> 2. What is the degree of confidence of the Fund's Board in the present management.

Tourtellot concluded, "It seems to me that the Foundation should, in the case of any grantee, be concerned with whether or not the active program of the grantee tends of carry out or distort the objectives for which the grant is made."

That a Newsom partner was asked to chair this committee along with two foundation staff members makes clear the deep involvement of the Newsom Company in the Ford Foundation's policies and actions. This involvement surfaced again in the fund's handling of the controversial Cogley Report.

THE COGLEY BLACKLISTING REPORT

One storm of protest over what the critics and some board members construed as "imprudent actions" arose over the John Cogley study of the blacklisting of artists accused of leftist leanings or of being Communists by the major networks and Hollywood producers before Kelly came aboard the fund ship. In September 1954, Dr. Hutchins hired John Cogley, a graduate of Loyola University and then editor of the liberal Catholic journal, *Commonwealth*, as director of the blacklisting study. The 2-volume study was completed in late December and in January was presented to Elmo Roper's committee on public relations. According to Reeves, "The volumes bulged with case histories of careers destroyed by inaccurate reporting of political sympathies; of professionals pressured into conformity or silence in order to get or hold jobs. Named in the report as powerful influences in 'clearing' seeking re-employment were several of the Fund's most profound antagonists." George Sokolsky, among others, had followed the Cogley study with avid interest and was waiting in the bushes to attack Hutchins and the fund.

On January 23, 1956, Roper's committee turned the Cogley study over to Earl Newsom. Ferry sent it to Newsom with a note, "This is a terrible chore to drop in your lap. But such is my respect and Elmo's for your judgement on such touchy matters that we agreed that nothing would be done until we had some expression from you." Reeves thought," If Newsom and his associates agreed to publication of the $100,000 report, there would be room later for considerably less adverse criticism from sensitive sources surrounding – perhaps including Henry Ford II." A week later Newsom replied to Ferry that he found the Cogley report "thorough, objective, and perceptive in delineating a deplorable situation." But he recommended that it not be made public, arguing, "It seems to me that such fears as we are dealing with here are overcome only by the normal evolutionary processes in the kind of democratic society we are committed to develop in this country. It is possible to give these evolutionary processes direction in some cases, but attempts to accelerate them usually result in setting back progress."

Newsom decided that the Cogley report was too hot to handle, undoubtedly another instance that irked Ferry and brought him to the conclusion that Newsom failed to see the things the fund could accomplish in furthering democracy. The buck was then passed back to the board of

directors. The board was faced with a tough decision because the Cogley
study was part of the fund's original mandate. The study had been widely
publicized, and the press was clamoring for copies. In February, the board
voted to ask Cogley to reduce the 2-volume report to 700 pages and to
submit it for review to representatives of the entertainment industry and the
professions for "the purpose of (a) of catching possible inaccuracies, and (b)
obtaining a statement or statements which might be used in connection with
the report." Cogley agreed but threatened to publish the report elsewhere if
there were further conditions. The issue was forced when the House
Un-American Activities Committee's staff demanded copies of the Cogley
report prior to publication. The board voted with several dissents that the
study be published. It appeared June 24, 1956, and 4 days later, Cogley was
subpoenaed to appear before the HUAC committee in closed session. This
was the beginning of a violent storm of controversy that broke around the
heads of Hutchins, Cogley, and the fund. By this time, Frank Kelly had
come aboard, and he used his political connections in Washington to
smooth the waves of criticism in Congress and in the press as much as he
could.

THE KIDDER MEADE MEMO

Another possible source of the friction between Earl Newsom Ping Ferry
could have been the memorandum, dated March 14, 1956—just as Frank
Kelly was taking charge of the fund's public relations. E. Kidder Meade, Jr.
wrote Newsom on "Fund for the Republic Grants to Expedite Desegregation in the South." Staffer Meade wrote Newsom:

> It is my understanding that this weekend the Fund's Board will consider a
> number of substantial grants for the purpose of "expediting" desegregation in
> the South. The funds, I am told, are not intended for improving racial
> relations but for immediate measures to accelerate integration.
>
> Having followed the segregation issue extremely closely I am disturbed by the
> Fund's plan for the following reasons:
>
> 1. Since the Virginia referendum in December and its constitutional conven-
>   tion last month, there has been a marked change in the South's attitude
>   toward compliance with the Supreme Court decision. The climate of
>   watchful waiting . . . has changed to one of open defiance. . . .
> 2. The South bears deep resentment to what it considers interference from
>   "outsiders," namely the "northern agitators for speed." The resentment is
>   growing more bitter. . . .
> 3. Conservative, middle-of-the-road and even liberal newspapers sensing the
>   temper of the debate, are beginning to counsel moderation. . . .

4. Granting of funds by the Fund for the Republic for the express purpose of expediting desegregation would be received, I suggest, with resentment and hostility throughout the South, both by the segregationists and integrationists, particularly if those funds were to be given to the NAACP for litigation purposes. (The NAACP is generally despised in the South among white people.)

In short, I cannot see any good coming out of these grants and I can foresee considerable harm, (including harm to the Ford Motor Company), and I don't think that the Fund can reason that since church groups are the main beneficiaries the project will be "safe in the arms of Jesus."

There is no evidence that Earl Newsom or his partners took these biased views of a Southerner seriously or passed them on to the Fund officials. If this were done, it would further reinforce Dr. Hutchins' view that Newsom viewed the foundation and the Fund for the Republic "as extensions of the Ford Motor Company public relations." Ferry fully, vociferously agreed with Hutchins' view. The concern of the Newsom organization and of Henry Ford II, understandably, was not in using these as instruments to promote Ford but rather to head off the backlash that controversial projects brought in this era of Communist hysteria.

One of the first steps Frank Kelly took as vice-president of the fund was to request that he be permitted to see the mail the company and Henry Ford II had received protesting grants of the foundation and the Fund for the Republic. Kelly asked Joseph Lyford of the fund staff to go through the files in Ford's New York office. Kelly reported, "Most of the letters came from two southeastern states, Alabama and Mississippi; most of them had racist slurs. Many did not refer to the Fund but expressed rage over the appearance of black people on the Ed Sullivan show, then sponsored by Ford." The letters did not provide any substantial reasons for Ford's turn against the fund. But turn against it he did.

Chairman Francis Walter of the HUAC Committee announced that a full-dress hearing on the affairs of the fund would begin early in 1956. Before that Henry Ford II had written Chairman Hoffman expressing strong objections to some of the fund's actions. Hoffman sent Ford a conciliatory letter and urged him to meet informally with the board before making any public statement. Hoffman's plea was ignored. On December 6, Fulton Lewis made public a letter from Ford to a New York American Legion Post in which he said, "Despite the fact that I have no legal right to intervene in the affairs of the Fund for the Republic, I have exercised my right as a private citizen to question the manner in which the Fund has attempted to achieve its stated objectives. Some of its actions, I feel, have been dubious in character and inevitably have led to charges of poor judgment."

Ford was responding not so much to his mail as to the heavy drumbeat of criticism from the right. According to Ashmore, "For months the chorus led by Lewis had been demanding that he issue a statement clarifying his position on the Fund and the *coup de grace* was delivered in an open letter to Ford from William F. Buckley, Jr., reproduced in a full page of his *National Review*." Buckley put the question to HF II, "What is your own judgment on these activities of the Fund that are at public issue?" Hutchins and the fund were now under assault from all sides. Just what role Earl Newsom had in this in his counsel to Ford and to the foundation was not revealed in the Newsom Papers.

The controversial grants were made, and Frank Kelly argued in the *Bulletin for the Study of Democratic Institutions*, dated November 1963, after asking the rhetorical question: "Was the Fund's grant-making program a success?" that:

> On balance, yes. It is doubtful, for example, that the Southern Regional Council would have survived without the Fund's support, and the race crisis in the South would have deteriorated still further without the agency's moderating influence. Important reforms, which ended some of the most flagrant abuses, can be traced directly to the impact of the reports on blacklisting and on the federal loyalty–security program, and other publications and activities for the Fund. Cumulatively, the Fund's program was a major factor in restoring calm and perspective in a time when the individual rights of all Americans were threatened.

A more objective observer concurred. Thomas Reeves summarized his evaluation of the Fund for the Republic in his book as follows:

> No corporate body during the years of the Fund's first phase even approached its efforts in what Hutchins accurately called "uncharted and dangerous territory." Fear was the great preventative. The most opulent foundations chose to ignore what were, in many ways, the most serious domestic problems of the fifties. No organization went beyond its [professed] belief in equal opportunities to pour hundreds of thousands of dollars into channels promoting racial equality. None tried as hard as the Fund to keep serious conversation alive. Dr. Hutchins is guilty of a rare understatement by asserting simply that the Fund for the Republic "did as much as any organization in those years to expand civil liberties."

THE CENTER FOR THE STUDY OF DEMOCRATIC INSTITUTIONS

By 1957, the fund had spent more than two thirds of its resources; this forced a reassessment of its function and its future. The board and a group of distinguished consultants concluded that the activities in which it had engaged dealt only with disturbing *symptoms* rather than with the basic issues affecting the American society. The program was redirected into an effort to "clarify the issues involved in maintaining a free and just society under the strikingly new political, social, economic and technological conditions of the second half of the twentieth century, and to advance the understanding of these issues by promoting discussion of them." Thus, the Basic Issues Program became the core activity of the newly created Center for the Study of Democratic Institutions.

The board chose to relocate the center from New York to Santa Barbara, California, for two reasons: one of economy and the other of function. According to the center *Bulletin*, "The Basic Issues Program required an operation that has been linked to that of a small university without students." Santa Barbara was also chosen because California supporters of the fund offered to make a substantial contribution toward purchase of a suitable facility. A final reason was that this location made possible an informal working relationship with the University of California through its Santa Barbara campus. Thus, the fund and the center for all practical purposes became one. The move to Santa Barbara was made on September 1.

Ferry was chosen to head the center's first major study, one on the American corporation. The study, *The Corporation and the Economy*, was published on October 26, 1959, and was divided into two sections. The opening section entitled "Notes" was by Ferry in which he declared that the large industrial corporation, although it had become one of the most powerful and pervasive institutions in American life and had attained the status of a 'private government,' did not have a clear understanding of its own goals." Frank Kelly sent a 15-page news release to editors and broadcasters throughout the United States with extensive excerpts from the report. Kelly knew that the media wouldn't use such a long release but sent it to demonstrate that the center participants had widely divergent views.

Kelly, in his *Court of Reason*, wrote, "In 1959 and 1960 a stream of controversial publications demonstrated that Hutchins and his colleagues had not retreated into a sanctuary. . . . The Center managed to disturb almost as many people as the Fund had done. To members of the Birch Society and other right-wing citizens it became known as 'Little Moscow on Eucalyptus Hill' because of its many criticisms of what was happening in America life."

FERRY BREAKS WITH HUTCHINS IN BITTER PARTING

Our interest in the center ends with the break between Dr. Hutchins and Ping Ferry, who had been staunch allies in the battle for civil liberties and decency in a most difficult time. At the center board's annual meeting to approve the 1969–1970 budget, Hutchins presented a reorganization plan that would place control of academic policy in a "faculty" made up of fellows who would approve all academic appointments. The board approved, and Hutchins initiated a plan under which he appointed the first two fellows and the two selected a third—a process continued until one was a unanimous choice. Ferry did not make the cut. On May 17, Hutchins wrote Ferry a letter that hit him across the heart. After explaining the elaborate process through which the new governing Fellows had been chosen, Hutchins wrote Ferry, "I am sorry to have to tell you . . . in view of our long association and all you have done for the Fund and the Center this is a very unwelcome duty. If you want to stay, I'll be glad to take up with the fellows any ideas you have about what you might do. If you want to leave, I'll guarantee financial arrangements satisfactory to you"

Ferry refused to accept the terms offered by Hutchins, and on November 16, 1969, he filed a lawsuit in Santa Barbara County charging that the fund had breached and terminated his contract illegally. He asked for general damages of $263,000 and exemplary damages of $400,000. The upshot of all this was that a year later Ferry accepted an out-of-court settlement of $100,000 spread over eight years. It was a bitter end to an exciting, challenging, and controversial career in which he had accomplished much for the betterment of society. To quote that fearless commentator, Elmer Davis, "This nation was not founded by cowards; nor will it be defended by cowards."

BACK TO THE FOUNDATION AND ENCO

A year after his assessment of the foundation's first 5 years in the memo to Gaither, Newsom followed up with a proposal to get the foundation favorably known in communities across the nation. In a confidential memo to Henry Ford II, Newsom proposed "that the Ford Foundation distribute to a hundred or more selected private colleges and universities in the United States 10 percent of the Ford Motor Company stock as *general endowment* grants; and that similar grants be made at regular intervals over the years if changing circumstances make this desirable. If the stock were to remain as it is, without voting rights, it would be given to the institutions in the form of non-transferable gifts." Newsom saw this endowment as a "move to strengthen education in the United States at its most vulnerable point by making higher education a partner in the economic growth of the county, and as a vote of confidence in those who administer the affairs of the great private educational institutions of this country." Newsom's memo came at a time when the foundation was feeling the heat of public opinion and was considering a "dump" of $570 million, or one fourth of its total capital. According to the foundation critic, Dwight MacDonald, in *The Ford Foundation: The Men and the Millions:*

> The philanthrophoids at Ford are reasonably intelligent and knowledgeable men and it is unlikely that it didn't occur to them that a more productive use could have been made of half a billion dollars than just giving it out, pro rata, to everybody. They were scared, or more accurately, Henry Ford II, Donald David [a foundation director] and the other trustees were scared, and the fear communicated itself, through channels, to the philanthrophoids who run the Foundation.

The Ford Foundation's need for public confidence and support and often the lack thereof continued in the years ahead. In a confidential memo to Earl Newsom dated June 26, 1956, Quigg Newton wrote:

> It is important that the Foundation operate in a climate of public confidence. Yet actions which involve deliberate risks of public misunderstanding are sometimes indicated in the fulfillment of our program. Moreover, we can not employ aggressive publicity-promotion techniques to "sell" the Foundation. The choice of operating outside the sphere of public attention is not available to us. . . . Moreover, in appearing to solicit public approval we might be inference seem to be conceding our susceptibility to public control.

Newton then suggested four "basic avenues of approach" in meeting the foundation's public relations needs:

1. Comprehensive and effective public reporting;
2. Intimate liaison with opinion leaders;
3. Analysis of immediate and long-range public implications of proposed actions;
4. Assumption of leadership initiative for a public relations program on the concept and function of private philanthropy in America.

Presumably, when Henry Ford II terminated Earl Newsom's counsel in 1957, it also resulted in the end of his involvement in the Ford Foundation's public relations. The previously quoted memo is the last in the Newsom Papers involving the foundation or the Fund for the Republic.

NOTES ON SOURCES

For the material in this chapter, I relied heavily on the Earl Newsom Papers in the Mass Communications History Center of the State Historical Society of Wisconsin and on three first-rate books: Harry Ashmore's comprehensive and insightful biography of Robert M. Hutchins, *Unseasonable Truths*, published in 1989 by Little, Brown and Company; Frank K. Kelly's memoirs, *The Court of Reason: Robert Hutchins and the Fund for the Republic*, published by The Free Press in 1981; and Thomas C. Reeves, *Freedom and the Foundation: The Fund for the Republic in the Era of McCarthyism*, published by Alfred A. Knopf, New York, 1969. Helpful as a contrarian's view was Dwight MacDonald's *The Ford Foundation: The Men and the Millions*, published by Regnal & Company in 1956. Also contributing to the strength and accuracy of this chapter were Harry S. Ashmore, John R. Newsom, John E. Sattler, who headed the New York public relations office of the Ford Motor Company for 30 years, W. H. "Ping" Ferry, and Martin Quigley, all of whom provided information or corrections of this first draft.

Permission to quote from Thomas C. Reeves' *Freedom and the Foundation: The Fund for the Republic in the Era of McCarthyism,* was granted by Random House, Inc. Permission to quote from *Unseasonable Truths* was granted by Harry Ashmore.

Epilogue

A PERSPECTIVE ON TODAY'S PRACTICE

With these thoughts I conclude this chronicle of the early years of public relations as a recognized vocation in the United States, told through profiles of the pioneer practitioners and agencies that gave this function—now worldwide in scope—definition, utility, and, to a degree, acceptance of its necessity in management.

The essentiality of public relations as a management function that Ivy Lee envisaged in the early 1900s becomes clearer each passing day as our global information society becomes ever more dependent on effective communications and on understanding the complexities of an interdependent, competitive world. An organization depends on its constituent publics for success or even survival, *internally and externally*. In 1991, people witnessed Marshall McLuhan's "Global Village" in all its power, glory, and worldwide impact, enthralled with war as theater presented 24 hours a day by CNN. It is also the public relations counselor's function to monitor the public opinion environment so that institutions can steer a safe and steady course through the winds and storms of the public climate. These storms come with increased velocity and frequency in this day of instant worldwide communication—a factor with which Ivy Lee, Pendleton Dudley, Edward L. Bernays, and the other pioneers did not have to contend.

Today any institution, private or public, that does not have an effective radar system to pick up problems while they are still on the distant horizon or communications machinery ready to respond to a crisis when it occurs lives at its peril. For example, the President of the United States and his

Secretary of Health and Human Services publicly excoriated the drug manufacturers for what they termed exorbitant prices charged for prescription drugs. The Pharmaceutical Manufacturers Association, which maintains a large internal public relations staff and retains outside counsel, quickly responded with a full-page ad placed in the nation's 40 leading dailies headed: "TO THE AMERICAN PEOPLE FROM THE PEOPLE WHO WORK IN PHARMACEUTICAL COMPANIES: We'd like to speak to you directly about our companies and the future of America's Healthcare System." The cost of placing this single ad was $500,000. This illustrates that the function has not changed essentially from the beginnings of defensive publicity and informative news releases but that the speed, sophistication, and costs of responding to public attacks have risen exponentially since the days of Theodore Roosevelt.

Today's public relations counselor is at the mercy of what Russian novelist Alexander Solzhenitsyn termed "the pitiless crowbar of events." The political-social-economic environment defines the need and the purpose of the public relations function and shapes public reception and interpretation of an organization's deed and deeds. Careful assessment of this ever-changing opinion climate is critical as the nation and world are undergoing a fundamental transformation from a fading Industrial Era to a Technology and Information Era and its Electronic Super Highway. Thus, it is necessary for the counselor to monitor, analyze, and influence the public climate if the organization is to sail safely to its goal through the reefs and shoals of today's world. Institutions and industries must constantly adjust and adapt to far-reaching, swiftly moving changes if they are to survive. Accurately monitoring these changes and helping management adjust to them has taken primacy over publicity in the evolution of public relations in this century.

The days when Ivy, Lee, Pendleton Dudley, John Hill, and their contemporaries could rely on their journalistic hunches and press clippings for their sense of the public mood are long gone. Today's technological advances, computer software programs, instant media analysis, and talk-show feedback have made the clip book obsolete. Today research information is quickly available to counselors and their executives through article content analysis, focus groups, phone and mail surveys, and before-and-after attitude studies. Providers of research services have taken public relations campaign results to the ultimate degree by introducing on-line, personalized information systems, focus groups to take the pulse of the public, and charting tools to help calculate the most cost-effective marketing mix. Several new types of research and evaluation techniques are in the incubation stage. These advances are a vivid reminder of how far the field has come since the days of The Publicity Bureau and its paid-for boilerplate news articles sent out to defeat president Theodore Roosevelt's railroad reforms. Today's successful counselor must be a sophisticated user of innovative research technology.

Observation of contemporary practice suggests that many practitioners have yet to measure up to their responsibilities in gauging public opinion and interpreting its significance to the policy makers of their institutions. This weakness remains some 70 years after Edward L. Bernays in his landmark book, *Crystallizing Public Opinion*, published in 1923, first set down the rationale for the function in management by introducing the two-way concept of public relations in contradistinction to the one-way publicity that then dominated the practice. Bernays developed the theory of public relations as a two-way mediating interpretation liaison between an organization and its constituent publics. One of today's concepts of the function is that stated by Tim Traverse Healy, distinguished British counselor, "Public Relations is aimed at producing a state of mutual understanding in which truth, dialogue, and public interest are paramount." The ethics of many of the pioneers and the ethics of today's practitioners make clear that this is the ideal, far from the norm.

As many shade the truth and deal in obfuscation as purvey accurate, useful information to the public via the news media. Reality says — as amply demonstrated in this volume — that the public relations counselor should be seen as the advocate, as John W. Hill did, not as a dedicated purveyor of truth to serve the public interest. Many counselors serve as advocates of institutions and causes in the same way lawyers serve their clients, to put the best possible face on the facts they can, regardless of merit or truth. Before the role of *advocate* comes the role of *adviser* in which the responsible practitioner seeks to persuade his management to adopt policies that serve the public interest and that of the institution in a mutually satisfactory way. The organization's policies and performance is the key to its acceptance in the public opinion marketplace.

In fact, the *public relations vocation*, or *business* as some prefer to term it, is still in transition toward the mature concept first enunciated by Edward L. Bernays. Public relations scholar James Grunig delineated four models of public relations practice. The oldest of these and one still widely practiced today is the press agentry model, given birth by P. T. Barnum in the 1830s to promote his circus and exhibits. The press agent abounds today in great numbers promoting movie stars, rock stars, country music singers, prize fighters, TV shows, professional sports teams, auto races, and so forth. Their goal is box office: selling books, selling records or CDs, creating celebrities, and promoting resorts or luxury cruises. The skillful Disney promotion of its theme parks and motion pictures epitomizes the best of today's press agentry. The hype of the football's Super Bowl epitomizes its power. The press agent strives for public attention, not public support or understanding. In the words of a longtime press agent friend of mine, "We stoop to anything but our stuff gets printed." Their task has been made easier today by the growth of publicity outlets that appeal to the lowest common denominator in public taste and hunger for program material.

The second oldest model was fashioned by Ivy Lee early in this century with his "Declaration of Principles," issued in 1906 when he was serving the anthracite coal operators in the UMW strike. This model places the public relations function in the role of an in-house journalist with the main purpose of disseminating factual information to influence public opinion.

Today, as Grunig noted, the public information model, found mainly in government agencies, relies on press releases and controlled media to disseminate information on the organization's policies and performance. The function continues to be too narrowly defined in government at all levels because of these sources of opposition: (a) the press that fears the function being used to control or conceal information; (b) the legislative bodies that fear its use by the Chief Executive to put pressure on them; (c) the "out" political party that decries the incumbent party's use of the function for political propaganda; and (d) the special interests that are opposed to a government program or proposed legislation, for example, the AMA's campaign against "socialized medicine" in the 1950s. Because of these pressures resulting in the narrowly defined concept of public relations, the function in government has not reached its full potential of usefulness, save perhaps in the highly sophisticated public relations machinery in the White House.

In Grunig's view, Bernays' concept was a two-way asymmetrical model whose purpose was scientific persuasion. Bernays and others of his time recognized that research on an organization's publics could help an organization target messages that would change attitudes and affect behavior. His work for Procter & Gamble in promoting the Ivory Soap sculpture contests in schools, designed to change children's attitudes toward bathing, is such an example. Influenced by his uncle Sigmund Freud, Bernays was the first to exploit the social sciences (e.g., psychology) in his efforts to persuade and thus influence human behavior.

The fourth model, which has emerged since the 1960s through the work of various educators, Grunig described as the two-way symmetrical model. This model uses research not only to shape messages but also to position the organization in rapport with its constituent publics. According to Grunig, practitioners of this model "serve as mediators between organizations and their publics," with a goal of mutual understanding as the principal objective. Study of Earl Newsom's concept of public relations, particularly after World War II in his work with Ford Motor Company and other clients, suggests that he was a pioneer of Grunig's symmetrical two-way model.

These models aside, the main thrust of today's public relations work is to set the public agenda through the dissemination of news or information through the multiplying channels of communication and entertainment. Most practitioners are employed — as they have been most of this century — to advance the interest of the employer by spotlighting the institution's favorable news and softening or suppressing what would be unfavorable to the employer if it became known. News is also used to deny and obfuscate news damaging to the employer. This was John Hill's tactic on behalf of the tobacco industry when news of the dangers of smoking began to appear. This is mostly a matter of emphasis and obfuscation. Few practitioners peddle untruths and survive any length of time. However, some skirt perilously close to the brink of falsehood.

The practitioner has another objective — one made necessary by the news media's lack of adequate manpower and outmoded news values. It must be readily acknowledged that the lack of reportorial and editorial manpower and the limits of news space or airtime are governed by the hard factors of economics, particularly in the print media as competition from television, cablevision, and telephone electronic information grows apace. Journalism's outmoded news values that emphasize sensationalism and violence could well be modified.

One must also acknowledge that today's busy reader or viewer has a limited amount of attention to news and public affairs as he or she is bombarded by newspapers, magazines, radio, TV, and some 150 cable channels, soon to be 500. This limitation of time on the part of the citizen greatly complicates the adequacy and perhaps the integrity of the information process. In his classic *Public Opinion* published in 1922, Walter Lippmann wrote that one of the main barriers to effective communication in society was "the "citizen's meagre time for paying attention to public affairs." That "meagre time" has diminished markedly in these intervening 71 years. The challenge for the communicator was never greater!

The public relations objective in the ideal sense is to inform the public of constructive, complex subject matter that the media have neither the news space nor expert manpower to report in sufficient depth — nuclear power, for example. In fact, public relations practitioners contribute much useful information to the public dialogue that otherwise would not see the light of day. However well intentioned, the practitioner faces increasing difficulty in getting his or her message through the filter of the traditional and new media of communication — now multiplying at a breathtaking rate. The traditional news values of the newspaper or magazine writer emphasize conflict not concord, the aberrational not the normal, the destructive not the constructive, and focus on newsworthy personalities rather than on the content of public issues. In the words of veteran journalist Martin Nolan, "The reporter has a vested interest in chaos."

And many come with a bundle of prejudices as did Ida Tarbell in unmasking the ruthless monopoly of the Standard Oil Trust and its ways of ruining competitors—her father had lost his fortune in his dealings with John D. Rockefeller. A veteran Associated Press executive, Conrad Fink, fears that Milton's marketplace of ideas is breaking down, that the self-righting process is seriously imbalanced. He fears that today's newspapers, in their fight for survival, are succumbing to the marketing influence as opposed to the journalistic instinct. The competition among all the news and entertainment media has become fierce as media enterprises multiply; as a consequence, there is a shift toward building audiences to sell to advertisers from the basic mission of newspapers, magazines, television and cable news, and the whole array of competitors.

Fink, now a professor of journalism at the University of Georgia, continued:

> Shareholder happiness depends on profits; profits depend on ratings; ratings depend on audiences; the cheapest, fastest, way to court mass audiences is to launch what might be called a Rising Tide of Crudity and Violence—"entertainment" programming that's often mindless, obscene, "entertainment" without conscience, without meaning; "entertainment" that rips and tears at our social fabric, the values, the institutions—*the very soul* of our society.

An example of the kinds of public relations problems that can arise from this lust for ratings is exemplified in the rigged crash demonstration NBC's *Dateline*, staged to prove that General Motors' heavy-duty pickup truck was unsafe. How GM converted this episode into a plus for the GMC pickup is told in chapter 21.

Given the news media's lack of adequate reportorial personnel—both in terms of numbers and in background knowledge—and lack of news space or air time, consider just one example of the counselor's problem in communicating to the public information in this complex age of technology and chemicals: Passage of the Superfund Amendment Reorganization Act by Congress in 1986 requires companies to inform the public about chemical emissions. Even if chemical companies fully understand how to present the facts to the news media, the problem of the journalists' limitations in understanding or caring about the company's particular risks remain. Writing in the *Public Relations Quarterly*, William C. Adams asserted out of long experience that practitioners "need to understand the whole is based on politics, power, and controversial issues, which encompasses more than just 'open and honest communication.' "

As previously stressed, the public relations practitioner and agency have inserted themselves into the nation's public information system—for good or ill. Seen through the prism of a long career in journalism, Conrad Fink saw this as for ill. He wrote:

> Our [public opinion] marketplace is under assault by manipulators of ideas — not *communicators* of ideas, but *manipulators*. Call them "public relations specialists" or "flacks" or "spin doctors," they serve good causes — the American Cancer Society is one — and with equal interchangeable skill and dedication, less worthy causes, such as the Tobacco Institute. Good cause, bad cause, they have one aim: they want to influence the media in their search for and delivery of facts and news, then to intervene in — to direct — the public's perception of facts and truth and thus to influence the national decision-making process. Add to these manipulators the heavily financed interest groups rampaging across our political and social landscape and we indeed have powerful forces actively engaged *not* in making the marketplace mechanism work, but rather, trying to distort it.

THE WASHINGTON POWERHOUSE

These special interests, their lobbyists, and their "manipulators" are daily on dramatic display in the nation's capital as they seek to pass or defeat regulation in the Congress, to initiate or eliminate government regulation in the federal agencies, and to dominate the public opinion power game, one played for high stakes. Writing in the *Columbia Journalism Review* Alicia Mundy vouched, "The use and abuse of journalists by P. R. flacks and lobbyists has long been a fact of life in Washington. In the past couple of years, though, media manipulation has been taken to a new level. . . . Media manipulation has evolved considerably since the days when a well-connected flack could place a story by simply calling up a columnist or editor."

Indeed the army of some 50,000 lobbyists and several hundred public relations agencies working the White House, the halls of Congress, and the myriad of governmental agencies today represents a quantum leap from the simple days when William Wolff Smith opened his publicity office in 1902 to send releases to the nation's newspapers to influence governmental action. His agency was born of the upheaval brought by President Theodore Roosevelt's Square Deal that sought to curb the abuses of the public by Big Business that had been accumulating for a quarter century. More sophisticated, but still simple by today's high-powered assaults of these special interests, was Ivy Lee's publicity campaign from 1912 to 1914 for the Pennsylvania Railroad and other railroads that finally won a freight rate increase from the Interstate Commerce Commission. Lee changed the ways of pressuring Congress with that campaign.

The injury these coordinated campaigns of public relations and legislative arm-twisting inflict on American people can be seen starkly in the iniquitous National Rifle Association's (NRA) successful efforts to block effective gun control in a nation awash with guns and the resultant murder and mayhem. Yet, public opinion polls repeatedly show overwhelming support for gun control laws. The NRA, with its large public relations staff and lobbyists, fights every gun control measure (even efforts to ban automatic weapons), no matter what its merit—all in the name of "sportsmen." Heavy contributions to legislators at the national and state levels are another weapon of the NRA that has effectively blocked control measures at the federal, state, and local levels for decades. The multiplying army of lobbyists and proliferating public affairs agencies in Washington is the Capital's largest industry. Their number grows as regulatory and tax laws increase and litigation steadily rises in the nation's courts.

A former executive of Hill & Knowlton's Washington office described today's political public relations in Washington this way:

> The real work is done behind the scenes. You have people of substance going to regulators and assistant secretaries, then you notify the press in advance that the government is taking a certain action, and why, and who you represent, and why your client deserved to have this regulation changed. You make your client's story a *government* story, showing how the government's action—by now a quiet *fait accompli*—has not only helped your client, but that it is good for the people. That's how you get the story out the right way to the media.

PRACTITIONERS AS FOREIGN AGENTS

As stated in chapter 4, the need for foreign governments to explain themselves and to promote trade, tourism, and political support in the United States became apparent shortly after the turn of the century when America shed its isolationism and moved onto the world stage in the wake of the Spanish-American War. These needs have intensified through the 20th century as nations grew more interdependent and a fiercely competitive world economy emerged. Today with the United States as the world's Super Power, caught in a highly competitive global economy and a world torn by ethnic rivalries and nations breaking up, the demands for U.S. political and economic support are many and intense. This has led to a boom in the business of public relations agencies pushing these foreign claims in the halls of Congress and in the public opinion—arena.

Hamilton Wright was the first publicity man to recognize the opportunities presented by the nation's move onto the world stage in the early 1900s. Wright's first major account was to promote American investment and tourism to the newly acquired Philippine islands. Wright's output of propaganda glorifying U.S. occupation and touting the Philippines' assets was prolific. From that day until the firm folded in the late 1960s, Wright and his two successors, son and grandson, served foreign nations almost exclusively in their promotional and public relations efforts.

Representation of foreign nations by United States agencies has had a stormy history. And today these practitioners find themselves once again under fire—from President Clinton to congressmen to Ross Perot. The stakes in this representation are high and often crucial for a South Africa under siege for its apartheid policies, for a Kuwait monarchy invaded by Iraq, for an Angolan rebel leader seeking U.S. arms, or for the victims of a now independent Serbia's brutal killings and "ethnic cleansing" of Croatia and Bosnia-Herzgovina in what once was Yugoslavia. Much of this stormy history is recounted in this volume.

The first intense controversies arose in the 1930s after dictator Adolf Hitler's seized power for the Nazis in Germany. Hitler's Nazi government used the two most prominent firms in the United States at that time—Carl Byoir & Associates and Ivy Lee and T. J. Ross—in an effort to moderate the growing anti-Nazi opinions then boiling up in this country. These stories are told in the Ivy Lee and Carl Byoir chapters. National concern about U.S. practitioners representing such a reprehensible government resulted in Congressional hearings and the passage of the Foreign Agents Registration Act of 1938.

Because of a number of revelations of questionable acts on the part of practitioners representing such clients as Ferdinand Marcos of the Philippines, the issue returned to the front pages in the early 1960s. Consequently, Senator J. William Fulbright, chairman of the Senate Foreign Relations Committee, ordered a set of hearings on these "Nondiplomatic Activities." Four public relations agencies were brought under the scrutiny of the Fulbright Hearings—Julius Klein, Harry Klemfuss, Selvage and Lee, and Hamilton Wright. The committee brought out testimony that showed how these firms used the media, particularly the Special Services branches of the defunct International News Service, United Press International, and United States Press Association, to peddle propaganda to the American readers. These hearings resulted in amendments to the 1938 Foreign Agents Registration Act that provided for greater and more explicit disclosure by agents engaged in political activities on behalf of foreign governments. These hearings were particularly damaging to the Hamilton Wright Organization, and were one factor leading to its demise in the late 1960s.

In the early 1990s, public criticism of public relations firms that represent foreign governments or their agencies arose anew, this time with demands that representation of foreign governments by U.S. principals be outlawed. Presidential candidate Ross Perot was most vocal with this demand. His fire was aimed mainly at the agents hired by Germany and Japan, America's chief economic competitors. Another cause of political concern was Hill & Knowlton's representation of the Bank of Commerce and Credit International (BCCI), which perpetrated the world's largest bank fraud. H&K was registered at the Department of Justice as a lobbyist for BCCI from 1988 to March 1990. It primarily worked to offset negative criticism of a BCCI affiliate, the First American Bank of Washington. William Von Raab, U.S. Customs Commissioner, testified in 1991 that "influence peddlers" had prevented federal regulators from moving in on BCCI. H&K forced Von Raab to admit in a letter that he did not have any evidence that H&K officials had pressured any government official. Nonetheless, the spate of unfavorable publicity about BCCI's crimes here and abroad enveloped Hill & Knowlton and again raised the legitimacy of a U.S. public relations firm's use of its First Amendment rights to represent the view of a foreign government or business. As of 1993, the files of the office of Foreign Agents Registration Act in the Department of Justice listed more than 800 lobbyists for 272 foreign governments. Again this is an exponential explosion of business from the early 1900s and the start of the Hamilton Wright Organization.

Another egregious example of this foreign representation by Hill & Knowlton in the early 1990s also added flames to the fires of protest of this public relations practice. Shortly after Saddam Hussein's Iraqi Army invaded oil-rich Kuwait in August 1990, the Kuwaiti monarchy retained Hill & Knowlton, Inc. to build support in the United States for rescuing the besieged monarchy. Hill & Knowlton, paid $12 million for this effort, set up a front called Citizens for a Free Kuwait. In a biography of Robert Keith Gray,[1] who has epitomized the unsavory in public relations practice this half century, entitled *The Power House,* Susan B. Trento wrote of H&K's Kuwait account:

> Everything came together on Kuwait. Every part of the intricate, well-oiled public relations and lobbying machine Robert Keith Gray had assembled was in place. Gary Hymel had Capitol Hill covered. Frank Mankiewiecz oversaw the massive machinery that dazzled the media. Gray had just made another one of his trademark reaches into the White House, hiring George Bush's

---

[1]Gray had years of experience lobbying for controversial clients, from "Baby Doc" Duvalier of Haiti to China in the aftermath of Tienamen Square Massacre. Gray was eased out or fired as head of H&K's Washington office on October 1, 1992. He was replaced by Howard Paster. A *Washington Post* reporter, Gary Lee, contrasted Gray's and Paster's styles this way, "In their approach to the art of power brokering, Gray is master of splashy publicity on behalf of himself and his clients while Paster has preferred to push his agenda behind closed doors." Paster quit H&K in January 1993 to become head of President Bill Clinton's Congressional Liaison staff.

former chief of staff, and friend, Craig Fuller, as president and CEO of Hill
& Knowlton Worldwide.[2]

H&K's office was then headed by the flamboyant self-promoter Robert
Keith Gray, who sent a memo to Citizens for a Free Kuwait calling for more
atrocity stories. (Alleged atrocities have been effective war propaganda
since the British used stories of German atrocities to inflame American
public opinion.) Hill & Knowlton quickly complied.

Nayriah, a 15-year-old Kuwait girl, shocked a public hearing of Congress's Human Rights Caucus on October 10, 1990, when she tearfully
testified: "I saw the Iraqi soldiers come into the hospital with guns. They
took the babies out of the incubators and left the children to die on the cold
floor." H&K sent its own camera crew to film this hearing that it had helped
cast and direct. It then produced a film that was quickly sent out as a video
release used widely by a gullible media. Too late some alert reporter
unmasked the story as a hoax and revealed that Nayriah was the Kuwaiti
Ambassador's daughter living in Washington. Once more the press served
as patsies for the public relations staged event. Arthur Rowse, author of
Slanted News, wrote at the time, "The press, which had shown little interest
in questioning the credibility of the atrocity reports when those reports were
having such a tremendous impact on U.S. policy, seemed reluctant to
reconsider the evidence — or its own reporting."

Another example of this work occurred when tiny Kosovo, threatened by
Serbian aggression after Yogoslavia's breakup, declared its independence
and adopted a U.S.-style constitution with a Bill of Rights; the document
was written in the United States by the public relations firm, Ruder–Finn.
James Harff, president of Ruder–Finn's global network, explained, "The
Kosovans knew their rights. . . . We helped the formulate the message in a
way that Americans could understand." This work of Ruder–Finn is
reminiscent of Edward L. Bernays' role in helping President Thomas
Masyrak proclaim Czecholovakia's independence in the United States in
1919 — and on a Sunday to get maximum press attention! Even public
relations history repeats itself! To build U.S. support for the threatened
new republic, Ruder–Finn staged an intensive publicity campaign and a
six-city U.S. tour in March of 1993. Ruder–Finn is perhaps the one agency
that is profiting from the breakup of Yugoslavia and the Serbian aggres-
sions of rapes, killings, and concentration camps. As of 1993, Ruder–Finn
represented not only Kosova but also Croatia and Bosnia-Herzegovina's
Muslim leadership. Again the objective is to move public opinion to embroil

---

[2]Craig Fuller later left H&K to become vice-president for public affairs of Philip Morris at
a salary of $500,000 a year and now spearheads that company's effort to head off more taxes
on tobacco and antismoking regulations.

America in that fratricidal conflict. Together as of March 1993, the three beleaguered republics have spent nearly $250,000 on U.S. public relations.

The Ruder–Finn agency is an old hand at foreign representation. It came under heavy criticism in 1976 when it hired Mrs. Marion B. Javits, wife of United States Senator Jacob Javits, to handle its Iranian Airlines account and thus represent the tyrannical Shah of Iran in the United States as his throne was toppling.

In 1993, the government of Mexico spent $30 million on lobbyists and public relations agencies to promote support for the trination North American Free Trade Agreement in the United States.

ETHICS OF TODAY'S PRACTICE — HAS IT IMPROVED?

Ethics of public relations has long been at the center of efforts to professionalize the field by the Public Relations Society of America (PRSA), the International Association of Business Communicators (IABC), the Council for the Advancement of Education (CASE), the National School Public Relations Association (NSPRA), and public relations educators. Each of these professional associations, and many others, has its codes of ethics. The PRSA has judicial machinery to enforced its Code Professional Standards, but over the years this code has been enforced unevenly or not at all. The phrases "generally accepted standards of good taste" and "truth and accuracy" have a lot of elastic in them. These professional organizations are voluntary associations and thus do not have the clout to enforce their codes. An accused member can simply resign from the organization, as Anthony Franco did in October 1986 when he was president of PRSA, after signing a Securities and Exchange Commission (SEC) consent order admitting "insider trading" on the information obtained from a client. Many others have taken this escape to keep from being censured by their colleagues. More than the practitioner's sense of ethics is involved in these decisions.

A distinguished Canadian counselor pointed out, "Unfortunately, these codes have little real value unless they are accepted in turn by the employers of practitioners and applied to the conduct of the institution itself." There are no watertight bulkheads in our industries and organizations. Even today the basic lessons of honesty and forthrightness have not been learned by many executives, in the corporate world and out. Take these few recent examples: The Sears scam of overcharging its customers in its auto shops; Exxon's disastrous response to the Valdez Oil Spill, the worst in the nation's history; Dow Corning's less than honest response to its crisis resulting from the ill effects of its silicone gel breast implant; or one that still haunts the nuclear power industry, General Public Utilities' series of blunders in handling the Three Mile Island disaster. To emphasize the importance of management, contrast these public relations blunders with that Johnson & Johnson's skillful handling of its Tylenol crisis. Such successful public relations takes a team—a forthright management and a competent counselor.

Codes of behavior will lack wholly effective means of enforcement until there is legal certification of practitioners. Public relations cannot be a true profession until there is *controlled access*—and that day is long distant.

The problems inherent in representing foreign governments discussed previously illustrate the dilemmas confronting all counselors and agencies. The competition for this business is keen. In a 1992 interview, Loet Velmans, former chairman of Hill & Knowlton, wistfully recalled when "the firm had the luxury of turning down clients, such as Ferdinand Marcos and South Africa." He told a writer for the *Columbia Journalism Review*, "Things have changed now. The competition is so fierce, hardly anyone turns away a client." Yet his successor Robert L. Dilenschneider wrote in *The New York Times* in December 1989 that "the clients we celebrate most are the ones we turn away. The bigger the account we reject, the more we celebrate it." Yet at the same time H&K was taking on as a client Tom Demery, then under investigation in the Housing and Urban Development (HUD) scandal and later indicted on several counts. Demery later pled guilty. Challenged by me on this contradiction, Dilenscheider, in a letter to me dated December 18, 1989, wrote "I am proud of our work on his [Demery's] behalf." Dilenschneider was forced out as chairman and chief executive officer of H&K in October 1991.

In the *Public Relations Journal* of November 1992 Daniel J. Edelman, founder of one of the top 10 international public relations firms, wrote, "We all know that power corrupts. There are signs that's happening to the public relations field, . . . this is a time of testing for public relations." Edelman whose firm is one of only four independents among the top firms, laid much of the blame for moral lapses on financial pressures brought by advertising agency owners on their PR subsidiaries. He has a point. In 1968, H&K was purchased by J. Walter Thompson, (JWT) for $28 million and thus became a profit center for JWT. Years later JWT was bought by a London mega-advertising–public relations firm, WPP. This intensified pressure on H&K to take any and every client. This explains Loet Velmans' wistfulness when "we wouldn't take on clients who would upset our most important people," as H&K did when it accepted the account of the National Conference of Catholic Bishops to wage an antiabortion campaign in 1990. This account, worth $3 million to $5 million, brought great internal dissension and the exodus of many of its top women executives. Several women executives at H&K offered their services free to groups supporting the prochoice movement. One H&K staffer even talked of subverting the campaign.

At the same time the firm took the bishops' account, it was also serving the Upjohn Company, maker of two abortion pills. Little wonder that in early 1992, Morley Safer asserted on CBS's *60 Minutes* that "public relations people believe they can sell anything given enough money, time, and access to the media." The disarray at John Hill's firm continued into 1992 when a group of employees quit the firm with what H&K charged in a lawsuit was "an audacious and outrageous theft" of its clients and staff members. In the early 1990s, the once dominant firm has lost clients and more than 100 employees through resignations and defections as well as firings. In 1993 it closed down several branches.

Edelman summarized these recent years thus:

> We have seen a series of developments that have cast a black cloud over the public relations field. . . . We have achieved so much in terms of growth and recognition, and, yes, even power. But if we abuse that power any further, the setback will be so great that it will be very difficult to recover. It's been a hard road getting to this point. But public relations is still quite fragile. . . . We must recapture the high standards of public relations practice that has enabled us to make so much progress. Let's not allow greed to blur our vision and our commitment to do the right thing. (pp. 30–31)

Bringing public relations purpose and respect is the challenge for the successors to Ivy Lee, Pendleton Dudley, William Baldwin III, Harry Bruno, Earl Newsom, and the other pioneers who built this vocation that is in transition to becoming a profession.

ONE FINAL THOUGHT

Little wonder there is today a public disgusted and alienated and even embittered with their government: this is reflected in the fact that in 1992 nearly 70% of the nation's voters voted for a change in our national government. There is a public that resents the dominance of the mass media in their lives and feels helpless to protect their jobs as the nation goes through a major transition, to protect their environment, to buy reliable goods at a fair price from the juggernaut of Big Business and Big Government.

Not since the Civil War has there been such estrangement between the races, between citizens and their governments, even between family members. This alienation, fear, and resentment can be found in every corner of the land and in every sector of society. Never in American history — save perhaps for the days of the Civil War — has the need for the practitioner's talents of persuasion, mediation, and conciliation been as great as they are today.

As the manipulation and misstatements of public relations practitioners contribute to this sense of malaise abroad in the land, they heighten public cynicism about all its major institutions. Public relations' complex and difficult tasks require broadly educated persons who are competent, have a compassionate concern for their fellow man, are sensitive to the difficulty of discerning the complex public opinion process, and most of all, have the guts to say no to their bosses.

Today's practitioners, in all seriousness, should ask themselves the question Earl Newsom raised for his contemporaries 30 years ago:

> I suggest that sober self-examination at this point requires that we come to an understanding of ourselves and what it is we really want to accomplish. This is not a problem that can be resolved by our society or by any committees thereof. It is purely a personal matter. Each of us lives but once, and each of us wants to spend his life constructively. . . . I am certain as can be that if each one of us establishes the highest standards for his own conduct, we shall eventually earn the status of a profession.

NOTES ON SOURCES

This essay is written largely out of my 57 years' involvement in the emerging vocation of public relations, beginning with my experience as press secretary to a gubneratorial candidate in my native West Virginia. It reflects a career devoted to advancing the knowledge, competence, and ethics of public relations. Other sources relied upon in this essay include the following.

James E. Grunig and Todd Hunt, *Managing Public Relations,* Holt, Rinehart, and Winston, 1984; Professor Conrad Fink's President's Lecture given at the University of Georgia, February 22, 1993, "Milton v. Gresham, The Battle for the American Mind"; William C. Adams, "The Role of Media Relations in Risk Communication," *Public Relations Quarterly,* Winter 1992-1993 (Grunig, Fink, and Adams are former students.) Alicia Mundy, "Is the Press Any Match for Powerhouse P. R.?" *Columbia Journalism Review,* September–October, 1992; Susan B. Trento, *The Powerhouse Robert Keith Gray and the Selling of Access and Influence in Washington,* St. Martin's Press, 1992, For an account of the use of atrocities in propaganda in World War I, see: J. M. Read, *Atrocity Propaganda, 1914-1919,* Yale University Press, 1941; Daniel J. Edelman,

"Ethical Behavior Is Key to Field's Future, *Public Relations Journal*, Vol. November, 1992; Robert J. Dilenschneider, *Power and Influence, Mastering the Art of Persuasion,* Prentice Hall Press, 1990 (his defense of taking the account of Tom Demery, who was convicted in the HUD Scandal, was in a letter to me, dated December 18, 1989.

Index

A

A&P, *see* Atlantic & Pacific Tea Company
Abraham and Straus, 330
Abrams, Frank W., 657
Ackerman, Carl W., 313, 314
Adams, William C., *277, 775*
Adelman, Moris A., 45, 154, *586, 587*
Advertising, 2, 62, 83, 115, 242, 323, 567, *see also*
      Lord & Thomas
  Bernays and, 200, 208, 215
  Carl Byoir and, 566, 576
  costs of, 70, 652–653
  Earl Newsom and, 639–640, 640, 652, 687
  Ivy Lee and, 66, 68–69
  John Hill and, 413, 420, 435, 441, 460, 472, 473,
      479, 486–487, 495
  Ku Klux Klan and, 396–399
  newspaper, *see* Newspapers
  politics and, 589, 602, 607–608
  product promotion, *see* Product promotion
  publicity and, 7, 24, 109, 396–397, 560
  radio, *see* Radio
  sponsored, 560, 572
  Steve Hannagan and, 254, 270
  tobacco industry and, 500, 501
  Whitaker and Baxter and, 601, 614–616
Advertising agencies
  political campaigns and, 589
Advertising Club, 215
AFL
  communist membership and, 431
  craft unions and, 240
  national health care and, 613
AFL–CIO, 240
African Americans, 373, 376
  Ku Klux Klan and, 387, 399
African-American education, 308, 309
  Fisk University, 312–313, 340
  Southern Education Foundation and, 340

  Tuskegee Institute, 309
Agent, *see* Foreign Agents
Aircraft industry, 267, 280, 281, 300, 301, *see also*
      Consolidated Vultee; Willow Run bomber
      plant; Aviation
  aircraft, 282, 284, 285, 287, 288, 425
  Aircraft Development Corp., 291–292
  Juan Trippe's Air Transport, 287, 300
  WWI and, 281, 284
  WWII and, 268–271
Airships, 291–294
  Hindenburg disaster, 292–293
Akin, Edward N., *91*
Aldrich, Winthrop, 138
Alexander, Herbert
  effects of TV and, 626
Allen, Frederic Lewis, *72,* 108, 198, *552, 586*
Allen, George E., *520*
Allied Laboratories, Inc., 301
American Association of Fund Raising Counsel
      (AAFRC), 89
American Association of Railraods, 129
American Butter Institute, 434
American Cancer Society, 489, 499, 502, *see also* Cigarettes
American Civil Liberties Union (ACLU), 310, 601
  Coal Operators and, 235
American Council on Public Relations, 216, 217, 339
American Federation of Labor (AFL), *see* AFL
American Federation of Musicians, 330
American Heart Association, 499, *see also* Cigarettes
American International Corporation (AIC), 312
American Iron and Steel Institute, 100, 118, 421, *see*
      also Steel industry
  labor relations and, 422
  public relations and, 423–424, 477
  unionization and, 461–462
American Legion, 306, 752
American Lung Association, 499, *see also* Cigarettes
American Magazine, 45, *72*
American Meat Institute (AMI), 99, 118

general news service of, 100
Meat Educational Program, 101
American Meat Packers Association (AMPA), 6, 99,
    100
American Medical Association, 326, 541
    anti-Truman plan campaign, 607, 612–621
        consequences of, 617–620
        political fallout from, 620–621
    National Education Committee and, 613, 614, 619
    socialized medicine and, 612–614
    voluntary health plans and, 614
American Mercury, 161, 185, *342*
American Museum of Immigration, 335–336
American Newspaper Publishers Association (ANPA),
    16, 50, 99, 100
American Petroleum Institute (API), 64, 100, 118, 441
American Red Cross, 114–116
    fundraising and, 34–35, 561–562
    publicity policy of, 66–69
    Red Cross War Council and, 64–65
American Road Builders, 79
American Tobacco Company, 126–128, *see also* Ciga-
    rettes; Tobacco Industry
    Lucky Strike promotion and, 208–212
American Trucking Association, 577
Americanism, Ku Klux Klan and, 387, 392, 401
Americans for Democratic Action, 613
Anderson, George, 99, 101
Andrews, Hannah Dunlop, 229
Anger, Charles W., 248
Anthracite Coal Operators, 45–46
Anti-Catholicism, 378, 393, 399
Anti-labor attitudes, 120, 235, 241, 432, 463, 465, 516,
    see also Labor disputes; Labor unions;
    strikebreaking
Anti-Saloon League, 27, 105, 319, 381
    prohibition and, 283
Anti-Semitic propaganda, 151
Anti-Semitism, 151, 205, 375, 378, 404, 534, 540, 550,
    660
    Henry Ford and, 690
    Henry Ford II and, 690–699
Anti-trust Act (Clayton), 565, 577
Anti-Trust Act (Sherman), *see* Sherman Anti-Trust
    Act
Arbitration, and labor-management disputes, 314, 464
Arbitration Society of America, 314
Archbold, John, D., 55–56
Architects, American Institute of, 79
Arena, 19–20
Armistice, 228
    aircraft industry, 281
Armstrong Committee, insurance companies and, 49
Armstrong, William A., 49
Army Air Corps, 284
Ashmore, Harry S., 750–751
    Unreasonable Truths, 738, 741, 749, *760*
Asphalt Trust, 46–47
Associated Press (AP), 4, 105, 223, 258
AT&T, 14, 15, 18, 19, 98
    public relations and, 18–19, 525–526
Atlanta Constitution, 378, 379
Atlanta Journal, 376, 386
Atlantic & Pacific Tea Company (A&P), 550

anti-chain store taxes and, 565–568
    litigation of, 570–574
Atlantic Monthly, 160, 206, *255*
Atlantic Refining Co, 639
Atomic Bomb, 130, 510–511
    Manhattan Project and, 130
Attorney General's office, Foreign Agents Registration
    Act and, 74
Atwell, William E., 570
Auerbach, Jerold S., *521*
Auto racing, 251
    Henry Ford and, 269
    Steve Hannagan and, 251, 253, 254, 255, 272
Automation, 356, 366
Automobile industry, 4, 4, 128–129, 197–200, 203–
    205, *see also* Automobile safety; Chrysler
    Corp.; General Motors; Ford Motor Co.;
    United Auto Workers
Automobile industry, 4
    air pollution and, 729–730
    Dodge Brothers, 128, 197–200
    John L.Lewis and, 247
    product promotion and, 106
    recession and, 712–713
    sales promotions and, 286
Automobile safety
    design research and, 724
    driver error and, 724
    Ford Pinto and, 701–703
    GM Corvair and, 713–715, 730
    GM pickup truck and, 732–733, 766
    legislation and, 722–723, 727
    pedestrian impact and, 723
    Ralph Nader and, 714, 723
    Ribicoff hearings, 717–718
Automotive News, 587
Avco, 424
Avco Manufacturing Corporation, 426–430
    ICBM missiles and, 429–430
    public relations and, 427–429
Aviation, *see also* Aircraft industry; Bruno, Harry;
        Bruno & Blythe
    aerial mapping and, 285
    Aeromarine Airways and, 282–283
    air freight services and, 283
    air races, 284, 287, 297
    airships, 291–294
    barnstorming publicity and, 280–283
    coast-to-coast transportation, 282, 294
    commercial, 106, 281, 283, 291, 294–295, 544
    fear of flying, 282, 283
    first nonstop coast-to-coast flight, 287
    gaining acceptance of, 138–139, 281
    historic flights and, 288–291, 295
    mail service and, 287
    Manufacturers Aircraft Association, 280–283
    monoplanes and, 279, 285
    publicity stunts and, 287
    publicizing safety and, 286
    Royal Flying Corps and, 280
    skywriting and, 284
    Wright Whirlwind Engine and, 287
Aviation Corps, 280, 286
Ayer & Sons, N. W., 7, 9

B

B & O Railroad, 23
Baer, George F., 46
Bahamas, tourism and, 450–451, 455–456
Bain, Herbert, 99, *103*
    meat industry and, 99, 100
Baker, Ray Stannard, *26*, 20–21, *9*
Baldwin, Beach & Mermey, *see also* Baldwin, W. H. III;
            Baldwin and Mermey; Mermey, Maurice
    Beach leaves firm, 329
    Campaign against sugar tariff, 318–321
    drug industry and, 323–327, 329–331
    Macy's Thanksgiving parade and, 315–316
    promoting free trade, 327–329
    promoting metals, 321–322
    radio broadcasting and, 314
Baldwin and Mermey, *see also* Baldwin, Beach &
            Mermey; Baldwin, William H. III
    AMI-Operation Unity campaign, 332–336
    broadcasters freedom and, 330
    Civitas and, 331–332
    drug industry and, 329–331
    other accounts of, 331
    partnership dissolved, 336
    promoting metals, 330
    promoting retail merchandising, 330
    Radio Free Europe and, 330
Baldwin, Roger, 235, 310
Baldwin, William H. III, 108, 188, 249, 303, 308–342,
            582, *see also* Baldwin, Beach & Mermey;
            Baldwin & Mermey
    American International Corp., and, 312
    background of, 308–311
    Baldwin, Beach & Mermey formed, 317
    character of, 308–310, 317, 320
    enlists in Naval Reserve, 311
    fighting McCarthyism and, 333–336
    fundraising and, 311–314
    Great Depression and, 317
    hires Maurice Mermey, 316
    improving race relations and, 312–313
    journalism and, 311
    labor–management disputes and, 314
    legacy, 341
    NAAPD and, 215–216, 302
    opens first office, 314
    Papers of, *192, 343*
    professional philosophies of, 317–318, 329, 331,
        336–339
    promoting retail merchandising, 315–316
    public service of, 308, 339–340
    with Robert L. Bliss & Co., 336
    social causes and, 312–314
Baldwin, William Henry, Jr., 308–310, 339
    African-American education and, 308–310
    Committee of Fourteen and, 309
Ball, George, 84
Ball, Richard A., 457
Baltimore & Ohio Railroad (B&O), 54
Bananas, 159, 196, 197
Bankruptcy Act, Chapter X
    McKesson Robbins and, 323
Banks

abuses by, 5
Great Depression and, 137, 204
labor disputes and, 241
patriotic appeals and, 228
Reconstruction Finance Corp. and, 204
Senate investigations of, 137–138
Barber, James David, *631*
Barbour, Robert L., *520*
Barmash, Isadore, 345, 348, 349, 356, 358, 361, 362,
        364, *370*
Barnhart, James J., 242
Barnouw, Erik, 625, 631, 681
Barrett, Edward, 444, 454, 455, 513, 518
Barrett, Edward W., *521*
Barrons, 186
Bart, Peter, *521*
Baseball, 266–267
    Albert Lasker and, 266
    Commissioner Landis and, 266–267
    Baseball Hall of Fame, 267
Baumgartner, J. Hampton, 23, *26*, 54
Baus, Herbert, 623, *632*
Baxter, Leone, 590, *see also* Whitaker, Clem; Whitaker &
            Baxter
    on lobbying, 609
    Papers, *631*
Beach, Brewster, 317, 329
Beals, Carlton, *552, 586*
Beckett, Henry, *157*
Beckley, John, 591
Bedford, Cotton A., 63–64
Beech, Ernest R., 697, 710
Beech Nut Packing Co., 196
Begeman, J., 573
Bekker, L. J. de, *157*
Belding, Don, 599
Bell, Luther K., 281
Bendiner, Robert, 581, *587*
Bendix, Vincent
    automatic washer and, 297–298
    Bendix Trophy and, 297
Bennett, Floyd, 288
Bennett, Harry, 270, 271
    Ford and, 682–684
Bennett, Richard, 162, 163
Bennett, Robert J., 540, 551, *552, 585–586*
Benny, Jack, 272
    canned laughter and, 665
Benton & Bowles Advertising, 323
Bergdorf Goodman, 348
Bernays, Edward L., 2, 108, 127, 159–224, *190, 191*, 526
    accomplishments of, 159
    Advertising Club and, 215
    art in publicity and, 195–196
    background of, 160–161
    Beech Nut Packing Co. and, 196
    Bernays–Byoir story, 165–167, 171–172
    birthday celebrations of, 159–160, 220, 221
    Calvin Coolidge and, 195
    campaign for public relations and, 181–182
    Cheney Brothers and, 195
    Chicago Museum and, 202
    clients in later years, 222
    Council on Public Opinion and, 216

Creel Committee and, 164–165, 171
criticisms of, 162, 166, 182–189, 203, 215, 367, 368
Czecholovakia independence and, 771
defends *Propaganda*, 184
Dodge Motor Car Co., and, 197–200
Doris Fleischman (Mrs. E. Bernays), 107, 168–170, *190*
education of professionals and, 219–220
engineering of consent and, 159, 186–188
from memoirs of, 162–164, 168
fundraising and, 220
General Electric and, 205–207
     investigation of IUE study and, 212–214
     Light's Jubilee and, 205–207
General Motors, 203–205
honors of, 221–224
journalism and, 162
letters of, 167, 187, 205
licensure and, 218–219
Liggett & Myers and, 207–209
Lithuanian campaign and, 166–167, 539–540
NAAPD and, 215–216
national highways and, 197
NBC and, 202
opens office, 167–168
philosophies of public relations, 159, 160, 170, 171, 176–181, 186–187, 214–218
praise of, 220–223
Procter & Gamble and, 194
propaganda and, 166, 182–186, 206, 214
PRSA and, 217–218, 220–221
radio broadcasting and, 200–202
radio's future and, 201
radium therapy and, 196
self promotion and, 160, 188, *190*, 203, 204, 215, 216
selling cigarettes to women and, 209–212
Sigmund Freud and, 161, 163, 170–176
sponsoring committees and, 162, 163, 208
The Wisemen and, 216, 508–509
theatrical press agentry and, 163–164
third party technique, 163
trade publicists and, 198–200
two-way concept and, 166, 176, 177
United Fruit Co., 196–197
Universal Trade Press Syndicate and, 199
view of self, 160
Waldorf-Astoria Hotel, 193–194
works, *190–191*
     Biography of An Idea, The, 9, 188–189, *190*, 211, *552, 586*, 635
     Contact, 182
     Crystallizing Public Opinion, 109, 176–182, 219, 221
     "Engineering of Consent," 186–187
     Engineering of Public Opinion, *190*
     Propaganda, 182–186
     Public Relations, 187, *190*
Bethlehem Steel Co., 118–119, 240–247, 462, *see also* Steel industry
Johnstown Citizens Committee and, 241–244
Senate Investigations and, 241, 243–246
strikebreaking and, 240–247, 463
B. F. Goodrich, 564
Biddle, Wayne, *307*

Big Business, *see also* Anti-labor attitudes; Automobile industry; Coal industry; Oil industry; Steel industry
Great Depression and, 350, 526, 563, 644
muckraking and, 6, 18, 42, 310
the press, 28–29
public opinion and, 18, 46, 569, 46, 137, 649–650
public relations, 46, 59
reorganizations of, 240
ruthlessness of, 4, 6, 8, 55
Bigelow, Cornelia, 41, 153
Bigelow, Lewis, 116
Biggers, John D., 563
Billingsly, Sherman, 265
Birchall, Frederick, 145
Birth of a Nation, The, 375, 383, 398
Biscayne Bay, 255
Black, Hugo, 129
     constitutionality of public relations and, 575, 580
Blacklisting, 753–754
Blee, Kathleen M., 381, *412*
Bloemaker, Al, 253, *277*
Blough, Roger M., 478, 481, *see also* Steel industry
Blumenthal, Frank H., 247, *250, 521*
Blumenthal, Sidney, 631, *632*
Blythe, Dick, 108, 282, 285, 291, *see also* Bruno & Blythe
     Lindberg and, 288, 290, 291
     retires from Bruno & Blythe, 293–294
B'nai B'rith
     Henry Ford II and, 694
     The Leo Frank Case and, 375
Boating, 295–298
     Doctor Seuss and, 296
     Gold Cup Regata and, 295, 296
     National Boat Show and, 295
     promoting 1st PT boat and, 300
     promoting boating facilities and, 296
Bok, Edward W., 63–64
Bonner, Charles W., 110, 214, 367
Boone, Julian, *520*
Boorstin, Daniel, 189
Borden Company, 79
Bourne, Leonard, 84, *91*
Bower, Robert T., *632*
Bowerfind, Edgar S., 423, 424, 468, 470, 476
Bowles, Chester, 310, 323
     OPA price controls and, 688–689
Bowles, Ruth Standish (Mrs. W. Baldwin, Jr.), 310
Boxing, Heavyweight, 257
     Gene Tunney Myth, 257–258
     Sharkey–Stribling fight and, 257
Boxwell, Paul, 427
Brakeley, George A.
     ACLU reports and, 235–236
     anti-labor campaigns of, 235, 241
     Budget Committee campaign and, 237
     loan drives and, 231
Brandenberg, George A., *632*
Brayman, Harold, *521*
Breech, Ernest, 705
Bridge, Charles, A., 50
Brisbane, Arthur, 57–58, 117
British Information Service, 83
Brooks, John Graham, *342*
Brooks, Robert R.R., *520*

Broughton, Averell, *520*
Broun, Heywood, *521*
Bruno & Blythe, *see also* Bruno, Harry; H. A. Bruno & Associates
    air races and, 284, 287, 297
    airships and, 291–294
    Bendix automatic washer and, 297
    Benxix Trophy transcontinental race and, 297
    building public confidence and, 289
    Ford Air Reliability Tour and, 285–286
    Lindbergh and, 288–291, 294
    move to Rockefeller Plaza, 297
    other clients of, 295, 298–300
    Papers, *307*
    Pittsburgh Plate Glass and, 296
    popularizing boating, 295–298
    promoting computers, 300
    promoting historic flights, 288, 295
    promoting war production, 298–299
    radio announcing and, 286
    unwarranted claims and, 287
    view of public relations and, 304
    Wright Whirlwind Engine and, 287
Bruno, Harry, 108, 138, 278–307, *see also* Bruno & Blythe; H. A. Bruno & Assoc.
    American Legion and, 306
    Aviation Corps and, 280, 287
    awards of, 306
    background of, 278–279
    barnstorming for aviation, 280–283
    critics of, 303
    death of, 306
    first client and, 284
    function of public relations and, 278
    good press and, 304–305
    Manufacturers Aircraft Association and, 280–283
    modern view of public relations and, 301
    monoplanes and, 279
    opens first firm, 284, 285
    Papers of, *307*
    praise of, 303–304
    professional ethics of, 302–306
    promoting skywriting and, 284
    publicity stunts and, 287
    Quiet Birdmen (QB) and, 282, 306
    retired, 306
    Royal Flying Corps and, 280
    The Lotus Club and, 305–306
    "Thieves of Thunder," 307
    Wings Over America, 280–282, 292, *307*
Bryan, William Jennings, 2, 50, 593, 624
Buck, Jane, 545, 557, 559, 564, *586*
Buckley, Christopher, 660
Budget Act, 237, 249
Buell, K.L., 109, 214
Bugas, John, 683, 704
Bureau of Education on Fair Trade and, 330
Burns, James McGregor, 630
Burtt, Everett Johnson, *520*
Bush, George
    campaign for Congress and, 627
    campaign for President and, 628
Bush Terminal Project, 79
Business, *see* Big Business

Business Organizations, Inc., 570–574
Business Week, 446, *521, 552, 587*
Butler, James J., *157*
Butler, Nicholas Murray, 101
Byoir, Carl, 252, 531–588, *587, see also* Carl Byoir & Associates
    anti-semitism and, 534, 540, 550
    background of, 532–535
    Bernays–Byoir story, 165–167, 171–172
    campaign for Lithuania and, 166–167, 539–540
    Carl Byoir & Associates born, 543–546
    Creel Committee and, 106, 536–540
    criticisms of, 544, 564, 573–574
    Cuban tourism and, 527, 542–544
    death of, 531, 581
    Freud and, 172
    import export business and, 540
    John Martin's Book and, 536
    journalism and, 532–534, 536
    Montessori program and, 535–536
    Papers of, *552, 586*
    philosophy of, 537
    political views of, 562
    promoting patent medicines and, 540–542
    techniques of, 539, 582
    third party technique and, 122
Byoir (Carl) & Associates, *see* Carl Byoir & Associates
Byrd, John, 288
Byrd, Richard E., 288

C

California
    chain store taxes and, 568–570, 622
    Goodwin Knight and, 603–604
    health insurance and, 606–607
    political parties and, 594–595
    political reforms and, 595
    political system of, 612, 622
    politics and, 603, 610–611
    Progressive reforms and, 590
    promotion of, 76, 78, 256
    Ronald Reagan and, 622–623
    Sinclair campaign for governor, 599–601
    tourism and, 76, 78
    utility referendum and, 597–599
California Chain Stores Association, 568–570
California League Against Sinclairism (CLAS), 600
Calitri, Princine, 280, *307*
Cameron, W. J., 206, 690
Campaign consultants, *see also* Campaign Management; New Politics
    effect on elections, 589, 629
    Spencer & Roberts, 589, 622–623
    subspecialists and, 589–590
Campaign contributions, 622
Campaign disclosure, 609–610
Campaign funds, 604
Campaign management, 526, 607, *see also* Campaign consultants; New Politics
    decline of the party system and, 590, 595, 631
    in older system, 622
    origins of, 593
Campaign trains, 2, 593, 624
Campaigns, Inc., *see* Whitaker and Baxter International

Campbell, Lawrence W., 242
Campbell Soup Co., 361
Campion, Frank D., 614, 618, *632*
Canada, 73, 669
Canadian Film Board, 83
Cannon, Joseph D., 235–236
Capers, T. Stanley, *224*
Capital punishment, 596
Capital Times, 307
Capone, Al, 256
Carl Byoir & Associates, *see also* Byoir, Carl
  A&P account, 565–568
  A&P litigation and, 570–574
  acquired by Foote, Cone, & Belding, 584–585
  appraisal of, 581–585
  B.F. Goodrich and, 564
  Chinese famine relief and, 551
  concepts of public relations, 563–564, 578
  criticisms of, 544, 564, 573–574
  Cuba and, 542–544
  Doherty hotel account and, 546
  fees of, 456, 546
  fighting polio and, 553, 555–563
  Freeport Sulphur Co., and, 564
  German Railroad account and, 73, 534, 547–551
    McCormack–Dickstein Committee and, 146,
      549–551
  Great Depression and, 547
  guiding principles of, 546
  Libby–Owens–Ford and, 563
  Nazi propaganda and, 146
  newspaper advertising and, 555–567
  North American Aviation and, 544–545, 547
  Patman hearings and, 568
  Railroad–Truckers Brawl, *see* Railroad–Truckers Brawl
  sponsored advertising and, 560, 572
  third party technique, 539, 564, 565, 571–572,
    574, 576, 579–581
Carl Schurz Assoc., 151
Carll, Charles, 270, 704, 709
Carnegie Corporation, 313
Carnegie Hall, 313
Carter, Burnham, 123, 148, 149
Carter Oil, 656
Carter, Richard, *586*
Carville, James, 589
Case, Clifford P.
  Fund for the Republic and, 748–749
Case, Francis, 443, 444
Casey, Robert P., 624
Castro, Fidel, 320
CBS, 200, 201, 658–668, *see also* Paley, William S.
  advertising and, 200
  E. R. Murrow controversy and, 658, 662–665
  expose on car safety and, 728
  mass appeal programs and, 201
  network reforms and, 663–665
  news funtions and, 661
  news policy and, 201–202, 658
  news promotion and, 660–661
  Paley image and, 666–667
  pay TV and, 667–668
  program listings and, 201
  quiz show scandal and, 658, 662–666

UNIVAC computer and, 300
CBS Foundation, 667
C.C. Dickinson Fuel Co., 236
Celebrities, 228, *see also* Hollywood
  in promoting Coolidge, 195
  in promoting hotels, 348
  in promoting products, 298
  in promoting radio, 198
  in promoting War bonds, 227–228
Central America, 79, 80, 197
Central Railroad (New York), 52
Chafin, Don, 121
Chain Stores, 550
  litigation of, 570–574
  price fixing and, 570
  public opinion and, 573
  taxes on, 565–574, 622
Chaplin, Charles, 228
Charles Bridge and, 50
Charles, Joseph, 591, *632*
Charnay, David, 575
Charnay Public Relations Agency
  Pennsylvania truckers and, 577, 581
Chase Manhattan Bank, 137–138
Cheney Brothers, 195
Chesterfields, 207, 208
Chiang Kai-Shek, 317, 551
Chicago Herald-American, 371
Chicago Museum of Science and Industry, 202
Chicago Tribune, 222, *307*
Chicago World's Columbian Exposition, 78
Chilean Nitrate of Soda Educational Bureau, 138, 139
Chinese government, 317, 551
Christy, Howard Chandler, 558, 560
Chrysler Corporation, 128–129, 200, *see also* Automo-
    bile industry
  Dodge Motor Car Co. and, 128–129
  engineering achievements and, 710
  labor strike and, 707
Chrysler, Walter P., 124
  Dodge Motor Car Co., and, 128–129
Church, David M., 241, *250*
Cigarette Research and Information Committee, 484–485
Cigarettes, *see also* Tobacco Industry; Tobacco Indus-
    try Research Committee
  anti-cigarette campaigns, 459, 482–484, 487–494,
    499, 662
  anti-smoking organizations, 499
  filters and, 494
  heart disease and, 458, 496
  Liggett & Myers and, 207–212
  lung cancer and, 196, 458, 482–483, 491, 494, 499
  Philip Morris and, 361–363
  research and, 482–485, 489, 494
  warning labels and, 499–503
  women and, 208–209, 284
CIO, 240, *see also* John L. Lewis,
  alleged communist domination of, 465
  auto industry and, 246
  Johnstown Committee and, 245
  Little Steel and, 247, 459–463
  national health insurance and, 613
Cipollone, Rose, 490–491, 500
Citizen's Committee for Reciprocal Trade and, 328

Citizens Union, 42
City Editor, 206
Civil liberties,, 235, 601, 737, 738, 310, *see also* Fund
    for the Republic
Civil Liberties Union, American, *see* American Civil
    Liberties Union
Civil Rights Movement, 310
Civitas, non-profit organizations and, 331–332
Clarke, Edward Young, *see also* Ku Klux Klan
    character of, 379–380
    criminal charges of, 409, 411–412
    described, 379
    the ministry and, 379
    publicity techniques of, 381, 387, 389, 392–400
    resigns from KKK, 409
    scandal and, 405–410
    speakers bureau program and, 392–394
    unfavorable press and, 403–404, 406, 407
Clarke, Joseph Ignatius Constantine, 55, 56
Clary, Thomas J., 22, *26*, 578, 579
Class warfare, 247
Clayton Anti-Trust Act, 565, 577
Cleveland, Grover, 40, 50
    Armstrong Committee and, 49–50
    political campaigns, 43–44, 48–50
Clinton, Bill, 589
    foreign agents and, 769
Commonwealth, 632
Coal industry, *see also* United Mine Workers; Colorado
    Fuel & Iron
    Anthracite Coal Operators and, 45–46
    Coal Operators and, 234–236
    Logan County strike, 119–123
Coca-Cola Company, 271, 272, 274, 322, 455
    sugar tariffs and, 318
Cochran, Jacqueline, 298
Cogley, John, study of blacklisting and, 753–754
Cohen, Abraham, 186
Cold War, Radio Free Europe and, 330
Coleman, McAlister, 246, 247
Collective bargaining, the steel
    industry and, 460, 480
Colliers, 72, 276, 467, 521, *734*
Collins, Francis A., 116
Colonial Williamsburg, J. D. Rockefeller III and, 670–671
Colorado Fuel & Iron Company (CF&I), *see also* Coal
    industry
    industrial relations and, 58
    Ludlow massacre and, 57, 109, 137
    miner's strike and, 57–60, 109, 119–123, 131
    U.S. Commission on Industrial Relations and, 58, 60
Columbia Broadcasting System, *see* CBS
Columbia Journalism Review, 522, 775
Commerce, *see* Interstate Commerce Commission
Commission on Industrial Relations, U.S., 131
    coal strike investigations and, 58, 60, 123
Commission on Infantile Paralysis Research, 559
Committee of Fourteen
    immigrants and, 309
    Macy's Thanksgiving parade and, 316
Committee on Public Information (CPI), *see* Creel
    Committee
Communists, and Communism, 235, 246, 383, 400,
    739, *see also* Red Scare

alleged at Ford Foundation, 751, 4399
alleged in Congress, 467
Crusade for Freedom and, 698–699
labor unions and, 431, 463, 465
Competition, unfair, 565, 570
Computers, Remmington Rand and, 300
Concepts of public relations, *see* Public relations concepts
Congress, *see* Congressional Committees
Congress of Industrial Organizations (CIO), *see* CIO
Congressional Committees
    House Committee on Nazi Propaganda, 144–146
    House Committee on Un-American Activities
        Cogley report and, 754
        Cox Committee (1952), 742
        McCormack–Dickstein Committee, 144–150,
            146–150, 549–551
        Republic Fund grants for desegregation and, 755
    House Subcommittee on Legislative Oversight
        CBS quiz show scandal and, 665–666
    McClellan Senate Committee
        natural gas price controls and, 444
    Senate Banking and Currency Committee, 137
        Chase Manhattan Bank and, 137–138
    Senate Civil Liberties (LaFollette) Subcommittee
        steel industry and, 243–246, 465–468, 473–475
    Senate Foreign Relations (Fulbright) Committee, 769
        defining objectionable PR activities, 74
        Hamilton Wright Organization and, 84–88, 317
    Senate Post Office and Post Roads Committee
        Little Steel strike and, 466
    Senate Subcommittee on Air and WaterPublic
        Works Committee
        General Motors, 729–730
    Senate Traffic Safety (Ribicoff) Subcommittee
        General Motors and, 717–718, 727
Congressional investigations, *see* Congressional Committees
Conservation, 13, 14
    National Conservation Association and, 32–33
    National Conservation Congress, 33
    T. Roosevelt and, 27
    White Conference of Governors on, 31–33
Considine, Bob, 289, *307*
Consolidated Aircraft, 425
Consolidated Vultee and, 267, 425–426
Consumers Union, 502
Coolidge, Calvin, 159, 290
    Ku Klux Clan and, 409–410
Cooper, Lee, Puerto Rico and, 84
Copper and Brass Research Assoc., 118
Copper industry, 117–119
    post WWI crisis and, 118
Copps, Joe, 254, 269, 272, 274
Corbett, Harvey Wiley, 79
Cordtz, Dan, 715, 726, *743*
Cornell University College of Agriculture, 161
Cornwell, Elmer E., 9
Coronet, 303, 327, *342*, 351
Corporate Institutes, 64, 99, 100, 118, 247
Corporate Management, 176, 602, 603, 726, 746–747
    explanation of policies to, 746–747
    formation of policies and, 155
    PR as a function in, 176
    public attitudes and, 727
Corporate Public Relations, 22–23, 514–515, *520*

Great Depression and, 526–527
Cosco, Joe, 522
Cosgrove, George, 164
Cosgrove, Ray, 427
Council For Tobacco Research (CTR), 496, 497
Counseling, origins of, 1–9
Counselor of Public relations, see Public Relations Counsel
Couzens, Frank, 269
Cox, Eugene, 742
Cravath, Paul D., 312
Creel Committee, 105, see also Creel, George
    Carl Byoir and, 106, 536–540
    Edward Bernays and, 164–166, 171
    Minutemen and, 69, 106
    Wilson and, 106, 165, 537, 699
Creel, George, 72, 552, 586, see also Creel Committee
    Ludlow Massacre and, 57
Creole Petroleum Company (Venezuela), 654
Crider, Mr., 701
Cronon, E. David, 520
Cuba, Republic of
    sanctions against, 320
    sugar tariff and, 319
    tourism and, 542–544
Culbertson, Ely, 348–349
Cunningham, Austin, 66
Cunningham, Noble E., 591
Curti, Merle, 3, 9
Curtiss–Wright Corp., 301
Cutlip, Scott M., 71, 91, 103, 189, 190, 522, 587, 681, 711, 775
    Fund Raising in the United States, 91, 586
    Lithuania's First Independence Battle, 191, 587
Cutting, R. Fulton,, 237

D

Daily Metal Trade, 418
Dairy industry
    dispute with Margarine industry and, 433–440
    prejudice against, 435
Dakin, Edwin F., 485
Daniel Guggenheim Fund for the Promotion of Aeronautics, 138
Daniels, J. J., 495
Daniels, Josephus, 118, 537, 538, 552, 586
Darr, E. A., 483, 494
Darrow, Richard W., 423, 457, 460, 503, 520
Davis, Elmer, 529–530
Davison, Henry F.
    the Red Cross and, 35, 65, 66, 114
    the YMCA and, 65
Dawes, Charles G., 237
De Grazia, Sebastian, 214
Debs, Eugene V., 235
Deegan, Thomas J., 455, 575
Deleanis, Leonard P., 113
delegation, 604
DeLorenzo, Anthony G., 714, 715, 732n, 733
    conflict with Newsom firm and, 717, 719–721, 724
    GM auto safety issue and, 719–720, 722–723, 726
    investigation of Nadar and, 725, 726
    Ribicoff hearings and, 718
Democracy, engineering of consent and, 187
Democratic Administrations, 44, 66
Democratic National Committee, 43, 44, 48, 66, 562

Democratic Party, 37, 204, 525, 557, 599
    campaign support and, 590
Democrats, 37, 385
Dempsey, Jack, 257
Department of Commerce, U.S., 105
Department of Justice, U.S., 490, 519, 770
    A&P and, 570–574
Department of State, U.S., 22
    foreign agents and, 85
Depression, see Great Depression
Desegregation, grants for, 754–756
DeSilver, Albert, 235, 236
Detroit, and the automobile industry, 270
Dewey, Thomas E., 624, 672
Dexter, Fellows, 41–42
Dial, 174, 179
Diamond, Edwin, 632
Dickey, C., 124, 146–147, 552, 563
    McCormack hearings and, 549
Dickey, Carl C., 543, 547, 548
Dickinson (C.C.) Fuel Co., 236
Dickstein, Samuel, 549, 550
Dilenschneider, Robert J., 773, 776
Dillon Reed & Co., 128
Dinnerstein, Leonard, 374, 375, 412
Direct Mail, Inc., 232, 243
Dirigibles, see Airships
Dirksen, Everett, 609
Disenschneider, Robert L, 514n
Doctors, and health insurance, 606
Dodge Brothers Motor Car Co., 197–200, see also Automobile industry
    Dodge Senior and, 198
    purchase by Chrysler of, 128
    Victory Six and, 198
Dodge, Cleveland H., 65
Dodge Motor Car Company, 128
Doherty, Henry L., 546, 563
    fighting polio and, 553, 555–563
Doll, Richard, 483
Dolly Sisters, 195
Donner, Frederick G., 714, 715
    GM safety issue and, 715–718, 724, 732
Doolittle, Jimmy, 139, 282, 297, 306
    cross country flight and, 287
Dorais, James J., 609
Dow Corning, silicone breast implants and, 772
Dreiser, Theodore, 175
Druck, Kal, 583
Drug industry
    abuses by, 447
    drug prices and, 762
    drug regulation and, 433, 445–450
    Lever Brothers and, 353, 355–356
    McKesson Robbins scandal and, 323–327
    patent restrictions and, 448
    Pepsodent and, 353–354
    Sterling Drug Company and, 329–330
    thalidomide scandal and, 448
Du Bois, Josiah, Jr., 151
Dudley, Pendleton, 7, 9, 38, 50, 72, 92–103, 103, 104, 153, 961, see also Pendleton Dudley and Associates
    background of, 92–93
    Dudley–Anderson–Yutzy, 101

early career and, 94–95, 97
education and, 93–94
evaluation of, 102, 102–103
journalism and, 95
letters of, *103, 104*
obituary, *104*
on origins of PR, 7, 97
Pendleton Dudley and Associates opened, 96
PRSA and, 102
The Wisemen and, 130, 509, 510
Dudley–Anderson–Yutzy (DAY), 101
Duke, David, 372
Dulles, Foster Rhea, *520*
Duncan, Robert J., 65, 226, 228, 232, *250*
DuPont, Pierre S. III, 333, 334
Durbin, William, *520*
Dutton, William S., *307*
Dyer (George L.) Advertising, 62, 115
Dyer, Gustavus W., 246
Dyer, Thomas G., 401, *413*

E

Earhart, Amelia, 295
Amelia Earhart Medal and, 306
Earl Newsom & Company (ENCO), *see also* Ford,
      Henry II
CBS Ed Murrow controversy and, 662–664
CBS image problems and, 666–667
CBS News and, 660–661
CBS quiz show scandal and, 662–664
   House hearings on, 665–666
clients of, 527
counseling political leaders and, 672–674
Ford Foundation, *see* Ford Foundation
Ford Motor Company, *see* Ford Motor Company
functions of, 640
GM's auto safety problems and, 716–719, 723–
      724, 729
GM's conflicts with, 717, 719–721, 724
GM's investigation of Nader and, 725–728
GM's position on auto safety
      legislation and, 722–723
GM's PR problems and, 716, 719–722, 726–727, 729
   suggested remedies for public distrust, 731–732
   suggested response at Pollution hearings, 729–730
GM's testimony at Ribicoff hearings and, 717–718
International Paper and, 640, 668–669
John Rockefeller III and, 640, 670–672
list of major clients, 680t
Newsom retires, 674
pay TV and, 667–668
philosophy of, 641, 644, 649–650, 708
product promotion and, 639
promoting Paley and, 659
PRSA and, 639–640
public opinion and, 644, 646
Radio Free Europe and, 673
research and, 641–642
services of, 641
staff of, 641–643
Standard Oil (NJ) PR campaign and, 644–657
   objectives for, 653–654
   Oil Cartel probe and, 654–657
   recommendations for, 650–654

reputation of, 644–645, 648–650
Earle, George H.
   Bethlehem steel strike and, 240–241, 244
Earle, Peter, 583, 585
Eastern Railroads, 22, 122, 129, 575, *see also* Railroad–
      Truckers Brawl
Eastern Railroads Presidents Conference, 575–577,
      580, 581
Edelman, Daniel J., 773, 774, *775, 776*
Edison Institute of Technology, 206
Edison, Thomas A, 2, 159, 47. 260
   Light's Golden Jubilee, 205–207
Editor & Publisher, 37, 50, 131, 133–134, 136, 144,
      153, 180, 185, 194, 207, 215, 221, 482
   criticism of Bernays, 185, 215, 221
   on IRT rate controversy, 131, 133–134, 136–137
   Ivy Lee obituary, 153
   praises Parker & Bridge, 44
   on press agentry, 180, 194
Education, 738, *see also* African-American education
   Ford Foundation and, 738, 741–742, 758–759
Educational television, 201
Edward Howard & Co., 113
Egypt, Answan Dam and, 81
Egypt, Aswan Dam opening, 81
Eisenhower, Dwight D., 248, 274, 516, 589, 672–673
   Cuban sanctions and, 320
   natural gas deregulation and, 444
   Presidential campaign and, 603, 624–626
Elco Company, 299–300
Elections, 589, 629
   returns and, 300
   steps to winning, 629
Electorate, The, 630
Electric Auto-Lite Co., 272
Electrical, Radio, and Machine Workers,
      International Union of, 212–214
Electricity, 2, 47, 260
Eliot, Charles W., 16–18, *25*, 308
   Harvard and, 11
   National Conservation Association and, 33
Elliott, John, 145
Ellsworth, James Drummond, 10–12, *25*
   AT&T and, 14, 15, 18, 19
   Publicity Bureau and, 14, 19
Emanuel, Victor, 424–426
   Avco Manufacturing Corp. and, 426–430
   Consolidated Aircraft and, 425, 426
   utilities and, 424
Emerson, Guy, 227–230
Employee relations, 110
Encyclopedia of Labor Conflict, 120
Engineering, public relations and, 110–111
Environmental Protection Agency, 674
Episcopal Church Pension Fund, 62, 63
Epstein, Leon D., 631, *632*
Equitable Life Assurance Society, 49
Esso Standard Oil, 656
Ethics, in public relations, *see also* Public Relations concepts
   Baldwin and, 338–339
   Bernays and, 171, 203
   Bruno and, 302–306
   Hill and, 450, 458, 475–477, 501–503
   Newsom and, 641, 644, 649–650

in professional organizations, 302, 339, 476, 504, 505, 508
the public interest and, 449
in public relations agencies, 772–774
tobacco industry and, 458, 482
unwarranted claims and, 287
Evening Journal, 133
Evening Journal, on IRT rates, 133
Evening Journal [O'Laughlin] and, 133
Ewing, Oscar, 613, 614, 619
Exxon (former name: *Standard Oil,* New Jersey)
Valdez disaster and, 64, 715, 772

F

Fairbanks, Douglas, 228
Fairchild, Sherman, 285
Fairchild, Sherman, aerial camera and, 285
Fairless, Ben, 480
Fairman, Milton, *104*
Farben (I. G.), *see* I. G. Farben
Faxon, F. W. Company, 182, *190*
Federal Bureau of Investigation, 510, 568
Federal Cigarette Labelling and Advertising Act, 500
Federal Communications Commission, 214, 500
Federal excise tax, 433, 434, 436
Federal Meat Inspection Act, 6
Federal Power Commission, 441
Federal Trade Commission (FTC), U.S., *104, 113*
Insull investigation and, 108, 183–184, 260, *113*
meat industry and, 99
Oil Cartel probe and, 656–658
patent medicines and, 541, 542
publications of, *588*
tobacco industry and, 501
Federated Department Stores, 358, 359
Fellows, Dexter, 41–42, *72*, 176
Feminism, Doris Fleischman and, 169
Ferry, W. H. "Ping," 642, 677, 740, 757, *760*
Corporation and the Economy, The, 757
Ford Foundation and, 736
Ford Motor and, 684–685, 694, 696, 704, 712
Fund for the Republic and, 749–750
Fund terminates contract of, 758
hired by Ford Foundation, 736
House hearings and, 742
minimizing critism of Foundation and, 739–740
split with Newsom and, 736
Standard Oil (NJ) and, 647, 655
supports Cogley Report, 753
supports desegreation grants, 754–755
supports Gaither report proposals, 745–746
Fifth Avenue Bus Co., 271
Fifth Avenue Hotel, 347–348
Finance, *see* Banks
Finances, economy of government and, 237
Fink, Conrad, 766
assault of public marketplace and, 767
President's Lecture, 775
First Amendment, 579
Fisher, Carl, 253, 254, 255, 257
Fisher, Thomas K., 665
Fisk, Frederick P., 18
Fisk University,, 312, 339
Fitzgerald Company, 750–751

Fitzgerald, Stephen, 642, 684
Flagler, Henry, 80
Fleischman, Doris E. (Mrs. E. Bernays), 107, 168–170, *190*
Edward L. Bernays Foundation and, 169
Fletcher, Frank Irving, 198
Florida Citrus Commission, 101
Florida (State), *see also* Miami Beach
tourism and, 80, 81
Flowers, Benjamin Orange, 5
Flynn, John T., 160, *191*
Flynn, Stephen, 557
Fokker, Anthony, 284
Wright Whirlwind Engine and, 287, 288
Fokker planes, 284, 287, 288
Fones, Jack Scott, 359, *370*
Fontaine, Andre, *733*
"Revolution of the Rouge," 696–697
Food Administration, 105
Food and Drug Administration, 448
Foote, Cone, and Belding, 258, 456, 531
acquires Carl Byoir & Associates, 584–585
anti-smoking campaign and, 488
Forbes, B. C., 72
Ford, Benson (Edsel Ford's son)
auto safety and, 702
Ford Foundation and, 694
Ford, Edsel (Henry Ford's son), 268, 270, 271, 683
financing North Pole flight and, 288
Ford Foundation and, 735
I. G. Farben and, 143
Ford, Edsel, Mrs., 682
Ford Foundation, 735–769, *see also* Ford, Henry II
charter for, 737
criticism of, 747
founding of, 735
Gaither Report and, 737
Jewish Theological Seminary award and, 694
link to Ford Motor Co. reputation and, 735–736, 739, 740
Newsom 1954 Assessment of, 747–748
philanthropic objectives of, 737
president of, 737–738
public approval of, 737–738
Publis relations, 738–739, 740–741
relationship to Republic Fund, 751–752
Republic fund disowned by, 748–750
right-wing opposition to, 739, 741, 742
testimony at House hearings and, 742
Ford, Guy Stanton, 538
Ford, Henry, 2, 254, 268–271, 683, *see also* Ford Motor Co.
anti-semitism and, 690, 691, 695
Ford Air Reliability Tour and, 285–286
Lights Golden Jubilee and, 205–207
Ford, Henry II (son of Edsel Ford), 269, 682–713, *see also* Ford Foundation; Ford Motor Company
assumes control of Ford Co., 683
assumes control of Ford Foundation, 735–736
background of, 682–683
"Challenge of Human Engineering," 687
Crusade for Freedom and, 698–699
ends Newsom account, 712–713
Foundation management style and, 741
Foundation policy and, 739, 742
Foundation reputation and, 740, 741, 755

Fund for the Republic and, 749, 755
good press and, 696–697
grant for auto research and, 701
Gridiron Club speech and, 697
hires Newsom, 683–684
image making campaign for, 687–688, 696–698
Israel and, 695
letter to UAW and, 685
magazine publicity and, 697–68
NCCJ and, 693, 694
objects to Fund's actions, 755–756
personality of, 684, 695–696
receives B'nai B'rith award, 694
speaks to managers of Ford Co., 746–747
testifies at House hearings, 742
United Jewish Appeal and, 693
Ford, Henry, Mrs., 682, 741–742
Ford Motor Company, 713–733, *see also* Automobile
       industry; Ford, Henry; Ford, Henry II;
       Ford Foundation
"American Road" Celebration and, 699–701
Arab League boycott of, 695–696
erases anti-Semite stigma, 690–696
Ford Foundation and, 746–747
Ford Pinto and, 701–703
improves internal PR dept., 710–711
Model A car and, 198
OPA price fixing and, 688–689
promotes auto safety, 701–703
UAW contract negotiations (1949) and, 703–709
UAW wage dispute (1941) and, 685–688
Willow Run bomber plant, 268–271
Ford Trimotor plane, 285
Foreign Agents, 74, 84, 86, *see also* Foreign interests
Agent defined, 72
controversies and, 769–770
disclosure of activities and, 74
investigated by Fulbright committee, 83–88, 768
need for, 768
Foreign Agents Registration Act (1938), 74, 769
list of lobbyists and, 770
Foreign interests, *see also* Foreign agents; foreign trade
German–American relations and, 144, 146
need for PR representation of, 73
Puerto Rico and, 83, 84
Foreign trade, *see also* Tariffs
promotion of, 75, 78, 327–329
Forestry, *see* Conservation
Formosa, 551
Forrest, John F., *342*
Fortnightly Clubs, 237
Fortune, 350, 455, 715, 726
Francisco, Don, 569, 599, 622
anti-Sinclair campaign, 599, 622
California Chain Stores Association and, 568–570
Franco, Anthony
(SEC) consent order and, 772
Frank, David D, 155
Frankfurther, Felix, on Bernays and Lee, 185
Free trade, 327
agriculture and, 320
Freeman, Andrew, *72*
Freeport Sulphur Company, 564
Freight business, *see* Railroad–Truckers Brawl

Freud, Anna, 161
Freud, Sigmond, 161, 163, 223, *see also* Bernays, Edward L.
book published in U.S., 170
criticism of theories in U.S. and, 174–175
influence on America, 175–176
letter to Bernays, 174–175
Freyermuth, George, 647, 651, 655, 678
Fronts, *see also* Tobacco industry; Hill and Knowlton, Inc.
anti-chain store tax campaign and, 565, 571–572, 574
Citizens for a Free Kuwait, 770
legality of, 570–572, 579–580
Pennsylvania railroad and, 211
Railroad–Truckers Brawl and, 574, 576, 579–581
Republican Party and, 600
sponsoring committees and, 162, 163, 208
Fry, Henry Peck, 402
Fuhrman, Candice Jacobson, 58–59, *72*
Fulbright Committee, *see* Congressional Committees
Fulbright, William J., 74, 317
Fulbright–Hickenlooper Amendment, 74, 87
Fuller, Craig, 771n
Fuller, Edgar I., 409, *412*
Fulton, William, *307*
Fund for the Republic, 736, 740, 746, *see also* Ford
       Foundation
Basic Issues Program of, 756–757
Cogley Report and, 754
disowned by Ford Foundation, 748–750
Fund for Democratic Freedoms and, 745–746
grants for desegregation and, 754–755
objectives of, 748–749
Fundraising, 139–140, 231–234, 313–314, *see also*
       American Red Cross
Chinese famine relief, 237, 551
Episcopal Cathedral and, 314
Episcopal Church Pension Fund and, 62, 63
Fisk University and, 312–313
guarantees of work to clients and, 85, 88–89
Harvard Endowment Campaign, 311–312
Ketchum brothers and, 112
Liberty Bond campaign, 31, 105, 226–228
Pitt Campaign and, 111–112
polio epidemic and, 551, 553–563
postwar WWI boom and, 248
Princeton Endowment Campaign, 139–140
Russia and, 347
Smith College and, 229
sponsoring committees and, 162, 163, 208
F. W. Faxon Co., 182

G

Gaither Report
Fund for Democratic Freedoms and, 745
objectives for Foundation, 737
Gaither, Rowan
as director at Ford Foundation, 739
Foundation charter and, 736–737
Galenson, Walter, *520*
Gambling, Bahamas and, 450–451
Garrett, Paul, 203, 205, 527
on Bernays CBS work, 205
General Motors and, 527, 638
The Wisemen and, 508, 509
Gas, *see* Natural Gas

Gaskill, William J., 124, 155
GE, *see* General Electric
Gearhart, Bertrand, 328, 329
General Asphalt Co., 46–47
General Dynamics, 300
General Dynamics Corp., 300, 301, 425
General Electric (GE), 205
    "Lights Golden Jubilee" and, 205–207
    v. the IUE, 212–214
General Mills
    Gold Medal Flour and, 139
General Motors (GM), 203–205, 713–733, *see also* Automobile industry
    auto safety and, 719–724
    auto safety legislation and, 722–723
    bank loans and, 204
    CBS controversy and, 733
    conflict with Newsom recommendations, 717, 719–721, 724, 731
    Corvair crisis and, 713–715, 730
    Great Depression and, 203, 204
    investigation of Nader and, 725–726
    management problems and, 726
    pickup truck crisis and, 732–733, 766
    PR counsel and, 35, 527
    PR policy in legal matters and, 714–715
    reply to CBS "Crash Program" and, 728
    research and, 710
    retains Newsom Co., 716
    Roche apology at Ribicoff hearings and, 727
    Senate Committee on Traffic Safety and, 717–718, 729–730
    unionization and, 246
Gentry, Curt, 384, *412*
George Harrison Phelps, 197, 199
George L. Dyer Advertising, 62, 115
George, Walter F., 183
Georgia
    anti-semitism and, 375
    Atlanta Bottle Club and, 373–374
    Atlanta Consitution and, 378, 379, 404
    Atlanta Journal and, 376, 386
    Harvest Festival and, 380
    Knights of Mary Phagan and, 375
    Ku Klux Klan and, 373–377, 393, 404
    promoting Atlanta and, 379
    (State), 373
    The Leo Frank Case and, 374–375
Georgia Power Co., 183
German Dye Trust, *see* I. G. Farben
German Railroads Tourist Bureau, 73, 146, 534, 547–550
Germany (Imperial), 280, *see also* Nazi Government
    Zeppelin disaster and, 291–294
Gerould, Mireille,, 641
Gimbel, Bernard, 455
Ginger, Ray, 72
Girdler, Reynolds, 576, 577
Girdler, Thomas, 247, 267, 421, *see also* Republic Steel
    aviation and, 425
    Bootstraps, 462, 469, *521*
    LaFollette Senate hearings and, 466–467
    Republic Steel and, 458, 462–470, 476
Glass, Dudley, 199
GM, *see* General Motors

Goebbels, Joseph, 149
Goering, Herman, 294
Gold Medal Flour, 139
Golden, L. L. L., *157, 530*
    on T. J. Ross, 125–126
Golden Trumpet Award
    Bernays and, 222
Goldman, Eric, 1, *9*, 39, 52, 61, *72*, 177, 180, 749
Goldwater, Barry, 622
Golin–Harris, 155
Gonser, Thomas, 355, 356
Goodman, Edwin, 348, 358
Goodman, Walter, 519, *521*
Goodyear Aircraft Corp., 301
    airships and, 291–292
Goodyear Tire & Rubber Co., 301
Goss, Bert, 422–423, 439, 449, *457*, 485, 492, 493, 503, *520*
Gossett, William, 704, 708
Governers, White House Conference, 31
Government, U.S., *see also* United States
    price fixing and, 688
    regulation and, 674–675
    size of, 526
Grace, Eugene, 241
Grace, W. R., 155
Granik, Theodore, *587*
Grant, Ulysses S., 373
Grant, U.S. III, 333
Gras, N.S.B, *9*, 650
Gray, Robert Keith, 770n, 771
Great Depression, The, 185, 198, 204, 232, 239, 352
    aviation and, 292
    banks and, 137, 204
    big business and, 350, 526, 563
    California and, 600
    chain store taxes and, 565
    political campaign management and, 526
    public relations and, 317, 525–527
    steel industry and, 422
    tariffs and, 320
Greater New York Fund, 115
    General Motors and, 203
Green, William, 240, 613
Greene, Harold C., 229
Greene, Jerome D., 16
Griffin, John A., 340
Groceries, and chain stores, 565
Groves, Leslie, 130, 510
Gruening, Ernest, 179, 183, *191*
Grunig, James, *775*
    4 models of public relations practice, 763–764
Guarantee of work to clients, and fundraising, 85, 88, 89
Gudgeon, Russell, 300, 301, 303
Guggenheim, David, 138
Guggenheim Foundation, 58, 138–139
    and Ivy Lee, 138–139
Guggenheim, Simeon, 118
Gulf Crisis, 64
Gumbrecht, A.C., 239
Gunther, John, *277*

H

H. A. Bruno & Associates Inc., 300–302, *see also* Bruno & Blythe; Bruno, Harry

H. A. Bruno & Associates Inc. 300–302
    clients of, 301
    incorporated, 300, 301
    international public relations and, 301–302
    role of, 301
    sale of, 306
    staff of, 301
Haas, Sidney, 196, 197
Hacker, Andrew, *586*
Hahn, Paul M., 484
Haldeman, H. R., 627
Hall, G. Stanley, 172
Hall, Stuart, 543
Hamel, George F., 449, *457*, 487, 518, *520*
Hamilton Wright Organization (HWO), 73–91, *see also*
        Wright, Hamilton I; Wright, Hamilton II;
        Wright, Hamilton III
    early clients of, 79–80
    free travel for journalists and, 87, 89
    Fulbright hearings and, 74–75, 84–88
    guarantees of work and, 88–89
    Heavyweight Boxing Championship, 257
    list of clients, 90t
    Pacific Exposition and, 78–79
    Philipine promotion of, 77–78
    pictorial publicity and, 82–83, 86–87
    political propaganda and, 75, 77
    promoting Florida and, 80–81
    PRSA and, 87–89
    tourism and, 75–81
Hammond, Donald, 239, 249, 518
Hammond, George, 559, 564, 581, 584, 585, *586*
    background of, 545
    defense of German tourist account, 550–551
    promoting President's Birthday Ball, 559
Hand, Ira, 295, 296
Hanley, Parke F., 230–231
Hannagan, Steve, 251–276
    auto racing, *see* Auto racing
    background of, 251–252
    baseball and, 266–267
    clients of, 271, 272, 275t–276
    Coca-Cola Export Corp., 251
    death of, 276
    failures of, 272–273
    focus of, 253
    Ford's Willow Run Plant and, 268–271, 425
    guiding principles of, 273
    Heavyweight Boxing and, 257–258
    Insull Campaign and, 259–263
    journalism and, 252–253
    later accounts, 271–272
    Lord & Thomas, *see* Lord & Thomas
    Miami Beach and, 251, 255–257
    obituaries, 277
    opens Steve Hannagan & Assoc., 263
    personality of, 456
    press agentry and, 252
    public relations and,, 251
    radio advertising and, 270
    review of career, 266
    Robinson–Hannagan Associations, Inc., 274
    sale of Hannagan agency, 274
    Sun Valley and,, 251, 264–266

women and, 265–266
WWII and, 267, 268
Hardenburgh, Wesley, *104*
Harding, Edward, 230
Harding, Warren G.
    Budget Act and, 237
    coal strike and, 120, 121
    and Miami Beach, 256
Hardwick, Thomas, 149
Harlow, Rex,, 216, 217, 339, 529
Harper's [Adelman], 587
Harper's Magazine [Walker & Sklar], *522*
Harriman, W. Averill
    free trade and, 328
    and Sun Valley, 264–265
Harris, Herbert, *521*
Harris, Leon, 343, 358, *371*
Harris, Richard, 446, *457*, *521*
Harris, Winthrop, and Company, 53
Harris, W.W., 62, 115, 116
    Lee, Harris, and Lee and, 62, 115
Hart, Russell M.
    memo on Foundation PR policy and, 740–741
Hartford Brothers, The, 565
Hartwell, Dickson, 266, 272, *276*, 574
Harvard Business Review [Baldwin], 327, *343*
Harvard Club, 221
Harvard Endowment Fund, 230
    John Price Jones and, 228–230, 311–314
    W. H. Baldwin and, 311–314
Harvard University, 11, 15, 16, 65
Hastings, Ned, 200
Haswell, Clayton, 223–224
Hate organizations, 377, *see also* Ku Klux Klan
Hatfield, George, 599, 603
Hawks, Frank, 295
Hawley–Smoot Tariff bill, 318
Hays, Samuel P., 72
Health insurance, *see also* National health insurance
    California and, 606–607
    voluntary, 607
Healy, Tim Traverse, 763
Hearst Corporation, 284
Hearst Magazine, 536
Hearst, William Randolph, 117, 132
    attack on IRT and, 132
    Lindbergh and, 292
    New York American and, 403–404
Hearst–Pulitzer War, 97
Heath, Burton, 84
Heavy construction, WWI and, 312
Heeney, Tom, 257
Heinrichs, E. H., 47
Held, Doris, 169
Hellman, Goeffrey, 348, 352, 366, *370*
Henderson, Elmer, 614, 616, 617
Henry, Barklie, 94
Henry Street Settlement House, 345, 346
Henry, Susan, 169, *192*
Hepburn Act, 8, 21, 23
Hereford, William R., 116
Hershey Chocolate Corporation, 318
Hess, John L., 365, *371*
Hickenlooper, Bourke, 74

Hiebert, Ray, 60, *71*, 118, 131, 137, 138
    Chase National Bank and, 138
Hiebert, Ray Eldon, 37, 42, 59, 63, *71*, 639
Higham, John, *412*
Highway, Public, and trucking, 577
Hill, Bradford, 483
Hill, George Washington, 124, 126, 188–189, 284
    American Tobacco Company and, 208–212
Hill, Harvey J., 65
Hill, John W., 108, 252, 267, 272, 414–523, 579, 582,
        see also Hill and Knowlton; Hill and
        Knowlton, Inc.
    as an author, 513–514
    anti-labor views of, 432, 463, 465, 516
    assessments of, 511–512, 518–519
    background of, 415–417
    Bernays and, 216
    death of, 415
    decides to enter public relations, 419–420
    early clients of, 420–421
    effort to organize counselors and, 503–506
    ethics and, 450, 458, 475–477, 495–496, 501–503, 518
    Hill Foundation and, 517–518
    honorary doctorates of, 416
    journalism and, 417–419
    obituary, *520*
    opens public relations office, 420–421
    Papers of, *277*, 451–452, *457*, 515, 518, *519–520*
    personal life, 512–513
    philosophy of, 514–515
    Political views of, 515–517
    PRSA and, 505, 507, 508
    The Wisemen and, 130, 508–511
    works
        Corporate Public Relations, *457*, 513, 520
        The Making of a Public Relations Man, 277,
            418–420, 444, *457*, *520*
Hill and Knowlton, 108, 112, 267, 272, 273, 420–424,
        see also Hill, John W.; Hill and Knowlton, Inc.
    American Iron and Steel Institute and, 421–424
    branches seperate, 422, 424
    Hill moves to New York, 421–422
    Republic Steel and, 423–424
    sold to J. Walter Thompson, 414
    strikebreaking and, 247
Hill and Knowlton, Inc. (N.Y.branch of Hill and
        Knowlton), 421–523, *see also* Hill and
        Knowlton; Hill, John W.
    aircraft industry and, 425–426
    anti-abortion campaign and, 773–774
    BCCI bank fraud and, 770
    campaign for Kuwait and, 770–771
    campaign to deregulate natural gas and, 441–445
        McClellan Senate hearings and, 444–445
    campaign to inhibit sale of margarine, 433–440
    campaign to thwart drug laws, 445–450
        Kefauver hearings and, 446–449
    campaign for tobacco and, 458–459, 483–496,
        501, 502, 679
        strategy of, 489, 492–496
        warning labels and, 499
    early accounts of, 422, 423
    effective drug legislation and, 433
    employee relations and, 426, 453

    ethics and, 458, 475–477, 495–496, 501–503
    fees of, 444, 468
    financial relations and, 430
    fronts and, 471–473, 476–477, 499
    HUD scandal and, 773
    influencing public opinion and, 485
    other accounts of, 454–456, 485
    philosophies and procedures, 451–454
    political campaigns and, 431–432
    product promotion and, 426–428
    Robinson–Hannagan Assoc. and, 450, 455, 456
    staff of, 422–423
    the steel industry and, 458–482, 475, 477
        campaign against unionization and, 433, 468–470
        LaFollette hearings and, 467–469, 474–475
        strikebreaking and, 469–472, 480–482
        The Ugly Bahamian Episode, 450–451, 455–456
Hiller, E. T., 185
    on manipulating public opinion, 185
Hindenburg,The, see airships
Hitler, Adolph, 140, 143, 146, 150, 534, 548
    anti-semitism and, 550
    industrialists and, 152–153
H. K. McCann Co., 227, 230
Hock, Henry J., Trade Press Syndicate and, 199
Hoffman, Paul G., 740
    Ford Foundation and, 737–738, 742
    Fund for the Republic and, 748
    right-wing attacks on, 739
    testifies at House hearings, 742
Hofstader, Richard, *9*
Hollywood, 86, 264, 272, *see also* Celebrities
    anti-Sinclair campaign and, 599
    blacklisting and, 753–754
Holman, Charles, 439
Holman, Charles W., 434
Holocaust, 149
Home Market Club, 13
Hoover, Herbert, 137, 196, 207, 321, 431, 515
    banking investigation and, 137
    Edison and, 206
    Great Depression and, 204, 525–526, 547
    press secretary and, *113*
    public relations and, 105, 525
    wartime food conservation and, 105
Hoover, J. Edgar
    anti-Red zeal of, 384, 465
    Justice Department and, 384
Hope, Bob, 354
Hopkins, John J., 300
House Banking and Currency Committee, 688
House Ways and Means Committee, 328
Howard, Roy W., 254
Howe, Louis McHenry, 525–528, 554
Hower, Ralph, 7, *9*
Hoyt, Edwin P., 211, *224*
HS 2 Navy Coastal Patrol planes, 282
Hughes, Judge Charles Evan, 115
Hull, Cordell, 327
Human relations, *see* Doris Fleischman
Humble Oil, 656
Humphrey, Hubert H.
    1968 presidential campaign and, 626–627
Hunt, Todd,, *775*

Hunter, Barbara, 92
Hussein, Saddam, 770
Hutchins, Robert M., 736, 740, 748, 757–758
    Cogley blacklisting report and, 753–754
    Ford Foundation and, 739
    Fund for the Republic and, 748–751, 757
    impudent actions of, 742, 751
    right-wing opposition to, 741
    testifies at House hearings, 742
Huxley, Gervas, 639
Hylan, John F., 132, 133

I

Iacocco, Lee
    Ford Pinto and, 702
Ianuzzi, Ralph R., Sr., 306
ICBM missiles, and shock tubes, 429–430
I. G. Farben
    German–American relationship and, 143–146
    House investigations of, 146–153
    Nuremberg trials and, 144, 151–152
    Standard Oil (N.J.) rubber patents and, 644–645
Ilgner, Max, 151, 152
Immigrants, 399, 400
    Committee of Fifteen and, 309
    in strikebreaking, 57
Immigration
    American Museum of, 335–336
Independent, 184
Indianapolis Speedway, 251, 253, 272
Industrial Home for Crippled Children, 112
Industrial relations, 58, 60, 123, 131, see also Labor dispute
Industrial Relations Advisory Committee, 704, 705
Industrialists
    courting the constituency and, 27, 319
    financing strikebreaking and, 241, 245, 246
    linking unionists to communists, 383
    National Citizens' Committee, 245–246
    as promoters, 285, 288
Industrialization, 1, 4, 38, 106, 107
Industry, see also Railroads; Steel industry; Automobile industry
    1920 business slump and, 100
    aircraft, 267–271
    anti-labor tactics of, 471–475
    arbitration and, 314, 464
    business codes and, 422, 459
    coal, 45–46, 57–60, 109, 119–123
    collective bargaining and, 460
    copper, 117–119
    ethics and, 772–773
    good press and, 304–305
    meat, 6, 99–101, 118
    oil, 30, 48, 55–56, 63–64
    Red Scare and, 235, 465
    research and, 118
    Samuel Insull, 259–263
    tobacco, 126–128, 207–212, 272
    trucking, 22
Infantile Paralysis, see Polio epidemic
Inland Steel, 462
Inquiry Magazine, 185
Insull, Samuel, 2, 113, 259–263
    acquitted of criminal charges, 263

imprisonment of, 262
indictments of, 261
National Electric Light Assoc. (NELA), 108
    utilities ownership and, 108, 113, 183–184, 424
Insull, Samuel Jr.(son of SI), 259–261, 263, 264
Insurance companies, 49
    and legislative influence, 49
    legislative influencing and, 49–50
Integration, see also African-American Education
    Sydenham Hospital and, 340–341
Integrationist, groups, 742
Interborough Rapid Transit (IRT), 41, 62, 131
    N.Y. Transit Commission, 133–137
    price gouging and, 132
    press accounts of, 132, 133, 136
International Harvester Company, 47
International Nickel, 321
International Paper Company (IP), 640, 668–66
International Psychoanalytic Press of London, 173, 174
International public relations, 551, see also Hamilton Wright Organization
International Public Relations Association, 218
International Union of Electrical, Radio, and Machine Workers (IUE), 212–214
Internationalism, 742
Internationalization, of advertising and public relations firms, 414
Interstate Commerce Commission, 767
    rail rates and, 20, 54, 59
IRT, see Interborough Rapid Transit
Irwin, James W., 51, 72, 158, 184–185, 191, 196, 224, 510, 511, 710
Ivory Soap, 194
Ivy Lee & Associates, 114, see also Lee, Ivy Ledbetter; Lee, Harris & Lee
    American Tobacco Co., and, 126–127
    becomes T. J. Ross & Associates, 154–155
    Chrysler Corp. and, 128–129
    confidentiality and, 125
    copper industry and, 118–119
    fundraising and, 139–140
    German Dye Trust (I. G. Farben) account, 143–153
    Guggenheim account and, 138–139
    I. G. Farben account, 140–153
        House investigations of, 144, 146–150
    IRT brings unfavorable publicity, 136–137
    IRT hearings and, 133–137
    IRT rates and, 131–137
    Ivy Lee & T. J. Ross Assoc., 74
    Pennsylvania Railroad and, 129–130
    product promotion and, 139
    Ross & Lee accounts, 156t
    Ross becomes partner of, 123
    Ross joins firm, 115
    staff of, 123–124

J

J. Walter Thompson Group, 108, 258–259, 414, 627
    buys Hill and Knowlton, 414, 456
    firm sold, 414
Jackson, Andrew,, 591–592
Jackson Hole project, 672
Jackson, Kenneth T., 382
James S. Twohey Associates, 641

Japan, atomic bomb and, 130
Japanese, 425
Jewish Daily Forward, Ivy Ledbetter Lee obituary, 144
Jews, 143, 144, 344, 550, *see also* Anti-Semitism
    German industrialists and, 145
    Ku Klux Klan and, 375, 399, 400
John Birch Society, 622
John Day Publishing Co., 637–638
John Price Jones Corp., *see also* Jones, John Price
    Bethlehem Steel Co. and, 240–249
    coal operators and, 234–236
    Direct Mail, Inc., and, 232, 243
    fundraising and, 226–228, 231–234, 237, 243
    goals of, 107
    incorporated, 230
    Johnstown Citizen's Committee and, 241–244
    McCann–Erickson partnership and, 234
    other early accounts of, 237–240
    promotional phamphlets, 231–232, 238–239
    publicity campaigns and, 231, 237, 241–246
    publicity philosophy, 239
    purpose of firm, 231–233
    sale of agency and, 248–249
    social causes and, 249
    staff of, 230
    statement of Standard Practice, 233–234
    strikebreaking and, 234–236, 240–249
    testimony at Senate hearings, 243–245
John Simeon Guggenheim Memorial Foundation, 138
Johnson & Johnson, Tylenol crisis and, 773
Johnson, Campbell, 498
Johnson, Hiram, 594
Johnson, Lady Bird, 335
Johnson, Lyndon B.
    American Museum of Immigration and, 335
    national health insurance and, 613
    smog control and, 730
Johnstown Steel Strike, 236
Joint Committee on Atomic Energy, 517
Jolson, Al, 195
Jones, C. S. "Casey," 282
Jones, Ernest, 173, 174, *191*
Jones, Jesse, 204
Jones, John Price, 107, 226–249, *250, see also* John
        Price Jones, Inc.
    anti-union views of, 241, 244
    background of, 227
    Consolidated Edison and, 228
    described, 248
    fundraising and, 226–229
    Guy Emerson and, 226, 227
    Harvard Endowment Fund and, 228–229
    John Price Jones firm incorporated, 230
    labeled a fascist, 246, 247
    Liberty Loan Drives and, 226, 227
    milk companies and, 228
    Papers, *249*
    philanthropy and, 227
Jones (John Price) Corp., *see* John Price Jones Corp.
Jones and Laughlin Steel, 462, 465
Jones, Price Jones *Papers, 249*
Jones, Stanley, 266
Jones–Costigan Act, 320
Journal of American History, 520, 521

Journal of the American Medical Association, 482–483
Journal-American, 307
Journalism, 2, 454, 455, *see also* Newspapers; News
        Media
    lust for ratings and, 766
    news values and, 765–767
    objectivity and, 25
    publicity and, 231
Journalist, Press agentry and, 2
Journalists
    cigarette debate and, 490
    crusading, 69
    free travel and, 87, 89
    muckrackers and, 5
J. P. Morgan & Company, 228
Justice Department, U.S., *see* Department of Justice

K

Kahn, E. J., Jr., *412*
Kefauver, Estes, 445, *521*
    Senate hearings on drug laws and, 445–449
Kelley, Lane, interview of Bernays, 222–223
Kelley, Stanley, 609, 596, 616, *632*
Kellogg, John Harvey, *521*
Kelly Air Mail Act, 287
Kelly, Frank K., 757, *760*
    desegregation grants and, 754–756
    Fund of the Republic and, 750–751
Kendall, Amos, 591–593
Kendrick, Edward, 658, 663, *681*
Kennedy, John F., 373, 628, 672
    TV debates with Nixon and, 626
    U.S. Steel and, 478
Kennedy, Robert
    Ribicoff hearings and, 717–718
Ketchum, Carlton, 107–108, 112, 226, 274
Ketchum, George, 107–108, 112, 226, 242, 274
Ketchum Public Relations, Inc., 111, 112, *113*, 273, 414
Keys, Melville, 544, 545, 547
Kilgore, Harley M., 648
Kindelberger, "Dutch," 270
King, Kerryn, 426, 427, 452, 511
Kirkley, Don, 245, 246
Kittle, William, 19–20, *26*, 28, 29–30, *35*
Klauber, Edward
    CBS news and, 202, 658–659
Klaw, Spencer, 574
Klein, Julius, 84
Klell, Norman, *191*
Klemfuss, Harry, 84
Knight, Goodwin
    political campaigns of, 603–604
Knowland, William, 604
Knowlton, Don, 421, 422, 452
Kraft Music Hall, 259
Ku Klux Klan (KKK), 108, 184, 246, 372–412, *see
        also* Southern Publicity Assoc.; Clarke,
        Edward Young; Tyler, Elizabeth; Sim-
        mons, William Joseph
    big buildup of, 386–391
    community opinion and, 393
    constitution of, 381–382
    dishonesty and, 393
    early history of, 373

exploiting fears and, 386, 387
image building and, 385–386
Lanier University and, 401–402
lawlessness and, 385–386, 388–389, 391, 402, 403
message of, 392
newsletter network and, 395
the press and, 376, 378, 379, 386, 397, 402–404, 406
principles of, 387, 394, 399–400
Protestant fundamentalism and, 387–388, 393
public relations techniques of, 388–393
  advertising and, 396–400
publications of, 399–400
reborn as Atlanta Bottle Club, 373–377
scandal hurts the cause, 405–410
secrecy and, 382, 388, 396
seeds for growth of, 383–385
Speakers Bureau and, 392–394
Stone Mountain and, 376, 383
symbolism and, 394
The Birth of a Nation, and, 375, 377, 398
"The Klansman's Creed," 388
women and, 378, 410
Kuchel, Thomas H., 622
Kulas, E. J., 420–421
Kuwait, 770–771

L

Labor, *see* Anti-labor attitudes; Labor disputes; Labor
      unions
Labor disputes, *see also* Coal industry; Labor unions
  arbitration and, 314, 464
  Bethlehem Steel strike, 240–249
  ethics and, 475–476
  Ford Motor Co. and, 685–688, 703–709
  General Electric and, 212–214
  IRT and, 62, 131–137
  Kennedy–Blough shootout, 478–482
  Little Steel strikes and, *see* Little Steel strikes
  musicians and, 330, 660
  Youngstown Sheet & Tube and, *see* Youngstown
      Sheet & Tube
Labor Film Corporation, 235
Labor unions, 235, 383, *see also* AFL; CIO; Labor
      unions; National Labor Relations Board;
      United Mine Workers; United Auto Workers
Labor unions, 235
  AFL, 240, 431
  the closed shop and, 461
  collective bargaining and, 460–462
  contractual guarantees and, 685–686
  job security and, 705
  Ku Klux Klan and, 387
  pension plans and, 703–709
  public opinion and, 62, 241, 462
  Red Scare and, 246–247, 383, 431, 463, 465
  right to organize and, 240, 422, 459
  steel industry and, 240, 333, 431, 461–464
Lacey, Robert, 684, 702, *733, 734*, 741,695
LaFollette, Robert M., Jr., 241, 247, *250, 521, see also*
      Congressional Committees
LaGuardia, Fiorella, 282, 319
Laissez-faire government, 2, 5, 8, 39
Lambert, W., *457*
Lamont, Thomas W., 228, 237

Landis, Kennesaw Mountain, 63
  baseball and, 266–267
Larson, Cedric, *72*, 538, *552, 586*
Larson, Henrietta, 650
Lasker, Albert, *see* Lord & Thomas
Lasker, Mary, 487, 488
Lasswell, Harold, 107
Lawrence, Bishop William, 62, 63
Lawrence, William H, *72*
Lawyer-lobbying, 8, 55
Lawyers, 56, 460
Lazarus, Fred, Jr., 358
Lead pipe, armored, 300
League for Industrial Democracy, 246
League of Women Voters, 328
LeBon, Gustav, 61, 636
Lee, Alfred McClung, *72*
Lee, Harris, & Lee, 62–64, 114, 116–118, 121–123, *see*
      also Harris, W.W.; Ivy Lee & Associates;
      Lee, Ivy Ledbetter
  American Red Cross and, 64–71, 114, 115
  Episcopal Church Pension Fund and, 62–63
  Red Cross and, 66–70
  staff of, 116–117, 123–124
  Standard Oil (New Jersey) and, 63–64
Lee, Ivy Ledbetter, 2, 7, 8, 14, 48, 53, *72*, 92, 107, *157*,
      176, 215, 228, 284, 996, *see also* Ivy Lee
      & Associates; Lee, Harris, and Lee; Parker
      & Lee; Selvage & Lee
  alleged anti-semitism of, 144–145
  anti-labor attitudes and, 120
  Asphalt trust and, 46–47
  aviation and, 138
  background of, 38–40
  coal strikes and, 45–46, 57–60
  concepts of public relations, 63, 67, 117, 153–154
  death, 140
  "Declaration of Principles," 45, 122, 764
  early career of, 40, 41, 42–43
  journalism and, 40–41
  legacy of, 153
  Nazi propaganda and, 148–149
  Nurenberg trials and, 144, 150–152
  obituaries, 144, 153, *157*
  opinion of publicists, 52
  Papers of, 53, *71*
  patriotism questioned, 140–143
  Pendleton Dudley and, 94–95
  policy of full disclosure and, 145
  public relations counsel and, 176–177
  relationship with clients and, 124–126
  reputation of, 143, 144, 154
  Rockefeller coal interests and, 55, 57–60, 59, 60, 62
  steel industry and, 118
  strikebreaking and, 57–60, 109, 119–123, 234. 235
  testimony for House Committee, 147–150
  testimony in House Un-American Activities hear-
      ings, 148–150
  testimony in IRT hearings, 134–135
  third party technique and, 122
  Two way concept and, 53–54, 61, 141
  visits Berlin, 145–146
  visits Russia, 141
  works

An Open and Above Board Trust, 47
City For the People, 42
Human Nature and the Railroads, 71
Publicity Some of the Things It IS and Is Not,
    71, 109, 419
The Problem of International
    Propaganda, 71
Lee, Ivy Ledbetter, Jr. (IL's son), 124
Lee, James Wideman II (IL's son), *71,* 123, 124, 128,
    145, 148, 152, 154
  on Chrysler account, 128
Lee, James Wideman (IL's father), 38–39
Lee, James Wideman, Jr. (IL's brother), 2, 53, 62, 115,
    154, 155
  background of, 52
Lee, Lewis (IL's brother), 115
Lee, Mrs., Ivy, 41, 154
Legislation, *see also* Regulatory legislation
  social, 606
Legislative influence, insurance companies and, 49
Legislative trends, advertising and, 567
Lehigh Valley Railroad, 50
Lennen & Mitchell, 202
LeNoire, Bill, 600
Lens, Sidney, *521*
Leonard, Colonel H.G., 29
Lever Brothers USA, 353, 355–356
Lewis, Craig, 674
Lewis, David, 1, *52,* 177, 207, *224,* 269, 271, *277,* 715,
    733, 734
  GM public relations dept. and, 715
Lewis, John L., 120, *see also* CIO
Lewis, John L. 120
  auto industry and, 246
  Johnstown Committee and, 246
  National Labor Relations Board and, 240
  steel industry and, 240, 459–462, 465
Libby–Owens–Ford (LOF), 271, 272, 563
Liberty Loan Drives, 31, 105
  celebrities and, 228
  John Price Jones and, 226–228
Liberty-engine planes, 282
Life, 457, 480
Liggett & Myers (L&M), 207–209, 498
  Chesterfield sales and, 208
Lilly, Robert J., *457*
Lincoln Center, 672
Lincoln Highway, 254
Lindbergh, Charles A., 108, 138
  alleged pro-German sympathies of, 290, 294
  antipathy to publicity and, 108
  Congressional Medal of Honor and, 290
  feud with the press and, 290, 294
  first transatlantic flight and, 288–290
  "The Lindbergh Line," 291
  transcontinental speed record and, 288
Lindley, Walter C., 571
Link, Arthur S., 8, 72, 538
Lippmann, Walter I., 107, 635
Lipsky, Abram, 180
Literaray Digest, 262
Lithuanian Independence, 166–167, 539–540
Little, Clarence, 487–489, 491
Little, Luther B., *9,* 593

Little Steel Strikes, 109, 246, 458–466, 476, *see also*
    Steel industry
  costs of, 464–465
  Senate investigations of, 460, 466–470
Little, Thomas, 155
Liveright, Horace, 172, 173, 175, 179
Liveright Publishing Corp., 221
Lloyd, James T., letter of, 30
Lobbying, 8, 609
  for foreign clients, 84
  for high tariff trade barriers, 29–30
  as political agitation, 27
  in political campaigns, 607
  of regulatory agencies, 29, 30, 441
  tobacco industry and, 496
Lobbyists
  utilities and, 183
  in Washington, 767–768
Lochner, Louis P., 145
Logan County Coal Operators, 119–123
Long, J. H, 109
Look, 698
Lord & Thomas, 261, 354, 531, *see also* Foote, Cone,
    and Belding
  American Tobacco Co., and, 128, 208, 487
  California anti-chain store tax and, 568–570
  California politics and, 599
  Ku Klux Klan and, 397
  Steve Hannagan and, 254, 258, 259, 261, 263
  Upton Sinclair and, 622
Low, Seth, 42
Lowell, Lawrence A., 228
Luckman, Charles, 353, 367
  Lever Brothers and, 355–356
  Pepsodent and, 354–355
  voluntary food conservation campaign and, 355
Lucky Strikes, *see* American Tobacco Co.
Ludlow Massacre, 57, 109, 137
Ludwig, Lore, 548, *552, 587*
Luxembourg Museum, 195
Lydgate, William A., 643, 668, 674, 702
  assessment of Nader investigation, 725
  GM's public relations needs and, 719, 723
  What America Thinks, 643
Lyon, Peter, *9*

M

MacArthur, Douglas
  Remington Rand and, 300
McCann Erickson Co., 227, 234
McCann, (H.K.) Co., 227, 230
McCarthy, Charles, 310–311
McCarthy, Joseph, 332, 662, 698
McCarthyism, *see* Red Scare
McClellan, John F., 441
McClellan Senate Committee hearings, 444
McClure's Magazine, 9
McClurg, A.C., 77
McCormack, John, 147, 149–150
  House investigation opening statement of, 147
McCormack–Dickstein Committee, *see* U.S. Congres-
    sional Committees
McCormick, Richard P., 591, *632*
McDonald, David J., 333, 334

MacDonald, Dwight, 759, *760*
McDonald, Forest, 261, *277*
McGinnis, Joe, 627, *632*
McGreary, Nelson M., 33, *35*
Machado, Gerardo, 317, 542, 543
McIntyre, Marvin, 556, 563
McIntyre, Robert B., *521*
McKesson Robbins, drug firm, 323
   scandal and, 323–327
McKinley, William, 2–4, 24, 593, 624
McMillan, Al, 574
McNamara, Robert S., 704, 705
   Ford auto safety and, 715–716
McWilliams, Carey, 596, 597, 602, 607, *632*
Macy's Department Store
   Thanksgiving Day parade and, 315–316
Mahan, Lynn, 684
Maltese, John A., *632*
Manhattan Project, atomic bomb and, 130, 510–511
Manning, Farley, 113
Manning, Reverand Dr. William, 97, 98
Manufacturers, fair prices and, 330
Manufacturing, *see* Avco Manufacturing Corp.
Mapes, John G., 422, 427, 435, 439, 440, 503
March of Dimes, 555
Marcos, Ferdinand, 769
Marcus, Stanley, 359
Margarine
   beneficial effects of, 434
   dispute with dairy industry and, 433–440
   federal excise tax and, 433, 436
   Rivers bill and, 440
Marketing, 6–8, *see also* Product promotion
Markey, Morris, 290
Markham, Baird H., 441
Marshall, George, 328
Marshall, Henry W., 252
Martin, Everett Dean, 636
Martin, Francis C., 241
Martin, Luis Munoz
   promoting Puerto Rico and, 83–84
Marvin, Thomas O., 10, 13, *25*
Marxist–Communist, agitation, *see* Soviet propaganda
Masaryk, Thomas G., *522*, 540, *586*
Mass production, 106, 639
Massachusetts Law Association, 222
Matchiabelli, Prince George, 348
Mathews, Herbert L., *586*
May, Alfred A.
   Ford's anti-Semitism problem and, 690
   "Memorandum for Ford Dealers," 691
Mayer, Louis B., 599
   Sinclair campaign and, 599, 622
Mayer, Raymond D., 338, 339
Meade, E. Kidder, 659, 660, 666
   memo on desegragation grants, 754–755
Meany, George, 334
Meat Industry, the, 6, 99–101, 118
Meigs, Merrill C., 259
Memorial Day Auto Race, 251, 253
Mencken, Henry L., 180
Mendelsohn, Harold, 630, *632*
Mermey, Maurice, 316–318
   Bureau of Education on Fair Trade and, 330

Merriam, Charles F., 621–622
Merriam, Frank
   campaign for governor and, 599–600
   Townscent Plan, 600
Metal industry
   in jewelry, 330
   nickel and, 321–322
Metropolitan Life Insurance Co., 182
Metropolitan Opera, 357
Miami Beach, 255
   Heavyweight Boxing Championship, 257
   tourism and, 255–256
Michael Rice & Co., 301
   partnership with H.A. Bruno & Assoc. and, 301–302
Michaelis, George V.S., 10–12, 23
   first PR firm and, 11
Michelson, Charles, 204, 525, 526, *529*
Michigan Christian Advocate, 186
Mickelson, Sig, 661
Military Training Camps Assoc.(MTCA), *see* Platts-
   burgh Training Camps
Miller, Karen, 494, 502, *520*
Mills, A.K. "Kay," 643
   Ford Motor Company and, 643
Milwaukee Journal, 223, 276
   tribute to Bernays [Haswell], 223–224
Miner's Lamp, 121–122
Mingos, Howard, 280–282, *307*
Mining, *see* Coal industry
Minneapolis Publicity Bureau, 199
Mitchell, Greg, *632*
Mitchell, John, 45, 46, *see also* Mining industry;
   United Mine Workers
Mock, James O., *72*, *191*, 538, *552*, *586*
Monoplanes, *Brumah II* and, 279
Monopolies, 1, 4
   exposing abuses of, 5
   Standard Oil Co., 63, 645
   sugar industry and, 320
Monroney, A.S., 84
Montauk Playground, 257, 272
Montessori, Maria, 535
Moody's Magazine, 47
Moon, Gordon A., *26*
Moore, Charley, 711–713
Morgan, Ephriam, 120–121
Morgan, J. P., 65
   International Harvesater Co. and, 47
   United States Steel Co. and, 4
Morgan (J. P.) & Co., *see* J.P. Morgan & Co.
Morgan, Keith, 553–559, 561
Morris, Markey, *157*
Morris, Roger, *632*
Morse, Samuel, 116
Morse, Sherman, 45, 46, *72*
   quotes I. Lee, 45
Moses, Robert, 197
Mosley, Shannon, 732
Motion pictures, 82, 83, 86, 87, 269
   newsreels, 82, 83, 559
   in promoting cars, 269, 699–700
   Samuel Insull and, 260
   short subjects, 86, 87
Muckraking, 3–6, 8, 19, 24, 49, 97, 380

big business and, 6, 18, 42, 537
defined, 5
magazines, 5
oil industry and, 64
railroads and, 20
role in growth of PR and, 97
WWI and, 66
Mullaney, Bernard J., 108, 260. 184
Mumford, John K., 72, 480
Mundy, Alicia, 775
Munsey's Magazine, 593
Murray, James, 619, 629
Murray, Philip, 480, 613
Murray, Robert K., *412*
Murrow, Edward R., 202, 658, 659, 667
    anti-network speech of, 663
    Person to Person controversy, 662–665
Musica, Phillip, 323
Myers, Theodore (POP), 253

N

N. W. Ayer & Sons, 7, 9, 258, 259, 261, 263
    publicizing Uneeda Biscuits, 7
NAACP, 613
Nader, Ralph, 727, 730
    campaign against GM, 714, 723
    investigated by GM and, 725
    Unsafe At any Speed, 730
Napolitan, Joseph
    Election Game, The, 627, 629, *632*
    Hubert Humphrey campaign, 626–627
    Shapp campaign and, 624, 626
Nation, 179, 368, 548, 597
National Aeronautic Association, 297
National Association of Accredited Publicity Directors
    (NAAPD), 215–216, 217, 338
National Association of Broadcasters (NAB), 330, 660
National Association of Engine & Boat Manufacturers,
    295, 296, 299, 301
National Association of Manufacturers (NAM), *250*
    anti-labor campaigns, 247, 467, 472
    Remington Rand formula for breaking strikes, 247, *250*
National Association of Public Relations Counsel
    (NAPRC), 102, 302, 338–339
National Biscuit Company, 7, 258
National Citizens' Committee, 245–246
National Coal Association, 235–236
National Conservation Assoc., 32–33, *see also* Conservation
National Conservation Association, 32–33
National Consumer's Tax Commission, 567, 574
National Foundation for Infantile Paralysis, 553, 555
National health insurance, *see also* Health insurance
    AMA anti-Truman plan campaign, 612–621
    background of, 613–614
    Bill Clinton and, 614
    Lyndon Johnson and, 613
    New Deal and, 613
National Highway Traffic Safety Board, 733
National Industrial Recovery Act (NIRA)
    business codes and, 459
National Labor Relations Board (NLRB), *250*, 422, 459
    General Electric and, 212–214
    union contracts and, 464–465
    union elections and, 463

Wagner Act and, 240, 247, 467
National monuments
    National Park Service and, 333–335
    Statue of Liberty and, 333–334
National Park Service, 333–335
    American Museum of Immigration and, 335
National Provisioner, *104*
National Public Relations Council (NPRC), 221
National Rifle Association (NRA), 768
National unity, 332–333
National Urban League, *see* Urban League
Nationalist China, 85, 86, 317
Natural gas, 441–445
    federal price controls and, 441–443
    Natural Gas and Oil Resources Committee and,
        441–442, 443
    Senate investigation of, 444
Nazi Government, 73, 74, 140, 143, 144, 146–149, 150
    German industrials and, 145
    German Railroads Tourist Bureau and, 547–550
    German–American Relations and, 144, 146
    Lindbergh and, 290, 294
    Nuremberg Trials of, 150–153
    Standard Oil of N.J. and, 645
    use of American PR firms and, 769
    Zeppelin company and, 293
Nazi Luftwaffe, 290, 294
Nazi propaganda
    dissemination of, 151
    House Committee investigation of, 144–153
    in the U.S., 144–153
Nazi war criminals, *see* Nuremberg Military Tribunals
NBC, 202
    GM pickup trucks and, 733, 766
    quiz show scandal and, 663
Neal, Virgil E., 540
Neely, Matthew M., 298
Nehru, Jawaharial, 223
Nelson, Jack, *413*
Neuberger, Maurine, 483–484, 487, 493, *521*
Nevins, Allan, 58, 72
New Deal, *see* Roosevelt, Franklin Delano
New Politics, 595, 622, 624, 626–631
    advertising and, 607–608
    campaign consultants, *see* campaign consultants
    campaign management, *see* Campaign management
    ethics and, 610, 767–768
    Nixon–Humphrey campaign and, 626–628
    polling and, 629, 630
    role of political parties and, 630
    technology and, 630
    television and, 432, 601, 624–626, 628–629
New Republic, 521, *521*, 573, *632*
New York, *371*
New York American, 72
    anti-KKK expose and, 403–404
    IRT and, 132
New York Central Railroad (The Central), 52
New York City Herald, 72
New York Evening Journal, 132
New York Globe, 227
New York Herald, Ku Klux Klan
    interviews and, 386
New York Herald-Tribune, 72, 211, 519, 521

IRT and, 132, 133
New York Journal, Ivy Lee and, 40
New York Press, 72
New York Sun, 230
New York Times, 27, 28, 41, 46, 89, 96, 119, 120, *157,*
188, 197, 198, 365, 371, 481, 489, 497–
498, *522, 587*
announces bombing of Japan, 130
coal industry and, 119, 120
E. R. Murrow interview, 664
interview of Bernays, 197
on IRT, 132
on PRSA suspension of Wright III, 89
on public relations, 181–182
report on Ivy Lee, 144
tobacco industry report, 497–498
Trinity church expose, 97
New York Times Book Review, 521, 660
New York Transit Commission, 133–137
New York Tribune, Doris Fleischman and, 169
New York University Dept. of Journalism, 219
New York World, 41, 42, 46, 49
expose of KKK and, 402–403, 405, 406
New York World Fair, 82
New Yorker, 290, 352, *379,* 627
Newcomb, Ellsworth, 303
Newmyer Associates, 642
Ford contract negotiations and, 708–709
promoting CBS and, 659
report on Quiz show hearings, 665
Newmyer, D. C., 642, 709
News media, 87, *see also* Newspapers; Journalism
competition and, 766
foreign agents and, 769
interest in chaos and, 765
lust for ratings and, 766
the public and, 774
use of by PR agencies, 87, 769, 771
News, values, 765
Newsom, Earl, 202, 221, 269, 503, 505, 527, 583, *760,*
see also Earl Newsom and Company
background of, 634–635
eulogy of, 676–677, *681*
interest in public opinion and, 635–636
legacy of, 679–680
Literary Digest and, 636, 637
Newsom, Palmer, & Wright and, 638
opens Earl Newsom & Company
Papers of, 658, *681, 712, 733, 759*
Pearl Buck and, 638
the person, 673–674, 675–675, 678–679, 684
philosophies, 641, 644, 676
product promotion, 639–640
promoting oil heating and, 637
PRSA and, 677–678
Newsom (Earl) & Associates, *see* Earl Newsom & Associates
Newsom, John R., 484, 643, *681, 733*
Newspapers, *see also* Journalism; News Media
advertising and, 7, 83, 397, 472, 486, 560, 566–
567, 608
AMA campaign and, 615–616
anti-press agentry views, 54, 180
anti-smoking campaigns and, 488

deceptive advertising and, 574–575
feud with Lindbergh and, 290, 294
hidden propaganda and, 608
Ku Klux Klan, *see* Ku Klux Klan
mass circulation and, 97
Pacific Exposition and, 78–79
polio campaign and, 557, 558
pressure on, 470
role in growth of PR, 97
sponsored advertising and, 560, 572
"tourches of freedom" parade and, 210
Truman takeover of steel mills and, 479
Newton, Quigg, 759
Nieman–Marcus, 359
Niese, Richard Bealle, 110
Nimmo, Dan, 595, 624, *632*
Nimmons, Richard T., 124
Nitrate (Anglo–Chilean) Consolidated Corporation, 139
Nixon, Richard, 604, 673
1968 presidential campaign and, 626–628
character of, 627–628
"Checkers" speech, 625–626
Harry Treleaven and, 627
presidential administration of, 628
television and, 625–626, 628
Non-profit organizations, Civitas and, 331–332
North American Aviation, 544–545
Nuremberg Military Tribunals, 150–153
I. G. Farben and, 151–152

O

O'Brien, Lawrence F., 627, 630
Ochsner, 483
O'Connor, Basil, 553, 554, 556, 558, 561
Odlum, Floyd, 298, 300, 426
Special Defense Trains and, 299
Office of Price Administration (OPA), 688
Office of Production Management (OPM), 298
Office of War Information (OWI), 270–271, 528
Ogilvy & Mather, 92
Ognibene, Peter J., 265, *277*
Ohio University, 220
Oil industry, *see also* American Petroleum Institute;
Standard Oil Co.; Standard Oil of New Jer-
sey; Exxon; Natural gas
Standard Oil of California, 608
Texaco and, 357, 426, 452
Olasky, Marvin N., 184, *191*
O'Laughlin, Edward T., on IRT strike, 133
Oldfield, Barney, 252–253
Oldine, John W., 199
Olson, Sidney, 738–739
O'Mahoney, Joseph C., *587*
One-way publicity, 176
Operation Bootstrap, 83, 84
Organized labor, *see* Labor unions
Orr, Thomas E., 115, 116
Otis Steel Company, 420
Oulahan, R., *457*

P

Pacific Gas & Electric (PG&E), 597, 598, 608
Pacific International Exposition, 78
Page, Arthur W., 527

Paley, William S., 155, 159, 200, 658, 659, *see also* CBS
  Congressional testimony of, 201
  E. R. Murrow controversy and, 662–665
  image making campaign for, 666–667
  network reforms and, 665
  personality of, 660
  quiz show scandal and, 662–664
Palmer, A. Mitchell, 119, 184, 235, 399
  Logan County coal strike and, 119
  Red Scare and, 184, 235, 384, 465
Palmer, Fred, 638, 717
  Earl Newsom & Co. and, 639, 641, 642
    Standard Oil (NJ) and, 647
  on Ford's 50th celebration, 699
  GM's position on pollution and, 729–730
  on GM's public relations needs, 719–721
  GM's safety issue and, 718, 719
Pan American Airways, 124, 271, 287, 300, 301
Pane, Marietta, *113*
Paper Box Makers Union, 235
Paper industry, 668–669
Parke Davis & Co., 316
Parker & Bridge, 44, 50
Parker & Lee, 37, 38, 43, 52, *see also* Lee, Ivy Ledbetter; Parker, George F.
  acclaimed, 44
  Armstrong investigation and, 49
  "Battle of the Currents" and, 47
  coal industry and, 45–46
  credo of, 44
  General Asphalt Co., 46–47
  International Harvester and, 47
  Ivy Lee and, 43
  Parker & Bridge, 44–50
  partnership disolved, 50, 53
  Pennsylvania railroad and, 48
Parker, Alton B., 37, 48
Parker, George F., 31, 37, 43, 44, 46–48, 51, *see also* Parker & Lee
  after Parker & Lee, 50–51
  "Battle of the Currents" and, 47
  Democratic National Committee and, 44
  in England, 44
  Grover Cleveland and, 48–50
  journalism and, 43
  Parker & Bridge and, 50
  Parker and Lee and, 43–49
Parrish, Harcourt, 123, 124
  on Ivy Lee staff, 117
  on promoting Lucky strikes, 127–128
Parrish, Wayne W., *191*
Patman, Wright, 550
  anti-chain store tax bill and, 566–568
  Anti-Trust Act and, 565
  attacks on philanthropic foundations of, 671–672
Pearl Harbor, 267, 268, 299, 329
  Dudley–Anderson–Yutzy, 101
Peck, G. R., praise for Ivy Lee and, 54
Pecora, Ferdinand, 137, 138
Pell, Arthur, 221
Pendleton Dudley and Associates, 92, 97, *see also* Dudley, Pendleton
  AT&T and, 98–99
  Dudley–Anderson–Yutzy formed, 101
  Florida Citrus Commission, 101
  founding of, 95–96
  meat industry and, 6, 99–101
  press agentry and, 99
  Trinity Church and, 97
  Woodrow Wilson and, 98–99
Pennsylvania Motor Truck Association, 575, 577, 578, *see also* Railroad–Truckers Brawl
Pennsylvania Railroad, 8, 128, 129–130, *see also* Railroad–Truckers Brawl
  freight rate increase and, 767
  Gap accident, 52
  Ivy Lee and, 8, 22, 48, 53, 129
Pepper, Claude, 620, 621
Pepperidge Farm, Inc., 360–361
Pepsodent, 353
  Bob Hope and, 354
Perot, Ross, foreign interests and, 769–770
Perry, James M., 595, 622, 623, *632*
Peters, Raymond W., *521*
Petrillo, James C., 330
Petroleum, *see* Oil industry
Pew, Marlen E., 215
Pharmaceutical industry, *see* Drug industry
Phelps Dodge and Co., 118, 301
Phelps, George Harrison, 197, 199
Philanthropy, *see* Ford Foundation; Fundraising
Philip Morris, 361–363, 498
Philippine Independence Fund, 51
Philippines, 51, 77–78
Phillips, Kevin, 628, *632*
Pickford, Mary, 228
Pictorial puclicity, *see* Motion pictures
Pierce, Daniel T., 47–48, 115
Pierce, James M., 534, 535
Pierce, Lyman, 111, 140
Pimlott, J.A.R., 177, *521*
Pinchot, Gifford, 27, 34, *35*
  Conservation and, 32–33
Pinkerton Detective Agency, 435–436, 437, 438
Plattsburg Training Camps, 34, 114
Plaza Hotel, 358
Poen, Monte M., *632*
Polio epidemic, 551
  Franklin Roosevelt and, 553–563
  United Fruit Co. and, 197
  Warm Springs Foundation and, 554–555, 558, 562
Political agitation, lobbying and, 27
Political apathy, Americans and, 604
Political campaign styles, 2, 592–593, 624–631
Political campaign techniques, 2, 432, 593–595, 600–603, 606–608, 610–616, 624, 629, 630
Political campaigns, 2, 34, 37, 525, 589, 628, 629, *see also* Campaign consultant; Campaign management; New Politics
  Andrew Jackson and, 591–592
  basic principles of, 605–606
  divorced from political parties and, 598
  Goodwin Knight, 603–604
  Grover Cleveland, 43–44, 48–50
  health insurance and, 606–607, 612–620
  Herbert Hoover, 525–526
  impact of technologies on, 630

ingredients of, 595
Nixon–Humphrey, *see* Nixon, Richard
Presidential press secretary and, 591
public opinion and, 591, 604–605
publicity and, 2–3, 593
Robert P. Taft and, 431–432
Seth Low Mayoral, 42
special interest appeals and, 593
Thomas Jefferson, 590–591
Upton Sinclair, 599–601
William McKinley, 24
Political Parties, 589–594
anti-party legislation and, 594
California reforms of, 594–595
decline of, 630, 631
history of, 589–595
impact of technology on, 630
independent voting and, 602
slavery and, 593
Political propaganda, 75–77, 611, 621
Politics, *see* New Politics
Pollay, Richard W., *522*
Polls
consumer, 566
in politics, 432, 629, 630
public opinion surveys, 728, 742
in public relations campaigns, 435
Pollution, air, 729–730
Pomer, Gerald, *521*
Poole, Ernest, 164, 165, *191*
Pope, Bayard F., 230, 232
Powers, Richard C., 384
PR Blue Book, 520
PR Week, 583
Pratt, John B., 235, 236
Press agentry
Press Agentry, 176, 303
Press agentry
compared to public relations, 24, 42, 109–110,
136, 176, 177, 180
compared to publicity, 42, 45
flavored with elegance, 350–351
modern, 763–764
newspapers and, 180
Pendleton Dudley and, 99
political, 51
Press Agents, goals of, 764
Press secretary, Presidential, *113,* 591
Price fixing, 570
Princeton Endowment Campaign, 139–140
Pringle, Henry F., 41, *157,* 171, 185, *191*
Printers Ink, 116, 134, *587,* 638, 644, 676, *681*
Product promotion, 7, 106, 258
auto industry and, 106
of foods, 7, 139, 196–197, 258
of home appliances, 426–428
in marketing campaigns, 7
to supplement advertising, 258
for trade associations, 639–640
Progressive Era, 7, 24, 27, 37–39, 374
political parties and, 590
Progressive, legislative reforms, 24
Prohibition, 106, 283, 539
Ku Klux Klan and, 387

propaganda and, 106
Propaganda, 106, 107, *see also* Bernays, Edward L.
government sponsored, 32–33
hostile, 469
House investigation of Nazi, 144–153
origination of, 183
political, 8, 75–77, 537, 611, 621
in strikebreaking and, 235, 247
to interpret American ideals, 165
unprincipled, 620
Protestant, fundamentalism, 387–388, 393
Proxmire, William, 609
Public consensus, 107
Public discontent, 774–775
Public Information, Committee on, 69
Public opinion, 179, 636, *see also* Bernays, Edward L.
auto safety and, 702
big business and, 18, 46, 137, 569, 649–650
content of publicity and, 63
federal excise tax and, 436
importance of, 117, 644, 646, 761–763
influencing, 33, 485, 604
Ivy Lee and, 117, 139
legislation and, 27
Lithuanian independence and, 166–167
organized labor and, 62, 241, 462–463
organizing, 33
political campaigns and, 591, 604–605
power of, 107, 111
public information model and, 764
publicity and, 33, 43, 63
sophistocated approach to, 43
Public Opinion Quarterly, 250, *250,* 320–321, 326,
338, 342, *342, 521, 522*
Public opinion surveys, 742
Public relations, *see also* Ethics; Public relations concepts; Publicity
ads to appeal for funds and, 242–243
agencies, *see* Public relations agencies
booming twenties and, 105–109
building public confidence and, 289
compared to press agentry, 24, 42, 109–110, 136,
176, 177, 180
compared to publicity, 109–110, 176, 177, 289,
301, 304
concepts, *see* Public relations concepts
corporate management, *see* Corporate management
costs, 133–134, 464–465, 608, 652–653
counsel, *see* Public relations counsel
definition of, 515
education and, 101, 219–220, 258, 281, 504–505, 529
employee relations and, 110
ethics, *see* Ethics, in public relations
function of, 278, 433, 763
"good press" and, 105, 304–305, 696–697
government regulation and, 674–675
Great Depression and, 317, 525–527
growth of, 105–113, 414
guarantees to clients and, 85, 88–89
influence of, 414, 629
lawyers and, 56, 460
mature concept of, 107, 338, 366, 528
merging with advertising and, 414, 420
origins of, 1–9, 97

over-selling and, 338
pioneers, 96
post WWI boom and, 308
post WWII boom and, 528–529
practice, *see* Public relations practice
as propaganda, 182–186
public consent and, 761–763
railroads and, 21–22, 54
replacing publicity and, 286
respectability and, 92
social causes and, 249
strategies of, 489
techniques, *see* Public relations techniques
Public relations agencies, *see also* Public relations
dilemmas of, 773
ethics and, 772–774
First Amendment rights, 770
Fulbright Committee investigation of, 74–75, 84–88, 769
McClellan Committee investigation of, 444–445
McCormack Committee investigation of, 146–150
NLRB investigation of, 212–214
peddling propaganda and, 769
public criticism of, 769
public relations practice, *see* Public relations practice
questionable activities of, 769–774
Public Relations, American Council on, 216, 217, 339
Public relations concepts, 24, 63, 153–154, 336–338, 353, 574, 578, 617, *see also* Public relations
application of social sciences and, 171
conglomerate agencies, 304
"Declaration of Principles," 45, 122, 764
engineering of consent, 159, 177, 186–188
mature, 107, 338, 366, 528, 761–763
one-way publicity, 176, 203, 287
policy of full disclosure and, 67, 145
press agentry and, 763–764
the press and, 25, 304
preventive public relations, 129–130, 366
public information model, 764
public opinion, *see* Public opinion
segmental approach, 166
social responsibility and, 641, 644, 649–650
sponsoring committees and, 162, 163
"the psychology of the multitude," 61
the truism of events and, 727, 730–731
truthful publicity and, 59, 61
two-way asymmetrical, 53, 61, 141, 166, 176, 177, 337, 449
two-way symmetrical, 764
Public Relations Counsel, *see also* Public relations
Bernays and, 160, 170, 176–181, 207, 214–218
booming 20's and, 236
certification and, 773
criticisms of, 179–180
definition of,, 181
development of, 57, 567
ethics and, *see* Ethics
functions of, 96, 106, 286, 514–515, 763
Great Depression and, 350
importance of public opinion, 117, 286, 644, 646, 761–763
impossible promises and, 287
introduction of term, 176

legal responsibility for clients, 571
licensure of, 218–219, 302–303, 773
manipulations of, 767–771, 775
National Association of (NAPRC), 102, 302
objectives of, 765
operational procedures of, 452–454
organizing of, 503–506
the profession of, 214–218, 763
seedbed era of, 1–9
social value of, 177
technological advances and, 762
WWI growth of, 226
Public Relations Journal, 84, 522, 603, 618, *632,* 773
Public relations practice, *see also* Public Relations
Agencies; Public Relations Counsel
constitutionality and, 575, 580
Grunig's 4 models for, 763–764
"Magna Carta" for, 129, 580
Public relations programs
decentralization of, 654
Public Relations Quarterly, 32, *36, 103,* 247, 338, *342,* 775
Public Relations Review, 91, 102, 183, 184, *522,* 587
Public Relations Society of America (PRSA), 102, 217, 302, 505, 529, 678
Code of Professional Standards and, *91,* 339, 476, 772
Counselors Academy of, 506–507
guarantee of results and, 88–89
licensure and, 218–219, 303, 506
Public relations techniques, *see also* Public Relations;
Publicity techniques
advertising, *see* Advertising
Church visitation, 291–292
client interviews, 428
community relations and, 429, 453
cooperating with the press, 52, 304–305, 322
courting the constituency, 27, 319
dazzling the clients, 350–351
diversionary, 600
employee relations and, 426, 453
exaggerating client's virtues, 367
fronts, *see* Fronts
lecturing and, 392–393, 435
letters and, 472–473
lobbying, *see* Lobbying
organizing consumer groups and, 567
polls, *see* Polls, and polling
press conferences, 428, 429, 435, 442
procedures of, 605–606
promotional pamphlets and, 78, 319, 325, 326, 337, 435, 600
research and, 435, 569, 641–642, 762–763
seminars and, 449, 450
staged events, 32, 539, 771
television, *see* Television
Publicists, 198–199, *see also* Publicity
1942 list of 6 top, 303
analysis of, 51
Great Depression and, 199–200, 350
politics and, 2, 589, 591
presidential campaigns and, 48–49
Publicity, *see also* Public Relations
as an element of public relations, 514
baseball and, 266–267
compared to press agentry, 42, 45

concept of truthful and, 61
criticism of, 28
definitions of, 109, 110
distinguished from advertising and
press agentry, 24, 109
marketing and, 6–8
merchants and, 288, 296
newsman's disdain of, 28
power of, 76, 107
religous organizations and, 110
respectability and, 92
shift to public relations of, 338
techniques, *see* Publicity techniques
Publicity Bureau, 10–22, *see also* Ellsworth, James
    Drummond; Small, Herbert
AT&T, 18, 23
clients and, 15, 23–24
criticism of, 19
first fixed fee and, 11
guiding concepts and, 24–25
Harvard account and, 16–18
Hepburn Act, 23
Michaelis, Ellsworth, & Stegman, 15
railroads and, 20
zenith years and, 20
Publicity campaigns, *see* Publicity; Publicity techniques
Publicity Club of Chicago, 222
Publicity Consultants, *see also* Sonnenberg, Ben
buildup of Charles Luckman, 353–356
buildup of John Snyder and, 356–357
firm closes, 363–364
firm opens, 349
Metropolitan Opera and, 357
Pepperidge Farm and, 360–361
Philip Morris and, 361–363
promoting Pepsodent and, 354–355
retail accounts of, 358–359
Sonnenberg's decision to close firm, 363–364
Publicity techniques, 84, *see also* Public relations techniques
advertising, *see* Advertising
art, 195–196, 453
barnstorming, 281–283
cartoons, 600
celebrities, *see* Celebrities
church visitation, 391–392
dropping leaflets, 381
motion pictures, *see* Motion Pictures
photographic appeals, 397–399
radio, *see* Radio
sloganeering, *see* Sloganeering
stunts, 284, 287
Puerto Rico, Commonwealth of,, 81, 271
"Operaton Bootstrap" and, 83–84
Purcell, David, 223

Q, R

Quigley, Martin, 642, 677, *760*
Ford Foundation and, 736, 740, 743–745
R. J. Reynolds, 483, 494
Racism, *see* Ku Klux Klan
Radio Advertising
for automobiles, 198
for Ford's war effort, 270
for Jack Benny, 272

for the Metropolitan Opera, 357
politics and, 569, 594
Seiberling Singers and, 314
Radio broadcasting, 479
AMA campaign and, 616
controversial, 658, 662
goals of, 201
labor disputes and, 330, 660
music strike and, 330
news programs, 201–202
polio campaign and, 558, 559
public relations and, 435, 442, 569
public service aspect of, 201
Radio Free Europe, Cold War and, 330
Radio and Television News Directors, 663
Railroad–Truckers Brawl, 22, 122, 129, 574–581
anti-trust investigation of, 577–581
Saroyan Papers and, 577–579
third party technique and, 576, 579
truck weight limitations and, 575, 576
Railroads, 20–23, *see also* Eastern Railroads Presidents
    Conference; Railroad–Truckers Brawl
American Association of Railroads, 129
Baltimore & Ohio, 54
government control of, 129–130
muckrackers and, 20
New York Central, 52
pioneers and, 76
and publicity, 48, 54
Publicity Bureau and, 8
rates and, 20, 54, 767
Southern Pacific, 48
Union Pacific railroad, 264
Rand, Remington, 247, 250
formula for strikebreading, 247, *250*
UNIVAC computer and, 300
Randall, Clarence, 479
Raskin, A.H., 481
Raucher, Alan, 9, *37*, 46, 47, *191*
RCA, 202
Bernays and, 202
NBC and, 202
Read, J.M., *775*
Readers Digest, *91*, *632*
Reagan, Ronald, 589
political campaigns of, 622–623
Reciprocal Trade Agreements (RTA), 327
Reconstruction Finance Corporation (RFC), General
    Motors and, 204
"Red Scare," 108, 235, 246, *see also* Labor unions;
    Communism
Congress and, 467
description of, 383–385
industry and, 235, 465
Ku Klux Klan and, 108, 398–399
McCarthyism and, 332, 662
public ownership of utilities and, 184
television and, 662
Redding, Charles W., 213
Reed, David, 142–143
Reef, Arthur, *521*
Reeves, Thomas C., 735, 746, 753, 756, *760*
Regier, C. C., *9*
Regulatory legislation, 260, 537

auto industry and, 722, 727
of drugs, 433
gun control and, 768
meat industry and, 6, 99, 99–100
of oil imports, 657
Progressive era and, 24
of railroad rates, 20, 54, 767
of utilities, 260
Reiger, C. E., 6, 9
Remington Rand, formula for strikebreaking, 247, 250
Reporter, 574, 581
Republic Steel, 246, 247, 421, 423, 424, see also Little
    Steel strikes; Steel industry
Republican Congress, 327
Republican National Committee, 34
Republican Party, 590, 591
    birth of, 593
    campaign support and, 590
    fronts and, 600
    Governor Merriam campaign and, 599
Republicans, 66, 120, 165, 599
    African Americans and, 385
    California and, 594–595
Retail Dry Goods Association, 330
Retailing industry, 315–316, 330, 348, 355, 358–359
Reuther, Walter, 704, 709
Review, 218
Ribicoff, Abraham, 714
Ribicoff Traffic Safety hearings, 717–718
    auto safety legislation and, 727
Rickenbacker, Eddie, 254
Riera, Julia, 587
Right-wing
    attacks on Ford Foundation and, 739, 741, 742
Riis, Jacob., 303
Riis, Roger William, 110, 214, 216, 303, 367–368, 371
Ripley, Joseph, 123, 124, 128, 154, 157
    interview with I. Lee, 45
Rivers bill, 440
Rivers, Mendel, 434, 436
Rixey, Limmian, 641
Robber-barons, 55
Roberts, William, 622, 623
Robinson, Claude, 216, 509, 513
Robinson, Joseph E., 565
Robinson, William E., 274, 455
Robinson–Hannagan Associates, 273, 274, 450, 455,
    456
Roche, James F., 716, 717, 718
    GM investigation of Nader and, 725–727
Rockefeller, David, 152
Rockefeller Foundation, 58, 126, 671
    Patman attack of, 671–672
Rockefeller, John D. III
    Colonial Williamsburg and, 640, 670–671
    Earl Newsom and, 640
    Jackson Hole project and, 672
    Lincoln Center and, 672
Rockefeller, John D., Jr., 61
    American Red Cross and, 114
    banks and, 138
    Bernays and, 163
    Colorado Fuel Strike and, 57, 58, 131
    finances North Pole flight, 288

    Ivy Lee and, 57, 58, 61, 62
Rockefeller, John D., Sr., 56, 58, 80, 137, 144
    Standard Oil Co. and, 55–56
    "tainted money" controversy, 55
Rockefeller, Nelson, 622
    role of, 21
Rollins, Arthur B., Jr., 529
Roosevelt, Eleanor, 163, 223, 340, 554, 613
Roosevelt, Franklin Delano, 163, 185
    aircraft industry and, 425
    fighting polio and, 553–563
        Birthday Balls for, 556–563
    foreign affairs and, 320
    "Good Neighbor" policy and, 320
    Great Depression and, 525–526
    industrial Code and, 422, 459
    national health insurance and, 613
    public relations and, 525–526
    regulatory legislation of, 537
    Supreme Court and, 320, 562
Roosevelt Raceway, 272
Roosevelt, Theodore, 21, 9, 31, 161
    battling the Trusts, 47
    coal strike (1902) and, 45
    conservation and, 31–33
    death, 140
    Federal Meat Inspection Act and, 6
    Office of Production Management and, 298, 299
    Progressive revolt and, 27, 767
    regulatory programs and, 537
    skill in public relations and, 3
    WWI Preparedness Campaign and, 34
Roper, Elmo, 641, 683
    Fund of the Republic and, 750, 753
Rose Polytechnic Institute, 112
Ross, Edward, 9
Ross, Irwin, 170, 191, 350, 370, 371, 441, 457, 521,
    527, 552, 586, 604, 608, 611, 632, 646
Ross, T. J., 123–130, 157, 158, see also Ivy Lee & As-
    sociates; Lee, Harris, and Lee
    background of, 115–117
    becomes Ivy Lee's partner, 123
    Bernays and, 188–189
    death, 155
    description of, 125
    Ivy Lee and, 153
    Manhattan Project and, 130
    philosophy of public relations, 126, 129–130
    PRSA speech, 126
    staff of, 116
    The Wisemen and, 130
    T. J. Ross & Assoc., 154–155
Ross, William, 632
Rovere, Richard, 627
Royal Flying Corps (RFC), 280, 285
Ruder–Finn (R&F), 363
    breakup of Yugoslavia and, 771–772
    Shah of Iran and, 772
Ruhr Chemical Co. of Germany, 128
Runyon, Damon,, 371
Russell, Charles Edward, 40–41
Russell Seeds Advertising, 254
Russia, 141–142
Ryan, Thomas Fortune, 47

S

Safer, Morley, 774
St. Louis Louisiana Purchase Exposition, 44
Sarnoff, David Sarnoff, 202
    RCA and, 202
Sarokin, H. Lee, 497, 498
Saroyan, Sonya, 577, 578, 581
Sattler, John E., *734*
Saturday Review, 125, 189, 290
Saunders, Frank, 356, 363
Savage, Jack, 284
Schackne, Stewart, 647, 651
Schlesinger, Arthur, 525, *529*, 592, 599
Schmiedke, Justin, 307, *307*
Schoonover, Jean Way, 92, *104*
Schreiber, George, 356, 364
Schriftgiesser, Karl, 72
Schurz (Carl) Association, 151
Schuyler, Philip,, *307*
Scriba, Jay, 276
Scribner's Magazine, 266
Searchlight, Ku Klux Klan and, 399–400
Securities and Exchange Commission, 772
Segmental approach, to public relations, 166
Seiberling Rubber Company, 314
Selvage, James, 113, 247, 463, 509, 511
Selvage and Lee, 113
    Fulbright Committee and, 84
    margarine industry and, 433, 434, 440
Senate Banking and Currency Committee, 137
Senate Foreign Relations Committee, *see* Congressional Committees
Seversky, Alexander P. de, 303
Seymour, Harold J., 230, 236, 237, 239, *250*
Shannon, David A., *521*, *529*
Shapp campaign and, Napolitan, Joseph, 624, 626
Shapp, Milton, 624
Shepherd, Morgan, 536
Sherman Anti-trust Act, 495, 503–504
    conspiracy to restrain trade and, 570–572
    legality of false fronts and, 570–572, 579–580
    negative advertising and, 495
    Railroad–Truckers Brawl and, 577
    Railroad–Truckers Brawl investigation, 571–581
    Standard Oil (N.J.) investigation, 645–646
    Standard Oil Trust investigation, 63
Shipp, Thomas Roerty, 31, *see also* Thomas R. Shipp and Co.
Shipp, Thomas Roerty, 31
    education of, 31
    promoting conservation and, 33
    promoting Plattsburgh Training Camps and, 34
    White House Conference of Governors and, 31–32
Shirer, William, 145
Shotwell, John M., 395, *412*
Siggal, Benjamin, 212, 213
Silicone breast implants
    Dow Corning and, 772
Simmons, William Joseph, *see also* Ku Klux Klan
    Atlanta Bottle Club and, 374
    background of, 374
    Clark & Tyler scandal and, 408–410
    Lanier University and, 401–402

Methodist ministry and, 374
    secrecy of, 377, 382
Simon, Elsie, *586*
Simon and Schuster, 188
Simpick, William M., 155
Sinclair Oil Co., 48, 115
Sinclair, Upton, 5, 6, 9, 100, *157*
    political campaign of, 568, 599–601, 622
    Poverty in California and, 599
Sklar, Paul, *191*, *522*, *587*
Slaughter, Jack, 641, 698
Slichter, Sumner, 704, 705
Sloan, Alfred, 527
Sloan, Alfred P., 203
Sloganeering, 600, 602, 603
    anti-health insurance campaign and, 606–607
    political campaigns and, 610–611
Small, Herbert, 10–13, 15, 24, *25*, *see also* Publicity Bureau
Small, Maynard, & Co., and, 13
Smith & Walmer, 27–31, *see also* Smith, William Wolff
    high-tariff barriers and, 29–30
Smith, Gerald L. K., 694
Smith, Henry Ladd, *586*
Smith, Rev. Rembert, 245
Smith, Sally Bedell, 201, *224*, 659, 662, 664, *681*
Smith, Steve, *225*
Smith, William Wolff, *see also* Smith & Walmer
    background of, 28–30
    clients, 29
    lobbying regulatory agencies, 29–30
    promoting high tariff barriers and, 29–30
    promotion of rifle practice and, 29
    Smith & Walmer, 27–31
    United States Tobacco Journal and, 29
    WWI and, 31
Smithsonian Magazine, 265
Snyder, John I., 356–357, 366
Snyder, John W., 688
Sobotka, Elsie Simon, 557
Social legislation, 606
Social Problems, *457*
Socialist, 246
Socialists, 40–41, 235, 236
    alleged connection to Ford Foundation and, 739
Socialized medicine, 612–613, 620
Sokolsky, George E., 516, *522*, 753
    attacks Ford foundation, 739
    propagandizing for steel interests, 471–472, 476, 516
    The American Way of Life, *521*
Solvay Chemical Co., 148
Sonnenberg, Ben, 343–370, *see also* Publicity Consultants
    accounts of, 350
    background of, 345–346, 368–369
    Ben Sonnenberg, Jr. and, 347, 353, 368–369
    character of, 344, 359–360
    criticism of, 367–368
    description of, 343–345
    early career of, 346–347
    Gramercy Park and, 351–352, 366
    hotel accounts of, 349
    last years of, 365–366
    philosophy of, 366–370
    Prince Matchabelli and, 348

public relations technique of, 350–351, 369–370
publicizing contract bridge and, 348–349
"Trader Horn" and, 347
Sonnenberg, Ben, Jr., 347, 353, 368–369
   Lost Property, 369, *370*
   Nation, 369
Sooth–Hawley Tariff Act, 318, 327
Sorensen, Charles E., 270, 271, 682, 717
Sosnowska, Nadia de (1st wife of H. Brune), 305
South Africa, 73, 85
South America, 79–80
South Bend Tribune, 136
South Bend Tribune, assessment of IRT affairs, 146
Southern Pacific Railroad, 48
Southern Publicity Association, 372, 377–381, 403, *see*
   also Ku Klux Klan
   publicity campaign of, 381, 383, 386–388, 392, 412
   repairing the KKK's image and, 388–392
   Searchlight and, 399–400
Soviet Russia, *see also* Red Scare
   Ford Foundation and, 747
   propaganda and, 144–153
   relationship to Ivy Lee and, 141–142
   Russian Revolution and, 235, 383
Space technology, 430
Spencer & Roberts, 589
   Nelson Rockefeller and, 622
   Ronald Reagan and, 622–623
Spencer, Stuart, 622, 623
Sperry Rand Corp., 301
Sponsoring Committees, *see* Fronts
Standard Oil Company, 55–56, 63, *see also* Oil industry
   tariffs and, 30
Standard Oil (New Jersey) (SONJ), 143, 296, 441, 640,
             644–657, *see also* Oil industry
   anti-trust actions and, 63, 645
   costs of advertising and, 652–653
   Creole Petroleum subsidiary and, 654–655
   history of, 650–651
   I. G. Farben and, 644–645, 648
   Newsom PR program for, 650–654, 654
   Oil Cartel probe and, 655–658
   oil imports and, 657
   public distrust of, 647–650
   public relations problems of, 646–648
   rubber patents and, 645–645
   toluol controversy and, 648, 650
   Truman Senate Committee and, 645
Standard Oil Trust, 63
Stanton, Frank, 660, 676
   conflicts at CBS and, 658, 662–665
   PR and CBS, 659, 666
   response to GM charges and, 728
   testifies at quiz show hearings, 665–666
Stanton, Rev. John H., 244–246
Starr, Kevin, 76, *91*
State Department, U.S., *see* Department of State
Statue of Liberty, 333–335
Steel industry, 4, 62, 267, 431, *see also* American Iron
         & Steel Institute; Little Steel Strikes; Re-
         public Steel; Bethlehem Steel; U.S. Steel;
         Youngstown Sheet & Tube
   employee representation plans, 460
   Great Depression and, 422, 459

Kennedy–Blough shootout and, 478–482
National Steel Co., 243, 245
Steel Workers Organization Committee and, 240,
   461–464
use of fronts, 471–473, 475–477
Stemple, Herbert, 662, 663
Stephenson, Howard, *521*
Sterling Drug Company, 329–330
Steve Hannagan & Associates, *see* Hannagan, Steve
Stevenson, Adlai, 625
Stevenson, Ward, 302
Stewart, Walter, 533–535
Stimson, Henry L., 34, 237
Stock Market Crash, *see* Great Depression
Stone, Melville, 179
Stratton, Samuel S., 522, *522*
Straus, Percy, 314
Street, Wolcott, 237
strikebreaking, 383, *see also* Labor disputes
   Remington Rand formula for, 247, *250*
Strobridge, R. L., 208
Subway Sun, 132, 133
Sugar industry
   smoking and, 210
   tariffs and, 318–321
Sullivan, Ray, 704
Sulzberger, Mr. and Mrs. Arthur Hays, 197
Sun Valley, 251, 264–266, 271
Supermarkets, *see* Chain Stores
Survey
   review of Bernay's book, 179
   review of *Propaganda* [Whipple], 185
Swift, G.E., 100
Swigert, J. Mack,, 482
Swinehart, Gerry, 551, 563, 564, 581, *586, 587*
   A&P and, 565, 574
   death of, 584
   international public relations and, 551
   Palm Beach Publicity and, 257
   polio campaign and, 557, 559
   popularizing Cuba and, 543
   promoting Quebec, 544
   Railroad–Truckers Brawl and, 575
Swope, Gerard, 327
Sydenham Hospital, 340–341

T

Taft, Robert P., presidential campaign of, 431–432,
       515–516
Taft–Hartley Act, 212
Tarbell, Ida, 56
Tariffs, 13–14
   Citizen's Committee for Reciprocal Trade and, 328
   Hawley–Smoot Tariff bill, 318, 327
   high tariff barriers and, 29–30
   Jones–Costigan Act, 320
   pro-low tariff groups, 328
   Reciprocal Trade Agreements and, 327–329
   Standard Oil and, 30
   sugar industry and, 318–321
Taxes, *see* Chain Stores
Taylor, Telford, 144
Teagle, Walter, 143
Technology

research, 763
Television, 201, 442, 453, *see also* New Politics
  Dwight Eisenhower campaign and, 624–625
  educational, 201
  E.R. Murrow controversy and, 662–665
  impact on government, 628–629
  quiz show scandal, 658, 662–664, 665–666
  Richard Nixon and, 625–626, 664, 628
  rigged reporting and, 733
Tenants rights, 97
Tenements, 8, 97
Thayer, M. J. B., 48, 53
  on Parker & Lee services, 48
The Lotus Club, 305–306
The Wisemen, 130, 216, 503
  formation of, 508–509
  Manhattan Project and, 510–511
Third Avenue Railway System, WEBJ and, 286
Third party system, 589
Third party technique, *see* Fronts
Third Reich, *see* Nazi government
Thirlkeld, Harold W., 230, 231
Thomas, Eugene, 327
Thomas R. Shipp and Co., 31–35
Thomas, R. J., 270
Thompson, Carl, 491, 493
Thompson, Charles W., 27, 28
Thompson, John W., 269
Thompson, Judge Floyd, 261
Thompson, J. Walter, 108, 258–259
Thornley & Jones, 241–243
Time, 123, 216, 221, 598, *633*
  on Hannagan, 256
T. J. Ross & Associates, 154–155
Tobacco Industry, 482–503, *see also* American Tobacco
        Co.; Tobacco Industry Research Committee
  cigarettes and, *see* Cigarettes
  Council for Tobacco Research and, 496, 497
  use of fronts, 208, 209, 490, 497–498
Tobacco Industry Research Committee (TIRC), 458–459,
        see also Tobacco Industry; Tobacco Institute
  congressional information program and, 491–492
  Dr. Little and, 487–489, 491
  funding of, 488
  Justice Department and, 490
  lawsuits and, 490, 497–498, 500
  lobbying Washington and, 496
  new media and, 488, 490, 493
  pro-cigarette campaign of, 489–496
  research and, 484, 486, 487, 491, 494
Tobacco Institute, 498–503, *see also* Tobacco Industry
        Research Committee
  advertising and, 500, 501
  stated purposes of, 499
Tobacco Research Council (TRC), 459, 498
Totalitarianism, government, 619
Tourism, *see also* German Railroad Tourist Bureau;
        Hamilton Wright Organization
  Bahamas, *see* Bahamas
  Cuba, *see* Cuba, Republic of
  Fulbright Hearings and, 84–88
Tourtellot, Arthur B.
  CBS and, 643, 668
  Earl Newsom and, 643, 655, 657, 660, 666

Ford Foundation and, 736
  Foundation deficiencies and, 743
  Foundation policy and, 751–752
Trade, *see* Foreign trade; Tariffs
Transcontinental Air Transport (*later*
  name TWA), 291
Transit Commission (N.Y.), hearings, 133–137
Treaty of Versailles, 106, 539
Treleaven, Harry, 627
Trento, Susan B., *775*
Trinity Episcopal Church, 8, 97
Trippe, Juan, 287, 300
Trucking Industry, *see also* Railroad–Truckers Brawl
  truck weight limitations and, 575–577
Trucks, *see* Railroad–Truckers Brawl
Truman, David B., *632*
Truman, Harry, 2
  campaign style of, 624
  national health insurance *see* American Medical
    Association
  Reciprocal Trade Act and, 327, 328
  seizure of steel mills and, 479–482
  on Standard Oil of N.J. and, 645
  supports federal excise tax, 436
  voluntary food conservation campaign and, 355
  war production and, 298, 299
Tucker, Richard K., *412*
Tuerck House, 740, 742
Tulsa World, 222–223
Tuskegee Institute, 309
Two-way technique, Bernays and, 166, 176, 177
Twohey, James, 685
  memo on Ford's OPA stand, 689–690
Twohey (James S.) Associates, 641
Tydings, Joseph, 609
Tylenol crisis, Johnson & Johnson and, 773
Tyler, Eliabeth ("Bessie"), 108, 109, 372, *see also* Ku
        Klux Klan
  background of, 373
  the press and, 403–404, 406, 407
  scandal and, 406–409
  Searchlight and, 399–400
Tyler, Elizabeth "Bessie," 108, 109

U

Udall, Stewart, 334
Underwood, Oscar W., letter of, 30
Unger, Craig, *371*
"Union busting," *see* Strikebreaking
Union Carbide and Carbon, and the Prest-O-Lite bat-
        tery company, 253
Union organizers, 119
Union Pacific Railroad, 264
Union Trust Company, 420
Unions, *see* CIO; Labor unions; United Auto Workers;
        United Mine Workers
United Auto Workers (UAW), 270, 642, 683, *see also*
        Automobile industry; CIO
  Ford contract negotiations (1949), 703–709
  Ford wage dispute (1941), 685–686
United Fruit Company, 80, 196, 197
  polio epidemic and, 197
United Jewish Appeal, 693
United Mine Workers Journal, 621

United Mine Workers(UMW), 45, 57–59, 120, *see also*
    CIO
    ACLU and, 235–236
    Anthracite coal strike and, 45–46
    Coal Operators strike and, 234–236, 240
    Colorado Fuel strike, 57–58
    membership of, 120
United Nations (UN), 124
United Press ((UP), 254, 317
United States, *see also* Government, U.S.
    communications with foreign nations and, 85
    economy and, 327
    foreign demands on, 768–769
    inflation and, 707
    isolationism and, 73
    Nuremberg trials and, 151–153
    oil imports and, 657
    social security and, 706
    Surgeon General and, 499, 500
    tobacco industry and, 482, 499, 500
    trade with Germany and, 550
    v. Krauch, 151
United Steel Workers Union, 333
United Transit Commission, 59
UNIVAC computer, 300
Universal Trade Press Syndicate (UTPS), 199
Untermeyer, Samuel K., 59, 131–132, 134–136
    Urban League and, 308–310, 313, 340, 696
U.S. Budget Office, promotion of, 237
U.S. Congress, *see* Congressional Committees
U.S. Department of State, *see* Department of state
U.S. Industries, 356–357
U.S. Information Agency, 528
U.S. Rubber, 115
U.S. Steel, 4, 706, *see also* Steel industry
    price increases and, 478
    public relations program of, 477–478
    union contract, 461–462
U.S. Supreme Court, 129, 320
    misleading advertising and, 500
    Railroad–Truckers Brawl decision of, 580
    right to organize and, 467
    seizure of private property and, 480
U.S. Tariff Commission, 13–14, 319
Utilities, 2, 47, *see also* Insull, Samuel; Insull, Samual Jr.
    FTC investigation of, 183–184
Uzzell, Thomas H., 116

V

Vail, Theodore N., 15, 18
Van Doren, Charles, $64,000 Question and, 662, 665
Van Hise, Charles R., comments on White House Con-
    servation Conference, 32, 33, *35*
Vanderbilt Hotel, skywriting publicity and, 284
Vanderbilt, William Henry, 46
Vanderlip, Frank A., 211
Victory Loan Drive, *see* Liberty Loan Drives
Viereck, George Sylvester, 146, 548, 550
    Foreign Agent Registration Act and, 548
    testimony for House investigation, 146
Voska, Emanual, 167, 540
Voting, and racism, 385
Vultee Aircraft, 300, 301, 425

W

Wade, Wyn, 379, 381, 383, 387, *412*
Wadsworth, Eliot, 65
Wagner Act, 240, 247, 467
Wald, Lillian, 345, 346
Waldorf-Astoria Hotel, 193–194, 211, 355, 557
Walker, Jimmy, 290
Walker, Strother H., *191, 522, 587*
Wall Street, 41, 97, 137
Wall Street Journal, 488
Walsh, Richard, 637, 638
Walsh, Thomas J., 183
Wanamaker, John, 288
Ward, Charles Sumner, 65, 111, 140
Ward, Rev. Harry, 235
Wardell, William J., 323, 324
Warm Springs Foundation, 554–555, 558, 562
Washburn, Charles, 176, 303, *307*
Washington, D.C.
    foreign agents and, 768–769
    lobbyists and, 767–768
Washington Post, 192
Waters, Robert S., 241, 243
Wattenberg, Martin P., 630, *632*
Weck, Alyce S., 145, *158*
Wecter, Dixon, 290, *307*
Wedemeyer, Albert C., 515, 516
Weinberg, Arthur, 5, *9*
Weinberg, Lila, 5, *9*
Weintraub, Oscar, 347–348
Weir, Ernest T., 243, 245, 472
West, George F., *71*
Westinghouse, George, 2, 47, 260
Whelan, Elizabeth M., *521*
Whipple, Leon, 185
Whitaker & Baxter International (Campaigns, Inc.), 589–
        633, *see also* Baxter, Leone; Whitaker, Clem
    advertising and, 607–608
    anti-Sinclair campaign, 599–601
    basic principles of, 604–606
    California health insurance and, 606–607
    California utility referendum and, 526, 596–599
    campaign for the AMA, 612, 613, 615–621
    campaign disclosure and, 609
    competitors of, 622–624
    ethics and, 610
    Goodwin Knight and, 603–604
    impact on American society, 590, 595, 621
    New Politics and, 595, 631
    other accounts and, 608
    Papers, 631, *631*
    philosophies of, 602–603, 629
    techniques of, 600, 602, 603, 606–607, 608, 610–
        612
Whitaker, Clem, 526, 590, *see also* Baxter, Leone;
        Whitaker & Baxter
    background of, 595–596
    belief in public opinion and, 602
    on campaign management, 602, 603
    journalism and, 596
    Leone Baxter and, 596–598
    lobbying and, 596
    Papers of, *631*

Whitaker, Clem, Jr., 607–609, *631*
    lobbying and, 6099
    Shirley Temple Black and, 624
White, Charlie, 463
White House, 195
White House Conference of Governers, 31–32
White, Theodore, 594, 598, 609–610, 631, *632*
White, William Allen, *9*
Who's Who, 34
Wiebe, Gerhard D., 189
Wiggin, A.H., 138
Wilder, R.H., 109, 214
Williams, Emlyn, 146
Williamsburg, Colonial, *see* Colonial Williamsburg
Willow Run bomber plant, 269, 269–271
    production problems of, 268, 270, 271
Willys–Overland, 271, 300
Wilson, Thomas E., 99, 100
Wilson, Woodrow, 34, 98–99, 114
    Bureau of the Budget and, 237
    Chinese famine relief and, 237
    Creel Committee and, 69, 106, 165, 537
    New Freedom reforms and, 380
    regulatory programs of, 537
    "The New Freedom," 8
    Versailles Peace Conference and, 165
    WWI, 34, 64–65, 69
Winchell, Walter, 558
Winkler, Allen M., 529
"Wisconsin Idea," 310–311
Wise, T. A., *457*
Wisehart, M. K., *157*
Witten, Evelyn, 306
Wittwer, Charlotte E., 32, *36*
Wolcott, Robert, 505, 506
Woman's Roosevelt Memorial Association, 140
Women
    cigarettes and, 208–209, 284
    Ku Klux Klan and, 378, 410
    suffrage and, 106, 539
Wood, Leonard, 34, 51, *71*, 78
Wood, Robert J., 584, *586–587*
Woodlock, Thomas F., 312, 326
Woodruff, Robert W., 272, 274, 322, 455
World War I (WWI)
    aircraft and, 281, 284
    American Red Cross and, 34–35, 64–70, 114–116
    Creel Committee, *see* Creel Committee
    heavy construction and, 312
    industrial expansion and, 107
    Liberty Loan drives and, 31, 105, 226–228
    Minutemen and, 31, 69, 106
    muckrakers and, 66
    Plattsburg Training Camps and, 34, 115
    preparedness campaign for, 34
    propaganda and, 537
World War II, 83, 101, 247

aircraft industry and, 267–271
atomic bomb and, 130
Manhattan Project and, 130, 510–511
National War Fund and, 230
Nazi propaganda and, 144–153
Office of War Information and, 270–271
Operation Pluto and, 300
public relations and, 527–528
Standard Oil (N.J.) controversy, 645
war bonds and, 528
war production and, 298–300
World's Columbian Exposition (Chicago), 78
Wright Aeronautical Corporation, 287
    Lindbergh and, 288, 290
Wright, Hamilton I, (aka Hamilton Mercer Wright), 74,
        76, 769–770, *see also* Hamilton Wright Orga-
        nization
    background of, 76
    Fulbright hearings and, 74, 84–88
    journalism and, 75, 76, 78–80
    Mrs. H. Wright, 87
Wright, Hamilton II, 81–90, *91*, *see also* Hamilton
        Wright Organization
    background of, 81
    foreign accounts and, 81–82
    Fulbright Hearings and, 74, 84–88
    Public Relations Society of America and, 87
    views of Fulbright hearings, 88
Wright, Hamilton III, 89, *see also* Hamilton Wright Or-
        ganization
    advertising and, 83
    PRSA censure of, 88–89
    resigns HWO, 90
Wright (Hamilton) Organization, *see* Hamilton Wright
        Organization
Wright, J. Handly, 422, 638
Wright, Milton, *521*

Y

YMCA, 65
    fundraising and, 65
    "The Pierce Plan," 111
    "The Ward PLan," 111
Young, James Harvey, *586*
Youngstown Sheet & Tube, 246, 462, *see also* Steel in-
        dustry
    Senate investigations of, 474–475
    strikebreaking techniques and, 470–475
Yugoslavia, breakup of, 771–772
Yutzy, Thomas D., 99, 101

Z

Zeppelin, Ferdinand, Count von, 291
    airships and, 291–294
Ziegfield Follies, 210
Ziegler, Ronald, 627